THE BIOGRAPHICAL
HISTORY OF BASEBALL

THE BIOGRAPHICAL HISTORY OF BASEBALL

Donald Dewey
and
Nicholas Acocella

Carroll & Graf Publishers, Inc.
New York

First Carroll & Graf edition 1995

Carroll & Graf Publishers, Inc.
260 Fifth Avenue
New York, NY 10001

Library of Congress Cataloging-in-Publication Data

Dewey, Donald, 1940–
  The biographical history of baseball / Donald Dewey and Nicholas
Acocella.—1st Carroll & Graf ed.
    p.   cm.
  ISBN 0-7867-0138-2 : $21.00 ($29.75 Can.)
  1. Baseball players—United States—Biography—Dictionaries.
2. Baseball—United States—History.   I. Acocella, Nick.
II. Title.
GV865.A1D45   1995
796.357'092'2—dc20
[B]   94-26564
                                                    CIP

Text designed by Terry McCabe

Manufactured in the United States of America

FOR
LAURA ACOCELLA
AND
THOMAS DEWEY

Introduction

On June 12, 1939, a dual ceremony was held in Cooperstown, New York. The more conspicuous one celebrated the opening of the National Baseball Hall of Fame and Museum. The second ceremony—implicit in the first—formalized major league baseball's move to enshrine itself as the national pastime and to charge an admission price for its past as well as for its present.

In the five and a half decades since that afternoon in Cooperstown, the history of baseball has lagged behind only the sport as a growth industry. Books, magazines, television documentaries, computer bulletins, newsletters, and academic treatises have charted the careers of all the Cincinnati milkmen who happened to drop by a ballpark and pitch a no-hitter in an 1882 exhibition game, while statistical research societies have furnished all the numbers necessary for demonstrating how many of those *Wunderkinder* were really better than Cy Young (give or take 500 victories). A more expansive school of historians has produced mountains of evidence that major league baseball, while not always aware of it, had a revolutionary impact on racism, management-labor strife, the Nazi threat, and other evils plaguing American society as a whole. A third concentration of writings in recent years has identified baseball with the securities of the nuclear family and the sublimations of the detonated psyche—a force for the continuity of sons relating to fathers and potential rooftop snipers redirecting their furies at umpires. As often purveyed, the history of baseball has been a cavalcade of reassurances in which every player who ever donned a uniform has earned a piece of glory, every owner who ever defended the principles of Attila the Hun has had his enlightened side, and every fan ever repulsed by the antics of a George Steinbrenner has remained basically grateful for the opportunity to debate the Yankees' pennant chances. One characterization of histories of the kind might be congratulatory.

It is not the intention of *The Biographical History of Baseball* to slap together another congratulatory tour of baseball's names and numbers. Although one of the book's assumptions is that the game has indeed served as a pastime for countless millions over twelve decades or more, and as such merits a cogent record of its development, *The Biographical History of Baseball* does not accept that nineteenth-century trivia has become twentieth-century significance merely for being recalled or that the journeyman players of the 1920s have turned into venerable all-stars simply for no longer being forgotten. The authors have a limited belief in the understanding achieved by progressively sophistic computations, nostalgic wish-fulfillment, or, conversely, the cynical attitudinizing of "nothing ever changes." We are not interested in electing people to the Hall of Fame, or even in reducing the number of those already on the premises. What we are interested in, on the other hand, is singling out those on and off the diamond who have been most responsible for developing baseball—primarily in athletic and business ways, but also in its larger cultural impact as a mass entertainment and in its smaller personal imprint as an arena for the imaginative, traumatic, and even tragic. The individuals listed in *The Biographical History of Baseball* have, in the view of the authors, done the most for consolidating the legitimacy, curiosity, respect, and criticism that the Hall of Fame and other repositories of baseball's chronicles and legacies have attracted over the years.

The Biographical History of Baseball is not a Who's Who. There has been no attempt to include every distinguished player and front-office executive in the annals of the game. The criterion for choosing entries has been one, and only one: For better or worse, has the subject influenced the game, the popularity of the game, or the image of the game? Has baseball become richer or poorer as a sport, a business, or an entertainment because of his or her involvement in it? Did he or she leave a game that was different from the one entered?

Of course, any player who ever singled in a run in the seventh inning of a mid-May contest has probably made a difference of some kind—maybe on his team's final standings, maybe in the emotions of somebody sitting in the bleachers. Similarly, any general manager who ever passed a sandlot game might have had a decisive say years later in signing up a prospect he saw there and who turned out to be of Hall of Fame caliber. Crushes and serendipities have been as much a part of the baseball fabric as anything else. But in seeking the historical perspective promised by their title, the authors had to decide that effectiveness on the field or efficiency in the office was not sufficient grounds for inclusion. Lew Burdette, to pick a name, won more than 200 games for the Braves and other teams in the 1950s and 1960s and, in the prime of his career, was the right-handed complement to Warren Spahn on two Milwaukee pennant winners. But for all his solidity as a starter and the impression he might have made on given County Stadium fans, Burdette was hardly unique in his abilities, so he has not been given an entry. George Zoeterman, by contrast, did not play a single game in a major-league uniform, but because his signing by the White Sox in 1947 prompted the only suspension of a big league franchise in modern times, he has been given an entry. Likewise, someone like John McHale has racked up an imposing number of

years in the administrations of National League and American League teams, completing trades, signing free agents, and ducking awkward questions, but his mere longevity as an organization man has not entitled him to inclusion. On the other hand, Joseph Danzansky never fulfilled his ambition to buy a franchise, but his efforts to do so caused so much turmoil and farcical manipulations that he has been included.

The subjects covered by *The Biographical History of Baseball* have mostly been drawn from the development of the National and American leagues. But since the history of the sport has hardly been exhausted by those two circuits, other entries owe their inclusion to their influence on a proto-major league (the National Association), the three nineteenth-century leagues (the American Association, the Union Association, and the Players' League) recognized as having been major, the one defunct twentieth-century league (the Federal League) accorded the same status, the more begrudgingly acknowledged Negro leagues, the minor leagues, and some foreign circuits. The individuals cited within these areas fall into the following—and sometimes overlapping—groups:

Hall of Famers. Admittedly, election to Cooperstown has allowed several figures to slip under the rope of restrictions against capable but otherwise uninspiring contributors to the sport. This has been particularly obvious with regard to players (e.g., Ted Lyons and Herb Pennock) who owe their election to the one-time preponderance of big city sportswriters among voters and to officials who owe their enshrinement either to the sport's penchant for consecrating every aspect of the founding of the National League (e.g., Morgan Bulkeley) or its tendency to commemorate fealty over an extended period (see Ford Frick). At the very least, however, the inclusion of all those who have received plaques at the Hall of Fame reflects Major-League Baseball's own estimation of its standards, priorities, and achievements. Beyond that, naturally, are the numerous players, officials, and others who have been indisputably seminal in their athletic or organizational accomplishments.

The Protagonists. Those who have been at the center of the game's defining dramatic moments.

The Innovators. In everything from playing

regulations and uniform gear to administrative and broadcasting structures, changes in the sport have been the result of an individual's insight, resolve, or, in some instances, misfortune.

The Record Holders. More markedly than in other professional sports, baseball has always prized primacies, superiorities, and durabilities as part of its competitiveness. In some cases (e.g., Roger Maris and Hank Aaron), changes in the record holder have occasioned more than a bigger number as a standard.

The Character Actors. Baseball has always been replete with thieves, hustlers, clowns, and buffoons whose antics have provided the color for a franchise, a season, or even an era.

The Suits and the Scouts. Not all front-office functionaries have been defined by their ability to blend into the background.

The Fans and the Media. Baseball has never been a tree falling in an empty forest.

The central contention of *The Biographical History of Baseball* is that we would be watching an entirely different game today—if we were watching it at all—were it not for the impact of the people discussed in the book. Credit them or blame them. History, too, has always been a partisan sport.

—Donald Dewey
Nicholas Acocella

A

HANK AARON (Hall of Fame, 1982)

Aaron ultimately prevailed over the racist lunatics who threatened him during his pursuit of Babe Ruth's career home run record, but he has had a much more difficult time erasing the impression that his feat was a sequel to Ruth's achievement rather than an improvement upon it. Baseball's vested interest in promoting its all-time icon has also served to reduce Aaron to a one-dimensional slugger, obscuring not only his all-around talents as a player but also his significant role as farm director of the Braves for many years. Because of this, Willie Mays and other contemporaries continued to insist into the 1990s that the right-hand-hitting outfielder with a drawerful of lifetime offensive records and a plaque in Cooperstown remained the game's most underrated figure.

Aaron broke in with the Milwaukee version of the Braves in spring training in 1954, after Bobby Thomson's broken ankle opened up a starting spot in the outfield. Over the next thirty-two years, Aaron batted .305, forging major league career records not only with his 755 homers but also with his 2,297 RBIs, 6,856 total bases, 1,477 extra-base hits, fifteen seasons of scoring 100 runs, 293 intentional walks, and 121 sacrifice flies. He batted over .300 fourteen times, won hitting titles in 1956 and 1959, led the National League in home runs and RBIs four times each, drove in 100 runs eleven times, had the most doubles four times, reached 200 hits three times, and had at least 40 home runs in eight years. His 3,771 lifetime hits trail only Pete Rose and Ty Cobb, while his 20 straight years of at least 20 home runs trail nobody. For all that, Aaron won his only MVP award in 1957 for leading the Braves to a pennant by pacing the NL in home runs (44), RBIs (132), and runs (118), batting .322, and slugging a round .600. It was also the first of three straight years that he won a Gold Glove as the league's premier defensive right fielder.

Although Aaron would eventually lose his franchise in fielding awards to Roberto Clemente, the Gold Gloves suggested the defensive qualities that both teammates and adversaries regarded as the equivalent to those of the Pittsburgh star and Mays. Before tearing up his leg in the 1960s, Aaron was also a superior base runner with a full complement of Negro league skills at forcing infielders to hurry throws and outfielders to make them to the wrong base. Aaron had only three opportunities to show off his talents under post-season pressures, but he made the most of them. In the 1957 World Series against the Yankees, he clouted 3 home runs and batted .393. In another meeting with the Yankees, the following year, he averaged .333. Against the Mets in the first National League Championship Series in 1969, he homered in each of the three games.

Especially during the feel good years in Milwaukee, Aaron seldom called attention to anything but his playing. With the Braves' move to Atlanta in 1966, however, the Alabama native began responding to all the inevitable questions about playing in the South by denouncing baseball's continuing aversion to hiring blacks as managers or general managers. After years of re-

1

Hank Aaron joined Babe Ruth in the exclusive 700-homer club with this swing in 1973. Photo compliments of the Atlanta Braves.

ceiving pooh-poohing reassurances that the situation was much better than it had been, he himself demonstrated that it wasn't by attracting threats on his life for challenging Ruth's "white man's record" in 1973. As bad as the poisonous scrawls and anonymous telephone calls were the ostensibly intelligent discussions held on radio and television programs about whether the Ruth record *should* be broken. The atmosphere of hatred was such that Aaron was assigned a bodyguard from the Atlanta Police Department. To complicate matters further, he ended the 1973 season with only 713 homers—one shy of Ruth.

With the Braves scheduled to open the 1974 season in Cincinnati, Aaron came under additional pressures when Atlanta owner William Bartholomay made it clear that he wanted the outfielder benched for the contests at Riverfront Stadium so the Ruth record could be broken at home for attendance purposes. This brought a

storm of criticism from traditionalists in the press and prompted Commissioner Bowie Kuhn to intervene with an order to have Aaron in the starting lineup for the opener against the Reds. Aaron responded by tying the record with his 714th home run in his first swing of the bat in the first inning, but that was it. Bartholomay got his wish when 53,775 poured into Fulton County Stadium on the cold and miserable night of April 8, 1974, and saw Al Downing of the Dodgers surrender number 715.

Only a few months after passing Ruth, Aaron got another lesson in baseball's race relations when Braves general manager Eddie Robinson ridiculed his candidacy as a successor to the fired Eddie Mathews as manager; moreover, Robinson broke with franchise tradition by giving Clyde King a multiyear contract, just in case Aaron got the idea that he would be a fallback choice in the immediate future. The King appointment effectively ended the slugger's ties to the Braves as a player, and after the season he agreed to return to Milwaukee, to the American League Brewers. He generated mild interest as a Brewers gate attraction in 1975, but made it clear prior to the start of the 1976 campaign that it was going to be his last. As it developed, his career as an active player ended sourly. On the final day of the season, he singled in his last plate appearance, and was then removed by manager Alex Grammas for pinch runner Jim Gantner. Gantner eventually scored with a run that would have enabled Aaron to break a tie with Ruth for second place in that category behind Cobb. Chagrined by the slugger's anger at having been lifted for Gantner, Grammas explained that he had only wanted to give him one last chance to run off the field to a standing ovation.

Following his retirement as a player, Aaron served for a number of years as farm director of the Braves. Those who bothered to see him as more than an emblematic presence credited him with the development of several prospects who directly or indirectly led to the revival of the franchise in the 1990s. On several occasions he also gave interviews putting his own name forward as a candidate for baseball commissioner; he never received a serious response.

By his own admission, Aaron has never been able to separate his satisfaction at retiring as baseball's greatest home-run hitter from the hatred he and his family were exposed to during pursuit of Ruth's record. In the same house where he keeps the ball that he hit off Downing, he has also put away an estimated five hundred letters warning him off belting number 714.

JIM ABBOTT

Abbott joined the California starting rotation in 1989 despite being born without a right hand. Although compiling only a 67–74 record with the Angels and Yankees in his first six seasons, the University of Michigan graduate has been among the most successful hurlers to graduate directly from college ball to the major leagues.

CAL ABRAMS

Abrams became the shame of Brooklyn when he was thrown out at the plate in the ninth inning

Jim Abbott overcame a birth defect that deprived him of a left hand and became a winning pitcher for the Angels in the early 1990s. Photo compliments of the California Angels.

of the final game of the 1950 season with what would have been the run to force a special playoff between the Dodgers and the Phillies for the pennant. Over the years, the bang-bang play on Richie Ashburn's throw to home after Duke Snider's single has been alternately attributed to Abrams's small lead off second, and third base coach Milt Stock's rashness in sending him home. In fact, the outfielder had little choice in trying to score since Pee Wee Reese, the runner behind him, was dashing up his back to get to third base.

BABE ADAMS

Adams had as flashy a rookie year for the Pirates in 1909 as he had a messy end with the same club seventeen years later. After a debut season that saw him win 12 games and post an ERA of 1.11, the right-hander stunned the Tigers in the 1909 World Series by throwing three complete-game victories for a Pittsburgh championship. Until 1926 he remained a mainstay of the team's staff, winning 20 games twice and usually fashioning an ERA under 3.00. In that final year, however, he became innocently involved in a bitter me-or-him showdown between coach Fred Clarke and Max Carey. The nub of the controversy was a Carey-led mutiny against Clarke's presence on the bench after the coach had compared the outfielder's effectiveness to that of the team batboy. Although a majority of the team refused to back Carey and another outfielder, Carson Bigbee, in the revolt, and Adams himself voted for keeping Clarke around, the coach wouldn't leave well enough alone, insisting that owner Barney Dreyfuss get rid of all those opposed to him. Mainly because Adams was on record for saying that "managers should manage and nobody else should interfere," the owner agreed with Clarke that the pitcher had also been part of the uprising. The upshot was that two of the A(dams) B(igbee) C(arey) Mutineers, as the Pittsburgh press branded them, were released, and Carey was sold to the Dodgers. The three players protested to National League president John Heydler, but Heydler, while absolving the trio of insubordination, also upheld the right of an owner to get rid of any player he wanted to. Adams, already forty-four and near the end of his pitching effectiveness, didn't attempt to catch on with another team.

DANIEL ADAMS

Among the candidates for the honorific title of Father of Baseball is Adams, a medical doctor and president of the Knickerbocker club from 1847 until 1862. As head of the oldest baseball team in the country, he was given the gavel at an 1857 convention of teams, and in that role established nine innings (rather than 21 runs) as the duration of a game. After that first meeting evolved into the National Association of Base Ball Players the following year, Adams chaired the rules committee, and in his three years in the position set the distance between the bases at 90 feet and from the pitcher's box to home plate at 45 feet. Adams had begun playing an early version of the game in 1839 for exercise and amusement, had a hand in making the Knickerbockers' balls and bats, and claimed to have been the first to move into the shortstop position, less to improve infield defense than to make it easier to relay the relatively light balls of the day from the outfield.

FRANKLIN P. ADAMS

A writer for the *New York Evening Mail*, Adams published one of baseball's most famous verses in 1910 under the title of "Baseball's Sad Lexicon." The work's popularity was key to the election of early-century Cub infielders Joe Tinker, Johnny Evers, and Frank Chance to the Hall of Fame; in fact, not one of the trio ever led the National League in double plays for his position. Adams's verse goes:

There are the saddest of possible words—
    Tinker to Evers to Chance.
Trio of bear Cubs and fleeter than birds
    Tinker to Evers to Chance.
Thoughtlessly pricking our gonfalon bubble,
Making a Giant hit into a double,
Words that are weighty with nothing but trouble—
    Tinker to Evers to Chance.

JOE ADCOCK

Although not on a level with his Hall of Famer teammates Hank Aaron and Eddie Mathews, Adcock accomplished a number of prodigious slugging feats while playing for the Braves in the 1950s. Among his 336 career blasts were four in one game against the Dodgers, the first ball ever hit completely over the left-field grandstand of Ebbets Field, and the first ball ever hit to the left-center field bleachers of the Polo Grounds (an officially estimated distance of 465 feet). In the July 31, 1954, game in which he tagged Brooklyn pitchers for four home runs, he also clouted a double to set a record for the most total bases in a game. The right-hand-hitting first baseman also hit the "nonhomer" that ended Harvey Haddix's 12-inning perfect game on May 26, 1959; when he passed Aaron on the bases in what he later admitted was a "daze," the hit was reduced to a double. As a pinch hitter in his seventeen-year career with the Reds, Braves, Indians, and Angels, Adcock also established the best career ratio for home runs, hitting a four-bagger every 12.75 times he came off the bench.

BOB ADDY

An outfielder for Chicago in 1876, Addy is credited with being the first player to slide into a base. He apparently pioneered the technique while playing for the Forest City Club of Rockford, Illinois, in the 1860s. A bit of an eccentric, Addy was forever contriving schemes he considered more worthy of his talents than conventional baseball; among them was an effort to popularize ice baseball in a Chicago skating rink he owned.

TOMMIE AGEE

There have been many great catches made by outfielders in World Series games, but Agee has been the only one to make two in the same contest. His diving grabs of drives up the alley by Baltimore's Elrod Hendricks and Paul Blair in the third game of the 1969 World Series saved the Miracle Mets in two crucial situations, helping pave the way to New York's eventual championship. Although usually put in the leadoff spot for his speed, Agee also had five straight years of more than 100 strikeouts, including a high of 156 in 1970. Only Bobby Bonds had a worse strikeout ratio among leadoff men.

DANNY AINGE

Long before Deion Sanders was holding up the Braves for contract concessions that would allow him to play professional football, Ainge was lavished with the same rights by the Blue Jays so he could pursue basketball. In 1979, the high school star made it clear that he preferred the court to the diamond, but Toronto was so insistent that it drew up a pact practically fitting baseball around the National Basketball Association schedule. After three partial seasons and a .220 batting average, Ainge dumped the major leagues for his first love.

EDDIE AINSMITH

Ainsmith's fifteen-year career as a backup catcher for the Senators and several other teams assumed secondary importance in 1918, when he appealed against being drafted into the military during World War I on the grounds that he was engaged in a patriotic endeavor since baseball was the national pastime. The appeal, engendered by Washington manager Clark Griffith, prompted a ruling from Secretary of War Newton D. Baker that baseball was an inessential amusement, with all its players and personnel subject to the draft. Prior to the Ainsmith case, players had been able to appeal their call-ups on a case-by-case basis. Earlier the same year, Yankee pitcher Happy Finneran had successfully argued that his ten years

of professional baseball had left him unequipped for seeking another job after getting out of the service and that he had to play to maintain his standing. At the heart of both the Ainsmith and Finneran cases was baseball's refusal to ask for a special exemption as an essential public entertainment, the way various branches of show business had. The ownership stance of asking the War Department to decide player-by-player aided Finneran, but ultimately worked against Ainsmith and anybody called up after him.

DALE ALEXANDER

By being traded from the Tigers to the Red Sox during the 1932 season, Alexander became the first major leaguer to win a batting crown while splitting his time between two teams. His overall average of .367 could not have come as a surprise to Detroit, since he had batted .343, .326, and .325 in his earlier seasons with the club and had also driven in more than 130 runs in two of the three years. Asked to explain the swap for outfielder Roy Johnson, manager Bucky Harris said that he couldn't stand watching Alexander's ineptitude around first base. As it turned out, Boston had little to crow about. In 1933, team physician Doc Woods decided to treat an Alexander leg injury with an innovative heat lamp treatment during a game, but then got so caught up in a Red Sox rally that he forgot about his patient. By the time he got back inside the clubhouse, Alexander had third-degree leg burns that later degenerated into gangrene. That was the end of his career.

GROVER CLEVELAND ALEXANDER (Hall of Fame, 1938)

There weren't many things that Alexander didn't accomplish during his twenty-year (1911–30) career—and not many that he wasn't forced to do afterward because of his physical ailments and his alcoholism. If the right-hander had one glaring statistical shortcoming, it was his failure to snatch the 374th victory that would have broken his tie with Christy Mathewson as the National League's all-time winner.

Alexander's biggest numbers include the following: six years of leading the league in wins;

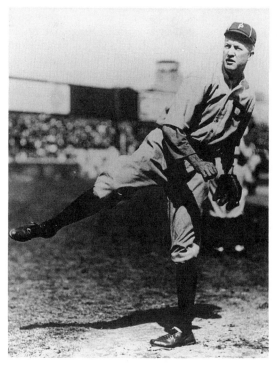

Plagued by epilepsy and alcoholism, Grover Cleveland Alexander nevertheless compiled a National League record 373 victories. National Baseball Library, Cooperstown, N.Y.

five years of leading in ERA; six years of leading in complete games; six years of leading in strikeouts; seven years of leading in shutouts, including a record-setting 16 in 1916; nine years of at least 20 wins, including three seasons in a row of more than 30; and two years of taking the pitching Triple Crown by setting the pace in victories, strikeouts, and ERA. Among Alexander's numerous records were the 94 victories he rolled up between 1915 and 1917. His ERAs between 1915 and 1920 were 1.22, 1.55, 1.86, 1.73, 1.72, and 1.91. Most astonishing, he achieved these numbers while pitching all but three of his major league seasons in hitter-friendly Baker Bowl and Wrigley Field.

As easy as his accomplishments often appeared between the lines, Alexander had a full quota of off-the-field demons. Even before joining the Phillies, he had to battle attacks of double vision to win 29 games for a minor league Syracuse team. Toward the end of the 1917 season he made

the mistake of informing Philadelphia's money-grubbing owner William Baker that he was about to be drafted, and was promptly sold to the Cubs. An accident while in military uniform rendered him deaf in one ear and prone to epileptic seizures—both conditions strengthening his dependence on the bottle. For a few years, Alexander kept all these disabilities at bay, winning two ERA crowns and posting two 20-win seasons for the Cubs, but by 1926 he was reeling off the field more frequently than he was reeling off victories on it. Waived to the Cardinals, he had enough left not only to provide key victories down the stretch for a St. Louis pennant, but also to hurl two complete-game victories in the World Series against the Yankees and then make a dramatic relief appearance in the seventh inning of the final game to strike out Tony Lazzeri with the bases loaded. Even the next year, he staggered through his problems for another 21 wins. From that point on, however, his waning effectiveness and the rising impatience of his employers before his drunkenness were synonymous. Even Baker's gate-inspired notion of bringing the hurler back to Philadelphia in 1930 went for nought when Alexander was belted around in three starts and six relief appearances. In the end, the club suspended the right-hander for showing up once too often under the influence. This final failure became even more poignant when research in the 1950s credited Mathewson with a 373rd win, creating the deadlock neither pitcher knew existed while they were active.

Alexander's post-major league life wasn't much better. At one point he grew a beard to join the House of David team; at another, he worked in a Times Square flea circus. None of these details emerged in *The Winning Season*, the Hollywood movie made of his life in 1952, with Ronald Reagan portraying the hurler.

DICK ALLEN

Allen was among the more conspicuous 1960s–1970s players who inhaled the social protest atmosphere of the period but who ended up exhaling it again in ways calculated to have him perceived as a reckless egotist. By accident as much as by design, he exposed a small army of hypocrites and toadies in the baseball establishment.

The right-hand-hitting slugger began his fifteen-year (1963–77) career with the Phillies, winning Rookie of the Year honors in 1964 for batting .318 with 201 hits, 29 home runs, 91 RBIs, 38 doubles, and a league-leading 13 triples and 125 runs scored. He contributed all that offense while playing third base for the first time in organized ball—an effort that didn't spare him catcalls from Philadelphia fans for also leading the league with 41 errors, especially after it became clear that the club was about to blow the pennant down the stretch. In 1965, his relations with Phillie fans got even worse when his offensive production dipped somewhat, he paced the National League for the second year in a row in strikeouts, and he began issuing his ever-more-frequent pronouncements on the state of baseball. The atmosphere got particularly heated after an early July game when he and backup outfielder Frank Thomas traded blows during batting practice over alleged racial remarks, Thomas came off the bench in the ensuing game to hit a key pinch-hit home run, and then returned to the clubhouse to be told he was being released because of his conflict with the franchise's chief young star. Philadelphia fans became so abusive—even throwing garbage at him—that Allen wore his batting helmet in the field.

Over the next few years he continued to be the team's major run producer and major headline while the Phillies began sinking to the lower depths of the standings. Most of his observations were along the lines of his ''Baseball is a form of slavery. Once you step out of bounds, that's it, they'll do everything possible to destroy your soul.'' At the same time, he developed a habit of skipping exhibition games and missing team planes with feeble excuses. In June 1969 there was a showdown of sorts when manager Bob Skinner fined the slugger for not showing up for a game against the Mets. When owner Bob Carpenter first hesitated to collect the money, then rescinded the fine on the grounds that there had only been some kind of ''misunderstanding,'' Skinner quit and Philadelphia fans went even wilder. The reaction became so hostile that Allen requested a trade. When he was accommodated

after the season, it was in the deal that helped change the economic structure of the game—the swap with the Cardinals that Curt Flood refused to accept.

Allen played only one season in St. Louis, but that was long enough to demonstrate that his power (34 home runs) was not compromised even by the distant fences of Busch Stadium. The following year, with the Dodgers, he and manager Walter Alston provided a season-long proof of how oil did not mix with water. In retrospect, however, even that tense season served as mere prelude to his next three years, in a White Sox uniform.

On the field, Allen swung his way to American League MVP honors in 1972 by batting .308 while piling up league-leading numbers in homers (37), RBIs (113), and walks (99). That came after he played tag with the White Sox right up to spring training, releasing announcements periodically that he was getting tired of being traded and was considering retirement. What ultimately talked him into reporting for his MVP season was the biggest contract ever awarded to a sports figure in Chicago. When his field performance attracted more than 1 million fans through the turnstiles of Comiskey Park for the first time in seven years, he received the biggest pact in the major leagues, while general manager Stu Holcomb and manager Chuck Tanner told anyone who would listen that the slugger was the franchise player. That didn't sit too well with right-hander Stan Bahnsen, who had been offered only a modest raise after winning 21 games, and several other Chicago players who saw their salaries slashed. To make matters worse, Tanner and Holcomb went out of their way during spring training in 1973 to keep a roster spot open for Allen's brother Hank, an outfielder of no particular talent. Hank Allen lasted for only a handful of at-bats into the season, but any relief in the clubhouse over that development dissipated in June when the franchise player, with 16 home runs already in the record books, fractured his fibula in a collision at first base and was sidelined for the rest of the season.

Allen's third and final year with Chicago was the most eventful of all. Although he came back in perfect health and began bashing the ball from Opening Day, he showed a gradually decreasing interest in the club's .500 fortunes as the season wore on. Whenever his hitting put the White Sox ahead in a game, however marginally, he persuaded the cooperative Tanner to yank him for the last couple of innings so he could avoid having to talk to sportswriters after the contest. Then, in early September, he called a club meeting and announced his retirement, effective immediately. Tanner's reply was to say only that Allen was "the greatest player I ever saw." He kept to that reaction even after the season, when the slugger said he had had another change of heart and would return the following year. The Chicago front office thought otherwise, trading him to the Braves for $5,000 and second-string catcher Jim Essian. When Allen declared that he wouldn't play for any club in the South, Atlanta was forced to trade him, and sent him to the Phillies. Obscured during all the late-season melodramatics was that even after walking away from the White Sox with three weeks to go, Allen ended up as the AL home-run king for the second time.

With the Phillies a second time, Allen contributed enough clutch performances from part-time first-base duty to help the team to an Eastern Division win in 1976. But he boycotted the clubhouse celebrations for the clinching in protest against manager Danny Ozark's decision to leave veteran second baseman Tony Taylor off the postseason roster. Although Mike Schmidt and other players also remonstrated against Taylor's exclusion, it was Allen who paid for it by being released shortly after making his only appearance in postseason play. He ended his career as a platoon first baseman with Oakland in 1977.

Allen, who lost much of his baseball earnings on breeding and betting on horses, provided one of the more memorable quotes on artificial turf when he told a newsman: "If horses can't eat it, I don't want to play on it." He also earned a baseball footnote on April 12, 1965, by hitting the first indoor home run in a regular-season game, his two-run blast defeating Houston in the newly opened Astrodome.

JOHNNY ALLEN

Allen was a model "rabbit ears" whose transparent sensitivity to heckling managed to undermine his effectiveness on the mound. It didn't

help, either, that he fueled his temper regularly with liberal doses of alcohol. After one loss with the Indians in the 1930s, the right-hander ripped apart a hotel lobby before dousing the desk clerk with the contents of a fire extinguisher; he responded to another defeat by thrashing his third baseman for having made a decisive error. Incidents of the kind were a mere prelude, however, to a game against Boston on June 7, 1938, when Allen stalked from the hill to the dugout rather than obey plate umpire Bill McGowan's order that he cut off the sleeve of his tattered uniform. With the fans growing ugly in Fenway Park, he sat stubbornly on the bench refusing pleas from manager Ossie Vitt and his teammates to snip off the offending sleeve before the game was forfeited to Boston. Finally, Vitt fined him $250 for leaving the mound without permission and told him he was out of the game. Allen promptly told Vitt to go to hell and announced his retirement. A couple of days later, Cleveland owner Alva Bradley met the team in New York and made the gesture of buying the controversial uniform from Allen for the $250 levied by Vitt. Bradley then had the garment put on display in the department store he owned in Ohio. Although the owner's move calmed Allen temporarily, it also underlined the chaotic relations between Vitt and his employers; the latter situation would degenerate a few years later into the revolt of the so-called Crybaby Indians.

LEE ALLEN

As historian of the Baseball Hall of Fame in the 1960s, Allen indefatigably pursued old ballplayers, tracking down the whereabouts of the living and uncovering the ultimate fates of the deceased in small towns across the country. A former Cincinnati sportswriter and public relations director of the Reds, he also wrote several highly regarded baseball histories.

MEL ALLEN

As the Voice of the Yankees, Allen parlayed a relaxed Alabama drawl and an unabashed rooting interest into a popularity rivaling that of the New York players whose onfield activities he described on radio and television from the 1938 World Series through the 1964 season. While his orotund style irritated almost as many people as his "homer" approach, to Yankees fans he was an indispensable link connecting several successive Bronx dynasties. As a result, his signature lines—introducing broadcasts with "Hi there, everybody"; following the flight of "Ballantine Blasts" with "Going . . . going . . . gone"; and punctuating just about everything but the most mundane incidents with "How about that"—became part of the New York vernacular. In addition, the sobriquets he popularized for almost every Yankee regular—from Old Reliable for Tommy Henrich, to the clunky Commerce Comet for Mickey Mantle—were efforts to impart some of his personal flair to a team that seemed to many a pennant machine. (Conversely, Red Barber was for much of the same period lending his sober approach to the often less-than-sober rival Dodgers.)

On the other hand, Allen's one-man-show approach annoyed several partners, including Jim Woods and Curt Gowdy, shortening their careers in the Yankee Stadium booth. As well, his hostility toward sharing play-by-play with what he considered unqualified former players, such as Joe Garagiola and Phil Rizzuto, won him no popularity contests in the Yankee front office. Allen's absence from the broadcasting booth during the 1964 World Series and his subsequent dismissal in December have been attributed variously to sponsor Ballantine's annoyance at a perceived aloofness, the Yankee front office's desire to project a new image, and the irritation on both their parts at Allen's undisguised on-the-air consumption of the product he hyped and after-hours taste for harder stuff. Coming on the heels of the firing of Yogi Berra as Yankee manager, however, the dismissal was a public relations catastrophe.

In 1978, Allen and onetime partner Barber were the first recipients of the Ford C. Frick award and a place in the broadcasters' corner of the Hall of Fame.

ARTHUR ALLYN, JR.

When Allyn bought the White Sox in 1961, it marked the end of the Comiskey family's involvement in the franchise. And nobody was more surprised than the Comiskey heirs.

The head of the Artnell conglomerate of oil and

clothing companies, Allyn purchased the majority interest in the franchise held by his father, Arthur Allyn, Sr.; Bill Veeck; and Hank Greenberg. The acquisition did not deter Chuck Comiskey, however, from selling his 46 percent interest in the team to Chicago insurance executive William Bartholomay as part of a grand scheme in which Bartholomay would also buy out Allyn to assume total control and give the organization presidency back to the family that had been running the White Sox since the founding of the American League in 1901. Unfortunately for Comiskey, Allyn rejected the Bartholomay offer; moreover, aware that their 46 percent would make for only a loud but ineffective minority, Bartholomay and his associates then sold their holdings to Allyn.

Allyn wasn't so fortunate in actually running the franchise for most of the 1960s. Although the club played .500 ball more often than not during the decade, it was a decidedly dull squad that attracted fewer and fewer spectators every year. The low point was reached on Opening Day in 1968, when a mere 7,756 fans showed up in the immediate wake of the assassination of Martin Luther King, Jr. Claiming that the black neighborhood around Comiskey Park was discouraging white fans, Allyn kept badgering the city for construction of a new downtown stadium. When his appeals continued to fall on deaf ears, he announced that the White Sox had agreed to play 10 home games in 1968 in Milwaukee's County Stadium—ostensibly to give the AL an incentive for including Milwaukee in its planned 1969 expansion, but mainly to find ammunition if he sought to sell the team to a Wisconsin group. The games in Milwaukee accounted for a third of Chicago's home attendance in 1968 and spurred Wisconsin lobbyists headed by Bud Selig to make an outright $13 million offer for the club. In the meantime, Texas millionaire Lamar Hunt made another approach with a similar offer and with the declared intention of moving the franchise to Dallas. But before Allyn could decide between the tenders, the league informed him that it would never approve any transfer out of the Chicago market. In the end, Allyn opted to sell 50 percent of his Artnell stock to his younger brother John and retire to Florida.

JOHN ALLYN

Allyn took over the White Sox from his brother Arthur in 1970 just in time to preside over the worst team (106 losses) in organization history. Things improved only minimally after that.

On the plus side, Allyn brought in Northwestern University athletic director Stu Holcomb to head baseball operations, Harry Carey as the team announcer, and Dick Allen as the most highly paid player ever to wear a uniform; on the minus side, he brought in Chicago, Carey, and Allen. Within a couple of years, the owner was having to mediate ongoing intrigues among Holcomb, personnel director Rollie Hemond, and manager Chuck Tanner, finally getting rid of Holcomb and Hemond. As for Carey, his initial popularity and role in bringing fans back to Comiskey Park was soon counterbalanced by repeated snipes at the team and individual players, leading Allyn to accuse him of discouraging attendance. In the meanwhile, slugger Allen was alternately winning league honors and taking off when the mood hit him.

By the middle of the decade, Allyn was pleading poverty before both the Internal Revenue Service and his brother Arthur, who went to court to claim $500,000 he still had coming from selling the franchise. The situation grew so critical that catcher Ed Herrmann was sold to the Yankees because Chicago couldn't pay him his salary, and outfielder Buddy Bradford was dealt to the Cardinals to meet the organization payroll. When Allyn went to the AL for help, he was greeted with an elaborate plan that would have forced him to sell the franchise to a Seattle group that included comedian Danny Kaye and that would have left Chicago open for still another move by Charlie Finley's Athletics, this time from Oakland. Allyn said no, deciding instead to close a fifteen-year circle by selling the club back to Bill Veeck, from whom his brother Arthur had originally bought the White Sox in 1961. Allyn retained a 25 percent interest in the second Veeck ownership.

FELIPE ALOU

The oldest of the three Alous, Felipe had the most extra-base power, topping the 20-homer and 30-double marks four times each. With the Braves in 1966, he led the National League in both hits and runs scored; two years later, he once again led NL batters in safeties. His seventeen-year career, which began in 1958 with the Giants, ended with three plate appearances in 1974 with the Brewers—enabling him to join Hank Aaron and Phil Roof as the only players to appear for both of Milwaukee's major league franchises in the second half of the century. While with San Francisco on September 10, 1963, Alou and his two brothers wrote a footnote to baseball history by making all three outs in an inning, against the Mets. Five days later, they also appeared together in the only all-sibling outfield. In 1992 Alou took over as manager of the Expos; among his charges were his son Moises and his nephew Mel Rojas.

JESUS ALOU

The youngest of the three Alous didn't have Felipe's extra-base punch or Matty's consistency but still managed to hit .280 over 15 seasons with four clubs. His most memorable game came on July 10, 1964, when, as a member of the Giants, he collected six hits off an equal number of Chicago pitchers, belting singles off Dick Ellsworth, Lew Burdette, Don Elston, Wayne Schurr, and Lindy McDaniel, and homering off Dick Scott. When the righty-hitting outfielder picked up his 1,000th hit, it not only made the Alous the only triumvirate of brothers to reach that mark but also assured them of first place in combined career hits for three or more siblings. Against the Alous' 5,094 safeties, for instance, the three DiMaggios managed only 4,853 and the five Delahantys a mere 4,217.

MATTY ALOU

The middle brother of the three Alous, Matty became the prize student of hitting coach Harry Walker in 1966, when, after batting .231 the year before, he raised his average to .342 to take the National League batting crown as a member of the Pirates. The lefty-hitting outfielder attributed the difference to Walker's insistence that he choke up on the bat. Alou kept the lesson in mind for the rest of his career, reaching the .330 mark in three additional years and averaging .307 for fifteen big league seasons. The 111-point improvement to the batting title is the biggest by a regular from one year to the next.

WHITEY ALPERMAN

Even among Bible hitters, Alperman was an extreme fundamentalist. As the regular second baseman for the 1909 Dodgers, he walked merely twice in 422 plate appearances to set the all-time mark for impatience.

WALTER ALSTON (Hall of Fame, 1983)

Working off twenty-three one-year managerial contracts between 1954 and 1976, Alston was an integral part of the Dodgers' gradual shift in identity from the blue-collar Brooklyn club that seemed to generate its glories and crises spontaneously to the buttoned-down-collar Los Angeles organization that seemed to have a wired-up producer behind even its most volatile events. His public image as a loyal, quiet, but intestinally strong tactician worked as a tempering influence both on those who wanted to believe that the Dodgers would always be the Dodgers whether on the East Coast or West Coast and those who were only too quick to accuse the franchise of going Hollywood.

Not that Alston always appreciated his role. From the day his appointment was announced in Brooklyn, and greeted by headlines of WALTER WHO?, to his final season in California, when he acted baffled by such innovations as free agency, he was seldom allowed to forget that he wasn't the most exciting figure to grace a dugout. Team owner Walter O'Malley, for instance, made a habit of surrounding him with such coaches as Leo Durocher, Charlie Dressen, and Bobby Bragan in the interests of ''creative tension.'' With Durocher, at least, the tension became a little too creative in the mid-1960s, prompting Alston to ream his coach on the bench in front of the team for second-guessing him. A typical O'Malley solution was to fire Durocher, but also to bounce Alston's right-hand man Joe Becker as a warning that a one-year contract was still a one-year contract. During Alston's tenure, the Dodgers won seven pennants and three World Series (including the only one won by Brooklyn, in 1955).

NICK ALTROCK

More noted as one of baseball's first professional clowns, Altrock had two 20-win seasons for the early-century White Sox. The southpaw posted 22 victories and an ERA of 1.88 in 1905, then came back the following year to help Chicago to a pennant with 22 more wins. Although his arm went the following season, he had a friendship with Clark Griffith to thank for the fact that he was picked up by the Senators in 1909. Altrock set a dubious record of sorts by appearing on the Washington roster ten times between 1912 and 1933, never once in that time getting into more than five games and usually just listed so he could make a questionable claim of being a five-decade player. His main value to the Senators, usually in partnership with Al Schacht, was in a pantomime act before games and between ends of doubleheaders. The original Sunshine Boys, Altrock and Schacht got into an argument early in their careers and went through their routine for years without talking to one another on or off the field.

SANDY AMOROS

Left fielder Amoros's startling one-handed catch of an opposite-field drive by Yogi Berra in the seventh game of the 1955 World Series squashed a late-inning rally by the Yankees and helped ensure the only world championship won by the Brooklyn Dodgers. Amoros made the grab after being put into the game for defensive purposes. Following his retirement, the Cuban outfielder became a symbol of the impoverished state many former major leaguers were reduced to because of inadequate pension and medical plans. His plight helped energize players in better financial circumstances to organize the Baseball Assistance Team.

SPARKY ANDERSON

The only manager to win world championships for teams in both leagues, Anderson has never quite convinced as either the latter-day Casey Stengel or the successful Gene Mauch that media pundits have alternately represented him as over the years. While he is not always at ease with the English language and is occasionally given to elaborate chess games with opposing pilots, his twenty-five years of steering Cincinnati and Detroit have been far more conspicuous for his Dodger-trained belief that Opening Day rosters should be changed as little as possible and for his view of starters as relievers who just happen to be on the mound at the beginning of games.

One of a handful of major leaguers who played regularly for one season (with the 1959 Phillies) but never appeared in a single game before or afterward, Anderson called the shots for the Big Red Machine between 1970 and 1978, winning five division titles, four pennants, and two World Series. Most of his field decisions with the heavy-hitting team involved knowing when to go to the bullpen because of a lack of dominating starters; it was because of his frequent trips to the mound that he earned the sobriquet of Captain Hook. For the most part, he remained aloof from the recurrent salary battles between his star players and the Cincinnati front office, generally winning their loyalty by consulting a circle of clubhouse veterans (Joe Morgan, Johnny Bench, Tony Perez, and Pete Rose) whenever some issue threatened club cohesion. If he had one notable failure in team relations, it was his inability to prevent the disastrous trade of Perez to the Expos following the 1976 season. When he himself was cut loose from the club after the 1978 season by newly installed general manager Dick Wagner, even the mayor of Cincinnati joined the outcry by charging that the Reds' front office had "gone bananas." At the time, Anderson's winning percentage of .596 was second only to Joe McCarthy's. Wagner justified the firing by saying that the Reds had grown too complacent.

Moving over to the Tigers during the 1979 season, Anderson found another club without deep pitching and used to banging its way to victory. Over his first eleven years at the helm, he kept the team above .500, winning a world championship in 1984 and an Eastern Division title in 1987; that gave him the record for managing in the most league championship series (7) and for winning the most pennants playoff series (5). He has frequently pointed to the 1987 win as his most satisfying achievement in baseball because of the aging and modest talents on the team. With such stars as Kirk Gibson and Lance Parrish leaving as free agents, however, the Tigers soon disin-

tegrated, exhausting Anderson in the process. Early in the 1989 season, he collapsed before the strain of what was going to be an arduous season and was sent home for three weeks; after some indications that he was about to announce his retirement, he returned to the club, but rarely lost an opportunity to tell interviewers that he could no longer manage "twenty-five hours a day." From the point of view of physical appearance, it was a little bit too late: It came to a shock to many, in fact, that the perennially gray and wrinkled Anderson did not complete his sixtieth year until 1994. He further solidified his position with Detroit during a couple of ownership changes by buying into the club.

In the name of boosting the self-confidence of prospects, Anderson has been embarrassed more than once by spring training evaluations of rookies (e.g., Chris Pittaro, Torey Lovullo, and Ricky Peters) as sure bets for the Hall of Fame. He also stubbed his toe in unloading Howard Johnson to the Mets in 1984 behind the view that the third baseman couldn't hit and didn't have the fortitude to last as a major leaguer. Behind the same ostensible aim of waking up his players, he has frequently gotten no farther than a couple of months into a season before declaring the Tigers dead in the division race. His penchant for extravagant assertions probably reached its low point following the 1976 World Series, when he called the Reds the greatest team in the history of the National League and mocked suggestions that Yankee catcher Thurman Munson could be compared to Bench.

MIKE ANDREWS

A second baseman for Oakland in the 1973 World Series, Andrews made two twelfth-inning errors that enabled the Mets to win the second game. When owner Charlie Finley then attempted to have the infielder declare himself physically unfit for the rest of the Series and to replace him on the roster with Manny Trillo, Athletic manager Dick Williams announced that, win or lose, he intended quitting as soon as the season was over. Even though Commissioner Bowie Kuhn turned thumbs down to Finley's ploy, the Oakland players showed their resentment of the owner by having the infielder's number sewn on their uniforms for the rest of the Series.

JOAQUIN ANDUJAR

Andujar saw vague conspiracies against him everywhere, but the one time he pointed a finger produced one of the ugliest incidents in postseason play. A journeyman for most of his thirteen-year (1976–88) career, the right-hander became a 20-game winner in 1984 and 1985 after Cardinal manager Whitey Herzog let him pitch on three days' rest; tiring toward the end of the latter season, he was ineffective in the League Championship Series against the Dodgers and was reduced to mopping up in the final Series game, with the Royals holding a commanding lead. Walking the first batter he faced and giving up a hit to the next, the Dominican decided to blame his—and the Cardinals'—fate on home plate umpire Don Denkinger, who had blown a ninth-inning call at first base the day before that had ultimately given Kansas City the game. Denkinger tossed both the pitcher and Herzog, but not before the former threw a tantrum on the mound. Herzog later blasted the hurler, and was quick to deal him to the Athletics in the off-season.

Playing out the string with Oakland and Houston over the next four seasons, Andujar continually blamed his decline on a "conspiracy" against him but never went into any detail. In fact, he suffered a severe injury while taking batting practice for the American League team, for which he would never bat under game conditions.

PETER ANGELOS

A Baltimore attorney who specialized in defending labor unions and pursuing workers' disability claims, Angelos headed the consortium that purchased the Orioles from the bankrupt Eli Jacobs in 1993 for $173 million. His high-profile partners included novelist Tom Clancy, film director Barry Levinson, sportscaster Jim McKay, and tennis player Pam Shriver. Described by some as the Steinbrenner-in-the-making and by others as the second coming of Charlie Finley, Angelos refused to sign the September 1994 owners' declaration that formally ended the season after the players' strike. According to the long-time defender of workers' rights, charges in the

document by his fellow owners that the players had not bargained seriously were "counterproductive." On the other hand, he made life miserable for manager Johnny Oates prior to the end of the season, and wasted little time in discharging him once play had stopped for the year. Angelos has also come under fire for listening too much to his young sons in formulating Orioles policy.

CAP ANSON (Hall of Fame, 1939)

Anson was to nineteenth-century field managers what Al Spalding was to club owners of the same era—coldly efficient, militarily strict, and highly successful. The fates of the two men were intertwined for the first decade and a half of the National League's existence: It was, in fact, only when the pitcher-turned-magnate withdrew from active involvement in the affairs of the Chicago club after the 1891 season that the first baseman-manager's fortunes began to decline.

Cap Anson was the soul—and spleen—of the Cubs for two decades. National Baseball Library, Cooperstown, N.Y.

Anson's jump from the National Association Philadelphia Athletics to Chicago paralleled Spalding's from the Boston Red Stockings in the events leading up to the founding of the National League in 1876. A right-handed batter, he won three batting championships, became the first major leaguer to record 3,000 hits (in comparatively short seasons), and finished with a lifetime average of .329. Anson was also durable, serving as a regular for all twenty-two of his National League seasons (in addition to five in the NA). He is the oldest major leaguer to hit a grand slam, knocking in 4 runs with one clout in July 1894 at age forty-two, and the second-oldest—at age forty-five—to hit a home run at all, connecting for two on October 3, 1897, the last day of his career.

After succeeding Spalding as manager in 1879, Anson won five pennants; compiled a .632 won-lost percentage during the 1880s; and was among the first to use more than one pitcher, employ the hit-and-run, and formalize spring training routines. A resolute disciplinarian, he barred even Spalding from the clubhouse when he thought necessary, and enforced his rules with fists. A temperance enthusiast, the manager administered a no-drinking pledge to the entire team in the owner's office in 1886. Anson was also a clever promoter, often dressing his players in outfits ranging from Native American garb to formal wear, and parading them through the streets of National League cities in open carriages to irritate local fans and stimulate them to buy tickets to the day's game. The extent of the public's identification of Anson with the franchise can be measured by the changes in its nicknames, from the traditional White Stockings to Colts when he launched a youth movement in 1886, and to Orphans after he left the team following the 1897 season.

The event that turned the Colts into Orphans was the accession to the club presidency of James Hart in 1892. Anson never got along with his new boss, so much so that he had refused to contribute toward the purchase of diamond cuff links Spalding had given Hart for handling travel arrangements on a goodwill world tour of ballplayers after the 1888 season; it didn't help, either, that the team had twice as many losing seasons as winning ones after Hart took over from Spalding.

Fired after the 1897 season, Anson indignantly refused Hart's offer to hold a benefit game for him. Out of organized baseball after a three-week stint as Giant manager in 1898, he then dabbled in the formation of abortive new leagues (the New American Association, of which he was briefly president in 1900, and the United States League in 1914); politics (he was elected city clerk of Chicago in 1905, but left office two years later under a cloud of financial scandal); and writing (his autobiography denouncing players who had sabotaged him and owners who had betrayed him). Especially after his political career ended, Anson fell on hard times, but nonetheless refused NL president John Tener's offer of a pension with the same scorn he had shown toward Hart's charity game.

Anson's literary endeavor confirmed the racist he was. He had been involved in a pair of ugly episodes in the 1880s, refusing to let his team take the field against clubs that included black players Fleet Walker and George Stovey. His memoir referred to Clarence Duval, the mascot and clown who was part of the 1888–89 world tour, as a "chocolate-covered coon" and a "no-account nigger."

JOHNNY ANTONELLI

Antonelli was the first of the postwar bonus babies to blossom into a star. After being carried on the Braves' roster for an obligatory two years and then being sent out for seasoning, he returned to the team in 1953 to win 12 games. But just when the club was on the verge of profiting from its initial investment of a $65,000 bonus, it swapped the left-hander to the Giants for Bobby Thomson. Antonelli proceeded to lead New York to the pennant in 1954 with 21 wins and a league-leading 2.30 ERA.

LUIS APARICIO (Hall of Fame, 1984)

Aparicio's eighteen-year (1956–73) career has generated more than one misconception. It is not true, for instance, that the right-hand-hitting shortstop, who spent most of his glory years with the White Sox, was the ideal leadoff man; on the contrary, he batted more than .280 only once, drew more than 53 walks only once, and had an overall on-base average of only .313. On the other hand, he was no mere spear-carrier in the revival of the running game in the late 1950s and early 1960s; years before Maury Wills appeared on the scene, the Venezuelan speedster broke all existing records by leading the American League in stolen bases in his first nine big league seasons. And although he ended up with fewer career steals than Wills, he also had a better success rate (79 percent to 77 percent).

In the field, Aparicio was the Ozzie Smith of his day, establishing career marks for assists and double plays along the way to nine Gold Gloves. Some of that achievement was due to his hardiness, since he played in at least 100 games in every one of his eighteen seasons. Another part of it was due to his longtime Chicago partner, second baseman Nellie Fox, the other half of Aparicio's double-play record. As key members of the 1959 Go-Go Sox, Aparicio and Fox regularly fashioned the wins of their pennant-bound club with little more than a single and stolen base by the shortstop, a ground ball to the right side by the second baseman, a sacrifice fly, and then nine innings of vacuum-cleaning defense. Aparicio provided some of the same leadership with the world champion 1966 Orioles. Ironically, however, he also literally fell down on the job with the 1972 Red Sox, when carrying a decisive run in late September, he flopped in the third-base coach's box, killing a rally, and dooming Boston to a second-place, half-game finish behind Detroit.

LUKE APPLING (Hall of Fame, 1964)

Before Ernie Banks came along, Appling was Chicago's most exasperated player—toiling for twenty years (between 1930 and 1950) as the shortstop for the White Sox without getting closer to the World Series than a couple of third-place finishes. As Comiskey Park's only consistent offensive light for two decades, however, he compiled a .310 batting average, going over the .300 mark 16 times. In 1936, the right-handed slap hitter reached a peak of .388, winning the batting title in a duel with Cleveland's Earl Averill by going 4-for-4 on the final day of the season; Appling took another batting crown in 1943. Although he never hit more than eight home runs in a season, his

.388 mark in 1936 sent 128 runners across the plate.

To the chagrin of the Comiskeys and other American League owners, Appling was as proficient at fouling off balls as he was at dropping them between opposition fielders. On one occasion he retaliated against Washington owner Clark Griffith's refusal to cough up passes for a group of friends by fouling off an estimated sixteen consecutive pitches into the grandstand at Griffith Stadium. On another occasion, Detroit hurler Dizzy Trout became so incensed at having more than a dozen deliveries wasted that he fired his glove at Appling in the batter's box. Defensively, Appling was so raw at shortstop when he came up that manager Lew Fonseca pressed the front office to deal him away. Mainly because the club didn't have a feasible alternative, he remained where he was, going on to lead the AL in assists seven years in a row and maintaining enough range that, in 1949 at age forty-two, he became the oldest starting shortstop in baseball history.

Appling's nickname of Old Aches and Pains derived in part from hypochondria and in part from rooming for many years with the White Sox trainer; in fact, the only serious injury he ever suffered was a broken leg in 1938. As a follow-up to the bizarre 1964 trade between Detroit and Cleveland of managers Jimmy Dykes and Joe Gordon, Appling and Jo-Jo White were also swapped in the first recorded exchange of coaches. Playing in the Cracker Jack All-Star Game of Old Timers at Washington's Robert F. Kennedy Stadium in 1984, Appling clouted a 275-foot home run into the left-field seats off Warren Spahn, thereby equaling or topping his long-ball production for eleven of his twenty seasons in a Chicago uniform. When he hit the ball, Appling was seventy-seven years old.

GEORGE ARGYROS

A California and Idaho real-estate tycoon, Argyros was a Charlie Finley without the imagination. Practically from the day that he bought the Mariners in 1981, he laid siege to the city of Seattle with complaints that he was nearing bankruptcy and threats to move the team. What he was mainly after was a bigger share of the proceeds from the Kingdome and an escape clause in his contract that would permit him to uproot the club without fear of lawsuits. In 1985 he achieved both objectives when King County buckled under. For the next couple of years he continued his threats to relocate, at one point even (prematurely) announcing that he was going to buy the Padres. He eventually sold the team to the Emmis Broadcasting Company in August 1989 at a tidy profit.

BUZZ ARLETT

Selected the premier minor league player of all time by the Society for American Baseball Research, Arlett's atrocious fielding limited his big league career to only one season. In nineteen seasons in the high minors between 1918 and 1937, the switch-hitter batted .341 and clouted 432 homers. (Having begun as a pitcher with the Pacific Coast League Oakland Oaks, he also won 108 games in his first five seasons.) While with the International League Baltimore Orioles in 1932, he twice knocked four home runs in a game.

Finally given a berth in the majors with the Phillies in 1931, Arlett hit .313 with 18 homers. But manager Burt Shotton kept looking for a place to hide his leaden glove and lack of range by moving him from the outfield to first base to a pinch-hitting role before finally giving up and letting him drift back to the minors.

HAROLD ARLIN

On August 5, 1921, Arlin became baseball's first play-by-play man when Pittsburgh radio station KDKA carried his broadcast, from a Forbes Field box seat, of an 8–5 Pirate win over the Phillies.

LIZZIE ARLINGTON

Taught to pitch by Boston hurler Jack Stivetts, Arlington became the first woman to appear for a professional team, in 1898, when Ed Barrow, president of the minor Atlantic League, hired her for exhibition games in several league cities. Born Lizzie Stroud, she chose what she considered a less humdrum name for her efforts to boost attendance during the doldrums of the Spanish-American War.

BOB ASBJORNSON

A backup catcher for the 1932 Reds, Asbjornson was given a day in his honor by fellow natives of Concord, Massachusetts, during a team trip to Boston. After receiving a hefty check in pregame ceremonies, he celebrated by hitting his only major league home run. After the game he discovered that the check had not been signed. When he brought it to the restaurant where he was due to be honored with more festivities, he discovered that no one had showed up.

RICHIE ASHBURN

Because he lacked the power of such National League contemporaries as Willie Mays and Duke Snider, Ashburn rarely received his due as one of the preeminent center fielders of the 1950s; a similar neglect has stymied his election to the Hall of Fame. A lifetime .308 hitter who occupied the leadoff spot for the Phillies from 1948 to 1959, the lefty swinger captured NL batting titles in 1955 and 1958, led the league by collecting 200 hits in three seasons, and paced the circuit twice in triples and four times in walks. His career 1,198 bases on balls and 2,574 hits fed a fifteen-year on-base percentage of .397. Defensively, Ashburn established the outfield records for most years (nine) with 400 or more putouts and most years (four) with 500 or more. But his single most important fielding play was an assist—in the final game of the 1950 season, when he snatched a single by Brooklyn's Snider and threw out Cal Abrams at the plate to cut down a run that would have forced a pennant playoff the following day; instead, the throw put Philadelphia in position to take the flag with Dick Sisler's three-run home run in the tenth inning.

Ashburn wound up his career with the first-year expansion Mets in 1962 by batting .306. He is the last regular to retire following a .300 season.

EMMETT ASHFORD

Ashford was the first black to umpire in the major leagues. Hired by the American League in 1966 after extensive minor league service, he lasted five seasons, just long enough to qualify for a pension. Theatrical in the performance of his duties and equally showy in his attire, Ashford nonetheless kept to himself off the field, rarely socializing with his fellow arbiters.

DAVE AUGUSTINE

Augustine never homered in 29 major league at bats, but he came legendarily close on September 20, 1973. Batting against the Mets in the top of the thirteenth inning, the Pittsburgh outfielder hit what appeared to be a tie-breaking round-tripper, only to have the ball bounce on the top of the fence and back into left fielder Cleon Jones's glove. Jones and third baseman Wayne Garrett relayed the ball home to nab runner Richie Zisk to end the inning. When New York won the game in the bottom of the inning and went on to win the division, Augustine's non-home run was pointed to as the turning point for the club.

GENE AUTRY

Autry stumbled into the ownership of the Angels in 1960, and he hasn't regained his feet yet. At the same time, his image of the genial

Gene Autry rode his early career as The Singing Cowboy into a broadcasting fortune and ownership of the California Angels. Photo compliments of Gene Autry.

singing cowboy of Hollywood and "Rudolph the Red-Nosed Reindeer" fame has succeeded in shifting all of the blame for the club's failure to reach a World Series on a parade of inept front office people and overrated players. In fact, before being forced by age to surrender practical boardroom control of the franchise to his second wife, Jackie, at the beginning of the 1990s, Autry was behind a series of chaotic management decisions that alternated between overpaying aging free agents and rushing untried rookies into the lineup. Little of this responsibility has been reflected in the annual *mea culpas* by managers and players that they had once again failed to win a pennant for the beloved cowboy.

Autry took over the expansion Angels through a broadcast contract he had signed with a consortium headed by Hank Greenberg, the originally projected owner of the new American League team. When other owners rejected the bid of the Greenberg group (mainly because it included the flamboyant Bill Veeck), Autry and partner Bob Reynolds were talked into moving in. Reflecting both his Hollywood career and a need to outheadline the market rival Dodgers, he has usually been open to players with marquee value, even if their activities off the field (for instance, Bo Belinsky) outstripped their talents between the lines. Decisions of this kind inevitably led to managers and general managers coming and going, with each new administration promising a reversal of the previous one's policies and the long-sought World Series victory for Autry.

EARL AVERILL (Hall of Fame, 1975)

Averill took one of the quieter walks into Cooperstown after a thirteen-year career in which he batted .318 with 238 home runs. One reason for the right-hand-hitting outfielder's low profile was that he spent most of his major league service with the also-ran Cleveland clubs of the 1930s. Another was that, aside from setting the pace in hits and triples in 1936, he never led the American League in any significant offensive category. On the other hand, he was in double figures in home runs in every one of his ten full seasons with the Indians. On April 16, 1929, he also became the first AL player to homer in his first big league at bat. Averill's most conspicuous foray into controversy occurred during the 1935 season, when he went up against the majority of his teammates in seeking support for unpopular manager Walter Johnson. Fans stirred up by daily reports of Johnson's dictatorial ways let loose with a couple of bottles against the outfielder, and he was booed unmercifully until Johnson was replaced.

BOBBY AVILA

Avila's 1954 batting average of .341 won him a Silver Bat, but it was tarnished by the fact that Boston outfielder Ted Williams hit .345 while falling short of the required number of at-bats. (A rule in effect between 1952 and 1956 required a hitter to have 2.6 official at-bats for every game his team played; Williams, having walked 136 times, came up 14 shy of the requirement.) In the World Series that year, the Cleveland second baseman faced off against National League leader Willie Mays of the Giants in the last such appearance of both leagues' batting champions.

After an eleven-year (1949–59) career, Avila returned to his native Mexico, where he served as mayor of Vera Cruz and commissioner of the Mexican League.

JOSÉ AZCUE

Catcher Azcue is the last major leaguer to sit out an entire season in protest over a contract offer. After working for a construction firm during the 1971 season, he settled his differences with the Angels and came back for the final campaign of his eleven-year career in 1972.

B

CARLOS BAERGA

On April 8, 1993, Cleveland second baseman Baerga became the only major leaguer to hit home runs from both sides of the plate in the same inning.

BILL BAILEY

Bailey is one of only two pitchers to endure ten consecutive losing seasons in the major leagues. After winning 4 and losing only 1 for the Browns in his rookie season of 1907, he never again got above .500, while laboring for the Baltimore Terrapins and Chicago Whales of the Federal League, the Tigers, and the Cardinals. The southpaw's lifetime record was 37-76. (The hurler who matched this feat was Ron Kline, in the 1950s and 1960s.)

HAROLD BAINES

On May 9, 1984, Baines ended the longest night game in major league history when he clouted a home run against Milwaukee in the twenty-fifth inning. The game, which began May 8 and went to a seventeen-inning, 6–6 tie before being suspended for resumption the next day, lasted eight hours and six minutes. A lefty-hitting outfielder who held most of Chicago's power records prior to Carlton Fisk, Baines was at the center of a controversial trade in 1989 in which he was packed off to Texas for outfielder Sammy Sosa, infielder Scott Fletcher, and pitcher Wilson Alvarez. White Sox owner Jerry Reinsdorf was so skeptical of the deal worked out by general manager Larry Himes that he embarrassed his

own front office executive when the Rangers came to Comiskey Park later in the season by staging ceremonies for the retirement of Baines's number.

DUSTY BAKER

Baker established the victory record for rookie managers in 1993 when his San Francisco Giants won 103 games. During his nineteen-year (1968–86) playing career, the right-hand-hitting outfielder was part of the only club quartet whose members each hit 30 home runs in a season. As a member of the 1977 Dodgers, Baker waited until his final at-bat on the last day of the season before clouting the round-tripper that allowed him to join Ron Cey, Steve Garvey, and Reggie Smith.

FRANK BAKER (Hall of Fame, 1955)

A deadball-era slugger, Baker led the American League in home runs in four consecutive seasons (1911–14) without ever compiling more than a dozen in one year; the lefty-swinging third baseman earned the nickname of Home Run for round-trippers he clouted to win the second game and to tie the third game of the 1911 World Series for the Athletics. Part of Connie Mack's $100,000 infield that helped win four pennants between 1910 and 1914, Baker batted .307 in a thirteen-year career while leading the AL in RBIs twice and triples once. After the 1914 season Baker flirted with the Federal League in an effort to get Mack to match the money the Feds were promising. Rebuffed by the Philadelphia owner-manager,

Baker sat out the 1915 season at his Maryland farm. Sold to the Yankees, he spent four seasons in New York before retiring again, to nurse his terminally ill wife, then returned for two final seasons, in 1921 and 1922, before calling it quits for a third and final time.

WILLIAM BAKER

A former New York City police commissioner, Baker ran the Phillies from 1913 to 1930—ran them right into the ground. As habitually hungry for quick cash as he was addicted to collecting every negative item ever published about one of his players for use in contract negotiations, he reduced the franchise to such straits that the club became known as the Phoolish Phillies. Particularly toward the end of his ownership reign, gamblers refused to take bets on the team unless they were wagers on their margin of defeat. The cigar box that became known as Baker Bowl was allowed to degenerate to the point that foul balls striking stadium beams released showers of rust on the stands below; fortunately for Baker and the organization's lawyers, there were seldom fans sitting in the lower stands to instigate lawsuits. As for the occasional star players who wore a Philadelphia uniform, they were viewed as good only for what money they would bring in sales to other clubs. In one of Baker's more notorious moves, he ordered that a screen be added to Baker Bowl's short right-field porch so that future Hall of Famer Chuck Klein wouldn't be able to break Babe Ruth's home run record and hold him up for a substantial raise. Not content with selling off his players, Baker also enlisted some sportswriter cronies to spread rumors that he had been forced into some deals because those departing had been acting ''suspiciously'' on the field. The suggestion in 1921 that traded outfielder Irish Meusel and fired manager Bill Donovan had been on the take finally forced Commissioner Kenesaw Landis to conduct an investigation and, after finding no grounds for suspecting anything illegal, to blast Baker publicly for inspiring the gossip. Baker died of a heart attack in December 1930 amid indications that other owners, tired of their paltry receipts from Philadelphia, were about to force him to sell the club.

LADY BALDWIN

Baldwin, who got his nickname because he neither smoked, swore, nor swilled, was less than delicate with opponents in 1886, when, pitching for the Detroit Wolverines, he set the National League season record of 42 victories by a left-hander. His dazzling fastball was attributable to his hop-skip-and-jump delivery, similar to that of a cricket bowler. The following year, confronted by new rules limiting hurlers to one step from a fixed position, he dropped to 13 victories and thereafter never again won in double figures.

NEAL BALL

Cleveland shortstop Ball made the major leagues' first officially recognized unassisted triple play, against the Red Sox, on July 19, 1909; in the previous year, while a member of the Yankees, he had committed 81 errors for a fielding percentage of .897, the worst figures in the majors in 1908.

PHIL BALL

A manufacturer of cold-storage units, Ball was among the first baseball owners to bring a personal fortune to the game; he also brought with him a penchant for litigation. A minor league player until he lost the use of his left hand in a Louisiana knife fight, Ball became one of the beneficiaries of the Federal League war when he swallowed a $182,000 loss, folded the St. Louis Terriers along with the rest of the FL after the 1915 season, and bought the Browns for another $250,000. His wealth, lavished on the Browns over eighteen years, provided the luxury of remaining essentially a fan with a very expensive hobby. After a nail-biting victory in May 1922, for example, he remonstrated with traveling secretary Willis Johnson for bothering him with ''unimportant details'' like the $12,000 visitors share of the gate.

In 1917 Ball lost his general manager, Branch Rickey, to the rival National League Cardinals, but not before getting an injunction compelling Rickey to honor his five-year contract by serving one additional day. With his next operations chief, Ball was a victim of his own generosity when Bob Quinn took a bonus handed him after a second-place finish in 1922 and invested it in a part ownership of the Red Sox. While the owner stayed, for the most part, out of personnel matters, he released one player for having breakfast in bed, because "I don't have time to eat breakfast in bed; he shouldn't either." On another occasion, Ball came to regret a remark that Doc Lavan and Del Pratt had deliberately lost a 1917 game against the White Sox, when the double-play combination sued him for $50,000. The matter was settled only through the intervention of American League president Ban Johnson and the subsequent trade of both players; ten years later, when Swede Risberg and other Black Sox were tossing around allegations about games thrown during the 1917 season, Ball went so far as to deny his earlier suspicions.

It was for Commissioner Kenesaw Landis that Ball reserved his most irascible moments. The animosity between the two dated to Landis's inattention, as a federal judge, to a lawsuit filed by the Federal League against the two older circuits, and was so intense that the owner refused to sign the judge's appointment as baseball commissioner, leaving Quinn to represent the Browns in the matter. The enmity reached its peak in 1930, two years before Ball's death, when he became the only owner ever to question Landis's powers in court, ostensibly over the Browns' right to keep outfielder Fred Bennett in the minor leagues but more generally over his right to run his business as he saw fit; the challenge was abandoned before the possibility that it would lead to the overturning of baseball's antitrust exemption.

DAVE BANCROFT (Hall of Fame, 1971)

Bancroft was known as Beauty for his agile shortstop play, but he was also a beautiful example of the way the Giants put a good face on their practical control of the Braves for many years. After three sparkling years in the Polo Grounds defensively and offensively (.318, .321, and .304), the man described by John McGraw as "the best shortstop in baseball" was dealt to Boston so he could manage the New England club. According to McGraw, the gift was made in the interests of "helping Matty"—the ailing Christy Mathewson, who had been installed as Boston president. What the New York manager did not say was that Bancroft's departure also gained the Giants outfielder

Billy Southworth; made room for Travis Jackson at the Polo Grounds; and, not least, assured more dubious trades between the two clubs for a few more years. Somewhat predictably, Bancroft went on to further good years in the field and at the plate, but found himself without the players necessary to raise the Braves above the nether regions. He concluded his sixteen-year (1915–30) career with a .279 average.

FRANK BANCROFT

Bancroft, who spent forty-three years as a manager and executive with major and minor league teams, introduced baseball to Latin America when he led the International League Worcester club on a tour of Cuba in 1879. The following year, when the same Brown Stockings entered the National League, Bancroft assumed the reins of the first of his record seven major league teams. While managing Providence in 1883, he conducted the first spring training for a major league club, taking the Grays to Washington, D.C. On September 18, 1893, as business manager of Cincinnati, a post he held for twenty-nine years, he persuaded groundskeeper Louis Rapp and Rosie Smith to be the principals in the first wedding ceremony performed at home plate. Bancroft also convinced baseball officialdom that Cincinnati, in tribute to the pre-NL Red Stockings, should have exclusive rights to play the first game of each season—a practice that generally lasted until 1994.

DAN BANKHEAD

Bankhead was the first black pitcher in the major leagues, debuting for the Dodgers on August 8, 1947. He was belted around, but emerged without a loss and also returned some of the favor with a home run in his first at-bat. The right-hander returned to Ebbets Field in 1950, when he won nine games, but most of the victories were slugfests that he was fortunate to survive.

SAM BANKHEAD

Bankhead was the first black to manage in organized baseball, piloting the Farnham club in the Class C Provincial League to a seventh-place finish in 1951. The brother of Dan, he also played shortstop for Farnham and had managed the all-black Homestead Grays in 1949 and 1950.

ERNIE BANKS (Hall of Fame, 1977)

Banks's most noted frustration—that he holds the record for most games (2,528) without ever appearing in a World Series—was shared in more than one way by the city of Chicago: He is also the only one to have made 2,000 appearances for a single team without a World Series.

Arriving in Wrigley Field with Gene Baker in 1953 as the Cubs' first blacks, Banks never again managed the .314 he averaged in a handful of at-bats that year, but started instead to demolish most of the franchise's power records. In thirteen campaigns he hit at least 20 homers, topping the 40 mark five times, and he drove in 100 runs in eight seasons. In 1958 and 1959 he won back-to-back MVP awards despite the fact that Chicago finished in fifth place both years. Indicative of his standing on the 1959 club, his league-leading 143 RBIs were 91 more than runner-up Bobby Thomson—the biggest such gap ever recorded between teammates. After doing most of his damage as a shortstop over his first nine years, he took his slower reflexes over to first base for the remainder of his career. Never quite the hitter he had been while turning the double play in the middle of the infield, he still managed three more years of 100-plus RBIs.

Already thirty-eight when the Cubs got their first real taste of a pennant race, in 1969, Banks performed ably enough to drive in 101 runs, but was also a key illustration of criticisms that Leo Durocher's insistence on playing his regulars every day ultimately cost the club the division title to the Miracle Mets. Durocher's defense was that Banks, in particular, continually came to him asking for rest, but then turned around to reporters and questioned why he was on the bench whenever the manager acceded to his requests.

Banks was voted the greatest player in franchise history for his 512 home runs and 1,636 RBIs. But however popular he was for his "Let's play two" attitude, Mr. Cub, as he came to be known, found himself on the outs for a while with the *Chicago Tribune* ownership that succeeded the Wrigley family, because of the organization's desire to become less identified with its losing years.

RED BARBER

Barber made baseball a game for the imagination as much as for the diamond. Brought to Cincinnati by Larry MacPhail in 1934, he was vital to exploding the prevailing wisdom that broadcasting games would devastate attendance. More than delivering basic radio play-by-play, Barber used his down-home twang and dry humor to underline the game's dramatic values and to personalize players who had remained little more than tin heroes or lifeless statistics in the sportswriting of the era. The consequences were twofold: an empathy by listeners who were able to project themselves into his detailed descriptions of field action, and a more human identification by the audience with the players involved in the action.

When MacPhail moved to Brooklyn in 1938, Barber went with him, immediately establishing the depth of his appeal by having even the crustier fans of the East accept such folksy phrases as "the rhubarb patch" (a field argument), "the catbird seat" (an advantageous situation), and "tearin' up the pea patch" (scoring runs in a batch). So sure was MacPhail of the Barber weapon that he unilaterally broke an agreement with the Yankees and Giants not to broadcast home games. While in Brooklyn, Barber also called the plays for the first televised game (August 26, 1939) and the first game televised in color (August 10, 1951). He also conducted the first televised player interview, getting Cincinnati pitcher Bucky Walters to demonstrate how he gripped various pitches.

Because of Barber's southern background, Branch Rickey used him as an early sounding board for gauging reaction to the decision of breaking the color barrier with Jackie Robinson. Barber had a much less confidential relationship with the Walter O'Malley regime that succeeded Rickey, and ended up leaving the Dodgers after O'Malley threw him a take-it-or-leave-it offer for taking on extra broadcasting duties in the 1953 World Series. For twelve years he worked in the Yankees' broadcasting booth, but that relationship also came to a brusque end when, on the last day of the 1966 season, he told the cameraman to pan the empty seats of Yankee Stadium to underline a point that bad teams did not draw fans.

CARL BARGER

For a brief period in 1992, Barger was the first executive since the dawn of the century who saw nothing wrong with heading the operations of two clubs simultaneously. Named as president of the expansion Marlins, he nevertheless held on to his presidency of the Pirates for some months with the argument that the Florida club was not due to take the field until 1993. Under pressure from other club owners who saw something questionable in an official making draft calculations for one team while sitting in the suite of another, Commissioner Fay Vincent finally insisted that Barger resign from Pittsburgh. Barger was felled by a fatal heart attack only hours before the expansion draft in the fall of 1992.

SAM BARKLEY

An infielder of modest talents, Barkley's efforts to escape from Chris Von der Ahe's St. Louis Brown Stockings in 1885 led to the firing of American Association president Denny McKnight and to the defection of the Pittsburgh Alleghenys to the National League. The trouble started when Von der Ahe agreed to trade the player to both Baltimore and Pittsburgh, and the second baseman signed contracts with both teams. The AA then stepped in to fine Barkley (but not Von der Ahe) and suspend him for the 1886 season on charges of ''dishonorable conduct.'' When league president and Pittsburgh stockholder McKnight rejected the recommendation, and Barkley, for his part, threatened to sue, the AA called another meeting, this time intending to censor its chief executive and discipline the player. McKnight foiled the plan by neglecting to inform Barkley of the second meeting and, pleading illness, failing to show up himself. The outcome was an out-of-court settlement that included a heftier fine, but no suspension, for Barkley; compensation in the form of an equally mediocre player for the Orioles; and a pink slip for McKnight. Within the year, the Alleghenys jumped to the NL.

AL BARLICK (Hall of Fame, 1989)

Barlick is the Red Schoendienst of umpires among Cooperstown residents. A competent but hardly influential National League arbiter for fourteen years between 1940 and 1955, he was voted a plaque by the Veterans Committee in the same year as the equally sturdy but unremarkable Schoendienst. Both elections prompted increased calls for the dissolution of the Veterans' Committee and the end of the cronyism involved in its annual selections.

ERNEST BARNARD

Barnard was baseball's first enthusiast for articulated working agreements between major league clubs and minor league organizations. As Cleveland vice president in 1910, a full decade before Branch Rickey turned the system into a science, he sold owner Charles Somers on the idea of concluding pacts with minor-level clubs in New Orleans, Toledo, Portland (Oregon), Waterbury (Connecticut), and Ironton (Ohio). Somers eventually had to pull out of the agreements, and then out of the Indians altogether, because of financial problems. Barnard himself remained in the hierarchy of the franchise as either vice president or president until 1927, but never again had access to Somers's kind of capital to return to his idea.

Barnard was also elected American League president in 1928, after the death of Ban Johnson, and served in that office until his own death in 1931.

DON BARNES

Barnes's ten years as principal owner of the Browns included the worst of times and the best of times; in between, only a world war prevented him from abandoning St. Louis and introducing major league baseball to the West Coast.

When the executors of the estate of Phil Ball offered a $25,000 bounty in 1936 for anyone who came up with a buyer for the franchise, Branch Rickey, the rival Cardinals' operations chief, proposed Barnes. The president of American Investment Company of Illinois, he teamed with longtime Browns employee Bill DeWitt to head a syndicate that took over the club for $325,000. Within three years, the never-too-successful club reached its nadir, finishing the 1939 season with a franchise-worst 43–111 record, a staggering 64½ games behind the pennant-winning Yankees. Finances were so desperate by the end of the decade that keeping the outfield grass trim became the responsibility of a goat.

When other American League clubs voiced concern in 1940 that they couldn't recoup their travel and hotel expenses for trips to St. Louis, league president Will Harridge suggested that the owners "go a little socialistic for their own good," and each sell a player to the Browns for $7,500. By this means, Barnes picked up an aging Eldon Auker, whose 16 wins made him the staff ace, and outfielder Walt Judnich, whose .303 average and 24 homers provided the club's only offensive threat. Not only did the organization go on the dole, but also individual players, strapped by paltry salaries, received off-season unemployment compensation of $15 a week. By the end of the 1941 season Barnes was forced to strip the franchise bare, abandoning five farm clubs and firing the entire scouting staff; this in turn dropped the value of club stock to 40 percent of Barnes's original purchase price. The AL had to intervene with a $25,000 loan to meet operating expenses.

Then, in early December, Barnes orchestrated a shift of the franchise to Los Angeles for the 1942 season. Cubs owner Phil Wrigley agreed to surrender not only his territorial rights to the California city but also his minor league park there. Anticipating improved road attendance, other AL owners gleefully agreed to the move; Barnes had a schedule drawn up including Los Angeles and priced the cost of air transportation to the West Coast for all teams; Cardinals owner Sam Breadon indicated a willingness to cough up cash and speed the Browns on their way so he could have St. Louis all to himself. All that was required was official ratification of the move at the AL's annual meeting on December 8. The bombing of Pearl Harbor the day before exploded the transfer plans.

Trapped in St. Louis, Barnes sold a controlling interest in the club to Richard Muckerman, head of the St. Louis Fuel and Ice Company, for $300,000, reducing himself to the position of minority partner. He nevertheless remained as club president long enough to be titular head of the team when it won its only pennant, in 1944.

ROSS BARNES

The National League's first superstar, Barnes was also the first player to sue his team. After leading the National League with a .429 average in 1876, he dropped to .272 in 1877 after the banning of his specialty, the fair-foul hit (a ball driven into fair territory just in front of home plate and spinning into foul ground out of the reach of defensemen). More devastating, however, was a muscular disorder that kept Barnes out of all but 22 of Chicago's 59 games. When club owner William Hulbert refused to pay his erstwhile star $1,000 of his $2,500 salary for the year, Barnes brought suit. He lost when a Chicago court ruled that no employer was obligated to pay for undelivered services.

CLYDE BARNHART

Pittsburgh third baseman Barnhart is the only major leaguer to hit safely in three games in one day. He did it against Cincinnati on October 2, 1920, in the last major league tripleheader.

GEORGE BARR

Barr was a National League umpire who, in 1943, made the mistake of calling a balk against the frequently hysterical Johnny Allen. Before the Brooklyn hurler could be pulled off him, Barr had almost choked from the way Allen was wrapping his tie around his throat. Largely because of the attack, ties were soon afterward dropped from umpiring garb.

Barr also opened the first umpiring school, in 1935.

JIM BARR

With San Francisco in 1972, Barr retired forty-one consecutive batters over two games for a big league record. Neither game was a no-hitter. The right-hander was otherwise known for his questionable taste in personal antagonists. As a member of the Angels in 1979, he got into a brawl with liquored-up broadcaster Don Drysdale after the onetime Dodger star had accused him of dogging it during California's American League Championship Series loss to Baltimore. Back with the Giants in 1983, he responded to being lifted from a game by flipping the ball to manager Frank Robinson and starting off the mound; Robinson grabbed him by the shirt and lifted him back to the hill with some words about mound decorum. Despite early indications that he would be the anchor of the San Francisco staff for the 1970s, Barr never won more than 15 games in a season and ended with a 101–112 record.

ED BARROW (Hall of Fame, 1953)

As manager of the Red Sox in 1918, Barrow converted Babe Ruth from the ace of his pitching staff to the most significant weapon in his offensive arsenal; as general manager of the Yankees, he reaped the full benefit of his move. After a successful career as a minor league manager, club owner, and league president (during which he discovered Honus Wagner), as well as a less successful season and a half as pilot of the Tigers, Barrow managed the Red Sox to a pennant in 1918, with Ruth's slugging leading the way. Ambivalent about what he had wrought, Barrow put himself on record first as fearing a lynching if he converted the best left-hander in baseball to an outfielder, then as insisting that Ruth should have batted .400 instead of swatting all those four-base blasts.

With the sale of Ruth to New York in 1920, Barrow realized that there was little in Boston's future but debts followed by more player sales, and, deciding he would rather be on the buying than the selling end, moved into the top job in the New York front office before the 1921 season. Within two months he had dipped back into the Boston well to come up with future Hall of Fame right-hander Waite Hoyt, catcher Wally Schang, shortstop Everett Scott, and pitchers Joe Bush and Sam Jones; he would return to the same source several times over the next year for third baseman Joe Dugan, righty George Pipgras, and Hall of Fame southpaw Herb Pennock. The immediate dividends were three consecutive pennants and dominance of the American League for a decade.

When the supply of Boston players dried up, Barrow brought in George Weiss in 1932 to head a farm system to be modeled on Branch Rickey's minor league chain for the Cardinals. Expensive as this player development system was, it led to

the next great Yankee era, in which the club won seven pennants between 1936 and 1943. Overall under Barrow's direction, the Yankees won fourteen pennants and ten World Series in twenty-five years. In 1940 there might have been a fifteenth flag, and an unprecedented eight in a row by 1943, but for Barrow's unwillingness to tarnish the Yankee image by admitting that the team needed the services of rookie Ernie Bonham. Finally promoted from the minors in August, the right-hander put together a 9–3 record, but New York finished third, only two games behind first-place Detroit.

As lavish as he was with owner Jacob Ruppert's money in developing and obtaining players, Barrow was equally stingy in doling it out to the same players. Basing his negotiating strategy on a conviction that underpaid players would hunger more for a World Series check, he would sit in a tattered sweater and offer take-it-or-leave-it deals. He drummed shortstop Leo Durocher not only off the Yankees but also out of the AL for daring to ask for a raise in 1929. He even insisted that Joe DiMaggio take a cut in salary out of wartime patriotism after having hit in 56 consecutive games in 1941.

As humorless and unimaginative as he was penurious, Barrow opposed virtually every innovation (except the farm system) that came along, spurning night ball and promotions as unnecessary for a winning club. This attitude made the arrival of champion promoter Larry MacPhail as his new boss in 1945 all the more galling. Kicked upstairs from the club presidency, a position he had held since the death of Ruppert in 1939, to a hollow chairman-of-the-board position, Barrow endured the ignominy of a title without authority or responsibility for only two years, refusing for the duration even to enter the newly—and flashily—renovated Yankee offices in midtown Manhattan.

DICK BARTELL

Dubbed Rowdy Richard for his belligerence with opponents and umpires, Bartell earned goat's horns in the 1940 World Series for a play that approximated Johnny Pesky's more famous delayed relay six years later. With the Tigers ahead, 1–0, and Cincinnati's Frank McCormick on second base in the seventh inning of the seventh game, the Detroit shortstop took a throw from right field and held the ball. Unable to hear over the enthusiastic home crowd, he failed to respond to cries of "Throw! Throw! Throw!" from his own bench and similarly frantic screams of "Run! Run! Run!" from the Cincinnati dugout, and missed an opportunity to make a play at the plate on McCormick, who had held up to see if the drive would be caught and was only halfway between third and home when Bartell got the ball. McCormick scored the tying run, with the Reds going on to win the game and the Series. Otherwise, Bartell batted .284, topping .300 six times, in an eighteen-year career with the Pirates, Phillies, Giants, and Cubs in addition to the Tigers.

WILLIAM BARTHOLOMAY

An Illinois insurance company executive, Bartholomay has managed to turn a series of initial miscalculations into profits for himself and his associates for some thirty years. His first apparent misadventure was in allying himself with Chuck Comiskey in the early 1960s in a labyrinthine scheme for taking over the White Sox; when that didn't work, he jettisoned Comiskey and sold his minority interest in the franchise for a substantial gain. In 1962 he headed a syndicate that purchased the Milwaukee Braves from Lou Perini and that, three years later, announced its intention of moving the franchise to Atlanta. This prompted a lawsuit headed by auto dealer Bud Selig that forced the Braves to spend a disastrous lame-duck season in Wisconsin and Bartholomay and his partners to spend rivers of money to fight the case in court. Finally arriving in Georgia in 1966, Bartholomay found even more local appreciation for his club because of the delay over the court battle, and was quick to make up for his lost 1965 revenues with the team's new television market. By 1976, however, the novelty of the Braves had long since worn off, and Bartholomay sold out to Ted Turner. To Bartholomay's own admitted surprise, Turner asked him to stay on—first as president, then as chairman of the board. He still held the latter post in the mid-1990s.

JOE BAUMAN

Bauman set a season record, for any level of organized baseball, by hitting 72 home runs for the Roswell Rockets of the Class C Longhorn League in 1954. The winner of four homer titles in his nine-year professional career, the first baseman played only one game above the A level and never reached the big leagues, largely because he was in the Navy for four years during World War II.

JIM BAUMER

Baumer made the mistake of making his major league debut at Yankee Stadium. Called up by the White Sox at the end of the 1949 season amid fanfare that he would be Chicago's shortstop of the future, he took the field in the bottom of the first inning, threw some warm-up tosses over to the first baseman, then looked around at the New York crowd, fainted, and had to be carried off the field. Although he got a sufficient grip on himself to play in a handful of games before the end of the year, he wrote another footnote to baseball history when he disappeared into the minors for the entire decade of the 1950s, not reappearing in the majors again until 1961, with Cincinnati.

BUZZIE BAVASI

Bavasi was Walter O'Malley's right-hand man for much of his thirty-year major league front office career, and was accused more than once of sharing the Dodger owner's sensitivity.

As general manager of the Dodgers, first in Brooklyn and then in Los Angeles, Bavasi thought nothing of selling off or even trying to farm out team veterans while informing the press before the affected players, or of building up one player in contract talks at the expense of talking another down. Another reported ploy was to leave players alone in his office with a phony contract on his desk so that visitors would think their offers were higher than teammates'. It was precisely to overcome such tactics that Sandy Koufax and Don Drysdale approached Bavasi as a tandem prior to the 1966 season, warning him that they intended sharing information on their individual pact negotiations. For most of his reign with the Dodgers, he relied on the organization's farm system for new blood, rarely entering into major trades except for a fourth starter and implementing O'Malley's disdain for free agents.

In 1969, Bavasi left the Dodgers to take over the expansion Padres. On the one hand, he fulfilled expectations by hiring a succession of managers with a Dodger background; on the other hand, clearly apprehensive about stirring up charges of collusion between the two Southern California teams in the National League, he went out of his way to avoid deals with Los Angeles. In fact, although they completed 100 or more trades in the first decade of their existence, the Padres completed only one in all that time with the Dodgers—a minor 1969 exchange of reliever Al McBean for shortstop Tommy Dean and minor leaguer Leon Everitt.

In the late 1970s, Bavasi was brought in by California owner Gene Autry to stop the franchise's financial bleeding. The appointment so irritated general manager Harry Dalton that he quit to go off to the Brewers, while Bavasi took over the Angels' baseball operations. In the typical chaotic style characterizing the California franchise, the usually fiscally responsible Bavasi then spent most of his tenure offering inflated free-agent contracts to second-line players; to that extent, anyway, he had traveled a great distance from O'Malley.

Bavasi's sons, Peter and Bill, followed him into baseball's executive suites.

DON BAYLOR

Baylor holds the major league career mark for getting hit by a pitch, working his way to first base the hard way 267 times. A right-handed slugger who played for six teams between 1970 and 1988, he became the first designated hitter to win an MVP award, in 1979, when he sparked the Angels to a Western Division title by batting .296, clouting 36 home runs, and leading the league in both RBIs (139) and runs (120). In his later years, he gained a reputation as a clubhouse leader who provided the extra push needed for winning teams; Boston, Minnesota, and Oakland all won pennants during his brief stays with them. After a couple of years of being passed over as a managerial choice (in at least one case for racial reasons), Baylor was given the reins of the first-year expansion Rockies in 1993. His skills as a hitting tutor became evident in the transformation

of Andres Galarraga into the National League batting champion.

GENE BEARDEN

Rookie Bearden was an unexpected hero of the Indians' last world championship. Despite his league-leading 2.43 ERA, it came as a surprise when manager Lou Boudreau chose him over Bob Feller and Bob Lemon to pitch the one-game playoff for the 1948 flag against the Red Sox. In the event, the southpaw notched his twentieth victory of the season with a 5-hit, 8–3 effort sparked by two homers from player-pilot Boudreau. In the ensuing World Series against the Braves, the knuckleballer hurled a complete-game shutout in the third game and earned a save in the sixth game. In six other major league seasons, Bearden was never better than a .500 pitcher for Cleveland and four other American League teams, ending his career with a 45–38 record.

GINGER BEAUMONT

Beaumont was one of the mainstays of the successful Pirate teams at the dawn of the century. Between 1901 and 1905, the lefty-swinging outfielder competed with teammate Honus Wagner for batting honors, winning the title in 1902 with a .357 mark and accumulating more safeties than the Hall of Fame shortstop or any other National League player from 1902 and 1904. He also led the league in hits in 1907 as a member of the Braves. Beaumont, who also stole at least 25 bases seven times, retired with a .311 mark over twelve seasons. As the Pittsburgh leadoff hitter in 1903, he was also the first man to come to the plate in a World Series.

GEORGE BECHTEL

Bechtel was suspended by the Louisville Grays during the 1876 season after teammate Jim Devlin accused the outfielder of wiring him a $500 offer to throw a game. Cited for drunkenness rather than dishonesty, he was blackballed despite an anonymous letter claiming that Bechtel's name had been forged on the telegram. At the end of the following season, the National League made his suspension permanent, along with those of Devlin and three other Grays accused of fixing games. Along with Bill Craver (also one of the

Louisville Four), Bechtel was part of the first recorded player sale, moving from the National Association Philadelphia Centennials to the Athletics of the same city, in 1875.

BOOM BOOM BECK

Beck was a journeyman right-hander who rode the elevator back and forth between the majors and minors between 1924 and 1945, squeezing in twelve years of big league service. The reasons for all his wanderings were implicit in the nickname fastened on him by teammates—the first boom suggesting the whack of the bat against one of his pitches, the second one the sound of the ball caroming off an outfield wall. Beck became part of Dodger lore in 1934, when in frustration at being removed from a game, he fired the ball toward the right-field wall at Philadelphia's Baker Bowl. A distracted and hung over Hack Wilson immediately charged after the ball, grabbed it, and shot it back to the infield on the assumption that it was another hit by an opposition batter.

ERV BECK

In the Opening Day game against Chicago on April 24, 1901, Indians' second baseman Beck doubled for the American League's first extra-base hit. The next day, he clouted the league's first home run.

JAKE BECKLEY (Hall of Fame, 1971)

Beckley's last appreciable record fell in 1994, when Eddie Murray surpassed him for most games played at first base. But for a twenty-year span from 1888 to 1907, the lefty slugger was one of the National League's main offensive threats, reaching the .300 level thirteen times and closing with a .308 average. Doing most of his damage for the Pirates and Reds, he also knocked in 100 runs four times and scored 100 runs in each of five seasons. A member of the Pittsburgh entry in the 1890 Players League, Beckley batted .324 and led the Brotherhood rebels in triples. His trade by the Pirates to the Giants in 1897 cost owner William Kerr mass defections in attendance and helped set into motion the deal that would bring Barney Dreyfuss from Louisville into the Pittsburgh front office. Beckley's career was almost short-circuited three years before his retirement when Jack Taylor, his drinking companion on the Cardinals, fell under a cloud for throwing exhibition games in 1903. Dreyfuss lobbied for banning both players, but St. Louis owner Stanley Robison resisted the move, realizing how severely such a purge would damage his club.

BO BELINSKY

No major leaguer received more publicity for doing less on a diamond than Belinsky. By the time he had wound up an eight-year career that included lengthy stays in the minors and on the disabled list, he had won a mere 28 games, only once managing more victories than losses. When he joined the Los Angeles (now California) Angels in 1962, however, the southpaw's reputation as a womanizer, pool hustler, and all-around bon vivant was just what the market-minded Angels needed in their rivalry with the Dodgers. When Belinsky reeled off five quick victories, one of them a no-hitter against Baltimore, the media fastened on to him as a symbol of the ''new ballplayer.'' Particularly avid for his company was aging Hearst columnist Walter Winchell, who saw the pitcher as an access to the starlets and actresses he wanted to bed down. With Winchell and every other gossip columnist worth his dirt chronicling his adventures, Belinsky did the town with the likes of Iran's Queen Soraya, and actresses Connie Stevens, Tina Louise, and Ann-

Bo Belinsky (far right) with gossip column pals Gypsy Boots and Mamie Van Doren. National Baseball Library, Cooperstown, N.Y.

Margret. The lengthiest relationship was with actress Mamie Van Doren, whose regular appearances at Dodger Stadium in low-cut outfits allowed the Angels to out-Hollywood the Dodgers.

Belinsky's chief nemesis during all the fun was manager Bill Rigney, who not only objected to the left-hander's gradually poorer performances on the mound but also to his influence on such teammates as Dean Chance. With the backing of general manager Fred Haney, Rigney thought he had solved his problem in July 1962 by completing a trade with Kansas City for reliever Dan Osinski for ''a player to be named later.'' Athletics' manager Hank Bauer, who wanted no part of the player to be named later, let Belinsky know that he was Kansas City-bound, prompting a brouhaha in the American League office. In the end, AL president Joe Cronin had to accept Belinsky's argument that there was something unethical about a player performing for one team while aware that he was headed for another, and ordered Haney and Rigney to send Ted Bowsfield to the Athletics instead.

Rigney tried again in 1963. After a relentless series of fines against Belinsky and Chance, the manager persuaded the front office that Belinsky's 1–7 record had earned him a demotion to the minors. When Belinsky realized that California's chief farm club was in Hawaii, he not only didn't object, he even refused a recall to Los Angeles in August because he was having so much fun on the islands. The air finally went out of the balloon during the 1964 season, when a punch-up with Los Angeles *Times* sportswriter Braven Dyer turned the media against Belinsky. Together with arm and drinking problems, the brawl greased the pitcher's slide from the Angels; he ended up drifting from one National League team to another before finally retiring in 1971.

BUDDY BELL

In eighteen years spanning 2,405 games, third baseman Bell never appeared in postseason play. That is the major league record for unfulfilled expectations in the era of divisional play. Bell labored for the Indians, Rangers, Reds, and Astros from 1972 to 1989.

COOL PAPA BELL (Hall of Fame, 1972)

While there is a wealth of apocrypha about Bell's swiftness, there is also enough documentation to strengthen the claim that the outfielder was the fastest man ever to play professional baseball.

In twenty seasons in the Negro leagues, Bell played for three of the greatest teams ever assembled: the St. Louis Stars (1922–31), the Pittsburgh Crawfords (1933–36), and the Homestead Grays (1943–46); these teams won a combined eleven championships with Bell as their center fielder. Given his nickname by Stars' manager Bill Gatewood for calmly striking out Oscar Charleston in a clutch situation, Bell moved from the pitching mound to the outfield in 1924 and averaged better than .300 sixteen times, reaching the .380 mark on more than one occasion. The switch-hitter also spent one season (1937) in the Dominican Republic and four more (1938–41) in Mexico, winning a Triple Crown in the latter country in 1940 for his .437 average, 12 homers, and 79 RBIs. In addition, he played winter ball in Cuba, Mexico, and California for twenty-one years. Even his Negro leagues career average of about .340 was eclipsed by a .391 mark in exhibition games against major league players.

One tall tale about Bell's running, made famous by Satchel Paige, is that he once got a hit up the middle but was declared out when his batted ball struck him as he slid into second. It was also Paige who cracked that Bell could throw the light switch and be in bed before the room was dark. (This actually happened, but only because of an electrical short in the wiring of the hotel where the pair was staying.) The fish stories aside, Bell once stole 175 bases in 200 games. There are also numerous eyewitness accounts of his going from first to third on a sacrifice bunt, scoring from second base on a sacrifice fly, beating out two-hoppers to the infield, and stealing two bases on one pitch. The most astonishing of Bell's feats occurred in an exhibition game against big league players when he scored from first base on a sacrifice bunt, so shocking Red Sox catcher Roy Partee and Indians' pitcher Bob Lemon that they became proselytizers of his myth; Bell was already several years past forty at the time.

Lured to the Dominican Republic in 1937 by Paige, Bell and other Negro league players were kept under armed guard in a compound in San Pedro de Macoris, where they were told that dictator Rafael Trujillo would be assassinated unless his team won the pennant; the club did, beating out Santiago on the final day of the season.

Bell's last four seasons were spent as a playing manager for minor black teams—the Detroit Senators and Kansas City Stars. In 1951 he refused Bill Veeck's offer to join the St. Louis Browns because he was forty-eight years old.

GEORGE BELL

Bell has been the most successful Rule V pickup by a team committed to keeping a drafted minor league player on its big league roster for an entire season. Purchased by the Blue Jays from the Phillies' farm system prior to the 1981 season, the right-hand-hitting slugger went on to have eight seasons with at least 20 home runs and four with a minimum of 100 RBIs. In 1987 the outfielder took MVP honors in the American League by batting .308 with 47 homers and a league-best 134 RBIs.

For a good part of his twelve-year (1981, 1983–93) career with Toronto and other clubs, Bell stirred controversy about his defensive limitations, especially in 1988, when Blue Jay manager Jimy Williams indicated that untried rookies Rob Ducey and Sil Campusano were preferable in the field to the previous season's MVP. Although both rookies failed and Bell was eventually shifted back to left field from his initial role as a designated hitter, his resentment of Williams carried through the season and helped make the Toronto clubhouse the most fractious in the major leagues. While with the White Sox in 1993, Bell and Bo Jackson got into such a public sulk about who should be the DH in the American League Championship Series against Toronto that neither player was offered a new contract with the White Sox following the season.

ESTEBAN BELLAN

Infielder Bellan was the first Latino to play at any level of organized ball in North America, appearing for Troy and New York in the proto-major league National Association in the early 1870s. He was also one of the fathers of Cuban baseball in the nineteenth century.

Johnny Bench was not only the greatest slugging catcher of all time but also the premier defensive backstop of his era. National Baseball Library, Cooperstown, N.Y.

JOHNNY BENCH (Hall of Fame, 1989)

Often cited as the greatest all-around catcher in National League history, Bench was a vital offensive and defensive cog in the Big Red Machine of the 1970s. Although more attention was paid to his hitting, his work behind the plate and with pitchers might have been even more significant, not least because of the mostly lackluster mound corps that Cincinnati had in the period.

Never one to hide his light under a bushel, Bench joined Cincinnati at the tail end of 1967 and saw enough to predict that he would be the NL Rookie of the Year in 1968. He was right—hitting just enough to beat out Jerry Koosman, catching a full schedule of 154 games, and becoming the first player at his position to cop rookie honors. It was also the first of ten straight seasons in which he would win a Gold Glove. At the plate, his best years were 1970 and 1972, when he was named the league's Most Valuable Player. In 1970 he led the circuit in both home runs (45) and RBIs (143), then repeated the trick two years later, with 40 homers and 125 RBIs.

The right-handed slugger won a third RBI crown in 1974, and all told topped the 100 mark six times. His 389 career home runs include 327 in the lineup as a catcher—the most ever by an NL receiver.

One of Bench's more conspicuous moments was in the 1976 World Series against the Yankees, in which he collected six hits over the first three games, then clouted two homers in the finale for a sweep. In the first game, he threw out New York's Mickey Rivers attempting to steal, and never had another Yankee base runner test his arm. The performance indirectly caused a mini-controversy when Reds' manager Sparky Anderson asserted that New York's Thurman Munson didn't belong in the same ballpark as Bench, the Yankees fired back, and then old Dodger Duke Snider chimed in with the opinion that Bench would have been only a backup to Roy Campanella.

Bench lingered in Cincinnati longer and more awkwardly than other members of the Big Red Machine. Declaring that he no longer wanted to catch, he persuaded manager John McNamara to allow him to close out his career as a third baseman. The result in 1982 was not only a club-leading 19 errors but also a marked lack of range that had pitchers moaning about having the fourteen-time All-Star behind them rather than in front of them. Bench finally called it quits after the 1983 season.

CHIEF BENDER (Hall of Fame, 1953)

The first Native American elected to the Hall of Fame, Bender was a pitching mainstay of the Philadelphia Athletics between 1903 and 1914, when he recorded the vast majority of his 210 career victories and led the American League in won-lost percentage three times. His jump to the Federal League Baltimore Terrapins in 1914 convinced Athletics' owner-manager Connie Mack that his four-time (in five years) championship team had become too expensive and too obstreperous, leading to one of the periodic dismantlings of the franchise. The pitcher played out the string with the Phillies in 1915 and 1916, and made a one-inning cameo appearance with the White Sox in 1925. An effective reliever as well as starter, Bender tallied six of his 21 wins in 1913, one of

only two 20-win seasons, out of the bullpen; he also led the AL in saves with 13 that year. A half Chippewa, the right-hander quietly suffered the use of his nickname but, calling himself Charley, never used it himself.

CHARLIE BENNETT

A popular catcher with the National League Detroit Wolverines in the 1880s, Bennett lost both his legs in January 1894 attempting to jump on a moving train in Wellsville, Kansas. Two years later, when Detroit entered the Western League, the club's home park was named Bennett Field in his honor. The Tigers used the field through their first eleven American League seasons, and Tiger Stadium stands on the same site.

EDDIE BENNETT

Born with a malformed spine, Bennett was the only man to wear the uniform of three different pennant-winning teams in three consecutive years. First adopted as a batboy-mascot by Happy Felsch of the 1919 White Sox, who thought rubbing Bennett's misshapen back would bring good luck, he filled a similar role for the 1920 Dodgers before moving, in 1921, to the Yankees. He stayed with New York through the 1920s, eventually becoming a full-time cheerleader while subordinates did the bat-carrying.

FRED BENNETT

When Bennett successfully appealed to Commissioner Kenesaw Landis in 1930 that the Browns had buried him in their farm system after only a brief stint with the big club, the outcome affected more than the outfielder's future. For Bennett, the decision meant free agency and an additional, relatively undistinguished, major league season. For the rest of baseball, it meant the validation of farm systems. In deciding the suit brought by St. Louis owner Phil Ball, a federal trial judge ratified the commissioner's broad authority to liberate individual players but upheld the essential legality of minor league networks. Realizing that further pursuit of his point might jeopardize baseball's antitrust exemption, Ball dropped the matter.

ROBERT RUSSELL BENNETT

Bennett composed the most elaborate music ever inspired by baseball. His 1941 *Symphony in D, for the Dodgers* consisted of four movements: *Allegro con brio* (''Brooklyn Wins''), *Andante lamentosa* (''Brooklyn Loses), *Scherzo* (''Larry MacPhail tries to give Cleveland the Brooklyn Bridge for Bob Feller''), and *Finale* (''The Giants Come to Town'').

ALLEN BENSON

A bearded pitcher from the House of David team, Benson was considered enough of a sideshow novelty that Washington signed him in 1934 as a quickie gate attraction. After getting pounded by the powerful Tigers, he asked for another start and for the right to shave off his beard. Senators' owner Clark Griffith agreed to the start but insisted that the beard made Benson ''special.'' The right-hander was banged around again, this time by the lowly Browns, and retired with a mark of 0–1 and an ERA of 12.10.

The House of David was a Michigan-based religious sect that spawned baseball teams for fundraising purposes at the beginning of the century. By the time Benson came along, it had fragmented into rival groups that sponsored teams at semipro levels, though with a common identity of long beards and shoulder-length hair.

RUBE BENTON

A fringe character caught up in the 1919 World Series scandal, Benton had either his imagination or his bad memory to thank for a one-year suspension. The southpaw's troubles began in the summer of 1920, when he accused Buck Herzog of having asked him to throw a 1919 game to the Reds that he was scheduled to start for the Giants; Herzog, a former Cincinnati manager then with the Cubs, retaliated by producing signed affidavits from several players declaring that Benton had boasted of winning $1,500 from the 1919 World Series because of his prior knowledge of the Black Sox fix. Summoned before the grand jury looking into the tainted Series, Benton admitted having won money in 1919, but insisted that it was only $20 and that his bets had been placed on the basis of nothing more than the general rumors of a fix. Once off the witness stand, he

reiterated his charges against Herzog, adding the particular that he had been approached in a Chicago bar and that one of the bartenders on the premises had heard every word.

For his part, National League president John Heydler just wanted the heavy-drinking Benton to go back to the mound for the Giants and let matters die, especially since the pitcher was not on the list of players outlawed by Commissioner Kenesaw Landis because of the Series fix. But with Benton periodically returning to his accusations against Herzog, Heydler finally had to agree in 1921 to go to Chicago with him to find the bartender. Once in the Windy City, however, the hurler claimed that he was disoriented by the interim replacement of saloons by speakeasies and couldn't remember exactly where Herzog had approached him. An infuriated Heydler then passed the word to NL owners that Benton would not be welcome on any league roster in 1922.

There matters stood until 1923, when Cincinnati owner Garry Herrmann decided that the left-hander's big 1922 season with St. Paul of the minor league American Association entitled him to another major league chance. When Herrmann went to Heydler, however, the NL executive repeated that Benton was ''morally undesirable.'' Deciding that Heydler had lost his objectivity because of the wild-goose chase to Chicago, Herrmann then went to Landis. The commissioner not only reinstated Benton but also took the opportunity to blast Heydler, Herrmann, and various sportswriters for having disparaged the pitcher's character without evidence. Benton won 14 games for the Reds in 1923.

JOHNNY BERARDINO

Berardino was the first player to rattle an owner by insisting that an agent handle negotiations for his services. In November 1947, the Browns' infielder was traded to the Senators for second baseman Gerry Priddy, but refused to go unless Washington owner Clark Griffith negotiated a new contract for the following season. When Griffith scorned the idea of having to deal with an agent, Berardino announced his retirement and his intention of trying to make it as an actor. Commissioner Happy Chandler stepped in to dissolve the trade, prompting Berardino to announce his unretirement. Three weeks later he agreed to a trade to the Indians when Cleveland owner Bill Veeck promised him not only regular playing time but also an introduction to a Hollywood producer. Never one to avoid a good publicity gimmick, Veeck also had his new infielder's face insured against accidents on the field. Retiring after the 1952 season, Berardino went to Hollywood, where he dropped the second ''r'' in his name and eventually began a thirty-year stretch as Dr. Steve Hardy on the daytime soap opera *General Hospital*.

MOE BERG

Berg has enjoyed a reputation as the most accomplished—and the most shadowy—backup catcher in the history of the game. Few of the receiver's accomplishments came in the batter's box. It was, in fact, Berg whom Mike Gonzalez was describing when he coined the phrase ''Good field, no hit'' while scouting the eventual .243 lifetime hitter for the Cardinals in the early 1920s.

After coming up with the Dodgers in 1923 as a slick infielder, Berg spent two seasons (1926–27) with the White Sox as a utility man, then found his niche as a second-string backstop, filling that role until 1939 with the Indians, Senators, and Red Sox as well as the White Sox; in only one of his fifteen big league seasons did he appear in more than 100 games. Along the way, he picked up degrees from Princeton University and Columbia Law School, and studied philology at the Sorbonne; however, his linguistic skills, which inspired the observation by Chicago teammate Ted Lyons that ''he can speak twelve languages, but he can't hit in any of them,'' did not involve proficiency in either Sanskrit, as he alleged, or in a dozen tongues.

The mystery surrounding Berg involved his self-proclaimed exploits as a spy for the United States both during and after his baseball career. His most famous supposed escapade while still active as a player was to take home movies of Tokyo from the roof of a hospital building during a 1934 barnstorming tour of Japan that, he claimed, were later used to plan the 1942 air raids led by General Jimmy Doolittle. Secretive about his avocation, he was nonetheless a frequent guest at embassy dinners and unhesitatingly introduced teammates to President Franklin D. Roosevelt.

His baseball career over, Berg worked for the OSS during World War II, tracking the whereabouts of German scientists. The information he gathered may or may not have enabled U.S. forces to capture Werner Heisenberg, the head of the Nazi atomic bomb effort, and several other noted nuclear physicists, in 1945. After the war, Berg rarely spoke of his experiences until the late 1960s when, out of financial necessity, he agreed to write a book. The project collapsed when, at a first meeting, the young editor assigned to the project glowingly praised the prospective author's movies on the mistaken assumption that he was about to sign a contract with Moe of The Three Stooges.

BILL BERGEN

Including all players who had at least 1,000 plate appearances, catcher Bergen was the worst hitter in baseball history. In 11 seasons for the Reds and Dodgers (1901–11), he averaged only .170 in 3,028 official at-bats. The fact that he was a first-string receiver for most of his career suggests what a defensive wizard he was.

MARTY BERGEN

Bergen, the brother of Bill Bergen, provided baseball with one of its more chilling stories at the close of the nineteenth century. A member of the Braves, he took to jumping the team for days at a time because, he said, his family needed him. His coming and going divided the club between those who warned the front office that he should be treated with kid gloves and those who resented what they perceived as favored treatment. With the sudden death of the catcher's son in 1898, however, his teammates overcame their rancor and united behind him, reminding him daily that he was vital to the team's success. This reaction boomeranged when Bergen announced that the players reminded him too much of his son in their love for him and returned to his regular journeys to his farm. By the end of the 1899 season, the clubhouse was united in the opposite way, warning owner Arthur Soden that they would not come back to Boston the following season if Bergen were still on the team. Their threat became academic on January 19, 1900, when Bergen used a razor and an ax to kill his wife, three-year-old son, six-year-old daughter, and himself. The only member of the Braves to attend the funeral was outfielder Billy Hamilton.

WALLY BERGER

Slugger though he was, Braves' outfielder Berger was the only position player in either starting lineup of the inaugural 1933 All-Star Game in Chicago who did not end up in the Hall of Fame. He made the team while in the midst of the second of his three seasons of 30 or more homers. In 1930, the right-hand-hitting Berger established the National League record (later tied by Frank Robinson) for rookie home runs by clouting 38 round-trippers.

YOGI BERRA (Hall of Fame, 1972)

As a player, Berra carried a public image as a lovable, cuddly figure with a propensity for malapropisms along with one of the most potent clutch bats in the American League; as a manager, he tended to show the crustier side of his personality, although this did not prevent him from winning a pennant with a New York club in each league.

Over a nineteen-year playing career (all but 4 games of it with the Yankees), Berra batted .285 with 358 home runs. The winner of three Most Valuable Player awards (1951, 1954, and 1955), the lefty-swinging catcher reached the 20-homer mark eleven times (ten of them in a row between 1949 and 1958); topped 100 RBIs five times; and holds records for appearing in the most World Series (14) and the most Series games (75), as well as for collecting the most Series hits (71). A notorious bad-ball hitter who once whacked a one-bounce delivery by Early Wynn for a double, Berra nonetheless connected often enough to keep his yearly strikeout totals between 12 and 38, and to lead an otherwise potent Yankee offense in RBIs every year from 1949 to 1955. He was particularly productive in late-inning situations, to the point that he was often walked in extra innings even though he represented the potential winning run.

A defensive liability when he first joined the club in 1946, Berra was often used in the outfield as well as behind the plate until manager Casey

Long before there were Berraisms, there was Yogi Berra the catcher. National Baseball Library, Cooperstown, N.Y.

Stengel hired Hall of Fame receiver Bill Dickey to tutor the young catcher. The mentor succeeded to the extent that his pupil established the record for consecutive chances without an error (950 between July 1957 and May 1959), and eventually became regarded as the best backstop in the league at pouncing on bunts and at calling a game. The most enduring image of the catcher is, in fact, of him with his limbs wrapped around Don Larsen, after having called the pitches in the right-hander's 1956 World Series perfect game.

The short, squat figure in that picture squared perfectly with the author of innumerable Yogisms. Among the most widely quoted are: "It ain't over till it's over''; "It gets late early out here"; "Nobody goes there anymore; it's too crowded"; "It's déjà vu all over again"; "The other teams could make trouble for us if they win"; "We made too many wrong mistakes''; "Why buys good luggage? You only use it when you travel''; "They were as close as Damon and Runyan''; and "You can observe a lot by watching." Although the unwitting witticisms endeared Berra to Yankee fans and others, the warm popular image was the creation of broadcasters Phil Rizzuto (an ex-teammate) and Joe Garagiola (a boyhood friend from St. Louis). In fact, the man who retired in 1963 and took over as the Yankee pilot the following year was a successful and somewhat grumpy New Jersey businessman with more baseball sense than his image allowed. Hired primarily to offset the widespread popularity of Stengel, who had signed on with the Mets after his firing by the Yankees, Berra made the 1964 season memorable for his altercation with infielder Phil Linz over a harmonica; his sourness that had both players and press running to general manager Ralph Houk for succor; an unexpected pennant; and an equally unexpected (but long-planned) firing in favor of Johnny Keane, whose Cardinals had just defeated Berra's Yankees in the World Series.

Joining Stengel's coaching staff in 1965, Berra served under four managers in Shea Stadium before succeeding Gil Hodges as pilot in 1972. Nominally in charge during the ''You gotta believe'' Mets pennant drive the following year, the manager lost points in the front office for allowing players a much freer rein in making on-field decisions than chairman M. Donald Grant thought wise. Grant fired Berra in August 1975 on the grounds that he had lost control of the club. Reemerging to pilot the Yankees a second time, in 1984, Berra brought a mediocre club home third and accepted owner George Steinbrenner's accolades and promises that he would have all of 1985 to bring another pennant to the Bronx; instead, he was replaced seventeen games into the season by Billy Martin in his fourth tour of duty. Vowing that he would not step foot in Yankee Stadium again until Steinbrenner was no longer in charge, Berra packed his bags and hasn't been back since.

BILL BEVENS

Prior to Don Larsen's perfect game in 1956, Bevens came closer than anyone else to pitching a World Series no-hitter. With only one out to go against the Dodgers in the fourth game of the 1947 Series, however, the Yankee right-hander yielded a double to pinch hitter Cookie Lavagetto that scored two runners and saddled Bevens with a 2–1 loss. It was the last game Bevens pitched in the major leagues.

HUGO BEZDEK

Bezdek was the most improbably successful manager in National League history. When he was drafted for the job by the 1917 Pirates after Honus Wagner had a change of heart about piloting the cellar club after only five games, Bezdek was the organization's business manager; before that, he had a been a star football player and wrestler in college, then football coach at the University of Oregon. If his charges were waiting for his inexperience to show up, they weren't disappointed when he signaled for such plays as having runners on second *and* third try to score on a suicide squeeze. But Bezdek got those glitches out of his system during the final months of the season, then returned to lead the Pirates over the .500 mark in both 1918 and 1919. But just when Pittsburgh players and sportswriters were warming to the unlikely manager, he quit baseball to coach the Penn State football team. Bezdek never went back to the major leagues, though he did end up taking three different college teams to the Rose Bowl and coaching the NFL Cleveland Rams.

LOU BIERBAUER

A second baseman with solid if unglamorous credentials over thirteen major league seasons, Bierbauer has been remembered mostly for his role in the naming of a franchise; less well known is that the episode resulted in the demise of an entire major league. Having jumped the American Association Athletics for the Brooklyn Players League club in 1890, the infielder's contract should have reverted to Philadelphia when the PL collapsed after one season. But when new Philadelphia owner J. Earl Wagner neglected to include the names of Bierbauer and outfielder Harry

Stovey on the list of those he claimed as spoils of the war, the pair went over to the National League, the former with Pittsburgh and the latter with Boston. Pittsburgh president J. Palmer O'Neill soon became J. Pirate O'Neill in the newspapers, and his club has been called after his less-than-flattering nickname ever since. Even more significant, the AA withdrew from the National Agreement over the piracy, precipitating a new trade war in which it was completely overmatched, and lasted only one more season.

IVAN BIGLER

Bigler's single appearance in a major league game, as a pinch runner for the 1917 St. Louis Browns, developed into a decades-long saga of arcane research. Listed in early editions of Hy Turkin and S. C. Thompson's *The Official Encyclopedia of Baseball*, his name was later thought to be a typographically erroneous rendering of Hall of Famer George Sisler's; recent investigation has established that Bigler actually did have the briefest of cups of coffee.

W. E. BILHEIMER

A St. Louis insurance executive, Bilheimer conceived the first Knothole Gang while a member of the broad-based local syndicate headed by James Jones that purchased the Cardinals in 1916. His scheme, advanced as an antidote for juvenile delinquency, allowed investors to reserve one bleacher seat for a young fan with every $50 of stock purchased. Adopted several years later as a pet project of general manager Branch Rickey, the program proved a valuable tool in building several generations of Cardinal fans.

STEVE BILKO

The only thing as popular as the arrival of major league baseball in California was Bilko. A bulky first baseman as noted for his gargantuan whiffs as for his occasional titanic blasts, he gained an enormous following among minor league fans in the Los Angeles area in the early 1950s. For that reason, the Dodgers in 1958 and the Angels in 1961 both made sure that he was aboard for their inaugural California seasons.

JACK BILLINGHAM

Billingham was as close as the Big Red Machine had to a pitching ace for more than one season in the 1970s. Although he never won 20 games, he came close in both 1973 and 1974, with 19 victories. The right-hander also holds the mark for the best ERA in World Series history for pitchers with at least 25 innings, having yielded only 0.36 run in seven games in 1972, 1975, and 1976. On Opening Day in 1974, Billingham gave up Hank Aaron's record-tying 714th home run.

MAX BISHOP

Known as Camera Eye for his mental picture of the strike zone, Bishop's skill at waiting out pitchers for walks boosted a lifetime .271 batting average to a .423 on-base percentage, the largest gap between the two statistics for players with at least 4,000 at-bats. The second baseman and leadoff batter for the Athletics from the early 1920s to the early 1930s, he collected 100 hits and 100 walks in seven seasons, with more bases on balls than safeties in six of those years; he also set a major league record by walking eight times in a doubleheader on May 21, 1930.

LENA BLACKBURNE

An infielder, primarily for the White Sox in the 1910s and 1920s, Blackburne later cornered the market on the Delaware River mud that is still used by umpires to take the sheen off new baseballs.

EWELL BLACKWELL

Although he finished his career only four games over .500 (82–78), Blackwell generated more dread among National League batters than any other right-hander in the late 1940s and 1950s. Labeled The Whip for a treacherous sidearm, buggy-whip delivery, he totally dominated the league for Cincinnati in 1947, at one point winning 16 games in a row on his way to leading NL hurlers in victories, strikeouts, and complete games. More astonishing, he came within two outs of duplicating teammate Johnny Vander Meer's 1938 feat of pitching successive no-hitters—holding the Braves hitless on June 18 and then getting one out in the ninth inning against

Ewell Blackwell had few peers in intimidating righthanded hitters in the 1940s. National Baseball Library, Cooperstown, N.Y.

the Dodgers on June 22 before Eddie Stanky managed a single. Although he had a couple of other good seasons of 17 and 16 victories for bad Reds teams, he was eventually undone by a kidney operation, an appendectomy, and an arm injury.

CLIFF BLANKENSHIP

Blankenship, a backup catcher for the 1907 Senators, had a drastic impact on the future of the franchise by breaking his finger. Unable to play, he was told to go to Kansas and Idaho to scout a couple of prospects. In Wichita he signed outfielder Clyde Milan; in Weiser he inked Walter Johnson.

STEVE BLASS

Blass suffered as mysterious an end to a dominating career as anybody in major league history. After anchoring the Pittsburgh staff for several years, including leading the National League in winning percentage in 1968 (.750, 18–6) and recording 19 victories in 1972, the right-hander showed up at spring training in 1973 completely unable to throw strikes. While his ERA blew up from 2.49 to 9.85, he was sent through a gauntlet of doctors, psychiatrists, hypnotists, and minor league pitching coaches for an explanation—all to no avail. Theories ran the gamut from some deep disturbance at watching teammate Bob Moose wild-pitch home the pennant-winning run for Cincinnati in 1972 to a profound trauma over the off-season death of Roberto Clemente. Whatever the cause, Blass was out of baseball after a final major league appearance in 1974.

RON BLOMBERG

When he came to bat for the Yankees in Boston's Fenway Park on Opening Day of 1973, the lefty-swinging Blomberg became baseball's first designated hitter. Otherwise a first baseman, Blomberg hit .293 in eight seasons, all but one of them with the Yankees.

VIDA BLUE

The least of Blue's accomplishments over a roller-coaster seventeen-year career between 1969 and 1986 were his battles with Charlie Finley, his reliance on a president of the United States for contract-negotiation advice, and his prison term for dealing drugs. Still, these episodes ultimately overshadowed the southpaw's 209 victories, three 20-win seasons, and eight straight years of at least 200 strikeouts.

Blue became a household name in 1971 when, pitching for Oakland, he took both MVP and Cy Young honors in the American League for a record of 24–8 and a league-leading 1.82 ERA. Having already spun a no-hitter in his rookie year of 1970, the lefty's performance was the biggest media event of the year—translated into a *Time* cover, several television commercials, and increased attendance whenever he was due to take the mound. Aware that part of the hurler's appeal was his unusual name, Finley pressed publicly and relentlessly to gild the lily by having him drop the Vida in favor of True, but Blue refused, in the process winning even more publicity. What he didn't reject, on the other hand, was an off-season observation by President Richard Nixon that he was the most underpaid player in the game. Blue promptly hired an agent to have Nix-

Southpaw Vida Blue's left arm made him a big winner in his rookie year; his name helped make him a media sensation. Ron Riesterer/Oakland Tribune.

2½ games. Once again in 1977, Finley sought to get $1 million for the pitcher, this time from Cincinnati, and once again Kuhn stepped in to say no, arguing that the Reds were already too dominant in the National League. Finally, before the 1978 season, Blue was sent packing to the Giants. The deal, which also brought the owner $300,000, set a major league record in its exchange of one player for seven—pitchers Dave Heaverlo, Alan Wirth, John Henry Johnson, and Phil Huffman, catcher Gary Alexander, shortstop Mario Guerrero, and outfielder Gary Thomasson.

Blue spent four seasons with the Giants before returning to the AL, with the Royals in 1982. What initially appeared to be only a deal for a pitcher who had seen his best days turned into a full-fledged scandal in 1983, when Blue was revealed as the principal source of drugs for teammates Jerry Martin, Willie Wilson, and Willie Mays Aikens. It also turned out that Blue was the main source of information to the police about club users, bringing him as many cold shoulders from players around the league as indignation from the Kansas City front office, which promptly released him. When Kuhn once again stepped into the fray to impose one-year suspensions on the four players, an arbitration panel allowed the order to stand only against Blue, as the pusher. All four players, however, ended up doing three-month terms after original felony charges had been dropped to misdemeanors. After his forced sidelining in 1984, the southpaw persuaded the Giants that he was undergoing rehabilitation, and returned to San Francisco for a final two seasons.

BERT BLYLEVEN

Blyleven set the gopher record for a season in 1986, when, as a member of the Twins, he yielded 50 home runs. The right-hander nevertheless managed to win 17 games. His negative mark was helped by having to pitch in the Metrodome, as well as by his league-leading 271 innings. During his twenty-two-year career (between 1970 and 1992) for the Twins and several other clubs, Blyleven compiled a 287–250 record, also joining the handful of pitchers to register 3,000 strikeouts (3,701). In 1977 he was a key figure in baseball's last four-club trade, involving the Rangers, Braves, Mets, and Pirates.

on's case made to Finley. This led to a spring training holdout in 1972, an eventual compromise agreement—and a disastrous season in which the unprepared hurler went only 6–10 and was booed constantly by the same fans who hadn't been able to get enough of him the year before. His main consolation for the year was in nailing down Oakland's pennant win over Detroit with four innings of brilliant relief in the American League Championship Series.

Blue rebounded in 1973 for another 20-win season, and settled in as the ace of the Athletics' staff for the next few years. Then, in 1976, with Finley unloading all his high-priced stars, he was sold to the Yankees for $1.5 million. Commissioner Bowie Kuhn put a hold on the deal (and another sale of pitcher Rollie Fingers and outfielder Joe Rudi to Boston), however, and for two weeks it remained in limbo until the transaction was canceled "in the best interests of baseball." The delay proved pivotal when Oakland ended up losing the division title to Kansas City by only

WADE BOGGS

The most consistent hitter of the 1980s, Boggs has gained as much attention for his near-fanatical rituals as for his lifetime .335 average—and even more for a scandal surrounding a long-running adulterous affair. The third baseman ranks nineteenth on the all-time batting average chart, with only Ted Williams among those with higher averages appearing in a major league uniform as late as 1961. The winner of five batting crowns (1983, 1985–88) while with the Red Sox, the lefty swinger is the only player in major league history to collect 200 or more hits in seven consecutive seasons (1983–89). Although often criticized as a one-dimensional spray hitter, Boggs has collected 100 walks four times; scored 100 runs seven times; and, moving from his customary leadoff spot to third in the batting order for a good part of the 1987 season, responded with 24 homers. Among his more impressive accomplishments has been reaching base 340 times in two different seasons; among the three players who had previously crashed that barrier, only Babe Ruth and Williams did so more than once.

Complementing an almost mechanical swing has been an array of rituals Boggs credits with his success: eating chicken before every game, running wind sprints at precisely 7:17 P.M. every evening, drawing a Hebrew letter in the dirt every time he steps into the batter's box, and following precisely the same path onto and off the field each inning. The 1988 revelation that Boggs had been involved in an extramarital affair for some years with Margo Adams added a human dimension to his image, but it was hardly a welcome addition, especially after Adams, who traveled with the Red Sox on the road, revealed the escapades of some other members of the team in a palimony suit. The predictable clubhouse tussles and calls for getting rid of the third baseman ended when he won his fifth batting crown. But after slipping to a .259 average in 1992, he was allowed to depart as a free agent to the Yankees, where he collected his eleventh and twelfth .300 seasons in his first two years in a New York uniform.

TOMMY BOND

An early curveballer, Bond is the only pitcher in history to win 40 or more games in three con-secutive seasons, in the process becoming the major leagues' first 100-game winner and pitching Boston to National League pennants in 1877 and 1878. The right-hander might have reached the century mark even sooner, except that while with Hartford in 1876, he accused manager Bob Ferguson of throwing games, only to be suspended for the final third of the season by club president Morgan Bulkeley, who sided with the pilot.

BARRY BONDS

Because of the record $43.75-million six-year contract that he signed with the Giants prior to the 1993 season, Bonds's on-field talents and contributions to winning clubs will never be described as invaluable, but he remained the single most dominant player in the game in the early part of the decade. A lefty swinger who had already captured three MVP trophies before the 1994 season, he was the primary offensive and defensive force in three straight Eastern Division titles of the Pirates between 1990 and 1992 and in San Francisco's 103 wins after he signed with the club as a free agent. Rather than sag under the money given him by the Giants, he turned in his greatest single-season performance by batting .336 and leading the National League in homers (46), RBIs (123), slugging percentage (.677), total bases (365), and on-base percentage (.458). With the hitting went the best defensive play in left field in the major leagues.

In his three previous seasons, with the Pirates, Bonds totaled 92 home runs and 333 RBIs. Especially in his final year in Pittsburgh, his on-field performance was constantly shadowed by two factors—his clear intention of leaving the club because of its claimed inability to compete with richer teams on the free-agent market, and his slumps in League Championship Series play that went a long way toward three consecutive losses of these series by the Pirates.

BOBBY BONDS

The father of Barry Bonds was a player of enormous parts who managed only a decent whole. In a fourteen-year career that extended from 1968 to 1981, the right-hand-hitting outfielder was the only major leaguer to combine power and speed to record five different seasons with at least 30 home runs and 30 stolen bases. At the same time, however, he struck out enough to take both first and second places for whiffs in a season, fanning 189 times in 1970 and 187 times in 1969. He also struck out at least 120 times in eight other years. Making Bonds's situation even more anomalous was the fact that, strikeouts notwithstanding, a parade of managers in both leagues insisted on using his speed for a leadoff hitter; this resulted in six different seasons of his scoring at least 100 runs, but, despite his slugging, only two seasons of 100 RBIs.

Bonds entered the major leagues with the Giants, becoming the first major leaguer in the twentieth century to hit a grand-slam home run in his maiden game. After San Francisco despaired of its own promotion of him as the second coming of Willie Mays, Bonds was dealt to the Yankees after the 1974 season in a controversial trade for Bobby Murcer that did neither of the sluggers much good. From that point on, Bonds was considered a power solution for several teams (Angels, White Sox, Rangers, Indians) that needed a year or less before deciding that his strikeout rate was too high a price to pay for his round-trippers and stolen bases; his travels and his power enabled him to set a record by hitting 30 or more homers in a season with five different clubs. It didn't help his case, either, that his raw numbers had made him one of the higher-paid players of the 1970s. He closed out his career with two painful years with the Cardinals and Cubs, during which it became obvious that leg injuries and his midthirties had robbed him of his speed.

ZEKE BONURA

Bonura was a slugging first baseman for the Senators in the 1930s whose defense usually had fans and teammates covering their eyes. One of his patented plays was to wave off pitchers on ground balls and lose the race to the first-base bag. His most ardent fan was Vice President John Nance Garner, who spent every free moment at Griffith Stadium and who insisted that Bonura come over for a hug and a handshake every time the slugger crossed home plate after a home run.

BRET BOONE

When he made his debut with the Mariners in 1992, second baseman Boone, grandson of infielder Ray Boone and son of catcher Bob Boone, became baseball's first third-generation major leaguer.

IKE BOONE

Boone was the greatest minor league hitter of all time, compiling an average of .370 in a career that spanned 1920 to 1937. A conspicuous liability in the field for his slowness afoot, the lefty-swinging outfielder failed to stick in the big leagues despite a .319 average in all or parts of eight scattered seasons with four clubs. His best major league marks were back-to-back .333 and .330 averages as a regular in 1924 and 1925 for the Red Sox; his best minor league year was 1929, when he hit .407 in 198 games in the Pacific Coast League.

JOE BORDEN

Calling himself Josephus the Phenomenal, Borden, while a member of the Philadelphia White Stockings, pitched the only no-hitter in the five-year history of the National Association, on July 28, 1875. The following year, on April 22, he won the National League's first game for Boston (a 6–5 victory in Philadelphia), then pitched the National League's first no-hitter, against Cincinnati, on May 23. The right-hander is still not officially credited with this last feat, however, because official scorer O. P. Caylor idiosyncratically recorded bases on balls as hits, and Borden allowed two bases on balls that day. Despite these feats, Borden had only an 11–12 record when Boston president Nathaniel Apollonio released him, and, in a ploy to get out from under the pitcher's $2,000-per-year contract, insisted that he work as a groundskeeper. The ex-pitcher took up his new duties until the owner offered a generous buyout, which Borden accepted and left baseball at age twenty-two.

HANK BOROWY

Nobody is more responsible for the last appearance of the Cubs in a World Series than Borowy. A right-hander for the Yankees, he had won 10 games by mid-July in 1945 when owner Larry MacPhail suddenly put him on waivers for reasons never satisfactorily explained. Chicago put in a claim, purchased him for $97,000, and then rode his 11–2 record the rest of the way to the National League flag. Not only did Borowy become the third twentieth-century pitcher (after Patsy Flaherty and Joe McGinnity) to win 20 games in a season split between two major leagues, but also his 2.13 ERA was the best in the NL. Most speculation around the deal has traced it to MacPhail's emergency need of cash.

BABE BORTON

Borton, who came to the Yankees as part of the 1913 deal that dumped Hal Chase on the White Sox, failed to live up to the standards established by his fellow first baseman. First, Borton was nowhere near the hitter Chase was, batting only .130 for the rest of the season. Second, when Borton got expelled from baseball for crooked play, it wasn't from the major leagues, as in the case of Chase, but from the Pacific Coast League, in a 1921 scandal that involved five of the circuit's eight teams.

GENE BOSSARD

Bossard was the most illustrious member of the first family of groundskeeping while employed by the White Sox between 1941 and 1983. Bill Veeck, for one, praised him for helping Chicago snatch a few extra wins every season. In 1967, for example, the area around home plate became known as Camp Swampy when Bossard dug up and watered the dirt as an aid to Chicago sinkerballers. Conversely, he used clay and gasoline to harden the soil if the opposition happened to be starting a sinker specialist. Other tricks included lowering or raising the bullpen mounds of adversaries to disturb their rhythm when they entered a game; keeping the grass long in front of slow-footed Chicago infielders; and adding more paint to the foul lines to tilt balls back into fair territory when the home team had gifted bunters.

Bossard's father, Emil, had held the same position with the Indians in the 1930s; Gene's son Roger succeeded him with Chicago in 1983; and other members of the family—Harold (with Cleveland in the 1960s), Marshall (also with Cleveland, in the 1970s), and Brian (with the Padres in the 1980s)—were similarly employed.

JIM BOTTOMLEY (Hall of Fame, 1974)

Bottomley was the first player to come through Branch Rickey's farm system—and almost the cause of its demise. Promoted to the Cardinals in 1922, the left-hand-hitting first baseman was told by Syracuse owner Ernest Landgraf to stay put until Rickey reached that city. What Landgraf didn't say was that despite his commitment to develop Bottomley for St. Louis as part of a deal in which the Cardinals owned half of the Syracuse franchise, he had had second thoughts and had threatened Rickey with putting the power hitter up for auction unless he received more money. With the validity of his farm system idea at stake, the St. Louis general manager got into an all-night bargaining and screaming session with Landgraf, at the end of which the Cardinals had to buy the other half of the minor league club to assure the delivery of Bottomley. It was a situation that Rickey and St. Louis president Sam Breadon didn't allow to happen again, insisting on total control or other contractual safeguards with the minor league teams in the franchise chain.

As for Bottomley, he had a sixteen-year career during which he averaged .310 and played a key role in four St. Louis pennants. Among his biggest years were 1925, when he batted .367 and led the National League in hits and doubles; 1926, when he led the way in doubles and RBIs; and 1928, when he took MVP honors for averaging .325 and setting the pace in doubles, home runs, and RBIs. In that season he also became the only player in major league history to swat 40 doubles, 20 triples, and 40 homers. Over his first nine seasons he never hit fewer than 31 doubles, and for another string of six years he drove in at least 100 runs. In 1924 he established a single-game mark of 12 RBIs—a record tied by St. Louis outfielder Mark Whiten in 1993.

LOU BOUDREAU (Hall of Fame, 1970)

Boudreau was so popular in Cleveland in the 1940s that he turned the quintessential populist Bill Veeck into the Grinch that Stole Baseball. And that was *before* the right-hand-hitting shortstop and manager led the Indians to one of its only two world championships.

After a couple of brief stints with the club at

the end of the 1930s, Boudreau took over short-stop in 1940, batting .295 and driving in 101 runs in his first full season. In the years that followed, he won a batting crown (1944), led the American League in doubles (1941, 1944, and 1947), and collected an MVP trophy (in 1948 for a .355 average with 18 home runs and 106 RBIs). In the field, he teamed with Roy Mack and then Joe Gordon to give the AL its steadiest double-play combination.

Boudreau the player was also Boudreau the manager as of 1942 and for most of the rest of his fifteen-year playing career, and that was where the trouble with Veeck began. Taking over the Cleveland franchise from John Sherwin and Alva Bradley in 1946, Veeck made little secret of his desire to replace Boudreau as pilot in favor of somebody (Casey Stengel was the most often-mentioned name) who would provide more color-ful daily quotes to the press. When the shortstop made it clear, however, that he would find it difficult to play for the Indians under another dugout boss, Veeck held his fire, since he had no intention of trading away his star player. But then, at the end of the 1947 season, the Browns stepped forward with an offer for Boudreau that would have included slugging shortstop Vern Stephens. As soon as Cleveland newspapers got wind of the proposal, however, Boudreau supporters organized protest demonstrations and circulated petitions demanding that Veeck leave town instead of their hero. Veeck ran all over Cleveland, going from bar to restaurant to bar, to admit as personally as he could that he had made a mistake while simultaneously denying that the St. Louis trade had been his idea. The upshot was that Boudreau was given an extension on his contract as player-manager, with Veeck grabbing the consolation prize of assigning his own coaches to the club.

In 1948, Boudreau paid back his fan support by leading Cleveland to its first pennant since 1920, dramatizing his own contribution by clouting two home runs in a special playoff game against Boston. The icing on the cake was a World Series victory against the Braves.

The years that followed were nowhere near as gratifying. Moving over to the Red Sox in the early 1950s as a manager with only a handful of at-bats left in him, Boudreau discovered a city slow to forget that he had defeated both Boston teams in 1948. He only made his situation worse by announcing before the 1952 season that no one then on the club, including local demigod Ted Williams, would be untouchable if the right deal came along. In 1955 he took over the Athletics in their first transplanted year in Kansas City, and was a largely negligible presence over the next couple of years as the franchise shipped its best players to the Yankees in one suspicious trade after another.

Boudreau's last opportunity to wear a uniform was in 1960, when he was asked to come out of the broadcasting booth to take over the Cubs. Despite not being able to lift the team out of the cellar, he demanded a two-year contract from Phil Wrigley at the end of the season and was turned down. While Boudreau returned to broadcasting Chicago games, Wrigley replaced him with his rotating managers scheme involving a handful of coaches.

JIM BOUTON

Bouton's early 1970s best-seller *Ball Four* scandalized both the baseball establishment and stiff-necked players by naming names in a diaristic narrative of the right-hander's experiences with the 1969 Seattle Pilots and Houston Astros and recollections of his years with the Yankees. Although most of the uproar over the book was because of its casual depiction of the sex-obsessed lives of major leaguers, it also unnerved front-office executives with its specific instances of settling rosters through racial quotas and of management hypocrisy in contract negotiations. Helped to the best-seller list by Commissioner Bowie Kuhn's clumsy attempts to have Bouton apologize for it, the book generated still more hypocrisy when it was attacked by Mickey Mantle and Billy Martin for "betraying" player confidences; while maintaining their public contempt of Bouton even decades later, Mantle and Martin didn't decline the help of ghostwriters to write their own (boastful) versions of major league womanizing and carousing.

Before becoming identified with his writing, Bouton had distinguished himself as a 21-game and 18-game winner for the pennant–winning Yankees in 1963 and 1964, respectively. Following his stint with Houston, he turned to sportscasting for several years, then tried to make a comeback as a knuckleballer with the 1978 Braves. Although the effort was buoyed by Ted Turner's cable superstation, it ended after one victory in five games.

BOB BOWMAN

Bowman threw one of the most resounding beanballs in baseball history when he decked Joe Medwick of the Dodgers in 1940. The St. Louis right-hander uncorked the pitch in Medwick's very first plate appearance against his former Cardinal teammates, less than a week after he had been purchased by Brooklyn for a whopping $135,000. It also followed an angry exchange between the players before the game, making it clear that there had been nothing accidental about the delivery. Aside from precipitating an ugly brawl between the Dodgers and the Cardinals, the beanball knocked out Medwick and made him a relatively more tentative hitter for the rest of his career. More than that, it caused enraged Brooklyn president Larry MacPhail to demand that the district attorney's office open an investigation into what he called Beanball, Inc.—the suspicion that all National League pitchers were deliberately throwing at Dodger hitters. As ludicrous as the charge might have sounded, it touched the right publicity nerve in the wake of the Murder, Inc., investigation, to the point that Burton Turkus, the prosecutor who had nailed Lepke Buchalter and his criminal associates, did indeed call in several Brooklyn and St. Louis officials for questioning. Still another consequence of the Bowman pitch was that it prompted MacPhail to order prototypes of batting helmets (actually, bands around the rim of uniform caps) for his players.

CLETE BOYER

Brooks Robinson had little on Boyer as a defensive third baseman, and there were years that he showed he was no automatic out at the plate, either. But Boyer's distinctions go beyond what he accomplished on the field. For one thing, he was one of seven brothers—the most in history—to have played in organized baseball; pitcher Cloyd and third baseman Ken also made the majors, while Wayne, Lynn, Ron, and Len had to

be satisfied with the minors. When Clete joined the Athletics in 1955, he also became a symbol of the Yankees' grip on the Kansas City franchise. Impressed by the infielder but not at all interested in carrying him on its roster for two years as a bonus baby, New York reached an under-the-table agreement to have the Athletics warehouse him while he was getting his feet wet, then grabbed him in a 1957 trade. Near the end of his career, with the 1971 Braves, Boyer got into a contract dispute with general manager Paul Richards, was released, and found himself able to latch on only with Hawaii in the Pacific Coast League. From there he became the first professional American player ever traded to the Japanese leagues.

ALVA BRADLEY

Bradley was Cleveland's longest-running owner, heading the organization through its all-but-invisible period of 1928 to 1946. Only once in that span did the Indians get within single digits behind the American League pennant winner, and that was in 1940, when the club folded in the last week of the season against the Tigers. Although he and his brother Chuck owned considerable prime real estate in the center of Cleveland, and made even more money from the profitable retail operations they installed on it, Bradley never spent a nickel when a penny would do. For years he refused to give the title of general manager to baseball operations chief Cy Slapnicka as an economy move and was inspired as much by thrift as intuition in giving the managing job to shortstop Lou Boudreau in 1942. By the mid-1940s, however, Bradley's penny-pinching had precipitated an organizational mess; typical of the team's foresight was that five members of the board of directors were widows who had little of their late husbands' interest in the Indians or in baseball. When the franchise's largest stockholder, John Sherwin, insisted on selling out to Bill Veeck, Bradley had little choice but to follow suit.

BOBBY BRAGAN

A Branch Rickey protégé, Bragan had a stormy career as both player and manager. To Rickey's stated disappointment, he was one of the handful of Brooklyn players who refused to play with

Jackie Robinson when the Dodgers announced their intention of breaking the color line in 1947. Although the Alabama-born infielder later said that he regretted his stand, some of the same racist charges were in the air during his stint as manager of the Braves in the 1960s. As a tactician, Bragan was a study in unorthodoxy, at one point in Pittsburgh putting his sluggers (especially Frank Thomas) at the top of the lineup because ''they're the only ones who know how to hit, so they'll get up more this way.'' He became the center of an even longer controversy in Cleveland, where local legend attributed him with putting a hex on the team in retaliation for being fired after the 1957 season. Although Bragan himself always said that the hex story was the fruit of a disc jockey's imagination, it gained sufficient currency (and promotion appeal) for the Indians to bring in a witch during the 1986 season to take the alleged spell off the team. The Cleveland firing also gave rise to one of baseball's more famous quotes, when Bragan related how general manager Frank Lane called him into his office and declared: ''Bobby, I don't know how we're going to get along without you, but starting tomorrow, we're going to try.''

RALPH BRANCA

Branca threw the most infamous pitch in National League history on October 3, 1951, when his one-strike delivery to Bobby Thomson in the ninth inning of the third game of a playoff duel was belted for a three-run homer and a pennant victory for the Giants over the Dodgers. The Brooklyn right-hander had been summoned from the bullpen to face Thomson after New York had put the tying runs on base against faltering starter Don Newcombe. In the decades since the blast, Branca and Thomson have made countless public appearances together to commemorate what many consider baseball's single most thrilling moment.

If Branca's presence on the mound cost the Dodgers a pennant in 1951, his absence from the hill cost the club another flag, in 1946. Furious that the pitcher had given him a hard time in contract negotiations, club boss Branch Rickey insisted that he be used only for mop-up duties for the first five months of the 1946 campaign. Only when Brooklyn was in dire need of another starter, in September, did Rickey cancel the order, permitting Branca to hurl a couple of shutouts over the final weeks of the season. When the Dodgers finished in a tie with the Cardinals, the pitcher was given a playoff game start but didn't fare any better against St Louis than he did against New York five years later; in fact, Branca holds the probably unassailable record of three losses (one in 1946 and two in 1951) in rare non-League Championship Series playoffs.

SAM BREADON

One of Branch Rickey's more neglected accomplishments was making Breadon seem like the junior partner in their running of the Cardinals in the 1920s and 1930s. In fact, the one-time automobile salesman held sway over the franchise as its boss of bosses for twenty-seven years, most of the time preferring to think of Rickey as an overpaid employee rather than as a minority shareholder. It was his money that financed Rickey's ambitious farm system, his temper that exploded when the farm system almost ruined the organization, and his long-simmering resentment that he wasn't perceived as the boss that led to Rickey's departure for the Dodgers in the early 1940s.

Breadon got involved with the Cardinals initially to keep an eye on his money, which had been disappearing down a rathole during the ''civic ownership'' phase of the organization in the late teens under James Jones. Soon after taking over as team president in January 1920, Breadon scored a financial and public relations coup by arguing that League Park had become dangerously decrepit and getting the city behind him in a campaign to have the Cardinals share the Browns-owned Sportsman's Park. When Browns owner Phil Ball rejected the idea of sharing quarters with what was then St. Louis's second team, Breadon took out newspaper ads urging readers to bring dirt to a quarry that he had leased to contribute to the construction of a new stadium. Terrified by the prospect of such a public demonstration, City Hall increased its pressure on Ball until he accepted the Cardinals as tenants. To put a ribbon on his victory, Breadon then turned around and sold the ramshackle League Park to the St. Louis Board of Education for $200,000 and some adjoining lots to other city agencies for $75,000. It was this money that seeded Rickey's farm system.

Breadon's baseball imagination encompassed more than his readiness to accept Rickey's ideas about building up a minor league chain of teams. It was Breadon, for instance, who began the practice of scheduling Sunday doubleheaders, in the conviction that people sought more than merely two hours of entertainment on their day off. He also lobbied for years for night baseball, first running into the wall of NL owners who thought the idea frivolous, then coming up against Ball, who was hardly ready to install lights in Sportsman's Park on the proposal of an unwanted tenant. It was in the context of such ongoing enmity between the two owners that Breadon always delighted in relating how Ball had enlarged Sportsman's Park in anticipation of big crowds for watching the Browns in the 1926 World Series, then gagged before the sight of the extra seating serving Cardinal fans instead.

The Cardinals' first taste of postseason action, in 1926, was not without problems for Breadon. Most of all, there was his personal dislike for manager-second baseman Rogers Hornsby, who was never reluctant to use his star status as a lever for more money. When Hornsby rejected a one-year contract for 1927, Breadon took on the entire city by trading him to the Giants for Frankie Frisch. Not only did Frisch win over St. Louis fans irate at Hornsby's departure by his aggressive play and by helping the team to another pennant in 1928, but also the experience persuaded Breadon that it would never be quite as difficult again to get rid of a manager, even after a winning season. This attitude was reflected over the years that followed in his abrupt derricking of the likes of Bill McKechnie, Gabby Street, Billy Southworth, and Ray Blades.

Despite presiding over clubs in the late 1920s and early 1930s that usually either won pennants or finished near the top, Breadon was so convinced that the Depression was going to linger and that the St. Louis market was going to become more prohibitive for two major league teams that he entered into negotiations for the sale of the club with Oklahoma oil millionaire Lew Wentz after the 1934 season. Even when those talks foundered on Wentz's refusal to accept his

estimates on the value of the Cardinal farm system, Breadon turned his energies to moving the franchise to Detroit. The obstacle there turned out to be threats by the Tigers that any such move would rekindle the early-century war between the leagues. In the end, the St. Louis owner fell back on the tried and true formula of building up his cash reserves by selling off star players—a tactic that in the case of the Cardinals was far less destructive than with other teams because of the prospects that kept arriving through the farm system.

In 1938, the Breadon-Rickey relationship began to unravel in the wake of Commissioner Kenesaw Landis's decision to release seventy-four St. Louis farmhands. In what was to be known as the Cedar Rapids Case, Landis defended his move by charging that Rickey had entered into ''secret understandings'' with minor league officials in violation of rules covering competitive opportunity. Although Landis never quite got around to making a formal presentation of the charges, Breadon resisted Rickey's urgings to file suit against the commissioner and refused to insist on the club's right to retain the services of the seventy-four players, the most noted of whom were outfielder Pete Reiser and infielder Skeeter Webb. To intimates, he claimed to have been embarrassed by the scandal and accused Rickey of endangering the very survival of the organization. For the next couple of years, Breadon thought nothing of publicly contradicting Rickey statements to the press. The final tear came in 1942, when he told Rickey of his intention of assigning sponsorship rights for radio coverage of the Cardinals to the Hyde Park beer company. When the abstemious general manager protested, Breadon reminded him who was the owner. Rickey got the message, and tendered his resignation in October.

Operating without Rickey didn't seem to faze Breadon. If anything, he appeared bent on being more royal than the king, completing countless trades that inevitably included some money for his pocket. The biggest setback over the final years of his reign came with the 1946 defection of several Cardinals, including prize southpaw Max Lanier, to the Mexican League organized by multimillionaire Jorge Pasquel. In defiance of the ban on the jumpers proclaimed by Commissioner

Happy Chandler, Breadon went to Mexico to negotiate with Pasquel for the return of his players. It proved to be a fairly academic exercise, since the Mexican had never really had any long-range plans for his league, but the trip aggravated Chandler, precipitating a lot of shouting behind executive doors. Breadon finally had enough of it all in 1947, selling out to lawyer Fred Saigh.

TED BREITENSTEIN

With catcher Heinie Peitz, Breitenstein formed the Cardinals' famed Pretzel Battery in the 1890s. The southpaw also pitched a no-hitter in his first major league start, for the American Association Browns on the last day of the 1891 season. In September 1894 he was fined $100 by St. Louis president Chris Von der Ahe for refusing to relieve in the second game of a doubleheader after having pitched 43 innings in nine days, including a complete game in the first half of the twin bill.

ROGER BRESNAHAN (Hall of Fame 1945)

A temperamental clone of his mentor John McGraw, Bresnahan brawled and battled his way through a seventeen-year career, almost all of it in the earliest years of the twentieth century. It was as much for his innovations in playing equipment as for his .280 lifetime average or the speed that made him one of the few catchers used in the leadoff spot that he earned a plaque in Cooperstown.

After a hospital stay necessitated by a beaning in 1905, Bresnahan took to wearing a protective helmet that was little more than a leather football helmet sliced in half; this "pneumatic head protector" failed to catch on. More successful were the receiver's efforts with shin guards. Surprised to discover in a collision at the plate that Philadelphia's Red Dooin wore papier-mâché protectors under his uniform, Bresnahan improved on the idea by sporting cricket leg pads on Opening Day of the 1907 season; while his inspiration met with initial scorn, less elaborate models were standard equipment within two years. The following year, he added padding to the inside rim of his catcher's mask to cushion the force of foul tips.

Traded by the Giants to the Cardinals in 1909, Bresnahan managed the club to financial if not artistic success—so much so that owner Helene

George Brett was the foremost exemplar of the Charlie Lau-style of hitting—and the franchise player for the Kansas City Royals. Photo compliments of the Kansas City Royals.

Britton presented him with a lucrative five-year contract in 1911. A year later, however, Britton fired him as pilot and traded his player contract to the Cubs because of money shorts; the manager's cause was not helped by charges that he had not fielded his best team in a key game against the Giants to give McGraw an edge in the pennant race against the Cubs and Pirates and by a subsequent four-letter-word defense of his innocence to the owner. It would be several years before he collected, in an out-of-court settlement, the $20,000 owed him. Known as the Duke of Tralee, especially in New York, where an Irish connection never hurt a player's popularity, Bresnahan was actually born in Toledo.

GEORGE BRETT

From the day he took over third base as a regular in 1974 to his retirement after the 1993 season, Brett was the franchise player for the Royals. A left-handed swinger with significant extra-base

THE BIOGRAPHICAL HISTORY OF BASEBALL

power, he posted a career average of .305, reaching the 3,000-hit level in 1992 and finishing his career with 3,154. Among his other offensive accomplishments was winning batting titles in 1976, 1980, and 1990—making him the only big leaguer to pick up a Silver Bat in three different decades. In 1980 he took MVP honors by leading Kansas City to a pennant with a .390 average; it was the highest mark in the major leagues since Ted Williams had hit .406 in 1941. Always more than a singles hitter, Brett led the American League in doubles twice, in triples three times, and in slugging average three times. In eight seasons he hit more than 20 home runs, and he topped the 100-RBI and 100-run marks four times each.

Franchise player or not, Brett had his uncomfortable moments in a Kansas City uniform. At the end of the 1974 season he broke down in tears when he heard that manager Jack McKeon had fired his hitting mentor, Charlie Lau. In 1978 Brett mainly sounded bitter when Whitey Herzog, who had rehired Lau after succeeding McKeon, did the same thing. Despite his own solid hitting, including three home runs in the third game of the 1978 American League Championship Series, he admitted to being devastated by the Royals' three straight losses to the Yankees in the playoffs between 1976 and 1978. When the club did finally make it past New York to the 1980 World Series against Philadelphia, he became the butt of nationwide jokes for a well-publicized case of hemorrhoids. Although he tried to make light of his ailment during the Series, his humor was in short supply the following season, when reporters kept referring to the condition. In one episode, he swung a crutch at a photographer who thought he was being cute about everything; in another, his slow recovery from an off-season operation to correct the problem caused him to break up a dugout toilet; in a third incident, he shoved a woman reporter.

On July 24, 1983, Brett was the protagonist of one of baseball's most farcical moments. In a game at Yankee Stadium, he hit what appeared to be a two-run home run off Goose Gossage with two out in the ninth inning to give the Royals a 5-4 lead. But then umpire Joe Brinkman agreed with New York manager Billy Martin's protest

that pine tar had been applied to more of Brett's bat than was legal, nullified the home run, called him out for the violation, and declared the Yankees the winner of the game. After an enraged Brett was pulled away from Brinkman, Kansas City filed an official protest with the league office, and won the argument when AL president Lee MacPhail decided that the pine tar regulation was too vague. A series of legal countermoves by the Yankees followed, but when these efforts to reverse MacPhail's decision failed, the teams took the field again in August to resume play from the moment of Brett's homer. With only 1,245 people in the stands to watch four outs and New York pitcher Ron Guidry pressed into service as a center fielder, Kansas City finally sealed its 5-4 win, but only after New York appealed—futilely—that Brett had missed each bag in circling the bases.

WALTER BRIGGS

After staying in Frank Navin's shadow for some seventeen years as a partner in the Tigers, Briggs spent an equal amount of time as the franchise's most visible executive. Taking over baseball operations after Navin's death in 1935, the former autobody builder presided over a Detroit pennant in 1940 and a world championship in 1945, but otherwise had to content himself with runner-up clubs that usually featured a lot of hitting and little pitching. On the other hand, he left himself open for more than one run-in with the commissioner's office, other owners, and fans.

Briggs's biggest crisis occurred in 1940, when Commissioner Kenesaw Landis cut loose ninety-one Detroit farmhands on the grounds that their careers had been stymied by a lot of devious paperwork. Although general manager Jack Zeller took the blame for the violations, Briggs's refusal to fire or even criticize his lieutenant suggested to many that he wasn't taken completely by surprise by Landis's charges. In 1941 the Detroit owner aroused the irritation of other major league owners by signing Dick Wakefield as baseball's first bonus baby; in language similar to later attacks on Ted Turner and George Steinbrenner for throwing big money at free agents, the owners fretted that the $52,000 and automobile given to Wakefield would set a dangerous precedent for other high school and college players targeted by major league teams. In 1946 Briggs provoked fan protests when he put slugger Hank Greenberg on waivers and managed to get him out of the AL to the Pirates. The move followed Greenberg's announced ambition to take over as Detroit general manager and the owner's insistence that the first baseman wasn't ready for such a position. There was little doubt that the old-boy network was at work in allowing Greenberg to pass through the league without any claims being made on him.

By the time Briggs died in 1952, he had formalized his distance from Navin in the most conspicuous way possible—rebaptizing Navin Field as Briggs Stadium.

GUS BRITTAIN

Brittain's major league career consisted of one game as a catcher and two appearances as a pinch hitter for the Reds in 1937. As far as manager Charlie Dressen was concerned, however, his offensive and defensive skills were beside the point, since his principal job on the team was to start brawls that Dressen deemed necessary for animating the team. Although Brittain held up his end of the bargain by jumping out of the dugout to precipitate several melees, Cincinnati still finished in the cellar.

HELENE BRITTON

Britton became the first woman to run a big league club when she inherited the Cardinals from her uncle Stanley Robison in 1911. After years of fighting off other National League owners who wanted her out of the exclusive male circle and of entrusting the franchise's day-to-day operations to others, including her husband, Schuyler Britton, she took over the team presidency herself in 1916.

Britton's ownership got off to a deceptive start in 1911, when unprecedented figures allowed her to liquidate organization debts and even show a profit. She was so gratified by the showing that she gave manager Roger Bresnahan a new five-year contract, with promises of 10 percent of the team's profits for its duration. She soon regretted her largesse. Aside from the fact that St. Louis played itself out of the 1912 race within the first month of the season, she began sinking financially

again under legal fees piling up over who was the legal executor of the Robison estate. Bresnahan made his position worse, first by coming under charges that he had thrown some games to the Giants to allow his mentor, John McGraw, to beat the Cubs and the Pirates for the pennant, then by defending himself in Britton's home with a tirade that she considered uncouth and inappropriate for her station. When she replaced Bresnahan with Miller Huggins, the outgoing manager initiated another legal wrangle for the money still due him on his five-year pact.

Suffragette Britton correctly calculated that attracting more women to Cardinals' games would bring in more men as well, and she achieved her goal by increasing the frequency of ladies' days and by hiring a crooner to perform between innings. Although hard-pressed herself, she even passed along part of her profits to the players when, in 1914, they delivered on her proposal to reward a third-place finish with 20 percent bonuses.

Britton's husband, Schuyler, did little as team president except follow her instructions and build a reputation as a kept man who liked to drink and womanize. When he returned home one night in a drunken state and smashed up the house, Britton initiated divorce proceedings and succeeded him as president. She personally transacted the franchise's only deal in 1916—the sale of pitcher Slim Sallee to the Giants for some urgently needed cash. Her heart no longer in the job, however, she summoned Huggins and organization attorney James Jones after the season, telling them she wanted to sell and giving them first crack at coming up with the purchase money. Jones proved to be the winner of the competition when he put together a coalition of scores of St. Louis businessmen for meeting the $375,000 asking price. It would take a number of years and threatened lawsuits, however, before Britton was able to collect all the money owed to her.

JOHNNY BROACA

Broaca predicted his own major league success, then walked away from it—for a pugilistic career. Playing for Yale University in the early 1930s, the right-hander told coach Joe Wood, a former Red Sox hurler, that he would take the mound only once a week because he was saving his arm for the major leagues. Inserted into the Yankee rotation in 1934, he won 39 games over three seasons. But with a starting assignment in the 1936 World Series imminent, he announced his retirement to become a boxer, predicting that he would one day fight Joe Louis for the heavyweight championship. While he did make two comeback attempts in baseball (with New York in 1937 and Cleveland in 1939), he never won a professional fight.

LOU BROCK (Hall of Fame, 1985)

Brock's 3,023 career hits and National League-record 938 steals over nineteen seasons (1961–79) assured him a place in the Hall of Fame, but he was anything but a traditional leadoff hitter. For one thing, the lefty-swinging outfielder struck out more than 100 times in nine seasons, and his lifetime total of 1,730 whiffs is only 27 fewer than contemporaneous leadoff man Bobby Bonds racked up. For another, Brock's .344 on-base average was 13 points lower than Bonds's .356 and a full 53 points behind such a non-Cooperstown leadoff man as Richie Ashburn. To a considerable degree, in fact, Brock's value at the top of the Cardinal lineups in the 1960s and 1970s had to be underwritten by two of the best second-place hitters in baseball history—Curt Flood and Ted Sizemore.

Joining the Cubs in the early 1960s, Brock

Lou Brock ran National League defenses ragged after being obtained by the Cardinals from the Cubs in 1964. National Baseball Library, Cooperstown, N.Y.

gained attention initially not so much for his speed as for his power, especially on June 17, 1962, when he became the only left-handed batter ever to clout a ball into the right-field side of the center-field bleachers in the Polo Grounds, an estimated 488 feet from home plate. Even after being traded to the Cardinals for Ernie Broglio in one of baseball's worst deals two years later, Brock remained indifferent enough to the vast dimensions of Busch Stadium to reach double figures in home runs on seven occasions. It was Brock's running game that became his signature, however. In 1966 he swiped 74 bases to lead the league in that category for the first of eight times; in 1974 he rolled up 118 steals, setting a new major league theft mark (later eclipsed by Rickey Henderson). Brock was even more devastating to opposition batteries in postseason play. In the 1967 World Series against the Red Sox, he stole a record seven bases while batting .414 with 12 hits; a year later, in the Series against the Tigers, he swiped another seven while increasing his average to .464 with 13 hits. Aside from tying Eddie Collins for most stolen bases (14) in World Series play, he also holds the record for the highest World Series batting average (.391) among players with at least 20 games.

Despite his contributions to the Cardinals for almost two decades, Brock was publicly embarrassed by general manager John Claiborne before the 1979 season when he was told he had only the month of April to show that he wasn't washed up. Although no longer the speed demon he had been, he responded with a .304 average that allowed him to retire with dignity at the end of the year.

Brock's 3,000 hits put him in some unwanted exclusive company. Aside from Collins and Dave Winfield, he is the only big leaguer to reach that plateau without winning a batting title; along with Al Kaline, Carl Yastrzemski, Robin Yount, and Winfield, he is the only one to amass as many safeties without ending up with a .300 lifetime average (his career mark was .293).

JIM BROSNAN

Brosnan's journal of Cincinnati's 1961 pennant-winning season, published as *The Long Season,* annoyed the baseball establishment for its less than reverential tone. Reds' owner Bill De-Witt, for one, forbade the right-handed reliever from any further writing, on the basis of ambiguous contract clauses warning against conduct detrimental to baseball. Brosnan had the same problem with the White Sox after being dealt to the American League after the 1963 season, but by then had foreseen the end of his pitching career and continued work on a second book, *Pennant Race,* in spite of front-office warnings. Somewhat lost amid all the humorlessness of De-Witt and his colleagues was that Brosnan had been a key factor in the 1961 pennant by winning 10 games and saving 16 others.

DAN BROUTHERS (Hall of Fame, 1945)

Brouthers, who played for eleven teams in eighteen nineteenth-century seasons plus a brief return engagement in 1904, has the highest batting average (.342) of any first baseman in the history of the game and the ninth highest among all players. The lefty's five batting crowns were won for four different teams—the Buffalo Bisons in 1882 and 1883; the National League and American Association Boston clubs in 1889 and 1891, respectively; and the Dodgers in 1892. He also led the NL in slugging in his first six full seasons, adding a seventh title in the AA.

BOBBY BROWN

A platoon third baseman with severe defensive limitations in the late 1940s and early 1950s, Brown spent as much time in the Army and in medical school as he did with the Yankees. Retiring in 1954 to practice medicine, he became a successful cardiac surgeon, but then left his practice to accept an appointment as American League president in 1984. In that role he was largely a bystander to the owner collusion, drug scandals, labor strife, and debates over television revenues and the future of the game that marked his tenure; he also stood by as AL owners spent his decade in office eroding the powers of the league presidency.

Brown was succeeded as AL president in June 1994 by University of Kansas chancellor Gene Budig.

JOE L. BROWN

The son of movie actor Joe E. Brown, Brown oversaw the revival of the Pittsburgh franchise in the late 1950s, remaining head of the team's baseball operations through its glory years in the 1970s. His most important moves as general manager were to be on the scene to succeed Branch Rickey when the latter's four-star farm club prospects began filtering into Pittsburgh in the late 1950s and to hire Danny Murtaugh as manager four different times to manage the club. Brown came back for a second stint in the 1980s, mainly to shake high salaries out of the roster so the Galbreath family would find it easier to sell the franchise.

THREE FINGER BROWN (Hall of Fame, 1949)

Brown was the National League's Ed Walsh in forging most of the senior circuit's ERA records. Among other things, Brown established the standard for one-season stinginess in 1906 by yielding merely 1.06 runs per nine innings; his fourteen-year (1903–16) ERA of 2.06 has been bettered only by Walsh and Addie Joss among all big league hurlers. The dominating hill force of the

Three Finger Brown exploited his handicap to give a novel spin to his pitches. National Baseball Library, Cooperstown, N.Y.

champion Cub teams in the first decade of the century, the right-hander gained his nickname from two childhood accidents on his Indiana farm. In the first mishap, he caught his index finger in a corn shredder and had to have it amputated above the knuckle; a couple of weeks later, he broke his third and fourth fingers, and they never grew straight. At the height of his popularity with Chicago, the corn shredder was the centerpiece of a tourist attraction in his hometown.

For six straight years between 1906 and 1911, Brown registered 20 wins, gaining a career-high 29 victories in 1908. In that year of Fred Merkle's boner, he kept Chicago in the running against the Giants by winning both ends of a doubleheader the day before the New York first baseman failed to touch second base and set off baseball's biggest stretch-run controversy. In the makeup game necessitated by Merkle's misadventure, Brown relieved starter Jack Pfeister in the first inning without bothering to warm up, going on to blank the Giants the rest of the way for a 4–2 Cub pennant. Coming in from the bullpen was nothing exotic for him: While racking up his 20 or more wins between 1908 and 1911, he also paced the NL in saves in each of the four campaigns.

Two years later, however, Brown, his skills eroded, fell victim to one of Cub owner Charles Murphy's periodic economy moves and was sold to a minor league team, engendering widespread sentiment that ten-year veterans should at least be afforded the courtesy of an unconditional release in such circumstances. Largely because of Brown, the Players Fraternity made this one of its key bargaining issues with major league owners. The hurler resurfaced with the Reds and later in the Federal League in 1914 and 1915. On his last legs in 1916, Brown took to the mound for the Cubs against the equally aged Christy Mathewson for one final face-off. Mathewson, then with the Reds, recorded the last of his 373 victories in a messy 10–7 affair.

PETE BROWNING

Despite his preeminence among American Association hitters, Browning's most enduring baseball legacy has more to do with the manufacture of his bats than with what he accomplished with them. Convinced that each of his bats contained

just so many hits, he nurtured and named them. When one of his favorites splintered during the 1884 season, the Louisville outfielder accepted an offer by woodworker Bud Hillerich to fashion a new one specifically tailored to Browning's taste. Other players were so impressed with the first so-called Louisville Slugger that the company, eventually called Hillerich & Bradsby, was launched on its way to becoming the largest producer of baseball lumber.

Browning, whose .341 lifetime average and three batting titles (1882 and 1885 in the AA, 1890 in the Players League) have never sufficiently impressed Hall of Fame electors, was as incapable of handling fly balls and liquor as he was adept at hitting fastballs. His defensive deficiencies and his reluctance to slide may have made him a one-dimensional player, but coupled with his endless and boisterous monologues in saloons around the league about his bats, his eyes, and his hitting accomplishments, they also made him the AA's biggest drawing card.

Afflicted with a chronic mastoid infection that left him deaf, he may have turned to drink as a painkiller. A decade after his retirement, inadequate medical treatment led to brain damage misdiagnosed as insanity, and Browning was committed to an insane asylum.

JOHN T. BRUSH

Brush, who owned three National League franchises between 1889 and 1912, was predisposed toward schemes. As president of the Indianapolis Hoosiers in 1889, he persuaded the NL to accept a classification plan ranking players from A to E—not on their on-field ability but on their personal habits; salaries were to be doled out accordingly: $2,500 for A-level players, $2,250 for B's, $2000 for C's, $1,750 for D's, and $1,500 for E's. Only the intervention of Players Brotherhood leader John Montgomery Ward averted a strike over the plan, but it was also a major reason why the players decided to form their own league in 1890. As part of the NL's effort to shore up the hard-hit Giants during the Players League war, Brush reduced his Indianapolis franchise to minor league status and transferred its entire roster to New York before the season; then, with the Giants' situation deteriorating daily, he forgave part of the payment in exchange for a minority interest in the club. His reward for this soldierly support was control of the NL's franchise in Cincinnati.

In Cincinnati, Brush soon fell to feuding with *Commercial-Gazette* sportswriter Ban Johnson. Johnson's criticism of the club was so irksome that Brush used his influence as owner of the Western League's Indianapolis club to have the sportswriter appointed president of that minor league in 1894, thereby getting him out from under foot (and also setting in motion the formation of the American League). The relationship between the two men didn't improve with Johnson's career change, however. Brush made a shambles of the WL by shuttling players between Indianapolis and Cincinnati, to the point that the two clubs became known disparagingly as Cincinnapolis-Indianatti. Johnson and the rest of the circuit fought equally hard to limit the effects of Brush's dual ownership, which was effectively the earliest example of a farm system.

It was also as Cincinnati owner that, in 1898, he pushed through the so-called Brush Plan "For the Suppression of Obscene, Indecent, and Vulgar Language Upon the Ball Field." While its principal tenet—suspension and possible expulsion for players charged with violations—was never enforced, the scheme left a legacy in attendant decisions to enforce it by employing two arbiters for every game and to pay for the increased umpiring staff by expanding to a 154-game schedule.

Brush's reputation for deviousness was never more evident than in the events that brought, first, John McGraw, and then himself to the Giants in 1902. When New York majority stockholder Andrew Freedman lost his appetite for the business, Brush, still a junior partner, began increasing his Manhattan presence. It was, in fact, to Brush that Baltimore executive John J. Mahon turned over the slightly more than 50 percent of the AL Orioles' stock that he had, with McGraw's contrivance, collected in the wake of the manager's sudden July departure from Baltimore and almost immediate reemergence in New York. The situation of an NL owner exercising effective control over an AL franchise got even stickier when two Baltimore players were transferred to Cincinnati and six more to New York. The substance of the plot became much less murky in September when Brush sold the Reds and, with McGraw acting as intermediary, bought controlling interest in the Giants from Freedman.

The New York owner and manager remained the last holdouts against an accommodation with Johnson's American League, even refusing to allow the Giants to meet the Red Sox in the 1904 World Series. For the final eight years of his reign, Brush, suffering from locomotor ataxia, a degenerative disease of the nervous system often brought on by syphilis, left most club operations to his manager.

STEVE BRYE

A mere .258 hitter in nine seasons, Brye had his most memorable moment in the major leagues when he was accused of helping to throw a batting race. On the final day of the 1976 season, the Minnesota outfielder misjudged a fly ball by Kansas City's George Brett that fell safely over his head and rolled to the wall for an inside-the-park homer. The hit turned out to be the difference in the batting race between Brett and Royals teammate Hal McRae. After the game, a seething McRae accused Twins manager Gene Mauch of having ordered Brye, normally a good fielder, to give an edge to Brett for racial reasons. Both Mauch and Brye initially denied any deliberate partiality, but the outfielder later admitted that most players around the league wanted to see Brett win the title—because McRae was a mere designated hitter.

BILL BUCKNER

First baseman Buckner had an outstanding twenty-two-year career, primarily with the Dodgers and Cubs, that included one batting championship and recorded him as one of very few players to have 200–hit seasons in both leagues. But on October 25, 1986, he ransomed those accomplishments away in the minds of most Boston fans by booting the Mookie Wilson grounder that enabled the Mets to climax an incredible come-from-behind victory against the Red Sox in the tenth inning of the sixth game of the 1986 World Series. In fact, Buckner had played the entire Series in hightops to protect his bad ankles, and for some months had been replaced defensively when Boston had a lead. Manager John McNamara never provided a reason why he decided to leave Buckner on the field for the fateful tenth inning.

DOC BUCKNER

Buckner was one of several black trainers that early-century teams used as masseurs and sought to hide from the public. Employed by the White Sox, he had to be concealed on segregated trains and in whites-only hotels after players insisted that they needed his ministrations on the road as well as at home. Hotel managers knew not to say anything if they wanted to keep the Chicago account.

BOB BUHL

Buhl has several claims to being the worst-hitting pitcher in the history of the game. His most famous mark was the all-time futility of going 0-for-70 in 1962 while splitting his time between the Braves and Cubs. That was no statistical fluke, however, for in nine of his fifteen major league seasons he couldn't reach the .100 mark, only on one occasion did he get as high as .200 (when he batted a mere 25 times in an injury-plagued season), and his lifetime average was .089. When he was on the mound, on the other hand, the right-hander fashioned back-to-back 18-win seasons for Milwaukee in 1956 and 1957, also posting the National League's top winning percentage in the latter year.

MORGAN BULKELEY (Hall of Fame, 1937)

The owner of the Hartford franchise in 1876, Bulkeley became the National League's initial president when his club's name was drawn first out of a hat in the original selection of league directors; more than six decades later, he was awarded a plaque in Cooperstown merely to balance the selection of Ban Johnson, the American League's founding president. Bulkeley was also the first club owner to move his team from one city to another, a step taken only after repeated denials that such a move was imminent. Despite inducements such as season tickets (another first) and prohibitions on the local press against printing scores until a game was over, crowds in Hartford were sparse; when they proved even more

sparse in Brooklyn in 1877, Bulkeley dropped out of the league. Subsequently he concentrated on building the Aetna Insurance Company that his father had founded and on a political career in which he rose from Hartford mayor to Connecticut governor to U.S. senator.

JIM BUNNING

Bunning was the mound equivalent of Frank Robinson from the mid-1950s to the early 1970s, at least insofar as excelling in both the American and National leagues; his considerable accomplishments have, however, failed to impress Hall of Fame electors as much as they have Kentucky voters. The right-hander was the first pitcher since Cy Young to win 100 games in each league, the first since the same Young to strike out 1,000 batters in each league, and only the third—behind Young and Tom Hughes—to fashion a no-hitter in each circuit. Pitching for the Tigers, he held the Red Sox hitless on July 20, 1958; for the Phillies, he went one better, hurling a perfect game against the Mets on June 21, 1964. Although finishing just shy of enough votes for a Cooperstown plaque several times, Bunning has represented a Kentucky district in the U.S. House of Representatives since 1986.

GLENN BURKE

A backup outfielder for the Dodgers and Athletics in the 1970s, Burke is the only major league player to admit that he was gay. Although not exactly blackballed, he was discouraged enough by baseball's homophobia to quit the game midway through the 1979 season. Before leaving, he contributed to on-the-field rituals by giving the first high-five. On October 2, 1977, Burke was the on-deck batter when Dusty Baker of the Dodgers clouted his thirtieth round-tripper—giving Los Angeles its record-making fourth player with at least that many homers. According to Burke, he just instinctively raised his hands to the sky, and Baker reciprocated with a high-five slap.

The former outfielder was felled by AIDS in 1994.

KITTY BURKE

If St. Louis manager Frankie Frisch had had his way, Burke would have been the first woman to bat in a major league game. On July 31, 1935, the Cardinals played their first night contest, against Cincinnati at Crosley Field. Because of the overflow crowd drawn to the novelty, hundreds of fans had to be accommodated behind ropes on the playing field. With the Cardinals leading, 2–1, in the eighth inning, nightclub singer Burke suddenly ducked under the rope, grabbed the bat away from Reds slugger Babe Herman, and went up to the plate against Paul Dean. As a lark, Dean underhanded the ball to Burke, who promptly swung and grounded out. Never one to ignore a possible edge, Frisch screamed that Burke's ground ball should count as an out. He lost the argument and later the game.

MIKE BURKE

Burke brought the first hint of flair to the Yankee front office in almost a quarter century when he assumed the club presidency in September 1966, but his stylishness was wasted on a franchise grown moribund under the previous owners and unable to rebound under a new regime unwilling to invest in the future. Worse, when he was finally able to assume an ownership position himself, he found himself with a senior partner whose flamboyance outdid his own.

A CBS vice president, Burke succeeded Dan Topping as chief executive of the New York club when its sale to the broadcasting giant became final. He immediately found himself between the rock of a talent vacuum left behind by Topping and partner Del Webb, who had stopped investing money in the team after they had decided to sell several years earlier, and the hard place of demands for immediate results by CBS chairman William Paley and company president Frank Stanton, who thought they were buying the premier franchise in baseball. Faced with an attitude that relegated the franchise to a mere line item in the budget of a megacorporation, he presided over the liquidation of a dynasty—trading Roger Maris to the Cardinals in December 1966 and watching as Whitey Ford retired in 1967 and Mickey Mantle followed him in 1968. He endured the situation for more than six years, until ordered by Paley either to buy the club himself or unload it on someone else. Forming a partnership with Cleve-

land millionaire George Steinbrenner, who arrived behind announcements that he would stick to his shipbuilding business and let professionals run the team, Burke was quickly disabused of any belief he may have had that he was one of the baseball people Steinbrenner had in mind when Gabe Paul was lured away from the Indians to run the franchise.

Burke's lasting legacy was keeping the club in the Bronx by negotiating the renovation of Yankee Stadium with New York City mayor John V. Lindsay. The project, which started as a $24 million face-lift and ended as a $120 million boondoggle, forced a two-year exile in Queens at the Mets' Shea Stadium, but headed off a potential permanent move to the New Jersey Meadowlands.

JESSE BURKETT (Hall of Fame, 1946)

Burkett is one of only four players (along with Ed Delahanty, Ty Cobb, and Rogers Hornsby) to hit higher than .400 in two consecutive seasons (for the Cleveland Spiders in 1895 and 1896); he also added a third batting title (for the Cardinals in 1891), while topping 200 hits in six different seasons. But the lefty outfielder irritated teammates and opponents alike with a disposition that won him the nickname of The Crab. References to his physical resemblance to Cleveland teammate and distant cousin Jack Glasscock, especially taunts about being the shortstop's son, seemed to annoy Burkett twice over. His carping while a coach with the 1921 Giants so angered team members that they specifically excluded him from a share of World Series money; manager John McGraw paid Burkett an equivalent amount out of personal funds.

JOHNNY BURNETT

Playing for Cleveland on July 10, 1932, Burnett smashed two doubles and seven singles in an 18-inning contest against the Athletics. The nine hits are the most by a player in a major league game of any length. Burnett was a lefty-swinging shortstop who averaged .284 in nine major league seasons.

WATCH BURNHAM

Despite a total lack of qualifications for the job, Burnham was appointed manager of the Indianapolis Hoosiers in 1887 solely because he had discovered that a National League franchise was available to the city. Within a month of Opening Day, he almost caused a rebellion among players by fining every one of them $5 for refusing to practice in uniforms dampened by a leaky roof. Worried about the reaction of club president Louis Newberger, Burnham forged a contrite letter from team captain Jack Glasscock. Seeing through the ploy, Newberger fired him, but then the resourceful ex-manager restored himself to favor by signing Larry Corcoran, once the ace of the Chicago pitching staff. The players' attitude failed to improve in Burnham's second tour, and after they learned the reason for his temporary departure, they directed their antagonism toward the president as well. With the possibility of an open revolt looming, Burnham was canned a second time and ended his major league managerial career with a record of 6 wins and 22 losses.

TOM BURNS

Burns collected two doubles and a home run for the Chicago White Stockings in an 18-run seventh inning against Detroit on September 6, 1883. The shortstop's contribution to the eventual 26–6 drubbing was the single best individual offensive inning in baseball history.

GUSSIE BUSCH

Busch used his 36 years (1953–89) as owner of the Cardinals not only to run his own franchise's affairs but also to have his beer products associated with just about every club in the National and American leagues. Prior to the organization of civic groups in the 1980s intent on breaking the identification of beer with baseball, his biggest frustration had been his failure to get the Cardinals' playing facility renamed Budweiser Park.

Busch took over St. Louis with the help of NL owners determined to get rid of Fred Saigh before he made a deal to transfer the franchise to Milwaukee. One of Busch's first moves was to purchase the Browns-owned Sportsman's Park and, failing at the Budweiser idea because of league sensitivities that it would have been too crass, to rename it Busch Stadium. His direct involvement in baseball matters was reflected in a chaos of

managers and general managers for most of the 1950s and the early part of the 1960s, with little to show for it until 1964 except two second-place finishes. On the other hand, he had consistently more financial room for maneuver than his predecessor, not only because of his beer company but also because the Cardinals were the only baseball team in town following the transfer of the Browns to Baltimore in 1954.

Busch's first significant crisis came in 1960, when first baseman Bill White protested the exclusion of black players from a public function held near the team's spring training camp in Florida. When a black newspaper in St. Louis got wind of the incident, it called for a nationwide boycott of Anheuser-Busch products as a means of getting the organization to pressure an end to Florida's segregationist policies in hotels and other public enterprises. With his dealers around the country warning of dire consequences, Busch gave St. Petersburg officials an ultimatum to provide integrated accommodations or face the loss of the team. That was enough for a local businessman to buy two of the best motels in the city and make them available to the Cardinals. Although the concession riled Florida racists, it also proved critical to clubhouse unity for the year, especially when such white stars as Stan Musial and Ken Boyer gave up their beachfront homes to move into the integrated hotels. The nucleus of the 1960 club would still be in place when the Cardinals returned to the World Series in 1964.

Busch invited other trouble after the 1962 season by bringing in the aged Branch Rickey as a special adviser. That led to two seasons of front-office intrigues involving Rickey; vice president Dick Meyer; general manager Bing Devine; and the latter's successor, Bob Howsam; what only Devine appeared to perceive before his forced resignation was that Busch was playing them off against one another so he could have the final say in the issue of the moment.

In 1966, Busch moved the team into the current facility known as Busch Stadium—a cookie-cutter industrial park with an artificial surface. Under the terms of his agreement with the Civic Center Redevelopment Corporation, which oversaw construction of the stadium and employed a bond issue to develop surrounding land, Busch ceded

St. Louis owner Gussie Busch enjoyed advertising his brewery's products by riding around the stadium named for him in a Budweiser wagon pulled by Clydesdales. Photo courtesy of Anheuser-Busch, Inc.

parking and concession stand revenues in return for a 25 percent interest in the group. Once free agency hit the baseball world in the mid-1970s, however, he began griping that the franchise wasn't realizing enough of a profit from the facility, and made two offers to buy it outright. Rebuffed both times, he upped the ante in 1981 to threats of selling the club if he couldn't get his own way. When reports began circulating that he had opened negotiations with a Missouri-based oil company for a sale, Civic Center caved in, selling him the stadium for an estimated (and cheap) $53 million. The high-handedness brought the club reams of bad publicity, but it remained the only baseball team in town.

Once Busch brought in Whitey Herzog as manager and general manager in 1980, he meddled less in the team's baseball affairs. Herzog ingratiated himself both on and off the field—in the former instance by winning a world championship and three pennants in the 1980s, in the latter by doing it mainly through shrewd trades instead of waving millions at free agents. But what not even Herzog could head off were the increasing incidences of Cardinal players (Lonnie Smith, David Green) admitting themselves to clinics for drinking problems, and the burgeoning movement to create alcohol-free zones in ballparks and to reduce the beer advertising that had become as ubiquitous as the major league logo. On one level, Busch's response was publicity campaigns emphasizing the historic roots of beer and the need to be "responsible" in its consumption; on another, he continued to play up the link between his industry and the sport, not least in his regular stunt of driving an old beer wagon around Busch Stadium before games and in having the organist play the "King of Beers" theme song instead of

"Take Me Out to the Ball Game" during the seventh-inning stretch.

Busch died on September 29, 1989, at age 90; he was succeeded by his son August Busch III.

JOE BUSH

Bush was one of the Yankee acquisitions from the Red Sox in the early 1920s who formed the nucleus of the first New York dynasty—and one of the few the club came to regret. A slightly better than .500 pitcher in his first ten seasons, the right-hander led the American League in won-lost percentage in 1922, his first year in New York, picking up 26 wins while setting the major league record for most victories without a shutout. He then proceeded to undo all his good work during the season by blowing a 2–0 lead in the eighth inning of the first game of the World Series against the Giants, and then blowing up at manager Miller Huggins for ordering him to walk Ross Youngs to get to George Kelly in the eighth inning of the fifth game. The pitcher's tirade was so loud that both patrons and sportswriters could hear the four-letter words, leaving him with little defense against accusations that he grooved the next pitch to Kelly, who converted the gift into a Series-winning two-run single. Bush's relationship with Huggins never recovered, and Bush was dealt to the Browns in 1925, starting what became a five-team odyssey over his final four seasons. He retired with a 194–183 record.

CHARLES BYRNE

The founder of the franchise that became the Brooklyn Dodgers, Byrne not only created the club, he also moved it from league to league until he found its permanent home in the National League. With the financial backing of Rhode Island casino operator Ferdinand Abell, he placed a Brooklyn entry in the minor Interstate League in 1883; switched to the major American Association the following year; and, in 1888, bought respectability by purchasing the entire New York Metropolitans club to get first baseman Dave Orr and outfielder Paul Radford, and by then handing

over $18,500 to the St. Louis Browns for pitchers Bob Caruthers and Dave Foutz and catcher Doc Bushong. The moves paid off in a pennant the following season, but the race exacerbated the already none-too-friendly relationship between Byrne and Browns owner Chris Von der Ahe. In spite of the player transactions completed between them, they disagreed on everything from league policy to the St. Louis president's intelligence. Their differences erupted at a winter meeting that deadlocked, with Byrne and Von der Ahe each controlling four votes, over the election of a new AA president. The Brooklyn owner broke the tie by withdrawing from the AA altogether and signing on with the NL.

Brooklyn won a second successive pennant in its first NL season, largely because higher-than-average salaries kept the team relatively intact during the Players League war. With the end of the Brotherhood, Byrne was eclipsed in front-office decision making by new partner and former PL backer George Chauncey; Byrne nevertheless remained as president until just before his death in 1898.

TOMMY BYRNE

In 1949, Byrne walked 179 batters in 196 innings, the worst ratio of bases on balls to innings pitched in major league history. The other side of the story is that the Yankee southpaw gave up only 5.74 hits per nine innings (the eighth-lowest total in history) and ended the year with a 15–7 record. Overall, Byrne averaged almost seven walks for every nine innings he pitched in his thirteen-year career (between 1943 and 1957), yet he won 85 and lost only 69 games for the four AL teams for which he pitched.

Byrne was also responsible for the so-called kimono ball, which he developed while on a tour of Japan in 1955. The delivery, made from behind the back and over the head, baffled the only batter—the Dodgers Pee Wee Reese, in an exhibition game during spring training in 1956—ever to face it, and was declared illegal on the spot by umpire Larry Napp.

C

FRANCISCO CABRERA

First baseman-catcher Cabrera vindicated the importance of the twentieth-fifth man in the seventh game of the 1992 National League playoffs when, with Pittsburgh one out away from the pennant, he came off the Atlanta bench to single in the tying and flag-winning runs for the Braves. It marked the first time that a League Championship Series game had ended with a home team coming from behind in its final at-bat. Cabrera had spent most of the 1992 season shuttling between Atlanta and the club's chief farm club in Richmond.

GEORGE CAHILL

The first night baseball game, a 16–16 tie played on September 2, 1880, at Nantasket Beach between employees of department stores Jordan Marsh and R. H. White, was a commercial for the one-year-old electric light staged by the Northern Electric Light Company of Boston. It remained for Cahill to produce the first night game in a major league stadium. On June 18, 1909, using a portable lighting system of his own invention, he illuminated Cincinnati's League Park sufficiently for two local amateur teams to play a game before 3,000 people. The demonstration impressed Reds president Garry Herrmann, but it would be another thirty years before Cincinnati general manager Larry MacPhail would install lights at the same site (although in a different stadium) and receive permission to play the first major league game after sundown.

LES CAIN

Cain won the only legal judgment requiring a baseball team to compensate a player for the rest of his life. In 1973, the Michigan Bureau of Workmen's Compensation upheld the Detroit southpaw's claim that manager Billy Martin had ruined his career by forcing him to pitch with a sore arm; the Tigers were ordered to pay him $111 a week for life. The two sides later agreed on a single lump-sum payment.

RAY CALDWELL

Caldwell was one of the numerous early-century pitchers who sacrificed his talent for a drink. Still hopeful that he could wring a successful season from the right-hander, Cleveland manager Tris Speaker proposed a bizarre bargain during spring training of 1920: If Caldwell stayed away from liquor otherwise, he could drink himself into oblivion every night following a starting assignment. The alternative would have been his immediate release. Caldwell accepted Speaker's terms and had his only 20-win season. The following year, the pitcher lapsed back into his earlier form and was released. On July 10, 1917, while with the Yankees, Caldwell threw a record 9⅔ hitless innings in relief to defeat the Browns in a 17-inning contest.

RICHARD CALIGUIRI

Caliguiri was the mayor of Pittsburgh who brokered the sale of the Pirates in 1986 to a coalition of private and public investors. Under the terms of the unusual arrangement, thirteen companies or individuals put up $2 million each, with the city committed to matching the sum with money raised through a bond issue. In fact, it took a number of years for the city to come up with its share of the investment; when it finally did, it was told that still more funds would be required to keep the team in Pittsburgh.

HELEN CALLAGHAN

Callaghan was not the biggest star in the All-American Girls' Professional Baseball League, formed during World War II by Cubs owner Phil Wrigley, but she was a major reason why the initiative was remembered years later. Her older son Kelly Candaele coproduced a 1987 television documentary on the league that directly inspired the Hollywood film *A League of Their Own*. Her younger son Casey Candaele rarely played a major league game for the Expos or Astros in the 1980s and 1990s without an announcer pointing out that the utility infielder-outfielder had learned the basics of the game not from his father but from his mother.

JOE CAMBRIA

Cambria was the pioneering scout who signed the Cuban and other Latin players who figured prominently on the Washington Senators roster in the 1940s and 1950s. He made his first trip to Havana in the mid-1930s after Senators owner Clark Griffith had pinpointed the Caribbean as a potential source of gifted (and cheap) prospects; Griffith had been optimistic about Latin players since managing a couple of them in Cincinnati some years before. It was largely because of Cambria's discovery of talents such as pitchers Connie Marrero, Pedro Ramos, and Camilo Pascual that other clubs, notably Brooklyn and Pittsburgh, also devoted more attention to Latin America.

DOLF CAMILLI

Camilli was a typical example of the solid players the Phillies auctioned off for almost thirty years in the desperate quest by three successive ownerships for quick cash. Dealt to the Dodgers for $45,000 after the 1937 season, the left-hand-hitting first baseman turned in four 100-RBI seasons for Brooklyn, including a 1941 pennant contribution of leading the league in both RBIs and home runs. Although normally soft-spoken, Camilli was as tried as most of his teammates by the antics of Brooklyn general manager Larry Mac-Phail, and on one occasion concluded a clubhouse contract talk with his employer by lifting him by his tie several feet off the floor. He also took the rivalry between the Dodgers and Giants extremely seriously, preferring to retire after the 1943 season rather than accept a trade to the Giants.

WILLIAM CAMMEYER

Cammeyer's introduction of the first enclosed ballpark, in 1862, paved the way for baseball to develop into a modern multimillion-dollar enterprise. Surrounding his Union Grounds, in Brooklyn, with a six-foot fence, the entrepreneur was able not only to charge admission but also to keep nonpayers from viewing his product. Union Grounds opened on May 15, 1862, with "The Star-Spangled Banner" being played at a ball game for the first time, and when within two years teams were paid a percentage of the gate, the death knell had sounded for amateurism in the game. Cammeyer later owned the New York Mutuals, a team plagued by allegations of gambling scandals throughout the life of the National Association and into the first year of the National League, in 1876. While one of the founding tenets of the NL was the extirpation of gambling, the Mutuals were expelled, after only one season, not for crookedness but for failure to complete their schedule. Seeking to cut his losses, Cammeyer refused to send his team on its last western trip, even after receiving a guarantee of $400 for the final five games in Chicago and St. Louis.

RICK CAMP

A right-hander with the Braves in the 1980s, Camp was at the center of baseball's most bizarre extra-inning game. In a 1985 night contest against the Mets that began on July 4 but ran well past midnight because of rain delays, the lifetime .074 hitter was forced to go to bat in the bottom of the eighteenth inning because Atlanta had run out of pinch hitters, and promptly hit his only major league home run—a three-run shot that retied the game. After the Mets came back with six runs off him in the top of the nineteenth inning, the

Braves responded with still another rally, pushing across two runs and putting two other runners on—once again for Camp. This time, however, he fanned, ending the game six hours and fifty-one minutes after it had started. Despite the fact that it was 3:55 A.M. when Camp went down, the Atlanta management decided to go ahead with a planned fireworks demonstration to celebrate the holiday—provoking outrage from nearby residents.

ROY CAMPANELLA (Hall of Fame, 1969)

Campanella became the last important piece of the Boys of Summer Dodgers when he went behind the plate in 1948; he also became a melancholy symbol of those teams in more than thirty years of public appearances in the wheelchair to which he had been confined following a devastating 1958 auto accident. Defensively, he is considered the standard not only for his era but, with the arguable exception of Johnny Bench, for the history of the National League. Offensively, he whacked 242 home runs in only ten seasons; these included a record-setting 40 as a receiver in 1953. Together with his handling of pitchers and clubhouse cheerleading role, his defensive and offensive talents netted him MVP trophies in 1951, 1953, and 1955.

Already twenty-seven when he completed the journey from the Negro leagues through the Dodger farm system to Ebbets Field, Campanella was bedeviled throughout his career by hand and leg injuries, accounting for precipitous drops in his production between MVP seasons. His most significant injury might have been the muscle pull he suffered on the last day of the 1951 season, sidelining him for the playoffs against the Giants that New York won on Bobby Thomson's home run. Although he never played for the California version of the Dodgers, the right-handed slugger triggered the biggest crowd in major league history when 93,103 fans showed up at Los Angeles Coliseum for an exhibition game on May 7, 1959, to pay him tribute. Reduced to being a paraplegic by his car accident, he nevertheless coached a couple of decades of Dodger catchers, including Steve Yeager and Mike Scioscia.

Prior to joining the Dodgers in Brooklyn, Campanella earned a historical footnote as the first black to manage in organized baseball when, during a 1946 game as a member of Nashua in the Class B New England League, pilot Walter Alston turned the team over to him after being kicked out. Campanella managed the squad to a 7–5 win.

BERT CAMPANERIS

Campaneris was the spark plug of the brawling Oakland teams in the early 1970s. A nimble defensive shortstop, he paced the American League in stolen bases six times, reaching a career-high 62 thefts in 1968, when he also led the league in hits. Campaneris was at the center of one of the ugliest incidents in League Championship Series play in 1972, when he responded to a suspected brushback by Detroit's Lerrin LaGrow by firing his bat at the hurler. Despite recommendations to the contrary, he was allowed to play in that year's World Series, serving a one-week suspension only at the beginning of the following season.

As a member of the Kansas City version of the Athletics on September 8, 1965, Campaneris, who had always boasted of his versatility, was encouraged by owner Charlie Finley to play a different position every inning in a game against the Angels as a gate attraction. Campaneris was smart to leave his catching stint to the ninth inning, since he had to be removed from the game with a damaged shoulder after a collision at home plate.

AL CAMPANIS

The last of the old executive guard that moved from Brooklyn to Los Angeles with the Dodgers, general manager Campanis sent the franchise—and major league owners in general—spinning when he unwittingly revealed the persisting depths of the sport's racism during a 1987 network television show. Interviewed on the ABC public affairs program *Nightline* on the occasion of the fortieth anniversary of Jackie Robinson's debut in the major leagues, Campanis spewed forth one stereotype after another about the mental and physical abilities of black players, declaring among other things that they ''may not have the necessities'' to be managers or general managers. Faced with a storm of nationwide criticism the following day, both team president Peter

O'Malley and his general manager issued apologies, but when that proved insufficient, Campanis was fired. Over the ensuing months, the Dodgers and every other major league franchise came under intense scrutiny for their minority hiring policies. Depending on the organization, there were meaningful or less meaningful hirings, but the overall impact of the *Nightline* interview was to point up the hypocrisy of baseball's commemoration of Robinson. Campanis had been a last-minute substitute on the television program for Robinson teammate Don Newcombe.

COUNT CAMPAU

A twenty-one-year minor leaguer who spent only parts of three seasons in the majors, Campau is the only player ever to lead two leagues in home runs in the same season. When the Minor International League folded on July 10, 1890, the outfielder's three homers was tops in that circuit; picked up by the St. Louis Browns for the rest of the season, Campau slugged 10 more four-baggers to lead the major league American Association as well.

BILL CAMPBELL

Campbell was the first reentry-draft free agent to be signed after the Messersmith-McNally decision cleared the way for free agency. Represented by agent LaRue Harcourt, the right-handed reliever got a four-year, $1 million pact from the Red Sox in November 1976; he had made $23,000 from the Twins the previous year. Although he turned in a career-high and league-high 31 saves for Boston in 1977, Campbell was soon afterward beset by arm miseries and never again broke into double figures in saves.

BUCK CANEL

The Argentine-born Canel pioneered Spanish-language broadcasts of major league baseball throughout the Western Hemisphere in the 1930s. In addition to delivering the play-by-play on decades of World Series games, he worked for some years with the Yankees. During World War II, Canel was also a Spanish-language radio interpreter of President Franklin Delano Roosevelt's speeches.

ROBERT CANNON

A Milwaukee judge, Cannon was the "legal adviser" to the players prior to the selection of Marvin Miller as executive director of the Players' Association. Recommended for the post by the owners, he was effectively a shill for their interests, and was never without a word of caution to the players lest they act as ingrates in pressing any of their then modest demands. In 1965 he saw little contradiction in sharing his counsel with the players while advancing his own candidacy for baseball commissioner.

JOSÉ CANSECO

The only 40–40 player in big league history, Canseco spent the first nine years of his career daring his antics to undermine his on-the-field abilities. With Oakland between 1986 and 1991, he clouted at least 31 home runs five times, including league-leading figures of 42 in 1988 and 44 in 1991; it was also in 1988 that he stole 40 bases. As an Athletic, the right-hand-hitting outfielder also drove in 100 runs five times. Along with that production, however, went a cocky personality that delighted in his numerous run-ins with traffic cops for late-night, high-speed joy rides; enjoyed the press and fan reaction to his assignations with the likes of rock star Madonna; and liked to put an adventurous face on brawls with his equally volatile wife, Esther.

Tiring of Canseco's perceived disruption of the team, Oakland traded him to Texas in the heat of a division race in 1992, even though all three players received in return (Ruben Sierra, Bobby Witt, and Jeff Russell) were in the walk year of their pacts. More disaster awaited with the Rangers in 1993, when Canseco, already suffering from arm twinges, persuaded manager Kevin Kennedy to allow him to pitch in a game; the result was a rotator cuff injury that sidelined him for all but 60 games and cost Texas a shot at the division title. Along with that went a divorce from Esther.

PAT CARAWAY

Caraway was a southpaw for the White Sox who won a relatively unexceptional 10 games in 1930. In one of his victories, however, he struck out Cleveland shortstop Joe Sewell twice. Sewell, the holder of every major league record for putting the bat on the ball, fanned only one other time the entire season.

HARRY CARAY

The original "holy cow" play-by-play sportscaster, Caray has managed to shill for four clubs and countless sponsors over five decades without letting listeners forget that his chief product was himself. Starting with the Cardinals in the 1940s, his often tart evaluations of home team players and their (mutual) employers have led him into a series of scrapes with humorless front offices—always with the rationale that he was "just a normal fan with a microphone." After pointing out once too often in 1969 that St. Louis was not what it had been, he was sent packing, ending up with Charlie Finley's Athletics for a year. When Finley had enough of Caray's on-air cracks, the Oakland owner agreed to trade his contract to the White Sox for that of the more obeisant Bob Elson. It was the start of something loud.

For his first few years in Chicago, Caray was as responsible as anyone for attracting the fans who showed up at Comiskey Park to watch generally mediocre clubs. One of his typically iconoclastic descriptions of the home talent came in one game when he set the outfield defense of the thumb-short Carlos May, the odd-looking Walt Williams, and the defensively inept Pat Kelly as "no thumbs in left, no neck in center, and no arm in right." By the middle of the 1970s, however, his jabs at several White Sox players, most notably home-run slugger Bill Melton, had created so much trouble in the clubhouse that owner John Allyn announced his intention of making changes in the broadcasting booth in 1976. But then Allyn had more urgent problems with his cash flow, and ended up having to sell out to Bill Veeck. For several weeks, Veeck, who had never particularly liked Caray's bluster, held off on a decision about rehiring him, but then finally yielded to an ultimatum by the announcer's station to hire him or look for another radio outlet. It was during their edgy years together that Veeck came up with the idea of having Caray punctuate the seventh-inning stretch with a ballpark sing-along of "Take Me Out to the Ball Game."

Caray moved over to Wrigley Field in the mid-

1980s after the new White Sox ownership of Jerry Reinsdorf and Eddie Einhorn began crowding out his airtime with their newly launched cable television operation. With the Cubs he has carried on all his trademarks—the seventh-inning sing-alongs, his barbs at what he considers overpaid players when they have failed in the clutch or made an error, and his flaunting of himself as the "typical fan." Caray's son Skip has been a broadcaster for the Braves for some years, and his grandson Chip is an announcer for the Mariners.

BERNIE CARBO

Carbo hit one of the most dramatic home runs in World Series history in 1975, when he came off the bench for Boston in the eighth inning of the sixth game and delivered a three-run shot against Rawley Eastwick of Cincinnati. The blast, his second pinch-homer of the Series, set the stage for the 12-inning marathon that would end when a shot by Red Sox catcher Carlton Fisk hit the Fenway screen. Carbo's reputation otherwise was as a member of the Boston band in the 1970s that went out of its way to taunt managers Darrell Johnson and Don Zimmer. The outfielder was something of a later-day Dusty Rhodes in his apparent obliviousness to game situations when he was sent up to pinch hit. On one occasion, after hitting a pinch grand-slam home run off a southpaw, the lefty swinger admitted that he hadn't realized the bases were loaded or even noticed with what arm the pitcher had thrown.

ROD CAREW (Hall of Fame, 1991)

The American League's most proficient batsman for most of his nineteen-year career between 1967 and 1985, Carew hit .328 for the Twins and Angels. With a crouched, open stance that would influence hitting coaches as much as players, the lefty-swinging second baseman-first baseman collected 3,053 hits and seven batting titles, including a 1977 average of .388 that threatened the .400 mark until well into September. One of the greatest bunters in baseball history, he was also, in his younger years, a nimble base stealer. In 1969 he stole home seven times, and would have tied Ty Cobb's major league record of eight but for a bowled-over umpire who failed to see that he had eluded a tag at the plate.

Carew left Minnesota after the 1978 season in one of the most protracted negotiations ever conducted. He might not have left at all if owner Calvin Griffith hadn't gotten drunk one night and boasted before a booster group that his franchise player had been a ''damn fool'' for accepting a two-year pact in 1977 that paid him the relatively low sum of $170,000 a year. Incensed by both Griffith's smugness and the feeling that the Minnesota owner had acted intolerably toward his Jewish agent, Carew demanded a five-year, $3.5 million contract at the next bargaining round, pointing out that he had approval rights on any deal that Griffith might try to make rather than see him just walk off as a free agent. When San Francisco came forth with an offer, Carew said he didn't want to play in the National League. California was next, and it offered the player satisfactory money but failed to satisfy Griffith with players. The Yankees were next, and Griffith was agreeable to the players, but Carew announced he had no intention of playing for George Steinbrenner. Only after intervention by Commissioner Bowie Kuhn did Griffith go back to the Angels and Carew end up in Anaheim.

MAX CAREY (Hall of Fame, 1961)

Carey is second only to Rickey Henderson for the most times (ten) in leading a league in stolen bases. A switch-hitting outfielder who spent most of his twenty-year (1910–1929) career with the Pirates, he swiped at least 30 bases fourteen times, retiring with 738 thefts. Carey also used his speed to pace National League hitters in triples twice and aggravated pitchers as well by drawing the most walks in the league twice. A lifetime .285 hitter, he batted over .300 in seven seasons, including a career high of .343 in Pittsburgh's world championship year of 1925. He also sparked the club in that season's World Series against Washington by getting 11 hits and batting .458.

A year later, however, Carey became persona non grata with owner Barney Dreyfuss after he attempted to stir up a team revolt against coach Fred Clarke; at issue were Clarke's sarcastic cracks about the outfielder's sudden offensive falloff and his urgings that Carey be benched. Packed off to the Dodgers in a midseason trade,

Carey played out the string for a couple more years, then was appointed Brooklyn manager in 1932. With the same crustiness that he had brought to his play, he talked the Dodger front office into a couple of deals—the acquisition of the bloated and perpetually hung over Hack Wilson, the trading off of Ernie Lombardi and Babe Herman—that haunted the franchise for the rest of the decade. He was eventually replaced by Casey Stengel when general manager Bob Quinn decided that the club needed a pilot less hostile to the New York press.

STEVE CARLTON (Hall of Fame, 1994)

The only pitcher to win four Cy Young awards, Carlton was the game's dominant southpaw for a good part of his twenty-four-year (1965–1988) career, to the point that there were no doubts as to who was meant by references to Lefty. Because of a midcareer decision to stop talking to the media and his practice of strengthening his hands and forearms by twisting them into buckets of rice, he was relentlessly portrayed as an oddball. That was half true: He *was* eccentric, but not because he refused to talk to the press or did strengthening exercises.

Carlton came up with the Cardinals in 1965, but it wasn't until he developed a slider during a team trip to Japan in 1968 that he suggested the pitcher he was to become. While on his way to a 17-win season in 1969, he tied the National League record for strikeouts in one game by fanning 19 in a losing effort against the Mets. In 1971 he recorded 20 victories for the first of six times. Unfortunately for St. Louis, the other five times weren't in a Cardinal uniform. Because of a contract dispute that involved less than $10,000, trade-frenzied general manager Bing Devine dispatched him to the Phillies in exchange for Rick Wise prior to the 1972 season.

It was in Philadelphia that Carlton attacked the record book, starting with a league-leading 27 wins in 1972 that accounted for a stunning 45 percent of the club's victories. He also struck out 310 batters during the year—the first of five times that he would pace the NL in that category—and completed pitching's Triple Crown by posting a 1.97 ERA. His other 20-win seasons were in 1976 (best NL winning percentage), 1977, 1980, and

1982; the Cy Young trophies were collected for these last three years and in 1972. His worst year in a Philadelphia uniform was 1973, when too much off-season banqueting after his triumphant 1972 campaign left him out of shape and contributed to 20 losses. It was mainly due to that experience that Carlton became a conditioning zealot, practicing isometrics and kung fu regularly as well as following his rice-bucket ritual. Aside from going 24–9 during the season in 1980, he beat the Royals twice during the World Series to secure the Phillies' only world championship.

In the mid-1980s, Carlton and Nolan Ryan jockeyed past each other almost weekly in first chasing Walter Johnson's all-time strikeout record and then in claiming the primacy. But while Ryan was getting another wind that would enable him to leave everyone in his wake, the Phillies' left-hander gradually ran out of gas. In 1986 he was released by Philadelphia, setting off an embarrassing three-year odyssey through the Giants, White Sox, Indians, and Twins. His overall 22–46 mark during this period, with accompanying ERAs rarely below 5 runs per 9 innings, took some of the juice out of his career numbers, leaving him with an overall record of 329–244 (.574), with a 3.22 ERA. On the other hand, he ended up with the most strikeouts (4,000) by an NL pitcher and the most (4,136) by a left-hander in either league.

Carlton lived as a recluse after leaving baseball, and media interviewers descending on him after his election to Cooperstown elicited observations along the lines of the conspiracy theories propagated by Lyndon LaRouche. At one time or another he has accused the federal government, Moscow, and a cabal of Jewish Swiss bankers of plotting to "keep humanity down." His longtime batterymate Tim McCarver has observed that Carlton has "a problem about being human."

BOB CARPENTER

Carpenter's takeover of the Phillies during World War II would have been a cause of grief in most franchises, but coming after decades of rum ownership by William Baker, Gerry Nugent, and William Cox, it seemed almost a relief. The club was actually purchased by Carpenter's father, Robert, Sr., a multimillionaire member of the DuPont family who made it clear from the start that his main interest in the purchase was to find something for his son to do. One thing that the younger Carpenter did in sitting in the club president's chair was to hire Red Sox farm director Herb Pennock to oversee baseball operations. The positive result of that was that Pennock was free to develop a Philadelphia farm system that eventually bore fruit with the Whiz Kids pennant of 1950. The negative result of it was that Carpenter grew increasingly resentful of the praise heaped on Pennock, so that when the veteran baseball man died of a stroke in 1948, he decided to handle the club's day-today affairs directly. Among the other things he handled were keeping the Phillies the most lily-white team in the National League; in fact, it wasn't until 1957, ten years after Jackie Robinson's arrival on the major league scene, that the club had its first black player in backup infielder John Kennedy, and not until 1960 that the team had its first black regular in second baseman Tony Taylor.

Because of Philadelphia's 1950 pennant win, Carpenter could not be dissuaded for years that he was only a middle reliever or a backup catcher away from taking another flag. He was abetted in his illusion by a series of front-office aides, most notably Roy Hamey, who were markedly timid traders. Until Johnny Callison in 1959, not a single star player was imported, while veterans such as Richie Ashburn and Del Ennis were allowed to show their age before being exchanged for second-liners. That the franchise didn't begin to flounder as it had in the Baker-Nugent-Cox days was primarily due to the 1954 transfer of the Athletics to Kansas City, leaving the Philadelphia market entirely to the Phillies.

After a decade of mostly nondescript managers, Carpenter brought in John Quinn as general manager, and he in turn hired Gene Mauch as field boss. With Dick Allen emerging as the first four-star prospect from the club's farm system in years, Mauch appeared on the way to securing Carpenter another pennant in 1964, but then directed one of the biggest stretch collapses in baseball history, enabling the Cardinals to pick up the marbles. Carpenter never again came so close.

RULY CARPENTER

The National League has Carpenter's zeal for fishing to thank for not having adopted the designated hitter rule. In 1979, the owner of the Phillies took off with his rod and reel on the eve of a league meeting scheduled to discuss, among other things, following the American League with the DH rule. Although baseball operations chief Bill Giles had been told to vote in favor of a DH proposal because of the presence of gimping slugger Greg Luzinski on the roster, he himself was opposed to the ninth batter and tried to reach Carpenter to pose his arguments again before the vote. When he was told the owner was out on a boat, Giles returned to the meeting and abstained, leaving the pro-DH forces one vote short. The DH question was never again raised at a league meeting.

Carpenter took over the Phillies in 1973 from his father, Bob Carpenter. It was a contradictory eight-year reign, especially where signing free agents was concerned. In 1978, for instance, he was so intent on signing Pete Rose that he agreed to the star's demand that he receive the highest salary of any player in professional sports; at the time, that meant bettering the contract of David Thompson of the NBA's Denver Nuggets. To get the money he claimed the organization didn't have, Carpenter entered into an agreement with local television station WPHL to guarantee $600,000 of Rose's annual payment. In the wake of the 1981 players strike, on the other hand, the Phillies owner professed himself as disgusted with ownership concessions, asserting that he no longer "recognized the game I grew up with" and predicting that the walkout would be the "final nail of the coffin" of the national pastime. Shortly afterward he sold out to Giles and the Taft Broadcasting Company for $30 million.

GARY CARTER

Carter gave smiling a bad name. Although recognized as the National League's best all-around catcher since the heyday of Johnny Bench, Carter was the constant target of snipings from teammates about his readiness to light up for the television cameras; originally nicknamed The Kid when he took over behind the plate for Montreal in the late 1970s, he was also known pejoratively as The Kodak Kid. Despite the criticism, Carter was one of the dominating sluggers in the NL through the 1980s, winding up with 324 home runs and 1,225 RBIs. He was particularly effective in clutch situations, batting over .400 for the Expos in both the 1981 divisional playoff with the Phillies and the subsequent League Championship Series with the Dodgers. As a member of the Mets in 1986, he turned the World Series against the Red Sox around by clubbing two home runs in the third game after Boston had taken the first two contests. More memorably, it was Carter who started New York's astonishing sixth-game comeback in the tenth inning after the first two batters had made out; his two-strike single led to the three runs that were climaxed by Bill Buckner's error at first base on Mookie Wilson's grounder.

When Carter signed with the Expos for a final season, in 1992, he reminded Montreal fans why he had been called The Kodak Kid in his earlier stay with the team when he insisted that part of the deal include an organization commitment to retire his number after the season. It was.

JOE CARTER

Carter had to create World Series history in 1993 before he gained overdue attention as baseball's most consistent slugger in the late 1980s and early 1990s. The right-hand-hitting Toronto outfielder seized center stage with a three-run home run in the bottom of the ninth inning of the sixth game that gave the Blue Jays their second consecutive world championship; the blast, off Philadelphia southpaw Mitch Williams, marked the first time that a World Series ended with a come-from-behind sudden-death home run. Carter's 33 homers and 121 RBIs during the 1993 regular season represented the fifth time in seven years that he topped the 30 level in round-trippers and the seventh time in eight seasons that he knocked across more than 100 runs. Between 1986 and 1994 his annual slugging averaged 30 homers and 110 RBIs, far and away the best in the major leagues.

Despite his formidable numbers, Carter found himself in three major trades within the first decade of his big league career. In 1984 he and fellow outfielder Mel Hall were dealt by the Cubs to the Indians for pitcher Rick Sutcliffe; for the

1990 season Carter was moved by Cleveland to San Diego in exchange for second baseman Carlos Baerga and catcher Sandy Alomar; and after the 1990 season Carter was returned to the American League with second baseman Roberto Alomar, landing with the Blue Jays for first baseman Fred McGriff and shortstop Tony Fernandez.

Alexander Cartwright is usually credited with being the first to set bases 90 feet from one another. National Baseball Library, Cooperstown, N.Y.

ALEXANDER CARTWRIGHT (Hall of Fame, 1938)

Cartwright became one of the putative parents of baseball when, in 1846, he wrote its first rule book, for the benefit of the Knickerbocker Base Ball Club that he and his friends had formed. The bank clerk's role in the development of the sport came to light in 1939, when his descendant Bruce Cartwright objected to published reports of the Abner Doubleday myth on the centenary of the supposed invention of the game. Although most of the Knickerbockers' refinements followed Cartwright's departure from the club, he has been credited with such innovations as settling on the four-base, diamond configuration of the field and the elimination of ''soaking'' (the practice of making a putout by hitting a batter or runner with the ball while he is between bases). For decades it was supposed that the first baseball game was a match played at Elysian Fields in Hoboken, New Jersey, on June 19, 1846, which the Knickerbockers lost to the New York Base Ball Club, 23–1, with Cartwright umpiring; recently, however, earlier games have come to light, and the most that can be said for Cartwright's efforts is that they formalized a game already growing in popularity.

As a baseball missionary, Cartwright's legacy is more secure. Traveling overland to the California Gold Rush in 1849, he organized games along the way (among mountain men and Native Americans as well as traveling companions) and on the West Coast. Moving on to Hawaii in 1852, he introduced baseball on the islands before it had become a rage even in Philadelphia.

RICO CARTY

Carty was the first star player to reach the majors from the Dominican mill town of San Pedro de Macoris. An injury-prone slugger, he spent 15 seasons moving from team to team, enjoying his best year in 1970, when he won the National League batting title as a member of the Braves. Although San Pedro de Macoris has gained a particular reputation for incubating shortstops (Rafael Ramirez, Julio Franco, Alfredo Griffin, Rafael Santana, Tony Fernandez, Mariano Duncan, José Uribe, José Offerman, et al.), it has also produced, in addition to Carty, such notable power hitters as George Bell and Pedro Guerrero as well as pitcher Joaquin Andujar. The town's baseball roots go back to an invasion by Cuban all-stars at the turn of the century.

GEORGE CASE

Speedster Case was the last major leaguer to promote cigarettes in full uniform, and the first to appear in a big league promotion by Bill Veeck. The right-hand-hitting outfielder batted .282 for the Senators and (for one year) the Indians between 1937 and 1947, and led the American League in stolen bases six times. It was because of the perceived inconsistency between Case's baserunning prowess and his nicotine habit that AL president Will Harridge, responding to protests from fans, canceled a series of magazine advertisements for Camels scheduled to appear early in the 1940 season; Case later made his endorsement in street clothes. In 1946, while with the Indians, Case raced Olympic track star Jesse Owens in an exhibition arranged by Veeck soon after assuming control of the Cleveland club; it was the only match race the outfielder ever lost.

DAN CASEY

An unlikely prototype for the hero of Ernest L. Thayer's "Casey at the Bat," lefty Casey never let his lifetime .164 batting average deter him from claiming that honor. His main proof, aside from his surname, was that in the late 1880s he had pitched for the Phillies, whose Huntington Avenue Grounds was in an area once known as Mudville. Casey cited as Thayer's source the events of a game against the Giants, but the date he gave turned out to be an off-day for the Phillies. As late as March 3, 1938, Casey, then in his midseventies, appeared on Gabriel Heatter's radio program *We the People* to press his claim to literary immortality.

HUGH CASEY

Reliever Casey threw the pitch that made Mickey Owen a goat in the 1941 World Series; he is also the only major leaguer to throw punches at Ernest Hemingway. The right-hander's sparring match with the novelist took place at Hemingway's Havana home while the Dodgers were in the Cuban city for spring training in 1942. Invited with several other members of the team by the writer for a few drinks, Casey drank enough to make him susceptible to a Hemingway challenge to put on boxing gloves. When the Dodger pitcher beat him, the ego-sore novelist proposed a duel with pistols or swords. It failed to materialize.

Owen's passed ball on a third strike to the Yankees' Tommy Henrich in the ninth inning of the fourth game of the 1941 Series, which led to a comeback victory for New York, may or may not have come on a spitball. But Casey got his revenge—of a sort. Six years later, he became the only hurler to win a Series game by throwing only one pitch; coming into the fourth game of the 1947 Series in the ninth inning with the bases loaded and one out, he got the same Henrich to bounce into a double play before Brooklyn scored two runs in the bottom of the inning to win the game, 3–2.

Casey compiled a 75–42 record, mostly for Brooklyn, in his nine-year career on both sides of World War II. In 1951 he committed suicide following his failure to patch up his marriage after years of heavy drinking and womanizing.

NORM CASH

Cash demonstrated the wonders of illegally hollowed-out bats in 1961, when he clouted 41 home runs, drove home 132 runs, and paced the American League in both batting (.361) and hits (193). The lefty-swinging first baseman also combined with Detroit teammate Rocky Colavito in knocking in 272 runs—two more than Roger Maris and Mickey Mantle managed as they were clouting 115 home runs. Although he had a couple of other seasons with conspicuous long-ball numbers, Cash never again hit as high as .290 over his seventeen-year (1958–74) career, never again had 100 RBIs, and never again had more than 168 safeties in a season. He later confirmed what opposition managers had been charging throughout the 1961 campaign—that he had hollowed out and reinforced his lumber.

FRANK CASHEN

Both with the Orioles in the 1960s and 1970s and with the Mets in the 1980s, Cashen distinguished himself with a front-office committee managerial style in which his was the final more than the first say. With Baltimore, the approach worked to the tune of two world championships, four pennants, and five division titles; with New York, it mainly produced disappointment in achieving only one world championship and two division titles. It was also Cashen who first hired

Frank Cashen earned his nickname from his habitual neckwear. Photo compliments of the New York Mets.

Earl Weaver and Davey Johnson as major league managers.

Dubbed The Bowtie for his habitual neckwear, Cashen entered the big leagues from the beer business when his employer, Jerold Hoffberger, bought the Orioles in May 1965. For most of the next decade, he presided over a consistently winning club, while developing such front-office executives as Joe McIlvaine, Al Harazin, and Lou Gorman. Shortly after the Orioles were sold to Washington attorney Edward Bennett Williams, Cashen came to a parting of the ways with Hoffberger, moving on to a position in the commissioner's office. In February 1980 he was signed by new owners Nelson Doubleday and Fred Wilpon to head baseball operations for the Mets.

His key moves on the way to the club's contending status in 1984 were a 1982 deal that brought pitching prospects Ron Darling and Walt Terrell from the Rangers, a 1983 trade that netted first baseman Keith Hernandez from the Cardinals, and the signing of Johnson as manager after the 1983 season. Although the Mets dominated baseball with a world championship in 1986, the club could manage only one more division title (in 1988) despite boasting some of the biggest names in the game. Part of the blame for the failure to establish a dynasty was laid to Cashen's penchant for white-breading the team, unloading a raucous talent such as Kevin Mitchell in favor of the nearly mute Kevin McReynolds. Bad trades didn't help either, nor did the executive's ongoing battle of wills with Johnson. In the 1990s Cashen eased himself out of the club's affairs at a pace that created considerable confusion about the future direction of the franchise.

PHIL CAVARRETTA

Despite a playing career that included a batting championship and an MVP trophy (both in 1945), Cavarretta cemented his place in Cubs lore mainly for being too honest. After two and a half seasons of managing dreary Chicago clubs, he was asked by owner Phil Wrigley in spring training of 1954 to assess the team's chances for the coming season. When Cavarretta replied that the Cubs didn't look much better than they had the previous year, he was summarily fired for being "defeatist." Brought up to the majors when he was still in his teens, Cavarretta was the only player who could claim to have been on a major league roster at the same time as both Babe Ruth and Hank Aaron.

O. P. CAYLOR

Journalist Caylor's wrath over the expulsion of the Reds from the National League in 1880 grew into a vendetta against the circuit and its founder-president, William Hulbert. Caylor's 1881 journey to St. Louis with a makeshift Cincinnati team for a series of games with the local Brown Stockings led directly to the formation of the American Association the following year. A cofounder of the league, he also managed the AA version of the Reds for two seasons (1885–86) and represented the loop in peace talks with the NL.

As sports editor of the *Cincinnati Enquirer,* Caylor straddled the line between observing and participating in the baseball affairs of that city for two decades. But as the manager and minority stockholder in the AA Metropolitans in 1887, his dual role caught up with him when he was refused admission to the league's annual meeting because he was also a journalist.

Caylor's permanent transfer to New York in 1890, as editor of *The New York Sporting Times,* was calculated to set up a weekly organ in support of the owners during the Players League war and to counter the influence of Francis Richter's *Sporting Life,* which endorsed the players' position. From this pulpit, he denounced the Brotherhood defectors as spoiled, greedy ingrates. Two years later, however, he turned his pen against the owners when every club released its personnel on the last day of the season and agreed not to sign each other's players only to avoid paying each man the two additional weeks salary their contracts stipulated.

BETTY CAYWOOD

Caywood was the first woman to be a regular part of an on-air baseball broadcasting team. Hired by Kansas City owner Charlie Finley on a dare in the late 1960s, she did mostly color commentary on events in the grandstands and dugouts.

CESAR CEDEÑO

Cedeño never lived up to predictions of a Hall of Fame production on the field, but he had few equals during his seventeen-year (1970–86) career for ending up on a police blotter. Between the lines, the outfielder sprang out of the box with Houston with two seasons of leading the league in doubles, two consecutive .320 years, another campaign when he clouted 26 homers and batted in 102 runs, and six consecutive marks of at least 50 stolen bases. Even when he was nearing the end of the trail, with the 1985 Cardinals, he proved to be the difference for a division title by replacing an injured Jack Clark in September and batting .434 in 28 games. But the right-hand-hitting Cedeño, whom Leo Durocher had habitually compared to Willie Mays (first positively, then negatively), rarely let an off-season go by without ending up in a courtroom. In 1974 he was convicted in his native Dominican Republic of the

involuntary manslaughter of his girlfriend; he got out of that scrape by paying a fine of a mere $100. In 1985 he attacked a heckler in the stands of the Astrodome; although charges weren't pressed, he was fined $5,000 by the Astros. In 1985 he paid out another $7,400 for drunk driving and property damage. In 1988 he was arrested for attacking another girlfriend, trying to take their child, and assaulting a number of policemen called to the scene by the woman.

ORLANDO CEPEDA

Cepeda's fine seventeen-year (1958–74) career has had to weather incessant reevaluation because of a tug-of-war over his Hall of Fame credentials. San Francisco's first grandstand hero when the Giants moved to California in 1958, the right-hand-hitting first baseman clouted 379 home runs and drove in 1,365 runs while compiling a .297 average. Included in the numbers were league-leading totals in home runs in 1961 and in RBIs in 1961 and 1968, a Rookie of the Year award in 1958, and an MVP trophy in 1967 for his crucial role in a pennant win by the Cardinals.

Cepeda's troubles with keepers of the flame started after his career was over, when he did prison time in his native Puerto Rico for drug dealing. Although his rehabilitation and community work have long eclipsed that episode, moralists among Cooperstown voters have continued to deny him his place among the sport's superstars. The situation got even stickier in 1993 when the Giants' front office launched an unprecedented Oscar-like campaign to get him elected. For the most part, sportswriters opposed to his election have insisted that his numbers are no better than two other right-hand-hitting first baseman equally denied Hall of Fame membership—Tony Perez (.279, 379 home runs, 1,652 RBIs) and Gil Hodges (.273, 370, 1,274). Conveniently left out of the argument is Hall of Famer George Kelly, who matched Cepeda's .297 but with only 148 home runs and 1,020 RBIs.

RON CEY

It was because of Cey's beaning by Goose Gossage of the Yankees during the 1981 World Series that the major leagues passed a regulation requiring batters to wear helmets with double earflaps.

A right-handed batter known as The Penguin for his hot streaks in the colder months, Cey was the third base part of the long-running Dodger infield that also included Steve Garvey, Davey Lopes, and Bill Russell. Cey had ten seasons of at least 20 home runs, including a career-high 30 in 1977.

HENRY CHADWICK (Hall of Fame, 1938)

The English-born Chadwick is the only writer in the Hall of Fame proper, having earned his berth by refining and proselytizing for the game over a career that spanned more than half a century.

A rounders player as a boy, Chadwick was the cricket reporter for *The New York Times* when he was converted to baseball in 1856. From initial nonpaying pieces he published in the *Times,* his output grew to include thousands of articles in newspapers and magazines as well as various annual summaries of the game, including those in the *Spalding Guide,* which he edited from 1881 until his death in 1908. Chadwick reinforced this body of work with service on the rules committee of every major amateur association and several professional leagues in his effort to convert baseball into a "manly" and "scientific" pursuit worthy of being called "a national sport for

Henry Chadwick wrote baseball's first rule book, and had little tolerance for people who questioned it. National Baseball Library, Cooperstown, N.Y.

America." Among his accomplishments were the collecting of historical and quasi-historical tales about the earliest days of the game; the development of a set of rules that attempted to blend the proper proportions of offense and pitching; the refinement of the box score into something very similar to what appears in newspapers today; the creation of a scoring system that has survived with very few changes; and the fostering of the mystique of statistics that still surrounds baseball.

For many, Chadwick had the title Father of Baseball applied to him even in his lifetime, but a $600 pension awarded to him by the National League for his long service on the Rules Committee so irritated Andrew Freedman that the Giants owner accused him of greed; Chadwick kept the pension, shunned the Polo Grounds, and recommended that others follow his lead for the rest of Freedman's reign. On the other hand, like most fathers, Chadwick could be cranky when the hobby horses he chose to ride were not everyone's idea of an ideal mount. As early as the 1860s, he complained that the ball was too lively. He advocated the addition of a tenth player, a right shortstop, arguing that "there is not a reasonable objection that can be made against it." He lamented the founding of the National League as "a sad blunder." He proposed that NL owners lower prices, not to spare the financially beleaguered fan but to generate less revenue as an excuse for lowering the salaries of, according to him, overpaid and pampered players. He complained that the emphasis on swinging for home runs was ruining the game—this in the 1890s. He castigated the influence of gambling and its potential for corruption so often and for so long that Harry Wright, for one, felt that he was alarming the public without cause. Chadwick declared the Players League a "terrorist" organization that forced players to join through high-pressure tactics. And he winked at Al Spalding's creation of the Doubleday creation myth, which he knew to be patently untrue.

At about the turn of the century, Father Baseball had become the object of so much derision in major league clubhouses that his annual pennant prognostications came to be regarded among players as the kiss of death for the teams he slated first.

ICEBOX CHAMBERLAIN

Chamberlain was the last ambidextrous pitcher in the major leagues. Following a 25-win season split between the Louisville and St. Louis entries in the American Association in 1888, he was the only player directly affected by a new rule permitting players only one glove per game. Throwing exclusively right-handed the following year, he won 32 games.

CHRIS CHAMBLISS

Chambliss hit 185 regular-season home runs, but none of them came close to the drama of his one postseason clout. The first baseman's solo blast, in the bottom of the ninth inning of the fifth game of the 1976 League Championship Series off Kansas City's Mark Littell, broke a 6–6 tie, gave the Yankees their first pennant in a dozen years, and created such havoc on the field that Chambliss couldn't touch home plate; he later had to reemerge from the clubhouse under police protection to make his game-ending run official. The lefty swinger spent seventeen seasons (between 1971 and 1988) with the Indians and Braves in addition to the Yankees, batting .279 and leading his league in an offensive category only once—pinch-hits in his final full season, 1986.

AARON CHAMPION

A Cincinnati civic booster and president of the local Red Stockings in 1869, the aptly named Champion decided to hire Harry Wright as club manager and to field the first openly all-professional team. Wright's recruits went on to record a legendary consecutive-game winning streak of 56 (or up to 130, depending upon whose research is used) games. The streak ended on June 14, 1870, after which Champion wired back to Cincinnati: "Atlantics 8; Cincinnati 7. The finest game ever played. Our boys did nobly, but fortune was against them. Eleven innings played. Though beaten, not disgraced." What the wire failed to reveal was that he and Wright had insisted on continuing a nine-inning, 5–5 tie and that the Brooklyn club had rallied for 3 runs in the home half of the eleventh after Cincinnati had taken a two-run lead in the top of the inning. The Red Stockings disbanded soon afterward because the sponsors could no longer afford the high sala-

ries their players' success could command; so strapped was the club at the end that its ballpark had to be dismantled and the lumber sold to stave off creditors. Nevertheless, the Red Stockings' play-for-pay-openly experiment encouraged similar moves by other clubs and led directly to the formation of the National Association, the first professional league, in 1871.

FRANK CHANCE (Hall of Fame, 1946)

Chance is less indebted than Johnny Evers or Joe Tinker to Franklin Adams for his election to the Hall of Fame. A lifetime .297 hitter, he was that rare species of a first baseman who could steal bases with consistency, leading the National League in that category with career highs of 67 thefts in 1903 and 57 in 1906. He was never averse to taking a walk or, as almost proved fatal, getting hit by a pitch to reach first base. As the Cubs playing manager from 1905 to 1912, Chance rolled up two world championships, four pennants, and two second-place finishes. Nowhere near as cantankerous as Evers or Tinker, Chance frequently took public stands on behalf of his players against the Cubs ownership, ultimately losing his job for his efforts. Not all of his charges were sardonic when they referred to him as The Peerless Leader.

Throughout his stay in Chicago, Chance relied on strong pitching and "little ball" tactics for winning. In common with other managers of the period, he had charge of his own deals, and his pickups of outfielder Jimmy Sheckard from the Dodgers and third baseman Harry Steinfeldt from the Reds proved crucial to his club's success. His main problem in the Windy City, however, was owner Charles Murphy, who sought any excuse to cut back on salaries and who battled his first baseman-manager almost annually over contract concessions. The crisis point in the relations between the owner and the pilot came after the 1911 season, when Chance was revealed as having developed a blood clot in his head from having taken too many fastballs in the skull. With his chief antagonist apparently out of the way in an intensive care unit, Murphy took to the newspapers to denounce several Cub veterans as drunkards and threaten their release. To the owner's chagrin, Chance got up out of his hospital bed to portray the alcoholism allegations as mere pretexts for cutting salaries. Although the press was won over to the manager's side, it didn't come as a shock when Murphy notified Chance abruptly during the 1912 postseason city series with the White Sox that he was through.

When the Yankees waved a $40,000 contract in front of Chance, Murphy, who still held his player contract, blocked the way until Reds owner Garry Herrmann gave the Cubs a player to sweeten the $1,700 waiver price from the Yankees. If the American League franchise had originally wanted him mainly to offset the popularity of John McGraw in the city, Chance proved to match the Giants manager mainly in an authoritarianism that had risen sharply after a hearing loss caused by all the beanings. It didn't help either that the Yankees were drifting around near the bottom of the standings or that Hal Chase, a former club manager, was still on the premises and still attracting suspicions about throwing games. When Chase wasn't mocking Chance's starched-collar ways or whiney voice (the result of his deafness), the manager was accusing the first baseman of selling his best efforts to gamblers. Although he received no backing from New York's owners in his accusations, Chance finally unloaded Chase in a trade to the White Sox, precipitating a shoving match with co-owner Bill Devery. That just about did it for Chance, and he was replaced during the 1914 season by twenty-three-year-old Roger Peckinpaugh.

Chance had one more year in a uniform, as manager of the cellar-dwelling 1923 Red Sox, before retiring as a dugout boss with a .593 winning percentage, the sixth highest in history.

HAPPY CHANDLER (Hall of Fame, 1982)

Chandler was never quite the pliable creature that major league owners expected him to be when they elected him to succeed Judge Kenesaw Landis as commissioner in 1945, but he wasn't the revolutionary that he painted himself as, either. At his best, he made the right enemies; at his worse, he tried to pass off their manipulations as part of some master plan of his own.

Chandler was given baseball's top administrative post in April 1945, after he had impressed several owners, and particularly Larry MacPhail

of the Yankees, with his defense of the sport's interests as a member of the U.S. Senate from Kentucky; he had been specially vocal in opposing moves to shut down the game as an inessential activity during World War II. The owners had even more reason to be satisfied in 1946, when Chandler ignored protests by Philadelphia first baseman Tony Lupien that his trade by the Phillies to a minor league club violated National Defense Act statutes protecting the jobs of military veterans; worked feverishly behind the scenes to thwart attempts by Robert Murphy's American Baseball Guild to unionize members of the Pirates; and blacklisted the major leaguers who had jumped to play in Jorge Pasquel's Mexican League. Although Chandler made a gesture of fining Cardinals owner Sam Breadon $5,000 for trying to negotiate separately with Pasquel, Chandler later admitted giving the money back to the St. Louis executive "because I had made my point."

It was with New York teams, however, that Chandler had his stormiest moments. Most conspicuously, there was Brooklyn president Branch Rickey's breaking of the color barrier in 1946 with the signing of Jackie Robinson. Rickey himself always voiced appreciation of Chandler's stand on the issue, which amounted more to noninterference than to support. In the Kentuckian's own eyes, however, that merited him at least as much recognition as Rickey for braving the antagonism of the other fifteen big league owners of the period. Chandler never tired of pointing out that he told reporters in 1946 that "if a black can make it in Okinawa and Guadalcanal, hell, he can make it in baseball"—if usually omitting the detail that he said it to newsmen for black dailies. In this as in other situations, Chandler showed more wiliness than depth of conviction—a stance that reflected his political reputation at home and that he would seek later to parlay into the Democratic Party's presidential nomination.

If he was only a minor player in the Robinson story, Chandler was very much the protagonist of the 1947 suspension of Dodger pilot Leo Durocher. The suspension followed a tangle of scandals linking Durocher to everything from underworld gambling activities to adultery. The announcement that the manager had to sit out the

1947 season inflamed a New York press that had always viewed Chandler as a boastful hillbilly who had usurped the commissioner's job from Ford Frick, the National League president who had started his career as a reporter. One typical comment was that "Chandler has found Durocher guilty of running a red light, so gave him the chair." Even years later, the harshness of the Chandler sentence for what was never a specifically cited violation prompted theories that Durocher was merely the fall guy for Rickey. One school of thought, for instance, said that Chandler had been carrying out the orders of the anti-integration owners in depriving Robinson of the dugout support he would have gotten in his rookie season from Durocher. Others discerned the hand of Dodger attorney Walter O'Malley, who had been making moves to force out Rickey and for whom the Durocher suspension might prove useful ammunition. But in view of Chandler's own ambitions and his admitted irritation at times at being unfavorably compared to his predecessor, Landis, it could also be plausibly argued that Chandler was intent on creating—and then immediately cleaning up—his own Black Sox scandal.

By 1951, it wasn't only the New York press that wanted Chandler out. The Braves were infuriated with him because he had declared infielder Jack Lohrke a free agent after some demotion irregularities, and the Cardinals were no happier after he rejected a request to let St. Louis play its Sunday games at night during the summer because of the city's sweltering temperatures. But Chandler's chief nemesis was Yankee co-owner Del Webb, whose gambling interests in Las Vegas and connections to the mob there and elsewhere sparked an official investigation by the commissioner's office. Unfortunately for Chandler, the man he entrusted with the probe, his private assistant Walter Mulbry, tipped off Webb, leaving the inquiry dead before it started. Under the impression that he still had enough owners in his camp in 1951, Chandler asked for an extension on his six-year contract, due to run out in 1952. He was stunned when the Yankees, Braves, and Cardinals mustered enough opposition to deny him a necessary three-quarters majority. Informed that he was going to be succeeded by Frick, Chandler commented: "Well, the owners

had a vacancy and I guess they decided to keep it."

SPUD CHANDLER

Toiling for the Yankees from 1937 to 1947, Chandler was the only pitcher besides Babe Ruth to post winning marks every season for a career lasting at least ten years. Chandler's career record of 109–43 also represents the highest winning percentage (.717) for pitchers with a minimum of 100 wins. Despite such prestigious numbers, the right-hander managed to lead the New York staff in victories only twice.

BEN CHAPMAN

A solid outfielder for the Yankees and other clubs in the 1930s, Chapman left his deepest impression on baseball as the bigoted Phillies' manager whose racist invective against Jackie Robinson in 1947 did more to unite the Dodgers than Branch Rickey's relentless sermons on brotherhood. Aside from objecting to Robinson on general racist principles, Chapman had special fits whenever someone referred to the Brooklyn star's running ability, since he himself had led the American league in steals four times.

FRED CHAPMAN

Chapman, four months shy of his fifteenth birthday, became the youngest player ever to appear in a major league contest when he was summoned from Reading and given the ball for the American Association Philadelphia club on July 22, 1887. With Cleveland ahead, 6–4, in the bottom of the fifth, a substitute umpire named Mitchell called Athletics batter Henry Larkin out for interfering with the catcher on an attempted steal of home. When the Spiders objected a bit too vigorously that it was the runner who should have been called out, Mitchell declared the game a forfeit. Chapman was denied the victory, however, and never appeared in another big league game.

RAY CHAPMAN

Chapman gained tragic singularity on August 16, 1920, when a Carl Mays fastball made him the only beaning fatality in major league history. The Cleveland shortstop lingered twenty-four hours before succumbing to a fractured skull. In the wake of the accident, numerous lunatics threatened to get even with Mays the next time the New York right-hander arrived in Ohio to play the Indians. The danger was overcome in good part because Chapman's ultimate replacement, Joe Sewell, sparked the club to a successful pennant run down the final weeks of the season. Chapman had been a fixture in the Cleveland lineup since 1913, enjoying his best season in 1917, when he hit .302 with 52 stolen bases.

JOE CHARBONEAU

The cocky Charboneau was baseball's ultimate one-year wonder. After taking Rookie of the Year honors for a .289 average and 23 home runs as a member of the Indians in 1980, the right-hand-hitting outfielder played only 70 more major league games, batting .211 and collecting only six more homers, before curveballs and back problems forced his retirement. True to character, Charboneau responded to being farmed out in 1981 by refusing to find an apartment in Charleston, West Virginia, insisting on sleeping at the minor league stadium because of his confidence that he would soon be called back to Cleveland. After a few weeks he went apartment-hunting.

OSCAR CHARLESTON (Hall of Fame, 1976)

No less an authority than John McGraw thought Charleston the greatest player in the Negro leagues. Compared to Ty Cobb for his aggressiveness both on and off the field, to Babe Ruth for his power hitting and fan appeal, and (at least early in his career) to Tris Speaker for his defensive skills from a short center field, the lefty swinger is credited with a batting average in the .350s over his twenty-seven-year (1915–41) career with the Indianpolis ABCs, Harrisburg Giants, Homestead Grays, Pittsburgh Crawfords, and other clubs. He topped the .400 mark in several seasons and led the league in homers six times.

Charleston also had something in common with his admirer McGraw: brawling. At one point or another, Charleston mixed it up with an umpire, a Dominican agent trying to recruit players from his team, a Ku Klux Klansman, and several Cuban soldiers (during one of his nine stints of winter ball in the country). Moving to first base in the latter part of his career, Charleston became

a playing pilot for several teams, including the famed Crawfords for the better part of the 1930s. He was felled by a fatal heart attack soon after leading the Indianpolis Clowns to a Negro American League title in 1954.

MIKE CHARTAK

Chartak helped demonstrate that patriotism isn't only the *last* resort of scoundrels. In 1942, the first baseman-outfielder was about to be sold by the Yankees to the Browns for $14,000 when Washington owner Clark Griffith remonstrated with New York that the prospect would benefit baseball and the nation as a whole if he were showcased instead in the wartime capital. The Yankees bought the argument, even selling Chartak to Griffith for a lower price of $12,000. The Washington boss promptly turned around and re-sold him to the Browns for the original $14,000.

HAL CHASE

Baseball's all-time crook, Chase managed to dodge enough bullets to stay around for a fifteen-year career despite repeated accusations by his managers and teammates that he threw games for profit. Charming and charismatic, he nevertheless developed a reputation for petty theft of cigars and other personal items, for cheating at cards, and for picking unnecessary fights on the field. Early in his career, Chase also showed a streak of vindictiveness; on one occasion he smashed all of New York teammate John Knight's bats after the infielder refused to loan him one. Despite all this, Chase wiggled out of one ticklish situation after another until forced out of baseball at the end of the 1919 season following a secret hearing and an equally quiet banning.

Dubbed Prince Hal for his defensive prowess, the lefty thrower was the premier first baseman of the deadball era. When allowing his performance to match his abilities, he exhibited a previously unseen flair at charging bunts even to the third-base side, throwing to third for force-outs, and turning the first-to-shortstop-to-first double play. At the plate, the right-handed hitter batted .291, posting the highest average in the National League in 1916 and pacing the Federal League in homers in 1915.

Signed by the New York Highlanders (later the

Whenever Hal Chase missed a ball, the whispers started that he had made a few more dollars. National Baseball Library, Cooperstown, N.Y.

Yankees) in 1905, Chase had his first run-in with management in September 1908 when, disappointed at not being named manager, he bolted the club in favor of the outlaw California League. Allowed to return after paying a nominal $200 fine, he was welcomed back by his teammates, who presented him with a silver loving cup, but immediately began undermining new pilot George Stallings. For his part, Stallings was the first to accuse Chase of throwing games, a charge neither American League president Ban Johnson nor New York chief executive Frank Farrell would countenance for fear of losing one of their bigger drawing cards. Chase finally succeeded Stallings as

pilot toward the end of the 1910 season but lasted only through the 1911 campaign. The arrival of Frank Chance to direct the club in 1913 brought another round of conflict. With the first baseman mocking the partially deaf Chance to the delight of teammates, and the manager telling columnist Heywood Broun that his first baseman was deliberately losing games, it came as no surprise when Chance traded Chase to the White Sox, for Rollie Zeider and Babe Bolton, only a few weeks into the 1914 season.

Chase stayed with Chicago barely long enough to claim reciprocity for the clause in his contract that gave owners the right to release a player with ten days' notice; eleven days later, he jumped to the Federal League Buffalo Blues. Hiding out in a hotel room to evade an injunction sought by Chicago owner Charlie Comiskey, Chase was served with papers in the second inning of his first FL game, but won the battle when a judge refused to make the injunction permanent, ruling that the reserve clause was "despotism" and "quasi-peonage."

Landing with the Reds in 1916, Chase began a new chapter of knavery by first establishing himself as the best player on the team—and the National League batting champion—and offering indications that he had reformed. It was, in fact, not until July 1918 that Reds manager Christy Mathewson grew suspicious of the frequency with which his usually sure-handed first baseman was making marginally errant tosses on plays in which the pitcher had to cover first. Suspended for the rest of the year, Chase was acquitted at a winter hearing before NL president John Heydler despite testimony by several Cincinnati pitchers that he had approached them about collaborating with him in his schemes. The exculpatory evidence included the fact that Chase had hit a home run to win one of the games he was accused of throwing, but the primary reason he got off was that chief accuser Mathewson was in France with the American Expeditionary Forces.

Chase found himself traded to the Giants in 1919 despite the fact that New York manager John McGraw had testified against him in the Heydler hearing. By June, however, McGraw had developed the same suspicions as Mathewson, and in August Heydler reopened his investigation with an announcement that he possessed a photographic copy of a $500 Chase check proving conclusively that he had bet against the Reds as part of a plot that also involved Cincinnati second baseman Lee Magee. Subsequent revelations had Prince Hal also conspiring with Giants third baseman Heinie Zimmerman to throw games with his new club. All three players were quietly blackballed from the NL: In the cases of Chase and Zimmerman, the Giants reached their objective by offering the players such laughable salaries that they effectively outlawed themselves by rejecting the contracts.

Chase's role in the Black Sox scandal has been obscured by his escape from punishment. His name was a constant refrain in the grand jury hearings that indicted the Chicago Eight, especially when it focused on meetings with gamblers Abe Attell and Arnold Rothstein to raise the money to pay the bribed players. Other testimony revealed that Chase had won an estimated $40,000 betting on Cincinnati in the 1919 World Series. Arrested in California, he was released almost immediately. The astonishing result of his involvement was that Commissioner Kenesaw Landis totally ignored him when it came time for formal banishment of the guilty; even more astonishing, Landis responded to a letter from Chase inquiring about his status by officially informing him that there were no charges against him.

By this time, however, Chase was persona non grata with all sixteen major league teams. Playing for (and owning part of) the San Jose team in the independent Mission League in 1920, he found time to become implicated in a gambling ring that controlled five of the eight clubs in the Pacific Coast League. He later drifted through several outlaw leagues in California and mining towns in Arizona before moving back to California, where he died in 1947.

TOM CHENEY

On September 12, 1962, Cheney set the record for the most strikeouts in a game of any length when, pitching for Washington, he struck out 21 Orioles in sixteen innings. He won only 18 other games in an eight-year career.

JACK CHESBRO (Hall of Fame, 1946)

Chesbro holds the twentieth-century record for most victories in a season, his 41 wins in 1904 boosting the Highlanders (later the Yankees) to within percentage points of first place on the last day of the season, only to have the pennant slip away because of an errant Chesbro spitball. The right-hander won only 199 games (and lost 131) in a eleven-year (1899–1909) career, almost exclusively with Pittsburgh and New York; he did, however, have five 20-win seasons. Chesbro is also the only pitcher to lead both leagues in won-lost percentage in this century, pacing National League hurlers with percentages of .677 (21–10) in 1901 and .854 (28–6) in 1902 and topping the American League with .774 (41–12) in his best-of-times-worst-of-times 1904 campaign. The New Yorkers entered the final day of that season needing a doubleheader sweep of the Red Sox to move past the Boston club into first place, but with two out, a runner on third, and the score tied, 2–2, in the ninth inning of the opening contest, the spitballer's next delivery sailed over the head of catcher Red Kleinow. For years afterward, Chesbro's wife campaigned to have the official scorer's call changed to a passed bill.

HILDA CHESTER

The raspy-voiced Chester was the most raucous of the Dodger fans who cheered on the team at Ebbets Field in the 1940s and 1950s. After she suffered the first of two heart attacks and was forbidden by doctors to keep yelling, she turned up in the bleachers with a frying pan and iron ladle, banging away from the first pitch to the last out. Dodger players later presented her with a cowbell, which became her most lasting signature. Chester was so enamored of Leo Durocher that she perjured herself during a trial over the Brooklyn manager's assault on a fan, claiming to the judge that the victim "called me a cocksucker and Leo came to my defense."

Although she could have sat anywhere in the park she desired, Chester generally preferred the center-field bleachers so she could be closer to her favorite players, Dixie Walker and Pete Reiser. On one celebrated occasion, she yelled for Reiser to pick up a note she dropped on the field and take it to Durocher. On his way to the dugout, Reiser paused to say hello to Dodger boss Larry MacPhail, sitting along the first-base line, then handed the note to Durocher. The manager read it, then ordered Hugh Casey to get up in the bullpen. Although starter Whitlow Wyatt had been sailing along up to that point, Durocher brought in Casey, who was promptly knocked around. After the game, a furious Durocher warned Reiser never to hand him another note from MacPhail during a game. The note had said, "GET CASEY UP, WYATT'S LOSING IT." That made Chester the only bleacher fan ever to change pitchers.

STEVE CHILCOTT

Chilcott came to epitomize the perils of the annual amateur draft after he was chosen by the Mets in 1966. The number one choice in the nation, the catcher never rose above the low minor leagues, in part thanks to an arm injury. By choosing Chilcott first, the Mets enabled the Athletics to draft future Hall of Famer Reggie Jackson.

EDDIE CHILES

As owner of the Rangers for most of the 1980s, oil millionaire Chiles saw that as little of his money as possible was spent on the team. Already seventy when he bought out Brad Corbett in January 1980 and with a reputation for America First bluster, he made it clear that he considered free agents the next worst thing to Communists, so allowed his front office to do little more than make endless deals involving second-stringers. By the middle of the decade, with his own fortune dwindling with the price of crude oil, he made the first of several attempts to reach an accord with Edward Gaylord of Gaylord Broadcasting as a buyer or majority partner—forays that were instantly thwarted by other American League owners who didn't want the media giant turning Texas into another national superstation entry. Chiles next sought to sell out to a New York-based syndicate, but that deal foundered on the refusal of the prospective buyers to guarantee that the Rangers would not be moved. But in 1988, after declaring his oil company bankrupt, he was less bothered by the commitment to remain in Texas, announcing that he intended selling his majority interest to a group that was very definite about shifting the club to Tampa. Minority owner Gaylord managed to hold up the sale—winning some points with the public, but still failing to overcome league resistance to his occupying the franchise's biggest executive chair. With Chiles clearly over a barrel, Commissioner Peter Ueberroth moved in to broker a sale to a consortium headed by George W. Bush, son of the president of the United States. Chiles complained loudly that Ueberroth was trying to run his business and threatened to go back to the Tampa group and start a court fight, but ultimately agreed to sell out.

HARRY CHITI

Catcher Chiti became part of Mets lore in 1962 when he was obtained from the Tigers in exchange for ''a player to be named later''; a few weeks later, he was sent back to Detroit as that player. Chiti was actually only one of several players effectively traded for himself; among the others have been first baseman Vic Power, catcher Brad Gulden, and pitchers Hoyt Wilhelm and Willis Hudlin.

EDDIE CICOTTE

It was Cicotte's testimony before a Chicago grand jury in late September 1920 that officially confirmed months-long rumors about the Black Sox scandal. The ace of the Chicago pitching staff at the time, the right-hander admitted having received $10,000 to throw the first game of the 1919 World Series against Cincinnati. His testimony followed published accusations the day before by professional gambler and former major leaguer Billy Maharg that the pitcher had been the first to indicate that several White Sox players were open to bribes because of their resentment against miserly Chicago owner Charles Comiskey. Along with the other members of the so-called Chicago Eight, Cicotte was acquitted at a 1921 conspiracy trial but was immediately banned from baseball anyway by Commissioner Kenesaw Landis.

Prior to his involvement in the fix, Cicotte had been among the American League's premier hurlers. In 1917 he had paced Chicago to a pennant with a league-leading 28 wins, then repeated the trick in 1919 with another 29 victories. Amid the swirling reports of an investigation in 1920, he won another 21 games. In the World Series against Cincinnati, however, it was his performance more than that of his coconspirators that prompted suspicions of something shady going on. In the opening game, he was battered out of the box in the fourth inning; in the fourth game, he deliberately cut off a perfect throw home by Joe Jackson that appeared likely to nail a Cincinnati base runner in a duel that ended as a 2–0 Reds' win.

BILL CISSELL

Some of Chicago's more superstitious fans have been prone to attribute the misfortunes of the White Sox over the years to the Cissell Curse. Cissell was an infielder who arrived at Comiskey Park in 1928 with predictions of being another Eddie Collins, but who developed a drinking problem that reminded people more of Tom Collins. For a couple of years after his nine-year career ended he worked as a laborer in the ballpark, solidifying the legend of a haunting presence. Cissell died of malnutrition at age forty-five.

JOHN CLAPP

Having jumped from the National Association Philadelphia Athletics during the 1875 season because the club refused to rescind a $200 fine, Clapp took advantage of the formation of the National League the following year to hold the first silent auction for a player's services; the winners, for $3,000, were the St. Louis Brown Stockings. Despite his refusal, in 1881, of a $5,000 bribe by Chicago bookmakers to throw games, the catcher was blacklisted for the 1882 season for dissolute behavior. As a manager, Clapp holds the distinction of having been in charge when three National League franchises—Indianapolis in 1878, Buffalo in 1879, and the Giants in 1883—played their first games; he was not hired for a second season by any of them.

JACK CLARK

Clark had one of his greatest baseball moments after his roller-coaster eighteen-year (1975–92) career was over. In 1994, the right-handed-hitting slugger was awarded more than $2 million by an arbitrator—the biggest slice of the fine money stemming from ownership collusion against free agents in the 1980s. It was a somewhat fitting conclusion for Clark, whose off-the-field involvements rivaled his diamond play for the Giants, Cardinals, Yankees, Padres, and Red Sox. The first star to blossom under the Bob Lurie regime in San Francisco, the outfielder represented Giants power in the late 1970s as he began piling up his 340 career home runs. Gradually, however, he also came to represent the club's disabled list with one injury after another, as well as the Born Again movement that occasioned continual clubhouse tensions and cost a couple of managers their jobs.

Traded to the Cardinals in 1985, Clark overcame the unfriendly distances of Busch Stadium in both 1985 (22 homers and 87 RBIs) and 1987 (35 homers and 106 RBIs) to spearhead two pennant wins. He climaxed his 1985 contributions by clouting a three-run home run off reliever Tom Niedenfuer in the ninth inning of the sixth and final game of the League Championship Series to forge a comeback victory. After a so-so season with the Yankees in 1988, he moved to San Diego, where his stay was marked by constant rifts with franchise star Tony Gwynn. At the center of the squabbles were Clark charges that Gwynn worried only about his personal statistics, and Gwynn retorts that Clark had too many imaginary ills. Worse awaited the slugger when he went off to Boston as a free agent. After belting 28 home runs in 1991, he hit merely 5 in 1992, and only 1 in homer-friendly Fenway Park. It emerged that he had been preoccupied all year with having to declare bankruptcy because of the failure of a miniature car racing enterprise.

FRED CLARKE (Hall of Fame, 1945)

Clarke played his entire twenty-one-year (1894–1915) career for Barney Dreyfuss, going from Louisville to Pittsburgh when the owner moved into the executive offices of the Pirates after the 1899 season. It was an alliance that was solidified through an almost equally long nineteen years as a player-manager and that helped Clarke save face during a player revolt.

The lefty-hitting outfielder broke in with the Louisville Colonels on June 30, 1894, collecting a debut record 5 hits (4 singles and a triple). Over the next five years in Louisville he dipped as low as .307 only once, averaging as high as .390 in 1897. A line-drive hitter who led the National League in doubles, triples, and RBIs once each, he could also run the bases, as attested to by his 506 career steals. It was, in fact, Clarke rather than teammates Honus Wagner and Rube Waddell who was considered the greatest gain for the Pirates when Dreyfuss folded the Louisville franchise in 1899 after ''trading'' his stars to Pittsburgh so they would be on hand when he took up half ownership of the club in the new century. Another part of the deal with incumbent Pittsburgh owner William Kerr called for Clarke to continue the double role of outfielder-manager

that he had been playing for the Colonels since 1897. Not that the pilot had a long honeymoon with Dreyfuss, however: A hard nose who was accustomed to defending himself on the field with his fists and who expected similar aggressiveness from his players, Clarke was scolded regularly by the puritanical owner for abusive language and other actions regarded as detrimental to the decorum Dreyfuss insisted on for the franchise. If the personality differences between the men didn't lead to a definitive clash, it was largely because Clarke was the most successful manager in the league in the first decade of the century, steering the Pirates to three pennants and four second-place finishes.

Clarke's longest stint with the club ended after the 1915 season, when it became clear that his retirement from playing (during which he compiled a .312 average) had also sapped him of enthusiasm for managing. He reappeared on the scene in 1925 as a Dreyfuss ploy for lighting a fire under manager Bill McKechnie. Variously described as a minority shareholder, an organization vice president, an assistant manager, and a coach, Clarke was a source of tension from Opening Day, all the more so when Dreyfuss began pointing to his return to uniform as a major reason why the Pirates were driving toward a pennant. Player resentment ran so high against Dreyfuss's ''spy,'' as he was labeled, that a majority of the club took the owner at his word that Clarke was an executive and voted not to give him a World Series share along with the other coaches. When McKechnie got wind of the snub, he talked the players into at least voting $1,000 for his unwanted shadow; Clarke trumped that move by returning the check after Pittsburgh had defeated Washington in the World Series.

The tensions boiled over in 1926. Knowing that outfielder Max Carey had been one of the strongest opponents of giving him any postseason money, Clarke was hard pressed to contain himself when Carey started the season in a slump; while urging McKechnie to bench the outfielder, he also suggested to a Pittsburgh newsman that the batboy would be of more help to the club in the lineup. Carey's response was to circulate a petition for Clarke's removal. Although the initiative failed, Clarke would not let it pass, demanding that Dreyfuss get rid of what the local newspapers began calling the ABC Mutineers (for pitcher Babe Adams, outfielder Carson Bigbee, and Carey). Although Dreyfuss knew that he was on slippery ground, especially where Adams's involvement was concerned, he accented what he termed Clarke's "historical significance" to the franchise, acquiescing in dealing Carey to the Dodgers and releasing Adams and Bigbee. When the owner also fired McKechnie for not containing the crisis, it appeared that Clarke would be back as manager. But then Dreyfuss, apparently less enthralled by historical contributions, also pressured Clarke into returning to retirement.

NIG CLARKE

On June 15, 1902, Clarke hit eight home runs for Corsicana in a Texas League game against Texarcana; in nine seasons in the majors, the catcher managed only six homers. Clarke also gets a footnote in the history of catching equipment: Although no one knew it at the time, he wore soccer guards under his uniform pants while playing for Cleveland in 1905; it would be two years before Roger Bresnahan openly wore shin guards for the Giants.

JOHN CLARKSON (Hall of Fame, 1963)

Clarkson's 53 victories for Chicago in 1885 is second only to Charlie Radbourne's 60 the year before for most wins in a season. The right-hander was, however, unable to produce the additional victory that would have won the 1889 National League pennant, losing to fifth-place Pittsburgh on October 5 in what was the first league flag decided in a season finale. Had Clarkson won, Boston would have had one more victory than the Giants, and, despite a lower won-lost percentage, would have been declared the champions; as it turned out, the two clubs had the same number of wins (83), but Boston, with two more losses (45 to 43), finished second. The situation compelled NL owners to change the rule granting first place to the team with the most wins (with a tie broken in favor of the team with the fewest losses) to one rewarding the team with the highest winning percentage.

Chicago's sale of Clarkson to Boston in 1888, one year after batterymate King Kelly had been shipped East for an identical $10,000, was among the major sources of player dissatisfaction that led to the formation of the Players League in 1890.

JIMMY CLAXTON

Claxton is one of several claimants to the title of being the first (secret) black to play in organized ball in the twentieth century. A southpaw pitcher, he joined the Oakland Oaks of the Pacific Coast League in May 1916 after identifying himself as an Indian. Although quickly dropped after an informer advised the team that it had signed a black, Claxton, who was in fact part Native American, was an Oak long enough to become part of a series of Zeenut baseball cards, the biggest name in the business before the Topps company. That made him the first black player on a baseball card.

ROGER CLEMENS

Clemens's right arm has brought him wide acceptance as the all-time Boston franchise pitcher. His most dramatic achievement was racking up a nine-inning-game record 20 whiffs against the Mariners on April 29, 1986. The dominant American League pitcher of the late 1980s and early 1990s, Clemens has taken Cy Young honors three times (1986, 1987, and 1991) and an MVP trophy (1986). The hurler has compiled three 20-win seasons, leading the AL in that category twice, and seven consecutive seasons of more than 200 strikeouts, including league-leading totals twice. He has also paced the AL in shutouts five times, ERA in four seasons, and winning percentage once.

ROBERTO CLEMENTE (Hall of Fame, 1973)

Except for batting average, few of Clemente's offensive numbers were as impressive as those of contemporaries Hank Aaron and Willie Mays, but there was hardly a player of the 1960s who did not regard him as the decade's third greatest outfielder. A right-handed swinger who spent his entire eighteen-year (1955–72) career with the Pirates, he won batting titles in 1961, 1964, 1965, and 1967; had at least 200 hits four times; had seven seasons of double figures in doubles, triples, and home runs; drove in 100 runs twice; and scored 100 runs three times. Along with his

Roberto Clemente cracks the 3,000th—and final—hit of his career. National Baseball Library, Cooperstown, N.Y.

of his death, the Hall of Fame waived the usual five-year waiting period for candidates and elected him right away; he was the first player from Latin America to be admitted to Cooperstown. An almost mythical figure in his native Puerto Rico, Clemente has had streets, ballparks, and buildings named after him in San Juan and other cities. The U.S. Postal Service made him the subject of a stamp, and several Puerto Rican players have requested uniform number 21 in his honor. Although often depicted during his career as a hypochondriac given to grousing through the 100-plus games he played in every one of his eighteen seasons, Clemente did in fact continually suffer from an arthritic spine caused by an automobile accident.

JACK CLEMENTS

Clements was the first known major league catcher to wear a chest protector—a piece of equipment he used as a rookie with the Union Association Philadelphia Keystones in 1884. His innovation did not catch on until Roger Bresnahan of the Giants began using a similar device after the turn of the century. Clements stayed around for a seventeen-year career, most of it spent with the Phillies, as the longest-running left-handed catcher.

TONY CLONINGER

Although six American League sluggers have accomplished the feat, pitcher Cloninger became the only National League player to hit two grand-slam home runs in a game when he connected with the bases loaded for the Braves in the first and fourth innings of a July 3, 1966, contest against the Giants. His mound record in a twelve-year (1961–72) career with the Braves, Reds, and Cardinals was 113–97.

DAVID CLYDE

The country's top draft pick in 1973, the eighteen-year-old Clyde was rushed to the mound by the Rangers after being signed to help create interest in a sagging team. When 36,000 fans showed up to watch him struggle through five innings to a debut victory on June 27, Texas owner Bob Short insisted the southpaw be kept in the rotation the rest of the year. In fact, Clyde's

steady bat (a lifetime average of .317) went a defensive skill that gained him twelve consecutive Gold Gloves and earned him a reputation as the league's best right-field arm for most of his career. As Pittsburgh's franchise player for many years, he rose from its cellar subsistence in the 1950s, to its 1960 championship against the Yankees, to more years of humdrum performances, back to the top of the league in the early 1970s. In both the 1960 World Series and in the 1971 postseason duel (against the Orioles) he had at least one hit in every one of the seven games; his clutch home runs in the sixth and seventh games of the 1971 Series, in which he hit .414 overall, netted him the MVP nod.

Clemente had a hide-and-seek start and a tragic end to his major league career. Originally signed by the Brooklyn Dodgers, he found his way to Ebbets Field blocked by Carl Furillo. Because he had been signed for more than $4,000, however, he was vulnerable to draft rules applying to minor leaguers in the 1950s, and, despite Brooklyn attempts to hide him by allowing him to play for top farm club Montreal as seldom as possible, was drafted by former Dodger boss Branch Rickey.

In his final game of the 1972 season, he collected his 3,000th hit. On New Year's Eve of that year, Clemente was killed in a plane crash while carrying food and medical supplies to Nicaraguan earthquake victims. Because of the circumstances

starts ended up accounting for one third of the club's home attendance. But they also proved destructive to the pitcher's development and self-confidence, and he ended up with a career record of 18–33.

TY COBB (Hall of Fame, 1936)

The only contradictions in Cobb were those brought to him by others. For himself, he was a virulent character who made little distinction among attacking baseballs, teammates, opponents, fans, or blacks who had never heard of the game's greatest hitter for average (.367). That he found unexpected allies in some of his worst moments was mainly a testament to his significance between the lines and the desire of others to profit from it.

Perhaps the most daunting of all the statistics attached to Cobb is that only eight players over the past half century have batted higher in a single season than he averaged over his entire twenty-four-year (1905–1928) career. Between 1907 and 1915, the left-hand-hitting outfielder won nine straight batting titles, then added another three later (although revisionist historians have challenged two of these crowns). Not counting his

maiden year for Detroit, when he had only 150 at-bats, he never hit below .320, and three times topped .400. He also left his mark on every other offensive category, leading the American League in doubles three times, in triples four times, in steals six times, and in slugging average eight times. Although he broke into double figures in home runs only twice, he even managed to lead the AL in that category when his 9 round-trippers in 1909 were high. Not that he couldn't hit the ball out of the park when he wanted. In a celebrated incident in 1925, the already thirty-nine-year-old Cobb, who had been fuming for years about the attention showered on Babe Ruth's slugging feats, told newsmen that he could have hit 30 to 40 home runs a year if he had so desired. When one of those present noted that his odd batting stance (he left several inches between his hands on the lumber) made that improbable, he went out and clouted three balls over the fence in a game to prove his point.

Cobb's hold on baseball's statistical imagination extended over generations to Lou Brock's surge over his 892 stolen bases and Pete Rose's conquest of his 4,191 hits. Still standing, however, are the primacies of his 2,245 runs scored

Ty Cobb played baseball with an aggressiveness that often verged on the homicidal. National Baseball Library, Cooperstown, N.Y.

and his lifetime swipes of home plate (54); nor has Rickey Henderson or anybody else duplicated his feat of stealing second, third, and home in the same inning on four occasions. As much as Rose, he attributed a sacred importance to numbers, even if it occasionally meant taking a backseat. During the 1926 season, for instance, the manager-outfielder took himself out of the lineup in June because his .392 average at the time was lower than that of three other Tiger outfielders—Heinie Manush, Harry Heilmann, and Fats Fothergill—who were all over the .400 mark. All four players eventually hit slumps, but Cobb stayed on the bench as long as he was hitting less than they were.

Then there was the other Cobb. The overture to what was baseball's ugliest great career was struck up in the summer of 1905, a few weeks before he joined the Tigers, when the Georgian's mother was arrested for the fatal shooting of his father. Police connected the killing to the woman's alleged infidelities, but a trial ruled otherwise, finding that the mother had mistaken the father for a burglar and fired in good faith. Even without the shooting on his mind, Cobb admitted years later, he had gone to Detroit in a decidedly edgy mood—first because he hadn't received any money from his sale by a South Atlantic League club in Augusta, and secondly because, as a southern Protestant, he fully expected trouble from a club dominated by northern Irish Catholics.

The first of the many Tigers to view Cobb's edginess as arrogance was left fielder Marty McIntyre, who showed his feelings for his freshman teammate by giving opposition catchers clear shots at throwing him out on attempted steals and by feinting after fly balls that would end up dropping and making center fielder Cobb look bad. After one such maneuver by McIntyre, pitcher Ed Siever attacked Cobb in a hotel lobby, accusing him of blowing a win for the hurler; Cobb's response was to knock down Siever and keep kicking him in the head until he was dragged away by teammates. The outfielder's isolation was so complete after that incident that he not only had to eat most of his meals alone, but also started packing a gun in case some of his teammates ganged up on him. By the middle of the 1906

season, the strain became too much for him, and he had to spend a month in a Detroit sanitarium for a nervous collapse.

Cobb's reputation as a racist has, if anything, been understated. In one 1907 episode, he got into an argument with a black groundskeeper about the condition of the club's spring training field in Augusta and ended up choking the man's wife when she sought to intervene. In 1909 he slapped a black elevator operator in Cleveland for being "insolent," precipitating a brawl with knives and a security guard's billy club. Although Detroit owner Frank Navin talked the hotel out of a civil suit, the Cleveland prosecutor's office pressed an assault charge, making it necessary for Cobb to miss Ohio games against the Indians for some time. In 1914 Cobb attacked a Detroit butcher for reputedly insulting his wife, then used the butt of his gun against a black shop assistant. The word "nigger" was not merely his single frame of reference for blacks, but also his handiest pejorative in his ongoing sniping at Ruth. In June 1924, the two superstars ignited a riot in Detroit when their mutual taunting led to a punch-up at home plate while a couple of hundred fans started smashing up grandstand seats.

Long before the Ruth episode, Navin had been tempted on a couple of occasions to trade his star player because of the chaos around him. In 1907 he went so far as to give his tentative agreement to Cleveland for a swap involving outfielder Elmer Flick, but the deal came to nothing when the Indians had second thoughts about importing The Georgia Peach's personality with his bat. On another occasion, Washington manager Clark Griffith boasted to intimates that he was near a trade for Cobb, but that, too, came to nothing. Navin had another reason to be lured by offers: Cobb's annual truculence at contract negotiations. It was after one such round of balky talks in 1908 that the outfielder explained his position to reporters as: "It isn't a question of principle with me. I want the money." Together with his diamond accomplishments, it was a stance that rarely failed to achieve its objectives. (As determined about money as he was about base hits, he later made a fortune by buying considerable stock in Coca-Cola for $1.18 a share.)

As Cobb continued to pile up his batting championships and the victims of his spikes-first slides into bases, other AL players and fans around the league went after him as bitterly as some of his teammates. On the final day of the 1910 season, St. Louis manager Jack O'Connor was so resolved to stop him from winning another hitting crown that he ordered his third baseman to play deep during a doubleheader so that Cleveland's Nap Lajoie could beat out enough bunts to capture the title. O'Connor was banned from baseball for the ploy. In 1912, a New York fan named Claude Luecker taunted Cobb for seven innings, until the outfielder charged into the stands and began punching and kicking him. After Hilltop Park police pulled him away, narrowly avoiding another riot, Cobb justified his assault by saying that Luecker had called him ''a half nigger.'' Informed that Luecker had lost four of his fingers in a printing press accident, he shrugged that he didn't care if the fan ''has no feet.''

What followed was one of several episodes in which the outfielder found unexpected solidarity. When AL president Ban Johnson suspended Cobb for the attack on Luecker, the other Tiger players sent a telegram to the league office warning that they would not take the field for a May 18 game against the Athletics if the ban were not revoked. When it wasn't, the players went through with their threat, forcing Navin and manager Hughie Jennings to scour Philadelphia for amateurs who could replace the major leaguers, thereby saving the owner a $1,000 fine. The amateurs were trampled by the Athletics, 24–2, and Johnson rushed to Philadelphia to warn the Detroit players they would all be blacklisted if they didn't play their next scheduled game, against Washington. Even with that threat hanging over them, the Tigers refused, not changing their minds until Cobb himself met with them and urged them to take the field. Because of his peacemaking efforts, he was given only a retroactive suspension and a $50 fine, while the other players were assessed $100 each. Those who explained their solidarity said either that nobody should be penalized for reacting to the insult of being called a ''half nigger'' or that no club should be forced to play without its best player. The incident otherwise had little impact on Cobb's relations with his teammates.

Cobb's siege mentality while playing in the North had the converse effect of making him even more popular in his native Georgia, where reports of his violent encounters only confirmed him as a southern David against the Yankee Goliath. That attitude proved beneficial to him prior to the 1913 season, when Navin refused to grant him a $2,000 raise. The owner changed his mind when Georgia senator Hoke Smith threatened to open an investigation into baseball's skirting of antitrust regulations. It was also Smith and influential Georgians like him who continually threw business opportunities (e.g., the Coca-Cola stock) Cobb's way. They made him even more of a hero in 1918, after he barely escaped with his life from an accident with poison gas in a military testing laboratory in France; the same mishap caused serious lung problems for Christy Mathewson for the rest of his short life.

After the 1920 season, Navin stunned Cobb and everybody else by naming him as manager. Like many other great hitters turned into dugout bosses, he knew what he could do, recognized similar talents in other budding or proven hitters, grew impatient when less talented position players couldn't emulate him, and had barely a clue about pitching. It was during his managerial reign, for instance, that the club was quick to trade Howard Ehmke (who won 39 games in his first two years elsewhere) and send Carl Hubbell back to the minors; on the other hand, he spotted Charlie Gehringer during a tryout, talked the club into signing him, and shepherded the future Hall of Fame second baseman through his fledgling years. As for the team as a whole, he managed five .500 seasons in six tries but was in serious contention only once. It was to remain a thorn in his career that he never played on or managed a world champion.

In October 1926, Navin sprang another surprise with the announcement that Cobb was resigning as manager and retiring as a player. A short time later, it emerged that both Cobb and Cleveland manager Tris Speaker had been forced out amid allegations by former Detroit hurler Dutch Leonard that the three of them plus Indians outfielder Joe Wood had conspired to fix a September 1919 game to assure the Tigers a third-place finish behind the White Sox and Indians. As evidence of his charges, Leonard sent two letters—one written by Cobb, the other by Wood after the reputed fix—to AL president Johnson. Over Johnson's insistence that the two resignations had closed the affair, Commissioner Kenesaw Landis intervened to conduct his own investigation. After traveling to California to interrogate Leonard, and despite the explicit indication in the Wood letters that Cobb had wagered on the 1919 game and an implication that the more serious allegation was also true, Landis ruled that the charges were unfounded, attributing them to Leonard's resentment that he had been released by Cobb in 1925 and denied a tryout with Cleveland by Speaker.

While the verdict led to a showdown between Landis and Johnson over the extent of a commissioner's authority, Cobb let it be known that he was entertaining suits against Leonard and Johnson over what he termed "absolute slander"; he also insinuated that the whole affair had been sparked by Navin as a ploy for breaking his multiyear contract. He dropped the suit idea around the same time that Landis emerged even stronger from his confrontation with Johnson. Landis, who had used far skimpier evidence to blacklist less renowned players accused of game-fixing, then persuaded both Cobb and Speaker to reject the several offers they had received from National League clubs and to stay in the junior circuit. Cobb signed with the Athletics, Speaker with the Senators.

Landis's suspect clearing of Cobb has been ascribed to his reluctance to undermine the reputations of baseball's luminaries. It was an attitude shared by others in 1936, when Cobb received the highest number of votes in the very first balloting for the Hall of Fame. Then, if not always in subsequent years, diamond ability was the only criterion for election to Cooperstown.

MICKEY COCHRANE (Hall of Fame, 1947)

Although he never led the American League in any offensive category and topped 20 home runs and 100 RBIs only once each, Cochrane is considered by many to be the greatest-hitting catcher of all time. In a thirteen-year (1925–37) career with the Athletics and Tigers, the lefty swinger compiled the highest lifetime batting average of any receiver (.320), with a personal high of .357 in 1930; he also clouted 30 or more doubles for seven consecutive years (1929–35).

Sold in 1934 for $100,000 in one of Connie Mack's periodic offloadings of stars, Cochrane took over the managerial reins as well as the backstop chores for Detroit, leading the club to pennants in his first two seasons and a world championship in his second year. Cochrane's playing career ended abruptly on May 25, 1937, when Yankee right-hander Bump Hadley fractured his skull with a beanball; Cochrane did, however, return to the dugout for the end of the 1937 season and into 1938.

ANDY COHEN

Cohen was one of several victims of the quest by New York teams to find a Jewish player at any cost to appeal to Jewish fans. To make matters worse, he succeeded Rogers Hornsby as the Giants' second baseman in 1928. As if that weren't enough, he stroked game-winning hits a couple of times in April, leading anti-Hornsby contingents in the press to post daily comparisons of his efforts at the Polo Grounds and the Hall of Famer's in Boston. Even the habitually sour Hornsby was moved to ask the Giants and the New York press to let up on Cohen. The infielder held down his starting job for only two years. He batted an acceptable .294 and .274, but with little clout and without much defensive range.

ROCKY COLAVITO

Colavito's trade by the Indians to the Tigers after the 1959 season initiated a Cleveland version of the Curse of the Bambino. One of the most popular players in Indians history, the right-handed slugger overcame the cavernous dimensions of Municipal Stadium to become the first Cleveland player to reach the 40 mark in homers more than once, leading the American League in that category (with 41) in 1958 and following up with 42 more in 1959. On June 10, 1959, the outfielder also became the last AL player to stroke 4 homers in a game. Despite these feats, Colavito was shipped to Detroit after the season for batting champion Harvey Kuenn. General manager Frank Lane justified the move to outraged Clevelanders by claiming that the Indians were looking more for consistency than power at the plate, but suspicions lingered that club officials feared the leverage Colavito's statistics and popularity gave him in contract negotiations. In the thirty-five years since the deal, the club has placed as high as third only once.

Colavito clubbed 139 homers in four years with the Tigers, turning in his best season (.290, 45 homers, 140 RBIs) in 1961. After the 1963 season he was shipped to Kansas City along with $50,000 for slap-hitting second baseman Jerry Lumpe in a deal even less fathomable than the Kuenn trade.

Reacquired by the Indians in 1965, Colavito still had enough clout left in his bat lead the AL in RBIs. Two years later, he ran afoul of general manager Gabe Paul with accusations that the front-office boss was forcing manager Joe Adcock to platoon him with Leon Wagner, and found himself forced out of Cleveland a second time (destination, Chicago). Playing out the string, Colavito bounced from the White Sox to the Dodgers to the Yankees over the next season and a half before calling it quits with a .266 average and 374 round-trippers.

It was with the Yankees, who had passed over the Bronx native fifteen years earlier, that Colavito ended not only his slugging career but also his two-game mound avocation. In three innings with Cleveland in 1958 and two and two—thirds more with New York a decade later, the shotgun-armed right fielder compiled a 0.00 ERA; grabbing the win in his second appearance, Colavito became the last position player to record a major league victory.

NATE COLBERT

Slugging first baseman Colbert was as close as San Diego got to a franchise player over the first several years of its existence, averaging 30 home runs a season between 1969 and 1973. Indicative of the club's problems, however, he hit the 100-RBI mark only once. Even more telling, in 1972 his 111 RBIs represented 22.61 percent of the Padres' runs—a major league record. Colbert's most conspicuous day on the field was August 1, 1972, when he clouted 5 home runs and drove in 13 runs in a doubleheader against the Braves.

GORDY COLEMAN

Coleman, the Reds' regular first baseman for a good part of the 1960s, was even more effective coming off the bench. His 40 hits in 120 at-bats (.333) represents the best average for pinch hitters with at least 100 plate appearances.

JERRY COLEMAN

As a Yankee second baseman between 1949 and 1957, Coleman had several moments in the sun. For one, he knocked a bases-loaded single in the eighth inning of the last game of the 1949 season to beat Boston out of a pennant; for another, he drove in the only run in the first game of the 1950 World Series against the Phillies, then singled home the winning run in the bottom of the ninth of the third game.

As San Diego's longtime broadcaster, Coleman has often sounded as though he needed introductions to players in the league less than five years. His relations with phrasemaking have been equally—if more humorously—distant. Sample Colemanisms over the years include:

"Those amateur umpires are certainly flexing their fangs today."

"There's a fly ball to deep center field. Winfield is going back, back.... His head hits the wall. It's rolling toward second base."

"Rich Folkers is throwing up in the bullpen."

"Somehow Pendleton managed to catch that.... Yes, with his hands."

"Grubb goes back, back, he's under the warning track."

"He slides into second base with a stand-up double."

"You have to wonder what Lasorda's thinking about. I wonder if Lasorda is wondering what he's thinking about."

"George Hendrick simply lost that sunblown pop-up."

"Benedict may not be hurt as much as he really is."

"And Kansas City is at Chicago tonight, or is that Chicago at Kansas City? Well, no matter, Kansas City leads in the eighth, 4 to 4."

"Enos Cabell started out here with the Astros. And before that he was with the Orioles."

JOHN COLEMAN

Right-hander Coleman holds the unapproachable records of yielding 772 hits and losing 48 games in one season, both as a rookie with the dismal Phillies in their inaugural season of 1883; somehow, he also managed to win 12 games that season. Two years later, on May 10, 1885, he did something else not to be seen again on a major league diamond: Called on to fill in for an injured right fielder in the sixth inning, Coleman, not scheduled to be in the lineup that day, played the rest of the game in street clothes.

His lifetime record in six seasons was 23–72.

VINCE COLEMAN

When he came up with the Cardinals in 1985, Coleman gave every indication of waiting for Rickey Henderson to shoot his wad before he climbed past the American Leaguer to claim all of baseball's steals records. After three disastrous years with the Mets in the early 1990s, however, the switch-hitting outfielder was hard put to find a team that wanted him as its leadoff hitter.

In his first six seasons with St. Louis, Coleman paced the National League in stolen bases, shattering previous rookie records with 100 thefts, then following that up with 107 and 109. Between September 18, 1988, and July 26, 1989, he established another mark for consecutive swipes when he filched 50 bases in as many attempts. But although Coleman's running figured prominently in 1985 and 1987 St. Louis pennants, he was pursued by charges from manager Whitey Herzog that he ran too often merely to add to his numbers and didn't have half the baserunning smarts of such teammates as Ozzie Smith and Willie McGee. A similar attitude was partly behind the decision of subsequent manager Joe Torre and general manager Dal Maxvill to let the speedster go on his way as a free agent after the 1990 season.

Coleman signed with the Mets for the 1991 season, initiating a marriage made in hell. For one thing, he spent more time on the disabled list than on the field over his three years with the club, attaining a high of 38 steals in 1993. For another, he alienated more than New York's baseball traditionalists with a lack of sophistication that extended on one occasion even to wondering aloud

who Jackie Robinson had been. In 1992 he was implicated with Dwight Gooden and Darryl Boston in the alleged rape of a woman near the Mets' spring training camp in Florida; although no charges were pressed in the affair, the episode hung more heavily over the unpopular Coleman than it did over his teammates. What turned out to be his last act for the Mets occurred in June 1993 when, following a game against the Dodgers, he hurled a lit firecracker toward some fans in the parking lot of Dodger Stadium. Coleman was suspended for the rest of the season, agreed to a plea-bargained reduction of original felony assault charges to a misdemeanor, and was sued by the family of a young girl injured by the explosive. After trying to get rid of him for some time, the Mets finally traded him to Kansas City after the season.

In the middle of all his other troubles in New York, Coleman drew another barrage of ridicule for his contention that the natural grass of Shea Stadium ''might keep me out of the Hall of Fame.''

EDDIE COLLINS (Hall of Fame, 1939)

The longest-running act among American League players, Collins batted .333 over twenty-five years of service for the Athletics and White Sox from 1906 to 1930. Mainly because of Ty Cobb's presence in the league at the same time, the lefty-hitting second baseman never won a batting title. On the other hand, he bested Cobb regularly as a base thief and was involved in many of the game's signal events in the first decades of the century.

When he first came up to the Athletics, Collins used the alias of Eddie Sullivan because he was still a student at Columbia University and in violation of intercollegiate rules covering student athletes. Manager Connie Mack soon moved him from the role of backup player to second base, where he became the keystone of the so-called $100,000 infield that also included first baseman Stuffy McInnis, shortstop Jack Barry, and third baseman Frank Baker. Between 1910 and 1914 Collins and his teammates steered Philadelphia to four pennants and three world championships. In that span, the infielder never batted below .322 and won the first of four steals titles by swiping

81 bases in 1910. He also paced the AL in runs scored three consecutive years. Following the Athletics' loss to the Miracle Braves in 1914, however, Mack began breaking up the team. One of the first to go was Collins, sold to Chicago for $50,000.

Even before he suited up with the White Sox, Collins became a a source of friction in the clubhouse because, while owner Charlie Comiskey was routinely slashing the salaries of some of his veterans, he had given Mack the $50,000 and then agreed to a five-year, $75,000 contract with a $15,000 signing bonus for the infielder. Some of the resentment was put on hold when Collins steadied the Chicago infield to return it to a contender's status and then provided field leadership for a pennant win in 1917. A four-games-to-two victory over the Giants in the World Series was climaxed when New York third baseman Heinie Zimmerman found himself in a one-sided rundown with Collins in the final game and ended up futilely chasing a world championship run across the plate.

By 1919, Collins's privileged contract situation had made him a minority in a clubhouse seething with resentment over Comiskey's miserly ways. While teammates such as Joe Jackson limited themselves to periodic complaints that they weren't making as much as Collins, others, such as shortstop Swede Risberg, expressed their contempt by refusing even to throw the ball to the second baseman during infield warm-ups. For his part, Collins didn't bother to disguise his satisfaction when the Black Sox scandal over that year's World Series with Cincinnati coughed up the names of most of the players who had been giving him a rough time; what he might have been less sanguine about, however, was that two of the eight men out, Jackson and third baseman Buck Weaver, significantly outhit him in the tainted games against the Reds.

With the team devastated by the bans imposed by Commissioner Kenesaw Landis on the Chicago players implicated in the World Series investigation, Comiskey came to rely on Collins even more over the first part of the 1920s, finally appointing him as a playing manager in 1925. After two years of lifting the team back up to the .500 level from the cellar, Collins returned to Philadel-

phia for a few years as a backup infielder before calling it quits. Aside from his offensive contributions over the years, he also ended up with most career fielding records for a second baseman, including the highest number of games (2,650), assists (7,630), and chances (14,591).

From 1932 to his death in 1951, Collins headed Boston's baseball operations for Tom Yawkey; although his long tenure as Red Sox general manager covered such important purchases as Jimmie Foxx from the Athletics and Ted Williams from the minor leagues, it also encompassed the period when the franchise didn't want to hear about black players. More often than not, in fact, it fell to Collins to put a good public face on the ostensibly benevolent Yawkey's resistance to integration. Among those he turned away after a Fenway Park tryout held to appease an aroused City Hall in the mid-1940s was Jackie Robinson.

JIMMY COLLINS (Hall of Fame, 1945)

Collins did as much as anybody to give legitimacy to the American League at the dawn of the century. After starring in Boston for the Braves at third base for several years in the 1890s, he jumped at an offer to become playing manager of the newly created Red Sox in 1901, taking along with him outfielders Buck Freeman and Chick Stahl. In the club's inaugural season, Collins not only steered the team to a second-place finish but also had his players performing excitingly enough to outdraw the Braves, two to one. In 1903 he guided Boston to its first pennant and then called the shots in the first World Series, defeating Pittsburgh, 5 games to 3, in a best-of-9 confrontation. Although John McGraw refused to meet a second Red Sox pennant winner in a World Series the following year, the publicity around his stand ultimately redounded to the reputation of Collins and his charges.

As a player, the right-hand-hitting Collins had five .300 seasons, led the National League in home runs in 1897, drove in 100 runs twice, and scored that many four times. As a manager he was a law unto himself, barring even Boston owners from the clubhouse if he thought they were infringing on his authority.

MARLA COLLINS

On July 22, 1986, Collins was fired by the Cubs after club officials learned that she had posed in the nude for a *Playboy* spread called "Belle of the Ball Club." For five years, the twenty-eight-year-old had worked for the Chicago club as a ball girl; her duties included sitting next to the visiting team's dugout, wearing shorts and a Cub T-shirt, and replenishing the home plate umpire's supply of baseballs.

PHYLLIS COLLINS

When Collins was appointed vice president of the National League in 1987, it marked the highest administrative position held by a woman in the circuit's history. She stayed at the post until replaced by Kate Feeney in 1994. The vice-presidential office calls for responsibility over, among other things, league pension and schedule matters.

EARLE COMBS (Hall of Fame, 1970)

The center fielder and leadoff batter for the Murderers Row Yankees of the 1920s, Combs batted .325 over twelve seasons (1924–35). Playing in the shadow of the likes of Babe Ruth and Lou Gehrig, the left-handed hitter had his best season in 1927, when he hit .356 and led the American League in hits and (for the first of three consecutive seasons) triples. It was in the bottom of the ninth inning in the fourth World Series game against the Pirates that year that Combs had his most dramatic diamond moment: With the bases loaded and two out, his feints and fakes toward the plate from third base so unnerved Pittsburgh pitcher Johnny Miljus that the right-hander uncorked a wild pitch to allow the game- and Series-ending run to score. Always plagued by injuries, Combs effectively ended his career in 1934 when he crashed into the center field wall in St. Louis's Sportsman's Park and fractured his skull.

CHARLIE COMISKEY (Hall of Fame, 1939)

As a manager, Comiskey provided a buffer between his players and an erratic, often penurious owner; as an even more tightfisted owner himself, he had no such intermediary. The result was baseball's most sensational scandal and the historical judgment that a good deal of the blame for the

Charles Comiskey learned too late that his notorious penny-pinching had a higher cost than that measured in dollars and cents. National Baseball Library, Cooperstown, N.Y.

1919 World Series fix rests in the Chicago owner's lap.

As a player, Comiskey popularized playing off the first-base bag, a technique he picked up from manager Ted Sullivan with the independent Dubuque Rabbits in 1879. He later became the first manager to win four consecutive pennants, for the American Association St. Louis Browns between 1885 and 1888. A .262 right-handed hitter in thirteen major league seasons, Comiskey ranks third among all big league managers in winning percentage (.608), having endured only one losing season (his last) in a twelve-year career with the Chicago Pirates of the Players League and the Cincinnati Reds, in addition to the Browns. With the Browns he spent as much time correcting the public utterances of the notoriously baseball-ignorant owner Chris Von der Ahe as he did making out lineup cards, and even more time trying to talk Von der Ahe out of levying inappropriate fines and completing damaging player transactions.

Comiskey served as a catalyst in getting Cincinnati owner John T. Brush to recommend local sportswriter Ban Johnson for the presidency of the Western League. Joining Johnson after the 1894 season as owner of the Sioux City club, Comiskey played a key role in the newly rechristened American League's assault on the

National League's monopoly, especially after moving his franchise into Chicago in 1900. Acceding to Cubs owner Charles Murphy's request that the new team not explicitly identify itself with Chicago, Comiskey retaliated by nicknaming the club the White Stockings, the original name of the NL team.

In winning the AL's first major league pennant a year later, Comiskey's White Sox outdrew the Cubs by about 150,000, but a rift developed between the owner and the league president in August, when Johnson expelled shortstop Frank Shugart. The episode was merely the first of a series of confrontations between the two most powerful figures in the AL. As in the Shugart incident, they patched up their differences after the suspensions of Chicago outfielder Ducky Holmes in 1905 and of playing manager Fielder Jones in the middle of a tight pennant race in 1907. But that was not the case in 1919, when Johnson resolved a dispute between the White Sox and the Yankees over the contract of pitcher Jack Quinn in favor of the New Yorkers. Thereafter, Comiskey was Johnson's sworn enemy, and Comiskey played a significant role the following year as part of the ownership group that humbled the league executive in a quarrel over whether the Red Sox could trade pitcher Carl Mays to the Yankees while he was under suspension. The animosity between the two men reached a point where, when a humbled Johnson retired in 1927, Comiskey refused even to sign the pro forma resolution thanking him for his contributions to the league.

Comiskey showed himself reluctant to share with his players the profits from Chicago pennants in 1906 and 1917, as well as from the club's generally successful first two decades. His 1919 pennant winners were woefully underpaid, some of them getting only half of what comparable players on other teams received; this made them ripe for the plucking by the gambling fraternity. The owner suspected skulduggery as early as the first game of the World Series against Cincinnati and knew conclusively, from at least two sources, of the actions of the Black Sox within weeks of the Series; he even withheld their World Series checks for a time. His subsequent public statement on the fix, issued in September 1920 during the grand jury investigation of the affair, was both an admission of his earlier knowledge and, in his offer of a $10,000 reward for anyone coming forth with information about the scandal, a sham.

The owner's purpose in suppressing information was to protect his investment in the offending players, all of whom except Chick Gandil he resigned for the 1920 season for uncharacteristically large salary increases. His complicity in the pilferage of the players' confessions from the district attorney's office made a conviction improbable, and his sole contribution to the 1921 jury trial of seven Black Sox was to explode in righteous denial before the allegation that he had jumped his contract with the Browns to join the PL in 1890—which, of course, he had.

The effect of the Black Sox scandal on Comiskey's subsequent career was to make him appear a martyr for suffering eleven more seasons without fielding a club that rose higher than fifth. When he died in 1931, there was some sentiment to rechristen one of the streets bordering Comiskey Park, which he had opened to much fanfare in 1910, Comiskey Road; local newspaper wags suggested a better name might have been Seventh Place.

CHUCK COMISKEY

Comiskey represents baseball's most pathetic boardroom tale. The grandson of the first owner of the White Sox, he waited twenty years to get his hands on the franchise that had been willed to him twice; then, suddenly impatient, he outsmarted himself for good. In one way or another, his father, mother, and sister all contributed to the failure of his ambition.

Comiskey's problems began in 1940, when his father, Lou, the son of Charlie Comiskey, died of a heart attack. Under the terms of his father's will, the White Sox franchise was left in trust to Chuck, then in his early teens, until he reached thirty-five. But because of ambiguities in other parts of the document, Lou's widow, Grace, had to go to court to take control of the team from the Chicago bank her husband had named as executor for fear that there wouldn't be any club for anyone to inherit. Grace ended up staying in charge until 1956, with Chuck's older sister Dorothy taking over as organization treasurer.

After finishing college, Comiskey served a two-year stint with one of Chicago's minor league affiliates; then, in the late 1940s, he moved into Comiskey Park as a vice president. His first significant move was to urge his mother to hire Frank Lane as general manager; shortly afterward, he clashed with Grace by backing Lane's demand that Jack Onslow be fired as manager and replaced by Paul Richards. Grace eventually relented, and for a couple of years Comiskey wasn't hesitant about telling everyone that the rise of the White Sox in the standings was due to his insistence on hiring Lane and Richards. Unfortunately, neither the local press nor his mother bestowed praise for the club's turnaround much beyond Lane and Richards—a point borne home when Grace refused her son's demand for a substantial raise. Infuriated by his mother's stand as well as by a passing disclosure that Lane had an attendance bonus, Comiskey resigned from his administrative position—a posture he maintained for six months. For the next two years he worked at peaceful coexistence with Lane despite his own resentment over the attendance bonus and the general manager's fury that Chuck had told Chicago newspapers about the incentive clause.

After Grace Comiskey found enough reasons to get rid of Lane in 1955, she divided day-to-day operations in the organization between Dorothy's husband, Johnny Rigney, and Chuck; at the same time, she made it clear that Dorothy had the ultimate say in corporate matters. That was how the situation remained when Grace died in 1956. Ignoring her son's expectations of finally succeeding her as president, Grace awarded Dorothy enough stock to give her practical control, with a second chunk going to Chuck, still in his early thirties, and a third block being put in trust for him until the thirty-five years originally stipulated by Lou. Comiskey, however, was not ready to wait another couple of years to assume majority control, so over the next eighteen months he and Dorothy dragged each other from courtroom to courtroom over everything from the validity of Grace's will to rival contentions about who had taken too much silverware from their late mother's house. Dorothy cracked first, but not in the way Chuck had anticipated: Instead of offering her brother the shares he didn't already have, she went looking for an outside buyer.

The farce went on for three years. At one point, both brother and sister sought to overturn a motion initially offered by Dorothy herself; at another point, an Illinois judge blasted both Comiskeys for attempting to turn the state's judicial system into a rumpus room; for the years 1957 and 1958, the White Sox had no formal president at all. Finally, in 1959, Bill Veeck took over Dorothy's share of the franchise.

Since he still had his significant minority holding, Chuck Comiskey remained on the premises, buoyed by the hope that Veeck's reputation for diving into things he couldn't handle would ultimately give him, Chuck, the power he had been promised since 1940. He appeared vindicated in 1960 when Veeck disclosed that his health would no longer permit him to operate the White Sox and that the club was up for sale. Aware that Arthur Allyn, Jr., the son of one of Veeck's partners, had the inside track on the majority holdings, Comiskey got too clever by half. First he sold his 46 percent interest in the franchise to a group headed by Chicago insurance executive William Bartholomay. The agreement between the sides was that, with the Comiskey shares accounted for, the Bartholomay syndicate would draw enough heavy investors to overwhelm Allyn with an offer to buy a majority interest right back, making a profit for the Bartholomay people and finally securing the president's chair for Charlie Comiskey's grandson. (It also formally severed the Comiskey name from the White Sox.) The scheme lasted only until Allyn said no; moreover, once he did, it was Bartholomay who ended up selling his 46 percent to Allyn. That gave Allyn the absolute control that Chuck had been promised by both his father and mother.

DAVE CONCEPCION

At the shortstop for the Big Red Machine in the 1970s, Concepcion was the first player to realize the new defensive possibilities offered by artificial turf by deliberately bouncing long throws to first base.

DAVID CONE

For a few years, Cone gave signs of being the Mets' payback for the horrendous trade of Nolan Ryan to the Angels. After being acquired from the Royals in 1987 for backup catcher Ed Hearn, the right-hander settled in at Shea as a mound force equal to that of Dwight Gooden. In his best season, 1988, he compiled a 20–3 record with a 2.22 ERA, striking out 200 batters for the first of four seasons. At the same time, however, Cone showed a tendency to undermine his hill efforts with explosions of temper. In one incident in Cincinnati, he became so enraged by a safe call at first base that he forgot to call time and raved at the umpire while two runs crossed the plate. The 1988 League Championship Series against Los Angeles also provided a showcase for the pitcher at his worst and at his best. Writing a column for a New York newspaper, the would-be sportswriter attacked the depth of the Dodger bullpen and was promptly tattooed by an awakened Los Angeles squad in the second game. After several days of Dodger hectoring and press criticism, however, he came back to hurl a masterful victory in the sixth game.

As one of the Mets' few bachelors, Cone never made a secret of his womanizing, leading to two ugly incidents. On the final morning of the 1991 season, he was informed that Philadelphia police were investigating rape charges against him; Cone took the mound at Veterans Stadium, tied the National League record for strikeouts in a game by fanning 19 Phillies, then came off the field to hear that no charges were being pressed. The following spring, in the midst of a number of scandals involving Met players at their Florida training camp, he was accused by two women of masturbating before them in the bathroom of a Met bullpen. This episode also evaporated behind questions about why the women had invited themselves to the bathroom in the first place.

Cone was traded to the Blue Jays as pennant insurance in August 1992; the deal prevented him from locking up his third straight NL strikeout crown. In 1993 he returned to the Royals as a free agent. In 1994, he took the American League Cy Young Award.

TONY CONIGLIARO

The Red Sox Impossible Dream of 1967 turned into a nightmare for Conigliaro. With Boston battling Detroit, Minnesota, and Chicago down to the wire in a torrid pennant race, the outfielder, who had busted 104 home runs in almost four seasons and who was working on a .287 average with 20 homers, took a fastball in the cheek from California's Jack Hamilton on August 18 and was put out on the sidelines for a year and a half. The good news was that he was able to return in 1969 to hit another 20 homers, following that up with 36 more in 1970. The bad news was that the righty slugger's eyesight had been permanently damaged by the beanball.

The Red Sox, keeping Conigliaro's degenerative condition secret, exacted a cynical revenge by peddling him to the Angels—the source of his problems. He lasted little more than a few months before retiring as much for the psychological effects of his injury as for his deteriorating vision. After an attempted comeback with the Red Sox in 1975, Conigliaro quit for good with a .264 lifetime average and 166 homers, but his life went from bad to worse when he suffered a debilitating heart attack in 1982. He died eight years later, at age forty-five.

JOCKO CONLAN (Hall of Fame, 1974)

Conlan is the only ex-player to become a Hall of Fame umpire. He began his arbiting career in 1935, when as a reserve outfielder for the White Sox he filled in for Red Ormsby, who had succumbed to heat prostration during a game in St. Louis. Bringing his trademark polka-dot bow tie back to the big leagues in 1941, Conlan remained in the National League for twenty-four years, becoming as noted for his frequent run-ins with the likes of Frankie Frisch, Jackie Robinson, and Leo Durocher as for his ability to call balls and strikes. Even in retirement, he would claim that the only two baseball people he didn't like were Robinson and Durocher, because the pair used foul language on the field. Conlan's most notable habit was using his left hand for all hand signs.

GENE CONLEY

While others have played two sports professionally, Conley has been the only one to do so with championship teams in both sports. Over eleven summers in the 1950s and early 1960s, the right-hander won 91 and lost 96 pitching for the Braves (in both Boston and Milwaukee), Phillies, and Red Sox; while with Milwaukee in 1957, he appeared (ineffectively) in the team's World Series victory over the Yankees. Over seven winters between 1952 and 1964, the six-foot, eight-inch Conley also played for the National Basketball Association Boston Celtics; during his hoop career, the Celtics won six NBA championships.

TOM CONNOLLY (Hall of Fame, 1953)

Connolly began an American League-record thirty-one-year career as an umpire after two and a half seasons with the National League. He officiated at both the first AL game in 1901 and the first World Series, between the Red Sox and Pirates in 1903. From the beginning of his AL tenure, Connolly provided the strong antirowdyism approach sought by league founder Ban Johnson, ejecting ten players in the circuit's first season. His most noted confrontation came with Orioles pitcher Joe McGinnity, who spat in Connolly's face and was suspended by Johnson as a result. After retiring in 1931, Connolly became umpire in chief for the circuit; he held the position for twenty-three years.

ROGER CONNOR (Hall of Fame, 1976)

The foremost home-run hitter of the nineteenth century, Connor is best remembered for hitting the first major league grand slam, on September 10, 1881; he did it while playing for Troy in a home game that took place across the Hudson River, in Albany. Another of his memorable clouts, while he was with the Giants, cleared the right-field wall at the first Polo Grounds, at 110th Street and Fifth Avenue, and so impressed a group of stockbrokers in attendance that they collected $500 and bought the first baseman a watch from Tiffany's. Although the lefty swinger led his league in homers only once (in the Players League in 1890), he ended his eighteen-year career with 136 four-baggers, the major league standard until Babe Ruth switched from pitching to the outfield.

CHUCK CONNORS

A first baseman for the Dodgers and the Cubs in the early 1950s, Connors was the most successful of the major leaguers who established a second career in show business. Aside from his popular television series *The Rifleman*, he appeared (ineffectively) in scores of motion pictures, most notably as the heavy in *The Big Country* and *Soylent Green*.

STANTON COOK

As president of the Cubs in 1992, Cook lit the fuse that exploded Commissioner Fay Vincent out of his chair. When Vincent announced a National League realignment plan for 1993 that would have moved Chicago and St. Louis to the Western Division and shifted Atlanta and Cincinnati into the Eastern Division, Cook went to court to block the proposed change. His main bone of contention—aside from what he saw as Vincent's strong-arm tactics—was that a shift to the Western Division would have inconvenienced eastern viewers of the club's WGN superstation, forcing them to watch more games at later Mountain and Pacific starting times and thereby threatening lower ratings and less advertising. The court issued a restraining order that effectively killed the Vincent plan and added another enemy against the commissioner in the ensuing pressure for him to step down.

Although Cook also took frequent aim at Vincent for what he regarded as the commissioner's lack of economic smarts in dealing with the Players Association, the Cubs' owner himself scandalized fellow major league executives in 1992 by personally offering an unprecedented contract to franchise star Ryne Sandberg that amounted to paying the second baseman $7 million a year for four years.

JACK COOMBS

Coombs was a pretty good (159–110 in fourteen seasons) pitcher and a very good one for two seasons; in World Series play, however, he was perfect. One of a succession of college-trained hurlers recruited by Connie Mack for the Athletics in the first decade of the century, the right-hander's 31–9 record in 1910 included a major league record 13 shutouts. The following year he paced American League pitchers again with 28 wins, though this time with only a single blanking. In three World Series—1910 and 1911 for Philadelphia and 1916 for the Dodgers—he won 5 games, the most by any pitcher without a loss.

MORT COOPER

Few pitchers in baseball history have stuck it to opposing batters as graphically as Cooper. In his glory years of 1942, 1943, and 1944, when he compiled 65 wins, the Cardinal right-hander went to the mound wearing the number of the victory he expected to record that day. In case batters missed the significance of the number, Mort's batterymate, brother Walker Cooper, tossed in reminders during the game.

BRAD CORBETT

Corbett's ownership of the Rangers in the 1970s prompted volumes of quotes about his incompetence—many coming from other owners and front-office officials. He was "a Charlie Finley without the imagination," "a George Steinbrenner with a drinking problem." Or: "Giving Corbett a baseball team is like giving a three-year-old a handful of razors," and "Corbett thinks the Texas franchise is a toy that he can play with or throw in a closet at will." An industrial parts manufacturer, Corbett invited the criticisms by working out trades behind the backs of his general manager and manager; by appointing rivals with the powers of a general manager so he could resolve the inevitable (and regular) conflicts; by agreeing to long-term contracts for players who irritated the manager, subsequently firing the manager and releasing the players; and by staggering through the press box denouncing the players on the field as "dogs." In one particularly notorious incident in 1978, he insisted that he would personally handle the final phase of a major trade between the Rangers and the Yankees after a briefing from his front office people. The swap, which cost Texas prospect Dave Righetti for worn-out bullpen ace Sparky Lyle, might have been more justifiable if the Rangers had also succeeded in obtaining second baseman Damaso Garcia, as had been projected. When the Yankees instead palmed off shortstop Domingo Ramos on him, Corbett told his astonished aides that he didn't see the difference between one Latin infielder and another. He was finally forced to sell out by other team investors in January 1980.

JACK CORBETT

The owner of the El Paso Texans of the Class C Arizona-Texas League, Corbett sued organized baseball when he was denied permission to sign banned players returning from Jorge Pasquel's Mexican League in 1946. His suit, for $300,000 in damages, was later combined with that of Yankee farmhand George Earl Toolson and resulted in a U.S. Supreme Court decision upholding baseball's antitrust exemption and right to police itself.

LARRY CORCORAN

The ace of the White Stockings staff in the early 1880s, Corcoran's dalliance with the Union Association in 1884 was cut short when Chicago president Al Spalding interpreted the pitcher's earlier request for an advance on a new contract as a legally binding commitment, effectively expanding the scope of the reserve clause. In his first five seasons (1880–84), Corcoran won 170 games, became the first pitcher to hurl three no-hitters, and led the White Stockings to three consecutive pennants.

PAT CORRALES

A backup catcher to Johnny Bench of the Big Red Machine and on three other National League teams in the 1960s and early 1970s, Corrales batted a mere .216; it was, however, as a manager that he suffered his worst baseball indignity. When he was fired by the Phillies on July 18, 1983, he became the only major league pilot axed while his team was in first place (with a 43–42 record). Philadelphia went on to win the NL pennant under Paul Owens. Corrales signed as Cleveland pilot less than two weeks after the dismissal.

FRANK CORRIDON

Although Bobby Mathews had thrown a spitball as early as the 1860s, it was Corridon's rediscovery of the wet pitch that led to its greatest popularity. The right-hander developed the pitch in collaboration with Providence teammate George Hildebrand in 1902. Moving later that season from the International League to the Pacific Coast League, he taught it to Sacramento teammate Elmer Stricklett. It was Stricklett who taught the pitch to future Hall of Famers Jack Chesbro and Ed Walsh.

CLINT COURTNEY

Called "the meanest man I ever met" by St. Louis teammate Satchel Paige, Courtney was also the first catcher to wear glasses and the first to employ the oversized mitt designed by Baltimore manager Paul Richards to make Hoyt Wilhelm's knuckleball more manageable.

Nicknamed Scrap Iron, Courtney lived up to his sobriquet in the culmination of a two-year feud with the Yankess on April 28, 1953. Bowled over at the plate as Gil McDougald scored the go-ahead run in the top of the tenth inning, the Browns catcher retaliated in the home half by badly spiking New York shortstop Phil Rizzuto while sliding into second base. The ensuing brawl resulted in a dislocated shoulder for umpire John Stevens, ejection and subsequent fines for six players, and a shower of bottles from the stands.

STAN COVELESKI (Hall of Fame, 1969)

Coveleski was one of the more consistent American League pitchers during his fourteen-year career (between 1912 and 1928), posting 20-win seasons four years in a row for Cleveland, from 1918 to 1921, then moving over to the Senators and winning another 20 in Washington's 1925 pennant-winning year. As both an Indian (1923) and a Senator (1925), he also led the AL in ERA. The right-hander's most brilliant efforts came in the 1920 World Series against the Dodgers, when he allowed only two runs in three complete-game victories. Coveleski's older brother Harry had three consecutive 20-win years, for the Tigers between 1914 and 1916. No other pair of brothers has had eight 20-victory seasons.

WILLIAM COX

Following William Baker and Gerry Nugent, Cox was the third owner of the Phillies during a lurid twenty-six-year period that saw the team get into the first division only once. A millionaire lumber magnate, he was practically handed the franchise by other league owners on the recommendation of National League president Ford Frick to put an end to Nugent's ramshackle way of operating. Cox was enthusiastic but little else.

At spring training in 1943, he showed how hands-on an owner could be by insisting on taking regular turns at pitching, fielding, and hitting, thereby earning the mockery of his players and tensions with manager Bucky Harris. Harris wasn't too much happier about the owner's normal postmidnight calls suggesting better ways to manage. Another early source of trouble was a former coach for the Hungarian Olympic team whom Cox insisted was necessary for getting the players into better shape. The coach turned out to be ahead of his time in announcing that he didn't want any of the players chewing tobacco, recommending instead that they partake of the orange slices he had laid out on the bench for every game. Unfortunately, once the game started, the coach had little interest in the proceedings, and when Harris caught him asleep on the bench, the manager had the excuse he had been seeking to get Cox to fire him.

Given such incidents, sportswriters covering the team were hardly surprised when Cox fired Harris midway into the season. What they hadn't been prepared for, however, was a revolt by the players and threats to sit out a game against the Cardinals unless Harris were reinstated. It required an appeal by the ousted manager before the players agreed to take the field. The incident might have ended right there if the exhausted Harris hadn't decided that he needed a drink with a couple of sportswriters before returning home. Between one raised elbow and other, he let slip that Cox was so naive about the skills of the team that he frequently bet on games. When the information got back to Commissioner Kenesaw Landis, Cox acknowledged that he had made "some small sentimental bets" without realizing that he had violated baseball's rules. When Landis told the owner to come back for another meeting with a lawyer, Cox read the writing on the wall and put the club up for sale. He was later formally blacklisted. Along with Horace Fogel, also of the Phillies, he is one of the only two major league owners to be banned from the game for life.

Before fading into the sunset, Cox had also solicited suggestions for renaming the Phillies as a symbol of the organization's break with its sorry past. Mrs. John L. Lucas got her proposal of Blue Jays accepted. Aside from a briefly used uniform patch, what this mainly brought was a letter from students at Johns Hopkins University asking the team not to use the school's nickname because it would "disgrace and dishonor" the collegiate Blue Jays.

ROGER CRAIG

Craig had practically four different identities after beginning his career with the 1955 Dodgers. For both the Brooklyn and Los Angeles versions of the franchise, he was a tightrope-walking right-hander who seemed to have a full count on every batter but who ultimately contributed significantly to three pennants. With the expansion Mets in 1962 and 1963, he lost a combined 46 games; in 1963 alone, he lost 18 in a row at one stretch, during which the team was shut out eight times. As a pitching coach with the Padres, Astros, and Tigers in the 1970s and 1980s, he was considered something of an alchemist in getting career performances out of journeymen, all the more so when he began teaching the split-finger fastball to his charges. Finally, as manager of the Giants between 1985 and 1992, he was credited with ending years of clubhouse rifts on the team by getting behind rookies Will Clark, Robby Thompson, and José Uribe and driving them to a division title in 1987 and a pennant two years later. While with the Tigers under Sparky Anderson between 1980 and 1984, Craig also popularized the trend of having coaches call pitches from the dugout. Between this habit and his weakness for pitchouts, his presence on the bench usually signified games as long as the ones he had once pitched for the Dodgers.

DOC CRAMER

Although he batted .296 over his twenty-year (1929–48) career, Cramer has the American League mark for the most at-bats in a season without a home run. As a member of the Red Sox in 1938, the lefty-hitting outfielder went to the plate a league-leading 658 times without reaching the seats. He had 37 career blasts.

DOC CRANDALL

Although others had been tried in the role before, Crandall was baseball's first successful reliever. After a year as a starter for the Giants in

1908, manager John McGraw used the right-hander primarily out of the bullpen for the next five seasons. In 1913 Crandall became the first hurler to make at least 30 relief appearances. He was nicknamed Doc by Damon Runyon because he was "first aid to the injured . . . the physician of the pitching emergency."

GAVVY CRAVATH

Cravath may have been baseball's most successful opposite-field power hitter. An outfielder for the Phillies in the years just prior to Babe Ruth's emergence as a slugger, the right-handed hitter took aim at the friendly right-field distance of Baker Bowl (officially 280 feet down the line, but suspected of being much less) to the tune of six National League home-run titles between 1913 and 1919. Indicative of the era's power standards, Cravath broke the 20-home-run mark only once, and won another title with a mere 8 round-trippers. On the other hand, he was a genuine clutch hitter, driving in 100 runs three times, leading the league in hits once, and setting the pace in slugging average twice.

BILL CRAVER

The only one of the so-called Louisville Four never specifically accused, let alone convicted, of selling games, Craver was blackballed for refusing to allow club officials to read his private telegrams, general misconduct, and "suspicious play." The evidence against the shortstop and field captain, given in a closed-door inquiry, consisted primarily of accusations by second baseman Joe Gerhardt and first baseman Juice Latham that he had deliberately rattled them into making errors; Gerhardt, however, recanted the next day, explaining that they had simply wanted to get rid of the irascible assistant manager.

Craver certainly carried a lot of baggage. In 1869, playing behind the plate for the Troy Haymakers, he protested an umpire's call so furiously that the entire team walked off the field in the sixth inning after the Cincinnati Red Stockings had tied the score at 17-all, reportedly to spare club owner John Morrissey the reported $17,000 he had bet on the Haymakers; that tie was the single blemish in Cincinnati's legendary consecutive-game winning streak. In 1870 he was suspended by the Chicago White Stockings and then banned for life by the amateur National Association of Base Ball Players for insubordination and gambling. In 1874, while with the proto-major league National Association Philadelphia White Stockings, he was implicated in the attempted bribe of an umpire. It therefore came as no surprise when the *Brooklyn Eagle* included him in its 1875 all-star "starting lineup of rogues." (That year he also became part, along with George Bechtel, of the first cash transaction for a player contract, moving from the Philadelphia Centennials to the Philadelphia Athletics.)

Nevertheless, at least in the Louisville affair, there is no real evidence that he played any part in the perfidy of his teammates. For his part, Craver unequivocally denied every allegation the Louisville club levied against him—except for late-night gambling and drinking, and refusing to allow the invasion of his privacy. After his forced retirement, he became a Troy policeman.

SAM CRAWFORD (Hall of Fame, 1957)

The only player to lead both leagues in both home runs and triples, Crawford also had an important role in assuring that there were two leagues to be led. It was in fact only when Cincinnati Garry Herrmann withdrew his objections to the lefty-hitting outfielder's defection from the Reds to the Tigers after the 1902 season that the owners of the National and American leagues hammered out their mutual coexistence agreement. What Herrmann lost was a career .309 batter who had paced the NL with 16 home runs in 1901 and 23 triples in 1902; what Detroit gained was the AL home run leader in 1908 (with a mere 7 round-trippers) and baseball's all-time triples king (with 312), who topped that category in five seasons. Crawford also led the AL in RBIs three times, reaching the 100 mark in six seasons. In addition, he scored the most runs in the junior circuit in 1907 and belted the most doubles in 1909. One asterisk to his extra-base power was that 50 of the speedy outfielder's 97 home runs were inside-the-park tears around the bases; another, attached to his career-high .378 average in 1911, is that he reached that level partly because of the introduction of the more lively cork-centered ball.

While with the Tigers, Crawford was a member in good standing of the anti-Ty Cobb faction, and had more than one scuffle with The Georgia Peach before calling it quits in 1917. Asked once to explain the antagonism to Cobb, he replied: "He's still fighting the Civil War and he sees us as just damn Yankees." For all that, Crawford was also one of the leaders of the team revolt against the suspension of Cobb in 1912 for hitting a fan.

GEORGE CREAMER

Second baseman Creamer was the fourth of five managers with the feckless 1884 Pittsburgh Alleghenys of the American Association. Lasting only 8 games, he established a major league mark for managerial futility by losing all of them. Player Creamer didn't help manager Creamer's cause: He batted only .183.

JOSEPH CREAMER

A wealthy physician who also worked for the Giants, Creamer was barred from baseball after the 1908 season behind accusations that he sought to bribe umpire Bill Klem. According to Klem, the doctor approached him before the winner-take-all makeup contest between New York and Chicago that had been necessitated by the Merkle boner and offered $3,000 if the arbiter would "call close plays the Giants' way." Creamer always denied the allegations.

JIM CREIGHTON

Baseball's first superstar, Creighton died in October 1862 at age twenty-one, four days after rupturing his bladder while hitting a home run for the Excelsior club of Brooklyn. Though nominally an amateur, he became the first paid player by accepting money from the Excelsiors surreptitiously in 1860. A hitting phenom, Creighton went through the entire 1862 season making only four outs. It was as a pitcher, however, that he revolutionized the game, first by employing (illegally) a snap wrist action to add speed to the required underhand delivery of the day, and then by learning to change speeds to fool hitters. Creighton is buried in Brooklyn's Greenwood Cemetery beneath an ornate stone monument featuring sculpted paraphernalia of the game, including a pair of crossed bats, a scorebook, a base, and a cap; the leitmotiv is topped by the carved word "Excelsior" and, above that, a granite baseball.

DODE CRISS

A pitcher-first baseman for the Browns in the first decade of the century, Criss amounted to the game's first professional pinch hitter insofar as 70 percent of his appearances over four years were the result of coming off the bench. In all four seasons between 1908 and 1911, he led the American League in both pinch-hits and substitute at-bats.

JOE CRONIN (Hall of Fame, 1956)

Cronin wore just about every uniform and suit there was to wear in baseball, but the only threads he sported with particular distinction were those of a player. A right-hand-hitting shortstop with extra-base power, he made his first mark with the Senators in 1929 after a couple of unimpressive trials with the Pirates. With Washington he drove in 100 runs five years in a row, led the American League in doubles and triples once each, and batted as high as .346. Before he ended his big league playing career in 1945 with Boston, he would rack up 100 RBIs three more times and build a lifetime .301 average.

From 1933, however, Cronin's hitting and wide-ranging defensive play had to share the spotlight with his managing. His biggest success as a pilot came in his very first year, when he led the Senators to a franchise-high 99 victories to finish ahead of the Yankees by a surprising 7 games. The following season, injuries and clashes with star players Goose Goslin and Alvin Crowder sent Washington skidding toward the bottom of the league. The campaign became even more of a nightmare when Cronin had to endure constant grandstand catcalls following an announcement that he planned to marry the niece of owner Clark Griffith in the fall. Griffith heard the jeering, too, and with the help of a $225,000 offer from Boston, decided that his playing manager would be under too much pressure to return the team to the top of the standings; the result was an October 1934 trade with the Red Sox that brought Washington shortstop Lyn Lary with the quarter-million dollars.

For his first eleven years at the helm of Boston, Cronin managed four second-place finishes, but nothing better despite the presence on the roster of such fellow future Hall of Famers as Ted Williams, Jimmie Foxx, and Bobby Doerr. Cronin's own stubbornness about remaining at shortstop in the face of a perceptible slowing down also led the club to sell hot minor league prospect Pee Wee Reese to the Dodgers. In 1946 Cronin finally returned to the World Series, but saw that accomplishment shorted in the seventh game when Enos Slaughter scored on Johnny Pesky's delayed relay to give the Cardinals the world championship. A year later, with the retirement of Eddie Collins, owner Tom Yawkey announced Cronin's promotion to general manager.

As the head of Boston's baseball operations from 1948 to 1959, Cronin was behind the decision to bring in another shortstop-manager, Lou Boudreau, to take over the dugout, but neither that move nor a regular series of second-line trades could get the Red Sox any higher than third in the 1950s. It was also during this period that the franchise became identified as the most reluctant in baseball to sign a black player. In fact, it was not until 1959 that Pumpsie Green broke the color line at Fenway Park, and that move just happened to coincide with Cronin's election as president of the AL.

As the league's chief official between 1959 and 1973, Cronin presided over the franchise shifts of the Senators to Minnesota, of the Athletics to Oakland, of the Pilots to Milwaukee, and of the second twentieth-century Washington team to Texas. In some of these financial maneuvers he had more than the customary passive role of a league president. At the league meeting that approved Washington's move to Minnesota, for instance, he rejected an attempt by Baltimore to reverse its initially positive vote on the grounds that it hadn't understood the significance of the ballot; if the Baltimore appeal had been accepted, Cronin's brother-in-law Calvin Griffith would have been blocked from transferring to the Twin Cities. After a couple of years of encouraging Kansas City owner Charlie Finley to explore the possibilities of moving the Athletics to California, Cronin had to act fast when the actual league vote approving a transfer to Oakland brought down the wrath of Missouri politicians. Disabused of the idea that Kansas City would accept some vague commitment for another major league team sometime in the future, he railroaded through a promise that the league would include the market in a 1969 expansion—a vow carried out with the creation of the Royals. By the same token, however, it was also Cronin who had the league rush to near havoc in accepting the bid by William Daley and Dewey Soriano for setting up the Pilots as the second new team in 1969.

FRANK CROSETTI

As a shortstop (1932–46), player-coach (1947–48), and coach (1949–68) for the Yankees, Crosetti picked up more World Series checks (23) than anyone else in the history of baseball. As a player, the right-handed hitter retired with a .243 average and eight league-leading totals in being hit by a pitch; as a coach, his grim visage became a fixture in the third-base coaching box. Severe and humorless, Crosetti was so irritated by the antics of Max Patkin that he clobbered the baseball clown one day.

POWEL CROSLEY

Crosley, who made his fortune in everything from broadcasting to manufacturing radios and automobiles, was talked into taking over Cincinnati in 1934 by Larry MacPhail, who wanted to get out from under the financial restrictions placed on him by the trust company into whose portfolio the franchise had fallen. His radio operation proved critical to MacPhail's pioneering use of Red Barber to air Reds games. In 1936, however, a simmering dispute between MacPhail and Crosley exploded when MacPhail slugged Crosley during an organization meeting; two days later, the general manager was out. At the height of the Red scare in the 1950s, Crosley changed the team's nickname to Redlegs lest some dim segment of the American public conclude that the occupants of Crosley Field endorsed communism. In the late 1950s he seriously pursued the idea of moving the club to New York to fill the gap left by the defecting Dodgers and Giants; he was ultimately dissuaded by a congressional investigation then going on into baseball's exemption from antitrust statutes and fears that another franchise

transfer might suggest that major league teams were more interested in money than market loyalty. Crosley died during spring training in 1961.

LAVE CROSS

Cross is the only player to play for four different teams in the same city: Between 1889 and 1907, he wore the uniforms of the American Association Athletics, the National League Phillies, the Players League Quakers, and the American League Athletics—all of Philadelphia.

TONY CUCCINELLO

Cuccinello was a casualty of the end of World War II. Two days before the end of the 1945 season, he was released by the White Sox and told he would not be invited back the following year because of the younger players expected to be released from the military. At the time, the third baseman had been locked in a duel with George Stirnweiss of the Yankees for the batting title. The .309-hitting New York second baseman ended up taking the crown by .00009 points, the smallest margin in baseball history.

CANDY CUMMINGS (Hall of Fame, 1939)

The most commonly accepted progenitor of the curveball, Cummings claimed to have received the inspiration for what was the first trick pitch as a teenager chucking clam shells in his native Massachusetts. The right-hander first used it in competition in 1866. After five seasons in the National Association, he made his National League debut with Hartford in 1876, pitching a shutout against St. Louis in which 24 of the 27 outs were pop-ups—21 of them to the catcher and another 3 to Cummings himself. Later that season, on September 9, he won both ends of the first major league doubleheader, besting Cincinnati by scores of 14–4 in the morning and 8–4 in the late afternoon. Joining the same Reds the following season, he quit with a midseason record of 5–14 following some abusive newspaper accounts of his diminished abilities. Although Cummings owes his place in Cooperstown largely to Henry Chadwick's verification of his claim to have thrown the first curveball, the historian also maintained from time to time that an unnamed Syracuse pitcher had beaten Cummings to the pitch by at least a decade. After retirement, Cummings served as the first figurehead president of the proto-minor league International Association.

NED CUTHBERT

Outfielder Cuthbert has been credited with being the first to steal a base, executing a theft of third against the astonished Brooklyn Atlantics while playing for the Philadelphia Keystones in 1865. The reason given for his innovation: There was nothing in the rules forbidding it.

KIKI CUYLER (Hall of Fame, 1968)

Of all the great outfields the Pirates have boasted over their history, the greatest of all should have been the 1927 array of Cuyler and the two Waner brothers. A .321 hitter over his eighteen big league seasons (1921–38), the right-hand swinger topped the .300 mark ten times, had at least 200 hits on three occasions, and in one season or another paced the National League in doubles, triples, runs scored (twice), and stolen bases (four times); for good measure, he also drove in 100 runs three times. But just as Lloyd Waner was joining his brother Paul on the Pittsburgh picket line, Cuyler got into a spat with

manager Donie Bush that mushroomed into one of the worst deals ever completed by the Pirates.

The trouble started when Bush, in an attempt to shake the Pirates out of an early-season slump, moved Cuyler from third to second in the batting order. Cuyler protested, claiming that he wasn't a good hit-and-run man and was better suited to driving in runs from the third hole, and backed up his argument by going hitless in a few games. Deciding that his authority was being questioned, Bush kept the lineup the way he wanted it, then fined Cuyler $25 for failing to slide to break up a double play in a game. This prompted shouting matches on the bench between the pilot and the outfielder, and stirred up both the press and the fans against Bush for being bullheaded. Bush appealed to owner Barney Dreyfuss, who backed him up completely, with the result that Cuyler was benched for the rest of the year and for the 1927 World Series against the Yankees.

It came as a shock to nobody when Cuyler was shipped off to the Cubs after the season. His revenge was to pick up his career where it had left off, playing a major role in Chicago's 1929 and 1932 pennants. The Pirates didn't really fare that badly, either: Between 1927 and 1930, they used three different outfielders in place of Cuyler, all of whom batted well over .300.

D

JAY DAHL

Dahl was the pitcher in the all-rookie starting lineup Houston fielded against the Mets on September 27, 1963. He lasted only three innings in a 10–3 thrashing and never appeared in another major league game. Two years later, at age nineteen, he was killed in a car crash; no major leaguer or ex-major leaguer has ever died at a younger age. The other starters in the contest were Rusty Staub (1B), Joe Morgan (2B), Glenn Vaughan (3B), Sonny Jackson (SS), Brock Davis (OF), Aaron Pointer (OF), and Jimmy Wynn (OF).

STEVE DAHL

Dahl was a Chicago disc jockey who, on July 12, 1979, helped create one of the most chaotic scenes ever played out in a major league ballpark. With the backing of Mike Veeck, son of White Sox owner Bill Veeck, he presided over a Disco Demolition promotion that invited fans to bring their passé disco records to Comiskey Park for destruction between games of a double header against the Tigers. No sooner had a pile of recordings been blown up than thousands of fans, some of whom had spent the first game firing vinyl through the stands, streamed onto the field, drinking beer, ripping up the turf, and improvising their own fires. After futile attempts by the senior Veeck to restore order, the police and fire departments had to be summoned. In the middle of the melee, which made it impossible to complete the doubleheader, Dahl himself simply stole away from the stadium. The following day, American League president Lee MacPhail awarded the second game of the twin bill to Detroit by forfeit.

HUGH DAILY

Despite having lost his left hand in a gun accident when he was a young man, Daily was the first pitcher to notch back-to-back one-hitters. In the first of them, on July 7, 1884, he also fanned 19 batters and lost a 20th when, under the rules at the time, catcher Ed Crane dropped a third strike and the batter reached first base. To compensate for his missing hand the pitcher used an adjustable wristpad, fastened at his elbow, that absorbed the impact of batted or thrown balls.

STEVE DALKOWSKI

Dalkowski was arguably the most anticipated prospect in baseball history. As a Baltimore farmhand at Kingsport of the Class D Appalachian League in 1957, he was clocked regularly at more than 100 miles an hour while averaging almost 2 strikeouts an inning. The other side of the coin, however, was that he walked 129 batters over the same 62 innings in which he fanned 121, leading to a record of 1–8 and an ERA of 8.13. He never pitched in the major leagues despite predictions from numerous people inside and outside the Orioles organization that he would make people forget Walter Johnson.

ABNER DALRYMPLE

The left fielder for the Chicago White Stockings in the 1880s, Dalrymple kept an extra ball inside his uniform, to be used on suitable occasions. He stole a home run from Boston's Ezra Sutton on a hazy day in 1880 by backing up against the fence and pulling the concealed ball out of his shirt as the game ball soared out of the park; the umpire, unable to see because of the fog, called Sutton out. The outfielder also led the National League with 501 total bases run, an official offensive category that existed only in 1880.

CLAY DALRYMPLE

Catcher Dalrymple has been the only major leaguer to challenge a nineteenth-century rule intended to discourage ambidextrous pitching. On July 17, 1969, while with the Orioles, he took up his normal position behind the plate with a mitt on his left hand and a fielder's glove in his back pocket. Questioned by umpire John Rice, Dalrymple explained that he intended using the fielder's glove for plays at the plate to take advantage of its greater flexibility. Citing the rule limiting players to one glove at a time, the umpire ordered the catcher to toss his spare back into the dugout.

HARRY DALTON

From his first official act as general manager of the Orioles, Dalton demonstrated a self-assurance bordering on cockiness that was to mark most of the rest of his career. Later the trait earned him both a hefty fine and a reputation for leaving chaos in his wake whenever he changed employers by taking with him most of the front-office talent on hand.

Assuming the duties of Baltimore general manager in December 1965, Dalton immediately asked the Reds to include another player in what was already a lopsided trade for outfielder Frank Robinson arranged by predecessor Lee MacPhail. The Orioles who won four American League pennants and two world championships between 1966 and 1971 were Dalton's creation, partly because he had been responsible as farm director for rearing most of their key players and partly for the judicious trades that brought outfielder Don Buford (in 1968) and pitchers Mike Cuellar (1968), Moe Drabowsky (1970), and Pat Dobson (1971) to the club.

Seeking new challenges, Dalton moved West in 1972 to give life to the sagging Angels, but

got caught, instead, between Gene Autry's ever-shifting priorities. After Dalton traded local hero Jim Fregosi to the Mets for Nolan Ryan in 1972, Autry decided to go with homegrown talent; this policy lasted until 1977, when the former singing cowboy switched direction again and laid out $5.2 million for free agents Joe Rudi, Bobby Grich, and Don Baylor. By then Dalton had already been whipsawed, in another typical Autry ploy, by the arrival on the scene of his successor, Buzzie Bavasi.

Taking over the Brewers in November 1977, Dalton inherited the nucleus of the team that would win the AL East second half in the strike-shortened 1981 season and the AL flag the following year; his contribution was the December 1980 trade that brought back-to-back Cy Young winners Rollie Ringers (1981) and Pete Vukovich (1982) to Milwaukee. A member of management's negotiating team during events leading to the 1981 strike, Dalton injudiciously went on the record with *Washington Post* columnist Tom Boswell to announce his hope that the owners were looking for a compromise, his fear that they were not, and his conviction that the players would accept a deal that would not require their "losing too much face." His candid assessment of the situation won him points with the players but a $50,000 fine from the Player Relations Committee, although the penalty was rescinded after the strike was settled.

It was also during his Milwaukee years that Dalton became noted for what came to be called The Dalton Gang, a clique of administrative staffers and scouts who had followed him from Baltimore to California to Milwaukee. Among them were Walter Shannon, Ray Poitevint, Dee Fondy, Bruce Manno, Julio Blanco-Herrera, and Walter Youse. Their departure from Baltimore with Dalton had crippled the Orioles' player development program, and their subsequent move from California would have done the same to the Angels had they concentrated on that area. Despite the fierce loyalty of his brain trust, Dalton never again came closer to another pennant than third place before being kicked upstairs to an inconsequential vice presidency in favor of Sal Bando after the 1991 season.

TOM DALY

Daly hit the first pinch-hit home run in the major leagues when he came off the bench to bat for ailing Dodgers left fielder Hub Collins in the ninth inning of a game in Boston on May 14, 1892; the utility man's heroics tied the game for Brooklyn. Collins died a week later of typhoid fever.

RAY DANDRIDGE (Hall of Fame, 1987)

Dandridge was a bowlegged third baseman who spent the better part of the 1930s setting the standard at his position in the Negro leagues, then almost all of the 1940s as a star of Jorge Pasquel's Mexican League. It was said of Dandridge that a truck could pass between his legs but that no batted ball ever did. Dandridge introduced the gimmick, later made famous by Dodger third baseman Billy Cox, of holding the ball just long enough to allow batters trying to leg out a hit to arrive a split second after his throw. The right-handed slap hitter is credited with batting averages in the .310s in the United States and the .340s in Mexico, but below .300 in Cuban winter ball.

In 1939 Dandridge jumped the Newark Eagles to play with the Vargas club in Caracas, Venezuela, then moved on to Veracruz, Mexico, batting higher than .300 in both places and helping both teams to win pennants. He almost completed the hat trick, topping .300 again for the Cienfuegos entry that finished a half game out of first place in the Cuban winter league.

The third baseman's stay in Mexico was interrupted in 1944 when Eagles owner Abe Manley had his draft exemption revoked to force him back to the United States. Two years later, with white North American stars receiving large amounts to play in the Mexican League, Dandridge forced a $10,000 bonus from Pasquel. In 1947 Bill Veeck tried to lure him north of the border to play for the Indians, but Dandridge refused to leave Mexico without a signing bonus. Signed by the Giants at age thirty-five, he was sent to their Triple-A farm club in Minneapolis, where he batted .362, .311, .324, and .292 in four seasons, taking Rookie of the Year Honors in 1949 and an MVP award in 1950 for his role in the Millers American Association championship;

several observers, among them Monte Irvin, claim that the New York club's refusal to promote him in 1950 despite the informal quota system then in effect for blacks cost the team a pennant. His primary function in 1951 was to prepare a young Willie Mays for his entry into the big leagues.

Dandridge is a member of the Mexican Baseball Hall of Fame as well as a Cooperstown honoree.

JOSEPH DANZANSKY

Danzansky's antics to keep one team in Washington and benighted efforts to attract another one showed how easy it was to paralyze major league owners. Owner of a chain of grocery stores and the president of the Washington Board of Trade, Danzansky first appeared prominently in 1971, when he offered Bob Short $8.4 million for the Senators. When the offer was judged too modest and the team appeared headed for Texas, Commissioner Bowie Kuhn and other American League owners urged the businessman to come up with more money so the nation's capital wouldn't lose its second club of the century. Aware that Kuhn and the owners were fearful that a move to Texas would encourage another congressional look into baseball's antitrust exemption, Danzansky played them along for months, periodically reporting new investment sources and getting them to apply more pressure on Short. Finally, however, Short ran out of patience and challenged everybody concerned for concrete evidence of the additional money. When Danzansky produced nothing to back up his boasting, Kuhn and the AL had no choice but to endorse the transfer of the Senators to Texas.

The episode was still in everybody's mind two years later when Danzansky entered into an agreement with San Diego owner C. Arnholt Smith to bring the Padres to Washington in time for the 1974 season. To demonstrate his commitment, he gave Smith a $100,000 deposit on a projected $12 million while waiting for National League owners to approve the sale. Not only didn't the owners give their approval because of opposition to abandoning the Southern California market, but also they initiated an eight-month circus of seeking, interviewing, and rejecting prospective buyers who would keep the club in San

Diego. In the meantime, Danzansky became the only outsider in baseball history to approve or veto trades, since his deposit money had bought from Smith the right to have the final say on all exchanges. Ever optimistic that he would be bringing the team to Washington in 1974, for instance, he turned thumbs down to a deal that would have sent Clay Kirby to St. Louis because the pitcher was from the capital and therefore a potential gate attraction. On the other hand, he permitted the Padres to sell pitcher Fred Norman to the Reds and infielder Dave Campbell to the Cardinals behind Smith's pleas that the club needed ready cash.

As the saga dragged on, Smith, becoming increasingly anxious about the threat of a federal indictment citing him for $23 million in unpaid taxes, decided to ignore his commitment to Danzansky and work out another arrangement with Marjorie Everett, main stockholder in the Hollywood Park racetrack. This prompted a lawsuit from Danzansky and trembling from NL owners; for the record, the latter said they were opposed to Everett's racetrack connections, but what they were mainly worried about was awakening congressmen again if Washington were denied a franchise in such a fashion. The upshot was that the owners vetoed the Everett bid and, turning full circle, indicated that they were ready to abandon San Diego and endorse Smith's original agreement. But then Danzansky popped up to announce that, together with the abuse he had suffered from both Smith and the league, the rising interest rates since he had first made his offer made in impractical for him to pursue any team ownership. He had his deposit refunded, and shortly afterward the Padres were sold to Ray Kroc.

ALVIN DARK

With the possible exception of Billy Sunday, no major leaguer mixed baseball and fundamentalist religion as extravagantly as Dark. Although the blend wasn't always evident during his fourteen-year career as a ferociously competitive shortstop for the Braves, Giants, and several other clubs, it was the glaring trademark of his stints as manager of the Giants, Kansas City Athletics, Indians, Oakland Athletics, and Padres. Even when he wasn't calling down heavenly vengeance on one of his employers, as he did with Charlie Finley, he was getting into other troubles with racist attitudes toward his players.

As a player, Dark became baseball's second Rookie of the Year (after Jackie Robinson) in 1948 by spearheading that season's pennant win by the Braves. Two years later, he and his double-play partner, Eddie Stanky, were traded to the Giants, where they proved to be the heart of New York's miracle 1951 win climaxed by Bobby Thomson's playoff home run. Again in 1954, Dark was a big reason for the Giants' pennant, not least for the deft bat-handling that made him about the best hit-and-run swinger of the period. After wandering around the National League for a few years, he got his first managerial job in 1961 with the transplanted Giants in San Francisco. A year later he led the club to another pennant, squeezed out of the Dodgers in a postseason playoff. In 1964, however, he came close to causing baseball's first twentieth-century racial strike when he accused San Francisco's black and Latin players of lacking the "mental alertness" of their white teammates and having "no pride" in their jobs. The remarks prompted most of the team's blacks and Latins to threaten an indefinite boycott until Dark was replaced. The situation was resolved only when Willie Mays, a teammate of the manager's in the Polo Grounds in the 1950s, interceded. Dark was fired at the end of the season—mostly because of the racial incident, but also because the front office dreaded the fallout from disclosures that the Bible-quoting pilot had been carrying on an adulterous affair with an airline hostess.

With the Kansas City version of the A's in 1967, Dark became enmeshed in another player revolt—this one aimed against team owner Finley. Although Dark had no part in a petition protesting Finley's niggardly ways, he was fired for not heading off the trouble; afterward, he called the uprising "one of the most courageous things I've ever seen in baseball." His next stop was in Cleveland in 1968, where he doubled as general manager. Mainly because of the players he had inherited, he steered the Indians to a rare first-division finish, but then found himself constantly outwitted by other general managers, leading to one transaction fiasco after another.

In 1974 Dark returned to Finley—and to an Oakland clubhouse where revolt was an everyday occurrence. The players so despised him for replacing Dick Williams, who had stood up to Finley, that Sal Bando, for one, openly declared that he "couldn't manage a meat market." Dark had enough wits, however, to turn a blind eye to the daily brawls that afflicted the Oakland clubhouse, and produced two division wins and a pennant. He also began to win some respect for his own run-ins with Finley over the owner's determination to pare the organization to the bone. In September 1975 Dark sealed his fate by telling a congregation of fundamentalists, "To God, Charlie Finley is just a very little, bitty thing. If he doesn't accept Jesus Christ as his personal savior, he's going to hell." Finley waited only until Oakland had lost to Boston in the American League Championship Series before announcing that Dark was being replaced because he was "too busy with church activities."

Although anxious to get back to the National League, Dark turned down an offer from the Cardinals on the grounds that his religious principles wouldn't permit him to work for a team owned by a beer company. Instead, he took over the Padres 48 games into the 1977 season. As soon as he told the San Diego players that they were prohibited from drinking beer anywhere in his presence, they, too, rose up in arms. Before the season was over, he had also alienated his pitching and hitting coaches by assuming most of their duties. Mainly because he preferred seeing Dark as a loner up against the odds, owner Ray Kroc insisted that he be retained for the following season. When tensions recommenced even in spring training, however, Dark was replaced by Roger Craig.

JAKE DAUBERT

In the preagent era, nobody was better than Daubert at getting an owner over a barrel during contract talks. As a member of the Dodgers, he won the National League batting title in both 1913 and 1914, each time serving notice on owner Charlie Ebbets that he would take his first baseman's mitt over to the Federal League if his salary demands were not met. They were. At the end of the 1918 season, which had been abbreviated because of World War I, Daubert read his contract meticulously enough to conclude that baseball ownership's ploy of prorating wages on the basis of the shortened schedule violated the pact, and asked for the full sum. When Ebbets took to the press to denounce him as "unpatriotic, selfish, and greedy," Daubert filed suit against the team. Panicky owners in both leagues pressured Ebbets to reach an out-of-court settlement lest a verdict come down against all of them. Ebbets sought to save face by trading Daubert to the Reds before the start of the 1919 season, but ended up sitting in the stands watching his former first baseman playing in that year's World Series.

HELEN DAUVRAY

A noted actress and the wife of future Hall of Famer John Montgomery Ward, Dauvray convinced Detroit owner Frederick Stearns and St. Louis boss Chris Von der Ahe to have a silver cup designed by Tiffany's, name it after her, and award it to the first team to win three postseason championship series between the National League and American Association pennant winners. Dauvray, Ward, and the trophy, the last accompanied by a round-the-clock hired guard, took in the entire 15-game, ten-city 1887 Detroit-St. Louis series, often attracting more attention than the two teams. Her union with the Giants shortstop, an early version of the Joe DiMaggio-Marilyn Monroe match, created a media sensation. Although it lasted longer than the marriage, the cup was retired when cooperation between the two leagues ended in 1891. Although no team won the required three series, each of the four yearly victors—the Wolverines in 1887, Ward's Giants in 1888 and 1889, and Brooklyn in 1890—was a National League club.

DONALD DAVIDSON

The four-foot-tall Davidson came close to aborting midget Eddie Gaedel's distinction in baseball. While serving as the batboy for the Red Sox in 1938, he was told by manager Joe Cronin to hit for Moe Berg. Umpire Bill Summers didn't share Cronin's sense of humor, however, and demanded that Berg take his turn. Davidson divided his batboy chores between the Red Sox and Braves. He ended up remaining with the Braves through their transfers to Milwaukee and Atlanta, moving up the ladder from team mascot to public relations director to traveling secretary.

MORDECAI DAVIDSON

Taking over ownership of the Louisville Colonels in 1888, Davidson launched a two-year tyranny that culminated in the first major league player walkout, in June 1889. The owner traveled with the club to maintain discipline, levied $100 fines for errors as well as rules infractions, left players on the road penniless, kept up a running attack on the team in the press, and changed managers capriciously (even serving two brief terms in the dugout himself). The strike, led by Pete Browning and Guy Hecker, lasted two days and ended only when the American Association confiscated the franchise and returned more than half of the fines Davidson had collected.

GEORGE DAVIS

After batting over .300 for nine consecutive seasons with the Giants, shortstop Davis jumped to Chicago in the rival American League in 1902 but, disillusioned with owner Charlie Comiskey's salary scale, retreated to New York the following year. After only four games, however, the peace treaty between the two leagues awarded the switch-hitter to the White Sox. Davis refused to report and sat out the rest of the schedule while his attorney, John Montgomery Ward, fought the decision in a lengthy but losing court battle.

HARRY DAVIS

A turn-of-the-century slugger with the Athletics and several other teams, Davis was the first player to lead a major league in home runs in four consecutive seasons. (Only Hall of Famers Frank Baker, Babe Ruth, and Ralph Kiner have duplicated or surpassed the feat.) After four nineteenth-century seasons with four National League clubs, the right-handed hitter became the first baseman for the powerhouse Philadelphia clubs of the first decade of the century. He won his four homer crowns between 1904 and 1907 without ever hitting more than 12 in a season; he also led the league in doubles three times, RBIs twice, and

triples and runs scored once each. He was manager of the Indians for part of the 1912 season, but his strict managerial discipline failed to boost the team out of the second division. Returning to the A's as a coach for the next fifteen years, he made token forays onto the field in several seasons, to run up a total of twenty-two years of service; the appearances didn't hurt his other career, as a Philadelphia city councilman, either.

MARK DAVIS

Davis has been the Cy Young Award's most anomalous recipient. A left-handed reliever of the Padres in 1989, he took the honor for leading the National League with 44 saves. That effort followed a brilliant second half in 1988 during which he compiled most of his 28 rescues on the season. Aside from that patch of bullpen dominance, however, Davis was not only bad, he was atrocious. Subtracting his 1988 and 1989 campaigns, for instance, he would have only 22 saves over 10 seasons, with an ERA of nearly 5 runs per nine innings.

RON DAVIS

While with the Yankees, Davis set a major league record for relief pitchers by whiffing eight consecutive Oakland batters on May 4, 1981.

SHERRY DAVIS

Davis became the first woman to work as a field announcer when she was hired by the Giants for Candlestick Park in 1993.

TOMMY DAVIS

Davis was the best hitter ever caught in baseball's revolving doors. Although a couple of other major leaguers have been traded more often, none can claim the two batting championships (1962 and 1963 for Los Angeles) and RBI title (1962) that the right-hand-hitting outfielder captured before changing uniforms twelve times. Following the Dodgers, he moved to the Mets, Astros, Cubs (twice), White Sox, Pilots, A's (twice), Orioles, Angels, and Royals. Some of the trades were in the interests of having Davis's bat on a pennant contender in September; others were motivated by the bad leg that slowed him up on the field.

WILLIE DAVIS

Davis's name is in the record book for having made three errors in the fifth inning of the second game of the 1966 World Series. Despite this, he was an outstanding center fielder, especially for the Dodgers from 1960 to 1973, and batted .279 over his eighteen major league seasons. Davis's speed was legendary; among other things, he once scored from second while opposition infielders were waiting to see if a ball along the third-base line would stay fair or roll foul.

Off the field, Davis exasperated a parade of front-office executives with his tangled financial affairs and endless loan requests. For their part, his managers distrusted his avowed conversion to Buddhism, especially after such assertions as "Nothing in baseball can make me unhappy. If we win, I am happy for myself. If we lose, I am happy because of the happiness it has brought the other guy."

ANDRE DAWSON

So anxious was Dawson to leave the debilitating artificial surface of Montreal's Olympic Stadium after eleven seasons with the Expos that he entered the collusion-tainted free agent market and signed a blank contract with the Cubs for the 1987 season. Chicago paid him a well-below-market $500,000; in return, the right-hand-hitting outfielder slugged 49 homers, drove in 137 runs, and became the only player ever to win an MVP trophy while playing for a last-place club. He is also the only player other than Willie Mays to compile both 400 homers and 300 stolen bases.

JOHN B. DAY

Day's career as a major league mogul began as a result of a chance meeting with Jim Mutrie, who, after watching Day pitch (badly) for a New Jersey club he had organized, offered to help the hurler-entrepreneur put together a winning team. Together they founded the New York Metropolitans; leased the original Polo Grounds, at 110th Street and Fifth Avenue, from James Gordon Bennett; fielded a team in the first professional game ever played in Manhattan (on September 29, 1880); and, for the next two years, ran one of the best and most profitable minor league teams in the country.

In 1882 Day flirted with the fledgling American Association but finally decided against sacrificing the certainty of exhibition games with National League teams for the uncertainty of membership in a rival circuit. Invited to join both warring organizations the following year, he avoided making a choice by entering the Metropolitans in the AA and forming an entirely new team for the NL. The new club, eventually known as the Giants, was made up in large part of players from the ousted Troy franchise. From the beginning, the older Mets were decidedly the lesser asset, relegated to the less desirable of the back-to-back fields at the Polo Grounds (or, worse, to Metropolitan Park, where the contents of the city dump underneath seeped upward). Dual ownership proved lucrative for Day but an irritant to the rest of the AA, especially when manager Mutrie began leaking the proceedings of association meetings to his boss. The irritation turned to pain when Day, deciding that all his stars should be consolidated on the team that could charge double the AA's 25-cent admission fee, transferred third baseman Dude Esterbrook and pitcher Tim Keefe from his pennant-winning Mets to the Giants after the 1884 season, then sold the Mets to a shady operator named Erastus Winman a year later.

Day had been a stalwart in the Union Association war of 1884, when he was the first to suggest blacklisting players who jumped their contracts; the Players League war four years later was another matter. Well liked by his players, he was blind to the possibility of even a strike by the Players Brotherhood, let alone the wholesale defection of virtually his entire roster to a new, employee-dominated circuit. He had, after all, just won two successive pennants, and completed construction on a new version of the Polo Grounds, at the foot of Coogan's Bluff in northern Manhattan. In late 1889, when star shortstop and Brotherhood organizer John Montgomery Ward offered him a job with the PL for the following season, he still didn't see the handwriting on the wall. The script became clear to him only after after the loss of court battles to prevent both Ward and catcher Buck Ewing from appearing for the PL. By midseason Day was in such desperate straits that other teams had to pump money into the franchise lest it fold altogether and leave the NL with no New York presence.

Outsmarted by his players in the events leading up to the war, Day was also outmaneuvered in its aftermath by Edward Talcott, the PL Giants' financial backer, who ended up with a larger chunk of stock than Day after a merger of the two teams. The new senior partner flexed his muscles early, insisting that the Giants play the 1891 season in Brotherhood Park, next door to Day's stadium, and that it become the third Polo Grounds. Then, when Talcott teamed with John T. Brush, former Indianapolis owner and one of the midseason angels, it spelled the end for both Mutrie, after the 1891 season, and, a year later, Day himself. In 1899 the former owner, bankrupt and in failing health, returned to manage the club for Andrew Freedman in a pathetic publicity stunt. An appointment as the NL's supervisor of umpires in 1900 was, in reality, an act of charity by former associates and didn't last all that long anyway. After that, Day disappeared until 1923, when he was discovered paralyzed in a Bowery room, unable to care for himself or his dying wife. The Giants held an exhibition game for his benefit, but he died a ward of the state a short time later.

DIZZY DEAN (Hall of Fame, 1953)

Dean so dominated the National League for five years that not even a career-abbreviating injury and a relatively meager 150 wins could prevent his election to Cooperstown. The Cardinal right-hander spun off 102 victories between 1933 and 1936, including 30 in 1934, which marked the last time a hurler in the senior circuit reached that plateau. He also paced the league four consecutive years (1932–35) in strikeouts. On the other hand, Dean was never unhittable, even in his best years: He got below 3 runs per nine innings only once while he was winning big and led the NL in hits yielded even as he was winning 28 games in 1935. On his way to what looked like another big season in 1937, Dean had his toe broken by an Earl Averill line drive in the All-Star game; Dean came back to the team too fast after the injury and, altering his motion to compensate for his discomfort, developed a sore arm. Prior to the 1938 season, the Cardinals traded him

to the Cubs for three players and $185,000. Although he pitched well in Chicago's drive to a pennant, he never again won in double figures. Following six years in the broadcasting booth, he was persuaded to come down to the mound one final time by the Browns in 1947, pitching four scoreless innings.

Dean's mangling of the English language as a broadcaster rivaled his earlier fame as a pitcher. When he didn't have runners "sludding" into bases, he was getting off such observations as: "Don't fail to miss tomorrow's game" (a broadcasting promo); "He's standing confidentially at the plate"; and "The players have returned to their respectable bases." As a player, he was able to laugh as much as his teammates when a headline announced the results of his examination for a possible concussion as, DEAN'S HEAD EXAMINED; X RAYS REVEAL NOTHING. Asked on one occasion to explain his success, he told a newsman, "The good Lord was good to me. He gave me a strong body, a good right arm, and a weak mind." In 1952, Dan Dailey stared as the pitcher in the Hollywood film *The Pride of St. Louis*.

Dean's brother Paul won 19 games for the Cardinals in both 1934 and 1935.

PAT DEASLEY

Catcher Deasley talked St. Louis Browns owner Chris Von der Ahe into signing him to a contract without a reserve clause for the 1884 season. When, assuming he was a free agent, the right-handed hitter solicited offers for the 1885 season, the American Association told him there would be none because his contract with the Browns had been a fraud. Having asserted the right to reserve the player even without a specific reserve clause, Von der Ahe then released him. Deasley eventually signed with the Giants.

EDWARD DEBARTOLO

The multimillionaire owner of shopping malls, banks, race tracks, hotels, and the National Hockey League's Pittsburgh Penguins, DeBartolo was stymied three times in the 1980s in attempts to buy an American League team because of his alleged underworld associations. After making a fruitless pass at the Mariners in early 1980, he worked out a $20 million deal with Bill Veeck to take over the White Sox later the same year. But over the next several months, AL owners raised one objection after another, pretending not to notice DeBartolo's formal concessions to each and every point. When the owners began leaking hints of the businessman's reputed gangster connections, Italian-American lobbying groups got into the act by accusing the league of ethnic prejudice. After the White Sox were awarded to Jerry Reinsdorf and Eddie Einhorn, DeBartolo turned his attention to the Indians, openly declaring that he intended moving the franchise to New Orleans. AL owners who had previously shown little opposition to such an idea immediately took up the cause of Cleveland fans, using it as a stick to discourage DeBartolo from pursuing the matter further.

DAVE DEBUSSCHERE

More than one athlete has tried to play two professional sports simultaneously, but DeBusschere was the only one who also attempted to manage in the bargain. A right-hander for the White Sox in 1962 and 1963, he spent the off-season playing for the National Basketball Association's Detroit Pistons. Still regarded as a top Chicago prospect, the six-foot, six-inch DeBusschere was farmed out to Indianapolis in 1964, where he posted the first of two successive 15-win seasons. But when the Pistons also made him a player-coach at age twenty-four, the right-hander began wilting under the pressure and eventually chose to concentrate exclusively on basketball. His baseball record in the majors was 3–4; as a hoop star he ended up in the Hall of Fame.

HARRY DECKER

A backup catcher for the Phillies in 1890, Decker spent some of his bench time designing the forerunner of the modern catching mitt. The first player to use what was called the Decker Safety Catching Mitt was New York receiver Buck Ewing.

ROB DEER

Deer made even Gorman Thomas and Dave Kingman look like contact hitters. In ten major league seasons (1984–93) with the Giants, Brew-

ers, and Tigers, the right-hand-hitting outfielder struck out 1,379 times in 3,831 at-bats—for a strikeout average of .360. (Runner-up Thomas whiffed 1,339 times in 4,677 appearances, an average of .286 percent.) In 1991 Deer also became the first player to hit 25 home runs without batting .200: He hit a mere .179.

ED DELAHANTY (Hall of Fame, 1945)

The only player to lead both leagues in hitting, Delahanty was the most accomplished of a record five brothers to reach the major leagues. A right-hand-hitting outfielder, he put together a lifetime .346 average and three .400 marks during his sixteen major league seasons, primarily with the Phillies during the 1890s. On July 13, 1896, Delahanty became the second player to hit 4 home runs in a game. After claiming a batting crown with Philadelphia in 1899, he won another in his first season with Washington, in 1902. Despite this, he jumped back to the Giants the following spring, only to be reassigned to the Senators when the two leagues established peace before the start of the 1903 season. Suspended in June for excessive drinking, Delahanty left the Senators in Detroit, scuffled with a conductor, was thrown off the train, and died—in what has never been firmly established as either an accident, a suicide, or a homicide—when he went over the International Bridge and into the Niagara River. The suicide speculation was abetted by a sizable insurance policy he had taken out with his daughter as beneficiary shortly before his death.

VIC DELMORE

Umpiring behind home plate for a Cubs-Cardinals game on June 30, 1959, Delmore precipitated the greatest field chaos since the Merkle boner of 1908. The trouble started when Stan Musial drew a walk in the fourth inning and Chicago catcher Sammy Taylor argued that the final pitch had ticked the St. Louis slugger's bat for a foul ball. Taylor became so embroiled in making his point that he neglected to retrieve the ball after it had glanced off him, and Delmore was so preoccupied with rebutting the receiver that he forgot about declaring the ball still in play. The first to realize what was going on were Musial, who went around first base and headed for second, and Cub third baseman Alvin Dark, who ran for the ball. Before Dark could get to it, however, a batboy picked up the ball and tossed it to the Wrigley Field field announcer, Pat Pieper. Seeing Dark charging toward him, Pieper instantly dropped the ball so that the infielder could retrieve it and fire down to second.

In the meantime, the still oblivious Delmore handed another ball to Taylor with an order to end his arguing. Taylor barely got his hand on it before pitcher Bob Anderson grabbed it away again and fired to second to get Musial. Although the Dark ball and the Anderson ball arrived practically simultaneously, Musial saw only the latter, which sailed wildly into center field; he promptly started for third, only to be tagged out by Chicago shortstop Ernie Banks, who caught the Dark throw. After a protracted argument, Musial was called out—erroneously because the ball was in fact dead as soon as the batboy touched it, irrelevantly because, after a protest, the Cardinals won the game anyway. As for four-year veteran Delmore, the fiasco weighed heavily in the decision at the end of the season not to rehire him.

BUCKY DENT

Dent's three-run home run off Boston's Mike Torrez in the seventh inning of the winner-take-all playoff game in 1978 provided the Yankees with a pennant-winning margin. Only his fifth homer of the year, the blow made Dent an instant darling of both female Yankee fans and Madison Avenue. When all the glory had settled, however, the shortstop had little to show for it except a fur coat commercial that irritated animal rights activists, a trade to Texas for another New York cover boy, Lee Mazzilli, and a stormy 89-game stint in 1989 and 1990 as one of George Steinbrenner's revolving-door managers.

JIM DERRINGTON

Derrington became the youngest pitcher to start a twentieth-century major league game when, at age sixteen years and ten months, he took the mound for the 1956 White Sox. Although he ended up the losing pitcher, he also singled to set the record for the youngest American League player to get a hit. After pitching a handful of games the following year, Derrington was de-

moted to the minors, never to return—washed up before his eighteenth birthday.

BILL DEVERY

A former New York City police chief, Devery had political connections that were reason enough for American League president Ban Johnson to ignore his reputation as a grafter and accept him as co-owner of the New York Highlanders (later the Yankees) in 1903. At first, Devery played silent partner to gambling kingpin Frank Farrell, preferring to concentrate on building a real-estate fortune with the payoff money he had accepted as head of the police department. After 1908, however, he was more active in club operations, siding with Hal Chase in his feud with manager Frank Chance to the point of engaging in a shoving match with the pilot after he traded the first baseman to the White Sox. In January 1915 Devery and Farrell, unable to build a winning team, sold out to Jacob Ruppert and Cap Huston for a profit of more than 250 percent on their original investment.

BING DEVINE

Devine is the Players Association's best argument against contentions that free agency has been responsible for undermining player loyalty to a team. Although other general managers (Branch Rickey, Frank Lane, Jack McKeon, etc.) have had greater reputations for being trigger-happy traders, the king of the hill was in fact Devine. Between 1969 and 1979, for instance, he completed or blueprinted no fewer than 193 deals (an average of 16 a year) for the Cardinals—and that includes only transactions at the major league level. In 1967, while running the Mets, he kept the door revolving so frantically between trades and call-ups that 27 pitchers and 27 position players ended up wearing the New York uniform at one time or another during the season. Fittingly, it was also Devine who brokered the clash between big league baseball and Curt Flood's challenge to the reserve clause. During an initial stint with the Cardinals in the late 1950s, he obtained Flood from the Reds in one of the franchise's best deals. In 1969, after returning to St. Louis from New York, he sought to send the outfielder to the Phillies in a headline-making swap involving, among others, Dick Allen and Tim McCarver. When Flood refused to report to Philadelphia, the stage was set for the years-long drama that would end in free agency and arbitration rights for players.

JIM DEVLIN

The winner of 65 games in the National League's first two seasons, Devlin was one of the infamous Louisville Four expelled from baseball for throwing games in 1877. With the Grays comfortably occupying first place by 5 1/2 games in mid-August, the right-hander, who pitched every inning on the schedule (the only time that has been done), lost 13 of his last 20 games. Meanwhile, Boston surged to the pennant by winning 20 of its last 21. A postseason investigation, prompted by anonymous tips from gamblers, uncovered a tangle of conspiracies, recriminations, and double crosses. Devlin admitted accepting, at left fielder George Hall's instigation, two $100 bribes to lose, first, an exhibition game in Indianapolis, and then a contest with the Cincinnati Reds, who were laboring under the threat of a suspension that would discount all their games from official standing. He further admitted lying to Hall about the amounts involved and to giving the outfielder only $25 of the gamblers' money.

The pitcher remained adamant to the end that he had thrown no *official* games and that he had never colluded with utility man Al Nichols. (Bill Craver, the fourth of the Louisville Four, came up only in Devlin's recollection of having shared his doubts with manager Jack Chapman about the shortstop's efforts in one game.) Although suspicions have lingered about Devlin's play in key losses to the Hartfords of Brooklyn and especially to Boston, no proof exists that these games were thrown. His explanations for the collapse—boils on his hand that made it impossible for him to grip his sinkerball properly, and poor hitting by his teammates—fell on deaf ears. The club suspended all four suspects indefinitely on October 30, 1877.

After the NL had made the suspension permanent at its annual meeting the following December, the ex-pitcher made repeated appeals for reinstatement to Philadelphia manager Harry Wright, Chicago stockholder Al Spalding, and NL president William Hulbert. All Devlin got for his trouble were a $50 handout from Hulbert (or so Spalding claimed), the proceeds from a benefit game (about $1,000) just before he died in 1883, and a league resolution promising not only never to commute the sentences of the convicted but also never even to hear further arguments on the case.

THOMAS DEVYR

Devyr was the central figure in baseball's first gambling scandal. Bribed by teammates Ed Duffy and William Wansley to throw an 1865 game against the underdog Brooklyn Eckfords, the shortstop temporarily escaped punishment when the New York Mutuals, run by the notorious Boss Tweed, managed to persuade the judiciary committee of the National Association of Amateur Baseball Players to drop the charges against him. On the other hand, Duffy and Wansley were banned, and when the case was reopened in 1869, so was Devyr. All three were reinstated by the full association the following year.

BILL DEWITT

DeWitt conducted a running fire sale of the Browns in the late 1940s and early 1950s. Given a chance later on to run clubs that didn't have to auction off players to pay the utility bill, he made one of the most meaningless, then one of the worst, trades in baseball history.

A Robert Hedges protégé, DeWitt started with the Browns as a teenage vendor, and then moved with Branch Rickey to the Cardinals, in 1917. In 1936 DeWitt joined a group assembled by Don Barnes to purchase the Browns from the estate of Phil Ball. Handling baseball operations while Barnes ran the financial side of the franchise, DeWitt presided over the dismal teams of the late 1930s; built the Browns' only pennant-winning team (1944), largely with the money provided by new partner Richard Muckerman; probably cost the club a second pennant, the next year, by insisting that one-armed outfielder Pete Gray stay in the lineup; and executed orders from a disgusted Muckerman to recoup losses after second-division finishes in 1946 and 1947.

What followed—between January 1947 and January 1949—were twenty deals, sixteen of which brought cash to the revenue-starved club. The carnage was interrupted only long enough for DeWitt and his brother Charley to buy Muckerman's almost 57 percent of the franchise behind claims that interests in Baltimore, Milwaukee, Los Angeles, and Dallas had offered more than the ostensible price tag of $1 million paid by the De-Witts. In actuality, the sale, mainly a reward for the deals DeWitt had engineered to recoup Muckerman's losses, was something of a junk bond corporate raid: a three-step process of borrowing heavily to make the deal, selling off the most valuable assets one at a time, then selling the shell of the structure.

To assume control of the club, the DeWitts put up only $75,000 of their own money, borrowed $300,000 from the American League (on condition that they keep the team in St. Louis), and let Muckerman hold notes on another $650,000. In an effort to retire some of the debt, DeWitt continued selling players; in ten of eleven major transactions between March 1949 and June 1951, he was on the receiving end of money. The only difference from his earlier binge was that now it was his own head that had to be kept above water. Together with the sale of the Browns' Toledo farm club to Detroit, the player sales netted more than $500,000. Finally, DeWitt sold the club to Bill Veeck in July 1951.

DeWitt resurfaced as president of the Tigers in October 1959. On the plus side of his eleven months in the job were swaps with Cleveland's Frank Lane for first baseman Norm Cash (for Steve Demeter) and outfielder Rocky Colavito (for Harvey Kuenn); even more memorable, if only for its ineffectiveness, was the swap of managers Joe Gordon and Jimmy Dykes he worked out in August 1960, also with Lane.

Moving on to the presidency of the Reds in November 1960, DeWitt inherited from Gabe Paul the team that would win the NL pennant in 1961, adding only an infield anchor in Don Blasingame three weeks into the season. In 1962 he negotiated the purchase of the club from the estate of Powel Crosley. His almost six years as Cincinnati owner are memorable mostly for guaranteeing that the club would be even better than it was by trading Frank Robinson to the Orioles in December 1965 for journeyman pitchers Milt

Pappas and Jack Baldschun. His rationale for the deal, one of the worst in baseball history, was that the slugger was "an old thirty." DeWitt sold the Reds to a group headed by Francis Dale and brothers William and James Williams in January 1968.

ROB DIBBLE

Fireballer Dibble gained prominence in 1990 when he teamed with southpaws Norm Charlton and Randy Myers in the Nasty Boys bullpen that helped Cincinnati to a world championship. As he moved into a more exclusive closer's role with the Reds over the next couple of years, however, the right-hander also showed that his hotheaded persona was not merely for intimidating batters, drawing numerous suspensions for firing balls at hitters, runners, and even in one instance at fans in the stands. When the suspensions proved ineffective, he was ordered into psychological counseling. At the beginning of the 1994 season, Dibble suffered a career-threatening rotator cuff injury.

BILL DICKEY (Hall of Fame, 1954)

One of the best catchers in American League history, Dickey's bat and defensive skills were major components of the Murderers Row New York lineups of the 1930s, while his teaching skills contributed to Yankee championship teams well into the 1960s. In his seventeen-year (1928–43, 1946) career, all of it with the Bronx club, the lefty swinger batted .313, topping .300 ten times, with a career high .362 in 1936 (the highest ever by a catcher who appeared behind the plate in at least 100 games). Between 1936 and 1939, Dickey reached the seats 20 times and drove in more than 100 runs each year. He also established a major league record (later tied by Johnny Bench) for catching at least 100 games in 13 consecutive seasons, and earned a reputation as the best handler of pitchers of his time.

Ordinarily mild-mannered, Dickey received an extraordinary suspension for an on-field fracas on July 6, 1932. After breaking Carl Reynolds's jaw following a home plate crash on a squeeze play, the receiver was slapped with a $1,000 fine and a suspension for the duration of the Washington outfielder's stay on the disabled list—an eventual thirty days.

Dickey succeeded Joe McCarthy as Yankee manager in May 1946, but quit in September when New York president Larry MacPhail hired Bucky Harris as a transparent manager-in-waiting. Dickey returned to the Yankees as a coach in 1949, his primary duty to work with Yogi Berra on his catching skills. As Berra later put it, ''Dickey learned me all his experiences.''

MARTIN DIHIGO (Hall of Fame, 1977)

Dihigo is the only player elected to halls of fame in three countries—his native Cuba, Mexico, and the United States. The most versatile and the most traveled of the Negro leaguers elected to Cooperstown, he was a star at every position on the diamond—so much so that, in the 1980s, he was voted by former teammates and opponents as the greatest second baseman of all time, while also receiving votes at third base and the outfield. A fifteen-year (1923–36, 1945) veteran of the North American black leagues, Dihigo also played in Mexico from 1937 to 1944 and from 1946 into the early 1950s. In addition, he played winter ball in his native Cuba for twenty-four years (1922–29, 1931–46) as well as in Puerto Rico and the Dominican Republic.

In North America, the right-handed Dihigo was primarily a position player; in Latin America, a pitcher. A consistent .300 hitter north of the border, he topped the .400 mark several times in Cuba. As a pitcher he won 115 games in Mexico (including the Mexican League's first no-hitter) and 119 in Cuba. He also managed several entries on both sides of the border.

A supporter of Cuban leaders Fidel Castro and Che Guevara, Dihigo was appointed minister of sport after the 1959 revolution and charged with converting baseball into an amateur sport in the country.

WALTER J. DILBECK

Spurned in an effort to purchase the Kansas City Athletics from Charlie Finley for $10 million and inspired by a Pentagon-sponsored trip to Vietnam, Dilbeck set out to take on the ''monarchical monopolists'' of organized baseball and bring the essence of American culture to the rest of the

world by founding the so-called Global League. Ignoring his lack of financing, he began a three-year shell game in 1966, changing the venue of putative franchises in the United States, Latin America, and Japan on whim; announcing he would not raid the major leagues, then changing his mind and approaching, among others, future Hall of Famers Don Drysdale and Roberto Clemente with fabulous offers; and claiming the support of Howard Hughes and his Hughes Sports Network. Dilbeck's main accomplishments were to entice former major league commissioner Happy Chandler to fill a similar post for the Global League; to sign future Cooperstown residents Johnny Mize and Enos Slaughter as a manager and coach, respectively; and to get, first Hall of Fame umpire Jocko Conlan, then veteran arbiter Bill McKinley, to be his supervisor of umpires.

The venture collapsed only three weeks after play began in May 1969. Paychecks bounced for teams representing both Japanese and North American cities (but playing in Caracas, Venezuela), and players were thrown out of hotels. Mize, Slaughter, and two full rosters were stranded in the Dominican Republic in the middle of a revolution. Dilbeck's later misadventures included serving time in a federal prison for income tax evasion.

POP DILLON

Of all ballpark inaugurals, none had the drama of the first game at Detroit's Bennett Park on April 25, 1901, when Dillon doubled home the winning run to cap a 10-run bottom of the ninth and give the Tigers a 14–13 comeback victory in their American League premiere. Otherwise, the left-hand-hitting first baseman had an undistinguished five-season career, batting .252 for four clubs.

JOE DIMAGGIO (Hall of Fame, 1955)

DiMaggio spent thirteen years (1936–42, 1946–51) with the Yankees, establishing himself as not only the greatest all-around player of his time but also as the enduring symbol of his era. As player, DiMaggio drew almost no criticism from any quarter. Fans, reporters, teammates, and opponents admired his wide stance and picture

Joe DiMaggio crosses home plate after tagging a home run in the fifth game of the 1949 World Series that clinched another championship for the Yankees. National Baseball Library, Cooperstown, N.Y.

perfect swing, his gracefulness afield, and his apparently unemotional approach to the game. As symbol, he entered literature as a personification of perfection for novelist Ernest Hemingway's fisherman in *The Old Man and the Sea;* popular culture as a metaphor for the good old days through Paul Simon and Art Garfunkle's lyric of ''Where have you gone, Joe DiMaggio?'' from their song ''Mrs. Robinson''; and show business as the husband of Marilyn Monroe. Through it all, he kept his eye on what he thought being Joe DiMaggio meant as intently as he ever did on a Bob Feller fastball.

With San Francisco of the Pacific Coast League in 1933, DiMaggio hit in 61 consecutive games, attracting a swarm of major league scouts until he damaged a knee getting out of a cab. Only the Yankees persevered after the injury, watching in gleeful expectation as he racked up a .398 average with 34 homers and 154 RBIs in his final minor league campaign, in 1935. Brought up to New York the following year, the right-hand-hitting outfielder went on to win two batting championships (1939 and 1940) and to pace the American League in home runs, RBIs, and slugging twice each. Along the way he picked up three MVP trophies (1939, 1941, and 1947), and concluded his career with a .325 average and 361 home runs while striking out a mere 369 times. Appearing

in 10 World Series, DiMaggio batted .271; in the 1947 Series against the Dodgers, he let his emotions show through for one of the few times on the diamond by kicking the dirt as he rounded second base after Brooklyn's Al Gionfriddo made a spectacular catch to rob him of extra bases. His most memorable diamond achievement was his 56-game hitting streak in 1941, a record made all the more impressive by the fact that after it was halted (only because of two sterling plays by Cleveland third baseman Ken Keltner on July 17), he launched another streak, which went on for 17 contests.

Hobbled by injuries late in his career, DiMaggio had a knack for returning from the disabled list with flair. On June 28, 1949, for example, after missing the first ten weeks of the campaign, he returned to the lineup and sparked a three-game sweep of the Red Sox with four home runs and nine RBIs. On the other hand, suffering from viral pneumonia, he took himself out of the pennant-winning game in the ninth inning against the Red Sox on the final day of the season after letting a Bobby Doerr drive go over his head for a triple.

His consistency and slugging aside, what made DiMaggio so admired among peers as well as the public was the seeming effortlessness of his classic swing and the equal ease with which he covered center field. Without flash or flourish, he used a knowledge of opposing batters and an ability to get a more than ordinary jump to arrive almost instinctively under fly balls. His most dramatic defensive play came when he tracked down a Hank Greenberg blast in 1939 behind the monuments in Yankee Stadium's center field, 460 feet from the plate; ironically, the play also marked one of his rare mistakes in the field, since he failed to realize that his spectacular catch was only the second out and neglected to make a throw back to the infield.

DiMaggio's relations with the Yankee brass varied with the occupants of the front office. He fought with Ed Barrow over money, holding out in 1938 until advised by prizefight manager Joe Gould to settle, then protesting again when Barrow used the limping excuse of World War II in an attempt to cut his salary after the feats of 1941. In 1947, he intervened with teammates on the verge of an insurrection against Larry MacPhail for fining players unwilling to attend promotional events and for insisting that the team travel on a decrepit C-54 transport plane. He largely ignored general manager George Weiss and dealt directly with co-owner Dan Topping, who made him the first $100,000 major leaguer, in 1949.

Under manager Joe McCarthy, DiMaggio flourished; he was just the kind of reticent, all-business performer McCarthy relished. The arrival of Casey Stengel in 1949 proved less happy. While parroting the veneration everyone heaped on the center fielder late in his career, Stengel pulled several embarrassing moves during the 1950 season, for example, dropping the aging star from his accustomed cleanup spot to fifth on one occasion and penciling him in at first base on another—neither time discussing the switch with the outfielder beforehand. Perhaps the most plangent moment involving the two was when the pilot sent Cliff Mapes out to replace DiMaggio in the field in the middle of an inning; in response, DiMaggio waved Mapes back to the dugout, then took himself out of the game after the end of the inning.

The Yankee Clipper's relationship with the fans was largely one-sided. As the successor to the gregarious Babe Ruth as the darling of the New York, he disappointed with his shyness, taking meals in his room and otherwise hiding from an adoring public. In his case, reticence was made synonymous with class, and viewed as an extension of his on-field behavior.

With his injuries finally catching up to him, DiMaggio refused a fourth six-figure contract and retired after the 1951 season because he could no longer live up to his own expectations. In retirement he became somewhat more mellow, more comfortable with his fame. His union with Monroe, the celebrity marriage of the half century, ended in divorce, but their continuing intimacy until her death and his devotion to her after it enhanced rather than tarnished his image. Not even performing in television commercials—for a coffee company and a New York bank—could taint the aloof dignity he had affected as a player. Also remaining was the old unwillingness to look ridiculous, leading him, after a time, to refuse to take part in Old-Timer games. And the self-assurance, too, never left: Told that old rival Ted Williams had said that he was the greatest player he had seen, DiMaggio accurately, if ungraciously, responded with an observation that Williams was the greatest *left-handed* hitter *he* had ever seen.

DiMaggio's brothers Dom and Vince also had substantial major league careers, the former as the leadoff batter and center fielder on the Red Sox in the 1940s and early 1950s and the latter as a free-swinging outfielder with several National League clubs in the late 1930s and 1940s.

BILL DINNEEN

Dinneen was the only major leaguer both to pitch and umpire a no-hitter. In fact, in his twenty-nine seasons (1909–37) as an American League arbiter, he called balls and strikes for six such masterpieces. His own came against the White Sox on September 27, 1905, while he was pitching for the Red Sox. The right-hander compiled a 170–176 record in twelve big league seasons (1898–1909) with four clubs. Dinneen was also the pitching star in Boston's 1903 world championship, winning 3 games against the Pirates in the first World Series.

BILL DOAK

In 1920 Doak, then a pitcher with the Cardinals, used the first glove with a preformed pocket and reinforced webbing.

LARRY DOBY

Aside from all the other obstacles he had to negotiate as the American League's first black player, in 1947, Doby also had to overcome a widespread impression that he was just one more of Cleveland owner Bill Veeck's box-office ploys. After an unspectacular start as a second baseman over the final weeks of his maiden season, the Negro leagues veteran began making his case in 1948 by moving to the outfield and batting .301 to help the Indians to a world championship. Over the next eight seasons the lefty slugger never hit fewer than 20 home runs, and twice paced the AL in the long-ball category. Unlike Jackie Robinson, who had broken the color barrier in the National League on Opening Day in 1947, Doby made no pledge about turning the other cheek, so that opposing teams got the message early that he would retaliate promptly against brushback pitches and deliberate spikings.

It was also Veeck who, as owner of the White Sox in 1978, named Doby as the AL's second black manager, after Frank Robinson. Doby lasted little more than a half season after replacing Bob Lemon.

BOBBY DOERR (Hall of Fame, 1986)

Except for his first two seasons, in 1937 and 1938, Doerr played his entire fourteen-year career with the Red Sox in the shadow of Ted Williams. Williams himself, however, always pointed to the second baseman as the indispensable Boston player of the 1940s. The right-handed hitter's most conspicuous offensive numbers were his six seasons of more than 100 runs batted in and his twelve straight years of between 23 and 37 doubles. Because of back problems, Doerr was one of few major league stars to play through most of World War II. He was also the only second baseman with as long a major league tenure never to have played even a single game at another position.

TOM DOLAN

For six of his seven major league seasons (between 1879 and 1888), Dolan was a light-hitting catcher; in the one season (1883 with the American Association St. Louis Browns) he played in the outfield he set a major league record of 62 assists.

DAVE DOMBROWSKI

After being named the first general manager of the expansion Marlins in September 1991, Dombrowski cleaned out his desk in a similar office in Montreal and then proceeded to clean out a good part of the Expos' franchise as well. The poaching of Montreal personnel for Florida became so serious that the franchise had to call on National League president Bill White to order an end to the defections.

While with the Expos, Dombrowski became noted mainly for his constant battles with manager Bob Rodgers over moves and nonmoves. Dombrowski resolved the conflict to his own satisfaction in 1991 by firing Rodgers and replacing him with Tom Runnells, but Montreal players were soon up in arms about Runnells's humorless boot camp approach to piloting. It took only a few weeks into the 1992 season for Dombrowski's successor, Dan Duquette, to get rid of Runnells in favor of Felipe Alou.

MIKE DONLIN

Whatever was right and wrong with the extravagant characters who played under John McGraw was right and wrong with Donlin. In a twelve-year career (between 1899 and 1914) interrupted more than once by forays into jail and show business, the left-hand-hitting outfielder vacillated between suggesting a Hall of Fame ability on the diamond and undermining the suggestion with off-field drunkenness and violence.

Donlin came into the majors originally with the Cardinals, for whom he hit .330 in half a season and where he met McGraw. In 1901 he jumped after his mentor to the American League's new franchise in Baltimore, where he hit .341. On the eve of the 1902 season, however, he decided he was smitten with actress Mamie Fields, and followed her and her boyfriend down a Baltimore street. When the boyfriend suggested he get lost, Donlin smacked him, then also clouted the actress for trying to intervene. Two days later, he was arrested in Washington, thrown out of the American League, and sentenced to several months in prison for assault. He was released in time to play a handful of games that year for the Reds, who had been persuaded by McGraw that he was worth the risk. He was, too, going on to lead the club in 1903 with a .351 average.

Over the first half of the 1904 season Donlin was even better, keeping neck-and-neck with Honus Wagner for the batting race by averaging .356. By then, however, he had so alienated Reds owner Garry Herrmann with his night escapades that the Cincinnati boss put him on waivers as a prelude to an arranged deal with the Browns. Instead, McGraw claimed him for the Giants. In 1905, Donlin batted another lusty .356, collected 216 hits, and led the National League with 124 runs scored. The only thing that remained the same over ensuing years was the .300 average.

In 1906 Donlin was arrested again, this time for brandishing a gun at a train porter while drunk.

Although Donlin spent only a night in jail, McGraw suspended him for the incident and his general alcoholic behavior for the beginning of the season. When he did get back in the lineup, the outfielder was moving along at a .314 clip when a broken leg ended his season. He spent his recuperation time falling in love with both vaudeville star Mabel Hite and show business. When McGraw wouldn't give in to his deliberately outrageous contract demands, he took the 1907 season off to tour the vaudeville circuit with his new wife, Hite. He came back to the Giants in 1908 (to hit another .334), but then once again staged a holdout lasting the next two seasons; as a consolation, he and Hite became more popular than ever on the stage.

In 1911 Donlin tried again with baseball, and though he started off at .333 over the first couple of weeks of the season, McGraw got tired of him and peddled him to Boston. With the Braves he hit .316; the following year it was .316 again, but this time with the Pirates. Pittsburgh owner Barney Dreyfuss was just about to follow the lead of Donlin's previous employers by unloading him when Hite died of cancer, sending the outfielder into a disabling depression and alcoholism. He was fished back by McGraw for a final shot in 1914 as a pinch hitter, but his skills were gone.

Donlin still had his show business career, however, and he ended up appearing in or producing a score of Hollywood silents over the next two decades; among those appearing in them was McGraw. The outfielder was known as Turkey Mike for his habitual strut; or, in the words of his favorite manager, "He was born on Memorial Day and he hasn't stopped parading since."

RED DOOIN

After the Black Sox scandal became public in 1920, Dooin revealed that he and several Phillies teammates had been offered bribes to throw late-season games to the Giants in 1908. The catcher embellished his role in the episode with a lurid tale of having been kidnapped by gamblers and escaping to rejoin the team in time to beat New York in the second-last game of the season, creating a tie with the Cubs and forcing a replay of the Merkle Boner game. Dooin also stands out for his initial reluctance to claim credit for his

major innovation, papier-mâché shin guards, which he wore under his uniform for two years for fear they would provoke cracks about his manhood; he admitted his cleverness only after Roger Bresnahan had begun wearing sturdier models openly. Also a pioneer in the effort to ban the spitball, Dooin blamed its unsanitary nature for Philadelphia pitcher Ad Brennan's tuberculosis in 1912. To emphasize his vigilance in defense of the public health, Dooin once doused a game ball with disinfectant.

TAD DORGAN

Cartoonist Dorgan picked up on Harry M. Stevens's introduction of frankfurters at the Polo Grounds in 1901 and commemorated the event in a newspaper sketch that included the first known use of the term "hot dog."

HERM DOSCHER

After an uneventful three-year career as a third baseman that ended with the Cleveland Forest Citys in 1882, Doscher agreed to do some scouting for the team during the off-season; at about the same time he signed to manage the Detroit Wolverines in 1883. When, on Cleveland's time, he began conscripting not only the players he had been sent to scout but also some former Cleveland teammates, his former employers had him blacklisted for double-dealing. The banishment lasted three years, until Doscher pulled some strings to have himself reinstated as an umpire. Doscher was also the older generation in the first father-son combination to play in the major leagues; his son Jack pitched for three National League teams from 1903 to 1908, compiling a record of 2–11.

ABNER DOUBLEDAY

Born in Ballston Spa, sixty-five miles northeast of Cooperstown, and reared in Auburn, eight-five miles northwest of there, Doubleday could not have been in the village with which his name has been linked in baseball lore when he was supposed to have devised the rules of the game because at the time he was a first-year student at West Point and ineligible for leave. Nor did the eventual Gettysburg hero make even passing mention of the sport in his extensive memoirs. His relationship to baseball, put forth in 1907 (solely on the basis of the recollections of nonagenarian Abner Graves) by a commission established by sporting goods manufacturer Al Spalding, was best described by Branch Rickey when, referring to the future major general's command to fire the first shot by the Union side at Fort Sumter in 1861, he said, "The only thing Doubleday started was the Civil War."

PATSY DOUGHERTY

Outfielder Dougherty was the first player to clout two home runs in a World Series game. He did it for the Red Sox in the second game of the very first Series, in 1903, against the Pirates. The lefty Dougherty played ten years (1902–11) with the Yankees and White Sox, as well as the Red Sox, compiling a .284 average.

LARRY DOUGHTY

Doughty was that rare baseball executive who was fired for publicly acknowledged incompetence. After serving as Pittsburgh general manager between 1989 and 1991, he was bounced by president Mark Sauer for what were referred to as "too many mistakes." Among Doughty's gaffes were neglecting the draft status of top organization prospect Wes Chamberlain, forcing his trade to the Phillies for benchwarmer Carmelo Martinez; prematurely identifying another prospect, outfielder Moises Alou, as a "player to be named later," necessitating his early departure for Montreal; spending more money than had been budgeted for journeyman right-hander Bob Walk while allowing first baseman Sid Bream, one of manager Jim Leyland's favorite players, to walk off as a free agent; and alienating Bobby Bonilla with several cracks before the slugger declared for free agency.

PHIL DOUGLAS

Douglas took one too many tongue-lashings from Giants manager John McGraw in 1922, so got even by getting himself banned from the major leagues. Smarting over one of the pilot's regular tirades, near the end of August, the right-hander fortified himself with alcohol, then wrote a letter to St. Louis outfielder Les Mann suggesting that he was ready "to go fishing" for the rest of the season if the Cardinals came up with

enough money to make it worth it. At the time, New York and St. Louis were running neck and neck in the race for the National League pennant. By the time Douglas sobered up, Mann had passed the letter along to Cardinal manager Branch Rickey, who in turn sent it to Commissioner Kenesaw Landis. As soon as he conceded his authorship, Douglas was outlawed from the game. The ban came less than a year after he had led the Giants over the Yankees with two World Series victories.

GEORGE DOVEY

Dovey and his brother John took over Boston's National League franchise in 1907; during their tenure, the club was known as the Doves. George died of a lung collapse in 1909, and a year later John sold the club to William Russell. The 1909 team was the worst in the seventy-six-year history of the Braves' franchise in Boston, compiling 108 losses.

AL DOWNING

Downing's seventeen-year (1961–77) career included leading the American League in stikeouts for the Yankees in 1963 and winning 20 games for the Dodgers in 1971. But that became yesterday's news on April 8, 1974, when he served up Hank Aaron's record-breaking 715th home run.

BRIAN DOYLE

Doyle lasted only four seasons (1978–81) in the major leagues and batted only .161, but in the 1978 World Series he might as well have been Willie Keeler. Replacing the injured Willie Randolph, the second baseman had the ultimate moment in the sun, hitting .438, scoring four runs, and driving in two more as the Yankees defeated the Dodgers in 6 games. The difference between Doyle's regular season and World Series batting averages—277 points—is the widest by any player with as many Series at-bats.

JOE DOYLE

Despite being the first American Leaguer (and the first twentieth-century pitcher in either league) to notch shutouts in his first two appearances (on August 25 and 30, 1906), Doyle was fated never to live up to that beginning. The right-hander finished his rookie season with a 2–2 record; never won more than 11 games in any of his five years with the Yankees and (briefly) the Reds; and, even though seven of his career 22 victories were shutouts, retired with a won-lost percentage of exactly .500. His nickname of Slow Joe referred to the pace of his deliberations on the mound.

LARRY DOYLE

Doyle's 1911 exclamation of "Goddamn! It's great to be young and a New York Giant!" served as am emblem of the arrogance and enthusiasm of John McGraw's early-century clubs. In that year's World Series, the second baseman tallied the winning run of the fifth game when he tagged up from third on a fly ball in the home half of the tenth inning; his slide, however, carried him around not only Athletics catcher Jack Lapp but home plate as well. Umpire Bill Klem kept his own counsel until all the Philadelphia players had left the field before calling a Giants victory; Philadelphia closed out the Series the next day, anyway. The left-handed batter closed his career in 1920 after spending all but one and a half seasons with New York. He won a batting crown in 1915 and finished with a lifetime average of .290.

MOE DRABOWSKY

Although he also had his moments on the mound in a seventeen-year career from 1956 to 1972, Drabowsky earned greater fame as a pioneering bullpen prankster. His specialty was the use of the bullpen phone to order food from establishments or to call long distance to find out the weather in Tokyo or Paris. His visits to Fenway park allowed him to tinker with the hand-operated scoreboard so that unwitting broadcasters were prone to telling their listeners how the Mets were doing against the Tigers or the Astros against the Indians. The right-hander's greatest moment of pitching glory came as an Oriole in the 1966 World Series, when he entered the first game in the third inning and fanned 11 Dodgers the rest of the way, including 6 in a row at one point.

Born in Poland, Drabowsky returned to the country of his birth in 1987 to assist in the creation of the first Polish Olympic baseball team. For many years, even after his retirement, Drabowsky stories were a staple of conversation among relief pitchers sitting in the bullpens of both leagues.

DAVE DRAVECKY

Dravecky put in eight seasons with the Padres and Giants in the 1980s, only to have his career end in a horrifying moment. Operated on for a cancerous growth on his pitching arm in 1988, the southpaw made a dramatic comeback the following season with a 1-hit, 7-inning stint against the Reds on August 10. But in his next start, against the Expos five days later, he was working on a three-hitter in the sixth inning when he delivered a pitch that fractured his humerus (the bone between the shoulder and the elbow) with a crack that echoed around the grandstand of Olympic Stadium. That November, following the discovery of another tumor, Dravecky retired with a 64–57 record. The arm was later amputated.

CHARLIE DRESSEN

After ending a modest eight-year career as a third baseman for the Red and Giants, Dressen hit his stride as one of the most knowledgeable managers and coaches in the game, with a special talent for stealing signs. He also initiated long yo-yo relationships with his frequent employer Larry MacPhail and his on-and-off crony Leo Durocher.

As manager of MacPhail's Reds in the mid-1930s, Dressen was particularly adept at instigating on-the-field brawls to cover the mediocrity of his players. When MacPhail was fired, he was out the door soon afterward for mouthing off to a host of Cincinnati sportswriters that his boss had gotten a raw deal. In the early 1940s, as a coach for the Dodgers under MacPhail, he abetted manager Durocher in the all-night drinking bouts and poker games that the team president and pilot considered essential to Brooklyn's success. On numerous occasions it was also Dressen's task to talk MacPhail out of his drunken firings of Durocher and to persuade Durocher to go back. But when Branch Rickey replaced MacPhail, Jolly Cholly (as sportswriters took to calling him) became the fall guy for Durocher, first being told that he was being fired for being a bad influence on the players, then being offered a new contract at a considerably lower wage.

Dressen swallowed his pride and stayed with

Rickey's Dodgers until MacPhail purchased the Yankees after World War II, then once again got caught between his perennial boss and the stormy manager. What ended up as an investigation into the gambling associates of both men was actually sparked by MacPhail's poaching of Dressen for a coaching job in the Bronx. After a tortuous investigation, Commissioner Happy Chandler found Dressen guilty of violating a contract with Rickey that stipulated that he could leave the Dodgers only for a managing post; he was suspended for thirty days before being allowed to take the coaching job with the Yankees. Appropriately enough, MacPhail sold out his interests in the Yankees not long afterward.

The next phase of Dressen's career began in 1951, when Walter O'Malley appointed him manager of the Boys of Summer Dodgers, at least in part because the new Brooklyn owner knew that the choice would irritate his predecessor, Rickey. Jackie Robinson and Pee Wee Reese, among others, called him the best manager they ever played for, and Dressen agreed. Known as a man incapable of forming a sentence without the word "I" in it, he added to baseball's compendium of famous quotations one day when, with Brooklyn on the short end of a 9–0 score early in a game, he told his charges, "Just hold them there, and I'll think of something." What he couldn't think of, however, was a way to stop the unprecedented Giants' drive against Brooklyn in 1951 that was climaxed by Bobby Thomson's ninth-inning home run in the final game of the playoffs. If other Dodgers were stunned by the defeat, Dressen was apoplectic before the fact that he had lost to a club managed by Durocher. After Dressen had led the team to a pennant the following year, he tried to use his success as leverage for obtaining more than a one-year contract. When his wife also wrote to O'Malley singing her husband's praises and demanding a longer pact, Jolly Cholly was replaced by Walter Alston.

Dressen went on to manage the Senators, Braves, and Tigers, and even rejoined the Dodgers in Los Angeles briefly as a coach under Alston.

CUTTER DREUERY

Although several pitchers had previously thrown a knuckleball using the upper joints of three fingers, career minor leaguer Dreuery was the first known practitioner of the fingertip pitch of more recent vintage. Already retired and working as a plumber, he taught the technique to Ed Rommel in 1920, after the rookie had been sent to the minors by the Athletics for lacking an out pitch other than the recently banned spitball; Rommel went on to a thirteen-year career as a mainstay of the Philadelphia pitching staff.

BARNEY DREYFUSS

Starting off as a bookkeeper for a distillery, Dreyfuss worked himself up to the longest-running executive act in the National League, maintaining personal control of the Pirates for more than three decades. He believed so ardently in his image as a benevolent, decorous man that he left himself open for an embarrassing confrontation with John McGraw that haunted him to his grave, and was so dedicated to his abstemious principles that he turned away future Hall of Famers because they indulged in the wrong habits. Given his longevity in NL ruling circles, the surprising thing about Dreyfuss was not that he used his standing to fill key league and team positions but that he didn't do it more often. In a sense, he was a Walter O'Malley without the cigars.

Dreyfuss bought his way into Pittsburgh from

Pittsburgh owner Barney Dreyfuss played a key role in the National League's acceptance of the American League as a partner in baseball's monopoly. Photo compliments of the Pittsburgh Pirates.

his position as owner of the NL Louisville Colonels, a franchise eliminated in the league's cutback from twelve to eight clubs after the 1899 season. As part of the deal with incumbent Pittsburgh owner William Kerr, Dreyfuss took over 50 percent of the team after engineering a mass movement of Louisville players to the Steel City. Because the Kentucky franchise was still formally in existence at the time of the transaction, the move of such future Hall of Famers as Honus Wagner, Fred Clarke, and Rube Waddell amounted to the most one-sided trade in baseball history; it became even more so a couple of weeks later when another future Cooperstown resident, pitcher Jack Chesbro, who had been sent to the Colonels to put a semblance of reason on the exchange, returned to the Pirates with the dissolution of Louisville. Mainly thanks to the players acquired in the dubious deal, Pittsburgh won pennants four times and finished second another four times in the first decade of the century. For his part, however, Kerr couldn't tolerate the suggestion that Dreyfuss had brought success to the organization, and went through a series of boardroom and court maneuvers aimed at getting rid of his new partner. This resulted in nothing more than an even more untenable position, from which Kerr was forced to sell his half of the club to Dreyfuss.

Like other NL owners, Dreyfuss had some bad moments when Ban Johnson began recruiting for the new American League in 1901. Although he didn't lose as many players (Chesbro was the key casualty) as other NL teams, he had to deal with the far more threatening possibility that Johnson would move his Detroit franchise to Pittsburgh to challenge the Pirates for fans. Not needing that development, he pressed successfully during the 1903 peace negotiations between the leagues for a commitment by Johnson to stay out of Pittsburgh. A few months later, however, the same Dreyfuss went farther than any other NL owner in legitimizing the new circuit when he endorsed public calls for his pennant-winning club to meet AL champion Boston in what was the first World Series. Although Pittsburgh lost the best-of-nine meetings, the owner professed himself so proud of the players that he added his personal profits to their pool so that they ended up with more money than the winning Red Sox. He was so committed to the World Series idea that the following year, when New York owner John T. Brush and manager McGraw refused to dignify the existence of Boston with another World Series, he set up an interleague series between the Pirates and their corresponding fourth-place finisher in the AL, the Indians.

The World Series wasn't the only issue that divided Dreyfuss and McGraw. In a 1905 incident that climaxed years of sniping by the New York manager, McGraw spotted the executive sitting behind the Pittsburgh dugout before a game against the Giants and challenged him to bet $10,000 on the outcome. When Dreyfuss ignored the taunt, he withdrew the challenge with some equally sarcastic crack about how the owner always welshed on his bets. Dreyfuss was so outraged by the attack on his character that he insisted that NL president Harry Pulliam suspend McGraw. Instead of letting the matter slide, Pulliam, a former Pittsburgh employee, did indeed announce a fifteen-day suspension and a fine of $150. In his turn at rage, McGraw accused Pulliam of being a toady for Dreyfuss and refused to go along with either the suspension or the fine. With the league's honor called into question, NL owners met, issuing a plague-on-all-your-houses verdict that included rapping Dreyfuss for misbehavior. The owner acknowledged years later that he would never get over the insinuation that he had indeed trafficked in some way with gamblers. In an even more righteous vein, he insisted he never regretted failing to sign Tris Speaker and Walter Johnson when he had a chance; Speaker's handicap was that he was a smoker, Johnson's that he had been brought to Dreyfuss's attention by a cigar salesman.

Managers came and went under Dreyfuss's ownership, but almost every one of them was portrayed as "resigning" rather than getting the ax, in line with the owner's proto-Dodger philosophy that all his employees constituted a "family;" by the same token, many of them were fished back a couple of years later as coaches or scouts. Through the teens and the twenties, Dreyfuss presided over several club uprisings against pilots, inevitably coming down on the side of the managers until he could dispense with them as easily as he had gotten rid of offending players; the most serious of the brouhahas involved outfielder Max Carey and coach Fred Clarke in the mid-1920s. The one crisis he could not weather, on the other hand, was the death of his son Samuel at age thirty-six in 1931. For months afterward, Dreyfuss went around in a daze, to the point that NL president John Heydler urged him to appoint somebody to take over the franchise on a daily basis. Suspicious of outsiders, he chose his son-in-law Bill Benswanger, who was an insurance company executive. Although Benswanger agreed to step in only temporarily, he found himself with a new profession when Dreyfuss contracted pneumonia after a glandular operation in January 1932 and, after a one-month battle, died. Benswanger ran the team until 1946, when he sold it to a consortium headed by banker Frank McKinney, realtor John Galbreath, and entertainer Bing Crosby.

DAN DRIESSEN

In the 1976 World Series against the Yankees, Driessen, a first baseman-third baseman for the Reds, became the first designated hitter for a National League team.

WALT DROPO

Dropo's 12 consecutive hits for the Tigers in 1952 both tied and bettered the major league mark set by Pinky Higgins with the 1938 Red Sox: Although both players officially went 12-for-12 in their streaks, Higgins also had two walks in the middle of this skein. Dropo, a right-hand-hitting first baseman, also stands as a model victim of the sophomore jinx. With the Red Sox in 1950, he was named American League Rookie of the Year for a .322 average, 34 homes runs, 101 runs scored, and a league-leading 144 runs batted in. A year later, however, he was down to .239 with merely 11 home runs, 37 runs scored, and 57 RBIs. In a fifteen-year wandering through several teams, Dropo reached the 20-mark in home runs in only one other season.

DON DRYSDALE (Hall of Fame, 1984)

Drysdale is the only National League starter to get into Cooperstown despite merely two 20-win seasons. A fixture in the Dodger rotation for most of his fourteen-year (1956–69) career, the six-foot, five-inch righthander was something of a Ewell Blackwell raised another notch—a whipping-motion intimidator who relished his modern National major League record of 154 hit batsmen and who kept hitters tentative enough to lead the NL in strikeouts three times and top the 200 level six times. It didn't hurt, either, that he was teamed with Sandy Koufax for the late 1950s and early 1960s in what was arguably the most daunting mound tandem in National League history. Drysdale's best year was 1962, when he paced the NL with 25 wins and 232 strikeouts—good enough for a Cy Young Award. Six years later, he hurled 58⅔ consecutive scoreless innings—a record later eclipsed by another Dodger right-hander, Orel Hershiser.

Prior to the 1966 season, Drysdale and Koufax directed their joint act against the Los Angeles front office after they suspected that general manager Buzzie Bavasi was playing them off against one another during contract negotiations. As soon as they made clear their intention of keeping one another fully informed of offers, the pitchers were called in for settlements. It turned out to be something of a bittersweet victory: Koufax had only one more season left in his arthritic left arm, and Drysdale's record after the negotiations was 45–48. When he retired after the 1969 season with a lifetime mark of 209–166 (and a 2.95 ERA), Drysdale broke the last link of Dodger players who had started out in Ebbets Field. Playing for Walter Alston for his entire career, he also holds the big league record for the longest tenure under one manager.

Drysdale was one of the best-hitting pitchers in baseball. In two different years he tied Don Newcombe's NL record of seven home runs, ending with 29 altogether. His postplaying days saw him announcing for several clubs, including the Angels, White Sox, and Dodgers. While broadcasting for California in 1976, he teamed up with manager Dick Williams in an ill-advised attempt to get owner Gene Autry to fire general manager Harry Dalton and give the job to him; the foray mainly led to Williams's ouster as pilot. Three years later, Drysdale got into a shoving match with Angels pitcher Jim Barr on a team flight, accusing the right-hander of showing the wrong attitude during Baltimore's relatively easy 1979

American League Championship Series win; manager Jim Fregosi finally had to intervene to tell Drysdale to stick to his play-by-play.

CLISE DUDLEY

As a right-handed pitcher, Dudley compiled an unimpressive 17–33 record in his five-year (1929–33) career with three National League teams; as a hitter he was just as bad, batting .185. But in his debut, on April 27, 1929, with the Dodgers, he became the first player to knock the first major league pitch thrown to him for a home run.

HUGH DUFFY (Hall of Fame, 1945)

One of Boston's Heavenly Twins (along with fellow outfielder Tommy McCarthy) in the 1890s, Duffy's hitting reached the ethereal in 1894, when he won an unofficial Triple Crown with 18 home runs, 145 RBIs, and an all-time-best .438 batting average while also leading the National League in doubles and slugging. While no asterisk mars his Cooperstown plaque, Duffy's record average came in a year when National League batsmen took full advantage of the new pitching distance of sixty feet, six inches, and collectively established another still unbroken record by hitting .309. After one additional spectacular season, a .352 average in 1895, pitchers began to readjust, and Duffy's (and the rest of the NL's) hitting dropped back closer to earth for the remainder of his seventeen-year career.

On August 7, 1901, while manager of the Brewers, Duffy punched out umpire Al Mannassau over a ninth-inning call that cost Milwaukee a loss. He escaped the lifetime banishment handed out by American League president Ban Johnson for similar offenses involving players and went on to a long career as a hitting instructor for the Red Sox; his most famous pupil was Ted Williams.

JOE DUGAN

When the Red Sox sold Dugan to the Yankees for $40,000 on July 23, 1922, New York filled its hole at third base with a .287 hitter and went on to win the pennant by a game over the Browns. The protests from St. Louis, whose National League fans had also been victimized by the Boston Braves' July trade of pitcher Hugh McQuillan to the Giants, compelled Commissioner Kenesaw Landis to prohibit interleague transactions after June 15 unless every other team in the league declined the players involved. This waiver rule remained in force for some sixty years.

BILL DUGGLEBY

A lifetime 92–104 pitcher at the turn of the century, Duggleby entered the record books when he became the only player ever to hit a grand-slam home run in his first major league at-bat, for the Phillies on April 21, 1898.

FRED DUNLAP

The premier player of the Union Association in 1884, Dunlap ignored the reserve clause in his contract with the National League Cleveland Blues and signed—for a then record $3,400—with the UA's St. Louis club. The second baseman hit a league-leading .412 and managed the Maroons to the pennant by 21 games.

JACK DUNN

A pitcher good enough to win 23 games for the Dodgers in 1899 before switching to the infield for the Phillies, Orioles, and Giants after the turn of the century, Dunn went on to become the most successful minor league club operator in the history of the game. After managing the International League Baltimore Orioles for three seasons, he purchased the franchise from Ned Hanlon in 1910 and began developing and selling players to the major leagues.

The Federal League war of 1914–15 gave Dunn a role in two of the most significant events in baseball history: the start of Babe Ruth's major league career, and baseball's exemption from antitrust legislation. The club president had struck a deal with the FL's Terrapins, whose largest share of stock was owned by Hanlon, that left his roster intact, but the local appetite for Baltimore's Federal team forced Dunn into temporary exile in Richmond, Virginia. Strapped for funds, he held a fire sale on his best players, including pitcher Ruth, who went to the Red Sox for a mere $2,500 after Connie Mack had passed on him for lack of funds. After the Feds faltered, Terrapin president

Carroll W. Rasin sought to work out a deal with Dunn, by either selling him the FL franchise or buying the IL franchise and hiring him as manager. Dunn settled for buying Rasin's ballpark and sat on the sidelines while the Terrapins engaged major league baseball in a court battle that did not end until 1922, when the U.S. Supreme Court declared baseball to be outside the reach of antitrust laws.

Dunn rebuilt the Orioles into the winners of seven consecutive IL pennants between 1919 and 1925, and resumed his lucrative relationship with Mack, shipping him such major figures on Philadelphia's 1929–31 pennant winners as pitchers Lefty Grove, George Earnshaw, and Rube Walberg, and infielders Joe Boley and Max Bishop. The sale of Grove alone brought more than $100,000, and endless complaints from the southpaw that he had to take a cut in pay to get to the majors. The Baltimore owner, however, lost his enthusiasm for the game when his son died in 1921, and never again set foot in the team's clubhouse.

RYNE DUREN

Yankee manager Casey Stengel said of Duren, "He takes a drink or ten, comes in with them Coke bottles, throws one on the screen, and scares the shit out of 'em.'' Whether it was the drinks, the poor eyesight, natural wildness, or cunning design, the hard-throwing right-hander's trademark warm-up toss on the screen behind home plate certainly kept American League batters edgy. Coming out of the bullpen for New York, Duren saved a league-leading 20 games in 1958 and followed up with 14 more in 1959, posted ERAs of 2.02 and 1.88, respectively, struck out a combined 183 batters in 152⅓ innings, and gave up a mere 89 hits. The rest of his ten-year career, with six teams in addition to the Yankees, was marked by plenty of strikeouts, even more drinks, and not much else. In retirement, Duren admitted to alcoholism and began a second career assisting others so afflicted.

LEO DUROCHER (Hall of Fame, 1994)

For more than four decades as a player, manager, and coach, Durocher was a boiling advertisement for the sly, the crass, the pugnacious,

Leo Durocher is sworn in during his trial for assaulting an Ebbets Field fan. Brooklyn Public Library—BROOKLYN COLLECTION.

and the hypocritical in major league baseball. From Babe Ruth to Judge Roy Hofheinz, he played everything from the stooge to the standup guy to the sneerer, earning a footnote to every major development in the sport along the way. Durocher won big and lost big, but most of all won and lost loudly. Even his nicknames were numerous—tabbed the All-American Out for his weak offensive play, C-note for an incessant need of cash to subsidize a high-stepping private life, and The Lip for his relentless hectoring of umpires and opposition players.

Durocher first came to the big leagues with the Yankees in 1925 for a single at-bat, not returning for good until three years later. A right-hand-hitting shortstop (he experimented briefly with switch-hitting), he won the open admiration of manager Miller Huggins for his defensive play and, even more, for a brashness that sometimes led him to call time in a crucial situation just so he could walk toward the batter's box to yell an insult at an opposing hitter that was guaranteed to upset him. Although he came to rely on Babe Ruth for protecting him during melees sparked by some of his insolent gestures, he had an uneasy relationship with the slugger—epitomized by Ruth's insistence on calling him the All-American Out. His relationship with club president Ed Barrow was even worse, and when he rejected a take-it-or-leave-it contract proposal after the 1929 season, he was summarily sent off to Cincinnati. It was while with the Reds between 1930 and the middle of the 1933 season that Durocher's regular visits to team owner Sidney Weil for $100 loans or advances on his salary gained him the nickname of C-note. It was also during this period that his habitually unpaid bills with restaurants and haberdashers started him on career-long visits to the commissioner's office, with Kenesaw Landis on at least one occasion offering to help him pay off a debt.

In the middle of the 1933 season, Durocher was traded to the Cardinals for pitcher Paul Derringer—a deal that put Durocher together with Branch Rickey for the first time. For the next four plus seasons he was the regular shortstop for the snarling and flamboyant Gas House Gang, even enjoying some unanticipated hitting success by driving in 70 runs two years in a row. Durocher attributed at least part of his improved play to the austerity budget that he was put on by Rickey: For his first couple of years in a Cardinal uniform, he received no more than $50 a week, with the rest of his salary being paid directly by club officials to creditors. His relations with manager Frankie Frisch, on the other hand, had little of the filial about them, and by the end of the 1937 season Frisch was issuing me-or-him ultimatums to Rickey. Durocher was packed off to the Dodgers amid reports that he was only the vanguard for Rickey himself moving to Brooklyn. Instead, the St. Louis executive stayed where he was, recommending instead that the top baseball job at Ebbets Field be given to Larry MacPhail.

If several of Durocher's baseball relationships were stormy, the one with MacPhail was a hurricane. Trouble arose almost immediately in 1938 after MacPhail signed Ruth as a coach and batting practice attraction, and the retired slugger decided he was being groomed as Burleigh Grimes's successor as Brooklyn manager. Throughout the season, the equally ambitious Durocher taunted both Grimes and Ruth about their baseball smarts, while MacPhail waited until he had his usual drinks in him before ranting that he would never turn the club over to an umpire-baiter such as his loudmouthed shortstop. Instead, it was indeed Durocher who was named to the helm of the Dodgers for 1939, with Grimes being paid off,

Ruth quitting in disgust, and MacPhail not remembering his previous declarations. As playing manager, Durocher brought enough electricity to the team to restore Ebbets Field fans as a twenty-sixth player. In one typical instance of the new enthusiasm, fans took up a collection to pay a $25 fine he had incurred for slugging Giants first baseman Zeke Bonura. The intention (called off only with the eleventh-hour intervention of National League president Ford Frick) was to change the money into pennies, then throw the coins onto the field and have league officials crawl around to retrieve them.

By Durocher's estimate, he was fired by MacPhail dozens of times during their five-year stay together in Brooklyn—usually after the executive had hit the bottle. In the event, however, it was MacPhail who quit the Dodgers first, resigning after the 1942 season to join the military. In his place came Rickey, who kept Durocher on the job despite some severe strains. In 1943, for instance, the pilot provoked a team revolt over an unwarranted suspension of pitcher Bobo Newsom and subsequent lies to the press about the incident. In 1945 Durocher maintained Rickey's support despite criminal charges of having teamed up with an Ebbets Field guard to beat up a heckling fan under the stands. More generally, there was the puritanical owner's distaste for Durocher's card playing, pool shooting, and womanizing. What emerged clearly only in 1947 was that Rickey had turned a blind eye to his manager's doings because of an overriding belief that he was the pilot best equipped for carrying out his plan for integrating baseball—a confidence more than borne out during spring training that year when Durocher stopped cold a protest by Dodger players against playing with Jackie Robinson.

But not even the frictions caused by racial integration were Durocher's biggest problem in 1947. Less than a week before the opening of the season, he was suspended for a year by Commissioner Happy Chandler for what was termed an "accumulation of unpleasant incidents . . . detrimental to baseball." The problems stemmed from three areas. The first was a series of charges and countercharges involving alleged offers from MacPhail (resurfaced as owner of the Yankees) for Durocher to leave the Dodgers to manage in the Bronx and the poaching of Brooklyn coaches by the former Ebbets Field executive. The second centered around Durocher's association with George Raft and professional gamblers close to the actor. The third involved Durocher's romance with actress Laraine Day, who was still legally married to someone else. The Raft and Day controversies became daily fodder for newspaper columnists, especially the priggish Westbrook Pegler. When Day and Durocher sought to end all the gossip about the adultery by flying off to Mexico to get her a quickie divorce and then returning to Texas to get married, Pegler did his part in whipping up Catholic organizations to withdraw from official promotions connected with the Dodgers. Although Chandler never publicly linked the romance with Day to the MacPhail and Raft stories, he made it clear that his suspension decision was based on elusive moral considerations more than on any solid evidence of specific wrongdoing.

Durocher did not react to the suspension well, especially after his one-year replacement, Burt Shotton, steered the Robinson Dodgers to a pennant; returning in 1948, Durocher took every opportunity to note that the flag winners had been "his" players. With the Robinson experiment successfully launched, Rickey began nudging him out the door in June. The pilot refused to take the hint, however, until he managed the NL All-Star team—a right given to him by Shotton's pennant win the previous year. When Rickey told him that Horace Stoneham was looking for a manager, Durocher made the most controversial leap between the Dodgers and Giants since Wilbert Robinson had gone in the opposite direction thirty years before. The pilot he was replacing in the Polo Grounds—Mel Ott—had been the target of the most famous of Durocherisms in 1946. As recorded by sportswriter Frank Graham, the exact quote was: "Do you know a nicer guy than Mel Ott? Or any of the Giants? Why, they're the nicest guys in the world. And where are they? In last place!" The observation was subsequently telescoped into the maxim "Nice guys finish last."

As with the Dodgers, with whom he won a pennant in 1941 after three seasons, Durocher needed four seasons with the Giants to field what

he boasted of as "his kind" of team. The last important piece of his 1951 winners was Willie Mays, whose initial failures at the plate elicited Durocher's most conspicuous success as a psychologist, when he reassured the outfielder that he would stay in the lineup "even if you go oh-for-the-rest-of-the-season." The relationship with Mays was also notable for representing one of the few instances in which Durocher showed a talent for piloting younger players. The 1951 campaign ended with Bobby Thomson's playoff home run against the Dodgers, climaxing the most dramatic comeback to a pennant in baseball history.

Durocher had more success with the Giants in 1954, when he captured his only World Series as a manager, in a four-game sweep of the heavily favored Indians. Otherwise, his eight years at the Polo Grounds were characterized by the most acrimonious chapter in the Dodgers-Giants rivalry, with field fights between the teams regularly following Robinson's taunts about Durocher's sex life with the much younger Day, or New York right-hander Sal Maglie's shaving of Brooklyn chins. He resigned his post near the end of the 1955 season amid increasing conflicts with owner Stoneham.

Durocher went to work for NBC as a sportscaster for a few years but had several opportunities to return to the dugout. In the late 1950s, negotiations over money stopped him from going to Cleveland. In 1960 he was called in by Stoneham to appraise the work of his successor Bill Rigney, with the understanding that his report on the club would merely be a prelude to returning to the helm; instead, after filing a tentative criticism of Rigney's relations with star Mays, he was left out in the cold in favor of Alvin Dark. Only a couple of months later, Durocher lost out to Rigney as the first pilot of the expansion Angels, largely because of Durocher's reputation for dealing most effectively with veteran teams. In 1964 he came the closest of all, when he reached a midseason agreement to take over the Cardinals, only to have incumbent manager Johnny Keane pull off a stunning pennant win. Instead, Durocher spent the first half of the 1960s as a Dodger coach under Walter Alston. That stint ended when, after more than one scene with Alston on the bench during the 1964 season about game strategy, he boasted to several reporters that he would have prevented the club's flop into sixth place.

Durocher got his next managerial chance with the Cubs in 1966, ending owner Phil Wrigley's College of Coaches experiment. At the press conference announcing his assumption of the job, Durocher contributed his second most famous Durocherism when he assured reporters that Chicago was "not an eighth-place team," as it had been in 1965; he was proved correct when the Cubs slipped to tenth in the first season under his command. But far more embarrassing for the manager of the 1951 club that had pulled off the Miracle at Coogan's Bluff was the 1969 campaign, when the Cubs held first place for 155 days during the season but still ended up finishing 8 games behind the Miracle Mets. Durocher himself came in for heavy criticism for the debacle—for getting rid of popular center fielder Adolfo Phillips without having an adequate backup; for playing his veterans into a bone-deep weariness; for keeping NL umpires in a state of agitation against the team through his incessant baiting; and even for leaving the team at two different junctures to attend to private business matters.

Worse followed. By 1971 Durocher had so alienated his players with personal attacks, dugout hectoring, and what many viewed as antiquated tactics ("Stick it in his ear!" cries to his pitchers and other beanball provocations from the Ebbets Field-Polo Grounds days) that relations between the sides were no better than an armed truce. Whenever the Players Association sought to apprise the Cubs of the latest developments on the labor-management front, Durocher first sought to prevent the meetings, then did his best to undercut the credibility of the union and Marvin Miller. While all this was going on, a gaggle of Chicago Republicans, with the help of the daily *Tribune,* sought to get back at a Democratic-appointed investigator-brother of Durocher's third wife by inventing links between the manager and a local gangster. This brought Commissioner Bowie Kuhn running—and then running away again when Mrs. Durocher made it clear that she would sue him if he played the *Tribune*'s games by suspending her husband. But although also supported through his travails by Cubs owner Wrigley, Durocher finally stepped down in July 1972.

Durocher's last dugout stint was just as dreary. With merely a month to go in the 1972 schedule and the Astros having a genuine shot at the Western Division title, owner Roy Hofheinz fired Harry Walker for somebody he described as "able to whip the horses down the final stretch." Durocher did the whipping as expected, but Houston players resentful of Walker's ouster barely managed a .500 record and finished 10½ games behind the Reds. The following year, player contempt for his methods was so obvious that, together with an intestinal ailment, it prompted him to resign before the season was over. As one of Durocher's last loyalists, Wrigley asked him back as pilot in 1975, but he held out for a general managership with Maury Wills coming along as the pilot, and was turned down.

Durocher's overall record for twenty-four years of managing was 2,019–1,709 (.542), with three pennants and one world championship. If nice guys finish last, he didn't always finish first, either.

PAT DUTTON

Dutton came closer than any other umpire to being an on-field fatality in a major league contest. Struck in the throat by a foul tip off the bat of Cincinnati's Jack Glasscock in a Union Association game against Wilmington on September 8, 1884, Dutton was revived only when a doctor rushed down from the stands to dislodge a broken jawbone blocking his windpipe.

JIMMY DYKES

Dykes established a mark for futility by managing for twenty-one years (between 1934 and 1961) without ever bringing a team home in first place; in stints with the White Sox, Athletics, Orioles, Reds, Tigers, and Indians, he never finished higher than third. For twenty-two years (1918–39) Dykes played all over the infield for the Athletics and White Sox, batting .280 overall with a personal best of .327 in 1929. In 1960 Dykes was half of the only manager-for-manager swap, moving from Detroit to Cleveland for Joe Gordon.

LEN DYKSTRA

The the delight of New York fans in the 1980s and Philadelphia fans in the 1990s, Dykstra carried on the Pete Rose tradition of the leadoff man as somebody who abhorred a clean uniform while attempting to reach base any way possible. To the chagrin of the baseball establishment, he also built his reputation as one of the National League's most versatile offensive players while almost matching Rose for off-field controversies and surpassing everyone for on-field exhibitions of how to get rid of chewing tobacco.

The brash, left-hand-hitting outfielder came up to the NL with the Mets in 1985, and in the middle of his first game told manager-first baseman Rose of the Reds that he intended playing for him someday. In 1986 Dykstra won over Shea Stadium for teaming with second-place hitter Wally Backman as ideal top-of-the-order hitters for the team that took few prisoners in its march to a world championship. He contributed conspicuously to the League Championship Series win over Houston by clouting a game-winning homer in the ninth inning of the third game and sparking a comeback rally with a triple in the ninth inning of the sixth game. He had two more home runs in the World Series against the Red Sox. Ultimately, however, home runs turned out to be a bone of contention between Dykstra and New York manager Davey Johnson, who pleaded futilely for the outfielder to cut down on his swing for two years and who then approved his trade to the Phillies in 1989.

Although the swap of Dykstra and reliever Roger McDowell in return for infielder-outfielder Juan Samuel turned out to be one of the best trades in Philadelphia history, it was so only after the Phillies had tried unsuccessfully to deal him back to New York and after a rib injury had persuaded the speedster that he could be more effective swinging half as hard. The result in 1990 was a league-leading 192 hits and a .325 batting average. He was even more productive in 1993, when he batted .305, leading the NL in hits (194), walks (129), and runs scored (143) while setting an all-time major league mark for plate appearances (773). In that year's World Series against Toronto, he belted 4 home runs and drove in 8 runs.

Dykstra'a impact on Philadelphia was also felt in 1991 and 1992, when his presence in the lineup produced twice as many team victories as was the case when he was sidelined. Unfortunately, he appeared in a mere 63 games in 1991 following an auto accident in which he and catcher Darren Daulton almost lost their lives while driving under the influence. In 1992 Dykstra broke his collarbone twice during the season on dives in the field, limiting him to 85 games. Aside from the drunken driving episode, Dykstra attracted league office attention for being involved in a high-stakes poker game and for allegedly abusing a Pennsylvania state senator in a restaurant. What has unnerved officials almost as much has been his addiction to chewing tobacco and his casual (and casually televised) disposal of globs of plug on the diamond, on his shoes, or on his uniform shirt. Protests over his chewing helped hasten the ban on smoking and chewing tobacco imposed on minor league players as of 1993.

E

JOE EARLEY

Earley was an Indians fan who wrote owner Bill Veeck in 1948 asking why the team never honored the average grandstand rooter. Veeck's response was Good Old Joe Earley Night, held on September 28. An estimated 60,000 fans flocked to Municipal Stadium to see Earley and his wife presented with a car and other gifts.

JOSEPH EASTMAN

Eastman was the head of the World War II Office of Defense Transportation who lent his name to baseball's Landis-Eastman Line. The line, accepted by Commissioner Kenesaw Landis, was drawn through the Ohio and Potomac rivers as the western and southernmost boundaries, respectively, for locating wartime spring training sites for every team except the Cardinals and Browns. The government order was aimed at saving fuel and decongesting railway lines. The biggest losers were the Dodgers, who had to shift their spring camp from Havana to frigid Bear Mountain in upstate New York, and the Cubs, who had to give up owner Phil Wrigley's private California island for freezing French Lick, Indiana.

CHARLIE EBBETS

Ebbets was both a sower and a reaper of Brooklyn baseball lore. An Horatio Alger who worked his way up from a scorecard vendor to the owner and president of the Dodgers, he also combined a miserliness and an extravagance that several times threatened to return him to his grandstand hawking. Not the least of his contradictory feats was having his death prove fatal to more people than to himself.

Taking over as president of the Brooklyn franchise following the death of Charles Byrne in 1898, Ebbets didn't need the national edginess caused by the Spanish-American War to discourage fans from coming to see the team; the club's miserable play had accomplished that without having to remember the *Maine*. In the interests of both attracting more fans and shoring up his own shaky financial footing, he entered into an 1899 agreement with Baltimore's Harry Von der Horst that would change the face of baseball for decades to come. In an era in which conflict of interest was a concept foreign to the sport, the pair devised an interdependent relationship between the clubs that brought to Brooklyn such star names as Ned Hanlon, Dan McGann, Hughie Jennings, Willie Keeler, and Joe Kelley. While retaining his title as president of the Orioles, Hanlon also became manager of Brooklyn, and delivered in a big way in 1899 by riding his fellow Baltimore transplants to a National League pennant. The victory came as a mixed blessing to Ebbets, who chafed under the idea that, as club president, he was making only a fraction of what Hanlon, his nominal underling, was taking in salary. The resentment continued to fester until 1902, when, with the help of $30,000 from Brooklyn furniture dealer Henry Medicus, Ebbets was able to buy out Von der Horst and his other partners and take complete control. Ebbets's first order of business was to call a board meeting at which he more than doubled his own salary as president and shaved Hanlon's to less than his own. Mainly because he didn't have other job offers, Hanlon rejected the unsubtle invitation to leave, remaining in Brooklyn for another three years of agitating the owner-president.

Between 1903 and 1914 Ebbets presided over the worst teams in Brooklyn franchise history, to some degree because of the defection of Keeler and other key players to the newly formed American League. Endangering the organization even more were attempts by New York Giants owner Andrew Freedman to get Brooklyn out of the league so he could have the metropolitan market to himself; among other maneuvers, Freedman used his City Hall connections to make sure that Brooklyn's Washington Park wasn't a site for one of the scores of new subway stations being planned for the outer boroughs. Ebbets's main strategy for staying afloat was thinking up what he termed "free entertainments" that would skirt the league's ban on paid admissions to Sunday games. In April 1904, for example, he announced no charge for a contest between Brooklyn and Boston; the only requirement was that fans had to buy scorecards—which just happened to be color-coded according to prices that corresponded to those for the seating in boxes, grandstands, and bleachers the rest of the week. The income from each Sunday games more than made up for the sparse attendance on other days.

Ebbets's most lasting contribution to the franchise came in a January 1912 announcement that he had been secretly buying up land in a Prospect Park area known as Pigtown and intended building a new ballpark there. But by the time Ebbets Field opened on April 5, 1913, Ebbets had had to weather more money problems by selling half interest in the franchise to contractors Edward and Stephen McKeever to finance completion of the project. Even Opening Day was less than glorious when he belatedly realized that the stadium had only one rotunda entrance and was ripe for tragedy with 24,000 people jamming the area at the same time; he had to spend more money cutting additional accesses into the walls.

Like other owners, Ebbets sought to stave off the threat posed by the Federal League in 1914 by offering his players multiyear contracts that would dissuade them from jumping; also like other owners, he sought to make up for that expense by slashing salaries across the board after the Feds went out of business and most of the pacts expired a year later. In Brooklyn's case, the result was a player revolt that died only when star outfielder Zack Wheat agreed to a new deal on the eve of the 1917 season. The cutback tactic seemed all the more sour because it came after manager Wilbert Robinson had led the club to its first pennant in sixteen years, in 1916. Robinson won another flag in 1920. In between the field successes, Ebbets's major accomplishment was finally forcing the repeal of blue laws in New York against playing on Sunday.

The 1920 pennant did nothing for Ebbets's growing reputation as New York City's chief penny-pincher and his worsening relations with the local press because of it. A typical lashing came from a *New York Herald* columnist covering the 1922 season opener who asserted that "President Ebbets was in the parade but dropped a dime just before the band signaled the start of the procession, and the parade passed on while he was searching for it." When the owner remonstrated against such a caricature, the columnist came back the following day to declare: "I was in error when I wrote that Squire Ebbets held up the Opening Day parade by searching for a dime that had dropped. The president of the Brooklyn club has informed me that the amount involved was fifteen cents." Caricature or not, it was an image that not only followed Ebbets into his grave but that also was affixed to the franchise as a whole for the next fifteen years.

Ebbets died at age sixty-five, on the eve of the 1925 season. After a pomp-filled funeral that included driving the hearse around Ebbets Field prior to a game and then to the former site of Washington Park, he was buried before hundreds of mourners who had to stand around in a cold rain while the gravediggers expanded the hole for the unexpectedly large coffin. One of the mourners was Edward McKeever, Ebbets's successor as Dodger president; because of an influenza that he picked up at the cemetery, however, McKeever also died, eleven days later, setting the stage for the era of Brooklyn's Daffiness Boys.

DENNIS ECKERSLEY

A starter for his first twelve seasons (1975–86) with the Indians, Red Sox, and Cubs, Eckersley enjoyed even greater success afterward as the ace of the Oakland bullpen. The transition from starter to reliever corresponded with even more dramatic changes in the right-hander's private life.

Starting out with Cleveland, Eckersley's solid status on the mound included a no-hitter against California on May 30, 1977. The following year, however, he was traded to the Red Sox, at least in part to ease the tensions caused when his wife left him for teammate Rick Manning. In Boston he threw himself into the bachelor's life; over his first five seasons he compiled an 87–50 record, but with his partying degenerating into alcoholism, he then slumped to 74–78 over the next seven years. After playing a key role in the Cubs' 1984 Eastern Division win, he was traded to the Athletics in 1987. Persuaded by pitching coach Dave Duncan to work out of the bullpen, a sobered Eckersley racked up at least 33 saves for six consecutive seasons—the only bullpen specialist ever to record such consistency. His trademark flowing locks still untrimmed, he earned saves in each of Oakland's four victories in the 1988 American League Championship Series. During the 1990 season Eckersley racked up 48 saves and an 0.61 ERA, allowing only 45 base runners in 73⅓ innings pitched. In 1992 he reached his career high of 51 saves to cop both the MVP Award and Cy Young honors.

WILLIAM ECKERT

Even for the shallow waters of a baseball commissioner, Eckert was out of his depth. A retired Air Force lieutenant general with no knowledge of the sport, he was recommended for the post initially in 1965 by General Curtis LeMay, the sword-rattling SAC commander who had been the first choice of major league owners. When Eckert's appointment was announced, a sportswriter (whose identity has changed depending on the telling) was heard to crack: "They went and got the Unknown Soldier."

In one sense, Eckert was not such a strange choice, since the owners had been looking for a military man to head the commissioner's office since 1951, when the election of Ford Frick had come after failed forays after other generals. Eckert also brought to the post a reputation as an able administrator who knew how to defer to the powers-that-be. In the event, however, he wasn't even much good at the paperwork, and teams had to detach some of their own front-office people to help him get through the day. Worse, Eckert stepped on the wrong toes in April 1968 when he supported the decision of Rusty Staub, Bob Aspromonte, Roberto Clemente, Maury Wills, and some other players not to play in spring training games after the assassination of Martin Luther King. The owners made sure he didn't repeat that mistake after the assassination of Robert Kennedy later in the year. Eckert was fired in December 1968 amid signs of a coming strike by players.

DAVE EGAN

Egan was a columnist for the Boston *Record* who so dedicated himself to making life miserable for Ted Williams that the Red Sox star rarely referred to him as anything but "that old drunken bastard." A pompous writer who liked to call himself The Colonel and affected the style of a rural philosopher, Egan blasted Williams for everything from not shaking hands enthusiastically enough with teammates after home runs to winning "cheap publicity" by reporting to the Marines for active duty during the Korean War. One of Egan's other hobby horses in the 1950s was tearing into the Red Sox for holding on to Williams rather than making room in left field for Faye Throneberry, a Boston farm prospect and brother of Marv. When pressed once on the fact that he kept up his screed despite never going to Fenway Park, Egan claimed that his absence from the ballpark enabled him to be more objective. It was also the *Record* columnist who, after Braves manager Casey Stengel was hit by a taxi in 1943, nominated the cabdriver as "the man who did the most for Boston" that year for sidelining the manager of the cellar-dwelling club.

DAVE EGGLER

The center fielder for Philadelphia in the first National League game on April 22, 1876, Eggler converted a fly ball into the first double play when he threw a runner out at the plate on the play.

HOWARD EHMKE

Ehmke was a washed-up 7-game winner when Athletics' manager Connie Mack chose him over aces Lefty Grove and George Earnshaw to start the opening game of the 1929 World Series against the Cubs. The move resulted in a 3–1 victory and 13 strikeouts, for a new World Series record. The choice of Ehmke was no whim on Mack's part, however; the pilot had counted on the right-hander's sidearm delivery foiling Chicago's predominantly right-hand-hitting lineup and had sent him to scout the eventual National League pennant winners toward the end of the season. Ehmke ended his fifteen-year career, after only one more season, with a 166–166 record.

DAVE EILAND

Eiland is the only pitcher who both yielded a home run to his first major league batter and clouted a four-bagger of his own when he got into the batter's box for the first time. With the Yankees in 1988, the right-hander was given a rude welcoming by Paul Molitor of the Brewers. As a member of the Padres in 1992, he tagged Bob Ojeda of the Dodgers for a homer in his first major league at-bat. That was also the only round-tripper Eiland ever hit in professional baseball.

JIM EISENREICH

Eisenreich's once-ballyhooed talents almost foundered altogether on the dangerous ignorance of the Minnesota front office. Hailed by Twins owner Calvin Griffith as a coming superstar in 1982, the left-hand-hitting rookie outfielder got no farther than a few weeks into the season when a facial tic and breathing difficulties forced him to the bench in a game against Milwaukee. The same symptoms plus involuntary vocalizations brought jeers from Fenway Park fans in another game, compelling Eisenreich to withdraw once again. For the next three years he spent most of his time on the disabled list for what was generally viewed as agoraphobia. When the Twins discovered in 1984 that he had been taking medication for Tourette's syndrome, they gave him an ultimatum to be treated for agoraphobia or return to the minors; instead, Eisenreich announced his retirement. After a couple of years of being treated for Tourette's, Eisenreich found

Minnesota unwilling to bring him back, but willing to sell his contract to Kansas City for the insulting sum of $1. With the Royals he worked his way back to a status as one of the best platoon players in the league. Signed as a free agent by the Phillies in 1993, he contributed a .318 average to the team's pennant win.

KID ELBERFIELD

A shortstop with six clubs between 1898 and 1914, Elberfield played a role in preventing the 1904 World Series from taking place and almost exploded the peace between the National and American leagues when his trade to the Yankees was engineered by AL president Ban Johnson to strengthen New York. Giants owner John T. Brush, who had reluctantly agreed to give up a prior claim he had on Elberfield's services, erupted when the shortstop turned up in New York instead of Detroit, where he could have done the Giants no box office harm. After failing in an effort to get an injunction against the move, Brush got his revenge on Johnson by refusing to allow the Giants to meet the Red Sox in the World Series in 1904.

Despite a temper that earned him the nickname of The Tabasco Kid, Elberfield was an innocent victim in his most noted field brawl. When Oriole pitcher Joe McGinnity protested a call by umpire Tom Connally a little too physically on August 21, 1901, Elberfield, then with Detroit, intervened to protect the arbiter and received a knockdown cuff from Baltimore's Mike Donlin for his pains. The fracas culminated in the shortstop's arrest; his attempted rescue by McGinnity and Baltimore shortstop Bill Keister; and the subsequent hauling of all three players, plus a fan named Allen, off to police court. Presiding judge Harry Goldman, who happened also to be a stockholder and officer of the Orioles, dismissed the cases against the players but fined Allen $20.

LEE ELIA

As manager of the Cubs in 1983, Elia had one of the more original views of the then boiling controversy over whether Wrigley Field should be equipped with lights. Infuriated that his humpty-dumpty club was the constant target of catcalls at home, he told reporters in August that Chicago fans were "garbage" and that "while 85 percent of the country is out working (during the day), the other 15 percent come here to boo my players." The owner of the Cubs, the circulation-reliant Chicago *Tribune,* decided that wasn't the best reason for switching to night baseball and showed Elia the door.

HOD ELLER

Eller, the anchor of the 1919 Cincinnati pitching staff, was approached by gamblers before that season's World Series to see if he would be interested in throwing his scheduled starts against Chicago. Although the right-hander reported the approach to manager Pat Moran, his disclosures that *both* teams had been at least initial prey for gamblers were lost in all the publicity attending the investigation of the Black Sox.

DOCK ELLIS

By his own account, Ellis was under the influence of LSD when he no-hit the Padres for the Pirates on June 12, 1970, and could remember nothing about the game when he saw a videotape some time later. For the right-hander, the no-hitter was the centerpiece of a stormy career that saw him sprayed with Mace by a stadium security guard on one occasion when he refused to show his identification and that pitted him relentlessly—and publicly—against managers perceived as too rigid and owners as cheap. While still with the Pirates in 1971, Ellis fumed over the admitted dread of his teammates whenever they had to face Cincinnati's Big Red Machine, finally taking matters into his own hands the next time he pitched against the Reds by hitting the first three batters to face him; walking the cleanup hitter on four high, inside fastballs; and then decking the fifth batter. At that point manager Danny Murtaugh removed him from the game but conceded at the end of the season that Ellis's demonstration had indeed worked to make the Cincinnati players edgier against the Pirates and to instill more confidence in the Pittsburgh clubhouse.

ELEANOR ENGLE

Engle's aspirations to play professional baseball were squelched in June 1952 when George

Trautman, the president of the National Association, the minor leagues' governing body, decreed that women could not be signed to baseball contracts. The stenographer and would-be shortstop had been signed by Dr. Jay Smith, president of the Harrisburg club of the Class B Interstate League; Engle's career ended after taking infield practice just once.

DEL ENNIS

Of all the hometeam sluggers booed relentlessly by Philadelphia fans over the years for encountering occasional slumps, none came in for more abuse than Ennis, a native of the city. For all that, the right-hand-hitting outfielder remained the thump in the Phillies' order between the mid-1940s and mid-1950s, winding up with 288 home runs. Seven times he hit at least 25 four-baggers and drove in 100 runs; in 1950 he provided a great part of the impetus to a Philadelphia pennant by leading the National League in RBIs. Before Mike Schmidt came along, Ennis held the franchise record for home runs, besting even Hall of Famer Chuck Klein.

CARL ERSKINE

Known to some of the Brooklyn faithful as Oisk, Erskine was the most popular pitcher on the Boys of Summer Dodgers. An overhand curveball specialist, the right-hander no-hit the Cubs in 1952, then had his best season in 1953, when he won 20. On the way to Ebbets Field one day in 1956, Erskine read an article quoting Giants scout Tom Sheehan as saying that Erskine was washed up because of recurring arm ailments. That afternoon the admittedly depressed Erskine pitched another no-hitter, against New York. As soon as the last out was recorded, Jackie Robinson, who had played the game with mysterious padding in his pants, pulled out the newspaper containing the scout's quotes and shoved it at Sheehan, declaring, "Stick this up your ass."

BILLY EVANS (Hall of Fame, 1973)

In 1906, Evans, at age twenty-two, became the youngest umpire in major league history; retiring after twenty-two years, he later served as general manager of both the Indians and Tigers to become the only Hall of Fame arbiter also to head a major league front office.

Evans was one of the few umpires ever suspended by American League president Ban Johnson. The penalty came for a confrontation with Tiger outfielder Davy Jones in June 1912, even though the planned fight between the two never materialized. On another occasion he did fight Ty Cobb, receiving a thorough thrashing while trying to insist that the brawl be conducted according to Marquis of Queensbury rules. In 1918 the official was the victim of one of the worst assaults ever to take place on a baseball field when he was struck on the head by a bottle thrown from the grandstand and knocked unconscious.

Evans turned in his blue uniform in 1927 to become general manager of the Indians. The most notable event of his nine-year tenure was an ongoing feud with manager Walter Johnson that bubbled over in May 1935 when the former pitching great unilaterally released veterans Willie Kamm and Glenn Myatt, asserting that they were the ringleaders of a plot to undermine him. Evans, doing a little undermining of his own, hired Kamm as a scout and publicly applauded a decision by the Giants to sign the thirty-eight-year-old Myatt. Evans quit a year later after refusing to take a pay cut from the strapped franchise. After serving as president of the Southern Association from 1942 to 1946, he closed out his baseball career as general manager of the Tigers from 1947 to 1951.

DARRELL EVANS

Evans may have hit the quietest 414 home runs in baseball history. It was in fact only toward the end of his twenty-one-year career as a left-hand-hitting third baseman and first baseman that he underscored his power skills by becoming the first player to hit at least 40 homers in a season in both leagues and then, in 1987, by becoming the first forty-year-old to wallop at least 30. Prior to these feats for the Tigers, Evans's chief claims to fame had been as one of the only trio of teammates (along with Hank Aaron and Davey Johnson) to hit 40 homers in the same season and as the only major leaguer on record to claim having witnessed a UFO landing.

JOHNNY EVERS (Hall of Fame, 1946)

Evers earned his nickname of The Crab much more than he did his place in Cooperstown. The chief beneficiary of the Franklin P. Adams poem that celebrated the supposed defensive superiority of the Cub infield at the dawn of the century, the left-hand-swinging second baseman left a long trail of irritated teammates, adversaries, front-office executives, and umpires in his wake over an eighteen-year playing career (between 1902 and 1929) and aborted attempts at managing. On the other hand, and despite the paeans of the Adams work, he never once led National League second baseman in double plays or fielding average, and paced his contemporaries in assists on only one occasion; he also made the most errors for a NL second baseman twice.

Like the Dick Bartells and Billy Martins of later eras, Evers was the sort of hustling infielder who was appreciated as a goad during winning seasons and detested as obsessive when the victories didn't come so readily. The former situation prevailed between 1906 and 1911, when Frank Chance's Cubs finished either first or second. Offensively, Evers was a slap hitter who reached the .300 mark twice, including a totally uncharacteristic .341 in 1912; his lifetime average was .270. He saved some of his best performances for the World Series, contributing significantly to two Chicago world championships in 1907 and 1908 by batting .350 each time and by topping that with a .438 mark for the Miracle Braves of 1914. It was also Evers who sent the league spinning in 1908 by noticing that the Giants' Fred Merkle had not touched second base on what appeared to be a winning base hit in a late September game at the Polo Grounds and called for the ball to record a force-out; his sharpness ultimately necessitated a makeup game in which the Cubs defeated the Giants for the pennant.

Personal relations were never Evers's forte, and, as in the case of Ty Cobb, his alienation from teammates ended up costing him physically. In 1905 his often cantankerous infield partner Joe Tinker stopped talking to him because of a banal mixup over an appointment to cab together to the ballpark; the second baseman and the shortstop didn't speak to each other for thirty-three years. Manager-first baseman Chance tinkered with the idea of moving Evers to the outfield just so he would not have to listen to his constant chattering and hectoring during games. Prior to the 1911 season, Evers suffered a nervous breakdown, causing him to miss most of the season. Matters didn't improve when he was named Chance's successor as manger in 1913. Tinker, still brooding about the taxi he had missed eight years earlier, declared that he was unable to play under his infield partner and had to be accommodated with a trade to Cincinnati. The players who stayed behind tangled with Evers in one row after another, some of them on the playing field. In one incident, Al Bridwell slugged him in the middle of an argument over how to play opposition hitters. In another, outfielder Tommy Leach ran all the way in from his position to the mound to take on the manager for what he had concluded had been ridicule of his defensive play.

Evers was fired as manager at the end of the 1913 season, but he didn't go alone. When he heard that Chicago president Charles Murphy was working on trading him to the Braves, Evers threatened to defect to the newly formed Federal League. That was enough for NL president John Tener to call Murphy on the carpet to lace into him for risking the loss of one of the league's stars to the Feds; together with previous administrative imbroglios, the incident was enough to force Murphy out as organization head. As for Evers, he ended up being traded to Boston anyway, and his field leadership proved invaluable to the club's 1914 world championship. Within a couple of years, however, Braves players were pressing for the removal of their frequently snarling teammate, and he was sent off to the Phillies, where he effectively ended his playing career in 1917.

In 1921 Bill Veeck, Sr., brought Evers back for a second managing tour with the Cubs, but it ended more quickly than even his initial stint after familiar run-ins with players; one of them, five-time 20-game-winner Hippo Vaughn, was so demoralized by his clashes with Evers that he quite baseball in the middle of the season. Evers returned to uniform for the White Sox in 1924, when he was one of owner Charlie Comiskey's stopgap managerial solutions for reassembling the franchise splattered by the 1919 World Series scandal. In his final appearance for the Braves, in 1929, he made an error on his only chance in the field and didn't come to bat.

Asked once what he thought of NL umpiring, Evers replied, "My favorite umpire is a dead one."

BUCK EWING (Hall of Fame, 1939)

Considered by many contemporaries to be the greatest player of the nineteenth century, Ewing became a focal point of the National League's battle against the Players League in 1890 when, despite his status as baseball's highest-paid player, he led the Giants in a mass defection to the New York entry in the new league. Federal judge William P. Wallace rebuffed Giants owner John B. Day's request for a federal court injunction to prevent Ewing from appearing for the identically named PL Giants, ruling that the reserve clause in the catcher's contract gave the club nothing more than the "prior and exclusive" right to make an offer for the following season. The singling out of Ewing probably saved his reputation among fellow players, since he had earlier expressed sympathy for Day's situation and had met with the owner secretly to discuss the possibility of declaring his intention to return to the NL after the inevitable demise of the PL; Ewing later claimed that he had been spying for the Brotherhood.

In his eighteen big league seasons the right-hand-batting receiver batted .303. He was a sufficiently swift base runner to be used regularly in the leadoff sport and slugger enough to top the NL in homers in 1883. It was, however, as a catcher, possibly the first to go into a full crouch behind the plate, that he outshone his contemporaries. Especially adept at throwing out runners, he was also something of a psychologist, using compliments and flattery to win over umpires both in his playing days and as a manager.

F

RED FABER (Hall of Fame, 1964)

Faber's twenty-year career (1914–33) was a little too synonymous with the White Sox. A favorite of owner Charlie Comiskey, the right-hander had four 20-win seasons by 1922, in the process also taking two American League ERA titles. For the next decade, however, he posted a record of 103–113, never once getting his ERA under 3.41 and prompting more than one manager to complain that he was in charge of "twenty-four players plus Faber." The pitcher's most visible moment of glory came in the 1917 World Series against the Giants, when he won 3 games to nail down a world championship. In the second game of the same Series, however, Faber pulled one of the biggest gaffes in postseason play when he sought to steal third base with teammate Buck Weaver already standing on the bag. Before ever taking the mound for Chicago, Faber was "loaned" to the Giants during an around-the-world barnstorming trip by the New Yorkers and the White Sox, and was belted around by his future teammates in the tour's concluding game in England before King George V.

ELROY FACE

Face was almost too successful for his own good with the 1959 Pirates. Because he compiled his 18–1 record as a reliever, critics have been quick to note that he blew numerous games for starters, yielding a batting average of .318 in the process. His reputation as a fireman hasn't been helped, either, by the record 21 homers he gave up over his career in extra innings. On the other hand, the right-hander was a major force in Pittsburgh's 1960 world championship by winning 10 and saving 24 during the regular season, then compiling another 3 saves in the World Series against the Yankees. In addition, Face led the National League in saves in both 1961 and 1962.

PAUL FAGAN

Heir to a California banking fortune and part owner of the San Francisco Seals, Fagan launched an all-out assault in 1946 to have the Pacific Coast League acknowledged as a third major league. His chief tactics were to dissuade other PCL owners from selling their players to the National and American leagues and to pay members of the Seals more than they would have made in the majors. The strategy worked only insofar as the San Francisco team ran roughshod over the PCL while the league as a whole broke all-time attendance records because of fan support for Fagan's scheme. Other owners, however, continued to make deals with major league clubs, insisting that they didn't have Fagan's funds for increasing player salaries or for getting into a lengthy war with the NL and AL. Conceding the failure of his plan, Fagan himself returned to selling players to the big leagues after the 1946 season. First baseman Ferris Fain, among others, protested when told he had been dealt to the Athletics, noting that his promotion to the AL was going to cost him money.

FRANK FARRELL

Farrell ran a network of two hundred gambling outlets at the beginning of the century and impressed American League president Ban Johnson by handing over $25,000 of his profits as a binder on a New York franchise in 1903. Taking over the AL spot vacated by Baltimore, Farrell and silent partner Bill Devery, a former New York City police chief, built Hilltop Park and put the Highlanders (later the Yankees) in business. Farrell's major contribution to the club was thawing relations between the Yankees and the rival Giants by inviting the National Leaguers to become temporary tenants in Hilltop Park after a fire destroyed the Polo Grounds in 1911; two years later, the Giants returned the favor, inviting the Yankees to leave the deteriorating rock pile in Washington Heights and share the luxury of a rebuilt Polo Grounds.

CHARLIE FAUST

Faust is the most legendary good luck omen in baseball history. Presenting himself to John McGraw before an early-season game in St. Louis in 1911, he told the New York manager that the Giants would win the pennant if he were allowed to pitch. Although he showed nothing during drills as a pitcher, batter, or fielder, McGraw kept him around for a few days, during which New York went on a winning run. With the players dubbing him Victory, he stuck around for most of the year, right into the World Series.

After the season, Faust took to the vaudeville circuit to explain how his presence had helped ensure a New York pennant. During both the 1912 and 1913 seasons he was called to New York during losing streaks, and on both occasions the club immediately started winning. By 1913, however, McGraw had begun entertaining doubts about what he had wrought, and he devoted more than one locker-room talk to assuring the players that they were capable of winning on their own. When the speeches fell on deaf ears, he made up his mind to tell Faust anyway that his services would not be required in 1914. But Faust disappeared before McGraw could get to him, not resurfacing until months later, in an Oregon mental institution. He died in 1915 in a Washington State asylum. As for the Giants in 1914, they finished 10 ½ games behind Boston.

The record books indicate that McGraw allowed Faust to take the mound in 2 games at the end of the 1911 season, when the pennant had already been clinched. He yielded a run in 2 innings in what was a burlesque performance by everybody, including the opposition Dodgers, except Faust himself.

CHUB FEENEY

Feeney served as president of the National League during the critical 1970–86 period, when relations between players and owners were radically redefined by the introduction of free agency and arbitration, when the drug crisis descended on Pittsburgh and St. Louis (among other teams), and when the Pirates and Padres underwent traumatic ownership changes as a last resort against moving. For all that, most obituaries following his death in January 1994 noted only that he had been opposed to introducing the designated hitter to the NL.

A nephew of Horace Stoneham, Feeney worked for the Giants with various titles from 1946 to his election as league president. In 1968 he was proposed by several NL owners as the next commissioner, but when a deadlock ensued between him and Michael Burke of the Yankees, Bowie Kuhn was elected as a compromise candidate. After stepping down as NL president for Bart Giamatti in 1986, Feeney was given a similar title with the deteriorating San Diego franchise. His refusal to sign free agents and various run-ins with players, the press, the fans, and even the club's own broadcasters prompted the regular appearance of SCRUB CHUB banners at Jack Murphy Stadium. Spotting one of them during Fan Appreciation Night in 1988, Feeney gave the bearers the finger, leading to his dismissal shortly thereafter.

DONALD FEHR

Fehr succeeded Ken Moffett in the top post of the Players Association in December 1985 just as the basic agreement between owners and players was about to expire. The union's former general counsel weathered that introductory storm, fending off the owners' demands (for limitations on salary arbitration and, for the first time, a salary cap) by leading a two-day walkout in the spring and finally agreeing to add a year to the length of service a player had to accumulate before being eligible for arbitration. Fehr also managed to steer through other controversies, including several collusion conspiracies against free agents (by emerging victorious from three arbitration hearings), Commissioner Peter Ueberroth's insistence on universal drug testing in 1985 (by countering with his own insistence that drug testing was an item to be negotiated), the expiration of the basic agreement in 1990 (by waiting out a spring training lockout by the owners to win an expansion of eligibility for salary arbitration), and the switch to a three-division format in each league in 1994 (by agreeing to the move only after winning concessions on the number of postseason games in whose revenue the players would share). As the pointman for the players in the 1994 strike, on the other hand, he became a figure of growing exasperation before the refusal of the owners to discuss anything but an imposed salary cap.

BOB FELLER (Hall of Fame, 1962)

Feller's brilliant pitching career for eighteen seasons between 1936 and 1956 was sandwiched between some brazen illegalities and a personal venality that would never qualify the right-hander as Mr. Charm.

On the mound, the Cleveland hurler left most of his contemporaries in the dust with six league-leading 20-win seasons and seven strikeout titles. His most dominating year was 1946, when he won 26, had an ERA of 2.18, completed 36 of 42 starts, threw 19 shutouts, and struck out a modern record 348 batters in 371 $\frac{1}{3}$ innings. Individual-game performances were equally striking. In his rookie year of 1936, while still in high school, he struck out 17 Athletics in one contest. That outing followed an exhibition game appearance in which, facing major league batters for the first time, he fanned eight Cardinals in three innings. On the last day of the 1938 season he struck out 18 Tigers to set the then record for the modern era. On April 16, 1940, he celebrated Opening Day by no-hitting Chicago (and thereby making the White Sox the answer to the trivia question of what club had all its players end a game with exactly the same batting average they had going into it). Before he was through, Feller would hurl two more no-hitters, to go along with twelve 1-

hitters. On the other hand, he would always admit to frustration at never winning a World Series contest; his 0–2 record in postseason play included a 1–0 loss to the Braves in the first game of the 1948 Series.

Feller's fastball and curve aroused awe in opposition hitters. They also prompted some widely circulated newsreels in the 1940s both demonstrating his velocity and providing graphic evidence that balls did indeed curve. Aside from his talent, the Indians pitcher was an obvious candidate for such promotional pieces because of the added popularity he had gained by enlisting in the Navy with the eruption of World War II and winning six citations during a four-year stint as a gun crew chief. For all that, his career with Cleveland was almost stillborn because of the transparent paperwork dodges general manager Cy Slapnicka resorted to in rushing the teenager to the major leagues in violation of baseball's age and schooling rules. When the owner of a minor league team in Des Moines filed a formal complaint against Slapnicka's tactics, arguing that he should have had first rights to Feller, Commissioner Kenesaw Landis, who had been very much aware of the Cleveland irregularities, reluctantly interceded to decide whether the pitcher should be declared a free agent. Landis's decision to leave him where he was stemmed from two considerations: Feller and his father both stated a preference for the Indians, and the two other main contenders for his services were the Yankees and Tigers—teams the commissioner regarded as already too talented for the good of competition in the American League. The Des Moines club owner received a sop indemnity of $7,500.

Although one of baseball's more articulate players for his era, Feller also had a long suit in crankiness against what he perceived as underappreciation of his talent or overappreciation of the skills of others. Nowhere was this clearer than in his constant criticisms of the significance of Jackie Robinson's breaking the color barrier in 1947. When he wasn't claiming that Robinson was at bottom ''a no-hit-good-glove'' player, he was trying to make the case that his own mound heroics were more important to the development of the game than racial integration. What Feller did not say, on the other hand, was that Robinson usually treated him as a batting practice pitcher during postseason games between major league and Negro league all-star squads and that he himself lost substantial money when these barnstorming tours became a thing of the past because of integration. Feller has never been averse, either, to picking up as much money as he could from autographs. In one particularly tawdry scene at Cooperstown in 1993, he arrived too late for a signing, but then stood on the sidewalk with an aide, hawking his signature to any passerby who had the money to pay for it.

HAPPY FELSCH

Felsch was one of the eight hapless White Sox players outlawed from baseball for involvement in the 1919 World Series game rigging. A right-hand-hitting outfielder, he played all six of his major league years with Chicago, batting .293. Like many of the ostracized players, he was enjoying a particularly good season in 1920 (career highs in batting, home runs, doubles, triples, and RBIs) when grand jury testimony by teammates Eddie Cicotte and Joe Jackson in late September led to his suspension for the remainder of the campaign.

Felsch was one of four Black Sox who confessed, in his case to accepting $5,000 but not to any direct action that led to the loss of the Series. In 1923 he sued White Sox owner Charlie Comiskey for conspiring to deprive him of a living, but failed to collect any damages; two years later, he collected $1,100 in an out-of-court settlement of a breach-of-contract suit.

TERRY FELTON

Felton is the most unsuccessful pitcher in baseball history. A right-hander for the Twins, he went 0–3 in 1980 and 0–13 in 1982—the 16 losses adding up to the most by any pitcher without a victory.

BOB FERGUSON

In a baseball career that lasted from 1864 until 1891, Ferguson served, at one time or another, as player, league president, manager, front office official, and umpire. As a player he became the first recorded switch hitter, when, playing for the Atlantics of Brooklyn on June 14, 1870, he moved across the plate to bat left-handed for the first time in his career to avoid the wide range and sure hands of Cincinnati Red Stocking shortstop George Wright; Ferguson's subsequent single drove in the tying run, and he himself later scored the winning run in the game, which broke the Red Stockings' legendary two-year winning streak. He also earned the sobriquet of Death to Flying Things for his sure-handedness as an infielder.

The manager-third baseman of the Atlantics in the National Association between 1872 and 1874, he was euchred into accepting the NA presidency by New York Mutuals owner Bill Cammeyer, and fulfilled Cammeyer's expectations by neglecting his club to run the league and thus allowing the Mutuals to assume the ascendancy among New York clubs.

One of the thornier baseball characters of the nineteenth century, Ferguson the player hit .271 in a seven-year National League and American Association career; Ferguson the manager, on the other hand, alienated his charges in a succession of managerial assignments in the late 1870s and 1880s. Most notable was his experience in Philadelphia in 1883, where his authoritarian ways provoked such hostility among Phillies players that he was removed from field command after only 17 games; he did, however, continue with the club in the unique position of second baseman-business manager. An even greater clash was averted the following year when several members of the Giants, who had endured Ferguson's temperamental fits while with Troy, refused to play for him, causing New York owner John Day to cancel the manager's contract even before Opening Day. In later years Ferguson became an umpire; in that role he once settled a dispute by breaking a player's arm with a bat.

RICK FERRELL (Hall of Fame, 1984)

Ferrell is usually the catcher on the all-time team of Hall of Famers who don't belong in Cooperstown. A Veterans Committee pick, he played through much of his eighteen-year career (between 1927 and 1947) deep in the shadows of Bill Dickey and Mickey Cochrane, rarely belonging to a first-division team. Usually cited for his defensive brilliance, he was actually only a notch above such contemporary American League journeymen as Luke Sewell, but made fewer enemies. Ferrell reached his offensive peak with the Red Sox in the mid-1930s after being obtained from the Browns in Tom Yawkey's first deal for Boston; in 1935 Ferrell batted .301, following that up with a .312 mark the following season. Mainly because of his brother Wes Ferrell's tantrums on the mound and in the clubhouse, Rick was traded with his sibling to Washington in 1937 in a swap that became known as the Harmony Deal for its anticipated impact on Boston.

WES FERRELL

Almost as many questions might be raised as to why Ferrell isn't in the Hall of Fame as to why his brother Rick is. After a couple of cups of coffee with the Indians in 1927 and 1928, the right-hander returned for good in 1929 and promptly became the only twentieth-century pitcher to post 20 wins in his first four seasons. Topping the 20-victory mark again in 1935 and 1936 for the Red Sox, he became the only hurler without a Cooperstown plaque to post six 20-win seasons in the twentieth century. (In fact, twenty-eight pitchers enshrined in Cooperstown have failed to record as many 20-win seasons.)

Ferrell was equally dangerous with a bat in his hands. He holds both the season (9) and career (37) records for home runs by a pitcher and had five seasons of at least 24 RBIs in his limited plate appearances. In 1933, when Cleveland outfielder Joe Vosmik was sidelined with injuries, Ferrell replaced him for 13 games, hitting .300 over the span. Ferrell's major problem with Hall of Fame voters has been his quick decline after his sixth 20-win season. For the last few years of his fifteen-year career he pitched for mostly humpty-dumpty teams and was batted around with regularity.

MARK FIDRYCH

Fidrych was as much of a shooting star as baseball has had in the past fifty years. A nonroster player with the Tigers in 1976, the right-hander didn't get into a game until five weeks into the season, but from there went on to fascinate the country with both his mound skills (19 wins, a 2.24 ERA, Rookie of the Year award) and idiosyncrasies. He talked to the ball, got down on his hands and knees to landscape the pitching hill, refused to pitch with a ball that had been knocked for a base hit, and ran over to shake the hands of his infielders after difficult plays. After some initial resentment that he might have been showing them up, even opposition hitters recognized that there was nothing false or calculated in the enthusiasm of the hurler who soon enough became known as The Bird. Fidrych also contributed critically to the Detroit coffers: In his 29 starts at home and on the road, he drew almost 900,000 fans, with his home starts accounting for 60 percent of the franchise attendance total. The phenomenon ended in the spring of 1977, when the pitcher tore up his right knee. After some signs in May that he had recovered from the injury, he developed tendinitis, shelving him for the rest of the season. He won only 4 more games for the Tigers, and called it quits in 1980.

CECIL FIELDER

The overweight Fielder looked so little like a major league player that the Blue Jays sold him to the Hanshin franchise of the Japanese Central League in 1989, after he hit only 31 home runs in four years of bouncing up and down to the minors and around the infield and outfield in search of a position. The right-handed slugger returned as a full-time first baseman, with the Tigers, in 1990 and became the first American Leaguer to top the 50-homer mark (51) since Roger Maris. Adding to the embarrassment in the Toronto front office, Fielder led the AL in four-baggers a second consecutive year in 1991, and paced AL hitters in RBIs for three consecutive years (1990–92), something no other player had accomplished since Babe Ruth's last season in Boston and his first two in New York.

ROLLIE FINGERS (Hall of Fame, 1992)

Although Hoyt Wilhelm beat him to the Hall of Fame, Fingers confirmed the new prestige of the relief pitcher in another, equally significant way: No sooner had he entered Cooperstown than his records for most saves (341) and most saves-plus-wins (430) were eclipsed immediately by first Jeff Reardon and then by Lee Smith. The right-handed Fingers was also the last of base-

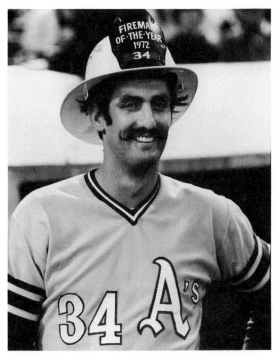

Rollie Fingers's handlebar moustache was the most flamboyant example of the facial hair encouraged by Oakland owner Charlie Finley. Ron Riesterer/Oakland Tribune.

ball's dominant relievers who went to the bullpen after failing in a big way as a starter.

Fingers made the first mark of his seventeen-year (1968–82, 1984–85) career as a member of the Athletics. When self-admitted nerves allowed him to finish only 4 of 35 starts over his first few years, he was assigned to the bullpen for good, teaming with southpaw Darold Knowles to give Oakland fearsome late-inning relief during its glory years in the early 1970s. Mainly because Fingers had to share the club's save opportunities, however, he never recorded more than 24 rescues for the A's. In 1976 owner Charlie Finley sold him and outfielder Joe Rudi to the Red Sox for $1 million apiece, but the deal was nullified by Commissioner Bowie Kuhn, who didn't like the image of Finley's fire sale of Oakland stars as a tactic against free agency. Signing with the Padres in 1977 as a free agent, Fingers racked up 72 saves in his first two years, but then began experiencing the arm miseries that would crop up at

increasingly frequent intervals for the rest of his career.

In 1980 Fingers became a prime exhibit of the trading reputations of Jack McKeon and Whitey Herzog when first he was swapped to the Cardinals in an eleven-player exchange and then, five days later, redirected to the Brewers in another, seven-man transaction. During the strike-shortened 1981 season, he picked up an American League-leading 28 saves and 6 victories to go with a 1.04 ERA to earn both MVP and Cy Young honors. In 1982 Fingers collected another 29 saves, but was forced to the sidelines with tendinitis at the end of the year; his absence in Milwaukee's subsequent World Series duel with the Cardinals was regarded as the difference in the seven-game St. Louis win. After missing all of the 1983 season with his arm problem, he came back in 1984 to notch another 23 saves for the Brewers by early July, but then was effectively sidelined for good by a herniated disc.

While with Oakland, Fingers was among those who responded most eagerly to Finley's offer of money for team members who grew mustaches; for the rest of his career, his wispy handlebar mustache was a trademark.

CHARLIE FINLEY

Blowhard, innovator, tyrant, and miser, Finley's two-decade (1961–80) run as owner of the Kansas City and Oakland versions of the Athletics marked one of the most erratic administrations in baseball history. By the time he stepped aside, it was difficult to say whether he was hated more by players, other owners, the baseball commissioner, the fans of two cities, or U.S. congressmen. What was beyond doubt was that the Indiana insurance executive had filled his own pockets while his enemies were taking turns to get at him. Syndicated columnist Jim Murray took Finley's measure when he called him ''a self-made man who worshiped his creator.''

In the 1950s and early 1960s there was hardly a franchise in either league with money shorts that didn't attract a Finley purchase offer. He finally realized his ambition when he forked over $2 million to the widow of Arnold Johnson after the 1960 season to take over Kansas City, which up to that point had been a laughingstock fran-

chise used by the Yankees as little more than a
farm team. In his first public act as owner, Finley
staged the burning of an old bus to point up his
claim that the era of the Yankee Shuttle was over;
he then promptly turned around and traded the
Athletics' best pitcher, Bud Daley, to the Bronx.
For Finley, contradictions of this kind were irrelevant; having little appreciable major league talent
on the field to boast of, he kept up dog-and-pony
shows to attract fans. Among other things, he
dressed his players in flamboyant kelly green and
gold uniforms, introduced livestock to Municipal
Stadium in promotions aimed at farmers, had his
team enter the ballpark on a mule train (and set
aside one of the animals as a mascot named Charlie O), sodded an area behind the outfield fences
for grazing sheep, installed a mechanical rabbit
behind home plate that popped up from the
ground to give balls to umpires, and insisted that
his players autograph all balls so that fans catching fouls and home runs would have "personal-
ized" souvenirs.

But when Finley wasn't making Kansas City
laugh, he was making it cringe. No sooner had
he taken over than he ordered his staff to end the
popular practice of personally delivering season
tickets. He so alienated fans with such moves that
the atmosphere was soon ripe for a campaign to
buy tickets to "save the A's"—precisely the cli-
mate that the owner had sought for extorting better lease terms for Municipal Stadium and then
for trying to persuade the American League that
he needed a bigger market than Kansas City for
survival. Throughout the early 1960s he was rumored as being on the verge of moving the team
to Dallas, Atlanta, or Oakland. More concrete was
a 1964 announcement that he had signed a condi-
tional two-year lease on Louisville's Fairgrounds
Stadium and formally petitioned the AL for a
move to Kentucky. Aggravated by the relentless
campaigns to go elsewhere and anywhere, the
other league owners rejected the bid by a 9–1
margin and ordered Finley to conclude a new pact
with Municipal Stadium or face expulsion from
the circuit. The Athletics owner responded by first
signing a new four-year lease for the stadium with
the city and then suing to reclaim rights to an
older contract that contained a critical escape
clause. Having muddied the waters sufficiently

*Charlie Finley and his mascot, Charlie O, socialized with all
of baseball's major personalities, including Casey Stengel.*
Ron Riesterer/Oakland Tribune.

with that tactic, he then announced that he was
putting the franchise up for sale. With Denver
and San Diego descending with offers and the
stadium-lease suit threatening to expose a lot of
dirty laundry, AL president Joe Cronin was em-
powered by the other owners to promise Finley
that a way would be found for moving the franchise out of Kansas City within three years; with
that, the owner withdrew his lawsuit and took the
club off the market.

Finley's last years in Kansas City were marked
by a revolt by players over what was seen as a
gratuitous fine against pitcher Lew Krausse. Before the tensions subsided, manager Alvin Dark
was fired for not disassociating himself from the
players' uprising, slugger Ken Harrelson was
given his outright release for being one of the
leaders of the rebellion, and Finley himself was
hauled before the National Labor Relations Board
to answer charges of having harassed his players.
Kansas City fans were still enjoying the almost-
daily revelations of some new Finley caper when
the AL dropped the other shoe, confirming that
the club would be shifted to Oakland for the 1968
season. Eleventh-hour negotiations to commit an
expansion club to Kansas City in 1969 did not
spare Finley an avalanche of attacks from Mis-

souri politicians at all levels; among the most vocal was Senator Stuart Symington, who called him "one of the most disreputable characters ever to enter the American sports scene."

The major difference between Finley in Kansas City and Finley in Oakland was that he had good teams in California. Otherwise it was the same pregame promotions of milking cows and chasing greased pigs, familiar tensions with star players over contracts, and meticulously timed complaints about how the franchise couldn't survive where it was located. The early 1970s were also Finley at his most creative where the playing and business of the game were concerned, although other owners were not always quick to accept his ideas. What they accepted was his call in 1973 for the use of a designated hitter to beef up offense; what they rejected was his promotion of an orange ball, again in the interests of giving batters an edge; what they left up to him was his use of a designated runner (Herb Washington)—an experiment that crashed after little more than one season. If the other league owners made one big mistake with Finley during the 1970s, however, it was in laughing off his proposal, following the Messersmith-McNally decision in 1975, that teams should routinely declare all their players free agents at the end of every year; according to Players Association director Marvin Miller, that in fact would have been the only sensible response by the owners to the abrogation of the reserve clause, but it was thwarted by a combination of automatic hostility to a Charlie Finley idea and simple lack of imagination.

Finley began his transfer tune in Oakland even as the club was tearing up the American League and individual players were tearing up one another in the clubhouse. Finley himself professed indifference to the often-savage scenes among the players and to their united contempt for him, pointing to three straight world championships as an acceptable trade-off; on the other hand, he wasn't so indifferent to what he viewed as modest attendance figures for the best AL team of its time. After initial hints that he was thinking of moving still again, this time to Toronto or Seattle, he let his trial balloon deflate for a couple of years. But then in 1974, with his popularity at an all-time low because of his crude attempt to have

infielder Mike Andrews placed on the disabled list during the 1973 World Series after making a couple of errors and the subsequent resignation of manager Dick Williams, Finley began a series of on-and-off romances with potential franchise purchasers from Toronto and Denver. At the same time, he returned to his Kansas City tactics of slashing costs, firing employees, and cutting back on ticket plans and promotions to help make his case to the league that he needed a bailout. When that produced no immediate results, he went on national television during the 1974 World Series between the Athletics and Dodgers to complain that Oakland couldn't support the club.

It got worse. After the 1974 season, pitching ace Catfish Hunter walked off as a free agent because Finley had neglected to fulfill a contract stipulation. In 1975 he failed in a headlined attempt to get rid of Commissioner Bowie Kuhn. In 1976, with the implications of the Messersmith-McNally decision sinking in, Finley began gutting his championship club before his stars made good on threats to walk away from him into free agency. When Kuhn intervened to thwart proposed sales of pitcher Vida Blue to the Yankees and outfielder Joe Rudi and reliever Rollie Fingers to the Red Sox for a combined $3.5 million, a furious Finley branded him "the village idiot" and sued to have the deals go through; he lost the suit. By 1977 some of his own players were demanding that the league take over team operations. Bay Area fans stayed away from the Coliseum to such an extent that the facility became known as the Mausoleum; even when Finley resorted to a half-price scheme for Monday-to-Thursday games, annual attendance dipped below the half-million level. The rights to broadcast coverage of A's games were given to a college radio station. The Coliseum scoreboard went untended, and amenities, from concession stands to rest rooms, were the worst in the major leagues since the dark ages of Ebbets Field in the 1930s.

Finley, however, kept making money. With a page torn from Branch Rickey's book, he completed only deals that brought him significant cash. If all this proved embarrassing to Kuhn and other AL owners, they could do little about it because of the building militancy of Oakland authorities against allowing the club out of its commitment to the Coliseum. Several times in the late 1970s, the Coliseum issue thwarted what otherwise appeared done deals to move the club to Denver, to shift it to New Orleans, or to have different groups buy out Finley and keep the team in Oakland. At one point, even Giants owner Bob Lurie agreed to contribute cash and several home dates to the Coliseum if it meant returning the Bay Area exclusively to San Francisco. But if none of the prospective arrangements worked out individually, they collectively began wearing down even Finley. Finally, on August 23, 1980, in failing health and admitting that he couldn't keep battling the league, the city of Oakland, and the Coliseum, he announced the sale of the franchise for $12.7 million to Levi Strauss & Company heads Walter Haas, his son Wally, and Walter's son-in-law Roy Eisenhardt. In bidding good-bye to Finley, AL president Lee MacPhail managed to keep a straight face in hailing him for "the new ideas" he had brought to the game.

HAL FINNEY

Finney ended his brief five-year career as a backup catcher for the Pirates in 1936 on the worst possible note. By going to the plate 35 times without a hit, he set the record for position players going hitless for an entire season.

BILL FISCHER

Pitching for Kansas City in 1962, Fischer went a record-setting 84⅓ innings without issuing a walk before Bubba Morton of the Tigers ruined the streak. It was just as well that the right-hander had his control, since he was belted around otherwise and closed the season with a 4–12 record.

RAY FISHER

Fisher was officially banned from baseball by Commissioner Kenesaw Landis in June 1921 without benefit of either formal charges, a hearing, or even a letter of explanation, because the right-hander had refused to sign a one-year contract with the Reds in favor of taking a coaching job with the University of Michigan. Three decades later, the Fisher file was unearthed in the commissioner's office; in it were various letters from Cincinnati officials claiming that the pitcher had refused a substantial salary increase, had ne-

gotiated with Michigan without permission, had applied for reinstatement, and had signed with an outlaw club while his case was being considered—none of which was true. Caving in to the vindictiveness of Cincinnati owner Garry Herrmann, Landis merely sent Fisher a terse telegram informing him of his fate. Fisher was eventually reinstated and worked as a spring training instructor for the Braves in 1960 and the Tigers from 1963 to 1965.

CARLTON FISK

Fisk gained his standing as one of baseball's greatest catchers at the same methodical pace that he ran games. It wasn't until the conclusion of his twenty-four-year (1969, 1971–93)) career that his numerous records for longevity together with his power feats put him in proper context. One reason for the belated acknowledgment was that the right-handed slugger had only two bust-out seasons, almost a decade apart. Even then he remained primarily identified with the Red Sox, although he actually ended up playing more years (thirteen to eleven) with the White Sox, for whom he also established various franchise long-ball marks.

Statistically, Fisk's most significant records are those for the most games (2,226) and most home runs (351) by a major league receiver. Other longevity marks include most seasons (24), most putouts (11,369), and most chances (12,417) by an American League catcher. Overall, he averaged .269 with 376 home runs and 1,330 RBIs. His single best offensive years were for Boston in 1977, when he hit .315 with 26 home runs and 102 RBIs, and 1985 for Chicago, when he clouted a career-high 37 round-trippers and knocked in 107 runs. Defensively, Fisk's greatest asset was his game-calling—an important ingredient of which was making sure that pitchers didn't rush their deliveries. To offset this danger, he developed a habit of rising from his crouch with practically every pitch before returning the ball to the mound—a time-consuming process that was pointed to in the 1980s as the main reason why White Sox games lasted substantially longer than those of other teams.

With both the Red Sox and the White Sox, Fisk had extremely high and equally low moments. One low point in Boston came in 1975, when he was singled out as a leader of the club faction bent on getting rid of manager Darrell Johnson. In that same year's World Series against the Reds, however, he entered postseason lore by "waving" a 12th-inning shot down the left-field line fair for a home run to give the Red Sox a sixth-game win. In 1976, Fisk and teammates Fred Lynn and Rick Burleson became involved in bitter, months-long contract renewal negotiations that attracted all the more attention because the three players were represented by agent Jerry Kapstein in what amounted to the first significant player-management bargaining duel since the advent of free agency. Although Kapstein ultimately won substantial raises for the trio, it wasn't until after the city's promanagement sportswriters had roasted the players, even accusing them and Kapstein of being partly responsible for the death of longtime Red Sox owner Tom Yawkey. The three contracts came back to haunt the franchise again with their expiration in 1980. While Burleson was quickly dealt off to the Angels, Fisk and Lynn again became entangled in protracted bargaining—a process that apparently so distracted general manager Haywood Sullivan that he failed to observe a mailing date for contract submissions, effectively making the two stars free agents. Fisk seized the opportunity to sign with the White Sox.

Fisk's first bad moments in Chicago came in 1985, when the loud, change-for-the-sake-of-change general manager, Ken Harrelson, decided to move him to left field to open up the catching spot for prospects Joel Skinner and Ron Karkovice. The experiment lasted only a few weeks into the season, when Fisk, embarrassed by his outfield play and backed by the team's pitching corps, returned behind the plate. His return wasn't so fast a few years later, however, when newly arrived manager Gene Lamont also thought Karkovice should do the brunt of the catching. Well into his forties and hobbled for some time by injuries, Fisk continued to insist that he should be the club's starting catcher—or if not that, at least treated with the respect due to somebody who had been so for many years. The sullenness on both sides eventually involved owner Jerry Reinsdorf, who was less subtle than Lamont about

declaring Fisk a relic. Only a few days after the veteran had broken Bob Boone's record for the most games by a catcher, Reinsdorf personally ordered Fisk's release.

ED FITZGERALD

Fitzgerald was the most recent player to make two separate appearances in a game. With the agreement of Cub manager Phil Cavarretta, the Pittsburgh catcher, who had already been used earlier as a pinch hitter, was permitted to go behind the plate in a late 1952 contest because of injuries to the Pirates' other available receivers.

MAX FLACK

Outfielder Flack was one of the handful of players who began their major league careers in the Federal League. In fact, in moving from the Chicago Whales to the Cubs after the 1915 season, he came into the National League as a tandem with Wrigley Field. In 1922 he gained another footnote to baseball history when, between games of a Cubs-Cardinals doubleheader, he was traded for outfielder Cliff Heathcote—the only deal ever made between games of a twin bill. Both players appeared in both games.

JOHN FLAHERTY

On April 12, 1992, Flaherty made his debut for the Red Sox in the first game of a doubleheader against the Indians. His batterymate, Matt Young, pitched eight hitless innings but ended up losing the game, 2–1. Although rule changes had recently barred such efforts from being considered no-hitters, Flaherty was the first catcher ever to break in by helping to hold opposition batters hitless for what amounted to a complete game.

JOE FLANNER

The editor of *The Sporting News,* Flanner epitomized the cozy relationship between the Baseball Bible and major league owners by drawing up the February 1903 peace treaty between the National and American leagues. A lawyer as well as a journalist, he even set the agreement into type in the newspaper's St. Louis office for forwarding to all interested parties. Not a single word of the Flanner document was changed before ratification by the leagues.

DANIEL FLETCHER

Fletcher tried to turn a 1910 postseason barnstorming tour of major leaguers into a third major league. Following the promoter's claim of having secured the services of dozens of players, the two established leagues fought back by denying the players permission to participate even in the exhibition games. Fletcher was deluged with returned checks from those he had recruited; Washington's future Hall of Fame pitcher Walter Johnson went so far as to deny a previous statement that he had accepted a $10,000 bonus for joining Fletcher. Deferring the inaugural of his league until 1912, Fletcher returned his attention to the barnstorming tour until that, too, collapsed with the withdrawals of Christy Mathewson, Ty Cobb, and Tris Speaker.

ELBIE FLETCHER

A first baseman for Boston and Pittsburgh in the 1930s and 1940s, Fletcher's entrée to the National League in 1934 came about because he won a newspaper contest to select the Boston high school player most likely to make it to the big leagues. The lefty won the prize, a trip to spring training with the Braves, as much because every member of his extensive family wrote to the paper recommending him as for his diamond skills.

On September 21, 1938, Fletcher's ordinarily superior defensive skills failed him epically when he called for a pop-up behind the mound and then watched the ball get carried into the distant left-field stands of Braves Field. It was only at that point that umpires acceded to game-long requests that the contest be suspended because of a hurricane that was ripping through New England and that would end up taking 600 lives.

ELMER FLICK (Hall of Fame, 1963)

Flick was once considered good enough by the American League to risk continued war with the National League, then considered good enough by the Tigers for a proposal of a straight-up trade for Ty Cobb. A left-hand-hitting outfielder who had few peers defensively, Flick, along with Nap Lajoie and Bill Bernhard, jumped to the AL Athletics from the Phillies during the interleague hostilities at the dawn of the century. When a Pennsylvania court enjoined them against playing

in the state for the junior circuit, AL president Ban Johnson persuaded Connie Mack to deal them to Cleveland, for whom they could at least play all scheduled games except those in Philadelphia and remain in the league. Flick's best years with the Indians were 1905, when he led the league in hitting and slugging average, and 1906, when his .311 mark included leading the AL in doubles, steals, and runs scored. In 1908 the Tigers were so concerned about the club rifts caused by Cobb that they offered him to Cleveland for Flick one-for-one. Indians owner Charles Somers said no, and had reason to regret it twice over—for Cobb's assault on the record books and for injuries that had Flick out of the league by 1910. The outfielder ended up batting .315 in thirteen seasons.

CURT FLOOD

Flood was as crucial to the economic rights of players as Jackie Robinson was to breaking the color barrier; unlike Robinson, however, Flood didn't benefit personally from his pioneering challenge.

A key part of the Cardinal teams that won three pennants in the 1960s, Flood refused to accept a trade to the Phillies in October 1969, saying he was getting tired of being treated like a commodity and declaring war on the reserve clause in court. With the backing of the Players Association and with former U.S. Supreme Court justice Arthur Goldberg arguing on his behalf, the outfielder pursued the case known as *Flood v. Kuhn* (Commissioner Bowie Kuhn) from January 1970 to June 1972 at district, circuit, and Supreme Court levels, gaining supporting testimony from, among others, Robinson, former owner and Hall of Famer Hank Greenberg, frequent owner Bill Veeck, and retired pitcher Jim Brosnan. On June 6, 1972, the Supreme Court came down against Flood by a margin of 5–3, with one abstention. But the language upholding baseball's exemption from antitrust statutes (the situation was described as ''anomalous'' and ''aberrational,'' among other things) was so riddled with ludicrous contradictions and rationalizations that it merely invited closer looks at the sport's status, setting the stage for the 1975 Messersmith-McNally rulings and the advent of free agency. The painful equivoca-

Curt Flood's challenge to the reserve clause represented a giant stride toward free agency. Cleveland Public Library.

tion of the Supreme Court decision also reinforced suspicions that Flood would have been vindicated much more directly if Goldberg, distracted by his gubernatorial campaign in New York, had put more energy and eloquence into his brief.

Flood's big league career effectively ended with his legal action, as he had known before getting into the suit. The one exception was a short stint with Bob Short's Senators in 1971 while the case was still pending, and that prompted a series of tortuous documents by all concerned attesting that his wearing a Washington uniform did not mean either that the commissioner recognized the player's right to reject the deal with Philadelphia or that the player accepted a subsequent exchange between the Senators and Phillies for his services. It all became academic after 35 at-bats, when Flood jumped the team.

Between 1958 and 1969, the right-handed hitter batted over .300 six times, topping the 200-hit mark twice and serving as the ideal cover batsman

for steals king Lou Brock. Defensively Flood was considered an equal to Willie Mays for the first part of the 1960s, and better when the Giants star lost a step toward the middle of the decade. Aside from the principle involved in the 1969 trade, Flood always made it clear that he didn't appreciate learning about it thirdhand from a newsman after twelve years in a St. Louis uniform and that he was particularly annoyed at having been shipped to Philadelphia, a city he had always viewed as racist.

HORACE FOGEL

Fogel was a Philadelphia sportswriter who, unfortunately for the cities of Indianapolis, New York, and Philadelphia, got to fulfill his dreams of becoming first manager and then president of a big league club. Although he was merely inept as the pilot of Indianapolis's 1887 entry in the National League, he came close to aborting a Hall of Fame career when, as manager of the Giants in 1902, he tried to convert Christy Mathewson into a first baseman. Even when Fogel was officially fired 41 games into the season, he still hopped back into the dugout from time to time to call the plays—and to get a closer look at his successor Heinie Smith's rival inspiration that Mathewson belonged at shortstop instead of first!

After being cast aside with the arrival of John McGraw in New York, Fogel returned to his notebook until resurfacing in 1909 as the front man for a business consortium taking over the Phillies. His first insight in his new position was that the club shouldn't be called the Phillies (or the Quakers, as they had also been known), but rather the Live Wires. To promote this cause, he sold or gave away thousands of watch fobs that featured the figure of an eagle carrying sparking wires. Mainly thanks to the pitching of Grover Cleveland Alexander, Fogel's Phillies (as fans continued to call them adamantly) weren't the worst team in the league; Fogel himself, however, had doubts about what was the best team. After one too many drunken accusations that the Giants had beaten the Cubs for the pennant in 1912 mainly because Cardinal manager Roger Bresnahan had not fielded his best nine against his former Giants' teammates and because league umpires were pro-New York, he was summoned to a league meeting to back up his charges. When he couldn't, Fogel was banished from baseball for having "undermined the integrity of the game," even though he had been put up to the charges by his financial backer, Cub owner Charles Murphy.

LEE FOHL

Fohl was the hapless choice to manage the Indians in name only while Tris Speaker actually called all crucial moves by using a hand code from his position in center field. The uneasy arrangement came to an end in 1919, when Fohl either misinterpreted or ignored Speaker's sign to leave in a Cleveland starter against Babe Ruth, deciding instead to bring in a reliever. When Ruth promptly smacked the first pitch out of the park, Speaker showed his anger to the grandstands so graphically that Fohl got up from his seat in the dugout and went upstairs to the team offices to submit his resignation. Speaker was then given the job in name as well as in power.

LEW FONSECA

Fonseca pioneered the use of film for detecting flaws in the swings of hitters and deliveries of pitchers. A batting champion for the 1929 Indians, the righty-hitting infielder initially got interested in the medium while playing a small part in the 1927 Joe E. Brown comedy *Slide, Kelly, Slide*. He was able to put his ideas into practice while managing the White Sox between 1932 and 1934. Fonseca later expanded his activities into providing an annual film review of American League highlights and a summary of World Series and All-Star games for the armed forces during World War II. When the National League joined the program in 1946, he was appointed head of major league baseball's motion picture division—a position he held until the formation of the Major League Baseball Promotion Corporation in 1968.

BARRY FOOTE

Foote's greatest claim to fame after ten major league seasons (1973–82) was that he was the highest-paid manager in minor league history. In 1984 he took over the Class A Fort Lauderdale club in the Yankee organization while working off an annual salary of more than $400,000 obtained a couple of years earlier when George

Steinbrenner gave him a multiyear pact as a backup catcher. Foote forced Montreal to play Gary Carter in the outfield for a couple of seasons in the 1970s, when the consensus of the front office was that he was the better defensive receiver.

RUSS FORD

The most successful early practitioner of the emery ball, Ford is the only pitcher besides Hall of Famers Christy Mathewson and Grover Cleveland Alexander to win 20 games and strike out 200 batters as a rookie. The right-hander followed his 1910 season (26–2, 209 strikeouts) for the Yankees with a 22–11 effort, then slipped to an AL-leading 21 losses in 1912. He later had a third 20-win season, with the Federal League Buffalo Blues in 1914, and ended his career a year later with an overall 98–71 mark.

WHITEY FORD (Hall of Fame, 1974)

Ford was a very good pitcher who became a great one simply by being allowed to pitch in a four-man rotation instead of every fifth day. In 16 seasons, all of them with the Yankees, the left-hander won 236 games and compiled a .690 winning percentage, the third-highest ever and the best among twentieth-century pitchers with 200 or more victories.

After a 9–1 rookie record in 1950 and two years in the Army, Ford quickly became the ace of the New York staff under manager Casey Stengel. Until 1960, the southpaw paced American League hurlers in victories and winning percentage once each and in ERA and shutouts twice apiece, but a 20-game season eluded him mostly because Stengel insisted that he was too small to pitch more than once every five days; in addition, the pilot often held him back from his regular turn for a big game in a subsequent series. The Yankee front office actually contemplated trading Ford to the Tigers for Al Kaline after a subpar 16–10 record in 1959, when a pulled tendon in his left arm was misdiagnosed as neuritis; a similar result in 1960 (12–9) did little to dispel a conclusion that the left-hander's career—at least with the Yankees—was just about over.

After Ralph Houk replaced Stengel, however, Ford worked every four days, posting records of

25–4 in 1961 and 24–7 in 1963 to lead the AL in both victories and won-lost percentage in both seasons, but also developing a reputation as a seven-inning pitcher. While the perception had validity (especially in 1961, when Luis Arroyo recorded 15 of his 29 saves in relief of Ford), it is also true that Ford topped AL hurlers in innings pitched for the only two times in his career in his two 20-win seasons.

Catcher Elston Howard dubbed Ford The Chairman of the Board for his uncanny ability to direct his fielders, but the pitcher and playmate Mickey Mantle called each other Slick for Stengel's reference to them as ''a couple of whiskey slicks.'' While he was often a prominent part of late-night Yankee carousing, Ford more often than not stayed in two nights before his scheduled starts and often convinced Mantle to stay in as well, thereby probably preventing the slugger from damaging himself even more than he did.

Especially in his later years on the mound, Ford became a master at doctoring the ball. Aside from developing a spitter, he came up with a scuffball with the help of a ring until umpire Hank Soar ordered him to remove the offending jewelry during a game; from that point on, it was Howard who provided the slash with a sharpened rivet on his shin guard. In addition, Ford learned how to throw a mudball from the Braves' Warren Spahn and Lew Burdette during the 1957 World Series. His mudder led to a rule preventing pitchers from reaching for the resin bag while holding a ball in his bare hand, a trick the left-hander had used to rub a moistened ball in the dirt.

Ford holds the World Series records for both most victories (10) and most losses (8), a result of having pitched for eleven pennant winners in his sixteen-year career.

GEORGE FOSTER

Foster was the cleanup hitter of the Big Red Machine in the 1970s, earning the pivotal spot by leading the National League in home runs in 1977 and 1978 and in RBIs in 1976, 1977, and 1978. His 52 homers in 1977 was the last time an NL slugger reached the 50 mark. The right-hand-hitting outfielder came up with the Giants in 1969, and his trade to Cincinnati in 1972 for shortstop Frank Duffy and pitcher Vern Geishert was the worst in the history of the San Francisco fran-

chise. In eighteen big league seasons, Foster hit at least 20 homers ten times, ending up with 348. Traded to the Mets in 1982, he had several trouble-filled years with the Shea Stadium faithful when he failed to produce the big numbers that he had for the Reds. During New York's 1986 pennant-winning season, he gave evidence of his isolation from his teammates by remaining on the bench during a violent on-field brawl with Cincinnati players. Shortly afterward, he accused manager Davey Johnson of benching him for racial reasons, even though his replacements, Kevin Mitchell and Mookie Wilson, were also black. A stupefied Johnson pressed successfully for his release a few days later.

RUBE FOSTER (Hall of Fame, 1981)

Foster wore four hats—as a winning left-hander, a highly successful manager, the owner of the Chicago Black Giants, and the founder of the Negro National League. As a southpaw, he was good enough to tutor Christy Mathewson in the screwball and to beat Rube Waddell in a 1902 game (one of 51 he won that year) to earn his nickname. In 1903 he posted a 54–1 record for the Cuban X-Giants, then beat the Philadelphia Giants four times in a postseason championship. The following year, he jumped to the Philadelphia club and led them to the first of three consecutive championships by beating the X-Giants 2 out of 3 in the playoffs.

Beginning his managerial career with the Leland Giants in 1907, Foster piloted the team to records of 110–10 (in 1907) and 128–6 (in 1910) before forming the Black Giants in 1911. His partner in the venture was John Schorling, a Chicago saloonkeeper and a son-in-law of White Sox owner Charlie Comiskey; the connection enabled the new team to play its home games in Comiskey Park. So dominant were the Black Giants that, for more than a decade, they won almost every national black championship.

During the winter of 1919, Foster organized the Negro National League, the first viable black major league. As president and secretary of the circuit until 1926, he ruled autocratically, taking 5 percent of the gate from every game in lieu of a salary; as manager of the Black Giants, he ruled it on the field as well, winning the championship in the first three seasons.

JAKE FOURNIER

Fournier was one of the rare Cardinal first baseman in the first half of the century who did *not* end up in the Hall of Fame. It wasn't for lack of hitting: In fifteen years (between 1912 and 1927) with St. Louis, Brooklyn, and a couple of other clubs, the lefty swinger averaged .318, winning both a home run and a slugging title in the bargain. Fournier also figured in a legendary Branch Rickey story. After purchasing the first baseman, the prudish Rickey called him up and asked: "Do you smoke?" Fournier said yes. Rickey: "Do you drink?" Fournier said yes. Rickey: "Do you like the ladies?" Fournier said yes. "Judas Priest, you must have horns!" Rickey cried, slamming down the telephone.

BUD FOWLER

Second baseman Fowler became the first black to be paid for playing baseball when he signed with an otherwise all-white New Castle, Pennsylvania, team in 1872. Fowler played for dozens of teams, several of which were part of white organized baseball, in a career that lasted until past the turn of the century. His birth in 1857, to migrant workers in Cooperstown, New York, is the only known nineteenth-century connection between baseball and that village.

DICK FOWLER

Right-hander Fowler won one game for the 1945 Athletics—a no-hitter over the Browns. He is the only pitcher to have accomplished this economical feat.

HOWARD FOX

Although officially Minnesota's traveling secretary, Fox was owner Calvin Griffith's chief line of communication to the team in the 1960s and 1970s; sometimes Griffith even knew what he was up to. Fox's chief antagonist for some time was Billy Martin, with whom he slugged it out in a Washington lobby in 1969; he was regarded as the architect of Martin's firing as manager after the season. Other Twins pilots also complained that the "orders" they ostensibly received from

Griffith through Fox had actually originated with the traveling secretary. When Griffith sold the franchise to Carl Pohlad in 1984, Fox was promoted for a brief time to organization president.

NELLIE FOX

Fox was one of the slowest players on the Go-Go Sox of the 1950s, and also the heart of the team. A lifetime .288 hitter, the lefty-swinging second baseman used one of the last of the slim-handled, wide-barreled bottle bats to win MVP honors in driving Chicago to a pennant in 1959. Four times during his nineteen-year (1947–65) career, he paced the American League in hits, also reaching the .300 mark six times. The quintessential contact hitter, 2,262 of his 2,663 safeties were one-basers, and he never struck out more than 18 times in a season. Defensively, he teamed with Luis Aparicio to forge the best middle infield in the AL in the 1950s and early 1960s. Fox's trade from the Athletics to the White Sox in 1949 for catcher Joe Tipton was arguably the biggest steal in Chicago franchise history. In 1985, the final year of his eligibility for election by sportswriters, Fox received 295 votes in the Hall of Fame balloting—2 shy of the necessary minimum; that was closest a nonmember has ever gotten to Cooperstown, and Fox's exclusion by such a slim margin attracted considerable attention to Hall of Fame entry requirements.

JIMMIE FOXX (Hall of Fame, 1951)

Foxx was the right-handed complement to Babe Ruth and Lou Gehrig as the most potent American League sluggers of the 1920s and 1930s. In fact, Foxx tied the two Yankee greats for the major league record of 100 or more RBIs in thirteen seasons and also established a record of his own by clouting at least 30 homers in twelve consecutive seasons. A lifetime .325 hitter in twenty seasons with the Athletics, Red Sox, and several other clubs, Foxx knocked 534 home runs (ninth on the all-time list), drove in 1,921 runs (sixth), and compiled a .609 slugging percentage (fourth). He won a Triple Crown in 1933 and led the AL in batting one other time, in home runs in three additional seasons, and in RBIs two more years. His 58 home runs in 1932 were as close as anyone came to Ruth's 60 until Roger Maris, and Foxx might have passed the 60 mark himself but for a wrist injury in August. Among his prodigious blasts were the first ever hit over the left-field second tier at Comiskey Park (and clear across West Thirty-fourth Place) and one that broke a seat in the distant Yankee Stadium left-field third deck.

Coming to the Athletics as a seventeen-year-old rookie receiver in 1925, Foxx backed up Mickey Cochrane behind the plate and tried his hand at third base before manager Connie Mack installed him at first in 1929, in time for the first of three consecutive pennants. (Foxx hit .344 in the three World Series.) By 1935, however, Mack had sold off most of his stars to deal with one of his periodic cash shortages, also asking Foxx to take a $6,000 pay cut for the 1936 season. When the slugger uncharacteristically exploded, Mack honored his request for a trade by selling him to Boston for $150,000 in December 1935. The first baseman went on to several productive seasons in Fenway Park and the tutelage of a young Ted Williams in 1939. As prodigious a drinker and spender as he was a hitter, Foxx choked to death on a piece of meat while dining with his brother in July 1967.

PAUL FOYTACK

On July 31, 1963, Angels right-hander Foytack endured the embarrassment of surrendering four consecutive home runs. The blasts were hit by Woodie Held, Pedro Ramos, Tito Francona, and Larry Brown of Cleveland.

JOHN FRANCO

Franco has been the most successful southpaw reliever in baseball history. As a member of the Mets in 1994, he posted 30 saves for a career total of 266, thereby eclipsing Dave Righetti's total of 252 for a left-hander. Between 1987 and 1989 for Cincinnati and as the ace of the New York bullpen in 1990 and 1991, Franco became the only National League pitcher to rack up 30 saves five years in a row.

TITO FRANCONA

Baseball's capricious rules for batting titlists claimed Francona as a victim in 1959, when the Cleveland outfielder averaged .363. Although that was 10 points higher than runner-up Harvey Kuenn, Francona was denied the crown because he fell one short of the required 400 official at-bats. In other years, the lefty swinger would have been able to take advantage of regulations requiring only 100 games, a formula combining at-bats with walks and hit batsmen into plate appearances, or artificially added plate appearances for reaching the minimum. In his fifteen-year career for a number of teams, Francona attained .300 in only two other seasons, closing out with a .272 mark.

HARRY FRAZEE

For more than seventy years, Frazee has been the twenty-sixth player for the Red Sox—the one who erases all the successes of his teammates and makes sure Boston never wins another world championship. Worse, he has done everything possible to guarantee that New York teams win what Boston should have, whether it be through his actual sale of Babe Ruth to the Bronx in December 1919 or through his haunting presence over Bill Buckner in Flushing in October 1986. In short, the Boston owner from 1917 to 1923 has been baseball's biggest ghost story.

A New York theatrical producer, Frazee bought the Red Sox from Joseph Lannin with more paper than cash. In fact, within only months of taking over the club, he had to hide behind no-comment replies to rumors that he had put the franchise back on the block merely to pay off what he owned Lannin. Unfortunately for future generations, however, Boston won the pennant and the World Series in 1918, permitting Frazee to think he could make a go of it. That illusion lasted only several months when losses from the Broadway plays he was producing persuaded him to sell off such noted players as Ernie Shore, Duffy Lewis, Dutch Leonard, and Carl Mays. Even the fact that Shore, Lewis, and Mays went to the Yankees served as a mere prelude in Boston agitation to the sale of Ruth for $100,000 plus a $350,000 loan. Frazee's immediate defense of the deal was that not even Ruth's burgeoning slugging after a few years of being a dominating pitcher had prevented the Red Sox from finishing sixth in 1919; what he didn't say was that the money received from New York went right back to Broadway to keep *No! No! Nanette* on the boards. The sale of Ruth was hardly the last transaction between the Yankees and Red Sox. With the critical assistance of Ed Barrow, who in 1920 went from being Boston manager to New York general manager, Frazee sent the likes of Waite Hoyt, Herb Pennock, Everett Scott, Wally Schang, and George Pipgras south at the beginning of the decade. Even more revelatory of the incestuous relationship between the teams was an October 1922 incident when the Yankees acknowledged that one of the conditions of their ''loan'' in the Ruth transaction was that they should be ''consulted'' before Frazee completed any deal with another club. This came to light when Colonel Jacob Ruppert protested a Boston-Detroit exchange that had brought pitcher Howard Ehmke to Fenway Park. Informed that New York had also been interested in Ehmke, Frazee's abject response was to claim that he had already cashed a Detroit check sent along with the pitcher, so he couldn't do Ruppert's bidding by canceling the deal.

Shortly after the Ehmke embarrassment, Frazee made a bigger mistake that ended up costing him the franchise. Anxious to cash another check, from Toronto of the International League for Frank O'Rourke, the owner forgot to secure waivers from the Phillies before shipping the outfielder to Canada. When Philadelphia protested, AL president Ban Johnson, with whom Frazee had been at loggerheads for some years, used it to round up other alienated AL owners and force the producer to sell out to a consortium headed by Bob Quinn. It was with the Quinn ownership that Frazee became more of a spiritual that material director of the Red Sox misfortunes.

GEORGE FRAZIER

Frazier is the only pitcher to lose 3 games in a World Series. The reliever did it in the Yankees' losing effort to the Dodgers in 1981; his ERA for the three games was 17.18. The right-hander did not feel the sting of owner George Steinbrenner until the following year when, toward the end of an August 3, 1982, doubleheader against the White Sox, Steinbrenner had Yankee Stadium public address announcer Bob Sheppard, the embarrassment apparent in his voice, offer each of the 34,000 fans present a free ticket to

any future home game for having endured a 1–0 loss followed by a 14–2 drubbing; Frazier, the final victim in the nightcap, sat on the mound, his head hung in humiliation.

JOHNNY FREDERICK

Frederick established the season pinch-hit power record in 1932 when he came off the bench for the Dodgers on six occasions to clout home runs. Although best remembered for this accomplishment, the lefty-hitting outfielder had raised other kinds of expectations in his rookie year of 1929, when he batted .328 with 24 home runs and a league-leading 52 doubles. Throughout his six-year career, in fact, he was considered more of a starter than a bench player, ending up with only 62 pinch-hit appearances.

ANDREW FREEDMAN

Even in a business noted for crooks, incompetents, misers, and paranoids, Freedman, who controlled the New York Giants from 1895 until 1903, stood out on all counts. A real-estate lawyer and bagman for Tammany Hall's Boss Croker, he characteristically accumulated Giants' stock for what amounted to an unfriendly takeover not in his own name but in that of James Bailey—without bothering to inform the future circus impresario. Taking over the organization in January 1985, he immediately canceled all free passes and demanded that the Brooklyn franchise pull out of the league and leave the entire New York market to him; when Brooklyn owner Charles Byrne ridiculed the notion, Freedman got his cronies on the City Council to make sure that none of the new subway lines planned for the city would go anywhere near Brooklyn's Washington Park.

The first conspicuous critic of Freedman's methods was Sam Crane of the *New York Commercial Advertiser*. When Crane accused the owner of trying to destroy the franchise, Freedman responded by voiding his press credentials and then alerting his ticket sellers not to allow him in the park even with a paid admission. When other New York writers came to Crane's defense, they were also put on his blacklist. Particular targets included the *New York Sun,* against which Freedman filed twenty-five unsuccessful lawsuits in five years, and *The New York Times,* whose beat writer the owner slugged for suggesting that he was the source of the franchise's problems. Freedman even engaged in a feud with venerable sportswriter Henry Chadwick, who ended up boycotting the Polo Grounds and urging his readers to do the same.

If anything, Freedman's relations with his managers and players were even worse than with the press. He employed twelve different managers—two of them twice each—in eight years, but couldn't lift the team above seventh place more than once. Among the pilots who came and went with dizzying rapidity were Harvey Watkins, an actor and errand boy for Bailey; John B. Day, a former Giants' owner who was down on his luck; Fred Hoey, a Tammany hanger-on who had no discernible baseball credentials; Horace Fogel, who tried to convert Christy Mathewson to a first baseman; Heinie Smith, who thought the future Hall of Fame right-hander would make a better shortstop than first baseman; and John McGraw, who would survive Freedman with the franchise by three decades. He alienated ace pitcher Amos Rusie over a $200 fine for a trumped-up charge, causing a rift that included a year-long sit-down by the right-hander. He overplayed an admittedly ugly anti-Semitic remark by former Giant Ducky Holmes into a firestorm that saw the National League suspend Holmes, players around the league threaten a boycott of Giants games, and a judge order the Baltimore outfielder's reinstatement.

Freedman's genius for making trouble reached its apex with his presentation in 1901 of a scheme, actually concocted by Cincinnati owner John T. Brush, to syndicate the NL by pooling all players and reassigning them to teams each season. The proposed trust called for the Giants to hold 30 percent of the stock; Boston, St. Louis, and Cincinnati to retain 12 percent each; and Philadelphia, Chicago, Pittsburgh, and Brooklyn to accept 10 to 6 percent each. The issue came down to a choice for NL president at the December 1901 league meeting, with Freedman and the three 12 percenters favoring incumbent Nick Young, and the four projected minority stockholders advancing the candidacy of Al Spalding. The comic opera affair ended with the election of compromise candidate Harry Pulliam, the demise

of the syndicate baseball scheme, and the end of the NL's patience with Freedman, who had been tolerated only because his Tammany connections had kept Ban Johnson's American League from entering the New York market. With the election of reform mayor Seth Low in 1901, however, Freedman's usefulness to other owners frayed at the edges. Although still in titular control of the franchise, he was a mere bystander to Brush's machinations to collapse the AL Baltimore franchise in the middle of the 1902 season and bring its manager, McGraw, and several of its stars to the Polo Grounds. Brush finally took over formal control of the Giants from Freedman in 1903.

M. C. FREY

A diminutive Swedish physician hired by the Reds in 1898, Frey was the first team doctor. Although he knew virtually nothing about baseball, Frey's reliance on massage to cure most ills proved popular with the players; despite his popularity, he quit after two years to become a jockey.

*FORD FRICK (Hall of Fame, 1970)

Frick's chief claim to being in the Hall of Fame was that, as the National League president in the 1930s, he was a prominent supporter of establishing the Cooperstown museum to help mark baseball's 1939 chimerical centennial. As both league president and later commissioner, on the other hand, he was rarely more than a mascot for major league owners. On one of the rare occasions that he did assert himself, the results were even worse, insisting in 1961 that the record books carry an asterisk if Roger Maris succeeded in surpassing Babe Ruth's mark of 60 home runs in a season.

Frick worked himself up to the game's biggest titles after working as a reporter and an NL public relations officer. He took over the NL office in 1934, remaining there until his election as commissioner in 1951. For the most part, his presidency was subordinated to the sway of Commissioner Kenesaw Landis—a relationship that Frick reversed when he himself moved into the commissioner's office, ruling again and again that issues brought to him were the prerogative of one of the leagues. His most visible moment as NL chief came in 1943, when he arranged the sale of the Phillies to lumber magnate William Cox; Cox was later blacklisted by Landis for placing bets on his own team.

Frick won the first of two seven-year elections as commissioner after big league owners had to concede failure in their attempts to find a military man for the post; his chief supporter as a compromise candidate was Brooklyn owner Walter O'Malley. It was hardly a coincidence that O'Malley reigned during Frick's tenure as the first among equals within ownership circles. The closest the two men had to a public disagreement was in 1958 over the ground rules for the left-field fence at the Los Angles Coliseum, Frick insisting that a second fence be erected behind a planned one only 250 feet away from the batter's box and that any ball dropping between the two would be declared ground-rule doubles; he lost that argument to the Dodger boss with the discovery of some arcane California earthquake regulation. On the other hand, he was a passive spectator to O'Malley's move to Los Angeles from Brooklyn, as well as to other transfers by the Giants, Braves, Athletics, Browns, and Senators.

In 1961 Frick used the excuse of the recently introduced 162–game schedule to announce midway through the season that anyone surpassing the Ruth record after a 154th game (the old schedule) would have an asterisk next to his name; at the same time, he declined to apply the same criterion to other records affected by the extra contests. What he also failed to mention was that he had been a relatively close associate of Ruth's and had even ghostwritten the slugger's autobiography. In some measure because of the asterisk ruling, only 23,154 were in attendance when Maris hit his 61st home run at Yankee Stadium in the 162nd game of the year. Commissioner Bowie Kuhn later deleted the asterisk.

It was also during Frick's tenure as commissioner that the Hall of Fame established a standing Veterans Committee for electing players and officials no longer eligible for voting by sportswriters. It was the Veterans Committee that elected him to Cooperstown in 1970. Later, the Hall of Fame named its special honors for broadcasting personnel the Ford C. Frick Award.

BOB FRIEND

Friend was a crucial vote in the Players' Association moves that led to the election of Marvin Miller as chief spokesman; it was, in fact only after Friend withdrew his earlier support from Robert Cannon, a mouthpiece for the owners, that the way was cleared for Miller's election by team representatives. On the diamond, Friend labored for long years as the closest that the dreary Pittsburgh clubs of the 1950s had to a franchise pitcher. His sixteen-year mark of 197–230 makes him the only major league hurler to have lost more than 200 games without winning at least 200.

DAN FRIEND

A southpaw by trade, Friend played left field for the Cubs for two-thirds of an inning against the Giants on August 30, 1897, and cost his team the game without ever touching the ball. With New York leading, 7–5, in the top of the ninth inning, Chicago manager Cap Anson was ejected from the game for arguing with home plate umpire Bob Emslie about the twilight playing conditions. The Cubs went on to score 5 runs and take the lead, but in the bottom of the ninth the regular left fielder had to go to first base to replace Anson, with Friend recruited for the outfield. The only problem was that he had already showered and dressed, so he took his position wearing a bathrobe over his street clothes and with only his uniform hat in place. New York manager Bill Joyce remonstrated so long with Emslie about the rule violation that the umpire finally realized that it had become too dark to continue and reverted the score to the 7–5 Giants lead in declaring the game over.

FRANKIE FRISCH (Hall of Fame, 1947)

One of John McGraw's balkier disciples, Frisch was a speeding arrogance in nineteen years (1919–37) of playing and sixteen years of managing (between 1933 and 1951) who always seemed to invite deflating. He never had any trouble finding someone to do the job.

A switch-hitting second baseman known as The Fordham Flash for captaining the baseball, football, and basketball teams at the Bronx university, Frisch took a couple of years to get his feet wet

Before he piloted the rambunctious Gas House Gang, the young Frankie Frisch was the darling of Giant fans and New York manager John McGraw. Photo compliments of Sharon Guynup.

with the Giants before bursting through with a .341 mark and a league-leading 49 steals in 1923. It was the first of eleven straight seasons in which he batted .300 and the first of three times that he would pace the National League in thefts. His other significant numbers include reaching 200 hits three times, cracking 30 doubles eight times, scoring 100 runs seven times, and driving in 100 runs three times. Defensively he was regarded as a whiz at second base, setting season records in 1927 for the most assists (641) and most chances accepted (1,059). The combination of superior hitting and fielding left him only a couple of votes short of an MVP trophy in 1927 but netted him the award four years later.

Frisch's son-father relationship with McGraw made for some stormy times on the Giants in the 1920s. In 1924 the infielder was implicated in an attempted bribe of Phillies shortstop Heinie Sand

but was ultimately exonerated in good part because of his manager's intervention with Commissioner Kenesaw Landis. McGraw wasn't so understanding otherwise, however, and Frisch's bearing as an acolyte acted only to make him the pilot's favorite whipping boy when New York stumbled on the field. In August 1926 Frisch finally broke under McGraw's hectoring and jumped the team for several days. After the season, McGraw traded him to the Cardinals in a stunning swap for Rogers Hornsby, deliberately throwing in journeyman pitcher Jimmy Ring so Frisch wouldn't entertain the idea that he was worth Hornsby straight up.

For the next ten years, Frisch was the field brain of the St. Louis club that evolved into the Gas House Gang in the 1930s. He was so determined to show up McGraw in 1927 that his dazzling hitting (.377), running (a league-leading 48 steals), and record-setting fielding were described by some teammates even decades later as the single greatest season they had ever seen a player enjoy. Another result of the performance was that it took Cardinal owner Sam Breadon off the hook with St. Louis fans who had vehemently protested the departure of Hornsby. For the first part of 1933, the fans appeared to have their cake and be able to eat it, too, when Hornsby returned amid rumors that he was about to begin a second tour of duty as manager. Instead, Breadon announced in July that Hornsby was being released, incumbent manager Gabby Street was being fired, and Frisch was taking over as player-manager.

Although the Gas House Gang was the most colorful NL team of the 1930s, it actually won its only pennant and world championship in 1934. Frisch's key contributions to the effort were another .300 season and a masterly manipulation of a pitching staff that, beyond the Dean brothers, was decidedly mediocre. In the seventh game of the World Series against the Tigers, Frisch cracked a bases-loaded double in the third inning that climaxed a seven-run outburst and put Detroit so far into the hole that disgruntled Tiger Stadium fans started pelting outfielder Joe Medwick with fruit, causing a near-riot. Over the next few years, while unable to steer the club any higher than second, Frisch himself was a series of miniriots over the predilection of such charges as Dizzy

Dean and Pepper Martin for sticking a pin in his ever-ready gruffness; rare was the week that he wasn't the target of a water balloon or that he wasn't threatening to trade one of the team cut-ups. But what also became clear from the incidents, especially from Martin's continued stay on the club, was that Frisch maintained slightly more room between egotism and pompousness than his mentor McGraw ever had.

After retiring as a player in 1937 with a .316 average, Frisch showed less interest in managing as well, and was replaced shortly afterward by Mike Gonzalez. Frisch reemerged as manager of the Pirates in 1940 for what turned out to be a seven-year stint, most of it during the war years, when organizations rarely blamed managers or wanted to hire new ones for the 4-F teams on the field. Frisch's best moment in Pittsburgh came in 1944, when he guided the club to an unexpected second-place finish. On the other hand, his tenure was marked by constant personality clashes with the team's best players (Arky Vaughan, Vince Di-Maggio, Bob Elliott) that both sent Frisch into deep brooding and prompted him to press for stupid trades. Team morale was considered so bad by 1946 that Robert Murphy, head of the American Baseball Guild, picked the Pirates as an ideal testing ground for his attempts to unionize major leaguers. Murphy didn't succeed, but not because of any player solidarity with Frisch.

Frisch's last uniform was that of the Chicago Cubs, whom he managed from the middle of 1949 to the middle of 1951. After some initial boasting that he and general manager Charlie Grimm were going to turn around the second-division franchise with some key trades, they made the mistake of getting into locked rooms with Brooklyn's Branch Rickey and Boston's Lou Perini, achieving nothing but giving away the Wrigley family's money for players who had mostly reached their level at Triple A. It was another trade in which he was not involved directly, however, that ended Frisch's tenure with the Cubs: After Wid Matthews announced the June 1951 deal that dispatched local favorite Andy Pafko to Brooklyn, the manager was overheard agreeing with most Chicago fans that the general manager had been swindled by the Dodgers. Frisch was fired shortly afterward.

For a while in the 1950s, Frisch had a sportscasting career linked to the televising of Giants games. It was from that forum that he became popularly identified with his signature moan of "Ooooh, those bases on balls!"

EMIL FUCHS

Fuchs was the most colorful of the early-century Boston Braves owners who got their hands on the franchise in good part because of John McGraw and who then showed their gratitude by agreeing to just about any trade the Giants' manager proposed. A former judge and assistant attorney general for New York State (and, before that, a lawyer who numbered among his clients Arnold Rothstein), he differed from such predecessors as George Washington Grant in actually living in Boston (rather than New York) and going out of his way to win over a New England press hostile to the years-long manipulations of the franchise from Manhattan. But most of the rest of his tenure as owner in the 1920s and early 1930s was marked by one fiasco after another, not least his stint as manager of the team in 1929.

While sitting on the bench, the Judge, as he preferred to be called, would make such moves as yanking a right-handed hitter in favor of a lefty even when the opposition had a southpaw on the mound; questioned about a decision of the kind, his usual reply was that he hadn't noticed who had been pitching. He didn't think too much of the squeeze play, either, lecturing his players that it wasn't "an honorable way" of scoring a run. National League umpires usually dreaded working Braves games because of another Fuchs habit: recounting long-winded stories to his charges in the middle of crucial game situations, the tales preventing batters from going up to the plate and adding an average half hour to Boston games. In the end, however, it was the Judge as owner rather than the Judge as manager that led to his demise.

Sinking under debt, Fuchs announced during the 1934 winter meetings that he intended converting Braves Field into a dog racing track and moving the Braves into Fenway Park. Unfortunately, he had failed to mention this to Red Sox owner Tom Yawkey, who promptly rejected any idea of sharing Boston's American League park.

The brooding Emil Fuchs often held up games to complete a windy story to his players on the bench. Cleveland Public Library.

When it emerged subsequently that the dog track idea had been pressed on Fuchs by Braves Field stockholders bent on evicting the baseball team because it was a losing financial proposition, the National League had to step in to mediate the crisis; one key consequence was that Fuchs was given six months to resolve his money problems or sell the club. The *coup de grâce* came when the Judge hired Babe Ruth—in his eyes as a gate attraction, but in the Bambino's as the club's imminent manager. When Ruth discovered that he had no chance of taking over the reins of the club, he lashed out bitterly at Fuchs and soon afterward announced his retirement. The controversy was the last straw for the league, which gratefully accepted the Judge's resignation as team president in July.

PAUL FUGIT

Fugit was at the center of the last baseball scandal involving collusion with gamblers to throw games. The first baseman-manager of the Houma club in the Class D Evangeline League in 1946, Fugit hit .327 with 23 homers and 130 RBIs and piloted the team to a championship. He also became involved in a conspiracy with Louisiana gamblers and teammates William Thomas, Leonard Pecou, and Alvin Kaiser, as well as Don Vettorel of the Abbeville team; all five were expelled from organized baseball. Although the incident occurred in the low minors, it sensitized the baseball establishment to the dangers of association with gamblers and, breaking as it did in December 1946, contributed to the harshness of Brooklyn manager Leo Durocher's one-year suspension for such associations the following spring.

DAVE FULTZ

A .271 outfielder for four teams between 1898 and 1905, Fultz attempted to make a larger mark by organizing the Base Ball Players Fraternity in 1912. Backed even at the beginning of the venture by a majority of players on thirteen teams, the New York University Law School graduate confronted the National Commission with the decidedly modest goal of assuring that both owners and players lived up to the terms of contracts; even at its most radical, the Players Fraternity never staked out a position more extreme than a request for a five-year limit on each player's reserve clause. The Commission, composed of the two league presidents and Reds owner Garry Herrmann, vacillated between ignoring the Fraternity and expressing a willingness to meet with its representatives as long as they were not accompanied by Fultz, whom they termed an outsider and an agitator. That approach lasted until November 1913, when about five hundred major and minor league players threatened not to sign their contracts for the 1914 season unless the Commission acted on their grievances; their victory—on such minor points as agreement to provide each player with a copy of his contract and written notification of the details behind trades and releases— had more to do with the impending threat posed by the Federal League than with any negotiating skill on Fultz's part.

The peace was only temporary, however, unraveling as soon as the Fraternity president refused to condemn the Feds. Fultz—and the players involved—emerged as victors in claims brought by pitcher Casey Hageman and first baseman Clarence Kraft, but the first came only after a protracted legal battle and the second only when the owners declined to test the players' will to participate in a strike called by Fultz. In its later years the Fraternity concentrated on improving conditions for minor leaguers. It was, in fact, in response to the rejection of demands made on their behalf in 1916 that Fultz made a fatal error—calling, for the second time, upon the organization's by then 1,215 members to strike. At first several hundred major leaguers, most notably Tris Speaker, were prepared to walk out in solidarity with the minor leaguers. Then, realizing that with the demise of the Feds they were risking permanent unemployment, enough of them signed contracts for the 1917 season to force Fultz to cancel the action. Although the Fraternity was to last on paper for another year, its effectiveness ended when Fultz released the strike's supporters from their pledges.

CARL FURILLO

Furillo was the quintessential blue-collar player of the Boys of Summer Dodgers. Despite falling merely 1 hit short of a career .300 average for fifteen seasons, winning a batting title, shining as a clutch hitter, and possessing the best right-field arm among his contemporaries, he seldom received the respect accorded his numerous Hall of Fame teammates. Part of the trouble stemmed from a tight-lipped personality that furnished neither the anger nor the geniality that made other Brooklyn players of the 1950s good copy. Another problem was the almost annual lull the right-hand-hitting outfielder fell into between early June and mid-July, when All-Star game voters were prone to selecting players on the basis of recent heroics. Aside from this regular slump, however, Furillo was, with Jackie Robinson, the Dodger most likely to curl an opposing pitcher's hairs by stepping into the batter's box with the game on the line.

Furillo's special cachet in the eyes of Brooklyn fans was his ferocious play against the Giants. This was never more apparent than on September 6, 1953, when, after being struck on the wrist by

Carl Furillo was so intent on overcoming a hand injury to play in the 1953 World Series against the Yankees that he insisted on taking fielding practice with his glove on the wrong hand. Brooklyn Public Library—BROOKLYN COLLECTION.

a Ruben Gomez fastball and jeered at by New York manager Leo Durocher, he charged into the Giants bench. With umpire Babe Pinelli shouting "Get him, Carl, get him!" Furillo swung at everybody around him. He emerged from the melee with a broken hand that sidelined him for the rest of the year—but that also allowed him to sit on a league-leading average that was not surpassed.

To a great extent, Furillo's defensive play, and especially his mastery of the right-field scoreboard in Ebbets Field, overshadowed his offensive skills. It was not unusual for him to throw out hitters at first base or to turn apparent singles into force-outs by getting the ball to second before a runner could advance ninety feet. His throwing darts earned him the nickname of The Reading Rifle, while his reading of line drives earned him the gratitude of Brooklyn clothier Abe Stark, whose right-field advertisement promised a new suit of clothes to any batter hitting the sign.

Furillo's fifteen years with the Dodgers were

framed at both ends by unhappy episodes. Along with Dixie Walker and Bobby Bragan, he was one of the chief resisters to the presence of Robinson on the club in 1947. Branch Rickey talked Furillo out of his posture, spreading the impression that the outfielder was an ignorant dupe of the other two players. In 1960, Los Angeles general manager Buzzie Bavasi demanded that the veteran accept a minor league demotion for what were termed ''temporary roster problems.'' Furillo not only said no, but following his outright release from the team, gave testimony before a congressional committee on the reserve clause and sued the Dodgers for breach of contract. Although he won the suit, he was effectively blackballed from baseball. This was borne home in 1962, when not even the newly created Mets, hungry for any player with an Ebbets Field background, could find room for him.

G

EDDIE GAEDEL

Gaedel was the star of Bill Veeck's most famous production. On August 19, 1951, between games of a doubleheader, the St. Louis owner celebrated the American League's fiftieth birthday with an oversized birthday cake out of which popped the three-foot, seven-inch Gaedel wearing a Browns' uniform with the number ⅛. The festivities were mere prelude to what followed, however, as Gaedel, armed with a toy bat and threatened by Veeck with a violent end if he used it, marched to the plate as a pinch hitter for leadoff batter Frank Saucier in the first inning of the second game. Assured by manager Zack Taylor that the midget had signed a valid contract, umpire Ed Hurley let Gaedel keep his appointment with baseball immortality—a base on balls issued by Detroit's Bob Cain, whose laughter as much as Gaedel's one-and-a-half-inch strike zone contributed to his wildness.

Veeck and Gaedel teamed together for several other stunts over the next decade. In 1960 Gaedel and three other midgets, all dressed as Martians, helicoptered onto the infield at Comiskey Park for a meeting with Luis Aparicio and Nellie Fox, then notified the crowd that they had arrived to assist the not overly tall double play combination in their struggle against the earthlings. The final Veeck stunt involving Gaedel was the employment of midget vendors on Opening Day of 1961 in Comiskey in response to fans who had complained that hot dog and peanut salesman blocked their view of the game. Gaedel died the following June; the only baseball figure in attendance at his funeral was Cain.

GARY GAETTI

Gaetti has been the most conspicuous case of a player not being offered a contract because of a production falloff attributed to a religious conversion. Minnesota's decision to let the third baseman walk off as a free agent after the 1990 season followed a couple of years in which he was criticized for spending more time reading the Bible than taking the extra batting practice and holding the clubhouse pep talks that had characterized his first several years with the Twins. Teammates had also admitted feeling more distant from the right-handed slugger they had once called The Rat for his grubby style of play and incessant badgering of opposition pitching. Gaetti declared himself a Born Again convert before the 1988 season. As a reanimated Christian he produced the highest batting average of his career (.301) that year, but also suffered a sharp decline in his power numbers that continued for the next several years—with the Twins, Angels, and Royals.

Defensively, Gaetti has been involved in a major league-record 7 triple plays, including 2 in a single game.

JAMES GAFFNEY

Gaffney was the most ambitious of the New York-based owners who ran the Braves for much of the first part of the century. A former policeman who had built up a fortune as a contractor through his use of Tammany Hall contacts, he was brought into the Boston franchise by John Montgomery Ward, a former Giant who needed some conspicuous financial backing for his grand plans for overhauling the team. In the event, Gaffney did most of the overhauling himself when Ward belatedly realized that other team owners were not ready to deal with the player-lawyer who had bested so many of them in courtrooms over contract disputes.

Gaffney's first innovation was renaming the club he had invested in; inspired by the nickname used by Tammany Hall politicians, he ended years of switches from Beaneaters to Nationals and from Doves to Rustlers by calling the team the Braves and redesigning uniforms so that they bore the profile of a Native American warrior. His second most significant contribution was in ordering construction of a new ballpark after the team had been playing for almost four decades in dilapidated South End Grounds. He had some personal ideas about what the new Braves Field should look like, too: Convinced that fans were more entertained by seeing runners scoot around the bases than by watching balls disappear into the outfield seats, he insisted that the park be spacious enough to encourage inside-the-park home runs. The result was a field that measured 420 feet down each foul line and 550 feet to dead center. It would not be until 1925, ten years after the park opened, that a Boston player would be able to reach the left-field seats even in batting practice; some weeks after outfielder Bernie Neis managed that feat, New York catcher Frank Snyder walloped the first official home run into the area. (The dimensions were later shortened.)

As for the teams that played within such grand confines, Gaffney quickly tired of Ward's inability to complete deals with other National League clubs and forced him out of the organization. Although nominally taking charge himself, he brought in George Stallings as manager and chief negotiator, giving the veteran baseball man a free hand to clean house with the cellar-dwelling team. The result in 1914 was the Miracle Braves world championship. But with the club not quite able to repeat in 1915 and faced with too many due notes over the construction of Braves Field, Gaffney decided to get out while the getting was good. A terse announcement in January 1916 said only that he had sold the franchise to a consortium of bankers and politicians for a price ''considerably higher'' than the $187,000 he had produced at Ward's urging.

JOHN GAFFNEY

Gaffney was the first full-time umpire. Whereas earlier arbiters had been locals paid $5 a game by the visiting team, he drew a salary and road expenses from the National League, eventually receiving more for his services than most players got for theirs. During a fourteen-year career that began in 1884 and ended in 1900 and that included service with the American Association and the Players League, Gaffney popularized the practice of working behind the plate; he moved behind the pitcher only when men were on base.

JOHN GAHERIN

Appointed in 1967 as the first head of major league baseball's Player Relations Committee, Gaherin made his mark by warning the owners that the reserve clause would not hold up and that they would eventually lose on the issue of free agency, and by arguing for a negotiated settlement on the issue. The former labor negotiator for the newspaper and airline industries was fired early in 1977 after reaching an accord on the details of free agency with the Players Association in the wake of the Messersmith-McNally case. Accused of having given away the store, he was essentially canned for failing to prevent what he had predicted would happen unless his bosses changed their approach.

ANDRES GALARRAGA

When Galarraga won the 1993 National League batting title as a member of the Rockies, it marked the first time that a player on a new expansion club led the way in any significant hitting category. The first baseman's .370 average was also the highest posted by a right-handed hitter in fifty-four years, since Joe DiMaggio's .381 in 1939. In his two previous seasons, the injury-afflicted and strikeout-prone Galarraga had batted only .243 and .219.

DANIEL GALBREATH

Galbreath took over as president of the Pirates from his father, John, just as the club was pulling up stakes after sixty-one years at Forbes Field and moving into Three Rivers Stadium. It proved a symbolic coincidence insofar as the stadium came to dominate his ownership.

John Galbreath, a Columbus realtor and horse breeder, had been in Pittsburgh's executive suites since 1946, when he joined Indianapolis banker Frank McKinney and entertainer Bing Crosby in purchasing the franchise from Barney Dreyfuss's widow. After buying out McKinney, Galbreath had entrusted the club's baseball affairs, first to Branch Rickey and then to Joe L. Brown, throughout the 1950s and 1960s. With only one pennant to show for all that time, however, Daniel arrived on the scene with a decidedly less passive approach. The good news was that Pittsburgh won Eastern Division titles in 1970, 1971, 1972, 1974, and 1975, as well as a world championship in 1971; the bad news was that the new president was far from satisfied with merely one World Series appearance, and pressured Brown to resign. Fraying Galbreath's nerves even more was the severe economic weather that hung over Pittsburgh for most of the 1970s, sharply reducing attendance.

In 1981 Galbreath decided to make Three Rivers Stadium the focus of his exasperation, and demanded that the city renegotiate its rental terms; among other things, he wanted City Hall to foot the bill for repairs, maintenance, and new access roads, claiming this was the only way for the franchise to reverse a reported $6 million in losses and prevent it from having to be sold or transferred to another city. As soon as the latter threat was aired, New Orleans Superdome general manager Cliff Wallace sought to lure the club to Louisiana—a bid that prompted the city of Pittsburgh to file a preventive suit.

Galbreath kept up the pressure over the next couple of years, winning nominal concessions here and there but never disavowing completely persistent rumors of an imminent move by the club from Pittsburgh. In 1983 he tried another revenue path by taking on Warner Communications as a 48 percent partner; but after only a few months of reports that the media giant's involve-

ment was a prelude to some pay-per-view scheme covering Pirate games, both sides abruptly announced that they wanted out from one another. Finally, in 1986, Galbreath sold the franchise to a local coalition from both public and private sectors headed by Mayor Richard Caliguiri.

DENNY GALEHOUSE

Galehouse contributed so mightily to Boston baseball lore that Red Sox fans presented him with the new first name of Why—as in Why Galehouse? The question was asked in 1948 after manager Joe McCarthy ignored his rested aces Mel Parnell and Ellis Kinder in favor of the journeyman right-hander for the winner-take-all playoff game that year against Cleveland. Galehouse was quickly battered around by the Indians, giving Cleveland the pennant.

JIM GALLAGHER

A sportswriter, Gallagher was hired as the Cubs general manager in 1941 after boasting that he could do better than the club's incumbent front-office people. He spent most of the next fifteen years making bad trades, skirmishing with perceived rivals within the organization, and being bounced up and down the franchise hierarchy. During his first few years as head of baseball operations, Gallagher also assured the hostility of the Chicago press toward the club by refusing to announce player transactions and even having beat writers informed of daily lineups through the field announcer just prior to the start of games. His reasoning was that local newspapers had attacked the franchise unfairly, so he owed them little cooperation. Most of the players Gallagher was talked out of by other general managers ended up on the Dodgers; prominent among them were future Hall of Famer Billy Herman and Eddie Stanky. Not that this won him gratitude from Brooklyn president Branch Rickey, who once described the official as "nothing more than a glorified office boy."

Even Gallagher had his moments. The first was in persuading owner Phil Wrigley that Chicago needed a farm system if it expected to compete in the National League. Although the minor league chain never achieved the productivity of the Brooklyn and St. Louis systems, it at least made the club less reliant on short-range deals. Gallagher was also nimble enough not to look a gift horse in the mouth when the Yankees offered him Hank Borowy in 1945—a move that was decisive in the team's last pennant. His own best deal was acquiring outfielders Hank Sauer and Frankie Baumholtz from the Reds in 1949.

During World War II, Gallagher offered a proposal that won the enmity of players and owners for diametrically opposed reasons. Arguing that the war would not only pare major league talent to the bone but would also leave a scarcity of good players after the hostilities because of expected casualties, he dusted off an early-century scheme for pooling those who remained among big league clubs. According to Gallagher, such a syndication plan should eventually lead to a rewriting of baseball contracts, including the elimination of the reserve clause. While players objected to the prospect of losing their contractual rights, owners blasted the idea as a threat to franchise integrity. For St. Louis owner Sam Breadon, for instance, the Gallagher proposal was "unthinkable, unworkable . . . an offspring of socialism that has no place in baseball."

PUD GALVIN (Hall of Fame, 1965)

As troublesome as he was effective in a fourteen-year career, primarily with the National League Buffalo Bisons and Pittsburgh clubs in three different leagues, Galvin was the major leagues' first 300-game winner. A holdout in 1880, the right-hander hid in a California outlaw league until Buffalo sent someone to retrieve him. Three years later he agreed to jump to the American Association's Pittsburgh Alleghenys but reneged under threats of legal action. Back with the Bisons, the disgruntled pitcher almost bolted again when he decided the team's new blue uniforms made him look fat. Between 1890 and 1892 Galvin faced Tim Keefe in the first four meetings of 300-game winners and the last such contests until Phil Niekro and Don Sutton opposed each other in 1986. Galvin ended with 361 victories.

CHICK GANDIL

If any of the Black Sox players can be said to be responsible for the scandal surrounding the 1919 World Series, it was Gandil. It was the first

baseman who planned the fix as early as August, initiated contacts with gamblers three weeks before the Series, and kept the plot moving in the face of various double crosses and defections. He was also the only one of the Chicago Eight not devastated by Commissioner Kenesaw Landis's 1920 ban of the implicated White Sox players, since he had already retired. Prior to his involvement in the scandal, Gandil had been a .277 hitter for Chicago, Washington, and Cleveland. In 1927 he resurfaced briefly to support charges by Swede Risberg, another of the outlawed White Sox players, that Ty Cobb's Tigers had thrown back-to-back doubleheaders to Chicago in 1917. The charges were dismissed by Landis but prompted a series of new regulations covering gambling in baseball.

RON GANT

Gant incurred the most expensive broken leg in baseball history in 1994 when the injury cost him $4 million. The outfielder was disabled by a motorcycle accident shortly after signing a one-year, $5 million pact with the Braves. Despite the fact that Gant had provided most of the right-handed power for three Atlanta division winners between 1991 and 1993, the team decided to cut its losses by paying him a required $900,000 before a March 15 spring training deadline and release him as a free agent.

While with the Braves, Gant had joined the select company of Willie Mays and Bobby Bonds as only the third big leaguer to hit 30 home runs and steal 30 bases in back-to-back years. In 1990 Gant bashed 33 homers with 32 thefts, then the following year went 34 and 32. He was signed by the Reds while rehabilitating in June 1994.

JOE GARAGIOLA

Garagiola was one of the first players to turn a mediocre playing career (1946–54) into the fodder for a successful sportscasting one. Especially after the publication of his best-selling *Baseball Is a Funny Game*, he became identified with the foibles of playing with such bad teams as the Pirates and the Cubs of the 1950s. Garagiola wasn't quite so comic, however, when he was one of the more conspicuous members of the Cardinal teams of the late 1940s who never missed an opportunity to spike Jackie Robinson or taunt the Brooklyn infielder from the bench; in the 1970s he also testified on the side of the owners against Curt Flood's challenge to the reserve clause. In recent years he has been a visible spokesman for the BAT assistance program for needy former major leaguers.

GENE GARBER

Except for 4 starts for the 1973 Royals, Garber walked out of the bullpen for his 931 appearances over nineteen seasons. His most publicized relief appearance came on August 1, 1978, when, as a member of the Braves, he fanned Pete Rose in his final at-bat to end the Cincinnati star's 44-game hitting streak. A year later, the sidewinding right-hander went into the record books himself for losing 16 games for Atlanta—the most ever suffered in a season by a reliever.

DANNY GARDELLA

For the first couple of years of his brief major league career in 1944 and 1945, Gardella mainly entertained sportswriters with his efforts to play the outfield, and his New York Giants teammates with an endless series of practical gags. He was such an inept defensive player that one wit thought it informative to add the word "unassisted" to a recording of his putouts; he was so committed to getting a laugh that he once spent a week portraying himself to a roommate as a would-be-suicide, then one morning threw open the window of their twentieth-floor hotel room and "hid" out on the ledge while raising blood-curdling screams of a suicide plunging to his death. But that Gardella ended in 1946, when he New York outfielder became one of the first major leaguers to accept cash from the Pasquel brothers and jump to Mexico.

Like the other jumpers, Gardella was banned from baseball for five years by Commissioner Happy Chandler; unlike them, he didn't take the ban, and after returning to the United States, filed a $300,000 suit in terms guaranteed to question baseball's exemption from antitrust laws. Although the basis for his suit was found invalid in a first go-round in July 1948, an appeals tribunal not only upheld his claim about the illegality of the Chandler blacklist but also issued a blistering indictment of the major leagues that effectively reversed the 1922 Supreme Court decision that declared that the sport did not engage in interstate commerce; a principal point of the ruling was that the radio and television coverage of games alone constituted an adequate definition of interstate commerce.

With a U.S. Supreme Court hearing on the Gardella suit imminent and fearing too many headlines until the final verdict, Chandler was persuaded by the leagues to drop his ban and announce an "amnesty" for players he now regarded as "basically good boys." The ploy worked: A few weeks later, Gardella settled out of court for $60,000. His own hopes of returning to the majors, however, were quickly scotched: He managed only one further at-bat—for the 1950 Cardinals.

WAYNE GARLAND

Garland received the first career-long contract after the coming of free agency, signing a $2.5 million, ten-year pact with Cleveland in 1976. When he told his mother the news, she replied: "You're not worth it." Many in Cleveland agreed with her when the right-hander, who had won 20 for Baltimore the year before, could manage only 13 victories and then suffered a rotator cuff injury, effectively ending his career.

STEVE GARVEY

The first-base anchor for the long-running Dodger infield (with Davey Lopes, Bill Russell, and Ron Cey) in the 1970s, Garvey managed the difficult trick of having one public image overwhelm appreciable diamond skills, then having a second public image completely contradict the first one. As a player for Los Angeles, he was second only to manager Tom Lasorda as a relentless flack for the "bleeding Dodger blue" way of playing baseball, honoring one's parents, and saluting the flag. Constantly portrayed as Mr. Clean, he had to labor for years to persuade cynical observers that he was in fact a durable performer (he still holds the National League record of 1,207 consecutive games played); a great clutch hitter; and, despite not having an arm, the savior of the club's infield defense through acrobatic leaps for the errant tosses of Lopes, Russell, and

Cey. The cynical observers included some of his own teammates, who referred to him as "Senator" for his political ambitions and with whom he got into more than one clubhouse scuffle over what was perceived as press favoritism for his willingness to accommodate reporters. On the other hand, he clashed with Lasorda following the 1977 World Series for showing enough sportsmanship to applaud Reggie Jackson on the field as the Yankee slugger was rounding first base after hitting his third home run in the final game of the postseason competition.

Typical of his ability to inspire public enthusiasm was his election as a write-in candidate to the starting lineup of the All-Star Game in 1974, the first time a player was chosen for the honor without having his name on the ballot; equally typical of his ability to take advantage of the spotlight was his MVP performance in the contest. In 1978 he became the first player to earn Most Valuable Player honors in two All-Star games. Moving on to San Diego as a free agent in 1983, Garvey was again in the limelight when he led the Padres to a come-from-behind victory over the Cubs in the following year's League Championship Series.

After his first, supposedly storybook marriage dissolved to national headlines, there came disclosures that Mr. Clean had spent his off-field hours impregnating two women while pursuing a third for marriage. This prompted Southern California bumper stickers declaring: STEVE GARVEY IS NOT *MY* PADRE.

ELMER GEDEON

An outfielder who had a handful of at-bats for the Senators in 1939, Gedeon was one of only two major leaguers killed in action in World War II. A member of the United States Air Corps, he was shot down over France in April 1944. The only other fatality during the war was Harry O'Neill, who died during the fighting at Iwo Jima. O'Neill had gone behind the plate as a late-inning defensive replacement in a single game for the Athletics in 1939.

JOE GEDEON

A light-hitting second baseman for three American League teams between 1913 and 1920, Ged-

eon became the "ninth man out" in the Black Sox scandal when Commissioner Kenesaw Landis banished him from baseball for "guilty knowledge" of the affair. A friend of Swede Risberg, the infielder had, at the Chicago shortstop's suggestion, bet on the Reds in the Series and sat in on a meeting with gambler Carl Zork and St. Louis theater manager Harry Redmon to discuss the plot. Redmon and Gedeon, then with the Browns, were "the St. Louis parties" White Sox owner Charlie Comiskey later admitted had informed him of the fix just after the Series. Gedeon later testified before the grand jury that indicted seven of the players and stood ready to appear at their trial but was never called. He was blackballed by Landis several months after the commissioner banned the eight White Sox players named in the affair.

LOU GEHRIG (Hall of Fame, 1939)

For all his accomplishments, Gehrig is still the most underrated player in the history of the game. He is almost always thought of as The Iron Horse, whose consecutive-game streak was ended by a disease later named after him, when not being remembered as "the guy who hit all those homers the year Babe Ruth hit 60." In fact, the left-hand-hitting first baseman retired with a prodigious batting record that could only have been obscured by the abruptness of its end and only overshadowed by the even more prodigious feats (partly made possible by having Gehrig bat behind him in the batting order) and outsized personality of his teammate and sometime rival. After Ruth's departure in 1934, Gehrig had to share the spotlight with, first, the anticipation surrounding the impending arrival of Joe DiMaggio from the Pacific Coast League, and then, from 1936 on, with the center fielder's actual presence. John McGraw and Mickey Cochrane also stole some of Gehrig's thunder—in the first case, on Gehrig's greatest day; in the second, in his greatest season.

In his seventeen-year (1923–39) all-Yankee career, Gehrig hit .340 (to Ruth's .342), slugged .632 (third on the all-time list behind Ruth and Ted Williams), drove in 1,990 runs (third behind Hank Aaron and Ruth), and knocked 493 homers. He reached the thirty-mark in homers ten times but failed to hit more than Ruth until 1934, the outfielder's last season with New York, and in 1931 was relegated to a tie (with Ruth) for the league lead when a baserunning lapse involving shortstop Lyn Lary negated one round-tripper. Gehrig topped .700 in slugging average three times, leading the American League in that category twice but losing out with such totals as .765 (the fourth highest ever) in 1927 and .721 in 1930—to the Bambino's .772 and .732, respectively. For twelve consecutive seasons Gehrig's batting average topped .300, and he parlayed his lone batting championship (1934) into a Triple Crown—a distinction never gained by Ruth and ignored by sportswriters, who selected Detroit's Cochrane as the AL's Most Valuable Player. The New York first baseman did win two MVP trophies (in 1927 and 1936) to Ruth's one, but one of them came only because Ruth had already taken the honors in 1923 and the rules of the day precluded anyone from repeating. Appearing in seven World Series, he was, if anything, even better than in regular-season play, ending up in the all-time top ten in every significant offensive category.

Among Gehrig's feats that neither Ruth nor anyone else ever matched are: thirteen consecutive seasons with both 100 runs scored and 100 RBIs, 200 hits and 100 walks in the same season seven times, a major league-record 23-grand-slam home runs, and the best ratio of homers (49) to strikeouts (31) of any player with 40 or more round-trippers (in 1934); he also holds an AL season record for his 184 RBIs in 1931. On June 3, 1932, Gehrig became the first American Leaguer to hit four homers in a game, following them in his fifth at-bat with his longest shot of the day but one that was caught by Al Simmons at the farthest reaches of center field at Philadelphia's Shibe Park; coincidentally, McGraw retired the same day after thirty-one years as Giants' manager, stealing all the headlines the following morning.

Throughout the 1920s, Gehrig and Ruth, despite the glaring differences in their personalities, had both a social and a business relationship: They hunted and played bridge together and made extra money barnstorming together in the off-season. A rift developed between them when Gehrig declined Ruth's suggestion that they both hold out

Lou Gehrig was the quiet hero of Yankee dynasties in both the 1920s and 1930s. Photo compliments of Sharon Guynup.

for more money in 1929, intensifying into a feud when Gehrig's mother commented that Ruth and his wife failed to measure up to her impeccable standards of child rearing. The two men did not speak for several years, until a long-retired Ruth, in a moment captured in one of the more memorable sports photographs, impetuously threw his arms around an already dying Gehrig during ceremonies held between games of the July 4, 1939, doubleheader to honor the Yankee captain.

The Gehrig myth, as it deals with his on-field performance, involves, almost exclusively, the consecutive-game streak that began when he pinch hit for shortstop Pee Wee Wanninger on June 1, 1925, and that did not end until he took himself out of the lineup on May 2, 1939. In between, he played in 2,130 consecutive games, but not in all of them at first base and not for nine innings in all of them. The streak at first base ended at 885 games on the final day of the 1930 season, when he played in the outfield. After another game in the outfield in 1933, Gehrig preserved the streak, despite an attack of lumbago, by appearing in the lineup as the shortstop and leadoff batter in a 1934 road contest only long enough to come to the plate once before taking an unaccustomed place on the bench; Gehrig being Gehrig, he singled to begin the game.

The rest of the legend involves Gehrig's sudden affliction with the rare and invariably fatal amyotrophic lateral sclerosis in 1939. Weak throughout spring training that year, he realized his problem was serious when teammates congratulated him after making a routine first-to-pitcher play; he ended his streak, and learned his fate at the Mayo Clinic several weeks later. The Hall of Fame waived its customary five-year waiting period and gave him entry immediately. On July 4, Lou Gehrig Day, in a moment captured in the Hollywood film *Pride of the Yankees* starring Gary Cooper, he delivered an emotional speech, ending with ''I may have been given a bad break, but I have an awful lot to live for. All in all, I can say on this day that I consider myself the luckiest man on the face of the earth.'' He died less than two years later, just weeks shy of his thirty-eighth birthday.

CHARLIE GEHRINGER (Hall of Fame, 1949)

If Ty Cobb had ever had an alter ego, it would have been his protégé Gehringer, dubbed The Mechanical Man for the unassuming way that he ripped apart American League pitching for nineteen years (1924–42) as a second baseman for the Tigers while saying practically nothing to anybody. The convergence of his diamond skills and personality was never more on display than near the end of his career, when the franchise sponsored a Charlie Gehringer Day at which the left-handed hitter was presented with a set of right-handed golf clubs. In the game that followed, he hit the first pitch thrown to him for a home run, banged out three other safeties, then won the contest by stealing home. Years later he admitted that he had learned how to play golf right-handed so as not to embarrass his well-wishers.

Gehringer came under Cobb's wing in 1924, when the then manager of the Tigers warned the prospect to ignore advice from every direction that he change his batting stance. Cobb was still in the dugout when the infielder won the second-base job with what turned out to be a mild offensive performance. From that point on, however, Gehringer compiled a career .320 average by hitting over .300 thirteen times (including a league-leading .371 in 1937), banging out 200 hits seven times, clouting 30 or more doubles ten times, ending up in double figures for triples seven times, scoring 100 runs twelve times, and knocking in 100 runs seven times. Defensively, he paced the

AL in fielding average six times, in putouts three times, and in assists a record seven times. His best years were 1929, when he led the league in eight offensive and defensive categories while batting .339, and 1937, when he took MVP honors for his batting crown, 209 hits, 40 doubles, 96 RBIs, and 133 runs scored.

In the 1930s, Gehringer was lumped together with Hank Greenberg and Goose Goslin as Detroit's G-Men—a takeoff on the enormous publicity being given at the time to the FBI's battles with notorious criminals. But he never quite lost his greater reputation as The Mechanical Man, especially after he averaged the same .320 in his three World Series appearances in 1934, 1935, and 1940 that he compiled in regular-season performances. His 10-for-20 in six All-Star games represents the highest average for any player with at least that number of at-bats.

Gehringer went into the service in 1942. In the early 1950s he served briefly as Detroit's general manager and was later kicked upstairs to a vice presidency.

PHIL GEIER

When Phillies owner John Rogers balked at the asking price of $1,500 for outfielder prospect Geier, the owner of the Fall River club in the New England League offered to add an infielder to the package. Geier went on to hit .249 in a five-year major league career (between 1896 and 1904) punctuated with frequent and lengthy trips to the minors; throw-in Nap Lajoie went on to the Hall of Fame.

BERNICE GERA

Gera was the first woman to umpire a professional baseball game—and quit immediately after her debut. The Queens housewife officiated at one contest in the Class A New York-Penn League on June 24, 1972, after fighting through the New York courts for the right to practice her profession. Resigning immediately after her first game, Gera placed the blame less on an ugly confrontation with Auburn manager Nolan Campbell during the contest than on the hostility of the league and other umpires and anonymous threats received in the weeks leading up to her lone appearance.

Bernice Gera calls out a runner in a 1968 semi-pro game.
National Baseball Library, Cooperstown, N.Y.

DICK GERNERT

When the Red Sox traded first baseman Gernert to the Cubs in 1959 in return for Dave Hillman and Jim Marshall, it marked the first modern interleague trade not requiring waivers.

CESAR GERONIMO

Geronimo's Gold Glove work in center field for the Big Red Machine in the 1970s was not matched by his hitting, leading to several dubious records. In the 1975 League Championship Series against Pittsburgh, he fanned in seven consecutive appearances—contributing significantly to his other playoff mark of going 30 straight at-bats without a hit. Somewhat more incidentally, he was Bob Gibson's 3,000 strikeout victim on July 17, 1974—then happened to be in the batting box again when Nolan Ryan chalked up number 3,000 on July 4, 1980.

BART GIAMATTI

The seventh commissioner of baseball, Giamatti found himself embroiled in the Pete Rose scandal for every one of his 154 days in office in 1989. By his own claims, on the other hand, he never spent a minute on the established collusion of National League owners against free agents while serving as president of the loop between 1986 and 1989.

A professor of Renaissance studies at Yale University and an unabashed Red Sox fan, Giamatti first came to the attention of baseball owners through his nonscholarly, often mawkish writings on baseball and through his truculence with unions while serving as president of Yale. Named NL chief in December 1986, he took office just as the league's owners—in common with those of the American League—were agreeing not to go after one another's eligible free agents as a ploy against further player salary increases. Asked once if such collusion didn't amount to an attack on the integrity of the game since it restrained clubs from putting the best available players on the field, Giamatti said only that he had never heard a whisper of any such conspiracy among the owners.

By contrast, he heard plenty about Rose. Already in 1988, as NL president, Giamatti suspended the Cincinnati manager for thirty days for pushing umpire Dave Pallone during an argument at Riverfront Stadium. Even as he was being sworn in as Peter Ueberroth's successor as commissioner on April 1, 1989, Giamatti was aware of stories that Rose's known addiction to gambling had included wagers on baseball games—an infraction that carried an automatic one-year suspension at best; but that if it also involved Reds games, threatened lifetime banishment. An investigation conducted for Giamatti by Washington lawyer John M. Dowd dragged on interminably, with columnists and television commentators uncovering more and more sordid details almost daily. Giamatti finally presented the all-time-hit leader with the charges against him on May 11. If the purpose of the delay had been careful preparation to avoid litigation, the commissioner was sorely disappointed because Rose immediately filed suit to bar Giamatti from passing judgment on him on the grounds that he had already made up his mind. The impasse was resolved on August 24 when the two men released a joint statement in which the manager accepted permanent banishment and abandoned his legal redress. For his part, Giamatti stipulated that he "will not make any formal findings or determinations on any matter including without limitation the allegation that Peter Edward Rose bet on any major league baseball games," then turned around in the press conference that followed and informally accused Rose of betting on major league contests—including Reds games. Eight days later the heavy-smoking Giamatti was felled by a fatal heart attack.

TED GIANNOULAS

Dressed as the San Diego Chicken, Giannoulas was the first of the grandstand mascots that became a staple of big league franchises in the 1970s. After some years of entertaining fans by cavorting atop dugouts and along outfield fences at Jack Murphy Stadium, he got into a squabble with the Padres over the patent rights on his costumed character and had to take it elsewhere in the majors and in the minors without reference to San Diego.

BOB GIBSON (Hall of Fame, 1981)

Gibson was a byword for competitiveness in his fifteen-year career with the Cardinals in the 1960s and 1970s. The asthmatic right-hander won 251 games (with an ERA of 2.91) in anchoring otherwise unstable St. Louis mound staffs, along the way becoming the first pitcher since Walter Johnson to strike out 3,000 batters. Gibson's grit was never more in evidence than in 1967, when he was sidelined for two months with a broken leg but then came off the disabled list to pitch three complete-game victories against the Red Sox in the World Series. In 1968 Gibson was the Pitcher of the Year in the Year of the Pitcher when he racked up 22 victories with a record-breaking 1.12 ERA; while assuring himself both the MVP and Cy Young awards for that effort, he also fanned 17 Tigers in the opening game of the World Series to set another record. Although his 35 strikeouts against Detroit established yet another World Series mark, he ended up on the losing end of a classic mound duel with Mickey Lolich in the deciding seventh game.

Even with his mound heroics, and conspicuous talents as a hitter and fielder (nine straight Gold Gloves between 1965 and 1973), Gibson generated almost as many tales for his fierce aggressiveness. In one spring training game against the Mets in the early 1970s, for instance, he and the equally competitive Tom Seaver startled players on both teams by hitting one another in a mutual declaration of war for the coming season. Intolerant of mound conferences, Gibson also chased his receiver, Tim McCarver, away on one occasion, telling him to "get behind the plate—the only thing you know about pitching is how hard it is to hit." Before joining St. Louis, Gibson played for the Harlem Globetrotters for a year.

JOSH GIBSON (Hall of Fame, 1972)

Gibson has been called the black Babe Ruth, but so impressive was his ability to hit for average as well as for tape-measure distances that, Ruth's own accomplishments in these areas notwithstanding, Gibson is regarded by some as the greatest hitter of all time.

The right-hand-hitting catcher has been credited with more than 900 home runs and a lifetime batting average higher than .350 in a career that lasted from 1930 to 1946. Included in the homer total were 9 league-leading figures in North America, 44 in only 450 at-bats in the Mexican League, and 13 in a mere 123 at-bats one winter in Puerto Rico; his lifetime average was built on several seasons when he topped the .400 mark, and two (1938 and 1939) in which he not only hit higher than .400 but also posted slugging averages in excess of 1.000. What's more, his round-trippers were rarely of the dime-store variety. Gibson hit the longest verified shot in Yankee Stadium, a blast that struck two feet from the top of the wall behind the center-field bleachers, some 580 feet from home plate; an eyewitness account by infielder Jack Marshall of the Chicago American Giants had him knocking one over the third deck next to the left-field bullpen in 1934 for the only ball ever hit out of Yankee Stadium. His blasts were measured regularly at more than 500 feet.

Gibson teamed with Satchel Paige on the Pittsburgh Crawfords for parts of the 1936 and 1937 seasons to form the most popular battery in black baseball history, but it was with the Homestead Grays that he earned his greatest fame. Missing only two of the Grays' nine consecutive Negro National League pennant-winning teams between 1937 and 1945 (he played in Venezuela and Mexico in 1940 and in Mexico in 1941), he attracted the attention of at least two major league owners, Pittsburgh's Bill Benswanger and Washington's Clark Griffith. Benswanger actually offered Gibson and first baseman Buck Leonard tryouts in

1939, but then, depending upon who is telling the story, either thought better of the consequences of trying to integrate the Pirates or was talked out of the move by Grays owner Cum Posey. It was also Posey, who years later forced Gibson to abandon the Mexican League by slapping him with a $10,000 lawsuit and claiming title to his house, even though he always claimed that his star slugger lacked the color to make his relatively high salary worthwhile.

Gibson's health began to deteriorate after he returned to the United States. In 1943 a brain tumor left him in a coma for ten days and with recurring headaches afterward. To kill the pain, he turned to drink while continuing to be a formidable threat at the plate if not as dominating as before. He was felled by a fatal stroke in January 1947, just after his thirty-fifth birthday and just before Jackie Robinson made his debut with the Dodgers.

KIRK GIBSON

Gibson hit the most Hollywoodian home run in World Series history as a member of the Dodgers in 1988, when he hobbled up to home plate with a severe leg injury in the bottom of the ninth inning of the first game and, with two strikes on him, belted a two-run blast to defeat Oakland's Dennis Eckersley. It was Gibson's only appearance in the Series, won by Los Angeles in 5 games. The club reached postseason play primarily because of Gibson's MVP season. The left-hand-swinging outfielder had signed with the Dodgers from Detroit that year after an arbitrator's ruling that he had been a victim of collusion among owners against free agents two years earlier.

FLOYD GIEBELL

Giebell was promoted from the minors by Detroit at the end of the 1940 season and immediately thrown into a pennant-vital game against Cleveland ace Bob Feller, on September 27. The rookie right-hander defeated the Indians, 2–0, to clinch the flag for the Tigers. Detroit manager Del Baker defended the move by saying he didn't want to ''waste'' one of his veteran pitchers against Feller with 2 games still left on the sched-

ule. As for Giebell, it was his third and last major league victory.

WARREN GILES (Hall of Fame, 1979)

As National League president between 1951 and 1969, Giles usually played Tweedledum to Commissioner Ford Frick's Tweedledee in rubber-stamping whatever Walter O'Malley or other influential owners wanted. Among other events that Giles presided over in relative silence were the franchise shifts of the Dodgers and Giants to California, relocations by the Braves from Boston and then from Milwaukee, and the 1962 NL expansion to include the Astros and Mets. In one of his rare public frothings, on the other hand, he lashed into his American League counterpart, Joe Cronin, in the late 1960s for breaking an agreement that committed both circuits to holding off on further expansion until the early 1970s. Cronin's decision to bring the timetable forward to 1969—made under heavy political pressure from Kansas City—disrupted an O'Malley schedule for expanding the leagues simultaneously, and the NL, too, was forced to push things ahead to 1969 to accommodate the Expos and Padres.

Prior to pushing paper in the league office, Giles had served as general manager and then president of the Reds. As Larry MacPhail's successor in Cincinnati in 1936, in fact, Giles was the one who put the final touches on the teams that won pennants in 1939 and 1940 and the world championship in the latter year. His most inspired moves as the head of Cincinnati's baseball operations in the prewar years included hiring Bill McKechnie as manager, obtaining third baseman-turned-pitcher Bucky Walters from the Phillies, and shortening the distances to the outfield walls of Crosley Field; the effect of the latter change was still being felt in the 1950s with the home run production of the first version of the Big Red Machine. During the war, when Giles saw his power show menaced by the significantly less resilient balata ball, he threatened to use his own balls at Reds home games unless Commissioner Kenesaw Landis and the Spalding company did something about the horsehided rock in use; it was largely because of the threat that the balata ball was phased out even before the end of the war.

Several noted front-office executives began their careers as assistants to Giles in Cincinnati; among them were Gabe Paul and Frank Lane.

WARREN GILL

First baseman Gill's single year of major league service for the Pirates in 1908 was enough to help set the stage for the most controversial gaffe in baseball history. In a September 4 game against the Cubs, he was on first base in the tenth inning of a scoreless contest when Owen Wilson singled in the winning run from third. Gill, however, went no more than 40 feet toward second before turning around and running into the dugout to celebrate with his teammates. Chicago second baseman Johnny Evers called for the ball with the intention of recording a force-out at second base, but umpire Hank O'Day had also run off the field. Chicago protested unsuccessfully that Gill's failure to touch second and Evers's force erased the winning run. Later that month, the same Evers and O'Day were key costars of an identical play that became known as Merkle's Boner and that forced an unprecedented makeup game between Chicago and New York for the National League pennant.

PAT GILLICK

Gillick built up the expansion Blue Jays according to a Dodger model but with significant Yankee pieces. In contrast to other front-office executives for new clubs, he also stayed around to tinker, then retinker with the original model.

Gillick's Dodger inspirations were largely the result of being hired for Toronto as player personnel director in 1976 by the organization's first president, Peter Bavasi. To get to Canada, however, he had to survive a protracted melodrama with George Steinbrenner to get out of the three months still left on a Yankees contract. For no better reason than that he didn't like his employees quitting before they were fired, Steinbrenner issued one demand after another, hoping that Bavasi would run out of patience and hire somebody else. Instead it was Gillick who lost patience, first threatening to go to *The New York Times* with the story and then rebuffing still another demand from the Yankees by telling George Steinbrenner to ''go fuck himself.'' Although one of the conditions made along the way was that he would not tamper with any Yankee personnel at his new post, raiding New York's minor league system became one of Gillick's most profitable exercises for the Blue Jays; among those he picked up in drafts or exchanges were second baseman Damaso Garcia and first basemen Willie Upshaw and Fred McGriff.

Like the Blue Jays as a whole, Gillick earned building approval through the mid-1980s, but then came under increasing attack for not being able to nudge the team up the final rung from contender to pennant winner; by the end of the 1990 season he had drawn the mocking nickname of Stand Pat for his inability to pull off any major deal. That ended in a flash with the off-season blockbuster acquisitions of slugger Joe Carter and second baseman Roberto Alomar from San Diego in exchange for McGriff and shortstop Tony Fernandez, and with another deal, which imported center fielder Devon White. It was the start of one big name after another arriving in Toronto: Dave Winfield, Jack Morris, and David Cone in 1992; Paul Molitor, Dave Stewart, and Rickey Henderson in 1993. The payback was back-to-back world championships and Gillick's consolidation as the longest-running executive for an expansion organization. He retired after the 1994 season.

JAMES A. GILMORE

The reason the Federal League was able to transform itself from a struggling minor league into a threat to the National and American leagues was the work of Gilmore. Elected president of the FL in 1914 as part of the strategy to gain major status, the millionaire coal dealer persuaded Charles Weeghman to take over a majority interest in the Chicago Whales from him, and Philip Ball of St. Louis and Robert B. Ward of Brooklyn to back clubs as well; Gilmore later brought oil magnate Harry Sinclair into the fold as an all-purpose angel. In 1914 Gilmore audaciously suggested that the Indianapolis Hoosiers, winners of the FL pennant, play a true world's championship against the World Series victor; a year later, he issued another futile challenge to the established leagues, this time with the twist that the three first-place teams—the Phillies, Red Sox, and Whales—engage in a round-robin World Series.

In January 1915 Gilmore initiated a federal lawsuit challenging the monopoly of the two established leagues, but the litigation stalled in the court of Judge Kenesaw Landis until the Feds had already reached a settlement with their adversaries. The terms of the accord allowed Ball and Weeghman to purchase the Browns and Cubs, respectively, and Sinclair to sell off players and come away from the venture with a profit. From his vantage point outside baseball, Gilmore declared in 1916: "There is no room for three major leagues. The reserve clause, to which I objected, is vitally important to clean promotion of the sport."

AL GIONFRIDDO

Gionfriddo's initial claim to fame was as the outfielder who brought Branch Rickey $100,000 of Pittsburgh's money as part of the Brooklyn executive's dumping of five players on the Pirates in May 1947. In the World Series that year against the Yankees, however, the speedster also speared a drive by Joe DiMaggio that prompted one of the Hall of Famer's rare shows of exasperation on the field. Gionfriddo was cut by the Dodgers prior to the 1948 season.

JACK GLASSCOCK

In a career that spanned seventeen years, Glasscock jumped leagues three times during the various nineteenth-century turf wars, and was part of the effort to form yet another league in 1894. Two-thirds of the way through the 1884 season, he and two other players left the National League Cleveland Forest Citys for Cincinnati of the upstart Union Association, Glasscock declaring, "I have played long enough for glory, now it is a matter of dollars and cents." A quality shortstop and lifetime .290 hitter, his defection provided a major boost for the Unions. After the 1889 campaign he agreed to leave the NL once again for the Players League, but Pebbly Jack became Judas Jack when he double-jumped back to the NL fold before the start of the next season. In 1894 Glasscock was active in trying to secure financial backing for a Cleveland franchise in the

abortive effort to revive the American Association.

KID GLEASON

The 1919 World Series scandal was something of a payback for Gleason, who came across as a markedly ineffectual Chicago manager after a twenty-two year (1888–1908, 1912) career as one of baseball's all-time snarling personalities. Aside from the fact that he admitted having turned a blind eye to clubhouse tensions throughout the 1919 season, he was even painted by some as an unwitting abettor of the Series fix by urging his players to spend their day off on the eve of the postseason meeting with Cincinnati at a racetrack. Claims of the kind died of their own absurdity, since Gleason was, in fact, the first to report suspicions about the performance of some of his charges to Chicago owner Charlie Comiskey. The accusations still marked quite a distance from the days when Gleason had been more known for spiking, rabbit-punching, or just beating up opponents. Originally a right-handed pitcher with the Phillies, he won 62 games between 1890 and 1891. When he developed a sore arm later in his career, he was converted to a lefty-swinging second baseman more known for defense than offense. Returning to Philadelphia as an infielder in 1903, Gleason was named team captain, and showed how seriously he took the honor by displaying a leather strap and knuckle-duster in his locker.

JOHN GOCHNAUER

The reason Gochnauer lasted two full seasons as Cleveland's shortstop could not have been his ability with either bat or glove. In 1902 and 1903 he put together back-to-back .185 batting averages, the two lowest ever for a player with 400 at-bats; in the latter season he made 98 errors, the most by any twentieth-century major league player.

FRED GOLDSMITH

Despite four 20-plus victory seasons with Chicago in the 1880s, Goldsmith was more noteworthy for demonstrating, on August 16, 1870, that a baseball could be made to curve. Challenged by baseball writer Henry Chadwick, the young right-hander set up two posts separated by twenty feet between the pitcher's box and home plate, and proceeded to throw several pitches that sailed to the right of the first one but to the left of the second. Convinced, Chadwick hailed Goldsmith as the inventor of the curveball—until several years later, when he learned of the earlier claims of Candy Cummings and switched his allegiance. Even though Goldsmith originally credited Yale University pitcher Charles Avery with teaching him the delivery, he later began believing his press clippings and changed his story. Thereafter a chagrined ex-pitcher complaining of having been denied official recognition for his accomplishment, he died in 1939 grasping a sixty-nine-year-old newspaper account of his encounter with Chadwick.

LEFTY GOMEZ (Hall of Fame, 1972)

Gomez was a standout on the staid Bronx Bombers Yankees of the 1930s as much for his zany wit as for his mound performance. In the latter category, he collected 189 wins in fourteen big league seasons (1930–43), all but one game of his career for the New Yorkers. The southpaw had two seasons (1934 and 1937) in which he took the pitching Triple Crown, leading the American League in victories, ERA, and strikeouts. He also topped 20 wins two other times, paced AL hurlers in strikeouts in one additional season, and placed first in shutouts on three occasions. Gomez's six World Series wins are the most by any pitcher without a loss. A notoriously bad hitter (.147 lifetime average), he nevertheless drove across the first run of All-Star competition in the 1933 contest and knocked in the winning run in the final game of the 1937 World Series against the Giants.

Most of the Gomez's barbs were self-deprecatory, many of them involving nemesis Jimmie Foxx, to whom he once refused to pitch, explaining to catcher Bill Dickey, ''Maybe he'll just get tired of waiting and leave.'' Dubbed Goofy by writer Bob Considine, Gomez once stopped a World Series game against the Giants to watch an airplane pass overhead. On another occasion he foiled a perfect double play by taking a ball hit back to him with a runner on first and firing it at second baseman Tony Lazzeri, who was sev-

eral feet from the bag, instead of to shortstop Frank Crosetti, who was covering, then explaining to the startled Lazzeri, ''I was just reading in the paper the other day what a smart fellow you were and I was curious to see what you would do in a spot like that.'' His most famous one-liner was, ''The secret of my success was clean living and a fast outfield.'' But his best was in response to Yankee owner Jacob Ruppert, who sought to slash his salary from $20,000 to $7,500 after a 12–15 record in 1935: ''You keep the salary, I'll take the cut.''

PRESTON GOMEZ

When he took over the Padres in 1969, the Cuban Gomez became the first Latin American to be signed to a regular managerial contract. With both San Diego and later Houston, he infuriated his bosses by yanking pitchers despite the fact that they had hurled eight no-hit innings. He defended the removal of both Clay Kirby in 1970 and Don Wilson in 1974 by noting that both pitchers had been trailing at the time because of a combination of walks and errors. More interested in the box office attraction of a no-hitter for a cellar team than in a relatively meaningless victory, the general managers of both the Padres and Astros used Gomez's win-at-all-costs view as a final excuse for firing him.

Gomez's other obsession was defending against stolen signs. To this end, he worked out separate signs for every one of his players.

RUBEN GOMEZ

Although he had a couple of good seasons as a starting pitcher for the Giants in the 1950s, Gomez gained more notoriety as one of manager Leo Durocher's beanball specialists and as a not especially valiant brawler. Known as El Divino Loco (The Divine Crazy) in his native Puerto Rico, he once plunked Dodger outfielder Carl Furillo with a pitch, prompting the Brooklyn star to charge into the Giants bench; went after Pittsburgh manager Danny Murtaugh with a bat; and slugged it out with teammate Willie Mays. Gomez's most notorious moment on the diamond, however, occurred in 1955, when he hit Milwaukee first baseman Joe Adcock with a pitch, tried to stop Adcock's charge to the mound by firing a second ball at him, and then fled more than 500 feet to the clubhouse in center field with the muscular Braves slugger in pursuit. Once in the clubhouse, Gomez grabbed an ice pick and sought to return to the field after Adcock, but he was knocked to the floor and disarmed by teammates.

In one of his calmer moments, Gomez sparked a revolt by black and Latin players on the Giants for road accommodations equal to those of white teammates. He had his most notable day on the mound at Seals Stadium on April 15, 1958, when he started the first major league game in California, going on to blank the Dodgers for the Giants, 8–0.

GLADYS GOODDING

Organist Goodding was the answer to a hoary New York riddle about the only person to have played for the Dodgers, the hockey Rangers, and the basketball Knicks. Hired by Larry MacPhail in 1942 after he had noticed her impact on Madison Square Garden spectators, she got into trouble almost immediately when she set Ebbets Field fans roaring by playing "Three Blind Mice" at the appearance of the umpires. The tune was especially aimed at umpire Bill Stewart, who worked as a hockey referee in the off-season and who had angered Rangers fans with some questionable calls the previous winter. After Stewart protested to the National League office, Goodding had to stick to more innocuous melodies.

DWIGHT GOODEN

Gooden's physical and drug problems in the 1990s threatened to reduce his once instant-legend status to that of a drawn-out potboiler. Equally important, however, was the impossible point of comparison that the Mets righthander established for himself in 1985—a performance that Hall of Famer Bob Gibson warned even then "will never be bettered by anyone, not even by Gooden."

Gooden burst onto the scene in 1984 with a 17–9 (2.60) mark that netted him Rookie of the Year honors; even more impressive were a rookie-record 276 strikeouts, earning him the sobriquet of Dr. K. He was even better in 1985, becoming the youngest pitcher (he was twenty-one) to win a Cy Young Award and the youngest to win 20 games (24–4, 2.53 ERA); for the sec-

Dwight Gooden became Dr. K in recognition of his rookie strikeout records, but then began striking out on his career. Photo compliments of the New York Mets.

ond straight year, he also paced the NL in strikeouts, this time with 268. He was so dominating during the season that Las Vegas bookmakers refused to accept bets on the Mets when he was scheduled to pitch.

From that point on, Gooden began disappointing the gods. In 1986 he again struck out 200, but declined to 17 wins. In 1987 he underwent therapy for drug abuse. In 1991 he suffered a rotator cuff injury that sidelined him for a good part of the season. In 1992 he was named with teammates Darryl Boston and Vince Coleman for allegedly raping a woman hanging around with the team in spring training (the charges were ultimately shelved). In both 1993 and 1994 he lost substantial time to other injuries. Even worse, he was suspended for sixty days in 1994 for having failed the drug tests he had been obligated to submit to since 1987, then failed a couple more while ostensibly undergoing treatment during his suspension.

By the mid-1990s, Gooden still had only his Cy Young season as a 20-victory year and had declined perceptibly enough in his strikeout rate to have lost his sobriquet as Dr. K. His sixty-day suspension in 1994 also cost him his decade-long standing as New York's franchise player. In part because of his various ailments and in part because of the wretched teams behind him in the early 1990s, he had also clouded some forecasts that he would end up with the NL's, if not baseball's, highest won-lost percentage.

BILLY GOODMAN

Goodman is the only twentieth-century player to win a batting title while serving as a utility man. The lefty swinger hit .354 for the Red Sox in 1950 while playing 45 games in the outfield, 27 at third base, 21 at first base, 5 at second base, and 1 at shortstop. The only other player to lead offensively while wandering around defensively was King Kelly in 1884 and 1886.

MARV GOODWIN

Although he was in no position to know it, Goodwin was at the center of one of the more ghoulish squabbles between teams over a player transaction. In September 1925 the right-hander was sold by the Cardinals to the Reds on the condition that he stick with Cincinnati for at least thirty days into the following season before the deal became final. Although he lost a couple of games for the Reds in the waning days of the 1925 season, the team reiterated its intention of having him on the roster in spring training. But then, on October 18, Goodwin, a flying instructor, became the first player to be killed in an air crash when his plane went down near Houston during a practice flight. Branch Rickey didn't let that deter him from demanding that the Reds make full payment of money and promised players for the pitcher. For its part, Cincinnati noted that since Goodwin hadn't lasted the stipulated thirty days into the 1926 season, the deal had been voided. Commissioner Kenesaw Landis finally had to step in and rule that the Cardinals were not entitled to anything in exchange for the dead pitcher.

GLEN GORBUS

Gorbus was a modest outfielder for the Reds and Phillies who hung on as long as he did because of his exceptional throwing arm. Responding to a challenge in 1957, he fired a ball an estimated 445 feet, 10 inches out of Connie Mack Stadium. There is no recorded instance of anyone hurling a baseball farther.

JOE GORDON

One of the American League's all-time power-hitting second basemen, Gordon almost had his eleven-year playing career (between 1938 and 1950) eclipsed by an antic trade while managing Cleveland in 1960. Mainly to create some interest in sagging teams, Indians general manager Frank Lane and his Detroit counterpart, Bill Dewitt, decided to swap pilots in the middle of the season—Gordon going to the Tigers for Jimmy Dykes. It was baseball's only swap of nonplaying managers.

As a player for the Yankees and Indians, Gordon clouted 24 homers or more in six seasons. In 1942 he took AL MVP honors for averaging .322 with 103 RBIs—one of four years in which he topped the 100-RBI mark. He had an even bigger year for the world champion Indians in 1948, with 32 home runs and 124 RBIs.

Aside from the Indians and Tigers, Gordon also had brief and unsuccessful stints managing the Athletics and Royals in Kansas City.

JOSEPH W. GORDON

The first, figurehead president of the New York Highlanders in 1903, Gordon indirectly contributed to the club's nickname because of the association of his own surname with the elite British military regiment known as the Gordon Highlanders. He was selected for his baseball position by chief stockholder Frank Farrell because, as New York City's Inspector of Buildings and the brother-in-law of former Giants owner and Tammany Hall stalwart John B. Day, he was politically well connected. For all that, Gordon lasted as club president only until 1907, and the name Highlanders survived only until 1913, when the club abandoned Hilltop Park (which had lent weight to the nickname because it was on one of the highest spots in Manhattan) and became known as the Yankees.

GEORGE GORE

A .301 hitter in fourteen seasons, mostly with Chicago and New York, Gore won a National League batting championship in 1880. But it is for his inestimable patience at the plate that he should be remembered. In 1886, when the Chicago outfielder became the first major leaguer to crack the century mark in walks, each of his 102 free passes required seven balls under the rules in effect at the time.

GOOSE GOSLIN (Hall of Fame, 1968)

It says something for the richness of Goslin's career that his reputation as one of Detroit's G-Men was only the final phase of his eighteen big league seasons. Brought to the big leagues by Washington in 1921, the lefty-swinging outfielder batted .300 over every one of his first full seven seasons, reaching a high (and a hitting title) in 1928 with .379. Unlike many of the other Senators in the period, Goslin hit with power, achieving double figures in doubles, triples, and home runs for five straight years, later doing it another three times before calling it quits. In five consecutive seasons between 1924 and 1928 he drove in 100 runs, including an American League high of 129 in 1924. Although initially gifted with one of baseball's strongest throwing arms, Goslin reduced his value to the club dramatically during spring training in 1928 when he got into a shotput contest with some high school athletes. The following morning he was unable to raise his arm, and he never completely regained the zip on his throws.

Mainly because of incidents such as that with the shotput, Goslin drew constant criticism for his work habits from newly installed manager Walter Johnson, prompting a 1930 trade to the Browns. With St. Louis he demonstrated that only the gigantic dimensions of Griffith Stadium had prevented him from being even more of a power hitter than he had been, racking up another three years of 100-plus RBIs with significantly more home runs. The Senators traded to get him back in 1933, whereupon he joined Ossie Bluege as the only Senator to appear in all three of the franchise's World Series (1924, 1925, 1933). Dealt off to the Tigers in 1934, Goslin played in two more fall classics, joining with Charlie Gehringer and Hank Greenberg as Detroit's G-Men. Goslin's last big year was 1936, when he averaged .315 with 24 home runs, 125 RBIs, and 122 runs scored. After a third, brief stint with Washington, in 1938, he retired with a .316 average.

GOOSE GOSSAGE

Gossage lasted longer in the major leagues than his fastball did. A dominating right-handed reliever in the late 1970s and early 1980s, especially with the Yankees, he was still wandering from one team to another in the mid-1990s, even taking his glowering, mustached visage to Japan for a year.

Gossage's first big year was with the White Sox in 1975, when he led the American League with 26 saves. He matched that number with the Pirates in 1977, then returned to the AL as a free agent in 1978, topping the 30 mark twice and pacing other firemen twice for New York. He became so indispensable to the Yankee bullpen that the team just about counted itself out of the division race in 1979 when he tore a thumb ligament in an early-season shower room tussle with teammate Cliff Johnson.

Signing on with the Padres as a free agent in 1984, Gossage got into the club's only World Series in good part because of his own 25 saves. Although he picked up another 26 rescues the following season, his relations with the ownership hit the skids when an edict came down banning beer drinking in the clubhouse after games. Noting that Jack Murphy Stadium was plastered with Budweiser signs, Gossage called the order "hypocritical," then went on to accuse owner Joan Kroc, the head of McDonald's fast-food chain, of "poisoning the world with her hamburgers." He was suspended until he agreed to make a humiliating apology, claiming that he and his family were regular customers at McDonald's.

After San Diego, Gossage moved on to the Cubs, the Giants, back to the Yankees, over to Japan, then back to the Rangers, Athletics, and Mariners. With his hard fastball long gone, he was used in his later years as a middleman who showed occasional zip.

HARRY GRABINER

Grabiner rose from a Comiskey Park peanut vendor to the linchpin of the White Sox organization. His diary of the year 1920, kept from public view until Bill Veeck used it as the basis of a chapter of his book *The Hustler's Handbook* in 1965, contains details of the Black Sox scandal, the ensuing cover-up, and the role played by his boss Charlie Comiskey. Most shocking was the revelation that Joe Jackson showed Grabiner $5,000 in cash immediately after the Series and told him where he got it. The executive's advice was for Jackson to go home and wait to hear from Comiskey; he never did.

Twenty years after the scandal, while the heirs of Charlie Comiskey battled each other in courtrooms over control of the team, Grabiner worked off an unprecedented ten-year contract behind various front-office titles to make sure there was a club to be had. In 1945 he sought to persuade Grace Comiskey to sell the franchise to him and Bill Veeck; when she said no, he ended his association with the White Sox and became a key member of the Veeck group that purchased the Indians shortly afterward. Grabiner attended to most of the organizational details, while Veeck went about his usual flamboyant promotions. The official's death shortly after Cleveland's 1948 World Series win contributed to the grieving Veeck's decision to sell the franchise.

JACK GRANEY

A .250-hitting outfielder with Cleveland between 1908 to 1922, Graney was the first player to go from the diamond to the broadcasting booth after his retirement. He ended up doing play-by-play of Indians games for 32 years.

CHARLIE GRANT

A black second baseman with the Columbia Giants of Chicago, Grant so impressed John McGraw with his skills during spring training in 1901 that the Baltimore manager tried to bring him into the American League. Concocting a bizarre tale that Grant was actually a half Cherokee named Chief Tokahoma, McGraw almost got away with his scheme until White Sox owner Charlie Comiskey pointed out that "the Cherokee of McGraw is really Grant, the crack Negro sec-ond baseman, fixed up with war paint and feathers," and threatened "to get a Chinaman of my acquaintance and put him on third" if McGraw persisted.

EDDIE GRANT

A third baseman for the Giants, Grant was the only big leaguer killed in action during World War I. A Polo Grounds monument in his honor stood in center field until the stadium was demolished in 1964. He is commemorated in New York today by the E. L. Grant Highway near the George Washington Bridge.

GEORGE WASHINGTON GRANT

Grant was one of several early-century owners of the Braves whose links to John McGraw helped reduce the Boston franchise to something of a major league farm club for the Giants. When he bought the team from a consortium headed by Percy Haughton after the 1918 season, the one-time film distributor and Wall Street speculator did so through McGraw's mediation efforts. At the same time, Grant was partnered with the New York manager in a bid to buy a Havana racetrack, and had both a Manhattan office and a Polo Grounds box adjoining those of Giants owner Charles Stoneham. Within months of taking over the Braves, Grant endorsed several deals with the Giants that benefited the latter much more than the former. When the Boston press turned on him over both the propriety of the exchanges and his refusal to move from New York to Massachusetts, he claimed the team had needed the cash it had received along with some mediocre players and that he himself didn't have the money to afford two residences. The low point of Grant's ownership came in 1921, when it was revealed that Boston manager Fred Mitchell had been liberally handing out fines against the smallest infraction of club rules, and that the penalties just so happened to cover most of Boston's traveling expenses. Grant finally sold out—at a substantial profit—to another McGraw crony, Judge Emil Fuchs.

M. DONALD GRANT

The board chairman of the Mets over most of the club's first two decades in the 1960s and

1970s, Grant became a byword for executive interference and was linked to all of the franchise's worst public relations moments. His unpopularity reached such a level at one point that bodyguards had to be assigned to him for fear of some lunatic fan attack. Even the fact that he had been the only member of the Giants board of directors to vote against the transfer of the franchise from New York to San Francisco in 1957 was ultimately interpreted as merely a no-lose tactic aimed at winning local plaudits.

As the chief adviser to original Mets owner Joan Payson, Grant was largely responsible for installing George Weiss as the team's first baseball operations chief—mainly because he was averse to bringing in Branch Rickey and his power demands. Grant stayed pretty much in the background until Weiss's departure in 1967, then insisted on two hirings—of manager Gil Hodges and of general manager Johnny Murphy—that would profit the team on one level and set the stage for relentless infighting on another. Shortly after the Hodges-Murphy tandem led the Mets to their 1969 world championship, the general manager died of a heart attack, and Grant, seething over the way he had been kept away from baseball decision making for three years, installed the reluctant Bob Scheffing as his successor. One consequence of the change was Hodges's tightened control over the clubhouse against both Grant and Scheffing. With most of the local press already lined up on the side of the popular Hodges, the chairman and the general manager didn't need another incident to lower their media image, but they created one anyway when, following the debacle trade of Nolan Ryan to the Angels in exchange for Jim Fregosi, Grant accused New York *Daily News* sportswriter Jack Lang of having "forced" the club into the deal.

With Yogi Berra replacing the deceased Hodges in 1972, Grant became even more embroiled in the club's daily affairs. Although the team would eventually win the National League pennant in 1973, its play was so desultory as late as August that one paper conducted a poll on who should be fired first—Grant, Scheffing, or Berra. In good part because he had negotiated the Ryan-Fregosi trade, Scheffing was the dubious winner, with Grant a close second. In 1975 Grant dragged

outfielder Cleon Jones before New York reporters to apologize for having been arrested in Florida on charges of having had sexual relations with a woman in a van. Jones proved even more useful to Grant a couple of months later when his refusal to take the field in the late innings of a game was the excuse the executive had been seeking for some time to fire the manager.

The nadir of the franchise was reached in 1975, following the death of Payson and the assumption of even more boardroom powers by Grant. Although formal control of the team passed to Payson's widower, Charles, his lack of interest in baseball prompted him to give the reins to his daughter Linda de Roulet. With Grant as her Richelieu, de Roulet invoked one austerity measure after another, not least the decision to ignore free agents. Grant's hard line on player salaries also led to the trading of Rusty Staub and an attempt to peddle franchise star Tom Seaver to the Dodgers in exchange for Don Sutton. De Roulet prevented the latter move when she was overwhelmed with calls and letters from Mets fans, but she could do nothing in 1977 when an anti-Seaver campaign fueled by Grant and *Daily News* sportswriter Dick Young led the right-hander to demand a trade to Cincinnati. In the wake of what was called locally the Midnight Massacre, Grant was bombarded by threats on his life and accepted a bodyguard for the rest of the 1977 season.

The end of of the trail came in 1978, when de Roulet made a surprise announcement that she was replacing Grant as the organization chairman. It emerged subsequently that the move had been inspired by Charles Payson, who had always distrusted Grant's influence on his wife and daughter. Grant went out fuming that he had never been appreciated by the Paysons, the players, the press, or the fans.

MUDCAT GRANT

The flamboyant Grant tried a precarious balancing act in the 1960s between pitching and singing. He reached double heights in 1965 when his league-leading 21 wins carried the Twins to the pennant, a pair of World Series victories almost toppled the heavily favored Dodgers, and he snared crooning engagements on several network programs. When his mound career began to falter over the next couple of years, however, the black right-hander came up against owner Calvin Griffith's neanderthal views on race relations. Told not only to cut out his singing but also to stop being seen in public with white women, Grant demanded a trade, and was accommodated by being sent to the Dodgers. He never quite repeated his 1965 success as either a pitcher or a singer.

ABNER GRAVES

One of hundreds of respondents to the plea of a commission established by Al Spalding in 1905 to settle the controversy over the origins of baseball, Graves recounted a tale of how his boyhood chum Abner Doubleday had reconfigured town ball for a prep school contest in Cooperstown, New York, in 1839, and, in the process not only invented a new game but also christened it "Base Ball." Ignoring the initial protests of historian and commission member Henry Chadwick, Spalding, ever anxious to deny that baseball had evolved from the British game of rounders, jumped at this "proof" that the game's beginnings were "free from the trammels of English traditions, customs, and conventionalities," no less so because Doubleday had been a noted Civil War general. It was, however, the beginnings of the general's military career that gave the lie to Graves's sixty-six-year-old recollections, since Doubleday, a West Point plebe in 1839, was not allowed to leave the citadel at the very time Graves had him in Cooperstown drawing a diagram of the first baseball field. The inconvenience of this fact notwithstanding, Spalding, in December 1907, had former National League president Abraham Mills, a wartime associate of Doubleday's and a pallbearer at his funeral in 1893, draft the commission's final report; the document became the foundation of baseball's myth of spontaneous domestic creation. While no one any longer subscribes to the fable, the Hall of Fame still displays a dilapidated old ball that was found in a trunk by Graves's son and was once claimed to have been used by Doubleday.

PETE GRAY

Gray was a one-armed outfielder for the 1945 Browns who aroused more resentment than admiration from his teammates. A subject of nationwide publicity and War Department propaganda for a successful minor league season in 1944, he was purchased by St. Louis for $20,000 behind adamant denials that the club was only looking for some freak attraction to outdraw the Cardinals in the city. Although Gray played well enough in spring training to make the team and drew praise in the clubhouse for dealing with his handicap, the tune changed when he showed himself capable merely of a powerless .218 season and, especially, when his relative nimbleness in taking off his glove and making throws in the field still provided a second more of incentive for opposition runners to take an extra base. As the season wore on, several Browns pointed to the opposition's baserunning as a major reason why St. Louis was hard pressed to repeat as American League pennant winners. Manager Luke Sewell also made it clear that he didn't appreciate front-office suggestions that he play Gray more than he had intended. The player most affected by those starts, Mike Kreevich, created enough turmoil in the clubhouse to be waived to Washington in the middle of the season. None of this did anything for Gray's already spiky personality, and he was generally represented as surly and uncooperative. He drove in only 13 runs in 234 at-bats, and was farmed out to Toledo the following year.

Years later, Sewell echoed the contentions that Gray's starts had cost St. Louis another pennant (the club finished in third place, six games behind Detroit) and insisted that good spring training or not, the outfielder should not have been in the major leagues.

RAY GREBEY

Succeeding John Gaherin as head of major league baseball's Player Relations Committee early in 1977, Grebey latched on to the issue of free agent compensation as a means of bringing down the Players Association and, according to Marvin Miller and others, earn enough plaudits to succeed Bowie Kuhn as commissioner. The former General Electric union buster was undone by his own strategy, though. Wrongly assuring the owners that they had won the right to compensation during negotiations in 1980, he misgauged the players' determination to preserve free agency, holding out for direct compensation to the club losing a free agent from the roster of the team signing him and thereby guaranteeing that there would be a strike in 1981. Grebey was replaced by Lee MacPhail as chief negotiator for the owners during the walkout, and was fired in April 1984.

DALLAS GREEN

Green's managing and front-office career has practically obliterated his eight years as a mediocre pitcher for several teams in the 1960s.

As a pilot, Green called the shots for the only World Series victory ever recorded by the Phillies, in 1980. Despite his carefully tended reputation as a booming backslapper and ass-kicker, however, he took a backseat at a crucial moment in that year's pennant drive to general manager Jim Owens, who lashed into the team during a clubhouse meeting for worrying about individual statistics and griping to every newsman available. Green's own bluster was more in evidence when he took over the Yankees in 1989, fired off some sarcastic cracks about the interference of George Steinbrenner, and was promptly fired with the owner's verdict that Green had been "one of the biggest mistakes I ever made." In 1993 Green resurfaced as pilot of the Mets, with the mandate of rebuilding the deteriorated club with young players.

Between his managerial stints, Green made a decidedly more enduring impression as head of baseball operations for the Cubs in the early 1980s. With his knowledge of the Phillies his main asset, he completed a series of trades with Philadelphia that brought such veterans as Keith Moreland, Dick Ruthven, Gary Mathews, Bob Dernier, and Larry Bowa to Wrigley Field; moreover, the deal that imported Bowa (in exchange for Ivan De Jesus) also brought franchise infielder Ryne Sandberg. All of the ex-Phillies played key roles in Chicago's 1984 Eastern Division title— the first time the franchise had experienced postseason play since 1945. For Windy City traditionalists, however, there was a significant trade-off for Green's tenure in the executive's incessant campaigning for the installation of lights in Wrigley Field. Mainly because of this issue, he was never a candidate for Man of the Year in Chicago,

and few tears were shed when he was forced to resign his post after the 1987 season. The first night game at Wrigley was played the following August.

PUMPSIE GREEN

In 1959, infielder Green became the first black player on the Red Sox, the last major league team to drop the color barrier. A backup infielder for the most part, he owed his celebrity otherwise to a Manhattan traffic jam that inspired him and pitcher Gene Conley to leave the team bus and, dispirited over a loss at Yankee Stadium, take a cab to the airport with the intention of flying to Israel. The plan was aborted by their lack of passports, but they wandered around for a couple of days before rejoining the team in Washington.

HANK GREENBERG (Hall of Fame, 1956)

For most of his thirteen-year career in the 1930s and 1940s, Greenberg was presumed to be carrying the Jewish people on his shoulders whenever he strode to the plate for the Tigers. That he ranked below only Jimmie Foxx as his era's greatest right-handed American League slugger has suggested to some that he might have been second to nobody if he had merely had to worry about opposing pitchers. For all that, he himself contended that he came up against more open anti-Semitism in his later days as a baseball executive than he had encountered on the diamond.

Greenberg made his first big impression on the AL in 1934, when he batted .339 while clouting 26 home runs, driving in 139 runs, and belting a league-leading 63 doubles. It was also toward the end of the 1934 campaign that his Jewishness became an issue for the sports pages when he admitted consulting a rabbi about whether he should get into uniform for Rosh Hashanah and Yom Kippur in late September. Mindful of the tense pennant race under way between the Tigers and the Yankees, the rabbi compromised by declaring that Greenberg should play on the happy occasion of Rosh Hashanah, but dedicate himself to prayer on the more somber Yom Kippur. The first baseman acquiesced, with his 10th-inning home run deciding the contest played on the Jewish New Year.

In 1935 Greenberg won the first of two MVP

awards by averaging .328, with AL-leading numbers in both home runs (36) and RBIs (170). Despite having more than 20 homers and close to 100 RBIs at the All-Star break that year, he was left off the AL squad by Detroit manager Mickey Cochrane amid whisperings of anti-Semitism. Then a broken wrist just about sidelined Greenberg for the World Series against the Cubs and, when it was rebroken at the beginning of the following season, he ended up missing most of 1936. The following year he came back with a vengeance, emerging as the biggest G of the so-called G-Men (along with Charlie Gehringer and Goose Goslin) with 40 homers, 49 doubles, 137 runs scored, and an astonishing 183 RBIs. In 1938 he led the league in homers for the second of four seasons by whacking 58 round-trippers—tying him with Foxx for fourth place behind Roger Maris's 61 and Babe Ruth's 60 and 59 for a season high.

Hank Greenberg was the biggest G in Detroit's fabled G-Men lineup. National Baseball Library, Cooperstown, N.Y.

Despite his team-leading slugging, Greenberg was never particularly close to Walter Briggs, and was given an abrupt ultimatum by the Detroit owner after the 1939 campaign to move to the outfield to make room at first base for defensively inadequate receiver Rudy York or expose himself to a $10,000 pay cut. Greenberg went to left field, where he put together another MVP season (he led the AL in home runs, RBIs, doubles, and slugging average), but most of his friends were critical of him for acting too much like a good soldier before the Briggs ultimatum. They could make the same complaint more literally in May 1941, when the newly converted outfielder was the first player from the American League drafted into the U.S. Army. He remained in khaki until just before the end of the 1945 season, again making it clear that he regarded himself as a role model not only for big league players, but for Jews more generally. When he did return to the Tigers, it was just in time to lead a sweaty flag battle down the stretch against Washington; he personally nailed down matters on the final day of the season by clouting a grand-slam home run.

After still another season of pacing the AL in homers and RBIs, in 1946, the thirty-five-year-old Greenberg applied for the job of Detroit general manager left open by the resignation of George Trautman. Briggs not only turned him down as unqualified, but with the obvious connivance of other AL owners, managed to get him waived out of the league to the Pirates. Speculation at the time attributed the owner with fears that Greenberg would call on his in-laws (the department store Gimbels) in an attempt to take over the Tigers franchise altogether. In his final season as a player, the righty swinger belted 25 homers and exerted a significant tutorial role on Pittsburgh prospect Ralph Kiner. Greenberg's lifetime numbers totaled out at 331 home runs, 1,276 RBIs, a batting average of .313, and a slugging percentage of .605.

In 1949 Greenberg joined the Cleveland front office under owner Bill Veeck, and was in position after the season to join with insurance executive Ellis Ryan in purchasing the franchise. For several years, Greenberg had to do little but add extra pieces to the winning clubs that were based on a Hall of Fame starting rotation of Bob

Lemon, Bob Feller, and Early Wynn. By the mid-1960s, however, Greenberg was under fire constantly for allowing the Cleveland farm system to go to seed and for adding little beyond aged veterans (Kiner, Sal Maglie, Billy Cox). Greenberg's chief response was to blame city newspapers for turning a still-respectable club into a mockery in the eyes of fans. If that didn't bring enough heat, he turned even previously sympathetic sportswriters against him during the 1957 season when he urged the organization's board of directors to move the franchise to Los Angeles before the Dodgers got there. Instead, the board majority voted to sell out to Cleveland banking and railroad magnate William Daley, leaving Greenberg with little alternative but to follow suit. Before going, he leveled one final charge at Cleveland fans and the press for being unable to support a big league team.

In 1959 Greenberg was back with Veeck as the key figures in a consortium taking over the majority interest in the White Sox. It wasn't too long, however, before Comiskey Park was mainly serving as an office for Greenberg and Veeck to lay plans for winning ownership rights to the expansion California franchise due to begin operations in 1961. They were so confident of being awarded the new club that they signed a tentative agreement to broadcast the Angels games over Gene Autry's KMPC and unloaded their interest in the White Sox to Arthur Allyn, Jr. But then reality raised its head in the form of Dodger owner Walter O'Malley and several AL owners, who made it clear that the Greenberg offer would be studied seriously only if Veeck were cut out. When Greenberg wouldn't throw over his partner, the California franchise was awarded to Autry.

Greenberg was among those testifying on Curt Flood's behalf when the outfielder challenged the reserve clause in court in the early 1970s.

BOB GREENWOOD

Greenwood was denied a win in his first major league start for the Phillies, even though Philadelphia won the game and no teammate appeared on the mound. On July 18, 1954, with the right-hander holding an 8–1 lead over the Cardinals in the top of the fifth inning of a game interrupted several times by rain, St. Louis manager Eddie

Stanky decided to stall. With darkness only minutes away and the rules of the day prohibiting turning on the lights in the middle of a contest, Stanky changed pitchers twice; when a call went out for the third reliever, however, umpire Babe Pinelli forfeited the game to Philadelphia—the last time a team has been so punished for delaying tactics. The Phils received a victory, but because the game had not lasted the regulation five innings, none of the players received credit for performances. Later in the season, Greenwood recorded his first—and only—major league win.

KEN GRIFFEY, JR.

On August 30, 1990, Griffey became the first major leaguer to get a hit in the same inning as his father. The ultimate baseball generational promotion saw Ken, Jr., and Ken, Sr., both left-hand-hitting outfielders for the Mariners, each single and score. Prior to their joint offensive performance, the Griffeys had been the only father-son combination to play together on the same club; a year before, they had been the only two generations active simultaneously in the major leagues. Griffey, Sr., retired after the 1991 season with a lifetime average of .296; the best part of his nineteen-year career had been spent as the left fielder for the Big Red Machine in Cincinnati. Griffey, Jr., hailed by many as the best player in the American League toward the mid-1990s, showed considerably more power and defensive skills. In 1993 the Mariners franchise player collected 45 home runs and drove in 109 runs while maintaining his five-season average above .300. Among the homers were those he banged out in 8 consecutive games between July 20 and 28 to tie a major league mark previously reached by Dale Long and Don Mattingly.

MIKE GRIFFIN

Lefty-swinging outfielder Griffin was the first player to hit a home run in his initial major league at-bat when he connected for the American Association's Baltimore Orioles in the first inning on Opening Day (April 16) in 1887. Within minutes, outfielder George Tebeau duplicated the feat, while playing for Cincinnati of the same league.

Calvin Griffith supported his uncle Clark in the Washington front office. National Baseball Library, Cooperstown, N.Y.

CALVIN GRIFFITH

Mocked even by his fellow owners as a neanderthal, Griffith said as much as anybody about the organizational mentality of the major leagues in the second half of the century by surviving for close to three decades as the head of the Washington Senators-Minnesota Twins. As in the case of Marge Schott, his crassness was frequently only an oversized mirror that his colleagues preferred not to look into to avoid seeing someone familiar. For better and worse, he was also one of the last owners who thought about nothing except baseball.

Griffith was born into the world as Calvin Griffith Robertson, but switched his second and third names when he was taken in by his uncle Clark Griffith; because he was already too old when he filed the request, he was never formally adopted by Clark, but was otherwise always treated as a son. From 1942 he took an active role in the affairs of the Senators, usually, but not always, doing as his uncle demanded. One notable exception occurred in 1953, when Calvin decided that Clark wasn't thinking clearly in supporting the move of the St. Louis Browns to Baltimore, since that would present Washington with a rival for its market; when Clark found out that Calvin had been speaking against the proposal at league meetings, he insisted on dragging his eighty-four-year-old bones to the final vote to make sure promises made to the prospective Baltimore owners were carried out. Clark died soon after, leav-

ing behind a will that gave Calvin practical control of the franchise, since his 26 percent interest was backed by another 26 percent from his rubber-stamping sister Thelma Haynes.

The team that Calvin inherited was the one that was first in war, first in peace, and last in the American League, and the one that served as an appropriate fantasy victor for the musical *Damn Yankees*. With no club to speak of on the field and little in the till, Calvin became a natural target of lobbying groups from Louisville, Minneapolis, Houston, Los Angeles, and San Francisco—all bent on either buying the team from him or inducing him to move from Washington. When the District of Columbia intervened to offer a new ballpark, he objected that the proposal site would have been in a heavily black neighborhood and would, in any case, have left him without the rental money and concessions from Redskins games at Griffith Stadium that had been keeping the franchise afloat. He stuck to that position against warnings from other AL owners that a move out of Washington would expose the major leagues to another investigation of the sport's exemption from antitrust statutes by congressmen irritated at losing a local team. In the end, the league had to accept Griffith's dried-up treasury as a reality and the feasibility of an offer made by the Minneapolis—St. Paul lobby; to put off any congressional consequences, a new Washington team was created as part of an expansion from eight to ten teams.

Minnesotans welcomed Griffith as a hero, especially when the team rose to second place in its second season. The players thought differently, most of all during bitter annual contract negotiations. In one particularly embarrassing instance, manager Sam Mele was practically forced to grovel before accepting a salary cut to return the following year. It was the same Mele who led the club to its first pennant in 1965, but little more than a year later, he was gone. In 1969 Griffith and Billy Martin kept saying how much they loved each other during the year, while all the time the owner was collecting evidence about the manager's night crawlings in order to get rid of him without alienating fans. Never one to understate a labor-management case, Griffith termed a 1970 strike by umpires "a disgrace to humanity" and savaged his fellow owners as "appeasers" for giving in too quickly on a 1972 players walk-out. His hard-line attitude was reflected in the fact that Twins players were involved in a number of significant contract firsts in the 1970s: Dick Woodson the first to benefit from binding arbitration, Jim Kaat and Jim Perry the first American Leaguers to insist on their five-and-ten trading rights, and Bill Campbell the first regular free-agent signee. It was Kaat who once described Griffith as "throwing quarters around like manhole covers"; lost to the ages, on the other hand, was the identity of the player who claimed that "swimming was invented the day Calvin came across his first toll booth."

Because of his aversion to free agents, Griffith allowed such stars as Rod Carew and Lyman Bostock to get away, and had trouble holding on to more than one manager who complained of not being able to send a competitive team out on the field. As cool as the fans and the press had become to him for these reasons, the atmosphere turned decidedly hostile after a reporter published excerpts of a speech that a drunken Griffith gave to a Lions Club affair in Waseca, Minnesota, on the evening of September 28, 1978. Amid a flood of racial invective, he said he was glad to have left Washington because the city had too many blacks who were more interested in wrestling than baseball; stunned that a black player like Carew had been stupid enough to accept the last pact he had given him; and annoyed that catcher Butch Wynegar had spent his spring training chasing his new wife around the bedroom instead of settling for one-night stands that would have allowed him to concentrate more on baseball. Carew, who had already been enraged by what he had seen as Griffith's anti-Semitic attitude toward his Jewish agent, got his revenge by forcing the club to trade him into a lucrative contract with the Angels; Minnesota fans got their revenge by staying away from Metropolitan Stadium and wearing TRADE CALVIN buttons.

By the late 1970s, even a good Twins team and a popular Griffith would have had a problem luring fans to the dangerously deteriorated Metropolitan Stadium. Although the facility had served a diplomatic purpose by being in Bloomington, a suburb that was neither Minneapolis nor St. Paul,

it became obvious even to the owner that he had to move. After once again contemplating a transfer to another state altogether, he swallowed his traditionalist baseball pride by accepting arguments for the construction of the indoor Metrodome in downtown Minneapolis. The biggest argument of all was financial: Since the Twins relied more heavily than other teams on fans traveling from distant places, the dome was a guarantee that they wouldn't be coming only to see snow piled up on the infield. With the help of an escape clause that allowed him to move out of the state if the franchise did not prove profitable over a three-year period, Griffith presided with a smile over the inauguration of the dome in 1982. What not even the Metrodome's roof could hide, however, was the worst club in franchise history, making Minnesota the only team in the majors that year unable to draw a million fans.

Over the next year or so, Griffith evinced decidedly mixed emotions about the fact that the sparse attendance was going to allow him to exercise the escape clause. In the end he decided to sell out to a consortium headed by banker Carl Pohlad. Much of the fight had gone out of Calvin through years of strife with his son Clark, who ultimately turned his back on the franchise. Calvin's total absorption in baseball had previously cost him his marriage, ostensibly because his wife had never gotten over being separated from the social and cultural whirl of Washington. As Griffith once told *Sports Illustrated;* "I like to look at magazines, read a few stories, read the captions. I don't like to socialize too much. You run into people who aren't athletic-minded. They're bookworms or symphony patrons, and that's all they want to talk about."

CLARK GRIFFITH (Hall of Fame, 1946)

Although associated primarily with the Washington franchise during his sixty-four-year career as player, manager, and owner, Griffith could claim an identification with the American League as a whole for his importance. As much as Ban Johnson and Charlie Comiskey, in fact, he was responsible for the very existence of the junior circuit in his unmatched recruitment of National League stars. If he sometimes came off as a poor cousin to Johnson and Comiskey, it wasn't for lack of desire to match their influence; on the contrary, during both world wars, Griffith relished the gratitude of both leagues for his indispensable role in seeing to it that baseball continued being played at all.

Griffith's numbers as a pitcher for the Cubs, White Sox, and several other teams at the turn of the century would have been sufficient in themselves to gain him consideration for Cooperstown. Between 1894 and 1899 the right-hander turned in 20 victories every season, also pacing the NL with an ERA Of 1.88 in 1898. Between his debut for the American Association's St. Louis franchise in 1891 and a final token appearance for the Senators in 1914, he put together a record of 240–141. Although he never again matched the mastery of his Cub years, he came through with a seventh 20-win season for the White Sox in 1901, also leading the league in winning percentage (.771). By then, however, Griffith was already paying attention to more than his personal wins and losses. As a representative of the Ball Players Protective Association, it was he who, the year before, had first received word of the NL's refusal to consider accommodating some of Johnson's then minor league AL clubs and who had quickly gotten to work persuading some of his Cub teammates to jump the NL after the season. As a reward for his efforts, he was named playing manager of Chicago's AL franchise; he repaid that confidence immediately not only by collecting 24 wins and steering the White Sox to the best record in the fledgling major league but also by creating enough excitement on the diamond to outdraw the Cubs by 150,000.

When Johnson needed a familiar name at the helm for the inaugural season of his AL entry in New York in 1903, he persuaded White Sox owner Comiskey that there might not be any league at all unless Griffith took over the club that was to become the Yankees. Griffith was again successful insofar as he helped consolidate the New York franchise, and he even led them to a couple of second-place finishes in his five-year tenure; on the other hand, he was gradually worn out by intrigues among club executives, especially when they began seeping down into the clubhouse, and he finally quit early into the 1908 season. After an unsuccessful bid to latch on as

manager of the Senators, he accepted the pilot's post with the Reds. Throughout his three-year return to the NL, however, Griffith never let Cincinnati owner Garry Herrmann or Washington boss Thomas Noyes forget that he would be available as soon as the Senators needed a new dugout boss. His biggest profit from piloting the Reds was the presence on the 1911 roster of Cubans Armando Marsans and Rafael Almeida; decades later, he would point to their abilities as the reason why he signed so many Latins during his reign in Washington (in reality, it was one of three reasons).

On October 27, 1911, Griffith finally realized his hopes by signing as manager of the Senators; moreover, the 10 percent interest he bought in the franchise instantly made him its single biggest investor. Predictions that he would have personality problems with Noyes became academic when the club president died suddenly in the middle of the 1912 season and was replaced by Ben Minor. Although as obstinate as Noyes on financial matters, Minor had few of his predecessor's airs about being a baseball genius, leaving Griffith even more of a free hand. He didn't waste any time waving it around. Convinced that the Senators needed only one more heavy hitter to rise from their already surprising second-place slot to the top of the AL, he cornered Detroit owner Frank Navin during the 1913 season and handed him a personal check for $100,000 for the services of Ty Cobb. When Navin voiced skepticism that Griffith could back up the paper, the Washington manager admitted that he couldn't, but promised that he would be able to within two weeks if the Tigers would sit on his proposal for that long. Griffith then went to work on hostile shareholders, outlining a plan by which he would place 100,000 tickets on sale for $1 apiece to raise the money needed for the purchase of Cobb. The outcome was still in doubt among the investors when Navin returned the check, saying that he had decided to hold on to Cobb. The Senators had to hold on to second place.

During World War I (and again during World War II), Griffith proved invaluable to both leagues in persuading the U.S. government not to eliminate baseball as a nonessential activity. In 1918, after league president Johnson had failed to gain deferments from military service for players (and in the process sharpened the antagonism of federal bureaucrats toward the big leagues), he worked out a deal with Secretary of War Newton Baker under which the players would perform pregame drills (with bats instead of rifles) in exchange for remaining exempt from the draft until Labor Day. The Washington manager also spearheaded a fund-raising drive to buy bats and balls for servicemen in Europe. Unfortunately for Griffith, however, none of this tap dancing on behalf of baseball as a whole endeared him any more to Senators stockholders, who were still waiting to celebrate their first pennant. By 1919, boardroom grumbling had turned to open calls for his replacement as manager. Griffith's response was to round up capital from the Metropolitan National Bank and from Philadelphia grain exporter William Richardson and to take over as both majority owner and president; a key part of the deal allowed him to speak for Richardson's holdings as well as his own.

Once he could no longer be taken for an employee, Griffith began brushing in the masterstrokes of a thirty-five-year franchise rule. Soon after the 1920 campaign, he stepped down as manager in favor of George McBride; from McBride to the arrival of Charlie Dressen in 1955, the club would be piloted only by those who had played or were still playing for it. In 1924 with Bucky Harris, and then in 1933 with Joe Cronin, he went to younger infielders as skippers for teams he regarded as only some enthusiasm and an odd arm or two away from the pennant; Harris won the franchise's first two pennants, in 1924 and 1925, Cronin its last, in 1933. Both managers also experienced the ups and downs of Griffith's zealous patronage when he insisted on squiring them around the nation's capital. In Harris's case it led to a marriage with the daughter of a U.S. senator, charges from sportswriters and his own players that he had become too stuck up because of his new circles, and a fast ride to the Tigers; in Cronin's case it led to marriage with Griffith's niece Mildred, taunts from the locker room and the stands that he was marrying into the family only to hold on to his job, and an even more celebrated deal with the Red Sox for $225,000 of Tom Yawkey's money.

Although Griffith was quick to stress that he had sold Cronin mainly because he didn't want the shortstop at the mercy of nepotism accusations, that didn't bother Griffith where numerous other members of his family were concerned. By the 1940s he had his nephew Calvin acting as his right arm; Calvin's sister Thelma working in the front office; and Calvin's brothers Sherry, Billy, and Jimmy all nearing executive positions. Later, retired Washington pitcher Joe Haynes, Thelma's husband, would also have a vice presidency.

If a Yankee Haters Club had existed in the 1930s, Griffith would have been president. Part of his resentment stemmed from the frequently vicious field fights that broke out between the teams; another important part had to do with New York's regular perch atop the AL standings between the wars. In a farcical attempt to exact some satisfaction from the Bronx, Griffith sprang a surprise resolution at the AL winter meetings in 1940 that prohibited a previous year's pennant winner from making trades with other clubs. Although there was enough of an anti-Yankee majority to get the resolution approved, it turned out to be a vain exercise twice over: first, because New York had been depending for years more on its own farm system than on trades for building flag winners; and second, because Detroit ended up winning the pennant in 1940. The Griffith resolution was overturned as soon as that year's World Series was completed.

During World War II the Washington owner again proved to be an effective diplomat in turning away some congressional calls for stopping baseball as an inessential activity. Far more established in the capital's political circles than he had been during World War I, he wasn't above discussing some of his own players with draft officials at power lunches; at the very least, it struck some other big league owners as curious that Washington players weren't receiving greetings from Uncle Sam as regularly as members of other teams. The war also increased the importance of Griffith's Latin card; since Cubans in particular remained exempt from draft registration until 1944, they appeared in appreciably growing numbers at Washington's spring training camps during the war. (Aside from the Marsans-Almeida experience and their status with the draft board, Latins also appealed to Griffith because they could be signed cheaply.)

The 1940s also saw Griffith outsmarting himself on several occasions. Prior to the 1945 season, for instance, he was so skeptical of the club's chances to contend seriously that he scheduled a slew of doubleheaders at Griffith Stadium in September to free Sunday dates for the NFL Redskins, from whom he exacted considerable rental and concession revenues; in the event, Washington lost out to Detroit by merely a game and a half, mainly because its pitching staff was worn thin by all the doubleheaders. In 1949 he learned that he had taken too much for granted with the stock of the Philadelphian Richardson; when the grain merchant's heirs sold their 40 percent stake in the franchise to a wheeler-dealer named John Jachym, Griffith needed to use every ounce of clout he had in Washington to round up the votes to beat back the only serious threat to his rule.

With his nephew Calvin taking over most of his tasks, beating off the Jachym power play turned out to be Griffith's last significant act. Until his death in 1955 at age eighty-five, The Old Fox, as he was known, became increasingly obsessed with his own Horatio Alger story, asking every visitor to his office to name others who had started out as players and ended up as owners (only the tactless would have submitted Comiskey as one answer). Asked on one occasion whom he most admired in America, Griffin replied; ''The Lone Ranger has been my guiding star—the sort of man I want to be.''

BURLEIGH GRIMES (Hall of Fame, 1964)

Grimes was the last of the legal spitballers, and there weren't many of his contemporaries who could think of any other compliment to throw his way. Known as Old Stubblebeard for his perpetual bad mood, the right-hander compiled five 20-win seasons in his nineteen-year (1916–34) travels through most of the National League. Four of his biggest campaigns came for the Dodgers in the 1920s after Brooklyn scout Larry Sutton recommended that he be obtained from the Pirates despite a grim 3–16 record for Pittsburgh in 1917. With the exception of his pivotal role in the Dodger pennant of 1920, Grimes's best efforts at Ebbets Field were generally for second-division

clubs. His single biggest year was in 1928, during a second tour with Pittsburgh, when he won 25 for a club that finished fourth. On the other hand, when he wasn't a staff ace, as with the Cardinals in 1930 and 1931, Grimes provided enough mound insurance to get his club into postseason play. His most conspicous moment in a World Series was in 1931, when he won the seventh game for St. Louis over the Athletics.

A master of the brushback as much as of the spitter, Grimes took particular delight in decking Frankie Frisch. On one occasion, after Frisch had accidently spiked him on a close play at first base and immediately apologized, Grimes waited for the Cardinal second baseman to get up again, and promptly beaned him. When the apoplectic Frisch protested that he had been sincere in his earlier apology, Grimes said that he knew that, but that Frisch had neglected to smile.

Old Stubblebeard's dourness was on full display when he replaced Casey Stengel as manager of the Dodgers in 1937, and employed his first meeting with the press to complain that he was making less money than his idled predecessor. Grimes worsened an already bad situation in 1938 when he ridiculed the idea that Babe Ruth, hired as a coach by general manager Larry MacPhail, could ever succeed him as manager. When Ruth, who had been deceived into such ambitions by MacPhail, decided he would get a jump on his plans by first reactivating himself as a player, Grimes won the ex-slugger's hostility for good when he insulted his mental and physical capabilities.

For many years after getting out of a uniform, Grimes held sway over the Veterans Committee of the Hall of Fame, where he gained a reputation for forging votes on his pet likes and dislikes.

RAY GRIMES

Grimes had his lumbago to thank for not receiving more attention for one of baseball's more productive streaks. As a member of the 1922 Cubs, the right-hand-hitting first baseman drove home at least one run in 17 consecutive games. He achieved the major league mark through two absences from the lineup because of a bad back. It was an ailment that would eventually abbreviate a more than promising career: In six years Grimes compiled a .329 average, including a high of .354 in 1922.

CHARLIE GRIMM

Through twenty years of playing between 1916 and 1936 and nineteen seasons of managing between 1932 and 1960, Grimm was a constant recourse but only a short-term solution. In 1920 the deft fielder and lifetime .291 batter appeared to resolve a decades-long quest by the Pirates for a solid first baseman. But although his tenure with Pittsburgh included a career year in 1923 of .345 with 99 RBIs, his after-hours antics with shortstop Rabbit Maranville persuaded humorless owner Barney Dreyfuss to trade both of them to the Cubs. The benefit to Grimm was that Chicago became his home for the rest of his playing career and that he starred in two World Series for the club, in 1929 and 1932, hitting an overall .364. Even better, he took over as pilot of the latter pennant-winning team in midseason after Rogers Hornsby had been ditched. But the managing job also marked the beginning of a yo-yo relationship with the Cubs for the best part of the next thirty-years.

Grimm's first nemesis was Chicago president William Walker, an ex-fish merchant who acted like one in regular screaming matches with his manager over what had or had not been done; like Larry MacPhail and Leo Durocher in Brooklyn a few years later, Walker regularly capped his rages by firing Grimm, then changed his mind after calming down. In spite of Walker's proclivity for terrible trades, Grimm came up with another pennant-winner in 1935, to a large extent because of his decision to step aside and hand first base over to nineteen-year-old rookie Phil Cavarretta. When Walker was replaced by Phil Wrigley, the manager's problem became yes-men who surrounded the owner and who always had a second guess about some field strategy. In 1938 Grimm had enough and submitted his resignation; Wrigley was so grateful that he didn't have to pull the trigger first that he gave the outgoing pilot a job as team broadcaster. Grimm stayed in the broadcast booth until 1944, when he was asked again to take over the dugout. He was at the helm of the Cubs when they made their last World Series appearance, in 1945.

After World War II the team declined precipi-tously, especially because of lack of hitting. In this context Grimm triggered one of baseball's more repeated tales. After receiving a telegram from a scout that read, "Spotted a pitcher who stopped a good team cold for nine innings; only one foul fly hit out of the infield," the manager purportedly wired back; "Forget the pitcher. Send the guy who hit the foul fly. We need hitters." By 1949, however, Wrigley had decided that the club's real problem was that Grimm and general manager Jim Gallagher had the wrong jobs, so while kicking Gallagher off to a less meaningful post, he brought in Frankie Frisch as the pilot and put Grimm in charge of baseball operations. The next six months were even more of a fiasco, with Grimm and Frisch making terrible deals and Gallagher jeering at them from the sidelines. Once again Grimm had enough of the franchise's politics, and resigned. After a couple of years of running the American Association Milwaukee Brewers in partnership with Bill Veeck, he succeeded Tommy Holmes as manager of the Braves.

No sooner had Grimm arrived in Boston than the franchise moved to his former stomping ground in Milwaukee; only in retrospect did owner Lou Perini admit that he had brought Grimm to Boston largely to acquaint him with the players he would be piloting in the city where he had gained substantial popularity. With the likes of Hank Aaron and Eddie Mathews in his lineup, Grimm moved Milwaukee into a contender's status over the next three years. But then in 1956 Perini decided that the low-key Grimm wasn't quite forceful enough, and replaced him with Fred Haney. Asked to take over the Cubs for a third time, in 1960, Grimm lasted little more than a month; behind an official explanation that his health wouldn't permit the daily rigors of piloting, he was traded back up to the broadcasting booth in exchange for Lou Boudreau. For those who had followed Grimm's career, it hardly came as a surprise that he was named as one of the revolving managers in Wrigley's College of Coaches the following year. In fact, Grimm never actually revolved back into the dugout.

HEINIE GROH

Groh helped breed generations of singles hitters with a specially designed bottle bat whose thick barrel and thin handle met without tapering. A defensive whiz at third base for Cincinnati between 1914 and 1921, he was the model contact hitter, batting below .280 only once in that span and attaining the .300 mark four times. Although Groh could wield his unusual club to hit the foul lines as well, leading the National League in doubles twice, he never hit more than 5 homers a season over his sixteen-year career.

GREG GROSS

Gross was baseball's most frequently used pinch hitter. Over seventeen (1973–89) seasons for the Astros, Cubs, and Phillies, he came off the bench for 588 official at-bats, hitting safely 143 times (.243). An outfielder when he was in the lineup, Gross was a pure singles hitter—whacking 5 home runs in one season but merely two others in the rest of his career, and managing more than 14 doubles in only one season.

LEFTY GROVE (Hall of Fame, 1947)

Grove had two careers—and a different personality during each of them. With the Athletics from 1925 to 1933, he was a flamethrowing hothead; traded to the Red Sox in 1934, he became a finesse pitcher with a more subdued demeanor to match. While he labored for Connie Mack in Philadelphia, the southpaw was the best pitcher in baseball and had the numbers to prove it: seven consecutive 20-win seasons, including 31 in 1931 and three other American League-leading totals; pacing the league in strikeouts in his first seven seasons; and back-to-back pitching Triple Crowns, topping AL hurlers in wins, strikeouts, and ERA in 1930 and 1931.

Grove's most notorious tirade followed a 1–0 defeat, on an error by substitute outfielder Jimmy Moore, as the left-hander sought his 17th consecutive victory in 1931. In the clubhouse after the game, Moore hid as the notoriously volatile Grove tore apart everything in sight, beginning with his own uniform and working his way up to several lockers, all the while damning the culprit who cost him a new AL record. The frightened outfielder emerged only when he realized that the object of the pitcher's wrath was regular left fielder Al Simmons, who had taken a few days

off and but for whose absence, Grove felt, the miscue would never have occurred.

In his first season in Fenway Park, however, Grove's arm went mysteriously dead, his record dropped to 8–8, his ERA exploded to 6.50, and his temper tantrums became even more monumental than the fits he had thrown in Shibe Park. But switching from a fireballer to a change-of-speeds craftsman, Grove became canny enough to notch one more 20-win season and to top AL hurlers in ERA four times; combined with the five ERA crowns he had won while with Philadelphia, this gave him a major league-record nine ERA season lows. At the same time, the man who had once trashed clubhouses around the league with regularity mellowed to the point that even a protracted quest for his 300th victory failed to ruffle him. Winning only 14 games in his final two seasons, Grove notched his 300th—and last—victory on July 25, 1941, stumbling home against the Indians by a score of 10–6.

RON GUIDRY

Guidry is best remembered for his career year of 1978, when he helped the Yankees to a stunning come-from-behind pennant win; if New York manager Billy Martin had had his way, however, the left-hander would have performed his heroics elsewhere. Convinced that the 5-foot, 11-inch, 160-pound Guidry wasn't big enough to be a winner in the majors, Martin had the Yankee front office shop him around throughout 1977 and into spring training of 1978 to, among others, the Cardinals (for Pete Vuckovich) and the Blue Jays (for Bill Singer). When there were no takers, Guidry went on to establish a record .893 winning percentage (25–3) for pitchers with 20 or more wins, lead the American League with a 1.74 ERA, and tie Babe Ruth's AL record of 9 shutouts by a southpaw—all in 1978. The left-hander also topped the 20-win mark on two other occasions, paced AL hurlers in ERA in one other season, and led all major league pitchers with 168 victories between 1977 and 1986. Guidry retired after an attempted comeback from elbow surgery in 1988; he would have retired sooner if not for the fact that he had been bankrupted by an embezzling agent.

TONY GWYNN

Gwynn has worked hard to gain his status as San Diego's all-time franchise player. Aside from compiling a .333 average and winning 5 batting titles since joining the Padres in 1982, the lefty-hitting outfielder has had to close his ears to the crashing of the organization around him on two occasions and pretend bafflement at being the source of season-long clubhouse conflict a third time.

A slap hitter who also gradually turned himself into one of the National League's best defensive right fielders, Gwynn won batting titles in 1984, 1987, 1988, 1989, and 1994; his .394 average in the abbreviated 1994 season was the highest by any NL player since Bill Terry's .401 in 1930. Gwynn has also paced the league in hits with more than 200 in four seasons and with 165 in 1994, and scored more runs than anyone else in 1986. While the Joan Kroc ownership deteriorated in the late 1980s, he remained the franchise's prize jewel, and went to the press on more than one occasion to blunt the possibility of being traded off. He showed the same attitude in 1993 when the Tom Werner ownership began holding a fire sale on such stars as Gary Sheffield and Fred McGriff—eleciting the admiration of many in San Diego for sticking with the franchise in miserable circumstances, but drawing some equal suspicion outside Southern California that he had grown too comfortable with his local popularity and preferred being a big fish in a small pond to playing with a contending club as just one of the cast.

In 1990 Gwynn was also at the center of months-long tensions with Jack Clark over the slugger's charges that he worried about his own hitting more than team victories. Although Clark received some backing in his allegations from Garry Templeton and other Padres, it was the accusers who were all wearing different uniforms a year later, while Gwynn went to work on another .300 season. Gwynn has attributed much of his batting success to his almost manic study of the videotaping of his plate appearances.

H

STAN HACK

Third baseman Hack was a perennial favorite with Cub fans, as much for his good looks and sunny disposition as for his .301 average over sixteen seasons. In 1935, vendors in the Wrigley Field bleachers did a vigorous trade in "Smile with Stan" mirrors, which the faithful used to reflect the sun in opposing batters' eyes.

HARVEY HADDIX

On May 26, 1959, Haddix pitched The Game. In what many consider the single greatest mound performance in baseball history, the Pittsburgh southpaw retired 36 consecutive batters through 12 innings, only to lose everything in the 13th on third baseman Don Hoak's throwing error, a sacrifice by Eddie Mathews, an intentional pass to Hank Aaron, and Joe Adcock's shot into the left-field stands that became a double when he passed Aaron on the bases but that nonetheless won the game for the Braves. It was also Haddix who, as a reliever, was credited with the victory in the final game of the 1960 World Series against the Yankees decided by Bill Mazeroski's home run.

CHICK HAFEY (Hall of Fame, 1971)

An early product of Branch Rickey's farm system, Hafey also later became a prime example of the St. Louis executive's trading philosophy. A right-handed hitter with some clout, the outfielder batted .317 over thirteen seasons between 1924 and 1937. In 1927 Hafey paced the National League in slugging average, then four years later led the circuit in batting with a .349 mark. No sooner had he won the batting title, however, than he was traded by Rickey to Cincinnati. It was a classic Rickey transaction; bringing the Cardinal executive a lot of cash for a player who had held out two years in a row and illustrating his view that it was better to trade a player at his crest or slightly past it (especially if, like Hafey, he was afflicted with an often debilitating sinus problem and questionable eyesight). Although Hafey went on to three more .300 seasons with the Reds, two of those years saw him plagued by shoulder injuries and appearing in very few games. As for Rickey, he had the consolation prize of Joe Medwick as his new left fielder.

CASEY HAGEMAN

Hageman's case against the Red Sox in 1913 was the first to gain the backing of the Players Fraternity. Demoted to the minors but promised that he would soon be recalled and that he would receive his major league salary in the interim, the right-hander appealed first to the Boston club and then to the governing National Commission when he was subsequently sent to an even lower minor league and his paycheck slashed. When neither Red Sox president Jimmy McAleer nor National Commission chairman Garry Herrmann would recognize his claim, Hageman went to union president Dave Fultz, who brought suit in New York State Supreme Court. The case took five years to resolve, by which time the Red Sox were being run by the perpetually strapped Harry Frazee, who refused to pay the court's judgment of $2,348 until threatened with a contempt citation.

JESSE HAINES (Hall of Fame, 1970)

Although he won 20 games three times for St. Louis in the 1920s, Haines was almost as known for providing three footnotes to the franchise history of the Cardinals. The most famous of these occurred in the seventh game of the 1926 World Series against the Yankees, when a bleeding hand blister forced his removal in the seventh inning, bringing on Grover Cleveland Alexander to strike out Tony Lazzeri with the bases loaded. The right-handed Haines was also an implicit testament to the effectiveness of Branch Rickey's farm system, since his acquisition from the Kansas City club of the American Association after the 1919 season marked the last time for twenty-five years that the Cardinals were compelled to make an outright purchase of a prospect. Lastly, Haines's eighteen years of service for the team between 1920 and 1937 was the longest by any pitcher in organization history and second only to Stan Musial among all players. Haines hung on with the club as long as he did partly because he was able to develop a knuckleball that prolonged his career but mainly because he was given a second role as an unofficial pitching coach; in fact, after his third 20-win season, in 1928, Haines never again won more than 13 games in a year and reached that level only twice over his final nine campaigns with the team.

ODELL HALE

Cleveland third baseman Hale recorded the most painful assist ever to start a triple play. With the bases loaded in the ninth inning of the first game of a September 7, 1935, doubleheader, Boston's Joe Cronin smashed the ball off Hale's head—directly into the hands of shortstop Bill Knickerbocker, who got the second out by tossing it to second baseman Roy Hughes, who relayed it to first baseman Hal Trosky to retire the side. Otherwise, Hale, who was called Bad News by pitchers wary of his slugging, was a right-handed hitter who batted .300 four times and drove in 100 runs twice in a ten-year career.

DICK HALL

In a nineteen-year career covering the 1950s and 1960s, Hall uncorked only a single wild pitch. His control was all the more remarkable in that he played his first couple of years for Pittsburgh as a third baseman and second baseman before becoming a bullpen ace for the Orioles.

GEORGE HALL

The first man to lead the National League in home runs (with 5 in 1876), Hall was at the center of the Louisville Crooks scandal a year later. When the left fielder confessed to club vice president Charles E. Chase in late October, the conspiracy (or rather conspiracies, since there were actually two separate illicit partnerships) unraveled, ending several months of rumor and speculation. Initially blaming the first plot on utility man Al Nichols, Hall admitted that he had cooperated in exhibition losses to teams in Lowell, Massachusetts, on August 30 and Pittsburgh on September 3, while claiming that he had refused to participate in throwing NL games. The second cabal, involving Hall and pitcher Jim Devlin, was responsible for losses to the NL Cincinnati Reds (on September 6) and the minor league Indianapolis Blues (on September 24); since Cincinnati was about to be suspended, games against the Reds had the force of exhibitions—or at least so Hall and Devlin argued. After first accusing Devlin of being the instigator, Hall admitted that he had actually been the one to approach both the pitcher and Nichols. The backbiting about who started what proved pointless when the NL banned all three, along with shortstop Bill Craver, for life.

BILLY HAMILTON (Hall of Fame, 1961)

No one will ever know how many times Hamilton stole a base, because until 1898 a runner received credit for a steal if he advanced more bases than the batter who advanced him. But however many of the 915 stolen bases recorded next to his name in a fourteen-year (1888–1901) career were earned by going from first to third on a single, Hamilton's .344 average and daring head-first slides, mostly for the Phillies and Braves, place him in the first rank of leadoff hitters and base runners. The left-hand-hitting outfielder crossed home plate more times in one season than anyone else (196 in 1894, in the Phillies' 132-game schedule), and averaged the most runs scored per game (1.06) in his career.

FRED HANEY

Haney illustrated the maxim that good players make good managers. After winning nothing but jeers for presiding over Browns and Pirates clubs that topped the 100-mark in defeats three times between them, he won nationwide plaudits for steering the Braves to successive pennants in 1957 and 1958, narrowly missing a third flag in playoffs against the Dodgers in 1959. As the first head of California's baseball operations in 1961, however, Haney's imprint was much more his own. On the one hand, his long friendship with Dodger general manager Buzzie Bavasi enabled him to go into the expansion draft with an up-to-date scouting report from Los Angeles, so that he was able to pick up such four-star prospects as Jim Fregosi and Dean Chance. On the other hand, he surrounded himself with a scouting network of old white cronies who were reluctant to go into the inner cities to look over black high schoolers, stagnating the franchise's farm system practically from the beginning. Haney was also conspicuously indecisive before the whimsical policy changes enacted almost annually by Angels owner Gene Autry and the circus stirred up by the antics of pitcher Bo Belinsky.

NED HANLON

It was as much Hanlon's instinct for timely trades and his genius for inside baseball as it was the fiery execution of his players that made the Baltimore Orioles a dominant force in the National League between 1894 and 1898. Hanlon, a fine defensive center fielder in the 1880s, took over a feeble Baltimore club in 1892 after having managed Pittsburgh entries in the NL and the Players League. His first move was to get rid of potential trouble by trading his predecessor, center fielder George Van Haltren, to the Reds for outfielder Joe Kelley. The following year Hanlon added shortstop Hughie Jennings; first baseman Dan Brouthers; and Willie Keeler, whom the manager converted from an infielder to an outfielder. Joining third baseman John McGraw and catcher Wilbert Robinson, the six future Hall of

Ned Hanlon poised to snare a fly ball (suspended from a string) for an early cigarette ad. National Baseball Library, Cooperstown, N.Y.

Famers formed the nucleus of the 1894 team, all of whose regulars batted over .300 and drove in more than 90 runs in the first of three consecutive pennant-winning seasons.

Later, Hanlon's moves took on an uncanny aspect. Typical was the sequence that began with switching Kid Gleason, a 15-game-winner on the mound in 1894, to second base. After Gleason hit .309 in 1895, Hanlon traded him to the Giants for Jack Doyle, who batted .339 and .354 the next two seasons. In 1898 Doyle and second baseman Heinie Reitz were shipped to Washington for first baseman Dan McGann, who enjoyed his only 100-RBI year; second baseman Gene DeMontreville, who hit 25 points higher than Reitz; and right-hander Doc McJames, who led the club with 27 victories in his only 20-win season.

While the Orioles never had pitching to match their everyday lineup, Hanlon was among the first to recognize that the new sixty-foot, six-inch distance between the mound and home plate, adopted in 1893, would mean wearier arms, sooner. To counter this, he instituted a three-man rotation that kept changing as pitchers wore out, held out, or were thrown out of the league. Perhaps his most spectacular feat was winning the 1894 pennant while juggling a mound corps that eventually numbered an unprecedented ten pitchers.

Hanlon was the progenitor of the clever and aggressive (and often illegal and brutal) style that characterized the Orioles. Outfielders hitting the cutoff man, pitchers covering first base on grounders to their left, runners taking the extra base, and McGraw and Keeler executing the hit-and-run became staples. Realizing that the new pitching distance also gave bunters and base runners an advantage, Hanlon had Oriole runners scampering around the basepaths on sacrifices, squeeze plays, and stolen bases. He encouraged cutting across the inside edge of the infield on the way from first to third and bumping opponents on the basepaths. Further, he did not discourage the vituperation and brawling that played such a large role in intimidating opponents, cheerfully reimbursing players for their repeated fines out of the handsome profits he realized from his 20 percent interest in the club.

In 1899 Hanlon moved his managerial skills—and most of his players—to Brooklyn while retaining the presidency of the Orioles as part of a new syndicate that controlled both clubs. A year later, when the NL cut its roster from twelve teams to eight, Hanlon clashed with Brooklyn president Charlie Ebbets, arguing for keeping the Baltimore franchise and abandoning Brooklyn. The collaboration lasted through 1905, but the outcome was evident as early as 1902, when after two pennants, in 1899 and 1900, Ebbets used his newly acquired controlling interest in the club to raise his own salary from $4,000 a year to $10,000 and to slash Hanlon's from $12,000 to $7,500.

CARROLL HARDY

Although he never drove in more than 36 runs in a season and ended an eight-year career with a .225 batting average, outfielder Hardy was called upon at one time or another to pinch hit for Ted Williams, Roger Maris, and Carl Yastrzemski.

BUBBLES HARGRAVE

Aside from Ernie Lombardi, his later successor as Cincinnati catcher, Hargrave is the only full-time receiver to win a batting crown. The right-handed hitter did it in 1926 with a .353 mark—one of seven times in his twelve-year career that he reached .300.

JACK HARPER

Harper incurred the wrath of Cub manager Frank Chance and was driven out of baseball for it. After winning 23 games twice (for the Cardinals in 1901 and the Reds in 1904), the right-hander beaned Chance early in the 1906 season. Vowing vengeance, the pilot traded pitcher Chick Fraser to Cincinnati to get Harper on his own club, cut his salary from $4,500 to $1,500, then used him in exactly a single game before releasing him at the end of the season. Harper appealed his treatment to the National Commission to no avail and, disgusted, he left the major leagues, with a 79–63 record.

TOMMY HARPER

Harper had his moments as a speedy outfielder, but none was as provocative as his departure from the Red Sox as a coach. In 1970, while with the Brewers, he showed uncharacteristic power, banging 31 homers while stealing 38 bases, to become the first American League player to reach the 30 mark in both those categories since Ken Williams of the Browns in 1922. Harper also led the AL in thefts twice and the National League in runs once in his fifteen-year (1962–76) career with eight teams.

After serving as a Boston coach for five seasons, Harper called attention to the lingering indifference of the franchise toward racial matters by suing the team in 1985 over its membership in a segregated Florida golf club where Red Sox brass and coaches (Harper excluded) would gather during spring training. The action was subsequently dropped, but on conditions never revealed; to this day both Harper and the Red Sox officials involved have declined to comment other than to say that their mutual silence was part of their accord.

KEN HARRELSON

Both on and off the field, outfielder Harrelson was considered baseball's chief fashion plate in the mid-1960s. On the field, he was the first player to wear batting gloves during a game, for the Kansas City Athletics in 1964; off the field, he helped popularize the period's craze for Nehru jackets. He was eventually cut loose by Kansas City after leading a player rebellion and calling owner Charlie Finley ''a menace to baseball.'' Finley was so infuriated with Harrelson that he didn't even expose him to waivers, but merely dropped him into free-agent status. The slugger then made his own deal with the Red Sox and enjoyed a couple of good years in Fenway Park before going on to various broadcasting and (short-lived) front office positions. With both the Red Sox and White Sox, his on-air comments have helped grease the skids for managers—not always to the surprise of his employer.

WILL HARRIDGE (Hall of Fame, 1972)

As president of the American League from 1931 to 1958, Harridge was the ultimate careerist—and statist. In 1911 he attracted the attention of AL founder Ban Johnson while employed as a clerk for the Wabash Railroad assigned to the league office in Chicago to handle arrangements for team transportation. After accepting Johnson's offer to become his private secretary, Harridge rose to league secretary upon Johnson's resignation in 1927, then succeeded Ernest Barnard in the top job in 1931. Lukewarm about night baseball and other innovations of his time, Harridge's most memorable decision was to negate midget Eddie Gaedel's appearance as a pinch hitter for the Browns in 1951 by erasing his name from official American League statistics. Since baseball was between commissioners at the time, St. Louis owner Bill Veeck had no place to go to appeal the decision. Gaedel's appearance was subsequently restored to the record book, but forever after the midget accused Harridge of ruining his baseball career.

BOB HARRIS

The violation of Harris's returning-GI rights by the Athletics in 1946 was the primary example of organized baseball's disregard for any law but its own and of the cozy relationship between major league owners and federal officials that made such disregard possible. A mediocre five-year big league right-hander, Harris returned from World War II only to be cut by Philadelphia in spring training of 1946. Some months later, he arranged a meeting with A's owner-manager Connie Mack for receiving the 1946 salary that was due him under the law guaranteeing returning veterans their jobs. The U.S. attorney, who should have been representing Harris, informed him at the meeting of what a great man Mack was and how much he meant to baseball, inducing the pitcher to accept a settlement for about two-thirds of what was due him. The federal prosecutor even prevailed upon Harris to pose with a beaming Mack for a photo opportunity.

BUCKY HARRIS (Hall of Fame, 1975)

Harris's presence in Cooperstown stems in part from his rookie managing success with the Senators in the mid-1920s and in part from his sheer availability as a pilot for another twenty-eight seasons. In fact, he won only one more pennant after his 1924–25 successes with Washington, with his overall record a decidedly modest 2,157–2,218 (.493).

As a player, Harris was a solid second baseman for the Senators through most of the 1920s. His most conspicuous moment with a bat in his hand came in the final game of the 1924 World Series against the Giants, when he banged a clutch two-run single in the eighth inning that tied up the contest and set the stage for Earl McNeely's pebble hit over the head of New York third baseman Freddie Lindstrom in the 12th inning. Washington's comeback world championship climaxed a year that began with the twenty-seven-year-old Harris being appointed manager and having to weather months of media and fan disapproval as Griffith's Folly. The following year, Harris led the Senators to another pennant, but had to put up with criticism even from American League president Ban Johnson when the club faltered in the World Series against Pittsburgh. For the next few seasons Harris was a constant target of Griffith Stadium boobirds, not only because of the team's drift downward but also because of press reports that his marriage to the daughter of a U.S. senator had made him snobbish and distant from his players. In 1929 he was scuttled in favor of Walter Johnson—the first of several occasions when Harris would lose a managing job to a high-profile diamond personality or future Hall of Famer.

Harris immediately moved to the Tigers as a playing manager; it was the start of another trend in which, despite the lack of success of the teams under his command, he ran off a string of twenty straight years without having to join the unemployment line. As the pilot of the Tigers, he presided over four of the grimmest years in franchise history, announcing his own resignation when he learned that the organization was considering replacing him with Babe Ruth. In 1934, Harris got in another year, as the dugout leader of the Red Sox—this time being shown the door for Joe Cronin. The trade-off was that he got to succeed Cronin with a second, eight-year stint with Washington. There were no 1924 miracles this time, however, and Harris managed only one first-division finish, finally resigning in 1942. For a chance of pace, he then went over to the National League, to the Phillies, lasting only a single season because of constant conflicts with owner William Cox. The climax to his brief tenure in Philadelphia came when he agreed to talk Phillies players out of a sitdown strike over his firing led by pitcher Schoolboy Rowe, then lingered at a bar with some sportwriters, disclosing between drinks that Cox had been betting on Philadelphia games. The revelation eventually led to the blacklisting of the executive.

After sitting on the sidelines for a couple of years, Harris returned to controversy in September 1946, when Yankee owner Larry MacPhail hired him for an unspecified front-office job. The appointment so angered acting manager Bill Dickey that he quit, and the way was open for Harris to go back to the dugout. In 1947 he steered New York to a world championship, but not without cost to his nerves because of the constant interference of the loose cannon MacPhail. At one point in the season, the pilot and Joe Di-Maggio had to talk the team out of an insurrection against the owner; after the World Series victory against the Dodgers, it was Harris himself who threw MacPhail out of the clubhouse for upbraiding outfielder Johnny Lindell for leaving the sixth game with a cracked rib. Although it might have seemed like an improvement at the time, MacPhail's departure from the organization and the arrival of George Weiss as general manager turned out to be worse for Harris. Despite keeping the Yankees in the 1948 pennant race down to the next-to-last day of the season, he was fired. Once again, his players protested; once again, he was pushed aside for a colorful name (Casey Stengel); and once again, he wasn't out of work very long.

Back with the Senators for the third time, in 1950, Harris squeezed out the last two .500 seasons the franchise would ever have, but accomplished little else. After five years, he was out the door again—his replacement this time being Charlie Dressen. Harris being Harris, he immediately latched on to another managing position, this time with a return engagement with the Tigers. Although he made up for his first stint with Detroit by keeping the club above .500 for two seasons, he finished fifth both times, making another change inevitable. The one difference, in what turned out to be his last dugout assignment, was that he was finally succeeded by someone with less box office cachet than he had: Jack Tighe.

JOE HARRIS

Harris's one moment of diamond glory wasn't really all that glorious, either. On September 1, 1906, the Red Sox right-hander dueled Philadelphia's Jack Coombs for 24 innings, thereby dividing the record for most innings pitched in an American League game. Unfortunately for Harris, he ended up a 4–1 loser. Even worse, he finished the year at 2–21 and his career at 3–30.

JACK HARSHMAN

A power-hitting first baseman in the minor leagues, Harshman was used almost exclusively as a pitcher in the majors. His power didn't vanish, however, as evidenced by the fact that 21 of his 76 hits (primarily for the White Sox in the

1950s) were home runs—by far the highest ratio of homers to safeties.

JOHN HART

As Cleveland general manager in 1992, Hart came up with management's most ambitious swerve around arbitration by signing twelve young Indians to long-term contracts. That disqualified them from salary arbitration for the duration. Among those inking the agreements were Carlos Baerga, Albert Belle, and Sandy Alomar.

FRED HARTMAN

Hartman achieved a measure of immortality by driving in the first two American League runs. The RBIs came when the White Sox third baseman singled with the bases loaded in the bottom half of the first inning of the AL's inaugural game, on April 24, 1901, off Cleveland righthander Bill Hoffer; otherwise, the right-handed hitter batted .278 in a six-year big league career with four clubs.

GABBY HARTNETT (Hall of Fame, 1955)

The National League's best all-around catcher in the first half of the twentieth century, Hartnett matched his American League contemporaries Bill Dickey and Mickey Cochrane in the curious fact that, for all his hitting ability, he never once led in any significant offensive category. On the other hand, his nineteen years (1922–40) with the Cubs and a final season with the Giants (1941) added up to a .297 average, 236 home runs, and 1,179 RBIs. His stellar years included 1930, when he batted .339 with 37 homers and 122 RBIs; and 1935, when he took MVP honors for swatting .344. Hartnett also hit the most famous home run in Chicago history when, on September 28, 1938, his twilight "homer in the gloamin' " in the ninth inning against Pittsburgh's Mace Brown enabled the Cubs to take a half-game lead over the Pirates that the Cubs never relinquished in their pursuit of a pennant. At the time, Hartnett was also the manager of the club.

Defensively, Hartnett had few equals in major league history—leading the NL in putouts four times, assists six times, and fielding average six times. The one asterisk to his defensive brilliance was in 1929, when what was diagnosed as a "dead arm" forced manager Joe McCarthy to sideline him in favor of Zach Taylor for all but pinch-hitting duties and a single game behind the plate. While doctors could offer no reason for the ailment, Hartnett's mother insisted that it was only a psychosomatic problem related to his wife's pregnancy; as soon as the Hartnett child was born during the off-season, the catcher had no more difficulty throwing.

In 1931 Hartnett created a flap when he was photographed with Al Capone in the Chicago mobster's box at Wrigley Field. The implication of the picture from a public relations point of view so distressed National League president John Heydler that he rushed through a rule forbidding players from socializing with fans before a game.

CLINT HARTUNG

Pitcher-outfielder Hartung has become synonymous with baseball's skeptical use of the term "phenom." When he joined the Giants in 1947, he was hailed by club publicists as a combination Christy Mathewson-Babe Ruth; over six seasons of moving back and forth between the mound and the outfield, however, Hartung managed a record of only 29–29 (with a 5.02 ERA), while hitting merely 14 home runs to go with his batting average of .238. Even Hartung's most noted diamond moment, in the 1951 playoffs against the Dodgers, was not due entirely to his baseball talent. After Don Mueller broke his ankle sliding into third base on the play immediately before Bobby Thomson's pennant-winning homer, manager Leo Durocher called in Hartung to take over as a pinch runner. Durocher later admitted that he had chosen the Hondo Hurricane over a couple of faster runners because of his fears that Brooklyn pitcher Don Newcombe would come after him for his game-long baiting, and he wanted the strapping Hartung between him and the Dodger right-hander.

ERNIE HARWELL

Harwell is the only baseball broadcaster ever traded for a player. He got his start as a major league announcer in 1948, when the Dodgers' Branch Rickey traded catcher Cliff Dapper to the minor league Atlanta Crackers to obtain his services as a complement to Red Barber and Connie Desmond. Later the Voice of the Tigers for thirty-two years, Harwell was dumped by Detroit owner Tom Monaghan after the 1991 season. Protests got him back for a more ceremonious farewell year, in 1993.

JOHN HASKELL

Umpire Haskell was American League president Ban Johnson's chief enforcer in his battle against field violence in the circuit's inaugural season and Haskell's only major league year of 1901. After a series of run-ins with John McGraw that resulted in a suspension for the Baltimore manager and a forfeited game for the club, Haskell turned up the heat. On August 5 he ejected Oriole first baseman Burt Hart for throwing his glove at the arbiter, then slugging him, after being called out trying to stretch a double into a triple; Johnson later suspended the rookie for life. White Sox shortstop Frank Shugart suffered the same fate after punching out Haskell and initiating a riot that required the intervention of police during an August 21 contest.

RON HASSEY

Although never known as a particularly deft defensive player, Hassey is the only catcher in history to have called the signals for two perfect games. As a member of the Cleveland Indians on May 15, 1981, he handled Len Barker's masterpiece against Toronto. On July 28, 1991, while winding down his career with Montreal, he was behind the plate for Dennis Martinez's immaculate no-hitter against the Dodgers.

BILLY HATCHER

As a member of the 1990 Reds, Hatcher lay ruin to a number of World Series records by collecting 7 straight hits against Oakland and by compiling 4 singles, 4 doubles, and a triple in 12 official plate appearances. The right-hand-hitting outfielder also drew 2 walks and was hit by a pitch in his club's 4-game sweep. While with the Astros in 1986, Hatcher clouted a 14th-inning homer in the sixth game of the National League Championship Series against the Mets that extended for another couple of innings one of the most dramatic postseason contests ever played.

PERCY HAUGHTON

A onetime Harvard football coach, Haughton took over as president of the Braves in 1912 and announced that he intended to stop the foul language used by players on the field. In a clubhouse talk to the team, he suggested that whenever a player was tempted to use a four-letter word to decry a strikeout or some other frustration, he think instead of the children in the stands and substitute the shout "Good!" The experiment in decorum lasted only until first baseman Sherry Magee had a ball bounce over his head into right field and began screaming "Good! Good!" Boston's tempestuous manager George Stallings had to be restrained by players on the bench from running onto the field to throttle Magee. Haughton decided to let the matter slide.

JOE HAUSER

Hauser is the only player to hit more than 60 home runs twice in organized ball. A lefty-swinging first baseman, he was brought to the majors by the Athletics in 1922 amid a great deal of ballyhoo that he would rival Babe Ruth for long-ball hitting. The closest he came to that in the majors was in 1924, when his 27 homers were second to Ruth's league-leading 46. The following year, Hauser snapped a kneecap during a spring training game—an injury that ultimately led to his return to the minors. In 1930, however, he belted 63 home runs for the International League Baltimore Orioles, then followed that with 69 round-trippers for Minneapolis in the American Association in 1933.

BILL HAWKE

Only a .500 pitcher in a three-year career with the Cardinals and Orioles, Hawke holds the distinction of having pitched the first no-hitter from the current mound distance of sixty feet, six inches. After his gem—a 5–0 victory over Washington on August 16, 1893—no pitcher would hold an opponent hitless for nine innings until more than four years later, the longest hiatus between no-hitters in major league history.

ANDY HAWKINS

Nobody ever gave up more runs without yielding a hit in a regulation effort than Hawkins.

Pitching for the Yankees against the White Sox on July 1, 1990, the right-hander carried a no-hitter into the bottom of the eighth inning, when his defense suddenly sabotaged him to allow Chicago to score 4 runs. Because the White Sox didn't have to bat again in the ninth, Hawkins was credited with an eight-inning no-hitter and a 4–0 loss.

Signed by the Yankees in 1989 after a moderately successful half-dozen years with the Padres, the right-hander became a .500 pitcher his first year in New York and worse in his second; he was out of baseball, with a lifetime record of 84–91, before the end of 1992.

PINK HAWLEY

An erratic right-hander, Hawley hit a National League record 195 batters—in only nine seasons (1892–1900) with four clubs. By contrast, it took Walter Johnson, the major league leader, 21 years to plunk 206 hitters.

BOB HAZLE

Few players blew onto the scene as loudly as Hazle did with the 1957 Braves. The left-hand-hitting outfielder, dubbed Hurricane by teammates, batted .403 in 41 games after being promoted from the minors in July, and was considered a savior of Milwaukee's drive to the pennant. Only a handful of games into the 1958 season, however, Hazle was packed off the the Tigers and was soon out of the majors altogether.

RICHIE HEBNER

Hebner holds the National League record for appearing in the most League Championship Series: eight. He also holds the mark for being on the most losing League Championship Series teams: seven. The left-hand-hitting third baseman had a lot to do with not making it eight-for-eight by cracking key home runs for Pittsburgh in the final two games of the 1971 postseason series against San Francisco. Five of Hebner's appearances were with the Pirates (1970–72, 1974–75), two with the Phillies (1977–78), and one with the Cubs (1984). A .276 hitter over eighteen major league seasons, he was the butt of endless jokes throughout his career for his off-season job as a grave digger. The humor had more of an edge to

it during his one season with the Mets, in 1979, when he spent most of the campaign berating the club, Shea Stadium, and New Yorkers in general, and got as good as he gave from the grandstands.

GUY HECKER

Hecker is the only major leaguer ever to lead his league in both pitching wins and batting average. Playing for Louisville of the American Association for all but one of his nine major league seasons, the right-hander topped AA pitchers with 52 victories in 1884. Two years later, he led the association with a .341 average. In the second game of an August 15, 1884, doubleheader, Hecker became the only player to score 7 runs in a game and the first of only two pitchers to hit 3 home runs in a single contest. (Jim Tobin of the Boston Braves tied the latter mark on May 13, 1942.) Hecker's effectiveness on the mound disappeared in 1887, when he strained his arm trying to adjust to a new rule limiting hurlers to one forward step in delivering the ball; he had always employed what was, in effect, a running start.

ROBERT HEDGES

Hedges had a long-range impact on the development of the major leagues when, as president of the Browns at the dawn of the century, he explored a prototypical version of the farm system. At the time, his chief aide was Branch Rickey. Although Hedges never exploited the system beyond moving a handful of players back and forth between the majors and the minors, behind what were described as ''gentlemen's agreements,'' Hedges's manipulations remained with Rickey as a means of building up a franchise.

A Cincinnati-based carriage manufacturer, Hedges rescued American League president Ban Johnson after one of the circuit's original teams, the Milwaukee Brewers, proved to be a financial disaster in 1901. With the club transplanted to St. Louis, Hedges turned it into a steady moneymaker despite the fact that the Browns never reached a World Series under his thirteen-year ownership. In 1905 he made Sportsman's Park the first concrete, double-decked stadium in either league. Hedges was as close to a mentor as Rickey ever had in the big leagues.

JIM HEGAN

Hegan was regarded as the defensive standard behind the plate in the American League for most of his seventeen-year (1941–42, 1946–60) career. Thanks to spending most of his time with the Indians, he handled more 20-game-winning seasons by pitchers (nineteen) than any other catcher in major league history.

HARRY HEILMANN (Hall of Fame, 1952)

Heilmann took a few years to get used to American League pitching, but after that he became one of the most potent offensive players in the game. The right-hand-hitting outfielder, who spent all but the final two of his seventeen big league seasons (between 1914 and 1932) with the Tigers, batted a career high of .403 in 1923—an average since eclipsed in the junior circuit only by Ted Williams's .406 in 1941. That was also one of four seasons in which Heilmann won the AL batting race. His batting crowns came in the odd-numbered years of 1921, 1923, 1925, and 1927, and his other three titles were also assaults on .400—coming in at .394, .393, and .398. He recorded four 200-hit seasons, eight with at least 40 doubles and 100 RBIs, and four with 100 runs. Heilmann, who batted .341 overall, is the only Hall of Famer who spent the brunt of his career with the Tigers never to play in a World Series.

SOLLY HEMUS

Hemus was to Eddie Stanky as Stanky had been to Leo Durocher. As both a middle infielder for St. Louis and Philadelphia in the 1950s and manager of the Cardinals from 1959 to 1961, Hemus sought to make up in provocative tactics and brawling what he lacked in natural talent. In his first year as St. Louis pilot, he was tossed from games eight times, and made it clear that he judged some of his players by their aggressiveness toward umpires as much as toward adversaries. Initially entertaining to local fans, Hemus alienated a good part of Missouri when he announced in 1960 that he was going to bench the enormously popular Stan Musial and give more playing time to young prospects. The outcry was so great, including threats to boycott home games, that he had to relent on his plan, for the most part sitting Musial down only for road games.

DAVE HENDERSON

In two games in 1986, Henderson had more dramatic RBIs than most players have in a career. With two strikes on him and two outs in the ninth inning of the fifth game of the League Championship Series, the right-hand-hitting Boston outfielder reached California's Donnie Moore for a two-run homer that gave the Red Sox a 1-run lead and saved them from pennant elimination. After California tied the game in the bottom of the inning, Henderson hit a sacrifice fly in the 11th inning that put his team ahead for good and started a 3-game comeback victory for the flag. The home run off Moore was Henderson's first hit of the playoffs; he had also helped the Angels to a lead earlier in the game by accidentally tapping a Bobby Grich drive over the wall for a home run.

In the ensuing World Series against the Mets, Henderson outhit everyone on both teams by getting 10 safeties in 15 at-bats; his most important blow was a home run in the top of the 10th inning of the sixth game that appeared to seal a Boston championship. It went for naught, however, when the Mets staged their own startling comeback in the bottom of the inning to pull out the contest and head for their 7th-game victory two days later.

RICKEY HENDERSON

Baseball's all-time leadoff man and stolen-base king, Henderson has suffered from stereotypes about black players as much as anyone in recent decades. Mainly because of his on-field arrogance and round-the-clock self-absorption, he has had his every poor performance put down to a caricatured laziness or racial bitterness. In fact, the right-hand-hitting outfielder has made a perfect set with Ty Cobb and Pete Rose in going out of his way to stick it to the opposition (as in patented snap catches) and in complaining constantly about teammates having more lucrative contracts than he has. The perception of Henderson the Dog has survived despite the adamant denials of two of his managers, Billy Martin and Tony LaRussa, not the most likely candidates for shielding an alleged jaker.

Henderson began demolishing the all-time steals record when he joined Oakland in 1979 and

Rickey Hnederson raises the trophy of his record 939th stolen base, on May 1, 1991. Ron Riesterer/Oakland Tribune.

swiped 33 bases. Over the next seven seasons he led the American League in thefts, establishing an all-time record for swipes in a year in 1982 with 130. Before slowing down in the early 1990s, he took four more stolen base titles while also pacing the league three times in walks, once in hits, and five times in runs scored. At the same time, he was boasting unusual power for a hitter usually slotted in the leadoff spot, turning in three seasons of 20-plus home runs; entering the 1995 season, he had a firm grip on the mark for leading off a game with a four-bagger by having done it 66 times. Henderson's best regular-season performance came in 1990, when he took MVP honors for batting .325 with 28 homers and 65 steals. He was never more devastating, however, than during the 1989 American League Championship Series, for Oakland against the Blue Jays, when he reached base 14 of 23 times; his performance included 6 hits, 7 walks, 1 hit-by-pitch, 5 RBIs, 8 runs scored, and 8 stolen bases. Going into the 1995 season he had a record 1,117 career steals.

Henderson was traded by Oakland to the Yankees in 1985. Despite some good seasons in the Bronx, he failed to spur the club into postseason play and became the target of more than one derisive headline for hamstring pulls. In 1989 he was traded back to the Athletics just in time for two pennants. Toward the end of the 1993 season he was swapped to the Blue Jays for pennant insurance; although Toronto won its second straight world championship, it did so without any significant contribution from Henderson, and he returned to Oakland for a third time as a free agent.

BOB HENDLEY

Hendley's most noted big league moment was a losing effort. As a member of the Cubs on September 9, 1965, the southpaw pitched a 1-hitter against the Dodgers, but lost, 1–0, because mound opponent Sandy Koufax was in the meantime fashioning a perfect game. Aside from Koufax, Hendley's greatest nemesis was Frank Howard, who over one span clouted 5 successive home runs off the lefty, made out a couple of times, then hit a sixth blast.

CLAUDE HENDRIX

Hendrix won 143 games for the Pirates, Chicago Whales (of the Federal League), and Cubs between 1911 and 1920, but he made a far bigger mark for being replaced by Grover Cleveland Alexander as the Cubs starting pitcher on August 31, 1920. Hendrix was scratched by club president Bill Veeck, Sr., following several phone calls and telegrams warning that the right-hander had been paid off to drop the game to the Phillies. After the story broke, Cook County District Attorney MacClay Hoyne summoned a special grand jury to investigate the incident—a probe that was eventually expanded to include allegations and rumors about the 1919 World Series. Hendrix, a two-time 20-game winner, got lost in the frying of larger fish, was released over the winter, and never appeared in another major league game.

TOMMY HENRICH

Henrich had his own initiative—plus an assist from Commissioner Kenesaw Landis—to thank for his eleven-year (1937–42, 1946–50) career with the Yankees. Convinced that he was being illegally hidden in the minor leagues by Cleveland general manager Cy Slapnicka, Henrich reported the infraction to Landis, who took one look at his bush league record and another at the Indians' manipulation of his contract and declared him a free agent. With the Yankees winning an eight-team auction for his services, Henrich went on to bat .282 and to lead the American League in triples twice and in runs scored once. The lefty-swinging outfielder-first baseman had his most memorable diamond moments in World Series play against the Dodgers: In 1941, he was at the plate when Mickey Owen let a third strike get away from him and reached first to begin a fourth-game-winning rally; in 1947, he drove in the winning run in three of the four New York victories; and in 1949, he ended a scoreless duel between Allie Reynolds and Don Newcombe with a ninth-inning, sudden-death home run in the first game.

BABE HERMAN

It was somewhat typical of Herman's career that stories about his most famous field moment—the 1926 game against the Braves in which he "doubled into a double play"—usually omit the particular that the hit also won the contest for the Dodgers. A left-hand-hitting first baseman-outfielder, he was in fact one of the best hitters in the National League in the late 1920s and early 1930s, averaging .324 over thirteen seasons. Especially for the two-year span of 1929–30, he ranked statistically with Bill Terry and Lefty O'Doul as the hardest outs in both leagues—turning in batting marks of .381 and .393, respectively, the latter second to Terry's .401.

Even though he led the league in errors at different positions in successive years (first base in 1927, the outfield in 1928), a good part of Herman's public image as a goof who was falling over his feet when he wasn't being hit on the head by fly balls represents inaccurate history, especially in the nostalgic misconception that he symbolized the Daffiness Boys—a term that originally referred not so much to the Brooklyn players on the field as it did to the bungling, quarrelsome executives who ran the club. The distinction was never more clear than in 1932, when the front office, irritated by Herman's threats to

sit out the season if his contract demands were not met, swapped both him and future Hall of Fame catcher Ernie Lombardi to Cincinnati. More than any other single transaction, the move doomed the Dodgers to the nether regions of the league for the rest of the decade. When he was forty-two and out of baseball for eight years, Herman was brought back to Ebbets Field as a wartime gate attraction in 1945. In what some saw as a deliberate crowd-pleasing move, he singled in his first at-bat—and then promptly tripped over first base.

BILLY HERMAN (Hall of Fame, 1975)

Herman had a way of making both his presence and his absence noticed. It was a tendency that announced itself with his very first at-bat for the Cubs, on August 29, 1931, when, facing Si Johnson of the Reds, Herman hit a foul in front of the plate that bounced back to knock him out and force his removal from the field on a stretcher. For the rest of the decade, however, the right-hand-hitting second baseman captured attention for his key offense and defense on three Chicago pennant winners. The span included seven seasons of .300 or better, with his best numbers coming in 1935, when he batted .341, scored 113 runs, and led the National League in both hits (227) and doubles (57). In 1941 his absence was noticed over the first weeks of the season in Brooklyn, which badly needed a second baseman to make a pennant run, and subsequently in Chicago, where newly installed general manager Jim Gallagher was talked into a one-sided deal with the Dodgers. In Ebbets Field, Herman sparked the Dodgers to the expected pennant with a .291 mark, but then came up practically absent again when a rib injury sidelined him for most of Brooklyn's loss to the Yankees in the World Series. In 1946 he was acquired by the Braves, contributing field leadership and a .306 mark to Boston's first finish in the first division in twelve years. The following year, Braves owner Lou Perini held an auction on his services, finally surrendering him to the Pirates, who wanted him as a playing manager. When Herman arrived in Pittsburgh, the first words out of his mouth were that the Pirates had paid too much for him—an accurate observation, since he was at the end of the line as an infielder, he couldn't pilot the club even to .400 ball, and the player obtained by Boston for him—Bob Elliott—went on to win the MVP trophy and lead the Braves to a pennant.

ENZO HERNANDEZ

A shortstop for the Padres in the 1970s, Hernandez holds the record for the worst clutch hitting in a season. In 549 official at-bats in 1971, he drove in merely 12 runs.

GUILLERMO HERNANDEZ

Hernandez provided one of the biggest and quickest payoffs for a trade when he won both the American League MVP and Cy Young Award for the Tigers in 1984. Detroit obtained the southpaw reliever from the Phillies in exchange for catcher John Wockenfuss and outfielder Glenn Wilson only a month before the start of the season. Hernandez, who had posted only 35 saves over seven preceding seasons, notched 32 for the Tigers to go along with 9 wins and a league-leading 80 appearances. The screwballer also picked up a save in the League Championship Series against Kansas City and two more against San Diego in the World Series to nail down Detroit's title. Over the next couple of years, he racked up 56 more saves.

KEITH HERNANDEZ

If not everyone has been ready to call Hernandez the best defensive first baseman in baseball history, nobody has been confident about naming someone better. He was the heart of the 1980s Met teams *after* he had won National League MVP honors, and his fielding brilliance was contained not only in his own range and catlike instincts but also in his attendant ability to hide the mediocrity of fellow infielders by covering much of their territory and pulling down their errant throws. Off the field, Hernandez's leadership was more of a sometime thing, especially in two periods years apart when he was linked to drugs and when he was mainly consumed by his own injuries. With the exception of Jackie Robinson and Roberto Clemente, however, nobody inspired more contemporaries to wear a uniform number in his honor; among those to adopt his No. 17 have been Mark Grace and onetime Mets teammates David Cone, Ron Darling, Bob Ojeda, and Darryl Strawberry..

Hernandez spent the first nine and a half years of his seventeen-year (1974–90) career with the Cardinals. In 1979, the left-handed swinger shared MVP honors (the only such tie) with Willie Stargell of the Pirates for leading the National League in batting (.344), on-base percentage (.421), doubles (48), and runs scored (116), while also banging out 210 hits and driving in 105 runs. He never again reached any of those category numbers, but he did have six more .300 seasons to contribute to a career .296 average. Despite being considered one of the bulwarks of the young St. Louis team that won the world championship in 1982, he was abruptly traded to New York the following year in exchange for pitchers Neil Allen and Rick Ownbey. In his initial explanation of the mystifying deal, Cardinal manager Whitey Herzog claimed that he had gotten tired of Hernandez's habit of doing crossword puzzles in the clubhouse; it wasn't until 1985 that real light was shed on the transaction, when the first baseman was called to testify in the Pittsburgh drug trials and he admitted that he had been a cocaine user. The degree of his popularity at Shea Stadium by that point was demonstrated when fans gave him a standing ovation in his first game after the testimony—a reaction that infuriated media moralists.

While in New York, Hernandez's off-the-record quotes to reporters about the latest dramas engulfing the team became enough of an open secret that almost as many people called him ''a team source'' as others referred to him as ''Mex.'' If many of the nonattributed observations were self-serving, they were equally effective in sending wake-up calls to dragging teammates, not least slugger Strawberry. More important, Hernandez could back them up with his continued deftness in the field and strong clutch hitting—indispensable ingredients for the Mets' rise to the world championship in 1986. His biggest hit of all came in the sixth inning of the seventh World Series game against Boston when, with the bases loaded and the Red Sox ahead, 3–0, he singled in 2 runs and set in motion the rally to a victory.

The ensuing years were not as glorious. Although the Mets won a second Eastern Division title, in 1988, Hernandez himself became bogged down with hamstring problems. In 1989 he traded punches with Strawberry during spring training after needling the outfielder about his hangovers and field performance. At this point the same reporters who had been hanging on Hernandez's every (anonymous) word for years began referring to him as The Dark Prince for his critical assessments of the team they were only too keen to publish, if still without attribution. Hernandez finished his career under contract to Cleveland, but rarely in an Indians uniform. Thanks to lingering leg problems, he played in merely 43 games through a two-year pact.

While it was recognized as an official statistic, Hernandez compiled the most career game-winning RBIs (129) and the most in a single season (24 in 1985).

GARRY HERRMANN

Hermann's twenty-five year reign (1902–27) as boss of the Reds demonstrated that outlandishness and pliability could coexist. A man with a taste for checked suits and pinky rings, he was known to some as The Walking Delicatessen for his habit of going everywhere with a supply of sausages that he would gobble down, whatever the setting. He was no stranger to taverns, either, and continually boasted of his ability to outdrink all comers. But behind the cartoon character was an owner whose partners included a Cincinnati political thug (George Cox) who got his way by threatening municipal or physical reprisals against anyone opposed to franchise desires and who delighted in humiliating Herrmann with public declarations that "When I whistle, you dogs come out of your holes."

The Cincinnati official was the prime mover in the National League's acceptance of the American League as an equal in 1903, surrendering his claim to future Hall of Fame outfielder Sam Crawford to effect the peace, and was considered reliable enough by his colleagues to be given the crucial swing vote on the three-man National Commission (the other members were the presidents of the two leagues) that dictated policy for all of organized baseball before Kenesaw Landis was chosen commissioner. Herrmann was, however, frequently criticized by his NL colleagues for siding too often with AL president Ban Johnson in interleague squabbles.

Garry Herrmann held the pivotal swing vote on baseball's National Commission prior to the formation of a commissioner's office. National Baseball Library, Cooperstown, N.Y.

Herrmann the clown and Herrmann the lawmaker came together in one incident when he cast the deciding vote obligating a San Francisco minor league team to pay for second baseman Eddie Colligan even though the infielder had been secretly hospitalized with a broken leg at the time of the sale. When the San Francisco owner, J. Cal Ewing, protested the decision, Herrmann replied that Ewing should have informed himself of Colligan's condition before accepting the deal. A few weeks later, the Cincinnati president received five barrels of sauerkraut COD from Ewing, only to discover after paying for it that it was completely rancid. When Herrmann protested to Ewing, the San Francisco owner blithely pointed out that Herrmann should have informed himself of the sauerkraut's condition before paying for it.

WILLARD HERSHBERGER

Hershberger has probably been the most noted of the numerous suicides that have afflicted the Cincinnati franchise over the years. A reserve catcher for the team in 1940, he severed his jugular vein with a razor in a Boston hotel room during a road trip. It emerged subsequently that the despondent Hershberger had alluded to his intentions in a conversation with manager Bill McKechnie, but that the pilot had regarded the threat as only a passing glumness. Some Reds players attributed the act to Hershberger's shock at having called for a pitch against Giants catcher Harry Danning a few days earlier that had ended up as a grand-slam home run and cost Cincinnati a key game; for his part, McKechnie never revealed the details of his talk with the catcher. The lack of a suicide note has tantalized newspaper reporters for more than a half century, prompting some bizarre theories that Hershberger might even have been murdered. Among other Cincinnati players to take their own lives were Cannonball Crane (chloral acid, 1896), Danny Mahoney (carbolic acid, 1911), Pea Ridge Day (gunshot, 1934), and Benny Frey (exhaust fumes, 1937).

OREL HERSHISER

Hershiser set a major league record of 59 consecutive scoreless innings for the Dodgers by preventing any opponent from crossing the plate between August 30 and September 28, 1988. He took Cy Young honors that year for his 23–8 record and National League-leading 8 shutouts.

BUCK HERZOG

John McGraw could never get enough of Herzog—except when he was around. A second baseman with more defensive than offensive abilities, Herzog was traded away by McGraw's Giants three times—once in managerial pique, once as a test of power between the pilot and the New York ownership, and once amid suspicions of World Series chicanery. The first deal, to the Braves in 1910, came after McGraw decided that the infielder's constant questioning of strategic moves indicated managerial ambitions best served in Boston. Braves manager Fred Tenney felt the same cramps, so he swapped Herzog back to New York the following year. Then, during the 1913–14 off-season, McGraw, who had always made his own trades, was informed after the fact that newly installed president Harry Hempstead had sent the second baseman to the Reds. This

prompted a McGraw ultimatum to Hempstead either to leave the baseball to him or replace him; Hempstead backed down.

The Cincinnati transaction finally allowed Herzog to realize his managerial ambitions, but little else. When the Reds finally got tired of his stewardship over cellar-dwelling clubs, they sent him back to the Giants once again—this time in the so-called Hall of Fame Trade of 1916 in which New York surrendered future Cooperstown residents Christy Mathewson, Edd Roush, and Bill McKechnie. Back in the Polo Grounds, Herzog held down second base without much comment until the 1917 World Series against the White Sox. When Chicago won the postseason contest after some dubious New York fielding at key junctures, McGraw let some intimates know that he suspected Herzog of having played out of position deliberately. Although charges were never brought against him, Herzog once again hit the trail after the World Series, going back to Boston. His name cropped up again a couple of years later in connection with other (unproven) game fix allegations.

WHITEY HERZOG

Herzog has achieved enough to deserve Gene Mauch's reputation as baseball's brightest dugout intelligence over recent decades, and also enough to merit Earl Weaver's fame for crustiness and gratuitousness.

A backup outfielder of no particular distinction for a number of American League clubs in the 1950s and early 1960s, Herzog made his first impression as a strategist as player development head for the Mets, for whom he groomed the team's formidable pitching staffs in the late 1960s. Annoyed that he was never given a shot as manager or general manager of the club, he moved on to Texas, where, as pilot in 1973, his first pronouncement was that the Rangers were "one of the worst teams" he had ever seen. Things went downhill from there, and after a season-long battle with owner Bob Short over the forced feeding of eighteen-year-old southpaw David Clyde as a major leaguer, Herzog was replaced in September by Billy Martin. He reappeared with Kansas City midway through the 1975 season, a prelude to the three consecutive division titles he would win while managing the Royals. All three times, however, his clubs fell to the Yankees in the League Championship Series—losses that Herzog did not suffer easily. After the 1977 playoffs, for instance, he blamed the defeat at least partly on slugging first baseman John Mayberry, hinting broadly that the player had been on drugs and demanding that he be dispatched elsewhere. Following the 1978 series, Herzog risked the disaffection of star players George Brett and Hal McRae by firing batting coach Charlie Lau, blaming him for trying to make the offense too homogenized. When Herzog could manage only a second-place Western Division finish the following year, he was fired.

In 1980 Herzog took over the Cardinals early in the season and so impressed owner Gussie Busch by keeping the club over .500 until August despite no front-line pitching that he was asked to leave the dugout before the end of the year for a bigger policy role, as general manager. In the latter role, he engineered several major swaps that imported the likes of relief ace Bruce Sutter to St. Louis. Once Herzog had completed his transactions, he left the front-office paperwork in the hands of Joe McDonald and returned to the dugout in 1981 for what would be a nine-and-a-half-year run. In that time he won three pennants (1982, 1985, and 1987) and one world championship (1982). Another postseason appearance was denied the club by the bizarre split-season formula employed in 1981 following the players strike: Although the Cardinals ended up with the best overall Eastern Division record, they finished a game and a half behind the Phillies over the first half and a half game behind the Expos over the second half.

Herzog's St. Louis teams were heavy on switch-hitting speedsters who could exploit to the full, offensively as well as defensively, the artificial turf at Busch Stadium. When he no longer had an ace reliever like Sutter, he pioneered the bullpen-by-committee system. His tactical agility earned him the sobriquet The White Rat, but it was a nickname that returned to haunt him in his last years with the club, when impatience with underachieving players was often interchangeable with surliness. He had several major clashes with players—most serendipitously when his fury at

an obscene on-field gesture by shortstop Garry Templeton prompted a swap for Ozzie Smith, most disastrously when he rushed Keith Hernandez off to the Mets. During his reign the Cardinals were also beset by an inordinate number of drug or drinking casualties (Hernandez, Lonnie Smith, and David Green) and sore-armed pitchers (Ken Dayley, Jeff Lahti, Danny Cox, Greg Mathews, and Joe Magrane). When the aged Busch assured him that he had a lifetime contract with the organization despite such problems, Herzog's barbed reply was, "Whose lifetime—mine or yours?" By the end of the decade he was complaining, "I can't get these guys to play for me"; shortly afterward, he resigned.

In 1991 Herzog resurfaced with what appeared to be carte blanche for reorganizing the Angels. He was disabused of that notion quickly, however, when owner Gene Autry's wife, Jackie, turned thumbs down to resigning Wally Joyner or offering big money to free agent Bobby Bonilla. Frustrated in trying to make the club an immediate contender, Herzog concentrated on rebuilding the California farm system, while filling the big league roster with over-the-hill players who came relatively cheaply. His greatest achievement with the team might have been hanging on until January 1994, before finally resigning.

JOHN HEYDLER

Heydler's main claim to fame while serving as National League president between 1918 and 1934 was in being the official who finally banned Hal Chase from baseball after years of charges that the first baseman had been throwing games. Otherwise, Heydler was mainly an appendage—not only to NL owners, but also to Commissioner Kenesaw Landis. Once Landis took office in 1920, in fact, league owners routinely went over Heydler's head to the commissioner if they didn't like the first answer. This was particularly clear in the early 1920s in the case of pitcher Rube Benton, whom Heydler wanted kept out of the game for his involvement in the 1919 Black Sox scandal; determined to have the hurler on his staff, Cincinnati owner Garry Herrmann not only won Benton's reinstatement from Landis but also had the commissioner scold Heydler publicly for trying to block the move. Heydler was also mostly a conspicuous silence during the deterioration of the Brooklyn and Philadelphia franchises in the 1920s and the ongoing dubiousness of Giants manager John McGraw selecting various owners for the Boston Braves. In the late 1920s, in an attempt to counter the publicity won by the American League because of Babe Ruth's slugging feats, Heydler proposed the adoption of a designated hitter rule but failed to win over enough NL owners to the innovation.

Prior to sitting behind a desk, Heydler had been an umpire. He quit that profession in 1898 in outrage over the verbal and physical abuse heaped on arbiters, especially by the Baltimore Orioles.

KIRBY HIGBE

Higbe was the only major league pitcher who owed some of his success to pinochle. Obtained by the Dodgers for the 1941 season after a couple of humdrum years with the Cubs and Phillies, he impressed manager Leo Durocher as being more interested in cards and liquor than in pitching. Himself no stranger to a card table, Durocher played a season-long pinochle game with the right-hander, offering to cancel 200 points of his continuous lead whenever Higbe pitched Brooklyn to a victory. By the time Higbe had erased his deficit with Durocher, he had led the National League with 22 wins and helped the Dodgers to a pennant.

PINKY HIGGINS

In 1938, Red Sox third baseman Higgins established the big league mark for most consecutive hits, with 12. The streak, which was later tied by Walt Dropo, included 2 walks. A right-handed hitter, Higgins had a twelve-year career between 1930 and 1946 for the Red Sox, Athletics, and Tigers, over which he averaged .292 as a batter. As Boston's manager from 1955 to 1962, he was all too comfortable with the pervasive franchise racism, once telling Boston beat writer Clif Keane that he was ''nothing but a fucking nigger-lover'' for observing that a young Minnie Minoso was the best all-around player in the league.

DICK HIGHAM

Higham is the only umpire ever expelled from baseball for corruption. On June 24, 1882, he faced a special National League meeting to consider charges that he had conspired with gamblers to fix games. When a handwriting expert hired by Detroit Wolverine president W. C. Thompson showed that Higham had penned incriminating letters, the umpire tendered his resignation. He later became a bookie and reappeared publicly only in 1889 as the victim of a Kansas City crowd that beat him for spreading malicious rumors about a bartender's wife.

JOHN HILLER

Hiller became baseball's all-time comeback player when he recovered from a 1970 heart attack to pace American League relievers a few years later. The Detroit southpaw's seizure, which led to the removal of seven feet of intestines to relieve a cholesterol problem, caused him to miss the 1971 season, but the following year he returned to post a 2.03 ERA in 24 games. In 1973 Hiller led the AL in both saves (38) and appearances (65). In 1974 he set a more mixed mark for decisions by a reliever, winning 17 and losing 14.

PAUL HINES

A superstar of the National League's first decade, Hines may or may not have made the first unassisted triple play (and the only one by an outfielder) and won the first Triple Crown. Playing for the Providence Grays on May 8, 1878, he made an impressive shoestring catch in short left-center field, then tagged third to retire, according to the rules of the day, the two runners, both of whom had already rounded that base; the confusion about the accomplishment arises from his subsequent throw to second base, which, while necessary to complete a triple killing under modern rules, was a superfluous gesture at the time. Further, the center fielder's .358 average, 4 homers, and 50 RBIs, also in 1878, are now recognized as league-leading figures; Hines got to wear only two of the crowns, however, because contemporary statistics show Abner Dalrymple of Chicago as the batting champion.

Unlike Babe Ruth's putative called shot in the 1932 World Series, the outfielder's prediction of a home run in a game in Boston attracted considerable press attention; before the game, he had marked the round-tripper next to his name in the fifth-inning column on the official scorer's sheet, then made good on his prediction. With less fanfare, he raced teammate Cap Anson to become the first major leaguer to stroke 1,000 hits; Hines ended the 1884 season with 1,027, Anson with 1 fewer safety. Finally, Hines is credited with having been the first to wear sunglasses in the field, a practice he began in 1882.

CHARLES E. HINTON

Professor Hinton unveiled his invention, the first pitching machine, in the Princeton University gymnasium on December 15, 1896.

DON HOAK

An infielder for the Dodgers, Reds, and Pirates among others in the 1950s and 1960s, third baseman Hoak's reputation as a hothead often slighted his baseball smarts. On April 21, 1957, while with Cincinnati, he even prompted a change in baseball's interference rules when, as the lead runner on second, he deliberately grabbed a potential double-play ball headed for the shortstop so he would be declared out but the twin killing avoided. Although this was the third time that season that a member of the Reds had pulled a similar ploy, Hoak's cavalier toss of the ball to Milwaukee shortstop Johnny Logan after his interference underscored the existence of the loophole; subsequently the two leagues ruled that both the runner and the batter are out when a runner willfully interferes with a play.

BUTCH HOBSON

Hobson's .899 fielding average for Boston in 1978 represented the first time since 1916 that a major league regular couldn't maintain a defensive average of .900. Suffering from severe elbow problems, the slugging third baseman had to traverse half the infield to make even routine throws to first; the situation became so dire that he pleaded with manager Don Zimmer to take him out of the lineup because of the damage he was doing to the team. The right-handed hitter lasted eight seasons (1975–82) with the Red Sox, Angels, and Yankees.

Gil Hodges ranked among baseball's elite for run production in the 1950s. Brooklyn Public Library—BROOKLYN COLLECTION.

GIL HODGES

As both a player for the Boys of Summer Dodgers and the manager of the Miracle Mets, Hodges was the guest of honor at a New York admiration feast for much of his career. But his popular image of a silent, forbearing Mr. Stalwart also obscured to some extent his ranking among the greatest midcentury sluggers and his tactical deviousness as a pilot.

Hodges's move from catcher to first base midway through the 1948 season (to make room in the Brooklyn starting lineup for Roy Campanella) corresponded with the power outburst that would give him 370 home runs over an eighteen-year career. Using the barometers of hits, home runs, runs batted in, runs scored, stolen bases, and batting average, the right-handed slugger was among the top five major leaguers in offensive production in the 1950s (the others were Stan Musial, Duke Snider, Richie Ashburn, and Mickey Mantle). Among other things, Hodges drove in more than 100 runs in seven consecutive seasons and hit at least 25 homers eight times. Four of the round-trippers came in a single game, against the Braves on August 21, 1950, marking the first time that anybody had accomplished that feat at night.

With the possible exception of Pee Wee Reese, Hodges was the most popular of the midcentury Dodgers, not least because he was one of the team's few year-round Brooklyn residents. Much of the borough went into mourning when he went hitless in 21 at-bats in the 1952 World Series against the Yankees and started the 1953 season by going only 14 for 75. Then, in June 1953, a priest named Herbert Raymond cemented the first baseman's place in the lore of Brooklyn by telling his parishioners: "It's too warm this morning for a sermon. Go home, keep the Commandments, and say a prayer for Gil Hodges." Within days, Hodges erupted for a season that eventually produced 31 home runs, 122 runs batted in, and a .302 average. In 1955 he even avenged his miserable 1952 World Series by driving in both runs in the 2–0 win by Johnny Podres in the seventh game of the Series that brought Brooklyn its one and only world championship.

A natural candidate for the expansion Mets in 1962, he kept things symmetrical by hitting the franchise's first home run, on April 11, but otherwise contributed little but nostalgia for New York's NL fans. The following year, he was traded to the Senators for outfielder Jimmy Piersall, and immediately announced his retirement to take over as Washington manager. Because he had still been technically active for the swap, Hodges narrowly missed gaining another baseball footnote when, in 1967, he was shipped back to Shea Stadium to manage the Mets in exchange for Bill Denehy and $150,000; no other retired player has come as close to being traded for active major leaguers twice in order to manage.

In New York, Hodges inherited the nucleus of the Miracle Mets—not least ace right-hander Tom Seaver. From the point of view of the standings, Hodges's influence on the team in 1968 seemed minimal; it even appeared perilously strenuous when he suffered a heart attack after the season. The following year, however, he offered numerous reminders that, his alter boy image notwithstanding, he had played under such masters of the devious as Leo Durocher and Charlie Dressen. What became the most noted of all Hodges's juiced-up tactics was the Shoe Polish Gambit: Like Dressen he always kept a couple of balls in the dugout smeared with shoe polish just in case there was ever an opportunity to argue that a New York hitter had been struck by a pitch. In the fifth game of the 1969 World Series against Baltimore, just such an opportunity arose with Cleon Jones at bat, and gullible umpires sent the outfielder to first base in what proved to be the turning point of New York's conclusive victory. It was also Jones who, on July 30 of the same year, had helped demonstrate Hodges's no-nonsense command of the team. After the outfielder had gone after a couple of balls with little energy, Hodges called time and walked ever so slowly out to left field where, against a deathlike silence from the Shea Stadium grandstands, he ordered Jones to accompany him back to the dugout. Many of the Met players said later that the episode was crucial to the team's victory.

With the death of general manager Johnny Murphy after the 1969 season, Hodges began to act almost as concerned with keeping intrusive board chairmen M. Donald Grant and new general manager Bob Scheffing out of the clubhouse as he was about keeping the team above .500. That not too much was made of this by the press attested to his popularity with the local media and his players. On April 2, 1973, Hodges was felled by a second, fatal heart attack while playing golf during a spring training break.

RUSS HODGES

Hodges was responsible for the single most memorable broadcasting call in baseball history after Bobby Thomson's home run in the 1951 New York-Brooklyn playoff. His hysterical call of "THE GIANTS WIN THE PENNANT! THE GIANTS WIN THE PENNANT!" even persuaded the tobacco company sponsoring the Giants broadcasts to put out a recording of his play-by-play of the bottom of the ninth inning.

ART HOELSKOETTER

In his four seasons with the Cardinals, Hoelskoetter set the standard for versatility. Between 1905 and 1909 he appeared in 78 games as a second baseman, 77 as a third baseman, 49 behind the plate, 28 at first base, 20 in the outfield, 16 at shortstop, and 15 on the mound; he ended his

career with a .237 batting average and a 2–5 won-
-lost record.

JEROLD HOFFBERGER

Hoffberger spent his 15 years as Baltimore owner alienating just about everyone who was not part of the Orioles' front office. The head of the National Brewing Company that had sponsored the club's games since 1962, his major contribution to the winning teams of the late 1960s and 1970s was the expansion of the club's farm system. On the other hand, his paternalistic approach led to continuing the organization's policy of releasing, trading, or leaving unprotected in expansion drafts every Oriole player representative from 1960 to 1968, when Brooks Robinson assumed the post.

In the events leading to the spring training strike of 1972, Hoffberger clashed repeatedly with Players Association chief Marvin Miller, who accused him of trying to compel players to desert the union. Whatever the truth of that specific allegation, Hoffberger was not quite the "hard-line reactionary" that Miller claimed; in fact, Hoffberger supported an increase in pension benefits, the main issue in the 1972 stoppage, and disagreed vocally with the tactics of Ray Grebey, head of the owners' Player Relations Committee. After the 1972 strike, Hoffberger boycotted owners meetings, not abandoning his stance until 1976, and then only to join forces with George Steinbrenner of the Yankees and Charlie Finley of the A's in an effort to oust Commissioner Bowie Kuhn.

When Baltimore failed to sell out its home games in the 1974 American League Championship Series, Hoffberger contemplated selling out but ran up against Kuhn's politically motivated fixation on putting a team in Washington. For his part, the Orioles owner was committed to staying in Baltimore, without even considering Kuhn's suggestion of a stadium between the two cities, or a Kuhn-inspired resolution at the December 1976 major league meetings calling on the Orioles to play "a suitable number of games" in the national capital. Hoffberger finally sold out to Washington attorney Edward Bennett Williams, the owner of the football Washington Redskins.

The sale was contingent on Williams's promise to keep the Orioles in Baltimore.

ROY HOFHEINZ

Hofheinz promoted indoor baseball by building the Astrodome; that was about as positive as it got with the judge.

Hofheinz bought into the Houston team in 1962 on the coattails of Robert E. Smith, then considered the richest man in Texas. Over the next couple of years, Hofheinz hocked everything he owned to buy out Smith in a series of bitter boardroom confrontations. Even before that, however, Hofheinz's reputation as a penny-wise, pound-foolish blowhard had undone the organization's first important hire, of Gabe Paul as head of baseball operations; Paul, who had resigned as general manager of the Reds to take the post with Houston, backed out as soon as he was informed of Hofheinz's eleventh-hour involvement with Smith. Paul's successor, Paul Richards, fared only minimally better, lasting through the 1965 season but with constant squabbling with the owner as the price. Even years later, Richards could reject a reporter's suggestion that Hofheinz was his own worst enemy by declaring, "Not while I'm alive he isn't."

Hofheinz was calling the shots when the Colt .45s changed into the Astros in moving into the Astrodome in 1965. Major league baseball's first indoor facility, it was trumpeted by Hofheinz publicists as the Eighth Wonder of the World and by Hofheinz himself as a cash cow for its potential to draw spectators for concerts, circuses, and conventions as well as for baseball games. Among the judge's inspirations for the plant was to introduce particularly long dugouts so he could sell more seats at higher prices with the come-on that they were directly behind the players. When players complained about losing fly balls in the dome's 4,500 plastic skylights, he ordered the skylights painted over, this in turn reducing the day lighting by 40 percent, killing the natural grass, and necessitating the first use of artificial turf, in 1966.

The painting over of the skylights was one of the few times that Hofheinz could be accused of listening to his players. With general manager Spec Richardson acting as his enforcer, his insisted on an All-American-Boy image for the team, imposing a strict dress code and curfews and fuming whenever a member of the club didn't take the opportunity of a media interview to say how devoted he was to the harmony of the organization. To help along this ''family'' atmosphere, Hofheinz refused to pay players by check, instead depositing their salaries in a local bank in which he had a significant holding. As he proudly pointed out to anyone who asked about the policy, the maneuver enabled the bank to hold on to the money a little longer and got the Houston players used to thinking about his institution when it came to money matters.

All of Hofheinz's financial deviousness and concern with image came together in an embarrassing explosion in 1975, when it was revealed that he could not meet $38 million in debts to franchise creditors. In a desperate move to stave off bankruptcy, he agreed to share power with creditor representatives on a three-man committee. There he found himself in a minority when the other two board members voted to oust Richardson. After a brief period of hanging on as a minority voice, Hofheinz sold the franchise to the creditors (the General Electric Credit Corporation and the Ford Motor Credit Corporation).

BILL HOLBERT

The original good-field, no-hit catcher, Holbert came to bat a record 2,335 times in a twelve-year career starting in 1876 without hitting a home run.

BOBO HOLLOMAN

Holloman pitched the most costly no-hitter in baseball history. A bulbous right-hander for the 1953 Browns, he was about to be farmed out after some disastrous relief efforts when he convinced owner Bill Veeck to give him a start. The first result was a May 6 no-hitter over the Athletics that made Holloman the only twentieth-century hurler to fashion such a gem in his initial starting assignment. The second result was that, having to hold on to the only gate attraction he had for the miserable Browns, Veeck had to exercise a $25,000 option on the pitcher. The third result was that, because of the money committed to Holloman, St. Louis was unable to put together the $31,500 earmarked for purchasing minor league

shortstop Ernie Banks. The icing on the cake was that the no-hitter itself came on a night that was so cold and rainy that Veeck announced before the start of the game that the 2,473 fans in attendance would be able to use their rain checks for another game as a reward for their hardiness. As for Holloman, his effort against the Athletics was his only complete game, and he closed out his single major league season with a record of 3–7 and an ERA of 5.23.

DUCKY HOLMES

Outfielder Holmes precipitated one of the ugliest incidents in baseball history. On July 25, 1898, while playing for the Baltimore Orioles against his former team, the Giants, he responded to a Polo Grounds heckler by shouting, ''I glad I don't have to work for no Sheeny anymore.'' New York owner Andrew Freedman took umbrage at this reference to his Jewish background and charged onto the field accompanied by security guards intent on removing Holmes from the park. The other Orioles responded by forming a bat-wielding circle around their teammate as the increasingly hostile crowd urged the guards to use their truncheons and Freedman demanded that umpire Thomas Lynch eject Holmes from the game. Instead, Lynch declared the game a forfeit to Baltimore and escaped to the visiting team's clubhouse.

Over the next few days, National League president Nick Young fined the Giants $1,000 for deliberately provoking a forfeit and suspended Holmes for the rest of the season, players around the league threatened to strike unless the suspension were lifted, and a Maryland judge granted an injunction barring the suspension. For his part, Freedman protested every game in which Holmes appeared for the rest of the year, but to no avail. One outcome of the episode was that it strengthened the obliviousness of baseball writers where ethnic questions were concerned; typical was the reaction of *The Sporting Life,* which declared itself aghast that Holmes should have been disciplined for ''the trifling offense of insulting the Hebrew race.''

OLIVER WENDELL HOLMES

U.S. Supreme Court justice Holmes wrote the Court's 1922 unanimous decision exempting baseball from federal antitrust legislation and establishing organized ball's right to regulate its own affairs.

The suit, *Federal Baseball Club of Baltimore v. National League,* accused the major leagues and the Federal League magnates who had capitulated to them of seeking to institute a monopoly and requested $900,000 in damages. The Baltimore interests pursued their cause through the federal courts for almost seven years, until May 29, 1922, when Holmes issued his often misunderstood decision. In fact, the jurist drew no distinction between sports and business, as is commonly assumed. The less quotable distinction he did make was between personal effort—what have come to be called service industries, including lawyers and doctors as well as performing artists—and trade or commerce, businesses that make, sell, or transport goods. In those limited and antiquated terms, baseball is not commerce, not subject to antitrust laws, and not liable to federal restraint in its business practices. Almost as an aside, Holmes also upheld the necessity of the reserve clause, even though baseball's counsel, mindful of the many legal losses on the issue, had not made it an essential part of their argument. Curiously, a year later, Holmes went through a tortuous distinction to rule that vaudeville *was* interstate commerce and, as such, subject to the same federal laws from which he had exempted baseball.

TOMMY HOLMES

Holmes had a career year in 1945—for both himself and for the twentieth-century Boston version of the Braves franchise. By batting .352 and leading the National League in hits (224), doubles (47), home runs (28), and slugging average (.577), the left-hand-hitting outfielder exposed the organization's perennial problems in offense by setting almost all of its major season records. In striking out merely 9 times, he also became the only major leaguer to win a home-run title while simultaneously proving to be the most difficult player in the league to fan.

JEROME HOLTZMAN

Chicago Sun-Times sportswriter Holtzman won the gratitude of relievers in both leagues for his successful campaign in the 1960s to have baseball formally acknowledge saves as an official pitching category.

RICK HONEYCUTT

Honeycutt has a late-season trade to thank for an ERA title. In August 1983, the Rangers swapped the southpaw to the Dodgers while he topped the American League with a 2.42 mark. In nine appearances with Los Angeles, he was battered around to the tune of a 5.77 ERA, but since that wasn't transferrable to the AL, he remained the junior circuit's stingiest hurler of the year.

HARRY HOOPER (Hall of Fame, 1971)

Hooper's .282 lifetime average and sterling right-field play helped the Red Sox to four pennants in the 1910s, but his greatest contribution to baseball was his role in converting Babe Ruth from a pitcher to an outfielder. He also played a major part in a threatened player strike during the 1918 World Series against the Cubs.

A left-handed leadoff batter for most of his seventeen-year (1909–25) career with the Red Sox and White Sox, Hooper possessed a reputation for defensive brilliance, especially after a bare-handed catch to rob Larry Doyle of the Giants of a home run in the final game of the 1912 World Series. Hooper is also the only player ever to lead off both ends of a doubleheader with a home run, a feat he accomplished on Memorial Day 1911 in a season in which he had only 4 round-trippers.

During spring training in 1918, the outfielder approached new manager Ed Barrow with a suggestion that Ruth was more valuable in the lineup every day than on the mound once every four days. Rebuffed at first on the ground that the fans would murder any pilot who tried to convert the best left-handed pitcher in baseball, Hooper kept at Barrow with arguments about the drawing power of Ruth's bat that finally had the desired effect on the manager, who was also a part owner of the club. Ruth got his first assignment as a position player, at first base, on May 6 before being moved to the outfield shortly afterward. Hooper's further role in the switch was to move to center field himself to assist the new left fielder in learning his position.

Upset by the low wartime attendance at the first 4 games of the 1918 World Series, Red Sox players asked Hooper to head a delegation of Boston and Chicago players to confront the members of baseball's ruling National Commission with an ultimatum to increase the players' share of the proceeds or risk a strike. But with American League president Ban Johnson reeling from a too-liquid lunch, Cincinnati owner Garry Herrmann delivering speeches about how much he had contributed to baseball, and National League president John Heydler saying nothing, Hooper and his associates realized they were getting nowhere, concluded they wouldn't get much farther with reporters or fans, and retreated.

Hooper, who is credited with the invention of the sliding catch, owes his election to Cooperstown to a concerted campaign by his sons and friends in the late 1960s.

BOB HOPE
Comedian Hope filled several file cabinets for many years with jokes about his minority holding in the Indians. Less known is that he also headed a syndicate to buy the Washington Senators in 1968, going so far as to name Bill DeWitt as his general manager. Hope pulled out at the last minute because of fears about an eye operation that he was scheduled to undergo. Hope's withdrawal left the field clear for Bob Short, who three years later moved the Washington franchise to Texas.

LOLLY HOPKINS
Hopkins was called Megaphone Lolly for her use of the instrument to inform everyone what she thought players were doing right and umpires were doing wrong during her regular trips to both Fenway Park and Braves Field in the 1930s and 1940s. "A positive fan" who cheered visitors as well as local heroes, the Rhode Island resident was rewarded with season passes by both Boston clubs.

BOB HORNER
Horner's nine years with the Braves from 1978 to 1986 were weighty in all senses of the word. The third baseman went directly from Arizona

State University to 1978 National League Rookie of the Year honors by belting 23 home runs. He followed that up with three seasons of at least 30 home runs, and on July 6, 1986, he joined the handful of players to tag 4 round-trippers in a game. On the other hand, Horner was in continual conflict with Atlanta owner Ted Turner over his own bulging waistline and contract demands, worsening his position with a series of sidelining injuries.

The first clash with Turner took place after Horner's rookie season, when he claimed that his six-figure signing bonus was part of his salary and that any negotiations for 1979 should begin from there; an arbitrator decided in the third baseman's favor in June 1979 but declined to grant his request of free agency. The worst clash between the two occurred in 1980, when the owner decided that he wasn't getting his money's worth from Horner's excess poundage and demanded that he be sent to the minors to play himself back into shape. The order provoked tensions with both Braves general manager John Mullin, who argued that even an overweight Horner was one of the best hitters in the league, and with the Players Association, which filed a grievance for "improper disciplinary action." Horner sat out for a few days, then went on to finish second in the league in homers. By the mid-1980s, however, hand and wrist injuries had finished 1978's number one draft pick.

ROGERS HORNSBY (Hall of Fame, 1942)
The career hitting gap between Ty Cobb's .367 and Hornsby's .358 was 9 points; the personality difference between the two greatest average hitters in baseball history was between the ugly and the obnoxious. The most potent right-handed batter ever to wear a National League uniform, The Rajah also had few equals, as either a player or a manger, in crassness and manic self-absorption. Even his one admitted vulnerability—gambling at the track—became a lever for ridiculing teammates, demeaning charges, and blackmailing franchises.

Hornsby's numbers were beyond debate. Although his seven batting titles were one less than Honus Wagner's, Hornsby's six straight between 1920 and 1925 for the Cardinals included three years of better than .400 and one season—1924—

Rogers Hornsby's personality won him fewer admirers than his hitting did. National Baseball Library, Cooperstown, N.Y.

of an all-time twentieth-century major league high of .424. In both 1922 and 1925, he won the Triple Crown. He was the class of the field in safeties four times, in doubles four times, in triples twice, in homers twice, in runs scored five times, in RBIs four times, in walks three times, and in slugging average nine times. He attained 200 hits seven times, 40 doubles seven times, 20 home runs seven times, 100 runs six times, and 100 RBIs five times. He reached the .300 level seventeen times, and his composite average between 1921 and 1925 exceeded .400. His overall on-base average of .434 was a point higher than Cobb's, and Hornsby's slugging average of .577 was 65 points higher than that of the Detroit star. Hornsby won MVP awards for St. Louis in 1925 and for Chicago in 1929.

With the numbers went enough abrasiveness and turmoil to keep not only Hornsby's various teams, but also the league offices, busy for a major part of his career. The first big ruckus came in 1923, when the second baseman decided that Branch Rickey might have had his virtues as a general manager but was far too much a theorist to serve as a dugout boss as well. For the next season and a half the two most visible members of the Cardinal franchise were constantly at one another, with Rickey's main rejoinder being ornately expressed suspicions that his hitting star wasn't always as injured as he often claimed and that he was merely trying to earn some extra time at the track. With the club still dithering in the middle of the league standings, however, owner Sam Breadon came down on Hornsby's side on May 30, 1925, firing Rickey as manager. Although he maintained his various front-office titles, Rickey insisted on selling all his stock in the franchise, and found a ready buyer in Hornsby, who managed to find the money with the help of a Breadon note to the bank.

In his first full year as manager, in 1926, Hornsby delivered by bringing the Cardinals their first pennant and then a World Series victory over the Yankees. But even as St. Louis was celebrating, Breadon was adding up his grievances against the city's new hero. To begin with, there was the owner's personal distaste when, on the eve of the postseason meeting with the Yankees Hornsby's mother died; the manager responded by declaring that he would skip the funeral to stay with the club in the World Series. If that left Breadon shaking his head, he had already had some practice a few weeks earlier, when Hornsby had refused to allow the club to play an exhibition game arranged by the owner on the grounds that full attention should be paid to the pennant race. Worst of all for Breadon was Hornsby's rejection of a one-year contract to return as playing manager in 1927, demanding instead a multiyear pact at a figure significantly higher than the proffered $50,000. Weighing personal dislike and financial grievances, Breadon took on the entire city of St. Louis by trading Hornsby to the New York Giants for Frankie Frisch and Jimmy Ring. Even when the crank phone calls and editorial blasts died down, the issue was kept alive by Hornsby's refusal to sell the stock he had purchased from Rickey unless he came out of the deal with a substantial profit. Because of a league rule against a player performing for one club while owning a piece of another, NL president John Heydler had to put together a deal under which his office, the Giants, and the Cardinals all threw money into a pot so that Hornsby came away with a $66,000 profit.

With the Giants in 1927, Hornsby got into Rickey-like clashes with John McGraw. Despite that, McGraw didn't hesitate to turn the team over to him when he was away for business or health reasons. In gratitude, Hornsby spent much of his time on the bench lecturing players on how McGraw did things the wrong way. Even a .361 average for the year didn't prevent Hornsby from being traded to the Braves after the season, for the rock-bottom price of catcher Shanty Hogan and outfielder Jimmy Welsh. With Boston in 1928, Hornsby batted another league-leading .387 and needed only a few weeks to persuade owner Emil Fuchs that he was a better manager than incumbent Jack Slattery. It took about the same amount of time for the other Braves players to begin petitioning Fuchs to get rid of his star infielder; among other things, they accused Hornsby of attacking them on the bench for ruining his RBI opportunities with weak hitting or inept baserunning. Although Fuchs was so relieved to have a gate attraction on his cellar dwellers that he responded to the protests by giving Hornsby a new six-year contract even before the end of the season, Hornsby himself saw little future with the Braves and persuaded the owner to trade him to the Cubs for a boatload of young prospects who would do the club more good in the long run. Fuchs also got $200,000 out of the deal.

Hornsby led Chicago to a pennant in 1929, but the next year, after replacing Joe McCarthy as pilot, he so ridiculed the heavy-drinking Hack Wilson that the slugger stopped hitting and was soon packed off to the Cardinals. When it also became clear that Hornsby's knowledge of pitching extended only to the fact that he could hit it, even the press began calling for his replacement as manager. If owner William Wrigley didn't go along, it was in considerable part because his manager owed the club tens of thousands of dollars advanced to him to cover track losses. After Wrigley died in January 1932, however, his son Phil decided that wasn't reason

enough to hold on to a bad pilot, and he switched to Charlie Grimm in July. When the Cubs won the pennant under Grimm, they made their feelings known about his predecessor by voting not a penny of World Series money to Hornsby. The Rajah promptly filed a protest with Commissioner Kenesaw Landis, who ruled that the players were free to vote as they wanted.

With his playing career all but behind him, Hornsby signed with the Cardinals again in 1933, as a pinch hitter. Rumors that he would be named manager were dispelled when he was released halfway through the season. He was immediately signed to manage the Browns by owner Phil Ball, who relished the prospect of outdrawing the Cardinals with one of the latter's emblematic stars. Ball was wrong several times over: Shortly after reaching the agreement with Hornsby, Ball died; his executors knew nothing about baseball and so were easily cowed into doing whatever the manager wanted; and one too many second-division finishes doomed the Browns in 1935 to a major league-record-low home attendance of 80,922. Things didn't get much better the following years except for the presence of a new ownership less willing to be bullied by Hornsby. Put on notice that his gambling habit would no longer be tolerated, Hornsby vowed to comply, unaware that he was being shadowed by Pinkerton detectives whenever he placed a bet. He was fired during the 1937 season.

For the next fifteen years, Hornsby managed in the minors, continuing to patronize whatever track was handy, lashing out at his players for being less entertaining than his sure things, and telling any small-town reporter who would listen that he never strained his eyes by going to the movies or reading a book. It was also in the minors that he was first recorded as taking a shower with one of his losing pitchers and urinating on him to show his displeasure. That he returned to the major leagues in 1952 was due to Browns owner Bill Veeck's willingness to try anything to annoy the Cardinals. But though he had the same intentions as Ball twenty years earlier, Veeck remained alive, and long enough to realize he didn't want Captain Bligh managing his team. Ironically, the owner came under more attack than Hornsby when the firing was announced in June because of suspicions that Veeck had merely been ridiculing the old man. The impression was solidified when the players presented Veeck with a two-foot loving cup for liberating them from the manager.

Hornsby had one more managerial stint left in him. No sooner had he been fired by the Browns than Powel Crosley decided that the NL's greatest hitter of all time was exactly what Cincinnati needed. Hornsby lasted through the 1953 season, when he was fired for all the usual reasons, including his shower specialty. Hornsby had the next-to-last laugh: Because he was still operating on Veeck's contract as well, his release at the end of the year meant that he collected 1954 salaries from two clubs he was no longer managing. But all that money, too, had been lost at the track by the time he was working as a coach for the Cubs in 1958 and 1959. His last connection with baseball was as a batting coach for the expansion Mets in 1962.

For someone whose big league career was identified with humorlessness, Hornsby had an atypical beginning, getting his first baseball job with a bloomer girl team that barnstormed through Texas with several male ringers who played in drag.

TONY HORTON

Horton's fragile self-esteem left him unprepared for the harsh give-and-take of salary negotiations in the pre-agent era. After a solid year with Cleveland (27 home runs and 93 RBIs) in 1969, he demanded a salary hike from $30,000 to $100,000. Alvin Dark, who had spent the season as manager telling the first baseman how invaluable he was to the club, changed gears in his second role as general manager to downplay the slugger's significance. After protracted talks, Horton finally agreed to a figure closer to Dark's proposal, but never overcame the criticism of his abilities raised during the bargaining. He moped through a good part of the 1970 season, then revealed how troubled he was when he ran out to his position after the final out of a game, compelling Dark to lead him back off the field. Horton was diagnosed as having suffered a nervous breakdown, never played another major league game, and was even ordered by his psychiatrist to stop watching televised games. Dark called the episode the saddest of his career, and pointed to

it as a reason why clubs should always have separate managers and general managers.

PETE HOTALING

Primarily an outfielder during his nine-year major league career with six teams, Hotaling was the first professional catcher to wear a mask. He adopted it in 1877 as a member of the independent Syracuse Stars.

CHARLIE HOUGH

Aside from its sheer length (twenty-five years through 1994), Hough's pitching career was noteworthy for reversing the usual transition from a starter to a reliever. In fact, it wasn't until the right-handed knuckleballer's fourteenth season, with the Rangers in 1982, that he became a fixture in a starting rotation rather than a bullpen specialist. It was because of Hough's butterfly pitch that Texas catcher Gino Petralli broke all American League passed-ball records in 1987—including most for a season (35), a game (6, on August 20), and an inning (4, on August 22).

RALPH HOUK

Houk is the only major league manager ever to win a World Series in each of his first two years as a pilot. In fact, he added a third consecutive pennant for the Yankees in 1963, but then got kicked upstairs, where he presided over the deterioration of the franchise. In subsequent managerial assignments—including a reprise with the Yankees and stints with the Tigers and Red Sox—he was unable to duplicate his early success. Through it all, he achieved the distinction of never having been fired.

The former third-string catcher (who played in only 91 games in eight seasons with the Yankees) was tabbed to succeed Casey Stengel at the New York helm in 1961 because of fears that some other club would snatch him away from the organization and benefit from the training course he had been undergoing as bullpen catcher, minor league manager, and big league coach at the Yankees' expense. Undoing the Stengel legacy of strict rules, extensive platooning, and irregular starting assignments for pitchers, Houk installed a regular lineup and a stable rotation, winning not only his trio of pennants but also the appreciation

Charlie Hough shows his grip on the knuckleball that kept him in the major leagues for 25 years. Photo compliments of the Florida Marlins.

of his players. Nor did it hurt that the 1961 team he inherited featured Roger Maris's 61 home runs and a club major league record 240.

Houk's promotion to general manager in 1964 was a failure: As a front-office figure, he was able to make little use of his ability to motivate players; instead, he spent too much time indulging those same players' gripes about successor Yogi Berra. Deciding well before the season was over that Berra had lost control of the team and had to go, Houk settled on Cardinals pilot Johnny Keane as the next Yankee manager. The plan hit a snag when both teams pulled themselves together to win pennants, presenting the general manager with the anomalous situation of having his team pitted in the World Series against one piloted by its next field chief. After the St. Louis victory in the Series, Berra was dumped, and

Houk was compelled to engage in a charade, denying that he even knew Keane had quit the National League club; within weeks, however, the switch was announced. His credibility already impaired by the treatment of Berra, Houk reached his public relations low by firing popular television broadcaster Mel Allen later in the year.

Soon after the takeover of the franchise by CBS in 1966, Houk stepped down from the front office for another tour in the dugout. His most notable achievement in almost seven seasons this time around was to bring a young and relatively untalented team into second place in 1970. The arrival of George Steinbrenner in late 1972 altered the franchise chemistry once again, and the new combination of elements would have produced an explosion had Houk not resigned after only one season. So tense was Houk working for Steinbrenner that he told players he had to get out or punch out his employer. Nobody doubted the possibilities in his rage, especially after he charged the mound in a game that year to snatch the cap off Gaylord Perry's head in search of the foreign substance he was certain the Cleveland right-hander was applying to the ball.

After five seasons (1974–78) in Detroit directing the breakup of a once successful but now aging team in favor of a young and not very good one, he spent two years as a consultant to the Tigers. Bored from too much golf, he went back to the dugout, this time with the Red Sox. Saddled with a front office so inept that it neglected to mail contracts to Fred Lynn and Carlton Fisk on time and lost the two stars to free agency because of the error, Houk was able to do no better than a tie for second place in the second half of the strike-induced split season of 1981. In fact, despite his reputation as a pitcher's manager, he was unable to bring any hurler up to even 15 wins in his four seasons in Fenway Park.

FRANK HOWARD

Between May 12 and May 18 in the 1968 season, Washington outfielder Howard joined baseball's all-time sluggers by swatting 10 home runs in 20 at-bats. The performance keynoted his years with the Senators, when his titanic shots were about the only reasons fans had to watch the team. Upon retirement, the six-foot, seven-inch

Howard became a manager and hitting coach whose on-bench lectures seemed to inspire rookies and drive veterans off the deep end. Mainly because many of his managers perceived him as having too much influence over younger players, he seldom lasted as a batting instructor on any team for more than a couple of years.

STEVE HOWE

Howe holds baseball's unofficial record for the most times (seven) suspended by a club or league. In the case of the southpaw reliever, the violations have centered around his use of cocaine since coming to the Dodgers in 1980 as a Rookie of the Year bullpen stopper. The repeated second chances—opportunities not made available to others—have raised questions about the sport's drug policies, not least in relation to the race of the player involved and the financial clout of the organization for which he plays.

After a series of unexplained absences, team fines, and suspensions with the Los Angeles Dodgers in the early 1980s, Howe was disqualified for the entire 1984 season while he received treatment. He returned to the Dodgers in 1985, but after falling back into his old habits, was released, then picked up by the Twins. After Minnesota also discerned evidence of continued drug use, he was cut loose again, ending up with the California League San Jose Bees (Class A), where another incident, with police, led to his suspension from organized ball in general. In 1987, Texas Ranger general manager Tom Grieve worked out a deal with Commissioner Peter Ueberroth under which Howe would be allowed to pitch for the Rangers top farm club in Oklahoma City but would not be promoted to Arlington without the express approval of the commissioner. No sooner was the ink dry on the accord than Grieve promoted the reliever to Texas, incurring a fine of $250,000. Worse, Howe once again admitted a relapse, and was again suspended from baseball.

The pitcher returned still again, with the Yankees in 1991. Midway through the following season, he was cited by authorities in his hometown in Montana for drug possession and dealing. Without waiting for a Montana court to hand down a verdict, Commissioner Fay Vincent kicked the hurler out of the game as an incurable recidivist. When the Players Association responded to a formal complaint by Howe by summoning Yankees officials to give testimony, Vincent decided that his authority was being usurped and warned New York general manager Gene Michael and another club official to adhere to his line or think about other employment. The upshot was that Howe pleaded *nolo contendere* in Montana, and the pitcher was reinstated with a big contract after the season.

Aside from all the other aspects of Howe's curious longevity as a major leaguer, there is also the diamond factor: After racking up 17 saves for the Dodgers in his maiden year, he has only twice again reached double figures in bullpen rescues and never saved as many as 20 games in a season.

BOB HOWSAM

Howsam was the architect of the Big Red Machine in the 1970s. A Branch Rickey protégé, his most significant moves in putting together the Cincinnati powerhouse were hiring Sparky Anderson as manager in 1970 and acquiring Joe Morgan, Jack Billingham, and George Foster in 1971 trades with Houston and San Francisco.

Howsam went to the Reds after a baptism by fire as general manager of the Cardinals in the mid-1960s. Succeeding Bing Devine largely on the say-so of Howsam's mentor Rickey, he fell into the middle of a power struggle orchestrated by St. Louis owner Gussie Busch and ending with Rickey's firing as a special adviser. After initially declaring his intention of quitting in solidarity with Rickey, Howsam stayed on long enough to complete a trade with the Yankees that brought Roger Maris to St. Louis—a key element in the club's 1967 and 1968 pennant wins.

Although generally hailed for building Cincinnati's wrecking crew in the 1970s, Howsam had his bad moments. One came when the organization's policy against signing free agents cost it the services of lefty Don Gullett after the 1976 season. Only a couple of weeks later, the executive invited criticism from prominent Reds players for trading first baseman Tony Perez to the Expos. Howsam was also attacked in some quarters for not carrying through on threats to sue Bowie Kuhn after the commissioner had nullified Cincinnati's $1.75-million purchase of Oakland south-paw Vida Blue on the grounds that, with Tom Seaver already a Red through a deal with the Mets, the acquisition of the lefty for pure cash would have turned the National League pennant race into an embarrassment.

Howsam stepped down from his post after the 1978 season, saying he wanted to reduce his workload because of age. But when his successor, Dick Wagner, made one unpopular move after another over the next few years, Howsam was called out of retirement in 1983 to salvage what was salvageable while negotiations were completed for the sale of the franchise to Marge Schott. His most significant moves in what turned out to be a two-year stay were signing free agent Dave Parker and bringing back both Perez (as a free agent pinch hitter) and Pete Rose (as manager).

DICK HOWSER

In his rookie 1980 season as a manager, Howser won 103 games and an American League East Division title for the Yankees (who established a new AL attendance record in the process)—and got fired for his effort.

The well became contaminated when owner George Steinbrenner publicly blasted the manager after New York dropped 3 straight games to Baltimore in early August; the contamination turned to poison when Steinbrenner blamed third-base coach Mike Ferraro for sending Willie Randolph to get tagged out at the plate on a bang-bang play in the final game of an American League Championship Series sweep by Kansas City. When the New York owner suggested that Don Zimmer, who had been filling the same role for the Red Sox, was welcome to switch allegiances at any time, Howser insisted that he had the final say on who his coaches would be. In November Steinbrenner announced Howser's departure behind some flimsy story about a Florida land deal that was too good to pass up.

Howser promptly turned up as pilot of the Royals after the players strike in 1981. There he boosted a foundering club into a half title in the AL West, finished second twice, and took two division crowns. In his final full season, 1985, the Royals also took the AL pennant by beating the

Blue Jays in the American League Championship Series and a world championship in defeating the Cardinals. After the All-Star break in 1986, however, it became public knowledge that Howser was suffering from a brain tumor. The organization kept up a front that he would be back, until spring training in 1987, when he stepped down. He died a couple of months later, at age fifty-one.

DUMMY HOY

Left deaf at age three from meningitis and mute because of his deafness, Hoy's disabilities prompted the introduction of hand signals to indicate balls and strikes—not by umpires, as is often claimed, but by his team's coaches. Widely regarded as one of the major leagues best center fielders during his twelve-year career, Hoy, on June 19, 1889, became the first outfielder to throw three runners out at the plate in one game. With a high-pitched squeaking sound he called flanking outfielders off fly balls, and he insisted that teammates learn to sign so he could participate in their off-field activities.

Hoy lived to be ninety-nine years old, and always claimed to have made the most spectacular catch in any professional league, when he jumped on a horse to run down a fly ball in Oshkosh in an 1886 minor league game.

WAITE HOYT (Hall of Fame, 1969)

Hoyt's career as a starting pitcher was ruined by relieving between starts, but he developed another one as a bullpen specialist. A schoolboy sensation from Brooklyn, the right-hander had a single-game tryout with the Giants in 1918 and a two-season apprenticeship with the Red Sox in 1919 and 1920 before moving down the Boston pipeline to the Yankees, where he won 157 games in ten (six of them pennant-winning) seasons. In 1927 he paced American League hurlers in wins (22), winning percentage (.759), and ERA (2.63), following that up with 23 victories in 1928. Overall he won 237 games in a twenty-one-year (1918–38) career with seven teams. In six World Series with the Yankees, the hurler won 6 games, and, in the 1921 Series against the Giants, he tied Christy Mathewson's record of 27 innings without yielding an earned run (although he did give up

2 unearned runs, one of them resulting in a 1–0 defeat in the eighth and concluding game).

Used regularly between starts, Hoyt had as many as 16 relief appearances, in 1925, while never dropping below 25 starts. In 1928, when he won 23 games, he also had 11 relief appearances and led the AL in saves with 8. In 1929 the wear and tear brought his record down to 10–9 and his ERA up to 4.24, after which he bounced from one team to another in both leagues before landing with the Pirates in 1933. In Pittsburgh he learned to husband his arm and became a bullpen ace, fashioning an ERA under 3.00 over four full seasons and part of another.

Articulate and talented, Hoyt was an amateur painter and a professional singer, appearing in the latter capacity at the Palace Theater and elsewhere on the vaudeville circuit. He was also a Broadway dandy and, after ending his career in 1938, used his connections to do regular radio work on New York stations. Moving to Cincinnati in 1942, Hoyt began a twenty-four-year stretch as Reds announcer, first on radio and later on television. In 1945 he disappeared for several days, initially claiming he had had an attack of amnesia, then announcing that he was suffering from alcoholism; when an outpouring of mail supported his continuing in the broadcast booth, Cincinnati had the anomalous situation of a publicly recovering alcoholic not only doing baseball broadcasts but also pitching the product of sponsor Burger Brewing Company. Hoyt's announcing trademarks were endless monologues on Babe Ruth and other former Yankee teammates, and an odd delivery of play-by-play in the past tense.

AL HRABOSKY

Hrabosky was the best act in the National League for several years in the 1970s and one of the worst acts in Atlanta in the 1980s. Especially in 1975 for the Cardinals, when he won 13 games and posted a league-leading 22 saves, the southpaw reliever known as The Mad Hungarian delighted the country with his Fu Manchu mustache and flowing hair, his perpetually infuriated looks, and his spastic switches from communing with the gods to pounding the rubber in a challenge to batters to get ready. This phase of the Hrabosky show ended in 1977, when the martinetish Vern

Rapp took over as manager of St. Louis and demanded that Hrabosky shave. After going through a disastrous season in the mood of a shorn Samson, the left-hander moved on to Kansas City, where he had another brief moment of glory, with 20 saves—according to the pitcher, mainly because of the Gypsy Rose of Death ring he wore to ward off werewolves. Ignoring the fireman's clear decline from his heyday in St. Louis, Atlanta's Ted Turner agreed to a free-agent contract that would pay him $170,000 annually for thirty years, the gimmick being an assurance that Hrabosky would have a place as a broadcaster on Turner's cable television network after his playing days were over. In fact, they were already over, with the reliever picking up a mere 7 saves in three years. Hrabosky and Turner later agreed to a buyout of the pact.

CAL HUBBARD (Hall of Fame, 1976)

Hubbard is the only resident of Cooperstown who is also a member of the college and pro football halls of fame. His American League umpiring career lasted from 1936 to 1951 before being interrupted by a hunting accident that affected the sight in his left eye. For the next fifteen years he served as a supervisor of the AL umpiring staff, returning to active duty sporadically between 1954 and 1962. On June 20, 1944, he became the first umpire to eject a pitcher (Nelson Potter of the Browns) for violating the rule prohibiting spitballs.

Hubbard earned his other Hall of Fame plaques as a tackle with Centenary and Geneva colleges and as a linebacker and end for the New York Giants and Green Bay Packers.

CARL HUBBELL (Hall of Fame, 1947)

Before a longtime organization star was referred to as a franchise player, he was known as a meal ticket, and nobody deserved the sobriquet more than Hubbell. A left-handed screwballer, he spent his entire sixteen-year (1928–43) career with the Giants, at one point in the 1930s ripping off five consecutive 20-win seasons, leading the National League in ERA three times, in shutouts once, in strikeouts once, and even in saves once. On July 17, 1936, he won the first of a record-shattering 24 consecutive games over two seasons. Equally famous was his 1934 All-Star Game performance when he struck out Babe Ruth, Lou Gehrig, Jimmie Foxx, Al Simmons, and Joe Cronin in succession. His postseason efforts were slightly more checkered: Although boasting an overall record of 4–2 with a 1.97 ERA as the Giants' ace in the 1933, 1936, and 1937 World Series, the southpaw managed it despite sharing the dubious record for yielding the most runs (7) in an inning.

Hubbell was originally signed by the Tigers, but was forbidden by Detroit manager Ty Cobb to use his screwball in a spring training tryout because it supposedly would hurt his arm. It was only after failing with the Tigers that he resumed throwing, in the Texas League, what Cobb had ridiculed as a ''butterfly pitch''; it was there that he was spotted by Giant scout Dick Kinsella. Hubbell's association with the Giants lasted well beyond his playing days: After running the organization's farm system for decades, he remained on the payroll as a scout until the mid-1980s.

NAT HUDSON

With Hudson, it was sink or swim in more than one way. A right-hander good enough to win 25 games for the American Association St. Louis Brown Stockings in 1888, he has generally been credited with developing the sinkerball. On the other hand, he thought nothing of leaving teammates flailing around when he decided to leave the club for periodic vacations that were possible because of his independent means. Hudson took one of his vacations just as St. Louis was about to begin the 1888 postseason championship series against the National League Giants; it turned out to be a crucial absence when the Brown Stockings lost 6 of the 10 games.

MILLER HUGGINS (Hall of Fame, 1964)

As manager of the Yankees throughout most of the Ruthian era, the dyspeptic Huggins was overshadowed by the outsized personality of his biggest star.

A second baseman for the Reds and Cardinals, Huggins led the National League in bases on balls four times and hit .265 in his thirteen-year (1904–16) career. Taking over as Cardinal pilot even before the end of his playing days, he was

offered an opportunity to purchase the club after the 1916 season, but found himself beaten to the punch when club attorney James Jones put together a coalition of St. Louis businessmen to buy out owner Helene Britton while the manager was off in his hometown of Cincinnati trying to raise the money for his own bid. After an 1917 season of seething over what he regarded as a fast shuffle by Britton and Jones, Huggins accepted an offer from New York owner Jacob Ruppert to take over the Yankees.

Huggins's New York career falls into three distinct chapters. The first, pre-Ruthian installment lasted three humdrum years. The second, from 1920 to 1925, brought three pennants, a World Series victory, and trouble with Ruth's off-field antics. The slugger's predilection for nightlife rubbed off on other players, most notably fellow outfielder Bob Meusel, causing constant friction not only between Ruth and Huggins but also involving co-owners Ruppert and Cap Huston. The 1922 season added clubhouse and dugout brawling to the list of Yankees activities, with Ruth and first baseman Wally Pipp going at it for a few rounds; pitcher Carl Mays and catcher Al DeVormer tangling; DeVormer switching sparring partners to fellow catcher Fred Hofman; and pitcher Waite Hoyt tussling with Huggins himself. Despite losing control of the team, Huggins managed to win the second of three consecutive pennants.

If 1922 was bad, matters were even worse in 1925. The year began with the manager getting thrown into a Daytona, Florida, jail for eight hours in a case of mistaken identity involving a hotel burglary. Ruth collapsed on the way home from spring training, but continued his all-night sprees even while recuperating from surgery; the manager reached the end of his patience when the home run king twice ignored signs, first bunting when told to swing away, then swinging away when told to bunt. With a seventh-place finish imminent, Huggins fined Ruth $5,000 and suspended him indefinitely for showing up late for an August 29 game in St. Louis. The confrontation concluded with Ruppert emerging from a closed-door meeting with Ruth to announce that ''Huggins is in absolute command.''

Despite the conflict with Ruth, Huggins actually liked the slugger. In fact, Huggins came down much harder on Meusel, who, he felt, never played hard enough to live up to his potential. But his true animosity was reserved for pitchers Joe Bush and Mays. Huggins never forgave Bush for shouting at him during the final game of the 1922 World Series, then serving up a fat pitch to George Kelly, who knocked it for a Series-ending base hit; and to his dying day Huggins remained convinced that Mays had sold out the 1921 Series.

The final phase of Huggins's tenure witnessed an unchallenged managerial authority and a chastened (but hardly reformed) Ruth contributing to three additional pennants and two more world championships. In 1929, however, an overconfident team never got started, frustrating its manager, who was ill for much of the season. Huggins died at age fifty of erysipelas on September 25 of that year.

JIM HUGHEY

A right-hander for five teams during the last decade of the nineteenth century, Hughey posted a career record of 29–80, giving him the worst winning percentage (.266) of any pitcher with at least 100 decisions. Part of his problem was that he pitched for the 1898 Browns and the 1899 Spiders—two of the worst teams in baseball history—for whom he dropped a combined 54 games; his efforts in the latter year produced the last 30-game-losing season. Indicative of his plight, Hughey managed to complete 100 of his career 113 starts. He never pitched a shutout.

WAYNE HUIZENGA

Few owners have asserted themselves as quickly within baseball's ruling councils as Huizenga did after entering the National League as head of the Marlins. Soon after the November 1992 expansion draft, he succeeded in blocking the all-but-done transfer of the Giants to St. Petersburg, thereby leaving his Miami-based franchise alone in Florida. Huizenga got his foot in the door of the major leagues by owning Blockbuster Video, which handles video production for Major League Promotions and is the sole retail and rental outlet for the sport's official line of videotapes.

WILLIAM HULBERT

For its first six seasons, the National League was virtually a one-man show, and the man was founder Hulbert.

Soon after the Chicago coal merchant and wholesale grocer became associated with the National Association White Stockings in 1874, he realized that this photo-major league was hopelessly flawed; a year later, after being selected club president, he staged a palace revolt. Incensed by the defection of shortstop Davy Force to the Philadelphia Athletics and NA's subsequent approval of the transfer, Hulbert retaliated by signing not only the Boston Big Four (pitcher Al Spalding, second baseman Ross Barnes, first baseman Cal McVey, and catcher Deacon White), who were in the process of leading the Red Stockings to a runaway pennant, but also Philadelphia third baseman Cap Anson. Knowing he could be expelled for tampering with another club's players during the season, he solved the problem with a series of preemptive moves. After recruiting the NA's St. Louis franchise and two strong independent clubs from Cincinnati and Louisville as a western half league, he presented a take-it-or-leave-it plan to four selected eastern teams (Hartford, New York, and the aggrieved Boston and Philadelphia) in a locked-door meeting.

What they took was a monopolistic scheme to control the best players and markets by setting up an association of clubs rather than players, which is what all previous baseball organizations had been. The new league limited membership with a franchise system that excluded cities with fewer than seventy-five thousand people, granted member clubs exclusive rights to their territories, and required teams to complete a predetermined schedule. The league, for its part, was committed to being vigilant against the influence of gamblers, ''hippodroming'' (crooked play), and ''revolving'' (the very offense Spalding and the others committed); a blacklist was to be maintained to keep offending players out of the league.

Even though Morgan Bulkeley of Hartford became the first NL president, Hulbert was in control from the beginning, expelling New York and Philadelphia for not completing their 1876 schedules, and, after assuming the league presidency himself in 1877, applying the same penalty to four Louisville players for throwing games. On the other hand, he applied the rules with something less than rigor when it suited his or the league's purposes (hastening, for example, to reorganize the Cincinnati franchise early in 1877 after its violation of the same rule for which New York and Philadelphia had been terminated late in 1876; then, for another, raiding the Reds for Charley Jones and other players). During Hulbert's brief reign the NL prospered, at least in part because restrictions on player mobility kept salaries from escalating. But with prosperity came imitation, but the league founder was not around to help meet the challenge of the American Association. On April 22, 1882, less than two weeks before the rival circuit played its first game, Hulbert suffered a fatal heart attack.

RANDY HUNDLEY

Hundley pioneered the use of the hinged flip-over mitt, which has given catchers more flexibility. Following his retirement in 1977 after fourteen years with the Cubs and three other teams, he also popularized the fantasy camp vacations for never-were major leaguers.

KEN HUNT

Hunt effectively ended his promising career by swinging a bat in the on-deck circle. Following an impressive 1961 rookie season for the Angels when he clouted 25 home runs, the right-hand-hitting outfielder stood flexing his back in the on-deck area in April 1962 when he suddenly snapped his collarbone. He never played a full schedule again.

RON HUNT

Hunt holds all the important National League records for being hit by pitches. A righty-swinging second baseman who liked to boast that "some people give their bodies to science, but I give mine to baseball," he was clipped 243 times over his twelve-year (1963–74) career with the Mets, Dodgers, Giants, Expos, and Cardinals. In 1971 he set the season record for being plunked 50 times; that was also one of seven straight seasons when the lifetime .273 hitter paced all big leaguers in getting to first base the hard way. Hunt's penchant for being hit enraged opposition

managers throughout his career, especially after his own admission that he wore special protective pads under his uniform, but umpires seldom found him violating the letter of the rules.

CATFISH HUNTER (Hall of Fame, 1987)

His Hall of Fame pitching credentials notwithstanding, Hunter's most lasting contribution to baseball was a result of his not getting paid.

In a fifteen-year (1965–79) career with the Athletics (in both Kansas City and Oakland) and Yankees, the right-hander won 234 games, fashioning five consecutive seasons over the 20 mark, leading the American League in victories twice, in winning percentage twice, and in ERA once. The ace for the Oakland dynasty of the early 1970s, he achieved initial prominence by pitching the first regular-season perfect game in forty-six years, on May 5, 1968, against the Twins. Weakened by diabetes and with his arm worn out, the right-hander later helped New York to three pennants and two world championships, pitching much of the time on little more than grit.

In 1974 Hunter agreed to a two-year contract calling for him to receive $100,000 a year, with half the amount payable directly by Oakland owner Charlie Finley into an annuity. When it was reported during the 1974 season that Finley had failed to make the annuity payment, Hunter refused to talk about it until after the World Series against Los Angeles; when the owner tried to hand the pitcher a check for the $50,000, he refused the payment. Immediately after the A's clinched the world championship, the Players Association claimed breach of contract and won free agency for Hunter after a hearing before arbitrator Peter Seitz. The hurler's liberation prompted a dual reaction from other owners: First they were shocked that he had won his case; then they lined up to make him extravagant offers. He eventually signed with the Yankees for $3 million. Although the universal right to free agency did not come until the following year, with the conclusion of the Messersmith-McNally case, Hunter's victory plainly illustrated how much the players had to gain from the elimination of the reserve clause.

Hunter's nickname was provided by Finley, who loved the promotional value of nicknames in general and the sound of this one in particular.

The owner had been a fan of George (Catfish) Metkovich, a journeyman first baseman-outfielder in the 1940s and 1950s.

HERB HUNTER

Hunter didn't have much of a career as an infielder for several teams in the late 1910s and early 1920s, but he was a living testament to how far Commissioner Kenesaw Landis would go when he decided not to like somebody. Hunter's attempts to organize a 1931 all-star tour of Japan were thwarted when Landis barred major leaguers from signing up. The reason? The commissioner accused Hunter of having let a team of Korean amateurs beat another all-star grouping of major leaguers during a 1922 tour of Asia. Landis ultimately permitted the 1931 junket, but only after replacing Hunter as tour leader with his personal representative, sportswriter Fred Lieb.

TIM HURST

Umpire Hurst is best known for his paean to his profession: "The pay is good, it keeps you out in the fresh air and sunshine, and you can't beat the hours." He also liked the power of his position, even going so far as to violate the first rule of umpiring by changing a call. When infielder George Moriarty protested a called strike, claiming that the pitch had been farther off the plate than the previous one, a called ball, the arbiter agreed and made both pitches strikes. What Hurst seemed to like most about his job, however, were the opportunities it offered for physical violence. While in the National League, his most notable victim was a Cincinnati fireman knocked cold when Hurst, returning fire from the grandstand, tossed a beer stein into the crowd; the umpire was fined $100.

Taking a year off to manage the Cardinals in 1898, Hurst earned a reputation as a rabid baiter of his former colleagues. He continued his confrontational ways after moving back into blue, in the American League in 1905. In one game, after tailing Clark Griffith to the dugout, he coldcocked the New York manager. Finally, in August 1909, when Hurst spat in the face of Philadelphia second baseman Eddie Collins and precipitated a riot, AL president Ban Johnson fired him. Hurst later became a boxing referee.

CAP HUSTON

Huston (full name Tillinghast L'Hommedieu Huston) was a half owner of the Yankees for eight and a half years but almost never got his way. A rumpled, hard-living Army Corps of Engineers captain and self-made millionaire, he made an odd couple with partner Jacob Ruppert, a polished socialite and honorary colonel on the staff of the New York governor. Brought together by Giants manager John McGraw to buy the Yankees, the two fell into conflict on almost every club matter from the beginning, when Huston (gauchely, in Ruppert's opinion) put up his half of the $460,000 purchase price in $100 bills.

The first major conflict between the partners was over the hiring of a new manager in October 1917. Ruppert wanted St. Louis pilot Miller Huggins; Huston preferred his drinking buddy Wilbert Robinson, who was piloting the Dodgers and whom Ruppert thought too old at fifty to handle the chore. The brewery magnate won, mostly because Huston was off in France with the Allied Expeditionary Forces, but the engineer never forgave his partner for the signing and spent the rest of their association trying to undermine the manager. It wasn't only Ruppert whom the engineer annoyed with transatlantic protests; he also irritated the rest of the baseball establishment with his letters to newspapers suggesting that the game be closed down and every able-bodied player shipped to the front lines.

Huston sided with Babe Ruth in his ongoing confrontations with Huggins, a preference made all the easier by the fact that the slugger and the co-owner often caroused together. After the Yankees lost a second consecutive World Series to the Giants in 1922, Huston lost patience, declaring that "Huggins has managed the Yankees for the last time." The threat backfired when general manager Ed Barrow, despite his close friendship with Huston, sided with Ruppert in a decision to stay with Huggins. With little alternative, Huston negotiated a $1.5 million buyout from Ruppert and severed connection with the franchise in May 1923.

Huston's major contribution to the club came as a result of his friendship with theatrical producer Harry Frazee, whose constant need for cash as owner of the Red Sox Ruppert and Huston satisfied in return for such future Hall of Famers as Ruth, Waite Hoyt, and Herb Pennock.

I

PETE INCAVIGLIA

Incaviglia made his most enduring contribution to baseball when he refused to sign with the Expos after being selected in the amateur draft of 1985 unless the team guaranteed to trade him. When Montreal broke the stalemate by trading the slugging outfielder to the Rangers, worried owners saw nothing but trouble ahead from other draft choices who didn't like the teams that had picked them. The result was the Incaviglia Rule, which bars clubs from trading amateur draft selections until at least one year after signing them.

In his rookie year for the Rangers, in 1986, Incaviglia established a first-year mark for strikeouts by fanning 185 times.

MONTE IRVIN (Hall of Fame, 1973)

But for Branch Rickey's refusal to offer compensation to the Newark Eagles for his services, Irvin might have beaten out Jackie Robinson for integrating the major leagues. Irvin had been the choice of many Negro league owners for that role, but three years in the Army during World War II had rusted his skills sufficiently to make Rickey balk at demands for $5,000 in exchange for his contract. As it turned out, Horace Stoneham of the Giants coughed up the $5,000; when Irvin asked for (and was refused) part of the payment, he became the first black player to receive a bad press for "greed."

Primarily a center fielder, the right-handed hitter won Negro National League batting titles in 1941 (.395) and 1946 (.404). He won another in the Mexican League (.397) after jumping the Ea-

gles in 1942 over a contract dispute. Playing for Vera Cruz, he also paced the circuit in homers (20) to win MVP honors even though he missed the first third of the season.

After debuting with the Giants in 1949, Irvin hit .312 with 24 home runs and a league-leading 121 RBIs in the miracle-pennant year of 1951 while also serving as mentor to rookie Willie Mays. In the ensuing World Series loss to the Yankees, Irvin hit .458 and stole home in the second game. But after breaking his ankle sliding into third base in a spring training game in April 1952, then reinjuring the leg the following year, he never was the same player. His overall average for seven seasons with the Giants and one with the Cubs was .293.

From 1968 to 1984 Irvin was a special assistant in the commissioner's office. He also served as chairman of the Hall of Fame's Special Committee on the Negro leagues after his own election to Cooperstown and shepherded the passage of Ray Dandridge, Martin Dihigo, Rube Foster, Judy Johnson, and John Henry Lloyd through that body.

ART IRWIN

In an effort to protect two broken fingers, Irwin, playing for the Providence Grays, invented the first fielder's mitt in 1885 by adding padding to a buckskin glove. The shortstop's most extraordinary double play became public only in 1931, when, after he had drowned while commuting between New York and Boston, it was learned that he had maintained two wives and two sets of children, one in each of the cities on the itinerary of his final boat ride.

J

BO JACKSON

Jackson's insistence on playing professional baseball and football simultaneously cost him stardom in both sports when he incurred a serious hip injury. Although he eventually returned to the diamond with an artificial hip, his drastically reduced speed erased predictions of being a dominant force in baseball, while making it impossible for him to reappear at all on the gridiron.

The right-hand-hitting Jackson joined the Royals in 1986 after winning college football's Heisman Trophy. The media attention focused on the outfielder created significant tension in the Kansas City clubhouse, especially after his assertion that he intended pursuing his football career with the Los Angeles Raiders as "a hobby." When he responded badly to teammates' criticism that he didn't take baseball seriously enough, he became a target of fan booing in Royals Stadium and did more striking out than hitting. By 1989, however, he had won over the fans with his power hitting and circus catches; in that year he clouted 32 home runs and drove home 105 runs while posing a constant steal threat. In 1990 Jackson appeared to be on the verge of an even bigger season until he separated his shoulder trying to make a diving catch in Yankee Stadium in July; before he was removed from the game, he had smacked 3 home runs in his only plate appearances. When he returned to the lineup in August, he belted the first pitch he saw from Seattle's Randy Johnson for his fourth consecutive home run.

During the 1990–91 football season, Jackson sustained his hip injury while playing for the Raiders. The Royals responded by releasing him on the eve of the season, insinuating that he would never be able to play again. But a short time later, Jackson signed with the White Sox. Although he was applauded nationally for his grit, he offered a melancholy spectacle trying to run, and ultimately decided to submit to a hip replacement operation. After missing the 1992 season, he returned to Chicago as a designated hitter in 1993, banging out 16 homers in part-time duty. During the League Championship Series against Toronto, both Jackson and alternate DH George Bell griped bitterly about who should be in the lineup; for his part, Jackson went hitless in 10 at-bats, including 6 strikeouts. He played for the Angels in 1994.

JOE JACKSON

Whether or not Jackson was ever actually asked to "say it ain't so," he did try to tell White Sox owner Charlie Comiskey that it was so, and was brushed off for his efforts. A year later, he became the most famous of the eight Chicago players banned for collusion in fixing the 1919 World Series against Cincinnati. The nearest thing to a consolation until his death thirty years later was knowing that he was the best hitter outside the Hall of Fame.

The left-hand-hitting outfielder came up originally with Philadelphia in 1908, but had little more than 40 at-bats over two seasons with Connie Mack. Convinced that the South Carolina-born Jackson was too uncomfortable in the eastern city, Mack dealt him to the Indians, where he

Joe Jackson's batting stance was emulated by many contemporaries, including Babe Ruth. National Baseball Library, Cooperstown, N.Y.

began putting together his lifetime .356 average. In his first full season, in 1911, he whaled American League pitching to the tune of .408, following that up with marks of .395 and .373 and pacing the league in one year or another in hits, doubles, triples, and slugging percentage. With the birth of the Federal League in 1914, Jackson received several offers to jump Cleveland, but stayed where he was on the advice of his wife, who handled all his business affairs. At least from a financial point of view, it proved to be an error when Indians owner Charles Somers became so desperate for cash that he sold the outfielder to the White Sox and to the penurious policies of Comiskey.

In a Chicago uniform, Jackson put together four more .300 seasons between 1916 and 1919, developing so much admiration for his offensive abilities among teammates and opponents that many of them, including Babe Ruth, acknowledged emulating his stance. Even in the tainted 1919 Series against the Reds, he was one of the hardest to read for any suspicious behavior because of his .375 average and a club-leading 6 RBIs. Shortly after the Series, however, Jackson and his wife wrote a letter to Comiskey confirming rumors of a fix and offering to provide details. But Comiskey, who was only too aware that any substantiation of the rumors would cost him the services of Jackson and other players of star quality, chose to ignore the letter. What he couldn't ignore was testimony from pitcher Ed Cicotte and Jackson before a grand jury on September 28, 1920, naming names and detailing particulars. It was allegedly after this appearance that Jackson was approached by a boy who pleaded with him to "say it ain't so, Joe."

In his testimony, Jackson admitted receiving $5,000 from professional gamblers—the basis for his subsequent ostracism from the major leagues by Commissioner Kenesaw Landis despite an acquittal of the Chicago Eight in a jury trial. On the eve of that trial, Jackson's admission and other confessions disappeared from the county prosecutor's office amid strong indications that the theft had been organized by gambler Arnold Rothstein with the full cooperation of Comiskey. The confession stayed lost until 1924, when Jackson filed suit against Comiskey for $18,000 in back pay; as miracles would have it, the Chicago boss was able to use the suddenly rediscovered documents to sustain his argument that Jackson had not lived up to the terms of a multiyear pact signed shortly before the 1919 season.

Before he was thrown out of the game in the final week of the 1920 season, Jackson had been enjoying one of his biggest years, averaging .382 with 218 hits; 42 doubles; a league-leading 20 triples; and, for the first time in his career, knocking in more than 100 runs. Such numbers have periodically marshaled groups into demanding that Cooperstown drop its moralistic objections and admit the outfielder as a bona fide Hall of Famer.

REGGIE JACKSON (Hall of Fame, 1993)

Jackson was Mr. October—and he wasn't too shabby in the other months of the season, either. On the other hand, the outfielder's braggadocio caused as much trouble with teammates as his bat did with opponents.

Although he managed to pass the .300 barrier only once in his twenty-one-year (1967–87) career, Jackson clouted 563 home runs (sixth on the all-time list) and is the only player to hit as many as 100 homers with three different clubs (the Athletics, Yankees, and Angels). The left-hand-hitting slugger paced AL hitters in homers four times, slugging three times, runs scored twice, and RBIs only once. Among his best individual seasons were 1973 (when he took MVP honors for Oakland with a .293 average and league-leading totals in slugging, homers, runs, and RBIs) and 1980 (when he reached a career high of .300 and reached the seats 41 times for the Yankees). The downside of his offense was a record 2,597 strikeouts—a category in which he topped the 100 mark eighteen times and led the American League five times.

Jackson, however, always seemed to save his

Reggie Jackson set records for World Series home runs and career strikeouts with his exaggerated swing. Ron Riesterer/ Oakland Tribune.

best for the autumn; he had plenty of opportunity to shine in postseason play, appearing for eleven division championships, six pennant winners, and five world championship teams. His World Series career batting average bested his regular-season mark by almost 100 points (.357 to .262), and in Series play he ranks in the top ten in almost every significant offensive category, including first in slugging (.755). His most memorable slugging feat was his 3 consecutive home runs for the Yankees in the sixth game of the 1977 World Series on three consecutive pitches off three different Dodger pitchers.

Jackson was one of the young players Charlie Finley took with him from Kansas City to the West Coast, where the A's won five AL West titles in the 1970s. He was also among the most restive of the brawling Athletics, tangling with Finley over the size of a salary increase after a stellar 1969 season (47 homers and 118 RBIs), with Dick Williams over the manager's dictatorial style, and (physically) with teammate Billy North. As free agency approached in 1976, Finley shipped Jackson and Ken Holtzman to the Orioles for Don Baylor and Mike Torrez. From the start, it was clear that Baltimore would not meet Jackson's demands for a three-year, $675,000 contract, and even when he settled for a one-year, $200,000 pact, the rest of the team became so unsettled that several other key players followed him into the first free-agent market after the season.

Jackson arrived in the Bronx with baggage aplenty. First, there were his claims that if he played in New York there would be a candy bar named after him; he may have wished no one had bothered when Yankee fans showered the field with free Reggie bars handed out on Opening Day of 1977. Then there was the resentment of teammates generated by the outfielder's statements about "the magnitude of me," a reaction that only got worse with the early-season publication of a magazine article in which he called himself "the straw that stirs the drink," disparaging any notion that Yankee captain Thurman Munson could fill such a role. Jackson only exacerbated the situation by pointedly ignoring the extended hands of teammates after hitting a home run the night the article appeared. When Jackson casually played a bloop single into a double on national television in June, manager Billy Martin sent Paul Blair to replace him in right field in midinning. The ensuing dugout scene showed the outfielder screaming at Martin, and the manager trying to break out of a cordon of coaches to get at the outfielder.

In the 1977 World Series, Jackson hit .450 and set records with 5 home runs, 25 total bases, and 10 runs scored. But matters disintegrated further the following year. Amid griping to owner George Steinbrenner, slumping, and being relegated to a DH role, he defied orders to bunt in a game against Kansas City, then some days later bunted when called on to swing away. The tension among the owner, manager, and slugger reached critical mass when Martin called Jackson a "born liar" and alluded to Steinbrenner's conviction for illegal campaign contributions. The cracks cost Martin his job.

Jackson himself departed from the Yankees in 1982 the way he had arrived, as a free agent. Steinbrenner admitted his mistake in letting him leave when the slugger led the AL (for the final time) in homers in his first season for California. After that, Jackson merely played out the string for four more years with the Angels and a final season with the Athletics.

TRAVIS JACKSON (Hall of Fame, 1982)

Jackson was so unassuming during his fifteen-year (1922–36) career with the Giants that even Ebbets Field fans usually didn't bother to boo him. The regular shortstop for the final phase of the John McGraw reign and most of Bill Terry's rule, Jackson squeezed six .300 seasons into his .291 lifetime mark. Defensively, Jackson began with an ouch, leading the league in errors in his first full season, but then went on to pace NL shortstops in assists four times. When leg injuries began slowing him up, he was shifted over to third base. Jackson's biggest RBI year—1934, when he topped the 100 mark for the only time—was the season that Terry had inflamed Brooklyn fans by inquiring if the Dodgers were still in the league. When even Jackson was greeted by catcalls at Ebbets Field, the New York manager understood how ably the Brooklyn front office had twisted his words to stir up the local faithful.

BILL JAMES

James was a high school English teacher in Lawrence, Kansas, when he began publishing *The Baseball Abstract* annually in 1977 and became the foremost sabermetrician. Perhaps the most popular of the statistical tools he developed was Runs Created, which strives to use statistical achievement in every offensive category to estimate how good a player is at generating runs for his club.

STUART JANNEY

Janney was the attorney for the directors of the Federal League Baltimore franchise in their protracted negotiations with the National and American leagues after the FL's collapse had left the Terrapins with what its owners considered an inadequate offer to liquidate. In those negotiations, Chicago White Sox owner Charlie Comiskey dismissed a Baltimore offer to purchase the St. Louis Cardinals for $250,000, calling the tender "the proper price for a minor league franchise" and referring to Baltimore as "a minor league city, and not a hell of a good one at that." When Brooklyn owner Charlie Ebbets added, "You have too many colored population to begin with. They are a cheap population when it gets down to paying their money at the gate," there was no place left for Janney to go except to the courts. The case was eventually decided by the U.S. Supreme Court, with Justice Oliver Wendell Holmes writing a majority opinion in favor or organized baseball's claim of exemption from federal antitrust legislation.

BROTHER JASPER

Jasper, a member of the religious order of Christian Brothers, has been credited with originating the 7th-inning stretch. The coach of the Manhattan College baseball team in the 1880s, he insisted that players and spectators at games sit with the decorum appropriate for young men at a strict Catholic college. But on one occasion in 1882, just as Manhattan was coming to bat in the 7th inning, he instructed students in the grandstand to rise and stretch to alleviate their heat-induced discomfort. The practice became a habit at the college's games and was passed on to major league fans during the frequent exhibition games the college squad played with the Giants at the Polo Grounds.

LARRY JASTER

Southpaw Jaster won 11 games for the Cardinals in 1966, but 5 of those victories were shutouts of the Dodgers. The only other pitchers to administer as many whitewashes to one team in a season were Tom Hughes of the 1905 Senators, who mastered the Indians, and Grover Cleveland Alexander of the 1916 Phillies, who dominated the Reds.

JOEY JAY

When he joined the Braves in 1953, right-hander Jay became the first major leaguer to come out of the organized Little League. It was a distinction he wore uneasily, and in later years he warned of the threats posed to children by overbearing parents and overly structured games for young people.

HAL JEFFCOAT

Jeffcoat was the last player to have separate appreciable careers at a major league level as a position player and a pitcher. Between 1948 and 1953 he played in at least 80 games five times as an outfielder for the Cubs. Discouraged that his offense was falling off from highs of .279 in 1948 and .273 in 1951, he developed a knuckleball that allowed him to return to Chicago as a pitcher in 1954. Used mainly as a reliever by the Cubs and then by the Reds, he turned in a better-than-even 39-37 record over a six-year period.

FERGUSON JENKINS (Hall of Fame, 1991)

Jenkins is the Ernie Banks of pitchers, his 284 victories in nineteen big league seasons making him the winningest pitcher who never appeared in a postseason game. The right-hander collected many more distinctions than that, however. Inserted into the rotation by the Cubs in 1967 after a deal with Philadelphia, he won 20 games for six consecutive years—a feat that had been considered implausible because of hitter-friendly Wrigley Field. In 1971 he took Cy Young honors for leading the National League with 24 victories; he also set an all-time mark by walking only 37 batters while fanning 263. Three years later, with

the Rangers, he paced American League hurlers with another 25 victories. A gifted hitter, he clouted 6 home runs one season; an equally nimble fielder, he holds the all-time mark for putouts by a pitcher (363).

Following his banner 1975 season with Texas, Jenkins turned in several more years of wins in the high teens, but his diamond performance was frequently overshadowed by his off-field antics and problems. With the Red Sox in 1976 and 1977, for instance, he gained more print for being one of the ringleaders (along with Bill Lee and Bernie Carbo) in the relentless taunting of manager Don Zimmer. Traded back to the Rangers in 1977 after Zimmer had accused him of falling asleep in the bullpen, he was stopped by a Canadian customs official in 1980 for carrying drugs, prompting a suspension by Commissioner Bowie Kuhn. Although the suspension was overruled by an arbitrator shortly afterward, the incident held up his election to Cooperstown for a while.

HUGHIE JENNINGS (Hall of Fame, 1945)

Jennings's animated and boisterous cheerleading, particularly his trademark ''Eeh-yah'' screech, were seen as positive components of team chemistry as long as things were going well; when they weren't, emphasis invariably shifted to his clubhouse sarcasm. The right-hand-hitting infielder brought a meager .136 batting average from Louisville to the Baltimore Orioles in a mid-1893 trade for Voiceless Tim O'Rourke and *his* .363 average. But then Jennings learned to avoid stepping into the bucket by keeping his back against a batting cage while teammate John McGraw threw to him over a winter that the pair spent as undergraduates at St. Bonaventure University. So effective was McGraw's tutelage that Jennings pushed his mentor over to third base and went on to establish a batting record for shortstops, with a .401 average in 1896. While barnstorming after spring training that same year, he showed his Oriole colors when he precipitated one of the ugliest incidents in that team's often unattractive history by starting a fight with a player with a member of the minor league franchise in Petersburg, Virginia. Pursued to their hotel by an irate mob of fans, the Baltimore players were whisked to the train station by police and cooler-headed locals, but not before the hotel lobby had been utterly trashed.

Shipped from Baltimore to Brooklyn in 1899 as part of the maneuvers of the syndicate that owned both clubs, Jennings flirted with the backers of the abortive new American Association, then became secretary of the Protective Association of Professional Baseball Players. After the rest of the leadership of the proto-union had been co-opted, he had to be content with minor league managerial assignments until Detroit owner Frank Navin rescued him in 1907. Managing the Tigers meant trying to manage Ty Cobb, and Jennings's first reaction was not even to try, offering the difficult outfielder to the Indians for holdout Elmer Flick. Turned down, the manager was forced to turn his attention to containing the furor over such incidents as Cobb's assault of a black groundskeeper and his wife, and to resolving his star's various feuds with other Detroit outfielders by repeatedly shifting him from one position to another to keep him as far away as possible from his foe of the moment. Jennings himself contributed to the turmoil by refusing to give up a whistle he began using in the third base coach's box when his voice gave out, and getting slapped with a two-week suspension for his insistence. Despite all the commotion, there were three consecutive pennants (1907–09) to point to. Only when the club began its long slide out of contention did Jennings vent his sarcasm on the Tigers. After hanging on for more than a decade after his last flag, he packed it in for health reasons in 1920.

Always accident-prone, Jennings was almost killed three times: by a beanball in 1897; from a dive into an empty swimming pool at Cornell, where he studied law in the off-season; and in a winter automobile accident that took the life of his companion. Despite failing health, he took a job as a coach on the Giants in 1921, and filled in as manager for an even more ailing John McGraw in 1924, when the New Yorkers won their fourth consecutive pennant, and again in 1925, when they failed to repeat. He then suffered a nervous breakdown that kept him out of baseball for the final three years of his life.

MANNY JIMINEZ

Jiminez had his appointment with history canceled by fireworks. As a member of the Athletics on July 4, 1964, the lefty-swinging outfielder walloped 3 consecutive home runs. He didn't get a chance at a fourth because the game was called as a tie after the ninth inning because of a commitment to celebrate Independence Day with a fireworks display. Jiminez, who had only 26 homers in his seven-year career, was one of the first natives of the Dominican municipality of San Pedro de Macoris to reach the major leagues.

TOMMY JOHN

Nobody had a more unexpectedly long career than John. While with the Dodgers in July 1974, the southpaw snapped a ligament in his pitching elbow, apparently ending his playing days. But then orthopedic surgeon Frank Jobe reconstructed the elbow using a tendon from the right forearm. After John sat out the 1975 season, he went on to complete a twenty-six-year career—the longest of any pitcher except Nolan Ryan. The Bionic Arm, as the hurler came to be called, ended up with 228 victories, those in his later years with the Yankees coming on sheer guile.

ALBERT JOHNSON

The financial backer of the Cleveland Players League club, Johnson spent the fall of 1890 meeting with National League owners over terms for the dissolution of the PL in a classic sellout of the players who had been his partners; as a freelance entrepreneur, he was also meeting with Cincinnati president Aaron Stern to complete a purchase of the Reds for the purpose of moving them into the PL. When the NL gave John T. Brush rights to its Cincinnati franchise and, at about the same time, the negotiations to abolish the PL succeeded, Johnson sought a buyout for his team without a league. Refusing to deal with Brush and rebuffed by the NL as a whole, he turned to the American Association. Awarded a franchise in that league, he promptly turned around and talked the NL into giving him $30,000 to deprive the AA of a foothold in the Cincinnati market. Johnson never got his money, though: Other PL investors he had brought into the Cincinnati deal questioned his right to sell, tying the transaction up in court until his death a decade later.

ALEX JOHNSON

Johnson was the first player to be put on the disabled list for emotional rather than physical reasons. The outfielder achieved the distinction in 1971 after two years of divisive incidents on the Angels that had several teammates attack him with fists, another draw a gun on him, and manager Lefty Phillips levy an astonishing twenty-nine fines against him in less than half a season. Among other things, Johnson regularly abused sportswriters covering the team, poured coffee into the typewriter of *Los Angeles Herald-Examiner* writer Dick Miller, insisted on playing the outfield within the shadow of a light tower on a hot afternoon, fired a soda bottle at pitcher Clyde Wright, and had periodic punch-ups in the batting cage with teammates. Through it all, the right-hand-hitting slugger argued that it was baseball's ''antiblack bias'' that painted him as a bad guy—a contention that scored mostly with general manager Dick Walsh, who was nervous about the franchise's sorry record with blacks. When Walsh finally suspended the outfielder, however, Players Association director Marvin Miller argued successfully before an arbitration panel that Johnson was suffering from acute mental distress and should be disabled with full pay.

When he felt like it, Johnson posed an appreciable threat at the plate. After being traded by the Reds to the Angels in 1970, he collected 202 hits and won the American League batting title with a .329 average. Following the arbitration panel's ruling, he was dealt to the Indians.

ARNOLD JOHNSON

In purchasing the Athletics from the Mack family and transferring them from Philadelphia to Kansas City for the 1955 season, Johnson gave the Yankees in particular, and baseball owners in general, a lot to be thankful for. An executive of the Chicago-based Automatic Canteen Company, he worked out deals so unsubtly with the Yankees during his ownership reign that Kansas City functioned as little more than a New York farm club on the major league level; between 1955 and 1960, for instance, the teams completed sixteen trades involving some sixty players, with such talents as Roger Maris, Clete Boyer, Ralph Terry, and Ryne Duren ending up in the Bronx. None of this should have come as a surprise to the other owners since, before purchasing the Athletics, Johnson had been the landlord of both Yankee Stadium and the Kansas City ballpark used by New York's chief farm club. But if AL owners, especially, had reason to resent the constant player traffic between New York and Kansas City, they and their National League counterparts had only gratitude in their hearts after Johnson had his attorneys press the Internal Revenue Service for a definitive ruling on the status of players as organization property; it is thanks to the IRS's response to the Johnson query that major league franchises are able to depreciate the value of player contracts over a number of tax years. Johnson died of a heart attack during spring training in 1960.

BAN JOHNSON (Hall of Fame, 1937)

Johnson created and nurtured the American League until it was the equal of the National. At the same time, however, he thrived on making and getting even with enemies—a flaw that eventually brought him down.

In 1890, Johnson succeeded O. P. Caylor as sports editor of the *Cincinnati Enquirer* and immediately started a feud with John T. Brush that made the Reds owner vulnerable to suggestions for getting him out of the city. Through the contrivance of Cincinnati manager Charlie Comiskey, Brush recommended Johnson for the post of president of the minor Western League in 1894. When Johnson proved to be more of a nuisance as a league executive than he had been as a commentator, Brush sought to unseat him, but Johnson survived the battle with sufficient authority to force Brush to sell the WL franchise he had in Indianapolis and that he was using a little too slickly to provide players for Cincinnati. Joined by Comiskey, who took over the Sioux City franchise in 1895, Johnson ran the most successful minor league in the nation for several years until deciding to go for the brass ring of major league status. Announcing a change in the circuit's name to the American League in 1900, he invaded several territories abandoned by the NL when it re-

American League founder Ban Johnson was at the center of just about every major controversy over the first couple of decades of the 20th century. National Baseball Library, Cooperstown, N.Y.

duced its roster from twelve to eight teams after the 1899 season, and transferred Comiskey's club from St. Paul (where it had gone after Sioux City) to Chicago. While recognizing the threat to its monopoly, the NL fought back only ineffectually, doing little more than making noises about reviving the American Association and threatening to blacklist defecting players.

Johnson had it all his way. He set up a wartime strategy of holding 51 percent of each franchise's stock and the leases on their ballparks in the league's name. He lined up millionaires, most importantly coal industrialist Charles Somers, to finance his undertaking. He supported umpires against the spread of the rowdyism that infected the NL, and he threw players out of his league for violence. He raided NL clubs for such future Hall of Famers as John McGraw, Jimmy Collins, and Nap Lajoie. He engineered trades to circumvent legal rulings that went against the AL; the most famous such deal sent Lajoie and Elmer

Flick from the Athletics to the Indians to get out from under an injunction against the pair appearing in Pennsylvania for anyone but the NL Phillies. His eight teams even outdrew the NL's in his second year of operation at a major league level.

By the end of the 1902 season, Johnson was synonymous with the AL, despite the embarrassing defection of McGraw, who became manager of the Giants and in the process trashed the AL Baltimore franchise. Johnson recouped his losses from this near-disaster by moving the Orioles to New York in a direct challenge to the Giants and raided the Pirates for, among others, pitchers Jack Chesbro and Jesse Tannehill to stock the new club. It was after this coup that Pittsburgh's Barney Dreyfuss led NL owners in suing for peace. Among other things, the settlement created the National Commission, consisting of the two league presidents and Cincinnati president Garry Herrmann, one of the prime movers in the NL's capitulation. With Herrmann more often than not voting with him, Johnson was the most powerful figure in baseball for more than a decade.

But it was also a series of votes on the National Commission that began to erode that power. In awarding George Sisler to the Browns instead of the Pirates in 1915, Johnson lost the support of Dreyfuss. In the Scott Perry case in 1918, Johnson irritated the rest of the NL when he refused to honor a commission vote awarding the pitcher to the Braves, then supported Connie Mack's courtroom efforts to keep the pitcher with the Athletics. That same year, what had over the years become a hot-and-cold relationship with Comiskey turned frigid when pitcher Jack Quinn was assigned to the Yankees in a dispute with the White Sox.

With new enemies snapping at his heels, Johnson won no new friends with his behavior in the face of a threatened strike during the 1918 World Series, showing up drunk at a meeting with a delegation of Red Sox and Cub players. The following year, he lost the support of Boston's Harry Frazee, already incensed over the league president's singling out Fenway Park as a hotbed of gambling, and New York's Jacob Ruppert and Cap Huston when he refused to let the Red Sox trade Carl Mays to the Yankees while the pitcher was under suspension. That decision set off a sequence of events that included a court order restraining Johnson from interfering with Mays's transfer to New York; a demand by Detroit owner Frank Navin for Johnson to throw out Mays's 9 wins for the Yankees and thereby award third place and the World Series money that went with it to the Tigers; and a bombardment of lawsuits by Ruppert and Huston alleging that the league president was trying to force them out of baseball and that he was guilty of a conflict of interest because he held stock in the Indians and really wanted Mays transferred to Cleveland.

The so-called Insurrectionists—Comiskey, Frazee, and the New York duo—carried the day in a showdown league meeting in February 1920 that finally sanctioned the Mays-to-New York deal and imposed a review committee to pass on all but the most routine league affairs. The Loyal Five teams caved in again the following November when the Insurrectionists joined the National League in insisting on the appointment of federal judge Kenesaw Landis as commissioner of baseball, holding out the threat of putting a rival team in Detroit and creating a twelve-team NL unless the rest of the AL went along.

With little to do after the superimposition of Landis, Johnson took out after the Black Sox. Even though his initial reaction on hearing of Comiskey's suspicions about some of his own players was, "That's the yelp of a beaten cur," Johnson took the inaction of Landis and the dropping of the first indictment against the Chicago Eight as an opportunity to win back some of his lost prestige and, not incidentally, embarrass Comiskey. Traveling two thousand miles in two months, Johnson lined up so much evidence that the Cook County district attorney had to bring another indictment. But Johnson's plans fell apart when a jury found the Black Sox not guilty on August 2, 1921, and Landis stole his thunder by banning them from baseball anyway.

Infuriated by the commissioner's show-stealing, Johnson spent his last years in office picking fights with Landis. One confrontation occurred in December 1924 after the league president had called for a federal probe into the events leading up to the banning of Giants outfielder Jimmy

O'Connell and coach Cozy Dolan and what he claimed as a whitewashing of other New York players involved. With Landis reminding them that they had pledged themselves not to contest any of his decisions in court, the AL owners publicly rejected their president's demand for an investigation. The end came two years later, in the wake of the Dutch Leonard-Ty Cobb-Tris Speaker affair, when Landis undid Johnson's quiet dismissal of the two future Hall of Famers behind accusations by the pitcher that they had bet on and fixed a game on September 25, 1919. After suffering a complete breakdown as the AL owners once again repudiated him in a January 1927 meeting, Johnson resigned the following July. He died on March 28, 1931, of diabetes.

CLIFF JOHNSON

A well-traveled catcher in the 1970s and 1980s who was much better off with a bat in his hands, Johnson holds the record for career pinch-hit home runs with 20. More notoriously, he had a hand in costing two teams relief aces. In 1979, while a member of the Yankees, he got into a shower room tussle with bullpen ace Goose Gossage that left the pitcher with a torn thumb ligament and New York with little chance of winning a division flag. When he signed with the Rangers as a free agent in 1984, his previous team, the Blue Jays, secured as compensation Tom Henke, the right-hander who would go on to be their Terminator for several seasons.

DAVEY JOHNSON

Despite his achievements as a Gold Glove second baseman for the Orioles in the late 1960s and early 1970s, Johnson has mainly been a disciple of the Earl Weaver school of Three-Run-Homers-Cure-Everything-and-Let's-Be-Arrogant-About-It-When-We-Get-One. As a player, some of his most illustrious moments involved the long ball. In 1972, playing for Atlanta, Johnson joined Hank Aaron and Darrell Evans as the only trio of teammates to hit 40 homers in a season, in the process tying Rogers Hornsby's season record for most home runs by a second baseman. In 1978, while winding down with the Phillies, Johnson became the first player to hit two pinch-hit grand-slams in a season. He is also the answer to the trivia question about the name of the player who walked out of the on-deck circle to greet both Aaron and Sadaharu Oh as they crossed the plate with the home runs that put them ahead of Babe Ruth's 714 career blasts. As the manager of the Mets between 1984 and early 1990, Johnson never hesitated to play the likes of Howard Johnson and Kevin Mitchell at shortstop in the interests of getting another slugger into the lineup, defense be damned.

It was also as the New York pilot that Johnson set the tone for what was perceived as the most arrogant National League club in years, especially after his preseason prediction in 1986 that the team would not only win the East Division but also "dominate" it. In fact, the Mets left the runner-up Phillies in the dust by an unprecedented 21½ games. Dynastic forecasts notwithstanding, that year's world championship turned out to be one of a kind. By the time he was replaced early in the 1990 season, Johnson had been conveying for some time the image of a bruised loser in the battle of egos with general manager Frank Cashen. For all that, however, Johnson still left Shea Stadium with one of baseball's all-time managerial winning percentages, and the curious lack of interest of other teams in hiring him raised suspicions that he was being blackballed for his readiness to talk back to his employers. When Johnson finally did get another job, in 1993, it was under the worst possible circumstances—replacing Cincinnati's popular Tony Perez, who had been fired after serving his purpose as a sop to critics of the organization's minority hiring policies. Johnson barely navigated through the rest of the season with a team in a state of near-mutiny over the treatment of Perez.

HOWARD JOHNSON

Aside from Bobby Bonds, Johnson is the only major leaguer to record three seasons of at least 30 home runs and 30 stolen bases, doing it for the Mets in 1987, 1989, and 1991. The third baseman also holds most of the power marks for National League switch-hitters. Entering the 1995 season, he had collected a senior circuit high of 202 homers, and also had the win-place-show spots for the most productive individual seasons for a switch-hitter by belting 38 round-trippers in

1991 and 36 each in 1987 and 1989. After pacing the NL with both his 38 homers and 117 RBIs in 1991, Johnson fell on lean times, in part because of injuries, and left New York to sign as a free agent with the Rockies in 1994. His power career at Shea Stadium had belied one of Sparky Anderson's more outlandish predictions; in dealing the young slugger from the Tigers to the Mets in 1985, Anderson tabbed him as a good defensive player who would never hit in the major leagues. In fact, most of Johnson's problems in New York stemmed from defense, especially after a series of managers started moving him off his natural third-base position to shortstop, right field, and center field. With Colorado he was sent to left field.

JUDY JOHNSON (Hall of Fame, 1975)

The best third baseman of the Negro leagues in the 1920s and 1930s, Johnson was known as the black Pie Traynor, but he hit for a higher average than the Pittsburgh Hall of Famer and his defensive play has been compared favorably to that of Brooks Robinson.

In a sixteen-year (1921–36) career with the Hilldale club of Darby, Homestead Grays, Darby Daisies, and Pittsburgh Crawfords, the righty-swinging Johnson was a regular .300 hitter, topping .400 in 1929. He also managed the Grays in 1930, discovering Josh Gibson along the way, and the Daisies in 1931–32. Johnson retired after Crawfords owner Gus Greenlee traded him and Gibson to the Grays after the 1936 season.

Connie Mack, an old admirer, hired Johnson as a scout in the late 1940s, but he switched to the Phillies after the post-Mack Philadelphia front office turned down his suggestions to sign Larry Doby, Minnie Minoso, and Hank Aaron. Johnson also worked for the Braves, whose center fielder Billy Bruton became his son-in-law.

KEN JOHNSON

Johnson is the only major league pitcher to lose a nine-inning no-hitter. Pitching for the Astros at home on April 23, 1964, the right-hander was beaten by Cincinnati, 1–0, on a couple of errors and a sacrifice fly.

LOU JOHNSON

Johnson was already in his thirties after many years of travels around the minor leagues when he blossomed into The Cinderella Man who animated consecutive pennants for the Dodgers in 1965 and 1966. A right-hand-hitting outfielder of modest defensive abilities, his clutch hitting down the stretch of both years made him a more popular figure with Los Angeles fans than some of the team's higher-priced stars. On September 9, 1965, Johnson was the only base runner in a duel between Sandy Koufax and Chicago's Bob Hendley. While Koufax was twirling a perfect game, Johnson walked and came around to score the game's only run on a steal and an error; later in the game, he had a bloop double off Hendley for the only hit of the contest.

WALTER JOHNSON (Hall of Fame, 1936)

Johnson has the most credible claim to the title of baseball's greatest pitcher. Although Cy Young won more games, Johnson's 416 victories (the most in the American League) over twenty-one seasons (1907–27) were for a team, the Senators, that lived in the second division and that didn't win a pennant until its ace was thirty-seven. Despite that kind of backing, the right-hander won more than 30 games twice, had 10 consecutive years of 20 wins or more, and led the league in wins six times, in ERA five times, and in strikeouts twelve times. Until Nolan Ryan and Steve Carlton passed him in the 1980s, he had the major league mark with his 3,508 strikeouts, accomplishing them almost exclusively with a sidearm fastball. His single greatest performance came in 1913, when he went 36–7 with a 1.09 ERA, yielding 6 hits per 9 innings and fanning 243 batters against a mere 38 walks. In that year he also hurled 12 of his major league-high 110 shutouts. Seven of his blankings occurred on Opening Day, for a record not likely to be broken. Another of Johnson's astounding numbers was ending up with a record of 38–27 in 1–0 games; all told, he lost 65 games in which Washington failed to score. It hardly came as a surprise when The Big Train, as he was known, joined Ty Cobb, Babe Ruth, Honus Wagner, and Christy Mathewson as

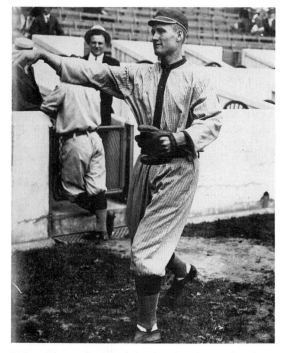

Walter Johnson dominated the American League for almost 20 years despite not picking up an effective second pitch until he was in the twilight of his career. National Baseball Library, Cooperstown, N.Y.

one of the Five Immortals elected to Cooperstown in the first year of balloting.

Johnson made his first splash for Washington during a 1908 weekend series against the Yankees, when he hurled 3 shutouts in a 4-game series. Despite catching on almost immediately as a fan favorite, he had one contract problem after another with Washington officials. Prior to the 1911 season, for instance, he walked out of spring training camp when club president Thomas Noyes refused to give him a salary equal to that of Ty Cobb ($9,000). When fans protested the possible loss of their mound star, Noyes used his newspaper connections to plant stories about how Johnson was headed for the Tigers. That only brought more vehement outcries, and the two sides eventually settled on a contract slightly less than Cobb's. During the 1914–15 off-season, there was an even bigger crisis when Noyes's successor as president, Ben Minor, told the pitcher that his "mere 28 wins" in 1914 did not entitle him to the same $12,000 he had received after winning his 36 games in 1913. Johnson was so furious that he promptly signed with the Chicago Whales in the Federal League. Without consulting Minor, manager and minority stockholder Clark Griffith went to Johnson's home and won the hurler back by promising to match the FL offer. In fact, Griffith had to get the money from White Sox owner Charlie Comiskey and then only through a heavy-handed warning to him that Johnson's FL presence in Chicago might ruin the White Sox.

By the early 1920s, Johnson appeared to have left his best diamond moments behind him, with not even his belated mastery of a curveball failing to prevent four years in a row without reaching the 20-win mark. But then in 1924, with the Senators smelling a pennant for the first time in their existence, he suddenly reverted to old form, winning 13 straight games down the stretch and winding up with league-leading numbers in both wins (23) and ERA (2.72). Although he had only a single win, and that in relief, in the World Series against the Giants, it turned out to be in the decisive seventh game, giving Washington a world championship. That wasn't his last World Series victory, either. In 1925 Johnson came back for still another 20-win season as the Senators won another pennant. When he wasn't driving the team on from the mound, he was ruining opposition clubs with his hitting: While always a competent batsman, he surprised even himself by setting an all-time-high batting average of .433 for pitchers, in 1925. The postseason duel with Pittsburgh brought both further glory and ugly disappointment. While Johnson won 2 games, including a shutout, he was also knocked around by the Pirates for 9 runs and 15 hits in the finale. Worse, a furious Ban Johnson, president of the American League, sent a bitter telegram to Washington manager Bucky Harris criticizing the decision to leave the right-hander in the entire game for what he called "sentimental reasons."

After retiring as a player, Johnson tried his hand at managing, with less than brilliant success. He piloted the Senators to two winning seasons in the early 1930s, but it took blazing finishes by the team to regain respectability after playing humdrum ball for most of these campaigns. Fired by Griffith for not showing enough animated leadership, he moved over to the helm of the Indians for three years, encountering hostility from a general manager (Billy Evans) who hadn't been told of his hiring, from players (Willie Kamm and Glenn Myatt) who objected to his high-handed ways, and finally from the fans. Especially after his release of Kamm and Myatt behind charges that they had sought to stir up a team plot against him, Johnson was booed whenever he stepped onto the field in Cleveland. At one point before being let go, he was so unpopular in Cleveland that extra police were assigned to the ballpark and beverages were dispensed in soft cups rather than bottles.

SMEEDERINO JOLLIANI

Smeederino Jolliani was the Italianized name of Smead Jolley, an outfielder for the White Sox and Red Sox in the early 1930s who could have used the designated hitter rule. Disturbed that Boston's large Italian-American community didn't have an ethnic hero at Fenway Park, Johnny Garro, editor of the Italian-language daily *Notizia*, decided to invent one with the name change. What Boston's cheering Italian Americans got to see was a left-handed slugger who averaged .305 over four major league seasons but who was so terrified of walls that he refused to chase fly balls anywhere near them. At Fenway he had an even greater nemesis in a left-field incline that usually had him tripping over his feet even when running toward the infield after a drive. As Chicago had previously, Boston added up the runs that Jolley had driven in and, weighing them against the ones he had allowed, dropped him.

BUMPUS JONES

Jones is often depicted as a brash youngster who presented himself to Reds manager Charlie Comiskey on the last day of the 1892 season as a pitcher the equal of anyone on the Cincinnati staff, proceeded to throw a no-hitter in his major league debut, and proved his feat was a fluke by managing only a 1–4 record and a 10.19 ERA the following year. In fact, the right-hander was a highly regarded prospect who had already won 27 minor league games before appearing in the Reds clubhouse; he faltered in 1893 because he was unable to adapt to the new pitching distance of sixty feet, six inches. What remains true from the familiar story is that Jones is the only pitcher to twirl a no-hitter in his first big league game.

CHARLEY JONES

An early slugger and good-time Charley, Jones managed to get involved in wrangles involving the two most powerful owners of the National League's first decade. In 1877, after league president William Hulbert had temporarily suspended the Cincinnati franchise, the outfielder signed with the Chicago White Stockings, owned by the same Hulbert, but only on the condition that the Reds remain out of the league for the rest of the year. After the right-handed power hitter had spent 2 games in a Chicago uniform, other league owners forced Hulbert to return his prize to the reconstituted Reds.

In 1880, Jones so exasperated Boston's Arthur Soden with his profligacy and demands for back pay that the owner suspended him, citing unsatisfactory performance and "conduct aggravating beyond the patience of most people." Jones, who was batting .300 with 5 home runs, and who had led the NL with 9 homers the year before, won a court judgment for the rest of his 1880 salary. Despite a second courtroom venture that resulted in a nasty, losing trial that made much of the outfielder's drinking, he remained on the blacklist until the American Association Reds allowed him to join the team in 1883. Three years later, Jones's wife ran into him with another woman on his arm and threw cayenne pepper in his eyes, temporarily blinding him and permanently damaging his eyesight.

CLEON JONES

Jones was the object of the two most humiliating incidents in Mets history. Although the right-hand-hitting outfielder was on his way to a franchise-high .340 average at the time, he gained the attention of manager Gil Hodges for not hustling after an extra-base hit in the first game of a July 30, 1969, doubleheader. Hodges proceeded to walk all the way out to Jones's position in left field and order him back to the dugout with him—a move that was later hailed by other Mets as the turning point in the club's pennant-winning sea-

son. In May 1975 he was dragged before the media by board chairman M. Donald Grant to apologize for having been seized by police in a Florida van on charges of having sexual relations with a woman in public. Although initial "indecent exposure" charges were eventually dropped for their absurdity, Grant insisted on collecting a $2,000 fine from Jones for "betraying the image" of the team.

FIELDER JONES

Best known as the manager of the world champion Hitless Wonder White Sox of 1906, Jones also holds the distinction of having scored the first American League run when he was singled home from third by Fred Hartman in the bottom of the first inning of the AL inaugural game of April 24, 1901, between Chicago and Cleveland. A lifetime .284 hitter for the Dodgers and White Sox in his fifteen big league seasons between 1896 and 1915, the center fielder later managed the Federal League St. Louis Terriers and the Browns, whom he quit on June 15, 1918, after the team had blown a 9th-inning, 6-run lead. He never returned to baseball.

NIPPY JONES

Jones's otherwise bland eight-year National League career was forgotten with his very last plate appearance. Pinch hitting for the Braves in the fourth game in the 1957 World Series against the Yankees, the right-hand-hitting first baseman jumped out of the way of a low fastball delivered by Tommy Byrne. When umpire Augie Donatelli called a ball, Jones and Milwaukee manager Fred Haney argued that he had been hit by the pitch and pointed out shoe polish smears on the ball. Donatelli awarded Jones first base; the Braves went on to rally, win the game, and eventually capture the Series.

RANDY JONES

Jones was so unexpectedly successful for the otherwise dreary Padres in the mid-1970s that he prompted rethinking in the National League about traditional platooning ploys. A sinker specialist, the southpaw won the ERA title in 1975, then came back the following year to take Cy Young honors for pacing the league in victories. In 1977, however, opposition managers defied custom by benching right-handed hitters against him and studding their lineups with lefty swingers who could neutralize the sinker. Jones never again had a .500 season, and his overall 100–123 record is the worst by any hurler with two 20–win years.

MIKE JORDAN

An outfielder for the 1890 Pirates, Jordan is the only player to have had 100 major league at-bats without reaching a .100 average. He managed merely 11 singles and a double in 125 plate appearances for an .096 average.

ADDIE JOSS (Hall of Fame, 1978)

Joss was such an overwhelming performer for the Indians in the first decade of the century that the Hall of Fame waived its normal condition of at least ten years of major league service for entry into Cooperstown. In his nine seasons (1902–10) with Cleveland, the righthander won 20 games four times, had at least 200 strikeouts six times, led the American League in ERA twice, and finished second to Ed Walsh for career ERA (1.88). Joss's single most memorable outing took place on October 2, 1908, when he hooked up against Walsh, defeating the Chicago right-hander, 1–0, while fashioning a perfect game.

Stricken with meningitis, Joss grew progressively weaker during the 1910 season, and died in April 1911. Anticipating a refusal to their request to be allowed to attend his funeral in Toledo because it coincided with the Indians' season opener in Detroit, the pitcher's teammates took off for the services without waiting for an answer.

After overnight stories that the club was in open revolt, Cleveland owner Charles Somers stepped in to calm AL president Ban Johnson and the Tigers, and the opener was played the following day—as Joss's teammates had requested in the first place.

BILL JOYCE

A major league third baseman for eight seasons in the 1890s, Joyce was half responsible for the term Texas Leaguer. He made his contribution to the baseball lexicon in 1889, while still in the minor leagues. When he and outfielder Art Sunday, both recently transferred from Houston of the Texas League, opened their first game for the International League Toledo club with back-to-back bloop hits, teammates jeered at the alleged source of the cheap hits.

BILLY JURGES

An often brutal shortstop for the Cubs and Giants in the 1930s and 1940s, Jurges almost got more than he gave early in his career. A second-year player with Chicago in 1932, he rejected the advances of one Violet Vallee, and received a bullet in the ribs and another in the hand for his trouble. After recovering from his wounds in little more than two weeks, he got into earnest about a seventeen-year career that earned him equal amounts of applause for his deft defensive work and protests over his murderous, waist-high take-outs at second base. A retaliatory beanball against his tactics around second base almost ended Jurges's career in 1940, but he stuck around for another seven seasons before retiring with a .258 batting average.

K

JIM KAAT

If Tommy John managed to hang on for twenty-six years thanks to his bionic arm, Kaat stretched his big league career to twenty-five seasons thanks to the quick pitch. A southpaw who was written off by several clubs in the 1970s and 1980s, he was the plague of concessionaires by forcing batters to keep their eyes on the mound whenever they were in the batting box. If this often led to unintentional toppers back to the pitcher, Kaat was ready with another of his talents—one that brought him a record 16 Gold Gloves.

Before becoming all guile, the left-hander was one of the dominant pitchers in the American League, compiling a circuit-leading 25 wins for the Twins in 1965, then going on to win 20 games in his only two seasons with the White Sox, in 1974 and 1975. In three other seasons he won at least 17 games, closing out with 283 victories. Kaat went from Minnesota to Chicago in 1973 after joining teammate Jim Perry as the first American Leaguers to invoke their five-and-ten rights (five years with one club, ten in the majors) to approve any transactions. It was a fitting climax to his years of contract wars with Twins owner Calvin Griffith, once described by Kaat as somebody who ''threw quarters around like manhole covers.''

AL KALINE (Hall of Fame '980)

Kaline was almost more curious for what he didn't accomplish than for what he did during his twenty-two-year (1953–74) career for Detroit. Among other things, the right-hand-hitting outfielder never led the American League in either home runs or RBIs, never hit 30 homers in a season, managed 200 hits only once, won only one batting title, and was never awarded an MVP trophy. His career batting average fell three points short of .300, and his home-run total was one shy of 400. On the other hand, Kaline established himself as the Tigers franchise player of the 1950s and 1960s almost as soon as he made his big league debut. Only a few days after his high school graduation, he took the field in a game against Chicago and threw out base runners at second, third, and home in successive innings—a foretaste of the 10 Gold Gloves he would accumulate. In 1955, at age twenty, he became the youngest player to win a batting title when he averaged .340. In 1959 he paced the AL in slugging average, and in 1961 in doubles. In 1968, after missing a good part of the season with a broken arm, Kaline was restored to the outfield for the World Series against the Cardinals, cracking 11 hits and driving home 8 runs in the seven-game Detroit victory. Ending up with 3,007 hits, he was the first member of the 3,000-hit club who failed to bat .300 for a career.

JERRY KAPSTEIN

As the first prominent player agent in the wake of the Messersmith-McNally decision in 1975, Kapstein became Public Enemy Number One for the baseball establishment and its media allies. He was particularly vilified in Boston in 1976, when his attempts to obtain new contracts for soon-to-be-free-agents Carlton Fisk, Rick Burleson, and Fred Lynn coincided with the hospitalization of Red Sox owner Tom Yawkey. When Yawkey died shortly after voicing his bafflement at the money being asked for his three players, more than one newspaperman in Boston suggested that Kapstein's demands had been a contributory cause. Among the agent's other clients that year were Wayne Garland, who signed one of the first big free-agent pacts, with Cleveland; Don Gullett, who left the world champion Reds to go to the Yankees; and Rollie Fingers and Joe Rudi, whom Oakland owner Charlie Finley sought (unsuccessfully) to sell to the same Red Sox for $1 million each. The son-in-law of Padres owner Joan Kroc, Kapstein was asked to assume the unfamiliar role of negotiating with prospective purchasers of the franchise in late 1989, eventually playing a role in the selection of Tom Werner as the new owner.

ED KARGER

No one took more advantage of an early-century rule authorizing abbreviated doubleheader nightcaps than Karger when, while a member of the Cardinals, he hurled a 7-inning perfect game against the Braves on August 11, 1907. In fact, his masterpiece was one of nine truncated twilight no-hitters tossed between 1903 and 1912. The southpaw pitched for six big league seasons with four clubs but compiled a lifetime record of only 48–67.

BENNY KAUFF

Kauff was the Ty Cobb of the Federal League, but never quite lived up to his own boast that he would "make Cobb look like a bush leaguer if I can play for the Giants." On the other hand, the fault was not entirely his own.

After a brief stint with the Yankees in 1912, the left-hand-hitting outfielder led the Federal League in hitting with a .370 average in 1914, also topping FL batters in hits, doubles, runs scored, and stolen bases. Transferred to the Feds Brooklyn club as part of a deal that saw the Indiana franchise moved to Newark, Kauff hit a 3-run homer to win the first game of the 1915 season; then, feeling slighted by his own team over a money matter, he crossed the East River to ink a pact with John McGraw's Giants. When

McGraw tried to use him in a game, however, Braves owner John Gaffney protested that the New York club had violated a prohibition against signing players already under contract to the FL. In the ensuing fracas, Boston manager George Stallings refused to let his team take the field, one umpire declared a forfeit of the game to New York, the other (after consulting with National League president John Tener) forfeited the contest to Boston, and the two teams played an "exhibition" game that Tener later validated as official after the fact. While McGraw blasted Tener and American League chief Ban Johnson for double-crossing him after encouragements to go after Kauff, the outfielder took the ferry back to Brooklyn, where he went on to repeat as FL batting champion, this time with a .342 mark.

With the demise of the Feds after the 1915 season, the Giants purchased Kauff in a more orthodox fashion. He went on to be a productive but hardly spectacular performer, reaching the .300 level twice (once in a part-time role) in five seasons. Although declining a $500 bribe from teammates Hal Chase and Heinie Zimmerman to throw a 1919 contest and reporting the incident to McGraw, Kauff fell afoul of both civil and baseball law when he was indicted in February 1920 for auto theft and for receiving stolen vehicles as part of a used-car business he operated with his brother. Without waiting for a trial, Commissioner Kenesaw Landis banished him prior to the 1921 season on the grounds that his presence on a major league playing field would "burden patrons of the game with grave apprehension as to its integrity." Even after Kauff's acquittal, with both McGraw and Tener serving as character witnesses, Landis refused to lift the ban, claiming that the trial was "one of the worst miscarriages of justice that ever came under my observation."

EWING KAUFFMAN

The head of Marion Laboratories who gained the Royals' expansion franchise in 1968, Kauffman served as the point man for major league owners in 1975 in their attempt to avoid going to arbitration over the free-agent claims of pitchers Andy Messersmith and Dave McNally. In a motion filed with a Missouri court, Kauffman claimed that the attack on the reserve clause integral to the Messersmith-McNally case fell beyond the purview of baseball's arbitration panel. Kauffman also argued that part of the basis of his investment in the Royals was the assumption that there would be no interruption of the reserve clause; failure to maintain it, he contended, jeopardized his investment unfairly. Both the arbitration panel and the Missouri court dismissed the claims.

Kauffman's tenure as Kansas City owner from 1968 to his death in 1993 was otherwise chiefly characterized by his seesawing business relationship with Memphis real-estate developer Avron Fogelman. When Kauffman's pharmaceuticals company suffered setbacks in 1983, he surrendered 49 percent of his interest in the Royals to Fogelman for $10 million; Fogelman also threw in another $1 million for the first option on buying the club altogether before 1991. A couple of years later, Kauffman picked up a little more money from the Tennessee businessman in exchange for making him a full 50–50 partner. But by 1990 it was Fogelman who needed cash after a downturn in the real-estate market; Kauffman obliged by advancing a $34 million loan that was secured by Fogelman's stock and that effectively returned him to sole ownership.

Prior to his death, Kauffman entrusted the team to a coalition of local businessmen and civic leaders to assure its survival in Kansas City. It was partly in recognition of this gesture that Royals Stadium was rebaptized Kauffman Stadium as of the 1994 season.

JOHNNY KEANE

Each of Keane's two managerial assignments—with the Cardinals and Yankees in the 1960s—ended abruptly, less for his performance than because of front-office machinations. After thirty-one years in the St. Louis organization, he became dugout boss in mid-1961, kept the team above .500 for that half-season and the next three full ones, and won a National League pennant in 1964. When Keane's friend and sponsor general manager Bing Devine was fired in July 1964, he resolved to quit at the end of the season, and made arrangements with Yankee general manager Ralph Houk to succeed Yogi Berra at the helm of the New York club. When both the Cardinals

and Yankees won their respective pennants, Keane was saved from complete embarrassment only because no one aside from the participants in the scheme knew he was going to take over the team his club beat in the World Series.

The circumstances of his hiring got Keane off on the wrong foot with the Yankees in 1965. His sanctimonious clubhouse lectures on proper behavior didn't improve matters. With players, press, and fans against him from the start, Keane's inflexibility and his secrecy (with Houk's complicity) about the extent of injuries to Elston Howard and Roger Maris merely hastened the inevitable. In 1965, for the first time in forty years, the Yankees fell below .500, and Keane was fired after a slow start the following May.

DAVE KEEFE

Keefe's invention of the forkball was the result of a childhood accident that cost the future major leaguer the middle finger on his right hand. The pitch helped him, however, to only a 9–17 record between 1917 and 1922 for the Athletics and Indians.

TIM KEEFE (Hall of Fame, 1964)

Keefe's career spanned the last year of the forty-five-foot pitching distance (1880) and the first of the sixty-foot, six-inch distance (1893); in between, from fifty feet, he was a workhorse with both the American Association Metropolitans and the National League Giants, winning more than 40 games once for each of the New York teams, and 30 or more in three other seasons. As a rookie, the right-hander compiled the lowest ERA (0.86) for any pitcher with 100 innings pitched, but finished the season with a mediocre 6–6 record for Troy. He came to New York following the NL's abandonment of the Troy franchise, but whereas once and future teammates Buck Ewing, Roger Connor, and Mickey Welch all went directly to the Giants, Keefe was assigned by John B. Day, who owned both clubs, to the Metropolitans. Keefe's most notable one-day accomplishment came on July 4, 1883, when he won both games of a doubleheader against Columbus, pitching a 1-hitter in the morning and a 2-hitter in the afternoon.

In 1885 Day decided to consolidate his stars

on the more profitable Giants, so he released Keefe and third baseman Dude Esterbrook from their Metropolitan contracts, shipped them on a Bermuda cruise to wait out the required ten-day period, then inked them to pacts with the Giants. The fallout from this fast shuffle led to, among other things, an early effort to establish ground rules for interleague player transfers.

Keefe picked up 172 of his eighth-ranking 342 victories in a half decade with the Giants. His best season was probably 1888, when he won a record 19 consecutive games (matched by fellow Giant Rube Marquard in 1912); led the NL in wins, won-lost percentage, and strikeouts; added 4 more victories against the St. Louis Browns in a postseason championship series; and designed the team's ''funeral uniforms,'' featuring black blouses with ''New York'' in large white letters stitched across the chest.

The pitcher served as secretary of the Players Brotherhood, despite tensions with organization president John Montgomery Ward, who had earlier married and separated from Keefe's sister-in-law. Keefe also formed a sporting goods company that manufactured the balls used in Players League games. After retirement, Keefe turned to umpiring but quit in the middle of his third season after being showered with bottles and having to leave the Polo Grounds under a police escort for calling several plays against the Giants.

WILLIE KEELER (Hall of Fame, 1939)

Often regarded as the quiet man on the rowdy Baltimore clubs of the 1890s, Keeler also earned a reputation as the greatest slap hitter of all time, compiling an eighth-ranking .343 average in nineteen seasons. A lefty-throwing third baseman with the Giants, he was moved to the outfield in Baltimore and went on to win the first of back-to-back batting crowns in 1897 with a .424 average, the highest ever by a lefty swinger. In one stretch he poked base hits in 44 consecutive games, a major league record that stood until Joe DiMaggio reached 56 in 1941 and that, among National League hitters, has been matched only by Pete Rose, in 1978. This season record is marred, however, by complaints against the Baltimore official scorer for awarding Keeler hits on dropped fly balls and unmistakably wild throws by in-

fielders. No defensive slouch, the right fielder made a diving, barehanded catch before crashing into a barbed wire fence in Washington, in June 1898, that John McGraw forever extolled as the greatest catch he had ever seen.

Only 5 feet, 4½ inches and 140 pounds, Keeler was dubbed Wee Willie, but limited size didn't preclude typically Oriole behavior when he was pushed too far. Needled unrelentingly by the same McGraw about defensive lapses during the 1897 season, the little outfielder took on his antagonist in a naked brawl on the floor of the clubhouse and shower room as teammate Jack Doyle stood guard over the fracas to prevent interference and prove himself right in his prediction that McGraw would be the first to cry uncle.

If there was a flaw in Keeler's skills, it was a lack of power. Almost 86 percent of his hits were singles, and the difference between his lifetime batting (.343) and slugging (.418) averages is the smallest among all players who hit at least .310. His famous dictum about hitting, a response to a suggestion by Abe Yager of the *Brooklyn Eagle*

Willie Keeler had more than one way to hit 'em where they ain't. National Baseball Library, Cooperstown, N.Y.

that he write about his batting philosophy, expressed his talent precisely: ''I have already written a treatise,'' he told the sports editor, ''and it reads like this: 'Keep your eye clear and hit 'em where they ain't; that's all.' ''

GEORGE KELL (Hall of Fame, 1983)

Kell's numbers are usually found with players who have just missed election to Cooperstown. A .306 hitter in fifteen years (1943–57) of major league service, the right-hand-hitting third baseman concentrated his two greatest efforts into 1949 and 1950—in the former season winning the batting title with a .343 mark, and in the latter averaging .340 and pacing the American League in hits and doubles for the first of two straight seasons. In 1950, as well, he broke the 100 mark in RBIs and runs scored for the only time in his career. Kell's best performances were with the Tigers, who obtained him in a 1946 trade with the Athletics. He later played with several other American League teams.

CHARLIE KELLER

Given the nickname King Kong for his brawny body and bushy brows, Keller figured prominently in two dramatic World Series plays. In the fourth game of the 1939 Series against the Reds, the Yankee outfielder barreled into Cincinnati catcher Ernie Lombardi while scoring the second run driven home by a Joe DiMaggio single in the top of the 10th inning. With Lombardi lying semiconscious about 3 feet from the ball and the rest of the Reds slow to react, DiMaggio also circled the bases to score. It was also Keller who drove in the winning run in the fourth game of the 1941 Series against the Dodgers after Brooklyn catcher Mickey Owen let a Hugh Casey delivery get away from him on a third strike to Tommy Henrich. Keller player thirteen seasons between 1939 and 1952, all but two of them for New York. He topped the 30-homer mark three times before retiring with a .286 batting average.

JOE KELLEY (Hall of Fame, 1971)

A .317 hitter in seventeen seasons with Baltimore (in both the National and American leagues), Cincinnati, and three other NL teams, Kelley was the master of the Oriole ploy of planting spare baseballs in the deliberately high outfield grass and using them as opportune occasions arose. The left fielder's gambit was discovered in a game against St. Louis, after he scooped up what appeared to be a Tommy Dowd single and threw to third to nail a runner trying to advance from first, only to face a wrathful umpire when center fielder Steve Brodie chased down the actual hit and fired the game ball to second base; the game was forfeited to the Cardinals. Kelley became manager of the Reds in the aftermath of a plot by Cincinnati owner John T. Brush and New York Giants manager John McGraw to destroy the AL Orioles in 1902. One element of the intrigue had Baltimore stockholder John J. Mahon collecting a majority of club stock and handing it over to Brush, who moved Kelley, as player-manager, along with outfielder Cy Seymour, to the Reds, and six others to New York. Mahon was Kelley's father-in-law.

GEORGE KELLY (Hall of Fame, 1973)

Kelly is one of Cooperstown's more dubious propositions. Gifted with a strong arm but clumsy on his feet, the right-hand-hitting first baseman batted .297 over sixteen years (between 1915 and 1932), spent most prominently with John McGraw's Giants. His best years were 1921, when he led the National League with 23 home runs and batted across 122 runs, and 1924, when he hit .324 with 21 home runs and a league-leading 136 RBIs. As solid a career as he had, Kelly stacks up nowhere near a significant number of non-Hall of Famers, among them Orlando Cepeda and Roger Maris. Of equal note, Kelly was a chief suspect in an October 1924 bribery scandal that led to the banning of New York outfielder Jimmy O'Connell and coach Cozy Dolan. Mainly because of his ungraceful fielding, Kelly was a prime target of New York sportswriters in his early years; later, however, he was portrayed by beat writers as the most approachable of McGraw's Giants.

KING KELLY (Hall of Fame, 1945)

The most frequently repeated of Kelly's escapades—that one day in the 1890s, he jumped off the bench, declared himself a replacement for teammate Charlie Ganzel, and caught a pop foul out of the catcher's reach to retire the side in a clutch situation—is almost certainly apocryphal. But almost everything else that has been said about Kelly is true:

- that he not merely won two batting crowns (in 1884 and 1886), but also played every position adequately, if not spectacularly, and shone both in the outfield and behind the plate;
- that he contributed pivotally to 9 pennants (2 of them in the same year) in sixteen seasons;
- that he made staggering amounts of money, sometimes through bizarre subterfuges in his contract, and spent it equally lavishly;
- that he turned down an even more staggering sum;
- that his popularity in Chicago has been matched only by that of Ernie Banks, eight decades later;
- that his unrivaled hold on Boston fans gave him the power to make and break franchises by his inclusion on and withdrawal from their rosters.

With Chicago, Kelly gave manager Cap Anson fits, once claiming that he was taking a day off to sweat off some excess weight, only to be discovered at a local racetrack. On the other hand, he led the White Stockings to five flags, thrilled crowds with the Kelly Spread (an early version of the hook slide that inspired the popular tune "Slide, Kelly, Slide"), and incited admiration for his ingenuity in thinking up such tricks as throwing his catcher's mask in the first-base path to trip batters. In 1887, Chicago owner Al Spalding was still able to ignore all these contributions when Kelly made salary demands he considered excessive, selling him to Boston for a then-sensational $10,000.

Meeting the right-handed slugger's $5,000 contract demand proved less difficult for Boston's Arthur Soden; he simply gave his new acquisition the official major league maximum of $2,000, then slipped him another $3,000 under the table for the use of his picture. Three years later, Kelly supplied the Players League with instant box of-

King Kelly was baseball's first matinee idol. National Baseball Library, Cooperstown, N.Y.

fice appeal by jumping to the Boston Reds as player-manager, and became the object of a National League scheme to wreck the PL by wooing him back. Approached by Spalding with a $10,000 bribe to defect from the union cause, he took a walk to consider the offer, then told his former boss, "I want the $10,000 bad enough, but I've thought the matter over, and I can't go back on the boys. And neither would you." In Spalding's version of the encounter, they shook hands, and Kelly accepted both the owner's congratulations and a $500 loan. The Reds went on to win the PL's only pennant.

With the end of the PL war in 1891, Kelly agreed to lend his cachet to the formation of an American Association franchise in Cincinnati. The Porkers lasted only 90 games, but Kelly made the brief experience interesting. Before games, he let a collection of veterans and rookies nobody else wanted pick the positions they wanted to play that day. On the field he led them in almost daily brawls. In the clubhouse he led them in regular postgame banquets. And on Sundays he led them directly from the ballfield to the local magistrate's court to be found not guilty of violating municipal blue laws prohibiting baseball on the Sabbath.

That adventure over in August, Kelly signed once again with the Reds, now part of the AA and locked in an attendance war against the Beaneaters. For four days, Boston fans poured into the AA club's Congress Street Grounds to see their returning hero, then went in equal numbers to the NL team's South End Grounds after Kelly succumbed to Soden's offer of a larger salary and a trip to Europe for him and his wife. Each team won its league's pennant, but Kelly won the fans for the NL entry.

After one more season (and one more pennant) in Boston and a final year with the Giants, Kelly, who had appeared in vaudeville from time to time, took to the stage full time. It was, in fact, on his way to a performance at Boston's Palace Theater that he succumbed to an attack of what was termed "typhoid-pneumonia" in 1894, several weeks shy of his thirty-seventh birthday. So reduced were his circumstances that NL owners raised $1,400 by subscription for his widow.

BOB KENNEDY

Kennedy had the longest uninterrupted run as one of Phil Wrigley's rotating managers in the Chicago owner's College of Coaches scheme in the early 1960s; Kennedy was, in fact, the Cubs pilot in everything but title from 1963 to the beginning of 1965. Later he went on to manage the Athletics in their inaugural season in Oakland in 1968 and to hold down several front-office jobs in the 1970s and 1980s.

Wrigley introduced the College of Coaches system in 1961 behind the argument that clubs required a change of managers during the season as much as starters needed relievers during games. What he didn't say was that he was exasperated by having had to make almost annual managerial changes and that it was cheaper to extend the duties of a coach than to hire a dugout boss. The coaches originally named to the managerial rotation were Rip Collins, Charlie Grimm,

Rube Walker, El Tappe, Harry Craft, Bobby Adams, Gordie Holt, and Vedie Himsl. Only Tappe, Craft, and Himsl from that group actually called the shots for any perceptible period. Along with Kennedy, Lou Klein and Charlie Metro were later added to the system, and took over as pilots for stretches.

BRICKYARD KENNEDY

Kennedy was the model small-town boy at odds with the big city. A four-time 20-game winner for the Dodgers at the end of the nineteenth century, he could never quite get the hang of Brooklyn or Manhattan. In his most legendary escapade, he set out one morning from his Brooklyn home to pitch against the Giants in the Polo Grounds, got lost, and ended up on a train heading for the Midwest. Asked how he had made such a mistake, Kennedy shrugged and said that a policeman he had asked for directions "heard I was from Ohio and figured that was where I should be."

W. H. KENNETT

Kennett was president of the Cincinnati Reds in 1880, when the National League decided to purge its rank of clubs that put immediate profits above the principle of long-term respectability. The Reds, whose German immigrant fans enjoyed beer at the ballpark and saw no reason not to play on Sunday, had never been in compliance with the National League's prevailing moral attitudes. League officials looked the other way until the *Worcester Spy* launched an editorial attack on the club both for selling beer and for renting its park for amateur Sunday games. The conflict came to a head in October 1880 when, with only Kennett dissenting, the league announced that at its next meeting it would pass legislation expelling any team that violated the bans on beer and Sunday ball; the next item on the agenda was the immediate expulsion of the Reds for breaking a law that had not yet been passed.

DICKIE KERR

Kerr's two victories over Cincinnati in the 1919 World Series were one of the few positives for Chicago, but he still ended up sharing the fate of the players outlawed in the Black Sox scandal.

After two subsequent seasons during which he posted a combined 40 wins, the southpaw demanded a $500 heftier raise than the team was about to grant, and backed up his position by sitting out the 1922 season. During that year he appeared in a semipro game against some of the blacklisted White Sox players, and for Commissioner Kenesaw Landis that was grounds for banning him from the majors as well. Kerr got the ban rescinded in time for the 1925 season, but by then he had lost his effectiveness.

BULL AND EDDIE KESSLER

The Kessler brothers set the standard for abusiveness among Philadelphia fans in the 1920s and 1930s by seating themselves on opposite sides of the infield and bellowing at each other about the inadequacies of both visiting and home-team players. They reserved their worst attacks for Philadelphian Jimmy Dykes, who became so distracted that Athletics owner-manager Connie Mack served up a bribe of season tickets for the brothers. When even that bit of uncharacteristic generosity failed, Mack took the Kesslers to court in an effort to get them off his infielder's back. In fact, only a trade to the White Sox in 1933 enabled Dykes to escape his antagonists, except, of course, when he returned to Shibe Park in a visitor's uniform.

HARMON KILLEBREW (Hall of Fame, 1984)

Killebrew was the most prolific right-handed power hitter in American League history, clouting 573 home runs in a twenty-two-year career between 1954 and 1975. His ratio of 1 home run for every 14.22 at-bats ranks behind only Babe Ruth (11.76) and Ralph Kiner (14.11). Originally brought up by the Senators as a third baseman, Killebrew spent most of his career with Washington and its successor franchise in Minnesota going to defensive positions (first base, the outfield) where his manager of the moment considered him least likely to hurt the team in the field. Through it all, he kept putting up numbers sufficient to lead the AL in homers six times, top the 40 level in round-trippers eight times, and deliver 100 RBIs nine times. In 1969 he took MVP honors for helping the Twins to a division title with his league-leading 49 homers and 140 runs batted in.

He also led the league in walks four times and topped the 100 mark in that category seven times.

Aside from his defensive limitations, Killebrew was very much a hit-or-miss offensive proposition—not only striking out more than 100 times in seven seasons and for never batting higher than .288 in a full year, but also for the streakiness of his long-ball hitting. In both 1962 and 1963, for instance, he endured slumps of seven weeks duration; he ended the dry spell in 1962 by belting 11 home runs in his final 11 games, in 1963 by knocking 7 in his last 6 games. Annoyed that he wasn't given the Minnesota managerial job at the end of 1974, Killebrew signed for a final, woeful year with Kansas City, when he batted only .199. Seeking to capitalize on the slugger's return to the Twin Cities and to help his ailing attendance, Twins owner Calvin Griffith staged a Harmon Killebrew Night on the Royals' first visit, but only 2,946 fans showed up. Things didn't get much better for Killebrew after retirement: Following some unsuccessful efforts at broadcasting, he went bankrupt and had to rely on personal loans to get along. The slugger was initially recommended to Washington by Idaho senator Herman Welker.

MATT KILROY

In his rookie season of 1886, Kilroy established an all-but-invulnerable record by striking out 513 batters for the American Association Baltimore Orioles. The next year, with the number of strikes for an out raised from three to four, his total dropped to 217, but he established a second major league record: 46 wins by a left-handed pitcher.

RALPH KINER (Hall of Fame, 1975)

Kiner came as close as anyone to being a one-man team. Brought up by the Pirates in 1946, the right-hand-hitting outfielder became the first National League rookie to lead the circuit in home runs in 40 years. In a career that spanned only 10 years, he bashed 369 home runs, including five straight seasons of at least 40, giving him second place to Babe Ruth for career long-ball frequency. More remarkable, Kiner accomplished his power feats (including leading the league in homers in every one of his seven seasons in a Pittsburgh uniform) in lineups that sometimes didn't even

Harmon Killebrew could do only one thing—but he did it more often than any other righthanded hitter in American League history. National Baseball Library, Cooperstown, N.Y.

seem to have a second major league player. The situation became so marked in the early 1950s that many fans didn't bother showing up at Forbes Field until the second inning, assuming that the first three Pirates would be retired in the first inning and cleanup hitter Kiner would be leading off in the second frame; by the same token, his final at-bat in the eighth inning usually signaled a mass exit. Given his lack of protection, it was hardly surprising that he received at least 100 walks seven years in a row; despite that, he still managed to drive in 100 runs five times.

Kiner credited his early survival in Pittsburgh (he had a ferocious strikeout rate) to Hank Greenberg, who was acquired in 1947 precisely for tutoring the slugger in a better appreciation of the strike zone. Equally emphatically, Kiner has attributed the end of his career in the Steel City to organization president Branch Rickey. Among the other things Rickey didn't like about his ostensible franchise player were Kiner's visibility in Players Association causes and the frequency of

his name in gossip columns linking him to Elizabeth Taylor, Janet Leigh, and other actresses. On another level, Kiner irked the executive for winning over Pittsburgh fans with the generally one-dimensional skills that Rickey had always preached against in dispensing his views about ideal players. For his part, Kiner didn't hesitate to describe Rickey as a hypocrite and a liar for his devious negotiating tactics. The thorny relationship came to an end on June 4, 1953, when Rickey packaged the outfielder to the Cubs in a ten-player deal that also brought the Pirates $150,000. To enraged fans, Rickey reiterated what he had previously told Kiner: that the Pirates could finish last without him as easily as with him.

Once out of Pittsburgh, Kiner fell prey to various leg injuries, and retired from the major leagues within three years. After serving as general manager of the Pacific Coast League franchise in San Diego for five years and being associated with several attempts to lure a big league club to California, he went into the broadcasting booth for the White Sox. In 1962 he became one of the original announcers for the Mets—a job he still had more than thirty years later. As a broadcaster, Kiner has frequently betrayed his Hollywood days in continually fumbling the names of even the most veteran players; throughout his seven-year stay with New York, for instance, Gary Carter seldom got through a game without being identified by Kiner as Gary Cooper. Kiner has also had trouble distinguishing third baseman Tim Wallach from Eli Wallach—to the point that the infielder's teammates also began calling him Eli.

SILVER KING

After averaging more than 30 wins a year in his first six full seasons, King lost his effectiveness when the pitcher's rubber was introduced in 1893. In his old delivery he had crossed from one side of the five-and-a-half-by-four-foot pitcher's box to the other; with his more restricted windup he managed only 25 victories in three more seasons. The right-hander also lost an opportunity to pitch the only Players League no-hitter, on June 21, 1890, when Chicago manager Charlie Comiskey elected to have his Pirates bat first in a home game against Brooklyn. Because King surrendered a run on errors in the seventh, the visiting Wonders did not have to bat in the bottom of the ninth, so the hurler had to be satisfied with eight innings of no-hit pitching.

DAVE KINGMAN

Kingman bids fair to hold in perpetuity the mark for the most home runs by a player not in the Hall of Fame. In sixteen years, the outfielder-first baseman clouted 442 balls out of the park—many of them titanic blasts that had public relations people scrambling after tape measures. The rest of Kingman had people scrambling to get away from him. Aside from being a worse-than-average fielder, he was the epitome of homer-or-nothing at the plate; his .204 batting average for the 1982 Mets was the lowest ever recorded for a home-run champion. His relations with the media were even worse than his consistency. In June 1986, for instance, he displayed his notion of humor by having a live rat delivered to a woman

sportswriter for the *Sacramento Bee*. That episode brought a fine and a decision by the Athletics not to offer him another contract despite the fact that he led the club with 35 home runs. When no other team signed him as a free agent, it gave Kingman the consolation prize of various records (35 homers, 94 RBIs) for a final career year.

ANDREA KIRBY

Kirby has done as much as anybody to prevent baseball players from having an interesting thought escape from their mouths during media interviews. A former television reporter in New York, she has been hired by a number of clubs to instruct major leaguers in showing themselves to best effect before the cameras. What this has usually meant is even more guardedness from players and managers about criticizing opposition players or suggesting that a clubhouse is not an extension of paradise.

GEORGE KIRKSEY

A public relations flack by profession, Kirksey was the idea man behind the Houston Sports Association lobby that brought major league baseball to Texas. Among his inspirations was to call the team (initially) the Colt .45s to firm up a pending advertising deal with the Colt Firearms Company. His ventures into contract negotiations, however, were another story. With no other Houston executive available, he had to handle the bargaining in the early 1960s with top-rated prospect Rusty Staub. Kirksey managed to sign Staub—but at twice the figure the organization had agreed to, plus sign the outfielder's brother to a three-year pact, plus agree to a scouting job for Staub's father. Kirksey was eventually squeezed out of his job with Houston after a number of years of being assigned to less and less meaningful positions.

CHUCK KLEIN (Hall of Fame, 1980)

Few players have depended on a ballpark as much as Klein relied on Baker Bowl. The Phillies' most potent offensive star prior to the arrival of Mike Schmidt, the lefty-swinging outfielder spent the overwhelming majority of his seventeen big league seasons (1928–44) taking aim at the friendly right-field wall of the bandbox, making clear his disaffection during brief stints with the

Cubs and Pirates. Between his rookie year and 1933, Klein racked up batting averages between .337 and .386. Within that period he also won a Triple Crown (in 1933, when he additionally paced the National League in doubles and slugging average), three other home run titles, another RBI title, scored the most runs in the league three consecutive years, and even stole more bases than anyone else once. When he was traded to the Cubs in 1934, on the other hand, Klein barely reached the 20 mark in home runs in his two seasons and had an RBI high of only 80. Reobtained by the Phillies during the 1936 season, he went back over the 100-RBI mark again.

Klein's power feats at Baker Bowl were a mixed blessing for cheapskate owner William Baker. Terrified that his star's slugging would make him intractable in contract negotiations, Baker had an extension placed atop the right-field wall in the early 1930s so that he wouldn't have to deal with somebody boasting Babe Ruth-like numbers. It was Baker's equally parsimonious successor Gerry Nugent who dealt the outfielder to Chicago in 1934 and to Pittsburgh in 1939 to pick up some quick cash. The tininess of Baker Bowl also helped Klein defensively, enabling him to set a never-approached twentieth-century record of 44 outfield assists in 1930. After hanging on as a would-be gate attraction in Philadelphia for a third stint, during World War II, he retired with an overall batting average of .320 and with exactly 300 home runs.

BILL KLEM (Hall of Fame, 1953)

Klem was to the no-nonsense umpire as Babe Ruth was to the slugging outfielder. For a record thirty-seven years (1905–41), Klem held sway over National League games with an autocratic bearing and encyclopedic knowledge of the rules that brooked little dispute from players, coaches, or managers. One of his more noted tactics during an argument was to draw a line in the dirt with his shoe and warn his adversary of the moment not to cross it. He didn't leave much leeway to his colleagues, either, and for his first sixteen years insisted on calling balls and strikes for every game; his acknowledged superiority behind the plate led other league arbiters to comply with his preference. On the rare occasion that he was questioned about one of his calls, he was content to reply, "I never called one wrong," only late in his career adding a tap to the left side of his chest and a qualifying "from here." Klem's reputation for honesty was such that when he accused New York Giants trainer Joseph Creamer of trying to bribe him before the final game of the 1908 season, a league meeting called to investigate the charge was little more than a formality before the physician was banned from baseball for life. On the other hand, Klem was the first umpire fined for unbecoming behavior during a World Series, running afoul of Commissioner Kenesaw Landis for responding in kind to Washington outfielder Goose Goslin's four-letter-word outburst. Among other things, Klem popularized the inside chest protector and the over-the-shoulder stance for calling balls and strikes. His records include the most World Series games (108) and being the oldest umpire (at sixty-eight) to work a major league game. After retiring from the field, The Old Arbiter, as he took to calling himself in his later years, served as the NL's supervisor of umpires until his death in 1951. Two years later he became the first umpire elected to the Hall of Fame.

EDDIE KLEPP

Klepp was Jackie Robinson in reverse. A white pitcher, he was signed by the all-black Cleveland Buckeyes in 1946 in an effort to integrate the Negro leagues the same year that Robinson was crashing through organized baseball's color barrier with Montreal in the International League. Klepp's experiences sound like a parody of Robinson's: Run off the field—and prohibited even from sitting in the Cleveland dugout—by racists during an exhibition game in Birmingham, he was forced to sit in the white section of the grandstand. Excluded from the team's road accommodations, Klepp was compelled to eat alone at whites-only restaurants and to sleep in whites-only hotels. He appeared in only a handful of games for the Buckeyes.

JOHNNY KLING

Kling was the regular catcher on the formidable Cub squads that dominated the National League in the first decade of the twentieth century. Deciding to leave the team in 1909 to pursue a career as a professional pool shooter, he was blamed for Chicago's second-place finish. Kling sought to return to the club in 1910, but during his year off had played a few games against outlawed players. The National Commission bent its rules for him and reinstated the receiver after imposing a $700 fine. When he did rejoin the Cubs, Kling contributed to still another pennant, but was the target of so much clubhouse resentment for his defection the year before that he was dealt away soon afterward.

TED KLUSZEWSKI

It was mainly because of Kluszewski's bulging biceps that Cincinnati thought it would be a good idea in the mid-1950s to go to sleeveless uniforms to gain a psychological edge on other teams. It worked to the extent that the 1956 team tied the National League record for most home runs in a season (221), but it didn't pay off in any pennants. Kluszewski himself was a somewhat contradictory slugger. Over his first five seasons, he hit a mere 74 home runs, not breaking out until 1953 with 40 round-trippers. In the power years that followed, he remained an unusually discriminating batter: While belting 49 home runs in 1954, he struck out only 35 times, following that up with a season of 47 homers and merely 40 strikeouts. On the other hand, the left-handed first baseman's fielding was deceptive: Although he led the league numerous times in fielding percentage, much of the mark was due to a modest range that kept him away from errors of ambition.

MICKEY KLUTTS

Klutts may have been baseball's most aptly named player. In eight major league seasons between the late 1970s and early 1980s, he appeared in only 199 games, mainly because of ten lengthy stays on the disabled list.

LON KNIGHT

The starting pitcher for home team Philadelphia on April 22, 1876, Knight threw the first pitch in major league history; he went on to lose the game, 6–5, to Boston.

RAY KNIGHT

Knight was one of the National League's best performers under pressure during his thirteen-year (1974–88) career. Installed by Cincinnati at third base in 1979 to replace fan favorite Pete Rose, Knight responded by hitting .318 and playing a major role in the club's unexpected division win. With the Mets in 1986, the right-hand-hitting third baseman had two of the most dramatic hits in franchise history. In the 10th inning of the sixth game of the 1986 World Series against the Red Sox, with two out and two strikes on him, he singled to reduce the New York deficit to a run and drove Kevin Mitchell around to third, from where he tallied on a Bob Stanley wild pitch; a few pitches later, Knight himself scored the winning run on Bill Buckner's error on the grounder hit by Mookie Wilson. In the seventh game, Knight hit a 7th-inning home run that put the Mets ahead to stay. After being voted the MVP in the World Series, however, Knight turned down a New York contract and ended up playing out his days for a considerably lesser sum with the Orioles and Tigers.

DAROLD KNOWLES

Knowles is the only pitcher to appear in every game of a seven-game World Series. The southpaw reliever did it for the Athletics in 1973, picking up saves in both the first and last games and not yielding a single earned run in a combined $6\frac{1}{3}$ innings.

LEN KOENECKE

Koenecke occasioned one of Casey Stengel's rare admissions of sincere regret. An outfielder for the 1935 Dodgers, he began to try manager Stengel's patience with such lapses as wandering off first base on a mistaken assumption that a third out had been made, and going to the wrong position in taking the field. On another occasion he got a hit-and-run sign, dribbled the ball in front of the plate, and stood arguing with the umpire that he had hit a foul while the catcher pounced on the ball and overthrew second base in an attempt to get the runner, the center fielder retrieved the errant toss to get the runner at third, and the third baseman fired back to the catcher to tag Koenecke for a double play. Exasperated by such incidents during a road trip, Stengel sent Koenecke back to Brooklyn from St. Louis on a train ahead of the rest of the team. But Koenecke left the train in Detroit and chartered an airplane to Buffalo, where he had friends. While over Canadian territory, he tried to wrest control of the plane away from pilot William Mulqueeny, who picked up a fire extinguisher and bludgeoned Koenecke to death. Two separate hearings in Canadian courts absolved Mulqueeny of any crime and found that Koenecke had drunk heavily during his stopover in Detroit. The hearings also floated the suggestion that the player had actually been bent on suicide in his attempt to take over the plane. Whenever Stengel mentioned the incident for the rest of his life, he blamed himself for not having recognized the signs of Koenecke's severe mental disturbance.

MARK KOENIG

Koenig was the indirect cause of Babe Ruth's "called shot" in the 1932 World Series between the Yankees and Cubs. Acquired from Detroit late in the season, the shortstop proved invaluable down the stretch with his nifty fielding and .353 average. Despite that, he was voted only a half share of the World Series pool by his teammates. When the Yankees began mocking the Cubs for their miserliness toward their own onetime teammate, tensions rose between the clubs, to the point that Ruth allegedly felt compelled to ridicule the National Leaguers by preannouncing a home run against Charlie Root in the third game. Root himself always denied that Ruth pointed to the center field bleachers before depositing a fastball there.

JIM KONSTANTY

Konstanty was the first National League pitcher celebrated as a reliever rather than as a failed starter who ended up being helpful from the bullpen. With the pennant-winning Phillies in 1950, he made 74 appearances out of the pen, winning 16 games and saving 22 others. Despite the fact that he hadn't started a game all year, he was handed the ball for the opening contest of the World Series against the Yankees; the right-hander allowed only 4 hits but lost, 1–0.

SANDY KOUFAX (Hall of Fame, 1972)

The most telling indication of Koufax's mastery of National League hitters in the 1960s was that he continually tipped his pitches and still couldn't be hit. One of the bonus babies of the 1950s who had to be carried on a major league roster for two seasons, the southpaw was no better than 36–40 after six years with the Dodgers. Even during his long orientation, however, he gave signs of what was to come by posting more strikeouts than innings pitched in three of those years, just missing the 200-K mark even when he managed only 8 wins in 1960. The turning point of his career came when catcher Norm Sherry noticed during a workout that Koufax's motion momentarily blocked his view of home plate. This helped produce a transition season in 1961, when the left-hander won 18 games and led the NL in strikeouts with 269, but still got roughed up for a 3.52 ERA and continued to issue too many walks (96). Then, over the next five years, he turned into one of the most dominant pitchers baseball has ever seen.

In all five seasons, Koufax paced the league in ERA; in 1963, 1965, and 1966, he won the Cy Young Award for leading in wins and strikeouts; twice he had the best winning percentage; twice he led the way for complete games and innings pitched; and three times he hurled more shutouts than anybody else. His 111–34 record over the span also included four no-hitters—one of them, a perfect game against the Cubs in 1965. If there was any fly in the ointment, it was an arthritis in his pitching elbow that first became noticeable in 1964 and that prompted Dodger physicians to go against the book the following year by advising the left-hander not to throw between starts. Then, in 1966, despite another glowing performance (27–9, 1.73), Koufax announced that the constant pain wasn't worth it and that, at age thirty-one, he was retiring. If unwillingly, this gave him two final entries in the baseball record book: the best performance by a pitcher in a final season and, five years later, the youngest player ever elected to Cooperstown.

CLARENCE KRAFT

Kraft was a first baseman of no particular distinction whose demotion to the minor leagues almost provoked baseball's first general strike. The trouble started when he was farmed out by the Dodgers to Newark of the Class AA International League in 1914. The National Commission, however, supported a prior claim by Nashville of the Class A Southern Association, even though the ruling body had reached an agreement with the Players Fraternity not to force players to perform at a level lower than the classification of the highest team that wanted him. American League president Ban Johnson justified the about-face with a contention that Nashville's claim predated the agreement and that it had never been made retroactive. Fraternity president Dave Fultz then called a strike of his five hundred or so members for July 22, forcing Brooklyn owner Charlie Ebbets to capitulate and send Nashville a $2,500 check for allowing Kraft to stay in Newark. Kraft's entire major league career consisted of 3 games with the Braves later in the 1914 season.

ED KRANEPOOL

Kranepool's eighteen years of service for the Mets between 1962 and 1979 represent the longest stint by any non-Hall of Famer with merely one club in a career. The left-hand-hitting first baseman owed much of his longevity to marriage with the daughter of one of the organization's directors. Although initially projected as a dominant National League first baseman, Kranepool achieved his most noteworthy success as a pinch hitter; he was especially effective coming off the bench between 1974 and 1978, when he banged out 57 hits in 144 at-bats for a .396 average. Otherwise, he never reached the 60-RBI level, and closed out his eighteen years in a Met uniform with a .261 mark.

LEW KRAUSSE

Krausse was the trigger for a team revolt against Kansas City owner Charlie Finley in 1967. The trouble started when Finley levied a $500 fine on the pitcher for alleged rowdyism on a team flight. Charging that Finley was merely seeking to save money on Krausse, Athletics players drafted a petition demanding that the owner put an end to his nickel-and-diming ways. The petition cost manager Alvin Dark his job and led to the release of slugger Ken Harrelson, one

of the drafters of the document. When the Players Association demanded a meeting with Commissioner William Eckert, Finley sought to block the move, this in turn leading to the association's first complaint with the National Labor Relations Board that a baseball owner was trying to harass its members. Under the threat of the NLRB's intervention, Finley and the association reached a compromise on general matters, but left it up to Krausse to pursue a hearing with Eckert on the fine. A few days before he was due to meet with the commissioner, however, the pitcher suddenly withdrew his appeal request. The decision followed a mysterious shooting incident at the hotel where Krausse and teammates were staying. A subsequent police report named only the hurler as having been questioned, saying that he had been cleared of any involvement. Signed as an eighteen-year-old phenom in 1961 for $125,000 by his father, a Kansas City scout, Krausse began his otherwise undistinguished career immediately thereafter with a 3-hit shutout of the Angels; thirty years earlier, his father, who had the same name, had made his debut with a shutout for the Philadelphia Athletics.

PAUL KRICHELL

By at least one yardstick, Krichell was the most successful major league scout ever. A backup catcher of little note with the Browns in 1911 and 1912, he served as a Yankee scout from 1920 until his death in 1957. Among his discoveries were five eventual Hall of Famers: Lou Gehrig, Leo Durocher, Tony Lazzeri, Phil Rizzuto, and Whitey Ford. He is the only scout to have inked so many future Cooperstown residents.

JOAN KROC

As soon as she took over the Padres after her husband's death in January 1984, Kroc made it clear that she wanted to unload the team. It was a quest, however, that took her the rest of the decade, mainly because of her condition that potential buyers undertake a formal commitment not to move the club out of San Diego. The low point of her hunt was in March 1987, when she announced that she had reached a $60 million sale agreement with Mariners owner George Argyros. The announcement turned out to be extremely premature, since Argyros still had not found a buyer for his Seattle franchise, and National League owners came out in chorus against the American League operator. It emerged subsequently that Kroc had been so hasty because her son-in-law, team president Ballard Smith, was divorcing her daughter, and she wanted him out the door as quickly as possible. Although Kroc got rid of Smith, she needed another three years before finally concluding a sale accord in April 1990, with a consortium headed by television producer Tom Werner. Prior to the deal, she had shown how serious she was about keeping the club in San Diego by opening negotiations to sell it to the city; she was talked out of the move by NL owners horrified by the prospect of a municipal ownership.

RAY KROC

Kroc exemplified the millionaire businessman who got into baseball counting on having a serious pastime and who ended up passing the time counting. When he took over the Padres in January 1974, the McDonald's fast food pioneer was already in his seventies and mainly interested, in his own words, in "going into the locker room to kick one player in the fanny and pat another on the back." He found the kicking part more instinctive on the very first game played under his ownership when he grabbed the public address microphone and blasted the Padres for "some of the most stupid ballplaying I've ever seen." Although the club didn't improve too much under such hectoring, San Diego fans flocked to Jack Murphy Stadium in greater numbers in the hope that the owner would put on another performance. For a couple of years he tried to return the fan interest by joining Ted Turner and George Steinbrenner as a no-holds-barred pursuer of free agents, but the club was still unable to break the .500 mark. When he drew a $100,000 fine for tampering with free agents Joe Morgan and Graig Nettles prior to the 1980 season, he declared himself disgusted with the whole business and turned most of the club's operations over to his son-in-law Ballard Smith. Kroc died in January 1984, a little more than nine months before the Padres captured their first flag.

TONY KUBEK

Yankee shortstop Kubek was felled by one of the costliest pebbles in baseball history. In the eighth inning of the seventh game of the 1960 World Series, a double-play ball off the bat of Pittsburgh's Bill Virdon took a bad bounce and struck him in the throat. After Kubek was carried off the field, the Pirates rallied for 5 runs, setting the stage for New York to tie the game in the top of the ninth and Bill Mazeroski to become a hero in the bottom of the frame.

Kubek, the American League Rookie of the Year in 1957, retired with a .266 average after the 1965 season at age twenty-nine because of chronic back and neck problems. He later became an outspoken broadcaster, doing both network games and working in the booth for the Blue Jays and Yankees. Unlike others in the broadcasting booth, he was particularly critical of owners, including his own employers.

BOWIE KUHN

Kuhn managed to survive more than fifteen years as baseball's commissioner, the second-longest tenure after Kenesaw Landis, despite annoying just about everyone connected with the game either by his decisions, half-decisions, or indecision. Presiding over an era that saw attendance in major league parks triple, he dealt with crises either by sidestepping the issue or by placating both sides; when he did make firm decisions, they tended, at best, to reinforce the status quo and, at worst, attempt to restore the status quo ante.

The National League's attorney when he was boosted into the commissioner's chair by Los Angeles owner Walter O'Malley in February 1969, Kuhn was faced almost immediately with the refusal of Cardinals outfielder Curt Flood to accept a trade to the Phillies and found himself the defendant in Flood's suit to have the reserve clause overturned. A hard-liner on the issue, Kuhn ignored a long history of legal precedent against reserving players in perpetuity and fought the case to a successful conclusion in the U.S. Supreme Court.

Turning his attention in early 1971 to the creation of a Negro leagues wing in the Hall of Fame, Kuhn made enemies on both sides of the issue: with the purists by failing to see any reason to include players who had performed outside the major leagues, and with the activists by ignoring that black players had been excluded through the racism of the day. Preoccupied by an obsession with returning baseball to Washington, D.C., after the second version of the Senators departed for Texas in 1972, he embarked on a series of misadventures that reached a climax when he tried to prevent the American League from expanding into Seattle and Toronto in 1977. His alternative—awarding new National League franchises to Toronto and Washington—was shot down by erstwhile patron O'Malley. The most visible result of Kuhn's fixation with Washington was the alienation of Baltimore owner Jerold Hoffberger.

With little time left over from these escapades, Kuhn played no part in the thirteen-day players strike of 1972. By his own choice, however, he was not so fortunate in the next labor-relations crisis. Realizing the futility of the owner-imposed 1976 lockout in spring training in the aftermath of the Messersmith-McNally arbitration decision on the reserve clause, he ordered the spring training camps opened on March 17, making no friends among his employers in the process. Learning his lesson, Kuhn stayed in the background during the 1981 players strike, largely at the request of the Player Relations Committee negotiator Ray Grebey. That made Kuhn the target of sports commentators, most notably columnist Red Smith, who regularly delivered such barbs as "This strike wouldn't have happened if Bowie Kuhn were alive today."

Not content with irritating owners wholesale, Kuhn also struck out at individuals. He earned the enmity of Charlie Finley for his veto of the Oakland owner's attempt to place second baseman Mike Andrews on the disabled list for errors made in the 1973 World Series. Negating Finley's 1976 cash deals for Joe Rudi and Rollie Fingers to the Red Sox and Vida Blue to the Yankees (as well as a later sale of Blue to the Reds) for not passing "the best interests of baseball" clause in the Basic Agreement did nothing to restore the relationship. Atlanta boss Ted Turner drew a one-year suspension for tampering with Giants outfielder Gary Matthews, also in 1976. But Kuhn's most lingering battle was with the Yankees'

George Steinbrenner. In November 1974 he suspended Steinbrenner for two years as baseball's punishment for a guilty plea in making illegal contributions to Richard Nixon's 1972 reelection campaign, but lifted the suspension during the 1976 lockout; later there were intermittent fines for Steinbrenner's criticisms of umpires and of staffers in the commissioner's office.

Kuhn's relations with some players weren't much smoother. Calling Jim Bouton to task for publishing *Ball Four* in 1970, the straitlaced commissioner questioned the credibility of the former pitcher's tales of player carousing; he helped make the book an instant best-seller not only by appearing to be censoring its contents, but also by (unsuccessfully) insisting that Bouton deny that they had ever talked about the book. In the same year, Kuhn suspended Detroit pitcher Denny McLain for two months for his involvement in a Michigan bookmaking operation, drawing fire for the halfway penalty. He made no such mistake in barring Hall of Famers Willie Mays and Mickey Mantle (in 1979 and 1983, respectively) from any involvement in baseball because of their employment by Atlantic City casinos; he made those proscriptions look even worse by grandfathering Steinbrenner and Pittsburgh boss Daniel Galbreath when, in 1980, forbidding baseball's owners from having any interest in racetacks or racehorses.

Kuhn's firmest position—and the cause of his most consistent defeats—was his insistence on mandatory drug testing for players, a proposition anathema to the Players Association. He was overruled in arbitration in all but one instance in which he suspended a player for drug use. The sole exception was the case of Vida Blue, who was convicted of dealing as well as personal use.

Kuhn was finally ousted not by AL owners, with whom he had had so much trouble over the years, but by the NL. The showdown came when he alienated Cardinals owner Gussie Busch in 1981 by refusing to intercede with the networks to get Budweiser beer, an Anheuser-Busch product, commercial time on broadcasts of sporting events. In the final vote for another term in November 1982, Kuhn carried the AL, eleven teams to three, but failed to secure the necessary two-thirds vote of the NL, gathering only seven yes votes from the twelve clubs. After the vote, the aged Busch banged the table with his cane, announcing gleefully, ''He should clean out his desk tomorrow.'' Kuhn, however, served out the rest of his term, until Peter Ueberroth was sworn in on October 1, 1984.

In the end, Kuhn offended as much by his stiff pomposity and last-minute wheedling as by anything he did. His lasting image is of a man in denial that anything had changed in baseball, or the world, even when he himself had been responsible for the changes. The most memorable illustration of this tendency was his sitting coatless and hatless, apparently oblivious to the freezing weather at Baltimore's Municipal Stadium, during the initial contest of the 1971 World Series—the first played under a new network contract, negotiated by Kuhn, that allowed Series night games for the first time.

JOHN KULL

''The man with a million-dollar arm,'' according to Connie Mack, Kull nonetheless pitched only 3 innings for the Athletics, in 1909. But that was long enough to set an unmatched standard for perfection: As a pitcher (a win and no losses), a batter (a single in a lone at-bat), and a fielder (an assist in his only chance) the right-hander left baseball with three 1.000 marks.

EMIL KUSH

The presence of Kush on the same Cubs staff as Bob Rush in the late 1940s prompted Wrigley Field fans to come up with a variation on the ''Spahn, Sain and pray for rain'' formula that helped the Boston Braves to a pennant in 1948. The Chicago version was ''Kush, Rush, and two days of slush.'' The right-hander never won more than 9 games in any of his six major league seasons.

BOB KUZAVA

Although Yankees second baseman Billy Martin drew all the headlines for his dash to snare Jackie Robinson's pop-up and record the final out of the 1952 World Series, it was southpaw Kuzava who retired the final 8 Brooklyn batters in the 7th game to preserve a 4–2 New York victory. His appearance in the game, coming in with the bases loaded and one out in the seventh inning, was more than a little surprising, since Ebbets Field and the Dodgers' predominantly right-handed lineup were supposedly lethal for lefties. Overall, Kuzava, who had also saved the final game of the 1951 Series, against the Giants, compiled a 49–44 record in ten big league seasons with eight clubs.

L

CHET LAABS

Laabs's 2 home runs in the final game of the 1944 regular season sealed the only pennant won by the St. Louis Browns. Although the right-hand-swinging first baseman had had his power moments earlier in his eleven-year career, the shots, off Mel Queen of the Yankees, were only his fourth and fifth of the year and brought his season RBI total up to a dismal 23.

CLEM LABINE

Although mainly the top reliever for the Boys of Summer Dodgers in the 1950s, Labine also pitched two of the most important shutouts of the era. In 1951 he was a 10–0 winner over the Giants in the only playoff game won by Brooklyn before Bobby Thomson's Shot Heard 'Round the World. In 1956 Labine took the mound in the World Series the day after Don Larsen's perfect game and blanked the Yankees, 1–0, for 10 innings. The right-hander also had the odd statistic in 1955 of going 3 for 31 at the plate, with all three hits home runs. Typical of the way the Dodgers cut their ties to some veterans, Labine was walking off the mound in Los Angeles one day in 1960 when he heard from the press box that he had been dealt to Detroit; he had been with the club eleven years.

BOB LACEY

A journeyman reliever in the 1970s and 1980s, Lacey might have been baseball's biggest sport. After surrendering a home run to Kansas City's Amos Otis on September 14, 1978, the Oakland right-hander joined several Royals at home plate to greet the outfielder after his tour of the bases. "Nobody ever hit one of my change-ups like that before," he said, shaking hands with Otis. "That's the way it's supposed to be."

LEE LACY

Lacy established the record for most consecutive home runs by a pinch hitter when he connected 3 times in a row for the Dodgers in May 1978. Del Unser of the Phillies tied the mark in June and July 1979. Lacy had a walk in the middle of his streak, while Unser achieved the feat in three consecutive plate appearances.

JEAN LAFITTE

Lafitte, a descendant of New Orleans pirate Jean Lafitte, is the only pitcher to throw a no-hitter but never a shut out. As a member of the Federal League Brooklyn Tip-Tops on September 19, 1914, he kept Kansas City hitless but not run-less in a 6–2 victory. While he won 36 games over five big league seasons, in none of them did he go the distance and give up no runs.

FIORELLO LAGUARDIA

In 1925, Congressman and future New York City mayor LaGuardia introduced federal legislation calling for a 90 percent tax on all player sales unless the player received half of the purchase price. Wondering whether he was "up against the same kind of proposition as I am when I am fighting the steel trust, the railroad, or other interests,'' The Little Flower watched his bill die without so much as a floor debate.

NAP LAJOIE (Hall of Fame, 1937)

Lajoie was the American League's biggest star before Ty Cobb, but had to be shifted from Philadelphia to Cleveland to keep him out of the clutches of the National League; in the latter city, his popularity was so great that the team was called the Naps in his honor.

A lifetime .338 hitter in twenty-one big league seasons (1896–1916), the second baseman was a stinging line-drive hitter with a reputation for gracefulness afield. A member of the 3,000-hit club (3,244 overall), the right-handed hitter led his league in batting and RBIs three times each; hits and slugging four times apiece; doubles five times; and home runs and runs scored once each.

Lajoie began his career with the NL Phillies. After five successful seasons, he jumped to the new American League Philadelphia franchise, established an AL record with his .422 average, and completed the century's first Triple Crown by also topping AL batsmen in homers (14) and RBIs (145). When the upstart Athletics outdrew his Phillies by almost two to one, owner John Rogers got the Pennsylvania State Supreme Court to grant an injunction barring Lajoie from playing in the state for any team but the Phillies. After only a single game in 1902 with the Athletics, Lajoie was shipped off to Cleveland in a ploy by AL president Ban Johnson to keep the drawing card in his own circuit.

The second baseman became an instant favorite of Clevelanders, so much so that a *Cleveland Press* poll in 1903 made the Naps an easy winner in a search for a new nickname to replace the original Blues; club owners Charles Somers and John Kilfoyl installed him as pilot two years later. Lajoie's biggest moment as a dugout boss came in 1908, when he led his namesakes to a second-place finish, a half game behind the Tigers, in the closest pennant race in AL history. On the other hand, when the pressures of managing affected his hitting to the extent that his average slipped below .300 for the first two times in his career, in 1907 and 1908, he decided that his dual role was hurting not only his own performance but the team as well, and he returned to the ranks after the 1909 season.

In 1910, relieved of the pressures of leadership, Lajoie responded with a .384 average to challenge Cobb for the batting crown, and had a big assist from St. Louis third baseman Red Corriden, who played deep enough to allow him to collect 6 bunt singles in a season-ending doubleheader. The Browns were so transparent in their partisanship that manager Jack O'Connor was banned from baseball; they were also ineffective in that they failed to accomplish their purpose of boosting Lajoie over the hated Cobb for the batting championship and the Chalmers automobile that went with it. The Chalmers company awarded a car to each of the batting stars, and there the matter rested until 1981, when *Sporting News* researcher Paul MacFarlane rechecked the records, discovered that one of Cobb's games had been counted twice and that the one-point margin in his favor should have been a deficit, and called for a correction. Commissioner Bowie Kuhn refused to honor the appeal, however, for fear of opening a Pandora's box of revised statistics.

Athletics owner-manager Connie Mack brought Lajoie back in 1915 as part of the illusion that he was not breaking up his four-time pennant winners. But the thirty-nine-year-old had lost his defensive magic, tying an AL record of 5 errors in a game, and batted only .280. After slipping to .246 the following year, he called it quits.

Along with Cleveland teammate Harry Bay, Lajoie was featured in the first motion picture of a baseball game—a postseason exhibition between the Indians and Reds in 1903.

GROVER LAND

As a catcher for the Brooklyn Tip-Tops of the Federal League in 1915, Land turned baseball's only pool break into a home run. Because he was working the game alone, umpire Bill Brennan did his officiating from behind the pitcher, and with a stack of baseballs on the mound behind him. Land succeeded in hitting a line drive into the pile, scattering balls all over the field. Because he had lost sight of the ball actually in play, the confused Brennan ruled an automatic home run, and then spent the next half hour trying to convince the opposition Baltimore Terrapins of his wisdom.

KENESAW MOUNTAIN LANDIS (Hall of Fame, 1944)

Usually portrayed as baseball's Abraham Lincoln, Landis was actually closer to Lyndon Johnson in trying to make an instant positive impression on his electors, accomplishing that, and then going on to rule with equal doses of whim and obstinacy. His greatest achievement as the first commissioner was to lift the odor of game fixes from the sport in the wake of the 1919 World Series scandal. His most enduring public relations triumph was to project himself as the defender of the helpless player and the foe of the greedy owner. His biggest failure was to act as the very opposite of a great emancipator by stifling all attempts to integrate the big leagues during his twenty-four-year (1920–44) reign.

Landis originally came to the attention of big league owners in 1915, when, as a federal judge in Chicago, he sat on a Federal League suit against the National and American leagues long enough to head off a legal test of the game's monopoly status. In 1920, following several scandals and disputes that bankrupted the credibility of baseball's ruling three-man National Commission, Cubs owner William Wrigley proposed Landis as commissioner. Although there was some initial skepticism about Wrigley's choice of a known Cubs fan for the new post, it disappeared rather quickly as the proportions of the Black Sox bribes became even more evident and as disclosures of other fixes triggered calls for outside policing of the major leagues. Landis accepted the position only after receiving an ironclad assurance that the owners would never publicly criticize his decisions or penalties.

The judge's very first rulings were geared to demonstrating that he was impartiality incarnate and that he was resolved to end gambling's encroachment on the game. Intervening in a dispute between the St. Louis teams over the rights to first baseman Phil Todt, he ruled in favor of the Browns despite the fact that owner Phil Ball had stood alone in refusing to sign the papers sanctioning his appointment as commissioner because

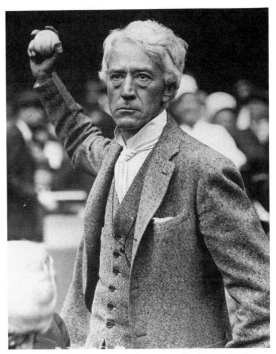

Kenesaw Landis knew how to be a politician as well as a judge. National Baseball Library, Cooperstown, N.Y.

of a resentment going back to the 1915 Federal League suit. If the Todt case established Landis's objectivity, his actions against players involved in the Black Sox scandal were equally definitive where the gambling question was concerned— even at the cost of ignoring due process. For the new commissioner, the important thing was not the August 2, 1921, jury verdict that acquitted the Black Sox of collusion in throwing games to Cincinnati in the 1919 World Series, but the statements of various witnesses that there had indeed been a conspiracy. Thus, a day after the jury announced its verdict, Landis banned the Chicago Eight from the big leagues, with the pronouncement that "no player who throws a ball game, no player that undertakes to throw a ball game, no player that sits in conference with a bunch of crooked players and gamblers where the ways and means of throwing a ball game are discussed and does not promptly tell his club about it, will ever play baseball." He later added Browns infielder Joe Gedeon for "guilty knowledge" of the affair.

Landis maintained his hard-line approach in the face of several reinstatement appeals from the affected players. Between 1921 and 1924 he also banned several other big leaguers—some of them on the basis of little more than his own arrogance. Giants outfielder Benny Kauff, for example, was blacklisted after being indicted for auto theft; when he, too, was sent home by a jury, the judge refused to lift his order, asserting that the verdict was wrong. Pitcher Ray Fisher was ostracized for taking a job at the University of Michigan instead of accepting a contract from the Reds. White Sox hurler Dickie Kerr was declared *persona non grata* because he pitched against a couple of the exiled Black Sox in an exhibition game.

Landis loyalists have contended that the lack of bans after 1924 demonstrated his success in cleaning up the sport; but the concentration of life sentences in his first four years has also been attributed to a desire for instantly projecting the commissioner's office as a higher forum than the league presidencies and for immediately conveying to the public that he was not just a new front for old habits. For sure, Landis showed little interest in banishments decided at a league level—never explicitly endorsing them, in one case (that of pitcher Rube Benton) annulling it as soon as he received a direct appeal, and in another (that of Hal Chase) explicitly assuring the infamous corrupter that he had a clean slate as far as the commissioner's office was concerned. The notion of justice tempered by public relations also seemed borne out by the fact that there were scandals later in the 1920s that appeared to incriminate some players as badly as those in the 1919 affair but that produced no new outlaws (although they were serious enough to prompt a baseball penal code relating to gambling). Also striking, with the exception of Joe Jackson, none of the players expelled by Landis was of Hall of Fame caliber; on the other hand, in 1924 and 1926, he was quick to exonerate such future Cooperstown residents as Frankie Frisch, George Kelly, Ross Youngs, Ty Cobb, and Tris Speaker of attempted bribery and game-fixing charges. The self-declared nemesis of all professional gambling also had nothing devastating to say about the well-known racetrack habits of Rogers Hornsby and John McGraw, even though Hornsby's addiction weighed on several of the teams for which he played.

Landis's high-handedness inevitably produced clashes with league presidents and owners. He spent a considerable part of the 1920s doing battle with AL president Ban Johnson, who never got over the discarding of his fiefdom on the three-man National Commission and who took every opportunity to undermine the authority of the commissioner's office. Johnson was finally forced to withdraw from the scene after he couldn't find a majority of owners to back him in 1926 charges that Landis had covered up for Cobb and Speaker in a game-fixing investigation. Then, as on several occasions before and afterward, Landis retaliated against the attacks on him with a one-two punch of high dudgeon that anybody would dare question his integrity, and sulky threats to resign if the owners didn't give him full and immediate support. Afraid of the reaction in the press if the judge walked off, the owners were always quick to cave in. On the other hand, it was an experience that their successors would keep in mind when choosing future commissioners.

Much of Landis's reputation as a paternalistic defender of individual players against greedy owners stemmed from his visceral opposition to the minor league farm team concept pioneered by Branch Rickey of the Cardinals in the 1920s; Landis, who prided himself on being a David up against various Goliaths bent on ruining the healthy ambitions of modestly fixed Americans, branded the farm chains ''a rape of small towns.'' In fact, his stance was not as risky as it might have been in subsequent eras for the simple reason that many owners without the money or the imagination of the St. Louis organization didn't like the system either, and were hardly disposed toward ganging up on him over the issue. He didn't have too much more to fear from the owners as a group when he went to bat for players who had been buried in the minors to the point of compromising their careers: If he angered the contract-holding team by ordering the player released, he equally pleased the clubs waiting to bid for the player's services. Even when he winked at regulations, as he did in allowing the Indians to hold on to Bob Feller in 1936 despite a number of glaring improprieties, he created front office allies as well as enemies—in that specific case, Cleveland and the other AL teams that saw the already talent-laden Yankees and Tigers ready to pounce on the right-hander if he were declared a free agent. The end result was that only one owner, Ball of the Browns, ever went back on the assurances given to Landis that his decisions would never be appealed in a courtroom, and that challenge fell before a judge who sanctioned the powers ceded to the commissioner.

If Landis had one special irritant, it was Rickey—not only for the farm system question, but for a sanctimoniousness that matched his own. The main character difference between the two was that Rickey was a genuine teetotaler who gave even his ruthless business smarts a rest on the Sabbath, while Landis never had to be asked twice after working hours to have a drink or recite the latest four-letter words that he had heard. Their biggest public explosion came in 1938, when Landis informed the Cardinals that he was granting free-agent status to seventy-four of the organization's farmhands because Rickey had entered into "secret understandings" with minor league operators aimed at denying the players competitive opportunity. Rickey immediately insisted that St. Louis owner Sam Breadon file suit so that the issue might be aired in a courtroom. The threat was effective to the degree that Landis never got around to conveying formal charges to the Cardinals; on the other hand, Breadon was so embarrassed by the accusation, and by his own awareness that something untoward had been going on, that he refused even to back Rickey in insisting on the franchise's rights to the seventy-four minor leaguers (among whom was future batting champion Pete Reiser).

In 1940 Landis issued a similar dictum against the Tigers, granting free agency to ninety-one Detroit farmhands and ordering the franchise to come up with $47,000 in damages for another fifteen players who had been buried in the minor leagues. Like the Cardinals, the Tigers didn't challenge the order.

As zealous as Landis seemed to be about the rights of minor leaguers, he was equally ardent about keeping the major leagues a strictly white domain. One of his very first diktats after assuming office was to eliminate postseason exhibition games between big league clubs and teams from the Negro leagues, permitting major leaguers to appear only as members of an all-star squad. He always denied that his order was aimed at protecting pennant-winning clubs from potential embarrassment at the hands of the black teams, and went on insisting to his dying day that he knew of no formal regulation prohibiting blacks from signing with the big league clubs. What he omitted saying was that he lashed into both the Pirates and the Senators in the early 1940s for even exploring the possibility of inking a couple of black players and that he blocked an ownership bid by Bill Veeck for the Phillies after being told that Veeck planned to break the color barrier. It was only with Landis's death in 1944 that Rickey began laying serious plans for desegregating the Dodgers.

Only a month after his death, Landis was elected to the Hall of Fame.

HOBIE LANDRITH

Landrith made two key contributions to the legend of the 1962 Mets. The first came when he was the expansion franchise's very first pick, and manager Casey Stengel explained the choice of the left-hand-batting receiver by saying, "If you don't have a catcher, you get a lot of passed balls." The second came midway through New York's initial season, when Landrith was traded to Baltimore for the most publicized Met clown of them all: Marv Throneberry.

TITO LANDRUM

Landrum hit baseball's most famous pawnshop home run when his 10th-inning blast in the fourth game of the 1983 American League Championship Series broke up a scoreless duel and enabled Baltimore to edge Chicago for the pennant. The outfielder had been dealt to the Orioles during the season by the Cardinals, and was reclaimed by St. Louis during spring training in 1984.

FRANK LANE

Lane earned his nickname of The Trader by completing 165 deals involving more than 400 major leaguers during a twelve-year run as general manager of the White Sox, Cardinals, Indians, and Athletics. Although many of the transactions stemmed from little more than a desire to net a headline, the majority of them ended up improving Lane's club of the moment. His most conspicuous successes were with the White Sox (1948–55), when he obtained southpaw Billy Pierce from the Tigers in 1948 for backup catcher Aaron Robinson, and when he acquired second baseman Nellie Fox from the Athletics in 1949 for backstop Joe Tipton. On the other hand, Lane was almost run out of Cleveland in 1960 for dealing away fan favorite Rocky Colavito to Detroit for Harvey Kuenn.

A Warren Giles protégé, Lane took over baseball operations for the White Sox against a background of squabbles among members of the Comiskey family for control of the franchise. Through such transactions as the acquisition of Pierce and Fox, he managed to bring the cellar-dwelling team up to regular first-division finishes by the early 1950s. He became so adept at player moves that he even entered baseball lore as one of the few executives to outwit Branch Rickey. In 1949, after getting Rickey to speculate on what he *might* ask for Dodger minor leaguer Chico Carrasquel if he would even consider trading the shortstop prospect, Lane waited a few days, then called the Brooklyn president and said he accepted the asking price. Rickey's disclaimers that he had never actually offered Carrasquel to Chicago got lost in a lot of double-talk about honoring one's word, with the result that the infielder went to the White Sox for two minor leaguers.

As one of the architects of the Go-Go Sox of the 1950s, Lane alternately drew praise and jealousy from franchise scion Chuck Comiskey, leading to periodic run-ins with the family. One of his more important mistakes, at least in the eyes of the Comiskeys, was coming out publicly in support of a Bill Veeck plan that would allow a visiting club to share in the revenues from local television coverage of games. He didn't endear himself to the family, either, for criticizing a miserly salary policy that prompted Paul Richards, the manager of the Go-Go Sox, to resign and go off to Baltimore. What turned out to be the breaking point in the general manager's relations with the owners took place near the end of the 1955 season when Lane, infuriated by an umpiring decision that went against Chicago, confronted

American League president Will Harridge at Comiskey Park and shouted obscenities about the caliber of the league's arbiters. The next day, Harridge fined Lane $500, while Chuck Comiskey denounced the executive for embarrassing the organization. Lane took the hint and resigned.

Moving over to the Cardinals for the 1956 season, Lane lived up to his reputation by completing twenty-six transactions in fewer than two years. Although the swaps (mainly involving such veterans as Alvin Dark and Del Ennis) boosted St. Louis to second place after three consecutive seasons of playing under .500, owner Gussie Busch made it clear that that wasn't good enough, causing Lane to resign behind a crack that he had no desire to work for "an irrational organization." Back in the AL, with the Indians, he completed almost sixty swaps at a major league level between 1958 and 1960. Among the most familiar names passing through Cleveland in the period were Billy Martin, Mickey Vernon, Jimmy Piersall, and Don Newcombe. As with Chicago and St. Louis, the overall impact of the deals was positive, with the Indians advancing from a fourth-place to a second-place showing.

If for different reasons, three of Lane's trades while in Cleveland stood out. In the first, in June 1958, he sent young slugger Roger Maris, pitcher Dick Tomanek, and first baseman Preston Ward to Kansas City in exchange for shortstop Woodie Held and first baseman Vic Power. The swap was denounced throughout the AL because it left Maris with a club—the Athletics—that operated as a major league affiliate of the Yankees. Lane, who had rejected a couple of direct offers from the Yankees for the outfielder and whose dislike for New York was such that a 1950 purchase of second-string receiver Gus Niarhos represented his only career deal with the Bronx, took the stance that he was not responsible for Kansas City's future decisions (which did indeed include sending Maris to the Yankees).

The fallout from the Colavito-Kuenn swap in 1960 was far worse. Lane's official justification for the exchange was that the Indians were in more immediate need of consistency at the plate than the long ball, but that rationale faded before statistics showing that Colavito was superior to Kuenn in just about every offensive category (including on-base average) except batting average. The actual trigger for the swap was Lane's fears that Colavito's power numbers and appeal to the fans would make him intractable in salary negotiations.

In August 1960 Lane pulled off his most antic trade by sending manager Joe Gordon to Detroit for Tiger pilot Jimmy Dykes. Lane had little compunction about admitting that the swap had been worked out with Detroit's Bill DeWitt mainly to revive interest in two decidedly also-ran teams.

Lane's last—and least successful—prominent position was as general manager of Charlie Finley's A's in 1961. He lasted only several months on a two-year contract, and ended up having to sue Finley to get the money due him.

BILL LANGE

A dazzling base runner with a .330 lifetime batting average, Lange's penchant for the high life of the Gay Nineties made him unpopular with Cubs manager Cap Anson but made Lange the darling of Chicago fans. The right-handed center fielder held out in 1897 so he could see fellow San Franciscan Jim Corbett defend his heavyweight boxing title against Bob Fitzsimmons in Carson City, Nevada; both pleased and chagrined when his demands were met almost immediately, Lange simply altered his tactics and leaked a story that he had sprained an ankle and would report as soon as possible—which turned out to be immediately after Corbett had been knocked out in the 14th round on March 17. Though compared favorably with Ty Cobb by contemporaries, the twenty-nine-year-old Lange quit baseball with a .330 average after seven seasons to marry a young woman whose father would not countenance a ballplayer as a son-in-law. The union ended in divorce.

MAX LANIER

Lanier's promising career stumbled over his decision to jump to Mexico in 1946. Because of his pivotal role in three St. Louis pennants between 1942 and 1944, when he posted 45 victories, the southpaw was considered the biggest coup in the major league raids by the Pasquel brothers. By his own admission, however, the pitcher went with the Pasquels because of fears that arm twinges he had kept secret from the Cardinals might end his big league career in any case. Faced with the five-year ban on the jumpers imposed by Commissioner Happy Chandler, Lanier tried to make ends meet upon his return from Mexico by organizing a barnstorming team of fellow defectors. He discovered the reach of Chandler's ban when even semipro and college teams declined to play his club. He eventually returned to the Cardinals for another three seasons but was no longer in peak form.

ERNEST LANIGAN

A nephew of the Spink brothers who founded *The Sporting News,* Lanigan was the first baseball encyclopedist. At various times a sportswriter, a club and league executive in the minors, and both historian and director of the Hall of Fame, he was the major proponent of including runs batted in as an offensive category. His most significant contribution to the history of the game was the publication of *The Baseball Cyclopedia* in 1922. He once confessed: ''I really don't care much about baseball, or looking at ball games. All my interest in baseball is in its statistics.''

JOSEPH LANNIN

As owner of the Red Sox in 1914, Lannin took the lead in American and National league efforts to stymie the insurgent Federal League by bankrolling minor league clubs that happened to share markets with the Feds. The tactic paid off in another way when the real-estate tycoon's good relations with Jack Dunn of Baltimore's International League Orioles enabled Boston to purchase Babe Ruth and Ernie Shore. Throughout his three-year tenure with the Red Sox, Lannin was accused of being far too close to AL president Ban Johnson. It was Johnson who eased his way into the Boston hierarchy, who arranged for him to deal holdout outfielder Tris Speaker to the Indians, and who came up with New York theatrical producers Harry Frazee and Hugh Ward when Lannin announced that he wanted to sell the franchise. The AL executive was thought to have taken away considerably more than a finder's fee for putting Lannin and Frazee together.

GENE LARKIN

Dogged throughout his somewhat humdrum career by his reputation as the first Columbia University student to reach the majors since Lou Gehrig, Larkin finally had a moment under the moon in the seventh game of the 1991 World Series when his bases-loaded pinch-single in the bottom of the 10th inning gave Minnesota the world championship over Atlanta. The hit ended a scoreless duel between the Twin's Jack Morris and the Braves' John Smoltz (for 9 innings) and Mike Stanton.

DON LARSEN

Larsen's perfect game against the Dodgers in the World Series on October 8, 1956, always bemused the right-hander, who otherwise had a less than scintillating career (81–91) and who was never shy about his rambunctious activities off the field. On the same day that he no-hit Brooklyn for the Yankees, for instance, his wife served him with divorce papers. His last service to New York came in a December 1959 trade that saw him go to Kansas City in exchange for Roger Maris.

Larsen's career turned around when Casey Stengel taught him the no-windup delivery that had so baffled the New York manager when he was a young outfielder and first encountered it at the hands of otherwise mediocre southpaw Patsy Flaherty. Right-hander Bob Turley, who came to the Yankees from the Orioles along with Larsen, was also helped by adopting the Flaherty style.

LYN LARY

Lary is usually charged with sloppy baserunning for costing Lou Gehrig the exclusive 1931 home-run title. But while it was true that he allowed Gehrig to pass him on the bases after the first baseman had reached the Griffith Stadium bleachers in an April 26 game against Washington, the fault lay more with manager Joe McCarthy than with the Yankee shortstop. The pilot's ambiguous signal to slow down convinced Lary that the ball, which had rebounded out of the stands and into the Washington center fielder's hands, had been caught. McCarthy, in a tacit admission of his mistake, removed himself from the coach's box for the rest of the season. The basepath mixup also cost New York the game.

TOM LASORDA

As Los Angeles manager since 1977, Lasorda has represented a fusion of the organization's assumptions of total loyalty and Hollywood's assumptions of relentless self-promotion. Just as Casey Stengel was the darling of the print media, so Lasorda has been the paramour of television, showing up not just on sports shows but also on talk programs and even variety hours to spout a well-rehearsed line of anecdotes, cracks, and homilies about the spiritual strengths of bleeding Dodger blue and working for the O'Malleys. Often lost amid all the huckstering have been Lasorda's abilities as a manager—considerable in many areas, but also circumscribed by his use of starting pitchers to excess and by mood swings that have ended up alienating many of the players he has been fond of embracing before the camera. For every player who has credited him with helping to shape or salvage a career, there has been another who has voiced relief at being out from under his bluster.

As a minor leaguer in the Dodger system, Lasorda established a number of pitching records in the 1950s, including the most victories (112) by an International League hurler; as a major leaguer, he lost his roster spot in Brooklyn to Sandy Koufax, had his trade to the St. Louis Browns canceled when American League owners forced out Bill Veeck, and lost his only four major league decisions, as a member of Kansas City in 1956. After coaching and managing in the Dodger system for years, he was named to replace Walter Alston in 1976. Lasorda's record from 1977 to 1993 showed six division titles, four pennants, and a pair of world championships. Until 1983, not even his managing abilities or 'round-the-clock promotion of the franchise had moved the organization from its traditional stance of offering pilots only one-year contracts; but when the Yankees refused to deny reports that they were interested in signing Lasorda as a combination manager-general manager, Peter O'Malley finally coughed up a three-year pact.

In terms of personnel, Lasorda's biggest achievement was the nurturing of southpaw Fernando Valenzuela in the early 1980s into the biggest gate attraction in the league. On the other hand, Lasorda has presided over a clubhouse that almost annually has exploded into rifts and fist-fights among star players; among those who have taken on Lasorda either directly or through the media have been Steve Garvey, Don Sutton, and Rick Sutcliffe. Lasorda also showed a marked crudity in responding to the 1994 release of Darryl Strawberry, chiding the drug-afflicted outfielder for not being as loyal as a dog who goes after a ball.

ARLIE LATHAM

In his seventy-six years in baseball, the puckish Latham served, at one time or another, in almost every capacity in the game, but he is best remembered for a pair of firsts—as clown and as coach. As the third baseman and leadoff hitter for the American Association St. Louis Browns from 1883 to 1889, he fashioned the first clown act on the diamond. Unlike his successors in the field, however, there was purpose beyond amusement in his pranks: His performances in the third-base coaching box aroused fans to join him in his constant hazing, camouflaged his sign stealing, and irritated opponents. Latham particularly liked mocking Chris Von der Ahe by wearing a bulbous red nose and mimicking the St. Louis owner's pompous strutting. An accomplished acrobat, Latham often turned cartwheels over the last twenty feet on the way to first base after a hit, and once, while playing for the Cincinnati Reds in the early 1890s, somersaulted over the head of dour Chicago manager Cap Anson. In 1889 Latham appeared as a song-and-dance man in a Broadway vehicle called *Fashions*.

Although Latham's playing days effectively ended in 1895, Von der Ahe, never one to shrink from a publicity stunt, brought his nemesis back the following year to play 8 games and manage 3 of them (all losses) for the then National League Browns. By this time, however, the third baseman's skills had so eroded that "to do a Latham" had become synonymous with waving ineffectively at a ground ball.

In 1909, Giants' manager John McGraw made Latham the first full-time coach. The hiring was, in part, a reward for his perpetuation of the old Oriole myth. (Latham had once said of his new employer: "He eats gunpowder for breakfast and washes it down with warm blood.") But the move

paid dividends, if not when Latham was activated for 4 games, and became, on August 18, the oldest player (at forty-nine) ever to steal a base, then when the Giants followed his instruction to steal a twentieth-century-record 347 bases on the way to the 1911 pennant.

Between 1912 and 1937 Latham lived in London where, when he wasn't hobnobbing with King George V and the prince of Wales (and trying to teach them baseball), he was organizing baseball leagues. Back in the United States, Latham worked at both the Polo Grounds and Yankee Stadium until his death, at age ninety-two, in 1952.

CHARLIE LAU

Lau provoked more passionate defenses and heated criticism than any other hitting coach. With his stress on balance and weight shifts and staying through the ball, he was able to claim particular success with George Brett, Hal McRae, and other members of the Kansas City Royals in the 1970s. Despite that, some baseball traditionalists in offensive theory have accused him and his chief disciple, Walt Hriniak, of ruining potential power hitters. They have also mocked the onetime catcher's own offensive abilities (a .255 lifetime average with a mere 16 home runs in eleven seasons) as a qualification for teaching others, asserting that his most successful students accomplished what they did in spite of rather than because of him.

The facts suggest otherwise. In his only year as Baltimore's batting instructor, in 1969, Lau had a team that averaged .265 with 175 home runs; the year before, the Orioles had hit .225 with 133 home runs. His 1970 charges in Oakland batted .249 with 171 homers; the year before, the club had also hit .249, but with 23 fewer round-trippers. When he went to Kansas City in 1971, Lau helped lift the team average by 6 points in his first season. When he took over as the batting coach for the Yankees in 1979, home runs increased by 25 over the previous year. Moving to the White Sox in 1982, he had a team that clouted 60 more home runs than it had in 1981, if partly because of the strike-shortened campaign. Overall, and notwithstanding his image as a tutor bent on having everyone hit singles through the middle or to the opposite field, Lau had twenty-seven of his charges blast at least 20 home runs in a season.

Lau's impact on his players was particularly evident in Kansas City, where players blasted both Jack McKeon and Whitey Herzog when the managers released him. In those instances, as with his other pilots in other cities, he got caught up in clubhouse jealousies because of player insistence on consulting him about more than just how to swing a bat. When he died of cancer in 1984, White Sox players paid tribute to him by wearing his initials on their uniform sleeves for the year.

COOKIE LAVAGETTO

Lavagetto delivered the most dramatic pinch-hit in World Series history in 1947, when he reached the Yankees' Bill Bevens for a two-out, 2-run double in the bottom of the 9th inning of the fourth game. The blow by the Dodger third baseman prevented Bevens from completing the first no-hitter in a World Series and also gave Brooklyn a last-gasp 2–1 victory. It was Lavagetto's last hit in a ten-year big league career.

ANDY LAWSON

With an undercapitalized bank account and an inflated sense of his own importance, Lawson set about to challenge the monopoly of the National and American leagues with the formation of the first Continental League in December 1920. Announcing that play would begin on May 1 of the following year, the promoter bounced around the country for several months issuing press statements at every stop about his successes, real and imaginary. The principles of his new circuit were ambitious. Franchises would represent states, not cities; ballparks would be built where old Federal League fields could not be acquired (he even offered to buy Fenway Park from perennially strapped Red Sox owner Harry Frazee); there would be no reserve clause; and as many players as possible would be assigned to clubs from home states. Players were to come from a variety of sources, including the ranks of those recently outlawed after the 1919 World Series scandal. More revolutionary, Lawson planned to tap the Negro leagues, where, he estimated, there were at least a hundred players who were the equal of major leaguers, and possibly even incorporate several existing all-black clubs in the CL. It was all very grandiose—and very unrealistic. The last Lawson was heard of was in a statement delaying the start of the season from May 1 to May 20.

JOHNNY LAZOR

Under rules then in force, Boston outfielder Lazor should have been awarded the 1945 American League batting title for batting .310 in 101 games. But then AL president Will Harridge stepped in to rule that since 17 of Lazor's games of a necessary minimum of 100 had been as a pinch hitter, the title should go to New York's George Stirnweiss for his .309.

TONY LAZZERI (Hall of Fame, 1991)

Lazzeri is the only Hall of Famer who is most famous for striking out. The second baseman for the Murderers' Row Yankees, he hit .292 in a fourteen-year (1926–39) career, almost all of it with New York. He reached the .300 mark five times, with a high of .354 in 1929; drove in 100 runs seven times; and reached double figures in homers ten times. Lazzeri's most glaring moment center stage came in the seventh inning of the seventh game of the 1926 World Series when, with the bases loaded and two out, he struck out against hung over St. Louis relief pitcher Grover Cleveland Alexander to permit the Cardinals to preserve their 3–2 victory. The only offensive category in which Lazzeri ever led the league was strikeouts, also in his rookie 1926 season.

BILL LEE

Lee's fourteen-year (1969–82) career was cut short by a field fight, media humorlessness, and his own penchant for staging one-man strikes in solidarity with teammates. He ultimately became the victim of an informal major league blacklist.

Lee's biggest years were with the Red Sox between 1973 and 1975, when he won 17 games three times in a row. At the same time, the left-hander was attracting off-the-field attention as one of baseball's few counterculture symbols for his dedication to yoga and for more than one hint that he had inhaled marijuana. It was in this context that teammate John Kennedy first dubbed him "Space-man"—a name writers thereafter used as shorthand for explaining their wariness of the pitcher's often enigmatic remarks. For his part, Lee wasn't above using the media for what he thought of as serious baseball purposes. On one occasion, he announced that he had thrown three spitballs to Tony Taylor of the Tigers to goad American League president Joe Cronin into fining him as he had previously penalized Texas pitcher Jim Merritt for the offense; according to Lee, the fine levied on the sore-armed Merritt had to be challenged all the way to the U.S. Supreme Court, indirectly if not directly. On another occasion Lee proclaimed his support of school busing in Boston for the avowed purpose of drawing the ire of racist fans and columnists who might have otherwise continued to dun the Red Sox with reminders of the Babe Ruth Curse during a stretch race against the Yankees.

Lee's demeanor kept him on the outs with such old-school managers as Eddie Kasko, Darrell Johnson, and Don Zimmer, and Lee succeeded on the mound as often as he did only after they had tried to bury him as a mop-up reliever. He became a particular nemesis of Zimmer after he joined with pitchers Ferguson Jenkins, Rick Wise, and Jim Willoughby and outfielder Bernie Carbo in a group calling itself the Loyal Order of the Buffalo Heads. The group's main activity was mocking Zimmer's ineptitude with the Red Sox pitching staff. Lee earned himself an extra demerit with Zimmer for once describing the pilot as a gerbil—an association that the veteran baseball man could never shed.

The turning point in Lee's career came in May 1976, when Yankee third baseman Graig Nettles dumped him on his shoulder during a field fight between the two teams. The resulting torn ligaments turned the southpaw into a junkballer—and gave Zimmer still further reason for ignoring him as much as possible. Only when Fenway Park fans began applauding his every appearance on the bullpen mound did the pilot relent, bringing him back into meaningful situations.

Lee was peddled to the Expos in 1979, and only a few days after reporting got caught up in another series of headlines because of a crack that he was fond of sprinkling marijuana over his pancakes in the morning. He was considered as still more of a ''character'' for being clipped by a taxi while jogging that season. On the hill, he won 16 games for Montreal in his first year, but then succumbed to a series of injuries over the next couple of years. In 1982 he burned his bridges with the Expos by walking out briefly on the team because of the release of second baseman Rodney Scott. Lee had staged similar protests while with the Red Sox over the trading away of Carbo and pitcher Sonny Siebert.

In his autobiography *The Wrong Stuff*, Lee cited San Diego manager Dick Williams and other baseball people as having told him that he would never pitch in the big leagues again because of an unofficial blacklisting encouraged by the Expos. Lee also accused Montreal of doing the same thing to Scott by, among other ways, spreading the rumor that the infielder was gay. In the book, Lee also admitted pitching a game for the Red Sox while under the influence of hashish.

MARK LEE

Lee didn't have much of a career with the Padres and Pirates in the late 1970s and early 1980s, but he had one of the more notable farewells to organized baseball. Toward the end of the 1982 season, the right-hander was told that he was being released by the Portland Beavers of the Pacific Coast League, but was also instructed to wait around in case he were needed for that night's game. After indeed being called in from the bullpen in the ninth inning, he got the first batter on a pop, the second on strikes, then called manager Tom Trebelhorn out to the mound and announced that he was quitting then and there, with the strikeout as his swan song. On the way to the dugout, he tossed his cap and uniform shirt onto the field. ''It was my way of saying,'' he explained later, ''that organized baseball didn't quite control *all* of me.''

RON LEFLORE

LeFlore is the only player to have led both leagues in stolen bases, accomplishing it with the 1978 Tigers and the 1980 Expos. The right-hand-hitting outfielder reached the majors thanks to Billy Martin, who met him while LeFlore was serving time for armed robbery. Despite his great speed, he lasted only nine years in the majors because of a combination of a ferocious strikeout rate, nagging injuries, and old-school managers who objected to his independent manner.

CHARLIE LEIBRANDT

For two straight years, Leibrandt's troubles in the 11th inning of the sixth game of the World Series spelled doom for the Braves. In 1991 the southpaw yielded a home run to Minnesota's Kirby Puckett to keep the Twins alive and set up their world championship victory the following day. In 1992 Leibrandt surrendered a 2-run double to Toronto's Dave Winfield that turned out to be the lock on a Blue Jay world championship.

BOB LEMON (Hall of Fame, 1976)

Lemon was Babe Ruth in reverse—a major leaguer who reached the Hall of Fame after starting his American League career as a position player. A twenty-six-year-old when he toed the mound for the first time in 1946, the right-hander went on to post 20 wins seven times, closing out a thirteen-year career spent entirely with Cleveland with 207 wins. His best seasons were 1950 and 1954, when he won 23 games each time. In the 1948 World Series, against the Braves, he notched 2 victories. As a hitter, Lemon's 37 career home runs rank him second to Wes Ferrell's 38 for career long balls by a pitcher. On April 30, 1946, he was the Indians' center fielder in Bob Feller 1–0 no-hitter over the Yankees. Two years later Lemon himself threw the first AL no-hitter at night, against the Tigers. In September 1949 he had another no-hitter going, against the Red Sox, until Boston manager Joe McCarthy protested that the sweat-stained bill of his cap was so discolored that he was no longer in uniform; the hurler obligingly changed to a new hat, but, his concentration broken, he lost the no-hitter. The next day Lemon took pregame practice in a fedora.

Following his retirement as a pitcher, Lemon managed the Royals, White Sox, and Yankees; with all three organizations, his fabled laid-back manner first earned him kudos for his patience and then cost him his job for lacking drive. In 1978, while piloting Chicago, Lemon was offered to the Yankees for Billy Martin by owner Bill Veeck in a straight-up trade of managers. Although the deal was rejected by New York, it triggered an outburst by Martin against New York owner George Steinbrenner that got him fired and opened up the Bronx job to the equally fired Lemon anyway. After steering the Yankees to a flashy come-from-behind pennant and World Series win, however, Lemon was devastated by the death of his twenty-six-year-old son in an auto accident, and he acknowledged that he was relieved when he was replaced by the same Martin in one of Steinbrenner's musical chair rounds the next season. He came back for another stint of managing New York in 1981–82.

MARK LEMONGELLO

Lemongello was the most crazed loser baseball has ever seen. Among his other reactions to being driven from the mound were to bite his shoulder until it bled and to beat on his pitching hand. When he was removed from his last starting assignment for the Blue Jays in 1979, the right-hander fired the ball at the head of manager Roy Hartsfield before marching into the clubhouse. Neither Lemongello nor his lifetime 22–38 record was ever seen in the majors again.

BUCK LEONARD (Hall of Fame, 1972)

Leonard was Josh Gibson's Lou Gehrig. A left-hand-hitting first baseman, Leonard batted cleanup behind Gibson on the Homestead Grays, slugging line drives for both power and average while Gibson specialized in Ruthian blasts. The similarity with Gehrig doesn't end there, either. Leonard, unlike most stars of the Negro leagues, spent virtually all of his career with one club, joining the Grays in 1934, before they were a power; staying through nine consecutive (1937–45) Negro National League pennants; and remaining until the demise of the franchise in 1950, two years after the collapse of the NNL. In addition, he played with all manner of injuries, including a broken hand in the black World Series of 1942 against the Kansas City Monarchs.

Having played over the years in Cuban, Puerto Rican, and Venezuelan winter leagues, Leonard moved to Mexico for the 1951 and 1952 seasons, hitting just about his career average, in the .320s, both years. Leonard turned down a contract offer from Bill Veeck to play for the Browns in 1952 on the grounds that he was too old and "didn't want to embarrass anyone or hurt the chances of those who might follow.'' His one shot in organized ball came in 1953, when he agreed to suit up for the Portsmouth club in the Class B Piedmont League, and hit .333 in 10 games. Two years later, Leonard played 62 games for Durango in the Central Mexican League, batting .312 with 13 home runs; he was forty-eight years old at the time.

DUTCH LEONARD

Leonard was the key figure in what was arguably baseball's most notorious cover-up of a game-fixing scandal and what was certainly the Waterloo for American League president Ban Johnson. The scandal ended up overshadowing Leonard's career year of 1914, when, as a member of the Red Sox, he established the major league ERA mark of a mere 1.01 while compiling a 19–5 record.

In the autumn of 1926, the retired hurler wrote a letter to Johnson asserting that he, Ty Cobb, Tris Speaker, and Cleveland outfielder Joe Wood had conspired to fix the last game of the 1919 season as a means of assuring a third-place finish for the Tigers behind the White Sox and the Indians. According to Leonard, Wood had also laid down bets for Cobb and Speaker on the September 25, 1919, contest. Johnson, never a fan of either future Hall of Famer, reportedly paid Leonard $20,000 for a couple of letters—one from Wood and the other from Cobb—that clearly implicated Cobb but nowhere mentioned Speaker. Within a month of one another, Cobb and Speaker were forced out as managers of the Tigers and Indians, respectively, to the undisguised delight of Johnson. (Wood had been out of the game for several years and drew almost no fire in the controversy.) Just as the two outfielders began musing aloud about filing lawsuits against everyone involved, however, Commissioner Kenesaw Landis initiated his own investigation, beginning with a trip to California to interrogate Leonard. Despite the suggestiveness of the Wood letters, especially where Cobb was concerned, Landis ruled that the fix charges against *both* stars were unfounded and were due solely to Leonard's resentment that Cobb had released him in 1925 and

that Speaker had declined to give him a tryout with Cleveland.

The commissioner's verdict was ridiculed by many, not least by Johnson. With his reputation at stake, Landis summoned a meeting of AL owners and asked them to choose between him and the league president. Before the session was ever formally convened, however, the owners persuaded Johnson to take a sabbatical, placed Detroit owner Frank Navin in charge of the league's day-to-day business, and publicly restated their confidence in the integrity of Landis. Johnson never regained his stature in league circles.

Leonard himself always insisted that the American League owners had supported Landis because they were afraid of losing such stars as Cobb and Speaker to the National League. In fact, after being dissuaded by Landis from pursuing lawsuits against Leonard and Johnson, Cobb signed with the Athletics and Speaker with the Senators.

DUTCH LEONARD

In contrast to an earlier namesake involved in a Detroit-Cleveland game-fixing scandal, the knuckleballer Leonard of the 1944 Senators ignored a $10,000 bribe to throw the final game of the season, defeating the Tigers and dooming them to finish a game behind the pennant-winning Browns. The following year, Leonard, Roger Wolff, Mickey Haefner, and Johnny Niggeling comprised the only starting rotation in major league history made up exclusively of knuckleballers.

JEFFREY LEONARD

Few players have had as much of a talent for irritating the opposition as Leonard, who seemed to thrive on accusations of showboating. During the 1987 National League Championship Series against the Cardinals, the San Francisco outfielder raised his act to a *casus belli* when he gave the ''dead arm'' trot to each of his 4 home runs, holding his left arm stiffly at his side as he rounded the bases; his accompanying number of having his batting gloves flop from his back pockets so annoyed umpires that a rule was thereafter enforced against having the gloves dangle. Amid all the consternation, Leonard became the first player in a League Championship Series to get an MVP nod despite being on a losing team. The right-hand-hitting slugger also had his own solution for dealing with catchers who sought to distract him in the batter's box: He made sure that receivers always saw the spot on his bat where he had carved the words "Fuck you."

On August 21, 1979, Leonard was the protagonist of the most protracted final out in baseball history. Facing the Mets' Pete Falcone as a member of the Astros, he hit what appeared to be a game-ending fly ball. But then the umpires ruled that New York shortstop Frank Taveras had called time before the pitch, so Leonard got a second chance and promptly singled. But then that plate appearance was also nullified when the umpires realized that first baseman Ed Kranepool, thinking that the original fly ball had ended the game, had not taken his position in time for the hit. As Leonard was called back to the plate for a third try, Houston announced it was playing the game under protest; immediately afterward, the outfielder again skied out. After the game, however, National League president Chub Feeney upheld the Astros' protest, ordering Leonard back to first base with his hit and the resumption of the game before a regularly scheduled contest the next day. Kevin Kobel finally ended matters by getting José Cruz on a grounder. The main victim of the fiasco was Falcone, who still had a 5–0 win but who lost his complete-game shutout.

BUDDY LEROUX

A real-estate wheeler-dealer and former Red Sox trainer, LeRoux entered into a partnership in 1977 with Boston scouting director Haywood Sullivan to purchase the franchise from the estate of Tom Yawkey. Nothing that followed over the next seven years was reminiscent of Yawkey's smooth forty-year control.

To begin with, LeRoux and Sullivan were so undercapitalized that they needed Yawkey's widow, Jean, not only to reject a higher offer from A-T-O, the parent of the Rawley Sporting Goods company, but also to add some of her own money to make their bid more credible. A-T-O promptly sued Yawkey on the grounds that she couldn't serve simultaneously as a purchaser and the executor of her husband's estate, but the will language was sufficiently vague to allow the LeR-oux-Sullivan offer to stand. For its part, however, the American League warned LeRoux and Sullivan not even to seek endorsement of the sale until they had obtained more solid financing. This the pair managed after many months by selling limited partnerships and by getting Yawkey to increase her financial presence in the new ownership.

No sooner had LeRoux and Sullivan settled into their new positions than they began going at one another. As the more visible head of baseball operations, Sullivan offered a better target, especially after a LeRoux confidant, Boston broadcaster Ken Harrelson, decided that Bucky Dent's playoff home run in 1978 would never have happened if Don Zimmer hadn't been the manager and Sullivan the general manager. During the 1980–81 off-season the bickering between the owners became so constant that it was viewed as the major reason for the club's failure to send stars Fred Lynn and Carlton Fisk their proposed contracts on time, in effect making them free agents. It was in the wake of the Lynn-Fisk snafu that one Boston sportswriter began referring to the organization's general partners as Dumwood Sullivan and Shoddy LeRoux.

The next act of the follies took place in June 1983, when LeRoux, claiming that he had a majority backing from the club's limited partners, staged a full-dress coup by bringing his administrative team into Fenway Park and declaring himself in charge. For two days the franchise operated under parallel administrations; then Sullivan and Yawkey secured a restraining order to evict the usurpers. For its part, the Massachusetts Superior Court decided some weeks later that LeRoux's move was illegal, but also resisted a plea by Sullivan and Yawkey that LeRoux and his fellow insurgents (representing about 42 percent of the stock) be forced to sell out. Not content with the ruling, however, LeRoux appealed it—only to regret his move a year later, when he *was* ordered to sell out.

W. R. LESTER

The sports editor of the *Philadelphia Record,* Lester proposed the general plan that set the distance between the mound and home plate back from fifty feet to the sixty feet, six inches it has been for more than a century. He offered his proposal following the 1892 season, when owners began complaining that pitching had come to dominate the game and that the lack of high-scoring games would eventually drive away spectators. As initially conceived, the plan would have pushed the mound back to sixty-five feet within a general broadening of the infield to ninety-three feet between bases. Meeting in New York on March 7, 1893, however, the owners found this too radical a change and compromised on the sixty feet, six inches. In 1892, only twelve players of the 184 who had appeared in at least 15 games batted .300; with the pitcher moved back ten feet, six inches a year later, sixty-five players reached the magic circle.

Lester himself batted .500 on two other proposals at the meeting. His call for the elimination of the flat bat was accepted, but the owners rejected another proposal, that all foul balls be charged as strikes. It was, however, only eight years later that the National League agreed to charging the first two fouls as strikes. The American League adopted the same rule in 1903.

DUTCH LEVSEN

On August 28, 1926, Indians' right-hander Levsen bested the Red Sox in both ends of a doubleheader by scores of 6–1 and 5–1. He is the last major leaguer to hurl two complete-game victories on the same day. He didn't record a strikeout in either game.

DAVID LEVY

Teenager Levy effectively ended the petty practice of big league clubs of chasing down balls hit into the stands. In August 1934 he suffered a fractured skull in an attack by Yankee Stadium ushers after he tried to dislodge a ball that Lou Gehrig had fouled into a screen. In 1937, a federal court awarded him $7,500 for his pain. Thereafter, front offices put out the word that patrons could keep any ball they could reach without interfering with a game.

ED LEVY

First baseman Levy joined the Yankees in 1942 amid a publicity circus aimed at drawing more Jewish fans to the Bronx. When he tried to tell team president Ed Barrow that Levy was his stepfather's name and that he had been raised as the very Irish Catholic Edward Clarence Whitner, the team executive shot back: "You may be Whitner to the rest of the world, but if you're going to play for the Yankees, you'll be Ed Levy." In less than 200 plate appearances over two seasons, Levy batted a mere .215, after which he was sent back to civilian life as Whitner.

DARREN LEWIS

Lewis holds title to the greatest fielding streak in baseball history. Before overrunning a single in late June 1994, the San Francisco center fielder had gone 392 consecutive games without making an error. No other position player has come close to such a streak, and even the record for pitchers, of 385 games, is held by Paul Lindblad, a reliever who was frequently called on to pitch an inning or less. Lewis's miscue was also the first in his major league career, going back to his debut with the Athletics in 1990. The streak was all the more remarkable for the outfielder's aggressiveness and for the unpredictable winds of his home field of Candlestick Park.

DUFFY LEWIS

Lewis's mastery of Fenway Park's hilly left field between 1910 and 1917 inspired decades of sportswriters to refer to the terrain as Duffy's Incline. Considered the defensive equal of longtime fielding companions Tris Speaker and Harry Hooper, Lewis also stroked .284 over eleven big league seasons. His most successful moments at bat came during the 1915 World Series, against the Phillies, when he drove in the deciding runs of the third and fourth games, then belted an 8th-inning home run in the fifth game to tie the score and set up a Boston world championship victory. The right-handed swinger also contributed 6 hits in 17 at-bats to the club's 1916 World Series win over the Dodgers.

Lewis earned another footnote in baseball history when he became the first player to pinch hit for Babe Ruth, in 1914. The outfielder left Boston in December 1918 in one of owner Harry Frazee's desperate deals with the Yankees for quick cash.

TED LEWIS

An ordained minister, Lewis justified jumping from the Boston Braves to the new Red Sox in 1901 by declaring the reserve clause illegal and immoral. The right-hander stayed with his new club only one year, however, quitting baseball entirely at age twenty-nine with a 94–64 record to accept a position teaching English at Columbia University. From 1927 until his death in 1936, he served as president of the University of New Hampshire. His favorite relaxation in Durham was discussing poetry while playing catch with poet Robert Frost in the backyard of the university president's house.

L'IL RASTUS

Rastus epitomized baseball's treatment of blacks early in the century. A teenager discovered sleeping in Bennett Park by Ty Cobb in July 1908, he was adopted by the notoriously racist outfielder as a good-luck charm for the Tigers. While Cobb himself was generally content to have Rastus around for self-confidence, other Detroit players refused even to enter the batter's box without running their hands through the boy's hair. Throughout the summer of the 1908 season, the players conspired in hiding Rastus on trains and under hotel room beds during road trips, convinced as they were that they couldn't win without him. By early September, however, the relationship between the club and its mascot had begun to founder. Aside from the fact that the Tigers started losing even with their good-luck charm on hand, there were charges that Rastus had stolen some equipment from the clubhouse and that he was endangering the ''image'' of the franchise by sneaking out of Cobb's room to parade his prestige before black bellhops. Told to hit the bricks, Rastus immediately offered his services to the Cubs, and was on the Chicago bench when the National Leaguers defeated the Tigers in the World Series. That was enough for Cobb to bring him back to Detroit in 1909, when the Tigers won another pennant. The Georgia Peach eventually brought Rastus home as a servant—an arrangement that lasted only a brief time before the teenager drifted off, never to be heard from again.

JOHNNY LINDELL

Lindell was a hard-drinking pitcher-turned-outfielder-turned-pitcher. The biggest hit of his twelve-year career was an 8th-inning homer on the next-to-last day of the 1949 season to give the Yankees a 5–4 victory, pull the team into a tie for first place, and put them in a position to win the first of Casey Stengel's pennants the next day. The right-handed hitter also batted .500 in the 1947 World Series for New York, but was blasted by owner Larry MacPhail for leaving the sixth game with a cracked rib; the attack, which led manager Bucky Harris to throw MacPhail out of the clubhouse celebration after the team had clinched the world championship, was one of a sequence of events that marked the owner's mental breakdown and departure from the club. Lindell's aggressiveness on the bases also led major league rulemakers to reconsider what was permissible in breaking up a double play after he chased White Sox second baseman Nellie Fox into left field to deliver a bone-crushing block; the play was a major factor in the passage of a 1950 regulation prohibiting bodily contact unless the fielder is in proximity to the base.

Lindell began his career as a hurler; despite a 2–1 record and a 3.76 ERA, he was converted to the outfield. A .273 lifetime hitter, he stayed with the Yankees into the 1950 season, when he was traded to the Cardinals. Released at the end of that year, he went to the Pacific Coast League, where he learned to throw a knuckleball. Accompanied by his personal catcher Mike Sandlock, he returned to the majors to compile a 6–17 record with the Pirates and Phillies in 1953 before concluding his career with a few pinch-hitting appearances the following year.

FREDDIE LINDSTROM (Hall of Fame, 1976)

Lindstrom was one of several Giants in the first decades of the century fated to be associated with a critical mishap; unlike Fred Merkle and Fred Snodgrass, he was the only one completely blameless. It was Lindstrom who, in the final game of the 1924 World Series against Washington, stood helplessly at third base as first Bucky Harris in the 8th inning and then Earl McNeely in the 9th inning hit bouncers that took pebble-aided hops into left field for what added up to a world championship for the Senators. Manager John McGraw and teammates were quick to absolve the third baseman of any responsibility.

From the time he broke into the majors in 1924, when he was only eighteen, the right-hand-hitting Lindstrom showed little awe of the older future Hall of Famers around him. While establishing his own credentials as a career .311 hitter over thirteen seasons, he was usually to be found in the middle of the rifts that beset the club as McGraw's control waned in the late 1920s. On one occasion Lindstrom told fill-in manager Rogers Hornsby that, as a tactician, The Rajah was a great hitter. Lindstrom was so certain of his own managerial skills that he went into a fury when McGraw passed him over as his successor in favor of Bill Terry in 1933; Terry wasted little time dealing him off to Pittsburgh. Although he was only thirty-one at the time, he became so disgusted with a muffed fly ball by a Dodger teammate in 1936 that he announced he couldn't play any longer with clowns, and retired.

Lindstrom's biggest years were for the Giants in 1928, when he averaged .358 with a league-leading 231 hits, and 1930, when he batted .379 with the same number of safeties.

PHIL LINZ

Linz's chief claim to fame was that he once tried to play "Mary Had a Little Lamb" on a harmonica. His foray into music occurred on the Yankee team bus on August 20, 1964, just after New York had lost a doubleheader to the White Sox. When an enraged manager Yogi Berra ordered Linz to "shove that thing up your ass," the infielder flipped the instrument in the general direction of the pilot, succeeding only in hitting teammate Joe Pepitone. For reasons never clear to the immediate participants, the incident was blown up as a turning point for New York's successful pennant drive. Most of the press took its cue from the team's rather prissy coach Frank Crosetti, who allowed as how the incident was the worst he had ever witnessed as a Yankee.

JOHN HENRY LLOYD (Hall of Fame, 1977)

Called the greatest player of all time by Babe Ruth, Lloyd was an itinerant shortstop in the Negro leagues who reminded more than one ob-

server of Honus Wagner, not least for the way both scooped glovesful of infield dirt with each ground ball. For his part, Wagner once stated that he "felt honored that they would name such a great player after me."

Lloyd played for twelve teams in a twenty-seven-year career that began in 1905, because, as he put it, "Where the money was, that's where I played." The lefty line-drive hitter averaged in the .360s, topping .400 in several seasons. He also spent twelve winters playing in Cuba. It was there, in 1910, that he had an encounter with the racist Ty Cobb, who was barnstorming with the Tigers. Outhitting the American League batting champion .500 (in 12 games) to .369 (in only 5 of the contests), the shortstop also nailed Cobb in three consecutive attempts at stealing second. Lloyd's answer to Cobb's spikes-high slides— metal shin guards worn under his socks—caught the American League baserunning champion totally by surprise. In his later years, Lloyd moved to first base, picked up the nickname Pop, and piloted several of the teams for which he played.

Ruth's assessment came in an interview with Graham McNamee, after specifically inquiring whether the broadcaster wanted him to restrict himself to the major leagues in answering a question about the identity of the best player in baseball.

WHITEY LOCKMAN

Lockman had the second biggest hit in the history of the New York Giants when his one-out double in the bottom of the ninth inning of the third playoff game in 1951 drove Brooklyn's Don Newcombe from the mound. It was because of the lefty-swinging first baseman's hit that Ralph Branca was called in to face Bobby Thomson. Following a fifteen-year career spent mainly with the Giants, Lockman replaced Leo Durocher as manager of the Cubs for a couple of seasons in the early 1970s. Lockman's most significant moment in that role came on May 8, 1973, when he was kicked out of a game and turned the reins over to Ernie Banks; it was the first recorded instance of a black managing even temporarily in the big leagues.

BILLY LOES

Although good enough to be a member of the starting rotation for several years for the Boys of Summer Dodgers, Loes gained more notoriety for a steady stream of quotes that marked him as one of the era's eccentrics. Asked prior to the 1952 World Series between Brooklyn and New York who would win, the right-hander said unhesitatingly that it would be the Yankees. In the same Series, he justified his bobble of a crucial ground ball by saying that he had lost it in the sun. Questioned on another occasion about why, despite all his talent, he never seemed to be able to win more than 14 games, he shrugged and said, "If you win 20, they expect you to do it every year." Loes is also the answer to the trivia question about the identity of the only major leaguer who was on the field when four different players accomplished the rare feat of hitting 4 home runs in a game. He was a member of the Dodgers when Brooklyn's Gil Hodges did it in 1950 and Milwaukee's Joe Adcock in 1954, of the Orioles when Cleveland's Rocky Colavito did it in 1959, and of the Giants when teammate Willie Mays did it in 1961.

TOM LOFTUS

Loftus is the only man to have managed teams in four major leagues. His career included stops in the Union Association (1884) with Milwaukee; the American Association (1888) with Cleveland; the National League (1889–91, 1900–01) with Cleveland, Cincinnati, and Chicago; and the American League (1902–03) with Washington.

JACK LOHRKE

A modest infield reserve, Lohrke was considered a good-luck presence by many of his Giants teammates in the 1940s and early 1950s. He had in fact picked up the nickname Lucky during World War II after arriving late for the flight of an army transport plane that crashed. As a minor leaguer in 1946 with a club in Spokane, he was pulled off a team bus with the news that he had been called up to the Pacific Coast League. The bus went on without him; a few miles later, it, too, crashed, killing nine members of the team.

MICKEY LOLICH

Lolich won 217 games in his sixteen-year career, but none of them was more important than the 3 victories he fashioned for the Tigers in the 1968 World Series against the Cardinals. Aside from giving his club the world championship, the wins defused angry racial tensions in Detroit that had been building since the assassination of Martin Luther King, Jr., earlier in the year. Despite notching 47 victories over the 1971 and 1972 seasons, the southpaw never won a Cy Young trophy.

ERNIE LOMBARDI (Hall of Fame, 1986)

Although he won two batting titles and averaged .306 in seventeen seasons for the Dodgers, Reds, Braves, and Giants, Lombardi's most impressive number might have been his 8 career steals. The right-hand-hitting catcher was so slow that opposition third basemen and shortstops regularly played on the outfield grass with little anxiety about being able to get him at first on a bunt or a topper. By the same token, his ten seasons of .300 or better were all the more creditable for including few cheap hits, since the defensive alignment against him also cut down on loopers over the infield.

Lombardi and Babe Herman were traded by the Dodgers to the Reds in 1932—one of the best swaps in Cincinnati history. After winning a batting crown in 1938 and helping the Reds to pennants in 1939 and 1940, Lombardi was traded to Boston in 1942 and promptly won his second hitting title. That production helped make him the biggest name affected by the salary cap that was in force in the major leagues during World War II. Because Boston could not pay him a raise that the organization itself admitted he was due, he was traded to the Giants, whose overall budget permitted the pay boost. (Under the war regulations, a player could not receive less than the lowest nor more than the highest salary paid by his team in 1942.)

DALE LONG

In May 1956, Long clouted home runs in 8 consecutive games. The record feat by the Pittsburgh first baseman was later tied by Don Mattingly of the Yankees and by Ken Griffey, Jr., of the Mariners.

HERMAN LONG

An acrobatic shortstop with five National League pennant-winning Boston teams in the 1890s, Long made 1,037 errors in his sixteen-year career, the most miscues by any major leaguer.

AL LOPEZ (Hall of Fame, 1977)

Lopez had most of the longevity records for catchers before the coming of Bob Boone and Carlton Fisk. A nineteen-year (1928, 1930–47) major leaguer for Brooklyn, Boston, Pittsburgh, and Cleveland, he was a defensive whiz with an unimposing bat (.261 lifetime). More than one manager cited him as a voice of sanity in the midst of dreary second-division seasons; in fact, only with the 1944 Pirates did Lopez play on a club that reached even second place. He turned his bench conversations to good purpose during his own managerial career, ending up with a .581 mark in seventeen years of piloting the Indians and White Sox in the 1950s and 1960s. In contrast to his playing days, he managed clubs to first- or second-place finishes twelve times. By guiding the Indians to a pennant in 1954 and the White Sox to a flag in 1959, Lopez interrupted what might otherwise have been sixteen consecutive American League championships for the Yankees.

TOM LOVETT

Lovett became baseball's first season-long holdout in 1892, when he refused to accept a salary cut from Brooklyn. The right-hander, who had won 53 games over the previous two seasons, took his stand in response to a National League-wide attack on player salaries after the dissolution of the Players League and the American Association. Lovett returned to the Dodgers in 1893 but could manage only an 11–11 record, for Brooklyn and Boston, over the next two seasons before retiring.

BILL LUCAS

Lucas was the first black to have a meaningful front-office position. As an employee of the Braves in the 1960s and 1970s, he worked his way up from farm director to director of player personnel and then acting general manager. At age forty-three, however, he died of a brain hemorrhage. Lucas was Hank Aaron's brother-in-law.

RED LUCAS

Lucas is the best pinch-hitting pitcher of all time. Although his total of 114 hits as a substitute batter has been surpassed by five players, none has been a pitcher; in addition, the lefty swinger held the record for almost thirty years, until Smokey Burgess passed him in 1965. As a hurler, Lucas fashioned a 157–135 record in a fifteen-year career with the Reds, Pirates, and other clubs in the 1920s and 1930s.

WILLIAM V. LUCAS

As the chief backer of the Union Association in 1884, Lucas threatened the monopoly of the National League and the American Association. His league, founded on a fuzzy combination of sound business sense and principled objection to the reserve clause and blacklisting, began by refusing to ask players to violate their contracts but soon evolved into an all-out war to get players to jump from the established circuits. With the enterprise doomed from the beginning by an inability to attract the best players and to keep franchises from dissolving, Lucas hastened its destruction by spending most of the available money on his own St. Louis Maroons and by such Louis XIV-like declarations as "I am the Union Association. Whatever I do is all right." The Maroons ran roughshod over the rest of the UA, winning the pennant by 21 games and putting together the highest won–lost percentage (.832) in major league history.

The UA ended after one year, with Lucas accepting a berth in the NL in 1885 and publicly embracing the reserve rule. Lucas himself was jobbed by both the Cleveland Blues, who sold him their franchise without turning over any players, and St. Louis Browns owner Chris Von der Ahe, who received reparations both for the damage he had suffered in the UA war and for allowing his territorial rights to be compromised. Von der Ahe proceeded to drive Lucas out of business in St. Louis by winning four consecutive AA pennants.

RON LUCIANO

Umpire Luciano was the most ostentatious example of a new breed of arbiters in the 1970s who seemed more interested in drawing attention to themselves than in perpetuating the traditional anonymity. His trademark gestures in calling an out—pumping his arm more times than many observers thought necessary, and making a shooting gesture with his fingers—so irritated Frank Robinson, among others, that in 1975 the Indians manager fined players for talking to him on the field. Luciano's chief nemesis was Orioles pilot Earl Weaver; their mutual disdain and reciprocal showboating, dating to their days in the International League (Luciano once ran Weaver out of 4 consecutive minor league games), reached a point where the American League office would not let Luciano work Baltimore games. Retiring after the 1980 season after thirteen years with the AL, Luciano parlayed his notoriety into new careers as the author of three books and a color commentator on NBC's *Game of the Week.*

CHARLEY LUPICA

There have been fanatical baseball fans, and then there was Lupica. On May 31, 1949, the Cleveland druggist climbed up to a platform atop a twenty-foot flagpole and announced that he intended staying there until the Indians, then mired in seventh place, repeated their 1948 world championship. After some initial efforts at getting him down, Cleveland police decided that Lupica was harmless, and Indians' owner Bill Veeck decided that he was the best advertisement the team could possibly have. The druggist remained on his flagpole perch 117 days, coming down only on September 25, when Veeck persuaded him that Cleveland's rise to the first division in fourth place was as good as it was going to get. The owner later presented Lupica with a new car in gratitude for the publicity he had generated around the country for the team.

TONY LUPIEN

Lupien challenged his trade to the minor leagues by the Phillies after World War II on the grounds that it violated the National Defense Act covering the reintegration of veterans into their jobs. Economic necessity forced him to settle out of court. The left-handed first baseman later signed with the White Sox for the final one of his six big league seasons.

THOMAS J. LYNCH

Former umpire Lynch became National League president in 1910 as a compromise candidate brought in to break a voting deadlock among NL owners. He was sponsored by Giants owner John T. Brush on the grounds that, as a former umpire, he was best qualified to perform the primary function of a league chief executive—the supervision of umpires. In fact, Lynch did far more than back up umpires with fines and suspensions of players and managers for various transgressions. Humorless and tactless, he irritated owners with his behavior, especially in levying a $500 penalty on Brooklyn boss Charlie Ebbets for hiding a player in the minor leagues. After his 1913 decision to ban Phillies' president Horace Fogel for claiming that umpires and Cardinals manager Roger Bresnahan had favored the Giants in the 1912 pennant race, Lynch was able to hang on for only one more year before he was fired in favor of Pennsylvania governor John Tener. What irked the outgoing president as much as his ouster were the facts that his successor would be making $25,000 to his $9,000 and that an official announcement of the change predicted that Tener would add "dignity and prestige to the office." Lynch's parting shot at his former employers was the hope that they might "inject some of that same dignity expected of him into yourselves."

FRED LYNN

Two protracted contract squabbles and a trade thwarted predictions that Lynn would put together a Hall of Fame career. The lefty-swinging outfielder certainly got more of a start on diamond glory than anybody else when, arriving in Boston in 1975, he became the first major leaguer to win Rookie of the Year and MVP honors in the same season. Four years later he won the batting title by averaging .333 while clouting 39 home runs and driving in 122 runs. In 1976, however, Lynn was one of three Red Sox players whose contract demands produced a Boston soap opera that ultimately prompted the removal of general manager Dick O'Connell. Although signed on that occasion, he was back in the same situation with the expiration of his pact in 1980, with more front-office confusion about mailing him his contract on time putting him in an advantageous position for approving any contemplated deals. When he finally okayed a trade to the Angels, he left behind a career average of .350 in Fenway Park and headed into another ten seasons in which, through a combination of different surroundings and nagging injuries, he would never again attain .300.

In 1988, Lynn triggered a change in waiver rules when he was obtained by the Tigers from the Orioles on the evening of August 31. Because he was unable to reach the city where his new team was playing before the stroke of midnight, he was declared ineligible for any postseason play for which Detroit might qualify. The publicity over the incident—and especially over Detroit owner Tom Monaghan's honesty in admitting that the outfielder had been unable to join his new teammates until the calendar had been turned to September—pressured the major leagues into eliminating the Cinderella waiver condition.

Lynn is the only player to have hit a grand-slam home run in an All-Star Game: He tagged San Francisco southpaw Atlee Hammaker in the 1983 contest.

BILL LYONS

Lyons was signed to a baseball contract for his singing voice. In the years immediately prior to World War I, pitcher Marty McHale assembled a foursome of Boston players, known as the Red Sox Quartette, that toured the vaudeville circuit in the off-season. When third baseman Larry Gardner decided show business wasn't for him, however, Lyons was drafted as a replacement. Because the team considered the group good publicity in its market war with the Braves, the Red Sox gave Lyons a formal player contract so no-body would question the legitimacy of the group's name. Aside from Lyons and McHale (dubbed by contemporaries The Baseball Caruso), the group included first baseman Hugh Bradley and pitcher Buck O'Brien.

TED LYONS (Hall of Fame, 1955)

Like Red Faber, Lyons followed up some dominating years with the White Sox with far too many seasons of mediocre or worse pitching for the franchise; unlike Faber, he came up with a solution near the end of his career that gave him a second wind. The right-hander joined Chicago in 1923 amid owner Charlie Comiskey's frantic attempts to put together another rotation after the Black Sox scandal. In both 1925 and 1927, Lyons paced the American League with 20-win seasons, then reached the mark again in 1930. For the rest of that decade, however, Lyons lost more than he won, and with earned-run averages that suggested it wasn't just the fault of the wretched clubs behind him. Then, in 1939, at the suggestion of manager Jimmy Dykes, he limited himself to pitching on Sundays, and turned in four straight seasons of winning ball, topping it off with the ERA crown in 1942. The experiment was successful not only artistically, but financially as well, with ''Sunday with Lyons'' proving to be one of Chicago's few gate attractions in the period. He closed out his active playing career with a few appearances in 1946, toting up a record of 260–230; thanks to his weekly regimen, his ERA of 3.67, already one of the highest in the Hall of Fame, wasn't still higher. As Lyons himself was forever telling sportswriters, he would have preferred to take off his uniform then and there, but Dykes's abrupt resignation after a contract squabble in 1946 led him to accept the managership of the club for a rather uninspired two and a half years.

M

CONNIE MACK (Hall of Fame, 1937)

No other individual has been so closely identified with one twentieth-century franchise as Mack was with the Philadelphia Athletics in their fifty-four years of very high peaks and very low valleys. Through a half century as manager and the entire lifetime of the team as at least part owner, he won nine pennants, but also finished dead last seventeen times as pilot, and eighteen overall. A key organizer of the AL in 1901, Mack outlasted all of his contemporaries. By the time he left the dugout after the 1950 season, just before his eighty-ninth birthday, he had become the venerable Grand Old Man of Baseball to some; to others, including members of his own family, he was little more than a senile object of derision.

A respectable catcher with Washington and Pittsburgh in the National League and Buffalo of the Players' League, Mack (born Cornelius McGillicuddy) averaged .245 between 1886 and 1896; his career as a first-string catcher ended in a home-plate collision with Boston's Herman Long in 1893. Appointed manager of the Pirates toward the end of the 1894 season, he soon developed his trick of freezing baseballs to deaden them for use when the opposition was at the plate; it was also in Pittsburgh, in 1895, that he was thrown out of a game for the only time in his sixty-one years as a major league player and pilot.

Following his dismissal in 1896, Mack threw his lot in with Ban Johnson's minor Western League, taking over its Milwaukee club in 1897. This left him well positioned when Johnson decided to challenge the NL in 1901. With the back-

ing of Ben Shibe, a partner in the A. J. Reach Sporting Goods company and a major stockholder in the rival Phillies, he created the Philadelphia franchise of the newly major AL in 1901; built its first ballpark, Columbia Park; and picked up a team logo, the white elephant, when John McGraw predicted that's what the Athletics would be. His biggest coup in the early going was signing future Hall of Famer Nap Lajoie away from the Phillies, but this was undone after only one season by a legal battle that necessitated the trade of the second baseman to Cleveland to get him out of the jurisdiction of Pennsylvania's courts. Despite the loss, Mack won the first of his nine pennants in 1902, following it up with another in 1905.

Early on, Mack showed a preference for college players, eventually discovering and developing dozens of them; in contrast, he rarely made trades involving front-line players, and when he did, they were almost always disasters. In different eras, he gave up Joe Jackson to the Indians for Bris Lord, Charlie Jamieson to the same club for Braggo Roth, George Kell to the Tigers for Barney McCoskey, and Nellie Fox to the White Sox for Joe Tipton.

After opening Shibe Park, the first steel and concrete stadium, in 1909, Mack won four pennants and three world championships between 1910 and 1914 with a team that featured the $100,000 Infield (Stuffy McInnis, Eddie Collins, Jack Barry, and Frank Baker). But he broke up the A's first dynasty for a combination of reasons: complacent players with large salary demands, indifferent fans, a stunning upset loss to the Miracle Braves in the 1914 World Series, and big-money overtures by the Federal League to some of the Philadelphia stars. It was at about this time that the manager (and, since 1913, half owner) developed his pet theory that a close second-place finish was better for business than a runaway pennant, because it kept patrons pouring through the turnstiles without drastically increasing salaries. After selling off his best players, Mack finished last every year from 1915 to 1921; the 1916 entry, which won only 36 games, was one of the worst teams of the twentieth century. During these lean years, Mack, sometimes known in the press as The Tall Tactician, became The Slim Schemer for his manipulations to keep Scott Perry despite a National Commission ruling that the pitcher belonged to the Braves, and for his role in the owner collusion to release every player in the majors rather than pay them for the final few weeks of the 1918 war-shortened season.

Rebuilding in the 1920s, Mack assembled a second dynasty, which brought him two world championships, in 1929 and 1930, and a final pennant in 1931. This time, the Depression did him

A wiggle of his scorecard was usually the extent of Connie Mack's expressivity while managing the Ahtletics. National Baseball Library, Cooperstown, N.Y.

in. When the bank that had been providing financing for the club called in a $400,000 note, he began selling off players once again. Future Hall of Famers Al Simmons, Mickey Cochrane, Lefty Grove, and Jimmie Foxx, among others, went to pay off the debt, and the club went back to the basement, this time landing last nine times and seventh twice between 1935 and 1946.

In 1946, a rapidly aging Mack made an eventually catastrophic miscalculation. Like King Lear prematurely dividing his kingdom, he gave each of his three sons 10 percent of the club. The most immediate problem this caused was that his second wife went into a public furor because her son, Connie, Jr., got only half of what the two sons from Mack's first marriage received, with the couple even separating for a time over the perceived injustice. Trying to rebuild again after World War II, he relied heavily on coaches Simmons and Earle Brucker. The manager was almost totally deaf and often napping on the bench; his mind would often wander, and he would call on sluggers long retired to get up and pinch hit. As often as not, players began to refer to him as The Old Man—but without the respect that had once been attached to the familiarity. The team's relative success in 1947—a fifth-place finish and the first record on the plus side of .500 since 1933—offered encouragement. But the following year, Mack vented his frustration over the lack of continued improvement by, among other things, publicly berating thirty-seven-year-old pitcher Nelson Potter and releasing him on the spot after the reliever blew a game in the ninth inning.

After the 1949 season, trouble erupted in the boardroom, which, in the Athletics' case, meant the family room. In October, Connie, Jr., and Shibe heirs Ben and Frank Macfarland engineered the release of coaches Simmons and Brucker in favor of former players Cochrane and Jimmy Dykes. The following May, the three completed their coup by moving eldest son Earle out as assistant manager, a position he had held since the late 1930s and from which he and everyone else assumed he would succeed his father. Dykes was inserted as assistant manager, with Cochrane becoming the club's first general manager. The victory proved only temporary, however, when Earle and his brother Roy bought out Connie, Jr., the

Macfarlands, and several other Shibe heirs in August and assumed control of almost 80 percent of the club's stock.

Mack retired on October 18, 1950. Publicly, the elder sons had maintained that their father could stay on as long as he chose; privately, they had applied pressure on him to step down. For the next four years, Mack remained a minority stockholder in the franchise he had created and played only a supporting role in the comic opera that followed the 1954 season as Earle and Roy tried to sell the franchise, accepting and then rejecting offers from various groups and, in the process, feuding over who should get the prize. In fact, the only offer of substance came from Chicago vending machine and real-estate magnate Arnold Johnson, who made no effort to disguise his intention of moving the club to Kansas City. Mack's penultimate involvement in club affairs was a sentimental plea before an AL meeting in October that other owners sanction an offer from a Philadelphia-based group that lacked the backing to complete the deal and reject Johnson's; in fact, he himself had already agreed to the Johnson proposal, and the rejection would have landed him in a major legal wrangle. The final act took place in November, in Mack's Germantown home, where Johnson presented the ailing nonagenarian with a check for $604,000 in exchange for his 302 shares in the club. The exchange was consummated with a handshake.

Mack holds the records for both most victories (3,731) and most losses (3,948) by a major league manager.

EARLE MACK

Mack was the first major leaguer to have his father (Connie) as a manager. As a member of the Philadelphia Athletics, he appeared in 5 games over three seasons (1910, 1911, and 1914) as a catcher, first baseman, and third baseman, collecting 2 hits in 16 at-bats. He later served as his father's longtime assistant manager, and actually ran the A's during Connie's extended illnesses in 1937 and 1939. Although long projected as the eventual manager of the team, Earle was deposed from his position by half brother Connie, Jr., and other stockholders in 1950, precipitating years of family and organizational strife that

didn't end until the team was sold to Arnold Johnson and moved to Kansas City following the 1954 season.

REDDY MACK

An otherwise forgotten second baseman, Mack illustrated a gaping hole in baseball's rules when, after scoring a run in a July 9, 1887, American Association game, he hung around home plate to nudge Brooklyn catcher Bob Clark, preventing him from making a play on two additional Louisville runners, who scored the apparent tying and winning runs. Umpire Wesley Curry disallowed both runs, however, even though there was no rule allowing for interference by anyone but a base runner, which Mack had ceased to be as soon as he crossed the plate. The rule book did not address this problem until 1904.

LARRY MACPHAIL (Hall of Fame, 1978)

With one glaring exception, MacPhail was the main driving force behind baseball's most significant innovations in the 1930s and 1940s. As general manager of the Reds, chief operating officer of the Dodgers, and part owner and general manager of the Yankees, he introduced night baseball to the major leagues, secured the first contract for continuous radio coverage of games, pioneered television coverage, and devised such popular fan promotions as Old Timers' Day. In addition, he was the first executive to fly his team regularly from city to city, the first to stress corporate seat purchases and season ticket plans as marketing devices, the first to build a stadium club for patrons who wanted more than hot dogs, and the first to hire women as ushers. But for all his accomplishments, MacPhail was also a ferocious opponent of baseball's single most important midcentury innovation: racial integration. This plus his general bluster, hot temper, and penchant for one cocktail too many created enough enemies to hold up his election to the Hall of Fame until thirty years after he had retired from the game and three years after he had died.

MacPhail was already approaching his fortieth birthday and was an automobile dealer when Branch Rickey, a law school classmate from the University of Michigan, asked him to help turn around St. Louis's financially troubled farm team in Columbus. MacPhail did it so well that he had Columbus outdrawing St. Louis in 1932; he did it so arrogantly, refusing to send Rickey second baseman Burgess Whitehead unless the Cardinals compensated him with five players, that he was tossed out on his ear at the end of the 1933 season. Only months later, however, Rickey recommended him for the general manager's position with Cincinnati. One of MacPhail's first maneuvers in arriving in the major leagues was to persuade Powel Crosley to buy into the franchise so he would have the capital necessary for drastically overhauling an organization that had gone to seed.

Under MacPhail, night baseball came to Cincinnati, and to the major leagues, on May 24, 1935. The main reason that other owners overcame their skepticism about the innovation was that they hadn't been making much money on their road trips to the city in any case. MacPhail being MacPhail, he wasn't content just to advertise the contest against Philadelphia and then nod to some technician at the appointed hour to switch on the lights. To begin with, there were military bands and fireworks displays, the latter culminating in configurations of the American flag and an enormous "C" with "REDS" in the middle. Then there was an elaborate presentation of special guests, who included George Cahill, an inventor who had staged a demonstration of the possibilities of night baseball as far back as 1909, and George Wright, the last surviving member of the fabled Cincinnati Red Stockings. Finally, a signal went to Washington, D.C., where President Franklin Delano Roosevelt gave to the go-ahead to MacPhail to light up the stadium by turning a key in a special switch installed in the White House. The Reds put the finishing touches on the evening by defeating Philadelphia, 2–1, before 20,422 spectators.

It was also MacPhail who introduced night baseball to New York City—first with the Dodgers on June 15, 1938, then with the Yankees on May 28, 1946. As in Cincinnati, he made sure that Brooklyn's encounter with history occurred with as much fanfare as possible, hiring Olympic star Jesse Owens to race several Dodgers around Ebbets Field before the game. Unlike Cincinnati, the Brooklyn game also improvised its own history when Reds southpaw Johnny Vander Meer

used the occasion to hurl his second consecutive no-hitter, a headline-making feat that did more than Roosevelt had done in 1935 to make the country aware of the novelty of night baseball.

There was one ironic note to the innovation: Although he had lobbied relentlessly for night ball, MacPhail had been dissatisfied with the scanty seven games other NL owners had agreed to commit to the experiment in 1935. Because he didn't consider these enough to cover lighting expenses, he was the only member of the Cincinnati board to vote *against* his own proposal.

Next to night games, MacPhail's biggest impact on baseball stemmed from his perception that the broadcast media could help rather than hinder stadium attendance. His vital ally in this belief was announcer Red Barber, whose radio play-by-play introduced the game to millions of people in the Ohio area, then later in New York. Subsequently, MacPhail and Barber were also involved in the first baseball telecast.

The profits from his innovations notwithstanding, MacPhail never endeared himself to boardrooms. One problem was his tactic of insisting that revenues be put right back into a team rather than divided among shareholders, while he himself enjoyed an appreciable salary and attendance bonus; another was his tendency to pursue this stratagem with bluster and fists. It was, in fact, following a punch-up with Crosley during a September 1936 meeting that MacPhail left Cincinnati. Landing with the Dodgers in 1938, he more or less followed the script he had followed in Cincinnati—the night game innovation, bringing in Barber, overhauling the ballpark right down to the ushers' uniforms, and completing a series of major trades aimed at returning the club to a contender's status. Just as the Reds players he had left behind in Cincinnati brought that franchise its first pennant in twenty years, in 1939, the Dodgers got into the World Series for the first time in more than two decades in 1941.

Once again, however, MacPhail's road to success was littered with bodies. He angered the Giants and Yankees by unilaterally breaking an agreement not to broadcast any games in the city for at least five years. He held Babe Ruth up to public ridicule by hiring him behind some vague promise that the slugger might one day be appointed manager, while being interested only in the Bambino's draw as a batting-practice performer. His love-hate relationship with Rickey was all love when he took on Branch Rickey, Jr., as the Brooklyn farm director and all hate when the younger Rickey began complaining to his father that it was a title without a meaningful job; all love when he purchased slugger Joe Medwick from Rickey's Cardinals; and all hate when the outfielder was beaned in the very first meeting between the clubs; all love when he consented to ''hide'' Cardinal free agent Pete Reiser in the Dodger farm system for a couple of years; and all hate when he decided that Reiser was needed in Ebbets Field. With the Brooklyn owners, it was the familiar story of gratitude that the franchise had paid off its debts and *seemed* to be registering a profit, but wonder at why every penny of the profits had to be channeled back into operating the team. Most of all, however, MacPhail's tenure with the Dodgers was marked by his volcanic relationship with Leo Durocher.

By Durocher's own estimate, he was fired as Brooklyn manager by MacPhail twenty-seven times between 1939 and 1942, almost always as the end of a shouting match liberally fueled by after-hours alcohol. On the final day of the 1939 season, for instance, the executive lauded his pilot before a packed Ebbets Field for having brought the Dodgers back to the first division, then after the game told him he was gone for having started a rookie pitcher who had almost cost the team a third-place finish. Following Brooklyn's pennant win in 1941, MacPhail and Rickey rushed up to 125th Street to climb aboard the team train for a gala welcoming at Grand Central Station, unaware that Durocher had arranged for the team to bypass the station lest some of the players get off and wander into Harlem saloons; he told Durocher he was through in the middle of the victory party. Again, after that year's World Series loss to the Yankees, MacPhail sank low enough into his cups not only to fire his manager but also to propose a roster-for-roster swap with the St. Louis Browns. Apropos of such incidents (which always ended with MacPhail sobering up and forgetting the firings), Durocher once said of his employer: ''There is no question in my mind that Larry was a genius. There is a line between genius and in-

sanity, and in Larry's case it was sometimes so thin that you could see him drifting back and forth.''

Between them, MacPhail and Durocher infused a swagger in Dodger players that made the club the most hated in the league. In one 1942 game, the Cubs knocked down 15 consecutive Brooklyn hitters. But after the team had blown a 10½-game lead to the Cardinals that season, raising the temperature of stockholders already aggrieved that they weren't receiving dividend payments, MacPhail resigned to enter the military. When he re-emerged in January 1945, it was as part owner of the Yankees.

Although he continued his flamboyant promotions (such as Nylons Day, for attracting women) in the Bronx, MacPhail also laid great emphasis on attracting a corporate clientele through such measures as setting aside more season tickets and opening a stadium club for businessmen and their guests; it was, in fact, under the veteran showman's ownership that the Yankees paradoxically gained their image as something of a bloodless General Motors of the sport. In 1946, the installation of lights in Yankee Stadium helped the franchise break the 2-million mark in attendance for the first time in baseball history. MacPhail's manner, however, continued to make enemies. Joe McCarthy and Bill Dickey both quit on him as managers. Joe DiMaggio and Charlie Keller were fined unfairly for not attending a team promotion. While MacPhail bragged about making the Yankees the first team to travel by air, the players protested his use of a rickety C-54 military transport that narrowly missed crashing a couple of times, forcing DiMaggio and manager Bucky Harris to step in at one point to head off a player insurrection. More trouble beckoned in 1947, when the owner got entangled in a mare's nest of charges about gambling associations and the poaching of coaches under contract to other teams—a scandal that also involved Durocher, Rickey, and Charlie Dressen and that ended up costing MacPhail a fine.

By the middle of the 1947 season, MacPhail was approaching a nervous breakdown even as New York was charging toward a world championship. He played out his last scene as a baseball executive at the club victory party, where he took a swing at both co-owner Dan Topping and general manager George Weiss. The next day, MacPhail sold his interest to Topping and Del Webb.

MacPhail's hostility to the desegregation of baseball was made up of one part racism, one part resentment that old foe Rickey had brought Jackie Robinson to the major leagues, and many parts financial calculations. To begin with, there was his corporate clientele marketing and a paucity of black executives to make the two compatible. Second, there were the extra dollars he had been making by arranging and promoting off-season all-star games between major leaguers and stars from the Negro leagues. Third, there was his stated fear that black ballplayers equaled black fans equaled depreciated franchises. Fourth, there was his pursuit of radio (and eventually television) advertising money and his apprehension that Madison Avenue would not be eager to go after a racially mixed demographic audience. It was also to gall him no little that the final nod to Robinson's arrival came from Happy Chandler, the commissioner whom MacPhail had pressed on the other owners soon after taking over the Yankees. As in the case of the first night game in Cincinnati, the executive whom Bill Veeck called ''the brightest, most imaginative guy in our business'' had ended up regretting his own inspiration.

LEE MACPHAIL

The son of Larry MacPhail, Lee was known as ''the man who says nothing'' by both admirers and critics. Brought into the Yankee organization when his father owned the team in the 1940s, Lee worked his way up to farm director, then moved around as general manager of the Orioles; special assistant to Commissioner William Eckert; general manager of the Yankees; and finally, in 1974, president of the American League for a decade. It was especially in this last post that his compliant behavior toward AL owners during confrontations with players over free agency and arbitration confirmed for many his talent for saying nothing. When his son, Minnesota general manager Andy MacPhail, helped guide the Twins to a championship in 1987, Lee showed little reluctance about admitting, ''I have been in the game for forty-two years and never won anything.''

GARRY MADDOX

Maddox was such a deft center fielder for the Giants and Phillies in the 1970s and 1980s that he inspired one of the game's most memorable quotes; as Mets broadcaster Ralph Kiner put it, ''Two thirds of the world is covered by water, the other one third by Garry Maddox.'' Despite that reputation, it was Maddox's error in the ninth inning of the fourth game of the 1978 National League Championship Series that gave Los Angeles a pennant over the Phillies. Because of a severe rash he picked up while fighting in Vietnam, Maddox was allowed to wear a beard even when team policies prohibited facial hair.

GREG MADDUX

Baseball's dominant pitcher over the first half of the 1990s, Maddux is also the only hurler to win the Cy Young Award in three consecutive seasons. The righthander picked up the trophies for the Cubs in 1992 and for the Braves in 1993 and 1994. Although he won 20 games in both 1992 and 1993, Maddux was even more overpowering in the strike-shortened 1994 campaign with his 16–6 record. His 1.56 ERA was more than two-and-a-half runs below the National League average—the greatest differential in major league history. He set another ERA record spread by finishing 1.09 runs per nine innings ahead of the major league runnerup, Steve Ontiveros of Oakland. Maddux joined Atlanta in 1993 after Chicago had dangled a take-it-or-leave-it free agent offer in front of him during the 1992 season.

BILL MADLOCK

Madlock won four batting titles during his fifteen-year (1973–87) career, but he was equally noteworthy as a crucial hired gun in the division wins of two teams and the world championship of a third. A right-handed spray hitter, the third baseman won his first two Silver Bats as a member of the Cubs in 1975 and 1976. The other two came with the Pirates in 1981 and 1983. All told, he turned in nine years of .300 or better for a career mark of .305.

Madlock's first significant contribution to a winning club came in 1979, when he was obtained by the Pirates from the Giants at the end of June; the transaction, which involved several players who had officially cleared waivers, just about put an end to the transparently artificial June 15 trading deadline that had been in effect for a half century. With Pittsburgh, Madlock averaged .328 for the rest of the year, following that up with a .375 mark in the team's victorious World Series with Baltimore. In 1985 he was obtained by the Dodgers from the Pirates under similar circumstances, proceeding to bat .360 over the final part of the regular season and to whack 3 homers and drive in 7 runs in the National League Championship Series against the Cardinals. Again, in 1987, he was looked upon as division victory insurance—going from the Dodgers to the Tigers, for whom he clouted 14 home runs and drove in 50 runs in little more than 300 at-bats as Detroit's designated hitter.

Madlock's departures were not always regretted by his managers. In Pittsburgh, his open criticisms of the organization, and of Chuck Tanner in particular, were portrayed by front-office flacks as ''poisonous'' to the club's younger players. In Los Angeles he didn't win many points from Tom Lasorda for suggesting more than once that not every member of the team was as committed to bleeding Dodger blue as the manager claimed.

LEE MAGEE

Magee became Hal Chase's Cincinnati teammate in 1918; soon afterward, Magee also became the crooked first baseman's accomplice, although not a very smart—or lucky—one. The outfielder-turned-second baseman, who had bounced around with five teams since 1911, approached a Boston gambler with Chase for a scheme to throw the first game of a July 25 doubleheader against the Braves. Each player put up a $500 check and accepted a promise of one-third of the gambler's winnings when Cincinnati lost. In the event, the Reds won the game, 4–2, with Magee scoring the winning run in the 13th inning after reaching base on a bad-hop grounder that broke Boston shortstop Johnny Rawlings's nose; in the aftermath, Magee foolishly stopped payment on his check, while Chase wisely let his clear. Magee's check eventually ended up in National League president John Heydler's hands as the chief evidence against him.

Magee inked a two-year deal with the Cubs the following year, only to be released after one season for being linked to Chase in unpublicized hearings before Heydler. The events became public only when Magee sued for the money owed him for 1920. He suffered further embarrassment when his claim—that his intent had been to bet on the Reds and that Chase had double-crossed him—didn't wash. The episode was the first public exposure of dishonesty on a major league field since the Louisville Four scandal of 1877.

SHERRY MAGEE

Outfielder Magee's long outs with men on third base were the reason Phillies' manager Ray Murray championed passage of the sacrifice fly rule in 1908. Since then, the rule abating an official at-bat when a run scores on a fly out has been reversed and reinstated several times.

GEORGE MAGERKURTH

Magerkurth had the shortest fuse of any umpire in major league history. In the very first game of his nineteen-year (1929–47) National League career, he tossed veteran Giants manager John McGraw. But it was Magerkurth's encounters a decade and more later with the Dodgers, and especially with manager Leo Durocher, that sealed his reputation. Relations between Magerkurth and the Brooklyn club became so bad that the parade celebrating the team's 1941 pennant included a coffin labeled ''Magerkurth.'' He once fined Durocher $50 for spraying him in the face with saliva, only to find at home plate the next day a bag filled with five thousand pennies collected by fans. On another occasion, a Dodger fan jumped out of the Ebbets Field stands to pummel him.

Magerkurth's most famous fight, however, was with Giants shortstop Billy Jurges, in 1939, during a dispute over whether a shot into the seats had been fair or foul. While neither of them had anything to do with the play, the umpire flattened the shortstop with one punch after Jurges spat in his face. The results of the ensuing melee included fines for both combatants and a ten-day suspension for the umpire. A more lasting consequence of the encounter was the attachment of screens on the foul poles to make such calls easier.

SAL MAGLIE

The dominant mound force for the Giants in the early 1950s, Maglie was known as The Barber for his ability to shave corners with his curve and chins with his fastball. Although the right-hander had only one 20-win season, when he led the league with 23 victories in New York's miracle pennant year of 1951, he developed a reputation for winning the big game because of his success against the perennially contending Dodgers. After several years of pitched battles against Brooklyn, he ended up as a Dodger himself in 1956, and his 13 victories were the difference in the club's pennant struggle with the Braves. In the final week of the season, with Milwaukee seeming to have an insurmountable lead, Maglie no-hit the Phillies, then, three days later, beat the Pirates. In that year's World Series against the Yankees, he was the tough-luck loser to Don Larsen's perfect game, 2–0. Before winding up his career in 1958, he completed the New York hat trick by also pitching for the Yankees. Maglie's success with the Giants followed a suspension for being one of the players who jumped to the Mexican League in 1946.

PETER MAGOWAN

Chairman of the Safeway supermarket chain, Magowan was allowed by National League president Bill White to bid for the Giants in November 1992 after an earlier sale had already been agreed to between outgoing owner Bob Lurie and a consortium based in St. Petersburg. The Magowan offer was actually $11 million less than what the Florida group had offered, but Lurie had little choice but to accept it after White and NL owners made it clear that they were not about to surrender the San Francisco market. Magowan sought to remove some of the odor from the deal by offering an unprecedented free-agent contract to slugger Barry Bonds—an addition that in fact kept the Giants in contention for the West Division title right down to the final day of the 1993 season.

BILLY MAHARG

Maharg's three claims to notoriety were all under an assumed name. First, he was one of the Philadelphia teenagers rounded up by the Tigers to play the Athletics on May 18, 1912, following the walkout of the regular Detroit team over the suspension of Ty Cobb. Second, he was the only one to reappear in the majors after that game— turning up with the Phillies for another single-game appearance, in 1916. Third, he was a critical whistle-blower in the 1919 Black Sox scandal. A gambler and occasional boxer, Maharg fancied spelling the name he was born with—Graham— backward.

WALTER MALMQUIST

Playing for York of the Nebraska State League in 1913, Malmquist batted .477—the highest average in organized baseball since the founding of the National League in 1876. The outfielder never made it to the big leagues.

JIM MALONEY

Maloney is the only pitcher to carry more than one no-hit game into extra innings. On June 14, 1965, the Cincinnati right-hander stumbled through 10 innings against the Mets, walking a no-hitter record 10 batters, before Johnny Lewis led off the 11th with a home run to defeat him. A couple of months later, on August 19, he pitched a 10-inning no-hitter against the Cubs. Maloney, who had a career record of 134–84 before arm miseries forced his retirement, also no-hitted the Astros, on April 30, 1969. The only Houston hitter who threatened the masterpiece was Johnny Edwards, whose looping fly ball in the sixth inning required a circus catch by Reds' shortstop Darrell Chaney. When he had been with Cincinnati, Edwards had been behind the plate for Maloney's first two no-hitters.

LES MANN

Mann had a creditable sixteen-year career as an outfielder that saw him wandering from one National League team to another, but he made a much greater impression on some people with his off-field activities. After playing regularly for the 1914 Miracle Braves, for example, he angered the NL establishment by becoming a prize catch for the insurgent Federal League the following season. Then, as a key member of the 1918 pennant-winning Cubs, he was in the forefront of a rebellion by Chicago and Boston Red Sox players that threatened to interrupt the World Series unless owners of the two teams were more generous in sharing the gate receipts. In 1936, Mann was also responsible for organizing the first team of baseball players to perform in the Olympics. (Earlier baseball demonstrations, at the beginning of the century, had been given by track-and-field athletes.) Because the Olympics in question were the games held in Nazi Berlin, the initiative was frowned on by major league baseball, which wanted to avoid the hot debate about whether the United States should be part of the Hitler extravaganza. With funds raised from private investors and the General Mills cereal company, Mann led a group of collegians and members of the Penn Athletic Club to Germany for a split-squad game. (Among the participants, only pitcher Bill Sayles later reached the major leagues.) Estimates varied on how many curious Germans packed Berlin Stadium to see the contest, with the lowest reported figure being 90,000. In his own subsequent report to major league owners, Mann himself claimed that the attendance was 125,000, which would make it the largest crowd ever to see a baseball game. For years afterward, however, the former outfielder had to spend considerable time refuting press charges that the amateur players had given the stadium the Nazi salute before playing ball.

FELIX MANTILLA

Mantilla was at opposite ends of the two most notorious errors of the 1959 season. On May 26, the Milwaukee shortstop led off the 13th inning of a game against Pittsburgh by hitting a grounder to Don Hoak that the Pirates' third baseman threw away; the miscue ended Harvey Haddix's perfect game. In the 12th inning on the last day of the season, Mantilla himself fired wildly to first after grabbing a bounding ball hit by the Dodgers' Carl Furillo; the misplay sent Gil Hodges home with the winning run for Los Angeles in the second game of the special playoffs for the pennant.

MICKEY MANTLE (Hall of Fame, 1974)

Named for Hall of Famer Mickey Cochrane and raised by his father to emulate his namesake, Mantle combined power and average as no other switch-hitter has before or since; nevertheless, it took a decade of spectacular slugging feats for

Mickey Mantle entertains Cooperstown fans in an exhibition game a few years before he earned a plaque of his own. National Baseball Library, Cooperstown, N.Y.

him to win forgiveness for a host of perceived sins, not the least of which was succeeding Joe DiMaggio in center field at Yankee Stadium.

In an eighteen-year (1951–68) all-Yankee career, Mantle knocked 536 home runs while averaging .298. Among his ten seasons above .300 and four with at least 40 round-trippers were league-leading totals in home runs four times, in slugging on three occasions, in runs scored in six seasons, and in walks in five different years. A Triple Crown (353, 52 homers, 130 RBIs) in 1956 won him the first of three MVP trophies, the others coming in 1957 and 1962. Mantle holds records for the most homers by a switch-hitter; for reaching the seats from both sides of the plate in a game ten times; and for the most round-trippers (18), runs scored, RBIs, and walks in World Series competition.

With an assist from club PR director Red Patterson, Mantle introduced the era of the tape-measure home run with a titanic blast off Chuck Stobbs on April 17, 1952, that traveled 565 feet over the back wall of the left-field bleachers in Washington's Griffith Stadium. Two later shots reached the filigree wrought-iron facade above the third deck in Yankee Stadium's right field; one, off Senators' right-hander Pedro Ramos on May 30, 1956, struck eighteen inches from the top of the facade and was as close as any major leaguer has come to hitting a ball out of the Bronx stadium; another, off the Athletics' Bill Fischer on May 22, 1963, landed just below the earlier one but was still rising when it caromed.

Despite muscular feats, Mantle was hardly a one-dimensional player. An excellent bunter, he was adept at dragging the ball left-handed for a base hit; his speed also enabled him to reach double figures in stolen bases in six consecutive seasons. In addition, his batting eye was good enough to make him one of the last two major leaguers to compile an on-base average higher than .500. (Ted Williams's .528 beat out Mantle .515 to lead the AL in 1957.)

Mantle accomplished all this even though hobbled by a succession of injuries that left teammates and opponents wondering how he managed to suit up, let alone excel on the diamond. The most celebrated injury was a torn knee he suffered stepping on an open drain in the Yankee Stadium outfield during the second game of the 1951 World Series. Perhaps his most statistically significant setback was an infection that resulted from a flue shot administered by a doctor recommended by broadcaster Mel Allen in early September 1961. With 53 homers at the time, Mantle continued to play every day but hit only 1 more the rest of the season, while teammate Roger Maris went on to establish a new major league record with 61.

For all his accomplishments in the face of physical adversity, Mantle was booed unmercifully after reaching the major leagues in 1951. Every year there was a new reason for the catcalls. In his rookie season, it was his slow start after an avalanche of favorable advance publicity and a temporary demotion to the minors. In 1952, it was because Mantle had been moved from right to center to take over for a retired DiMaggio. In 1953, it was because he had failed the physical examination for the armed forces. In 1954, it was because he lacked the panache of New York rival Willie Mays of the Giants. Even after Mantle's Triple Crown year, the boobirds were all over him for every strikeout (and there were 1,700 of them in his career) and for the temper tantrums that led him to smash dugout water coolers or whatever else was handy after a failure at the plate. Manager Casey Stengel's regular pronouncements that "every year he ought to lead

the league in everything" didn't help matters, either.

Attitudes toward him in both the press and the grandstand changed with the arrival of Maris, and especially during their 1961 race after Ruth's record; then it was Maris who became the public whipping boy. But by then Mantle had begun to slow down, the victim of too much late-night carousing as much as of the accumulated effects of his various injuries. The hard living was linked to a fear that he, too, would contract the hereditary Hodgkin's disease that killed his grandfather, father, and later a son, all before age forty. Even at age thirty-seven, when he retired, Mantle was already cracking, "If I'd known I was going to last this long, I'd have taken better care of myself when I was younger." Despite the sentiment, Mantle did not enter a rehabilitation program until 1994.

MOXIE MANUEL

Every pitcher ever lifted for a pinch hitter has reason to be grateful to Manuel. Removed in the eighth inning of a game against the Yankees on June 14, 1908, he watched as the White Sox rallied to come from behind and win the game; afterward, American League president Ban Johnson established the precedent of awarding a victory to the hurler taken out in such circumstances rather than to his successor on the mound.

HEINIE MANUSH (Hall of Fame, 1964)

Manush never let being traded bother him. In his seventeen-year career between 1923 and 1939, the lefty-swinging outfielder captured a hitting title with one team, led the American League in hits for a second one, and paced American Leaguers in both hits and triples while with a third club. The lifetime .330 batter started out with the Tigers, with whom he won the batting crown with a .378 mark in 1926. In good part because of a clash with manager George Moriarty, he was dealt to the Browns for the 1928 season, matching that .378 high, banging out a league-best 241 safeties and 47 doubles; he wasn't so bad the following year, either, in averaging .355 with another 204 hits and another league-leading 45 doubles. Swapped to the Senators in the middle of the 1930 season because of St. Louis's need of power hitter Goose Goslin, Manush found Griffith Stadium equally appealing, going five straight years over .300, collecting two more 200-hit seasons, and remaining in double figures in both doubles and triples. Before he was finished, he would also register two seasons of 100 RBIs and six years of at least 100 runs scored.

RABBIT MARANVILLE (Hall of Fame, 1954)

No member of the Hall of Fame invites as much of a reaction of "You had to be there" as Maranville. A .258 batter over twenty-three years (1912–33, 1935) with five National League clubs, the shortstop-second baseman had enough range to top middle infielders in putouts six times, assists four times, double plays five times, and fielding average three times, but also had seasons of 74 and 65 errors—high even for miscues of ambition. What has never been debated about Maranville, on the other hand, was his flair (he patented the basket catch before Willie Mays) and his standing as one of the game's greatest practical jokers. Any list of his diamond antics would have to include: going up to bat by crawling through the legs of the home plate umpire; sticking eyeglasses on umpires in the middle of arguments; and, on the pretext of administering first aid to a scratched arbiter, "discovering" one facial nick after another until he had completely covered his victim in iodine. His off-field exploits (usually fueled by alcohol) ran the gamut from walking on the ledges of high-rise hotels and dangling teammates from upper windows to pursuing a modest stage career of singing, telling jokes, and demonstrating his catches at the belt buckle.

Maranville came up with the Braves and teamed with Johnny Evers to give the club the best middle infield defense in the league in its 1914 championship season. His next stop was Pittsburgh, where he even managed solid offensive years of .294 and .295, but also turned so unruly off the field that he caused one change of managers and thought nothing of involving even prim owner Barney Dreyfuss in his gags. As a member of the Cubs in 1925, Bill Veeck, Sr., decided the best solution for the antics was to make Maranville the manager—an experiment that lasted only a few weeks when the infielder took his players out to celebrate every win as

Rabbit Maranvile's clowning infuriated owners, exasperated managers, and delighted fans. National Baseball Library, Cooperstown, N.Y.

though it were a World Series victory, engaged in a headline-making fight with a Brooklyn cabdriver, emptied a spittoon on fellow train passengers, and made life hell for traveling secretary John Seys. In between subsequent travels to the Dodgers, Cardinals, and (again) Braves, Maranville cured his alcoholism, so that when he returned to Boston, his constant needling of owner-manager Emil Fuchs was at least a sober commentary. For all practical purposes, Maranville's career ended when he broke his leg in a collision at home plate in spring training of 1934, causing him to miss the entire season and retire after an ineffective comeback effort in 1935; so painful were the multiple fractures he suffered in the play that he called on on-deck hitter hitter Shanty Hogan to knock him out. The catcher accommodated him with a single punch.

FIRPO MARBERRY

Baseball's first great relief pitcher, Marberry led the American League in appearances six times and in saves five times in the 1920s and early 1930s while working for the Senators. The right-hander was pushed into the bullpen role by the fact that Washington's chief starters of the period were all over thirty-five and prone to running out of gas in the late innings. He owed much of his effectiveness to what became known locally as Marberry Time—the twilight hours in which the late innings of afternoon games were usually played in the capital. An unrepentant fastballer, Marberry played a key role in Washington pennants in 1924 and 1925, and then again in Detroit's 1934 flag. For all his speed, however, he had relatively few strikeouts, breaking the 100 mark only once in his fourteen-year (1923–36) career; for the most part, his heavy ball produced pop-ups by opposition batters. Paradoxically, his record as a starting pitcher (94–52) was extraordinary. Marberry, whose real name was Frederick, gained his nickname from his resemblance to the heavyweight fighter who once knocked Jack Dempsey out of the ring.

JUAN MARICHAL (Hall of Fame, 1983)

Marichal was the best right-hander in baseball for most of the 1960s, turning in a record of 154–65 (.703) for the Giants between 1963 and 1969. Thanks to the presence in the league of Bob Gibson and Sandy Koufax, however, Marichal never won a Cy Young Award. His career record of 243–142 (with 2.89 ERA) included six 20-win seasons and pacing the National League in ERA (2.10) in 1969.

On August 22, 1965, Marichal was involved in one of the most violent brawls in diamond history after he attacked Dodger catcher John Roseboro with his bat. The trouble was ignited by the hurler's belief that Roseboro was returning the ball to Koufax by way of his ear in retaliation for some alleged knockdown pitches. When Marichal whacked the receiver with his bat, a free-for-all ensued. Marichal was later fined $1,750 and suspended for nine days. The suspension cost him 2 starts, and San Francisco ended up losing the pennant to Los Angeles by 2 games.

Marichal's pinpoint control was such that he established the record for the most strikeouts per walk, fanning 3.27 batters for every free pass.

ROGER MARIS

When Hank Aaron was chasing Babe Ruth's career home run record, he had to deal with morons of an anonymous kind; when Maris was chasing Ruth's season home-run mark, he at least knew that the moron was sitting in the commissioner's office. Moreover, Commissioner Ford Frick's insistence on asterisking the slugger's 61st home run in 1961 has ultimately had the converse effect of pointing up the negligible difference in establishing major league marks established within the former 154-game schedule and the newer 162-game slate.

Maris took a controversial path to his 1961 celebrity as a member of the Yankees. Originally brought to the major leagues by the Indians in 1957, the lefty-swinging right fielder was traded the following year to the Athletics by Frank Lane in a move that was widely seen as a prelude to a second swap, to New York. Even normally somnolent American League president Will Harridge, already under fire for allowing Kansas City to operate as a big league farm club for the Yankees, was moved to caution the Athletics not to send the outfielder to the Bronx for at least eighteen months. Kansas City owner Arnold Johnson took the pledge, and at one point was on the verge of dealing Maris to the Pirates in exchange for Bill Mazeroski, but finally succumbed only a few hours after the eighteen-month period expired.

Maris's first year in pinstripes, in 1960, netted him the first of two consecutive MVP trophies for belting 39 home runs and pacing the league in RBIs (112) and slugging percentage (.581). That performance was quickly eclipsed, however, by the circus atmosphere surrounding his 1961 effort. In pure numbers, he tagged 61 home runs and led the AL in both RBIs (142) and runs (132). What went less noticed (except by his teammates and adversaries) was that he also consolidated his standing as one of the game's best all-around players—fielding, throwing, and running as intelligently as athletically. Far more conspicuous was the media caravan that grew longer the closer Maris got to Ruth's fabled number and his growingly sullen reactions to being the center of national attention. Making everything worse were the Frick ruling and the clear preference of Yankee rooters for Mickey Mantle, who ended up with 54 homers on the season, to surpass the Bambino before the outsider from Kansas City did. In the end, Maris became so frayed by the various pressures that he began losing his hair.

Maris finally broke the record with a blow into the right-field seats off Boston's Tracy Stallard in the last game of the season before a Yankee Stadium crowd of merely 23,154. The modest attendance was attributed to the slighted significance given to the feat by Frick's asterisk. When longtime New York fan Sal Durante sought to give Maris the ball he had caught in the stands, the star declined, insisting that Durante should get the $5,000 posted for the ball by a California restaurateur. He would say later that Durante's generosity meant more to him than the media pressures and the catcalls from the pro-Ruth and pro-Mantle fans.

In 1967 Maris was dealt to the Cardinals, for whom he played a key role in back-to-back pennants before retiring. In the 1967 World Series against the Red Sox, he batted .385 with 7 RBIs.

RUBE MARQUARD (Hall of Fame, 1971)

On the mound, on the stage, and in team lore, Marquard was the most accomplished of John McGraw's starstruck Giants in the early part of the century. A fastballing southpaw, Marquard had three successive 20-win seasons between 1911 and 1913, topping the National League in winning percentage and strikeouts in 1911 and in victories (26) in 1912. In the latter year, he also won a record-breaking 19 consecutive games, and was denied a 20th by scoring rules of the day that didn't recognize his right to a victory for being on the hill as a reliever when his team overcame a deficit to win. For all his accomplishments with New York, however, Marquard remained very much the club's second pitcher behind Christy Mathewson.

Off the field, the pitcher was one of several Giants of the period whose name was as likely to pop up in show business columns as on the sports page. He toured the country with Blossom Seely, the reigning queen of vaudeville, then later married her after being chased through several states by her estranged husband and a succession of process servers. Marquard also appeared in the Hollywood film *Nineteen Straight* with Maurice Costello.

After his three big years with New York, Marquard was waived to the Dodgers, where he rejoined former Giants coach Wilbert Robinson and contributed more sting to the city rivalry between the clubs. Although Marquard never again won 20, his 13 victories and 1.58 ERA in 1916 played a big role in a Brooklyn pennant, and he came back the following season with 19 wins. Marquard's overall record was 201–177, with a 3.08 ERA.

MIKE MARSHALL

Marshall should have been one of the most influential pitchers of the 1970s, but his maverick behavior tended to alienate even those who were awed by his stamina on the mound and impressed by the fervor of his ideas off it. He has also spawned conflicting stories about his role in organizing the players' strikes of the 1970s.

A right-handed reliever who specialized in a screwball, Marshall began his fourteen-year (1967, 1969–81) career with the Tigers, moving on to eight other teams before he called it quits. In 1974 he became the first fireman to win the Cy Young Award, when his 15 victories, 21 saves, and record 106 appearances provided the backbone for a Los Angeles pennant. He had been obtained by the Dodgers from the Expos prior to the season in a controversial trade for outfielder Willie Davis; as the closer for Montreal the year before, Marshall had racked up another 14 wins and 31 saves while establishing the previous National League mark of 92 appearances. While with Minnesota in 1979, he also set the standard for American League appearances by a pitcher by going to the mound 90 times.

Marshall attributed his durability to his own theories on physical conditioning, acquired while gaining a doctorate in the physiological field of kinesiology. This put him constantly at loggerheads with managers and pitching coaches, and was the single most important reason for his regular travels from one club to another. What especially alarmed some of the older guard was his influence on young hurlers, who only had to see his effectiveness to begin raising questions of their own about the tried and true methods of developing hurlers. But although Marshall was always glad to share his insights on conditioning, he also unnerved many of his would-be disciples with a more general skepticism of the role of major leaguers in American society. For himself, for instance, he insisted on being regarded primarily as an educator rather than a ballplayer. He also had little use for the questions of sportswriters, once describing them as "useless at best." He could be equally severe with fans, objecting on principle to signing autographs and occasionally querying an autograph-seeker on the relevance of his quest to anything meaningful.

Teams that weren't put off by Marshall's ideas on conditioning and public relations were quick to jettison him because of his union activism. But although one of the Players Association's earliest advocates of militancy in dealing with owners, the pitcher has always been coy about the reasons why he cast the only negative vote on the 1976 free-agency agreement. According to Association director Marvin Miller, Marshall was simply misguided in initially objecting to any accord that didn't demand all-out free agency rather than permitting it only after six years of big league service. Another reading of the vote, however, has attributed it to a Marshall-Miller tactic for allowing the latter to present himself to owners as a moderate alternative to more radical views from within the Association. The most glaring instance of Marshall's paying for his union militancy occurred in 1980, when he was cut by the Twins despite overcoming a bad start to yield only a run in 12 innings. The Players Association filed a grievance to obtain the full amount of salary still due on the reliever's contract, and Minnesota owner Calvin Griffith settled before the case went to the National Labor Relations Board.

PAUL AND NANCY MARSHALL

The Marshalls were 1993 season ticketholders in San Diego who filed an unprecedented class-action suit against the Padres for trading away their best players. The basis of the action was a form letter written to ticketholders by club president Dick Freeman before the season, promising that San Diego would contend for years to come with a nucleus of young stars who would not be dealt away. Soon afterward, the team began to pare its payroll by trading off outfielder Darrin Jackson, shortstop Tony Fernandez, and third baseman Gary Sheffield. The suit by the Marshalls was eventually settled out of court, with the Padres committed to liberalizing their refund policy and the plaintiffs withdrawing a demand that the franchise vow not to trade slugger Fred McGriff. Five days after the agreement was reached, McGriff was traded to Atlanta.

BILLY MARTIN

As both a player and a manager, Martin excelled under pressure—on the field. Once in a clubhouse or a bar, however, he became one of baseball's model studies in self-destruction. Unfortunately for the man who always wanted to be thought of as a Yankee, he found more than one accomplice in pursuing his bent.

A light-hitting second baseman for eleven seasons between 1950 and 1961, Martin saved his most memorable moments as a player for the World Series. His most conspicuous performances were a game-saving shoetop catch of a Jackie Robinson pop-up with the bases loaded in the seventh game of the 1952 World Series against the Dodgers, and, a year later, a record 12 hits, including an RBI single to drive in the Series-ending run, against the same Brooklyn club. But weighing against him, at least in the eyes of New York general manager George Weiss, were his truculence on the field (Clint Courtney and Jimmy Piersall were notable sparring partners in his playing days) and his late-night carousing off it (usually with Mickey Mantle and Whitey Ford in tow). When the infamous Copacabana incident occurred, during a Martin birthday party on May 16, 1957, Weiss blamed Martin, even though it was outfielder Hank Bauer who flattened a patron of the nightclub. Not even the support of manager Casey Stengel could prevent a trade of the infielder to Kansas City.

Out of New York, Martin bounced around for four and a half more years, landing with six different clubs without distinguishing himself, other than by an assault on Jim Brewer that left the Cubs southpaw with a broken jaw and Martin with a lawsuit that took nine years to settle. Remaining with the Minnesota organization after his retirement in 1961 (with a .257 career batting average), he got his first managerial shot in 1969 after a season-long barrage of mail and phone calls from fans calling for the promotion of the popular coach. Despite a divisional title, his relationship with Calvin Griffith began to sour when the Twins' owner became convinced that his frequent scenes with umpires were to gain personal headlines. It was destroyed for good when Martin worked over pitcher Dave Boswell after getting hit accidentally while trying to break up a barroom fight.

It was the same story in Detroit: Two successful years and another division title with a veteran club were followed by a series of petty altercations with general manager Jim Campbell. Martin was finally dismissed after admitting that he ordered Tiger pitchers to throw at Cleveland batters in retaliation for Gaylord Perry's spitballing. Soon afterward, Martin arrived in Texas behind owner Brad Corbett's statement that he would fire his mother to hire him; he departed a year and a half later, after taking a young club from last to second, then taking heat in 1975 to win immediately after Corbett traded three young pitchers for Perry and picked up several other veterans who failed to produce.

Then began the Yankee psychodrama with owner George Steinbrenner and slugger Reggie Jackson.

Martin returned to Yankee Stadium as manager to complete a third-place finish in 1975, then took a relatively untempestuous pennant in 1976. Despite this success, Steinbrenner and general manager Gabe Paul engineered a series of off-season deals that irritated the touchy manager, sending Martin favorites Oscar Gamble and Dock Ellis elsewhere; displacing a third, Fred Stanley, with the acquisition of Bucky Dent; and saddling the manager with an unwanted Ken Holtzman. The straw that broke the camel's back, however, was the free-agent signing of the strutting Jackson. The inevitable explosion took only a few months in coming, during which players conspired against Martin, Steinbrenner fired the manager at least five times and threatened to do so on dozens of other occasions, and everyone resented Jackson's incessant blather about "the magnitude of me" and celebration of himself as "the straw that stirs the drink." The manager didn't help matters by dropping Jackson from the cleanup spot and penciling him in as a designated hitter. After Jackson played a bloop single into a double in a nationally televised game on June 18, Martin sent Paul Blair out to right field to replace him midinning. The cameras caught the next act: Martin being restrained in the dugout from attacking his near-hysterical outfielder.

This scene was mere prelude to what would follow in 1978. Defied by Jackson, who one day disobeyed a sign to bunt, and then on another, bunted on his own with a two-strike count, and betrayed by Steinbrenner, who was discussing a manager-for-manager trade with the White Sox, an overwrought Martin told reporters in late July that "the two of them deserve each other—one's a born liar, the other's convicted." Martin was promptly fired. This was followed only weeks later by an announcement to a stunned packed house on Old Timers' Day at Yankee Stadium that successor Bob Lemon would be promoted to the front office in 1980, with Martin coming back as manager. With that timetable pushed up by six months, Martin was back in the Yankee dugout in June 1979, only to be taunted throughout the rest of the season by Steinbrenner with the necessity for good behavior. In October the manager got into a fistfight in a Minnesota hotel with a marshmallow salesman named Joseph Cooper and was fired by Steinbrenner for the second time.

Arguably, Martin's greatest success came not in his adopted hometown of New York but during his stay in his birthplace of Oakland; at the very least, the experience with the A's highlighted most graphically both his greatest managerial strength (an aggressive offense) and his greatest failing (an inability to handle a pitching staff). Hired by Charlie Finley in 1980, he took over a team with a talented outfield and a lusterless infield, taught it what became known as Billy Ball (emphasizing the hit-and-run, the suicide squeeze, double and even triple steals, and stealing home), and finished second. Given responsibility in 1981 for personnel decisions by the Haas family, who bought the team from Finley, the manager used the same tactics to turn a first-place finish in the first half of the split season into a West Division win. The end of his enchanted period with the A's began in the middle of the 1982 season, however, with Martin once again creating the irrational scenes that always prefaced his departures. This time it was a demand for a five-year extension on his contract and an office-destroying tantrum after an early August loss that included screaming into a phone at various club officials about the delay on his new pact. As if that weren't enough, club president Roy Eisenhardt had Martin's overuse of young starters Rick Langford, Steve McCatty, Mike Norris, Matt Keough, and Brian Kingman—and their resulting sore arms—to point to when he fired the manager in October.

Martin eventually returned to manage the Yankees for all of 1983, most of 1985, and part of 1988 in what became an obsessive quest to please Steinbrenner sufficiently to be named to the post permanently. Rumors of his return for a sixth tour continued right up to his death in an automobile accident on Christmas Day 1989. Most final analyses of his life cited alcoholism, an insatiable appetite for young women, and a need for dominance (sometimes physical, sometimes psychological) as contributing to his inability to handle success.

J. C. MARTIN

Martin's sole at-bat in World Series play produced an explosion and a turning point victory for the 1969 Miracle Mets. Pinch hitting in the bottom of the 10th inning of the fourth game with New York and Baltimore deadlocked at 1–1, the lefty-swinging catcher bunted down the first-base line with runners on first and second. Orioles' pitcher Pete Richert fielded the bunt and fired to first, but the ball struck Martin's wrist and caromed into foul territory, allowing pinch runner Rod Gaspar to score the winning run from second. The Orioles jumped all over home plate umpire Shag Crawford that Martin had run to first illegally within the baseline, but the protest was to no avail despite the apparent legitimacy of their charge. The Mets clinched their championship the next day.

PEPPER MARTIN

Martin was the rambunctious heart of the Gas House Gang teams of St. Louis in the 1930s. A right-hand-hitting third baseman, he averaged .298 in thirteen seasons between 1928 and 1944 with the Cardinals and double that in his ability to aggravate managers and St. Louis general manager Branch Rickey with his penchant for doing anything for a laugh. On the field, Martin's strong suit was the kind of daring baserunning that enabled him to lead the National League in steals three times. He batted .290 or higher eight times and scored 100 runs in three seasons. Martin had his greatest offensive moments in two World Series: In the 1931 duel against the Athletics, he went 12-for-24 with 5 stolen bases, a home run, and 4 doubles; in 1934 he helped defeat the Tigers by going 11-for-31.

Martin's notions of daring extended to never wearing an athletic supporter when he played. His ideas of leisure included trapping snakes for a St. Louis zoo and racing cars; the latter pastime usually caused him to miss batting practice at home games, driving manager Frankie Frisch into regular spouts of fury until his third baseman took the field and showed little effects from his morning derring-do. A beaning of the infielder inspired Rickey to call him The Wild Horse of the Osage, one of several tags dreamed up by the executive in the 1930s to give more box office color to his players.

BUCK MARTINEZ

Martinez suffered the most productive career-ending injury in baseball history. On July 9, 1985, the Blue Jays catcher fractured his leg tagging Seattle's Phil Bradley on a play at the plate, then fired wildly to third in an effort to nail Gorman Thomas. With left fielder George Bell retrieving the ball and throwing home as Thomas rounded third, the prostrate receiver held his ground and completed an unlikely double play. Although he returned in a familiar role as backup receiver in 1986, Martinez batted only .181 and hobbled into retirement at the end of the season.

DENNIS MARTINEZ

Martinez went from the bottom of a bottle with the Orioles in the early 1980s to the status of a national hero in his native Nicaragua for fighting his alcoholism and becoming one of the National League's top winners with the Expos in the late 1980s and 1990s. His biggest moment in a Montreal uniform came on July 28, 1991, when he twirled a perfect game against the Dodgers. El Presidente, as he is known, moved on to the Indians as a free agent in 1994, and started the inaugural game at Jacobs Stadium.

BOBBY MATHEWS

Although credit for inventing the spitball usually goes to Frank Corridon (in 1902), Mathews had been known to load up the ball as early as 1867, while still a teenage pitcher for the Lord Baltimore club. Four years later, the right-hander won baseball's first professional league game when he shut out the National Association Cleveland Forest Citys for the Fort Wayne Kekiongas, 2–0, in what would remain for four years the lowest-scoring NA game.

EDDIE MATHEWS (Hall of Fame, 1978)

Half of the greatest one-two home-run combination in the history of baseball, Mathews was destined to be eclipsed among third basemen in Cooperstown by Mike Schmidt as much as he was in Braves lineups by Hank Aaron. Nevertheless, Mathews's slugging records and able glove make him the runner-up only to Schmidt as the major leagues' greatest all-time power-hitting third baseman. Among other feats, Mathews shares with Schmidt the record for most consecutive seasons (9) in the NL with at least 30 home runs. With teammate Aaron between 1954 and 1966, the lefty-hitting Mathews amassed 863 long balls, four more than the combination of Babe Ruth and Lou Gehrig between 1923 and 1934.

The only member of the Braves to play with the franchise in Boston, Milwaukee, and Atlanta, Mathews nevertheless had to find out through a reporter that he had been traded to the Astros for the 1967 season after fifteen years with the organization. When the Atlanta press chided the front office for such shabby behavior, the club sent a letter of apology to ''Edward'' Mathews. (His first name is Edwin.) He came back to manage the team in the closing weeks of the 1972 season but lasted only until midway through 1974.

CHRISTY MATHEWSON (Hall of Fame, 1936)

Mathewson was the only one of the National League's great early-century pitchers who would have received the *Good Housekeeping* Seal of Approval. In studied contrast to his vulgar, tobacco-chewing contemporaries, he was a Bucknell graduate who had headed two college literary societies, sung for the campus choir, and attracted attention for his championship play in everything from football to checkers; as a member of John McGraw's rowdy Giants over the first seventeen years of the century, he was publicized as such a model of clean living (he was rarely asked to pitch on Sundays, in respect for his religious principles) that he inspired fictional baseball heroes for children and was considered personally responsible for attracting women and entire families to the Polo Grounds. Mathewson also happened to be good enough to rack up 373 victories, tying him with Grover Cleveland Alexander for the NL record, and to win election to Cooperstown in 1936 as one of the Five Immortals.

The right-hander reached the Giants before McGraw did, and it was almost Mathewson's undoing. In December 1900 he was traded by Cincinnati to New York for the worn-out Amos Rusie in what has been called the worst swap in baseball history; in fact, however, the deal was engineered by Reds' owner John T. Brush shortly before his own departure for the Polo Grounds, so that, whatever else the transaction involved, Cincinnati miscalculation was not one of its ingredients. Even though Mathewson immediately produced the first of his thirteen 20-win seasons for the Giants, that wasn't good enough for Horace Fogel and Heinie Smith, the clowns who managed New York over the first half of the 1902 season and who vied with one another in seeking to convert the mound star to first base and then to shortstop. Only with McGraw's arrival at the end of the year did the experimenting come to an end. Between 1903 and 1914, Mathewson's lowest victory total for a season was 22. Four times he topped the 30 mark, and five times he paced his contemporaries in strikeouts. His single greatest year was 1908, when he set the league standard for wins (37), ERA (1.43), complete games (34), strikeouts (259), and shutouts (12).

Mathewson was no less formidable in World Series games, employing his famous fadeaway (screwball) to record the most shutouts (4) and complete games (10) in Series history. His stellar

Christy Mathewson had to overcome ludicrous attempts to turn him into an infielder to become the most successful pitcher in National League history National Baseball Library, Cooperstown, N.Y.

moment in October competition came in 1905, when he shut out Connie Mack's Athletics three times in five days for a New York championship. His overall ERA in 11 World Series appearances was 1.15.

From the moment that McGraw took over the Giants in 1902, he indicated that there would be one set of rules for fellow college graduate Mathewson and another set for the rest of the players. The negative side of this for the pitcher was that he was assessed fines twice as heavy as those for his teammates if discovered in the crap games McGraw had banned from the clubhouse (''Matty should have known better''); the positive side was that McGraw and his wife came to regard him as

a son, even insisting that the Mathewsons share an apartment with them for an extended period. With his teammates, Mathewson was regarded as the ultimate stand-up guy—a perception that he more than confirmed in September 1908, when he stood alone on the planet in insisting that Fred Merkle had touched second base before veering off into the dugout and into baseball history for the game's most notorious bonehead play. His standing with adversaries was such that Cub manager Frank Chance saw nothing ludicrous in offering the Giants $50,000 for the hurler even as the two clubs were clawing at one another down the stretch of the same 1908 season: ''Of course, I didn't expect McGraw to say yes,'' Chance conceded later, ''but what did it cost me to dream?''

When Mathewson finally *was* dealt, it was back to the Reds in 1916 so that, his pitching career over, he could realize an ambition to manage. The transaction became known as the Hall of Fame Trade because it also exported future Cooperstown residents Edd Roush and Bill McKechnie to Cincinnati in exchange for infielder Buck Herzog. Mathewson appeared to be on the verge of building the club a respectable pitching staff when he was called into military service. While working in a chemical lab in France, he was exposed dangerously to an explosion of poisonous gas, weakening his lungs. After a protracted recovery and a return to the United States, he was helped by McGraw to the presidency of the Braves, but was soon spending more time battling the tuberculosis that took up residence in his lungs. Mathewson died during the 1925 World Series, at age forty-seven.

GARY MATTHEWS

Few free agents created as much trouble as Matthews did in 1976. No sooner had he been signed away from the Giants by Ted Turner than Commissioner Bowie Kuhn smacked the Atlanta owner with a tampering charge, levying a $10,000 fine and stripping the Braves of their first-round amateur draft pick in January. When the dissatisfied Giants brought further tampering evidence to Kuhn, the commissioner increased his penalties to a one-year suspension of Turner and the loss of Atlanta's June draft selection as well. Turner responded by suing Kuhn, but fared only marginally better in the courtroom. Although a judge returned the draft picks to the Braves, he upheld Kuhn's right to impose the fine and suspension.

In New York, meanwhile, ace right-hander Tom Seaver pointed to the Atlanta signing of Matthews as evidence that the Mets were not serious about seeking free-agent hitters. The criticism soon blew up to a regular war of words between the future Hall of Famer and franchise chairman M. Donald Grant, preparing the ground for the year's dramatic trade of Seaver to the Reds.

As for Matthews, the right-hand-hitting outfielder averaged .283 with decidedly mild power numbers for the Braves in 1977.

DON MATTINGLY

First baseman Mattingly has played more seasons (thirteen) for the Yankees without appearing in postseason play than anybody else in the history of the franchise. The lefty swinger won the American League batting championship in 1984 with a .343 mark, then followed that up with MVP honors in 1985 for batting .324 with 35 homers and league-leading numbers in both RBIs (145) and doubles (48). In 1987 he set records for hitting 10 home runs over 8 consecutive games and for clouting 6 grand-slammers in the season.

Mattingly's production fell off sharply with the advent of the 1990s, in good part because of recurring back problems. Acknowledged as the team leader by fellow players, he was humiliated by manager Stump Merrill and owner George Steinbrenner in 1992 when he was ordered to get a haircut in terms that ludicrously suggested that his curls were one of the reasons for New York's dismal season. The episode prompted the first of several Mattingly threats to quit baseball with or without a postseason ring.

GENE MAUCH

Mauch is either the smartest man in baseball never to win a pennant, or the most expert at pulling defeat out of the jaws of victory. In twenty-six years of managing the Phillies, Expos, Twins, and Angels between 1960 and 1987, the onetime infielder piloted his clubs to only two division titles. Worse, even the division wins (with California in 1982 and 1986) ultimately

served to solidify his reputation for falling down inches away from the finish line. In 1982, the Angels took the first 2 games of the American League Championship Series from the Brewers, then lost 3 in a row; in 1986, the club had the Red Sox on the ropes in the 9th inning of game five with one out to go, only to have Dave Henderson hit a home run and Boston rumble back for 3 consecutive wins.

Mauch first attracted the reputation of a loser with the 1964 Phillies, when the team lost 10 games in a row down a September stretch run, allowing the apparently dead Cardinals to sneak through for the flag. Much of the blame for the foldup was attributed to the manager's insistence on going only with Jim Bunning and Chris Short as starters over the end of the season. With Minnesota in the mid-1970s, he used his "little ball" tactics of the first-inning sacrifice, the stolen base, and the hit-and-run to pull the team out of the depths of the West Division, but again presided over August and September skids. For all that, numerous players who have been on Mauch teams have singled him out as the most insightful manager they ever played for.

DAL MAXVILL

Maxvill might as well have thrown away his bat in his fourteen-year career in the 1960s and 1970s as a slick-fielding shortstop. A career .217 hitter, he set several marks for offensive ineptitude. With the Cardinals in 1970, for example, his 89 total bases marked a major league low for players in at least 150 games. Two years before that, he established the record for most at-bats in a World Series (22) without getting a hit.

CHARLIE MAXWELL

Mainly because of his prowess against the Yankees, outfielder Maxwell gained a reputation in the 1950s as the Sunday Home-Run Hitter. Although 40 of the Detroit slugger's 148 career home runs were indeed blasted on the seventh day, he also had 23 blows against New York, a staple weekend home attraction for the Tigers. Maxwell always attributed much of his reputation to a Sunday, May 3, 1959, doubleheader against the Yankees, when he reached the seats in his final at-bat in the first game, then clouted 3 more homers in the nightcap. As a rookie with Boston in 1951, the left-handed Maxwell hit three pinch-homers—against future Hall of Famers Satchel Paige, Bob Lemon, and Bob Feller.

RUDY MAY

May had his moments over a sixteen-year career (between 1965 and 1983), but one of them wasn't when he was told he had been traded by the Yankees to the White Sox in 1983. Informed of the deal, the left-hander said he was pleased because he didn't like New York manager Billy Martin and had never relished playing for him. A few hours later, May was informed that some administrative problems in the Chicago front office had caused the deal to be canceled. He appeared in only 15 games for Martin's Yankees in 1983. The southpaw's best seasons were with Baltimore in 1977, when he won 18 games, and with New York in 1980, when he led the American League with his 2.47 ERA.

CARL MAYS

Right-handed submarine baller Mays is most often associated with the only fatal beaning in major league history—that of Cleveland shortstop Ray Chapman. But Mays was also the booty in an internecine war that almost wrecked the American League before the Yankees could fully claim his services, then made the club wish it hadn't bothered.

A two-time 29-game winner with the Red Sox by 1919, Mays stalked off the mound at Chicago's Comiskey Park after working only 2 innings of a July 13 game. Accepting the pitcher's claims of an injury and personal problems, Boston owner Harry Frazee saw no reason not to trade him to the pennant-contending Yankees soon afterward; AL president Ban Johnson took exception, however, claiming that the league could not allow a player to be rewarded for such a tantrum. The ensuing fracas saw lawsuits flying back and forth, three club owners threatening to jump to the National League, and the other five magnates caving in to their blackmail. With Johnson humbled and his power seriously curtailed, Mays went on to win 26 games for New York in 1920 and another (league-leading) 27 the following year.

In the 1921 World Series against the Giants,

however, the pitcher aroused the suspicions of, among others, New York manager Miller Huggins and team co-owner Cap Huston by blowing a lead in the 8th inning of game four. After the game, sportswriter Fred Lieb carried a tale to Huston about an eyewitness who had seen Mays's wife signal him on the mound that a payoff had been made just prior to a 3-run outburst that put the Giants in the lead. A subsequent investigation by Commissioner Kenesaw Landis turned up nothing. Huggins, on the other hand, never doubted the truth of the accusation and used the hurler infrequently over the next two years. Huggins did, however, leave him on the mound to endure a 20-hit, 13-run drubbing by Cleveland on July 17, 1923. After that, Mays spent five years with the Reds, including a last 20-victory season, and one with the Giants.

Chapman's death occurred on August 16, 1920, after Mays struck him on the head with a pitch in the Polo Grounds. The beaning brought numerous death threats to the pitcher from Indians' fans, but there were no physical attacks on him. Mays himself showed little mental scarring from the tragedy, proving as effective on the hill after it as before it.

WILLIE MAYS (Hall of Fame, 1979)

When Leo Durocher observed that only the great players could hit, hit with power, run, field, and throw, he had Mays in mind. Although the outfielder shared the limelight during his twenty-two-year career for the Giants and Mets (between 1951 and 1973) with a host of other superstars, few of them exceeded his accomplishments at any of the five, and none performed as consistently at his level in all five. What's more, he not only did it all, he also did it with a flair and a style seldom matched in baseball history.

Mays could hit: The right-handed slugger stroked a career total of 3,283 safeties for a lifetime average of .302 including ten seasons above .300 and one batting crown. He could hit with power: He finished his career with 660 home runs (third behind only Hank Aaron and Babe Ruth), including seventeen seasons of more than 20 and two topping the 50 mark. In a contest against the Braves on April 30, 1961, he joined the select group of hitters with four round-trippers in one

Willie Mays was arguably the most gifted all-around player in the history of the game. National Baseball Library, Cooperstown, N.Y.

game. He also posted six season slugging averages above .600, five of them league-leading totals. Mays could run: He led the National League in stolen bases in four consecutive seasons at the end of the 1950s and is the only player in major league history to compile more than 400 homers and more than 300 stolen bases. He could also hit in the clutch: He drove 1,903 runs across the plate (although he never led the league in RBIs) and clouted a record 22 extra-inning homers.

Mays could certainly field. The best center fielder of his—and perhaps of any—era, he covered the vast outfield spaces of the Polo Grounds as if they had been designed with him in mind, and won 12 consecutive Gold Gloves beginning with the first such awards in 1957. Most people point to his back-to-the-plate snare of Cleveland's Vic Wertz's 460-foot blast in the first game of the 1954 World Series as his greatest defensive play. Connoisseurs, among them Branch Rickey, have pointed to one he made in Pittsburgh's Forbes Field when he caught up with a 400-foot hooking line drive off the bat of Rocky Bridges, and, with his back to the infield and the ball trailing down and to the right, reached out and caught it barehanded at knee level.

Mays could also throw. While virtually everyone remembers the catch off Wertz, fewer recall that, after it, Mays whirled and threw on a line to second baseman Davey Williams with enough

force to drive himself to the ground and enough accuracy to hold Larry Doby, on second, to one base and to send Al Rosen scurrying back to first. Perhaps Mays's greatest defensive play came against the Dodgers on August 15, 1951, just as the Giants had begun the stretch drive that would bring them from 13½ games behind Brooklyn to a tie and then to Bobby Thomson's miracle home run. In the 8th inning, with the score tied, the center fielder picked a Carl Furillo drive off his shoetops, spun in the air, and threw a three-hundred-foot perfect strike to nail Billy Cox at the plate. Brooklyn manager Charlie Dressen, flabbergasted for once, could only say, "I'd like to see him do that again."

But the numbers and the eye-opening defensive plays tell only part of the story. Arriving in the major leagues four years after the smashing of the color line, Mays completed the revolution begun by Jackie Robinson. Mays's flash and dash, so common in the Negro leagues, took big league fans by surprise. It wasn't just the belt-high basket catches or the cap flying off his head with every moderately hard run in the outfield or on the bases (a touch Mays later admitted he embellished by choosing headgear one size too small); it wasn't even that he could go from his exploits at the Polo Grounds to a stickball game on the streets of Harlem. The extra factor was that, in contrast to the businesslike demeanor of other stars of the 1940s and 1950s and even to the fierce intensity of Robinson, Mays was having fun of a kind that was communicable to fans. What he shared with Robinson, on the other hand, was his view of baseball as a contact sport—a trait he displayed in his particular penchant for slowing down around third base to draw a throw, then crashing into the catcher.

The best player of his generation got off to a slow start, making a lone hit in his first 25 at-bats after being asked to abandon his .477 batting average with New York's Triple-A farm club in Minneapolis and join the Giants in late May 1951. Although that hit was a homer off Warren Spahn, a despondent Mays had to be talked by Durocher out of appeals to be sent back to Minneapolis. Mays went on to take Rookie of the Year honors for his part in the Giants pennant drive that year, and an MVP Award in 1954 for his batting crown

(.345), 41 homers, and 110 RBIs in the Giants' last pennant-winning year in New York.

The darling of New York fans, their collective Say Hey Kid, Mays came in for something of a surprise when the franchise resettled in San Francisco after the 1957 season. First of all, there were racial incidents. The seller of the house he wanted to buy tried to back out of the deal at one point behind pressure from neighbors; then, when the sale was finally completed, a brick was tossed through the living room window. More lasting was the preference of Bay Area fans for rookies Orlando Cepeda (in 1958) and Willie McCovey (in 1959), who carried none of the perceived tarnish of New York. It didn't help, either, that manager Bill Rigney predicted that Mays would top Babe Ruth's 60 home runs, bat .380, and drive in 150 runs, or that Mays himself gave too many interviews stressing the good old days under mentor Durocher in the Polo Grounds. Mays didn't quite live up to Rigney's predictions, but his career-high .347 average, NL-leading totals in runs scored and stolen bases, 29 homers, and 96 RBIs in 1958 hardly merited the boos that greeted him regularly; at the end of the Giants' first season on the West Coast, local fans voted Rookie of the Year Cepeda the team's Most Valuable Player.

The club's move to Candlestick Park in 1960 presented additional problems. Hitting into the stadium's unpredictable winds proved frustrating; playing defense against the elements was almost impossible until the center fielder discovered that, if he stood stark still for five seconds after a ball had been hit, he could gauge the direction in which the wind would take it.

It wasn't until the pennant-winning season of 1962 that San Franciscans warmed up to Mays. What it took was an 8th-inning homer on the last day of the season to pull the club into a tie for first with Los Angeles, 2 round-trippers to win the first game of the playoffs against the Dodgers, and a crushing line drive that tore reliever Ed Roebuck's glove off and keyed the game-winning rally in the third and final contest. Mays's prestige among teammates had, on the other hand, always been high, and he used it to quell an uprising over some racist remarks by manager Alvin Dark. Mays cooled tempers by pointing out to furious black and Latin teammates that, whatever Dark's

racial views, they had never prevented him from presenting a lineup that had a majority of minority players.

In May 1972, Mays returned to New York in a trade with the Mets for pitcher Charlie Williams and some cash, and received a hero's welcome, especially after homering against the Giants in his first Shea Stadium game in a Met uniform. His skills seriously diminished, he lasted just long enough to appear in the 1973 World Series against Oakland, first embarrassing himself by falling on his face in pursuit of a game two line drive that sparked a game-tying rally, then redeeming himself with a single to put New York back ahead.

In later years, Mays ran up against criticism from the Mets for not showing up often enough for his coaching duties, got into a demeaning squabble with the Giants over a mixup about giving his uniform to the Hall of Fame, and was suspended from baseball by Commissioner Bowie Kuhn for his employment by Bally's Atlantic City casino. His public appearances often showed a sour man who felt vaguely cheated by the course of his baseball travels. What remained the same was his philosophy about playing: "When they hit it, I catch it; when they throw it, I hit it."

BILL MAZEROSKI

The best defensive second baseman in the National League in the 1950s and 1960s, Mazeroski gained even greater fame for the 9th-inning, seventh-game home run that gave Pittsburgh a World Series victory over the Yankees in 1960. That moment of glory was made possible only because his father-in-law, Pittsburgh manager Danny Murtaugh, succeeded in voiding a trade that would have sent the infielder to Kansas City after the 1958 season. Murtaugh's remonstrations also helped ensure another significant diamond event, since the Athletics player ticketed for the Pirates in exchange was Roger Maris, who would have found spacious Forbes Field a far more forbidding arena for hitting home runs than Yankee Stadium.

JIMMY MCALEER

A swift center fielder primarily with the National League Cleveland Spiders in the 1890s, McAleer became one of American League presi-

Pursued by a gleeful fan, Bill Mazeroski scored the winning run of the 1960 World Series. Photo compliments of the Pittsburgh Pirates.

dent Ban Johnson's chief lieutenants in his battle to gain respectability for the junior circuit, then one of his principal problems.

The bond between McAleer and Johnson developed when the manager succumbed to the president's importuning to take control of the AL's St. Louis franchise in 1902; as pilot of the Browns, he recruited, among others, Hall of Famers Jesse Burkett and Bobby Wallace from the rival Cardinals. After launching the Browns and serving a brief stint with the Washington Senators, McAleer, with Johnson's secret financial backing, formed a partnership with former AL secretary Bob McRoy that purchased a half interest in the Red Sox in December 1911; another silent partner was a Chicago banker who was also manager Jake Stahl's father-in-law. Trouble started when McAleer insisted, over Stahl's objections, on starting rookie Buck O'Brien in the sixth game of the 1912 World Series. Even though the right-hander lost, Boston's championship victory the next day calmed tempers.

What was not forgotten so quickly was the treatment, prior to the sixth game, of Boston's Royal Rooters, who suffered the indignity of being turned out of their cheering section when the Red Sox sold their seats to other patrons. Led by Mayor ''Honey Fitz'' Fitzgerald, the enraged boosters marched around the park until McAleer sent mounted police to herd them behind the left-field fence. The public relations gaffe led to a boycott of the seventh game by the Royal Rooters and others, reducing the crowd to half that of previous games.

The following season, the club president and his manager once again found themselves on opposing sides, this time involving clubhouse factionalism between Masons and members of the Knights of Columbus. Faced with a choice between his old ally and the continued financial goodwill of Stahl's father-in-law, Johnson hinted publicly that Stahl would soon be moving up to the front office. In retaliation, McAleer replaced Stahl, whom he suspected of supporting the Masonic faction, with Irish-Catholic catcher Bill Carrigan. In so doing, McAleer won the battle, but he also provoked Johnson into delivering the decisive blow of the war—arranging the sale of McAleer's and McRoy's interests to Joseph Lannin while the club president was off on a postseason world tour.

GEORGE MCBRIDE

McBride holds the records for both the lowest batting average (.218) and slugging average (.264) for major leaguers with at least 4,000 at-bats. Despite such near-invisible numbers, the shortstop's defensive abilities kept him in the major leagues for sixteen years between 1901 and 1920. One ball he didn't catch, however, cost him a managerial career. At the helm of Washington in 1921, he suffered partial facial paralysis after being struck by a batting-practice line drive; the injury led to a breakdown, and he never returned as a dugout boss.

JACK MCCARTHY

In the top of the 1st inning on April 24, 1901, while a member of the Indians, McCarthy bounced a ground ball off White Sox third baseman Fred Hartman for the first American League base hit. In 1904, with the Cubs, McCarthy scooted home from third during a game, in the process breaking his ankle on a long-handled broom that the plate umpire had cast aside after wiping off the dish. The injury prompted both leagues to dispose of the domestic brooms in use until then and to replace them with the pocket whisk variety. McCarthy recuperated sufficiently quickly to become the only player to begin three outfield-to-catcher double plays in the same game when he foiled three attempted sacrifice flies by the Pirates on April 26, 1905.

JOE MCCARTHY (Hall of Fame, 1957)

McCarthy is the most successful manager in major league history, compiling a .615 winning percentage in twenty-four years of piloting between 1926 and 1950. Because he spent sixteen of those years with a powerhouse Yankee club that won eight of his nine pennants, he was tagged by Jimmy Dykes as "a push-button manager." On the other hand, even with the Cubs and the Red Sox, McCarthy never finished out of the first division; moreover, he handled a potentially explosive situation involving an envious Babe Ruth with tact and patience.

Hired by Bill Veeck, Sr., to manage the Cubs in 1926, McCarthy, who had never played in the major leagues and whose most advanced managerial assignment until then had been in the American Association, drew fire from Grover Cleveland Alexander and other players as a bush-leaguer. Once he had convinced Veeck to dispose of the future Hall of Fame right-hander to the Cardinals, McCarthy showed just how valuable his minor league experience had been by recommending that Chicago pick up Hack Wilson and Riggs Stephenson from the AA. After two fourth-place finishes and one third-place season, the purchase of slugger Rogers Hornsby from the Braves put the club over the top by 10½ games in 1929.

Despite his pennant win, there were recurrent rumblings throughout the 1930 season that McCarthy was on his way out, mainly because of his testy response to owner William Wrigley's criticism of Chicago's losing performance in the World Series against the Athletics; most of the reports had him going to the Braves as part of a secret agreement in the Hornsby deal. Instead, he

ended up with the Yankees, where he instituted in the clubhouse the same coldly professional atmosphere that prevailed in the front office. Card playing was banned. There was a dress code. Players were expected to arrive at the park clean-shaven. Nevertheless, he won over the Yankee players—all except Ruth, who had grown increasingly vocal about his desire to manage the Yankees and who had now been passed over for a National Leaguer who had never even played in the big leagues. McCarthy's approach to the slugger's frustration was to bide his time, reprimanding others for the same infractions he passed over in silence when Ruth was the culprit. The inevitable showdown came after the 1934 season, when the slugger demanded that owner Jacob Ruppert and general manager Ed Barrow fire McCarthy and install him in his place. By then, however, McCarthy had won his first world championship (in 1932)—in the middle of a record streak of 308 games (between August 1931 and August 1933) without being shut out. The brass rejected Ruth's demands, even after McCarthy offered to step down, and peddled Ruth to the Braves.

Even without Ruth, McCarthy's Yankees rolled to seven more pennants and six additional world championships between 1936 and 1943. The honeymoon ended in January 1945, when the flamboyant Larry MacPhail purchased a controlling interest in the Yankees. The new owner's razzle-dazzle, not to mention his interference, made the club's fall to the depths of fourth place (and a "mere" 81 victories, McCarthy's lowest season total) in 1945 intolerable for the manager, whose stomach ailments sent him home to upstate New York in May. MacPhail was able to talk him into returning, but the reconciliation lasted only until May 1946, when McCarthy, unable to cope with MacPhail's antics, a still-foundering team, and constant battles with left-hander Joe Page, quit for good.

After turning down Branch Rickey's offer to manage the Dodgers in 1947 while Leo Durocher was serving his one-year suspension, McCarthy turned up as pilot of the Red Sox in 1948. In Boston he lost the 1948 pennant when he started right-hander Denny Galehouse instead of rookie southpaw Mel Parnell or veteran Ellis Kinder against the Indians in a single-game special playoff to break the regular-season tie between the two clubs; the following year, he finished second to New York by a single game when his team failed to beat the Yankees in the last 2 games of the season, the second defeat coming when he pinch hit for starter Kinder in favor of a worn-out Parnell. McCarthy's last year and a half with Boston were marked by impatience with rookies, testiness with veterans he felt were coddled by owner Tom Yawkey, a greater-than-ever suspicion of the press, and a tendency to rely too much on the whiskey bottle kept for him on the end of the bench by trainer Gus Froelich. McCarthy resigned in June 1950.

TOMMY MCCARTHY (Hall of Fame, 1946)

McCarthy owes his Cooperstown plaque more to having been paired with teammate Hugh Duffy as Boston's Heavenly Twins in the 1890s than to his lifetime .292 batting average and .887 career fielding figure. The only future Hall of Famer to debut in the 1884 Union Association (with the Boston Reds), he played for thirteen seasons, mainly with the American Association St. Louis Browns and the National League Boston Beaneaters. The outfielder's specialty play was trapping a pop fly to get a force-out of a runner who was a greater threat on the basepaths than the batter. McCarthy's habit of feigning possession of the ball by tipping it from hand to hand while running toward the infield has won him erroneous credit for prompting a rule change permitting a runner to tag up and run as soon as a fly ball makes contact with a fielder; while he practiced the deception, the prohibition against advancing until a ball had been caught cleanly actually remained in effect until 1920.

TIM MCCARVER

McCarver has not had to make jokes about his lousy catching career to further his standing as one of baseball's more articulate broadcasters. In twenty-one years (between 1959 and 1980) spread among the Cardinals, Phillies, Expos, and Red Sox, the left-hand-hitting receiver managed a .271 mark while developing a reputation as one of the canniest game-callers of his period. His biggest moment offensively came as a member of the 1964 Cardinals, when he went 11-for-23 (.478) in

a World Series victory over the Yankees. In 1966 he became a rare catcher to lead a league in triples.

McCarver's major defensive liability was his arm—a deficiency that was largely neutralized in his final years as the regular catcher for Steve Carlton because of the southpaw's pickoff move. McCarver himself was the first to admit that his playing career was extended by a good five years because of Carlton's insistence on throwing to him and gave rise to his crack that he and the pitcher would someday be "buried sixty feet, six inches away from one another." As an announcer for both the networks and the Mets, McCarver has been praised for his astute insights into game situations and criticized for a frequently pedantic tone. His on-air observations have led to more than one clash with players and managers.

GEORGE MCCONNELL

McConnell was the unwitting cause of increasing pressures for the outlawing of the spitball. While pitching for a minor league team in Buffalo, he was scouted by Cubs manager Frank Chance as a possible addition to the Chicago rotation. Although the right-hander hurled a 2–0 shutout, Chance was so alarmed at the discovery that three Buffalo catchers had been hurt handling McConnell's serves and so repelled at the sight of fielders having to wipe off their hands whenever they touched the ball that he became an influential spokesman in major league executive circles for banning the pitch. McConnell eventually wound up on the Cubs, but only after Chance had stepped down as manager. In 1915, as a member of Chicago's entry in the Federal League, McConnell employed his spitball to rack up a circuit-leading 25 victories.

BILL MCCORRY

McCorry was the Yankees traveling secretary in the 1940s and 1950s who cost the club the services of Willie Mays. Sent out to provide a second opinion on the eighteen-year-old outfielder, who had received rave notices from regular scout Joe Press, McCorry reported back that the prospect couldn't hit a curveball. Chided some years later by John Drebinger of *The New York Times* for his seeming misevaluation, McCorry betrayed his conformity to the racism that pervaded the Yankee front office of the time: "I got no use for him [Mays] or any of them," he declared. "I wouldn't arrange a berth on the train for any of them."

WILLIE MCCOVEY (Hall of Fame, 1985)

Nobody ever hit a ball harder than McCovey, and nobody ever had a career so punctuated by other Hall of Famers. Brought up to the Giants in July 1959, the left-hand-swinging first baseman debuted by rocking 2 triples and 2 singles in a game against Robin Roberts. After the game, McCovey attributed his success to the batting tips he had picked up in Phoenix from Ted Williams; after his career twenty-two years later, McCovey had the same number of home runs (521) as Williams had. In the interim, there were Rookie of the Year honors in 1959, an MVP trophy in 1969, three years of leading the National League in home runs and slugging average, two years of setting the pace in RBIs, a league high in walks, and a major league record in intentional passes (45 in 1970).

Despite his splashy beginning in his rookie year, McCovey was bounced around for a couple of seasons after that, including return trips to the minors, because of the presence at first base of Orlando Cepeda. Depending on the San Francisco strategy of the moment, the two were moved back and forth between first base and left field, until Cepeda was finally traded to the Cardinals in 1966. During their joint stay on the team, the two sluggers were also rivals for the affections of Giants fans—both of them regarded as native sons more than Willie Mays, who had moved to California with the team after glory years in New York. McCovey's popularity was never more in evidence than on Opening Day in 1977, when, returning to the club after a few years with the Padres and Athletics, he was reduced to tears in the batting box by an endless ovation. At age thirty-nine, he responded by winning Comeback Player of the Year honors with 28 home runs. His 521 career blasts are the most by a left-handed hitter in the NL.

CLYDE MCCULLOUGH

In 1945, McCullough became the only major leaguer to miss an entire regular season but still appear in the World Series of the same year. He achieved the distinction by being discharged from the Army just before his club, the Cubs, met the Tigers in the series. McCullough, who had a fifteen-year National League career as catcher, made out in his only appearance against Detroit.

WILLIE MCGEE

McGee is the only player to be traded in midseason from one league to another and still win a batting crown. The switch-hitting outfielder did it in 1990, when a late August swap sent him from the Cardinals to the Athletics. Although his overall average including his Oakland at-bats was lower than that of National League runner-up Eddie Murray of the Dodgers, he was awarded the title because of his .335 mark with St. Louis. McGee also won the NL hitting race in 1985, a year in which he took MVP honors for playing a critical role in the Cardinals' pennant win.

TIM MCGINLEY

McGinley was the Boston catcher in the very first National League game, played against Philadelphia on April 22, 1876. In that role he became the first major leaguer both to strike out and to score a run.

Willie McCovey is greeted by Willie Mays as he crosses home plate after one of his 521 career homers. National Baseball Library, Cooperstown, N.Y.

DAN MCGINN

McGinn had only a 15–30 record as a reliever, but he had 2 of the most memorable hits in Montreal history. On April 8, 1969, he hit the expansion franchise's first home run (and the only one of his career), off Tom Seaver. A few days later, the southpaw pitcher singled across the winning run to give himself the victory in the first big league game played in Canada.

JOE MCGINNITY (Hall of Fame, 1946)

There wasn't much that McGinnity didn't cram into his ten years of major league service from 1899 to 1908. Among other things, the right-hander was a prominent actor in the turn-of-the-century shenanigans involving two Baltimore clubs and the National League's two New York franchises, won more games than Christy Mathewson even when the latter posted 30 victories, and starred in some of baseball's most notorious brawls.

McGinnity forged a career-long alliance with John McGraw as a member of the NL Orioles in 1899, when, as a rookie, he led the circuit with 28 wins. He racked up the victories in a Baltimore uniform only because he had agreed to a McGraw request to hide his curve until April 15—the date by which Ned Hanlon had to choose the Oriole players he wanted to take with him to Brooklyn as part of a syndicate scheme that saw the same people running the two clubs. When the Baltimore franchise was folded at the end of the year, McGinnity went over to Brooklyn anyway, where he again paced NL hurlers, with 29 victories. Hanlon barely had time to savor that triumph when McGraw returned to Baltimore as manager of the American League franchise in the city, and McGinnity jumped back to his mentor, this time not leading the league but still throwing 26 victories. Then came the second boondoggle, when McGraw himself helped arrange the dissolution of the Orioles' franchise by moving to the Giants as manager in 1902, taking McGinnity (among others) with him. Dividing his season between the teams and the leagues, the hurler posted 21 victories, but that turned out to be only a prelude.

Between 1903 and 1906 McGinnity won 114 games for New York, racking up 31 in 1903 and 35 the following season; in the latter year he also paced the NL in both winning percentage (.814) and ERA (1.61). In 1903 and 1904 he combined with Mathewson for a staggering total of 129 wins, in each of the two years edging his fellow Hall of Famer in the victory column. Two more 20-win seasons followed, in 1905 and 1906. Having worked in an iron foundry, he was known as Iron Man even before becoming a mound workhorse who holds the twentieth-century NL season record for innings pitched (434 in 1903); in addition, he pitched both games of a doubleheader five times and possesses a record for hurling 2 complete-game victories on the same day three times—all 6 wins coming in the same month (August 1903). His overall career record was 247–144, with a 2.64 ERA.

McGinnity's success didn't come quietly. He was fined by the NL on numerous occasions for having instigated field and grandstand brawls. On one occasion, NL president Harry Pulliam accused him of "attempting to make the ballpark a slaughterhouse." Pulliam made the charge with some reason: At the peak of his career, McGinnity had the frightening big league record of hitting one of every nineteen batters he faced. His reputation was such that even when an explosion of violence wasn't his fault, he was still fingered as its catalyst; typical was a 1908 episode in Boston when the pitcher and McGraw went to the aid of a Braves fan being roughed up by security guards and, despite having most of the spectators on their side during an ensuing melee, were arrested for fomenting a riot. It was also McGinnity who was the first Giant who realized what the Cubs were up to after Fred Merkle's failure to touch second base in September 1908; he grabbed the ball that would have forced out the first baseman and fired it into the stands in what turned out to be a futile attempt to stave off the consequences of Merkle's Boner.

BILL MCGOWAN (Hall of Fame, 1992)

McGowan was the Lou Gehrig of umpires. During his thirty years (1925–54) with the American League he put together a record streak of 2,541 consecutive games—a stretch of 16½ seasons without an absence.

John McGraw was still in his early thirties when he decided to retire as a player and concentrate on managing the Giants. Cleveland Public Library.

JOHN MCGRAW (Hall of Fame, 1937)

McGraw and his Giants held sway over baseball at the beginning of the century with a dynastic consistency that only the Yankees ever matched on an organizational level and that nobody ever equaled on an individual basis. Between 1903 and 1931, the Little Napoleon of managers compiled ten pennants, eleven second-place finishes, and six other first-division showings. But over and above the statistics of his piloting record, McGraw imbued the game with a personality—tough and often vicious, insightful and often innovative, enigmatic and often suspect—that defined the contours of the national pastime for generations. In the context of his earlier, electrifying playing career, of his run-ins with every luminary of the sport for more than four decades, and of his practical administrative impact on more franchises than his own, even his managing of the Giants accounted for only part of his significance.

For the first decade of his major league life,

McGraw was a left-hand-hitting third baseman for Baltimore—initially with the American Association Orioles (1891), then with the National League franchise operating under the same nickname (1892–99). After breaking in with a couple of passable seasons, he came in to his own in 1893 with an average of .321, 101 walks, and 123 runs scored. That turned out to be his lowest batting mark for nine years, with a high of .391 coming in 1899. It was also the first of three times that he would draw 100 bases on balls and the first of five seasons that he would score 100 runs. Thrown into the mix were two seasons of more than 70 steals. When he retired as an active player in 1906, McGraw had a .334 batting average.

But, as with his career as a dugout boss, McGraw's numbers as a hitter were the least of it. As a prize pupil of manager Ned Hanlon, he embodied the old Oriole style of play in all its legal and illegal aspects. In the former category, he teamed up with Willie Keeler to perfect the hit-and-run play, mastered the Baltimore Chop, and elevated the squeeze play to an art; in the latter category, he never got closer than ten feet to second base when going from first to third if an umpire had his back turned, grabbed the belts of opposition runners when they were tagging up from third, and continually interfered with catchers on throws to nab would-be base stealers. More than any of his teammates, with the possible exception of shortstop Hughie Jennings, McGraw was also identified with the intimidation tactics (honing spikes in full view of opponents) and incessant invective unleashed against adversaries and umpires characteristic of the Baltimore squad. If there was a brawl on the field, the Oriole nicknamed Muggsy was sure to be in the middle of it. The worst such melee took place in Boston on May 16, 1894, when fans became so caught up in a fistfight between McGraw and Tommy Tucker that they didn't notice that South End Grounds was burning down around them. On the other hand, McGraw also gave lie to the legends that would grow up around the Orioles in later years about how they were too tough ever to allow physical problems to stop them from playing: In 1895 he played in only 96 games after being felled by malaria, and in 1896 he appeared in only 23 games because of a typhoid fever attack. Questioned sardonically about these ailments on one occasion, McGraw, who rivaled Jennings and Wilbert Robinson in telling tales of the supposedly invincible Baltimore clubs, said with a shrug, "I came back, didn't I?"

Under the syndication scheme worked out in 1899 between the Orioles and Dodgers, McGraw was left behind in Baltimore as a playing manager while Hanlon took most of his best players off to Brooklyn. As expected, Hanlon's Dodgers won the pennant, but McGraw collected some unplanned consolation prizes. For one thing, he managed to hold on to right-hander Joe McGinnity by persuading the rookie not to display his curve until it would be too late for him to be included in the Hanlon exodus to Brooklyn; future Hall of Famer McGinnity ended up leading the league with 28 victories. If that wasn't enough to irk Hanlon, McGraw managed it by swinging a couple of deals on his own that allowed Baltimore to remain a respectable fourth; by continuing the kind of field melees that kept attention focused on his club; and, most annoying of all, by outdrawing the superior Dodgers on the road.

With the dissolution of the NL Orioles after 1899, McGraw moved over to the Cardinals for a season, but only after holding out for a contract without a reserve clause option. Despite regular appeals by St. Louis that he stick around as playing manager, he held to his original intention of returning to Baltimore in 1901 to assume that double role for the new American League's franchise in the city. Along with Robinson, he also invested in the fledgling club. Trouble started even before the opening of the season when McGraw partisans, representatives of the old Hanlon Orioles, and city marshals clashed over the right of the new AL team to the park used by the defunct NL squad. In the end, McGraw and his followers were evicted from the site, and the franchise was forced to build a new facility. Two weeks into the season, the manager ignited a year-long war between the team and umpires, involving protracted field tantrums, fines, and suspensions. AL president Ban Johnson, who had promised that his clubs would behave more decorously than those in the NL, held his fire only to

avail himself of some of McGraw's contacts for planting a franchise in the New York market.

The truce with Johnson ended quickly in 1902. On Opening Day, McGraw was thrown out for protesting a call. A few days later, he punched a visiting Dodger official for trying to lure outfielder Jimmy Sheckard to Brooklyn. At the end of April, McGraw got into a war of attrition with umpire Jack Sheridan, during which McGraw was hit by a pitch in five successive at-bats but not allowed to take first base. When he sat down in the batter's box to protest the fifth plunking, he was kicked out of the game by Sheridan. Ignoring the immediate circumstances around the ouster and agreeing that the umpires had reason for their hostility to the pilot, Johnson earned McGraw's enmity for good by suspending him for five days.

McGraw's revenge was thorough. In mid-June he met secretly with Giants' owner Andrew Freedman to plot his escape to the Polo Grounds and to take the Oriole players with him. Step one saw him deliberately provoke a late June argument with umpire Tom Connally, prompting an indefinite suspension from Johnson. McGraw then went to the Baltimore board of directors and suggested that, since he was so much trouble to everyone, he would cancel some $7,000 in chits from covering club traveling expenses if the team would tear up his contract. Step three was selling out his interest in the team and signing a four-year contract with the Giants. Step four was persuading Robinson and other minority shareholders to sell out as well, putting a majority interest in the club in the hands of various fronts for the Giants ownership long enough (twenty-four hours) to gut the Orioles of McGinnity, Roger Bresnahan, and others for the Giants, while also authorizing the dealing of Joe Kelley and Cy Seymour to the Reds. Before Johnson could step in, Baltimore was reduced to tatters. Step five came later, as Cincinnati owner John T. Brush, who had masterminded the plot, sold his interest in the Reds and took over the Giants.

Within ten minutes of his first meeting with Freedman and the Giants at the Polo Grounds, McGraw had released nine players and announced the end of a plan by his immediate predecessors, Horace Fogel and Heinie Smith, to convert Christy Mathewson into an infielder. Although

McGraw didn't accomplish much in the standings over the remainder of the 1902 season, it was an informative enough period to permit him to guide the club from the cellar all the way to second place in 1903 and to take his first pennant in 1904. His success was the result of several ingredients whipped into an original whole: an eye for baseball talent and a freedom from front-office restraints to go after it; his nerve-wracking Old Oriole style of play that kept opponents constantly on the defensive; a deliberately tendered image of the Giants as couldn't-lose swaggerers, which only made other teams press more against them; and constant umpire baiting aimed at getting the next call. Little Napoleon, as he had begun being called in Baltimore, was also a master psychologist, both in seeming to play up to the superstitions of his charges while tactfully turning them to the club's advantage, and in channeling most of his confidence-building to players who were being pilloried by the fans or the press for perceived shortcomings. In the former category, he manipulated the bizarre saga of Victory Faust as the club's good-luck charm between 1911 and 1913; in the latter category, he could not have been a more staunch defender of Fred Merkle after the first baseman's infamous baserunning lapse in 1908, or of Fred Snodgrass after the outfielder's error in the 1912 World Series had given the Red Sox a world championship.

McGraw's reign at the Polo Grounds was broken down into two major periods. In the pre–World War I years, he owed most of his achievements to pitching staffs that included eventual Cooperstown residents Mathewson, McGinnity, and Rube Marquard, as well as such solid starters as Red Ames and Jeff Tesreau; he also pioneered the frequent use of relievers, most notably Doc Crandall. Over the same period, the only position player with superior credentials was catcher Bresnahan. With the arrival of outfielder Ross Youngs in 1917, however, McGraw's squads became far more offensively oriented, becoming identified with the likes of Frankie Frisch, George Kelly, Dave Bancroft, Casey Stengel, Travis Jackson, Hack Wilson, Bill Terry, Freddie Lindstrom, Rogers Hornsby, Edd Roush, and Mel Ott. What was common to both McGraw creations was the pugnacious personality the manager strove to give

them—not only in the interests of intimidating opponents, but also of improving ticket sales. Typical was his decision to have special uniforms designed in 1906 that proclaimed the 1905 World Series victors over Philadelphia as WORLD CHAMPIONS. It was in these togs that the team traveled by horse and carriage from their hotels to visiting ballparks, infuriating the local population along the way. In the odd circumstance that crowds figured to be kept down by bad weather or by a host club out of the pennant race, McGraw would send telegrams from the team train requesting police protection upon arrival because of some "anonymous threats"; the sight of police reinforcements at the station was generally enough to boost ticket sales.

Field fights were incessant, and as often as not involved fans jumping down from the stands to join in. As for McGraw himself, he was blamed for inciting two riots of Polo Grounds fans against umpires in 1907; arrested for fomenting a riot in Boston in 1908; arrested for joining umpire Cy Rigler in a brawl against some Cuban fans in a Havana bar in 1911; chased off a New Jersey field by fans wielding sticks and rocks after protesting a call in an exhibition game against a black team in 1912; beaten up by Philadelphia fans for attacking pitcher Ad Brennan in 1913; fined for slugging umpire Bill Byron under the stands in Cincinnati in 1917; and accused of attacking Philadelphia pitcher George Smith in 1922. In addition to all these personal incidents, there was never any doubt in the NL office that the manager's temperament was the catalyst for the regular series of fracases involving New York players.

When he wasn't mixing it up with opponents and umpires, McGraw was going after league owners. In one instance, he began shouting across the field at Brooklyn's Charlie Ebbets, who was sitting next to the Dodger dugout; when Ebbets stood up and demanded to know whether McGraw had called him a "bastard," the manager replied, "No, I called you a son of a bitch!" Although few owners were spared such scenes (again, largely in the interests of getting an opponent to press against the Giants), McGraw's favorite target was Barney Dreyfuss, the prim boss of the Pirates. The messiest scene between the two occurred in 1905, when McGraw began shouting about Dreyfuss's (nonexistent) gambling debts and refusal to pay them, Dreyfuss insisted that NL president Harry Pulliam fine and suspend him for the slander, McGraw accused Pulliam of being a Dreyfuss puppet, and the other owners had to step in to deliver a plague-on-all-your-houses verdict. The incident forged an almost irrational animosity in McGraw toward Pulliam, to the point that McGraw even snickered when the NL official committed suicide a few years later in the wake of another anti-Giant ruling over the Merkle boner. As for Dreyfuss, he never bothered hiding his contempt for the Giants' manager over more than a quarter century, accusing him of everything from cultivating shady associates to attempting to pilfer Pittsburgh players by advising them to reject contract offers so they would become more attractive as trade commodities (among those named in this context was Pie Traynor, in 1924).

Dreyfuss had a point when it came to McGraw's associates. One of his partners in a New York pool hall in 1908 was professional gambler Arnold Rothstein. Rothstein was also close to Charles Stoneham, the bucket shop operator who bought the Giants in 1919 and advanced McGraw the money to buy a piece of the franchise. Both Stoneham and McGraw had interests in racetracks. Between the late 1910s and the mid-1920s, the Giants were also at the center of more game-fixing or bribery scandals than any club outside the White Sox. The Phillies and Pirates accused the Giants of throwing the 1916 pennant to the Dodgers. McGraw helped accused fixer Hal Chase get out of a mess over his play with the Reds, the signed him for New York in 1919; when Chase began acting equally suspicious as a Giant, the manager got rid of him—and third baseman Heinie Zimmerman—by offering contracts so ludicrous they had to be rejected. In 1922, pitcher Phil Douglas was exiled for soliciting a bribe from the Cardinals. In 1924, outfielder Jimmy O'Connell and coach Cozy Dolan were blackballed for making an illegal approach to Philadelphia shortstop Heinie Sand.

Particularly curious during all the scandals to hit the Giants was Commissioner Kenesaw Landis's attitude toward McGraw and the organiza-

tion. Aside from demanding that the manager and Stoneham divest themselves of their racetrack holdings, Landis was usually quick to squash suggestions that the New York brain trust was involved in anything untoward. This became especially noticeable in the aftermath of the Sand case, when the commissioner wasted little time exonerating stars Frisch, Kelly, and Youngs of collusion in the affair even though he never bothered to interview McGraw. When Dolan went to court to win vindication as an equally innocent party, Landis left the country on a lengthy vacation before he could be called to testify. All the time that the commissioner was expressing confidence in the Giants' best players, McGraw was helping to keep the sorely tested NL together by arranging for one New York contact after another to take over the Braves franchise in Boston. It was also McGraw who had brought together Jacob Ruppert and Cap Huston to purchase the Yankees in 1915. Aside from the gratitude of league officials, the manager's mediation efforts earned the Giants an unending supply of talented players from the Braves in one-sided trades and annually increased rents from the Yankees as tenants at the Polo Grounds.

As innovative as he had been in such areas as making extensive use of a bullpen and hiring full-time coaches, McGraw never accepted the brand of slugging baseball introduced by Babe Ruth, adding a new-versus-old theme to the 1921, 1922, and 1923 World Series duels between the Giants and the Yankees. He admitted savoring the Giants wins' in the first two Series as much as anything he had ever accomplished, just as he couldn't deny a particular sourness after the Yankees triumph in 1923. For their part, the Ruthian Yankees found themselves thrown out of the Polo Grounds—and thus built Yankee Stadium—because of the pilot's embarrassment and irritation that his own team was being outdrawn by the home-run-attractive AL club.

After winning the last of his three world championships in 1922 and the last of his ten pennants two years later, McGraw became increasingly distracted on the bench and began turning over the club for long periods to the likes of Jennings, Bancroft, Stengel, and Hornsby. One special cause of distraction was a Florida land deal

McGraw had been inveigled into endorsing in the newspapers; when it turned out to be a scam, depriving investors of some $100,000, he spent years paying back as much of the money personally as he could even though he was never formally charged or even sued for being part of the hustle.

By the late 1920s, McGraw had been sapped of much of his energy by minor ailments and the deaths of his closest friends—Jennings, Mathewson, journalist Sam Crane, and Youngs. This made McGraw even more alternately distant and authoritarian with his players, fueling constant speculation that he was ready to step down. Instead, he hung on until June 3, 1932, when he called Terry into his office and offered him the job as his successor.

Less than two years after he retired, McGraw died of uremia in a New Rochelle hospital at age sixty-one. His final record as a manager was 2,840–1,984 (.589). His most enduring eulogy was an observation by Connie Mack that "there has been only one manager, and his name is John McGraw."

TUG MCGRAW

McGraw's cry of "You gotta believe" became the rallying cry of the pennant-winning Mets in 1973. It also served as an example of the southpaw reliever's quick footwork, since it was initially uttered as a sarcastic crack to a late-season locker room pep talk given to the Mets by board chairman M. Donald Grant, whose baseball smarts were rarely recognized by anyone working for him. McGraw made the observation stand up by registering 25 saves during the year, most of them down the stretch drive and all of them followed by his trademark slapping of his glove against his thigh. The bullpen ace also had a lot to do with Philadelphia's world championship in 1980, returning from the disabled list in July and yielding only 3 earned runs over more than 52 innings for the rest of the year; he picked up two additional saves in the League Championship Series against Houston, and 2 saves and a win in the World Series against Kansas City. The redheaded fireman was a feast for reporters with such observations as describing his fastball as a Peggy Lee—as in, "Is That All There Is?"

'NUF SAID MCGREEVEY

The unofficial leader of the rabid Boston loyalists known as the Royal Rooters from the 1890s to the early 1910s, McGreevey's expertise in all questions touching upon baseball was universally acknowledged throughout the Hub City. The saloonkeeper's opinion, once expressed, halted further debate; it was " 'Nuf said." The Royal Rooters wrote parodic lyrics to popular songs to mock the opposition. Pittsburgh outfielder Tommy Leach credited their rendition of "Tessie, why do I love you madly?"—"Honus, why do you hit so badly?"—with contributing to teammate Honus Wagner's .222 batting average in the 1903 World Series.

DEACON MCGUIRE

McGuire is the only position player to appear in twenty-six major league seasons. The catcher, who hit .278 in a career that included stops with twelve teams, had his best years with the National League Washington Senators in the 1890s; it was with that team, in 1895, that he became the first receiver to set up behind the plate in every one of his team's games. On July 27, 1907, as manager of the Boston Red Sox, he sent himself up to the plate and became the oldest player to hit a pinch-hit home run. Five years later, on May 18, 1912, while coaching for Detroit, he became the oldest man to catch a major league game when he was activated during the one-day strike by the Tigers players over Ty Cobb's suspension; the forty-six-year-old got a hit in 2 at-bats and made 3 putouts and 3 assists.

BILL MCGUNNIGLE

McGunnigle is the only manager to win two consecutive pennants in two different major leagues; he has the added distinction of getting fired immediately afterward. The pennants came for Brooklyn—in the American Association in 1889, and the National League in 1890. The firing came about when Brooklyn Players League backer George Chauncey acquired a share of the NL club in 1891, and convinced new partner Charles Byrne that John Montgomery Ward should also move over from the PL as pilot.

MARK MCGWIRE

McGwire obliterated all rookie power records when he blasted 49 home runs for the 1987 Athletics. The right-hand-hitting first baseman burned a few more record book entries when he hit at least 32 homers in each of his next three seasons. In the early 1990s, McGwire was dogged by a series of foot injuries.

BILL MCKECHNIE (Hall of Fame, 1962)

Following a modest eleven-year career as a third baseman for several teams before 1920, McKechnie hit his stride as a National League managerial standby, accumulating twenty-five years of piloting during which he won four pennants and two world championships. Although represented as a hard-nosed disciplinarian, he frequently found himself in untenable positions between his players and employers and, almost as often, reacted with a marked passivity.

McKechnie got his first taste of managing while still playing with the 1915 Newark Peppers of the short-lived Federal League. After the league folded and he wound up his playing career with a few more years in the NL, he was hired by Pittsburgh owner Barney Dreyfuss in 1922 with two specific mandates: to polish the skills of third-base prospect Pie Traynor, and to reimpose discipline on a club that had become notorious for its antic ways. McKechnie succeeded with Traynor, but had considerably less luck with Pittsburgh's two resident clowns—shortstop Rabbit Maranville and his roommate, pitcher Chief Moses Yellowhorse. At one point McKechnie became so exasperated with the practical jokes of the pair that he insisted on rooming with them on the road; that led to folly when he returned to their shared hotel room one evening, found the two players sleeping off one of their regular drunks, and opened the drawer of a bureau to be smacked in the face with a couple of dozen terrified pigeons. Faced with McKechnie's inability to deal with his charges but otherwise satisfied with his managing efforts, Dreyfuss got rid of Maranville, Chief Yellowhorse, and a third prankster, Charlie Grimm, then brought in Fred Clarke. Although Clarke had various titles with the organization, his main task was to be a prefect of discipline.

In 1925, McKechnie skippered the Pirates to a world championship; on the other hand, he was helpless to stem the player resentment against Clarke, manifested at the end of the year when the team voted not to award him a World Series share. Although McKechnie squeezed a compromise out of the players for giving his ostensible coach a nominal sum, Clarke rejected the gesture and went to war on the players the following year. The upshot was a player mutiny in 1926 that ended with outfielder Max Carey being traded, outfielder Carson Bigbee and pitcher Babe Adams being released, Clarke being pensioned off, and McKechnie being fired for not having shown enough authority during the crisis.

In 1928, McKechnie popped up in the Cardinals' dugout after spending the previous year with International League Rochester. With such future Hall of Famers as Frankie Frisch, Chick Hafey, and Jim Bottomley under his command, he won the pennant, then watched as the Yankees rolled to a 4-game sweep in the World Series. Behind the argument that the team hadn't been prepared adequately for taking on Murderers' Row, St. Louis owner Sam Breadon returned McKechnie to Rochester after the season, turning the Cardinals over to Billy Southworth. Midway into the 1929 campaign, however, Southworth's martinet ways while the Cardinals were floundering caused Breadon to have another change of heart, and he switched the St. Louis and Rochester pilots. For a couple of months, McKechnie kept the club at a .500 level, but then began to take time off to run for public office back in his hometown in Pennsylvania. Knowing that Breadon was furious with his part-time manager, the Braves asked for permission to talk to McKechnie about taking over in Boston the following year, and the Cardinal owner was only too glad to get rid of the future alderman.

McKechnie piloted the Braves for eight dreary years, during which the club got no higher than fourth place and, in 1935, established a franchise-low record of 38–115 (.241), finishing 61½ games out of first place. For a while he even served as club president while the organization tried to undo decades of mess caused by owners foisted on it by John McGraw of the Giants. Just before a new front office under Bob Quinn was about to fire him, McKechnie submitted his resignation to take over the Reds. For the first seven of his nine years in Cincinnati, he kept the club above .500, in the process winning a pennant in 1939 and beating Detroit for a world championship the following year.

STEPHEN MCKEEVER

McKeever was the daffiest of The Daffiness Boys. A Brooklyn contractor, he and his brother Edward gained half ownership of the Dodgers in 1913 as the price for putting up the money to complete construction on Ebbets Field. A windy man, he liked to be referred to as The Judge—not for any juridical standing, but because of his intimacy with the borough's Democratic Party bosses and his proprietorial air on social occasions.

McKeever never disguised his desire to run the Dodgers—or his exasperation when one opportunity after another to do so was thwarted. In April 1925, for example, he and Edward had it out over who should succeed Charlie Ebbets even as the team president's body was still being waked. Although Edward got the best of that argument, his victory lasted literally only a few days because he contracted pneumonia at Ebbets's funeral and died shortly afterward. The Judge was already dusting off the president's chair when he was informed that the Ebbets heirs were throwing their support behind manager Wilbert Robinson as the new organization head. From that point on, The Judge let everyone know that he had found an exception to his frequent boast that he had never met a man he didn't like. It was, in fact, because of the relentless conflict between McKeever and Robinson that sportswriters began referring to the team's front office as The Daffiness Boys. While the organization went to seed around them in the 1920s and early 1930s, McKeever sat in the club offices in downtown Brooklyn banging his cane on the desk with endless denunciations of the manager-president, while Robinson kept shaking his head from separate quarters at the St. George Hotel.

By the beginning of the 1930s, the situation had become so desperate that National League president John Heydler named a brother-in-law of U.S. Supreme Court chief justice Charles Evans

Hughes to referee brawls. Even when Robinson was forced out, however, there was little appreciable improvement in the organization, with creditors descending regularly and office phones repeatedly shut off for nonpayment of bills. McKeever's one consolation was that, at age seventy-eight and with nobody else willing to take the job, he finally claimed the presidency before a divided board of directors. What was never really clear to his aging mind through a good part of the 1930s was that the board considered him only a figurehead, maneuvering him at will. He died in 1938, shortly after Larry MacPhail arrived and began raising the franchise from the gutter.

JACK MCKEON

Although dubbed Trader Jack for his readiness to complete ambitious deals, McKeon had equal experience in managing for franchises that were falling down around his ears. Sometimes he himself got a jump on matters by causing havoc in the clubhouse.

McKeon's first managing stint was with the Royals in 1973, steering the team to a second-place finish in his maiden year but also precipitating a near-revolt in 1974 when he fired popular hitting coach Charlie Lau. Among others, George Brett, Steve Busby, and Fred Patek accused him of jealousy over Lau's regular tips—about pitching as much as hitting—to the players.

With Oakland in the late 1970s, McKeon was in and out of the dugout while Charlie Finley dismantled the franchise by disposing of the club's remaining stars and allowing the Coliseum to fall into such disrepair that it was known as the Mausoleum. From there he moved South, to San Diego, where he had an oasis of success between two periods of chaos.

Taking over as general manager from the fired Bob Fontaine in 1979, McKeon gradually accumulated power as owner Ray Kroc distanced himself from the franchise and as organization president Ballard Smith fought a publicity war with Dave Winfield over resigning the outfielder as a free agent. By 1982 McKeon had gained enough leverage to bring in Dick Williams as manager and to embark on a series of deals that would earn him his nickname and the Padres a 1984 pennant. Among the players acquired by

McKeon within a two-year period were first baseman Steve Garvey, third baseman Graig Nettles, and pitchers Goose Gossage and Ed Whitson. What generally went unnoticed among the executive's building reputation, however, was that his key acquisitions (Garvey, Nettles, and Gossage) were signed as free agents, while his most conspicuous swap of the period—obtaining shortstop Garry Templeton from the Cardinals—cost San Diego Ozzie Smith.

McKeon's deals after the 1984 pennant earned similar results. A 1987 trade with the Mets that exported outfielder Kevin McReynolds to New York brought potential slugger Kevin Mitchell, but also a couple of mediocre minor league players who had better Shea Stadium notices than abilities; when Mitchell spent more time hanging around with toughs from his old neighborhood than delivering on the field, he was traded to the Giants, where he finally fulfilled his long-ball promise. McKeon's one consolation was that the deal with San Francisco brought one-year wonder—and Cy Young winner—Mark Davis.

In 1988, McKeon also had to tote up manager Larry Bowa as a failure, and returned to the dugout himself. For the next few seasons he wore two hats as Joan Kroc became more frantic about selling the club. When she finally succeeded in April 1990, the new owners, a consortium headed by television producer Tom Werner, discovered that McKeon was about the only one in the organization who knew what was going on. Before Werner felt confident enough about holding the reins, McKeon talked him into giving a multiyear pact to Greg Riddoch as manager and confined himself to his front-office duties. That lasted about a year, when he was ousted in favor of Joe McIlvaine.

AMERICUS MCKIM

When McKim agreed to form a Kansas City club to succeed Altoona in the Union Association in 1884, he accepted the most humiliating terms ever imposed on a franchise: The team's games were included in their opponents' records, but the Unions, as the team was known, could not win the pennant no matter how many games they won. The owner's revenge was that he made a $7,000 profit at the end of the season, while UA angel Henry V. Lucas lost about $100,000.

DENNY MCKNIGHT

A cofounder and the first president (1882–85) of the American Association, McKnight guided the always unstable league through turf wars with the National League (in 1882) and the Union Association (in 1884), only to be undone by his association with the Pittsburgh club. The president of the Alleghenys until 1884 and a stockholder thereafter, he was accused of partisan behavior in a dispute over the rights to infielder Sam Barkley in 1885, and summarily fired. His departure made a weak league even weaker, especially after the Alleghenys transferred to the National League in 1887 in protest over the AA's treatment of their former official.

DENNY MCLAIN

McLain's off-field activities as a player and his postretirement involvement in a string of felonies have cast long shadows over his status as the last 30-game winner in the major leagues. With one 20-game season already under his belt, the right-hander became the cover boy of baseball in 1968, when he went 31–6 (with an ERA of 1.96) to lead the Tigers to a pennant and take both MVP and Cy Young honors. The following year he led the league again with 24 victories, and shared a second Cy Young prize with Baltimore southpaw Mike Cuellar.

But that was only part of the story. Already in 1967, McLain raised some eyebrows when he claimed a mysterious foot injury down the stretch in a heated four-team pennant race; at the time, he had been well on his way to another 20-win season. In 1969, even as he closed in on his second Cy Young trophy, the hurler clashed often with manager Mayo Smith over the latter's role in getting pitching coach Johnny Sain fired; ultimately, McLain began showing his displeasure by missing workouts between starts and arriving at the park only shortly before games were due to start. The tension with Smith went on display nationally at that year's All-Star Game, when McLain, the scheduled starter for the American League, showed up late for the pregame hoopla in Washington, then left the capital altogether to return to Detroit for a dental appointment after rains had forced a one-day postponement of the contest. By the time he got back to Washington the next day, Smith had given the start to the Yankees' Mel Stottlemyre.

In 1970, McLain drew two suspensions from Commissioner Bowie Kuhn and a third from the Tigers, reducing his season to 14 games and a record of 3–5. The first Kuhn punishment came in February, when the pitcher was implicated in an investigation of a Michigan bookmaker who had profited from the Tigers' loss to the Red Sox in 1967, the year that McLain had incurred his mysterious foot problem. When writers tried to ask him about the investigation during spring training, McLain dumped ice water on them, causing the team to act. Kuhn's second suspension came at the end of the season, after McLain had been accused of waving a gun in a Chicago restaurant. The Tigers finally had had enough, and traded him off to the Senators in October.

After leading the AL in losses in 1971, McLain hung on for another year with the Athletics and Braves before quitting with an overall record of 131–91. In 1984 he was convicted of a series of federal charges covering everything from racketeering and extortion to distributing cocaine, and given a lengthy prison term.

DRAYTON MCLANE

A major stockholder in the Wal-Mart Corporation, McLane purchased the Astros from John McMullen for a reported $115 million in July 1992. His first important hire was Bob Watson, the first black general manager in the major leagues.

BILLY MCLEAN

McLean has the best claim to being called the first professional umpire. He was a former prizefighter, and his ability and fairness while officiating in the National Association led the National League to pay him $5 per game. His career, with the American Association as well as the National League, lasted ten years, between 1876 and 1890. A Boston resident, he regularly walked to games in Providence, setting out at 4 A.M.

JACK MCMASTERS

A former conditioner for professional prizefighters, McMasters became the major leagues' first full-time trainer when he tended to the minor

ailments of the American Association's Brooklyn Bridegrooms in 1887.

JERRY MCMORRIS

McMorris emerged as the head of the Colorado franchise in 1993 after scandals and public relations concerns forced the withdrawal of a couple of predecessors. A millionaire who accumulated his fortune by building the nation's largest private trucking company, his additional asset was an association with Denver that two penciled-in predecessors, Michael Monus and John Antonucci, didn't have. Monus, head of the Ohio-based Phar-Mor drugstore chain, had to step aside when the FBI filed charges against him for embezzling company money. The fallout from that scandal, coming at a time when the Rockies were trying to establish their regional identity, bounced back against Antonucci, chief executive officer of the Superior Beverage Group, also headquartered in Ohio. McMorris's ascension was aided no little by the pressures brought to bear on the organization by Peter Coors, head of the locally based brewing company.

JOHN MCMULLEN

McMullen had a zigzag fourteen-year (1979–92) run as owner of Houston that had more than one feature in common with the earlier administration of Roy Hofheinz. A New Jersey shipbuilder and naval architect, McMullen headed a consortium that rescued the Astros from years of being operated by creditors. To show that the new group was willing to spend, he signed Nolan Ryan to a big free-agent contract and brought back the popular Joe Morgan. On the other hand, McMullen's regime showed a near-fatal obtuseness in the case of pitcher J. R. Richard, interpreting as laziness what turned out to be symptoms of a coming stroke. The resultant publicity over the Richard case served as an embarrassing indictment of baseball's persistent stereotypes of black players.

Although the signing of Ryan and Morgan proved critical to Houston's 1980 division win, McMullen undid most of his good work a couple of weeks after the season by firing general manager Tal Smith, claiming that the move was necessitated by an attendance clause in Smith's contract that the organization couldn't continue to honor. In an uproar over the firing of the man considered the architect of the club's success, some of McMullen's limited partners banded together to buy him out. When that didn't work, they went to court to obtain a charter change that turned the franchise from a partnership into a corporation. Under the terms of the reorganization, McMullen had to accept a three-man administrative committee for major corporate decisions.

For the next several years, McMullen maintained a relatively low profile while new general manager Al Rosen put together most of the club that won the West Division title again, in 1986. By the middle of the decade, however, he was also making sounds about selling the franchise—assertions that would be heard for another six or seven years before he acted on them. In the meantime, to make the club more attractive to prospective buyers, he ordered the trading or nonresigning of such high-salaried players as Glenn Davis and Dave Smith, reaping a small bonanza when American League clubs in division races shipped such young talents as Jeff Bagwell, Pete Harnisch, and Steve Finley to Houston for the older Astros. It was also about this time that the franchise took the lead in offering bona fide major leaguers such as outfielder Pete Incaviglia and pitcher Doug Jones minor league pacts to come to spring training as nonroster players, then revaluing their agreements if they made the team.

In July 1992, McMullen finally sold out to Drayton McLane for a reported $115 million.

FRED MCMULLIN

McMullin was a utility player for both the White Sox and the Black Sox. One of the eight players banned from baseball for involvement in the 1919 World Series fix, he became involved in the plot only after overhearing a locker-room discussion between conspirators Chick Gandil and Swede Risberg and demanding a piece of the action. Even though he came to the plate only twice in the Series (and singled in one of those at-bats) and was the only one of the conspirators not reindicted after a mysterious loss of evidence caused the original charges to be thrown out of court, he was, nevertheless, banished with his seven teammates by Commissioner Kenesaw Landis. Never

appearing in more than 70 games in a six-year career, he had his most conspicuous moment on the diamond at Fenway Park in 1917, when he and Buck Weaver, later to be another of the Chicago Eight, slugged it out with gamblers who invaded the field in an attempt to force a forfeit that would protect their bets. He was praised afterward by American League president Ban Johnson for defending the integrity of the game.

DAVE MCNALLY

McNally really did it for the principle in associating himself with Andy Messersmith in the 1975 challenge that ended baseball's reserve clause and opened the way for free agency; in fact, the southpaw had already announced his retirement before seconding the Messersmith action and refused to be talked out of his decision even with the promise of big money offered by a free-agent market. Although he left the game from Montreal after a fourteen-year (1962–75) career, McNally was otherwise completely identified with Baltimore, turning in four straight 20-win seasons between 1968 and 1971. His single best year was 1968, when he won 22, struck out 202, and etched an ERA of 1.95. In 1971 he paced the American League with his .808 (21–5) winning percentage.

McNally also performed conspicuously for the Orioles, both as a pitcher and a hitter, in postseason competition. Among his appearances in League Championship Series and World Series he posted 9 victories while registering an ERA substantially below 3 runs per 9 innings. At bat he homered off the Mets' Jerry Koosman in the 1969 World Series; then, a year later, McNally swatted the only World Series grand-slam hit by a pitcher, against Cincinnati's Wayne Granger.

JOHN MCNAMARA

McNamara's eighteen-year managing career between 1969 and 1991 ended up being dominated by the lingering question that has become part of the lore of Red Sox futility in postseason play: Where was Dave Stapleton in the sixth game of the 1986 World Series?

Debuting as a major league pilot with the Athletics in the last few weeks of the 1969 season, McNamara was around to watch the conclusion of Reggie Jackson's first big year, then, in his first full season, was told by owner Charlie Finley to bench the slugger because of a salary squabble. Unable to mediate the differences between the two, the pilot was sent packing, accompanied by accusations that he was too nice. After three humdrum seasons and part of a fourth (1974–77) with the Padres, he was put in the unenviable position of succeeding Sparky Anderson with the Reds in 1979. McNamara surprised everyone by winning a division title with aging veterans and untested rookies, then was surprised himself when the Reds' NL-best record for the strike-shortened 1981 season proved useless because the team finished second in both halves under the convoluted split-season format. He was gone in mid-1982, with the team headed for a franchise-worst season.

McNamara's two years (1983–84) with the Angels were most notable for the number of injuries with which he had to contend; next came his fateful assignment with the Red Sox. He made his contribution to Boston's postseason jinx when he left backup first baseman Stapleton on the bench in the 10th inning of the sixth game. A hobbled Bill Buckner then let a dribbler off the bat of Mookie Wilson go through his legs for the error that scored the winning run and provided the impetus for the Mets to clinch a world championship in the seventh game. McNamara never explained his decision; instead, he defended Buckner and pointed the finger at Calvin Schiraldi, who gave up several key hits in the final rally, and at Bob Stanley, who sent home the tying run with a wild pitch.

McNamara got a pink slip from the Red Sox during the All-Star break in 1988, with the team playing barely .500 ball. His final piloting job was with the Indians in 1990 and the early part of 1991.

GRAHAM MCNAMEE

McNamee was baseball's first network play-by-play man. A singer by profession, he was originally hired by New York's WEAF to broadcast the 1923 World Series between the Giants and the Yankees. With the National Broadcasting Company (NBC), he began making his calls from coast to coast in 1926.

BID MCPHEE

Widely acclaimed as the best second baseman of the nineteenth century, McPhee played 14 seasons before becoming, at the start of the 1896 season, the last player to capitulate to the fashion of wearing a glove in the field. The result was a .978 fielding average—a record for second baseman that stood for almost 30 years. McPhee, a lifetime .272 hitter over eighteen seasons with the Reds in the American Association and National League, retired after the 1899 season holding almost every defensive record at his position; the marks included 529 putouts in 1886—a peak yet to be approached.

GEORGE MCQUILLAN

Pitching for the Phillies in 1907, McQuillan got off to the best start of any pitcher ever, yielding not a single run in his first 25 big league innings. A quality starter for three more seasons, he topped 20 wins in 1908 and led the National League in ERA in 1910.

HAL MCRAE

McRae became so noted for his roll blocks into middle infielders while playing for the Royals in the 1970s and 1980s that the regulation outlawing the maneuver became known as the McRae Rule.

CAL MCVEY

McVey was one of the original Big Four (along with Al Spalding, Ross Barnes, and Deacon White) whose move from the Boston Red Stockings to the Chicago White Stockings after the 1875 season signaled the death of the National Association and the birth of the National League. As a member of the first all-professional Cincinnati Red Stockings, he was involved in what were probably the two most significant plays in that club's history. On August 27, 1869, he hit a foul tip that the Troy Haymakers argued was a third strike, then used the dispute as a pretext to storm off the field, preserving a 17–17 score so that gambling associates would not have to pay off on a possible Cincinnati victory; the tie was the only taint in the Red Stockings' fabled winning streak. On June 14, 1870, with the Red Stockings ahead by 2 runs in the 11th inning, a Brooklyn fan jumped on McVey's back as he stooped to pick up a drive in right field; the batter picked up a run-scoring triple, and the Atlantics went on to score 2 more runs and hand the Red Stockings their first loss.

JOE MEDWICK (Hall of Fame, 1968)

Medwick's snarling personality was almost as conspicuous as his offensive abilities in his heyday with the Gas House Cardinals in the 1930s. When he wasn't tattooing National League pitchers, he was going after his own hurlers with fists for such perceived slights as staying in the batting cage too long or suggesting that he might have run a little harder after a line drive. Among those he squared off with at one time or another were Dizzy and Paul Dean, Tex Carleton, Ed Heusser, and Bob Bowman. More often than not, the right-hand-hitting outfielder's bat sealed over the brawls.

Medwick's greatest season was 1937, when he won the Triple Crown with 31 home runs, 154 RBIs, and a .374 average; the offensive explosion—which also included pacing the league in slugging average, doubles, runs scored, hits, and at-bats—marked the last time that an NL player swept the major hitting categories. He also led the league in doubles and RBIs in both 1936 and 1938. In the 1934 World Series against Detroit, he aided a St. Louis victory with a .379 mark. That became secondary, however, to the chaos that ensued in the seventh game after the Cardinals had built a virtually insurmountable 9–0 lead before the Tigers' home fans. Zeroing in on Medwick because of a 6th-inning hard slide he had made into Detroit third baseman Marv Owen, the fans vented their frustration by pelting Medwick with fruit and eggs. Commissioner Kenesaw Landis finally had to pull the outfielder from the field to enable the game to be played to the end.

In more than one way, Medwick was a typical creature of Cardinals general manager Branch Rickey. A gem of the St. Louis farm system, he was called up to the majors in 1932 after Rickey had disposed of another future Hall of Famer, Chick Hafey, in line with his theory that it was better to get rid of stars before they began to decline. In 1940, Medwick himself fell before the same philosophy, when Rickey dealt him to the Dodgers. It was also the St. Louis executive who

fabricated out of whole cloth Medwick's nickname of Ducky, claiming that some woman in the stands had been struck by the player's odd walk. The outfielder hated the nickname, but could do little about it when Rickey's public relations ploy of making characters out of his players proved successful with fans.

Only days after he joined the Dodgers in 1940, Medwick was beaned by old Cardinal nemesis Bowman. Although Medwick still had a few .300 years left in him, he never again hit with the power he had shown in St. Louis. Medwick ended up with a .324 average for his seventeen big league seasons.

BILL MELTON

A slugger with the White Sox in the 1970s, Melton's one-dimensional talents drew so much criticism from team announcer Harry Caray that owner John Allyn cited it as the major reason for the sparse attendance at Comiskey Park in the period. Melton had previously become a gate attraction by becoming the first White Sox player, in 1971, ever to lead the American League in home runs. In 1975, the third baseman appeared to have had the last laugh when Allyn announced that he was getting rid of Caray; shortly afterward, however, the owner sold out to Bill Veeck, and Melton himself ended up being peddled to the Angels. In July 1970 the righty swinger tied a slew of major league marks by striking out 7 times in a doubleheader, 10 times in three consecutive games, and 12 times over four consecutive appearances.

RUBE MELTON

Melton was in the middle of one of Larry Mac-Phail's more obvious finagles in 1940. Although touted for some time by Branch Rickey as a prized Cardinals prospect, he stayed in the minors because other clubs had grown gun-shy of the St. Louis executive's windy claims. When Brooklyn's MacPhail finally tried to purchase him, Rickey set the price at $30,000. MacPhail not only rejected the price as exorbitant, but made a passing remark that he would wait and acquire the right-hander more cheaply. Shortly afterward, the cash-desperate Gerry Nugent of the Phillies bought Melton for $7,500, then immediately turned around and sold him to the Dodgers for $15,000. A howling Rickey went to Commissioner Kenesaw Landis with charges that MacPhail and Nugent had conspired on the deal and that the Brooklyn president had even advanced the original $7,500 to Nugent. Declaring that he agreed with Rickey that "something was smelly," Landis canceled the deal between Philadelphia and Brooklyn, ordered the Phillies to keep Melton for at least two years, and censured both MacPhail and Nugent. After two seasons of a combined 10–25 record, the pitcher was sent on to Ebbets Field, where he only provided more evidence that Rickey had indeed once again outsmarted his rivals.

MARIO MENDOZA

It was bad enough that Mendoza batted only .215 in nine seasons as a shortstop for the Pirates, Mariners, and Rangers between 1974 and 1982, but then George Brett noticed it. According to the Kansas City star, the cutoff point in the Sunday paper listings of big league batting averages was "The Mendoza Line"; the point is usually at .200. After retiring as a player, Mendoza went to work in the California Angels system—as a hitting coach.

FRED MERKLE

Merkle holds the patent on disastrous mistakes by a rookie. The Giants' first baseman gained baseball infamy on September 23, 1908, in the 9th inning of a deadlocked contest between New York and Chicago with first place at stake. With Moose McCormick on third base with the winning run and himself on first after delivering a clean clutch single, Merkle failed to touch second base after Al Bridwell singled home what appeared to be the tie-breaker. When Chicago second baseman Johnny Evers saw him veer off the basepath and go running to celebrate with his teammates, he screamed for center fielder Solly Hofman to throw him the ball. New York coach Joe McGinnity, realizing what the Cubs were up to, braved a cluster of fans to retrieve the ball and, seeing Chicago shortstop Joe Tinker charging him, threw it into the left-field stands. Another ball was thrown onto the field, and Evers grabbed it, stepping on second to record the out. But when

the infielder appealed to umpire Bob Emslie for the force-out call, the latter claimed he hadn't been watching Merkle and passed the buck to colleague Hank O'Day. O'Day agreed with Evers, but refused to say so because of the thousands of New York fans swamping the Polo Grounds field. Only later that evening, in a conversation with National League president Harry Pulliam, did the arbiter recommend the out call.

Pulliam sat on his verdict for days, even allowing the Cubs and Giants to play again. Only with the visitors out of town did he rule that the tie stood and that the clubs would have to meet in a makeup contest after the regular season if the game could have an influence on the pennant race. In fact, the game proved decisive when the two clubs finished in a dead heat. Chicago ended up winning the makeup game and claiming the pennant.

Merkle had his defenders, most of them pointing out that touching second base in such a situation had been a very sometime thing until then. Manager John McGraw was particularly quick to diffuse blame on the nineteen-year-old rookie for the ultimate Chicago flag, noting that the Giants had plenty of other opportunities over the last week of the season to claim the championship. Merkle received his most extravagant support from Christy Mathewson—the only person in the Polo Grounds that day to insist that he actually did touch second.

The September 23 game was the first one that Merkle started. For the rest of his sixteen-year career (which concluded with a .273 batting average) and later in retirement, he refused to grant interviews on the subject of his baserunning lapse.

ANDY MESSERSMITH

Messersmith's successful challenge to baseball's reserve clause in 1975 signaled the start of the free-agent era. The right-hander assumed his originally unintended pioneering role following the 1974 season, when his league-leading 20 wins and .769 winning percentage failed to gain him the contract he had sought with the Dodgers. When the club unilaterally renewed his existing pact, Messersmith, backed by the Players Association, resolved to play through the 1975 campaign and then enjoin Los Angeles from automatically

Free agent pioneer Andy Messersmith wore number 17 to promote Atlanta owner Ted Turner's superstation WTBS. Photo compliments of the Atlanta Braves.

extending its option still another year. Joined in the action by Montreal southpaw Dave McNally, the hurler was vindicated by arbitrator Peter Seitz, who destroyed the century-old reserve clause by ruling that clubs did not have the right to renew contracts perpetually through one-year option clauses.

Following the Seitz decision, Dodger owner Walter O'Malley attempted to put a good face on his legal defeat by claiming that he was still interested in resigning Messersmith; at the same time, however, he was laying plans for black-balling players who took advantage of their free-agent status. The scheme was undone when Atlanta's Ted Turner signed Messersmith.

In addition to the Dodgers and Braves, Messersmith also pitched for the Angels and Yankees during his twelve-year (1968–79) career. A basic fastball-curveball pitcher, he had a second 20-win season, for California in 1971. A stipulation in his contract with Atlanta was that he wear the

number 17, becoming in effect a living billboard for Turner's TBS superstation.

GEORGE METKOVICH

Metkovich was a journeyman first baseman-outfielder in the 1940s and 1950s who never lived down an accident that ruined an initial tryout with Casey Stengel's Braves in 1940. At spring training that year, he spent an off-day fishing, caught a catfish, and while standing on his catch to remove a hook, got speared in his foot by the fish's fin. Subsequent surgery to remove the fin cost him his chance with the Braves and led Stengel to proclaim, "We got a first baseman who gets attacked by a catfish!" Labeled as Catfish for the rest of his career, Metkovich wound down his playing days with the grim Pittsburgh clubs of the early 1950s, where he himself became known for the odd, ridiculous quote. One day, for example, after waving futilely at another in a long series of line drives whizzing by him, he turned to the first-base umpire and shouted for all to hear, "Don't just stand there! Get a glove and give me a hand!"

BING MILLER

Miller provided the decisive blow on the only occasion that a home team has come from behind by more than a single run in the bottom of the 9th inning of a final World Series game. A steady if unspectacular outfielder with the Athletics in the late 1920s and early 1930s, he singled in the winning run in the decisive fifth game of the 1929 World Series. His shot off the Shibe Park wall to score Al Simmons, in the same inning as a 2-run homer by Mule Haas to tie the score, gave Philadelphia a 3–2 victory and a world championship.

BOB MILLER

One of the most well-traveled players in baseball history, Miller player for ten teams (two of them twice) in a seventeen-year (1957, 1959–74) career, most of it as a reliever. In 1970, 1971, and 1973, the right-hander wore three different uniforms in the same season. Miller's low point came as a member of the expansion Mets in 1962, when only a victory in the waning hours of the campaign prevented him from going 0–12. On the other hand, he was a key member of the Dodger relief corps in the mid-1960s, even leading the National League in appearances in 1964. Miller is the only pitcher to enter a game twice with the bases loaded and nobody out, throw a pitch, and get a triple play. (Only two other pitchers have accomplished this even once.)

JOHN MILLER

Miller is the only player to have homered in his first and last major league plate appearances. The right-hand-hitting outfielder reached the seats for the 1966 Yankees and the 1969 Dodgers. They were his only home runs in 61 official at-bats.

MARVIN MILLER

More than any other individual, Miller was responsible for the dizzying economic gains of players in the 1970s and 1980s, establishing the posture for taking advantage of the free-agency and arbitration decisions that destroyed the reserve clause and revolutionized the game's labor-management relations. As the executive director of the Players Association between 1966 and 1984, his astute organization of members also served as a model for major league umpires, while his negotiating successes with owners proved an indispensable premise for every recent development in the sport, from the increasing role played by player agents to the billions of dollars reaped through television contracts and merchandising markets.

Miller took the Association job in 1966 after working for some sixteen years as a researcher, economist, and legal consultant for the United Steelworkers of America. Major league players voted him into office by a margin of 489–136 after years of entrusting their affairs to Robert Cannon, an ownership toady mostly interested in becoming baseball commissioner. The vote came in the face of attempts by National League owner Warren Giles and others to paint Miller as a labor goon and only after initial attempts even by player representatives to flank him with Richard Nixon as a general counsel. Indicative of the wars on the horizon, Miller made it clear from his first meetings with the players that he regarded the Association as a union in the fullest sense and

not merely a professional guild with pension concerns. It was an attitude that was to amuse, scandalize, and finally terrify owners over the next two decades as their various ploys for dividing players fell apart.

Miller negotiated five major contracts with ownership representatives. The first, worked out in 1967, increased management contributions to the pension fund and raised the minimum salary of major leaguers from $7,000 to $10,000, but was mainly significant for having the owners concede to demands for collective bargaining. A 1969 negotiation session was thornier, with little progress reported on salary and pension issues until Miller threatened a strike at spring training camps. When the owners returned to the bargaining table, they recognized the Players Association as an official negotiating party in all matters except individual salaries and granted players the right to use agents in talks about their contracts. Years later, Miller himself would admit to some reservations about the entry of agents on the scene, warning players not to become employees of their own representatives and suggesting that 4 percent, not the customary 10 percent, was a fair fee for their services.

When the owners played hardball in 1972 over another basic agreement contract, Miller secured strike empowerment by a 633–10 margin, then closed down spring training camps for thirteen days and kept the players out of nine regular-season games until Commissioner Bowie Kuhn and the owners got the message. Both sides ultimately claimed victory with a compromise on salary and health benefits matters, but Miller walked off with the biggest prize in getting an extension on the arbitration principle, allowing major leaguers with only two years of service to seek binding arbitration in wage disputes. In the years that followed, arbitration emerged as the players' most powerful weapon in dealings with management.

Prior to the 1975 Messersmith-McNally decision, Miller attempted to work out an accord on the reserve clause that would have saved the owners some face. But they ignored the advice of even their chief negotiator, John Gaherin, to go for a compromise, suffering total defeat when arbitrator Peter Seitz handed down a verdict that effectively ended the contractual peonage of

THE BIOGRAPHICAL HISTORY OF BASEBALL

major leaguers. They also laughed off the counsel of one of their own, Oakland's Charlie Finley, who proposed that the clubs go Seitz one better by declaring every player a free agent—an approach that, according to Miller, would have been a logical countermove. Instead, after some useless courtroom challenges and a brief lockout, the owners came back to the table in 1976 to work out a pact that enabled the players to declare for free agency after six years in the big leagues.

The 1976 agreement stuck in the craw of Kuhn and several owners; they were especially irritated by the stipulations that provided for only amateur draft selections as compensation for clubs losing free agents. By 1981, with the stiff-necked Ray Grebey succeeding Gaherin as spokesman for the owners, compensation was being publicized as the principal problem between the Players Association and management. That was false on two counts: first, because it was a squabble primarily between the owners of small-market and large-market franchises concerning their respective resources for hanging on to or signing free agents; second, because Grebey and Kuhn, especially, were bent on using compensation issues as a pretext for breaking the union. As with past ploys, it didn't work, but this time that became obvious only after the players staged a fifty-day walkout during the 1981 season to defend their earlier bargaining gains. The nearest thing to a consolation prize for the owners was the creation of a compensation pool of unprotected minor leaguers and major league veterans for satisfying a team that had lost a free agent. The consolation lasted no more than four years: In 1985, after some bad publicity stemming from the White Sox grab of Tom Seaver from the Mets, the owners themselves asked that the pool idea be abandoned in favor of a return to a compensation system involving amateur draft choices.

Miller retired as Players Association director in 1982. Less than a year later, however, he was asked back on an interim basis when his successor, former federal mediator Ken Moffett, estranged the players with both his secretive style and what were perceived as giveback tactics. Only with the election of Donald Fehr in 1984 did Miller step down for good. What he left behind were the greatest financial gains by any

American union for such a short period in the country's history. Between 1876 and 1976, for instance, major leaguers averaged slightly less than seven times the standard U.S. salary; by the early 1990s, following the Association negotiations in the era of free agency and arbitration, big leaguers were averaging fifty times more than other American workers.

STU MILLER

Miller was the first reliever to win Fireman of the Year honors in both leagues. A right-handed junkballer who threw slow, slower, and slower still, he racked up the most saves for the Giants in 1961 and for the Orioles in 1963. In 1958, his 2.48 ERA for San Francisco was the lowest in the league. Miller provided the most graphic demonstration of the atrocious playing conditions at Candlestick Park when, in the middle of a delivery, he was blown off the mound by a gust of wind in the 1961 All-Star Game. He ended up as the winning pitcher in the contest.

A. G. MILLS

The third president of the National League, Mills made his most significant contribution to the game by defining, in two internecine wars with upstart leagues, the extent to which the NL would share its monopoly. Succeeding to the presidency in 1882, he inherited a league so unstable he refused to list the franchises on his letterhead. Mills settled the struggle with the American Association the next year by convincing its leaders that a trade war senselessly gave players an opportunity to extract higher salaries by playing one league off against the other. The so-called Harmony Conference he convoked for February 17, 1883, resulted in the first National Agreement specifying the governance of baseball.

With the peace shattered again after the formation of the Union Association in 1884, Mills directed the battle by, among other things, expanding the reserve rule to include eleven members of each club, even though he admitted privately that the rule was "technically illegal," and endorsing the AA's expansion to twelve clubs to control the contracts of as many players as possible. At first Mills favored wooing back defectors, but with the May 1884 passage of the

Day Resolution, calling for the permanent black-listing of contract-jumpers, he locked himself into the opposite position so securely that it would eventually cost him his job. When the victorious NL turned around and not only reinstated the players on the blacklist but also offered a franchise to Union Association angel Henry V. Lucas, Mills resigned.

RUPERT MILLS

Nobody was ever more adamant about two sides living up to a contract than Mills, a first baseman for Newark's entry in the Federal League. After both the team and the entire league dissolved after the 1915 season, he announced that he had no intention of following the lead of other players in accepting buyouts for contracts extending into 1916. When he insisted on total payment for the second year of his contract, team owner Patrick Powers sought to ridicule his stance by demanding that the player do seven-hour work sessions by himself every day through a nonexistent season. But Mills did just that, showing up for sixty-five days at the club's erstwhile field for ''practice.'' Only after he had collected at least that proportion of the $3,000 due him did he agree to join a minor league team. A .201 hitter in 1915, Mills never played another major league game.

MINNIE MINOSO

One of the most popular figures ever to wear the White Sox uniform, Minoso has had his actual career with the team blurred by both faulty memory and quick-buck hustling. Although associated for many with the Go-Go Sox of the 1950s, for instance, the right-hand-hitting outfielder was not part of the club that won the 1959 flag, having been traded to Cleveland a year earlier. Minoso did most of his running for the team in the first part of the decade, leading the American League in steals in 1951, 1952, and 1953. During his first stint at Comiskey Park, the Cuban native also paced the league in doubles once, triples three times, and being hit by pitched balls six times; he reached the .300 mark on five occasions. Back with the White Sox a year after their pennant, he led the AL in hits and drove in 100 runs for the fourth time; at the time, Minoso was officially

pushing forty, though with rampant speculation that he was in fact several years older. In the crowd-pleasing style that had marked his first tenure with Chicago, he clubbed 2 home runs in the 1960 season opener, allowing Bill Veeck to set off the $350,000 exploding scoreboard that the owner had installed during the off-season. It was the first use of such a promotional device in the big leagues.

Most of the rest of Minoso's career was marked by the same public relations ploys. After wandering to the Cardinals and Senators for a couple of seasons, he returned to Chicago a third time in 1964, for what was supposed to be his swan song. But then, in both 1976 and 1980, Veeck brought him out of retirement for a few at-bats as a designated hitter so he could claim to be a five-decade player. When the same hype was tried again in the 1990s by owner Jerry Reinsdorf, with Minoso at least seventy, Commissioner Fay Vincent said no.

GREG MINTON

As a workhorse reliever for the Giants in the late 1970s and 1980s, Minton went a record 269⅓ innings without yielding a home run. The streak was finally broken by John Stearns of the Mets in 1982.

PAUL MIRABELLA

Southpaw Mirabella was the only player to return to the majors in a serious way after playing in the Florida Senior League of retired big leaguers. His 44 appearances for the 1990 Brewers dramatized, for many, the dearth of available left-handed pitchers. Another southpaw, Daniel Boone, appeared in a couple of games for the Orioles after the collapse of the Senior League in 1989–90.

BOBBY MITCHELL

Mitchell was the first left-handed pitcher in the major leagues; debuting in 1877 with the Cincinnati Reds, he lasted only four seasons and compiled a 20–23 record.

JACKIE MITCHELL

When she was signed by the Chattanooga Lookouts of the Southern Association in 1931,

Jackie Mitchell with her Chattenooga sponsor Joe Engel. National Baseball Library, Cooperstown, N.Y.

Mitchell gained the highest rung ever climbed by a woman player in organized baseball—at least technically.

Taught to pitch by Hall of Famer Dazzy Vance, the seventeen-year-old Mitchell, a right-hander, faced the Yankees in an exhibition game on April 2, 1931, and proceeded to strike out both Babe Ruth and Lou Gehrig. Although some sportswriters insisted that the two sluggers had only been clowning around, a number of New York players said that was not the case, that their only instructions had been not to hit back through the middle. A couple of days after the exhibition contest, Commissioner Kenesaw Landis voided Mitchell's contract with Chattanooga, claiming that baseball was too rough for women.

JOHNNY MIZE (Hall of Fame, 1981)

Mize was in the long tradition of Cardinals' first basemen who didn't let their power affect their consistency. Over a fifteen-year career between 1936 and 1953 that also included big mo-

ments with the Giants and Yankees, the lefty slugger led the league in home runs four times and, in 1939, won the batting title with a .349 mark. Aside from the fact that he batted over .300 in his first nine big league seasons (leading to a career average of .312), Mize demonstrated his batting eye by striking out more than 50 times in only one season. Although his brawny frame won him the name of The Big Cat early in his career, he also had sufficient speed to lead the NL in triples in 1938. Among his records are those for most home runs in a season for a National League left-handed batter (51 in 1947) and most times (6) hitting 3 home runs in a game.

Like Ralph Kiner, the man with whom he had to share two of his home-run titles, Mize was no Branch Rickey fan. In 1935, prior to his first major league season, he was peddled to Cincinnati on a trial basis, but when Larry MacPhail discovered that the first baseman had a bad leg, was promptly returned to St. Louis general manager Rickey. After the 1941 season, in which Mize hit .317 and drove in 100 runs, Rickey dealt him to the Giants with the view that the slugger had seen his best days. It was with the New Yorkers in 1947 and 1948 that he hit a combined 91 homers. In 1949 the Yankees purchased him from the Giants, mainly to head off the Red Sox from making a similar move. Over the next five years, he played a key role in five Yankee championships, especially coming off the bench.

Asked once about his greatest disappointment in baseball, Mize admitted that it was his failure to "out-Rickey Rickey." This stemmed from the fact that his original contract with St. Louis had been signed by his father, who at the time had not been his legal guardian. In similar cases, players had been declared free agents.

KEN MOFFETT

The first thing Moffett did after being elected executive director of the Players Association in December 1982 was tell the player representatives who had given him the job—and who, along with other major leaguers, had waged a highly successful walkout in 1981—that "No one ever wins a strike." The next thing he did was go on vacation. On the job only three months, the formal federal mediator praised owners for signing what was in fact a terrible television deal, failing to realize that his observation might jeopardize a pending suit by the Association requesting a role in future negotiations with the networks. Moffett blundered further by supporting a joint drug program with the commissioner's office, long a sore spot among members of the Association. His gaffes caught up with him after a member of his staff confiscated a harsh memo from predecessor Marvin Miller, who had been retained as a consultant to the group. Moffett was fired after only eleven months on the job and eventually was replaced by former chief counsel Don Fehr.

PAUL MOLITOR

In fifteen seasons with the Brewers, Molitor ended up playing regularly at every position except catcher and pitcher at one point or another. In addition to his natural versatility and the hitting and running skills that demanded his presence in the lineup, his mobility was often dictated by injuries that opened up his most recent position to the latest rookie promoted by Milwaukee. In the 1982 World Series against the Cardinals, he was the first major leaguer to get 5 hits in a game in the Fall Classic. Molitor's next World Series appearance was in 1993, when, as a free-agent acquisition for Toronto, he took Most Valuable Player honors.

TOM MONAGHAN

The head of the Domino's Pizza chain, Monaghan ran the Tigers between 1984 and 1992—at first quietly, then crassly. For the first several years of his ownership, he was mainly conspicuous for benefiting from the collusion that kept free-agent outfielder Kirk Gibson part of the club in 1985 and pitching ace Jack Morris on the staff after that. In the early 1990s, however, Monaghan's attempts to pressure the city of Detroit into building him a new ballpark backfired twice over—first by arousing traditionalists who viewed Tiger Stadium as third only to Wrigley Field and Fenway Park as a venerable emblem of the game, then by chilling voters, who in March 1992 rejected proposals for new municipal taxes to pay for a modern facility. He didn't win any more plaudits by firing popular announcer Ernie Harwell after the 1991 season for criticizing the Ti-

gers' play. Then in August 1992, Monaghan was in such a hurry to shake the franchise that he fired team president Bo Schembechler by fax and organization chairman Jim Campbell by phone while the latter was attending Hall of Fame induction ceremonies in Cooperstown. A week later, Monaghan announced agreement to sell the Tigers to rival pizza magnate Mike Ilitch of Little Caesar's. Indicative of the kind of organization Monaghan ran is the fact that during his eight years of control only infielder Travis Fryman emerged from the farm system to be an everyday player for Detroit.

RICK MONDAY

Monday was the first player picked in the inaugural free-agent draft of college and high school players, in 1965. Selected by Kansas City, the left-swinging outfielder went on to a nineteen-year (1966–84) career that never quite fulfilled expectations of a premier slugger with Gold Glove defensive abilities. Although he ended up with 241 home runs, he reached the 20 mark only three times and never drove in more than 77 runs; on the other hand, he fanned at least 100 times in eight seasons. Monday's biggest baseball moment came in the 9th inning of the finale of the 1981 National League Championship Series, when his home run off Montreal's Steve Rogers gave Los Angeles a pennant. On April 25, 1976, he also won the hearts of red-white-and-blue Americans by stopping demonstrators from burning a flag during a game at Dodger Stadium.

ROBIN MONSKY

Monsky's sex discrimination suit against the Braves in 1986 was a result of her difficulties with manager Chuck Tanner, who objected to the media information director's practice of including unflattering statistics in the pregame fact sheets distributed to reporters. Barred both from the clubhouse and from traveling with the team, Monsky charged in August of that year that the manager's underlying objection was to a woman holding a position of authority. Fired in January 1987, she settled with Atlanta out of court in June 1989.

DONNIE MOORE

The Angels' bullpen ace of 1986, Moore served up a 2-run home run to Boston's Dave Henderson in the 9th inning of game five of the American League Championship Series, setting the stage for a comeback pennant win by the Red Sox. The right-hander never recovered from the blow, and within a couple of years was drifting around the minor leagues. On July 18, 1988, he shot his estranged wife (she recovered) and then put a bullet in his own head. Friends said that Moore had never stopped blaming himself for blowing California's pennant.

WILCY MOORE

Moore became a thirty-year-old rookie with the Yankees in 1927 after New York general manager Ed Barrow bought him sight unseen after reading about the sinkerball specialist's 20–1 record in the Class B South Atlantic League in an August 1926 issue of *The Sporting News*. Finishing 30–4 for Greenville in 1926, the right-hander repaid the executive's confidence by winning 19 games (13 of them in relief) for the Yankees in 1927 and saving 13 more. Injuries plagued the rest of Moore's six-year career, with the Red Sox as well as the Yankees, and he retired with a 51–44 record. He also notched 2 wins and a save in three World Series appearances.

BOB MOOSE

Moose was the mainstay of the rotation for the winning Pittsburgh teams between 1969 and 1972. But his progress was brutally curtailed when he unleashed a wild pitch in the bottom of the 9th inning of the decisive fifth game of the 1972 National League Championship Series, enabling Cincinnati to tally the pennant-winning run; thereafter, he reached the .500 mark only once. Moose was killed in a car accident at age twenty-nine.

JOSÉ MORALES

Coming off the bench for the Expos in 1976, Morales collected 25 pinch-hits for a season major league record. That was also one of four times during his twelve-year travels that the righty swinger led the league in pinch-hits.

PAT MORAN

Moran became the first big league manager to win pennants with two different clubs, piloting Philadelphia to a flag in 1915 and leading Cincinnati to a world championship over the Black Sox in 1919. In nine seasons at the helm of the Phillies and Reds, he finished below third only twice. The onetime backup catcher died during spring training in 1924 of Bright's disease complicated by his heavy drinking.

JOE MORGAN (Hall of Fame, 1990)

Of all Cincinnati's Big Red Machine stars of the 1970s, Morgan had the biggest reputation as a winner. Aside from his critical offensive and defensive roles on the Reds, the left-hand-hitting second baseman had a major impact on the Astros, Giants, and Phillies after joining them in the 1980s; in fact, it wasn't until his swan song as a member of the Athletics in 1984 that his presence failed to improve the fortunes of a club.

Offensively, Morgan was a force in just about every significant category. His biggest years in 1975 and 1976—when he won consecutive MVP Awards for Cincinnati—saw him bat .327 and .320, tag 17 and 27 home runs, produce 94 and 111 RBIs, compile slugging averages of .508 and .576, steal 67 and 60 bases, and walk 132 and 114 times. He reached the 100 mark in both walks and runs scored eight times, stole at least 40 bases nine years in a row, and was in double figures in two-base hits over his last sixteen seasons. In his eight seasons with the Big Red Machine between 1972 and 1979, his on-base average was .410. His 268 career home runs include the mark (266) for second basemen. It was his single in the seventh game of the 1975 World Series that erased the practical significance of Carlton Fisk's dramatic home run in the sixth game, sealing a world championship for the Reds. Defensively, Morgan used the smallest piece of leather in baseball to win Gold Gloves every year between 1973 and 1977.

Moving back to the Astros, his original major league team, in 1980, a perceptibly slower Morgan still managed to spark Houston to its first postseason appointment; although the club went down to the Phillies in the League Championship Series, his 11th-inning triple in game three produced a 1–0 victory. Playing for Frank Robinson with the Giants in 1981 and 1982, Morgan helped lift the club from the nether regions of the West Division, but ultimately had to settle for a home run on the final day of the 1982 season to knock Los Angeles out of contention and hand the half pennant to Atlanta. Despite Robinson's energetic support, he failed to win a raise from San Francisco general manager Tom Haller after the season, making his trade to Philadelphia a foregone conclusion. Reunited with Big Red Machine teammates Pete Rose and Tony Perez, Morgan slugged 16 home runs—the majority of them down the stretch—to key a division win, and then a League Championship Series victory, for the Wheeze Kids.

Following his retirement after the 1984 season with Oakland, Morgan turned down a couple of managerial offers in favor of becoming a broadcaster.

GEORGE MORIARTY

A light-hitting third baseman for the Yankees, Tigers, and two other teams between 1903 and 1916, and later a feisty American League umpire for twenty-two years, Moriarty left his most lasting impression on the game during a two-year hiatus in his second career. Taking over Detroit's managerial reins from Ty Cobb in 1927, the former arbiter decided that his charges were insufficiently schooled in the art of stealing home. Using the experience he had gained in executing the play successfully 11 times in his playing days, Moriarty proceeded to display his technique at every opportunity—including in hotel lobbies around the league where, on various occasions, he knocked over patrons and decorative plants with his graphic demonstrations.

During the 1945 World Series between the Cubs and Tigers, Moriarty gained headlines for taking on the Chicago bench and its relentless Jew-baiting of Detroit star Hank Greenberg. An embarrassed Commissioner Happy Chandler, however, ended up fining the umpire as well as several Cub players for calling attention to anti-Semitism.

JACK MORRIS

Morris holds the record for the most consecutive starts on Opening Day, having inaugurated the season fourteen times in a row for Detroit, Minnesota, and Toronto between 1980 and 1993. The ace of the Tigers in the 1980s, the right-hander posted a major league-high 162 victories in the decade. Morris also pitched one of the most memorable games in World Series history when he fashioned a 10-inning, 1–0 victory for the Twins in the finale of the 1991 championship meeting with the Braves. Little more than twenty-four hours after the triumph, however, he filed for free agency, souring fans who had been listening all year to his profusions of gratitude that he had been able to pitch in his hometown. He moved on to the Blue Jays, where his league-leading 21 wins spearheaded another drive to a world championship despite an ERA of 4.04. After another injury-riven season with Toronto, he signed with the Indians, where he had to watch Dennis Martinez break his Opening Day streak in the inaugural game played at Jacobs Field.

DICK MOSS

In November 1994, player agent Moss announced plans for the formation of the United Baseball League as an alternative to the National and American leagues. The initiative attracted significant attention because it was outlined during the impasse in player-owner negotiations that had caused an interruption of the 1994 season. According to Moss and co-founder Robert Mrazek, the United Baseball League would be launched in 1996 with eight charter franchises in cities still to be determined. One of the key features of the plan calls for host cities to receive a 15 percent share of their clubs, 15 percent of the capital gains if the teams are sold, and additional guaranteed percentages of parking and luxury suite revenues.

LANNY MOSS

When Moss was appointed general manager of the Portland Mavericks of the Class A Northwest League in 1975, she became the first woman hired to run a club in organized ball.

JOHNNY MOSTIL

For several years in the 1920s, Mostil was a one-man Go-Go Sox, prompting Comiskey Park fans into a "Steal! Steal!" chant whenever he reached first base. The right-hand-hitting out-fielder listened to the crowd enough to pace the American League in stolen bases twice while running up a ten-year batting average of .301. Defensively, he was fast enough to be the only big league center fielder ever to catch a fly ball in foul territory, a feat he accomplished in a spring training game.

Mostil almost put an end to his own career in 1927, when he attempted suicide with a razor and remained unconscious in a hospital for several days. The official line was that he had been depressed by a painful jaw condition, but it emerged subsequently that he had been discovered having an affair with teammate Red Faber's wife and had been threatened by the pitcher. Mostil recovered from his self-inflicted wounds to put in another full season.

MANNY MOTA

Mota holds the all-time mark for pinch-hits with 150. Curiously, however, he never once led the league in that category, and got as many as 15 in a season only twice. After several seasons as a starting outfielder for Pittsburgh, Mota did most of his substitution work for the Dodgers in the 1970s. In both 1980 and 1981, he was activated from a coaching position to add to his total, going 3-for-8.

GEORGE MUIR

Muir was traveling secretary for the 1899 Cleveland Spiders, who set every major league record for futility: a 20–134 record, a .130 won-lost percentage, finishing 84 games out of first place, and an unfathomable 35 games out of eleventh in the twelve-team National League. At the end of the season, the members of the Spiders presented Muir with a diamond locket inscribed to ''the only person in the world who had the misfortune to watch us in all of our games.''

HUGH MULCAHY

A member of the Phillies' rotation in the second half of the 1930s, Mulcahy was known as Losing Pitcher Mulcahy even before his career mark of 45–89 left him with the worst percentage (.336) of any twentieth-century pitcher with at least 100 decisions. He also lived up to his name

by becoming the first major leaguer drafted into the military for World War II.

TONY MULLANE

Known as The Count for his good looks and suavity, Mullane played pawn in one of the more sordid demonstrations of nineteenth-century owner chicanery. In 1884, after two 30-win seasons, the right-hander, ignoring the reserve clause in his contract with the American Association St. Louis Browns, jumped to the Union Association St. Louis Maroons, but backpedaled when threatened with blacklisting. However, when Browns owner Chris Von der Ahe realized that he would have to come close to matching the Maroons' offer, he shuffled Mullane off to the Toledo Blue Stockings, in a threefold stroke of shrewdness: First, it kept Mullane out of the Unions' hands; second, it preserved the Browns' salary structure; and third, it gave the small-market, expansion Blue Stockings a bone fide star. At the conclusion of the season, which witnessed the demise of both the UA and the Toledo club, Von der Ahe reclaimed the pitcher, paid him an advance on his 1885 salary, and whisked him off to a secret hotel room to wait out the mandated ten days before a contract could be signed. Mullane escaped, signed with the AA Cincinnati Reds, and was slapped with a fine and a one-year suspension for flaunting the rules.

One of very few pitchers known to have thrown with either arm, Mullane also holds a major league record for surrendering 16 runs to Boston in the 1st inning on June 18, 1894; at the end of the carnage, Baltimore catcher Wilbert Robinson left the game, while Mullane stayed around until the 7th inning. Despite such outings, he posted five 30-win seasons and won 20 on three occasions.

WILLARD MULLIN

Mullin was a cartoonist for the *New York World-Telegram* who inspired two of the most noted nicknames for National League teams in the 1930s. In one cartoon, he depicted a band of grubby Cardinals going across railroad tracks with clubs in their hands toward a gasworks. Although Leo Durocher has often been credited with dubbing his club The Gas House Gang, Durocher himself said that he was inspired by the Mullin cartoon. A couple of years later, the cartoonist came up with an Emmett Kelly-like tramp as a symbol of the Dodgers, leading the team to be known as the Bums. Mullin drew the figure as commentary on a franchise that had deteriorated to the point that even its office phones had been shut off for nonpayment of bills. The most famous version of the Bum character was published following Brooklyn's 1955 World Series victory, with the headline NOW WHO'S A BUM?

VAN LINGLE MUNGO

Mungo's melodious name wasn't backed by a lyrical personality. Regarded as Brooklyn's franchise hope in the early 1930s, the right-hander gradually succumbed to the bad luck and bad teams undermining most of his mound appearances and eventually became better known as a drinker and a brawler. Mungo probably reached his low point at the start of the 1936 season when, after promising that he would keep a leash on his temper, he yielded a run to the Giants in the 1st inning of the Opening Day game, got thrown out for arguing in the 2nd inning, came right back the next day to lose, 1–0 on an error, then lost a third game on what should have been a pop fly to end the contest. Following the third fiasco, Mungo announced that he was tired of playing with amateurs and jumped the team. Manager Casey Stengel talked him back to the Dodgers, and he went on to 18 wins—and 19 losses—that season. A couple of years later, the pitcher had to be smuggled out of Cuba when he broke the team's curfew rules, ended up with a hotel singer whose husband objected to a late-night tryst, and got into a bloody knife fight.

THURMAN MUNSON

For eleven seasons (1969–79), catcher Munson was the heart of Yankee teams bad and good until he was killed in an airplane crash on August 2, 1979. The American League Rookie of the Year in 1970 for his .302 average, the righty batter went on to post three more .300 seasons between 1975 and 1977, also recording at least 100 RBIs in each of those years and taking MVP honors in 1976. He was even better in October, topping his overall regular-season average of .292 by 65

points in 30 postseason contests, including an average of .373 in three World Series.

Moody with reporters and fans but the team leader and captain in the clubhouse, Munson became a rallying point against free-agent acquisition Reggie Jackson in 1977, especially after the appearance of the outfielder's *Sport* magazine interview claiming to be "the straw that stirs the drink" and charging that Munson "can only stir it bad." Yankee brass had attempted for years to talk the receiver out of virtually commuting from Yankee Stadium to his home in Canton in a private plane; the fatal crash came while he was practicing takeoffs and landings.

MASANORI MURAKAMI

The only Japanese to play in the major leagues, Murakami had a 5–1 record in 53 relief appearances and a single start for the Giants in 1964 and 1965. He returned to Japan when his father insisted that the honor of the family required that he pitch in his homeland.

TIM MURNANE

Murnane was the first major leaguer to turn to sportswriting to earn a living after his playing days were over. A professional first baseman before the founding of the National Association in 1871, he appeared in the first National League game on April 22, 1876, recording the first major league stolen base in the contest. As a journalist, he rose to be sports editor of *The Boston Globe*, a position he held when he died in 1917.

CHARLES MURPHY

As president of the Cubs between 1906 and 1913, Murphy put the finishing touches on the club that won four pennants in five seasons and then applied the touches that finished most of the team's pivotal players. Acting as a front man for Cincinnati magnate Charles Taft, Murphy appointed first baseman Frank Chance as Chicago manager, then backed a series of trades completed by the pilot for converting the runner-up Cubs into a flag winner. By 1911, however, the executive had tired of his regular contract battles with Chance and other Chicago regulars and was looking for a way to get rid of them. He found it when he claimed to have collected reports of numerous incidents of Chicago players taking the field in either drunken or hungover states; when Chance denounced the allegations as merely a ploy to save money on salaries, he was on his way out the door.

Murphy promptly replaced Chance in 1913 with Johnny Evers—a choice that promptly led Joe Tinker to demand (and obtain) a trade. When he then sought to get rid of Evers as well at the end of the season by trading him to the Braves, the second baseman threatened instead to jump to the Federal League. That brought National League president John Tener running with warnings that Murphy was helping the Feds stock themselves with NL stars. Tener pressured Murphy to unload his minority interest in the Cubs on Taft and depart the scene.

DALE MURPHY

Murphy may be one case of a player who wore out his eligibility for Cooperstown by being too nice. The People's Choice since moving in as an Atlanta regular in the early 1980s, the right-handed slugger collected back-to-back MVP Awards in 1982 and 1983 while in the midst of leading the National League in home runs, RBIs, and slugging average twice, topping the 30-homer level six times, and driving in 100 runs five times. But although his numbers played a large role in the Braves division win in 1982, they could do little over the rest of the decade to prevent the club's plunge to the won–lost depths. Even with the relentless losing wearing on him, however, the Mormon Murphy refused to walk away as a free agent, also rejecting suggestions that he press for a trade to a winning team. While this made him only more popular with the fans and the front office, it also gradually seeped the energy out of him, to the point that the team's own announcers began lamenting on the air that he couldn't play with a contending club. By the time a trade was finally made—to the Phillies in 1990—the outfielder was just about done. Ironically, it was almost immediately upon his departure that the Braves once again rose to the top of the West Division. Murphy ended up with 398 home runs, declining to hang on with the Rockies in 1993 to reach the 400 mark.

JOHNNY MURPHY

Murphy held the major league records for most victories in relief (73) and most saves (107) until the advent of the era of the closer in the 1960s. After a cup of coffee in 1932 and one season (1934) as a starter for the Yankees, the right-hander became a bullpen specialist, and virtually a private caddy for ace southpaw Lefty Gomez. Murphy's best year was 1941, when he led the American League in both saves and relief wins, and recorded an uncharacteristically low (1.98) ERA. One of the very few quality players to retire during World War II, he returned to New York in 1946 after a two-year absence to win 4 games and save 7 more. After a final season with the Red Sox, he retired with a 93–53 record. The general manager of the Mets in the late 1960s, Murphy died in January 1970, only months after the club's Miracle world championship of 1969.

LIZZIE MURPHY

On August 14, 1922, Murphy became the first woman to take the field against a major league team, when she played 2 innings at first base in an exhibition contest against the Red Sox. Aside from her Fenway Park appearance, Murphy barnstormed with amateur and semipro clubs for some eighteen years (1918–35).

MORGAN MURPHY

Murphy had a steady career as a backup receiver in the 1890s, but a more short-lived one as a buzzer operator. Playing for the Phillies in 1898, he set up a wire leading from the third-base coaching box to the clubhouse where, after glimpsing an opposing catcher's signals, he buzzed a shock code to his third-base coach; the coach in turn relayed the information to Philadelphia batters. Murphy's scheme came a cropper in a game against Cincinnati, when Reds third-base coach Tommy Corcoran uncovered the wire under the dirt and alerted the umpire.

ROBERT MURPHY

A former National Labor Relations Board lawyer, Murphy took it upon himself to form the American Baseball Guild in 1946. Choosing blue-collar Pittsburgh as his battleground, he applied for permission to hold a vote on forming his first local among the Pirates, but when owner Bill Benswanger stalled, announcing on the June 5 deadline that he needed more time to study the proposition, militant players pushed for a strike. Murphy blinked, however, calculating that by compromising he would win both the public relations battles and a favorable hearing for an unfair labor practices case he had filed with the NLRB. With the strike deadline postponed two days, Benswanger exerted his influence with players in a clubhouse meeting; when the vote came, the Guild managed a majority but not the two-thirds necessary for a job action.

The strike threat over, major league owners retaliated by establishing a minimum salary, providing spring training expense money ("Murphy money," as it came to be known), and funding a pension program for the first time. With the Guild's issues co-opted, twelve players didn't even bother to show up for an August 20 referendum on whether to unionize the team, and those who did, cast ballots voted overwhelmingly not to organize. The lawyer's final observation on the episode was: "The players have been offered an apple, but they could have had an orchard."

TOM MURPHY

Murphy was the first groundskeeper to tailor a playing field to the skills of a home team. Conspiring with Baltimore manager Ned Hanlon in the 1890s, Murphy sculpted the baselines at Oriole Park to incline toward fair territory to keep bunted balls in play, and packed the ground in front of home plate and around the infield to a concretelike hardness, in the first case to increase the height of Baltimore chops, in the second to give Oriole speedsters a better footing.

EDDIE MURRAY

Murray's power feats have gained only a begrudging acceptance in the media because of his years-long coolness to the press. Unlike Steve Carlton and others, Murray has made the situation even worse by influencing younger players to adopt a similar attitude toward sportswriters, winning for himself a reputation as clubhouse poison. Slighted by all the bitchery on both sides has been the most consistently productive career by any

major league switch-hitter, including Mickey Mantle.

Murray spent the first twelve years of his career with the Orioles, winning Rookie of the Year honors in 1977 for bashing 27 home runs and driving in 88 runs while averaging .283. Over the next eight seasons he never clouted fewer than 25 round-trippers except in the strike year of 1981, when his 22 blasts gave him a share of the league lead. He also drove home more than 100 runs five times, helping to set an unprecedented pattern of compiling at least 75 RBIs in every one of his eighteen seasons going into 1995. His lowest RBI total (84) would also have been higher but for the strike-shortened 1981 campaign, when his 78 RBIs was the league's best. At the end of the 1994 season, his lifetime power numbers showed 458 home runs and 1,738 RBIs.

Murray's final years in Baltimore were clouded by tensions with owner Edward Bennett Williams over a contract extension and by the subsequently regular attacks on the first baseman by the *Sun*, the city's only conspicuous newspaper and regarded as close to the Orioles' boss. It was because of the *Sun* snipings that the previously communicative slugger turned sour on the media. Traded to the Dodgers for the 1989 season, he continued to produce on the field, but came up against media-happy Tommy Lasorda before and after games, and was soon carrying his tag as a clubhouse pollutant. At the end of the 1991 season, the Dodgers let Murray walk off as a free agent, and he walked to the Mets. Over the next two years, while driving home a combined 193 runs, he was cited constantly as a bad influence on Bobby Bonilla and other New York players; it didn't help, either, that his once-superior defensive skills had degenerated almost pathetically. It came as no surprise when he was once again allowed to walk off as a free agent, at the end of the 1993 season, this time signing with Cleveland.

Despite his many games as a designated hitter with the Orioles, Murray established the new record for appearances at first base early in 1994 when, as a member of the Indians, he surpassed Jake Beckley's eighty-seven-year-old standard and concluded the season with 2,394 contests. Murray also entered the 1995 season with the record for most career assists by a first baseman (1,842).

IVAN MURRELL

Murrell, an outfielder for San Diego, Houston, and Atlanta between 1963 and 1974, was about the worst pinch-hitter who ever came off a bench. His overall numbers of 21–180 (.117) included seasons of 2–35, 3–33, and 5–36.

DANNY MURTAUGH

Murtaugh was the only manager who didn't need George Steinbrenner's whims to pilot the same club four times. Because of an umbilical relationship with general manager Joe L. Brown, Murtaugh was called on to take over the Pirates from 1957 to 1964, for part of 1967, in 1970 and 1971, and from 1973 to 1976. Each of his exits was prompted more by a heart condition than by front-office dissatisfaction. In his combined fifteen years at the helm, Murtaugh won world championships in 1960 and 1971 and East Division titles in 1970, 1974, and 1975. Unlike other field bosses, he went out of his way to play down his importance to winning, making a preseason ritual of telling his clubs, "If you keep it close in the 8th inning, I'll lose it every time, so make sure we have a big lead by then." What Murtaugh's humor concealed was an ability to get the best out of teams that varied widely in talent but that generally reflected his preference for lumber company sluggers.

As a player, Murtaugh had a modest nine-year career as a second baseman in the 1940s for the Phillies, Braves, and Pirates. His main distinction as a player was ending up with the most steals (only 18) in the National League in 1941 despite being promoted to the majors by Philadelphia with the season already half over.

STAN MUSIAL (Hall of Fame, 1969)

The most popular player ever to wear a Cardinal uniform, Musial went through seventeen seasons of his Cardinal record twenty-two-year career between 1941 and 1963 before his average dipped below .310, then found the energy to bounce back for another .330 season. Not the least of his accomplishments was compiling a higher career mark (.331) than comparable National

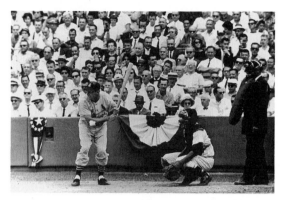

Stan Musial's unorthodox crouch was a feared sight to National League pitchers in the 1950s. Fred Roe.

League titlist Honus Wagner (.329), and that without compromising his overwhelmingly superior power numbers.

Dubbed Stan the Man by admiring Brooklyn fans, the lefty-swinging outfielder-first baseman amassed seven batting crowns, eight years of leading the league in doubles, five years of leading in triples, six years of leading in base hits, and six years of leading in slugging. He knocked in 100 runs ten times, scored 100 runs eleven times, and reached 200 hits six times. Although he never paced the league in home runs, he topped the 30 level six times, ending up with 475. In 1948 he missed a Triple Crown by a lone homer but led the NL in hitting with his career-high .376 as well as in slugging, hits, doubles, triples, runs, and RBIs; only two other players (Tip O'Neill in 1887 and Joe Medwick in 1937) reached the top of the lists in as many significant offensive categories. If there was one flaw in Musial's game, it was his running: He never swiped more than 9 bases in a season. In 1943, 1946, and 1948, he was awarded the league's MVP trophy.

Musial's charisma was aided by an odd batting stance that was all crouch and coil, giving him the appearance of a clamp gripping an invisible shelf. His popularity as much as his offensive prowess got him picked for twenty-four All-Star Games; even in 1957, when Cincinnati fans stuffed the ballot boxes to elect Reds' players to seven positions outside pitcher, they conceded that first base belonged to Musial. His six homers in All-Star competition are a high, as are his 8 extra-base hits and 40 total bases. The first player to appear in more than 1,000 games at two positions, he was sufficiently consistent at the plate to maintain a career average higher than .323 in every month of the season. He also managed the odd feat of dividing his 3,630 lifetime hits evenly between 1,815 at home and 1,815 on the road.

In 1946 Musial became the prime target of Jorge Pasquel's attempts to lure American players to Mexico. Commissioner Happy Chandler asserted later that Musial's refusal to abandon the Cardinals removed most of the threat from Pasquel's raids; at the very least, it enabled Chandler to outlaw the players who did go without fear of costing the major leagues a superstar. In 1960, St. Louis manager Solly Hemus provoked the wrath of St. Louis when he announced that he intended benching the aging star to give more playing time to rookies; Musial himself helped smooth over the minicrisis by proposing that he do most of his sitting on the road. In 1962 he was dragged into another controversy when franchise adviser Branch Rickey suggested that his .330 comeback that year at age forty-two was the last hurrah and that he should retire; Musial allowed as how Rickey's advice was "embarrassing," and the uproar chilled the executive's relations with other St. Louis front-office people for good, but in fact it turned out to be an accurate prediction, with the star retiring after a .255 performance the following season.

In 1967 Musial agreed to succeed Bob Howsam as Cardinals general manager, mainly at the urging of field manager and former roommate Red Schoendienst. Musial stayed in the job for a single pennant-winning season, making him the only general manager to preside over a flag in his lone year of front-office service. As a long-standing member of the Veterans Committee of the Hall of Fame, he was regarded as the main reason for Schoendienst's election to Cooperstown.

JIM MUTRIE

The holder of the second-highest won–lost percentage (.611) among managers with more than two years of service, Mutrie was the first to call the New York National League club the Giants, in an exuberant reference to the height of several players on his 1885 squad. In the clubhouse Mutrie was known as a player's manager, but in league counsels he was more commonly referred to as a double-dealer. The former reputation was a result of his genial backseat approach, sporting his trademark stovepipe hat, cheering his charges from the stands, and leaving the actual direction of field activity to a succession of field captains, most notably catcher Buck Ewing. Mutrie earned the latter accusation for leaking private information to the National League while managing the American Association's New York Metropolitans.

In 1884 Mutrie challenged the NL-pennant-winning Providence Grays to a postseason series with his own first-place Metropolitans, but lost all 3 games of the first officially sanctioned interleague championship series. The following year, he ended up in the NL himself after the AA fined and suspended him for his part in transferring third baseman Dude Esterbrook and pitcher Tim Keefe from the Metropolitans to their NL rivals in New York. The expulsion prompted John B. Day, who owned both franchises, to transfer the manager to his NL organization as well.

In the 1920s, Mutrie, in reduced circumstances, worked as a ticket taker at the Polo Grounds until Giants' president Charles Stoneham found out who he was and pensioned him off generously.

N

JIM NABORS

A right-hander with the 1916 Athletics, Nabors went 1–20 for the worst record by any pitcher with 20 decisions in a season. Indicative of the Connie Mack cellar-dwellers, that made him merely third in losses on the staff. Nabors had only five more decisions in his brief career—all losses.

FRANK NAVIN

Navin was an insurance company bookkeeper who gained control of the Tigers in record time and maintained it for more than three decades. He was a key player in just about every major dispute that affected the American League in the early going, and functioned as president of the league for a period. Many of his conflicts stemmed from having Ty Cobb on his club and having AL president Ban Johnson as an on-and-off ally.

Navin got involved with the Tigers in 1902, when his employer, Detroit insurance man and railroad contractor Samuel Angus, was awarded the franchise by Johnson in its second year of existence. At first it seemed like a brief involvement when Johnson sought to move the franchise to Pittsburgh for the larger Pennsylvania market, but that plan was ditched with the peace agreement reached between AL and the National League in January 1903. With Angus preoccupied with other business ventures, Navin had the influential say in the hiring and firing of several early-century managers; he continued to have it after William Yawkey bought out Angus in 1904.

When Yawkey revealed that he didn't have enough money to purchase star prospects, Navin formalized his own role by advancing the cash and taking over as team president. From that position he felt strong enough to oppose Johnson's dictum against extroverted managers who would give the AL the same raucous image that the NL had, hiring Old Oriole Hughie Jennings to take over the team in 1907. Jennings immediately piloted the club to three straight pennants—the only ones that Navin would enjoy for almost a quarter century.

From the day Cobb joined the Tigers on August 30, 1905, he became Navin's chief antagonist—especially, but not only, in bitter annual contract talks. Partly because of these arduous encounters, but also because of the numerous on-field and off-field acts of violence by Cobb, the executive was always open to a trade offer for his star, but could never finalize anything because other AL clubs were apprehensive about importing so much trouble into their clubhouses. One of Navin's worst crises with Cobb occurred in 1912, when Tiger players refused to take the field in a game against Philadelphia unless Johnson rescinded a suspension and fine levied on the outfielder for slugging a New York fan. Terrified by the prospect of having to pay a $1,000-a-day fine of his own for not fulfilling the schedule, Navin ordered Jennings to scour Philadelphia to find amateurs for the game, signed them to one-day contracts, and then watched them get drubbed by the Athletics. The crisis ended only when

Cobb himself appealed to teammates to end their protest.

Navin found his third compliant partner in the boardroom in 1919, when Yawkey died of a stroke and his heirs sold out to auto-body builder Walter Briggs. With Navin's holdings in the franchise up to 50 percent, he was confirmed as president by Briggs. Again, though, it initially appeared to be a short-term victory because of another attack that threatened the survival of the Tigers. This time the trouble arose from Johnson's resistance to a Cubs-inspired proposal to name Kenesaw Landis as baseball's first commissioner. The Chicago initiative had the backing of the seven other NL teams, plus the White Sox, Red Sox, and Yankees. When Navin came out in support of Johnson more vocally than other AL loyalists, the pro-Landis teams concocted a scheme that would lead to the creation of a twelve-club NL—the incumbents in the senior circuit, their three AL allies, and a brand-new Detroit franchise. Navin wasn't *that* loyal to Johnson: He quickly brokered a conference of all existing clubs and forced the AL president to read the writing on the wall, leading to Landis's election.

One of Navin's more unorthodox moves was naming Cobb as manager in 1920. Despite the star's frequently virulent relations with teammates, Navin's hunch was that the Tigers respected Cobb's baseball ability enough to play for him, especially with his relative mellowing over the years. Navin was proved right to the extent that Cobb kept the pitching-short club over .500 in five of his six years as dugout boss and supervised a clubhouse no worse than several others around the league. When the explosion came, in fact, it had more to do with his own relations with Cobb. In October 1926, Navin announced that Cobb was stepping down as manager and retiring as a player. The surprise move came in the wake of accusations by former Detroit pitcher Dutch Leonard that he, Cobb, Cleveland manager Tris Speaker, and Indians outfielder Joe Wood had fixed a September 1919 game. Although Landis stepped in to quash the charges with suspicious alacrity, Cobb had in the meantime accused Navin and Johnson of being behind the scandal in an attempt to break his multiyear contract with

the club, and threatened to sue. Thanks to Landis, the suit was never filed, but the incident ended Cobb's association with the Tigers. It also put a practical end to Johnson's tenure as AL president. Stung by charges that he had covered up the Leonard allegations, Landis demanded a showdown with Johnson and AL owners, making it clear that he would resign if he didn't receive full vindication. He did, and Johnson took off for a sabbatical from which he never truly returned; for some months, Navin was put in charge of the league's day-to-day affairs.

Navin's last moments of glory were partly the result of a miscalculation by Babe Ruth. Determined to get a box-office name to manage the club in 1934, the owner offered the job to Ruth, who had been talking of nothing else for years but piloting a team. But face to face with the only serious managing proposal he would ever receive, the slugger asked Navin to hold off until he returned from a series of personal appearances he had scheduled in Hawaii. Deciding that Ruth's interest was too vague, Navin purchased catcher Mickey Cochrane from the Athletics for $100,000 and named him manager instead. Cochrane then proceeded to win two pennants in a row, the first for the franchise since 1909. A month after the team won its only world championship during his reign, in 1935, Navin died of a heart attack.

RON NECCIAI

As a nineteen-year-old rookie on May 13, 1952, Necciai pitched the dream game, striking out 27 batters in a 7–0 no-hitter for Bristol of the Class D Appalachian League. Since one batter had grounded out in the second inning, it took an error by the catcher on the 26th strikeout to give the right-hander the opportunity to record number 27. Promoted ten days after his gem, Necciai left behind a 4–0 record, with only 2 earned runs and 109 strikeouts in 43 innings. With Burlington of the Class B Carolina League, he gave up 1.57 earned runs every 9 innings and struck out 172 batters in 126 innings, earning yet another promotion despite a 7–9 record. Finally advanced to the parent Pittsburgh Pirates to add a gate attraction to the end of their last-place season, Necciai struck out only 18 batters in 52 innings, racking up a 1–6 record with a 7.04 ERA.

BOB NEIGHBORS

A shortstop for the 1939 Browns, Neighbors was the only major leaguer killed in action in the Korean War.

GRAIG NETTLES

While carving a niche for himself as a formidable power hitter in twenty-two big league seasons (1967–88), Nettles became equally renowned for his glib observations on playing for George Steinbrenner's Yankees. Asked once about the continual chaos afflicting the team, Nettles declared, "When I was a little boy, I wanted to be a baseball player and join the circus; with the Yankees, I've been able to do both." Noting on another occasion that the previous year's top American League reliever, Sparky Lyle, had been displaced in the New York bullpen by free-agent pickup Goose Gossage, Nettles observed, "From Cy Young to Sayonara."

On the field, Nettles cracked 20 home runs in eleven of his seasons, pacing the AL in that category with 32 in 1976. While in the Bronx, the lefty-hitting third baseman contributed to five East Division titles, four pennants, and two world championships. His personal *bête noire* in his pinstripe years was slugger Reggie Jackson, with whom he traded ugly punches during a World Series victory dinner and about whom he once said, "The best thing about being a Yankee is getting to watch Reggie play every day; of course, the worst thing about being a Yankee is getting to watch Reggie play every day."

For a good part of his career, Nettles was considered second only to Brooks Robinson defensively at third. His four dazzling fielding plays against the Dodgers in game three of the 1978 World Series were eerily reminiscent of Robinson's defensive brilliance against the Reds at the beginning of the decade.

DON NEWCOMBE

Although he was the dominant pitcher on the Boys of Summer Dodger teams in the 1950s and is the only major leaguer to have taken Rookie of the Year, Most Valuable Player, and Cy Young awards, Newcombe could never overcome a reputation for not winning the big game. The right-hander's troubles started in the opener of the 1949

World Series, when he yielded a 9th-inning home run to Tommy Henrich to lose, 1–0. After that, Newcombe was the loser to Dick Sisler's home run in the 10th inning of the final game of the 1950 regular season, the exhausted pitcher who had to yield to Ralph Branca in the 9th inning of the final game of the 1951 playoff against the Giants, and the perennial batting practice target of the Yankees in World Series competition. His overall record in Series play was 0–4, with an ERA of 8.59. Often overlooked, however, was his clutch pitching down the stretch of the 1949 pennant drive, when he even started both ends of a doubleheader to keep Brooklyn in contention. Newcombe was also one of baseball's greatest hitting pitchers, ending his career with 15 homers and a .271 mark. An admitted alcoholic for a good part of his career, he has worked for the Los Angeles Dodgers for some years as a counselor to players with drinking problems.

HAL NEWHOUSER (Hall of Fame, 1992)

Nobody was elected to Cooperstown more begrudgingly than southpaw Newhouser. Although his 207 career victories included four years of 20 wins and he is the only pitcher to have captured back-to-back MVP trophies, he was belittled for years by critics who noted that he did most of his pitching during World War II, when major league talent was at a minimum. But in fact, Newhouser also compiled 82 wins between 1946 and 1949, when there was no such talent scarcity. Indicative of the franchise's priorities over the years, he is the only Detroit pitcher to have reached the Hall of Fame.

BOBO NEWSOM

Newsom was either the best bad pitcher or the worst good one in baseball history; he was certainly the player who changed uniforms the most times, with several of his departures caused by his swagger and bombast. The right-hander never ran into a fact—especially about his own abilities—that he couldn't exaggerate, or a lie that he couldn't defend indignantly as a fact.

In a twenty-year career between 1929 and 1953, Newsom won at least 20 games three times, but lost 20 in an equal number of seasons; for the Browns in 1938, his first 20-win season, he established a major league record for the highest ERA (5.08) of any 20-game winner. He concluded his career with a 211–222 record to become one of only two pitchers to win more than 200 games—and lose more than he won. (The other was Jack Powell.) With all this, Newsom considered himself the best pitcher in baseball and would announce this assessment to anyone willing to listen.

Newsom changed teams a record seventeen times in his career, never lasting more than two full seasons in a row with the same club, and was traded in the middle of a season an astounding eight times. The hurler served a record five terms with the Senators; for lack of any other logical reason for his recurrent pursuit of a hurler who seemed to save his most mediocre years for Washington, club owner Clark Griffith once asserted that he always looked forward to his nightly pinochle games with Newsom. The pitcher also did three stretches with the Browns, and two each with the Dodgers and Athletics, as well as individual stints with the Cubs, Red Sox, Tigers, Yankees, and Giants. He earned his nickname from a habit of calling all teammates Bobo, since he was never around long enough to learn any of their names.

In the eight-year period between 1937 and 1944 alone, Newsom changed teams nine times. Traded by the Senators to the Red Sox in mid-1937, he took to chasing Boston shortstop-manager Joe Cronin back to his position, complaining that player-pilots were more of a nuisance than the bench variety, because they had less distance to travel to annoy him; he was traded to St. Louis at the end of the year. Two years later, he irritated Browns bench boss Fred Haney by warming up in the bullpen on his own in a game against the Yankees and bringing the abuse of the crowd down on the pilot's head when he called for someone other than fan favorite Newsom to enter the game; once again he was traded at season's end, this time to the Tigers. When he complained loudly about having his salary slashed by two thirds before the 1942 season as a wartime economy measure, he was peddled back to the Senators. Shipped to Brooklyn by Griffith in mid-1942, Newsom tangled with Leo Durocher the following season over a passed ball that the

Dodger manager charged was a spitter and drew a suspension even though he was leading the club in victories at the time; when shortstop Arky Vaughan threatened to lead a walkout of players over the false charge, front-office chief Branch Rickey had to step in. The payoff was that Newsom was once again sent packing, once again in the middle of the season, back to the Browns. Knocked around early in his first nine starts for St. Louis, the pitcher was passed back to Washington, where he completed his only three-team season. Acquired by the Athletics in time for the 1944 season, Newsom lived up to his reputation for the unexpected when he stood up Connie Mack at what the Philadelphia owner-manager had planned as a dramatic contract signing before a winter baseball writers' dinner.

The other side of the story is that Newsom often pitched well for some awful teams—and did it with grit. In 1936, for example, he had his kneecap smashed by an Earl Averill line drive in his second start of the season for Washington, finished the game, then spent the next six weeks on crutches. On Opening Day of the following season, Newsom brashly traded autographs with Franklin D. Roosevelt—even though the president hadn't asked for his—then, once the game began, got knocked unconscious by a throw from third baseman Ossie Bluege; once again Newsom finished the game, after a brief application of a cold towel. When he finally got to pitch for a winner, the Tigers in 1940, his father died from a heart attack just after witnessing Newsom beat the Reds in game one of the World Series; his reaction was to go out and win the fourth game, and pitch well enough to win the seventh but come up on the short end of a 2–1 score.

The controversial hurler's observation on the owners he worked for was, characteristically, a malaprop: "Those maggots are nuts."

AL NICHOLS

Although he made only six appearances for the Louisville Grays in 1877, Nichols was one of four members of the team blacklisted for throwing games—a scandal that led to the collapse of the franchise. Purchased in July as a backup infielder, he served as go-between with gamblers while teammate George Hall delivered losses in 2 exhibition losses. Nichols may also have suggested that they bring Jim Devlin into the conspiracy, but Hall appears to have double-crossed him and proceeded to do business with the pitcher as a duo. Suspected of foul play early on by manager Jack Chapman, the infielder left the club before the end of the season and became fair game in the private inquiry subsequently held by club officials. Center fielder Orator Shaffer, for example, reported that Nichols had admitted betting on games and a willingness to throw games. Although banned along with Devlin, Hall, and shortstop Bill Craver, Nichols was the only one of the four to play professional baseball again; he reappeared, under an assumed name, with the Brooklyn Franklins in 1884, and was probably the Williams who played for Jersey City of the Eastern League in 1886.

KID NICHOLS (Hall of Fame, 1949)

Nichols was the best thing that happened to the Boston Beaneaters during the Players League war of 1890. Signed to bolster a depleted roster, the fastball specialist went on to what was probably the greatest decade-long pitching performance, winning an average of almost 30 games through the 1890s. He reached a career total of 361 victories without ever developing an off-speed pitch, led Boston to five pennants, and topped the NL in victories in three of his seven 30-win seasons. His most awkward moment on the mound came on August 6, 1891, when Cap Anson was awarded first base for jumping from the right to the left side of the plate, so distracting the young right-hander that he couldn't pitch; the rules of the day required the pitcher to deliver the ball no matter what, and umpire John McQuaid gave the Chicago manager-first baseman a free pass for Nichols's ''refusal'' to comply. Nichols's average 29-plus wins in the 1890s is a major league high for a decade.

BILL NICHOLSON

Long before grandstands were resounding with ''LOOOOUUUU'' or ''MOOOOKIE'' for every appearance by a favorite player, Nicholson was setting off a stadium call of ''SWISH'' whenever he strode to the plate. Originally inspired by the hulking outfielder's classic strikeout form, it be-

came a call of respect when Nicholson tore up wartime pitching as a member of the Cubs to lead the National League in home runs and runs batted in in both 1943 and 1944. The only other player to accomplish that tandem in back-to-back years was Mike Schmidt, and he had the benefit of the strike-shortened 1981 season.

GEORGE NICOLAU

Nicolau was the arbitrator who ruled in the Players Association's favor on the second and third collusion cases. In 1988 he found the owners guilty of collusion against seventy-nine players and awarded new-look free-agency status to twelve others. Two years later, in July 1990, he similarly decided that a data bank set up by owners through which they could share information about offers to available players constituted a violation of the right to an unrestricted free market of seventy-six members of the 1987 class of free agents. Among the players involved were Paul Molitor, Jack Morris, Dave Righetti, Mike Witt, and Jack Clark. By the time these two cases, plus Collusion I (decided by Thomas Tuttle Roberts), had been settled, the cost to major league owners would run to more than $100 million.

PHIL NIEKRO

Although the knuckleballer Niekro won 318 games over twenty-four major league seasons, he also holds a number of negative records. They include ties for the major league marks for the most consecutive seasons (four) leading a circuit in losses and for the most years (three) leading a league in runs allowed. More predictably, his knuckleball has earned him all the significant National League records for career, game, and inning wild pitches. The right-hander is also the last hurler to win and lose 20 games in the same season (1978).

Niekro's close ties to Atlanta owner Ted Turner caused a great deal of friction with manager Joe Torre in 1983, prompting a me-or-him ultimatum from the pilot. Although Niekro ended up a temporary loser by not being offered a new contract and then wandering around the American League for several years, Turner always insisted that he would be back in a Braves uniform for his final mound appearance. He was, in 1987, but had to withdraw after yielding 6 hits and 6 walks in 3 innings. In December 1993, Niekro was named manager-coordinator of the Colorado Silver Bullets, the first all-women's team to compete regularly against minor league clubs made up of men.

Niekro's younger brother Joe, who also used a knuckleball more than other pitches, was one of the NL's best hurlers in the late 1970s and 1980s. The Niekros hold the records for both most wins (579) and most years of big league service (46) by two brothers. They also hold the mark for the most combined losses (478).

BOB NIEMAN

Called up by the Browns in September 1951, Nieman put his name in the record books by becoming the only major leaguer to hit home runs in his first 2 at-bats. The right-hand-hitting outfielder had as many as 20 homers in only one of his twelve big league seasons.

RICHARD NIXON

Nixon courted—and was courted by—baseball before, during, and after his years as president of the United States. In the 1960s, he was approached by player representatives Robin Roberts and Jim Bunning to succeed Robert Cannon as attorney for the Players Association; the idea died when Marvin Miller refused to work with him. While in the White House between 1969 and 1974, Nixon popularized the ritual of receiving world championship teams; it was during one such encounter that he spurred Oakland pitcher Vida Blue into demanding more money from Charlie Finley. Despite being disgraced by the Watergate scandal, Nixon's name remained on the lips of major league owners whenever a league presidency or the commissioner's job had to be filled, not least because of his regular presence at Shea Stadium and in Gene Autry's box for California home games. His closest formal tie to the game came in 1985, when he accepted an arbitration role in a threatened strike by umpires; he averted the job action by granting the umpires a 40 percent raise, with the expansion of the League Championship Series from a best-of-5 to a best-of-7 formula. Nixon was also known for his regular notes to players whom he perceived as struggling against adverse circumstances. Among the

recipients of his letters was Luis Aparicio, when the shortstop was going through a dire slump in the 1960s, and George Brett, when the Kansas City third baseman was awaiting the verdict on his pine tar home run in the 1980s.

BILLY NORTH

The only thing North could do better than run was start locker-room fights. The center fielder for the brawling Athletics of the 1970s, he was in one major confrontation after another with teammates because of cracks about their abilities or their criticisms of his. The most serious battle took place on June 5, 1974, when North and Reggie Jackson went at it so violently that catcher Ray Fosse felt compelled to break it up; what he got for his trouble was a crushed disc in his neck that required surgery and sidelined him for the year. North was also one of the Oakland players most prone to giving the American League advice on how to handle A's owner Charlie Finley, such as when North warned in 1977 that if the league didn't immediately take over the club, Finley would walk away with the whole Bay Area, leaving behind a shambles of a franchise. On the field, the switch-hitting speedster led the AL in steals in 1974 and 1976, and teamed with Bert Campaneris for the most aggressive top of the order of the period.

JACK NORWORTH

It was while riding in a train past the Polo Grounds in 1908 that Norworth got the inspiration to write "Take Me Out to the Ball Game," first sung by diva Nora Bayes, the lyricist's wife. Neither Norworth nor composer Albert Van Tilzer, who wrote the music, attended a major league game until decades after the song had become baseball's anthem.

LOU NOVIKOFF

Novikoff came up to the Cubs in the early 1940s ballyhooed as another Babe Ruth, but managed only 15 home runs in four seasons. Aside from being unable to cope with National League pitching, he was undone by a phobia of the ivy growing on Wrigley Field's outfield walls. Despite a parade of doctors and psychologists brought in to reassure him that he had no particular vulnerability to the vine, Novikoff found it easier to chase after caroms off the wall than to plunge after any long shots while still in the air. When he refused to be convinced even by teammates who chewed some of the ivy to show him it was harmless, the outfielder was farmed out.

GERRY NUGENT

Nugent was an affable shoe salesman who married the personal secretary of ruinous Philadelphia owner William Baker, thereby putting himself in a position to take over the Phillies in 1933. To considerable surprise (and some titters), Baker left most of his stock in the team not to his wife, but to May Mallon Nugent; Baker's widow did the same thing following her death a few years later. Gerry Nugent, who had quit the shoe business a couple of years earlier to work in the Philadelphia front office and had risen to organization president amid all the chaos of the Baker reign, distinguished himself from his predecessor only in his personality: Whereas Baker had been hard pressed to hide a cutthroat demeanor, Nugent managed to maintain his cordiality while justifying one astounding player sale after another. Among the others he dealt off (usually behind the argument that the alternative would have been moving the team to another city) were Chuck Klein, Don Hurst, Dolf Camilli, Bucky Walters, Claude Passeau, Spud Davis, Dick Bartell, and Kirby Higbe. The result was that the club remained last or next to last for every year of his ownership. About the only positive news for the franchise in the period was the move out of dilapidated Baker Bowl; even that decision carried an asterisk, however, when the Phillies had to accept being tenants of the Athletics in Shibe Park.

Nugent missed his last chance for glory in 1942 when, faced with an ultimatum from other National League owners either to upgrade his operation or sell out, he considered a revolutionary proposal from Bill Veeck to break baseball's color line unilaterally and stock the team with Negro leagues stars. But then he and Veeck informed Commissioner Kenesaw Landis of their idea, and the league took over the team before it could be accused of countenancing antisegregationist acts. It was under league auspices that the Phillies were sold to lumber magnate William Cox.

JOE NUXHALL

On June 10, 1944, Nuxhall took the mound for Cincinnati at age fifteen years, ten months, and eleven days, making him the youngest major leaguer of the twentieth century. In two-thirds of an inning, the lefty surrendered 2 hits and 5 walks, retiring for the season with an ERA of 67.50. He returned to the Reds eight years later, remaining with them through the 1950s; his best year was 1955, when he won 17, leading the National League in winning percentage and shutouts. After ending his sixteen-year career in 1966, Nuxhall went into the Cincinnati broadcasting booth.

O

REBEL OAKES

Oakes was testimony to the informal blacklisting of players active in the Federal League. After five solid seasons with the Reds and Cardinals, the left-swinging outfielder moved to the FL Pittsburgh Rebels as a player-manager and provided the club nickname from his own. Seeking to improve on a seventh-place finish in 1914, club owner Edward Gwinner provided Oakes with a bankroll to raid other teams. While all FL players were officially reinstated to organized ball for the 1916 season, Oakes, despite his lifetime .279 average, was among those ignored because of his aggressive recruiting of players from the established leagues.

PETE O'BRIEN

First baseman O'Brien signed with Seattle as a free agent for the 1990 season after turning down offers from the Tigers and Phillies because of his stated fear that the two clubs might be contenders. He remained at peace with the Mariners into the 1993 season, when a sudden midseason spurt led a few observers to think that the team might win the West Division. Around the same time, O'Brien announced his intention of retiring.

DICK O'CONNELL

Nobody had a more embattled run as general manager than O'Connell did for the Red Sox between the mid-1960s and mid-1970s, and absolutely nobody returned to the post in the circumstances that he did in the 1980s.

After serving as the team's business manager for some years, O'Connell was made head of Boston's baseball operations in 1965. His first significant move was to hire Dick Williams, who managed the club beyond all expectations to the Impossible Dream pennant of 1967. Mainly because of frictions involving owner Tom Yawkey and star outfielder Carl Yastrzemski, O'Connell had to get rid of Williams a couple of years later, igniting several years of dim dugout leadership and the gradual evolution of the team's identity as "twenty-five players who took twenty-five cabs" after games. The general manager added to the oppressive air by evoking the Curse of the Bambino in dealing relief specialist Sparky Lyle to the Yankees in a swap for bit player Danny Carter.

In 1976, O'Connell met his Waterloo. With the winds of free agency blowing around the franchise, he hemmed and hawed throughout the season on renegotiating the contracts of star players Fred Lynn, Rick Burleson, and Carlton Fisk. At the same time, however, he turned around and announced that the Red Sox were ready to pay Charlie Finley $1 million each for Oakland reliever Rollie Fingers and outfielder Joe Rudi. Although Commissioner Bowie Kuhn ultimately scotched the deal with the Athletics, its mere possibility strengthened the hands of the three Boston players in the salary talks, especially when the local media and protesting fans began asking why the club had money for Fingers and Rudi but not for Lynn, Burleson, and Fisk. Making matters even worse was scouting director Haywood Sullivan, who was so bent on getting O'Connell's job that he leaked the particulars of the negotiations with the three Boston players, then led the tsk-tsk chorus about the inflated salary demands. When later in the year O'Connell also became the first front-office executive to offer a big contract to a free agent (reliever Bill Campbell), Sullivan closed the net by persuading owner Jean Yawkey that the general manager should be allowed to spend only what she personally approved. O'Connell didn't hang around Boston's offices too long after it was announced that Sullivan, Yawkey, and onetime club trainer Buddy LeRoux had formed a new owner partnership.

In 1983, O'Connell came back as part of LeRoux's administrative coup attempt against Sullivan and Yawkey. For two days, O'Connell sat in the club's offices with the title of general manager—the same one that Sullivan was brandishing. A Boston judge finally put an end to the farce by issuing a restraining order against LeRoux and O'Connell. O'Connell was long gone from the scene when the ownership squabble was worked out many months later.

JIMMY O'CONNELL

O'Connell starred in major league baseball's last big fixing scandal. An outfielder for the 1924 Giants, he approached Philadelphia shortstop Heinie Sand near the end of the season, offering $500 if the infielder did not bear down during an upcoming series with New York. Within twenty-four hours, the naive O'Connell was in Commissioner Kenesaw Landis's office, saying that he had been put up to the approach by Giants' coach Cozy Dolan and star players Frankie Frisch, Ross Youngs, and George Kelly. Although Frisch, Youngs, and Kelly all adamantly denied having any part in the attempted bribery, Dolan offered no better defense than that he couldn't remember whether he had urged O'Connell to tempt Sand. Landis banned the coach and the outfielder for life, but exonerated the three future Hall of Famers.

JACK O'CONNOR

O'Connor despised Ty Cobb enough to get himself thrown out of the major leagues. The manager of the cellar-dwelling 1910 Browns, he ordered third baseman Red Corriden to play deep throughout a doubleheader on the final day of the

season so that Cleveland's Nap Lajoie might dump enough bunt hits to beat Cobb for the batting race. In fact, Lajoie collected 8 hits during the day, 6 of them bunts that Corriden was unable to field. When American League president Ban Johnson heard of the finagling, however, he threw O'Connor out of the league, sending St. Louis pitching coach Harry Howell along with him for offering the official scorer a new suit if he would change a ruling on one of Lajoie's at-bats. Cobb won the batting title by a point anyway.

PADDY O'CONNOR

A backup catcher of no particular distinction at the beginning of the century, O'Connor was probably responsible for Leo Durocher's lengthy career as a player and a manager. While managing a minor league team in Hartford in 1925, O'Connor was inundated by complaints of a clubhouse thief going through players' pockets. Suspecting that the culprit was Durocher, he planted a marked bill in a pair of pants and then followed his shortstop after the game to a nearby hotel. As soon as Durocher handed a hotel restaurant waiter a bill to pay for his meal, O'Connor had the evidence he needed. But despite demands by a number of players that Durocher be denounced to the league (a move that would certainly have led to a lifetime ban from organized ball), O'Connor worked out a compromise under which Durocher would continue to play for the pennant-contending club, after which he would be sent packing. As soon as Hartford won the league flag, O'Connor made good on his promise—by selling Durocher to the Yankees. The thefts were not mentioned to New York.

HANK O'DAY

O'Day was never far from controversy as a pitcher, umpire, manager, or member of a rules committee. His single most notorious moment in any role came in September 1908 when, as an umpire, he called Giants' rookie first baseman Fred Merkle out for not touching second base after what appeared to be a game-winning hit in a Giant-Cub game. The decision ultimately necessitated a replay of the game in what amounted to a playoff that enabled Chicago to win the pennant. An arbiter for most of the time between

1895 and 1925, O'Day represented the National League for the first World Series, in 1903.

Before donning blue, O'Day had had a seven-year (1884–90) pitching career in which he posted three 20-loss seasons and one with 20 victories. He even managed for parts of two seasons—for the Reds in 1912 and the Cubs in 1914—compiling an overall record a single game under .500. The initial success of his Cincinnati club stoked suspicions that former umpiring colleagues were favoring O'Day's Reds—an allegation that evaporated when the team began losing regularly.

O'Day saved his most acrimonious moments for meetings of the rules committee, on which he sat for years. His 1920 disagreement with sportswriter Fred Lieb over a possible modification in the scoring of sudden-death home runs with men on base was indicative of his crustiness. Insisting that "you can't score runs after a game is over" and that a batter should be credited in such circumstances with only the number of bases required to score the winning run, he accused Lieb of trying to accumulate more homers for his friend Babe Ruth. Lieb's counterargument, that a fair ball hit into the seats was a homer no matter what the circumstances, carried a majority. The ruling was not made retroactive, however, and Ruth was not awarded what would have been a 715th round-tripper for a 9th-inning blast with a man on first on July 8, 1918.

EMMETT O'DONNELL

Major General "Rosey" O'Donnell was elected baseball commissioner at a meeting of league owners on August 21, 1951. The appointment had to be voided, however, when President Harry Truman refused to release O'Donnell from his duties as commander of bomber forces in the Korean War. A subsequent owner vote endorsed Ford Frick as commissioner.

O'Donnell had won the favor of the owners mainly because his military background would have been a public relations coup in a period when congressmen were challenging baseball's reserve clause. The owners had initially sought General Douglas MacArthur as their chief spokesman, but he declined for reasons of age. So intent were they on drafting a military man that they subsequently considered giving the post to Erle

Crocke, Jr., the head of the American Legion. Crocke put himself out of the running with one too many remarks about how the State Department was run by fellow travelers who didn't want to win in Korea. O'Donnell had thus emerged—briefly—as a compromise candidate between MacArthur and Crocke.

LEFTY O'DOUL

O'Doul was a legend on one coast, but only an explosive short story on the other.

After trying to make it as a pitcher for the Yankees and Red Sox between 1919 and 1923, O'Doul returned to the Pacific Coast League where, partly thanks to a sore arm, he gained renown as one of the circuit's all-time sluggers. Back with the Giants in his new role as a lefty-swinging outfielder in 1928, he contributed a .319 average, but was regarded as too slow and old (he was then thirty-one) by manager John McGraw, and traded to the Phillies. Within the comfortable confines of Baker Bowl, O'Doul proceeded to win the National League batting title in 1929 with a .398 mark; he also banged out 254 hits—the league record (tied a year later by Bill Terry) for the most safeties in a season. After a .383 campaign in the lively ball year of 1930, he was turned into one of Philadelphia owner William Baker's cash cows by being shipped to Brooklyn for negligible players and a conspicuous sum of money. With the Dodgers he won a second batting title in 1932, with a .368 mark. O'Doul's eleven years of major league service, which include his first four seasons as an American League hurler, saw him bat .349 overall; not counting the mound years, his mark was .352.

With the end of his big league career, O'Doul returned to the PCL, where he added to his West Coast reputation as the manager of the San Francisco Seals, the mentor of Joe DiMaggio, and the proprietor of a popular restaurant. Both before and after World War II, O'Doul was also a key figure in the consolidation of baseball in Japan.

JOE OESCHGER

On May 1, 1920, Oeschger locked up with Brooklyn's Leon Cadore in the longest game in major league history—a 26-inning 1–1 tie. The Boston right-hander went the distance, as did Cadore. Along the way, Oeschger set another record, of hurling 16 consecutive scoreless innings in a game. The 1920 contest lasted fewer than four hours and involved the use of only three baseballs.

BOB O'FARRELL

A twenty-one-year catcher for the Cardinals, Cubs, Reds, and Giants from 1915 to 1935, O'Farrell provided the most unusual conclusion to a World Series by throwing out Babe Ruth on an attempted steal in the 9th inning of the final 1926 game. O'Farrell was already popular with St. Louis fans for his gritty receiving, and his play helped persuade owner Sam Breadon to name him as Cardinal manager in 1927 as a hedge against the outcry over the trading of player-pilot Rogers Hornsby. Although O'Farrell guided the team to an even better record than it had compiled under Hornsby, he was fired after only a season for failing to win another pennant. O'Farrell batted .273 during his lifetime.

CURLEY OGDEN

Ogden's career added up to only an 18–19 record in five big league seasons, but he played a pivotal role in the most elaborate deception in World Series history. In the decisive game seven of the 1924 World Series against the Giants, Washington manager Bucky Harris unexpectedly picked the right-hander as his starter. But when the third New York batter, lefty-hitting Bill Terry, came to the plate, Harris yanked Ogden for southpaw George Mogridge. Harris's ploy had been aimed at seeing whether John McGraw would replace Terry with the platooning right-hand-hitting first baseman George Kelly. McGraw didn't bite, Terry remained in the game, and the Giants even took a 3–1 lead well into the contest, but Washington ended up pulling out the world championship anyway.

NOVELLA O'HARA

O'Hara was a fanatical San Francisco fan who tried to buy herself a pitcher from the team. The object of her affections was John Pregenzer, a right-hander who made token appearances for the Giants in 1963 and 1964. When she first heard that San Francisco had purchased Pregenzer's contract from a low minor league for a mere $100, O'Hara offered the club $110 for him. Rejected there, she organized a fan club for the pitcher that grew to a claimed three thousand members, among them Peace Corps Director Sargent Shriver. When plans for a John Pregenzer Day at Candlestick Park were aborted by his demotion to the minors, O'Hara whipped up a Bring Back John Pregenzer Day. A San Francisco restauranteur who had counted on a guest appearance by the pitcher posted a sign proclaiming "John Pregenzer was going to eat here."

STEVE OLIN

The bullpen stopper for the Indians in 1991 and 1992, Olin was killed in a grisly boating accident during spring training of 1993, sending the rebuilding club into a collective depression from which it failed to recover for the rest of the season. Fellow right-handed reliever Tim Crews also died in the crash, with southpaw Bob Ojeda suffering severe injuries as well. The accident marked only the beginning of the devastation of the Cleveland bullpen: In November 1993 lefty Cliff Young was killed in a truck crash, and early in 1994 right-handers Jerry DiPoto and Matt Turner went down with cancer and Hodgkin's disease, respectively.

TONY OLIVA

Nobody had a Hall of Fame career so clearly aborted by injuries as Oliva did. A lifetime .304 hitter over his fifteen years (1962–76) with the Twins, the lefty-swinging outfielder established a record by becoming the first American League rookie to win a batting title, in 1964, then cemented that feat by claiming a second Silver Bat the following year. In 1964 as well, he entered the record books as the league's first rookie to get 200 hits, and he tied Hal Trosky's first-year record of 374 total bases. No singles hitter, Oliva threw 32 home runs and an AL-leading 43 doubles into the mix. It was the first of five years in which he set the pace for safeties and the first of four campaigns in which he would lead in doubles. Along the way to a third batting championship in 1971, however, Oliva was beset by shoulder and leg injuries; before his career was up, he would have seven knee operations. It was mainly because of Oliva that Minnesota owner Calvin Griffith cast a decisive vote backing Charlie Finley's proposal for a designated hitter.

DIOMEDES OLIVO

Next to Satchel Paige, Olivo was the oldest rookie in baseball history—and without the extenuating circumstances of having been barred for racial reasons. When he joined the Pittsburgh bullpen in 1960, the right-hander admitted only to being in his "early forties." A few years later, when he would have been in his "middle to late forties," he threw a no-hitter in the International League, making him the oldest pitcher to fashion such a masterpiece on the higher rungs of organized baseball.

PETER O'MALLEY

O'Malley's buttoned-down ways with the Dodgers since the 1970s have been more a change of style than of substance from the way his father ran the franchise. The main difference between the two is that, in good measure because of the success of the Wharton School of Business attitudes that he brought to Los Angeles, the younger O'Malley has never enjoyed the dominance over other National League owners that Walter did; too many of them learned a long time ago that they had to be like him. Peter's biggest crisis occurred in 1987, after longtime front-office executive Al Campanis blithely told a national network television audience that blacks didn't have "the necessities" to hold important jobs in baseball. After a first stab at trying to quell the resultant uproar through a mere apology, O'Malley fired Campanis, then hired former basketball star Tommy Hawkins to a newly created public relations post in the hope of showing that the Dodgers weren't bigoted.

WALTER O'MALLEY

For almost three decades, O'Malley reigned as the General Motors of baseball: What was good for him was good for the rest of the National League (and sometimes even the American League). As owner of the Dodgers, he brought the major leagues to California, made sure that a succession of commissioners and league presidents didn't bring teams anywhere that he didn't want them, and called most of management's sig-

Walter O'Malley and Mrs. John Smith put their best faces on buying out Branch Rickey for control of the Dodgers on the latter's inflated terms. Brooklyn Public Library—BROOKLYN COLLECTION.

nals in the bitter labor wars with players in the 1960s and 1970s. But his long series of defeats in his dealings with the Players Association also underlined how he ultimately proved more successful in building up his own franchise as a flourishing megacorporation than in imposing his will on others to any long-term advantage.

A corporation lawyer with a Tammany Hall tinge, O'Malley bought into the Brooklyn version of the Dodgers in 1944, as a partner with Branch Rickey and John Smith of the Pfizer chemical company. For several years, O'Malley remained largely in Rickey's shadow as the club president engaged in his regular tussles with manager Leo Durocher, broke the color barrier with Jackie Robinson, and put together pennant-winning teams in 1947 and 1949. What emerged clearly even during this period, however, was O'Malley's distaste for the headlines that Rickey appeared attached to. By October 1950 O'Malley had accumulated enough power within the organization to have the final say on whether Rickey should be given a new contract as the chief baseball man in the franchise. Knowing that he was probably going to be turned down on a renewal, Rickey offered instead to sell his holdings; to make sure that O'Malley paid heavily for the privilege of buying them, he worked out a sideline deal with real-estate developer William Zeckendorf for the latter to present himself as a competitive bidder to jack up the selling price. Chalking it up to part of his boardroom education, O'Malley persuaded the Smith estate to contribute to a substantial Rickey profit to get rid of the executive and to head off Zeckendorf.

As owner and president, O'Malley brought in Buzzie Bavasi and Fresco Thompson to oversee what turned out to be the peak performances of the Boys of Summer Dodgers. During this period, O'Malley initiated a three-decade policy of granting only one-year contracts to managers; when Charlie Dressen objected to the policy in 1953, he was fired and replaced by Walter Alston. Where O'Malley found it harder to get his way, on the other hand, was in his demands for New York City to build Brooklyn a new ballpark, ideally in the downtown area near a Long Island Railroad terminus. His chief arguments for the new facility were the limited seating capacity of Ebbets Field (only 32,111) and the lack of adequate parking for accommodating the white, middle-class, Long Island fans who were perceived as the franchise's most reliable long-term customers. But even after he scheduled several Dodger games in Jersey City in 1956 and 1957, as a sign of how serious his move threats were, New York City refused to consider the downtown Brooklyn site for a park, and in fact wasn't even all that concrete in its commitment to an alternative location in Queens (where Shea Stadium is now situated).

O'Malley's October 8, 1957, announcement that he was shifting the Dodgers from Brooklyn to Los Angeles formalized the most traumatic franchise move in baseball history, and only partly because of the simultaneous transfer of the Giants from New York to San Francisco. Unlike the Giants, the Dodgers had been making money; more important, they had become so integral to Brooklyn that the community's subsequent eco-

nomic and social decline was laid by many to the departure of the club. The enduring bitterness of borough residents toward O'Malley because of the team's defection has been captured best in the apocryphal story of the Brooklynites who privately listed their choices for the three most evil people of the twentieth century and who, in comparing their choices, discovered that each had written down Hitler, Stalin, and O'Malley.

Although he had been studying the feasibility of moving into Los Angeles since Lou Perini had opened his eyes to the consequences of air travel for baseball by shuffling the Braves from Boston to Milwaukee in 1953, O'Malley actually completed all the practical preparations for the transfer in months. To secure economic and political collateral, he acquired Phil Wrigley's Wrigley Field in Los Angeles, traded minor league franchises with the Cubs owner, and then made the grand gesture of deeding his newly obtained stadium to the city. In return, the city gave him title to the Chavez Ravine section of Los Angeles with its substantial fuel deposits, plus $4.7 million to help get construction under way on a new park. The sweetheart deal caused an uproar among political opponents of City Hall, but it was sanctioned by a city referendum organized in June 1958—if by the unexpectedly small margin of 345,435 to 321,142. The generous city contribution aside, Dodger Stadium was the first privately financed major league park to be built since Yankee Stadium in 1923. The city's last direct contact with the project was in ousting the eighteen hundred Chicanos living at the Chavez Ravine site.

After four years in Los Angeles Memorial Coliseum, O'Malley moved the Dodgers into Dodger Stadium in 1962. From its bright blue paint to its painfully polite personnel, the facility fulfilled his intention to being the Disneyland of baseball. If there was a downside to the new quarters, it was that he had to share the park for four seasons with the AL expansion Angels. His consolation was an astronomical rent that infuriated Angels' owner Gene Autry. Then again, Autry also partly owed O'Malley for coming into possession of the Angels franchise in the first place, since it had been the Dodger boss who had screamed most effectively before initial indications that the expansion club would be awarded to a consortium that included veteran showman Bill Veeck. Having no desire to compete with Veeck for the Southern California market, O'Malley had used his influence to promote Autry as a worthier bidder.

For the most part, O'Malley left team personnel decisions up to Bavasi. One exception was in the coaching area, where the owner delighted in surrounding the taciturn Alston with such boisterous egotists as Leo Durocher, Charlie Dressen, and Bobby Bragan—all in the name of what he called "creative tension." He also personally demanded that Bavasi get rid of Maury Wills after the shortstop did not accompany the team on a postseason tour of Japan in 1966, and was second to no owner in dispatching players who served as Dodger representatives for the Players Association and in ignoring free agents.

In the 1960s, O'Malley was a prime mover in the election of compliant major league administrators—a role that he had played in the boosting of Ford Frick to commissioner and that he continued with the likes of NL president Chub Feeney and commissioners William Eckert and Bowie Kuhn. O'Malley wasn't happy that former Brooklyn partner Rickey used the threat of a third major league to win NL expansion membership for the Mets and Astros, but regained some of his leverage by successfully advising New York not to hire the authoritarian Rickey as head of baseball operations. That detail taken care of, he offered the Mets the nostalgic gate attractions of Gil Hodges, Duke Snider, and other former Brooklyn Dodgers in the name of helping the league as a whole prosper. By his own timetable, the senior circuit was not to have expanded again until sometime in the 1970s, but he was forced into pressing for the addition of Montreal and San Diego in 1969 after the AL announced its intention of going to twelve teams and two divisions that season. His consolations were considerable: a substantial territorial payment for giving up the Dodgers' top minor league team, in Montreal; first dibs in moving the Triple A club into the New Mexico market for Albuquerque; and the seeding of a new major league rivalry with the Padres. It was also part of the O'Malley persona that appearances be maintained as much as possible, so that, although it was Bavasi who went

off to run the new San Diego franchise, player transactions between the two Southern California teams were practically nonexistent.

By 1970, O'Malley had turned most day-to-day Dodger business over to his son Peter. From his new position as the chairman of the board, Walter proved especially conspicuous as the chief strategist for the owners in their dealings with the Players Association. At first his strategy was simple: Say no. But as a disciple of Tammany Democrats who understood the advantages of dealing with one labor voice, he eventually accepted the Association as a collective bargaining unit. After the 1972 season, he demonstrated the cynical lengths of that attitude by getting rid of the only four Dodgers who had voted against empowering the union with a strike threat earlier in the year; according to O'Malley, it would have been nice if all twenty-five players had voted against the strike, but since they hadn't, the four who had were potential clubhouse troublemakers.

O'Malley wasn't so subtle after the 1975 Messersmith-McNally decision that effectively scrapped the reserve clause. After several court challenges proved futile, he sought to organize the owners in a blacklist against players seeking free agency. That scheme was aborted when Atlanta owner Ted Turner signed Messersmith. O'Malley was only briefly more successful in imposing a lockout on spring training camps in 1976; as soon as he saw that the tactic was only uniting the players even further, he called it off, merely shrugging when Kuhn went around claiming credit for the change of mind.

O'Malley died in 1979, less than a year after he had fulfilled a goal of attracting 3 million fans to the ballpark that had gained the nickname of the Taj O'Malley. He left a personal estate valued at $20 million to his children, a family trust estimated as equal to that, plus a controlling interest in the Dodgers that was put at some $240 million by the beginning of the 1990s. Moreover, there were the oil and gas deposits in the land beneath Dodger Stadium. By any standard, O'Malley's move from Brooklyn amounted to the greatest business coup in baseball history. For some, it also consolidated his standing next to Hitler and Stalin.

MICKEY O'NEIL

A backup catcher for the 1926 Dodgers, O'Neil asked manager Wilbert Robinson to allow him to coach third base for an inning in an August game against the Braves. He stood in the box as, a few minutes later, Babe Herman came to bat with the bases loaded and doubled off the right-field wall of Ebbets Field. The blow sent Hank DeBerry home from third, but then chaos ensued. Dazzy Vance lumbered from second around third, then retreated to third. Chick Fewster hustled from first around to third. As for Herman himself, he tore all the way around to third—where he found Vance and Fewster waiting for him. Boston promptly tagged out Fewster and Herman, and the latter went into baseball history for having "doubled into a double play." O'Neil didn't coach another inning until he was with Cleveland four years later.

BUCK O'NEILL

In 1962 the Cubs signed O'Neill as the first black coach in major league history. A longtime player and manager for the Kansas City Monarchs, O'Neill had originally signed with the Cubs as a scout in 1956. He had earned points with the Cubs for urging the signing of Monarch slugger Ernie Banks. As an organization scout, O'Neill also recommended the signing of another Hall of Famer, Lou Brock.

TIP O'NEILL

O'Neill is the only one ever to lead a major league in batting average, doubles, triples, and home runs in the same season. The outfielder won his quadruple crown in 1887 while leading the St. Louis Browns to the third of their four consecutive American Association pennants. His 1887 season average was officially listed for decades as .492, with walks regarded as hits in that season only. But even after the statistical fastidiousness of the late 1960s had corrected the aberration, his astonishing 225 safeties (in 124 games) produced a .435 average. The outfielder's presence in the St. Louis lineup was the result of the first major front-office blunder. A rookie pitcher with the AA New York Metropolitans in 1883, O'Neill was slated for transfer to the National League Giants the following year, a seemingly simple transfer,

since John B. Day owned both clubs. But the owner and manager Jim Mutrie overlooked a rule that prohibited a club from signing a player until ten days after his release from another team, so O'Neill became free to sign with the Browns.

JACK ONSLOW

Onslow's limitations as a strategist for the 1949 White Sox led to one of the organization's greatest trades. Criticized by his players all year for being outwitted by rival managers, Onslow exploded one day against catcher Joe Tipton, prompting a few punches before order was restored. Under Onslow's demands that Tipton be traded, general manager Frank Lane unloaded the receiver on the Athletics—in exchange for second baseman Nellie Fox. Onslow was fired in 1950, but only after Chuck Comiskey informed his family that he would quit the franchise if a new manager weren't found.

JIM O'ROURKE (Hall of Fame, 1945)

Known as Orator Jim for his verbosity and rhetorical flourishes, O'Rourke earned Cooperstown honors for his .310 average over nineteen seasons. The righty-swinging outfielder got the first National League hit—a two-out single for Boston in the first inning of the league's initial game, on April 22, 1876. As a player, O'Rourke was a devoted supporter of the Players Brotherhood. By the time the Brotherhood had evolved into the Players League, in 1890, he already had a long history of defiance of the authority of owners; in 1877, for example, he had objected to a new rule requiring players to purchase their own uniforms and, when Boston owner Arthur Soden backed out of an agreement to exempt him, refused to sign a new contract until fans chipped in to pay for his work clothes. After his big league days, however, O'Rourke became a successful lawyer and minor league official, and denied having played any part in the Players League. His final major league game was also his most famous. When New York manager John McGraw allowed him to catch the first game of a doubleheader, on September 22, 1904, the fifty-two-year-old not only became the oldest man ever to play a full big league game, but he also got a hit in 4 at-bats and scored a run in what became a pennant-clinching game.

PATSY O'ROURKE

O'Rourke showed little as a second baseman for the Cardinals in 1908, but he always showed up as a scout for the Phillies in the 1930s—and that was the trouble. As Philadelphia's one and only talent evaluator in the tawdry organization run by Gerry Nugent, O'Rourke had even this distinction diluted by the owner's refusal to spring for any train tickets that might have allowed him to look over prospects. The upshot was that O'Rourke did little but attend Philadelphia's home games—a routine that became so predictable that manager Jimmie Wilson sardonically announced to the bench during every game that it was time for his ''O'Rourke check,'' to make sure the scout was in his seat.

DAVE ORR

Orr's .342 lifetime batting average would have placed his name ninth on the all-time list and on a Hall of Fame plaque but for his having played only nine seasons, more than half of them with the American Association New York Metropolitans. So highly regarded were the lefty swinger's abilities that Brooklyn owner Charlie Byrne purchased the entire New York roster to acquire his services in 1888. The first baseman's career was cut short by a stroke, brought on partially by his excessive weight.

JORGE ORTA

Orta collected 1,619 hits in a sixteen-year (1972–87) career with the White Sox, Royals, and other teams, but none was as important as a dribbler wide of first base in the 9th inning of game six of the 1985 World Series between Kansas City and St. Louis. Although a toss from Cardinals' first baseman Jack Clark to pitcher Todd Worrell appeared to be in time, umpire Don Denkinger called Orta safe, opening the gates to a comeback victory by the Royals that ultimately proved to be the turning point of the Series.

ROBERTO ORTIZ

The Cuban Ortiz was not particularly gifted as an outfielder or hitter, but he kept his place on the Washington roster in 1950 as an interpreter for Latin pitchers Connie Marrero and Sandy Consuegra.

MARTY O'TOOLE

Because spitballer O'Toole loaded up for his out pitch by slobbering all over the ball with his tongue, Phillies' first baseman Fred Luderus rubbed the game ball with liniment when Philadelphia faced the Pittsburgh right-hander in a 1912 game. After 3 innings, the Pirates had to replace O'Toole.

PATSY O'TOOLE

O'Toole was the classic foghorn-voiced fan—and the only one ever to have his seat changed by a president of the United States. From his customary perch atop the Detroit dugout, he spent twenty-five years bellowing, ''Boy, oh, boy, oh, boy, oh, boy. Keep cool with O'Toole,'' and punctuating the irritating refrain by hollering ''You're a bum'' at every visiting player and ''You're a great guy'' at every member of the Tigers. Attending the third game of the 1933 World Series, O'Toole had a seat just a few rows behind that of Franklin D. Roosevelt, who, after being exposed to several O'Toole blasts, had him removed to the other side of the field.

MARY OTT

The Horse Lady of St. Louis, Ott turned her equine shrillness on Cardinals' opponents for almost three decades. Among her favorite targets were the Dodgers in the 1940s. Capable not only of nuancing her braying to reflect just about every human emotion but also of downing prodigious quantities of beer, she once estimated that it took her about 3 innings to get a visiting pitcher sent to the showers when she put all of her animal energy into the effort.

MEL OTT (Hall of Fame, 1951)

As brilliant a career as Ott had in twenty-two years (1926–47) in a New York uniform, he remains almost as noted today for being the subject of Leo Durocher's crack that ''nice guys finish last.'' What Durocher actually said, in a conversation with broadcaster Red Barber prior to a 1946 game between the Giants and Dodgers, was:

Mel Ott's distinctive leg kick has had only a few imitators, and none at all with his power numbers. National Basebal Library, Cooperstown, N.Y.

''Look over there. Do you know a nicer guy than Mel Ott? Or any of the other Giants? Why, they're the nicest guys in the world. And where are they? In last place!'' The telescoped version of the quote about the then New York manager appeared the following day in the *New York Journal-American* in a story by Frank Graham.

In sheer baseball terms, the left-hand-hitting Ott had already carved a niche before replacing Bill Terry as manager in 1942. Only sixteen years old when he made his debut in the Polo Grounds in 1926, the outfielder went on to become the first National Leaguer to pile up more than 500 home runs; his career total of 511 round-trippers was accompanied by 1,860 RBIs and a .304 average. Six times he paced the National League in homers, between 1929 and 1942 failing to hit at least 25 only once. His season RBI count was equally impressive—totaling at least 100 nine years in a row. As prolific as he was as a slugger, Ott was equally popular with the fans, especially in con-

trast to the stern visages of his mentor-predecessors John McGraw and Terry. Helping Ott's popularity along was a batting stance that saw him elevate his front foot almost to the knee of the other leg when stepping into a pitch.

As a manager, Ott presided over mostly second-division teams that knew how to do only what he did—hit the long ball. The 1947 club, for example, set the NL record with 221 home runs, but had little more to show for it than a fourth-place finish. Although he tried to inject some fire into his managing style—levying fines liberally; blasting players publicly; even becoming, in 1946, the first pilot to be thrown out of both games of a doubleheader—he lasted as long as he did only because of the sufferance of Giants' owner Horace Stoneham and his fan support. When Ott was finally replaced as pilot midway in the 1948 season, it was by Durocher.

MICKEY OWEN

Owen's reputation as a solid defensive catcher was marred forever by the passed ball in the 9th inning of game four of the 1941 World Series that allowed Tommy Henrich to reach first base and that sent the Yankees on their way to a comeback victory over Brooklyn. He himself always downplayed suggestions that Hugh Casey's two-strike pitch to Henrich was a spitball, observing that he should have caught it anyway. Earlier that same year, Owen underscored his defensive abilities by setting the National League season record for most consecutive chances (476) by a catcher without an error.

Mickey Owen chases the third strike passed ball thrown to Tommy Henrich, shown running to first base, that cost the Dodgers the fourth game of the 1941 World Series. Photo compliments of Sharon Guynup.

After nine years with the Cardinals and Dodgers, Owen became one of the first recruits of the Pasquel brothers for the Mexican League in 1946, signing on as a playing manager for Vera Cruz. Within weeks, he thought better of the Mexican venture and took a $250 cab ride to El Paso to escape, but returned amid a flurry of threatened lawsuits, only to be fired at the end of the year. Permitted to return to the big leagues in 1949, Owen wound up his career as a backup receiver for the Cubs and Red Sox.

RAY OYLER

Oyler's lack of hitting assumed near-legendary proportions in the 1960s. The ultimate gloveman, he demonstrated that pennant winners didn't need offense at shortstop in 1967, when he batted an hallucinating .135 in 111 games for Detroit. Manager Mayo Smith knew to quit when he was ahead, however: In the World Series against the Cardinals, he preferred sticking outfielder Mickey Stanley at short to make room for Al Kaline rather than suffer through any more Oyler at-bats with the world championship on the line. In 1969, the righty swinger was adopted by desperate Pilots' fans for a Ray Oyler Fan Club; he responded to the Seattle welcome by hitting .165. In six major league seasons he averaged .175, reaching the .200 mark (barely) only once.

DANNY OZARK

Ozark may have been the managing fraternity's most hapless winner. Despite steering the Phillies to three consecutive East Divisions titles between 1976 to 1978, he was seldom portrayed as anything but an extremely dim bulb. The image was affixed to him for good in 1975, after the Pirates had defeated Philadelphia in a late September game to clinch that season's East Division title, and Ozark, standing only a short distance away from where the Pittsburgh players were celebrating, told reporters that he was going to stick with his rotation "because we're not out of this thing yet." The manager's approximate command of clichés also fueled ridicule; among the more-often cited ones attributed to him are:

- "I have always had a wonderful repertoire with my players."
- "Even Napoleon had his Watergate."
- "I don't want to get into a Galphonse-Aston act."
- "I will not be cohorsed."

Even worse was when Ozark sought to be witty. Asked once why he never gave straight answers, he replied: "You'll have to ask these people who are always calling me a fascist—a guy who says one thing and means another."

P

JOHN PACIOREK

In a September 29, 1963, game against the Mets, Paciorek collected 3 hits and 2 walks in 5 plate appearances. Forced into premature retirement by a back injury, the outfielder left baseball with the most hits of any player with a 1.000 batting average.

ANDY PAFKO

Despite a solid seventeen-year career with the Cubs, Dodgers, and Braves, Pafko's two most memorable moments on the field were the stuff of embarrassment and shock. On April 30, 1949, while playing the outfield for Chicago, he made what appeared to be a diving catch on a liner by St. Louis's Rocky Nelson to end a 3–2 contest. When umpire Al Barlick ruled instead that the ball had only been trapped, an enraged Pafko kept after the arbiter, not realizing until too late that Nelson was circling the bases for an inside-the-park home run and a Cardinal victory. Alluding to Chicago catcher Gabby Hartnett's famous Homer in the Gloamin' in 1938, the local wits tagged Pafko's failure to ask for time the Homer in the Glove. On October 3, 1951, the then-Brooklyn outfielder gained even more dubious fame by being photographed against the wall of the Polo Grounds looking up at Bobby Thomson's playoff-winning home run.

JOE PAGE

The bullpen ace of the Yankees in the late 1940s, Page held the single-season record for most saves (27 in 1949) until the beginning of the age of the relief specialist in the 1960s. He was also the immediate cause for the resignation of the most successful manager in major league history.

A mediocre starter with a blazing fastball, unlimited potential, and a devil-may-care attitude when he came up to New York in 1944, the southpaw engaged in a running battle with manager Joe McCarthy over his daytime indifference and nighttime carousing. Page shuttled between Newark and the Bronx for two years, and his lack of discipline finally got to McCarthy, who quit as dugout boss in May 1946 after a shouting match with the pitcher aboard an airplane.

Converted to a reliever by Bucky Harris the following year, Page led the American League in saves and relief victories in both 1947 and 1949. The southpaw took pleasure in beating the Red Sox, especially after McCarthy became their manager in 1948, and particular pleasure in his uncommon success against Ted Williams, for what he saw as his contribution to the Joe DiMaggio side of the ongoing debate over which was the greater hitter. In fact, Page's most memorable appearance was on the penultimate day of the 1949 season, when he entered the game in the 3rd inning, walked 2 batters with the bases loaded to give Boston a 4–0 lead, then pitched 1-hit ball for 6⅔ innings as New York came back to win, 5–4, on its way to the pennant.

Released in 1950 after he tore a muscle in his throwing arm, Page's career was over—except for a brief reappearance with the Pirates in 1954—with a 57–49 record and 76 saves.

SATCHEL PAIGE (Hall of Fame, 1972)

As a pitcher, Paige was without peer; as a legend, only Babe Ruth was in his league.

Even without the tall tales that grew up around it, the right-hander's career read likes fiction. For one thing, Paige was even more of an itinerant than other Negro leaguers. In his first two years (1926–27) as a professional, with the Chattanooga Black Lookouts, he jumped the team twice, to play for the New Orleans Black Pelicans and the Baltimore Black Sox. He lasted only three seasons (1928–30) with the Birmingham Black Barons and only one (1931) with the Cleveland Cubs. After winning 63 games in two years (1932–33) with the fabled Pittsburgh Crawfords, he drifted off to pitch for a white semipro club in North Dakota and stayed there through the 1935 season after the Negro National League banned him for his defection. Returning to the Crawfords in 1936, Paige was practically shanghaied to Santo Do-

mingo, where he won a politically charged championship for dictator Rafael Trujillo's team in 1937. Sold by the Crawfords to the Newark Eagles in 1938, he refused even to negotiate with Eagles' owner Effa Manley and took off for the Mexican League, where he developed the first sore arm of his career and suffered a permanent ban by the NNL.

Paige was signed next by the Kansas City Monarchs' road team (rebaptized Satchel Paige's All-Stars), with whom he worked the kinks out of his arm and was promoted to the parent American Negro League varsity squad. Even while contributing to six NAL pennants with the Monarchs between 1939 and 1948 and winning 3 games in a sweep of the Homestead Grays in the 1942 black World Series, he was more of a pitcher for hire, rented out to semipro teams for a day at a time. He also did the customary winter league tours in Puerto Rico, Cuba, and California. Finally, between and after major league stints (in 1948–49, 1951–53, and 1965), he barnstormed virtually nonstop until 1967, when he wasn't on the roster of the Miami International League club (1956) and Portland's entry in the Pacific Coast League (briefly in 1961).

The numbers Paige amassed in this forty-two-year career are staggering, even if necessarily estimated: Appearing in more than 2,500 games for about 250 teams (the vast majority of them one-day employers), he racked up 2,000 victories (100 of them no-hitters) and earned upward to $40,000 a year, several times what other black players of the period took home and more than most contemporary big leaguers. He beat teams of white major leaguers regularly, including 4 wins against Dizzy Dean in 6 1934 contests. Paige's single best game was probably one in which he struck out 22 white major leaguers in a 1930 barnstorming contest.

As the oldest rookie in major league history, with the Indians in 1948, Paige proved to be more than one of Bill Veeck's stunts, contributing a 6–1 record and a 2.48 ERA toward a Cleveland pennant; he followed that up with a 4–7, 3.04 effort the next year. Rehired by Veeck in 1951, he spent three seasons with the Browns, pitching creditably in relief and as a spot starter. The hurler closed out his major league career with a

Satchel Paige's mound skills, durability, and instinct for self-promotion combined to create a legend that epitomized the Negro leagues for many. Photo compliments of Sharon Guynup.

single appearance for the Athletics in 1965, yielding only a hit in 3 innings as the oldest man ever to take a major league mound. His overall record was 28–31 with a 3.29 ERA and 32 saves.

Throughout his career, Paige did nothing to discourage his elevation into the realm of folklore. From a vagueness about the year of his birth (probably 1906) and the inspiration for his nickname (probably involving suitcases he carried for tips as a child in his hometown of Mobile), he graduated to (possible) exaggerations of his pitching prowess. Whether (or how often) he summoned his outfielders to sit behind him on the mound while he struck out the side or fulfilled advertised promises to strike out the first 9 men he faced in a game is irrelevant. What is relevant is that fans believed he had—and paid for the possibility of seeing him do it again. Even in the majors, he was a significant drawing card: More than two hundred thousand people paid to see his first three starts in the big leagues, in the process setting attendance records for night games in both Cleveland and Chicago. In St. Louis, Paige and Veeck contrived to provide a rocking chair in the bullpen for Paige's use between appearances.

Paige had names for his various pitches. His fastball was Long Tom (or, alternatively, the bee ball, jump ball, or trouble ball). The tales of his speed took on mythic proportions. Even Paige's own fabulous accounts of his velocity were outdone by Negro leagues catcher Biz Mackey, who claimed that a particularly high-powered Paige fastball actually disappeared on the way to the plate. His most famous delivery, however, was the hesitation pitch, which he developed in the 1940s and offered after deliberately pausing as his forward foot hit the ground; so disorienting was the discontinuity of his motion to opposing batters that the American League banned the pitch after Paige introduced it in the big leagues in 1948.

As a barnstormer, Paige refused to play in towns where the black players on his team could not stay in local hotels or eat in local restaurants. He was also given to sardonic observations about how to keep young and to train. Among them were: "Go very light on the vices, such as carrying on in society. The social ramble ain't rest-ful." "Avoid running at all times." "Don't look back. Something might be gaining on you."

Ultimately, Paige's ability, longevity, and showmanship gave the Negro leagues much of whatever visibility they had in the white world. Among those who called the right-hander the best pitcher they ever saw were Dean, Joe DiMaggio, and Charlie Gehringer. Fittingly, Paige was the first of the Negro leagues stars admitted to the Hall of Fame.

DAVE PALLONE

Scurrilous press reports put an end to Pallone's ten-year (1979–88) umpiring career in the National League—and to the possibility that he might be fired for one of a couple of valid reasons. A scab hired during the 1979 strike by major league umpires, Pallone was retained after settlement of the labor dispute despite constant hostility from his colleagues, mockery from players, and a penchant for dubious calls that marked him as one of the more incompetent men in blue. Mainly to save face for its own original hiring, the league kept him around through regular diamond explosions until 1988, when a protracted argument with Cincinnati manager Pete Rose almost caused a riot at Riverfront Stadium. The clash led to a thirty-day suspension of Rose and censures against Reds broadcasters Joe Nuxhall and Marty Brennaman for their on-air attacks against the umpire. The incident took on added resonance a short time later, when Pallone was falsely linked to an upstate New York investigation of sex crimes committed against teenage boys. By the time police spokesmen got around to dismissing the initial media reports, Pallone had admitted that he was gay. While the admission suggested deeper insinuations in the macho notions about baseball sustained by Nuxhall and Brennaman in their blasts, it also offered the league a more convenient excuse for terminating the arbiter. A couple of years later, Pallone published a book filled with arch hints about the number of gay major leaguers who were in the closet.

JIM PALMER (Hall of Fame, 1990)

For the better part of his nineteen seasons (between 1965 and 1984) with the Orioles, Palmer was the franchise pitcher; for almost as long, he was the bane of manager Earl Weaver's existence.

The right-hander's career was almost derailed by arm miseries, a shoulder ailment, and back problems after a 15–10 record in 1966, his first full big league season. So serious were Palmer's difficulties that the Orioles left him off their protected list in the 1969 expansion draft, but neither newly created team, the Royals or the Pilots, thought him worth the risk. But after spending most of 1967, all of 1968, and the first six weeks of the 1969 season on the disabled list, he returned to hurl a no-hitter against the Athletics four days after being reactivated and went on to pace American League hurlers in winning percentage (.800, 16–4) for the first of two times. The following year, Palmer posted the first of eight 20-win seasons, a total topped in the AL only by Walter Johnson and matched only by Lefty Grove; in three of those years Palmer led the league in wins, while also setting the pace in ERA twice. His best efforts involved Cy Young seasons in 1973 (22–9, 2.40), 1975 (23–11, 2.09), and 1976 (22–13, 2.51). Palmer was released in May 1984 after a battle with the Baltimore front office, which had suggested several times that he retire. In 1991, after already being inducted in Cooperstown, he attempted a comeback but failed to make the club in spring training.

Almost from the moment Weaver joined the Orioles in the middle of 1968, the pilot and Palmer were at loggerheads. At the root of their differences was Palmer's aversion to the much-vaunted Oriole fundamentals that Weaver, as a manager in the club's farm system, had a hand in developing, and Weaver's stated suspicions that the pitcher's various loudly proclaimed ailments were psychosomatic. Palmer's side of the running dialogue between the two—which often seemed designed as entertainment—included sarcastic cracks about how long he would be side-lined ("You never know with psychosomatic injuries") and disparaging remarks about the intelligence of managers in general and Weaver in particular ("Most pitchers are too smart to manage"). Palmer's summary of the relationship ("I don't want to win my 300th game while he's still here; he'd take credit for it") proved irrelevant; although the manager left after the 1982 season,

the hurler had a 268–152 record when he was forced off the roster less than two years later.

CHAN HO PARK

Park became the first Korean major leaguer when he took the mound for the Dodgers in the 9th inning of an April 9, 1994, game against the Braves. The fact that the right-hander yielded 2 runs was quickly forgotten when Atlanta's Kent Mercker completed a no-hitter in the bottom of the inning.

DAVE PARKER

Parker set the tone for his stormy nineteen-year (1973–91) career by wearing a Star of David "because my name is David and I'm a star." A left-hand-hitting outfielder who epitomized the lumber company Pirates of the 1970s, he won successive batting titles in 1977 and 1978, paced the National League in slugging average in 1975 and 1978, and collected the most hits in 1977, the most doubles in 1977 and 1985, and the most RBIs in 1985. The lifetime .290 hitter was awarded the NL's MVP trophy in 1978.

For all his slugging feats, however, Parker was equally adept at attracting controversy—sometimes, but not always, through his own doing. In the early 1980s, the fact that he was one of the game's first million-dollar players (in a contract covering five years) drew the ire of a city enmeshed in grave unemployment problems; the same Pittsburgh fans who were amused by Willie Stargell's balloon proportions attacked Parker vehemently for his own expanded waistline and, in one notorious incident, showered him with batteries and other objects after he had made a fielding lapse. Moving over to Cincinnati as a free agent in 1984, he rediscovered the clout he had lost after a couple of seasons of leg injuries, excess weight, and fan harassment, but also came into constant conflict with manager Pete Rose over his defensive nonchalance and elaborate styling whenever he belted a ball out of the park. The relationship was fractious enough for Parker to be one of the few players who voiced delight when Rose was suspended for betting on games.

Parker's worst hours came when he was named as a cocaine user in Pittsburgh's drug trials. His own admissions of involvement led the Pirates to file suit against him for the return of some of the salary he had made while snorting. A protracted legal battle over whether he had violated the "physical condition" clauses of his contract ended with an out-of-court settlement. Parker concluded his career by moving around as a designated hitter for the Athletics, Brewers, Angels, and Blue Jays.

JORGE PASQUEL

The millionaire president of the Mexican League, Pasquel and his four brothers staged a serious raid on major league rosters in 1946 with offers of extravagant salaries for North American players willing to play south of the border. The first prominent player to go along was Browns' shortstop Vern Stephens, who signed a two-year pact at $25,000 a year. Otherwise, Pasquel largely zeroed in on the Cardinals and Giants, picking up (among others) pitchers Max Lanier, Fred Martin, and Sal Maglie, infielder Lou Klein, and outfielder Danny Gardella. Pasquel also offered Stan Musial a five-year pact at $30,000 a year, but the St. Louis star decided to accept instead a $13,000 contract form the Cardinals. When Commissioner Happy Chandler announced that the jumpers would be banned from organized baseball, the defectors began drifting back to the United States. Their return trip hardly mattered, since the importation of high-priced baseball talent had, from the first, been a bread-and-circuses campaign tactic on behalf of Miguel Aleman's candidacy for the presidency of Mexico. With the politician's success in the 1946 election, Pasquel allowed baseball to assume a lesser priority in his affairs.

ROY PATTERSON

When rain washed out 3 of the 4 scheduled games on April 24, 1901, White Sox right-hander Patterson became the winner of the American League's first game by beating Cleveland that day, 8–2.

GABE PAUL

Paul always knew when it was time to leave. As the top front-office official for the Reds, Astros, Indians (twice), and Yankees over more than three decades, he built winners when he worked for an owner with deep pockets, patched over problems (sometimes of his own creation) when he didn't, and always moved on before a bad situation got worse.

Promoted to Cincinnati general manager in 1952, Paul had already served in various front-office capacities since 1919, as the protégé of Warren Giles with both the International League Rochester club and the Reds. Paul's most notable achievement as Cincinnati GM was putting the finishing touches on the second-biggest Red Machine. His trades for center fielder Gus Bell, third baseman Ray Jablonski, and role players Smokey Burgess and George Crowe, along with the drafting of future Hall of Famer Frank Robinson in 1953, completed the ensemble that tied the National League record with 221 home runs in 1956 while finishing third. He also put together the less spectacular 1961 outfit that won the NL pennant.

Paul quit the Reds in late 1960 after a series of disagreements with Powel Crosley over the owner's efforts to move the team to New York, and signed a three-year pact to run the soon-to-be-expansion Houston club. Within months of Paul's putting his name on the document, however, Robert E. Smith and Judge Roy Hofheinz were brought in as new principal owners, and Paul needed only one look at the erratic Texas millionaires to decide that his future lay elsewhere.

That elsewhere was Cleveland. In his first tour of duty with the Indians (1961–72), Paul spent most of his time searching for a succession of buyers. With owner William Daley near bankruptcy and putting out feelers about moving the club to Seattle, Paul took advantage of the backlash to the suggested move and put together his own syndicate to buy the team in 1963. Suffering the same cash shorts as his predecessor, he sold out in August 1966 to frozen-food magnate Vernon Stouffer. In 1972 Stouffer was out and sports entrepreneur Nick Mileti was in. Paul survived the changes for no apparent reason other than to provide institutional continuity: In making more than a hundred deals involving major league players, he failed to give the club a winning record more than twice in thirteen years. The last of those deals raised some eyebrows when he shipped third baseman Graig Nettles to the Yankees for four uniforms in late November 1972, then jumped off the sinking ship just before yet another sale of the club by following Nettles to New York in January 1973.

Paul's major burden in the Yankee front office was to play mediator in the three-sided lunacy that prevailed among owner George Steinbrenner, manager Billy Martin, and slugger Reggie Jackson. Paul's trades brought Lou Piniella, Chris Chambliss, Willie Randolph, and Mickey Rivers, among others; Paul also reached into Steinbrenner's bank account to sign Catfish Hunter and Jackson as free agents. But just when Paul seemed on the verge of convincing the public that he was the only one of the ''baseball people'' parading through the Yankee front office with any credentials at all, he proved powerless to prevent the ill-considered June 1976 deal that shipped pitching prospects Tippy Martinez and Scott McGregor and catcher Rick Dempsey to Baltimore for Ken Holtzman and four bodies. Two pennants and a world championship later, Paul had enough of the constant strife and went back to Cleveland in December 1977 as a minority owner and president.

Anything but triumphal, his return began with a franchise bailout of owner Ted Bonda engineered by transportation tycoon Steve O'Neill that was seen as temporary until Paul could come up with yet another savior. When he wasn't queering sales he himself had arranged (in one noted case because he refused to abide the activism of prospective owners Neal Papiano and James Nederlander in their pursuit of free agent Dave Winfield and a trade for Red Sox outfielder Fred Lynn), he was adding the names of limited partners to the masthead for quick infusions of cash. His own efforts where the roster were concerned was a repeat of his old pattern, making no fewer than fifteen trades in 1978 alone (and almost seventy in seven years), most of them amounting to rearrangements of the furniture. Through the 1980s, Paul collected pitchers to whom he gave big raises (most notably, Rick Sutcliffe) before unloading them because the Indians couldn't afford their salaries. When O'Neill died in 1983, his heirs began clamoring even more loudly for an angel to rescue them. It was at about this time that bumper stickers began to appear in Cuyahoga County declaring, SAVE THE TRIBE, FIRE THE CHIEF.

Paul was unable to satisfy his partners' demands: Yet another sale, this time to Wall Street lawyer Dave LeFevre, fell through after protracted negotiations and litigation. Paul did, however, satisfy fans by selling his 5 percent interest in the club to LeFevre, and retiring in December 1984. The Cleveland legacy he left after two stints totaling nineteen years was a financial situation at least as bad as when he first arrived and a single third-place finish—in 1968.

GENE PAULETTE

Paulette was blacklisted by Commissioner Kenesaw Landis in March 1921, two weeks after the Black Sox had suffered the same fate. The first baseman's offense was his association with St. Louis gambler Elmer Farrar, who had given him a loan that had never been repaid; the incriminating evidence was a letter from the player to the gambler offering to throw games in exchange for more money. Traded from the Cardinals to the Phillies in mid-1919 while the subject of rumors about the Farrar connection, Paulette initially escaped punishment by signing an affidavit affirming that he had done nothing wrong. When his letter fell into Landis's hands, however, he was finished. In six big league seasons with four clubs, the right-handed hitter averaged .269.

JOAN PAYSON

The original owner of the Mets when the expansion team joined the National League in 1962, Payson was more missed in her absence than particularly assertive by her presence. For most of her tenure with the organization until her death in 1975, she presented the organization's genial face as the reverse side of devious board chairman M. Donald Grant and sour president George Weiss. The image was fastened to her practically from the club's first season, when she disclosed that she would have preferred giving it the nickname of Meadowlarks rather than Mets. At the same time, it helped her through potentially troublesome publicity when her investments in racehorses were contrasted with the pious rejections of ownership bids in San Diego, Cleveland, and Chicago because would-be purchasers also had money in racetracks. With Payson's death, the franchise lurched toward self-destruction under her widower, Charles; their daughter Lorinda de Roulet; and Grant.

DICKEY PEARCE

In twenty-two years of professional play beginning with the Brooklyn Atlantics in 1856, Pearce exercised considerable influence on the development of the game by originating the bunt and by popularizing the placement of the ninth man between second base and the third baseman. On June 29, 1876, as the shortstop for the St. Louis Brown Stockings, Pearce started the first major league triple play. In addition to the bunt (or tricky hit, as it was called), he is also credited with the invention of the fair-foul hit.

ROGER PECKINPAUGH

A seventeen-year shortstop with the Indians, Yankees, Senators, and White Sox between 1910 and 1927, Peckinpaugh derived most of his celebrity from his 9–8 record as New York manager at the end of the 1914 season; since he was only twenty-three at the time, he went into the books as the youngest pilot in big league history. He later served a couple of terms as manager of Cleveland.

TERRY PENDLETON

Pendleton gave new definition to leadership during the 1993 season when he suddenly walked off the field and into the clubhouse in the middle of an inning to protest teammate Marvin Freeman's refusal to deck some opposition batters. According to Pendleton, the hurler was remiss for not retaliating for several Atlanta batters who had been hit or knocked away from the plate during the game. Although both the Braves management and the National League did a lot of tsk-tsking about the third baseman's gesture, its main consequence was to consolidate his standing as the club's field and clubhouse leader.

Signed as a free agent by the Braves in 1991 after seven seasons with the Cardinals, Pendleton served as a catalyst for Atlanta's becoming the first club in NL history to go from last to first in one year. The switch-hitter took MVP honors on the season for his league-best .319 average and 187 hits. Pendleton's biggest moment as a Cardinal came in a late September 1987 game,

when his 9th-inning home run off Mets' reliever Roger McDowell stemmed what appeared to be a St. Louis collapse before onrushing New York and ultimately proved to be the turning point in a division win.

HERB PENNOCK (Hall of Fame, 1948)

Left-hander Pennock was the exception among the players picked up by the Yankees from the Red Sox in the early 1920s; whereas others, such as Babe Ruth, Joe Bush, Carl Mays, and Joe Dugan, were demonstrably at the top of their games when they were shipped from New England to New York, Pennock was perceived as washed up at age twenty-nine after two consecutive losing seasons. Instead, he went on to pace the American League in winning percentage in his first year with the Yankees, record two 20-win seasons, and notch a 5–0 record in four World Series. In twenty-two seasons (between 1912 and 1934) with the Athletics as well as the Red Sox and Yankees, he won 240 games overall.

After his playing days, Pennock directed the Red Sox farm system and served as general manager of the Phillies from 1944 until his death in 1948. In the latter role, he was largely responsible for assembling the Whiz Kids club that won the National League pennant in 1950.

H. C. PENNYPACKER

Appointed president of the Philadelphia Athletics in 1888, Pennypacker presided over perhaps the most precipitous fiscal slide of any major league team. Showing a $30,000 profit in 1889, the Athletics should have been sufficiently healthy to survive the onslaught of the Players League the following season, despite heavy defections among players. Instead, on September 17, with the club in the red for $17,000, Pennypacker disbanded the organization and released all the players, blaming the competition from the PL. The truth emerged only when the American Association took over the franchise and discovered that Pennypacker had been paying himself and team secretary William Whitaker exorbitant salaries.

JOE PEPITONE

As a seventeen-year-old out of Brooklyn, Pepitone gave a hint of things to come by blowing his $20,000 1958 signing bonus with the Yankees on a car and a boat. Arriving with the Yankees in 1962 as the backup first baseman to Bill Skowron, the lefty swinger had to dissuade some admirers in his old neighborhood from breaking Skowron's legs so the local boy could take his place in the lineup. Eventually assigned a starting role in 1963, he held down the first-base job until 1969 except for two years (1967 and 1968), when he moved to center field in a switch of positions with an ailing Mickey Mantle.

Ordinarily a slick fielder and the winner of three Gold Gloves, Pepitone had his most memorable moment on the diamond in the 7th inning of game four of the 1963 World Series, when he lost a throw by third baseman Clete Boyer in the crowd's white shirts and allowed Jim Gilliam to go all the way to third; minutes later, Gilliam scored the Series-winning run on a sacrifice fly. Pepitone's memorable moments off the field were even more embarrassing. He regularly frequented after-hours spots while carrying a bow and arrow. Haunted in his last years with New York by multiple ex-wives and loan sharks, he jumped the team three times in 1969 and was traded to the Astros after the season. After bouncing around with three National League clubs, he left the big leagues after twelve seasons (1962–73) with a .258 average.

Signing with the Yakult club of the Japanese Leagues in 1973, Pepitone became so much the ugly American—wearing his hair long, griping about the high prices and food, partying through the night, playing in only 14 games before quitting with a .163 average, and skipping out on a $2,000 phone bill—that his surname became the Japanese eponym for a player who goofs off. In 1989 he served two months of a six-month jail term on drug and gun charges before the Yankees hired him as part of a work release program.

PASCUAL PEREZ

One of the most flamboyant pitchers of the 1980s, Perez was undermined by a drug problem and by a refusal of major league teams to accord him the same repeated chances given to such other cocaine users as Steve Howe. Originally brought to the majors in 1980 by Pittsburgh, the righthander first attracted notoriety after being traded to Atlanta in 1982 and losing his way to Fulton County Stadium for a starting assignment because he kept driving past a highway exit. In 1984, after a couple of years of indications that he was becoming the staff ace, doubts were raised about the driving story when he admitted to a drug problem. Perez underwent rehab and returned to the National League with Montreal in 1987, establishing himself as one of the game's great flakes by performing such antics as trying to pick off runners by throwing to first base through his legs. His wafer-thin physique and dreadlocks made him a fan favorite at Olympic Stadium, but he chose (against most advice) to sign with the Yankees as a free agent in 1990. A combination of injuries and a relapse into drugs ended his career in 1991, though some also wondered why New York was ready to forgive and forget in the case of the repeated offender Howe but not in that of the twice-fallen Latin Perez.

TONY PEREZ

Perez had his best playing years in a Cincinnati uniform, but he gained equal notoriety for his unexpected departures from the club. The first exit came after the 1976 season, when the first baseman-third baseman was traded to the Expos after thirteen years of heavy RBI duty for the team that had developed into the Big Red Machine. The swap was denounced by such teammates as Joe Morgan and Pete Rose as lethal to Cincinnati's field leadership, and proved to be so when the Reds took a two-year vacation from postseason competition. While with Cincinnati, the right-hand-hitting Perez had put together six seasons of more than 100 RBIs, enjoying his best campaign in 1970 with 40 home runs, 129 RBIs, 107 runs scored, and a .317 batting average. After roaming around for another decade as a member of the Expos, Red Sox, Phillies, and (again) Reds, he retired with a twenty-three-year (1964–86) sum of 379 home runs, 1,652 RBIs, and a .279 batting mark.

Perez's second, uglier departure from Cincinnati came in 1993, when he had been on the job only a few weeks as manager. His abrupt replacement by Davey Johnson strongly suggested that the Latin star had been hired initially only to help blunt the fallout from revelations of owner Marge

Schott's racist hiring policies and had been bounced as soon as the front office thought the worst of the controversy was over. Several Cincinnati players called for a strike after the Perez firing, but satisfied themselves with just calling in their efforts for the remainder of the season.

LOU PERINI

Perini's transfer of the Braves from Boston to Milwaukee in 1953 signaled the start of the franchise moves that would both extend the major leagues geographically and introduce havoc in the minor leagues. The intrigues and procrastinations behind the uprooting of the Braves also underscored the lengths to which big league owners would go to get rid of unwanted members of their circle.

Perini and fellow construction industry millionaires Joseph Maney and Guido Rugo bought into the Braves in 1941 and needed a mere couple of years to gain total control. Known as The Three Little Steamshovels, they embarked on an ambitious spending program directed at both raising the club to the heights of the National League and winning Bostonians away from the Red Sox. Their biggest setback came on Opening Day in 1946, when an estimated five thousand fans had their clothing ruined by freshly painted seats at Braves Field; for the rest of the year, lawyers and accountants had to pore over more than thirteen thousand damage claims. Their biggest success was a 1948 pennant—the first by the team since the Miracle Braves of 1914. Then things started to go downhill.

Mainly because he was committed to a long-term contract with Billy Southworth, Perini backed the manager in a conflict with star infielders Alvin Dark and Eddie Stanky, trading them away in what was the first of several ruinous deals. Within a couple of years, the club was back to thinking of .500 as a lofty goal, and Bostonians were back to Fenway Park. Although he always adamantly denied it, Perini and his brothers kept their hands busy by buying out Maney and Rugo so they would be able to move to Milwaukee without any interference. For a couple of years, their intended move was embroiled in a controversy with both leagues, with both Bill Veeck of the Browns and Fred Saigh of the Cardinals also

holding talks with Milwaukee interests for a possible transfer. In the end, however, Perini prevailed—first because he had territorial rights to the Wisconsin city through a minor league team there, and second because the other owners were determined to get rid of both Veeck and Saigh and blocked any move by the two St. Louis owners to resolve their own money problems through a switch.

Although the Braves received an ardent welcome in Milwaukee, Perini was never quite as popular. His first problem was his procrastination before finally making the move—interpreted by locals as an attempt at gaining an even better deal from the county than that offered through the free construction of County Stadium. He alienated other sectors by refusing to move his residence from Boston—increasing the image of a carpetbagger who could leave Milwaukee if a better deal were offered elsewhere. The owner didn't win any points, either, with his ban on bringing beer into the ballpark, forcing fans to buy their brew at inflated prices from concession stands. When the club began to slip toward the second division in the early 1960s, sportswriters such as Russ Lynch of the *Milwaukee Journal* warned that Milwaukee's scant potential for a lucrative television contract was almost surely going to push Perini into pulling up stakes again. Lynch was half right: A television package offered by Atlanta did lead to the club's defection to Georgia after the 1965 season, but by that time Perini himself was no longer the chief decisionmaker of the franchise. Worn out by narrowing revenues and constant criticism, and dismayed that none of his children had his enthusiasm about running a big league club, he sold out in 1962 to a Milwaukee-Chicago syndicate headed by Illinois insurance broker Bill Bartholomay.

The last word on Perini's ownership fell to Dodger president Walter O'Malley, who acknowledged that the move from Boston to Milwaukee had opened his eyes to the real impact of air travel on major league baseball. Four years after Perini's transfer, O'Malley was shifting his club from Brooklyn to Los Angeles.

GAYLORD PERRY (Hall of Fame, 1991)

In his twenty-two years (1962–83) in the major leagues, Perry practically had two careers—as the pitcher who logged 314 victories, and as the professional coquette who might or might not have been using a spitball. Long before he revealed his technique for loading up his pitches, the right-hander made it clear that the doubts he had planted in opposition hitters and managers with his every delivery had become as vital to his arsenal as the spitball itself.

The only hurler to win the Cy Young Award in both leagues (with the 1972 Indians and the 1978 Padres), Perry wore eight different uniforms during his travels, usually being traded away upon some organization's conviction that he was finished. In fact, there was little reason to think he would ever get started, having compiled a record of only 24–30 by the time he was twenty-eight. His 239 wins from age thirty to his retirement at forty-five put him behind only Cy Young and Warren Spahn for victories by a pitcher past thirty. Along the way Perry had five 20-game seasons and eight years of at least 200 strikeouts. Despite racking up 3,534 strikeouts, however, Perry never once led a league in that category. As a member of the Giants on September 17, 1968, he pitched his only no-hitter, a 1–0 victory over Bob Gibson of the Cardinals. As a member of the Indians on July 3, 1973, Gaylord and his brother Jim Perry became the first siblings to start against one another in an American League game; Gaylord took the loss.

The only time Perry was actually caught doctoring the ball was on August 23, 1982, while with the Mariners; he was fined $250 and suspended for ten days.

SCOTT PERRY

Although Perry led the American League in losses twice, the right-hander was good enough for Philadelphia owner-manager Connie Mack to risk a new war with the National League over him. After bouncing from the Browns to the Cubs to the Reds without achieving much distinction, Perry found himself the property of the Class A Southern Association Atlanta Crackers, who sold his contract to the Braves in 1917. Refusing to report, he jumped to an outlaw league only to discover that Atlanta had resold him to the Athletics; this time he went and was given enough work

to finish the 1918 season with 21 wins and an AL-leading 19 losses.

When Boston president Percy Haughton protested what he considered the illegal reassignment of the pitcher, the case was referred to the National Commission. When the ruling there favored Boston, Mack secured an injunction preventing the pitcher from joining the NL club. This got NL owners fuming over dragging an intramural contest into court, league president John Tener suggesting a cancellation of the World Series, the owners refusing to go that far, and Tener resigning. The matter was finally settled when Mack agreed to pay Boston $2,500 in compensation.

JOHNNY PESKY

As with Bill Buckner, Pesky's solid career is doomed to remain overshadowed by a single World Series moment—in his case, a hesitation on a relay throw that enabled Enos Slaughter to score from first base and give St. Louis the 1946 world championship over Boston. As a shortstop in the 1940s, however, the lefty swinger broke from the gate with more hitting consistency than any other American League player at his position, racking up averages of .331, .335, and .324 in his first three seasons and leading the AL with more than 200 hits each year. Although he would never again hit that high, he did have three other years of better than .300, closing out his ten-year career between 1942 and 1954 with a .307 average. Pesky inherited the starting shortstop role from manager Joe Cronin in 1942 after Cronin had refused for a couple of years to acknowledge his failing defensive skills.

GARY PETERS

Southpaw Peters was about the best the White Sox had on the mound for a few years in the 1960s, especially in 1963, when he took Rookie of the Year honors, and in 1964, when his 20 wins paced the American League. In May 1968, he had another impact on the club after manager Eddie Stanky inserted him into the sixth slot in the lineup—the highest in the starting order a pitcher had hit in decades or, outside of stunts, has hit since. Stanky's move, in the name of shaking up a torpid lineup, inflamed an already dissident clubhouse and just about ended his reign. For a pitcher, Peters was an above-average hitter, managing a .222 mark in fourteen seasons.

JOHNNY PETERS

A shortstop with Chicago in 1880, Peters was the first "player to be named later" when he was sent to Providence after the season to complete a trade for catcher Lew Brown.

FRITZ PETERSON

Peterson announced baseball's most singular trade in 1972 when he told reporters that he and Yankee teammate Mike Kekich had decided to trade lives my moving in with each other's family. He eventually married Susan Kekich, but the relationship between Kekich and Marilyn Peterson did not last. Both pitchers were later dealt off to Cleveland, though in separate trades. After his retirement, Peterson became head of the Baseball Chapel.

FRED PFEFFER

The popular second baseman of Chicago's Stone Wall Infield (along with Cap Anson, Ned Williamson, and Tom Burns) in the 1880s, Pfeffer later got involved in an abortive effort to form a new league. In 1894 he joined with Louisville pilot Billy Barnie, Pittsburgh manager Al Buckenberger, and several monied parties to establish a new American Association. The circuit died without playing a single game, or even signing a single player, for several reasons, not the least of which was the NL's frontal assault on the threat. Unlike Barnie and Buckenberger, who capitulated early, Pfeffer refused to cooperate with NL inquiries, telling the owners that since he didn't pry into their business affairs, they had no right to intrude on his. Suspended and exiled to a coaching job at Princeton University, the infielder let it be known that he still wanted to play. When ten thousand fans petitioned the NL with threats of a boycott, and Louisville president Fred Dresler sent him a contract in defiance of the banishment, the league retreated, settling for a $500 fine that was raised by Pfeffer's friends.

Pfeffer has also been credited with being the first middle infielder to cut off a throw to second

and throw home to spoil the front end of a double steal.

BABE PHELPS

Phelps did two things very well: hit and imagine illnesses. On the first score, he holds the record for the highest batting average (.367 in 1936) by a catcher with at least 300 at-bats, had another part-time season (1935) batting .364, and broke the .300 mark three other times in his twelve-year career. One the other hand, he became a progressively more serious neurasthenic, begging out of games regularly with the Dodgers in the late 1930s and early 1940s. One of his personal medical theories, which accounted for sharp mood swings, was that if his heart missed one or two beats, he was all right, but that if it missed four, he was about to die. According to Brooklyn manager Leo Durocher and others, Phelps often showed up for games in a haggard state because he had spent the night sitting up listening to his own heartbeat. The catcher burned his bridges with the Dodgers in 1941, first by refusing to report to spring training in Havana because it entailed getting on a boat, then by jumping the club before a crucial series because he said he wasn't feeling well.

DAVE PHILLEY

A switch-hitting outfielder for several American League clubs in the 1940s and 1950s, Philley came into his own at the end of the latter decade as a premier pinch hitter. With the Phillies in 1958 he banged out 8 consecutive hits coming off the bench, then added a 9th straight in his first 1959 appearance for a big league record. With the Orioles in 1961, he set the AL pinch-hitting mark with 24 safeties. An overall .270 batter for his eighteen years of major league service, Philley averaged .299 as a pinch hitter.

DEACON PHILLIPPE

A much-underrated right-hander at the beginning of the century, Phillippe won the very first World Series game when he hurled Pittsburgh to a 7–3 triumph over Boston on October 1, 1903. It was the first of five appearances for him in the best-of-9 matchup; he also won the only other 2 games captured by the Pirates, while going down to defeat twice. With Louisville in 1899 and then with Pittsburgh for the next twelve seasons, Phillippe had five 20-win seasons, finishing up with 186 victories and a 2.59 ERA. When the Pirates set a major league record in June 1903 by hurling 6 consecutive shutouts, he contributed 2 of them. Phillippe's mere 363 bases on balls in 2,607 innings gave him the lowest ratio of walks per 9 frames (1.25) of any pitcher working from the modern mound distance of sixty feet, six inches.

E. LAWRENCE PHILLIPS

In 1902, Phillips introduced the concept of a regular public address announcer by walking around Washington's American League Park and using a megaphone to relay lineups to fans. Wolfie Jacobs had clarified some rules decisions to fans through the use of a megaphone in Boston the previous year.

RICHIE PHILLIPS

A Philadelphia lawyer, Phillips has been the head of the Major League Umpires Association since the late 1970s. He scored particular success in 1979, when he kept arbiters on the picket line for the first seven weeks of the season while negotiating significant salary increases, annual no-cut contracts, per diem traveling money, and a midyear two-week vacation for members. On the other hand, he failed to pressure the league offices to fire eight scab umpires who donned blue during the strike, leading to many years of continued tensions between the strikers and nonstrikers. Phillips also threatened umpire walkouts in 1984 and 1985 over postseason working conditions, and again in 1991 over a new contract; eleventh-hour settlements were arrived at in all three cases, but in 1991 not before retired and minor league umpires had to be called in to work Opening Day. As the profession's most authoritative spokesman, Phillips has been blamed often for the arrogance and short tempers of arbiters in recent years. He has only fueled the charges with a personality that brooks little argument.

OLLIE PICKERING

When he stepped into the batter's box in the top half of the 1st inning on April 24, 1901, Pickering, the Cleveland center fielder, became the first American League batter; he flied out to Chicago center fielder Dummy Hoy.

JOHN PICKETT

Pickett is the only major leaguer who ever needed teammates to testify that he was minimally qualified before he could collect his salary. Cut by the Orioles in mid-1892 after a three-year career, the right-hand-hitting second baseman sued for the balance of his annual salary. While Baltimore claimed that he did not have the requisite skills to play in the big leagues, Pickett dragged a bunch of fellow players into court to swear under oath that he had demonstrated ordinary skills and won a judgment of $1,285.72. His lifetime batting average was .252, but he was hitting a mere .213 at the time of his release; he never played in the major leagues again.

JACK PIERCE

Pierce, a Brooklyn restaurateur, was the most fanatical of Ebbets Field fans. With a devotion that bordered on idolatry, he attended almost every home game of the Dodgers in the late 1930s and most of the 1940s to cheer on third baseman Cookie Lavagetto. Pierce didn't come empty-handed either—toting along two big cartons of balloons, a helium tank, a giant banner, and two bottles of scotch. Camped in a third-base box, Pierce would belt down his scotch, scream out the name "COOKIE," then puncture one of his inflated balloons for emphasis. When Lavagetto was drafted during World War II, Pierce turned his attention to Joe Medwick, but with slightly less enthusiasm.

JIMMY PIERSALL

Piersall came as close as anybody to awakening baseball to the possibility that some of its "colorful" stars might have been deeply troubled men. Following a nervous breakdown while a member of the Red Sox in 1952, he described some of the emotional stresses he had been under in the best-selling book *Fear Strikes Out;* the autobiography, which laid heavy emphasis on a win-at-all-costs father, was later adapted for the screen, with Tony Perkins portraying the outfielder. Because he had branded himself with his acknowledged breakdown, Piersall was a constant target

Jimmy Piersall responds to heckling fans with a universally recognizable gesture. Photo compliments of Sharon Guynup.

of abuse from opposition players and fans; matters got so bad for him in 1961 during a return trip to Fenway Park as a member of the Indians that Massachusetts legislators were moved to introduce bills outlawing fan profanity at sporting events within the state.

Piersall did little to discourage the abuse; on the contrary, he delighted in mocking the game's traditional symbols and promotional rituals, providing still more fodder for pundits who treated his excesses as an extension of his breakdown. In Yankee Stadium, he urinated on the Babe Ruth monument that once stood in the outfield playing area. In Comiskey Park, he fired baseballs at Bill Veeck's scoreboard, with the avowed purpose of short-circuiting the fireworks that were set off whenever a Chicago player hit a home run. After being traded to the Mets in 1963, he celebrated his 100th home run by circling the bases backward.

As a broadcaster for the White Sox after his

retirement, Piersall found himself in hot water constantly—with the league office, and with players and umpires. On one occasion he almost cost the club a forfeited loss by giving the finger from the press box to umpire Joe Brinkman. After calling Veeck's wife "a colossal bore" during an interview, he almost came to blows with the owner's son. Piersall *did* come to blows with a Chicago-area reporter who questioned his sanity and with a Red Sox official who questioned a Piersall boast about the talent on a White Sox team. Veeck, who was forever vacillating between Piersall's popularity with fans and a personal aversion to the man, instigated a referendum on whether he should be kept in the broadcasting booth, and was chagrined to have to announce an overwhelming yes vote. During pregame comments on another evening, the club announcer advised Chicago fans to stay away from the ballpark because of inclement weather, prompting still another scene with Veeck. Another suspension came during the subsequent ownership of Jerry Reinsdorf and Eddie Einhorn, when Piersall told a television panel that all ballplayers thought of their wives as "horny broads who . . . wanted to get married and wanted a little money." It was because of remarks such as this that he had to surrender a part-time coaching job with the White Sox.

Lost amid all the controversies was a seventeen-year career (between 1950 and 1967) that, at least in the 1950s, established Piersall as one of the AL's peskiest leadoff men and most talented center fielders.

LIP PIKE

Pike was one of the first players to be acknowledged as a professional. While others had certainly been paid before 1866, Pike, along with two teammates on the ostensibly amateur Philadelphia Athletics, was ordered that year to appear before the judiciary committee of the governing National Association of Base Ball Players to answer charges that he had accepted $20 for his services. Although the matter was dropped when nobody bothered to show up for the hearing, the incident exposed for the first time the widespread practice of paying supposedly amateur players. The outfielder later became the first Jewish major leaguer (with the St. Louis Brown Stockings in 1876) and the first Jewish manager (with the Cincinnati Reds the following year).

BABE PINELLI

After playing a solid third base of the Reds for most of the 1920s, Pinelli switched to umpiring, remaining with the National League for twenty-two years (1935–56). His last game calling balls and strikes was Don Larsen's perfect effort for the Yankees against the Dodgers in the 1956 World Series. Even decades later, Dale Mitchell, the Brooklyn pinch hitter who took a halfhearted swing at Larsen's final delivery of the game and was rung up by Pinelli for the 27th out, insisted that the arbitrator had missed the pitch. According to the disgruntled Mitchell, Pinelli ''should have retired before the game, not after it.''

LOU PINIELLA

Called Sweet Lou for the smoothness of his right-handed swing and not for his disposition, Piniella attracted attention in about equal amounts for his studious quest after a flawless cut at the plate and his tantrums when he did not achieve it.

After brief stints with the Orioles and Indians, Piniella arrived with the Royals in 1968 to take the American League Rookie of the Year award. But it was with the Yankees from 1974 until his retirement in 1984 that he attracted the most attention. Although he topped .300 six times and batted .291 overall (and even higher in five League Championship Series and four World Series), his most vivid moment on a diamond came when, playing right field in the 1978 playoff game against the Red Sox, he lost a 9th-inning drive by Boston second baseman Jerry Remy in the sun but decoyed everyone into believing he would make a routine catch; base runner Rick Burleson could advance only one base after the ball bounced, and was unable to score the tying run on Jim Rice's subsequent fly ball.

Promising a calmer, sweeter Lou, Piniella succeeded Billy Martin as New York pilot in 1986. The only discernible difference in his temperament, however, was that he stopped trashing bat racks and water coolers when he struck out in favor of tossing the rack's contents onto the field when he disagreed with an umpiring call. His

rages became even more common the following year, when the club slipped from second to fifth, with predecessor Martin questioning his every move from the broadcasting booth. For all that, Piniella was the only New York manager to survive two full seasons in the 1980s, before being kicked upstairs to the front office in late 1987 so Martin could return to the dugout for his final tour with the Yankees. In the gavotte of managerial changes under owner George Steinbrenner, the change lasted only until the following season, when he was sent back to the bench to succeed the again-fired Martin.

In 1990, in his first season as Reds manager, Piniella won a West Division title, beat the Pirates in the League Championship Series, and took a world championship with a startling World Series sweep of the Athletics. When the club slipped to fifth place the following year, there were rumors of his imminent departure, but instead he assumed a strong say in player procurement. A second-place finish in 1992 failed to satisfy owner Marge Schott, however, especially since the team's collective salary had swelled by $35 million because of players recommended by Piniella. The manager's case was not helped when he squared off against Rob Dibble in a clubhouse brawl after the bullpen specialist objected truculently to being removed from a game.

Taking over the Mariners in 1993, Piniella led the club to a fourth-place finish with an 82–80 record—only the second time in franchise history that the team had finished above .500 and so high in the standings.

EDDIE PLANK (Hall of Fame, 1946)

Plank was a deliberate southpaw who annoyed opponents and spectators with the slow pace of his games; he annoyed Athletics owner-manager Connie Mack even more by jumping to the Federal League in 1915.

Coming off the Gettysburg College campus in 1901, Plank notched seven 20-win seasons for Philadelphia over the next fourteen seasons, recording more than 23 percent of the victories by a team that won six pennants and fell out of the first division only twice in the period. He was, however, a World Series Jonah: Although he held the opposition to a 1.32 ERA in seven Series appearances, he lost 5 games (against only 2 victories)—4 of them when the A's were shut out. He also missed the entire 1910 Series with a sore arm.

The southpaw's desertion to the Feds was such a bitter pill for Mack that the A's boss speeded up the dismantling of his powerhouse four-time pennant-winning team as a result. After a final 20-win year for the St. Louis Terriers and the collapse of the Feds, Plank was assigned to the Browns. Traded to the Yankees two years later, he refused to report and retired with 327 wins, the most by a big league left-hander until Warren Spahn.

JOHNNY PODRES

Possessor of the best change-up of his era and the hero of the 1955 World Series, Podres never won 20 games, reaching a career high of 18 for the 1961 Los Angeles Dodgers. Even when he led the National League in ERA (2.66) and shutouts (6) for the 1957 Brooklyn version of the franchise, he managed a record of only 12–9. As far as Ebbets Field denizens were concerned, however, the southpaw could just as well have retired after his seventh-game, 2–0 victory over the Yankees in 1955, giving the Dodgers their only world championship in Brooklyn. There would probably never have been a seventh game if Podres hadn't also won the 3rd game for Brooklyn after the Yankees had taken the first 2 contests. The 2 wins were all the more surprising in that the lefty's record during the 1955 season was 9–10, with a very visible 3.95 ERA.

CAL POHLAD

A Minneapolis banker, Pohlad ended the sixty-five-year ownership of the Washington Senators-Minnesota Twins by the Griffith family when he put together a group of buyers to purchase the franchise in 1984 for more than $44 million. Although he endorsed the signing of expensive free agents for a few years, helping the Twins to world championships in 1987 and 1991, he began tightening the purse strings in 1993 as part of the strategy of small-market owners to force revenue-sharing on television contracts and a player salary cap. Pohlad is often listed as one of the hundred wealthiest people in the United States.

PAM POSTEMA

Postema's thirteen years as a minor league arbiter was the longest umpiring tenure for a woman in organized baseball; the circumstances of her dismissal aroused suspicions that sexist attitudes and not her ability to call balls and strikes were the reason she never reached the big leagues. Released from her contract in December 1989 after seven years at the AAA level and several spring tryouts in the majors, Postema was given no reason why neither the National League nor the American League had expressed interest in her services, but there were suggestions that neither league wanted to be bothered with providing separate facilities for a woman umpire or with the inevitable conflicts that would arise from resentment by some players.

NELSON POTTER

Although the spitball had already been outlawed for almost a quarter century, it wasn't until July 20, 1944, that anyone enforced the rule, with umpire Cal Hubbard throwing Potter out of a game for going to his mouth while he was on the mound for the St. Louis Browns. The right-hander was later fined and suspended for ten days.

JACK POWELL

Powell has the most wins of any major league pitcher with a losing record. His 245 victories with the (Cleveland) Spiders, Cardinals, Browns, and Yankees included four 20-win seasons; his 256 defeats were compiled by losing in double figures in every one of his sixteen major league seasons (1897–1912) despite a career ERA of only 2.97.

JAKE POWELL

Powell was responsible for throwing one of the ugliest lights on baseball's racism prior to the arrival of Jackie Robinson in the majors. Interviewed by Bob Elson in Chicago on a July 1938 pregame radio show, the Yankee outfielder asserted that he had spent his off-season as a Dayton, Ohio, cop "cracking niggers over the head." Although Elson immediately cut off the interview, Powell's remark ricocheted around the country for the next several weeks. While black dailies from coast to coast demanded that the player be banned from both baseball and police work in Ohio, the baseball establishment and the mainstream press sought to interpret the incident as nothing more than an attempt at "jocularity." Even when Commissioner Kenesaw Landis finally sensed the depth of the anger of the black community and suspended Powell for ten days, he insisted that the crack had been made "carelessly, not purposely." For his part, Yankee president Ed Barrow called the remark a "thoughtless blunder," but also provided assurances that he had spoken with "two of my colored servants and they seem to feel that it was just an unfortunate mistake that cannot happen again."

Before calls by several black groups for organizing a boycott against Yankee owner Jacob Ruppert's beer products, the team prevailed upon Powell to visit a Harlem-headquartered newspaper and issue an apology. Like most of the rest of the case, this, too, was ignored by most white papers; it was only when Powell returned to action at Griffith Stadium after his suspension and was greeted by boos and bottles that mainstream dailies focused complete attention on the episode, largely in the interests of denouncing the bottle throwers as being worse than the outfielder.

Powell had an eleven-year career with the Yankees, Senators, and Phillies in the 1930s and 1940s, batting .271 overall. He began going downhill after fracturing his skull while chasing a fly ball in a 1940 game. In 1948 he was arrested in Washington for passing bad checks, and shortly afterward committed suicide in his cell.

VIC POWER

Power's flamboyant style of playing first base was exactly what the Yankees weren't looking for in breaking the team color barrier, so they traded him to Kansas City in 1954 and put racial integration on hold for another year until the low-key Elston Howard was ready. On the other hand, the Power deal was the only one of dozens between New York and the Athletics in the 1950s that benefited Kansas City more than the Bronx. As deft as he was flashy, the Puerto Rican native ended up collecting seven Gold Gloves and leading American League first basemen in fielding three times. No slouch with a bat either, Power batted over .300 three times and concluded a

twelve-year run with a .284 average. While with Cleveland on August 14, 1958, he stole home twice in a game—the only time that has been accomplished in the major leagues since Walter Gautreau of the Braves did it in 1927. The thefts were aided by an element of surprise: Power stole only a single other base that year and never swiped more than 9 in a season. Even after the major leagues had been integrated for some time, Power remained a particular target of redneck harassment, in part because he was married to a light-skinned, redheaded Puerto Rican.

MIKE POWERS

Powers sustained the first fatal injury on a major league field during the opening of Shibe Park on April 12, 1909. A backup catcher with four teams for eleven seasons before and after the turn of the century, he was behind the plate for the ballpark inaugural only because he was Eddie Plank's personal receiver. In the 7th inning he crashed into a wall while chasing a pop foul but remained in the game. Immediately afterward, however, he had to undergo surgery for internal injuries. Two weeks and two more operations later, Powers died of gangrene of the bowels.

AL PRATT

A former National Association pitcher, Pratt was tending bar in a Pittsburgh saloon in October 1881 when he overheard two visitors from Cincinnati, Justus Thorner and O. P. Caylor, lamenting that no one had shown up for a meeting they had called to discuss the possibility of forming a new major circuit. The American Association was born after the pair acted on Pratt's suggestion that they seek out local sportsman Denny McKnight; in 1882 Pratt became the first manager of the Pittsburgh entry in the new league.

GERRY PRIDDY

Priddy became the focal point of clubhouse tensions on the 1947 Senators when he refused to sign a statement that the team stood squarely behind manager Ossie Bluege. The declaration had been fashioned by Bluege himself after weeks of press reports that the players were in full revolt against the pilot. Owner Clark Griffith immediately stepped in to quash the statement, then, after the season, traded Priddy to St. Louis and fired Bluege. On his way to the Browns, Priddy got in the last shot by promising that he would have his best year in the majors without the distractions of the Washington organization; in fact, his next two seasons were the best in his career, the second baseman topping the .290 mark twice.

CHARLES PRINCE

Boston blueblood and Harvard graduate Prince attempted to challenge the National League in Boston twice—first as backer of the Players League Reds in 1890, then as owner of an American Association franchise of the same name in 1891. He failed both times despite pennant-winning seasons in both leagues. The first venture flopped even though the Reds had recruited almost the entire roster of the NL Beaneaters; in the peace talks that followed the season, Prince growled about the PL's readiness to fight on while privately maneuvering to gain an American Association franchise. His second foray was doomed when he acceded to conditions by Beaneaters owner Arthur Soden that Prince charge the NL admission of fifty cents and not use Boston as part of the club name. Even with these handicaps, Prince signed King Kelly in midseason and looked as if he might make a go of it; but when the Hub City favorite moved over to Soden's club 4 games later, Prince, the Reds, and, as it turned out, the entire association were through. Prince quit as club president when his board of directors retaliated against Soden by lowering ticket prices to twenty-five cents, and had to sit on the sidelines as the AA unraveled behind demands to return Kelly.

LOU PROCTOR

Proctor was a Western Union telegraphist in Boston who inserted his name into the box score of a May 13, 1912, game between the Browns and the Red Sox. Several newspapers, including *The Sporting News,* recorded him as having gone 0 for 1 as a pinch hitter—a prankish failure that was recorded in early editions of *The Baseball Encyclopedia.*

DOC PROTHRO

Prothro wasn't much as a third baseman in the 1920s, but he was even less than that as a manager. His record of 138–320 (.301), for the Phillies between 1939 and 1941, is the worst by a big league manager with at least two full seasons.

HUB PRUETT

Pruett was a mediocre southpaw who went 14–18 for the St. Louis Browns between 1922 and 1924. On the other hand, he was a Hall of Famer when he faced Babe Ruth, striking out the Yankee slugger 13 of the 21 times that he faced him.

KIRBY PUCKETT

The most popular player ever to don a Minnesota uniform, Puckett was the offensive backbone of the club's world championships in 1987 and 1991. Although quickly establishing his credentials as an offensive force in his maiden 1984 season, the fireplug-built outfielder also managed to get through 557 at-bats without tagging a single home run—a statistic that turned even more anomalous later in the decade, when he walloped at least 24 homers three years in a row. The right-handed swinger also won the American League batting title with a .339 average in 1989—one of five seasons in which he reached 200 hits and one of four in which he paced the league in that category. In 1993, Minnesota fans came close to protest demonstrations when the organization's stance on resigning free agents had Puckett only hours away from signing with the Red Sox; at the eleventh hour, however, owner Carl Pohlad signed him to one of the most lucrative contracts in the game. Puckett's most nationally visible moment came in the 11th inning of game six of the 1991 World Series, when his home run off Atlanta southpaw Charlie Leibrandt kept the Twins alive for a seventh game, which they would also win.

HARRY PULLIAM

The president of the National League between 1903 and 1909, Pulliam owed his position to Pittsburgh owner Barney Dreyfuss; he owed his tragic end in good part to John McGraw.

A minority partner with Dreyfuss of the Louisville Colonels in the 1890s, Pulliam moved to Pittsburgh as organization secretary when the Kentucky team was dissolved at the end of the decade. After season-long tensions in 1900 between major stockholders Dreyfuss and William Kerr, Pulliam became a *casus belli* when Kerr tried to have him removed from his position. Knowing that the attack on Pulliam was just a preliminary skirmish for pushing him out as well, Dreyfuss countered ably enough to force Kerr to sell out and take over the Pirates completely. Three years later, Dreyfuss had gained enough influence in league councils to impose Pulliam as president of the circuit. In that role, he endorsed his rabbi's call for the first World Series in 1903 and also made an enemy for life when he scolded McGraw for not being willing to have his Giants meet the Red Sox in a 1904 Series.

In 1905, Pulliam made another big mistake when he gave in to a Dreyfuss demand that McGraw be fined and suspended; the Giant manager's sin had been to taunt the prim Pittsburgh owner about (nonexistent) gambling habits and debts in public before a Pittsburgh-New York game. When McGraw flatly refused to serve fifteen days on the sidelines or to pay an ordered $150, throwing in charges that Pulliam heard only his master's voice, other NL owners stepped in quickly before the episode threatened the league as a whole. The Solomonic verdict was that McGraw should abide by the suspension and fine,

Dreyfuss should be censured for unbecoming behavior, and Pulliam should be congratulated for acquitting himself responsibly. It all went for nothing when McGraw continued to ignore the suspension and fine orders, and Pulliam, trying to end his daily pillorying in the New York press, ultimately let the matter die.

Worse followed in 1908 after the Merkle Boner debacle. When Pulliam ruled—belatedly—that the New York first baseman's failure to touch second base had nullified an apparent Giants victory, McGraw exploded in further rage against the NL president, leaving him little room for still more contempt when a makeup game at the end of the season necessitated by the Merkle misadventure cost New York the pennant. Throughout the off-season, New York sportswriters stirred up by McGraw lashed out at Pulliam unmercifully. The official finally cracked. Making it clear to several intimates that McGraw in particular had worn him down, Pulliam took a six-month leave of absence, but after returning, blew his brains out in the New York Athletic Club on July 28, 1909, at age thirty-nine. An official league announcement attributed the suicide to the fact that the executive had been "broken in health from overwork in his long fight to maintain a high standard of baseball." The only team not represented at the funeral was the Giants. Informed of what had happened, McGraw commented, "I didn't think a bullet to the head could hurt him."

Q

TOM QUALTERS

A right-hander for the 1954 Phillies, Qualters spent the entire season with the team without getting into a single game. He was neither injured nor suspended, but a bonus baby who had to be carried for two years on the major league roster. Steve O'Neill and Terry Moore, who split managing duties during the year, shared a resentment at losing a pitching spot to the bonus rule, and refused even to drop the hurler into a laughter. Philadelphia finished in fourth place in 1954, 22 games behind the Giants.

JOE QUEST

A light-hitting second baseman for six teams in the 1870s and 1880s, Quest's contribution to the baseball lexicon was the term ''charley horse.'' He applied the label to a leg injury to teammate George Gore when the center fielder pulled a muscle trying to steal second base in an 1882 game. The day before, Quest had been the only one of several Chicago players in attendance at a local racetrack who refused to bet on a heavy favorite named Charley, who justified the infielder's doubts by pulling up lame in the backstretch after having run most of the race several lengths in front of the field.

In 1907, two decades after he had left baseball, Quest was suspected of peculation while employed by his old manager, Cap Anson, then the Chicago City Clerk; his response to the accusation was to disappear completely and permanently.

BOB QUINN

As an owner, general manager, or combination of the two, Quinn was baseball's all-time loser. Operating from the front office of the Browns, Red Sox, Dodgers, and Braves almost continuously between 1917 and 1944, the executive saw his clubs compile an overall won–lost record of 1,726–2,357 (.423), without a single pennant among them. Only four of the squads broke .500, while nine of them couldn't even reach .400.

Quinn began his administrative career with the Browns, taking over as general manager under owner Phil Ball, who prided himself on not interfering in baseball decisions. Ball was so ecstatic over an unexpected second-place finish by St. Louis in 1922 that he handed around bonuses to his top aides; Quinn promptly used his money to buy into the Red Sox. Although initially hailed in New England for taking over from Harry Frazee, the owner who had sold Babe Ruth and numerous other Red Sox stars to the Yankees, he was soon presiding over a club that was even worse than those run by his predecessor. The ill-advised deals with New York didn't stop either; one of the worst was the 1930 dispatch of future Hall of Famer Red Ruffing to the Bronx. Managers came and went so regularly that one of them, Marty McManus, got considerable mileage out of a crack that he had been offered the job while in church with Quinn and instantly had another reason to feel humbled.

Like Frazee, Quinn spent much of his time in Boston scrambling after cash. Some of his financial shorts stemmed from the 1926 death of his chief backer, Indiana glassworks millionaire Palmer Wilson. In the same year, a fire destroyed a substantial part of Fenway Park, necessitating costly rebuilding. With the crash of the stock market in 1929, the usually hotheaded Quinn became even more so in having to rely even more heavily on creditors, at one time or another threatening to sell every player on his roster and to shutter Fenway Park and move into Braves Field to save on overhead expenses. Hardly a visionary in the best of times, his daily turmoils led him to ridicule an idea before its time in 1931: that the Red Sox become the first club to offer telecasts of their games. But even as he was laughing at the notion of undermining his already thin attendance with television coverage, he was dipping into his own insurance policies to help meet the organization's payroll. When Tom Yawkey came along in 1933 with an offer to buy the club for little more than its debts of $350,000, Quinn accepted.

When Quinn was general manager of the Dodgers in 1934 and 1935, his major contributions were continuing the sideshow antics of the incompetent regime known as The Daffiness Boys, hiring Casey Stengel as the manager, and blowing up a casual remark by Giants pilot Bill Terry into a declaration of battle between the teams. It was in fact out of personal irritation that his trading prowess was being questioned that Quinn made Terry's ''Is Brooklyn still in the league?'' a war cry that echoed across the East River and that dramatized the Dodgers' knocking the Giants out of the 1934 pennant race on the final weekend of the season.

After the 1935 season, Quinn was asked by the National League to take over as president of the Braves because of regulations prohibiting chief stockholder Charles Adams, a heavy investor in a racetrack, from holding the office. Quinn's first move with still another franchise staggering under financial problems was to poll local sportswriters for a new team name in an effort to get away from the New York Tammany Hall connotations of Braves. After sorting through such proposals as the Basements and the Bankrupts, he decided on the Bees; he also changed the name of the team stadium from Braves Field to National League Park. These cosmetic alterations made,

Quinn then sent one humpty-dumpty club after another onto the field and, as in Brooklyn, brought in Stengel as a sideshow. There was also the usual series of players-for-cash deals—in this instance keeping the franchise so visibly afloat that a group of Boston businessmen backed Quinn in 1941, when he bought out Adams's 73 percent holding.

Quinn barely got through World War II as the owner of his second Boston franchise. By 1943, three of his backers—construction industry millionaires Lou Perini, Guido Rugo, and Joseph Maney—had bought up a controlling interest in the team. Quinn remained as president until 1944, before being demoted to minor league director and being replaced as head of the organization by his son John Quinn. Before losing his place to Perini and his partners, Bob Quinn changed the name of the team back to the Braves and the name of the ballpark back to Braves Field.

JACK QUINN

Quinn lasted long enough as a big league pitcher (twenty-three years between 1909 and 1933) to become the oldest hurler both to win a major league game and to finish a World Series game, and the oldest player to hit a home run. A dispute over his contract also helped push American League president Ban Johnson from power.

Quinn's best and worst years came for the Baltimore Terrapins of the Federal League, when he won 26 games in 1914 and then slipped to a league-leading 22 losses the following year. After the collapse of the Feds, the spitballing righthander went to the Pacific Coast League, where he pitched for the Vernon club until World War I forced the circuit to close down in July 1918. When the pitcher signed with the White Sox and Vernon simultaneously sold his contract to the Yankees, the two major league clubs locked horns over who had the rights to his services. Even though Quinn appeared in 6 games for Chicago in late 1918, the National Commission ruled in New York's favor, with Johnson voting against Chicago owner Charlie Comiskey. The owner became so irate—more at what he took as a betrayal by his old friend than over the loss of the hurler— that the two became implacable enemies, with

Comiskey joining Johnson's growing number of enemies and plotting his overthrow at every turn.

Quinn went on record 18 wins for the Yankees in 1920 and another 18 for the Athletics in 1928. On June 27, 1930, still with the A's at age forty-seven, he hit the last of his 8 career homers; later that season he pitched the last 2 innings of game three of the World Series. He recorded his final victory, for the Dodgers, on August 14, 1932, at age forty-nine, while leading the National League in saves for the second consecutive year. Quinn retired with 247 victories—and a record for having been the teammate of thirty-one eventual members of the Hall of Fame.

R

DICK RADATZ

Radatz was the greatest strikeout pitcher in baseball history. Although he had only three imposing years as a reliever for the Red Sox, in the 1960s, the right-hander averaged 9.67 strikeouts per 9 innings over his seven-year career—a ratio better even than Nolan Ryan's 9.42. In 1964 Radatz established the major league mark for whiffs by a reliever, fanning 181 batters in 157 innings. In the fastballer's glory years (1962–64) for otherwise wretched Boston clubs, he averaged 69 appearances, 26 saves, 13 wins, and a 2.17 ERA annually.

CHARLIE RADBOURNE (Hall of Fame, 1939)

The winner of 311 games in his career, Radbourne was a formidable hurler before 1884, having led the National League in won–lost percentage in 1881, strikeouts in 1882, and wins in 1883. In 1884, however, the Providence right-hander, already known as Old Hoss for his durability, had what may have been the greatest season by a nineteenth-century pitcher, winning an all-time record 60 games and leading the league in strikeouts and ERA.

Difficult when sober and impossible most of the time, Radbourne was suspended in mid-July after an on-field temper tantrum over a balk call; returning, he made everyone forget that he had been flirting with the Union Association by offering to pitch every day for the rest of the season after mound partner and rival Charlie Sweeney departed for the Unions. The underhand hurler proceeded to complete his next 35 starts, winning 30 of them and turning a close pennant race into a rout. By the end of the season, the pitcher was unable to raise his arm above his head and got ready for the day's game by light tossing a few feet and gradually increasing the distance of his tosses. After beating the American Association's New York Metropolitans 3 straight in postseason championship play, Radbourne's reward was a blank contract, which he famously filled in with a modest raise. Less well known is that during his iron man streak he collected Sweeney's salary as well as his own.

A .235 lifetime hitter, Radbourne hit 9 homers. The first of them, in the bottom of the 18th inning off Stump Weidman of the Detroit Wolverines on August 17, 1882, handed John Montgomery Ward a victory in what is still the longest 1–0 game concluded by a sudden-death home run; Radbourne played right field that day.

FREDERICK RAH

Rah designed dandelion-colored baseballs with the idea that they would be safer for batters than the white variety coming out of the shirts of outfield spectators. Larry MacPhail of the Dodgers obtained league permission to use them in a game in 1938 and in 3 more games the following year, but then abandoned the experiment. Thirty years later, Charlie Finley of the A's pressed for a similar switch to yellow balls, but without success.

WILLARD RAMSDELL

Ramsdell didn't let team loyalty stand in the way of $50. As a member of the Cubs in 1952, the knuckleball specialist drew a walk off Carl Erskine in the 5th inning of what turned out to be the Brooklyn hurler's first no-hitter. In the 9th inning, with merely three outs to go to the masterpiece, Ramsdell was informed that he would be the Chicago representative on a postgame show that paid $50—provided no other Cub got on base. The right-hander openly cheered for Erskine to strike out teammate Eddie Miksis so he could collect the money for his postgame show. Miksis went down swinging.

TOAD RAMSEY

Ramsey was the first knuckleballer, a pitch he called a drop curve. Pitching for the Louisville Colonels of the American Association on June 23, 1887, Ramsey struck out 17 Cleveland batters. Although record books cite Roger Clemens's 20 whiffs of the Seattle Mariners as the strikeout record, Ramsey's accomplishment remains noteworthy because, under the rules of the day, he had to get four strikes on a batter to record a whiff.

LENNY RANDLE

Randle's attack on Ranger manager Frank Lucchesi during spring training in 1977 ranks as one of the ugliest assaults by a player on a pilot. The infielder sprang at Lucchesi while the dugout boss was talking to reporters, hitting him with a left-right combination, then continuing to hammer him on the ground until pulled away by teammates. Randle's only explanation was that he had gotten tired of Lucchesi calling him a "punk"— an accusation denied by the manager from his hospital bed, where he had to be treated for a concussion, a broken cheekbone, and a lacerated lip. Randle was fined $10,000 and suspended thirty days by Texas, and subsequently arrested on felonious assault charges. The criminal count was eventually reduced to a misdemeanor carrying a fine of $1,000, by which time Randle had been peddled to the Mets. The episode didn't do much for Lucchesi's image, either, and he was fired in June behind claims by owner Brad Corbett that he had become helpless to control a dissension-filled clubhouse.

RICHARD RAVITCH

Ravitch triggered the firing of Commissioner Fay Vincent in 1992 when he took over as the chief labor negotiator for major league owners. He took the post only after making it clear that he wanted a free hand in dealing with the Players Association, with no intrusions from anybody inspired by "the best interests of baseball." With Milwaukee owner Bud Selig taking over as a temporary commissioner, Ravitch labored for months to work out an agreement among owners for a television revenue-sharing scheme that he viewed as an indispensable premise for entering into negotiations with the Players Association and demanding a cap on big league salaries. He then became the owners' chief spokesman for the salary cap demand that precipitated the 1994 players' strike on August 12 and the premature end of the season.

DAVE RAYMOND

Better known as the Philly Phanatic, Raymond wore a home uniform in Philadelphia longer than anyone except Mike Schmidt. For sixteen years through 1993, Raymond cavorted on the field and in the stands of Veterans Stadium in the flouncy, big-bellied attire of a green anteater that looked more appropriate to *Sesame Street* than to a ballpark. The specialties of his performances were mocking umpires and opposition players, leading fans in ridiculous dances, and "swallowing" spectators with his oversized beak. Another constant of the mascot's act was to speed over the artificial surface of the field in a scooter, chasing groundskeepers and coaches out of his way. Raymond's explanation for the effectiveness of his antics was that he had been raised by a severely hearing-impaired mother with whom he had to learn extravagantly physical communication skills.

AL REACH

One of the earliest paid players (with the Eckford club of Brooklyn in the early 1860s), the British-born Reach built one of the great baseball fortunes, both as a team owner and sporting goods manufacturer. As part owner and president of the Phillies from the team's inception in 1883 until 1902, he was responsible for the construction of

Huntington Avenue Grounds, the first concrete stadium, which opened in 1887. Reach's partnership with Ben Shibe encompassed both a jointly owned half interest in the Phillies, and full control of the sporting goods company that bore Reach's name. Incorporated in the late 1870s, the firm sold out to competitor Al Spalding in 1892, although the Philadelphia branch continued under its founder's operating control. This cozy relationship got even cozier when partner Shibe accepted the presidency of the upstart American League Athletics in 1901 and, perhaps more significantly, the contract to produce AL balls. The only one who seemed to be concerned about this obvious conflict of interest was John Rogers, the holder of the other 50 percent of the Phillies, and he grew even more concerned after the A's began raiding the Phillies for such stars as Nap Lajoie, Elmer Flick, and Bill Duggleby. After two years of lawsuits and mutual recriminations, all three stockholders sold out to a group headed by stockbroker Jimmy Potter. A. J. Reach and Co. continued to manufacture baseballs—for both leagues—until well into this century, even though the NL balls carried the Spalding imprint. Similarly, Reach published the annual American League guides, while Spalding did the National League books.

JACK REED

Reed's home run in the top of the 22nd inning was the decisive blow in the longest game in American League history, a seven-hour affair, on June 24, 1962, in which the Yankees defeated the Tigers, 9–7; the round-tripper was the outfielder's only homer in the major leagues.

JIMMY REESE

Nobody in baseball has worn a uniform longer than Reese, who died at age eighty-eight in 1994 while still serving as a coach for the Angels. Once an outfielder for the Yankees and a roommate of Babe Ruth, the New York native first wore togs in 1917 as a batboy for the Los Angeles Angels of the Pacific Coast League. His subsequent seventy-seven years encompassed three seasons with the Yankees and Browns (for a career batting average of .278); decades of managing and coaching in the minors; and, from 1972 until his death,

conditioning coach and fungo hitter for California.

PEE WEE REESE (Hall of Fame, 1984)

Reese owed his sixteen years (between 1940 and 1958) in a Dodger uniform to the vanity of another Hall of Fame shortstop. Ready for promotion to the major leagues from the Boston farm system in 1939, he was kept where he was because Red Sox shortstop-manager Joe Cronin wasn't ready to admit that his best years were behind him. Purchased by the Dodgers, the right-hand-hitting Reese took a finishing course from still another Cooperstown shortstop-manager, Leo Durocher, then went on to captain the Boys of Summer teams through the 1950s.

In terms of diamond skills, Reese was the classic playmaker—hitting behind the runner, bunting, and turning the double play with agility. In an era that didn't think too much of the stolen base, he paced the National League in that category in 1952; he also topped the league in walks in 1947 and in runs scored in 1949. As much as in his physical skills, however, Reese was invaluable to Brooklyn in his leadership qualities—and never more so than when Jackie Robinson broke the color barrier in 1947. After acknowledging his own misgivings about playing with Robinson, the Kentuckian infielder ended up turning the tide for his teammate's brutal orientation in 1947 when, amid some particularly violent hectoring from the Boston bench, he walked over from his shortstop position and put his arm around Robinson. One small footnote to the relationship between the two players was that, in six of the ten seasons they played together, Reese stole more bases than Robinson.

CHARLIE REILLY

An otherwise undistinguished third baseman for eight seasons, Reilly stroked the first major league pinch-hit—a single for the Phillies in the 9th inning on April 28, 1892.

JERRY REINSDORF

Reinsdorf emerged as a Walter O'Malley-like first among equals with major league owners in the early 1990s, especially after leading the successful campaign to dump Commissioner Fay

Vincent. At the very least, the White Sox owner felt invulnerable enough in his position after the September 1992 ouster of Vincent to tell reporters that the time had come to "run the business for the owners, not the players or the umpires or the fans."

A real-estate magnate, Reinsdorf and his partner Eddie Einhorn took over the Chicago franchise in 1981 after the American League had blocked previous owner Bill Veeck's attempts to sell to Edward DeBartolo. Reinsdorf's first move was to sign catcher Carlton Fisk, who had been rendered a free agent by Boston's failure to send him a contract by a necessary deadline. It was to prove a pivotal pickup in that Fisk went on to establish various franchise power records, but would also ultimately serve as a case in point of the owner's crassness when it came to players or other employees he no longer wanted around.

Although the White Sox won a division title in 1983, Reinsdorf had very few other satisfactions for quite some time. For one thing, there was the mid–decade purchase of the Cubs by the *Chicago Tribune*, which meant that Chicago's chief newspaper and its associated radio-television network devoted about twenty words to the city's National League entry for every one it spent on the White Sox. In 1984 Reinsdorf annoyed several other owners by indirectly causing the demise of the free-agent compensation pool by plucking Tom Seaver from the Mets; although New York itself assumed an ambiguous stance in the loss of its right-hander, smaller-market teams had seen the pool as a way of obtaining better prospects for departed free agents than those offered subsequently by the amateur draft. The owner also had to settle for a Pyrrhic victory when he appointed machine-gun-mouthed Ken Harrelson as general manager in 1985 in an attempt to beat the Cubs to the local sports headlines; he got the headlines, but they were mostly about such misguided Harrelson moves as switching the heavy-footed Fisk to the outfield and the ensuing protests by White Sox pitchers at losing one of the game's most astute receivers.

More than anything else, however, the Reinsdorf-Einhorn ownership was consumed throughout a good part of the 1980s by its demand that the city provide a new stadium for the White Sox.

While municipal and state legislators got bogged down in one argument after another, the pair grew less subtle in threats to leave Chicago for Florida. By the beginning of 1988, St. Petersburg had begun construction on a $140 million dome that would seat forty-three thousand. On June 27, only three days before the deadline that the Illinois legislature had for approving a new Comiskey Park, Florida officials revealed that Reinsdorf had taken a fifteen-year lease on the dome and had already hammered out an agreement for the fourth-best television package in the major leagues. With Illinois governor James Thompson finally pulling out all the stops to save the franchise for the state, the legislature put the finishing touches on the construction bill with literally only minutes to spare. The second Comiskey Park opened in 1991 directly across the street from the old facility, with Reinsdorf maintaining the air of somebody who would not have been completely disappointed if he had had to go through with his threat to move to Florida.

His successful pressuring of the Illinois legislature together with an ambitious cable sports network launched a few years earlier to carry White Sox games put Reinsdorf at the center of baseball's financial strategy sessions at the start of the 1990s. He figured prominently in the selection of Richard Ravitch as the owners' chief negotiator—a choice that took on new meaning when Ravitch insisted on *carte blanche* in dealing with the Players Association; what this meant ultimately was no interference from the commissioner's office. When Vincent stubbed his toe with several other teams, the Chicago boss had enough support for the commissioner's ouster and a redefinition of his job to a CEO who served at the sufferance of the owners. Reinsdorf's chief ally in all the boardroom maneuvering, Milwaukee owner Bud Selig, was appointed pro-tem commissioner.

With regard to his own franchise, the Chicago owner invited a series of public relations gaffes in the new decade. The most short-lived was an attempt to bring back Minnie Minoso as a stunt so that the 1950s star, in his seventies, could claim to have played in six decades; even the White Sox players protested that gambit. In 1993 Reinsdorf climaxed years of a strained relationship with Fisk by first allowing him to appear in a game so that he could establish the record for most games by a catcher, and then releasing him a few days later. Prior to spring training in 1994, with most attention on the prospects for the White Sox to repeat their 1993 division title, he threw a publicity bombshell by announcing that retired basketball great Michael Jordan would be in camp for a tryout. Reinsdorf, who also owned Jordan's former Chicago Bulls, feigned surprise when even manager Gene Lamont voiced his irritation at such a distraction, but clearly relished the media circus that ensued.

PETE REISER

Legal roadblocks kept Reiser from getting to the Dodgers until 1940; once in Brooklyn, he confronted an incredible series of physical obstacles that prevented him from fulfilling predictions of being a superstar.

Signed by the Cardinals before his sixteenth birthday, Reiser was hidden through subterfuges such as listing him as scout Charley Barrett's chauffeur until he was of age. Even then, when St. Louis boss Branch Rickey got caught shuffling players from one minor league affiliate to another, Reiser was among the "slaves from the St. Louis chain gang" freed by Commissioner Kenesaw Landis in 1938 for illegal contract manipulations. The shortstop-turned-outfielder then signed as a free agent with the Dodgers, but he was kept in the lower minors by general manager Larry Mac-Phail as part of a secret deal with Rickey whereby the Brooklyn organization would hide him for the three-year waiting period before he could be legally transferred back to St. Louis. It was only through the intervention of Dodger manager Leo Durocher and Bill Killefer, the pilot of the Dodgers' Eastern League affiliate in Elmira, that he escaped becoming the player to be named later in the deal that brought Joe Medwick from St.

Pete Resier steals home in a 1942 game with an expression that typified his approach to the game. Photo compliments of Sharon Guynup.

Louis to Brooklyn. Reiser finally came up with the Dodgers in 1940.

In 1941, Reiser's .343 average made him the National League's youngest (twenty-two years old) batting champion ever; the lefty hitter (he also tried switch-hitting later in his career) paced NL hitters in doubles, triples, and slugging as well, despite two serious beanings, by Ike Pearson of the Phillies and Paul Erickson of the Cubs. The next year Reiser suffered a fractured skull crashing into the center field wall in St. Louis on July 2; he still managed to pick up the ball and relay it back to the infield before being carried off the field on a stretcher for one of eleven times in his career. Reiser was back as a pinch hitter two days later to drive in the winning run in an extra-inning game—and to pass out rounding first base and wind up back in the hospital. Three weeks after that, he was in the lineup again. Hitting .383 at the time of the accident, he finished the season with a .310 average and a league-leading total in stolen bases.

After three years of military service during World War II, Reiser broke an ankle sliding back into first base on a routine pickoff play with two days left in the 1946 season; his second league-leading total in stolen bases held up in his absence, but without him, the Dodgers ended the season in a tie with the Cardinals and lost a best-of-3 playoff. Early the next season, he had his second dramatic encounter with an outfield wall, this time in Ebbets Field, when he misjudged the distance to the fence because it had been shortened during the off-season. Paralyzed for ten days and out of uniform for five weeks, he bumped into pitcher Clyde King during batting practice shortly after returning and revealed a previously undetected blood clot that required surgery and kept him sidelined for all but the last two months of the season; when he was in the lineup, he averaged .309. In the World Series against the Yankees that year, he fractured an ankle still again but kept playing and set up the winning run in Bill Bevens's near-no-hitter when he was walked intentionally; pinch runner Eddie Miksis replaced him and scored minutes later on Cookie Lavagetto's double.

The injuries—and, even more so, the efforts to play despite them—finally caught up with Reiser

in 1948, when he played in only 64 games. After four more seasons of bouncing from the Braves to the Pirates to the Indians, the sometime switch-hitter retired at the end of 1952 carrying a .295 lifetime batting average and providing endless speculation about what he would have achieved had he been able to avoid outfield walls.

JOE RELFORD

A twelve-year-old black batboy for the Fitzgerald club of the Class D Georgia State League, Relford was the youngest person ever to appear in a professional baseball game. On July 19, 1952, with Fitzgerald losing, 13–0, to Statesboro, manager Charlie Ridgeway responded to taunts from the crowd insisting that he ''put in the batboy'' by sending Relford up in the 8th inning to bat for outfielder Ray Nichting, a .330 hitter at the time. The pinch hitter grounded out, then went out to play center field, where he made a running catch. Relford, Ridgeway, and umpire Ed Kubrick were all fired for the stunt.

MERV RETTENMUND

As a pinch hitter for the 1977 Padres, Rettenmund reached base 37 times in 86 plate appearances to set a big league record. He had 21 hits and 16 walks.

ED REULBACH

Reulbach spent the meat of his thirteen-year (1905–17) career pitching for the Cubs in the shadow of Three Finger Brown, so he never quite achieved the distinction due him for two 20-win seasons, three consecutive years of leading the National League in winning percentage, and an overall 182 wins with a 2.28 ERA. On the other hand, the right-hander was only too well known to the Dodgers: In 1908 he defeated Brooklyn no less than a record nine times. Two of the victories were registered on September 26, when Reulbach became the only pitcher ever to hurl shutouts in both ends of a doubleheader.

JERRY REUSS

Reuss got into five League Championship Series with the Pirates and Dodgers in the 1970s and 1980s, but might have wished he hadn't. His 0–7 record is the worst in playoff history.

ALLIE REYNOLDS

Reynolds's overall contribution to the Yankees' pennants of the late 1940s and early 1950s have been obscured by the fact that he is one of only three pitchers to toss two no-hitters in the same season. A decent but hardly overpowering right-hander with the Indians between 1942 and 1946, he came to New York only after Joe DiMaggio persuaded owner Larry MacPhail, who considered Reynolds ''gutless'' and incapable of winning the big game, to make a deal for second baseman Joe Gordon. Proving MacPhail wrong, Reynolds led the American League in winning percentage in 1947, but was kept from a 20th win—and a big salary increase—by being pulled out of the rotation after notching his 19th with two weeks remaining in the season.

Reynolds's most impressive season was 1951, when he won 17 games (including the two no-hitters), paced AL hurlers in shutouts, and appeared in relief 14 times, earning 7 saves. Neither no-hitter came easily. In the first, on July 12 against the Indians, he fell flat on his butt delivering a pitch to Bobby Avila before striking out the Cleveland second baseman for the final out; in the second, on September 28 against the Red Sox, he watched as catcher Yogi Berra dropped a foul pop off the bat of Ted Williams, then retired the Boston slugger for the final out on an almost identical play. The latter gem also clinched the pennant for the Yankees. Despite all this, general manager George Weiss tried to cut his salary because he had completed only 16 of his 26 starts.

In later years, Reynolds claimed that going back and forth between starting and the bullpen shortened his career, but in fact he responded with his only 20-win season in 1952 and league-leading totals in strikeouts and shutouts. He quit two years later with a 182–107 career record.

FLINT RHEM

Although Rhem was hardly the only potential diamond star done in by alcoholism, he had some of the most creative excuses for neglecting to show up for his scheduled starts. With the Cardinals in the 1920s, for example, he explained that he had not gotten to the Polo Grounds in time to face the Giants because he had been kidnapped, brought blindfolded to New Jersey, and then forced at gunpoint to drink a bottle of whiskey.

BILLY RHINES

A right-hander with a more-than-modest 114–103 record in the 1890s, Rhines was the first submarine pitcher. In his rookie season of 1890, with the Reds, he won 13 of his first 14 starts and 28 games overall while posting the lowest ERA in the National League. Managing one more 20-win season and another ERA title for the Red, Rhines never developed into a consistent winner because of injuries.

DUSTY RHODES

Rhodes was a hard-drinking outfielder for the 1950s Giants who became almost as known for his all-night binges with manager Leo Durocher and owner Horace Stoneham as for the respectability he brought to pinch hitting. In fact, most of his on-field reputation stemmed from the single, pennant-winning year of 1954, when he came off the bench during the season to hit .333 and then devastated the Indians in the World Series with a pinch-homer and a couple of pinch-singles, ending up with 7 RBIs for the 4-game sweep. Otherwise, the lefty swinging Rhodes had a career average of only .186 (40 for 215) as a substitute batter.

KARL RHODES

Rhodes is the only player to hit home runs in his first 3 at-bats in a season. He did it as a member of the Cubs on Opening Day in 1994; all three blasts were off Dwight Gooden of the Mets. The lefty-swinging outfielder walked and singled in his other two plate appearances on the day.

KEVIN RHOMBERG

Rhomberg showed some promise as a hitter with the Indians in the early 1990s, but he ended up psyching himself out of a major league career. Arguably the most superstitious player in baseball history, he had a particular aversion to being touched last, and whenever anyone even grazed him, he would insist on touching that person back. When the American League got wind of this tic, opposition players went out of their way to bump him, pat him on the shoulder, or just bounce a ball at him, and then run off, with Rhomberg in pursuit. On one occasion, a teammate tapped him with a ball, then fired the ball over an outfield fence; the outfielder immediately climbed the fence to get the ball so he could touch it back. After a while, even fans got into the act with letters that usually said little more than ''Ha, ha, you touched this letter last.'' Rhomberg's reaction was to answer each and every letter from his ill-wishers. Aside from his touching mania, the Cleveland prospect refused to make right turns, so that even when he was thrown out on a grounder, he would make a counterclockwise turn rather than simply veer off toward the first-base dugout.

JIM RICE

The left-field successor to Hall of Famers Ted Williams and Carl Yastrzemski in Fenway Park, Rice posted Cooperstown-caliber numbers of his own for a dozen of his 16 years (1974–89) with the Red Sox.

After a cup of coffee in 1974, Rice was edged out for Rookie of the Year honors by teammate Fred Lynn in 1975 despite a .309 average, 22 homers, and 102 RBIs. The right-handed slugger went on to top .300 six times, stroke 200 hits four times, knock at least 20 homers in eleven seasons, and drive in 100 runs eight times. His efforts included three league-leading totals in round-trippers and two each in slugging and RBIs. Rice's 406 total bases in 1978—when he took MVP honors for pacing the American League in slugging, hits, homers, triples, and RBIs—was the highest total in the big leagues since Stan Musial's 429 in 1948 and the highest in the AL since Joe DiMaggio's 418 in 1937; no major leaguer has had as many as 400 since. So potent was Rice's bat that year that several teams followed Kansas City's lead in using four out-fielders against him.

Bristling over being assigned regular desig-nated hitting chores in 1988, Rice fell to feuding with manager Joe Morgan the following year. Then, when Morgan sent light-hitting shortstop Spike Owen in to bat for him, Rice exploded and began shoving the manager, in full view of the rest of the team and some beat reporters. With

elbow surgery limiting Rice to only 56 games in 1989, the outfielder responded to his release on November 13 by blasting both Morgan and the Boston front office for the way he had been treated.

Noted for his strength, Rice once broke a bat despite failing to make contact on a checked swing. No speedster, he holds a major league re-cord for grounding into 36 double plays, in 1984. His final statistics include a .298 batting average and 382 home runs; the latter figure, as well as his totals in hits, total bases, and RBIs, ranks third among all Red Sox hitters behind only Williams and Yastrzemski.

SAM RICE (Hall of Fame, 1963)

Rice showed up on the Senators in 1915 as a pitcher, tossed a complete-game victory, then was told to get an outfielder's glove. The diminutive lefty hitter's mistake had been to put on a show in batting practice, where he had struck manager Clark Griffith as having more of a future as an everyday player. By the time he finished his 20-year career, Rice had an overall average of .322, never once averaging below .293, and reaching that nadir only in his final season, at age forty-four. Relishing the gaps of spacious Griffith Sta-dium, he strung together ten straight seasons of at least 30 doubles and 10 triples; he also attained the 200-hit level six times, leading the American League in safeties twice. Even when he made an out, it usually wasn't for lack of contact: In nearly 10,000 at-bats, he struck out only 275 times.

Rice proved comically solemn about the most controversial moment in his playing career. In game three of the 1925 World Series against Pittsburgh, he chased an 8th-inning line drive by Earl Smith into an overflow crowd, disappeared for long seconds, then reemerged, holding the ball. When umpire Cy Rigler ruled a fair catch, Pirates owner Barney Dreyfuss jumped down onto the field in protest, precipitating a long argument. After the game (won by the Senators, 4–3), Rice refused comment other than to declare: ''The um-pire said I caught it.'' That would have ended the story then and there except for the outfielder's occasionally tantalizing remarks over the years that he had left a letter about the catch that was to be opened only after his death. When the missive was finally opened in 1974, it turned out to be pure bathos. "At no time did I lose possession of the ball," it only said.

J. R. RICHARD

Richard was a glaringly tragic example of white baseball's attitude toward black players. The National League's most dominating mound force in the late 1970s, the Houston fireballer turned in consecutive seasons of 20, 18, 18, and 18 wins, in the process becoming the first NL right-hander to record 300 strikeouts (in 1978) and then doing it again the following year. In 1979, he also paced the league with his 2.71 ERA, and seemed on his way to bettering that in 1980 (10–4, 1.89) when he suddenly collapsed of a stroke. Only in the aftermath of the seizure, which ended Richard's career, did it emerge that he had confessed to feeling sluggish for some time but had been talked out of his concern by Astros officials. The incident bred a nationwide debate about whether baseball people in general, and not just the Houston management, would have been more responsive to the hurler's sluggishness if it had not fit so neatly into stereotypes about "lazy blacks."

PAUL RICHARDS

Richards is usually recalled as the designer of the oversized catcher's mitt intended to spare Baltimore receivers from breaking every record for passed balls while Hoyt Wilhelm was on the mound. Less well remembered are Richards' sometimes bizarre tactical moves as a manager, and his successes as a general manager with expansion and transferred franchises.

A backup receiver with the Dodgers, Giants, and Athletics for four years in the 1930s, Richards retired to manage in the minor leagues, but returned to catch for the Tigers during and just after World War II. Quitting as an active player for good with a .227 batting average, he again piloted minor league teams until becoming dugout boss of the White Sox in 1951. He won as many as 94 games (in 1954) in Chicago, but never finished higher than third behind Casey Stengel's Yankees and Al Lopez's Indians.

In 1955 Richards took on the challenge of a dual role as field leader and general manager of the Orioles, who were only one year removed from their earlier existence as the St. Louis Browns. Given a $250,000 fund for player procurement by owner Clarence Miles, Richards spent $700,000 within two years—a spree that led a Baltimore executive to observe: "Paul was the only man in baseball who had an unlimited budget and exceeded it." Most of the money went to sign young players, including five bonus babies, who had to be carried on the major league roster. Having clogged the roster with the inexperienced and the unproductive, Richards began bending the rules by placing players on the disabled list without cause and hiding new recruits by having them use aliases. The results were, in the first instance, a ruling by Commissioner Ford Frick that a doctor's note would be required to place a player on the DL, and in the second, hefty fines for the club and Richards personally.

The Frick ruling converted Richards to a trading policy, and with a vengeance. On November 18 and December 1, 1954, he completed the largest trade in baseball history in two stages. The key elements in the eighteen-player deal were pitchers Don Larsen and Bob Turley and shortstop Billy Hunter, who went to the Yankees for, among others, catcher Gus Triandos, outfielder Gene Woodling, and shortstop Willie Miranda. Richards' hectic quest for a radical turnaround in the team's fortunes almost produced an even bigger deal: In 1956 he offered Kansas City general manager Parke Carroll a twenty-five-for-twenty-five swap of complete rosters, a deal that fell through mainly because Carroll could not reach Athletics owner Arnold Johnson before the June 15 trading deadline passed.

The following November Richards was forced to choose between his two titles. Electing to remain in the dugout, he displayed his penchant for esoteric tactics. He had already made it a practice, while with the White Sox, to move his starting pitcher to third base only long enough to allow a relief pitcher to retire one batter; on September 11, 1958, he went himself one better, listing three pitchers in his starting lineup, only to be foiled by a first-inning rally that required him to pinch hit for one of them. In 1960 he told leadoff hitter Jerry Adair to bat out of order in the hope that he would run the count to 3–0 and Richards could run the pitcher up to the plate to complete the walk before anyone noticed; in the event, he outsmarted himself when Adair singled home two runs but had his at-bat voided when Tigers' manager Jimmy Dykes appealed to the umpires.

It was also in 1960 that Richards revealed the oversized mitt, fifty inches in circumference, for use in handling Wilhelm's knuckleball. The innovation followed performances in which two Baltimore catchers had each allowed 3 passed balls in an inning within a week. However, after the 1964 season, the ''pancake mitt'' was outlawed. His most notable achievement while with the Orioles was bringing the club—sparked by his Kiddie Korps rotation of Chuck Estrada, Milt Pappas, Jack Fisher, and Steve Barber—into second place.

Quitting Baltimore before the end of the 1961 season, Richards moved to Houston. In the expansion draft for the new Colt .45s, he concentrated on younger players, leaving the more familiar names to the Mets, and stocked the rest of the organization with high school and junior college prospects. The strategy paid off when Houston finished eighth in 1962, ahead of not only New York but also Chicago. His biggest find for the club was Rusty Staub. Midseason in 1964, Richards replaced manager Harry Craft with Lum Harris, with owner Roy Hofheinz warning that the new pilot had better produce when the team moved into the Astrodome in 1965. When the 1965 Astros won a game less than the 1964 Colt .45s, Hofheinz fired both Harris and Richards. Even twenty years later, Richards would remain bitter enough over the incident to reject a reporter's suggestion that Hofheinz was his own worst enemy be remarking that ''not while I'm alive he isn't.''

Richards' next stop was Atlanta, where he produced a divisional title in 1969, in good part by acquiring third baseman Clete Boyer from the Yankees and first baseman Orlando Cepeda from the Cardinals. On the other hand, the Cepeda deal turned sour when the first baseman became injury-prone after only two productive season, and Joe Torre, who went to St. Louis in the deal, won an MVP award.

After leaving the Braves in 1973, Richards reappeared to manage the White Sox in 1976. His condition for coming out of retirement was that he not have to take part in any of new owner Bill Veeck's promotional stunts, changing his mind only for a Bicentennial replication of the The Spirit of '76 on Opening Day. The price he exacted from Veeck for carrying the thirteen-star flag (while the owner, of course, played the one-legged fife player) was permission to end the scene with a recitation of the little-known fourth stanza of the ''The Star-Spangled Banner'' that confirms the survival of the flag left in doubt by the more familiar first stanza. The White Sox finished in sixth place, and Richards retired for good at the end of the season.

BOBBY RICHARDSON

A slick-fielding Yankee second baseman for twelve seasons (1955–66), Richardson saved his most potent offense for World Series play. The .266 lifetime hitter holds several Series batting records: most RBIs (12 in 1960 against the Pirates), after knocking in only 26 in the regular season; most runs driven in in a game (6) in game three in 1960; and most hits (13 in 1964 against the Cardinals, since tied by Lou Brock and Marty Barrett).

SPEC RICHARDSON

Richardson did such a bad job as head of Houston's baseball operations for a decade that the National League entrusted him with taking emergency administrative control of the Giants. While serving as a right-hand man to Judge Roy Hofheinz between the mid-1960s and the mid-1970s, Richardson saw to it that no Astro player made a public utterance contradicting the All-American pretensions of the franchise or attempted to hold out for a significant raise. In the meantime, he was making one disastrous trade after another—getting rid of the likes of Joe Morgan, Mike Cuellar, Rusty Staub, Jerry Grote, and Dave Giusti, while importing such sluggers as Lee May, Donn Clendenon, and Curt Blefary to the homer-unfriendly Astrodome. Richardson was finally bounced as general manager in 1975.

After working a few months in the commissioner's office, Richardson was sent by the NL to San Francisco to try to make some order out of the administrative mess left by Horace Stoneham, the disenchanted Giants owner for whom even signing monthly checks had become a burden. Richardson stayed on for several years even after Bob Lurie had purchased the franchise from Stoneham, but spent most of his time sitting on his hands while managers Joe Altobelli and Dave Bristol warned futilely of the problems being created in the clubhouse by baseball's most localized Born Again movement.

PETE RICHERT

There was nothing Richert could do subsequently to match his major league debut. Entering a game for the Dodgers with two out in the 2nd inning on April 12, 1962, he stuck out the first 6 batters he faced; the only blot on his record was a passed ball that required him to record 4 whiffs to retire the side in the 3rd inning. The southpaw spent thirteen seasons (1962–74) with five clubs, reaching his crest as a stopper for the Orioles in the 1969 and 1970, when he saved a combined 25 games.

LEE RICHMOND

Despite a lifetime losing record (75–100), Richmond managed to cram several firsts into his six-year career: He was the first left-handed curveballer, the first medical student to play major league baseball, the first pitcher to win 20 games with a last-place club (the Worcester Brown Stockings in 1881), the victim of the first grand slam (surrendered to Roger Connor of Troy on September 9, 1881), and the first to toss a perfect game. The last achievement—on June 12, 1880, against Cleveland—occurred after the pitcher had stayed up all night at a pregraduation party at Brown University, played in an early-morning baseball game between his alma mater and Yale, and skipped lunch to reach Worcester in time for his starting assignment. The southpaw's effort was saved by a right-field-to-first-base putout in the 5th inning and interrupted by a seven-minute, 8th-inning thunderstorm.

FRANCIS RICHTER

As the founder and editor of the Philadelphia-based weekly *Sporting Life* from 1883 until 1917, Richter was as much a participant in as a commentator on the turbulent comings and goings of nineteenth-century franchises and leagues. He helped form the American Association in 1882; supported the Players League in 1890; played an active role in attempts to resuscitate the AA in 1895 and 1900, and to create a major league National Association in the latter year; promoted the Players Protective Association in the late 1890s; and encouraged the forces behind the Federal League in 1914–15. His so-called Millennium Plan, broached in 1887, met with initial approval in all quarters. Calling for all major league players to be dropped into a common pool annually and then doled out "impartially" among clubs as a means of equalizing competition, the scheme would, according to Richter, end labor disputes and boardroom conflicts and lead to "a thousand years of peace and harmony." Five years later, both sides welcomed Richter's services as a go-between in the amalgamation of the NL and AA. In 1907, NL owners thought sufficiently highly of Richter to offer him the league presidency, which he declined. Five years after Richter left *Sporting Life* in 1917, his successor, Edgar Wolff, converted the once-powerful baseball newspaper into a monthly dealing exclusively with bowling and billiards.

TEX RICKARD

Rickard was the malaprop field announcer at Ebbets Field in the 1940s and 1950s. On one occasion he told the crowd that "a small boy has been found lost." Asked by the plate umpire another time to have fans remove their jackets from an outfield railing, Rickard declared: "Will the fans along the left-field railing please take off their clothing." Dodger players on the bench vied with one another to exploit Rickard's unfamiliarity with newly promoted prospects, leading him to identify pitchers on the loudspeaker as bandleaders Wayne King and Spike Jones.

BRANCH RICKEY (Hall of Fame, 1967)

Even without his two most significant contributions to baseball, the development of the farm system and the racial integration of clubhouses, Rickey would probably have ended up in Cooperstown. In a half-century-plus as a player, college instructor, manager, executive, owner, and league founder, there was hardly an aspect of the game that he did not influence, alter, or perfect.

When Branch Rickey put his hand into his pocket, it wasn't to take out money, but to make sure it stayed where it was. National Baseball Library, Cooperstown, N.Y.

By turns pedantic, sanctimonious, and ruthless, he battled everyone from Kenesaw Landis to Walter O'Malley, provided career opportunities for everyone from Larry MacPhail to Jackie Robinson, and devised everything from spring training sliding pits to the Vero Beach camp that mushroomed into Dodgertown. All the while, he never stopped padding his own pockets, raining biblical adages on the people around him, and padding his pockets some more. Once compared to Mohandas Gandhi for being "a combination of your father and Tammany Hall," the teetotaling lawyer was baseball's ultimate Mahatma—hold the passive resistance.

Rickey's least impressive role was as a player. A lefty-swinging catcher, he got into 117 games for the Browns and the Yankees between 1905 and 1907—long enough for his .239 average and

bad throwing arm to convince him to pursue a law degree. Before he left New York, however, he strapped on the tools for a June 28, 1907, game in which an American League-record 13 runners stole on him. He was a much more respected presence at the University of Michigan, where he undertook the baseball coaching job after dropping out of the major leagues at age twenty-six. Aside from winning various championships for the school, he was acclaimed as an instructor in the finest points of the game, to the point that several big league managers dropped by to audit his sessions when they were in Michigan for games against the Tigers. Of the numerous future big-leaguers who passed through his hands at the university, the most accomplished was first basemen George Sisler. It was, in fact, Rickey who, as a member of the Browns' front office in 1914, persuaded Sisler to challenge an ambiguous contractual arrangement he had with the Pirates and who then signed the future Hall of Famer for St. Louis.

Rickey was drawn back to the Browns by Robert Hedges, the millionaire franchise owner who offered him an open assignment as an administrative factotum for dealing with emergencies. The emergencies ended up covering everything from scouting to managing, with Rickey doing most of the team's signing and dealing by 1914 and its piloting by the end of the 1913 season. Although he could not get the club above fifth place, he continued to impress Hedges for his money smarts and his meticulous instructional programs. Rickey was equally impressed by Hedges, especially with the owner's ideas on developing a minor league system that would feed players to big clubs. It therefore came as a shock when Hedges, apprehensive about the outcome of the 1915 Federal League suit against the National and American leagues, decided to sell the Browns before he was charged with being part of a monopoly. Rickey barely got along with Hedges's successor Phil Ball, particularly after the new owner bounced him from the dugout, insisting that he concentrate on the franchise's administrative affairs. In 1917, with a new ownership in place with the Cardinals, Rickey asked out of his contract to accept an offer as president of the Browns' city rivals. Although Ball initially took the position that he would never stand in the way of somebody who no longer wanted to work for him, he was talked into a harder stand by AL president Ban Johnson, winning a court injunction to block the move. The maneuver died quickly, however, when Johnson and the Browns were portrayed in the press as the heavies of the situation. Needing all the good publicity he could engender in his rivalry with the Cardinals, Ball let Rickey go, creating in the process his chief nemesis for the next decade.

Rickey moved into the Cardinals franchise just long enough to establish himself as a ferocious contract negotiator with players, then went off to the military as a major in the same World War I chemical testing department that recruited Sisler and Ty Cobb and where an explosion shortened the life of Christy Mathewson. When Rickey returned to the Cardinals after the war, he found the franchise in such disarray that he persuaded his own parents to invest in it to help ensure its survival; during one spring training, he had the players wear only one uniform in order to keep another one ready for Opening Day, there being no money even for regular washings. The financial crisis began to abate only in 1920, when automobile salesman Sam Breadon moved in as the majority owner. Although Breadon also insisted on Rickey's title as organization president, the trade-off was the acquisition of a business partner who was ready to spend to improve the franchise.

Even before Breadon had come along, Rickey had invested some money in several minor league clubs. It wasn't until Breadon gave him more than $25,000 from the sale of League Park (the team had moved in as tenants of Ball at Sportsman's Park), however, that he had the wherewithal to indulge his project of the farm system that Hedges always claimed was a necessity for money-poor clubs. As he noted, even when a St. Louis scout was the first to discover raw talent, a minor league operator, college coach, or parent would waste little time in contacting representatives of such affluent clubs as the Giants or Cubs to disclose Rickey's interest in the prospect and dicker for a better offer than that being made by the Cardinals. It was thus in the name of thwarting this process that Rickey persuaded Breadon to purchase an 18 percent interest in the Houston

club of the Texas League, then even larger parts of an Arkansas team in the Western Association and the Syracuse franchise of the International League. What started as a trickle soon became a flood: Before farm system foe Landis began intervening, Rickey and Breadon had deals with more than thirty clubs around the country and even controlled two entire leagues (the Arkansas-Missouri League and the Nebraska State League).

As Rickey found out to his chagrin, however, even a substantial minority investment in a club was not always a guarantee that his minor league pipeline would function smoothly. Following the 1921 season, he "called up" from Syracuse the very first product of his farming policy, first baseman Jim Bottomley, only to be held up to a ransom by the owner of the New York state team. With the validity of his entire project at stake, he had to journey to Syracuse to negotiate the purchase of the rest of the International League organization to ensure the delivery of Bottomley. From that experience on, the St. Louis executive made sure that there were no more financial or legal loopholes in his arrangements with minor league operators.

Next to his playing, Rickey was weakest at managing—according to his contemporaries, because of a tendency to try to intellectualize relatively simple situations. Rickey himself, however, did not share such evaluations of his dugout skills, and was irritated when Breadon emulated Ball in removing him from the dugout and confining him to front-office duties; in fact, he was so annoyed with the 1925 managerial switch to Rogers Hornsby that he insisted on selling all his stock in the organization. Nevertheless, he maintained his positions as vice president and business manager, from that vantage point watching his farm system supply a steady flow of talent to Sportsman's Park, a great deal of it of Hall of Fame caliber. Between 1926 and 1942, Rickey's farm chain development scheme delivered four world championships, six pennants, and five second-place finishes. Aside from furnishing the St. Louis varsity, the minor league clubs provided trading material for desirable players on other major league teams and allowed Rickey to indulge his pet philosophy of unloading a player at or just after his peak to get maximum value for him. The exchanges became only more frequent after Breadon agreed in the mid-1930s to give Rickey 10 percent of every cash transaction he worked out. This led to periods when the Cardinals obtained practically no bodies, but just checks for their players.

Although never the best of friends, Rickey and Breadon worked off one another successfully for most of the 1920s and 1930s. Frictions were never far away, however. For his part, Rickey never completely hid his snobbishness around the relatively uneducated Breadon, and was never sure that the owner was as God-fearing as he should have been. On the other hand, Breadon was never completely comfortable with Rickey's religiosity (he had always observed the Sabbath even as manager, turning the club over to others for the day), especially when it seemed to leave room for some shady dealings with minor league operators that he preferred not to know too much about. The first big conflict between the pair came in 1938, when Landis announced that he was summarily releasing seventy-four organization farmhands because of contractual irregularities. Rickey wanted to fight back by breaking a pact with Landis prohibiting teams from ever contesting his decisions in court, but Breadon, more embarrassed by than innocent of any collusion in what became known as the Cedar Rapids Case, refused to go along; despite the lack of formal charges from Landis, the owner even declined to petition the commissioner's office to keep the minor leaguers.

Over the next few years, the rip in the Rickey-Breadon relationship caused by the Cedar Rapids Case grew to a gaping hole. The breaking point finally came during the 1942 season, when Breadon announced that Hyde Park Beer had been signed as a sponsor for the club's games on radio. When Rickey objected that a brewery wasn't an appropriate sponsor for games heard by tens of thousands of children, Breadon gave vent to his doubts about the convenient latitude of Rickey's religious principles. Soon after St. Louis's 1942 World Series victory over the Yankees, the Mahatma rendered his resignation.

Only a few weeks later, Rickey landed on his feet, as president of the Dodgers. He took over from Larry MacPhail—a onetime law school classmate, the most prominent of a dozen protégés that Rickey spent his career recommending for positions he didn't want, and already an on-again, off-again nemesis who was destined to become even more of a snapping hound from hell within a few years. Mainly because of MacPhail's easy way with bar bills, Rickey received a cold shoulder from New York sportswriters. His most immediate problem during World War II, however, was talking himself into retaining the services of Leo Durocher despite one excuse after another that the fractious Brooklyn manager gave him for being fired. In what was eventually explained by his belief that Durocher was the ideal pilot for running the first racially mixed club in the majors, Rickey abided a team revolt over some gratuitous Durocher fines and follow-up lies to the press; felonious assault charges against the dugout boss and an Ebbets Field security man stemming from the beating up of a grandstand heckler; and regular reports about how the players were losing money in card games to the skipper and his chief coach, Charlie Dressen.

By the time World War II ended, Rickey had two further incentives for proceeding with what became known as The Great Experiment. The first was the death of Landis, who, in addition to hating farm systems, had also systematically stymied any thoughts about allowing blacks in the big leagues. The second was his own financial investment in the Dodgers. In 1944 he joined with corporation lawyer Walter O'Malley and John Smith of the Pfizer chemical company in the first of several stock purchases that would give the trio 75 percent of the franchise within a couple of years. As Rickey laid it out to O'Malley and Smith, the fastest way of enriching their investment with the benefits of a consistently winning team was to outflank the Cardinals by signing blacks as well as whites.

The Rickey plan began taking shape May 7, 1945, when he announced the formation of the Brown Dodgers as Brooklyn's entry in the Black United States Baseball League. The announcement elicited little reaction, despite his cryptic references during a press conference to black players who might someday play in the big leagues. Five months later, he dropped the first veil by disclosing that Jack Roosevelt Robinson, a shortstop for a Negro league team in Kansas City, had signed to play with Brooklyn's farm club in Montreal, thereby knocking down the first of organized baseball's racial barriers. Most of what followed seemed to have been scripted too neatly even for Rickey. Robinson was the sensation of the International League. Rickey set up 1947 spring training quarters in Havana—a city far more physically suggestive of racial equality than any in the United States at the time. Several Dodgers saw what was coming and tried to organize a protest against playing with a black, but were quickly sat on by Durocher. Landis's immediate successor, Happy Chandler, endorsed the move, so NL president Ford Frick also got into line and warned other league teams not to go through with any threats to boycott games against Brooklyn. Only a short time after Enos Slaughter had made one of the greatest runs in World Series annals to give the Cardinals a world championship, the Dodgers were the most talked-about franchise in baseball. Robinson, who shared with Rickey a college degree and an aversion to alcohol, turned the other cheek as promised against shouts, spittings, and spikings. The right-hand-hitting first baseman was named NL Rookie of the Year and sparked the Dodgers to a pennant. As Rickey was fond of saying in other contexts, in a popular paraphrase of a thought expressed by Louis Pasteur, his "luck was the residue of design."

The one unexpected development for the Brooklyn official in 1947 was that the manager for the regular season was longtime assistant Burt Shotton rather than Durocher, who had been suspended by Chandler before Opening Day for a series of incidents that added up to loose living, that brought moralistic censures from pulpits and editorial pages, and that were reduced in the commissioner's office to "actions detrimental to baseball." Rickey himself added to the headline-making by accusing MacPhail, who had resurfaced as an owner of the Yankees, of being seen with the same kind of gambler that Chandler had accused Durocher of frequenting. But what rankled the Dodger executive most of all were strong indications that Durocher had been negotiating with MacPhail behind his back to jump to the Yankees. With the Robinson experiment launched

successfully and the club under fire from religious groups for employing a morally dubious manager, Rickey had little compunction about pushing Durocher toward the Giants in 1948 and installing Shotton as his full-time pilot.

Rickey spent the rest of the 1940s putting into place the final pieces of the club that became known as the Boys of Summer. By 1950, however, his relations with O'Malley had soured to the point that he doubted he would receive an extension of his contract as baseball operations chief. Deciding to beat O'Malley and the Smith estate to the punch, he first offered to sell his interest in the team to his partners, then set up real-estate developer William Zeckendorf as a rival straw man for demanding a higher price. Zeckendorf ended up with more than $1 million for doing nothing more than nodding that he was thinking of buying into the club, while Rickey made three times as much as O'Malley had initially offered him for his stock.

Just as he had wasted little time in moving from the Cardinals to the Dodgers, so Rickey waited only a few weeks before going from Brooklyn to Pittsburgh. In the short term, his six-year stay with the Pirates was a disaster, with the club taking up permanent residence in eighth place with a level of talent that was barely of high-minor league caliber, let alone up to a major league standard. In addition, he made a personal crusade of downplaying the abilities of the franchise's only legitimate all-star, outfielder Ralph Kiner. On one level, Kiner irritated Rickey for his visibility in Players Association causes, his regular presence in gossip columns as an escort of Hollywood actresses, and his annual contract demands and denunciations of the executive as a miser and a hypocrite; on another level, the slugger galled him for winning over Pittsburgh fans with the generally one-dimensional skills (power) that Rickey had always preached against in dispensing opinions about the ideal player. Behind the crack that the Pirates could finish in last place without Kiner as easily as with him, he dealt off the outfielder to the Cubs in June 1953 for six undistinguished players and $150,000.

What did not emerge clearly until Rickey had severed his ties with Pittsburgh after the 1955 season was that his signing and drafting philosophy of recruiting hundreds of cheaply paid prospects with the hope that at least a few of them would work out, had in fact enriched the franchise with such future stars as Bill Mazeroski, Dick Groat, Vern Law, Bob Skinner, and Frank Thomas. It was also Rickey who plucked future Hall of Famer Roberto Clemente out of the Dodger farm system.

After remaining on the Pittsburgh payroll as a consultant for a few years, the then-seventy-eight-year-old Rickey was talked into heading the would-be Continental League by New York Attorney William Shea. Ostensibly aimed at becoming the first new major circuit since the Federal League in 1915, the main impact of the Continental League was to force the NL into expanding in 1962 with the addition of the Mets and Astros. Despite his age, Rickey made it clear that he was interested in heading the baseball operations for the New York team; that goal was thwarted when both O'Malley and franchise chairman M. Donald Grant warned Mets owner Joan Payson against Rickey's protean sense of power.

Rickey's wiles were not especially on display when he took a job as a consultant for Cardinals owner Gussie Busch after the 1962 season. What he realized too late was that Busch had thrown him in with front-office executives Dick Meyer and Bing Devine as he might have thrown a fox in a henhouse, but with the fox defanged and declawed. The fabled Mahatma fell into one political trap after another—at one point embarrassing Stan Musial by suggesting that he retire, at another recommending that the 1964 team (then on the verge of starting a surprising rise to the pennant) be overhauled by dispensing with veterans. One of his last public acts in the baseball world was attending the team's 1964 victory dinner, where he was snubbed by both players and executives. A couple of days later, he was informed by Busch that his services were no longer required. On the other hand, still another of his protégés, Bill Howsam, took over the franchise's baseball affairs.

CY RIGLER

A National League umpire for twenty-nine years beginning in 1906, Rigler was the first arbiter to use hand signals to indicate balls and strikes.

BILL RIGNEY

Rigney owed most of his big moments to the Giants. After winding up an eight-year career as a backup infielder, he succeeded his mentor Leo Durocher as manager for the team's final two seasons in New York in 1956 and 1957, then went to San Francisco with the franchise. When the expansion Angels joined the American League in 1961, he was chosen over Durocher as their first pilot on the grounds that he would have more patience in dealing with the team's collection of untested rookies and retreads. He ingratiated himself to owner Gene Autry by showing up at the expansion draft with detailed scouting reports given to him by his former San Francisco boss Chub Feeney; together with similar intelligence collected by general manager Fred Haney from the Dodgers, the reports enabled the Angels to draft far more astutely than the new Washington Senators franchise.

Rigney stayed at the helm of California through the 1960s, waging regular battles over the organization's reluctance to part with headline-making hurler Bo Belinsky and over a development policy that seemed predicated on Autry's moods. After telling reporters on numerous occasions that he was sticking it out only because of his friendship with Autry, Rigney was bounced without too much ceremony in 1969. He then moved over to Minnesota, where he was initially treated as a leper because of succeeding the popular Billy Martin, but then led the Twins to a second consecutive West Division title in 1970 with a record a game better than his predecessor's club. In 1972 he fell victim to some Calvin Griffith logic, when the Minnesota owner announced that he was out in favor of Frank Quilici because the Twins had "always played better under Italian managers"— a reference to Cookie Lavagetto, Sam Mele, and Martin. Rigney then returned to the Giants for a final humdrum season, in 1974.

JIMMY RING

Ring's honesty brought Hal Chase to his first major accounting for suspicious play. In 1918, while both were with the Reds, the right-hander was brought into a tie game only to have the first baseman amble over and suggest that, since he had a big bet on the game, there might be something in it for Ring if Cincinnati were to lose. Ignoring the suggestion but losing the game anyway, then finding an envelope stuffed with money in his locker the next day, the hurler reported the incident to manager Christy Mathewson. It was only because the pilot was in the army in France and couldn't appear at the postseason hearing on the episode before National League president John Heydler that Chase got out from under the charges, even though Ring testified against him.

Ring, who compiled a 118–149 record in twelve National League seasons (1917–28), was the throw-in Giants manager John McGraw sent to the Cardinals for Rogers Hornsby after the 1926 season lest Frankie Frisch, the primary bait, think he was Hornsby's equal.

CAL RIPKEN, JR.

By the mid-1990s, Ripken's quest to break Lou Gehrig's record of playing in 2,130 consecutive games had begun to overshadow the Baltimore shortstop's offensive and defensive gifts. Against the backdrop of a debate about whether he might have been a better player if he had taken a day off here and there, the right-hand-hitting slugger turned in his eleventh season of at least 20 home runs and seventh of at least 90 RBIs in 1993. Entering the 1995 season, he had also consolidated his record for the most home runs (310) by a major league shortstop. Defensively, Ripken's mere 3 errors and .996 fielding average in 1990 sit alone in a big league showcase.

Ripken began his games streak on June 5, 1982; by the start of the 1995 season, it had grown to 2,009 contests. Even more impressive were the 8,243 consecutive innings he played between June 5, 1982, and September 14, 1987; that skein came to an end when his father, Cal Ripken, Sr., then managing the Orioles, deliberately took him out of the September 1987 game. By 1990, many critics were pointing to Ripken's declining batting average as evidence that he was being worn down by his longevity streak. In 1991, however, he rebounded with a .323 average, 34 home runs, and 114 RBIs—good enough for his second American League MVP trophy. He was awarded

the first one in 1983 for helping the Orioles to a world championship with regular-season contributions of a .318 average, 27 homers, 102 RBIs, and league-leading numbers in hits (211), doubles (47), and runs scored (121).

In 1987, Ripken and his brother Billy, a second baseman, were the first siblings to be managed together in the major leagues by their father.

SWEDE RISBERG

Risberg's offensive and defensive performance in the 1919 World Series against Cincinnati did nothing to prevent him from being banned as one of the eight Black Sox. The shortstop managed only a single and a triple in 25 at-bats for an .080 average while leading both teams in making 4 errors. In 1927, Risberg came to the fore of another baseball scandal when he charged before Commissioner Kenesaw Landis that the White Sox had won the 1917 pennant in significant part because Ty Cobb's Tigers had thrown two consecutive doubleheaders to his team. He was backed in his allegations by Chick Gandil, another of the Chicago Eight. But a Landis investigation prompted a parade of about forty other witnesses from the two teams that were unanimous in refuting the accusation. The defense offered was that, in common with the practice of the period, Chicago players had taken up an end-of-the-season collection for Detroit pitchers who had defeated the runner-up Red Sox in a key September series. Landis accepted that version of events and issued a series of new regulations putting an end to the practice and threatening expulsion for players wagering on games.

MICKEY RIVERS

For most of his fifteen seasons (1970–84) in the American League, Rivers was a good center fielder and leadoff batter, and for two of those years (1976 and 1977 with the Yankees), he was a great one; however, his ''ain't no sense worryin' '' approach to life and baseball drove more than one general manager to conclude that he was too much trouble. The lefty swinger sparked the Yankees to three consecutive American League pennants (1976–78) with his slashing line drives and dashing baserunning after strolling to the plate with the gait of an aged grandmother. Although he averaged .312 and .326 in the first two pennant-winning years (and .295 overall), the outfielder's chronic losses at the track and incessant marital problems led him to demand more and more frequent salary advances with less and less understanding of why his subsequent paychecks were reduced. Rivers's difficulties with his estranged wife reached a low point when the pair engaged in a demolition derby in the players' parking lot at Yankee Stadium; his mathematical abilities reached their nadir with his observation on Yankee owner George Steinbrenner, manager Billy Martin, and himself: "Me and George and Billy are two of a kind." On the other hand, Rivers once deflated one of Reggie Jackson's regular symphonies to himself by telling the slugger that he didn't even know how to spell IQ.

EPPA RIXEY (Hall of Fame, 1963)

Rixey's lifetime mark of 266–251, between 1912 and 1933, has made him a prime target of critics of Cooperstown's standards. In fact, he was a classic hard-luck hurler for two generally bad teams who still had the most victories by a National League southpaw until Warren Spahn came along. Even when Rixey led the league in losses for the Phillies in 1917, he did so with an ERA of 2.27. The year before, when Philadelphia had finished second, he won 22 while posting an ERA of 1.85. Dealt to Cincinnati in 1921, in one of owner William Baker's habitual transactions for quick cash, Rixey posted three more 20-win seasons, including a league-leading 25 in 1922. In two other years, he won 19 games.

PHIL RIZZUTO (Hall of Fame, 1993)

Rizzuto's long wait to gain entry to the Hall of Fame, the heavy-handed campaign waged on his behalf by Yankee owner George Steinbrenner and others, and the actual circumstances of his election were almost enough to bury the merits of his case.

Playing for New York from 1941 to 1956 (with three years off for military service during World War II), the right-hand-hitting shortstop averaged .273. His career year in 1950 earned him American League Most Valuable Player honors on the basis of personal highs in batting (.324), slugging (.439), hits (200), doubles (36), runs scored (125),

and walks (92). Practically reinventing the art of bunting, the Scooter, as he came to be known, had his most vivid diamond moment when he squeezed Joe DiMaggio home on a high, inside pitch in the 9th inning to win a September 17 contest against the Indians and put New York in first place to stay. Defensively, he was the premier AL shortstop of his era, making up for a relatively weak arm by playing shallow to take advantage of extraordinary lateral movement. He led the AL in fielding, double plays, and putouts twice each and in assists once.

Callously released by general manager George Weiss on Old Timers' Day in 1956, Rizzuto declined any public criticism of the move, winning points that he cashed in the following year by being assigned to the club's broadcasting team. Since then, he has won more fame for his television persona than for his accomplishments on the diamond. His broadcasts include an avalanche of birthday and anniversary greetings to friends and acquaintances; regular exclamations of "Holy cow!" before even mildly unusual diamond action; distracted rejoinders of "Huckleberry" when corrected by broadcast partners for one of his inevitable lapses of memory or diction; recountings of his various phobias (snakes, flying, spiders); on-air tastings of the canoli and other delicacies sent by fans; and references to his idiosyncratic method of scoring a game, including the invention of the WW code—for "Wasn't Watching."

Rizzuto's most popular characteristic is his stream-of-consciousness stories that often as not overwhelm the action on the field or trail off, uncompleted, into a between-innings commercial; many of these have been collected in book form as free verse. On one occasion, Rizzuto ignored the fact that the Yankees were in the process of blowing a 5-run lead in favor of recounting how Walter Cronkite had once corrected his grammar, including his pronunciation of the name of the city of Moscow; when partner Tom Seaver pointed out that pronunciation had nothing to do with grammar, Rizzuto responded with, "I know, but I forgot the story I was going to tell." On another, he presented partner Frank Messer with a bizarre series of free associations that bounced from séances to the ballet to tables flying in barroom brawls to mysticism to Mystic, Connecticut, to Boston's Mystic River.

Steinbrenner's public disparaging of the Veterans Committee every time it failed to put Rizzuto's name on a Cooperstown plaque was more embarrassing than helpful; in fact, he was not elected until teammate Yogi Berra, old friend Pee Wee Reese, and former broadcasting colleague Bill White joined the committee.

ROBIN ROBERTS (Hall of Fame, 1976)

Roberts was the Phillies pitching staff for most of the 1950s, and demonstrated it not only in six straight 20-win seasons, but also in a like number of years of hurling at least 300 innings. A hard thrower, he paid little attention to the record-breaking 502 homers he yielded over his nineteen-year (1948–66) career, especially since the majority of them were bases-empty shots without the game being on the line. The right-hander's best effort came in 1952, when he led the National League with a 28–7 mark; he lost the MVP award that year simply because a Philadelphia writer who didn't like him left his name off the ballot altogether. It was the first of four consecutive seasons that he paced NL hurlers in victories. When his fastball started picking up pauses, Roberts was dealt to the Orioles, where pitching coach Harry Brecheen added a change-up to his repertoire; the result in 1962 was the second-best ERA (2.78) in the American League. Roberts' single biggest game was the finale of the 1950 season, when he went 10 innings to defeat the Dodgers, 4–1, on Dick Sisler's home run and earn entry to his only World Series. Always active in union causes, it was Roberts who introduced Marvin Miller to player representatives in 1966.

THOMAS TUTTLE ROBERTS

Roberts was the arbitrator who decided the first collusion case against free agents. In September 1987 he ruled that 139 players had been denied their right to an unfettered market after the 1985 season, and granted second-look free agency to seven of them (including Kirk Gibson and Carlton Fisk). The total damages collected by the injured parties eventually totaled more than $10 million.

BOB ROBERTSON

Robertson is the only National League player to have hit 3 home runs in a League Championship Series game. The Pittsburgh first baseman did it in game two of the 1971 Series against the Giants.

CHARLIE ROBERTSON

Robertson was the author of baseball's most unlikely perfect game. The right-hander twirled his masterpiece for the White Sox in his third major league start, against the Tigers, on April 30, 1922. The performance was particularly startling in that Robertson never had a winning season in eight big league campaigns, ending up with a career record of 49–80 and a 4.44 ERA. Detroit stars Ty Cobb and Harry Heilmann protested throughout the game that the Chicago hurler was using illegal substances on the ball, but failed to persuade the umpires.

SHERRY ROBERTSON

Because he was Clark Griffith's nephew and Calvin Griffith's brother, Robertson wore a Washington uniform for ten seasons between 1940 and 1952. Ballyhooed during his minor league days as a hitting machine with speed, he ended up with a .230 average and a mere 32 stolen bases for all his big league service. When the family finally persuaded him that his playing days were over, Robertson took over as the Senators' farm director. Aside from his brother Calvin (whose surname was also Robertson originally), his front-office colleagues included his brother-in-law Joe Haynes as vice president, his brother Jimmy as head of concessions, and his brother Billy as head of operations for Griffith Stadium. His sister Thelma, Haynes's wife, shared control of the club with Calvin.

BROOKS ROBINSON (Hall of Fame, 1983)

Robinson's defensive brilliance at third base was such that he ended his twenty-three-year (1955–77) career with Baltimore as the first major leaguer to hold every lifetime fielding mark for a position—encompassing assists (6,205), putouts (2,697), double plays (618), and fielding average (.971). Thrown into the mix were Gold Gloves every year from 1960 to 1975 and league-leading

Brooks Robinson revolutionized defensive play at third base.
National Baseball Library, Cooperstown, N.Y.

numbers in fielding average eleven times and in both assists and putouts eight times. Although Robinson's defensive abilities were no secret in the American League through the 1960s, they did not become a national assumption until the 1970 World Series against Cincinnati, when his snatches of balls hit by Tony Perez, Tommy Helms, and Johnny Bench in game three moved Bench to crack that he was going to become a left-handed hitter so he could hit to the right side of the infield.

Robinson's fielding usually overshadowed his offensive abilities. In 1964 he added a .317 mark with 28 home runs and a league-leading 118 RBIs to his defense to win the AL MVP award. On five other occasions the right-handed hitter also topped the 20 level in four-baggers and three other times had a minimum of 90 RBIs. On the other hand, his slowness afoot produced a mere 28 stolen bases and helped him to the league record hitting into the most double plays (297).

Robinson became so critical to the Orioles (his length of service is the record for a player with one club) that teammates insisted that he become player representative in 1968 for their own protection. The union-busting organization had traded away or released every previous representative since 1960.

FRANK ROBINSON (Hall of Fame, 1982)

Robinson developed such a reputation as a no-holds-barred hustler on the diamond that his prodigious slugging sometimes seemed like an afterthought. But typically he trumped even the attention focused on him as the first black manager in the majors by tagging a home run in his first at-bat as a playing pilot.

The right-hand-hitting Robinson holds most of the significant records for duplicating feats in the National and American leagues, not least winning MVP recognition in both circuits. He began his assault on the record book with Cincinnati in 1956, clouting 38 home runs to tie Wally Berger's NL rookie mark. In his first seven years with the Reds, Robinson dipped as low as 29 home runs only once, along the way picking up MVP honors for leading the club to a 1961 pennant with a .323 average, 37 homers, 124 RBIs, 117 runs scored, and a league-leading .611 slugging average. The following year he was even better, averaging .342, knocking 39 balls into the seats, driving in 136 runs, collecting 208 hits, and pacing the NL in doubles (51), runs scored (134), and slugging average (.624). Before he was finished with his twenty-one-year career, he would compile 586 homers, 1,812 RBIs, and 1,829 runs scored to go with his .294 average and .537 slugging percentage.

Despite hitting another 33 home runs and registering triple figures in both RBIs and runs in 1965, Robinson impressed Cincinnati president Bill DeWitt as "an old thirty," so the Reds executive traded him after the season to Baltimore in exchange for pitchers Milt Pappas and Jack Baldschun and outfielder Dick Simpson. Robinson responded by winning the Triple Crown for the Orioles with a .316 average, 49 home runs, and 122 RBIs; he also piled up AL-leading numbers in slugging (.637) and runs (122). In spearheading a Baltimore world championship, he also put on display as never before his image as the ultimate team player, as likely to produce a victory by taking out an infielder to thwart a double play as by reaching the seats. It was also in 1966 that more than one AL manager admitted fining pitchers for throwing at Robinson and making him even more aggressive. He added some sprinkles to the cake by also taking MVP honors for Baltimore's 4-game sweep over the Dodgers in the World Series.

Although he never again reached his 1966 numbers, Robinson was at the heart of three more Baltimore pennant winners, in 1969, 1970, and

Frank Robinson's bat was only the most obvious of the weapons he used to devastate opponents. Photo Compliments of the Baltimore Orioles.

1971. He then became the centerpiece of other headline-making trades involving the Dodgers, Angels, and Indians, with his best twilight performance coming with California in 1973, when he reached the 30 mark in home runs for the last time. Along the way, he shattered all records for players jumping back and forth between both leagues: Among other things, he was the first to hit 200 home runs in both circuits and the first to hit All-Star Game home runs for both sides.

Throughout his playing career, Robinson never hid his ambition to manage; as he subsequently admitted, however, until his trade to the Orioles, he had never been particularly eager to gain pioneering status as the game's first black dugout boss. On the contrary, the star described at the time by *The Sporting News* as a ''Grade A Negro'' even refused to join a Baltimore chapter of the NAACP unless he received assurances that he would not be called on to make public appearances while active as a player. He began changing his attitude after encountering the unwritten rules of Baltimore's segregated housing and finding little support from the team. Within a couple of years he became one of the game's most outspoken critics of such racist niceties as the league's systematic failure to penalize white pitchers who threw at black hitters. By the time he was on the Angels in 1973, he was widely touted as the most likely candidate to break the managerial color ban—a forecast that did nothing for the nerves of incumbent California pilot Bobby Winkles. Winkles became so hostile to Robinson's presence that he first demanded that general manager Harry Dalton trade him, then upped the ante by calling a meeting to tell Angels players that he had made the request. The tactic backfired when Dalton fired Winkles instead.

Still, Robinson never had a chance of breaking the color barrier with a team located in conservative Orange County. Rather, the opportunity came with the Indians in 1975. To add drama to the occasion, Robinson, in the lineup as the team's designated hitter, walloped a home run in his first at-bat in the first inning of Opening Day. He remained at the helm of Cleveland for two and a half years—a stint that was distinguished largely by his run-ins with Gaylord Perry, John Ellis, and other players because of both his sharp tongue and his penchant, common among Hall of Fame sluggers, for expecting others to perform as he had. For the next few years, he coached for the Angels and Orioles, prompting regular reports that he was going to take over both clubs. Instead, he again pulled off a twin-league feat by being named the NL's first black manager when he was signed to pilot the Giants in 1981. He remained in San Francisco four and a half years, showing considerably more restraint toward his players than he had displayed in Cleveland but also knocking heads regularly with general manager Tom Haller about the latter's timidity about pulling the trigger on deals.

In the wake of the furor caused by Al Campanis's racist observations on the abilities of blacks to hold down executive positions, Robinson was hired by Baltimore as a special presidential assistant after the 1987 season. Against his declared wishes, he returned to the dugout at the beginning of the 1988 season while the club was wading its way through 21 consecutive losses from the starting gate. The onetime firebrand startled everyone with his philosophical patience as the wretched club wound its way toward a franchise-record 107 defeats, then provoked a surprise of another kind when he turned the team around to finish within 2 games of East Division titlist Toronto in 1989. Robinson returned to his front-office position in 1991.

JACKIE ROBINSON (Hall of Fame, 1962)

Next to Babe Ruth, no single player in the twentieth century had as much impact on baseball as Robinson. Most obviously, he was Brooklyn president Branch Rickey's choice in 1945 for breaking the color barrier. But, almost as striking, Robinson also introduced a daring style of play to the major leagues that made him as much of a direct antecedent to stars such as Pete Rose as to subsequent blacks such as Willie Mays.

Rickey's selection of Robinson as the vehicle for openly challenging baseball's color ban was controversial for more than racial reasons. For one things, his professional career consisted of only one season with the Kansas City Monarchs of the Negro National League, where he had performed ably but not spectacularly. Second, he was already twenty-six years old. Third, although one of UCLA's greatest athletes, he had distinguished himself in football, basketball, and track more than in baseball. Fourth, he was a player in search of a position, all scouting reports at the time agreeing that he lacked the arm for being the shortstop he was for Kansas City. By Rickey's own testimony, Robinson emerged as the chief candidate through a combination of raw athleticism, fierce competitiveness, superior intelligence, and mental toughness. It couldn't have hurt, either, that he was as much of a teetotaler as Rickey, that he was used to playing on integrated teams from his days at UCLA, and even that he shared the birth date of Branch Rickey, Jr., the Brooklyn president's much-doted-upon son. Robinson was formally signed to a Dodger contract on October 23, 1945, and assigned to the Montreal Royals farm club for the following season.

During his single year in Montreal and for his first few seasons in Ebbets Field, Robinson generally endured the racial taunts of fans, opponents, and even some teammates with the forbearance he had promised Rickey. Robinson's fiery play on the field netted Rookie of the Year honors in 1947 and an MVP trophy in 1949 for the .311 career hitter. His single greatest performance came on September 30, 1951, when he made an acrobatic catch in the bottom of the 9th inning in Philadelphia to rescue Brooklyn from pennant elimination, then homered in the 13th inning to force a playoff against the Giants. Robinson's apparent off-field stoicism in the middle of such diamond dash gradually won over the baseball establishment and forged a model that other black players were to be measured against for some time. On the other hand, any departure from Robinson's initial behavioral model quickly laid bare the sport's persisting racism, most often through front-office or media criticism that the perceived mistakes of an individual black player were liable to compromise the opportunities accorded to his entire race. This patronizing attitude had a couple of long-range consequences: It effectively kept the big leagues out of the reach of some of the most flamboyant players in the Negro leagues (and of some who simply weren't married or part of a model family), and it imposed a higher standard of playing excellence for blacks than for whites. For years, even decades, to come, a black player's road from the minors to a parent club was to prove almost as rocky as the one that had led from the Negro leagues to a big league organization, and for similar reasons.

Once he had established himself in Brooklyn, however, there was not too much that stymied Robinson. One important factor in his development as a major leaguer was that he was playing in a city already heated to passionate and frequently bitter levels by the long-standing rivalries between the National League Dodgers and Giants and between both of them and the American League Yankees. Robinson's dynamic presence boiled the water over the rim of a pot that already contained the likes of Leo Durocher, Larry MacPhail, Charlie Dressen, and other volatile tempers in a continuous bubbling of scandals, controversies, and vows of vengeance against somebody or other. He excited Brooklyn fans not only by contributing his bat, glove, and speed to the confrontations against the Giants and Yankees, but

A stunned Jackie Robinson (shown standing behind second base) watches as Bobby Thomson is mobbed by teammates after scoring the pennant-winning run in 1951. TV Sports Mailbag.

also by embarrassing the opposition into the kinds of mental and physical errors that led them to beat themselves. Or as Durocher once noted: "You want a guy that comes to play. But [Robinson] didn't just come to play. He came to beat you. He came to stuff the goddamn bat right up your ass."

The results of Robinson's aggressiveness were not totally translatable into his career statistics. Of the thirteen second basemen inducted into the Hall of fame by 1994, for example, his lifetime .311 average ranked him only seventh. Due to his relatively brief stay in the big leagues (1947–56), he compiled fewer hits than any of the others and topped only the mediocre-hitting Johnny Evers in most key categories. On a seasonal basis, he never hit 20 home runs or 40 doubles, and he drove in 100 runs only once. And although he led the NL in stolen bases twice, he reached the 30 mark on only one occasion. What the numbers do not convey are what Rickey called Robinson's "thinking man's game." His speed, for instance, was deployed not primarily for stolen bases but for running the opposition into defensive mistakes. As a member of the power-hitting Boys of Summer Dodger teams, his thefts tended to be surgical cuts in late-inning situations rather than mechanical charges from base to base. Then there were the prancings and shoutings to the opposition pitcher, causing balks, wild pitches to the plate, and wild throws over to the first baseman; the threatening moves toward the next base to pull out of position both infielders and the outfielders backing them up; and the endlessly taunting, jockeying advances toward the next base on routine pop flies and singles for the purpose of daring outfielders to throw behind him. These "tricky ball" tactics, a staple for years in the Negro leagues, flew directly in the face of white baseball's traditional wisdom about riling the opposition. As someone who was already playing in a pressure cooker because of his race, Robinson pursued his antagonistic kind of game with the self-assurance that his determination was stronger than anyone else's and that, pressure pitted against pressure, he wouldn't be the first one to crack.

But that was not all. If Robinson brought his Negro league education to the majors, he also brought along the instincts and talents from his extraordinary athletic career at UCLA. With the same indifference to retaliation that he displayed with his psychological taunting, he never hesitated to throw rolling blocks into opposition infielders or, in some cases, opposition pitchers who went after bunts that he deliberately laid down along the first-base line. Playing in the field, particularly at second base or third base, he defied runners to knock him down. For the sturdy, muscular Robinson, baseball was very much a contact sport. It was not the least of Rickey's insights that he had foreseen this all-consuming kind of play as a spontaneous, productive outlet for the turmoils and frustrations that Robinson endured privately as a major leaguer; it was not the least of Robinson's strengths that there was very little of the gratuitous in his aggressiveness and that his on-field actions didn't precipitate any more physical brouhahas than did those of his white teammates.

By the mid-1950s, with numerous other blacks established as major league stars, Robinson had begun to go public with his grievances about baseball's discriminating practices. This reawakened the old critics who had been opposed to integration from the start, and also stirred earlier supporters into charges that Robinson was an ingrate or that he was losing sight of the turn-the-other-cheek philosophy that had been crucial to his gaining a foothold in the majors. More indirectly, he also drew reprimands from other black players who didn't want him rocking the boat. With his skills also on the wane, his outspokenness led to increasingly frequent comparisons—and unfavorable ones—to Mays, Roy Campanella, and Ernie Banks, all of whom were embraced by the media as black stars who embodied the "joy" of the game. In effect, Robinson's new and often angry candor represented a second beachhead for black players, and one that once again left him as something of a lonely pioneer. It was to take many more years for black players to follow him down this road than had been needed to follow him into the major leagues.

Robinson's playing career came to an end following the 1956 season, when he chose to retire rather than accept a trade to the Giants. In 1994 the Rookie of the Year Award was redesignated the Jackie Robinson Award.

WILBERT ROBINSON (Hall of Fame, 1945)

Robinson's career was one of the most picaresque in major league history, providing him with signal moments as player, manager, coach, and team president; he even umpired a game in an emergency in 1898. Along the way, he got involved in the political intrigues of three leagues and, more fatefully, in the emotional ups and downs of John McGraw.

A catcher by trade, Robinson began his seventeen-year (1886–1902) career with the American Association Athletics, remaining with the team as a backup receiver until he was peddled to the league's Baltimore entry in 1890; it was there the following year that he first became a teammate of McGraw. At the end of the 1891 season, the AA Orioles became the National League Orioles with the collapse of the former circuit, and Robinson moved in as the first-string backstop with a good glove and an awakening bat. A lifetime .273 hitters, he had four .300 seasons, including a career-high .353 in 1894; on June 12, 1894, he

Your Uncle Wilbert on the porch of his Georgia home following his forced retirement from the Dodgers. Cleveland Public Library.

also became the first of two major leaguers (Rennie Stennett was the other) to collect 7 hits in a 9-inning game.

Aside from his defense and offense, Robinson served the club in two fundamental ways: first by personifying the Old Oriole way of playing by resorting to such ploys as throwing his mask in the way of opposition base runners, and secondly by acquiring the raw material from which he would enchant generations of listeners with stories about the grittiness of his teammates. As much as anybody, Robinson was responsible for the exaggerated—if not false—image of the NL Orioles as macho cutthroats who were avid to play as long as they had at least one limb functioning; in fact, Robinson's career itself was proof of the exaggeration. For example, between 1895 and 1898, while the Orioles were winning two pennants and finishing second on two other occasions, he was sidelined with a variety of ailments and appeared behind the plate in only 267 games, with backup receiver Bill Clarke taking over in 256 contests. Robinson finally recanted all his years of Oriole puffery after watching the Yankees sweep the Cardinals in the 1928 World Series; telling columnist Dan Daniel that the Murderers' Row New Yorkers "would have beaten our brains out," he brought down the wrath of McGraw and other old Baltimore teammates.

Because he was already thirty-six, Robinson was not one of the Baltimore players transferred to Brooklyn in 1899 as part of an elaborate syndication scheme for common control of the two franchises. Instead, staying behind with manager-third baseman McGraw, Robinson contributed enough Old Orioleism to field fights and other ruckuses to embarrass the syndicators by having fourth-place Baltimore outdraw pennant-winning Brooklyn on the road. That moral victory achieved, he and McGraw then signed with the Cardinals, making it clear from the beginning that they intended to be part of Baltimore's new American League franchise in 1901. They carried through on their intention, even becoming minority investors in the team. That became important in 1902, when they used their stock as a stepping-stone for another labyrinthine scheme aimed at getting McGraw and some of Baltimore's top players to the Giants. As the good soldier in the finagling, Robinson stayed behind as McGraw's managerial successor to play out the schedule with a roster largely contributed by other AL teams. When what was left of the Baltimore franchise was sold to New York's Frank Farrell and the Orioles were transformed into the Highlanders, he retired from baseball for some years to run a local meat concern.

In 1911 Robinson was back in uniform for McGraw at the Polo Grounds, serving as the big leagues' first full-time pitching coach. As in Baltimore and St. Louis, another important part of the job was playing the good cop to McGraw's bad cop where umpires were concerned. As Robinson liked to tell people in his later years, the routine was instinctive, with McGraw ranting and screaming as nastily as he could until Robinson would introduce himself with some patented, good-natured smiles, assuring the arbiter in question that "Mac just says things, he really likes you." The same roly-poly soft-soaping was directed regularly against sportswriters, and most of them fell for it, making Robinson almost as popular as McGraw with sports cartoonists. For his part, the more jaded Damon Runyon insisted on referring to him only and always as Your Uncle Wilbert.

Robinson's twenty-two-year friendship with McGraw ended abruptly after the 1913 World Series when the exasperated pilot, looking for anybody at all to blame for the Giants' loss to the Athletics, decided that the main culprit had been his first-base coach for sending the leg-sore Fred Snodgrass to second in a futile steal attempt in the final game. If Robinson was stunned by his firing, he got over it quickly enough when the Dodgers came along to offer him their managerial slot for the 1914 season. It was the start of several things: Robinson's eighteen-year stay as the Brooklyn pilot, his often bitter rivalry with the across-the-river McGraw, and even the popular designation of his team as the Robins.

In his third year at the helm at Ebbets Field, Robinson steered Brooklyn to a pennant. The win was all the sweeter in being clinched in a late September game against the Giants; it came all the more suspiciously when several New York errors contributed to it, prompting a seething

McGraw to stalk off the field before the end of the contest. Although McGraw kept his version of peace, runner-up Philadelphia demanded that NL president John Tener investigate whether the known sympathies of several of the Giants for Robinson had contributed to their errors. Tener dismissed the accusation, and it was about the last time that the league's New York teams would ever be charged with trying to help one another. In 1920 Robinson led the club to another pennant, and again the victory came under a cloud—this time from an ambitious Brooklyn district attorney who sought to make political hay with an investigation similar to that under way into the 1919 Black Sox scandal. These charges also died before they got beyond first base.

Through the first half of the 1920s, Robinson's chief nemesis was the miserly ways of owner Charlie Ebbets. Relations between the club officials grew tenuous enough for Robinson to consider a move to the Yankees as pilot—a prospect that died only when Jacob Ruppert decided against the advice of his partner Cap Huston and hired Miller Huggins instead. With Ebbets's death in 1925, however, Robinson realized what a real enemy was when, to his announced surprise, the Ebbets heirs voted for him as club president over more than eager half-owner Stephen McKeever. The resentful McKeever immediately declared war on the manager-president, creating so much organizational chaos that the franchise executives were lumped together by the press as The Daffiness Boys.

Robinson's attempt to wear two hats also cost him the benevolence of New York sportswriters. The first rupture appeared when the *Brooklyn Eagle,* close to McKeever, criticized the selection of Robinson as president as confirmation that "the common sense of the common people is a common fallacy." Even sharper was a clash between Your Uncle Wilbert and the *New York Sun* after the paper had run a cartoon in 1926 mocking the high salaries of Brooklyn's unproductive stars and contrasting them with the pittances being earned by the club's only productive players. When Robinson called the paper to protest the publication of player earnings, *Sun* sports editor Joe Vila doubled the poison not merely by reporting the call but also by ordering the paper never again to print either Robinson's name or the term Robins for the team. It was from that point on that the *Sun* (and later other New York dailies) recognized the Brooklyn franchise more regularly as the Dodgers.

By 1930, the Robinson-McKeever feud had left the club in such disarray that other NL owners insisted that league president John Heydler do something to restore order. Heydler's compromise solution was to have Robinson given a new two-year contract as manager but have him resign as president so that a new board of directors could start with a fresh slate. The board included two McKeever votes, two from the Ebbets-Robinson faction, and the deadlock-breaking presence of Walter Carter, a brother-in-law of U.S. Supreme Court chief justice Charles Evans Hughes. It proved to be the beginning of the end for Robinson. A year later, with the Dodgers still stumbling on the field and in the boardroom and with other NL owners still complaining that their trips to Ebbets Field were a waste of time because of the sparse attendance in a rundown facility, Carter used his tie-breaking vote to propose that Robinson be replaced as manager by Max Carey.

With the help of former Yankee owner Huston, Robinson took over as manager and president of the Atlanta franchise in the Southern Association for a year, but then fell down a flight of stairs, sustaining serious injuries. While recovering from the fall, he died in a hospital of a heart attack at age seventy.

YANK ROBINSON

Robinson's dirty pants almost led to a strike by the players on the 1889 St. Louis Browns. Ordered by owner Chris Von der Ahe to change the soiled flannels before the start of a game on May 2, the second baseman sent a clubhouse boy to his hotel for a fresh pair; but when the young man couldn't get back into the ballpark, Robinson launched a profane tirade against the ticket taker barring his way. Von der Ahe fined the player $25, which he refused to return even after the offer of an apology. When Robinson bolted the team, claiming that the owner had, through previous clashes, already fined him enough to build a house, and the executive retaliated with threats of suspension and blacklisting, the rest of the team

refused to board their train in protest. Only the intervention of manager Charlie Comiskey persuaded them to proceed to their Kansas City destination while he talked Von der Ahe into reinstating Robinson.

FRANK ROBISON

Originally a Cleveland streetcar operator, Robison was an ardent promoter of syndicated ownership of major league clubs. Denied permission by the National League to sell the Cleveland Spiders to interests in either Detroit or Toronto during the 1890s, he instead purchased the St. Louis Browns in early 1899 and cannibalized the Spiders, transferring, among others, future Hall of Famers Cy Young, Jesse Burkett, and Bobby Wallace to his new team. With Robison's brother Stanley in nominal charge, the Spiders suffered through the worst season-long performance on the major league level—a 20–134 (.130) record, including an unequaled 24 consecutive losses while managing no winning streak longer than 2 games. Originally dubbed the Leftovers, Discards, and Castoffs in the press, the team quickly enough became the Wanderers and Exiles when the Robisons began a wholesale shifting of home games to the road, permitting local fans only six opportunities to see the club after July 1. At the end of the 1899 season, the Robisons accepted $25,000 for what amounted to a mercy killing in the dissolution of the team as the NL cut back from twelve to eight clubs.

With his new operation in Missouri, Robison became an ally of Andrew Freedman in the New York owner's syndication scheme in 1900. Even though that effort died of its own weight, the St. Louis owner resurrected it at the time of the reconciliation between the National and American leagues; the newest version called for one eight-team league organized as a holding company with eight wholly owned subsidiaries. "What people want is good baseball," he told reporters, 'they don't care who owns the clubs.'' Robison's most lasting contribution to the game was his suggestion to establish a purse for the first- and second-place teams in each league—a plan he sought to impose as part of an across-the-board 20 percent pay cut for players; in 1911, minus the salary reduction, the proposal became the basis for the later sharing of World Series money among the top four clubs in each league. Robison died in 1908; Stanley continued to run the Cardinals until his death in 1911.

JOHN ROGERS

A successful Philadelphia lawyer and half-owner of the Phillies from 1883 until 1902, Rogers, the author of the standard player contract of his time, considered eliminating the reserve clause from future agreements after the National League lost court battles to the Players League over the services of New York stars John Montgomery Ward and Buck Ewing and Phillies' infielder Bill Hallman. Instead, Rogers rewrote the clause sufficiently tightly that, after future Hall of Famer Nap Lajoie bolted to the American League Athletics in 1901, a local court granted an injunction prohibiting his appearance in an A's uniform anywhere in Pennsylvania. Rogers eventually sold out before the 1903 season because of the AL anyway, when the conflicting involvements of his partners Al Reach and Ben Shibe snapped already strained relations among the three.

BILLY ROHR

Rohr came within a strike of becoming the first twentieth-century pitcher to hurl a no-hitter in his major league debut. Facing New York at Yankee Stadium on April 14, 1967, the Boston southpaw got all the way down to a full count in the 9th inning when Elston Howard ruined the masterpiece with a single. Although Rohr held on for a 3–0 shutout, he pitched only one more complete game and was out of the major leagues, with a 3–3 lifetime record, after only two seasons.

BARRY RONA

As general counsel to the owners' Players Relations Committee in 1985–86, Rona maintained that sharing information did not violate the letter of the prohibition against acting in concert in negotiating with free agents; the September 1987 decision by arbitrator Thomas Tuttle Roberts against ownership collusion disagreed with him. In 1994, another arbitrator decided in Rona's favor after the Players Association had denied him the right to represent players as an agent; Daniel Collins ruled that there was no specific proof that Rona had been involved in the collusion effort, that he was merely performing a lawyer's duty to represent his client ably, and that he could work on behalf of the two dozen or so athletes under contract to his new employer, Bienstock Sports.

BUDDY ROSAR

Rosar set the standard for catching perfection in 1946, when, as a member of the Athletics, he handled 605 fielding chances over 117 games without making an error. The streak reached 147 games before ending in May 1947.

PETE ROSE

Rose's obsession with numbers and money over his twenty-four-year (1963–86) playing career were fitting for somebody dubbed Charlie Hustle; what wasn't so expected was that baseball's most prolific hitter would be denied his place in the Hall of Fame by a commissioner who had built an intellectual altar to his diamond virtues.

Rose began his assault on the record books as the first piece of the Big Red Machine in 1963, when, as a second baseman for Cincinnati, he took National League Rookie of the Year honors for batting .273 and scoring 100 runs for the first of ten times. A lifetime .303 batter, his subsequent achievements included three hitting titles (1968, 1969, and 1973); fifteen years of averaging .300; leading the league in safeties seven times and in doubles five times; and reaching the 200-

Pete Rose acknowledges the hometown Cincinnati crowd after singling for his record-breaking 4,192nd hit, on September 11, 1985. Photo compliments of the Cincinnati Reds.

hit plateau an unprecedented ten times. The switch-hitting leadoff man's most productive year was 1973, when he was designated NL MVP for his .338 batting crown, 36 doubles, and 115 runs. His most magnetic season was 1978, when he pursued Joe DiMaggio's 56-game hitting streak before national cameras, finally having to settle for tying Willie Keeler's NL mark of 44 games. In 1985 he caused another media event by pursuing Ty Cobb's all-time hit record, finally surpassing the Detroit star with a single off San Diego's Eric Show for his 4,192nd hit on September 11.

Rose closed out his career with 4,256 safeties. He had an additional 45 hits (and a .381 average) in League Championship Series for another record. He also went into retirement with marks for the most games played (3,562) and most at-bats (14,053), a second-place finish for doubles (746), and a fourth-place standing in runs (2,165). While hardly a power hitter, Rose did whack up to 16 home runs in a season, and drove 3 balls out of the park in an April 1978 game against the Mets at Shea Stadium. While never particularly speedy (in 1975 he had 662 official at-bats but not a single stolen base), his belly flops became a personal trademark and an incentive for a whole generation of players to eschew sliding feet-first in favor of head-first dives into bases. While not especially gifted defensively, his doggedness and intense work habits permitted managers to move him around over the years from second base to the outfield to third base to first base; he ended up being elected to the All-Star team seventeen times at five different positions.

The immediate Rose persona was a pit bull as capable of dispatching close friend Ray Fosse to the disabled list for two months after a home-plate collision in the 1970 All-Star Game, as he was accustomed to fielding his position and returning to the dugout at the conclusion of every inning on a run. It was a quality that some identified with a winning attitude and that others ascribed to mania, but that, at least in baseball terms, translated into seven division titles, six pennants, and three world championships. The worst fallout from his rugged style occurred during the 1973 National League Championship Series, when his hard slide into second base

precipitated punches with Met shortstop Bud Harrelson and then mass disorder in the grandstands of Shea Stadium. Only when Met players begged fans to control themselves did Cincinnati lose a fleeting hope of winning the game by forfeit.

Off the field, Rose could spit out at a moment's notice statistics covering not only every facet of his play but also those pertaining to others with whom he was in competition for one offensive category or another. The only numbers of equal importance to him were those relating to his salary—a source of friction on more than one occasion during his career. On the eve of the 1977 season, for instance, he complained bitterly that the Reds had given shortstop Dave Concepcion a five-year, $1 million contract, dropping leaden hints that he would leave the team as a free agent at the end of the season if he didn't get considerably more than the infielder. That minicrisis ended when general manager Bob Howsam was overwhelmed by letters and phone calls demanding that a deal be worked out with the local hero. Two years later, however, Cincinnati braved fan reaction by dropping out of the bidding fairly early for Rose's free-agent services. For most of the off-season he was wined and dined by several NL teams—offered a racing stable by the Pirates, a national identification through Ted Turner's cable network by the Braves, and a chance to become king of the mountain in New York by the Mets. In the end, Rose dismissed the horses, decided he didn't need the exposure provided by Turner, and told the Mets he didn't "play for losers," coming down in favor of the Phillies. To get the infielder-outfielder, however, Philadelphia had to borrow heavily from a television station to meet a demand that Rose's contract make him the highest-paid player in any sport (a primacy then held by David Thompson of the NBA Denver Nuggets).

With the Phillies, Rose proved to be a spark plug in the franchise's only world championship, in 1980. On the other hand, he was mortified when he was benched in favor of Tony Perez during the 1983 World Series against Baltimore. After beginning the 1984 season with the Expos, Rose realized an often-stated ambition of being swapped back to the Reds so he could take over his old club as a player-manager. As a pilot, he

brought together all his field instincts and an encyclopedic knowledge of both players and the rule
book to guide the club to four consecutive second-place finishes between 1985 and 1988. Although most expectations were that he would be
an able motivator but something of a disaster in
shaping a pitching staff, there were extended periods when just the opposite was the case. His
worst moment on the field as manager came in
1988, when he engaged in such a protracted argument with umpire Dave Pallone that he was suspended for thirty days for provoking a near-riot
by Riverfront Stadium fans. But all that turned
out to be a mere prelude to the crisis that was to
keep him out of the Hall of Fame.

In spring training in 1989, Commissioner Bart
Giamatti confirmed press reports that he was
looking into the possibility that Rose had been
betting on baseball games and that he was in debt
to various bookmakers for an estimated $500,000.
The months that followed were a circus of accumulating evidence about Rose's addiction to betting on sports events, independent investigations
linking him with ambiguous figures around the
country, and repeated denials by Rose that he had
ever wagered on baseball. Eventually the media
pressure became so great that he decided not to
lead the Reds up to Cooperstown for the annual
exhibition game played after induction ceremonies lest he divert attention from former teammate
Johnny Bench, one of that year's inductees. Then,
finally, with a suit challenging Giamatti's authority losing wind as it bounced from courtroom to
courtroom, Rose announced on August 24 that he
would abide by the commissioner's decision to
ban him permanently from baseball.

Although the behind-doors accord between the
two sides made no mention of Rose's alleged betting on baseball (an important concession in view
of the possible criminal charges for such activities), Giamatti was unable even to get through
his initial press conference without reiterating his
belief that Rose had indeed been wagering on
games, including Reds' games. For his part, Rose
continued issuing denials in this regard, and also
spurned suggestions for a long time that his monumental losses to bookmakers (estimated in the
millions) indicated an addiction to gambling. His
public image didn't improve when, barely a week

after agreeing to his banning, Giamatti suddenly
died of a heart attack, prompting charges from
a lot of glib columnists that the chain-smoking
commissioner had been done in by Rose. He lost
still more of his faithful when, clearly desperate
for money, he stepped up his appearances at card
shows to sell his autograph at inflated prices and
became a regular on home-shopping networks for
peddling the trophies and memorabilia he had accumulated over the years.

In the summer of 1990, a federal court found
Rose guilty of tax evasion and sentenced him to
several months' imprisonment. On top of that, the
committee charged with overseeing Hall of Fame
election procedures made him ineligible for consideration as a member of Cooperstown. The decision—based on Hall of Fame regulations about
the moral character of candidates—made little
mention of the fact that the museum was already
honoring racists like Cap Anson, assailants like
Ty Cobb, drunkards like Rabbit Maranville and
Grover Cleveland Alexander, and numerous others who should have come up as short of this
criterion as Rose. Like Giamatti, who had once
talked of Rose as the perfect major leaguer, the
committee decided that what Charlie Hustle had
achieved between the white lines had become
irrelevant.

AL ROSEN

Rosen squeezed a lot into what were essentially
only seven big league seasons. As a rookie third
baseman for Cleveland in 1950, he led the American League in home runs with 37, also topping
the 100 mark in RBIs, runs, and walks. It was
the first of five consecutive seasons of 100 RBIs,
including league-leading numbers in both 1952
and 1953. In the latter year, the right-handed slugger also won his second home-run title, with 43
blasts, and came within a point of Mickey Vernon
for the batting title. There was some sentiment in
Cleveland for Rosen to protest the outcome because two members of the Senators had intentionally committed baserunning gaffes to prevent
Vernon from coming to bat one more time. The
third baseman declined, even though he had collected his own 3 hits on the final day of the season after ignoring a patent invitation by Detroit
infielders to lay down as many bunts as he wanted

to claim the Triple Crown; one of the two outs he made that day came when he deprived himself of a fourth hit by running over first base without touching the bag.

In 1954, playing for the pennant-winning Indians all season with a broken finger sticking out of his glove, Rosen could manage only 24 home runs, but again batted .300 and drove home 100 runners. It turned out to be his last joyful season. Over his last two years, Rosen attracted boobirds whipped on by press insinuations that there was something dark about the fact that a Jewish player was allowed to play through a horrendous slump on a team in which one of the owners (Hank Greenberg) was also Jewish. The ugliness reached its climax in 1956, when Rosen was hooted for leaving a game with a broken nose. Manager Al Lopez was so disgusted by the grandstand reaction that he resigned after the season. Rosen went with him, having averaged for his seven full campaigns 27 home runs and 102 RBIs.

After his playing days, Rosen became a front-office executive for the Yankees, Astros, and Giants. With New York in the late 1970s, he was a mostly silent presence who collected a lot of useless high-priced free agents at owner George Steinbrenner's whim. As head of Houston's baseball operations for the first part of the 1980s, he presided over a West Division title in 1980. Moving on to San Francisco in 1986, he put together a division winner in 1987 and a pennant-winning club in 1989.

ROSEY ROSWELL

Longtime Pittsburgh announcer Roswell had the most distinctive home-run call of any baseball broadcaster. Whenever a ball started toward the outfield seats, he would proclaim, ''Open the window, Aunt Minnie, here she comes,'' then key a sound effects recording of glass shattering.

ARNOLD ROTHSTEIN

Rothstein has been charged with fixing the 1919 World Series, but the accusation is only part of the story. The foremost American gambler of his time, a friend of Giants owner Charles Stoneham, and a partner in several business ventures with New York manager John McGraw, Rothstein was approached by two different gambling fac-

tions with plans to buy the Series. One, consisting of former major leaguers Billy Maharg and Bill Burns and ex-featherweight champion Abe Attell, he ignored; the other, including gamblers Sport Sullivan and Rachael Brown, he bankrolled. The Maharg-Burns group, which the players had approached initially, bluffed that it had Rothstein's support, but when it failed to make promised payoffs on time, the White Sox players played game three on the level, handing the conspirators heavy losses in their one-game-at-a-time wagers. Rothstein and Sullivan, betting on the Series as a whole, escaped this particular setback but became concerned when Chicago won games six and seven. To settle matters, they threatened Lefty Williams, who was knocked out in the 1st inning of game eight.

After making his killing, Rothstein appeared voluntarily—feigning outraged virtue—before the grand jury investigating the episode, then arranged with Chicago owner Charlie Comiskey's lawyer Alfred Austrian to purloin the confessions and immunity waivers of four of the Black Sox from the state's attorney's office. The gambler's grand jury performance was convincing enough for him to avoid being indicted with the players. What's more, none of the principal gamblers involved ever stood trial, and, with the confessions unavailable at their trial, the players were found not guilty.

After Rothstein was murdered in November 1928 for welshing on losses in a poker game, the FBI found papers in his files indicating that he had laid out $80,000 to facilitate the Series fix.

EDD ROUSH (Hall of Fame, 1962)

Roush had some of the most curious—and curiously overlooked—numbers of early-century National League players. A left-hand-hitting outfielder who did his damage with a 46-ounce bat, he compiled a .323 average in 18 seasons (between 1913 and 1931) spent mostly with the Reds and the Giants. In 1917 and 1919 he won the NL batting title; in 1918 he took league slugging honors; in 1923 he hit the most triples in the league. Perhaps most impressive of all, Roush had a ten-year streak of never hitting below .321—the highest minimum for so long by any NL player except Honus Wagner. Abetting him in such consistency was an eye that saw him strike out merely 260 times in his career. On the other hand, Roush was a model case of a hitter surrounded by outs: Despite his lifetime batting average and on-base percentage (.369), he never once scored 100 runs or batted in 100. Although his lack of long-ball power (his home-run peak was 8 in 1925) explained the latter, the fact that he scored as many as 90 runs only twice attested to one of baseball's all-time stranded base runners.

Roush arrived in the National League with the Giants in 1916 as one of the players picked up by John McGraw from the disbanded Federal League. After only a few at-bats in the Polo Grounds, Roush was dealt to Cincinnati for Buck Herzog in the so-called Hall of Fame Trade; accompanying him to the Reds were fellow future Cooperstown residents Christy Mathewson and Bill McKechnie. It was Roush who alerted Cincinnati officials to attempted bribes of Reds players prior to the 1919 World Series and who insisted to his dying day that some of his teammates had played as suspiciously as the White Sox during the blackened Series.

When Roush wasn't tagging NL pitchers, he was playing tag with Cincinnati owner Garry Herrmann in annual contract negotiations; it was in fact a rare season that Roush didn't miss spring training in a holdout tactic. Despite his star player's popularity in Cincinnati, Herrmann finally had enough of the yearly tug-of-war in 1927, sending the outfielder back to the Giants. It was good timing on the owner's part, since Roush, one of the league's most reliable defensive outfielders, was then under lingering criticism for making an unlikely error in a late September game that had doomed the Reds' pennant chances. On the other hand, he held out with New York as well and actually sat out the entire 1930 season, after which he was sold back to the Reds.

DAVE ROWE

An outfielder by trade, Rowe was pressed into service as a pitcher by the Cleveland Forest Cities on July 24, 1882. He pitched a complete game, but yielded 29 hits and 7 walks—and established a major league record by giving up 35 runs. The journeyman also established another record of du-

bious honor by playing for seven different teams in his seven major league seasons. He left a different kind of mark by agreeing to drop a lawsuit against Chris Von der Ahe in exchange for the support of the St. Louis Browns owner in getting the American Association to lift the blacklist on players who had defected to the Union Association in 1884.

JACK ROWE

Shortstop Rowe, the brother of Dave, played 75 games for the National League Buffalo Bisons in 1882, and put the ball in play in every one of his 308 official at-bats, a season record for plate appearances without striking out.

BAMA ROWELL

Second baseman Rowell inspired novelist Bernard Malamud's climactic scene in *The Natural* when he smashed the Bulova clock atop the right-field scoreboard in Ebbets Field as a member of the Boston Braves on Memorial Day in 1946. The blow shattered the clock and showered Brooklyn outfielder Dixie Walker in glass. In the novel by the Brooklyn-born Malamud, the home run was hit by fictional hero Roy Hobbs and won a pennant for the New York Knights. In reality, Rowell had to wait forty-one years even to collect the watch that Bulova had promised anyone who hit the clock.

PANTS ROWLAND

The manager of the pennant-winning 1917 Chicago White Sox, Rowland, as president of the Pacific Coast League, petitioned the major leagues for equal status in 1946 to head off any future encroachment on his turf either through expansion or transferred franchises. Denied that privilege, he later championed a vote to desert the National Association of Professional Baseball Leagues unless the player draft were abolished; the National and American leagues felt sufficient pressure to grant the West Coast minor league a promotion from Triple-A status to a vaguely defined open classification that included exemption from the major league draft. The league existed in this limbo between the major and minor leagues until 1958, when the incursion by what Rowland had called the ''vultures,'' in the form of simultaneous moves by the Dodgers and Giants to California, curtailed any future ambitions of the PCL.

JOE RUDI

Rudi's two biggest moments in a sixteen-year (1967–82) career took place in the World Series as a member of Oakland. In 1972 he made a circus catch in left field in the 9th inning of game two to preserve a 2–1 victory over Cincinnati and send the Athletics barreling toward a championship. In 1974, the right-hand-hitting outfielder tagged Dodger relief ace Mike Marshall for a 7th-inning homer in the final game to produce another championship. Although he never hit more than 22 home runs and never reached the 100 RBI mark, Rudi led the American League at one time or another in hits, doubles, and triples. In 1976 he and reliever Rollie Fingers were sold to Boston by Charlie Finley for $1.5 million apiece, but the deal was scotched by Commissioner Bowie Kuhn, who objected to the garage sale atmosphere in which the Oakland owner was unloading his star players.

MUDDY RUEL

Ruel scored the most important run in the sixty-year history of the Washington Senators. A catcher who traveled from team to team in the American League over a nineteen-year career between 1915 and 1934, he doubled to begin a rally in the bottom of the 12th inning in game seven of the 1924 World Series against the Giants, eventually scoring when Earl McNeely hit an apparent double-play ball that bounced over Freddie Lindstrom's head. The run sealed the only world championship won by Washington. Ruel whacked his double after New York catcher Hank Gowdy had tripped over his mask going after an easy foul pop. A lawyer when he wasn't crouching behind the plate, Ruel is also credited with having coined the phrase ''tools of ignorance'' for referring to a catcher's gear.

RED RUFFING (Hall of Fame, 1967)

Ruffing's trade from the Red Sox to the Yankees in May 1930 hardly looked like a steal at the time; as it turned out, the deal became the last of New York's raids in New England for future Hall of Famers.

In slightly more than six seasons with Boston, Ruffing compiled a 39–96 record, leading the American League in losses in both 1928 and 1929, and with an ERA as low as 3.89 only once. After moving to the Yankees, he became the club's right-handed ace throughout the 1930s, winning at least 20 games in four consecutive years (1936–39) and leading the league in victories, winning percentage, and strikeouts once each and in shutouts twice. He also won 7 World Series games.

Originally a power-hitting outfielder, Ruffing turned to pitching after losing four toes in a mining accident; he didn't lose his ability with a bat, however, hitting .269 with 36 homers during his big league career. Suffering from a flying phobia as a result of experiences in the Army Air Corps during World War II, Ruffing was the only member of the 1946 Yankee squad excused from traveling on a rickety team plane. After a final season with the White Sox in 1947, he retired with 273 victories.

VERN RUHLE

Ruhle was the protagonist of what should have been the first triple play in a League Championship Series. Pitching for the Astros in game four of the 1980 League Championship Series against the Phillies, the right-hander speared a soft liner and threw to first to complete what appeared to be a double play. Philadelphia manager Dallas Green protested that the ball had been trapped, and during an ensuing argument Houston first baseman Art Howe realized that nobody had called time, so he grabbed the ball and stepped on second to catch another Philadelphia base runner who had wandered off. To resolve the confusion, umpire chief Doug Harvey consulted with National League president Chub Feeney who, ignoring the fact that time hadn't been called as Howe had rightly observed, ruled a double play and sent the Phillies' runner back to second base.

JACOB RUPPERT

Millionaire socialite and brewer Ruppert bought a half interest in the Yankees in January 1915 as a promotional stunt. His scheme was to rename the team the Knickerbockers after his brewery's best-selling product, but the sports editors of New York's daily newspapers refused to go along because the name was too long to fit into their headlines.

Ruppert and his partner, Cap Huston, had tried separately to buy the Giants and were brought together by John McGraw, the manager of the National League club. They spent money lavishly, most of it going to the Red Sox for established Boston players, but they differed over just about everything else except their animosity toward AL president Ban Johnson. Tangling with Johnson over their right to purchase pitcher Carl Mays from the Red Sox in 1919 because the right-hander was under suspension at the time, they helped reshape the governance of baseball by breaking the executive's dictatorial control over the league, forging the new office of commissioner of baseball, and agreeing to fill it with Kenesaw Landis.

The appointment of Miller Huggins as manager in 1918 triggered irreparable tensions in the Yankee boardroom, with the partners sniping at each other until Huston finally sold out in 1923. Ruppert's telegram to the team at the time—declaring "I am now sole owner of the Yankees. Miller Huggins is my manager," should have served as a warning to Babe Ruth and other anti-Huggins players on the team, but it didn't. After being slapped with a suspension and a $5,000 fine by Huggins in 1925, Ruth appeared at Ruppert's office with a him-or-me ultimatum, only to be chastened by the owner's unequivocal public declaration that "Huggins is in absolute command."

Ruppert's most solid contribution to the franchise was the construction of Yankee Stadium in 1923. As early as 1919, Ruppert and Huston had approached Giants owner (and Yankee landlord) Charles Stoneham with a suggestion that both teams abandon the Polo Grounds and build a new 100,000-seat joint home. Instead, Stoneham, irritated over the Yankees' success and Ruth's popularity, issued a subtle eviction notice disguised by the logic that, with separate parks, both clubs could schedule additional profitable Sunday dates. Meanwhile, AL president Johnson, with little to do since the appointment of Landis as commissioner except plot against his enemies, tried to buy the Yankees' Polo Grounds lease with the intention of doing Stoneham's dirty work of evicting the tenants and leaving them homeless for the 1923 season. For his part, Ruppert, as a hedge against a huge rent increase on what amounted to a year-to-year lease at the Polo Grounds, had already bought the Bronx site where Yankee Stadium would be built. Yankee Stadium opened on April 18, 1923, with a 4–1 Yankee victory over Boston, the margin provided by a 3-run homer by Ruth.

Leaving front-office affairs in the hands of Ed Barrow and dugout matters to Huggins and later Joe McCarthy, Ruppert presided over the first ten Yankee pennants and seven World Series victories during his twenty-four-year ownership. The honorary colonel died on January 13, 1939, at age seventy-one. A lifelong bachelor, he bequeathed the baseball portion of his $100 million estate to two nieces and to Helen Winthrope Weyant, a chorus girl whose name had never before surfaced publicly.

AMOS RUSIE (Hall of Fame, 1977)

Known as The Hoosier Thunderbolt for his blazing fastball, Rusie has often been credited with causing the removal of the mound from fifty feet away from home plate to sixty feet, six inches in 1893. At the very least, he was the first modern hurler who, taking advantage of the recent license given to overhand pitching, so dominated National League hitters in the early 1890s that baseball officialdom sought to restore some balance between offense and pitching. The right-hander spent eight of his ten major league seasons with the Giants, arriving in and departing from New York as a result of wily deals engineered by John T. Brush. While a member of the Giants, Rusie posted four consecutive 30-win seasons (1891–94) toward his eventual 246 career victories; he also led the NL in ERA twice (1894 and 1897) and in strikeouts five times (1890–91 and 1893–95). Equally conspicuous were his five straight years (1890–94) of pacing the league in walks, establishing along the way the modern single-season record of 218 free passes in the first year of the new pitching distance.

As contentious in salary negotiations as he was formidable on the mound, Rusie was a frequent

Amos Rusie's brilliant career will always be overshadowed by the fact that he was dealt for Christy Mathewson. National Baseball Library, Cooperstown, N.Y.

holdout, sitting out the entire 1896 season over a $200 fine and suing Giants owner Andrew Freedman for $5,000 in a case that wasn't concluded until other NL owners chipped in for a $3,000 settlement lest the fractious issue of the reserve clause be raised in a courtroom.

After his rookie season of 1889, with Indianapolis, Rusie had been part of a package put together by Hoosiers' owner Brush to shore up the Giants in the war against the Players League in 1890; in return for surrendering his franchise, he received a promissory note that quickly became a part interest in the New York club when Giants owner John B. Day couldn't pay up. The same Brush, by 1900 in charge at Cincinnati, traded Christy Mathewson to acquire Rusie for the Reds. Knowing he was about to buy controlling interest in the Giants from Freedman, Brush instigated the

deal not only to rid himself in advance of a proven thorn to ownership (and a pitcher who had been sidelined all of 1898 and 1899 with a torn shoulder), but also to obtain in return a highly regarded prospect whom he had paid a mere $100 to acquire from a Norfolk minor league club. Mathewson went on to a Hall of Fame career with the Giants; Rusie ended his with an 0–1 record for the Reds in 1901. For Cincinnati, it was the worst trade in the history of the franchise; for Cincinnati's—soon to be New York's—owner, it was the best of his career.

BILL RUSSELL

Converted from the outfield, Russell ended up plugging the Dodger hole at shortstop throughout the 1970s and well into the 1980s. He also ended up plugging his share of spectators behind first base with an arm that contributed to the National League lead in errors twice and to 29 to 39 miscues in eight different seasons. Although never involved in any of the drug scandals of the period, Russell was proffered a contract by the Dodgers in 1985 that stipulated regular urine tests. Representatives of the players' union and major league owners later agreed that such a move by Los Angeles violated mutual understandings in dealing with addicted players and ordered the clause canceled.

WILLIAM RUSSELL

In partnership with Boston publishers Louis and George Page, Russell, a New York lawyer, bought the Braves in December 1910 for what turned out to be eleven months of hell. Bickering constantly with the Pages about on-field and off-field decisions, he ceded to the strain, and died of a heart attack in November 1911. During his tenure the team was sometimes called the Rustlers.

BABE RUTH (Hall of Fame, 1936)

Widely regarded as both the best and the most influential player of all time, Ruth scaled dizzying statistical heights, and did it with a flair that brought the adjective "Ruthian" into the language. His feats at the plate compelled changes in equipment, style, strategy, and salaries, altering the game forever in each of these areas. The cir-

As a Red Sox southpaw before becoming the Sultan of Swat, Babe Ruth proved he knew more about pitching than how to hit it. Photo compliments of Sharon Guynup.

national League Baltimore Orioles late in the 1914 season, he soon became the best left-hander in the American League, winning 65 games in his first three full years and leading the AL in ERA in 1916. In the course of winning 3 World Series games (against no losses), in 1916 and 1918, he shaped a 0.87 ERA around 29 consecutive scoreless innings (a record that stood for forty-two years). He later pitched 5 games for the Yankees, all victories, for a career record of 94–46.

Initially reluctant to alter Ruth's role, Boston manager Ed Barrow finally succumbed to the importunings of team captain Harry Hooper and others in 1918 for getting the pitcher's already potent bat (a .325 average in 1917) in the lineup more often. Patterning his batting stance after that of White Sox star Joe Jackson, Ruth moved to the outfield (and, on occasion, first base) between starts, averaged .300, hit 11 homers, and gave a hint of what was to come by leading the American League in both slugging average (.555) and strikeouts (58) while compiling a mound record of 13–7 (2.22). Appearing as a position player regularly for the first time in 1919, the lefty swinger hit .322, slugged .657 (to lead the AL for the second of seven consecutive seasons and thirteen times overall), topped AL hitters in RBIs for the first of six times and runs scored for the first of eight, and established a new major league mark of 29 homers. He also pitched often enough to win 13 games while losing only 5.

The Ruth persona was firmly established early on. On June 23, 1918, he was ejected for assaulting umpire Brick Owens, who had called a base on balls on the opposing Senators' first batter; the ouster led to a 26-batter "perfect" game by reliever Ernie Shore. That July Ruth jumped the team in a dispute about whether he should return to a regular spot in the rotation, threatening to play in an industrial league rather than return to the Red Sox. Habitually disregarding training rules, he came close to a fistfight with Barrow in 1919. In both 1918 and 1919, he held out, in the latter year ending up with more money than any other big leaguer except Ty Cobb.

On January 3, 1920, Boston owner Harry Frazee, in an effort to make up for losses in his theatrical productions, sold Ruth to the Yankees for $100,000 (double the highest previous amount

cumstances around his departure from Boston for New York in 1920 shifted the destinies of both franchises, and in the process seeded both one of the sport's great rivalries and one of its great myths. As undisciplined in his personal life as he was talented professionally, his Rabelaisian personality provided the final ingredients for a legend that transcended baseball.

Although it was his unexcelled hitting that eventually elevated him to stardom, Ruth began as a pitcher. Joining the Red Sox from the Inter-

paid for a player)—plus a $350,000 loan secured by a mortgage on Fenway Park. The sale eventually gained the aura of a curse on the New England franchise that has lasted into the 1990s; more tangibly, it marked the beginning of both the Yankee dynasty and the modern, live-ball era of baseball.

Over the next fifteen seasons with New York, Ruth not only rewrote the record book in a way that exhausted superlatives, but also redefined the game. In 1920 he broke his own home-run record by clouting an eye-popping 54, then eclipsed that mark the following year with 59, slugged 60 in 1927 to create a threshold that would not be crossed until Roger Maris's 61 in 1961, and knocked another 54 in 1928 for a record four seasons with more than 50. He topped the AL in homers a record eleven times, swatted 40 or more a record eleven times, and averaged more than 50 round-trippers a year between 1926 and 1931. Sixty years later, he still had more four-baggers (714) than anyone except Hank Aaron. Even if Ruth didn't actually call his home run in game three of the 1932 World Series against the Cubs (as claimed by *New York World-Telegram* writer Joe Williams and maintained by teammate Joe Sewell for some six decades), he would have had a shot at being right if he had; in what was arguably his most impressive feat of all, he reached the seats an average of eight and a half times every 100 at-bats.

Also in 1920, Ruth established a still-standing mark with his .847 slugging average, following that up with the second-highest figure (.846), in 1921. Overall, he owns six of the ten highest season slugging averages, leading the AL in that category a record thirteen times; his overall mark of .690 is also a record. In 1923 he established still another big league standard with 170 walks, topped that category an unrivaled eleven times, and heads the all-time list for free passes with 2,056. Even Ruth's reputation for monstrous strikeouts bears scrutiny. Unlike the free-swinging power hitters of more recent times, he never, for example, whiffed more than 93 times in a season; also unlike modern sluggers, he made enough contact to compile a .342 career batting average.

The Bambino's home-run totals become even more impressive in the context of his era. When

he reached the fences 29 times in 1919, the next-highest total was Gavvy Cravath's National League high of 12, while the *team* high was the Yankees' 45. When he popped 54 in 1920, the runner-up was George Sisler with 19; moreover, Ruth's personal total that year was higher than that of every major league team except the Phillies, and represented almost 1 of every 9 four-baggers hit. Earning the title The Sultan of Swat, he broke Roger Connor's career mark of 136 round-trippers in 1921, reached 700 in 1934 (when only two other players had as many as 300), and retired with 714 (more than twice as many as the then-runner-up on the all-time list).

Ruth's prodigious slugging not only allowed him to tower over the game; it also changed the sport in substantive ways. In anticipation of better things to come, the owners outlawed doctored pitches such as the spitball and created the lively ball, which made it possible for the overall major league batting average, which had hovered around .250 in the 1910s, to jump to about .285 by 1921. In deference to the shift in emphasis, most managers stopped playing the inside game of trying to score a run at a time and switched to a quest for the big inning; as a result, the number of runs scored annually in the major leagues jumped from fewer than 9,000 per year in the 1910s to almost 12,000 in the 1920s and to more than 13,000 in 1930. In emulation of Ruth, other hitters switched to longer, heavier, thinner-handled bats. In adoration of him, fans turned out in record numbers, with the Yankees becoming the first club to reach the 1 million mark in attendance, in 1920.

Perhaps even more impressive, Ruth altered the salary structure of baseball, if only by a trickle-down effect. It cost Yankee owners Jacob Ruppert and Cap Huston $41,000 to sign him for the 1920 and 1921 seasons. In 1922 he accepted a five-year contract calling for the then-unheard-of annual salary of $52,000, "because," as he said, "I always wanted to make a grand a week." The amount rose to $70,000 with a three-year pact in 1927, and to $80,000 on another three-year deal in 1930. (It was after signing the latter contract that he was reportedly told that he was earning more than President Herbert Hoover and allegedly replied, "Why not? I had a better year than he did.") In addition, he made large amounts from endorsements, barnstorming, movies, and vaudeville shows.

Again, comparisons help. After Ruth's retirement in 1935, the highest salary in the game belonged to Lou Gehrig, who was making $30,000. Nevertheless, Ruth's salaries, as gargantuan as his home runs, helped jack up major league wages across the board, so much so that teammate Waite Hoyt said years later that every ballplayer and his family should give thanks for Ruth's existence.

Ruth appeared in ten World Series, seven of them for New York. In the 1923 and 1928 games, he put together slugging percentages of at least 1.000. In both 1926 and 1928 he hit 3 homers in a game. On the other hand, he suffered two of his most embarrassing diamond moments in Series play: getting cut down trying to steal second by St. Louis catcher Bob O'Farrell for the last out of the 1926 Series, and striking out on a quick pitch by Bill Sherdel of the Cardinals in 1928.

Besides conquering new heights in power hitting and income, Ruth set new standards for intransigence and intemperance. His difficulties with baseball authorities were at their worst in 1922 and 1925. No sooner had the 1921 World Series ended than he found himself in trouble with Commissioner Kenesaw Landis for flouting an old baseball rule prohibiting World Series participants from barnstorming. Although the trip was canceled for poor attendance after only a few days, and Ruth accepted a $3,000-per-week offer to hit the vaudeville circuit, Landis, still incensed at the defiance involved in even starting the tour, suspended the slugger and teammate Bob Meusel for the first thirty-one days of the 1922 season. Even before serving the sentence, Ruth ran afoul of Landis again. The distractions of training in New Orleans proved so compelling that even the usually compliant sportswriters of the day began filing stories about the team's partying, led by Ruth. One dispatch, under a headline announcing ''Yankees Training on Scotch,'' inspired Ruppert and Huston to hire a detective, who ingratiated himself with the players and persuaded Ruth and several others to attend a party at a Joliet, Illinois, brewery and to pose for a group picture. The incriminating evidence found its way into the hands of Landis, who invaded the Yankee clubhouse to issue admonitions about cavorting with bootleg-

gers. After getting back into uniform, Ruth climbed into the stands on May 25 to go after a heckling fan and was fined $200, suspended for a game, and forced to give up his nominal title as Yankee captain. On June 19 he drew a three-day suspension for protesting a call by umpire Bill Dinneen a little too strenuously, then had two days added to the banishment when he went after the umpire the next day.

Ruth's appetite for fast cars, willing women, and huge quantities of food and alcohol was protean. In 1920, outfielder Ping Bodie, nominally a road roommate, noted that he mainly shared hotel accommodations with the star's suitcase. But on the way north from spring training before the 1925 season, the carousing exacted a price. Feeling ill, the 270-pound outfielder got off the train in Asheville, North Carolina, and collapsed. Hustled back onto the train, he passed out again and cracked his head open. Reports of his death appeared as far away as London even as the team announced that he was undergoing emergency abdominal surgery. Reporters and others around the team suspected that Ruth's problems were a result not of the immediately rumored food and liquor, but of a third excess: women. Speculation about which combination of venereal diseases he had contracted reached Ruthian proportions, but the postoperative scar he carried was clearly abdominal.

Ruth's illness, which kept him out of the lineup until June 1, won him no sympathy from manager Miller Huggins. On the contrary, Ruth's unaltered habits both during his recuperation and after he returned to the lineup only increased the pilot's annoyance. Huggins continued to seethe when Ruth stayed out all night on a trip to Cleveland and even when he twice ignored signs—first bunting when he had been instructed to swing away, and then swinging away when told to bunt. The breaking point came on August 29, when Ruth showed up late for a game in St. Louis; with prior approval from Ruppert and Barrow, Huggins slapped Ruth with a $5,000 fine, the largest in history up to that time, and an indefinite suspension. In a fury, Ruth laid the blame for the team's languishing in seventh place on the manager and laid down an ultimatum: ''Either he quits or I quit.'' Returning to New York, the slugger was confident of victory but emerged chastened from a closed-door meeting with Ruppert, apologized to Huggins in front of the entire team, and never again publicly challenged the manager's authority.

Thwarted by Ruppert in his desire to succeed Huggins, who died toward the end of the 1929 season, Ruth deeply resented the appointment of pitcher Bob Shawkey and became bitter over the selection of Joe McCarthy in 1931. For his part, the new manager bided his time, let Ruth pick his spots to play, and ignored his violations of the rules. Ruppert and Barrow had no such compunction, cutting the aging slugger's salary to $52,000 in 1933 and to $35,000 in 1934. Ruth himself forced the issue of his future when, after the 1934 season, he virtually demanded that the owner and general manager fire McCarthy and give him the manager's job. The brass rejected the demand, even after McCarthy had offered to step down; instead, Ruppert suggested that Ruth take the pilot's job with the Yankees' top farm club in Newark. When Ruth refused, the owner felt free to orchestrate a deal that sent Ruth to the Braves in a position that the outfielder was led to believe would carry front-office responsibilities and eventually control of the dugout, but that Ruppert knew was mere window dressing.

It took Ruth only a couple of weeks into the season for him to realize that he was only a drawing card for the last-place Braves. On May 25, in a game against the Pirates, he summoned up what was left of his hitting prowess and clouted 3 homers and a single to drive in 6 runs. After striking out 3 times against Syl Johnson of the Reds in a subsequent game and a final at-bat against the Phillies, he retired on June 2.

In 1938 Ruth signed as a coach with the Dodgers under circumstances similar to those of the Boston fiasco; his relationship with Brooklyn ended bitterly following declarations of alternate desires to make a comeback as a player and to succeed Burleigh Grimes as field boss. Both notions were dispelled by the appointment of Leo Durocher as Dodger manager for the 1939 season.

The Legend of the Babe transcended baseball: Japanese soldiers fighting in the Pacific during World War II, for instance, taunted their American foes by shouting "Fuck Babe Ruth." The

myth also endured beyond the Babe's departure from big league diamonds. Central to that myth was Ruth's purported affection for children. He actually did call on sick children in hospitals, the most noted episode being the speedy recovery of a suburban New Jersey boy named Jimmy Sylvester following such a visit. It was equally true—and equally typical—that, a year later, Ruth had no recollection of the event.

JIMMY RYAN

Ryan's clubhouse needling proved the undoing of two Chicago managers in the 1890s. With Cap Anson, the japes were calculated to undermine the longtime pilot's authority and eventually get him fired. Anson's successor Tom Burns was, however, an unintended victim. When the new manager appointed Ryan team captain for the 1898 season, the rest of the players refused to accept the decision and threatened to strike before the season opener in Louisville unless the honor go to outfielder Bill Lange instead; in yielding to the demand, Burns surrendered any possibility of controlling the team and lasted only two seasons.

Ryan also became the first player ever issued an intentional pass when the Giants, riding a 4-run lead, walked him—with the bases loaded—in an 1896 contest to get to George Decker; Decker struck out.

JOHNNY RYAN

Ordinarily an outfielder for the Louisville Grays in 1876, Ryan took to the mound just once, but nevertheless established himself as the original Wild Thing. In 8 innings of relief work on July 22 of that year, he yielded 22 hits—and established a never-broken record of 10 wild pitches.

NOLAN RYAN

Starting with his unprecedented twenty-seven years (1966, 1968–93) as an active player, Ryan tore up the baseball record books with his career. Equally significant, at least until injuries plagued him over his last couple of seasons, his compilation marks were not merely the result of a pitcher hanging on with accommodating organizations, but also reflected a craftsman still looked upon well into his forties as a staff anchor. The right-

Nolan Ryan's fastball and intensity on the mound were contributing factors in his record seven no-hitters. Photo compliments of the Texas Rangers.

hander attributed both his endurance and his performance to the training methods of the Mets' farm system in the 1960s and to his own rigorous daily exercises, which left him few idle moments around a ballpark. Still another factor was Ryan's ongoing flexibility—evolving from a strict fastballer with only an approximate notion of the strike zone, to a fastballer with a masterly curve, to an occasional spitballer and headhunter whose almost mythical reputation afforded him protection from umpires. It was in this latter connection that White Sox third baseman Robin Ventura gained surprising vocal support from American League hitters in 1993 when he charged Ryan on the mound after taking a pitch too close to the skull. Although most coverage of the ensuing melee centered on the forty-six-year-old hurler's ability to use his fists, the episode also made it

obvious that many hitters resented what they considered a separate set of umpiring rules for Ryan.

Ryan's numbers were endless. By the time he had taken off his Texas uniform for the last time after the 1993 season, he had established the records for most strikeouts (5,714), most no-hitters (7), highest strikeout-ratio-per-9-innings with at least 1,000 innings (9.42), and most consecutive starting assignments (595). Along with these peaks went such other records as the most walks allowed (2,795) and the most grand slams permitted (10). On a seasonal basis, he set a modern mark with his 383 strikeouts while pitching for California in 1973—one of eleven seasons in which he led a league in whiffs. He also set the pace for shutouts three times and earned-run average twice. What might have been his most overpowering performance of all took place within an eight-day period in 1972, when he ripped off 3 wins by striking out 15 Rangers, 16 Red Sox, and 16 Athletics. Two years later, he had his highest strikeout game against Boston, fanning 19. His 7 no-hitters broke down into 4 for the Angels (2 in 1973 and 1 apiece in 1974 and 1975), 1 for the Astros (1981), and 2 for the Rangers (1990 and 1991).

Ryan critics, who grew thinner on the ground as he returned to the mound year after year, usually jumped on the fact that he won 20 games only twice (for California in 1973 and 1974), usually had a won–lost mark hovering near .500 (324–292 overall), and led the league in walks eight times. What the skeptics usually overlooked was that he was usually the ace of mediocre teams. His only World Series appearance was as a young reliever with the 1969 Mets, and he totaled only 6 games in League Championship Series. Perhaps more striking, he never won a Cy Young Award.

Over his career, the right-hander was also at the center of several notable front-office and clubhouse incidents. His trade from New York to California for Jim Fregosi during the 1971–72 off-season ranks as one of the worst deals in major league history. In 1977 he came back to haunt the Mets a second time with reports that his higher salary with the Angels had become a bone of contention between Tom Seaver and the New York ownership; Seaver not only denounced the claim by *Daily News* columnist Dick Young, but also demanded the trade that landed him in a Cincinnati uniform. While with the Angels, Ryan accused southpaw Frank Tanana of compromising his training by so living it up between starts that the team was unable to adopt a four-man rotation that would make both of them more effective; Tanana's retort was that a four-man rotation had been the cause of his sore arm and that the club was ruining its entire staff merely to accommo-

date Ryan. In 1981 Ryan became the first $1 million pitcher in signing a four-year pact with the Astros worth $4.5 million. In 1989 he signed a $2 million free-agent pact with the Rangers. As with the earlier contract with Houston, the team more than made up for that outlay with the crowds drawn for every Ryan appearance to see whether he would pitch another no-hitter, break a new strikeout record, or simply pass another of his numerous milestones.

S

FRED SAIGH

Saigh got into baseball by buying the Cardinals from Sam Breadon at the end of the 1947 season; he got out of it by going to jail. When he took over the club, the lawyer was partnered with Robert Hannegan, a longtime associate of Franklin Delano Roosevelt who had also served as U.S. Postmaster General. When Hannegan died in 1948, Saigh moved quickly (some said ruthlessly) to buy up the rest of the team from his widow. His most prominent act as owner, president, and general manager was to lead the move to dump Happy Chandler as commissioner after the 1950 season; his pet peeves against Chandler were that the commissioner had permitted racial integration and had denied a request that the Cardinals be allowed to play home games at night during the summer because of the torrid weather in St. Louis. Two years later, Saigh's chickens came home to roost when he was charged with federal income tax evasion. Accepting the advice of his attorneys, he pleaded *nolo contendere* with the understanding that he would be given only a heavy fine and a suspended sentence. When sentencing came due, however, the judge who had reportedly agreed to the deal had been replaced by a hard-liner, who sentenced Saigh to fifteen months in prison. Some linked the bench switch to politicians who had never forgiven Saigh for his reputed hustling of Hannegan's widow. Chandler loyalists then got in their innings by blocking Saigh's attempt to sell the Cardinals to a group in Milwaukee. Facing his jail term and needing money to put off his back taxes, he was ultimately forced to sell out to the Anheuser-Busch brewery for a lower price than that offered by the Milwaukee group.

JOHNNY SAIN

As good as he was as a pitcher for the Braves in the late 1940s and Yankees in the early 1950s, Sain became equally controversial as a pitching coach for a number of teams between the late 1950s and the mid-1980s. Although numerous hurlers in his charge credited Sain with turning around their careers, almost as many managers and general managers came to resent Sain for his autonomous hold over a succession of mound staffs, his endorsement of four-man rotations and skepticism of the value of pitchers running, his usually acerbic views of the organization he was working for, and his occasional pointers to players about to enter into contract negotiations. The result was a nomadic coaching career that included the Kansas City Athletics, the Yankees, the Twins, the Tigers, the White Sox, and two stops with the Braves. Through it all, he tutored seventeen pitchers into 20-win seasons for the first time in their careers.

As a pitcher, the right-hander was the dominant reason for the Braves' 1948 pennant—one of three straight years he won 20 games. There were, however, two asterisks to the noted evaluation of the 1948 team's pitching corps as "Spahn, Sain, and pray for rain." For one thing, it was Sain, not the future Hall of Famer Warren Spahn who fashioned Boston's key wins down the stretch; for another, manager Billy Southworth didn't bother

412

with any prayers over the final three weeks, sending out his two aces practically every day between September 6 and September 27.

LENN SAKATA

Utility infielder Sakata occasioned one of the most bizarre innings in baseball history. On August 24, 1983, he was pressed into service as a catcher for Baltimore in an extra-inning game against Toronto when only 1½ games separated the teams in the East Division standings. The first batter up for the Blue Jays in the 10th inning singled off Orioles' reliever Tippy Martinez and, with no fear of Sakata's arm, took a big lead off first base; he was promptly picked off by Martinez. The second batter did exactly the same thing, and was also picked off by the Baltimore southpaw. The third batter, figuring he must have at least had the odds on his side, followed suit—and was also caught napping by Martinez. Sakata later hit a home run to win the game, effectively ending Toronto's run on Baltimore for the division flag.

JUAN SAMUEL

Samuel's defensive and contact limitations seemed secondary when he burst on the scene for the Phillies in the 1980s as the only player to reach double figures in each of his first four years in doubles, triples, home runs, and steals. But his four consecutive seasons of leading the National League in strikeouts (including the rookie record of 168 in 1984) and leaden glove both at second base and in the outfield came to the fore after he was traded to the Mets in 1989 for local favorite Lenny Dykstra and Roger McDowell. Samuel was soon bouncing around from team to team as a backup player.

RYNE SANDBERG

In June 1994, Sandberg walked away from a long-term contract worth as much as $16 million, claiming he had ''lost his competitive edge.'' What he had certainly lost was the largest sum of money ever pending on a big league contract.

Practically since being acquired by the Cubs from Philadelphia prior to the 1982 season, Sandberg had been the most popular player in Wrigley Field since Ernie Banks. In 1984, the righty-swinging second baseman took National League MVP honors for pacing Chicago to an East Division title with a .314 average and the circuit's top numbers in triples and runs scored; in 1990 he led the NL with 40 homers. Sandberg retired with the highest lifetime fielding average (.990) by a second baseman. It wasn't the result of playing it safe, either, since he had picked up ten Gold Gloves along the way for showing the widest range at his position. For one record 123-game period over the 1989 and 1990 seasons, he did not commit a single error.

An injury in 1993 had reduced Sandberg's power production to 9 homers and 45 RBIs, and when his average fell to .238 in the first few months of 1994, he dropped the bombshell of his retirement. The decision seemed motivated at least in part by marital problems; a week later, the infielder's wife filed for divorce.

DEION SANDERS

Sanders went Bo Jackson one better by playing baseball, football, and the media *simultaneously,* but with more glitter than charm. Unlike Jackson, he also went through a few seasons in the late 1980s and early 1990s playing his baseball and football owners off against one another in a cash grab that still somehow left him more petulant than those vying for his services as a center fielder or combination defensive back-punt receiver.

Already under contract to the NFL Falcons, Sanders made his first stab at baseball with the Yankees in the late 1980s. The period was notable for two 1989 incidents that rattled baseball traditionalists. In one game, after hitting his first major league home run, he stopped at home plate and deliberately bent over to tie his shoe with his rear end to the mound. In another contest, he hit a lazy infield pop, took a few steps out of the batter's box, then veered off to the New York dugout—prompting White Sox catcher Carlton Fisk to give him an embarrassing tongue-lashing in front of twenty thousand fans. Although he claimed that he learned his lesson about hustling from the Fisk lecture, he was cut loose by the Yankees because of the certainty in the front office that he would ultimately choose football over baseball.

Instead, Sanders spent the next few years choosing both, and within the same Atlanta market. Egged on by the financial possibilities of replacing Jackson as the country's top two-sports star, he engaged in a series of contract battles with the Braves that made it impossible for the club to count on him over the second half of the season. In 1992 he enraged manager Bobby Cox by playing with the Falcons in the afternoon and then, shadowed by CBS cameras, returning to suit up for the Braves for an evening National League Championship Series game against the Pirates; although Cox had ample opportunity to make Sanders the first player ever to perform in two professional sports on the same day, he deliberately chose not to. When the publicity ploy was denounced by Tim McCarver on the air, Sanders responded by attacking the announcer with ice water on three occasions in clubhouse celebrations for Atlanta's eventual win over Pittsburgh. He was let off with a laughable fine by National League president Bill White.

By 1994 Sanders, known as Neon Deion for the ropes of gold jewelry around his neck, seemed to have settled in as Atlanta's leadoff hitter, but in May the Braves traded him to the Reds for Cincinnati center fielder Roberto Kelly. The swap followed complaints that Sanders was not a team player, with other Braves complaining particularly about his not bothering to show up for promotional events obligatory for the entire team.

RON SANTO

One of the National League's preeminent sluggers for most of his fifteen-year career (342 home runs, 1,331 RBIs), Santo gained almost as much attention for his off-field conflicts as for his diamond exploits. After a number of years of being regarded as a clubhouse leader for the Cubs, he fell victim to the pressures exerted by manager Leo Durocher during the club's 1969 pennant battle with the Mets, at one point turning on teammate Don Young for a key misplay in a game in what he later admitted was "the worst thing I ever did in baseball." Two years later, he had to be grabbed by teammates before throttling Durocher for the manager's false accusation that he had been holding up the Cubs to organize a Ron Santo Day at Wrigley Field. Following the 1974

season, the right-hand-hitting third baseman became the first major leaguer to insist on his five-and-ten rights by turning down a completed trade to the Angels and forcing the Cubs to send him to the crosstown White Sox.

BOB SAVERINE

Saverine had the longest day of any hitter in American League history on June 8, 1966, when he went hitless in 12 at-bats in the course of a doubleheader. The Washington second baseman's futility matched that of Red Schoendienst, who also went 0–12 in a doubleheader for the 1947 Cardinals.

EDDIE SAWYER

Sawyer managed the Whiz Kid Phillies to the pennant in 1950, but gained almost as much attention from the way he walked away from the team in a second tenure at the end of the decade. After piloting the club to a cellar finish in 1959 and seeing little improvement during spring training the following year, he waited only until Philadelphia had lost its Opening Day game before announcing his resignation. Said Sawyer: "I'm forty-nine and I want to live to be fifty."

PAT SCANTLEBURY

When he joined the Reds in 1956, pitcher Scantlebury became the last player to reach the majors from the Negro leagues. He was already thirty-nine, and lost his only decision.

AL SCHACHT

Schacht dubbed himself The Clown Prince of Baseball for his pregame act that was half pantomime, half anecdote. A member of the Clark Griffith circle, he had a 14–10 record in three years of pitching for the Senators, later going on to coach for the team.

GERMANY SCHAEFER

While he was not the only one to pull this trick and no one has ever identified the exact game in which he did pull it, Schaefer once stole first base. Executing the intended first part of a double steal, probably in 1908 against the Indians, the Detroit second baseman failed to draw a throw from the Cleveland catcher. Safe at second, he reversed tracks on the next pitch and went back to first. When this, too, failed to produce the desired result, he stole second again, and the runner on third finally scored either because the bewildered Cleveland pitcher held the ball too long or the catcher finally made the throw. (A variant has Schaefer perpetrating the reverse theft against Washington, in 1911, while with the White Sox; in this version, the Senators catcher wisely holds the ball and the runner on third never scores.) Schaefer's cunning is often credited with causing a new rule declaring a runner out if he runs the bases in reverse order, but this regulation did not appear in the books until 1920, a year after its supposed progenitor had retired.

RAY SCHALK (Hall of Fame, 1955)

Schalk's .253 batting average, the lowest compiled by any member of the Hall of Fame, has put him on many people's "Why him?" list, but he was the standout defensive catcher of his day. It also didn't hurt his Cooperstown credentials that he was the most vociferous of the White Sox players in condemning their Black Sox teammates.

When he retired in 1929 after eighteen years of service, with all but a handful of his games for the White Sox, Schalk held a host of fielding records for receivers; his marks for the most seasons pacing catchers in putouts (9) and fielding average (8), as well as for double plays (221) and most twentieth-century assists (1,811), are still in the record book. In addition, he is the only man to have been behind the plate for four no-hitters, one of which was Charlie Robertson's perfect game in 1922.

The righty-swinging Schalk did the best hitting of his career (.304) in the tainted 1919 World Series against the Reds, but spent most of the autumn in a fury. He got thrown out of game five in the 6th inning for pushing umpire Cy Rigler after a close play at the plate, more incensed with center fielder Happy Felsch for dropping a fly ball and pitcher Lefty Williams for ignoring his signs than with Rigler over the call. Later, he dragged Williams aside and worked him over with his fists for complicity in the plot. That winter the catcher dropped a few hints in an interview that several White Sox players would not be back with the team. Proven wrong, Schalk lent his name to the official complaint against the Black Sox as an injured party who had been defrauded by their behavior, and celebrated with Red Faber and Dickie Kerr when an indictment was handed down.

Schalk later managed the White Sox for a season and a half. As a rookie pilot in 1927, he expected the team to contend, but the attempted suicide of center fielder Johnny Mostil, grief-stricken over an affair with a teammate's wife, sank the White Sox chances. Years later, the death of former Chicago infielder Bill Cissell in 1949 prompted Schalk to help organize Baseball Anonymous, a benevolent society to assist needy ex-major leaguers.

JACK SCHAPPERT

Although he had only one major league season, Schappert used it to establish himself as baseball's first headhunter. The right-hander was so notorious that other American Association owners convinced the Browns' Chris Von der Ahe to drop him after the 1882 season; it was in fact due to the right-hander's penchant for hitting batters that the league decided, in 1884, to award hitters first base when struck by a delivery.

MABEL SCHLOEN

Schloen turned a successful career as a catcher into an equally successful one as a stage performer. Nicknamed Lefty even though she threw and batted right-handed, she played in the 1920s for the semipro East Rutherford (New Jersey) Cubs, for whom she once caught Walter Johnson for 3 innings in a Fenway Park exhibition game. Schloen also put on the catching gear for several exhibitions held by the Eastern League Providence Grays; while in a Providence uniform, she called the signals for another future Hall of Famer, Rube Marquard.

When Schloen wasn't crouching behind home plate, she was hitting the vaudeville circuit in such shows as *Follies* and *Powder Puff Frolic*. Her act included comedy skits about baseball—a particular she publicized to the maximum by showing up at a local game on the afternoon before an evening performance. She had less success with several silent film appearances.

Schloen attracted national attention in October 1926, when she announced that Johnson was going to drop a ball to her from the top of the Washington Monument in a reenactment of the feat accomplished in 1908 by the pitcher's one-time batterymate Gabby Street. Although Washington police refused her permission for the stunt, Schloen milked the situation for weeks, ending up with more publicity than she would have gotten had she gone through with the display.

ALLIE MAY SCHMIDT

A church worker in St. Louis, Schmidt was responsible for one of baseball's most distinctive emblems. While overseeing the decorations for a February 1921 social function to which St. Louis vice president Branch Rickey had been invited, she was struck by the sight of two cardinals perched on a snowy limb outside the church hall and created cardboard cutouts of the bird for each table. Although the St. Louis team had been called the Cardinals for some years, Rickey was so taken with the cutouts that he proposed that bird figures be added to its uniforms the following year.

HENRY SCHMIDT

Right-hander Schmidt broke in with a flourish when he posted 21 wins as a rookie for the 1903 Dodgers. Confessing that he was uncomfortable pitching in the East, however, the native Texan then retired, making him the only hurler to win 20 games in his lone big league season.

MIKE SCHMIDT (Hall of Fame, 1995)

Not even the fact that he was baseball's best all-around third baseman saved Schmidt from regular catcalls from Philadelphia fans during his eighteen-year (1972–89) career with the Phillies. More philosophical than such previous boobird targets as Del Ennis and Dick Allen, however, the right-handed slugger gradually won over the fans even when he was going bad. In fact, a poll conducted after his retirement named him as the greatest player in the history of the franchise.

Schmidt had one of the slowest starts any major leaguer had to a Hall of Fame career when he batted merely .196 and struck out 136 times in 1973, his first season as a regular. But the next year, he won the first of eight National League

Mike Schmidt powered more home runs than any other third baseman. Photo compliments of the Philadelphia Phillies.

home-run titles and the first of five slugging percentage crowns. Among his other conspicuous numbers were clouting at least 30 home runs thirteen times (and more than 40 three times), driving in 100 runs eight times (four times as the NL leader), and drawing 100 walks seven times (four times the league best). On April 17, 1976, he joined the handful of sluggers to belt four home runs in a game, in a Wrigley Field contest against the Cubs. Schmidt's biggest offensive weakness was the strikeout—leading the league in that category four times, including a glaring 180 whiffs in 1975. In the field, he was one of the first third baseman to overcome the even greater precariousness of his position provided by artificial turf, winning ten Gold Gloves and turning the most double plays six times and registering the most assists on seven occasions. Overall, he clouted 548 home runs (seventh on the all-time list) and drove in 1,595 runs while batting .267. His MVP awards in 1980, 1981, and 1986 made him one of four NL players to capture that honor as many times.

Aside from his inaugural season and the 1980 World Series against Kansas City, Schmidt's roughest moments came in the postseason. In going only 8-for-44 (.181) in the 1976 National

League Championship Series against Cincinnati and in the ensuing 1977 and 1978 championship games against Los Angeles, he was targeted by both fans and the media as the main reason for Philadelphia's failure to win three pennants. He was equally ineffective in the 1980 National League Championship Series against Houston (5 for 24, .208), but then won MVP honors by going 8-for-21 (.381) against the Royals for the Phillies' only world championship. In the 1983 World Series against Baltimore, he gave his worst postseason performance of all, managing only a single in 20 at-bats and striking out 6 times.

In the clubhouse, Schmidt had more than one clash with his manager. In 1976 he objected to Danny Ozark's exclusion of the veteran Tony Taylor from the postseason roster; in 1980 he was among the Philadelphia players singled out by Dallas Green and general manager Paul Owens as being more interested in personal statistics than in being a team player; and in 1983 he blasted Owens for taking it on himself to succeed the fired Pat Corrales and then depending too much on his coaches for every game move.

WILLARD SCHMIDT

Schmidt took a long time getting the message. A right-handed reliever with the Reds in 1959, he became the only player ever to get hit with a pitch twice in an inning. Back on the mound the next inning, he got hit by a line drive on the pitching hand that forced his removal from the game. Although he seemed to recover from the liner, appearing in 36 games during the season, he was never quite as effective as he had been, and dropped out of the league after seven years with Cincinnati and St. Louis.

RED SCHOENDIENST (Hall of Fame, 1989)

Schoendienst was a solid second baseman for nineteen seasons (1945–63) whose election to the Hall of Fame suggested to many that the Cooperstown museum has a side door. Certainly, in his heyday the switch-hitting leadoff man for the Cardinals and Braves was overshadowed at his position by first Jackie Robinson (elected) and then Nellie Fox (not elected); more embarrassing, Schoendienst's overall numbers were not much better than such a contemporary as Johnny Tem-

ple. A lifetime .289 hitter, Schoendienst had his biggest impact in 1957, when a midseason trade from the Giants to the Braves allowed him to spark Milwaukee to a pennant with a league-leading 200 hits. His best personal performance was for St. Louis in 1953, when he batted .342 and narrowly lost the batting race to Carl Furillo, who was sidelined over the final weeks of the season with a broken hand. Despite batting in the leadoff position for good-hitting teams most of his career, the redheaded infielder scored 100 runs only twice, and after a rookie season in which he paced the league with 26 stolen bases, only once again reached even double figures in thefts.

On the other hand, Schoendienst has no rivals for the length of time spent in a St. Louis uniform. After appearing for the Cardinals as a player in all or parts of fifteen seasons, he went to the coaching lines for the team in 1963 and 1964, took over as manager for another unprecedented twelve years in 1965, then returned in 1979 for another string of fifteen years as coach or fill-in pilot. His closest associate for decades, starting with their years together as roommates, was Stan Musial, who was a power on Cooperstown's Committee on Veterans when it tapped Schoendienst for a plaque.

MARGE SCHOTT

Since taking over the Cincinnati franchise in 1984, Schott has appeared alternately as a female George Steinbrenner, a Sinclair Lewis-type bean counter, and a racist ignoramus. At the same time, her often brutal handling of front-office employees, on-and-off draconian budget cutting, and casual conversational references to "niggers" and "sneaky Jews" have greatly discomfited other owners for being merely more publicized illustrations of some of their own activities and attitudes. The unease was particularly visible during the winter of 1992–93, when other owners dragged their feet for months in investigating Schott's discriminatory hiring practices; although they finally decided that she had been guilty of at least "racially and ethnically insensitive language" on numerous occasions, they resisted calls for forcing her to sell her interest in the Reds in favor of a $25,000 fine and a slap-on-the-wrist suspension that lasted little more than ten months; unchastened, Schott declared in May 1994 that she didn't want any of her players wearing earrings because "only fruits wear earrings." Even the early 1993 public relations gesture of hiring Tony Perez as manager to pad over past crudeness toward Latins had little meaning: first, because the organization simultaneously hired a host of former managers (Davey Johnson, Jack McKeon, and Bobby Valentine) to stick in the wings; second, because Perez was fired barely weeks into the season. Other episodes involving Schott have included stripping her general manager of his Riverfront Stadium seat so she could sell it to the general public; insisting that players cavort with her pet dog on the field before games; cutting back on training room and medical supplies to the point that the club physician quit; and resisting even minimal decorations in the exquisitely institutional Riverfront Stadium on the grounds that they would cost money.

PAUL SCHREIBER

Nobody waited for a second cup of coffee longer than Schreiber. A right-hander who appeared in a combined 10 games for the 1922 and 1923 Dodgers, he made his next major league appearance as a Yankee an astonishing twenty-two years later, in 1945. After adding another 2 games to his résumé, he retired for good, having neither won nor lost.

HOWIE SCHULTZ

A platoon first baseman for Brooklyn for a good part of the 1940s, Schultz led the National League in nicknames for the six feet, seven inches that made him the only major leaguer exempt from military service because of his height. Among other things, he was known as Stretch; The Steeple (he was as religious as he was tall); and, thanks to a Willard Mullin cartoon, The Leaning Tower of Flatbush. Schultz also had two dramatic at-bats in the 1946 playoffs against the Cardinals. In the 9th inning of the first game, with the Dodgers trailing by 2 runs and having runners on first and third, he singled to right to cut the margin to a run, but St. Louis right fielder Enos Slaughter threw out Bruce Edwards attempting to go from first to third. In the second game, Brooklyn went into the 9th inning trailing, 8–1, scored

3 runs, and had the bases loaded when Schultz pinch hit against Harry Brecheen. After lining a drive foul by less than a foot, he went to a full count, then struck out on a change-up.

HERB SCORE

The Gil McDougald line drive that struck Score in the face on May 7, 1957, may have been one of the goriest accidents on a major league field, but it didn't end the southpaw's big league career; a less dramatic torn elbow tendon early the following season did. After winning 16 games and leading the American League in strikeouts with an American League rookie record 254 whiffs in 1955, Score came back the following season to notch 20 wins and raise his strikeout count to 263—another pace-setting performance. Although he lingered with Cleveland for two years after the elbow injury, and also tried to make it with the White Sox, the left-hander's lost fastball doomed him to a 17–26 record in his last five years.

MIKE SCOTT

Scott was pitching guru Roger Craig's prime pupil in learning the split-finger fastball; the pitch transformed him from a so-so right-hander to the ace of the Houston staff in the second half of the 1980s. On September 25, 1986, he clinched a West Division title for the Astros by no-hitting the Giants.

VIN SCULLY

Aside from the O'Malley bloodline, sportscaster Scully has served as the most important continuum for the Dodgers from Brooklyn to Los Angeles. A protégé of Red Barber when he first occupied an Ebbets Field broadcasting booth in 1950, his mellifluous play-by-play on the radio has come in particularly handy before protests over the Dodgers' limited television coverage on the West Coast; an early 1990s poll of Dodger fans even went so far as to name him as the franchise's most valuable member.

Scully's television coverage of network games has not been received with equal enthusiasm; aside from a faintly patronizing tone toward teams that he does not see on a regular basis, he has lent himself a little too easily to the "themes" imposed on games before they are actually played. His worst moment in this regard came in the 1986 World Series, when Mets and Red Sox fans took turns at accusing him of being slanted against their team. In fact, Scully was mainly busy trying to shoehorn in the network's preestablished motif of the moment (an imminent New York defeat, an imminent Boston loss, a comeback New York win) without especially alert concern for the contradictions unfolding in front of him. He only made matters worse by claiming, after decades of working for the O'Malleys, that he has never had a personal interest in the outcome of a game.

Among the more noted Scullyisms over the years was his report that the prognosis for an injured player was that he would be "day to day"; after a beat, he added, "Aren't we all?"

TOM SEATS

Seats was a southpaw for the 1945 Dodgers who was able to go the mound for his starts only after being fed liquor by manager Leo Durocher. When teetotaling Brooklyn president Branch Rickey found out about Durocher's cure for the hurler's nerves, he got rid of Seats despite the lefty's second-best-on-the-staff 10 wins.

TOM SEAVER (Hall of Fame, 1993)

Probably the most popular pitcher ever to toe a slab in New York, Seaver still had an unusually stormy relationship with the team with which he

Grazing the ground with his right knee generated Tom Seaver's arm speed—and left his uniform dirt-stained. Photo compliments of the New York Mets.

was identified for much of his career as The Franchise. When he wasn't leaving the Mets in one of the most emotion-racked trades in baseball history, he was leaving them because they hadn't protected him in suspicious circumstances against the compensation pool draft or not joining them in favor of broadcasting for the Yankees. Two of the right-hander's most significant diamond moments—hurling his only no-hitter and notching his 300th victory—also took place while he was wearing a uniform other than that of the Mets.

Seaver's twenty-year career began with Rookie of the Year honors for his 16 wins and 2.76 ERA for New York in 1967. He had reached Shea Stadium through sheer luck—via a special lottery drawing overseen by the commissioner's office after his earlier signing by Atlanta had been ruled a violation of amateur drafting rules; losing out to the Mets in the drawing were the Phillies and Indians. After his rookie season, he won another 16 games in 1968, striking out a minimum of 200 batters for the first of nine consecutive seasons. Then came the even bigger numbers. In 1969 he led the National League with 25 wins—the first of five 20-win seasons and the first of three times that he won the Cy Young Award (the other years were 1973 and 1975). In 1970, 1971, and 1975, Seaver recorded the lowest ERA in the league, ending up with a career ratio of 2.86 to go with his 311 victories against 205 losses. He also paced NL hurlers three times in winning percentage and in strikeouts five times. His single most overpowering moment on the mound came on April 22, 1970, when he struck out the last 10 San Diego batters to come to bat in a record-tying, 19-whiff performance. He concluded his career with 3,640 strikeouts.

Aside from turning around the previously lowly Mets into a contender in the late 1960s, Seaver was a forceful clubhouse presence, at one point early in the world championship season of 1969 turning on his teammates for celebrating the fact that they had reached the .500 mark. The prize pupil of manager Gil Hodges, he was also unusually articulate with the media—a talent initially welcomed, but later turned against him by Dick Young and other stiff-necked sportswriters who didn't share his negative views of the war in Vietnam and positive appreciation of Marvin Miller's militant Players Association. Another nemesis was professed fan M. Donald Grant, the chairman of the board of the Mets, who first sought to get rid of the pitcher in the wake of the 1975 Messersmith-McNally decision, fearing that the franchise favorite would hold up the club for millions to sign again. When word leaked of Grant's attempts to deal Seaver to the Dodgers for righty Don Sutton, there was such an avalanche of protests that the team quickly negotiated another contract.

In 1977, similar tensions had a different outcome. Annoyed that the Mets had done nothing to sign outfielder Gary Matthews or other offensively gifted free agents, Seaver questioned Grant's commitment to putting a winning team on the field. That was opening enough for Young to jump in with almost daily attacks on the hurler, culminating in a June 15 column that attributed Seaver's criticisms of the organization to nothing more than his wife's envy that Nolan Ryan was making more money from the Angels. A devastated Seaver asked for a trade away from Grant and Young, and was accommodated by being shipped to Cincinnati for outfielders Steve Henderson and Dan Norman, pitcher Pat Zachry, and infielder Doug Flynn. New York reaction to what became known as the Midnight Massacre (slugger Dave Kingman was traded away in another deal the same day) ran the gamut from rage to fury. While Seaver broke down in tears before the television cameras, fans picketed Shea Stadium, others canceled season tickets, and cranks made so many menacing calls to Grant's office that he went around for the rest of the year with a bodyguard.

Seaver remained with the Reds until 1982, enjoying his best moment on June 16, 1978, against the Cardinals, when he hurled his only no-hitter. Prior to the 1983 season, he was traded back to the Mets, precipitating a New York Love-in when he went to the mound to oppose Philadelphia on Opening Day. He went through the rest of the year pitching well for a bad team, and was rumored to be a top candidate for the team's managerial position in 1984. Instead, the job went to Davey Johnson, who in one of his first public statements emphasized that he wanted to bring his young pitchers from the International League (Dwight Gooden, Ron Darling, and Walt Terrell)

with him to New York. It was in light of this stated intention that some writers subsequently interpreted an avowed Met "mistake" in leaving Seaver off the protected forty-man roster and exposing him to a draft in the compensation pool by the White Sox. While the pitcher once again questioned the ways of the Mets front office, general manger Frank Cashen lashed out at the White Sox for being insensitive to the feelings of New York fans, and Johnson didn't say much of anything. It was mainly because of Chicago's grab of Seaver that the compensation pool was eliminated soon afterward.

Seaver's last big moment as a player in New York came on August 4, 1985, when, as a member of the White Sox, he notched his 300th victory against the Yankees at Yankee Stadium. The following year, he was sold to the Red Sox for pennant insurance; although injuries kept him off the active roster, he was in the Boston dugout as the Mets came from behind to defeat the Red Sox in the 1986 World Series.

After retiring as a player, Seaver teamed up with Phil Rizzuto to do Yankee telecasts. Regular reports that he was about to rejoin the Mets as either a broadcaster or front-office executive seemed to die merely in being reported or in some persisting gap between having once been the franchise pitcher and the pitcher the franchise wasn't always eager to have.

PAT SEEREY

Of the twelve major leaguers who have hit four home runs in a game, the least likely has been Seerey, who accomplished the feat for the White Sox against the Athletics on July 18, 1948. The overweight outfielder entered the history books little more than a month after Cleveland had despaired of his strikeout rate and fielding lapses and traded him to Chicago. Seerey's shots came in the course of an 11-inning game; only he and Mike Schmidt have needed extra innings to join the 4-home-run club. Aside from his performance against Philadelphia, the right-handed slugger performed for Chicago as he had for Cleveland— sandwiching the occasional long ball between strikeouts and errors. The following year he was out of the league, retiring with 86 home runs and

485 strikeouts in less than 2,000 at-bats and a career average of .224.

PETER SEITZ

Seitz was the impartial arbitrator who, on December 23, 1975, ruled that Los Angeles righthander Andy Messersmith and Montreal lefthander Dave McNally could not be tied to their teams by an automatic turnover of baseball's reserve clause. The decision effectively authorized all players to become free agents one year after the expiration of the specific duration of their contracts. Seitz announced his verdict after some weeks of hinting to both Players Association chief Marvin Miller and owners' representative John Gaherin what his ruling would be, suggesting that they seek a compromise before it was too late. Although both Miller and Gaherin were in favor of compromise negotiations, the latter could not persuade the owners of such a course. The key part of the Seitz declaration said: "The grievances of Messersmith and McNally are sustained. There is no contractual bond between these players and the Los Angeles and Montreal clubs, respectively. Absent such a contract, their clubs had no right or power, under the Basic Agreement, the uniform player contract, or the Major League Rules to reserve their services for their exclusive use for any period beyond the 'renewal year' in the contracts which these players had heretofore signed with their clubs."

FRANK SELEE

The first long-term successful manager who had never played in the major leagues, Selee won five pennants for Boston in the 1890s, built the Cub roster that won four pennants under successor Frank Chance between 1906 and 1910, and holds the fourth-highest won-lost percentage (.598) among managers with more than two seasons on the job. Among Selee's skills was relocating players to the positions where their talents were most suitable; those he shifted included Bobby Lowe (from an outfielder to a second baseman), and Fred Tenney and Frank Chance (both from catcher-outfielders to first basemen). The manager surrendered the helm at Chicago to

Chance in mid-1905 after discovering he was suffering from tuberculosis.

BUD SELIG

Selig has been Mr. Baseball in Milwaukee for thirty-five years, but this role as acting commissioner around the events of the 1994 players strike made him Mr. No Baseball for the rest of the country.

The automobile dealer's quest to bring major league baseball to Wisconsin began when, as a charter member of the group that resisted the departure of the Braves in the mid-1960s, he forced the club to spend an unhappy lame duck year in Milwaukee before its inevitable departure to Atlanta. He also played a prominent part in convincing the White Sox to play 10 home games in the city in 1968, as well as in the boosterism that had those 10 games account for one-third of the White Sox' total home attendance for the year. Denied an expansion franchise in 1969, Selig headed a group (including Robert Uihlein of Schlitz breweries, Ralph Evinrude of the outboard motor company, and meatpacker Oscar Mayer) that bought the expansion Pilots in 1970 for an overpriced $10.8 million with the intention of moving them to Milwaukee as the Brewers. Even after the American League accepted the offer during the 1969 World Series, however, legal action in Seattle kept the deal up in the air until March 31 of the following year. His most dramatic act as owner was the November 19, 1977, firing of manager Alex Grammas and general manager Jim Baumer and replacing them with George Bamberger and Harry Dalton, respectively; the arrival of what became known as The Dalton Gang of front-office staffers ushered in the franchise's most successful seasons. For twenty-five years Selig has run the Brewers within a strict budget, managing to win a second-half title in the split season of 1981 and an American League pennant in 1982 but also having to endure many lean seasons because of an inability to keep blossoming players in the free-agent era.

Selig was White Sox owner Jerry Reinsdorf's chief ally in dumping Commissioner Fay Vincent in 1992. Asked to fill in as interim commissioner, Selig has resisted suggestions that he assume the position on some terms other than as a caretaker;

the other major league owners have, for their part, been in no hurry to name an outsider as his permanent successor. For the most part, the functioning of major league baseball without a commissioner for two years showed little appreciable difference from baseball with someone in that position. One dubious difference manifested itself in June 1994, after Selig suspended Mets pitcher Dwight Gooden for two months for failing a drug test. The action raised questions about the Milwaukee owner's latitude for dealing with AL players having a direct bearing on the field fortunes of the Brewers.

In his double role as a team owner and acting commissioner, Selig became for many a symbol of the counterproductive tactics of the owners in the 1994 labor conflict with the players. Rather than win sympathy for his side, his bumpkinish manner and mechanical repetitions of the owners' line gave credence to the view that he was merely a mouthpiece for others, especially Reinsdorf.

JOE SEWELL (Hall of Fame, 1977)

No one who played in the major leagues for any length of time struck out less often than Sewell. In a fourteen-year (1920–33) career, the lefty-hitting infielder whiffed a mere 114 times in 7,132 official at-bats, including three full-season totals of only 4 and one 109-game year with just 3. He joined the Indians in September 1920 to play shortstop after Ray Chapman was killed by a Carl Mays beanball and replacement Harry Lunte was injured on Labor Day. Sewell went on to record averages higher than .300 nine times, bang out at least 40 doubles on five occasions, and drive in more than 100 runs twice. Moved to third base in 1929, he was released following the 1930 season (after batting .289) and closed out his career by playing third for the Yankees from 1931 to 1933. Sewell's lifetime average was .312.

RIP SEWELL

Sewell was a crowd-pleasing right-hander for the Pirates during the World War II years for a blooper that was dubbed the eephus ball. The name was the creation of Pittsburgh outfielder Maurice Van Robays, who explained that "an eephus ain't nothin', and that's what that ball is." Sewell added the pitch to his arsenal as the result of a December 1941 hunting accident that forced him to deliver the ball with a banged-up toe held upward. The tantalizingly high arc to the slow pitch caused as much trouble for umpires as it offered entertainment to fans. It was, in fact, only after Pittsburgh complained to the league office that umpires were automatically recording the delivery as a ball that umpire Bill Klem ordered Sewell to give him a special demonstration and, satisfying himself that it did indeed enter the strike zone, passed the word that it should be judged like any other pitch. The eephus's most dramatic moment came in the 1946 All-Star Game, when Ted Williams became the only player ever to hit one for a home run. For Sewell, however, it had a far more significant effect in turning him into a winner: After leading the National League in losses in 1941, he used his new pitch to win 17 in 1942, a league-leading 21 in 1943, and another 21 in 1944.

Sewell's days in Pittsburgh were not always so pleasant. In 1946 he was the chief team spokesman against the unionizing efforts of Robert Murphy's American Baseball Guild. When the Murphy initiative failed, the pitcher was presented with a watch by Commissioner Happy Chandler for his promanagement stand—a ceremony that only increased tensions in the Pittsburgh clubhouse between pro- and antiunion factions.

BOBBY SHANTZ

Nothing else Shantz accomplished in his sixteen-year (1949–64) career—including his MVP year in 1954—was as spectacular as his 9 consecutive no-hit innings in relief in his second major league appearance. With only two-thirds of an inning of major league experience under his belt, the left-hander replaced Carl Scheib in the 4th inning on May 6, 1949, for the Athletics, set down the Tigers without a safety through the 12th inning, and recorded his first major league victory despite giving up 2 hits and a run in the 13th inning. He took MVP honors for fifth-place Philadelphia in 1952 with an AL-leading 24 wins. Injuries relegated Shantz to the bullpen thereafter, but he had enough left to lead the league in ERA (2.45) in 1957, his first year with the Yankees. After bouncing around with five National League teams in his last four seasons, he retired with a 119–99 career record.

BILL SHARMAN

Basketball Hall of Famer Sharman is the only player ever to be thrown out of a baseball game without appearing in one. The future Boston Celtic had been called up to the Dodgers from the minors and was in the visitors' dugout at Braves Field in Boston on September 27, 1951, when umpire Frank Dascoli cleared the bench in retaliation for the abuse he had been taking over a close play at the plate that had gone against Brooklyn. Sharman later went back to the minors without ever getting his name into a box score.

BOB SHAW

Shaw won 108 games for several teams in the 1950s and 1960s, but had his biggest impact on the game as a member of the 1964 San Francisco Giants when he taught Gaylord Perry how to throw the spitball. The right-hander had his own delivery problems as a member of the Braves on May 4, 1963, when he committed a record-setting 5 balks in a single game.

WILLIAM SHEA

Shea was a New York lawyer prominent in the organization of the Continental League following the 1957 departure of the Giants and Dodgers to California. Mainly a stalking-horse for forcing an expansion of the National League, the Continental League spawned the Astros and Mets, and the latter named their Flushing Meadows stadium after Shea.

TOM SHEEHAN

Sheehan became the oldest rookie manager in major league history in June 1960 when he took over the Giants two months past his sixty-sixth birthday. He had worked for many years as an organization scout, and returned to that role after going 46–50 (.479) as San Francisco's dugout boss.

FRANK SHELLENBACK

Nobody suffered from the 1920 ban against spitballers more than Shellenback. Because he had been farmed out after two mediocre seasons with them, the White Sox forgot to include him on the list of practicing spitballers who were exempt from the regulation. Not able to use his best pitch, the right-hander never made it back to the majors. Shellenback had his consolations, however. For one thing, he won 315 minor league games over the next twenty years. While coaching for the Red Sox in the early 1940s, he had on his staff Nelson Potter, later to be the first major leaguer suspended for throwing a spitball since the adoption of the 1920 rule. Shellenback was also the pitching coach for the Giants in the 1950s when Sal Maglie, Ruben Gomez, and others were accused of putting more than mustard on the ball.

BERT SHEPARD

Shepard was a minor league pitcher who lost a leg when he was shot down over Germany in World War II. Hired as a coach by Washington in 1945 as a public relations gesture, he was brought into a laugher against the Red Sox on August 14, proceeding to yield only one run in 5⅓ innings. The left-hander was also able to maneuver well enough on a wooden leg to come to bat 3 times. Shepard never appeared in another major league game.

LARRY SHERRY

Sherry is the only pitcher to figure in four winning statistics in a World Series. In the 1959 Series against the White Sox, the Dodger reliever chalked up 2 wins and 2 saves. Los Angeles might never have gotten that far if the right-hander hadn't been called up in the closing weeks of the season. In a year that ended with a special playoff against the Braves, Sherry won 7 games and saved 3 others down the stretch.

BEN SHIBE

A partner of Al Reach in both a sporting goods business and the Phillies, Shibe effectively sacrificed the latter venture for the former when he agreed, in 1901, to become half-owner and president of the American League Athletics as well. His motivation for double dipping in the Philadelphia market was a commitment by AL president Ban Johnson to give the Reach firm exclusive manufacturing rights to league balls. Although Reach and Shibe were compelled to sell their share of the Phillies after the 1902 season, the industrial partnership continued until Shibe's death in 1922. The company profited greatly from

Shibe's patents on the machines that wind the yarn in baseballs and that punch the stitching holes in their covers; he also designed the cork-and-rubber-centered ball that replaced the rubber-only core and that sent batting averages soaring in 1911. Shibe's association with the A's also lasted the rest of his life, and Shibe Park, the first concrete and steel stadium, was named for him when it opened in 1909.

BEN SHIELDS

Shields has more wins—4—without a loss than any other pitcher. The lefty's perfect record took 13 appearances over four seasons (1924–25 with the Yankees, 1930 with the Red Sox, and 1931 with the Phillies); his lifetime ERA was a less-than-perfect 8.27.

BILL SHINDLE

In 1890, Shindle made 115 errors (modern sabermetrics have run the figure up to 122), a season total officially recognized as the highest for any player at any position. The footnote to this record is that Shindle was the regular shortstop for the Players League Philadelphia Quakers that year, whereas in his twelve additional major league seasons he was almost exclusively a third baseman.

ART SHIRES

If Shires wasn't the most violent player in baseball history, it wasn't for lack of trying. For openers, his brief four-year career was bracketed by an attempted killing and a killing.

A cocky first baseman, Shires joined the White Sox at the end of the 1928 season, got 4 hits in his first game, and so impressed manager Lena Blackburne that he was appointed team captain for the following year. Blackburne began to have second thoughts at spring training when his ostensible field leader knocked him down for suggesting that bright red party hats were not appropriate attire for batting practice. On two other occasions during the season, Shires used his fists to respond to Blackburne threats, also belting Chicago traveling secretary Lou Barbour in a dispute over hotel accommodations. Despite Shires's .312 batting average, he was suspended by the club, amassing fines of $3,000. To make up for

the money he lost on baseball, Art the Great, as he liked to call himself, hooked up with boxing trainer Jack Blackburn for several fights. He won his first bout against a construction worker, lost his second to professional football player George Trafton, won or lost a few more depending on the memory of the judges, but succeeded in making enough money to erase his White Sox fines and then some. The show came to an end, however, when he challenged Hack Wilson of the Cubs to a ring meeting and Commissioner Kenesaw Landis stepped in to ban major leaguers from any kind of organized boxing.

When his fight money dried up, the disgruntled Shires demanded a $25,000 contract from Charlie Comiskey; after more than one accusation that the Chicago owner was a cheapskate, he settled for $7,000. Once his hitting fell off in 1930, Comiskey was only too pleased to trade him away to the Senators. Shires the ballplayer had one big shot left in him: After telling Washington reporters that he was playing in the city where ''phony politicians think it's their job to cheat the country,'' he went out and got 3 hits to beat his former teammates from Chicago. It made for his last big headlines on the sports pages.

There were other pages in the newspaper, however. Even before coming up with the White Sox in 1928, Shires had fired a ball at a black spectator in Waco prior to a Texas League game; although the man was severely injured, no charges were pressed. In 1948 he was charged with murdering a longtime friend. Despite his own admission that ''I had to rough him up a good deal because he grabbed a knife and started whittling on my legs,'' Shires was acquitted because of medical testimony that said the victim had actually died of natural causes brought on by preexisting conditions of pneumonia and cirrhosis of the liver.

ERNIE SHORE

Except for Lou Gehrig, no player was more associated with Babe Ruth than Shore. The right-hander was on the same minor league team as Ruth in Baltimore from where they were both dealt to the Red Sox for $8,000 for the 1914 season. Together they helped pitch Boston to pennants in 1915 and 1916, also fashioning superb performances in the World Series of both years. On June 13, 1917, their association was cemented for good when Ruth walked the leadoff batter in a game against Washington, got ejected for protesting, and was replaced by Shore. In what amounted to the greatest relief appearance ever turned in at a major league level, Shore watched the Senators' runner get thrown out and then retired the next 26 batters for what is considered a perfect game. In December 1918 the pitchers became linked still again when Shore was traded to the Yankees by Boston owner Harry Frazee, who was desperate for cash. The trade would turn out to be only the first in a decade-long New York stripping of Fenway Park's best talents; the most notorious of the deals occurred in January 1920, when Ruth followed Shore to New York.

BOB SHORT

Short was responsible for bringing American League baseball to Texas—and leaving Washington without it, again. A Minnesota hotel entrepreneur and onetime treasurer of the Democratic National Committee, he bought the second twentieth-century version of the Senators in January 1969, then spent the next three years trying to hide his inept club by importing distracting gate names. Among his key moves was hiring Ted Williams as manager, trading for the scandal-ridden former 30-game winner Denny McLain, and signing Curt Flood while the outfielder was still in the midst of challenging baseball's reserve clause. All the while, Short was also setting the stage for transferring the franchise to Texas: He defaulted on rent payments for Robert F. Kennedy Stadium on the grounds that he was out of money, and he challenged Commissioner Bowie Kuhn and AL owners to come up with a buyer who would make up his original $9 million outlay plus another $3 million for the expenses he had incurred along the way. After various buyer-candidates were turned down for one reason or another, Kuhn and the league had little choice but to approve the shift to Dallas-Fort Worth after the 1971 season.

In Texas, Short distinguished himself mainly by insisting that manager Whitey Herzog stick David Clyde, a raw eighteen-year-old just out of high school, in the Rangers' 1973 rotation. On the positive side, the left-hander's starts accounted for almost one-third of the club's 686,000 attendance during the year; negatively, the forced feeding proved to be too much for Clyde, and he never won more than 8 games in a season. In September 1973, Short fired Herzog for Billy Martin, telling newsmen that "if my mother were managing the Rangers and I had the opportunity to hire Billy Martin, I'd fire my mother." Martin didn't have much time to act flattered: A couple of months later, Short sold out to a consortium headed by industrial parts manufacturer Brad Corbett.

BURT SHOTTON

A slap-hitting outfielder for some fourteen seasons, Shotton had stints with the St. Louis Browns and Cardinals that were only the start of his long career as Branch Rickey's right-hand man. Even while still active, he managed the Cardinals on Sundays in Rickey's stead because of the latter's rigid observance of the Sabbath. It was on the Mahatma's endorsement that Shotton later managed Philadelphia (to preside over the worst team in Phillies' history) and got coaching jobs with Cincinnati and Cleveland. More dramatically, he was Rickey's choice to manage the Dodgers after Leo Durocher was suspended for the 1947 season. When the Giants sought Shotton's services the following year, Rickey said no, allowing them to hire Durocher instead. Although he remained at Brooklyn's helm through the 1950 season, Shotton wasn't particularly visible at Ebbets Field: Because he declined to wear a uniform, he had to remain on the bench, sending coaches out to change pitchers or argue with umpires.

WILLIAM SIANIS

Sianis was a Chicago saloonkeeper who put a hex on the Cubs after Wrigley Field refused to admit him for the 1945 World Series against Detroit in the company of his pet goat. The team has never appeared again in a World Series. In 1994, one of the original goat's descendants was flown from Milwaukee to the ballpark to break the spell of 10 consecutive home losses by the club; it didn't work any magic that day, but the Cubs finally won a home game a couple of days later. Sianis's Billy Goat Tavern was the model for a series of comedy routines on television's *Saturday Night Live*.

AL SIMMONS (Hall of Fame, 1953)

Despite his foot-in-the-bucket batting stance, Simmons became a feared slugger and the player Connie Mack chose as the one who, if cloned nine times, would make up the perfect team.

The right-hand-hitting outfielder hit .334 in twenty seasons between 1924 and 1944, leading the American League in batting with averages of .381 in 1930 and .390 in 1931. He also paced AL batters in hits twice (among his six 200-hit seasons), RBIs once (among twelve 100 RBI performances), and runs scored once (among six seasons topping the century mark in that category). Simmons also reached double numbers in home runs thirteen times, including three seasons with more than 30. His most memorable diamond moment came in Philadelphia's 10-run 7th inning in the fourth game of the 1929 World Series; with the A's trailing, 8–0, he homered to lead off the inning, then singled in the tying run as the team batted around on its way to scoring a record 10 runs in the frame.

Unloaded by Mack after the 1932 season, Simmons spent three productive years with the White Sox before being sold to the Tigers, managed by former teammate Mickey Cochrane. Cochrane figured Simmons as insurance for a third consecutive pennant, in 1936; when that failed to materialize despite Simmons's .327 average and 112 RBIs, the pilot's acerbic tongue went to work on the outfielder, who responded in kind.

From 1937 to 1941, Simmons drifted from the Senators to the Braves to the Reds and back to the Athletics, posting some relatively good batting averages during increasingly limited service. He even returned, with Boston and the A's (again), during World War II with a loudly announced pursuit of his 3,000th hit, eventually falling short by 73 safeties.

TED SIMMONS

Simmons came close to beating Andy Messersmith and Dave McNally to the punch in challenging the reserve clause. Emboldened by Curt Flood's suit against the automatic option in baseball contracts, the St. Louis receiver announced that he intended playing the 1972 season without a pact, then declaring free agency afterward. He held out until August 9, when he agreed to a two-year contract covering 1972 and 1973.

The switch-hitting Simmons had a twenty-one-year (1968–88) career for the Cardinals, Brewers, and Braves, batting .285 and knocking in more than 100 runs three times. After retiring as a player, he served for a brief period as general manager of the Pirates, but became so aggravated at having to dump high-salaried stars such as southpaw John Smiley for budgetary reasons that he suffered heart stress and had to quit.

HARRY SINCLAIR

Oil millionaire Sinclair was lured into backing the Federal League in the circuit's second year of operation. Taking over the pennant-winning but unprofitable Indianapolis franchise and moving it to Newark in 1915, he arrived with plans to use the New Jersey city as a gateway to the New York market. It didn't turn out quite that way, but Sinclair, who was once described as having half the money in the world with John D. Rockefeller holding the other half, made a good show of it. First, he offered Giants manager John McGraw $100,000 to pilot the Peppers. Then, following the 1915 season, he took over the foundering Kansas City Packers and announced his intention of combining the two clubs into a New York entry in 1916. He went so far as to apply to the city for permits to close off streets at the proposed construction site of a new $800,000 stadium, and to unveil designs by architect C. B. Comstock for a double-decked grandstand with no obstructing posts. Challenging the owners of the three established New York clubs, he offered to "stand at the Battery and match any of them in pitching dollars into New York Harbor. We'll see who quits first."

It was all a giant bluff. And it worked. In the ensuing peace treaty, Sinclair was awarded a direct $100,000 buyout and the right to sell off FL players to American League and National League clubs. As a result, he was among the few backers of the Feds to emerge with a profit. Sinclair later became a central figure in the Teapot Dome Scandal, allegedly bribing Secretary of the Interior Albert B. Ball in 1922. While acquitted of conspiracy charges, Sinclair was found guilty of contempt of Congress and sentenced to three months in jail.

BILL SINGER

Singer had 20-win seasons for both the Dodgers and Angels, but his greatest impact was on a team for which he never played. Prior to the 1977 season, the right-hander was traded by the Blue Jays to the Yankees for a New York prospect. But when Toronto realized that Singer was on the cover of the expansion franchise's first media guide, it called off the deal so as not to give the impression of instability in its inaugural year. The New York prospect who should have gone to Canada was Ron Guidry. Singer had a 2–8 mark in 1977, then retired.

While with the Dodgers in 1969, Singer was the first pitcher formally credited with the new computation category of save. Saves compiled before that season were ascribed retroactively.

DICK SISLER

A lefty first baseman-outfielder who never hit more than 13 home runs in any of his eight major league seasons, Sisler banged the most dramatic homer in Philadelphia history in the 10th inning of the final game of 1950. The 3-run, opposite-field blast off Brooklyn ace Don Newcombe gave the Whiz Kids the pennant. In 1964 Sisler came under other pressures when he had to take over as Cincinnati manager from the cancer-ridden Fred Hutchinson during a four-team brawl for the pennant. Because Hutchinson's condition made the Reds the sentimental favorite around the country, Sisler took a lot of gratuitous press criticism when he could lead the team only to second place. As the son of Hall of Famer George Sisler, he once told reporters, he was "used to the expectations of others."

GEORGE SISLER (Hall of Fame, 1939)

Considered by many the greatest defensive first baseman of all time, the .340-hitting Sisler was no slouch at the plate either. But none of his considerable on-field exploits contained the high drama and intrigue of his circuitous route to the Browns, for whom he was the all-time franchise player.

George Sisler was as noted for his baserunning as for his hitting. National Baseball Library, Cooperstown, N.Y.

Signing with the Akron team of the Ohio-Pennsylvania League when he was only seventeen years old, Sisler became the ostensible property of the Pirates when club owner Barney Dreyfuss purchased his contract in 1912. In the meantime, however, he elected to attend the University of Michigan, where he became the foremost college player of the period, under coach Branch Rickey. With Sisler's graduation approaching, Dreyfuss pressed his claim with the National Commission. Advised by Rickey, Sisler argued against the Pittsburgh claim on the grounds that he had been underage when he signed the Akron contract, was declared a free agent in January 1915, and signed with the Browns, whose manager at the time was none other than Rickey. The fallout from the Commission's decision was that Dreyfuss soured on its erratic governance of baseball and later joined with the forces seeking to replace it with a single commissioner.

Sisler arrived in St. Louis as a southpaw pitcher, posting a 4–4 record (with an ERA of

2.83) in 1915, while playing first base part time. Shifted to first permanently the following year, the lefty swinger went on to a fifteen-year career in which he batted over .400 twice (and no lower than .341 between 1917 and 1922); established the major league season mark for most base hits (257, in 1920); averaged an AL high of .420 in 1922; and, in addition to the pair of .400-plus batting crowns, paced American Leaguers in stolen bases four times, in hits one additional year, and in triples and runs scored once each. Defensively, Sisler's career record of 1,528 assists held up for almost sixty years, until broken by Keith Hernandez. Sisler was a master of the 3–6–3 double play, pulling off 13 of them in 1920. His most astonishing play came in a game against the Senators, when he charged an attempted squeeze bunt by Roger Peckinpaugh, tagged the batter as he ran to first, and threw home to catch the runner coming from third for a double play.

Sisler's lifetime average of .340 might have been even higher but for an attack of sinusitis that caused an infection in his optic nerves and left him with double vision for more than a year. After sitting out the 1923 season, he returned in 1924 to bat higher than .300 six more times (with the Senators and Braves as well as St. Louis), but was never again the dominant force he had been.

SEYMOUR SIWOFF

As general manager of the Elias Sports Bureau in the 1960s, Siwoff pioneered the use of computers in assembling sports statistics. His innovation made possible the breakdown of player statistics into almost every conceivable subcategory: how batters performed against right-handers and southpaws, in day and night contests, on grass and artificial surfaces, and in late innings. Between 1985 and 1993 he published *The Elias Baseball Analyst,* a popular compilation of such breakdowns. Elias, the official statistician of the National and American leagues, has been compiling figures since 1916.

JOEL SKINNER

Catcher Skinner was the first player picked up (by the White Sox from the Pirates) in the short-lived compensation pool created in the early 1980s as a means of giving something back to teams that had lost free agents. The scheme—which made vulnerable any club engaging in free-agent signings—ended after a couple of years, partly because of the uproar caused when the same White Sox snatched New York favorite Tom Seaver away from the Mets.

ENOS SLAUGHTER (Hall of Fame, 1985)

Baseball's model hustler, Slaughter batted an even .300 in nineteen seasons with the Cardinals, Yankees, and other teams. In one season or another, he led the National League in hitting (1942), RBIs (1946), hits (1942), doubles (1939), and triples (1942 and 1946). The lefty-swinging right fielder also had a strong arm, coming up with a critical assist in the 1946 playoffs against the Dodgers when he nailed a runner at third in the 9th inning of a 1-run game. In that year's World Series against the Red Sox, Slaughter entered major league lore in the 8th inning of game seven by scoring from first on a Harry Walker double after Boston shortstop Johnny Pesky hesitated on a relay throw to the plate; Slaughter's slide across the plate, captured in a memorable photograph, gave St. Louis the world championship. As a member of the Yankees in 1956, he provided another indelible picture when he was pulled away from a melee with the White Sox with his jersey ripped off his chest and his cap askew.

ROY SMALLEY, SR.

Smalley became such a notorious presence at shortstop for the Cubs in the 1950s, that Wrigley Field fans were given to chanting an updated version of the Tinker-to-Evers-to-Chance refrain: "Miksis to Smalley to Addison Street." In 1950, the infielder reached his nadir with 51 errors and a .945 fielding average.

AL SMITH

Being a member of the 1959 pennant-winning White Sox was not all roses for Smith. Booed for a good part of the season for some shoddy defense and lackluster hitting, the left fielder became so depressed that Chicago owner Bill Veeck decided to buoy his spirits by staging Al Smith Night at Comiskey Park, allowing anybody named Smith or its similars free admission. Before thousands of fans sporting buttons that declared ''I'm a Smith and I'm for Al,'' he dropped a late-inning fly ball that allowed Boston to edge Chicago, 7–6. In that year's World Series against the Dodgers, his humiliation went national when he was photographed being drenched by a cup of beer from the left-field stands as he stood against the wall watching a Charlie Neal homer. Smith, who batted a solid .272 over twelve major league seasons, was the only player outside of Early Wynn who represented the American League in the two World Series of the 1950s that did not include the Yankees; he was also a member of the 1954 Indians.

ELMER SMITH

An outfielder for the 1920 Indians, Smith hit the first World Series grand-slam home run. He did it in the 1st inning of game five against Brooklyn's Burleigh Grimes.

LEE SMITH

Smith entered the 1995 season with 434 saves—the most by any major league reliever. The right-hander forged ahead of Jeff Reardon and Rollie Fingers despite being written off by four different teams as finished at various points in his fifteen-year career. His biggest seasons were with the Cardinals in 1991 and 1992, when he led the National League with 47 and 43 saves, respectively. St. Louis let him go to the Yankees near the end of the 1993 season, and New York declined to offer him a multiyear free-agent pact—both clubs contending that he had seen his best days. Smith had heard the same talk when the Cubs traded him to the Red Sox in 1988 for mediocre pitchers Al Nipper and Calvin Schiraldi; with Chicago, Smith had posted at least 30 saves four years in a row and led the NL in that category a fifth time. An identical refrain was heard in 1990, when Boston had to choose between Smith and Reardon, decided the former was less promising, and dealt him to the Cardinals. Smith signed as a free agent with Baltimore for the 1994 season and with California in 1995..

LONNIE SMITH

Smith is the only player to appear in the World Series for four different teams. The right-hand-

hitting outfielder performed for Philadelphia in 1980, St. Louis in 1982, Kansas City in 1985, and Atlanta in both 1991 and 1992. In game seven of the 1991 Series against the Twins, he pulled one of the biggest gaffes in the history of postseason play when he led off the 8th inning of a scoreless duel by singling, then was decoyed by Minnesota second baseman Chuck Knoblauch into breaking his stride around the bases on a subsequent double by Terry Pendleton. The hesitation made it impossible for Smith to get beyond third base, where he was ultimately stranded, and the Twins ended up winning the game—and the world championship—in the 10th inning, 1–0. While a speedster who swiped as many as 68 bases in a year, Smith gained the nickname of Skates for his regular tumbles in the outfield while pursuing fly balls.

OZZIE SMITH

Touted as the greatest defensive shortstop of all time, Smith nevertheless had his most dramatic diamond moment with a 9th-inning, game five-winning home run in the 1985 National League Championship Series. The switch-hitter's blow off Los Angeles right-hander Tom Niedenfuer came batting left-handed for the Cardinals as a graphic on the Busch Stadium scoreboard was telling the crowd (and announcer Vin Scully was informing the television audience) that he had never reached the seats from the left side of the plate in his major league career. The home run helped set up a pennant win for St. Louis in game six.

Brought to the majors by San Diego, Smith established the major league mark for most assists by a shortstop (621) in 1980. With both the Padres and (since 1982) the Cardinals, he earned the sobriquet The Wizard of Oz by winning thirteen consecutive Gold Gloves (1980–92), making 500 or more assists in a record eight seasons, and leading the National League in both assists and chances accepted a record eight times. An accomplished acrobat who regularly did pregame flips on the field until advised by doctors to stop, Smith has used his tumbling ability to good purpose: He customarily throws on the run, and dives for ground balls, bouncing to his feet and throwing in a seemingly seamless motion. His most noted defensive play was on a bad-hop grounder up the middle by Atlanta's Bob Horner: Diving to his left with his glove outstretched, Smith reached back, caught the ball barehanded after it bounded up behind him, and threw Horner out.

A baserunning threat as well, the shortstop averaged more than 34 thefts in his first sixteen seasons. While with San Diego in 1980, he stole 57 bases to join Gene Richards (61) and Jerry Mumphrey (54) as the only trio of teammates to pilfer more than 50 in the same season.

As a member of the Padres in the late 1970s, Smith was so badly paid that he took out an ad asking for work as a gardener. With the Cardinals in the early 1990s, he ran into so much reluctance by the front office to give him a new multimillion-dollar contrat that he became a *cause célèbre* in St. Louis, with fans finally pressuring general manager Dal Maxvill to offer the popular infielder another pact.

REGGIE SMITH

On the field, Smith was a solid slugger for most of his seventeen-year (1966–82) career who established several switching-hitting records before the coming of Eddie Murray and Howard Johnson. Off the field, however, the outfielder figured prominently in the clubhouse friction that characterized the Red Sox in the early 1970s and the Dodgers at the end of the decade. With Boston in particular, Smith was a vocal critic of Marvin Miller's union tactics, joining with teammates Carl Yastrzemski and Butch Hobson in stressing their gratitude to owner Tom Yawkey; this led to some physical confrontations in the Boston locker room, most notably with Bill Lee. With Los Angeles in the 1970s, Smith groused over the preferential media treatment given regularly to Steve Garvey despite numbers that were at least the equivalent to those of the popular first baseman. When Don Sutton took up his cause and pointedly told newsmen that Smith was the most valuable player on the club, the pitcher and Garvey ended up swapping punches.

Between the lines, Smith clouted 30 home runs in 1971 and 1977; in the latter year, he was one of four record-setting Dodgers to reach the 30-homer plateau. On August 25, 1981, he was a principal in a bizarre fight when he screamed out from the bench for Pittsburgh right-hander Pas-

cual Perez to stop brushing back so many Dodger hitters, Perez charged off the hill after the inning, the two players led both teams into the runway behind the Pirates' dugout, and there began pushing and shoving while sixteen thousand fans in Three Rivers Stadium stared at an empty diamond. It took the umpires ten minutes to get the teams back into their dugouts; since the fracas was considered "private," nobody was ejected.

TAL SMITH

Smith created a new baseball occupation when he formed a company to handle arbitration hearings for major league front offices in late 1980. Attracted to the head-to-head confrontation of arbitration even though he had lost his only two cases while serving as general manager of the Astros from 1975 to 1980, he first offered his services to the Athletics, winning out over pitcher Mike Norris and outfielder Tony Armas. By 1982 Smith was handling eight cases for a variety of clubs—and winning seven of them. While his winning percentage dropped to a more realistic .500 in ensuing years, Tal Smith Enterprises soon took over representation of thirteen of the twenty-six major league organizations in arbitration.

Smith went into his consulting work after building up the Houston team that won the West Division title in 1980. He was fired soon after the League Championship Series because owner John McMullen couldn't afford the attendance clause in his contract. In 1984 he branched out to do an appraisal of the Red Sox for Haywood Sullivan and Jean Yawkey as part of their buyout of Buddy Leroux in the ownership of the franchise. In February 1989, Smith was hired to bring order to the Padres front office following the resignation of club president Chub Feeney at the end of the 1988 season, while owner Joan Kroc concentrated on finding a buyer for the club.

WENDELL SMITH

Smith played a major role in most midcentury events leading to the racial integration of baseball. While covering the Kansas City Monarchs for a Pittsburgh daily in 1945, he arranged for Jackie Robinson and two other Negro league players to have a tryout with the Red Sox. Although it was an empty exercise primarily aimed at defusing

City Hall pressures on owner Tom Yawkey for desegregation, Smith immediately afterward tipped off Dodger president Branch Rickey about Robinson. Rickey later hired him to accompany Robinson on road trips during the infielder's rookie year.

As a reporter for the Chicago *Herald American* in the late 1940s, Smith became the first black sportswriter to have a byline in a major white newspaper. In the 1960s, he wrote an investigative series that effectively put an end to Jim Crow housing in baseball spring training camps. In 1994, he was inducted into the writers' wing of the Hall of Fame.

JEFF SMULYAN

The chief of the Emmis Broadcasting Company, Smulyan bought the Mariners from George Argyros in August 1989. The agreement committed him to keeping the club in Seattle, but Smulyan wasted little time in launching a three-year-long lament about how lack of television prospects doomed the franchise no matter how greatly attendance improved during his ownership. Although he adamantly denied having bought the club to move it to the Emmis headquarters in Indianapolis, he did acknowledge in 1991 that he had been holding talks with officials in St. Petersburg for moving the Mariners to Florida. The admission set in motion months of negotiations involving the Seattle-based Nintendo company for keeping the team in Washington State. Smulyan finally sold out in June 1992 to a consortium in which Nintendo held a 49 percent interest.

DUKE SNIDER (Hall of Fame, 1980)

The greatest left-handed power hitter in Dodger history, Snider has also nevertheless had to put up with muttering about his achievements. The first reservation has stemmed from the fact that he was the third-best center fielder in New York in the 1950s, after Willie Mays of the Giants and Mickey Mantle of the Yankees. A second criticism has arisen from his place in a lineup of otherwise right-handed batters in the Ebbets Field teams of the era, allowing him to escape for the most part from the southpaw pitching that gave him fits. All that said, Snider was baseball's most prolific home-run hitter of the 1950s, clouting 326

round-trippers. Included in that total were five straight seasons (tying Ralph Kiner's NL record) of 40 or more blasts and a league-leading 43 in 1956. He also drove in 100 runs six times (with NL highs three years in a row). Although he struck out more than any other NL batter three times, Snider was no all-or-nothing hitter: He paced the league in hits in 1950, averaged .300 or better seven seasons, and finished with a career mark of .295. Snider's prowess with a bat was on display in the postseason: In both 1952 and 1955, he hit 4 home runs in the World Series. While not gifted with the speed of a Mays or a Mantle, and given to allowing hits to roll out to him, he was an exceptional defensive outfielder. His leaping catch of a Yogi Berra drive against the Yankee Stadium auxiliary scoreboard in game five in 1952 ranks as one of the greatest fielding plays in World Series history.

Nobody was more affected than Snider by the Dodger move from Brooklyn to Los Angeles following the 1957 season. Instead of the friendly right-field wall of Ebbets Field, he had to deal with the Yellowstone distances of the Coliseum, and his production declined precipitously. After falling into a platoon role with the Dodgers, he was sold to the Mets in a gate-appeal move by the expansion New York franchise. He managed one more season of 14 home runs, but, by his own testimony, spent most of the year sitting on the bench next to Casey Stengel and listening to the manager's nostalgic tales of the days when the Yankees and Dodgers faced off regularly in the World Series. The outfielder ended his eighteen-year career in 1964 with a short stint with the Giants.

His debut in 1947 was in the same game in which Jackie Robinson broke the color line; while Robinson went hitless, Snider got a pinch-hit single. In 1956, he himself attracted notoriety for telling *Collier's* magazine that he played baseball for money. The declaration horrified baseball executives and sportswriters for, in the words of one of them, "disillusioning young fans."

FRED SNODGRASS

Although he was in the National League for nine years, Snodgrass might just as well have played only in the 1912 and 1913 World Series as far as baseball history is concerned. The Giants' outfielder is most remembered for dropping the Clyde Engle fly ball in the 10th inning of the final game of the 1912 Series that opened the door for the Red Sox to produce a comeback championship win; in fact, he also did both better and worse than that. The better was a circus catch of a drive smacked by Harry Hooper immediately after the error on the Engle fly; the worse was that Snodgrass had also misjudged a liner by Tris Speaker in the opening game of the Series that led to another Boston win. If nothing else, the outfielder's error in the final game earned him the vociferous support of manager John McGraw, who, responding to charges that Snodgrass had committed what was termed The $30,000 Muff (the difference between the winning and losing shares), immediately announced a raise in salary for the besieged player. McGraw wasn't feeling as generous a year later, however, when Snodgrass was thrown out trying to steal second at a climactic moment in the World Series against the Athletics. The play prompted a tirade by the manager against first-base coach and longtime friend Wilbert Robinson for having sent the sore-legged outfielder in the first place. Robinson was fired for the decision and soon after moved over to manage Brooklyn, ushering in eighteen years of bitter rivalry between the former cronies. Before his legs went on him, Snodgrass was New York's swiftest runner, swiping as many as 51 bases one year.

LOUIS SOCKALEXIS

A member of the Penobscot Native American Indian tribe, Sockalexis had created a legend even before he reached the major leagues; it was, in fact, his exploits in amateur Maine summer leagues in the early 1890s that inspired rival manager Gilbert Patten to write his Frank Merriwell stories under the pseudonym Burt L. Standish. A hard drinker by the time he joined the Cleveland Spiders in 1897, Sockalexis silenced the war whoops that greeted him around the league by tearing National League pitching apart until, sporting a .338 batting average and little else, he hurt his foot in a fall or jump from a whorehouse window during a Fourth of July celebration. Thereafter, his drinking no longer under control,

Louis Sockalexis, pictured here in the uniform of a Poland Spring, Maine, amateur club, inspired the nickname Indians for the American League Cleveland franchise. National Baseball Library, Cooperstown, N.Y.

the phenom appeared sparingly for the rest of that season and parts of two more. In 1915, two years after the outfielder's death, Cleveland fans memorialized him by choosing Indians as the nickname of their American League club in a *Cleveland Press* ballot. The name and attendant logos have stuck for eight decades despite periodic accusations that they have fostered racial stereotyping.

ARTHUR SODEN

The leader of the Triumvirs (along with James Billings and Arthur Conant) who owned the National League's Boston franchise for three decades, Soden was the author of the first reserve rule binding a player to his club in perpetuity, and a sufficient presence in NL councils that he was elected interim league president when William Hulbert died in 1882. Soden also had a well-earned reputation as the quintessential skinflint. The reserve clause, introduced in September 1879, failed to win enthusiastic approval from the owners, who initially applied it to only five players on each club. Realizing that the rule's net effect was to depress salaries, the skeptical soon enough became converts and, within ten years, joined in extending the restriction to virtually every player.

Reserving players fit Soden's pathological penny-pinching. Among his economies over the years were charging players' wives admission to the ballpark, removing the press box to make room for more paying customers, and bringing his lunch in a brown bag every day of his tenure with the team. His frugality also manifested itself in club policies such as ignoring requests to sign new players and issuing dividends so rarely that small stockholders invariably became disgusted enough to sell out to him. On one occasion at least, he was generous with some remarkably prescient advice: After the Players League folded in 1890, Soden told PL organizer John Montgomery Ward that he should have advised his followers to play the 1890 season without signing their contracts, forcing the owners either to accept a break in the chain of automatic contract renewals or to suffer the wrath of the public by locking out the vast majority of major leaguers.

MOSES SOLOMON

A left-hand-hitting outfielder, Solomon was one of the New York Giants' periodic attempts to find a Jewish player who would appeal to the city's large Jewish population. In addition, manager John McGraw hoped he would help offset the popularity of Babe Ruth, and to that end encouraged sportswriters to refer to him as The Rabbi of Swat, a takeoff on the Yankee star's epithet of The Sultan of Swat. Unfortunately for the Giants and McGraw, Solomon managed only 8 plate appearances in 1923 before being demoted back to the minors. Although he managed a double and 2 singles in his at-bats, he was a catastrophe defensively, and never returned to the major leagues.

CHARLES SOMERS

Nobody was more vital to the creation and early survival of the American League than Somers. Although he was primarily owner of Cleveland, the coal magnate's open purse and belief in the aims of AL president Ban Johnson also provided seed money for the Athletics and Browns, supplied the capital for the White Sox to build Comiskey Park, and was used to pay off the bills accumulated by the Red Sox for some years. Somers's crucial role was so conspicuous that,

though he had only a brief formal tie to the club, Boston carried the nickname of Somersets for a while. In a less grateful mood a few years later, some newsmen in Cleveland noted the owner's coal mining background and the dissension of some local players over their salaries to dub the team the Molly McGuires—making Somers the only baseball personality to inspire nicknames for two different teams.

Over and above his liberal outlays of cash, Somers's most valuable contribution to the AL's survival was his ability to bluff. Encountering Cardinals' owner Frank Robison on a train in December 1902, he euchred his companion into believing that the AL had already secured a ballpark site for its embryonic New York franchise. Robison swallowed the deliberate overstatement and, concluding that there was no further use in fighting the junior league, reported his news and his conclusion to an NL meeting; his surrender was a major turning point in the senior league's decision to accept the AL as a coequal.

Over the first half of his reign as Cleveland owner (1901–15), Somers endeavored to stay in the background, taking only a vice-presidential title (initially because of his simultaneous involvement in the Red Sox) and leaving day-to-day affairs in the hands of president John Kilfoyle. Somers's loans around the league, however, made Kilfoyle's job easier in obtaining players. When Connie Mack couldn't keep future Hall of Famers Nap Lajoie and Elmer Flick because of a Pennsylvania court order, for instance, the Athletics manager sent them to Somers; some years later, the still-helpful Mack would send along Joe Jackson. Somers took over the presidency in 1908 because of Kilfoyle's deteriorating health, and, in a move with long-range consequences for the franchise, he brought in onetime college coach and *Columbus Dispatch* sports editor Ernest Barnard as his chief assistant. He eagerly accepted Barnard's recommendation for setting up a minor league chain by investing heavily in clubs in New Orleans, Toledo, Portland (Oregon), Westbury (Connecticut), and Ironton (Ohio). Somers also wasn't above getting Red Sox owner John Taylor drunk and, between one sip and another, prying away the game's most successful pitcher, Cy Young, in a one-sided deal.

Somers encountered his first big problem when he rebuilt the League Park grandstand with non-union labor and the American Federation of Labor called a boycott of all Cleveland games, at home and on the road. Only the intervention of Johnson prevented the conflict from becoming a leaguewide disaster. The bottom began falling out altogether in 1914, with the rise of the Federal League and its threats to move into Cleveland. To head off that move, Somers shifted his Toledo minor league franchise to the city, so that local fans would have some kind of baseball without the Feds even when the Indians were on the road. What that mainly achieved was showing Clevelanders that Toledo was a better club in its league than Cleveland was in the AL, aggravating already serious attendance problems. Finding himself overextended by almost $2 million, Somers engaged in a fire sale of his players; among those netting him some money were his two prizes from the Athletics: Lajoie and Jackson. But it was all too little, too late, and creditors ended up taking away all of Somers's baseball properties except the minor league club in New Orleans. Acting as an agent for the creditors, Johnson then arranged the sale of Cleveland to James Dunn, the head of a Chicago-based railroad construction firm.

DEWEY SORIANO

Soriano was the chief operating officer of the expansion Seattle Pilots—and the chief reason why the franchise disappeared after only one season, in 1969. As a minority partner to Cleveland-based William Daley, he persuaded the American League that he would make the Pilots commercially viable by having minor league Sicks Stadium enlarged as a temporary playing site, by winning voter approval for a new domed stadium, and by quelling any legal problems from the displaced Pacific Coast League club by paying a $300,000 indemnity. In the event, he ended up fighting with the city throughout the season about the pace of the expansion work, to the point that Mayor Floyd Miller threatened to evict the team; the bond issue was not approved until after the Pilots had ceased to exist; and the indemnity to the PCL club was not paid until years after that. And that was only the beginning.

Even as he was telling everybody that Sicks

Stadium would house the club for two years at the most, Soriano inked a five-year agreement for use of the ballpark. Even though he admitted that the Pilots were probably going to be the worst team in the league for a couple of years, he announced the highest ticket prices in baseball. Even as he was talking about enlarging the club's spring training quarters in Tempe, Arizona, lawyers were suing the organization for nonpayment of its first-year bills. It didn't take long for AL owners to realize that they had made a major mistake. Still insisting that they wanted to remain in Seattle, however, they rejected an offer from a group in Milwaukee to buy the team, entertaining offers instead from a rogues' gallery of Washington-based entrepreneurs whose common characteristic was that they turned out not to have the funds they claimed; in fact, one of them didn't even have the money necessary to cover a single day of payroll.

With Daley and Soriano refusing to put another penny into the team, the league had to finance the Pilots' spring training in 1970. That contribution broke the dissenters on the move to Milwaukee. After another lawsuit looking into Soriano's claims of being bankrupt, the AL approved the creation of the Milwaukee Brewers for the 1970 season. One of the major consequences of the fiasco was that it prompted serious enough lawsuit threats by the abandoned city of Seattle that the league had to make a commitment to create the Mariners.

BILLY SOUTHWORTH

Southworth's passage from a thirteen-year playing career (between 1913 and 1929) to thirteen years as a manager was like Dr. Jekyll's transformation into Mr. Hyde. A genial, outgoing outfielder who batted .297 overall and who played a big hand offensively in the Cardinals' 1926 world championship, he showed up as such a martinet when St. Louis tapped him as manager three years later that owner Sam Breadon farmed him back to Rochester in midseason following incessant player complaints. Although he mellowed somewhat in his later years, he also developed a severe drinking problem that took the luster off some of his best efforts as a dugout boss for the Cardinals and Braves in the 1940s.

As a player, Southworth arrived in St. Louis in 1926 after stints with the Indians, Pirates, Braves, and Giants. While he had no appreciable power, he batted over .300 four times during his journeying, led the National League in triples in 1919, and was considered a deft fielder. Some of his travels were the result of controversial trades. When the Pirates dealt him to the Braves in 1921, it was for the popular Rabbit Maranville—a fact that Boston fans were slow to forget with their constant booing; when the Braves sent him to the Giants in 1924, it was so that future Hall of Famer Dave Bancroft could pilot Boston and consolidate New York manager John McGraw's hold on the New England club. In the 1926 World Series for St. Louis, Southworth batted .345 to help edge the Murderers' Row Yankees in seven games.

After his first bitter taste of managing in 1929, Southworth piloted minor league teams until he was hired as a coach by Bill Terry of the Giants in 1933. The relationship got no farther than spring training when the two got into a fistfight over personnel disagreements, leading to Southworth's return to the minors for a second time. He popped up again with St. Louis in 1940, mainly as Breadon's eleventh-hour solution to getting rid of Branch Rickey confidant Ray Blades as manager. A kinder, gentler Southworth—at least when he was sober—remained at the helm for the next six years, reeling in three pennants, two world championships, and two second-place finishes with clubs that played above .600 every season. By the end of the war, however, not even such a record was enough to prevent Breadon from seeking to cut his manager's salary because of general financial shorts in the franchise, and Southworth took the opportunity to skip off to Boston.

With the Braves, the drinking got still worse and the authoritarian airs came back in full force, but owner Lou Perini was only too quick to ignore them as the club ended decades of wretched play to go up the ladder to the top of the league. It was during the flag year that the pitching-short Southworth acknowledged that his rotation plans consisted of "Spahn, Sain, and pray for rain." Once they had their pennant, Perini and general manager Bob Quinn also went after player salaries, but with the added twist of emphasizing that

only Southworth was indispensable to the franchise. It was a tack that only increased clubhouse agitation, and the pilot himself worsened an already bad situation by issuing new rules in spring training in 1949 that left the players with little to do but play games and then return to their rooms. Alvin Dark and Eddie Stanky, the double-play combination that had been pivotal for the team's success in 1948, took it upon themselves to ask Southworth to ease up on his drinking, but instead of interpreting the duo's request in the light of their almost obsessive religious backgrounds, he took it as a final confirmation of press reports that Stanky was jockeying for his job.

In August 1949, Southworth had what was officially described as a nervous breakdown, and asked to be relieved of his post for the remainder of the season. Totally unsympathetic, the players voted him only a half share of their fourth-place World Series money. Despite the deteriorating morale of the club, Perini let the three years still remaining on Southworth's contract determine his course of action: Instead of replacing the manager, he traded away Dark and Stanky to the Giants and got rid of several other players fingered as rebels. Southworth came back in 1950 for another fourth-place finish, but in June 1951 told Perini that his health was more important to him than guiding another also-ran club and finally quit.

WARREN SPAHN (Hall of Fame, 1973)

Already twenty-five when he won his first game for the Braves in 1946, Spahn went on to post the most victories (363) of any left-hander in the history of the game. His biggest numbers included thirteen 20-win seasons (tying him with Christy Mathewson for the most in the National League), most career shutouts by a southpaw (63), and the NL leader in wins eight times, strikeouts four times, and ERA twice. He didn't pitch a no-hitter until he was thirty-nine, but then followed up a 1960 masterpiece against the Phillies with a second one, against the Giants in 1961. Spahn also won four World Series games, carrying 3 of his starts into the 10th inning. An offensive threat as well, he was often used as a pinch hitter, and ended up with 35 home runs over his twenty-one-year career.

Warren Spahn's characteristic high kick helped him amass 363 career victories. National Baseball Library, Cooperstown, N.Y.

If there was one stain on Spahn's record, it was his inability to beat the Dodger teams that dominated the NL in the late 1940s and 1950s; in 1952 and 1953, for instance, he had an 0–7 record against Brooklyn, after which he was generally kept away the right-hand-hitting Ebbets Field lineup. In his final appearance against his old Dodger nemeses, in the 1959 playoff game between Milwaukee and Los Angeles that ended up settling the pennant race, he came in as a reliever against pinch hitter Carl Furillo with the bases loaded, threw one pitch, and had a circus catch from Hank Aaron to thank for a mere sacrifice fly instead of a grand slam.

AL SPALDING (Hall of Fame, 1939)

Starting as a seventeen-year-old pitching phenom and ending at the center of a titanic struggle over the future of the National League, Spalding cut a dominant figure in the development of nineteenth-century baseball.

While a member of a provincial Rockford, Illinois, club, the right-hander first achieved national attention by handing the Washington Nationals the only defeat of their 1867 tour through the Midwest. He went on to post 207 victories (against only 56 losses) in the five years of the National Association, including a 57–5 record for the Boston Red Stockings in 1875; his contract for the next season with Chicago already known, he was undefeated at home for that entire season despite the animosity of Boston fans. After his defection to William Hulbert's White Stockings effectively created the National League, Spalding pitched the circuit's first shutout, a 4–0 blanking of Louisville on April 25, 1876, and followed it up two days later with a repeat performance to become the first pitcher to open his big league career with two whitewashings. His 47–13 record brought Chicago the first NL pennant; he also managed the club.

Retiring two years later because of an injury, Spalding devoted his attention to the sporting goods company he had started with his brother J. Walter and to purchasing stock in the Chicago club at Hulbert's encouragement. When the club and league president died in 1882, Spalding purchased a majority interest in the team and took over active control. His ten-year regime was marked by a paternalistic approach designed to keep players' salaries down and their standards of deportment up. Toward the first end, he encouraged the formation of the League Alliance of NL-affiliated independent clubs, and sold fan favorite King Kelly for $10,000 when the catcher-outfielder's salary demands rose to levels he was not prepared to pay; toward the latter, he hired detectives to trail his employees, and insisted that they take a no-drinking pledge effective over the winter as well as during the season. Part of the money he saved on salaries he put into a renovation of Lake Front Park that included the first private boxes; the boxes featured armchairs for comfort, curtains for privacy and protection against the wind, and a personal suite with a telephone.

Spalding struck a markedly selective attitude toward efforts to break the NL's monopoly. For instance, he agreed to have his club meet the Cincinnati Reds, winners of the first American Asso-

Al Spalding never let facts get in the way of his determination to make baseball a purely all-American game. National Baseball Library, Cooperstown, N.Y.

ciation pennant in 1882, in a postseason championship series before a settlement had been reached with the rival league. Two years later, during the Union Association war, he incurred the wrath of NL president A. G. Mills for surreptitiously backing a profitable effort by Samuel Morton, one of his employees, to funnel players to the Unions; he also rented Lake Front Park to the UA Browns for several games. Years later he took a beneficent approach to the American League's decision to challenge the NL. The Players League, on the other hand, he regarded not as a struggle among capitalists but as open rebellion. After an initial blunder in telling Players Brotherhood organizer John Montgomery Ward that his demands for an end to player sales and the Brush Classification Plan were sufficiently important to merit immediate attention, Spalding directed the NL's wartime strategy: taking legal action against defecting players, pumping money into faltering clubs, attempting to win ex-employee Kelly back

to the fold, and conducting a massive public relations campaign to discredit the players. He also orchestrated the final assault, getting PL financial backers to admit their heavy losses while keeping silent about the not inconsiderable damage to the NL, keeping the players out of the settlement discussions, and rearranging franchises and owners to suit the need of the hour.

Spalding's greatest genius was, perhaps, in publicizing the game—through the quasi-official annual Spalding *Guide;* through a 1907 commission that snatched Abner Doubleday from the obscurity of Civil War histories and placed him at the center of a creation myth for baseball; and through an autobiography he published in 1911. The most spectacular of his publicity efforts was a six-month, around-the-world tour in 1888–89 that brought baseball to thirteen countries, on every continent except Antarctica.

The tour probably would have included the South Pole, too, if there had been anyone there to purchase the uniforms, balls, bats, gloves, and other equipment the millionaire peddled through A. G. Spalding and Brothers. At bottom, all his other roles were geared toward increasing the profits from the sporting goods company that eventually became an international monopoly by gobbling up competitors such as A. J. Reach and Wright and Ditson.

Spalding's last appearance on baseball's center stage was also his least successful. Retired since 1891, the sporting goods executive was called on in December 1901 to undo the damage caused by New York owner Andrew Freedman's syndication plan. The choice was a curious one, since Spalding himself had been the force behind the dissolution of the AA in 1891 and the creation of "one great league," and more recently had sounded out AL president Ban Johnson about a consolidation of the two leagues along lines not unlike what Freedman was proposing. With the issue hinging on an election for league president, Brooklyn, Chicago, Philadelphia, and Pittsburgh (the four clubs with nothing to gain from Freedman's scheme) supported Spalding for NL president for twenty-five ballots, while Boston, Cincinnati, New York, and St. Louis (the beneficiaries) voted for incumbent Nick Young. The deadlock was broken—and Spalding elected, four votes to none—only after the prosyndication faction had left the room. What followed was *opéra bouffe*, with Spalding confiscating league records from Young at 4:00 A.M., announcing a quorum at the next day's meeting because a minor official of the Giants was standing in the doorway, evicting Freedman from baseball, scurrying out of New York to avoid an injunction restraining him from serving in the office, and finally resigning the following spring.

Spalding returned to California, where he died in 1915.

THE SPANISH LADY

The Spanish Lady was the name given to the devastating flu epidemic that claimed an estimated 25 million lives around the world between 1916 and 1918; in the United States the death toll was put at 500,000. The emergency sanitary laws invoked to combat the disease provided a critical justification for outlawing the spitball. In the atmosphere of the period, even apparently unrelated ailments, such as a diphtheria attack suffered by spitballer Ad Brennan, were ascribed to the handling of spittle-covered baseballs.

JOE SPARMA

Sparma's wildness indirectly prompted a refinement of one of the game's basic rules. Convinced that Sparma was unable to issue an intentional walk without hitting the backstop, Montreal manager Gene Mauch assigned one of his infielders to a spot behind the catcher during a 1970 game while the right-hander delivered four wide ones. The National League subsequently intervened to rule that only a catcher could be standing in foul territory with the delivery of a pitch.

TRIS SPEAKER (Hall of Fame, 1937)

For somebody who batted .344 and revolutionized outfield defensive play during his twenty-two-year (1907–28) career, Speaker came in for a lot of rejection. After Speaker's unimpressive trial with the Red Sox in 1907, Boston owner John Taylor turned down his contract demands, Pittsburgh owner Barney Dreyfuss didn't want him because he smoked, and Giants manager John McGraw claimed he already had too many

The best defensive center fielder of his day, Tris Speaker was also second only to Ty Cobb among contemporary hitters. Photo compliments of Sharon Guynup.

outfielders. Taylor only took him back to help pay off some spring training expenses by leasing him to a minor league franchise in Arkansas. Rejections of a more dramatic kind awaited him after he had established himself as one of the American League's great early-century players.

Speaker batted over .300 eighteen times, including a league-leading .386 in 1916, and three other seasons when he reached the .380 mark. At one time or another, he paced his contemporaries in hits (twice), doubles (eight seasons), home runs (once), RBIs (once), and slugging average (once). He had 200 or more hits four times, at least 50 doubles four times, scored 100 runs seven times, knocked in 100 runs twice, and stole a minimum of 30 bases seven times. His lifetime 792 doubles are the most in baseball history, while his 3,515 safeties rank him fifth behind Pete Rose, Ty Cobb, Hank Aaron, and Stan Musial. Defensively, Speaker was the game's first important "reader," moving to his left or right even as the pitch was on its way home. This ability enabled him to play so shallow that he was able to pull off four unassisted double plays, take pickoff throws from the pitcher and catcher, throw batters out on balls hit up the middle, and even turn the pivot on a double play. The Gray Eagle, as he was known, led AL outfielders in putouts seven times, in assists three times, in double plays five times, and in fielding average twice. His 448 career outfield assists remain a benchmark figure.

While with Boston, Speaker was a major force in the club's 1912 and 1915 world championships. On the other hand, he was also prominent in clubhouse tensions in that period between Protestant and Catholic factions on the team; the rift particularly pitted Speaker and Joe Wood against Bill Carrigan and Heinie Wagner, and helped prompt a franchise sale and a couple of managerial switches. Following the dissolution of the Federal League in 1915, Red Sox owner Joseph Lannin adopted the general boardroom ploy of slashing player salaries to redress the inflated wages paid two years earlier to prevent defections to the Feds; Speaker's refusal to accept a cut led to a tug-of-war that lasted through the off-season and spring training right up to Opening Day in 1916. It was then that Lannin announced that he had completed a deal sending his star to the Indians. The Yankees, among others, protested the transaction because of the suspected involvement of AL president Ban Johnson and the latter's pressures on Lannin to offer Speaker to his friend Cleveland owner James Dunn.

In Cleveland, Speaker was effectively a playing manager. Rarely did nominal Indians' pilot Lee Fohl make a move in the lineup or with the starting rotation without consulting his center fielder; Fohl even made pitching changes during games on the basis of prearranged signals from Speaker in the outfield. The star also had a big say in front-office transactions, and wasted little time in acquiring some of his former Boston teammates; among them was clubhouse ally Wood. Although the Indians showed marked improvement after Speaker's arrival, their failure to reach the top rung increased tensions between the outfielder and Fohl. This was especially so after Speaker's suspension for the rest of the season after throwing a punch at umpire John Connolly in a late August

game in 1918 prevented Cleveland from making up a 2-game deficit and finished as runner-up to Boston in the pennant race. The breaking point came during an August 1919 game against the Red Sox, when the pilot either ignored or misinterpreted the signals from his outfielder and brought in reliever Fritz Coumbe to pitch to Babe Ruth. When Ruth homered, Speaker let everyone in the ballpark know how he felt about Fohl's strategy. Fohl submitted his resignation that very day, forcing Speaker to take over the club in title as well as in function.

With his new title weighing on him, Speaker slumped enough over the final weeks of the 1919 season to cost Cleveland its shot at another pennant. The following year, however, he rebounded with a .388 average and guided the club to its first pennant. The victory didn't come cheaply. For one thing, there were rumors throughout the season that the same White Sox players who were being investigated for selling out the 1919 World Series were on the take again for assuring a Cleveland pennant. For another, Speaker was devastated by the August 16 tragedy in which Indians' shortstop Ray Chapman was beaned by New York's Carl Mays, and died shortly afterward. Amid the reports of the new gambling manipulations, the death of Chapman, and the lynch mob atmosphere in Cleveland when Mays and the Yankees came to town late in the season, Speaker admitted to having "lost some of the taste" for the pennant run. Nevertheless, the club won the flag, and then topped Brooklyn, 5 games to 2, in a best-of-9 World Series.

Speaker remained at the helm through the 1926 season, when he received his biggest rejection of all. At the end of the year, Cleveland announced that he was stepping down as manager and retiring as a player because of charges by former Detroit pitcher Dutch Leonard that he had conspired with the hurler, Wood, and Ty Cobb to throw a 1919 game for assuring a third-place finish for the Tigers. The smoking gun in the accusations were notes written by Wood and Cobb to Leonard alluding to bets placed on the contest in question. Although the correspondence never mentioned Speaker by name, and he denied any involvement, he had to wait through long weeks of executive intrigue while AL president Johnson and Commissioner Kenesaw Landis came to contradictory conclusions before being semicleared. He ended up playing two final seasons for the Senators and Athletics.

J. G. TAYLOR SPINK

A character out of *The Front Page,* Spink inherited the fiscally shaky *Sporting News* from his uncle Alfred H. Spink in 1914; by his death in 1962, the weekly had become The Bible of Baseball. By turns abrasive and sensitive, contentious and sentimental, Spink stormed through the baseball world for almost four decades, working the phones seven days a week at all hours to track down stories. An ally of Ban Johnson against Commissioner Kenesaw Landis, Spink helped the American League president in his pursuit of leads in the Black Sox scandal.

Spink's publication created its own Most Valuable Player awards in 1929 after the two leagues abandoned similar honors, and continued the practice even after the Baseball Writers' Association started its more widely recognized prizes in 1931. Similar *Sporting News* recognition followed for Rookie of the Year (in 1946), Pitcher of the Year (1948), and Fireman of the Year (1960). His son C. C. Johnson Spink took over as publisher of the newspaper until it was sold out of the family in 1977. In later years, the weekly rarely found reasons to criticize owners in their battles with players on contractual matters. Its regular team reports were also infamous for being bland rehashes of the daily filings of beat writers, with little attempt at analysis or original reporting of important issues.

KARL SPOONER

Spooner was the flashiest of flashes when he debuted for Brooklyn in the last week of the 1954 season with back-to-back shutouts of the Giants and Pirates, striking out 27 batters along the way. But the following year the southpaw developed a sore arm and won a mere 8 games. His final big league appearance was in game six of the 1955 World Series, when he was knocked out in the 1st inning by the Yankees. Even his two shutouts had asterisks next to them insofar as the Giants were blanked the day after clinching the pennant and the Pirates were the worst team in the league.

CHICK STAHL

Stahl's womanizing led to one of baseball's more grisly suicides. An outfielder for the turn-of-the-century Braves, he had little trouble attracting Baseball Annies when he emerged as one of the club's steadier bats. His popularity only increased when he jumped with Jimmy Collins to the newly created Red Sox in 1901 and made the American League team an instant success. In 1906, Stahl succeeded Collins as Boston manager for a few games, and was then offered a contract to return as pilot the following year. During spring training, however, he continually changed his mind about accepting the job, indicating some deep stress. Then, one evening, Collins returned to the room they shared to find Stahl dying of a lethal dose of carbolic acid. Stahl's last words as reported by Collins and another player—''Boys, I couldn't help it; it drove me to it''—remained enigmatic until 1986, when a Boston magazine revealed that the outfielder had been overwhelmed by guilt for having married one woman in November 1906 even as he was finding out that he had impregnated another, who was demanding a walk down the aisle. In addition, according to the magazine, a third woman had twice tried to shoot him for leaving her in the lurch.

GEORGE STALLINGS

Stallings was as schizophrenic a personality as ever had anything to do with baseball. Polite to the point of courtliness away from the diamond, he bordered on the savage when he put on a uniform. Although mainly associated with the Miracle Braves of 1914, he had already disenchanted scores of players, front-office executives, and umpires before ever reaching Boston.

After a couple of cups of coffee as a catcher with the Dodgers and Phillies in the 1890s, Stallings got his first managerial shot in Philadelphia in 1897. Only twenty-eight at the time and still trying to hang on as a receiver, he was a walking profanity who spent as much time establishing regulations and lashing into his players as he did trying to outwit opposing clubs. The result was a team revolt that led to his firing during the 1898 season. After a couple of seasons of managing Detroit in the minor Western League, Stallings found himself in perfect position when the club was elevated to major league status in the first year of the American League; it didn't hurt that he was also half-owner of the franchise. Stallings always claimed that he was the first one to dub his players Tigers after having them don black-and-yellow striped socks, though other sources attribute the nickname to *Detroit Free Press* sports editor Philip Reid.

Stallings's stay in Detroit was even stormier than his Philadelphia experience. While AL president Ban Johnson tried to pass off his circuit as a decorous alternative to the brawling National League, Stallings drew fine after fine for his constant invective against rival players and incessant baiting of umpires; he interrupted this performance only to accuse his partner Jim Burns of financial irregularities and to open secret negotiations for shifting the Tigers to the NL. Faced with an ultimatum from Johnson, Stallings finally agreed to sell his interest in the franchise—an opportunity that the AL executive used to get rid of Burns as well. It was partly because of this antagonism that Johnson turned a deaf ear in 1909 and 1910 when Stallings, back as manager of the Yankees, became the first pilot to accuse the notorious Hal Chase of throwing games. With New York's ownership also circling the wagons around one of the junior league's biggest stars, the manager suffered the indignity of being replaced by Chase himself.

Moving over to Boston in 1913, Stallings inherited a club that had not risen above sixth place for a decade. He did nothing to alter that in his first year, when he piloted the Braves to another cellar finish. Once again, he was at almost daily odds with the few stars on the club, sometimes to the point of clubhouse blows; by this point, in fact, he had picked up the nickname of Bonehead—not because of his own mental deficiencies, but because that was his ordinary term for summoning players. At the same time, however, a slightly older Stallings also began showing that he could be as encouraging to rookies as he was impatient with veterans, and more than one first-year player praised him for building up self-confidence. Another of the manager's talents was sign stealing—an area where he had few rivals over the opening decades of the century. On the other hand, he had such extraordinary supersti-

tions about paper that opposition pilots regularly assigned bench players to sneak up behind the Boston dugout and shred newspapers to distract him.

Stallings began Boston's greatest season in 1914 by leading the club to a mere 4 wins in its first 22 games. In July, the Braves couldn't even win an exhibition game against a team of soap company employees. But in one of the greatest comebacks in baseball history, Stallings's charges ran roughshod over the league in the second half of the season, winning 52 of their final 66 games. The Miracle Braves completed their startling season by sweeping the heavily favored Athletics in the World Series.

For a couple more years, Stallings kept the team competitive, but against the background of increasing chaos from the franchise's executive suites and a parade of John McGraw-inspired owners who were never reluctant to pass on Boston's most promising players to the Polo Grounds. On more than one occasion, Stallings himself sought to acquire the club, but was turned down; although the reason given was usually insufficient funds, it was actually because he was a distrusted outsider to the cozy New York-Boston entente. In 1920 he finally had enough of pleading futilely for the franchise to purchase decent players and took owner George Washington Grant up on a challenge to quit if he didn't like the way the organization was being operated.

EDDIE STANKY

Stanky was never quite able to get out from under the backhand compliment of Branch Rickey, who once asserted that the second baseman "can't hit and can't field . . . all he can do is beat you." But Stanky could very much hit, as witness the .320, .285, and .300 seasons he had between 1948 and 1951 and the fact that neither his predecessors nor his successors on the Cubs, Giants, or Braves neared his offensive production. In addition, he led the National League in walks three times, on-base percentage twice, and runs scored another time.

Overriding these achievements, however, was the image of The Brat—the no-holds-barred scrapper who kicked balls out of the hands of infielders (most notably, Phil Rizzuto's in the

1951 World Series between the Giants and Yankees) and who never saw a diamond situation he couldn't worsen by starting a fight. If these qualities were essential to Stanky's play on the pennant-winning Dodgers in 1947, Braves in 1948, and Giants in 1951, and were openly encouraged by his mentor Leo Durocher, they were equally destructive during his subsequent managing career. As pilot of the Cardinals in the mid-1950s, he became an embarrassment to the front office with his constant baiting of umpires and regular premature trips to the showers. With the White Sox in the 1960s, he managed to alienate most of the city of Chicago by blaming his mediocre team's showing on the media, compromising his coaches by turning them into spies on players, insisting on martinet disciplinary rules, getting opposing teams up for their visits to Comiskey Park by ridiculing their managers and personnel, and publicly scorning his front-office bosses.

In June 1977, the Rangers hired Stanky to replace Frank Lucchesi, but after sitting in the dugout for a single game (a victory), Stanky returned home with the announcement that he wasn't up to dealing with modern players.

WILLIE STARGELL (Hall of Fame, 1988)

Stargell was Reggie Jackson without the twenty-four-hour-a-day preening. Dubbed Pops in his later years for his expansive manner and expanded midsection, the lefty-swinging outfielder-first baseman rolled up a Reggie-like 475 home runs in his twenty-one-year (1962–82) career with the Pirates and, like his American League counterpart, established his own circuit's record for strikeouts with 1,936. Along the way, Stargell paced the NL in home runs twice, and RBIs, doubles, and slugging average once each. In six campaigns he belted at least 30 home runs— some of which were titanic blasts. Of the 18 balls hit out of Forges Field in sixty-one years, for instance, 7 of them came off his bat; he has also been the only player to hit a ball completely out of Dodger Stadium, and he did it twice.

Although he was already thirty-eight, Stargell was at his best in Pittsburgh's world championship season of 1979: After hitting 32 homers during the regular season to gain half an MVP award with Keith Hernandez, Stargell completed the hat

Willie Stargell's ebullience as much as his slugging made him the leader of the "We are Family" Pirates. Photo compliments of the Pittsburgh Pirates.

trick by also taking MVP honors for both the National League Championship Series against Cincinnati and the World Series against Baltimore. Overall in the two postseason series, he collected 5 home runs and 13 RBIs. More than contributing with his bat, however, Stargell was the soul of the "We Are Family" Pirates of 1979—a role he played to the hilt by awarding gold stars to teammates who had distinguished themselves by game efforts and who proudly wore their prizes on their helmets throughout the season.

RUSTY STAUB

Staub was one of the few players who did not make his time with the Expos sound like enforced exile in Siberia; as a result, *LE Grande Orange*, as fans came to call him for his carrot hair, was probably the most popular player ever to wear a Montreal uniform. As an active member of the Players Association in the 1970s and 1980s, on the other hand, he wasn't always popular with front offices. In 1968, for instance, he raised the hackles of his Astros employers by being one of the most visible spokesmen for demands that teams suspend spring training games in the wake of the assassination of Martin Luther King, Jr; though Houston's chief offensive threat at the time, he was packed off to Montreal after the season. On other occasions, he irked the Mets with demands for a long-term contract (and was traded to Detroit) and the Tigers by sitting out spring training over a contract impasse (and was sent back to the Expos).

A lefty-hitting first baseman-outfielder, Staub is the only major leaguer to have collected at least 500 hits for four different teams (Houston, Montreal, New York, and Detroit) and the only one apart from Ty Cobb to bang a homer before he was twenty and after he was forty. In Staub's waning years, during a second stint with the Mets, he became one of the game's most potent pinch hitters, at one point in 1983 tying Dave Philley's record of 8 consecutive pinch-hits in a season. He is one of the few sports stars whose association with the restaurant business goes beyond merely lending his name to an enterprise, being in fact a very hands-on owner of a New York eatery and priding himself as a wine connoisseur.

GEORGE STEINBRENNER

Within three years of Steinbrenner's taking over as The Boss of the Yankees, the team returned to the top of the standings for the first time in more than a decade, winning three consecutive American League pennants and two world championships. Everything else about his more than two decades in the Bronx has been a nightmare.

The head of Cleveland's American Ship Building Company arrived in the Bronx in April 1973 after paying (a bargain) $10 million to CBS for the club and asserting that "We plan absentee ownership. I'll stick to building ships." Into 1974 he kept his word, if only because he was busy defending himself against an indictment for illegally contributing $100,000 to President Richard Nixon's 1972 reelection campaign. Pleading guilty in August 1974, Steinbrenner was fined $15,000 by the courts and suspended from all club operations for two years by Commissioner Bowie Kuhn. Steinbrenner in exile proved almost as ubiquitous as Steinbrenner in power, however, sending taped messages into the clubhouse and almost certainly approving major player moves, such as the 1975 signing of free agent Catfish Hunter for $3 million. Kuhn ignored these probable violations of the ban and reinstated the owner, in March 1976, five months prematurely—shortly after the Yankees had switched sides to cast the deciding vote in awarding the commissioner a second term.

The advent of free agency in 1976 gave Steinbrenner further opportunity to throw money around. His first acquisition, of Cincinnati lefty Don Gullett, also set a pattern of recruiting high-priced pitchers who would develop physical or psychological disabilities that restricted their usefulness. Following Gullett would be Andy Messersmith (1978), Luis Tiant (1979), Rudy May (1980), Rick Reuschel (1981), Doyle Alexander (1982), Bob Shirley and John Montefusco (1983), Ed Whitson (1985), Britt Burns (1986), Steve Trout (1987), Andy Hawkins and Rich Dotson (1988), and Tim Leary (1990).

The acquisition of Gullett was eclipsed, however, by the signing of future Hall of Famer Reggie Jackson, a move that set manager Billy Martin fuming for his exclusion from front-office decision-making. Tensions simmered among the owner, the manager, and the slugger throughout the 1977 season—failing to explode only because of the constant mediating of club president Gabe Paul. With Paul gone back to Cleveland in 1978, however, the owner stepped up the pace of his phone calls to Martin to tell him what he was doing wrong (mainly not batting Jackson cleanup). The open Martin-Jackson feud had Steinbrenner increasing the frequency of his trips to New York, ostensibly to set matters right, but accomplishing little besides fanning the flames. Third baseman Graig Nettles summed up the attitude of Yankee players toward the owner: "The more we lose, the more he'll fly in. And the more he flies in, the better chance that there'll be a plane crash."

What followed was Steinbrenner-directed comic opera: the firing of Martin in the wake of references to Jackson as a "born liar" and to Steinbrenner as "convicted"; the hiring of Bob Lemon as his successor; and an announcement to a stunned Old Timers' Day crowd that Martin would be back in the dugout in 1980, with Lemon moving up to the front office. Meanwhile, the team launched a stretch run that ended with Bucky Dent's 3-run homer to beat the Red Sox in a single-game playoff for an AL East title, then went on to a world championship. Steinbrenner brought Martin back in 1979, a year earlier than announced, for a season of haranguing reminders about remaining on good behavior, then dismissed him a second time after a postseason fight with a marshmallow salesman.

Dick Howser followed Martin in the door of the manager's office in 1980 and right out again after winning 103 games but losing the American League Championship Series to Kansas City in 3 games. Then came an eleven-year-long parade of fourteen managerial changes, with Martin returning for three additional tries at pleasing The Boss. Coaches were even more expendable in the Steinbrenner cosmos; in 1982 alone, there were three batting coaches and five pitching coaches. The front-office picture was no clearer. In rapid succession, Cedric Tallis, Gene Michael, Bill Bergesch, Murray Cook, Clyde King, Woody Woodward, Lou Piniella, Syd Thrift, and Michael again headed baseball operations.

Unsurprisingly, the roster changed with head-spinning regularity. For half of the 1978 season, for example, Steinbrenner saddled the team with Jim Spencer, Jay Johnstone, and Gary Thomasson, all lefty-swinging outfielder-first baseman-designated hitters; as if that were not sufficient folly, Spencer's contract carried a provision, inserted at Steinbrenner's insistence, that the player would start every game in which the Yankees faced a right-handed pitcher. In 1982, the managing partner decided that the team's future success would be based on a slash-and-dash offense, so he signed Dave Collins as a free agent, then changed his mind and got Roy Smalley, Jr., from the Rangers to provide power. Lost in the shuffle was Dent, and partly as a result nineteen players rode the infamous Columbus shuttle, with pitcher Dave LaRoche making four round trips. The confusion reached its apex in 1991, when general manager George Bradley kept busy offering second baseman Steve Sax a contract extension that would make him untradeable for a couple of years, while vice president Pete Peterson was trying to peddle the infielder to make room for prospect Pat Kelly.

Young players suffered the most in the turmoil. Right-hander Jim Beattie and shortstop Bobby Meacham were among the more conspicuous victims, the former finding his courage as well as his ability questioned in Steinbrenner-seeded headlines for giving up 4 runs in 3 innings in a key game in 1978, the latter summarily dispatched to Columbus when his error cost the Yankees the fourth game of the 1984 season.

Always a bully, Steinbrenner regularly called front-office staffers a few minutes after 5:00 P.M. to make sure they were still at their desks. Failing to understand the purpose of spring training, he would become hysterical over exhibition losses to the Mets. Regularly congratulating himself for having restored "the Yankee tradition," he would nonetheless publicly apologize for team losses, most notably after a defeat by the Dodgers in the 1981 World Series. On the other hand, he did not apologize for a claimed run-in with two Dodger fans in an elevator; rather, he displayed his bruised knuckles as a badge of honor, even though there was much speculation that the victim of the fisticuffs had been the elevator itself.

Steinbrenner did not confine his outbursts to employees and phantoms. In January 1983 he called White Sox owners Jerry Reinsdorf and Eddie Einhorn "the Abbott and Costello of baseball" in response to charges of irresponsibility for signing ex-White Soxer Steve Kemp to a $5.5 million, five-year contract; Kuhn fined him $5,000 for the crack. In spring training of the same year, the owner accused umpire Lee Weyer of being under instructions from NL president Chub Feeney to call all close plays for the NL team; the fine for this was $50,000. In 1983, Steinbrenner's outbursts against AL president Lee MacPhail for reversing the umpires' decision in the "pine tar" incident and awarding George Brett a homer cost Steinbrenner a $250,000 fine and $50,000 in legal fees. In 1987, the owner won a court case brought by the Umpires' Association over an accusation that arbiter Dallas Parks was incompetent. Two years after that, Steinbrenner took on his own fans when he had Yankee Stadium security guards confiscate signs saying ''George Must Go.'' Only an action brought by the American Civil Liberties Union prevented a recurrence.

George finally did go, when Commissioner Fay Vincent discovered that he had paid Howard Spira, a professional gambler, $40,000 to dig up dirt on outfielder Dave Winfield, with whom Steinbrenner was feuding. Vincent was about to suspend the owner for two years when he offered to remove himself indefinitely from club affairs, provided the word ''suspension'' was not used in the official decree. The Yankee Stadium announcement of the arrangement was greeted by a standing ovation.

A battle with the commissioner's office followed over who would be allowed to assume the role of managing partner of the franchise. The public disarray of the organization, even after agreement was reached on installing Steinbrenner's son-in-law Joseph Molloy, led other AL owners to pressure Vincent for a specific date for Steinbrenner's return. In one of his final pronouncements as commissioner, Vincent announced that the owner could resume full control of the club in March 1993.

The Return of George II was a quieter affair than the first restoration. Preoccupied by the impending bankruptcy of American Ship Building, Steinbrenner was uncharacteristically content with garden variety egomania and bullying. Only later did it become clear that he had been borrowing heavily against more than $500 million in contracts with the cable Madison Square Garden Network and WABC Radio—initially to try to salvage his shipbuilding interests, then to increase his already considerable profits. He also began stepping up threats to end ''Yankee tradition'' altogether by moving the club out of New York because of the city's failure to throw more public money into improving the facilities around Yankee Stadium.

BILL STEMMEYER

Stemmeyer established an unapproachable record for wildness in 1896, when he uncorked 64 wild pitches in only 41 games. The Braves' right-hander still managed to post 22 victories.

CASEY STENGEL (Hall of Fame, 1966)

The earliest public perception of Stengel as a clownish buffoon gave way to that of a gifted raconteur whose Stengelese made more sense than was immediately apparent; this, in turn, yielded to one of a venerable old man wisecracking his way through otherwise frustrating seasons with an expansion club. What was often lost in all three views was a shrewdness that made Stengel a millionaire from oil and banking interests and the guile of the only manager ever to win five successive world championships or even five straight pennants—not to mention a mean streak that surfaced more frequently as he grew older.

Stengel arrived in the major leagues as a left-hand-hitting outfielder with the Dodgers in 1912. Before he was through as a player fourteen seasons later, he would wear the uniform of five National League clubs, put up a lifetime .284 average, and gain a well-deserved reputation as a zany. Like protégé Billy Martin decades later with

Before Casey Stengel became the Old Professor, he was the Young Hothead. National Baseball Library, Cooperstown, N.Y.

the Yankees, he would do his best work in World Series play, posting a .393 average in three Series. In the 1923 Series, in a losing cause for the Giants, he batted .417; won the first game with a 9th-inning inside-the-park home run, the first four-bagger ever hit in Yankee Stadium in post-season play; and reached the seats in the 7th inning of game three to hand the National Leaguers a 1–0 victory. His emerging persona was evident in such antics as carrying a flashlight onto the field to convince an unimpressed umpire that it was too dark to continue a game, and doffing his cap to release a bird for the delight of the crowd. More important, however, he became a devoted acolyte of Giants manager John McGraw.

Warren Spahn summed up Stengel's managerial career with the claim that he played for the pilot "both before and after he was a genius." His references to stints with the Braves and Mets under Stengel are only a partial truth. For one thing, Stengel showed little evidence of genius in piloting the Dodgers either. For another, more positive thing, he showed flashes of minor league brilliance by winning pennants with the Toledo Mud Hens (American Association), Milwaukee Brewers (AA), and Oakland Oaks (Pacific Coast League). He also demonstrated, early on, the cunning (typically disguised as tomfoolery in the retelling) that would mark his later years when, as outfielder-manager-president of the Eastern League Worcester club in 1925, he got out from under all three jobs by releasing himself from the first, firing himself from the second, and resigning from the third to take over the McGraw-owned Mud Hens in 1926; in fact, the entire escapade was an elaborate ploy to gull Worcester owner Judge Emil Fuchs out of compensation for his player contract.

After two years as a Dodger coach, Stengel took over as dugout boss in 1934. His first big league managing job lasted three years, and it had its moments. For one, the Stengel-led club took two late 1934 games from the Giants that cost the New Yorkers the pennant, fulfilling general manager Bob Quinn's wildest hopes when he took New York manager Bill Terry's spring question about whether the Dodgers were still in the league and used it to whip up Brooklyn fans against the Giants. For another, Stengel brought the daffiness

of the front office down to the field in ways calculated to charm newsmen and help fans avert their eyes from the team's second-division finishes, such as by protesting the continuation of a game in inclement weather by coaching at third base holding an open umbrella, and by staging races between his players so he could make a few dollars from reporters. For a third, the daffiness took on a life of its own, with center fielder Frenchy Bordagaray chasing his cap rather than a fly ball, and right fielder Hack Wilson, on the assumption that it was yet another line drive, hurriedly retrieving a ball thrown in frustration by pitcher Boom Boom Beck against the wall of Philadelphia's Baker Bowl.

Seven years (1938–43) at the helm of the Braves was more of the same. That phase ended when the manager, in response to a question about a spring training play, unloaded a classic bit of Stengelese on an unamused Lou Perini, who was about to elevate himself from a minor investor in the club to its principal owner. Not too many laughed when, just before Opening Day in 1943, Stengel was run over by a taxi and missed the first two months of the season with a broken leg, nor when columnist Dave Egan nominated the cabbie as the man who did the most for Boston baseball in 1943.

When Stengel succeeded Bucky Harris as Yankee manager in 1949, after several seasons with clubs in the high minors, kind observers regarded the move as a crowd-pleasing sideshow that would last as long as it took to rebuild the club; the unkind thought it a disaster. It turned out to be neither. General manager George Weiss spent considerable time convincing co-owners Del Webb and Dan Topping to accept his choice. Stengel vindicated his old friend by turning in his best managerial effort in his first season, winning the pennant over the Red Sox by only a game on the final day of the season by juggling lineups to compensate for seventy-one injuries and platooning at almost every position. He also made uncannily successful decisions, often going "against the book," such as when he allowed righty-swinging outfielder Johnny Lindell to bat against Boston right-hander Joe Dobson in the 8th inning of the penultimate game, even though Lindell had been platooned with lefty hitter Gene

Woodling all year and had been removed for a pinch hitter in several previous at-bats against Dobson; Lindell homered to break a 4–4 tie.

His first world championship under his belt after besting the Dodgers in 5 games, Stengel saw no further reason to defer to the Yankee old guard, as he had in 1949 by keeping George Stirnweiss and Charlie Keller in the lineup until injuries made them expendable. The dictatorial, acerbic Stengel, kept in check in 1949, reemerged in 1950 to alienate most of the veterans. His relationship with Joe DiMaggio was particularly strained. Although the manager went out of his way to declare the center fielder the best player he had ever managed, he also seemed to look for ways of humbling the future Hall of Famer, whose lack of respect for the manager was no secret. On various occasions, Stengel had Topping persuade the star to move to first base, an experiment that lasted only a game; dropped him from cleanup to fifth in the batting order and sat him down for "a rest" without discussing the moves beforehand; and sent an embarrassed Cliff Mapes out to replace him in the field in midinning. In the last instance, DiMaggio waved his substitute back to the bench disdainfully, then took himself out of the game at the end of the inning. By the end of the season, DiMaggio was barely acknowledging Stengel's presence, but it hardly mattered to the manager, who won a second pennant and World Series.

It was with younger players that Stengel had his greatest successes. Martin and Whitey Ford arrived in 1950. Then, in 1951, the organization ran the first of its pre-spring training instructional camps; Mickey Mantle, Gil McDougald, and pitcher Tom Morgan joined the big league club directly from the camp the first year, with others following regularly. Even though Mantle was to become the jewel in Stengel's crown, DiMaggio's successor in center field had to endure constant barbs from the manager for a perceived disparity between his potential and his productivity. Even years later, he mused about what might have happened had he left Mantle a shortstop instead of converting him to the outfield, speculating that he would have been greater than Honus Wagner.

Through 1960, Stengel won ten pennants (tying him with McGraw for the most ever) and seven World Series (matching Joe McCarthy's total), using his standard approach of riding his players when they were doing well and heaping praise on them when they were losing. He also evolved into The Old Perfesser, holding forth until all hours of the night in bars around the AL with what he called "my writers." The key to his charm was the highly developed art form that came to be known as Stengelese, a personal jabberwocky of rambling double-talk, gibberish, non sequiturs, and catchphrases that left his audiences alternately amused, bewildered, and mildly better informed. Those subjected to his monologues required a dictionary informing them that a "butcher boy" was a chopped ground ball, a "whiskey slick" a carouser, and "the Youth of America" the current crop of rookies. The U.S. Senate Subcommittee on Monopoly and Antitrust had no such word book when Stengel delivered a vintage dose of his private language in a July 1958 hearing on baseball's exemption from federal antitrust laws.

But as he grew older, Stengel became increasingly impatient with "the Youth of America." For several years, Topping and Webb were anxious to replace him before some other team snatched Ralph Houk away from the Yankee farm club in Denver. An opportunity arose following the 1960 World Series loss to the Pirates, with Stengel coming in for widespread criticism for getting only two starts out of Whitey Ford and getting Ralph Terry up in the bullpen four times before he came to the mound in time for Bill Mazeroski's decisive home run. Two days after the conclusion of the Series, Stengel officially "retired," while putting up no pretense that the change had been his idea. "I'll never make the mistake of being seventy again," he complained.

Two years later, Weiss, in his new role as president of the embryonic Mets, hired Stengel as manager of the expansion club, making him the only man ever to wear the uniform of all four twentieth-century New York clubs. Stengel's job was less to direct the sorry collection of veterans that compiled one of the worst records in baseball history than to promote his Amazin' Mets as better entertainment than the Yankees. For nearly four years, hardly a day went by without the sports pages reporting some bizarre (or bizarrely stated) observation from him on the sorry state of his team. The brilliance of his public relations performance endeared the incompetent Mets to The New Breed fans, who relished the incompetence as much as its promotion. "Can't anybody here play this game?" became as much a trademark Stengel tag line as "You could look it up." Behind assertions that he was interested in building the team into a winner, he wisecracked his way through three tenth-place finishes and part of another.

But when he wasn't winning public relations points for the Mets, Stengel was snoozing on the bench or castigating his players. Of infielder Jerry Lumpe's offensive abilities, he said, "He's a great hitter until I play him." Catcher Chris Cannizzaro, whose name Stengel invariably mispronounced, came in for this assessment: "He's a great catch, that Canzoneri. He's the only defensive catcher who can't catch." The psychologically disturbed Jimmy Piersall he described as "great but you gotta play him in a cage." Catcher Greg Goossen entered all the books of baseball's greatest quotations by being described as "only twenty and with a good chance in ten years of being thirty." Everyone laughed—except the players.

In 1965, a broken wrist forced the seventy-four-year-old manager to turn the club over to coach Wes Westrum temporarily. Then, in late July, after a banquet the night before an Old Timers' Game, another fall fractured his hip. Everyone but the New York players regretted his consequent retirement. Stengel lived for more than a decade after being pensioned off by the Mets. The inscription on his grave is one of his most quoted lines: "There comes a time in every man's life, and I've had plenty of them."

RENNIE STENNETT

Stennett is the only twentieth-century player to get 7 hits in a 9-inning game. The Pittsburgh second baseman rapped out two doubles, a triple, and four singles in a 22–0 rout of the Cubs on September 16, 1975. The game was the most one-sided shutout in baseball history.

GENE STEPHENS

Stephens was known throughout his eight-year career with the Red Sox as a defensive caddy for Ted Williams. But on June 18, 1953, in the course of a 17-run 7th inning, the lefty-swinging outfielder also became the only twentieth-century major leaguer to get 3 hits in an inning.

VERN STEPHENS

Stephens was a slugging shortstop who proved the power of contrition. While with the Browns, the righty hitter signed a five-year, $175,000 contract to play for the Mexican League in 1946. After only 2 games south of the border, however, his father and St. Louis scout Jack Fournier drove to Mexico and whisked him across the Rio Grande disguised in the former's clothes. He avoided the suspension imposed on the other jumpers when Commissioner Happy Chandler reinstated him at once, ostensibly on the grounds that, since he had not signed with the Browns for 1946 before he took off, he had not broken a valid contract; in fact, Stephens had violated the supposedly sacrosanct reserve clause. The infielder played fifteen (1941–55) big league seasons, mostly with the Browns and Red Sox, compiling a .286 career average and 247 homers, and leading the American League in homers once and in RBIs three times.

RIGGS STEPHENSON

Stephenson's .336 lifetime average is the highest among twentieth-century players eligible for the Hall of Fame but without a plaque in Cooperstown. Primarily a second baseman with the Indians from 1921 to 1925 and an outfielder with the Cubs between 1926 and 1934, the right-handed hitter's chronic shoulder ailments made him too much of a defensive liability to be a regular with Cleveland. His potent bat kept him in Chicago's lineup, however. In the Cubs' pennant-winning season of 1929, he combined with future Hall of Famers Hack Wilson and Kiki Cuyler to form the only outfield in major league history in which each of the trio drove in 100 runs. (Wilson had 159 RBIs that year, Stephenson 110, and Cuyler 102.)

LESLIE STERLING

Sterling became the first woman public address announcer in the American League when she succeeded the deceased Sherm Feller in Fenway Park in 1994.

AARON STERN

Other major league owners were as venal as Stern, but none was foolish enough to leave so extensive a paper trail chronicling his rapacity. As president of the American Association Reds when the traveling world championship series of 1887 was about to come to Cincinnati, he wrote to the club treasurer: "In the game between Chicago and St. Louis use no turnstiles—if they ask for our turnstiles, say they are out of order"; he added that he wanted nothing said about money collected at a downtown ticket agency so that he could keep the full amount rather than the 20 percent due him. Three years later, Stern, having switched the Reds to the National League and severely damaged by the Players League war, swore up and down that he would never sell out, and, if he did, it would be for cash. Within weeks, he unloaded the franchise for $40,000, half of it in promissory notes, to a consortium of PL backers headed by Al Johnson.

HARRY STEVENS

Stevens was a paid informer for Cincinnati who, in 1914, cost the franchise both a manager and baseball's greatest player. In protest over an order that Stevens would be accompanying the club on road trips to report on player antics, manager Joe Tinker refused to sign a contract and was sold to the Dodgers. Then, during the season, Reds boss Garry Herrmann decided to get more for his money than his spy's bland reports, so he dispatched Stevens to Baltimore to make recommendations on two players owed to Cincinnati by the minor league Orioles. Although he had absolutely no experience as a scout, Stevens endorsed the acquisition of shortstop Claude Derrick and outfielder George Twombly. He also recommended that the club not bother with pitchers Ernie Shore and Babe Ruth.

HARRY M. STEVENS

Dissatisfied with the scorecard he had purchased for an American Association Columbus Colts game in the 1880s, the English-born Stevens won a contract to design and hawk an im-

proved version, supposedly originating the cliché "You can't tell the players without a scorecard" in the process. After expanding to other cities and branching out into food and drink, Stevens won an exclusive concession contract at the Polo Grounds in 1893 and, using his new connections in the city, soon was operating in Madison Square Garden as well. By 1911 he was so wealthy that he was able to loan Giants owner John T. Brush the money to rebuild the Polo Grounds grandstand after a fire. His innovations include the introduction of the hot dog (at the Polo Grounds in 1901) and serving drinks with a straw (so thirsty patrons would not have to tilt their heads back and possibly miss a vital play while sipping his soda and beer). Stevens's multimillion-dollar business today includes concessions at racetracks and hotels as well as sports arenas and stadiums; the company's most recent baseball contracts have been with Candlestick Park, Shea Stadium, and Fenway Park.

DAVE STEWART

Stewart was the classic case of a journeyman getting off at the right stop for once. After wandering around from the Dodgers to the Rangers to the Phillies as a long reliever between 1978 and 1986, the right-hander landed in Oakland with manager Tony LaRussa and pitching coach Dave Duncan, who decided he was better suited as a starter. The result was four straight 20-win years. With the Athletics and then later with the Blue Jays, Stewart also racked up a record 10 victories between League Championship Series and World Series.

In 1988, the Year of the Balk, Stewart was saddled with a major league mark of 16.

ERNIE STEWART

Stewart, a five-year veteran American League arbiter, was fired in 1945 for attempting to organize an umpires' union.

SAMMY STEWART

Based on what he actually did for the Orioles in 1981, Stewart won the American League ERA title. But under a rule stipulating that the number of innings pitched be rounded off to the nearest complete inning, he lost the honor to Oakland's

Steve McCatty. On September, 1978, the right-hander set a new standard by striking out 7 consecutive batters in his major league debut.

DAVE STIEB

Toronto's best pitcher for most of the 1980s, Stieb played three years of tag with no-hitters. In back-to-back games in September 1988, the right-hander got two outs in the 9th inning before yielding his first hit. On August 4, 1989, he went himself one better (or worse) by throwing a perfect game until the 27th batter, Roberto Kelly of the Yankees, lashed a double. In that same season, he threw two more one-hitters. Stieb finally ended his quest on September 2, 1990, by no-hitting the Indians. The game also ended his dominance as an American League pitcher; shortly afterward he was injured and, after having won in double numbers ten times, never again posted more than 4 victories in a year.

TONI STONE

Stone was the first woman to play in the Negro leagues. A high school softball player, the twenty-two-year-old second baseman hit .243 in 40 games for the Indianapolis Clowns of the Negro American League in 1953 in what was largely a publicity stunt to attract fans after the best black players had been skimmed by the majors. Traded to the Kansas City Monarchs in 1954, she was replaced on the Indianapolis roster by nineteen-year-old Connie Morgan, the second female Negro leaguer.

CHARLES STONEHAM

Stoneham's seventeen-year (1919–35) ownership of the Giants was a daredevil act over potential indictments and lawsuits that exposed more than had been intended. His survival owed mainly to his Tammany Hall connections and to adversaries who were as legally dubious as he was.

When he purchased the club from Harry Hempstead and the John T. Brush estate in January 1919 for $1 million, Stoneham was depicted in New York's buddy-boy press as a Wall Street broker; actually, he was the proprietor of a string of bucket shops for off-market speculation. One of his partners in the latter venture was Arnold Rothstein, the professional gambler who shortly afterward became implicated in the Black Sox scandal. On the other hand, Stoneham was also a close associate of Governor Alfred E. Smith and most of the powers-that-be in the state's Democratic Party. It also helped that he had cultivated local hero John McGraw for years; in fact, his first act as owner of the Giants was to give the manager a piece of the club and add a vice-presidency title to his standing in the organization.

Through most of the 1920s, Stoneham was content to endorse the McGraw moves that produced four pennants and led to a succession of future Hall of Famers taking the field in the Polo Grounds. His most nervous moments came in 1924, when a handful of players was accused of trying to get Philadelphia shortstop Heinie Sand to throw a game, and in 1927, when newly acquired Rogers Hornsby was sued by the Kentucky Gambling Commission for some $70,000 in unpaid wagering debts: Both episodes reminded too many people of his own gambling connections, prompting unfounded rumors of some imminent investigation of the franchise by Commissioner Kenesaw Landis. In the event, Stoneham's biggest headache turned out to be minority stockholder and city magistrate Francis X. McQuade.

Between 1928 and 1933, Stoneham and McQuade took turns at legal suits over the owner's charges that the since-fired club treasurer had sought to "destroy" the Giants, among other ways by trying to draw McGraw into a plot to find the organization new ownership. McQuade retaliated by offering evidence that Stoneham had been using franchise money for years to finance his other ventures, not least his periodically investigated bucket shops. But those charges would have been more persuasive if, for his part, Stoneham hadn't countered with equally compelling proof that McQuade had used his position as treasurer to "borrow" money for his own private purposes. With the various trials entertaining everybody in the city except McQuade and the owner's political and business associates, an appeals court finally took the high road by ruling that, whatever had ensued during McQuade's stint as organization treasurer, it was secondary to the fact that his simultaneous standing as a city magistrate precluded such activities as being an officer of a baseball club. (McQuade's name, but not Stoneham's, had also figured prominently in the Seabury Commission's 1931–32 probe of corruption in the Tammany administration of Mayor Jimmy Walker.)

Stoneham died in 1935, leaving the club to his son Horace.

HORACE STONEHAM

Like Tom Yawkey, Stoneham kept a nice-guy reputation through a forty-year (1936–75) reign as an owner; unlike Yawkey, he was still on his feet when he was overwhelmed by the changes brought by free agency.

When he took over the Giants from his father, Charles, in 1936, Stoneham was known mainly as a hard but convivial drinker who talked baseball into the wee hours with his favorite players and others he regarded as part of the franchise family. The only thing that really changed over the years was that he became as knowledgeable as he was garrulous, in good part because of his all-night sessions in the late 1940s and early 1950s with manager Leo Durocher. What he didn't realize until after the fact was that Durocher used the gab and drinking fests to find out who Stoneham's favorite players were and then play them into the ground if he didn't share the owner's opinion. Among the players disposed of in this way were outfield sluggers Willard Marshall and Sid Gordon.

In the mid-1950s, Stoneham began issuing regular warnings to New York City and the National League that he would be forced to move to another city if he didn't get a new stadium. Unlike the similar warnings coming from Brooklyn's Walter O'Malley at the same time, Stoneham's had some basis in economic reality because of a sharp attendance drop at the Polo Grounds and the third serving the franchise was receiving after the Dodgers and Yankees from local broadcasting rights. The fact that the Polo Grounds was in Harlem did not help attract the carriage trade, particularly after a spectator was killed in 1956 by a sniper firing into the stadium from a rooftop across the street. By the beginning of the 1957 season, the question wasn't so much whether Stoneham would move the Giants, as where he would move them. For some weeks, the likely destination seemed to be Minneapolis, where the

club had its chief farm team. But then in May, the NL gave its formal approval for the Dodgers to move to Los Angeles and the Giants to San Francisco if there were unable to conclude local deals. With O'Malley turning on the pressure (the league had made it a condition that both clubs move if one did), Stoneham went before his board of directors on August 19, 1957, and got an 8–1 vote in favor of moving to San Francisco.

Stoneham took some time to get used to California. He was especially sharp in rejecting suggestions that the club change its name to the Seals, arguing somewhat defensively that "it's one thing to move a team, another to erase a glorious past." He was also as appalled as Willie Mays that San Francisco fans did not take to the Polo Grounds star for quite a number of years, preferring such local heroes as Orlando Cepeda and Willie McCovey because they had no trace of New York about them. What he never got used to was Candlestick Park—or to the fact that he had been given a guided tour of the land for the facility in the early afternoon, a couple of hours before the arrival of the daily winds that made it the worst outdoor stadium in the major leagues. Although the park was little more than an obstacle during the club's regular winning seasons in the 1960s, it became a decisive reason for fans to stay home when the play on the field turned mediocre in the early 1970s, to the point that attendance figures began dipping below those registered in the final years at the Polo Grounds.

By 1972, Stoneham was talking about selling out. It ended up taking more than four years, but not for lack of trying. Prospective buyers came and went amid demands by Mayor George Moscone that any deal contain a commitment to keep the club in San Francisco, the threatened alternative being a lawsuit. Stoneham paid lip service to the commitment, then in 1975 announced that he had concluded an accord with a Canadian beer company bent on moving the Giants to Toronto. For its part, the NL appeared ready to sanction the move just to get rid of Stoneham; for a couple of years, in fact, San Francisco's finances were so chaotic under the owner's drinking and casual attention that the league had been forced to delegate Spec Richardson as its representative to make sure checks were issued on time. But once again Mayor Moscone managed to thwart the deal. It was only then that real-estate developer Bob Lurie stepped forward with the money to buy the club and a commitment to keeping it in the Bay Area. As for Stoneham, he confessed to being relieved at getting out of a "world or agents and boardroom accountants where there's no more personal touch."

CARL STOTZ

Together with Bert and George Bebble, Stotz started the Little League in Williamsport, Pennsylvania, in 1939. Then consisting of only a handful of local teams, the Little League has grown to include 2.7 million participants, mostly in the United States but to one degree or another in eighty other countries as well.

GEORGE STOVALL

A competent first baseman for a dozen years, Stovall was in the forefront of a threat by Cleveland players to strike in April 1911 so they could attend the funeral of teammate Addie Joss. After conferring with club president Charles Somers and manager Deacon McGuire, American League president Ban Johnson thought better of his original decision to order the players to the field. Other Stovall disputes with management had less favorable outcomes. For example, four years earlier, he had been suspended for throwing a chair at McGuire's predecessor, Nap Lajoie. Late in the 1913 season, Stovall was fired as Browns' manager for spitting at umpire Charlie Ferguson and told he would be paid for not showing up to play first base for the rest of the season as well. A subsequent war of nerves with St. Louis owner Robert Hedges had the ex-manager honoring his contract by appearing at the ballpark every day, the owner refusing a request for an outright release, and the player becoming the first to jump to the Federal League, with the observation that "no white man ought to submit to be bartered like a broken-down plow horse."

HARRY STOVEY

Though ignored by Hall of Fame electors, Stovey was nonetheless the game's first great slugger. Among his accomplishments were being the first player to break double figures in home

runs in a season (14 with the American Association Philadelphia Athletics in 1883) and leading all major leaguers in homers during the 1880s (with 90). As good a base runner as he was a slugger, Stovey was the first to wear sliding pads, an innovation he came up with to protect a bruise on his leg. While the first baseman-turned-outfielder had his best seasons in the AA, he indirectly contributed to that league's demise. When the Players League folded after the 1890 season, Stovey, who had jumped to that circuit's Boston Reds, should have been returned to the Athletics, his 1889 club; the A's, however, left him off their protected list on the assumption that he would remain with the Reds, who were about to be absorbed into the AA. Taking advantage of the player's technical free-agent status, the National League Boston Beaneaters signed him, precipitating a new interleague war, one that the AA was ill equipped to fight.

For a century, record books credited Stovey with a .404 average in 1884, but the actual figure was .326. Chicanery by the Philadelphia official scorer, aimed at giving him the batting crown over New York's Dave Orr, may account for the discrepancy. Stovey was actually born Harry Stowe, but he played under a pseudonym to spare his genteel mother the embarrassment of seeing the family name in the sports pages.

MONTY STRATTON

Stratton's back-to-back 15-win seasons in 1937 and 1938 with a darting fastball that he called the "gander" seemed to mark the beginning of a brilliant pitching career for the White Sox. In November 1938, however, the right-hander accidentally shot himself while hunting, leading to the loss of a leg. Stratton's tenacity allowed him to return to the mound at a minor league level for a few games, but it was more of a psychological than a physical victory. He was the subject of a popular 1949 film with Jimmy Stewart.

DARRYL STRAWBERRY

Strawberry's titanic blasts for the Mets in the 1980s were subsequently eclipsed by numerous off-field incidents and his penchant for putting his foot into his mouth. Called up to New York in 1983, he sprang out of the gate faster than any other power hitter in history, never dipping below 26 homers in a year over his first nine seasons. Along the way, the lefty-swinging right fielder won Rookie of the Year honors (1983), paced the National League in round-trippers and slugging average (1988), and reached the 200-homer plateau sooner than any other big leaguer (at age twenty-seven in 1989). The only thing longer than some of Strawberry's drives was his tongue—especially in his annual predictions that he intended carrying the team with a "monster season," his attacks on teammates; and his endless declarations of new awareness for having overcome alcoholism, a bad marriage, an irreligious life, bad companions, and then, closing the circle, an obsession with the religious life. In between were episodes with the police over gun-carrying and wife-beating charges.

Feeling rebuffed by Mets general manager Frank Cashen, Strawberry signed as a free agent with the Dodgers in 1991. After one passable season, he was sidelined for most of the next two years with a herniated disc that ultimately required surgery. Shortly after making another pronouncement in spring training of 1994 that he was ready to carry the Dodgers with one of his monster seasons, he was admitted to a rehab clinic because of a second bout with drink and drug problems. Within weeks, the Dodgers bought out his contract, a solution Strawberry accepted because he was also having trouble with the IRS. Dodger manager Tom Lasorda's parting shot came as a guest on a cable TV show when he responded to a caller's accusation that Strawberry was a "dog" with this tasteless crack: "You're wrong. A dog is loyal and runs hard after balls."

Strawberry signed with the Giants in June, after undergoing rehabilitation, then in December found himself indicted on federal income tax evasion charges arising from a wide ranging investigation of fees paid to players to sign autographs at memorabilia shows.

GABBY STREET

Street had an eight-year (1904–12, 1931) career as a catcher and put in another six seasons managing the Cardinals and Browns, but he is mainly remembered for catching a ball dropped from the top of the Washington Monument. The stunt was arranged in August 1908 by Pres Gibson, a theater critic who wanted to demonstrate that his crony Street was the best defensive catcher in the league at the time. Gibson took thirteen balls to the top of the 555-foot-high monument and, with a crowd in attendance, dropped them one at a time down to the waiting Street. Because of high winds, the first 12 balls either caromed off the side of the monument or fell completely beyond the receiver's reach. On the very last drop, however, Street made the catch. Whether or not the demonstration proved Gibson's case about Street's defensive abilities, it certainly wasn't offense that kept the catcher around: He batted only .208 for his career. Taking over the Cardinals in 1930, Street became one of the few managers to win pennants in his first two years of managing.

CUB STRICKER

A light-hitting second baseman with several clubs in the 1880s and 1890s, Stricker had his best day at the plate on July 29, 1883, when he went 4-for-4 while playing for the American Association Philadelphia Athletics against Louisville's Guy Hecker. It also turned out to be his worst day on the basepaths, when Hecker picked him off first a record three times in the game.

CURTIS STRONG

Strong was a Philadelphia caterer whose drug-trafficking trial in Pittsburgh in 1985 shed glaring light on the widespread use of drugs among major league players. Among those who testified during the proceedings (all under grants of immunity) were such stars as Keith Hernandez, Jeffrey Leonard, Lonnie Smith, and Dave Parker. All admitted having bought one kind of drug or another from Strong or one of his codefendants, with Hernandez raising the most hackles in baseball circles by estimating that up to 40 percent of his big league contemporaries had used cocaine at least once. Trial testimony disclosed that Strong and other pushers had enjoyed almost total access to the clubhouse and team flights of the Pittsburgh Pirates for a six-year period beginning with the team's championship year of 1979. At one point, a law enforcement witness disclosed, the FBI had even wired the club mascot, the Pirate Parrot, to gain evidence against the pushers and the players.

Despite the consistency of such testimony, Chuck Tanner, the Pittsburgh manager throughout the period in question, denied ever noticing anything untoward. When he did not return to manage the Pirates in 1986, the most benign interpretation was that he had lost touch with his players.

DICK STUART

In a period when the major leagues boasted such brilliant defensive first basemen as Gil Hodges, Vic Power, Bill White, and George Scott, Stuart gained equal fame as Dr. Strangeglove for his fielding ineptitude. Nevertheless, he also managed to lead the American League in both assists and putouts in 1963—an anomaly he was usually the first to asterisk by noting that he also committed the most errors that season for a first baseman. A classic all-or-nothing slugger, he hit at least 23 home runs six times in his ten-year career with six teams, and was the first player to hit 30 home runs and drive in 100 runs in a season in both leagues. When he signed with the Angels in 1969, he also became the first player to return to the majors after playing in Japan.

MOOSE STUBING

As a coach for the Angels in 1988, Stubing took over for fired manager Cookie Rojas for the final 8 games of the season, losing them all. That established the twentieth-century record for most managerial losses without a win and tied the overall mark set by George Creamer of the Pittsburgh Alleghenys in 1884.

JIMMY ST. VRAIN

A left-handed pitcher but a right-handed batter for the 1902 Cubs, St. Vrain was so useless at the plate that manager Frank Selee suggested during a game against Pittsburgh that he try to hit from his natural southpaw side. From this unfamiliar vantage point, he did indeed make contact with a grounder to shortstop Honus Wagner. St. Vrain ran as fast as he could—to third base.

ED SUDOL

A twenty-year National League arbiter, Sudol gained recognition as the Extra-Inning Umpire. His reputation would not have been possible without the assistance of the Mets, who were involved

in three marathons in which Sudol called balls and strikes: a 23-inning contest with the Giants on May 31, 1964 that lasted seven hours and 24 minutes, longer than any other NL game; a 25-inning affair with the Cardinals on September 11, 1974; and a 17-inning game, also against St. Louis, on April 19, 1976.

CLYDE SUKEFORTH

A backup catcher in the National League in the 1920s and 1930s, Sukeforth became Branch Rickey's middleman during the secret maneuvers to break the color ban with Jackie Robinson. Never told explicitly what was in the offing, Sukeforth was sent to Chicago to scout Robinson for the all-black New York Brown Bombers Rickey was touting to confederates as a new venture. Finding Robinson sidelined with a sore shoulder, he brought him to New York instead, and fretted over the fact that he had never seen the prospect play before the deal with Brooklyn was consummated.

Sukeforth declined a couple of opportunities to manage the Dodgers in the 1940s, preferring to stay in the background as a troubleshooter or coach. But he was thrust into unhappy prominence during the 1951 playoffs against the Giants when, asked by Charlie Dressen who was ready to come in to face Bobby Thomson, he reported from the bullpen that Carl Erskine had just bounced a curve and that Ralph Branca looked sharp. Sukeforth was fired by Rickey's successor Walter O'Malley after Thomson reached the seats against Branca.

BILL SULLIVAN

As promotions director of the Boston Braves in 1946, Sullivan devised the first team yearbook. The *Braves' Sketch Book* sold an estimated twenty-two thousand copies.

DAVE SULLIVAN

Objections to Sullivan's umpiring by St. Louis Browns manager Charlie Comiskey resulted in the only forfeited game in postseason championship play. In the sixth inning of the second game of the 1885 series played between National League and American Association champions, the umpire hesitated in calling a fair ball on a slow roller by

Chicago's Ned Williamson. The hit put the White Stockings ahead, 5-4, but Comiskey, having already protested Sullivan's work on several earlier plays, pulled his team off the field and accepted a forfeit rather than what he felt was theft by a National League partisan. Both teams later agreed to disregard the forfeit, but when the Series ended in a 3-3 standoff with one tie, Chicago manager Cap Anson decided unilaterally to reinstate the second game and declare his club world champions. Sullivan never officiated in another major league game.

TED SULLIVAN

A successful baseball promoter of nineteenth-century baseball, Sullivan earned his niche in the game's history when he had Charlie Comiskey experiment with playing wide of the fist-base bag and with stretching for throws from other infielders. After coming up with these innovations as the founder and manager of the Dubuque Rabbits in 1878, Sullivan formed the minor Northwestern League to give his club more structured competition. His major league career included managerial assignments with the American Association St. Louis Browns in 1883, when, under his direction, the club racked up 53 wins against only 26 losses before repeated clashes with owner Chris Von der Ahe forced him to depart. He also guided the Union Association St. Louis Maroons to victory in their first 20 contests of the 1884 season before moving on to pilot the Kansas City Unions.

While organizing a succession of profitable minor league teams, Sullivan championed ladies' days, night games, the importation of English football, and the exportation (to England) of American baseball. Along the way, he picked up a reputation as a "queer genius," as the weekly *Sporting Life* labeled him for his suggestion that pitchers should be omitted from the batting order. In later life he published two books on the game, *Humorous Stories of the Ball Field* (1903) and *History of the World's Tour* (1914), and several plays with baseball plots. Sullivan has also frequently been cited as the first to dub baseball enthusiasts "fans." He claimed it was his personal abbreviation for what his onetime boss Von der Ahe called "fanatics."

ED SUMMERS

The most successful of the old-fashioned knuckleball pitchers who used the top joints of their fingers rather than their fingertips to flick the ball, Summers established an American League rookie record by posting 24 wins for the Tigers in 1908. The fingertip knuckler was not used in the major leagues until 1920, when Ed Rommell arrived with the Athletics; he learned the pitch from a plumber named Charles Dreuery.

BILLY SUNDAY

A speedster, mostly with the Cubs, from 1883 to 1890, Sunday is reported to have stolen second, third, and home on consecutive pitches to win a game; despite such heroics, he is best remembered as a fiery Prohibitionist orator. Converted suddenly in 1887, the outfielder retired after the 1890 season to devote himself exclusively to evangelism. Often beginning his temperance lectures by executing a perfect hook slide onto the stage, he roused audiences with descriptions of how he would punch, kick, and bite the plague of demon run until, "old and fistless and footless and toothless," he would "gum it to death until it goes home to perdition and I go home to glory." Another of his obsessions in his various crusades was the violation of the Sabbath with the playing of baseball games.

JIM SUNDBERG

Catcher Sundberg was a key figure in the disheveling of the Texas franchise in the late 1970s and early 1980s. It was when the defensively brilliant receiver was offered a six-year contract by Brad Corbett that other stockholders united to force the erratic owner to sell the franchise. A couple of years later, Sundberg exercised his contractual rights by refusing a trade to Los Angeles that would have brought the Rangers pitchers Orel Hershiser, Dave Stewart, and Burt Hooten. Sundberg was eventually dealt to the Brewers for the .182-hitting Ned Yost.

RICK SUTCLIFFE

Sutcliffe is the only pitcher to win a Cy Young Award for a team he joined in midseason. On June 13, 1984, the right-hander was peddled by the Indians to the Cubs in exchange for outfielders

Joe Carter and Mel Hall. He went on to fashion a 16-1 record for Chicago in its East Division win. Sutcliffe was traded under bumpier circumstances in 1981, when the Dodgers sent him to Cleveland for Jorge Orta; the swap followed his trashing of manager Tom Lasorda's office after being informed that he was being kept off the Los Angeles roster for the National League Championship Series because of injuries. In 1979 he won Rookie of the Year honors for the Dodgers with 16 victories.

BRUCE SUTTER

Sutter's arbitration win prior to the 1980 season alerted major league owners that they had more to worry about than free agency. With the Cubs for only four seasons when his case was heard, the relief ace's award of $700,000—double the team's offer—effectively recognized diamond stardom regardless of the length of big league service. The decision brought the ire of other owners down on the Cubs for not reaching an agreement with the right-hander prior to arbitration—an irritation that gradually became more academic with subsequent rewards. The forkball specialist found himself in an advantageous position after leading the National League in saves in 1979. He repeated that performance four more times during his twelve-year career, including 1982, when his bullpen work helped steer the Cardinals to a world championship. It was after Sutter's defection to the Braves as a free agent in 1984 that St. Louis manager Whitey Herzog made the first extensive use of a bullpen by committee to nail down victories.

DON SUTTON

Sutton's career was more whole than parts. In twenty-three seasons (1966–88) with the Dodgers and four other clubs, the right-hander won more than 20 games only once (21 in 1976), paced National League hurlers in ERA (2.21 in 1980) and in shutouts (9 in 1972) only once each, never led his league in any other category, never pitched a no-hitter, and never won a Cy Young Award. On the other hand, he became a 300-game winner (324), the only one to have only one 20-win season, and one of the baseball's top five strikeout

pitchers (3,574), the only one never to rack up league-leading totals in the category.

Eluding the disabled list for his entire career, Sutton ranks on several all-time lists for durability: third in games started, seventh in innings pitched, and tenth in shutouts. A teammate of Hall of Famers Sandy Koufax and Don Drysdale, he nevertheless has the most wins (233) of any Dodger pitcher, in either Brooklyn or Los Angeles.

An accomplished scuffballer, Sutton was ejected from a game against the Cardinals on June 14, 1978, after umpire Doug Harvey collected three similarly doctored balls. After threatening a lawsuit against both Harvey and the National League for threatening his ability to earn a living, the pitcher was let off with a warning but no suspension.

EZRA SUTTON

Sutton made the first major league error when he threw wildly past first base after fielding a ground ball in the first National League contest, on April 22, 1876. After one season with Philadelphia, Sutton moved to Boston, where, for more than a decade, he built a reputation as the best third baseman of the nineteenth century.

LARRY SUTTON

Although his baseball background had consisted of little more than a few years as an umpire for a minor league in New Jersey, Sutton was responsible for the signing of just about every top player on the Dodgers in the years immediately before and after World War I. Having convinced owner Charlie Ebbets that he knew talent when he saw it and that he was free to roam over the country for a salary that was close to free, Sutton, a professional printer, dug out of the minors for Brooklyn such major league stars as Casey Stengel, Jake Daubert, Otto Miller, and Jeff Pfeffer. Even more impressive, Sutton signed future Hall of Famer Zach Wheat and recommended that Ebbets trade for two other eventual Cooperstown residents—pitchers Dazzy Vance and Burleigh Grimes.

CHARLIE SWEENEY

Sweeney was helping to pitch Providence to a National League pennant when, on July 21, 1884, he got drunk during an exhibition game, left the park, and failed to show up for practice the next morning. Sent to the mound for the afternoon's game anyway, the right-hander sulked his way through 7 innings, refusing to acknowledge manager Frank Bancroft's first order to turn the pitching duties over to someone else, then storming off the field in the wake of a second, more insistent command; he left the team to blow a 6-2 lead with only eight men on the field. The hurler fumed right into the arms of Union Association angel Henry V. Lucas, signing a contract with that league's St. Louis Maroons that made him the best-paid moundsman in the game. The question is still open whether the stormy nature of Sweeney's defection was the result of an alcoholic pique or a premeditated sham to cover his intentional contract-jumping. What there is no question about is that Sweeney is the only pitcher ever to play a major role on two pennant-winning teams in the same year. His 17-8 record provided the Grays with a significant first-half boost toward their flag; his 24-7 second-half mark made the difference for the Maroons, who captured the UA banner in the league's only season.

LEO SWEETLAND

Sweetland's 1930 ERA of 7.71 is the highest for any pitcher in a season with enough qualifying innings. It wasn't all the fault of the Year of the Hitter, either: In five major league seasons for the Phillies and Reds, the southpaw's best ERA was 5.04.

STUART SYMINGTON

Of all the U.S. senators who have threatened baseball with an investigation into its exemption from antitrust statutes, Missouri Democrat Symington got the quickest action. Outraged at the 1967 American League decision to allow Charlie Finley to move the Athletics from Kansas City to Oakland, he rejected generic promises from league president Joe Cronin that another team would eventually move into the city, asking for a specific calendar. With most of the AL owners already headed home from the meeting that had approved the franchise shift, a panicked Cronin managed to reassemble a bare quorum for an extra session, where it was decided that Kansas City would have a new team by 1969. The second thoughts had a ricochet effect in the National League, where equally vague plans for an expansion sometime in the 1970s were scrapped in favor of admitting San Diego and Montreal in 1969. Symington denounced Finley on the Senate floor as "one of the most disreputable characters ever to enter the American sports scene," and didn't shy away from comparing the Athletics boss's impact on Kansas City to that of the atomic bomb on Nagasaki.

T

WILLIAM HOWARD TAFT

Taft became the first president of the United States to throw out the ceremonial first pitch on Opening Day, when the longtime fan tossed a ball to Walter Johnson before a Washington-Athletics game on April 14, 1910. Vice President James Sherman, also in attendance, was knocked unconscious when a foul ball off the bat of Philadelphia's Frank Baker struck him on the head.

After leaving the White House, Taft became a factor in the guerrilla war between American League president Ban Johnson and dissident AL owners. In 1918, the former national chief executive was put forward by Boston's Harry Frazee as a candidate for a proposed post of baseball commissioner to supplant the National Commission—the first time such a suggestion had surfaced.

EDWARD TALCOTT

A principal backer of the Players League New York Giants in 1890, Talcott made an initial mistake in meeting with National League representative Al Spalding after the season to discuss mutual problems, then compounded the error by blurting out the extent of the PL's financial losses. Spalding, keeping the NL's equally desperate situation to himself, negotiated a complete PL capitulation. In 1892, after assuming a minority interest in the NL Giants, Talcott lost twenty of his shares in a wager on the team's final place in the standings to Brooklyn manager John Montgomery Ward.

FRANK TANANA

Tanana had more major league starts (616) than any other pitcher who never had a 20-win season. In his twenty-one years (1973-93) with six big league clubs, he won 240 and lost 236, with a personal high of 19 victories for the Angels in 1976. Coming down with a sore arm the following year, the southpaw blamed his woes on manager Dave Garcia's indulgence of Nolan Ryan's preference for a four-man rotation, even though the introduction of the designated hitter made that approach obsolete; Ryan's rebuttal was to accuse Tanana of living it up between starts. Whatever its cause, this and later arm miseries forced Tanana to convert from a flamethrower to a junkballer, accounting for his longevity.

The hurler's most memorable performance came in the final game of the 1987 season, when he delivered an American League East championship to Detroit with a 1-0 victory over the Blue Jays. An American Leaguer for all but part of his last season, Tanana is the only player to complete twenty major league seasons without coming up to the plate; the streak was broken after he signed with the Mets in 1993.

CHUCK TANNER

Tanner's genial persona over eighteen consecutive years (1970-87) of managing didn't disguise his obtuse handling of various crises under his command—some of his own making. With the White Sox between 1970 and 1975, his problem was the players he alienated by making it clear

President William Howard Taft is greeted by Walter Johnson after becoming the first chief executive to throw out the ball on Opening Day, on April 14, 1910. National Baseball Library, Cooperstown, N.Y.

that they were very secondary to slugger Dick Allen. With the Athletics in 1976, he lost clubhouse authority by not protesting owner Charlie Finley's season-long attempts to sell off would-be free agents even as the club was fighting for the West Division lead in the American League. As pilot of the "We Are Family" Pirates between 1977 and 1985, Tanner, by his own claims during the 1985 Pittsburgh drug trials, never noticed any of the dealers who not only invaded the locker room regularly but also took team flights. With the Braves in 1985 and 1986, his main concern was public relations assistant Robin Monsky, whom he insisted be fired for not saying "more positive" things about the cellar-dwelling team in press releases.

On the question of wins and losses, Tanner took his only world championship with the 1979 Pirates. He steered five other teams to second-place finishes. After the 1976 season he was one of the rare managers swapped for an active player, when Finley sent him to Pittsburgh for catcher Manny Sanguillen.

RANDY TATE

A right-handed pitcher for the 1975 Mets, Tate went to the plate 41 times without getting a hit.

That made him statistically the worst lifetime hitter in baseball history.

BILLY TAYLOR

No proof of the effects of expansion is necessary beyond the details of the career of right-hander Taylor. Pitching for the St. Louis Maroons in the Union Association in 1884, he won 25 and lost only 4; after defecting to the American Association Philadelphia Athletics in midseason, he won another 18 games while losing 12. The UA, a third major league, and the AA, which increased its membership from eight to twelve teams that year, added hundreds of players to major league rosters for that one year. In none of his six other major league seasons did Taylor win more than 4 games.

DUMMY TAYLOR

Deaf-mute Taylor spent almost all of his nine major league seasons (1900-1908) with the Giants and taught manager John McGraw the fundamentals of signing. Both were once ejected from a game by Tim Hurst, who knew enough signing himself to understand that what the pitcher and manager were flashing between the mound and the dugout had less to do with what pitch to throw than with the quality of Hurst's umpiring.

HARRY TAYLOR

A former first baseman for three teams in the 1890s, Taylor became the attorney for the Players Protective Association during the 1900 season just as the American League's raids on the National League were about to provide the players with some leverage in their dealings with owners. Turning up the heat under a pot of player resentments, Taylor offered the NL owners several proposals: reciprocity in the ten days' advance notice required to release a player; club responsibility for doctor fees for injured players; player consent for any trade, sale, or demotion to the minors; and creation of an impartial arbitration panel to settle disputes. When the demands were rejected, a majority of NL players agreed not to sign contracts for the 1901 season. But then, with Taylor returning to his native Buffalo to take care of other legal business, the owners called another meeting with union president Chief Zimmer.

When the owners got Zimmer (and later Taylor) to sign off on mere cosmetic changes, the budding union's power was effectively nipped. Within five years, almost all of the association's leaders had been co-opted and Taylor accepted an offer to become president of the minor Eastern League.

JACK TAYLOR

Of all baseball records, Taylor's mark of 188 consecutive complete games is probably the most unassailable; what was less so was Taylor's reputation for honesty once he took the mound.

From June 20, 1901, when he was with the Cubs, to August 9, 1906, in his third season with the Cardinals, the right-hander was never removed for a relief pitcher. Aside from the 188 complete efforts in that stretch, he also finished another 15 games from the bullpen, for a total of 1,727 innings thrown without respite. Because he was on mediocre teams, Taylor's overall record for ten seasons was only 152-139. He did, however, have a career ERA of only 2.66.

In 1904 Taylor came under fire for comments about accepting money to lose a game in the 1903 postseason Chicago city championship against the White Sox. After denying the charges and being exonerated by the National Commission, the pitcher was immediately confronted by additional allegations that he had thrown a regulation game while with St. Louis in 1904. Admitting only to heavy drinking the night before the game, he was slapped with a $300 fine by the National League but was exonerated of the more serious charge. When the pitcher refused even to pay the fine, a suspiciously consenting Cardinal manager Kid Nichols suggested that the club make good on the levy to keep Taylor from talking about the incident; others recommended getting rid of both Taylor and drinking companion Jake Beckley. Instead, the league adopted a policy of doing nothing until the problem went away.

JOHN TAYLOR

Taylor was a particularly pathetic example of a millionaire operating a baseball team as a toy. The son of *Boston Globe* publisher Charles Henry Taylor, he was given the Red Sox by his father in 1904 mainly to prove that he could do more than live it up at night and sleep late in the morning. He took the mandate seriously enough to enter the clubhouse to lecture the players whenever they lost. When manager Jimmy Collins barred him from the locker room, he stationed himself in a passageway between the field and the locker room to get his remarks in anyway. On two occasions, American League president Ban Johnson, who had brokered the sale of the club to the Taylors, was called in to dissuade Collins from resigning over the owner's interference. A third try failed, and Collins was succeeded by a parade of pilots over the first decade of the century who either resigned on the same grounds or were fired for talking back to Taylor.

Another source of grievance for the succession of managers was Taylor's insistence on completing deals. Among his transactions were swapping future batting king George Stone to the Browns for a washed-up Jesse Burkett, unloading Collins to the Athletics for .239-hitting Jack Knight, and sending future National League home-run champion Gavvy Cravath to the White Sox. The biggest storm of all blew in Boston after he dealt Cy Young to the Indians; it emerged subsequently that he agreed to the transaction in the middle of an all-night drinking session with Cleveland owner Charles Somers. Taylor also so alienated rookie Tris Speaker that the future Hall of Famer offered his services to two other clubs before Johnson again stepped into mediate a new contract for the outfielder in 1908. The AL official finally persuaded the elder Taylor to sell out to Jimmy McAleer and Bob McRoy.

PATSY TEBEAU

As the manager and third baseman-first baseman for Cleveland in the 1890s, Tebeau proved almost the equal of the more famous contemporary Baltimore Orioles. In competition, Tebeau's Spiders won half a pennant in the National League's split season of 1892, finished second twice in the decade, and beat Baltimore in one of the two Temple Cup Series in which the two teams faced each other; in aggressiveness, Tebeau rivaled the worst of the Orioles. His attack on umpire Jack Powers on August 18, 1889, required a squadron of policemen to be stationed along the foul lines before the game could be completed. He throttled Cleveland sportswriter Elmer Pasco

for his comments about the Spiders after the losing 1896 Temple Cup Series. Most notoriously, the manager was jailed and fined $200 earlier that year for assaulting an umpire for calling a game because of darkness. Claiming he had been denied due process, Tebeau won an injunction canceling both the fine and a threatened boycott by other teams.

KENT TEKULVE

The underhanding Tekulve couldn't hang on long enough to beat Hoyt Wilhelm's record of 1,070 pitching appearances, but he did manage to chalk up various longevity marks for a fireman. Most prominently, every one of his 1,050 turns on the mound were as a reliever (Wilhelm had 62 starts). The right-hander, who as a member of the Pirates in the late 1970s and early 1980s led the National League in appearances four times, also racked up his numbers over five fewer seasons than the Hall of Fame knuckleballer. Tekulve had his best years for Pittsburgh in 1978 and 1979, when he posted back-to-back efforts of 31 saves. In the latter year he also contributed to a world championship for the Pirates. Facing the Orioles in the 1979 World Series, he saved 3 of the 4 Pittsburgh wins.

WILLIAM TEMPLE

The president of the Pittsburgh franchise in 1892, wealthy sportsman Temple donated the two-and-a-half-foot Temple Cup to be awarded to the winner of a postseason championship match between the first- and second-place finishers in the expanded twelve-team National League. Winners of the cup included the New York Giants in 1894, the Cleveland Spiders in 1895, and the Baltimore Orioles in 1896 and 1897. The original idea behind Temple's donation was that the trophy would become the property of the first club to win three series. No team took permanent possession, however, because neither the fans nor the players took the games seriously, and the contests were dropped after four years. Even Temple recognized the ultimate folly of his good intentions when Boston and Baltimore players filled the cup with wine and passed it around the table like a communal goblet at a dinner after the 1897 series.

GARRY TEMPLETON

In 1979, Templeton became the first switch-hitter to record at least 100 hits from eash side of the plate, in a season. For the Cardinals shortstop it proved to be his last big act in a sixteen-year (1976-91) career that saw him decline from leading the National League in hits once and in triples three straight years to surviving as little more than a journeyman. His most trouble-riven season was 1981, when, exasperated by the heckling he had been receiving for what was perceived as lackadaisical play, he gave Busch Stadium fans the finger, prompting manager Whitey Herzog to pull him down the steps of the dugout and shove him on the bench. Templeton was subsequently admitted to a hospital for depression, but that didn't save him from being shipped to San Diego after the season in return for Ozzie Smith—an exchange that proved pivotal for St. Louis's winning teams over the next decade. Templeton also raised establishment hackles when he declined to go to an All-Star Game as a backup selection, declaring; "If I ain't startin', I ain't departin'."

GENE TENACE

Tenace had one of the biggest World Series ever enjoyed by a major leaguer, as a member of the 1972 Athletics. After clouting homers in his first 2 at-bats in the first game, against Cincinnati, he went on to add 2 more homers and compile 9 RBIs as the key offense in his team's world championship. In the American League Championship Series played before the meeting with the Reds, the right-hand-hitting catcher went hitless in his first 16 at-bats, but then singled home the pennant-winning run against the Tigers in his final plate appearance. An otherwise modest hitter with above-average power over his fifteen-year (1969-83) career, Tenace had a seeming aversion to putting the ball in play: In addition to striking out at least 90 times seven years in a row, he walked 100 times in six seasons, leading each league in that category once (for the 1974 Athletics and the 1977 Padres).

JOHN TENER

Tener was the first former player to become president of a major league. The right-hander's primary contribution to the game during his play-ing days as a 25-31 hurler was his service as secretary of the Players Brotherhood in 1890. Pursuing a political career after hanging up his uniform, he became a congressman and, in 1912, was elected governor of Pennsylvania. Two years later he was chosen as National League president because of the desire of league owners to have a more prestigious chief executive than incumbent Thomas Lynch.

With his gubernatorial term overlapping his league presidency for two years, Tener issued a predictable fine and suspension on John McGraw for belting an umpire and even more predictable pronouncements against the Federal League and the Players Fraternity. What wasn't predictable, however, was his reaction to a failure of league owners to back him in a controversy with American League president Ban Johnson. Relations between the two league executives had never been cordial, but when Johnson supported Philadelphia owner Connie Mack's decision to ignore a National Commission ruling awarding the disputed services of pitcher Scott Perry to the Braves and fight the matter in court, Tener recommended an all-out war, starting with the cancellation of the 1918 World Series. When NL owners refused to back him to this degree, he resigned in August 1918. The move came as a surprise to everyone except Tener himself, who had once lamented that his power was restricted to supervising umpires and signing the official league ball.

FRED TENNEY

The slickest-fielding first baseman between the reigns of Charlie Comiskey in the 1880s and Hal Chase in the 1900s, Tenney initiated the first-to-short-and-back-to-first double play, first executing it on June 14, 1897, against Cincinnati. After anchoring the infield for Boston pennant winners in 1897 and 1898, the lefty also managed the team, first, in 1905, under a contract that induced him to dash into the grandstand in pursuit of foul balls to assure the franchise profit that would earn him a bonus, and later, in 1907, as a minority stockholder who took his ball-hoarding craze to the extreme of accusing umpire Bill Klem of stealing the club's balls, and trying to search him to prove the point. When senior partners George and John Dovey fired him as manager after the 1907 season, Tenney's demand for a 25 percent profit on his share of the club brought him only an unexpected trade to the Giants. Even as a Giant he refused to sell his Boston equity for less than he thought fair, despite National League president Harry Pulliam's objections to a player on one team holding stock in another. In his first season in New York, Tenney affected the outcome of one of baseball's legendary games by taking a day off because of a backache; his absence caused Fred Merkle to make his first start of the season, and 9 innings later, Merkle's boner entered baseball history.

JERRY TERRELL

Terrell was the lone dissenter in the Players Association's 967-1 vote authorizing the 1980 spring training strike; the Kansas City infielder cited his religious convictions as the reason for his breaking ranks with his fellow players.

BILL TERRY (Hall of Fame, 1954)

The last National Leaguer to reach .400 (.401 in 1930), Terry was that rare RBI producer not especially noted for home runs. Even with the friendly right-field porch of the Polo Grounds in front of him for his entire fourteen-year (1923-36) playing career, the lefty-swinging first baseman reached the 20 mark in homers only three times, but still managed to use the gaps to drive home 100 runs six seasons in a row. He also scored 100 runs eight times and had at least 200 hits in six different seasons, tying Lefty O'Doul's NL record of 254 safeties, in 1930. Terry closed out with a lifetime average of .341.

Like his successor Mel Ott, Terry played the last several years of his career with the added job of manager. Unlike Ott, his prickly personality never got him public relations points. Even in being named John McGraw's successor in 1932, he had problems with coach Dave Bancroft, who quit because he wanted to be manager, and third baseman Freddie Lindstrom, who sulked the rest of the season for the same reason and then was traded away. Terry's own first appointment of Billy Southworth as a coach ended badly when the two got into a fistfight in spring training the following year. Despite the turmoil, he reanimated

the sagging franchise with a World Series win in 1933 and pennants in 1936 and 1937.

Terry gained a special place in the Giants-Dodgers rivalry during the 1934 winter meetings thanks to an off-the-cuff remark made to Roscoe McGowan of *The New York Times*. After discussing the deals made by other NL clubs at the busy gathering and noting that the Dodgers hadn't completed any trades, he wondered aloud if "Brooklyn is still in the league." Dodger officials used it as a rallying cry for their misbegotten club, making it sound as if Terry had been referring to Brooklyn's playing abilities. The upshot was that, on the final weekend of the season, Brooklyn defeated New York twice to allow the Cardinals to snatch the pennant.

Because he considered himself "a Giant first and last," Terry turned down several lucrative offers to jump to other teams as a dual manager-general manager. Even when he stepped aside for Ott after the 1941 season, he stayed in the organization for a while as minor league director. In the mid-1950s he sought unsuccessfully to buy the club to keep it in New York.

ERNEST L. THAYER

First published under a pseudonym in the *San Francisco Examiner* on June 3, 1888, Thayer's poem "Casey at the Bat" became a sensation almost a year later, when matinee idol De Wolf Hopper recited it, for the first of some ten thousand times in his career. Hopper gave his reading as an encore to a New York performance of a long-forgotten play called *Prince Methusalem* attended by members of the New York Giants and Chicago White Stockings. Over the years there have been almost as many claimants to the authorship of the poem as there have to being "mighty Casey" himself. Among those demanding writing credit was George D'Vys, who maintained that he had taken the name of Casey's club from his own Mudville Nine of Somerville, Massachusetts, that he had been inspired by seeing King Kelly strike out with the bases loaded in August 1886, and that he had submitted the work to *The Sporting Times*. The issue of that paper containing a garbled version of "Casey" was, however, dated later than the *Examiner*'s version and specifically credits the San Francisco paper.

The first to proclaim himself the prototype of the failed hero was O. Robinson Casey, the president of the Syracuse Society for the Prevention of Cruelty to Animals. His claim to have struck out in circumstances similar to the fictional Casey's, while playing for Detroit against Minneapolis in 1885, was, however, patently spurious, since Minneapolis had no major league team in 1885, and he himself never played for Detroit—or any other major league team. Later self-entrants in the noncontest were pitcher Dan Casey and his brother, outfielder Dennis Casey. For his part, Thayer maintained until his death in 1940 that the filler for which he had been paid $5 had no basis in fact.

FRED THAYER

While serving as captain of the Harvard University club in 1877, Thayer designed the first catcher's mask, for temmate Jim Tyng.

BOBBY THIGPEN

Right-hander Thigpen set the record for saves in a season in 1990 when, as a member of the White Sox, he marched in from the bullpen to close out 57 victories.

HARRY THOBE

Thobe was a retired bricklayer from Oxford, Ohio, who served as an unofficial mascot for the Reds in the late 1930s and early 1940s. He showed up regularly at Crosley Field wearing a white suit with red trouser stripes, one shoe to match the color of the suit and the other that of the stripes, and a straw hat with a red band; he also carried an umbrella of the same colors. Well into his seventies, Thobe would dance a jig through entire games while cheering on the home team.

BILL THOMAS

Between 1926 and 1952, right-hander Thomas won 383 games—the most by any pitcher in minor league history. He never wore a big league uniform.

DANNY THOMAS

Thomas spent parts of only two seasons (1976-77) with the Brewers before his devout observation of The World Wide Church of God's prohibition against any form of labor between sundown Friday and sundown Saturday cost him his career. Unwilling to hold on to a six-day-a-week outfielder, even if he had been a first-round draft pick with power and speed, Milwaukee sent him back to the minors to stay. Three years later, Thomas died a suicide in an Alabama jail cell while awaiting trial on a rape charge.

FRANK THOMAS

Thomas's slugging feats in the 1950s and early 1960s were overshadowed by a thumb and a fist. After hitting 23 or more homers for six years with the cellar-dwelling Pirates and then clouting 34 for the Mets in their inaugural season, he finally got into meaningful games when New York traded him to Philadelphia as pennant insurance in 1964. After a hot start for the Phillies, he broke his thumb in early September, sidelining him for the rest of the year; when Philadelphia did a swan dive in the stretch run, the first baseman-outfielder's injury was pointed to as a major reason. In July of the following year, Thomas got into a punchup during batting practice with Dick Allen; in the ensuing game against Cincinnati, Thomas came off the bench to deliver a late-inning home run to tie the contest, then returned to the clubhouse to be told that he was being placed on waivers because of the run-in with Allen.

FRANK THOMAS

Thomas was as responsible as anyone for the record explosion of home runs in the abbreviated 1994 season. It was the first baseman, supported by his White Sox employers, who protested successfully against a 1993 order from American League president Bobby Brown for umpires to return to the traditional strike zone between the knees and the shoulders. As adept at walking as hitting homers, Thomas argued that the Brown order disoriented hitters after years of counting on a smaller strike zone. AL umpires soon returned to squeezing the plate against pitchers—a salient factor in the unprecedented outburst of long balls through the first four and a half months of the 1994 campaign. Only the players' strike called on August 12 prevented both leagues from establishing new home-run benchmarks.

One of general manager Larry Himes's happy draft picks in the late 1980s, Thomas took MVP honors in 1993 for leading the White Sox to a West Division title. Dubbed the Big Hurt, the right-hand-htting slugger batted .317 with 41 home runs and 128 homers. He also walked 112 times, giving him 372 bases on balls over a three-year stretch. In the strike-shortened 1994 season, he took another MVP trophy for driving Chicago to the top of the Central Division.

LUCILLE THOMAS

Thomas became the first woman to buy a professional baseball team when she acquired the Western League's Wichita franchise in 1930. The builder of a fortune through a chain of movie theaters and drugstores, she promptly moved the club out of Kansas to Tulsa, Oklahoma.

ROY THOMAS

A speedy center fielder for the Phillies at the turn of the century, Thomas's skill at intentionally hitting foul balls (he reportedly fouled off 22 consecutive pitches on one occasion) prompted the National League to declare, in 1901, a batter's first two foul balls strikes; the American League adopted the same standard in 1903. Despite the new ruling, Thomas led the NL in walks seven times between 1900 and 1907.

HANK THOMPSON

Thompson was the only black player to break the color ban on two clubs. In 1947 he debuted with the St. Louis Browns shortly after Larry Doby had become the first black in the American League. In 1949 Thompson broke the Giants' whites-only policy. The left-hand-hitting second baseman and third baseman was the odd man out when Leo Durocher drastically revamped his lineup in 1951 to make room for Willie Mays and gear up for the team's comeback drive to the pennant. Thompson forced his way back into the lineup in subsequent years, however, clouting a combined 50 home runs in 1953 and 1954.

SAM THOMPSON (Hall of Fame, 1974)

Thompson was the first National Leaguer to bang out 200 hits (203 in 1887), winning a batting championship in the process. In a fifteen-year career, with the Detroit Wolverines and Philadelphia Phillies (as well as an 8-game encore with the Tigers at age forty six), he led the NL in home runs and RBIs twice each, drove in 100 runs eight times, and topped .300 seven times. His career-high average came in 1894, when he batted .404, but finished third in the batting race behind Hugh Duffy (.438) and Tuck Turner (.416).

BOBBY THOMSON

Thomson's 3-run home run off Brooklyn's Ralph Branca in the 9th inning of the third playoff game on October 3, 1951, was the most dramatic hit in baseball history. The one-strike clout climaxed the Giants' miracle drive to the pennant after dropping behind the Dodgers by as much as 13 ½ games in August. The home run also cast into the shadows Thomson's otherwise solid career as New York's chief clutch hitter in the late 1940s and early 1950s; among other things, he had also homered in the first game of the 1951 playoffs against Branca to provide a win.

Indirectly, and even unwillingly, Thomson helped launch the careers of the National League's two greatest outfielders. In 1951, he was moved out of center field to third base to make room for Willie Mays; in 1954, as a member of the Braves, he broke an ankle in spring training, forcing Milwaukee to keep Hank Aaron on the team.

JUSTUS THORNER

Thorner is the only man ever to head three clubs in the same city in three different major leagues: the National League Cincinnati Reds in 1880, the American Association Reds in 1882, and the Union Association Outlaw Reds in 1884. In 1882 he devised a scheme to play the NL champion Chicago White Stockings in the first interleague championship series despite an AA ban on just such contests. Releasing all his players on October 1, even though their contracts had another two weeks to run, he allowed a local entrepreneur to sign the same players to barnstorm-

Despite being voted the greatest all-around athlete of the first half of the twentieth century, Jim Thorpe had only a modest baseball career. Photo compliments of Sharon Guynup.

ing contracts and arrange the match with Chicago. AA president Denny McKnight saw through the subterfuge and short-circuited the plan with a fine and threats of expulsion for the Reds—but not before the two clubs had traded shutouts.

JIM THORPE

The first athlete to win the Olympic decathlon (in 1912), Thorpe had a modest six-year career between 1913 and 1919 with the Giants, Reds, and Braves. A right-hand-hitting outfielder, he batted .252 with only 29 stolen bases. He was initially signed by John McGraw as a gate attraction, and drew crowds just to watch him take batting practice. He was later forced to return his Olympic medals because he had played baseball professionally in a low minor league in 1909. Thorpe's most conspicuous moment in the major leagues came on May 2, 1917, when he drove in the winning run for the Reds against Jim Vaughn

in the 10th inning after the Chicago southpaw had matched Cincinnati's Fred Toney in the only double-no-hit game in major league history.

SYD THRIFT

No one thought more highly of Thrift as a baseball executive than he did. As general manager of the Pirates under the public-private consortium that purchased the team from the Galbreath family in 1986, he went a long way toward undoing the shabby image of the franchise in the wake of the Pittsburgh drug trials the previous year. In three years he hired Jim Leyland as manager; acquired Bobby Bonilla (from the White Sox), Doug Drabek (from the Yankees), and Andy Van Slyke and Mike Lavalliere (from the Cardinals); and promoted slugger Barry Bonds to the varsity. The result was a jump from sixth to second in the National League East over the same period.

Never one to hide his light under a bushel, Thrift let everyone know that he was the one responsible for what he called ''resurrecting the dead.'' Following the 1986 season, he demanded that he be given greater control over the organization as a whole, but organization chairman Malcolm Prine declined, spurring a round of peacemaking sessions before the board in 1987. Finally, with the board having to choose between Prine and the general manager who was making good on his promise to reanimate the franchise, it threw its weight behind Thrift. Prine resigned, Carl Barger took over as president, and Douglas Danforth was elected chairman of the board.

The club finished second in 1988 and drew a franchise-record attendance of more than 1.8 million. On the other hand, the second-place finish was a full 15 games behind the Mets, giving Danforth and Barger an excuse to get rid of Thrift for futile acquisitions of aging backup players that exceeded budget limits.

The following year, Thrift put in a five-month appearance as a senior vice president of baseball operations for the Yankees, abandoning a four-year contract in August over the vague definition of his job in the crowded New York executive suite. He resurfaced for a couple of years as assistant general manager of the Cubs under Larry Himes.

MARV THRONEBERRY

The symbol of the ineptitude of the expansion Mets in the early 1960s, Throneberry owed his derisive moniker of Marvelous Marv to a sincere outburst by team owner Joan Payson, who exclaimed after a game-winning home run by the first baseman: "Wasn't that marvelous of Marv?" Throneberry made the sarcasm inevitable with such feats as legging out a triple and being called out for having failed to tag second base; when manager Casey Stengel began to protest the call, he was told not to bother because his hitter had also neglected to touch first. Stengel himself added to the legend when, presiding over a clubhouse birthday party for his benighted player, he announced that the club would have bought a birthday cake "but you would have probably dropped it." The marketing of the Throneberry image was so overwhelming that it obscured the fact that he played a mere 130 games for the Mets over a season and a fraction. Perhaps more ironic, he actually had a better fielding average than other New York infielders over that period. Like Joe Garagiola, Bob Uecker, and others, Throneberry later sought to cash in on his playing infamy by doing beer commercials, but he himself admitted to never being at ease with a reputation that contradicted onetime hopes as a Yankee prospect that he would be the next Mickey Mantle.

JAMES THURBER

The author's short story "You Could Look It Up," which appeared in *The Saturday Evening Post* in 1941, involved a baseball team so desperate it hires a midget to pinch hit; the tale inspired both Bill Veeck's most famous stunt and Casey Stengel's signature tag line.

ALLAN W. THURMAN

Thurman was a man of rectitude—and was punished for it. In October 1890, the minority stockholder in the Columbus Solons put forth a proposal to combine the National League, the Players League, and his own American Association into two leagues that became the basis of the final settlement among the three. For his trouble, he earned the sobriquet of The White-Winged Angel of Peace and the AA presidency. The position turned sour when, as chairman of the three-man National Board established to settle interleague disputes, he cast the deciding vote endorsing the piracy of Lou Bierbauer and Harry Stovey by Pittsburgh and Boston, respectively, from the AA's Philadelphia club. Fired from the presidency, Thurman became a nonvoting (because he represented no league) member of the board, and watched as the AA declared war anew on the NL, was defeated after only one season, and was absorbed into a twelve-club NL.

LUIS TIANT

Tiant gained attention for one of the most unorthodox deliveries in major league history, but he also happened to be a four-time 20-game winner described by teammates as the glue of the Boston clubs of the 1970s. A portly right-hander, he dazzled opponents over his nineteen-year (1964-82) career by swiveling practically all the way around to center field before unleashing pitches at one of numerous possible release points. The motion was so disorienting that American league umpires had to reach a special agreement for not calling the hurler regularly for balking.

The Cuban-born Tiant arrived in the major leagues with Cleveland, but was hard put to attract the spotlight because of the simultaneous promotion of strikeout king Sam McDowell. The 1968 season was typical: Although he won 21 games, struck out 264 batters, led the AL with 9 shutouts, and posted the league's lowest ERA (1.60) since Walter Johnson's 1.49 in 1919, he was overshadowed by both another McDowell strikeout-leading effort and by Denny McLain's 31 victories. As soon as Tiant led the AL with 20 defeats the following year, on the other hand, he was peddled to Minnesota, where a torn rib cage muscle started him on the road back down to the minors for a couple of years. Fished back up by the Red Sox, Tiant again led the AL in ERA in 1971 with a 1.91 mark, then went on to 20-win seasons in 1973, 1974, and 1976. He also starred in the 1975 World Series against Cincinnati, hurling 2 complete-game victories and pitching into the 7th inning of a third contest before tiring.

The gregarious, cigar-wielding Tiant was the very opposite of the "twenty-five players, twenty-five cabs" reputation affixed to the Boston clubs of his era, most teammates agreeing that he provided a necessary buffer among clubhouse factions. It was in this context that, informed that the Yankees had signed the hurler as a free agent in 1979 after Boston had failed to make a serious offer, Carl Yastrzemski moaned that ''they have cut out our heart and soul.'' For his part, New York owner George Steinbrenner admitted that one of the reasons he had gone after Tiant was for its impact on Boston morale.

Tiant closed out his career with an overall record of 229-172 (ERA 3.30).

MIKE TIERNAN

An outfielder for the Giants, Tiernan once hit a home run that brought the fans in two stadiums to their feet. The incident occurred on May 12, 1890, when he hit a shot that cleared the centerfield fence of the Polo Grounds, then landed in the outfield of adjoining Brotherhood Park, where a Players' League game was under way. Spectators in both parks applauded as Tiernan rounded the bases. The long ball ended a 13-inning scoreless duel between Kid Nichols and New York ace Amos Rusie.

JOE TINKER (Hall of Fame, 1946)

Unlike his double-play partner Johnny Evers, Tinker at least led the National League in twin killings once, and also paced senior league shortstops in fielding average four times and in assists twice. On the other hand, he also committed more than 60 errors in three seasons.

With Evers doing most of the shouting and nagging, Tinker was relatively silent during his first eleven years with the Cubs at the beginning of the century: there was nothing even relative about it toward Evers, after Tinker decided that his infield partner had offended him in a 1905 mixup over a taxi, refusing to speak to him for thirty–three years. As a batter, the shortstop wasn't particularly loud, either, averaging .263 over fifteen seasons.

In 1913 Tinker underwent a change. To begin with, he objected so strenuously to the appointment of Evers as manager that he demanded a trade. He was sent to Cincinnati, where he became a playing manager who made it clear from the start that he wasn't accustomed to associating

Joe Tinker (left) combined with Johnny Evers in a legendary double play combination even though the keystone pair didn't speak off the field for decades. National Baseball Library, Cooperstown, N.Y.

with losers. When owner Garry Herrmann turned down a couple of his trade suggestions, Tinker went to the press with charges that the franchise was more interested in saving money than in fielding a winner. That gained him the support of Reds fans, but little else. When he was informed before the 1914 season that the organization intended sending a spy on road trips to report on the activities of the players, Tinker refused to sign a new contract. Herrmann retaliated by replacing him as pilot with Buck Herzog and selling him to the Dodgers. Rather than report to Brooklyn, however, Tinker jumped to the Federal League's newly formed club in Chicago as playing manager. As field boss of the Whales, he assembled a team good enough to outdraw the Cubs in both 1914 and 1915; in the latter year, he guided the FL entry to the closest pennant win in major league history, Chicago beating out St. Louis by a percentage point on the final day of the season.

With the folding of the Feds after the 1915 season, Whales' owner Charles Weeghman, who had purchased the Cubs, brought Tinker along to pilot the team with which he had started his big league career. It proved to be a generally unhappy experience, and Tinker was fired for Fred Mitchell after a single season.

JIM TOBIN

As a member of the Braves on May 13, 1942, Tobin became the only twentieth-century pitcher to hit 3 home runs in a game. As a hurler with Boston, Pittsburgh, and Detroit, he had slightly less success, compiling a career record of 105-112.

BOBBY TOLAN

Tolan came closer than anyone else to threatening the reserve clause before Andy Messersmith and Dave McNally finally undid the rule in 1975. Refusing to sign his 1974 contract with the Padres, the outfielder filed two grievances in October of that year, one seeking free agency for himself and the other insisting on a clarification of the one-year-at-a-time right of a club to renew player contracts forever and on their own terms. Even though he later signed a retroactive, two-year contract with San Diego in December, the second grievance remained in place until it was voluntarily withdrawn by Players Association head Marvin Miller. Miller's move was calculated both to take the heat off arbitrator Pete Seitz, who had recently decided the Catfish Hunter case in the player's favor, and to encourage the owners to negotiate an end to the offending contract clause.

Tolan, who began his career with the Cardinals in 1965, was the original center fielder of the Big Red Machine in the early 1970s and a .300 hitter who also led the National League in stolen bases in 1970. An injury that kept him on the disabled list for all of the 1971 season curtailed his production thereafter. Released by the Padres after his two-year deal expired, the lefty hitter played on the pennant-winning Phillies of 1976, drifted to the Pirates, then to Japan in 1978, before playing a final season with the Padres in 1979. He averaged .265 in his thirteen big league seasons.

FRED TONEY

On May 2, 1917, Toney pitched a 10-inning no-hitter for the Reds, defeating Cub left-hander Hippo Vaughn, who didn't give up a hit until the 10th inning. The double no-hitter ended with a single by Cincinnati's Larry Kopf; the game ended minutes later when Kopf moved to third on an error and scored the game's only run when Vaughn wasn't quick enough in fielding Jim Thorpe's tap to the box and throwing it back to catcher Art Wilson.

Right-hander Toney won 137 games in a twelve-year career with four National League teams between 1911 and 1923.

GEORGE EARL TOOLSON

Toolson was a pitcher in the Yankee farm system who refused to accept a demotion from Newark to Binghamton and sued on the grounds that the reserve clause was a monopolistic practice that prevented him from advancing himself in his chosen profession. The case, coupled with similar suits brought by Dodger farmhand Walter Kowalski and minor league operator Jack Corbett, reached the U.S. Supreme Court in November 1953. The High Court, by a seven-to-two majority, found in favor of organized baseball, upholding the 1922 precedent that exempted baseball from federal antitrust statutes. The Court's reasoning was not that baseball was not "commerce," the 1922 rationale for the exemption, but that the remedy for the problem had to be legislative (even though Congress had chosen not to act in the thirty-one years since the original decision).

DAN TOPPING

Topping was half of the partnership that owned the Yankees in the period of their greatest successes and that sowed the seeds of their worst failures. Starting as a quarter-owner while Larry MacPhail ran the franchise from 1945 to 1947, the multimillionaire and the equally wealthy Del Webb bought MacPhail out following the senior partner's nervous breakdown. While Topping held the title of president until 1966 (after he had sold most of his interest in the club to CBS), he almost always deferred to the judgment of his front office in player personnel matters. This hands-off policy extended to tacit support of general manager

George Weiss's refusal to put a black player in a Yankee uniform until 1955, even though Topping employed black players on the Brooklyn Dodger football team he owned.

The co-owner was more active in the selection of managers. A great admirer of Joe DiMaggio, he talked the Yankee Clipper out of retiring twice, offered him the post of dugout boss in 1949, and tried to persuade him to return as a coach and potential successor to Casey Stengel (Weiss's choice in 1949) in 1954. The forced retirement of both Stengel and Weiss after the 1960 World Series was Topping's doing. So, too, were the hiring of Ralph Houk and Roy Hamey to fill the vacated jobs. Even more damaging was Topping's scheme to install Yogi Berra in the dugout for the 1964 season, while kicking Houk upstairs to succeed Hamey as general manager.

As if those moves were not enough to sink the dynasty, with bad publicity overwhelming whatever good reasons there may have been for the Houk-Hamey succession and bad chemistry demolishing the intended public relations coup of the Berra-Houk move, Topping and Webb decided in 1962 to sell—and to stop spending money until they could find a buyer. Although the Yankees won three more pennants (1962-64)—making a total of fifteen since Topping and Webb had become partners—the signs of decay were inescapable, with the big league club populated with injured and aging stars and the farm system so barren that the top four affiliates finished last in 1963.

When negotiations to sell to the Lehman Brothers stock brokerage house fell apart over an unfavorable tax ruling, Topping turned to CBS, which purchased 80 percent of the club for $11.2 million in 1964. This set off league fears that the media conglomerate would interfere with baseball's lucrative television contract and that the wrath of the U.S. Congress or Justice Department would threaten baseball's antitrust exemption. Only with assurances that Topping and Webb would continue to run the club for five years did the other owners relax and approve the move. The promise of gradual departure was written on water: Webb sold his remaining 10 percent to CBS in February 1965, while Topping held out only until September 1966.

SALOMON TORRES

Few rookies have broken into the major leagues as inauspiciously as Torres did in 1993. Called up by the Giants in September to fill a hole in the starting rotation, the right-hander suffered 4 losses in the team's final 18 games. They were the only defeats in that span for San Francisco, which lost the division title on the final day of the season to Atlanta.

MIKE TORREZ

Torrez won 185 games in an eighteen-year career, but he will be most remembered for two pitches. The first, delivered to New York shortstop Bucky Dent in the 1978 playoff at Fenway Park, resulted in a 3-run home run that cost the Red Sox the pennant. The second, thrown to Houston shortstop Dickie Thon early in the 1984 season, fractured the cheekbone and impaired the vision of the Astros star, reducing him to a second-line player.

CESAR TOVAR

On Minnesota teams that featured the likes of Hall of Famers Harmon Killebrew and Rod Carew, Tovar regularly won the nod from adversaries as the club's most valuable player. An all-purpose infielder-outfielder, he motored the team to division titles in 1969 (.288, 45 steals, 99 runs scored) and 1970 (.300, 30 steals, 120 runs scored, and a league-leading 36 doubles and 13 triples), then came back in 1971 to pace the American League in hits (204) while batting .311. On May 18, 1969, Tovar and Carew stole home in the same inning against an inattentive Mickey Lolich of the Tigers. Minnesota feeling for Tovar was demonstrated in 1967 when, despite having batted only .267, he received a first-place vote from a Minneapolis sportswriter for AL MVP, thereby depriving Triple Crown winner Carl Yastrzemski of a unanimous victory. On September 22, 1968, Tovar was allowed to play a different position each inning; as a pitcher, he surrendered only a walk while striking out Reggie Jackson.

DAVID TRACY

The midcentury St. Louis Browns were so bad that owner Bill DeWitt hired the hypnotist Tracy to use his expertise to instill some self-confidence in the players. On June 6, 1950, shortly after Tracy's arrival, the Browns were savaged by the Red Sox by a score of 20-4. The following day, June 7, Boston won by a margin of 29-4. The day after that, June 8, Tracy was sent packing.

ALOYSIUS TRAVERS

Travers was a nineteen-year-old Philadelphian who was drafted by the Tigers on May 18, 1912, to pitch a major league game against the Athletics because Detroit players had walked off on strike in response to the suspension of Ty Cobb. With other amateurs from Philadelphia and Tiger coaches behind him, Travers pitched all 9 innings of a 24-2 shellacking administered by the Athletics. He later entered the priesthood.

CECIL TRAVIS

No major leaguer's career was more damaged by World War II than Travis's. For nine seasons before Pearl Harbor, the third baseman-shortstop for the Senators averaged .327; in 1941, while Ted Williams was batting .406 and Joe DiMaggio was hitting in 56 consecutive games, the lefty swinger topped both Hall of Fame sluggers and everyone else in the American League with 218 base hits. Suffering frozen feet in the Battle of the Bulge, Travis was never the same hitter after the war; over three postwar seasons, his career average dropped to .314 before his retirement after the 1947 season.

PIE TRAYNOR (Hall of Fame, 1948)

As player (seventeen years), manager (five and a half years), and broadcaster (thirty-three years), Traynor spent his entire big league career with the Pirates. Originally a shortstop when he joined the club in 1920, he was moved to third base because of Pittsburgh's acquisition of Rabbit Maranville, going on to become the first player at that position to be elected to Cooperstown in the normal sportswriters' ballot. Although he led the National League only once in an offensive category (tied for triples in 1923), he ended up with a .320 average and batted in 100 runs on seven occasions; in 1928 he set the record for power thrift by batting in 124 runs but with only 3 home runs. He was also the proverbial contact hitter, never striking out more than 28 times a season in his

Pie Traynor's bat and glove made him the premier third baseman of his era. Photo compliments of the Pittsburgh Pirates.

seventeen-year career. Defensively, he led in assists three times, double plays four times, and putouts seven times. Traynor's playing career effectively came to an end in 1934, when he broke his arm in a field collision, but, as Pittsburgh manager, he spotted himself at first base and as a pinch hitter for a couple of more seasons. He got his nickname from his habit as a child of saying he wanted a pie when a priest rewarded him for chasing after balls hit by a parish team.

GUS TRIANDOS

Statistics citing the 1950s Baltimore catcher as the slowest man in baseball history lie: He was even slower. According to the record, Triandos's theft of only a single base in 1,206 major league games stands as an all-time low for players with at least 1,000 appearances. But the heavy-footed slugger's single swipe, in a late-season 1958 game against the Yankees, was an uncontested steal of second at the end of a New York pounding of Baltimore; more recent scoring rules do not credit runners with steals in such situations.

On the other hand, Triandos was the first catcher to call no-hitters in both leagues—being behind the plate as an Oriole for Hoyt Wilhelm's masterpiece in 1958 against the Yankees, and as a Phillie for Jim Bunning's perfect game in 1964 against the Mets.

HAL TROSKY

Trosky appeared headed for a Hall of Fame career with the Indians in the 1930s until he got sidetracked by one of the game's most notorious managers and then by his own headaches. After six straight seasons of at least 100 RBIs, the right-hand-hitting first baseman emerged as one of the leaders in the revolt against manager Ossie Vitt in 1940. The player uprising came after years of Vitt's public mocking of his team to reporters and other incidents that caused some players to start brawls in the hope that the manager would try to get into the mix. When Cleveland dailies got wind of the trouble, they began referring to the team as the Crybaby Indians—a tag that was gleefully picked up in the grandstands around the American League. For their part, Trosky and the other players sought to outmaneuver Vitt even on the field by designing their own codes for steals, bunts, and other plays in defiance of the tactics preferred by the pilot. Although Vitt was fired after the 1941 season, the tensions did nothing for Trosky's chronic migraine condition, and he had to retire before the 1942 season.

DIZZY TROUT

After fourteen solid big league seasons (1939–52) that included two 20-win seasons for the Tigers, Trout made the mistake of looking overpowering in an old-timers' game five years after his retirement. Convinced by the Orioles that he still had something, he made two appearances on the mound for Baltimore in 1957, failed to get out of either inning in which he relieved, and called it quits for good with a season ERA of 81.00. Trout's finest season was 1944, when he won 27 games and led the American League in ERA and shutouts. He followed that up in 1945 by posting 4 wins over the last eleven days of the season for pennant-winning Detroit.

DASHER TROY

Troy's contract jumping from the Detroit Wolverines to the Philadelphia Athletics and back again in 1882 was the immediate cause of the first war between the National League and the American Association. Until Troy's double defection, the two leagues had merely eyed each other warily without either firing the opening shot. The second baseman defended his desertion of the Athletics by claiming that he had not known the AA planned to play Sunday games. In retaliation the association opened its doors to players blacklisted by the NL.

VIRGIL TRUCKS

Trucks was as much of a no-hitter specialist who ever toed the pitching mound. After hurling at least one masterpiece in every minor league in which he played, the right-hander tossed two no-hitters for the Tigers in 1952. What made that doubly remarkable was that he managed only 3 other victories while losing 19 during the season; of his other wins that year, one was a one-hitter and another was a two-hitter. Trucks spent eleven of his seventeen big league seasons (between 1941 and 1958) with Detroit, but had his only 20-win year in 1953 while dividing his time between the Browns and White Sox.

TOMMY TUCKER

Tucker's .372 batting average, for the American Association Baltimore Orioles in 1889, is the highest ever for a switch-hitter. But he is known less for his hitting than for an inflammatory combativeness, both verbal and physical, that earned him the enmity of umpires and opponents alike during his thirteen-year career. The first baseman's most memorable physical encounter came after he spiked Baltimore's John McGraw on May 15, 1894; the tussle that followed so distracted fans that no one noticed a fire, reportedly begun in a pile of peanut shells, until it was too late to stop the complete destruction of the grandstand at Boston's South End Grounds. Several months later, on July 17, Tucker's antics in the third-base coach's box failed to impress the umpire sufficiently to get the arbiter to call the game for rain; it did, however, impress the Philadelphia fans who attacked Tucker and broke his cheekbone.

TED TURNER

Turner's acquisition of the Braves in January 1976 opened a new chapter in baseball's relations with television, particularly with regard to cable coverage. Although he has never quite succeeded in his announced goal of making Atlanta "America's Team" through TBS coverage, his very articulation of the aim underscored the thinking of entrepreneurs for whom specific metropolitan geographics and market numbers are only casually compatible. In one sense, this has made him less a business pioneer than only an especially grandiose follower of Walter O'Malley; in another sense, Turner has gone beyond O'Malley in making his franchise as much of a national media event as a local sports operation.

Turner's first move after buying the Braves was to sign free agent Andy Messersmith even as O'Malley was organizing other owners to blackball the pitcher and any other player who sought to declare free agency after the 1975 decision by arbitrator Peter Seitz. His second move was to skirt the owners' lockout of 1976 spring training camps with a technicality by inviting minor leaguers down to Florida on schedule. On the other hand, he went along with other owners on a contractual prerogative permitting clubs to slash by 20 percent the salary of any player who announced his intention of playing out his option year. In the first blush of his ownership, he also played—literally—to the grandstand with such stunts as jumping out onto the field to welcome a Braves' player at home plate after a home run, and joining the ground crew in sweeping the infield in the 5th inning.

In 1977 Turner decided that the best way to distract attention from a bad club was to manage it himself with the help of coach Vern Benson. The stunt lasted a game (a 16th straight loss by the Braves); then National League president Chub Feeney cited an old regulation prohibiting managers from owning stock in the club that employed them and ordered regular manager Dave Bristol back on the job. Turner went from the dugout to court, where he was contesting a fine and suspension levied by Commissioner Bowie Kuhn for his alleged tampering with free-agent outfielder Gary Matthews. The highlight of the legal proceeding was the threat by the Braves owner to give Kuhn's attorney "a knuckle sandwich" for his cross-examining techniques; otherwise, the suspension against him was upheld, and he put baseball behind him for a year, concentrating instead on winning the America's Cup.

In the late 1970s and early 1980s, Turner came under frequent attack from other owners for his lavish contract offers to free agents who were something less than all-stars. In 1979, for instance, he agreed to pay reliever Al Hrabosky $170,000 annually for thirty years; Hrabosky ended up with seven saves over three seasons. In 1980 he inked Claudell Washington for five years for a sum barely falling short of $5 million; up to that point in his career, the outfielder had never hit more than 13 home runs in a season and had averaged .300 only once. In his five and a half years with Atlanta, he proved to be a solid but unspectacular performer, most noted for inspiring grandstand signs declaring WASHINGTON SLEPT HERE. It was also during this period that Turner wined and dined Pete Rose behind the argument that his TBS cable operation would make Charlie Hustle a household name across the nation. Rose ultimately signed with the Phillies.

Until Atlanta surged to the top of the West Division in the early 1990s, Turner had been for some years more conspicuous for his low profile around the club than for his presence. His principal public forays in connection with the team in the 1980s had been in relation to pitcher Phil Niekro: in denying that the knuckleballer had been a spy in the locker room for him during Joe Torre's managership, in allowing the hurler to go off as a free agent, and in bringing him back for a final mound appearance in 1987. At the same time, however, he was forming a nucleus of hardliners with the owners of the Cubs, Mets, and Yankees against revenue-sharing plans that would have cost him the financial edge provided by his TBS broadcasts.

During postseason games in the 1990s, Turner and his wife, Jane Fonda, showed little sympathy for calls by Native Americans to eliminate the so-called Tomahawk Chop by fans at Fulton County Stadium, but were, on the contrary, shown on networks other than TBS joining in on the Atlanta rally ritual.

TUCK TURNER

As the fourth outfielder for the Phillies in 1894, Turner got into enough games for his .416 average to qualify for the batting crown. The switch-hitter had two problems, however: Hugh Duffy's league-leading .438 and three regular Philadelphia outfielders—Ed Delahanty, Billy Hamilton, and Sam Thompson—who hit a combined .401 for the season. Turner's .416 is the highest average never to be rewarded with a batting title.

WILLIAM MARCY TWEED

From 1860 to 1871, the notorious Boss Tweed, head of New York's Tammany Hall and champion grafter, was president of the Mutual Club of New York. For the better part of its existence, the team was theoretically amateur, although Tweed provided players with no-show patronage jobs in the coroner's office or the street department that cost the taxpayers about $30,000 a year. As with everything Tweed did, the Mutuals operated on a lavish scale, conducting a grand tour through the south in the spring of 1869. The club was formed originally by members of New York City's Mutual Hook and Ladder Company Number 1.

JIM TYNG

A pitcher and catcher on the Harvard University club in the late 1870s, Tyng's mishaps behind the plate persuaded him to wear the first catcher's mask, designed by teammate Fred Thayer, in a game against the Live Oaks of Lynn on April 11, 1877. In 1879, while pursuing his career as a lawyer, Tyng responded to Boston manager Harry Wright's late-season request to pitch for the Red Stockings; his two losses in three appearances handed the Providence Grays the pennant. In 1888 he returned to the National League to pitch an inning for the Phillies, again at Wright's behest, but only after the manager had agreed to a contract that named the lawyer director of athletics for Huntington Street Grounds, the Phillies' park, thus allowing him to escape the social stigma of being a professional ballplayer.

U

PETER UEBERROTH

Money come, money go was the main motif of Ueberroth's four-and-a-half year term as commissioner, between October 1984 and April 1989. With a decidedly CEO approach to his job, the former head of the 1984 Los Angeles Olympic Organization Committee played a prominent role in negotiating lucrative television contracts with CBS and ESPN, as well as in persuading large companies to cough up substantial fees so they could be called "official sponsors" of Major League Baseball. The underbelly of these deals was that the contract with CBS ended the traditional season-long *Game of the Week* while creating implosively unrealistic criteria for television revenues, and the sponsorship associations soon overwhelmed the game with specific plugs for everything from the call to the bullpen for a relief pitcher to the simple reading of a lineup.

Where individual franchises were concerned, Ueberroth pressured the Cubs into installing lights at Wrigley Field and blocked a couple of sale moves by Texas owner Eddie Chiles until the franchise could be peddled to George W. Bush. It was also during Ueberroth's reign that major league clubs stepped up their plaints that they were losing money, to the point where only the New York teams and the Dodgers sometimes seemed to be financially profitable. At the height of this public relations ploy against player salary demands, Ueberroth suggested to the owners the collusion tactic against free agents that would end up costing several of them millions, as well as star players.

On nonfinancial matters, Ueberroth was even less successful. His tough rhetoric against the sport's drug problem notwithstanding, he had little legal choice but to accept a significantly watered-down rehabilitation-discipline program advanced by the Players Association. Even emptier were his periodic pronouncements to pressure owners into ending discriminatory hiring practices against minorities for managing and front-office jobs.

BOB UECKER

Uecker made a second career as a broadcaster by ridiculing his first one as a big league catcher. A .200 hitter in six seasons with the Braves, Cardinals, and Phillies, the righty swinger has primarily aimed his humor at his anemic offensive output, his inability to handle Phil Niekro's knuckleball, and Philadelphia fans. In addition to his regular platform as a longtime Brewers broadcaster, he has written a book, *Catcher in the Wry;* appeared on late-night talk shows with some regularity, in numerous beer commercials, and in the television situation comedy *Mr. Belvedere;* and played himself in a couple of films with baseball themes.

Among Uecker's often self-deprecating putdowns are:

"Instead of having the word 'powerized' on my bats, they said, 'For display only.' "

"When I went to bat with three men on and two out in the ninth, I looked over in the other team's dugout, and they were in street clothes."

"The way to catch a knuckleball is to wait until the ball stops rolling and then to pick it up."

"I made a major contribution to the Cardinals' pennant drive. I came down with hepatitis. The trainer injected me with it."

"Philly fans are so mean that one Easter Sunday when the players staged an Easter egg hunt for their kids, the fans booed the kids who didn't find any eggs."

"The cops picked me up on the street and fined me $500 for being drunk and $100 for being with the Phillies."

"The highlight of my baseball career came in Philadelphia's Connie Mack Stadium when I saw a fan fall out of the upper deck. When he got up and walked away, the crowd booed."

"The average age in Sun City, Arizona, is deceased."

GEORGE UHLE

Uhle was among the earliest major league practitioners of the slider and named the pitch for its motion. The right-hander led the American League in victories twice, while playing for the Indians, and concluded his seventeen-year career (between 1919 and 1936) with 200 wins for four clubs. Uhle holds the season record for hits (52) by a pitcher, averaging .361 in 1923. He is also the only major league pitcher to appear behind the plate, donning the tools of ignorance for a game for Cleveland in 1921.

V

BOBBY VALENTINE

In October 1994, Valentine became the first American hired to manage in Japan, when he was signed by the Lotte Orions of the Japanese Pacific League. In conceding unprecedented control over a Japanese franchise by a foreigner, the Orions also signed former American League infielder Lenn Sakata as pilot of the team's top minor league affiliate for facilitating Valentine's personnel decisions. In the late 1960s and early 1970s, one-time National League infielder Don Blasingame was widely recognized as the de facto manager of the Nankai Hawks, but he was never given the title formally. Valentine went to Japan after a promising playing career was cut short by a leg injury and after managing the Texas Rangers for all or part of eight lackluster seasons.

FERNANDO VALENZUELA

There have been few debuts to match that of Valenzuela, the best and most popular Mexican major leaguer. After yielding no earned runs in 18 innings of relief work for the Dodgers in 1980, the southpaw won his first 8 games in 1981, 5 of them shutouts; tied the major league rookie record of 8 shutouts despite working in the strike-shortened season; became the first rookie ever to lead the National League in strikeouts, with 180; and was the only pitcher to take both Rookie of the Year and Cy Young honors in the same season. The screwballer's success combined with an unathletic physique and an unorthodox delivery in which he glanced skyward before releasing the ball to create Fernandomania, the name given to the international excitement generated by his every start. While millions of Mexican radio listeners and television viewers on both sides of the border tuned in Los Angeles's Spanish-language networks, millions more coast-to-coast viewers

Fernando Valenzuela was baseball's biggest gate attraction in the early 1980s. National Baseball Library, Cooperstown, N.Y.

477

took in his appearances on network television, and Dodger Stadium filled to capacity for eleven of his starts. Thanks in good part to Valenzuela's outings, the team drew 2.3 million fans despite the loss of 25 home dates to the strike. In Mexico, his popularity spawned a comic strip.

Over the next several years, Valenzuela was the most effective Dodger left-hander since Sandy Koufax. In 1986 Valenzuela established a big league mark of 44 ⅓ innings without yielding an earned run at the start of a season, then went on to lead the NL with 21 wins. A shoulder injury in 1988 limited his effectiveness until his release before the 1991 season. After an abortive comeback with the Angels in 1991 and a year in the Mexican League in 1992, he joined the Orioles in 1993. He showed flashes of his old form, but became a financial casualty after the season. In 1994, Valenzuela surfaced again, with the Phillies.

CLARENCE VAN BUSKIRK

Van Buskirk was the architect who designed Ebbets Field, which opened in Brooklyn on April 5, 1913, for an exhibition game between the Dodgers and the Yankees. Despite the legendary status that the park would gain, it initially threatened to be only a firetrap because of Van Buskirk's failure to provide for more than a single rotunda entrance and exit. Only after seeing the chaos engendered by having thousands of fans crowding through the single entrance did Brooklyn owner Charlie Ebbets have Van Buskirk cut other points of access into the walls.

DAZZY VANCE (Hall of Fame, 1955)

Of all the players in the Hall of Fame, Vance may be the most unlikely. Already thirty-one before he won his first big league game, for Brooklyn in 1922, the right-hander had spent the previous decade moving from one minor league club to another, failing miserably in trials with the Pirates and Yankees, and then coming up with a series of arm injuries that jeopardized even his journeys around the boondocks. When Dodger scout Larry Sutton recommended that he be acquired after a winning season for a minor league team in New Orleans, owner Charlie Ebbets refused until the pitcher became part of the price

for the player he truly wanted from the Louisiana squad, catcher Hank DeBerry. The odds against the fastballer becoming one of the premier pitchers of the 1920s didn't get any shorter with his presence in Ebbets Field, with the Dodgers a less than mediocre second-division club that had little more than one unexpected second-place finish to show for his tenure.

Despite all these obstacles, Vance won 20 games three times (including a career-top 28 in 1924), led the National League in ERA three times, and struck out more batters than any other NL pitcher seven years in a row. In 1924 he took MVP honors for achieving the pitching Triple Crown in wins, ERA, and strikeouts. He also made an unwilling contribution to the rule book when his ploy of fraying his pitching sleeve to distract batters was outlawed. Off the field, the high-living Vance gained the nickname of the Big Four for a clique of Dodgers he put together whose main purpose was to watch the sun rise from off-limits locations and mock the chaos of the Daffiness Boys front office.

JOHNNY VANDER MEER

Vander Meer had two extraordinary boosts to a Hall of Fame career but was unable to take advantage of them. The more noted thrust was his never-equaled feat on June 11 and June 15, 1938, of throwing back-to-back no-hitters against the Braves and Dodgers, respectively. Less well known is that the Cincinnati southpaw was second to no National League pitcher in overpowering the puny lineups that came to bat during the World War II years; before he himself was drafted, he led the league in strikeouts three consecutive seasons. For all that, however, Vander Meer also had to deal with his own team's modest offense, never winning more than 18 games and concluding his career 2 games under .500 (119-121).

Vander Meer's second no-hitter was also the first night game in Brooklyn. Although the contest itself was never at issue, with Cincinnati leading, 6-0, he had to escape the perils of Pauline in the 9th inning after walking the bases loaded. After a visit to the mound by Reds' manager Bill McKechnie that aroused the boos of 38,748 fans, the left-hander concluded matters by getting Ernie

Koy to tap into a force-out at home and Leo Durocher to hit a soft outfield fly. He did not surrender a hit until the 4th inning of his next game, when Debs Garms of the Braves connected safely.

ARKY VAUGHAN (Hall of Fame, 1985)

The Arkansas-born Vaughan's election to Cooperstown has almost remedied his standing as the most underrated shortstop in National League history. Mainly because he led the league in errors with Pittsburgh in 1932 and 1933, he was perceived for a while even by his supporters as a one-dimensional, offensive infielder. In fact, many of his errors were miscues of ambition, and his range was wide enough to lead the circuit in both assists and putouts on three different occasions despite such slick-fielding contemporaries as Leo Durocher, Billy Jurges, Dick Bartell, and Eddie Miller. On the other hand, the right-hand-swinger's hitting was never in question, starting with the fact that he averaged .300 every one of his ten seasons with the Pirates—a franchise feat not even accomplished by such other Hall of Famers as Honus Wagner and Paul Waner. Usually among or at the top of seasonal leaders in doubles, triples, and runs scored, Vaughan hit a career high of .385 in 1935—not only a franchise record but also a plateau not topped in the NL until strike-shortened 1994. Although he reached double figures in home runs only twice, he was the first major leaguer to hit two balls out of the park in an All-Star Game, in the 1941 contest.

For the most part, Vaughan was regarded as low-key, but he left both the Pirates and Dodgers after fighting with his manager. In Pittsburgh he got into a season-long feud in 1941 with Frankie Frisch over playing time; this precipitated one of the worst trades in franchise history when he was dealt to Brooklyn for four dim lights. After a couple of solid seasons with the Dodgers, he sparked a revolt against manager Durocher after the pilot had talked out of both sides of his mouth over a suspension of pitcher Bobo Newsom; according to Vaughan, the incident demonstrated that Durocher was capable of lying about any of his players. Although Branch Rickey finally restored something like peace, the future Hall of Famer announced his retirement after the 1943 season at age thirty-one because he couldn't tolerate Durocher.

When Durocher was suspended for the 1947 season for a mountain of other matters, Vaughan returned to Brooklyn to contribute a .325 average to the team's pennant victory. Jackie Robinson also credited the southern-born shortstop with providing him with moral support through the worst days of racial baiting by other teams. Vaughan's career average of .318 is second only to Wagner's .327 among shortstops.

BILL VEECK, JR. (Hall of Fame, 1991)

Even Veeck himself conceded that, whatever else he accomplished, he would be most remembered as the man who sent a midget up to bat. In fact, Eddie Gaedel's single plate appearance, while the most famous of Veeck's stunts, was hardly among his significant contributions to the game. Far more important were his innovations in baseball's financial operations—almost all of them initially deplored by other owners. In ownership stints with the Indians, Browns, and White Sox (twice) between 1946 and 1980, Veeck also

The mere mention of the flamboyant Bill Veeck's name was usually enough for other major league owners to patch over their differences and join together against the greater enemy. National Baseball Library, Cooperstown, N.Y.

gained the distinction of being the last person to purchase a big league franchise without a fortune independent of baseball.

Veeck's start in baseball—as a stockboy and vendor—came about because his father was president of the Cubs in the 1920s. After Veeck, Sr., died in 1933, the son went to work in the Cubs front office, originally in ticket sales but eventually as treasurer; in the latter capacity, he was responsible for planting the ivy that still adorns the walls of Wrigley Field. Veeck's first independent venture, in partnership with Charlie Grimm, was as owner of the American Association Milwaukee Brewers, which turned out to be a proving ground for Veeck's promotional genius. Giveaways of everything from six live squab to a two-hundred-pound block of ice kept fans laughing—and coming. His most widely discussed present was a left-handed pitcher—hidden inside a birthday cake—that manager Grimm had been requesting for some time. Veeck's most lasting contribution as a minor league operator was the institution of a rule prohibiting adjustable fences—passed the day after the Milwaukee owner unveiled a gadget for raising the height of the Milwaukee fence upward in the visiting team's half inning and downward when the home team came to bat. Not incidentally, Veeck also took a moribund franchise, won three pennants with it in five years, and sold it for a $275,000 profit in 1945.

In 1943, while still maintaining control of the Brewers, Veeck secured sufficient backing to purchase the Phillies from a bankrupt Gerry Nugent. His intention was to revitalize the feeble club with Negro leagues stars, making the franchise immediately competitive, not to say revolutionary. His mistake was informing Commissioner Kenesaw Landis of his intention, killing the project instantly. Within days, the National League took over the Philadelphia franchise and turned it over to William Cox. Veeck also launched an effort to buy the Yankees in 1945, but lost out to the Larry MacPhail-Dan Topping-Del Webb triumvirate.

When The Sport Shirt, as he came to be called for his customary attire, finally did purchase a major league club—Cleveland, in June 1946—Veeck was, at forty-two, one of the youngest men ever to do so. And he did it with a creative piece of financing, called a debenture-common stock group, that involved investors putting up money partly to buy stock and partly as a loan to the organization; remuneration to the partners then became nontaxable loan repayments rather than taxable dividends. In late 1947 he broke new ground of a different sort by making Larry Doby the first black player in the American League.

Veeck almost undid all of his good work in 1948 by trying to trade popular shortstop-manager Lou Boudreau to the Browns. As soon as the newspapers got word of the proposal, Boudreau supporters organized protest demonstrations and petitions demanding that Veeck leave town instead of their hero. When he realized what he had wrought, Veeck ran all over Cleveland, going from bar to restaurant to bar, to admit as personally as he could that he had made a mistake while simultaneously denying that the deal had been consummated or even that it had been his idea to begin with. Popular opinion ran against the owner until he gave Boudreau a new two-year contract in his dual role. The playing manager rewarded this vote of confidence, on the part of Clevelanders if not of his boss, by winning the franchise's first pennant and world championship since 1920 and establishing a new major league season attendance record. A key contributor (a 6-1 record) to the team's success was Negro leagues star Satchel Paige, who became the oldest rookie in history when Veeck signed him. A noncontributor was Joe Earley, for whom Veeck staged a "night" after the fan protested that Veeck honored everyone except the average "Joe."

The highlight of the rest of Veeck's tenure in Cleveland was a ceremonial burial of the 1948 world championship flag as soon as it became clear that the team could not overtake the Yankees and Red Sox late in the 1949 season. Soon afterward, needing money to settle divorce proceedings his wife had brought, he sold out to insurance executive Ellis Ryan and protégé Hank Greenberg.

Less than two years later, Veeck reemerged as owner of the Browns, with the express intention of driving the Cardinals out of the city that the two clubs shared. Woefully underfinanced, he managed mostly to annoy the NL club's owner,

Fred Saigh, by hiring any number of ex-Cardinals and decorating Sportsman's Park, which the clubs shared but the Browns owned, with Brownie memorabilia. The Gaedel stunt took place on August 19, 1951, and Veeck, never one to let an absurdity rest, was still arguing with AL president Will Harridge over whether Gaedel's at-bat should be included in the record book when he staged Grandstand Managers' Day five days after Gaedel walked on four pitches. With Veeck, former Athletics manager Connie Mack, and four thousand fans each holding a placard with a green ''yes'' on one side and a red ''no'' on the other, publicity director Bob Fischel held up cards with proposed moves—steal, change pitchers, and the like—to which the grandstand managers flashed their opinions. With regular manager Zack Taylor puffing a pipe and resting in a rocking chair on the sidelines, the fans called an excellent game: The Browns triumphed, 5-3, to end a 4-game losing streak.

Veeck's St. Louis undoing—and that of the franchise—began immediately after the 1952 season, when he proposed that AL clubs share local radio and television revenue with visiting clubs. Voted down, 7-1, he refused to sign releases to allow broadcasts of games in which the Browns were the visiting team. The rest of the league retaliated by changing the schedule to eliminate lucrative Friday night games in St. Louis. While contemplating a suit over this collusion, Veeck learned that Saigh, who had been indicted for tax evasion, had sold the Cardinals to the Anheuser-Busch breweries. Realizing that the resources of his new NL rival were overwhelming, he decided to move his own franchise. Assured by other AL owners that his proposed relocation to Baltimore was a done deal, he nevertheless found himself on the short end of a 6-2 vote at the winter meetings. Petitioning again after a disastrous lame duck season in 1953, he was informed without equivocation that the transfer would be approved only if he stepped aside.

After abortive attempts to buy the Athletics in 1954 and the Tigers in 1957 (as well as the Ringling Brothers Circus and a Cleveland NBA franchise), Veeck popped up in 1959 at the head of a group willing to get between Chuck Comiskey and his sister Dorothy Rigney, who owned

both the White Sox and the world's record for interfamilial lawsuits. Veeck's syndicate purchased Dorothy's 54 percent of the club and inherited Chuck's animosity and the endless litigation through which he expressed it. Chuck was only a sideshow, however, to the Go-Go Sox pennant and to more of the familiar Veeck antics, one of them involving Gaedel helicoptering onto the field for a conversation with Chicago double-play combination Luis Aparicio and Nellie Fox.

A year later, however, Veeck began suffering anew from a leg that had been crushed by an artillery piece during World War II and that had already been amputated to the knee. Told that the rest of his leg had to come off and that he was suffering from stretched blood vessels in the head that required complete rest, Veeck stayed around only long enough to install baseball's first exploding scoreboard and to put players' names on the backs of their uniforms. He then sold out to Arthur Allyn, Jr., the son of one of his perennial partners.

A decade and a half later, in December 1975, after an abortive effort to acquire the Orioles, Veeck repurchased the Chicago club from Allyn's bankrupt brother John. The deal ended speculation that the franchise would be moved to Seattle to settle a suit against the league for deserting Washington State after the 1969 season, and that Charlie Finley's A's would pull up stakes in Oakland and replace the White Sox in Chicago. Other AL owners were bruised by his intervention, and Veeck only angered them more by setting up shop with general manager Rollie Hemond in a hotel lobby and making four trades within full view of spectators. Two weeks later, however, arbitrator Peter Seitz introduced the age of free agency by ruling for the players in the Messersmith-McNally case. Veeck's career as a baseball owner—and the possibility of anyone else without extensive outside money becoming one—were effectively over. The irony of the situation was that Veeck had always regarded the reserve clause as stupid at best and illegal at worst; he had, in fact, testified on behalf of Curt Flood's effort to overturn the rule in 1972, probably the low point of his popularity among other owners.

Still, the once-again White Sox owner hung on for five seasons. During that time, his best gimmick was a Bicentennial-inspired ''Spirit of '76'' parade on Opening Day 1976, featuring himself as the peg-legged fifer. (''If you've got the guy with the wooden leg,'' he remarked at the time, ''you've got the casting beat.'') His best idea was a ''rent a player'' scheme for taking over other clubs' stars in their option years. His best season was 1977, when leased sluggers Richie Zisk and Oscar Gamble powered the team to 90 victories and third place. His best sentimental gesture came in 1976, when he reactivated fifty-four-year-old ex-White Sox star Minnie Minoso, who picked up his last big league hit in 8 at-bats and who could say he had played in four different decades. His worst sentimental gesture came in 1980, when he reactivated the four-years-older Minoso, who went hitless in 2 at-bats to say he had played in five different decades. His longest surviving idea was having announcer Harry Caray sing ''Take Me Out to the Ball Game'' during the 7th-inning stretch. His most copied idea was having players take curtain calls after hitting a home run. His least copied idea was having the team play briefly in short pants. The worst idea of his career was Disco Demolition Night, June 12, 1979, when a disc jockey's stunt of blowing up disco records between games of a doubleheader resulted in thousands of fans jumping onto the field, policemen trying futilely to restore order, firefighters abandoning efforts to put out the blazes caused by exploding platters, and umpires declaring the second game forfeit to the visiting Tigers. Veeck finally gave up and sold the club to Jerry Reinsdorf and Eddie Einhorn in January 1981.

By the mid-1990s, several teams had come around to the conclusion—adamantly resisted during Veeck's day—that baseball had to provide more bread and circuses to keep fans attracted. Owners also had to look more seriously at the concept of revenue sharing that they had been so quick to mock forty years earlier. Their belated awareness underlined the fact that, for all his twitting of the stuffed shirts in the game's executive suite, Veeck never surrendered his profit priorities, but merely preferred hacking his own trails to reach them.

BILL VEECK, SR.

A sportswriter given to criticizing the club, Veeck took over baseball operations for the Cubs in 1918 on a dare, accepting owner William Wrigley's challenge to do a better job. In his first two years he handled a pair of explosive situations deftly but failed to duplicate the 1918 pennant win for more than a decade.

Veeck's baptism of fire came at the end of his first season as front-office boss, when he released Lee Magee in the wake of evidence that the second baseman had conspired to throw games while with the Reds the year before. He even managed to get Cincinnati owner Garry Herrmann and Brooklyn boss Charlie Ebbets to kick in $2,500 each to Chicago for having passed along what they suspected were damaged goods when Herrmann sold Magee to the Dodgers and Ebbets traded him to the Cubs. The episode became public only months later, and then only because Magee sued for the salary owed him on a two-year contract.

The following year, Veeck's initial reaction to suggestions of a fix in an August 31 game against the last-place Phillies was to switch pitchers from Claude Hendrix to Grover Cleveland Alexander and to conduct a quiet investigation. Both efforts failed when the Cubs lost anyway and his former colleagues in the press got hold of the story. When the executive invited the local chapter of the Baseball Writers' Association to join him in investigating the affair, Chicago papers, most vocally the *Tribune,* kicked up such a fuss that State's Attorney MacClay Hoyne was forced to begin the grand jury investigation that soon turned its attention to the much larger Black Sox scandal.

Veeck continued to run the Cubs until his death in 1933, winning pennants in 1929 and 1932.

MICKEY VERNON

Vernon was a rare offensive light in the dim Washington clubs of the 1940s and 1950s. A lifetime .286 hitter for his twenty-year career between 1939 and 1960 with the Senators and several other teams, he took the American League batting title in both 1946 (.353) and 1953 (.337), also leading the circuit in doubles twice. The lefty-swinging first baseman's second batting crown was helped along by generous teammates on the final day of the 1953 season. With Vernon and Cleveland's Al Rosen separated by less than a point, the Washington star received word in the dugout that Rosen had picked up 3 hits in 5 at-bats in a contest against the Tigers in his quest for a Triple Crown. Some quick arithmetic showed that Vernon's 2-for-4 against the Athletics would be enough to give him the title, but that if he made one more out it would go to Rosen. To make sure Vernon didn't get another opportunity at the plate, Washington catcher Mickey Grasso doubled but was then conveniently picked off and outfielder Kite Thomas was tagged for the third out when he walked around first base toward second after hitting a single.

After wandering around the majors as a pinch hitter for several teams, Vernon was named the first manager of the expansion Washington Senators in 1961. His tenure was marked mainly by clashes with general manager Ed Doherty, whose development policy for the new club effectively excluded black prospects.

ZOILO VERSALLES

As the Twins shortstop in 1965, Versalles led the American League in both strikeouts and errors—and was rewarded with an MVP trophy. It also helped that he was regarded as the heart of the pennant-winning club for setting the league pace for most defensive double plays, plate appearances, doubles, triples, and runs. Indicative of his importance (or of the scarcity of other candidates), he took the honor with more than 100 votes more than the runner-up, teammate Tony Oliva.

JOE VILA

The sports editor of the *New York Sun,* Vila was more responsible than anybody else for popularizing Brooklyn's team as the Dodgers. Although the nickname Trolley Dodgers had been used on occasion for years, it had never gained any official status and had, since Wilbert Robinson's arrival as manager in 1914, been eclipsed by the more common Robins. But when Robinson and Vila got into a dispute in 1926 over a *Sun* article that had printed the salaries of Brooklyn's players, the editor ordered his staff never to use Robinson's name or the nickname Robins in any story. A couple of other papers, in solidarity with their colleague, also began using Dodgers more

frequently. The rival Robins disappeared altogether after Robinson departed in 1931.

FAY VINCENT

Vincent's arrival in the commissioner's chair came about because of the death of Bart Giamatti in September 1989; his departure almost exactly two years later marked the death of the office of commissioner as it had existed since the selection of Kenesaw Landis in 1920. In between, Vincent consistently used liberal arguments to make authoritarian points.

Vincent had been a corporate lawyer, chief executive officer of Columbia Pictures, and executive vice president of Coca-Cola before signing on as old friend Giamatti's deputy commissioner. In his first year as Giamatti's successor, he spent most of his time on the investigation and subsequent suspension of Yankee owner George Steinbrenner for paying gambler Howard Spira $40,000 to provide dirt on New York star Dave Winfield. Even after Steinbrenner volunteered to step aside indefinitely as managing partner of the club, Vincent had to deal with lawsuits filed by franchise limited partners seeking first to reinstate him, then to allow Leonard Kleinman, also implicated in the Spira nastiness, to succeed him. The Steinbrenner case did not go away until Vincent announced a reinstatement in July 1992, effective the following March.

In the meantime, Vincent incurred the wrath of his employers by intervening in the thirty-two-day spring training lockout that postponed the start of the 1990 season for a week. Joining the discussions in February, he had little impact on the eventual solution other than to restart the talks after they had stalled, but his intervention in the domain of the Player Relations Committee came back to haunt him in June 1992, when several owners attempted to strip him of all authority in labor relations.

The commissioner's handling of Steve Howe's most recent drug involvement brought more criticism. Vincent suspended the Yankee left-hander indefinitely after he pleaded guilty to possession of two grams of cocaine in June 1992. When the Players Association filed a grievance over the penalty and hearing officer George Nicolau suggested that Vincent define the length of the suspension, he reacted by expelling the pitcher permanently. With Howe accepting three years' probation as his punishment from the courts, Nicolau overruled his banishment from baseball. Convinced that his authority was being challenged, Vincent summoned New York manager Buck Showalter, general manager Gene Michael, and vice president Jack Lawn to his office and threatened to discipline them for failure to support baseball's drug policies in their testimony at Howe's grievance hearing. The Players Association responded by filing an unfair-labor-practices suit.

Vincent had already alienated several powerful clubs by going before a U.S. Senate subcommittee and attacking the influence of cable superstations, then made his situation even worse by insisting on realignment of the National League in the interests of more geographic sense. The rearrangement would have moved the Braves and Reds to the East Division and shifted the Cubs and Cardinals to the West. Ten of the twelve NL clubs agreed, but one of the dissidents, the Cubs, had little to gain from the move except a later starting time for most of their road games; a consequent smaller audience on their WGN superstation; and lower profits for the *Chicago Tribune,* which owned both the club and the television station. Chicago consequently blocked the move, and, when Vincent imposed his plan anyway, took the issue to court and won.

With several owners calling for his head because he had overstepped the bounds of his office, Vincent declared on August 20, "I will not resign—ever." Two weeks later, he was handed a vote of no confidence by a margin of two to one. Four days after that, he resigned "in the best interests of baseball," to be succeeded by an awkward arrangement in which Brewers owner Bud Selig took over as acting commissioner.

Throughout his tenure, Vincent was given to populist pronouncements that made him sound like the chief critic of the owners. At the same time, he anguished publicly over such social ills as drug taking. When push came to shove, however, his remedies smacked of the same disregard for due process that he claimed to be surprised by in his dealings with the owners.

OSSIE VITT

Vitt piloted the so-called Crybaby Indians who blew the 1940 pennant mainly because they were more preoccupied with outwitting him than the Tigers. Although statistically one of Cleveland's most successful managers, the onetime infielder brought most of the trouble on himself by indulging a penchant for criticizing his players to the press and the Cleveland front office, but rarely to their own faces. Another frequent tactic was jeering at players from the dugout after they had committed an error or surrendered a big hit. By the middle of the 1940 season, Vitt's relations with the team had degenerated to the point that players were marching into general manager Cy Slapnicka's office demanding either a trade or a new skipper; for his part, outfielder Jeff Heath acknowledged starting fights on the bench for the sole purpose of seeing whether Vitt would attempt to break them up. Mainly because of the manager's close ties to a couple of Cleveland newsmen, the dissatisfaction of the players was portrayed in the press as nothing more than whining—a perception that led soon enough to the tag of Crybaby Indians. Fans in Detroit and other cities took to pelting the Indians with everything from jars of baby food to baby bottle nipples. Through it all, such team leaders as first baseman Hal Trosky, pitcher Mel Harder, and catcher Frankie Pytlak began running parallel games through a private set of signs when they didn't agree with Vitt's tactical calls. The upshot was that the totally demoralized club finished a game behind Detroit. Vitt was fired at the end of the year.

BILL VOISELLE

Voiselle gained more attention during his nine-year (1942-50) National League career for his uniform number than for his pitching. A native of Ninety-six, South Carolina, that was also the number on his back when he won 21 games for the 1944 Giants, in the process leading the league in strikeouts. Although he never again won 20, the right-hander contributed 13 pivotal victories to the pennant-winning Braves in 1948; as much as anybody, in fact, he was the "rain" in the season's popular cry of "Spahn, Sain, and pray for rain."

WILLIAM VOLTZ

In 1885, Philadelphia sportswriter Voltz tried to form the first benevolent protective association that would establish a fund for sick and needy players. The idea came a cropper because players generally suspected that Voltz, an outsider, was not on the level.

CHRIS VON DER AHE

Von der Ahe built a dynasty in one league and destroyed it in another. Although his initial interest in baseball was in selling beer at Sportsman's Park, he quickly came to understand that a winning club attracted more patrons, who bought more beer, and that the only way to assure big, thirsty crowds was to own a winning club in an organized circuit.

At the top of his game, Von der Ahe financed the St. Louis Browns, who won four consecutive American Association pennants between 1885 and 1888, and did it with flair. For one thing, there were his personal style and appearance: checkered slacks, spats, and diamond stickpins; a brace of ever-present greyhounds named Schnauzer and Snoozer; referring to himself as The Boss President in a comic book German accent; and a bulbous nose turned scarlet from sampling many of his own wares. For another, there was his abysmal ignorance of even the grosser points of the game. On one occasion, for instance, he told a group of visiting dignitaries that his ballpark had the biggest diamond in the world; informed by manager Charlie Comiskey that all diamonds were the same size, he amended his boast to possessing the biggest infield. For a third, there was his lavish spending: Among his indulgences were a sequence of very expensive and very public mistresses and a life-size statue of himself that eventually found a final resting place over his grave; among his business expenses were private trains and first-class accommodations for his winning teams; among his generosities were giving the Browns players the full proceeds of the 1885 postseason championship games and half the take from the 1886 Series.

With the beneficences, however, came equally lavish abuse and fines for routine errors, demands that team members live in rooming houses he owned and drink in his establishments, and insis-

tence on a willingness to play exhibition games on off-days (he once laced into the team for refusing to meet the black Cuban Giants, accusing them of spite against him and not "honest prejudice"). Moreover, when the players performed below the standards he had set, Von der Ahe turned vindictive, refusing to share any of the income from the losing 1887 "World Series" against the Detroit Wolverines, then selling pitchers Bob Caruthers and Dave Foutz and catcher Doc Bushong to Brooklyn for $18,500.

Despite the deals, a feud festered between Von der Ahe and Brooklyn's Charles Byrne, who regarded the St. Louis owner as a buffoon. The climax came in a September 1889 series between the two clubs. The first game ended in a fiasco, when, with St. Louis leading in the 8th inning and darkness approaching, Von der Ahe set up a row of lighted candles in front of the visitors' bench. After fans knocked over several candles with beer cups and started a small fire, Comiskey refused to let his team take the field in the 9th inning, prompting a barrage of beer bottles and a forfeit win for Brooklyn. When Von der Ahe refused to allow his team to play the next day as well, the Browns forfeited that game as well. The eventual upshot was a cancellation of the first forfeit, a Brooklyn pennant, a subsequent struggle over the selection of a new AA president, and a walkout by Byrne (and Aaron Stern of Cincinnati) into the National League.

The full measure of Von der Ahe's foolishness and crudity was revealed when he considered joining the Players League the following year, only to be rejected by PL organizer John Montgomery Ward.

With the AA all but ruined by the PL war and the ensuing battle for supremacy with the NL, Von der Ahe botched an assignment to persuade association clubs to join their stronger rival in 1892 in a twelve-team league, ultimately bearing responsibility for a buyout that cost considerably more than it should have. Von der Ahe's NL career was a travesty. Losing Comiskey to Cincinnati in 1892 eliminated the buffer he had always enjoyed between himself and the players; what's more, the team plummeted to the depths of the expanded league. To compensate for the club's failure as a drawing card, he became an impresario, installing a carousel and carnival rides in the outfield and sponsoring band contests, boxing matches, and horse races in the park; Von der Ahe called his enterprise the Coney Island of the West. Another scheme, to sell betting pools at games, was short-lived. He also changed managers—twelve times between 1895 and 1897—at a crazed pace, even taking over himself for parts of each of the three seasons.

In 1898 everything caught up with Von der Ahe: The park burned down, his wife sued him for divorce, his son took him to court over a property matter, and he himself ended up in a Pittsburgh jail after Pirates owner William Nimick had him kidnapped by private detectives and shanghaied to Pennsylvania over a seven-year-old debt. Financially ruined, Von der Ahe was unable even to sell his club because a Missouri court had appointed a receiver to dispose of the team. One of his last legacies was that of being the first owner to install a tarpaulin to protect the field from rain.

W

RUBE WADDELL (Hall of Fame, 1946)

Waddell's "colorful" career is a prominent example of the casual treatment baseball historians have given to players with emotional disturbances. The left-hander's erratic behavior, both before and while he was the American League's premier southpaw of the first decade of this century, was, in fact, triggered by either severe psychological problems or a case of at least mild retardation; whichever it was, the condition was compounded by alcoholism.

While the southpaw compiled a relatively modest 191-145 record in a thirteen-year career (between 1897 and 1910), he also racked up four consecutive 20-win seasons for the Athletics, topping the AL with 26 victories in 1905; seven league-leading strikeout totals, including a career-high 349 in 1904 that stood as the big league mark for more than sixty years; and a stingy 2.16 lifetime ERA. Possessed of a fastball compared favorably with Walter Johnson's, Waddell would wave everyone but the catcher off the field in exhibition games and face batters without a defense behind him. In one regulation game against the Tigers, he called his outfielders in to the edge of the infield grass and then struck out the side.

Waddell's unpredictable behavior was largely childlike, at least in the beginning. He held up the start of games to play marbles in the street. He was easily distracted by toys and pets. He was even more easily sidetracked by fishing, taking off without notice for days at a time to a favorite hole. Most of all, he loved fire engines and firefighters, missing games to follow them several times. Less benign, he wrestled alligators for a fee in the off-season.

Bouncing back and forth between the National League and the minor Western League from 1897 to 1901, Waddell ran afoul of every manager for whom he played, and was suspended several times for both on-field tantrums and off-field zaniness. Philadelphia manager Connie Mack, who had been Waddell's pilot for part of the 1900 season while both were with the WL Milwaukee club, was the only one who could deal with him, doling out his salary in small amounts and indulging his unauthorized absences. Lured by Mack away from a team improbably named the Los Angeles Looloos in late June 1904, the lefty won 24 games and struck out a league-leading 210 batters to pitch the A's to their first AL pennant. After going 26-11 in 1905, he missed his only opportunity to appear in a World Series—and a much-heralded matchup with the Giants' Christy Mathewson—when he injured his left shoulder in a playful train-station tussle with fellow pitcher Andy Coakley over the latter's straw hat. Never the same pitcher thereafter, Waddell became increasingly unstable and violent—so much so that several teammates refused to report for spring training in 1908 unless Mack traded him. The decision to ship the pitcher to the Browns before the start of the season was made easier by a fit he had thrown after blowing a 7-1 lead in a late September 1907 game against the Tigers. Waddell was out of the big leagues by August 1910 and dead, at age thirty-seven, in 1914.

DICK WAGNER

Wagner might not have been the most unpopular general manager ever to sit in a National League front office, but he was close. Replacing Bob Howsam in Cincinnati after the 1978 season, his first move was to fire Sparky Anderson as manager of the Big Red Machine, and his second was to allow Pete Rose to sign with the Phillies as a free agent. Protests in the city ran all the way to City Hall, where Mayor Gerald Spring suggested that the executive had "gone bananas." Although he justified the moves by claiming that the Reds had grown complacent under Anderson and that Rose had overpriced himself, and found a degree of vindication in 1979 when John McNamara piloted the team to a division title, it soon enough emerged clearly that Wagner's brief from the franchise was to dismantle the Big Red Machine. In short order, he traded Ken Griffey and George Foster and evinced little interest in re-signing Joe Morgan or Dave Collins. When these moves brought only more protest from fans and criticism from the media, owners William and James Williams defiantly backed their general manager by giving him a new five-year pact. The gesture only worsened attendance at Riverfront Stadium and led then-minority partner Marge Schott to crack that "if they want to fill the ballpark, they should have an I Don't Like Dick Wagner Night." In the event, Wagner lasted only midway through his pact before the Williams brothers got rid of him for not making winners out of his cheaply assembled team.

In September 1985 Wagner resurfaced as general manager of the Astros, and was in place when the team put together by his predecessor Al Rosen won the 1986 West Division title. A year later, however, Wagner was forced to step down when manager Hal Lanier persuaded the ownership that he couldn't work with the executive.

HONUS WAGNER (Hall of Fame, 1936)

One of the Five Immortals elected to Cooperstown in the inaugural-year balloting, Wagner had his lack of flair and extravagant anecdotes to blame for later-day wonder that some early-century spectators regarded him as superior to Ty Cobb.

Of all the stunning numbers next to Wagner's

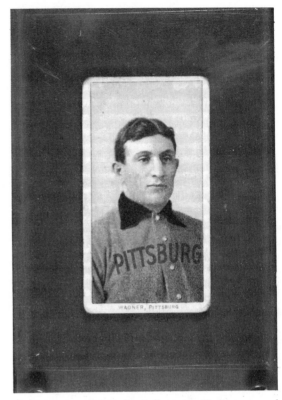

Honus Wagner's 1910 baseball card sold for a record $451,000 in 1990. Compliments of Glenn Stuart from Mr. Mint.

name, the most astonishing is probably his better-than-.300 averages in his first seventeen big league seasons with Louisville and Pittsburgh, not dropping below that level until he was forty years old. His career average of .327 encompassed an NL record eight batting titles, 3,418 hits, 643 doubles, 252 triples, 101 homers, 1,735 runs, 1,732 RBIs, and 722 stolen bases. He led the league in RBIs four times, in slugging six times, and in doubles eight times. Despite bowlegs that prompted a sportswriter to describe him as "a hoop rolling down the baselines," Wagner also paced the league in stolen bases on five occasions, attaining a high of 61 in 1907. Defensively, he spent several seasons moving around from first base to third base to the outfield before settling in as a shortstop in 1903. It was the only weak part of his game: Even allowing for the lower defensive standards of the day and his league-leading double-play turns in five seasons, he never committed fewer than 49 errors in his first eight years at the position, taking consolation only in the fact that none of those performances represented the league's worst. His defense also presented his most colorful side, as he scooped up what seemed like shovelsful of dirt in fielding each ground ball hit to him.

The right-hand-hitting Wagner moved from Louisville to Pittsburgh as part of the mass transfer of Colonels players following the folding of the Kentucky franchise after the 1899 season. Because of his aversion to tobacco, he was a favorite of the abstemious Barney Dreyfuss, and the club owner never needed encouragement to contrast the character of his shortstop with that of rowdier stars. (Wagner's dislike of tobacco also prompted his objections to a baseball card with his image issued in 1910 by Piedmont cigarettes; the card was removed from circulation, ultimately making it so rare that hockey star Wayne Gretzky paid $451,000 for one copy of it in 1990.) On more than one occasion, Wagner stepped into the breach to manage the Pirates for a few games after Dreyfuss had fired a pilot, but when he was offered the job officially in 1917, he declined the post after suffering 4 losses in 5 tries. The decision prompted some strains with the owner that were never resolved in Dreyfuss's lifetime. Wagner left the Pirates after 1917, going on to coach baseball at Carnegie Tech and to open a sporting goods store with Pie Traynor. When the Depression hit, however, Wagner was reduced to bankruptcy—a fact that he did his best to hide from Dreyfuss. Only when sportswriter Fred Lieb revealed the extent of the former star's plight did Bill Benswanger, a Dreyfuss son-in-law who had taken over the club with the old man's death, bring him back as a coach. Wagner remained a tutor with the club for twenty years, always sidestepping attempts to have him take over as manager.

J. EARL WAGNER

With his brother George, Wagner set the standard for fast-and-loose club ownership based on robber baron principles. Beginning with a financial rescue of the Players League Philadelphia Quakers in July 1890, the wholesale butchers traded their franchise for an American Association entry from the same city. Their single most notable moment in the AA was contributing to its demise by neglecting to include on their reserve list Harry Stovey and Lou Bierbauer, whom Boston and Pittsburgh, respectively, pirated, precipitating a new war with the National League. Accepting a $56,000 buyout from the NL after the AA folded, they applied $16,000 of the amount to the purchase of the Washington Senators in an expanded twelve-team NL. The Wagners hit their stride in Washington—selling any quality player who could bring them their price; moving home games away from disgusted Washington fans and to other cities for the larger crowds available there; and, in 1885, detaching manager Gus Schmelz from the club to run The Texas Show, a clone of the Buffalo Bill Wild West Show they owned. Showing far more interest in profiteering than in winning ball games, the Wagners allowed themselves to be bought out again, this time for $46,500, when the NL cut back to eight teams in 1900. Their total take over ten years was $230,000; their only winning seasons were their first two in Philadelphia.

EDDIE WAITKUS

Philadelphia first baseman Waitkus was the inspiration for Bernard Malamud's episode in the novel *The Natural* in which Roy Hobbs is shot by a woman he invites to his hotel room. During a 1949 road trip to Chicago, Waitkus was cut down by Ruth Ann Steinhagen, who subsequently admitted that she had loved the player from afar and was determined that nobody else would have him. Waitkus recovered from a serious chest wound and ended up playing eleven big league seasons.

CHARLIE WAITT

The first player to wear a glove in the field, Waitt appeared in 83 major league games. Ordinarily an outfielder, he first donned a tight-fitting, fingerless glove while playing first base for the National Association St. Louis Brown Stockings in 1875.

DICK WAKEFIELD

Wakefield became baseball's first bonus baby when he signed a contract with the Tigers in 1941 for $52,000 and an automobile. For a while, Detroit seemed to have struck gold with the outfielder, especially when he came close to winning the batting title in 1943 and used an extended leave from the Navy in 1944 to provide crucial slugging in the club's pennant battle with the Browns. Not one to hide his bat under a bushel, Wakefield was discharged from the Navy in time for the 1946 season and promptly challenged Ted Williams to a $1,000 bet that he would win the batting crown. Commissioner Happy Chandler immediately summoned both outfielders to tell them he didn't like the sound of that. It proved academic when neither of them won the crown: Williams lost despite an average of .342, while Wakefield's mere .268 started his slide toward a part-time status on several teams.

DIXIE WALKER

Known as The Peepul's Cherce, Walker was the most popular of the pre-Boys of Summer Dodgers in Ebbets Field. Part of the lefty-swinging outfielder's appeal lay in the troubled route he had taken to Brooklyn, another part in his team-leading offense. His tenure with the club ended sourly, however, when he asked to be traded rather than have to play with Jackie Robinson.

Walker originally came up with the Yankees in 1931. Although he could hit, and was regularly praised in print by manager Joe McCarthy, he was squeezed off the team by the arrival of Joe DiMaggio and other New York farmhands, taking his bat first to the White Sox and then to the Tigers. Just as he was settling in as a reliable .300 batter, his career was jeopardized by an arm injury and subsequent operation. In 1939, Brooklyn general manager Larry MacPhail picked him up cheaply, gambling that even the defensive shortcomings caused by his bad arm would be minimized by the short right-field wall in Ebbets Field. MacPhail got much more than he bargained for. In seven of his eight season with the Dodgers, Walker batted over .300, including a National League-leading .357 in 1944. In 1945 he paced the league with his 124 RBIs. The lifetime .306

hitter also recovered enough to his arm strength to lead the NL in assists one year.

Walker's off-field performances were not as smooth. In 1941 he got into spring training tussles with both MacPhail and manager Leo Durocher over their announced intention of starting the season with the aging Paul Waner in right field. When five thousand fans signed a petition urging Walker's return to regular duty, MacPhail threatened to bounce Durocher if he gave in to the outcry. The issue became academic when Waner quickly showed his age, and Walker's .311 average helped the team to a pennant. The following season, he ridiculed a MacPhail warning in midseason that the Dodgers were about to blow a big lead to St. Louis, offering to bet $500 on another Brooklyn pennant. The executive promised to rid himself of so much arrogance, and appeared on his way to doing so when his forecast proved accurate and the Cardinals did overcome Brooklyn; but then MacPhail quit the club to enter the military. In 1943 the outfielder earned Durocher's enmity by siding with Arky Vaughan in a clubhouse brouhaha, prompting the manager to promise that Walker would be gone by the end of the year. He wasn't.

With Branch Rickey's signing of Robinson in 1946, however, Walker's days began being numbered more seriously. Because of his Georgian background, he was a frequent target of reporters bent on underscoring the folly of Rickey's experiment. He kept his peace through most of 1946, content to note that Robinson in Montreal was not Robinson in Brooklyn, but then read the writing on the wall when Rickey announced that the Dodgers would be training together with their chief farm club in Cuba in 1947. Walker then circulated a petition among teammates aimed at protesting Robinson's imminent promotion—an initiative that was first squelched by Durocher, then by Rickey. When Walker demanded a trade to another club, Rickey said he would think about it. He continued to think about it while both Walker and Robinson played major roles in a 1947 pennant. Then, after the season, Walker was traded to Pittsburgh. The press played into Rickey's hands by insisting that the swap was only the result of Walker's racist views; in fact, it also had a great deal to do with the fact that the outfielder had seen his best years. He stayed with the Pirates for two years before retiring. In the meantime, the players obtained by Rickey for Walker—pitcher Preacher Roe and third baseman Billy Cox—were providing further foundation for the Boys of Summer.

Walker's father, also named Dixie, pitched briefly for Washington between 1909 and 1912; his uncle Ernie had a couple of cups of coffee as an outfielder with the Browns at about the same time; and younger brother Harry had an eleven-year playing career in the big leagues.

FLEET WALKER

Walker's presence on the American Association Toledo Blue Stockings in 1884 defied the unwritten rule that barred black players from major league baseball. A better-than-average catcher, he had joined Toledo in 1883, while the club was still part of the minor Northwestern League. When Chicago came to town on one occasion for an exhibition game, White Stockings manager Cap Anson refused to allow his team to take the field against a black man; Toledo manager Charlie Morton responded by threatening that there would be no game without Walker, even though the catcher had a sore hand and had been scheduled for a day off. Weighing the relative merits of Chicago's share of the gate receipts against his racist principles, Anson played the game against the minor league Blue Stockings. Walker was no stranger to such treatment. Two years earlier, while with an independent Cleveland club, he had been kept out of a game in Louisville when future major leaguers Fred Pfeffer and John Reccius walked off the field rather than compete against him.

Life in the AA was more of the same. Among Walker's teammates, the worst attitude belonged to mound ace Tony Mullane. When he wasn't deliberately bouncing balls in the dirt, Mullane was ignoring his receiver's signs; the two finally reached a tacit agreement to dispense with signs altogether. Without recanting the racist attitude behind his behavior, Mullane later credited his batterymate with being "the best catcher I ever worked with." Fans in Louisville were particularly abusive, once even attacking Walker in the street after a game. A potentially uglier incident,

Fleet Walker was already dead 23 years by the time Jackie Robinson followed him and his brother as the first black players in the major leagues. National Baseball Library, Cooperstown, N.Y.

a threatened mob assault in Richmond, was averted only because Walker was released because of injuries before the team arrived in the Virginia capital for a scheduled game. There would not be another acknowledged black player in the majors until Jackie Robinson in 1947.

His major league career over, Walker played minor league ball for five more seasons, most notably when he teamed with left-hander George Stovey to form the first all-black battery in organized ball, for the International League's Newark Little Giants in 1887. Once again, Anson refused to allow his team to take the field against black players for an exhibition game, on July 19, 1887; unlike the previous confrontation, this one ended in the benching of Walker and Stovey. Coincidentally, on the same day, the IL voted not to accept any more black players and became the first circuit to state formally its intention of running a segregated operation.

In later life, Walker published *Our Home Colony,* an account of race relations in America. Among the conclusions he reached in his 1908 booklet were that blacks could never achieve justice in a United States whose history had been so tainted with racial injustice (even though he himself had been acquitted in 1891 by an all-white Syracuse jury of the stabbing murder of a white man who had accosted him), and that the only solution was the complete ''separation of the races by Emigration of the Negro from America'' to Africa.

HARRY WALKER

The younger brother of Dixie Walker is the only National League player to win a batting crown despite a midseason trade from one senior circuit club to another; he averaged .363 for the Cardinals and Phillies in 1947. He and Dixie are also the only brothers to take batting titles.

Walker started his eleven-year career with St. Louis in 1940, but the lefty-swinging outfielder's lack of power did not make him an organization favorite. Still, it was in a Cardinal uniform that he had his single most important hit, when he doubled in the 8th inning of the seventh game of the 1946 World Series against the Red Sox; when Boston shortstop Johnny Pesky hesitated with his relay throw, Enos Slaughter came all the way around from first base to score what proved to be the world championship run. Walker achieved most of his hitting title the following year in a Philadelphia uniform, also pacing the NL with his 16 triples. He closed out as a player with a .296 average.

Walker had three stints as a manager—with the Cardinals in 1955, with the Pirates between 1965 and 1967, and with the Astros between 1968 and 1972. None of his clubs ever got higher than third. On the other hand, he became a renowned batting coach, especially when working with the kind of slap hitter he had been; his most prominent pupil was Matty Alou, who won a batting title after several off-season sessions with him. Still, Walker's managing had its moments. While with St. Louis, he traded blows with his Cincinnati counterpart Birdie Tebbetts during a field melee. Later, with the Astros, Walker earned the grudging respect of some players for interrupting his regular, windy monologues on the techniques of hitting to display more strategic smarts than he was generally credited with. On the other hand, several black players on Houston, notably Joe Morgan, criticized him for Neanderthal racial views.

Walker was called The Hat because of repeated tugs at the bill of his cap while getting ready to hit.

RUBE WALKER

As pitching coach for the Mets in the late 1960s, Walker popularized the five-man rotation. Although the concept proved suitable to New York's starter-rich pitching staff, it came under increasing criticism in later years for both encouraging the use of mediocre fifth starters and for pampering the arms of the other four members of a rotation. One of the chief critics of Walker's philosophy was Nolan Ryan, a principal reason why the Mets went from a four-man to a five-man rotation to begin with.

WELDAY WALKER

The younger brother of Fleet, outfielder Walker was the second black to appear in the major leagues, joining his sibling on the American Association Toledo Blue Stockings for a handful of games in 1884. Four years later, Welday Walker lodged a protest with the president of the Ohio State League for having formally banned blacks. ''There should,'' he pleaded, ''be some broader cause—lack of ability, behavior, and intelligence—to bar a player, rather than his color.''

MURRAY WALL

In 1959, Wall pitched for a team to which he didn't belong. Swapped by the Red Sox to the Senators for Dick Hyde, he took the mound for Washington to pitch an inning, after which he was told that the deal had been canceled because of Hyde's sore arm.

BOBBY WALLACE (Hall of Fame, 1953)

Wallace is high on everyone's list of Hall of Fame questionables. A .266 hitter in twenty-five major league seasons (1894–1918) with the Cleveland Spiders and two St. Louis franchises, his most idiosyncratic claim to fame was that he briefly interrupted his playing career between June 1915 and August 1916 to become an American League umpire.

Starting as a right-handed pitcher with the Spiders, Wallace compiled a record of 24–22 in three seasons. Moving to third base in 1897, the right-handed hitter posted career highs with a .335 average and 112 RBIs. A shortstop for the rest of his career, he had a second 100-RBI year in 1899 for the Cardinals and another .300 season in 1901. With the Browns as of 1902, he never hit higher than .287. On the other hand, the club thought enough of his defensive skills to offer him a $32,500, five-year, no-trade contract to woo him away from the Cardinals; the pact made him the highest-paid player in the game at the time.

Wallace was the first AL shortstop elected to the Hall of Fame. His was one of six inductions endorsed by the Veterans Committee in the first year of the panel's balloting.

DICK WALSH

Walsh was probably the most despised general manager in baseball history. Moving into the Angels' front office after the 1968 season with an extraordinary seven-year contract, he soon earned himself the nickname of The Smiling Python for actions that were variously described as paranoid, dictatorial, and hypocritical; a greater consensus, including the vote of California owner Gene Autry, formed around the opinion that he was also a liar. Among Walsh's moves with the team were: threatening to tell a pitcher's wife about an adulterous affair unless he signed a proffered contract; refusing to allow star shortstop Jim Fregosi to undergo a needed foot operation because he didn't want to incur the expense of purchasing another infielder; and lying that the Red Sox had not informed him of outfielder Tony Conigliaro's delicate physical condition before concluding a trade with the Angels. Walsh was so hated by most of the players that he became the target of their batting-practice line drives if he made the mistake of venturing onto the field before a game; he also had to quit the clubhouse after a couple of incidents, with the batboy intervening to escort him to safety. Autry finally unloaded him long before even the midway point in his contract.

Ed Walsh was the major leagues' last 40-game winner. National Baseball Library, Cooperstown, N.Y.

ED WALSH (Hall of Fame, 1946)

Walsh was a great pitcher but an even greater technical adviser. On the mound, the cocky right-hander won 195 games with the White Sox between 1904 and 1916, in the process establishing the career-record ERA of 1.82. In 1908 he enjoyed what was probably the best year by any twentieth-century pitcher—setting another perduring mark of 464 innings pitched while leading the American League in victories (40), shutouts (11), starts (49), complete games (42), saves (6), and strikeouts (269). His ERA of 1.42 represented the third time in five straight seasons that he permitted fewer than 1.88 runs per 9 innings. His 40 wins were also the last time a major league hurler gained that plateau.

Walsh's herculean efforts were necessary insofar as the team behind him didn't come by its reputation as the Hitless Wonders by accident. In 1910, for instance, when he led the league in losses with 20, the White Sox batted .211; as for Walsh, he suffered the 20 defeats despite as astonishing ERA of 1.27. After his brilliant 1908 season, he was given a modest raise by owner Charlie Comiskey, but decided it wasn't enough of a hike and sat out the first month of the 1909 season in protest. Shortly after he rejoined the club, Comiskey asked him to accompany architect Zachary Taylor Davis on a tour of the site where the owner was building his new stadium. It was thanks to Walsh's suggestions that Comiskey Park opened in 1910 with foul lines stretching 363 feet; for the next eighty years, the stadium was a pitcher's paradise.

Because of his confident, not to say often overbearing, personality, Walsh was thought to have been the model for the narrator in Ring Lardner's *You Know Me, Al.*

BILL WAMBSGANSS

In the fifth game of the 1920 World Series against Brooklyn, Cleveland second baseman Wambsganss snared a line drive off the bat of pitcher Clarence Mitchell and turned it into the only unassisted triple play pulled off in postseason competition. In the 1940s, Wambsganss managed one of the all-women teams organized by Cubs' owner Phil Wrigley, serving as the prototype for the Tom Hanks role in *A League of Their Own.*

LLOYD WANER (Hall of Fame, 1967)

Although overshadowed by his older brother Paul, Waner was a pesky leadoff man for most of his eighteen years (between 1927 and 1945) with the Pirates and a scattering of other National League teams. His .316 lifetime mark included 11 seasons of .300 or better, four of at least 200 hits, and three of 100 runs scored. Although the lefty outfielder was in the Pittsburgh tradition of Bible hitters ("Thou shalt not pass") and was reluctant to accept a base on balls, he struck out as much as 20 times only twice, and had a few years in which he held his strikeouts down to single-digit numbers. Little Poison, as he was known, combined with his brother to post the highest batting average by far of big league siblings.

PAUL WANER (Hall of Fame, 1952)

Like Honus Wagner and Arky Vaughan, Waner didn't know what less than a .300 average was while wearing a Pittsburgh uniform. Arriving in the majors in 1926, the left-hand-hitting outfielder

did not drop below .300 until his thirteenth season. A notoriously heavy drinker whose imbibing never affected his hitting, Waner would sober up by doing backflips for fifteen or twenty minutes. Big Poison, as he as called by contemporaries, won three batting titles with averages that went as high as .380; his overall mark for twenty big league seasons of 3,152 hits was .333. Waner reached the 200-hit level eight times, and paced the National league in doubles twice, triples twice, and RBIs once. Batting ahead of potent Pirate RBI men, he scored 100 runs nine times, leading in that category twice. Picked up by the Dodgers as a gate attraction during World War II, he batted .311. Even though he was pushing forty, he was still considered enough of a good idea for the Giants and Yankees to give him similar shots, but by then he had exhausted his hitting prowess.

ARCH WARD

Ward was the sports editor of the *Chicago Tribune* who pressed successfully for the playing of the first major league All-Star Game, in 1933. The journalist lobbied for the contest as part of Chicago's Century of Progress Exposition. A formula devised by Ward and major league teams provided for the all-stars to be chosen by both fans and league managers John McGraw and Connie Mack. The selection method has gone back and forth over the years, including exclusive managerial choices (1935–46); fan selection of position player starters, with the pitchers and substitutes left to the managers (1947–57); major league players, managers, and coaches making all the picks (1958–69); and fans selecting the position player starters (1970 to the present). The inaugural game, played in Comiskey Park on July 6, 1933, was won by the American League, 4–2. The starting pitchers were Lefty Gomez of the Yankees and Bill Hallahan of the Cardinals. The crucial blow was a 2-home run by thirty-eight-year-old Babe Ruth in the 3rd inning off Hallahan. Frankie Frisch homered for the losers.

JOHN MONTGOMERY WARD (Hall of Fame, 1964)

In each of three separate baseball careers—as player, union organizer, and lawyer-executive—

JOHN MONTGOMERY WARD
1878 — 1894
PITCHING PIONEER WHO WON 158,
LOST 102 GAMES IN SEVEN YEARS.
PITCHED PERFECT GAME FOR PROVIDENCE
OF N.L. IN 1880.
TURNED TO SHORTSTOP AND MADE 2,151 HITS.
MANAGED NEW YORK AND BROOKLYN IN N.L.
PRESIDENT OF BOSTON, N.L. 1911-1912.
PLAYED IMPORTANT PART IN ESTABLISHING
MODERN ORGANIZED BASEBALL.

The long memory of the baseball establishment kept any reference to John Montgomery Ward's role in the Players League off his Cooperstown plaque when he finally gained admission to the Hall of Fame in 1964. National Baseball Library, Cooperstown, N.Y.

Ward was more successful in his less visible efforts than in more salient undertakings.

As a player, he is best remembered as an outfielder-shortstop, primarily with the Giants in the 1880s and early 1890s; in fact, his performance as a position player—a lifetime .275 average and a conspicuous paucity of league-leading totals—was inferior to his pitching. Before a sore arm curtailed his mound career, he was Providence's regular hurler, contributing to the Grays' first pennant, in 1879, with league-leading totals in wins (47) and strikeouts (239); the year before, the right-hander had led the NL in ERA, and the year after, he led in shutouts (in a second 40-win season). He also put together the fourth-lowest career ERA (2.10) of all time; collected 165 lifetime

victories against 100 losses; and fashioned the second perfect game, against Buffalo on June 17, 1880.

As both the president of the Players Brotherhood, which he helped form in 1885, and the driving force behind the Players League in 1890, Ward fought on the wrong issues and with the wrong allies—and, as a result, lost the war. From the beginning, he limited his cause by admitting that salaries were excessive, contracts sacrosanct, the blacklist not without merit, and the reserve clause a necessary evil to protect owners from themselves; refusing an offer of affiliation with the Knights of Labor didn't help either. Although there was no end of discussions about salary limitations and the reserve clause, there was little movement in either side's position until, with Ward away on Al Spalding's 1888–89 around-the-world promotional tour, the NL passed Indianapolis owner John T. Brush's Classification Plan; the scheme solidified the salary scale but based it on player behavior rather than performance, edging an already tense situation closer to critical mass. The explosion came with the sale of Deacon White and Jack Rowe to Pittsburgh. Although likening the player sales to slavery and the reserve rule to the Fugitive Slave Laws, Ward, who had vetoed his own sale to Washington in 1889, talked his cohorts out of striking over the White and Rowe cases and into forming a new league.

The PL, an artistic success but a fiscal disaster, ultimately failed for three reasons: First, the rebels overvalued their victories in a series of lawsuits brought by owners, with Ward the defendant in the first of the test cases; second, they overestimated the attractiveness of the vast majority of quality players recruited from the established leagues; and third, and most significantly, they failed to realize that the financial backers they had enlisted ultimately had more in common with the NL owners than with the players. The bond between the monied interests on both sides became apparent at a series of postseason meetings, unwisely initiated by Ward himself, at which the players were shut out of the settlement.

Ward spent the two seasons after the collapse of the PL as player-manager in Brooklyn. Traded to the Giants for the same double role, he ended up owning stock in both clubs as part of a unique deal in which Brooklyn's compensation was a share of New York's gate receipts. Retiring after the 1894 season, Ward, who had earned a law degree in the 1880s, won acclaim for his representation of Amos Rusie and the *New York Sun* in noted cases against Giants owner Andrew Freedman. Less successful were Ward's forays into baseball's executive suites: a candidacy for NL president, in 1910; the presidency of the Braves for about half of the 1912 season, a position that quickly foundered on the twin rocks of resentment by the old guard, who blocked his player moves, and criticism from Boston owner James Gaffney, who jumped all over him for failing to improve the club immediately; and an appointment as business manager of the Federal League's Brooklyn Tip-Tops, in 1914, that lasted only until Ward realized that the powers behind the latest upstart league were more interested in worming their way into the established circuits than in altering the corporate face of baseball.

For all that, the long memory of the baseball establishment kept Ward out of the Hall of Fame until almost four decades after his death, and, when he was finally given a plaque, it carried no reference to the Players League.

ROBERT B. WARD

The owner of the Brooklyn Federal League franchise, Ward came as close as anyone to introducing night baseball before its actual debut in 1935. The millionaire owner of Tip-Top Bakeries, ready for a fight to the finish after two money–losing seasons in 1914 and 1915, started construction on five eighty-five-foot light towers at his Washington Park for night games to be played in 1916. A 1915 postseason exhibition between FL players and local semipros was to have been the trial for four-night-a-week regularly scheduled games the following year. But on October 19, Ward suffered a fatal heart attack; with the Feds tottering, his brothers accepted a buyout from organized ball and turned the ballpark over to the Dodgers.

LON WARNEKE

Warneke is the only man ever to play and umpire in both a World Series and an All-Star Game.

As a right-hander for the Cubs and Cardinals between 1930 and 1945, he won 193 games, including three 20-win seasons. He reached the World Series with the Cubs in both 1932 and 1935, winning 2 games and losing 1, and appeared for the National League in three All-Star games. Returning to the National League as an umpire in 1948, he saw service in the 1954 Series and the 1952 All-Star Game.

HERB WASHINGTON

Washington was Oakland owner Charlie Finley's experiment in designated running. With the Athletics in 1974, he didn't appear in a single game as a hitter or fielder, being used exclusively as a substitute runner. The experiment proved to be less than a success when the former indoor track star managed only 29 steals in 45 attempts, a below-average 64 percent. Washington was released early the following season after swiping 2 more bases in 3 tries.

BOB WATSON

Watson became the first black given the title of general manager when he was put in charge of Houston's baseball operations following the 1993 season. The appointment came after a nineteen-year (1966–84) career during which the first baseman-outfielder averaged .295, including seven seasons of .300 or better and two of at least 100 RBIs. Watson is the only player to have hit for the cycle in both leagues, having accomplished the feat for the 1977 Astros and the 1979 Red Sox. On May 4, 1975, he also became part of baseball promotional history by scoring the one-millionth run in the major leagues. The benchmark tally came on a home run by Milt May, who came close to postponing the milestone by almost passing another runner on the bases.

BUCK WEAVER

Weaver didn't even have the consolation of some spending money before he was outlawed by Commissioner Kenesaw Landis for his part in the 1919 Black Sox scandal. Unlike the other seven Chicago players affected by the ban, he was never accused of being part of the conspiracy, but only of knowing about it and not reporting it. Landis insisted on his hard-line approach through several requests by the third baseman in later years for reinstatement. Even his .324 average in the games against Cincinnati was adjudged irrelevant. After his blacklisting, Weaver sued Charlie Comiskey for the balance of his money on a three-year contract. The case dragged on until 1924, when the White Sox owner settled out of court.

Prior to his association with the 1919 scandal, the switch-hitter had been among the American League's premier third basemen. He batted over .300 twice, including his 1920 average of .333 while he was waiting for the other shoe to drop in the investigation of the tainted Series. In 1917 Weaver duked it out with gamblers in Fenway Park when they invaded the field to protect their bets against what was clearly going to be a Boston win over Chicago.

EARL WEAVER

As manager of the Orioles' top farm team, in Rochester, New York, Weaver wrote the organization's instruction book that called for victory based on good pitching, good defense, and 3-run homers; promoted to pilot the parent club, he used the book to dominate the American League East for more than a decade.

In the first of his two stints as Baltimore's field boss, from mid-1968 through 1982, Weaver's clubs finished fourth twice (including once in the second half of the 1981 split season), third once, second seven times (including the first half of 1981), and first six times. His half-dozen years at the top of the AL East yielded four pennants and two world championships. True to the franchise's philosophy in that span, he managed twenty 20-game winners; fashioned a nonpareil defense built around Hall of Fame third baseman Brooks Robinson, shortstop Mark Belanger, and center fielder Paul Blair; and molded a potent offense featuring Cooperstown residents Brooks and Frank Robinson and first baseman Boog Powell. Weaver abhorred bunting, claiming its place was "at the bottom of a long-forgotten closet." A firm believer in the odds, he used an elaborate set of index cards detailing every player's performance against every opponent; this allowed him to use platooning in inspired ways, most notably with left fielders Gary Roenicke and John Lowenstein from 1979 and 1982.

An accomplished umpire baiter, Weaver employed a trademark backward-turned-cap to facilitate face-to-face confrontation at close quarters without violating the rule prohibiting contact with an umpire. The tactic did not prevent him from being ejected a record ninety-one times (including both ends of a doubleheader) and suspended six times in his final seven seasons. An infamous chain-smoker, he was ejected from one 1969 contest against the Twins even before it started for puffing away in the dugout; the next day, he left the dugout to deliver the lineup card with a candy cigarette in his mouth, eating the confection before reaching home plate. Perhaps his most noted encounter with an umpire was his refusal to let his team take the field in the middle of a September 1977 game in Toronto until what he considered a dangerous tarpaulin in the Blue Jays' bullpen was removed; the tarp stayed where it was, and the Orioles forfeited the game.

Weaver's most famous running feud was with ace pitcher Jim Palmer. The manager described his problem with the Hall of Fame hurler by comparing what he considered the right-hander's imaginary ailments to the Chinese calendar: "The Chinese tell time by the 'Year of the Horse' or the 'Year of the Dragon.' I tell time by the 'Year of the Back' and the 'Year of the Elbow.' This year it's the 'Year of the Ulnar Nerve.' "

Mainly as a favor to the Orioles, Weaver came out of retirement for a second managerial stint, in the mid-1980s, but showed little enthusiasm for the task.

DEL WEBB

For an owner of the Yankees, Webb spent an inordinate amount of time worrying about baseball in his native West; he spent a lot less time worrying about his associations with the gaming industry.

Originally a minority member (along with Dan Topping) of the Larry MacPhail triumvirate that purchased the Yankees from Jacob Ruppert's estate in 1945, Webb took over a half share of the club after MacPhail's nervous collapse following the 1947 World Series. Three months earlier, mobster Bugsy Siegel had been gunned down in his girlfriend's apartment, and Webb, whose construction company was building the Flamingo

Hotel in Las Vegas for Siegel, had taken a piece of the project to protect his investment. Commissioner Happy Chandler, taking a dim view of the development, ordered the builder to divest himself of his holdings in either the Flamingo or the Yankees. In response, Webb joined with Cardinals' owner Fred Saigh in leading the effort to oust Chandler. Ford Frick, Chandler's successor, took the more accommodating position that the Yankee executive should cash in his Las Vegas chips as soon as possible without making a financial sacrifice.

Back on the East Coast, Webb was well ahead of Topping in accepting general manager George Weiss's proposal to hire Casey Stengel as field boss in 1949; he was also more reluctant to dispose of Stengel in 1960. Otherwise, he mainly concentrated on his construction business—except when owning the Yankees could help that business. In 1951, he persuaded Giants' owner Horace Stoneham to switch spring training sites, with the National League club relocating to St. Petersburg for one spring, and the American Leaguers switching to Phoenix so Webb could parade his prize possession before his western friends. As an added attraction, the Yankees ran an instructional camp for prospects before spring training proper; the camp served as a showcase for, among others, Mickey Mantle, Billy Martin, Gil McDougald, Tom Sturdivant, and Tom Morgan.

With much of his business centered around Los Angeles, Webb consistently hyped an AL franchise in the West Coast city. In 1954, with the Browns on the verge of pulling out of St. Louis in favor of Baltimore, Webb blocked the move, pushing through a league resolution committing the franchise to the California city instead; when it took only twenty-four hours for league owners to realize that the California resolution would result in a massive lawsuit from the Baltimore interests, the Yankee co-owner then sponsored a successful vote promising LA a franchise in the near future. A year later, when the Athletics became available, Webb worked both sides of the street, telling everyone concerned in California that he was doing everything he could to secure them the club while working with Arnold Johnson to transfer the team to Kansas City, where he had the inside track on a contract to enlarge the minor league stadium to be used by the Athletics.

When Webb turned down Topping's offer to sell his share of the Yankees in 1962 because he couldn't give the organization his full attention, the partners decided to sell at the earliest possible date and to spend as little as possible in the interim. That date was 1964, when CBS took over an 80 percent interest in the franchise. Webb sold his remaining 10 percent in February 1965.

In the early 1970s, Webb sought to make a comeback by purchasing the White Sox. The deal never got off the ground because he refused to divest himself of his holdings in several Las Vegas casinos—a precondition imposed by Commissioner Bowie Kuhn.

EARL WEBB

Webb established the major league season mark for doubles when he took an extra base 67 times while playing for the Red Sox in 1931. In none of his other six big league seasons did the lefty-swinging outfielder get more than 30 two-baggers.

CHARLES WEEGHMAN

Weeghman, who had made a fortune running a chain of lunch counters, took over the Chicago Federal League franchise from league president Charles Gilmore in 1914 after being promised that his $26,000 investment would be the full extent of his commitment. Before he was through, however, he and his fish wholesaler-partner William Walker would lay out $412,000 to support the Whales. The largest chunk of their money went to build Weeghman Park, on the city's North Side.

Weeghman emerged from the Federal war as one of the victors, when he was permitted to purchase the Cubs for $500,000. The ballpark entered the NL with Weeghman in 1916. By 1918, the money-short businessman had surrendered most of his stock for loans by chewing gum magnate William Wrigley; in 1926, the facility originally built as an FL showcase was rechristened Wrigley Field.

Weeghman was the first major league owner to surrender all balls hit into the stands to the fans without a battle; he introduced the practice when he moved to the NL in 1916.

George Weiss (right) prospered when mentor Ed Barrow was squeezed out of the Yankee front office by Larry MacPhail (left). Photo compliments of Lee MacPhail.

AL WEIS

A .219 lifetime hitter, Weis was the improbable offensive hero of the Miracle Mets' 1969 World Series victory over the Orioles. The second baseman drove in the winning run in the 9th inning of the second game with a single, and tied the final contest with a 7th-inning homer that positioned New York to win it in the 8th inning. The switch-hitter averaged .455 for the five games. Weis hit only 7 regular-season homers in ten years (1962–71) with the White Sox and the Mets.

GEORGE WEISS (Hall of Fame, 1971)

There never was anybody in baseball better at winning pennants or making money from them than Weiss; as for making it fun, he just didn't get it.

In 1920, at age twenty-four, Weiss sold his family's store and bought the Eastern League New Haven franchise. He first attracted the attention of Yankee general manager Ed Barrow by refusing to pay the New York club its share of the gate receipts for an exhibition game because Babe Ruth, the central attraction, had not made the trip to Connecticut. An infuriated Barrow appealed the matter to Commissioner Kenesaw Landis, who sided with Weiss.

After serving as general manager of the International League's Baltimore Orioles from 1929 to 1931, Weiss was hired by Barrow to build a farm system as a less expensive alternative to purchasing players. He succeeded so brilliantly that, during his sixteen-year tenure in the job, the Yankees paid cash for only five minor league players, two of whom were Tommy Henrich and Joe DiMaggio. The acquisition of DiMaggio, from the Pacific Coast League's San Francisco Seals, was particularly noteworthy in that the farm director went over his reluctant boss's head to owner Jacob Ruppert in his enthusiasm for the outfielder, whose injured knee had cooled Barrow's ardor.

By the time Weiss was promoted by new majority owners Dan Topping and Del Webb to head baseball operations in late 1947, the Yankees had the best run and most productive minor league chain in baseball, and Weiss had a well-deserved reputation as a drill sergeant. So interested was he in maintaining excellence in every detail that he once gave Frank Lane, then operating New York's top farm club, in Kansas City, demerits for failure to wash the windows on the telephone booths in the lobby of the club's offices.

The first significant move in New York by the excruciatingly formal general manager was to bring in the exhaustingly effusive Casey Stengel as manager in 1949; the pair, friends since both had been in the Eastern League in the 1920s, became an odd couple in forging the team that brought ten pennants and seven world championships to the Bronx between 1949 and 1960. Weiss wanted Stengel for his ability to work with young players, a skill that dovetailed with his own ability to sign the best young talent in the country.

Implementing the philosophy that "There is no such thing as second place. Either you're first or you're nothing," Weiss's Yankees ran roughshod over the rest of the American League for more than a decade, while he did pretty much the same to the players who made the pennants possible. His brutally cold-blooded approach to the business of baseball calcified the image of the 1950s Yankees as a corporate machine. His aloofness led him to negotiate directly only with top stars, leaving the handling of other contracts to assistant Roy Hamey. Weiss's salary battles, especially with pitchers Vic Raschi and Allie Reynolds, were acrimonious. Because of a profit-sharing plan instituted by Topping and Webb, Weiss was not above subterfuge in holding down salaries: When Phil Rizzuto demanded $50,000 after winning AL Most Valuable Player honors in 1951, Weiss offered $35,000. In a meeting to settle the difference, Weiss acceded but, claiming that his secretary was not around to type a new document, persuaded the shortstop to sign the one at hand and have it supplemented with an immediate check for $15,000. The following year, however, negotiations between the two began at the $35,000 figure on the official document.

There was no room for perceived troublemakers on Weiss's Yankees. Billy Martin, regarded as a bad influence on stars Mickey Mantle and Whitey Ford, was traded after the infamous Copacabana fracas in May 1957 even though the second baseman wasn't involved in what happened. Players to be released were notified by telegram. Rizzuto fared worst of all, receiving his walking papers an Old-Timers' Day in 1956 after a protracted conversation in which Weiss took him through the entire roster, soliciting the infielder's advice on how to make room for recently acquired Enos Slaughter.

Weiss provided Stengel with a steady stream of fresh young talent—supplemented by reinforcements from the Athletics, after their relocation to Kansas City from Philadelphia in 1955. (He treated the major league club pretty much as he had the Yankee top farm club when it was in the Missouri city, stripping it over the years of, among others, Clete Boyer, Ryne Duren, and Roger Maris.) The successes notwithstanding, Weiss also missed a few, refusing to sign both Herb Score and Frank Lary because neither was what he called "a Yankee type."

The worst blot on Weiss's record, however, was his unwillingness to affront what he saw as the delicate sensibilities of Yankee Stadium patrons by putting a black player in pinstripes. Always maintaining that the organization was searching for a black capable of making the team, Weiss, with enough drinks in him, betrayed his reasons for carrying an all-white roster for five years after Jackie Robinson stepped over the color line: "Boxholders from Westchester don't want that sort of crowd," he once said. "They would be offended to have to sit with niggers." This

attitude led to the trade of flashy first baseman Vic Power to the Athletics in December 1952, ostensibly because he was a hotheaded showoff (and, rumor had it, fond of white women), but mainly because he was good enough to make the team.

Weiss only compounded the problem by converting Elston Howard, the only remaining black in the system, from an outfielder to a catcher in 1954, seemingly setting him up to be blocked from the parent team by future Hall of Famer Yogi Berra. Even when Howard forced his way onto the big club by winning the International League MVP award in 1954, the Yankees made no effort whatsoever to compel still-segregated facilities in the South, and even in some major league cities, to accept Howard. The general manager came in for yet another bashing by the press for insisting that Howard skip an exhibition game in Birmingham, Alabama, rather than cancel the contest in the face of a state law that prohibited blacks from competing with whites on the same field.

Forced to retire in November 1960, Weiss left less noisily if not less bitterly, than Stengel, who had suffered a similar fate a few weeks earlier. Resurfacing two years later as president of the expansion Mets, Weiss once again hired Stengel as manager, this time for the exact opposite reason he had lobbied for him to take over the Yankees. In the earlier instance, he had wanted Stengel for his skills with young players; now, having opted in the expansion draft for a clubhouse full of worn-out players familiar from the glory days of the departed Dodgers and Giants, he wanted the very clownishness he had asked everyone to ignore fourteen years earlier—as a cover for the very bad team he was about to put on the field.

When the New Breed fans responded more enthusiastically than he could have imagined, Weiss, for whom winning was a compulsion, missed the point. His response to the fabled banners unfurled by Met fans to cheer their antiheroes was to complain about "these noisy people with their bedsheets. Where do they come from? Why don't they keep quiet?" True to form, however, when he retired, this time voluntarily, in 1966, the essential ingredients of the Miracle pennant of 1969—Tom

Seaver, Jerry Koosman, Nolan Ryan, and Tug McGraw—were already part of the organization; equally true to form, only one of them, outfielder Cleon Jones, was black.

CURT WELCH

Welch's 10th-inning steal of home to win the final game of the 1886 "World Series" for the American Association's St. Louis Browns became fabled as the $15,000 Slide. The play was, in fact, a John Clarkson pitchout that, depending on the account, either sailed over the head of Chicago Catcher King Kelly or glanced off his mitt, the slide being a mere embellishment. As for the gate receipts for the 6 games of the winner-take-all set, they were just under $13,000.

MICKEY WELCH (Hall of Fame, 1973)

Welch was the co–ace (with Tim Keefe) of the Giants' mound staff in the 1880s—and the team's poet laureate. As a pitcher, Welch won 308 games in a thirteen-year career, including nine seasons of more than 20 and four of more than 30. Although never a power pitcher, the right-hander established a major league mark by striking out the first 9 batters he faced, on August 28, 1884. One of the three future Hall of Famers (along with Roger Connor and Buck Ewing) to come to the Giants from the ousted Troy franchise in 1883, he felt a personal loyalty to New York owner John B. Day and refused to join the Players' League in 1890, although by then his skills had seriously eroded.

As a poet, Smiling Mickey, as he was known, had but one subject matter: beer. (He even dedicated his phenomenal 44–11 season, in 1885, to his favorite beverage.) His most popular work off the mound, which he set to music, also hinted that beer wasn't the only painkiller available to players in his day:

Pure Elixir or malt and hops
Beats all the drugs and all the drops.

TOM WERNER

Werner headed the syndicate that purchased the Padres from Joan Kroc in April 1990 for an estimated $90 million. A television producer, he made his first imprint on the game by asking Roseanne Arnold, one of his sitcom stars, to sing

"The Star Spangled Banner" before a home game. When Arnold's painfully screeching rendition was booed by the fans, she returned the compliment by grabbing at her crotch and throwing vulgar gestures at the grandstands. Although the baseball establishment professed itself scandalized by the episode, it was relatively more silent in 1993 when Werner proceeded to break up a pennant-contending roster behind the argument that the franchise could not afford the high arbitration salaries that were imminent for such stars as Gary Sheffield and Fred McGriff. Although Werner himself denied it, some commentators saw the fire sale as an ownership ploy aimed at dramatizing the allegedly precarious economic situations of smaller-market franchises. Werner finally sold a controlling interest in the club to software millionaire John Moores for $80 million in December 1994.

VIC WERTZ

One of the premier sluggers in the American League in the 1950s, Wertz is most often remembered as the batter who swatted the 440-foot drive in the first game of the 1954 World Series that Giants center fielder Willie Mays turned into The Catch. What is not recalled as often is that the blast would have been Wertz's fifth hit in the contest. In the latter part of his career, the lefty-hitting first baseman continued to menace pitchers despite having to wear a leg brace to offset some physical degeneration caused by polio.

ZACK WHEAT (Hall of Fame, 1959)

The National League's most dangerous left-handed hitter for most of his nineteen-year (1909–27) career, Wheat would almost certainly have had even bigger numbers than his .317 lifetime average if the lively ball had come along a little earlier. Although the Dodger outfielder won a batting title in 1918 and had already batted .300 seven times before 1920, he became even more menacing to pitchers afterward, going three straight seasons of .375, .375, and .359. Aside from providing most of the Brooklyn offense for close to two decades, Wheat was also the franchise's most popular player, with teammates as much as with fans. This became particularly clear after the 1915 season, when he led a player revolt against owner Charlie Ebbets's attempts to slash team salaries because of the dissipated threat of the rival Federal League; by the same token, when he was talked into accepting a contract, the uprising died.

Wheat's up-and-down relations with manager Wilbert Robinson in the 1920s eventually led to his release after the 1926 season. Initially Robinson was so convinced of the outfielder's smarts that he turned the day-to-day piloting of the club over to Wheat while he himself sat in the stands for what he called "a cooler appraisal" of NL clubs; when the Dodgers began stumbling, however, Robinson returned to the dugout, drawing Wheat's irritation because of the clear vote of no confidence.

HARRY WHEELER

Outfielder Wheeler is the only player in major league history who played for five different teams in one season. His 1884 odyssey included 5 games for the St. Louis Browns (American Association), 14 for the Kansas City Unions (Union Association), 20 for the Chicago Browns (Union Association), 17 for the Pittsburgh Stogies (Union Association), and 17 for the Baltimore Monumentals (Union Association). He batted .244 overall, and never again appeared in a big league contest.

PETE WHISENANT

A vagabond outfielder who played with ten clubs in eight seasons in the 1950s and the early 1960s, Whisenant is the only player ever to appear in the box score for a team that had already traded him. Sent up to bat as a pinch hitter for the Indians in the seventh inning of the second game of a doubleheader at precisely 6:35 P.M. on May 15, 1960, he was just as quickly removed from the game as part of a lefty-righty gambit after White Sox manager Al Lopez changed pitchers. When Chicago went on to lose the game, Lopez protested that Whisenant had been ineligible because, prior to the day's games, Cleveland had issued a press announcement—for release at exactly 6:00 P.M.—that the outfielder had been traded to the Senators for shortstop Ken Aspromonte; and that, even though he had not seen a single pitch, his formal insertion into the game

had affected the outcome because it had necessitated a change in pitchers. The protest was denied by American League president Joe Cronin on the grounds that the two clubs had intended for the trade to be effective after the contest. Whisenant holds the further pinch-hitting distinction of having connected for all 5 of his 1957 home runs (while playing for the Reds) as a substitute swinger—3 of them off Cardinal left-hander Vinegar Bend Mizell.

BILL WHITE

White's three distinct careers in baseball have made him about as nimble a personality as the sport has seen. As a player, he was a slick-fielding first baseman who held reign over the position between the eras of Gil Hodges and Keith Hernandez. Offensively, White was an alley hitter with .300 averages four times; his most impressive feat at the plate came on July 17–18, 1961, when he collected 14 hits in back-to-back doubleheaders. While with St. Louis in 1960, White's protests at the exclusion of black players from public functions at the club's Florida spring training site mushroomed into a nationwide call for the boycotting of Anheuser-Busch products and demands that the state desegregate its hotels and restaurants or face the loss of big league teams.

Upon retirement, White went into the broadcasting booth, most notably serving as a combination goader and straight man for Phil Rizzuto's antic pronouncements during Yankee telecasts. White's broadcasting style included a lot of pregnant silences and monosyllabic sarcasm, suggesting someone who wanted to say much more than his prudence dictated. The same qualities came to the fore when, in 1989, he was selected as president of the National League, making him the highest-ranking black in the game's history. Although he was given to the same macho observations about umpires trying to take center stage and pitchers being too intimidated to throw inside as he had grunted during his broadcasting career, there was little practical follow-up to his attitude in setting league policy. He also took a hit in 1992 for unilaterally delaying the sale of the Giants to a Florida group and allowing a Bay Area consortium to purchase the franchise for a lower price. On more than one occasion, White declared that he was fed up with his post, and even formally resigned on March 31, 1993. But a year later he was still on the job because of the organizational chaos created by the owners' refusal to elect a permanent commissioner.

White's breaking point came during a January 1994 ownership meeting that passed a number of resolutions that he told newsmen were inimical to the game; among the moves were a decision to diminish further the already dubious powers of the league presidents, approval of rotating advertising signs behind home plate, and greater empowerment of the executives from small-market clubs determined to take a hard stance in new contract negotiations with the players. In reiterating his intention of stepping down, White made it clear that he had become disgusted with his job. He was finally replaced, in March 1994, by Leonard Coleman, the executive director of major league baseball's marketing development department.

DEACON WHITE

Catcher-third baseman White was a member of both nineteenth-century Big Fours, whose transfer from one team to another destroyed, in the first instance, an entire league, and in the second, a National League franchise. With pitcher Al Spalding, first baseman Cal McVey, and second baseman Ross Barnes joining White, the first quartet devastated the National Association, leading Boston to 71 wins against only 8 losses in the league's last season, then effectively abolished it altogether by jumping to Chicago and thus precipitating the formation of the National League. The second unit—including first baseman Dan Brouthers, second baseman Hardy Richardson, and shortstop Jack Rowe in addition to White—was sold to Detroit by Buffalo in September 1885. When NL president Nick Young voided the deal, the four refused to return to the financially faltering Bisons and sat out the last weeks of the season; a crisis was averted only because the Buffalo franchise folded at the end of the year, allowing the second Big Four unimpeded passage to the Wolverines, who won the 1887 pennant with the quartet leading the way.

In 1889 White got into still another transaction hassle when he was sold by Detroit to Pittsburgh after he had already committed himself to managing the Buffalo club in the International League. He refused to report to his new employer until the Alleghenys gave him a bonus and a raise, and even then only after Players Brotherhood president John Montgomery Ward had advised him to honor his contract and not spoil the union's more dramatic plans. White's complaint against the reserve clause—"No man can sell my carcass unless I get at least half"—expressed a major rallying point for the Players League in 1890.

White paired with pitcher-brother Will as the first sibling battery, with Cincinnati in 1878. The receiver also pioneered in several other areas: Playing for the Cleveland Forest Citys on May 4, 1871, he was the first batter—and collected the first base hit, a double—in a professional league (the National Association) game. He has been credited (along with Nat Hicks) with being the first catcher to move up directly behind the batter, a position he had staked out with men on base as early as 1875; he and Spalding developed the quick pitch; and, in collaboration with Detroit manager Jim O'Rourke, White designed the first primitive, all-rubber chest protector, in the early 1880s. He got his nickname from those who said he had the manners of a church official.

SOL WHITE

An infielder with several minor league teams and numerous black ones in the 1880s and 1890s, White dodged enforcement of the color line to appear on an integrated team as late as 1895. The cofounder (with sportswriter H. Walter Schlichter) and manager of the Philadelphia Giants from 1902 to 1910, White built such a great team that opponents in a proposed 1905 postseason series for the world championship of black baseball took one look at the Giants' 134–21 record and stayed home. The following year, after a 108–31 season, the manager challenged the winners of the Cubs-White Sox World Series to a true championship series but never received a reply. White's most enduring legacy to baseball was the 1907 publication of *Sol White's Official Baseball Guide*, the primary source for information about early black baseball. The book, a patchwork of fact, legend, playing tips, and verse, included the prediction that the color barrier would soon fall; White lived until 1955.

WILL WHITE

That White is one and a half answers to the trivia questions of who was the first player to wear glasses on a diamond and who made up the first brother battery has obscured his mound accomplishments. Among other things, he was the first pitcher to win 200 games, in 1884 with the American Association Cincinnati Reds; his 1879 totals of 75 complete games and 680 innings pitched for the National League Reds are among the baseball records least likely to be broken; and he kept the powerful Chicago White Stockings from scoring an earned run in the first two post-season interleague championship games ever played, in 1882. The right-hander also tried managing the AA Reds, in 1884, but quit, with a record of 44–27, claiming he lacked the temperament to be a pilot. He first wore spectacles in 1877 while with Boston, and tossed his first pitch to brother Deacon the following year, for the Reds.

WILLIAM WARREN WHITE

As secretary of the Union Association in 1884, White was the first to invoke "the best interests of baseball" when he committed the new league to that standard in a letter to the *New York Clipper*.

EARL WHITEHILL

Whitehill is the only major league pitcher to win 200 games with an ERA higher than 4.00; in seventeen major league seasons (1923–39), mostly with the Tigers and Senators, the southpaw put together a record of 218–185 while giving up 4.36 earned runs every 9 innings.

MARK WHITEN

On September 7, 1993, Whiten tied three of baseball's most conspicuous power records on what was arguably the greatest offensive day by a major league hitter. Facing the Reds in the second game of a doubleheader, the Cardinal outfielder joined the handful of players to clout 4 home runs in a game, in the process also tying Jim Bottomley's sixty-nine-year-old mark of 12

RBIs in one contest. Because he had also driven in a run in the first game, Whiten additionally tied Nate Colbert's twenty-one-year-old record of 13 RBIs in a doubleheader.

ROBERT WHITLOW

Whitlow was an Air Force colonel who was brought in as "athletic director" of the Cubs in the early 1960s as part of owner Phil Wrigley's managerial experiment with a College of Coaches. As conceived by the Chicago boss, Whitlow's position was to have been second only to his own in the organization, with even general manager John Holland reporting to him. For his part, the colonel was supposed to have infused the franchise with radical reforms borrowed in part from the military and in part from university administrative structures. The notion lasted only as long as it took Bob Kennedy to assert his authority as the first coach of coaches and to order Whitlow to stay clear of his players. In having to announce the departure of the military man, Wrigley claimed that his ideas had been "too far ahead of their time." But aside from his installing an auxiliary fence in the center-field bleachers, nobody in Chicago could put a finger on what Whitlow's ideas had been.

ALAN WIGGINS

Wiggins was the first major leaguer known to have died from AIDS. He succumbed in 1991 after having his once-promising career aborted by repeated drug problems. With the Padres in 1983 and 1984, the second baseman put together 136 steals.

HOYT WILHELM (Hall of Fame, 1985)

Wilhelm's twenty-one-year career between 1952 and 1972 was long enough to give him the record for most games (1,070) by a pitcher and to make him the first active player eligible to collect his pension. Only a week shy of his forty-ninth birthday when he was cut loose by the Dodgers, the right-handed knuckleballer was the first reliever to be elected to Cooperstown. In spite of that precedent, however, he never once led the league in saves, although picking up 20 or more in three successive years for the White Sox in the early 1960s. On the other hand, Wilhelm does hold the record for most wins (123) in relief, is the only rookie ever to lead a league in ERA (2.43 with the 1952 Giants), and picked up another ERA title with the Orioles in 1959.

Already twenty-nine when he was brought up by the Giants, the hurler evoked little patience from most of the teams he played with—in part because of his age, in part because of the knuckleball that terrorized catchers (and caused most of the passed-ball records now standing). His most noted escape from premature retirement came in 1958, when Baltimore manager Paul Richards gave him one final chance to stick with the club after a succession of disastrous relief outings; Wilhelm responded with a 1–0 no-hitter against the Yankees. It was also Richards who designed a special pancake catcher's mitt for Orioles receivers who had been complaining about having to catch Wilhelm.

Before he was finished in the big leagues, Wilhelm had bounced from the Giants to the Cardinals to the Indians to the Orioles to the White Sox to the Angels to the Braves to the Cubs, back to the Braves and, finally, to the Dodgers. In his first at-bat for the Giants in 1952, he hit a home run; he was still looking for his second one twenty-one years later.

BILLY WILLIAMS (Hall of Fame, 1987)

Williams did for the Cubs from the left side of the plate what Ernie Banks did from the right side, if with slightly less power and slightly more consistency; the difference was that Williams finally got away from Chicago in his twilight years and managed to play in a postseason series. After a couple of late-season appearances in 1959 and 1960, the outfielder had the first of his thirteen straight years of 21 or more home runs in 1961, reaching a career high of 42 in 1972. Despite his power, however, Williams was no hit-or-miss proposition, winning the batting championship in 1972, reaching the .300 mark five times, compiling 200 hits on three occasions, banging out 30 or more doubles seven years, and ending with a career batting mark of .292. He also scored 100 runs five times and drove in 100 runs three times. From 1963 to 1970 he was the National League's Iron Man, appearing in a record 1,117 consecutive games—a frontier later surpassed by Steve Gar-

vey. Although he shared Banks's plight of never being on a pennant-winning club during his sixteen years with the Cubs, Williams did manage to get into a League Championship Series as a designated hitter for the Athletics in 1975. That was the good part; the bad part was that he went hitless in 8 plate appearances.

CY WILLIAMS

One of the most productive sluggers of the late 1910s and early 1920s, Williams was the victim of the first Williams Shift. His dead pull hitting, although ideally suited to Philadelphia's Baker Bowl, encouraged opposing managers to bunch defenders on the right side; Cleveland manager Lou Boudreau later used a similar tactic against Red Sox slugger Ted Williams.

In a nineteen-year (1912–30) career with the Cubs and Phillies, Williams hit .292 and reached the seats 251 times, with highs of .345 (in 1926) and 41 round-trippers (in 1923). He was such a standout defensive center fielder that his flankers in left and right saw little reason to move for anything not hit directly at them; in mock recognition of this, local sportswriters once decided that he club's slogan for the 1920s was "GET IT, CY, GET IT."

DIB WILLIAMS

A second baseman for the Red Sox in 1935, Williams developed a mental block against being able to score from third on a grounder or a fly ball. The problem became so acute that Boston manager Joe Cronin had to send in a pinch runner whenever he considered Williams's run important.

DICK WILLIAMS

One of baseball's all-time abrasive personalities, Williams shares the twentieth-century record with Jimmy Dykes for managing the most major league clubs (six). A key difference from Dykes is that he reached the World Series four times with three of the teams.

Williams got his first managerial shot with the Red Sox in 1967, turning it to gold with the Impossible Dream pennant. It was also the first display of a personality that tilted between that of a hard taskmaster and a martinet with little variation. When Boston failed to repeat in 1968, the martinet took over from the taskmaster in imposing a number of petty rules and fines for perceived infractions—a gradually demoralizing process that ended only when the pilot included franchise star Carl Yastrzemski on his Bad Boy list and owner Tom Yawkey came running with a pink slip.

In 1971, Williams resurfaced as pilot of the Athletics, turning his instinctive distance from players into an asset by ignoring their contempt for him and their relentless goadings of one another over inferior performances. He was also capable of waging his brand of psychological warfare on opponents. In game three of the 1972 World Series against the Reds, for example, his gesticulations toward both first base and on-deck hitter Tony Perez, apparently indicating an order of a belated intentional walk, so fooled batter Johnny Bench that reliever Rollie Fingers was able to sneak a third strike past the Cincinnati slugger. As with Yastrzemski in Boston, Williams had some of his worst troubles in Oakland with franchise star Reggie Jackson. But when Jackson complained to Charlie Finley during the 1973 season that the pilot and his coaches had become dictatorial, the owner did the opposite of Yawkey by extending the contracts of the entire brain trust.

The contract extension aside, Williams didn't like Finley any more than the players did, and the existence of a common enemy helped blunt the hostility of some of the players toward him. The three-way Mutual Lack of Admiration Society came apart at the seams during the 1973 World Series against the Mets, when Finley sought to have second baseman Mike Andrews placed on the disabled list after making a couple of crucial errors. Although the ploy was thwarted by Commissioner Bowie Kuhn, the incident prompted Williams to call a clubhouse meeting and announce his intention of resigning as soon as the World Series was over. He made good on the threat after another Oakland world championship, and attracted immediate attention from the Yankees. Holding the ace of another year on Williams's contract, Finley demanded various New York regulars in exchange for the services of his erstwhile manager. The Yankees said no, then

signed Williams to a contract anyway, precipitating months of courtroom squabbles and late-night meetings at the office of American League president Joe Cronin. In the end, Williams had to sit home for the final year of his pact with the Athletics.

A subsequent stint with the Angels from the middle of the 1974 season to the halfway point of the 1976 campaign was equally troubled. With the California front office continually shifting gears on him as it had with his predecessors, Williams began taking out his frustrations on his players. When he wasn't shouting at them on the field or in the dugout, he was ignoring their simplest requests, making each and every one of them feel responsible for his broken promise prior to the 1975 season that he would never pilot a last-place club. Early in the 1976 season, he chilled relations with just about everybody in the organization by naming second baseman Jerry Remy and pitchers Nolan Ryan and Frank Tanana as ''the only major leaguers'' on the club. A short time after that, he sought to get owner Gene Autry to dump general manager Harry Dalton in favor of Angels broadcaster Don Drysdale. After a final dugout clash with slugger Bill Melton, Williams was sent walking.

Popping up in the National League with the Expos in 1977, Williams followed the usual script, raising the club to the status of a serious contender, but so alienating his players that he had to be replaced by Jim Fanning just before reaching the playoffs in 1981. With San Diego the following year, he began a four-year tenure that peaked with a Padre pennant in 1984. After a disappointing 1985 season, however, he clashed with general manager Jack McKeon over the firing of longtime confidant and third-base coach Ozzie Virgil. Although owner Joan Kroc stepped in and ordered Virgil rehired, Williams and McKeon sniped at each other through the off-season, with the manager complaining in particular about being forced to carry coach Harry Dunlop, whom he described as a front-office spy. On the very day that pitchers and catchers reported to spring training camp in 1986, the club announced that it had brought out the remainder of Williams's contract.

Next to his days with the Angels, Williams

spent his most miserable years in the dugout as pilot of the Mariners between 1986 and 1988. By the middle of his second year, he was admitting to newsmen that he had lost his taste for managing a decidedly bad team; by June 1988 he was telling everyone who would listen that he intended retiring at the end of the year. When staff ace Mark Langston approached him to ask if he didn't think he was hurting the club by blanketing the clubhouse with his lame duck airs, Williams responded by calling the southpaw "gutless." Shortly afterward, the front office told him to stay home for the rest of the year. In twenty-one seasons of managing, he ended up with a record of 1,571–1,451 (.520).

As a utility outfielder-infielder for the Dodgers, Orioles, and other clubs between 1951 and 1964, Williams batted .260.

EDWARD BENNETT WILLIAMS

When Williams, the ultimate Washington insider, took over the Orioles in August 1979, the purchase was seen by many as the first step in the transfer of the club to the District of Columbia; instead, the lawyer and owner of the NFL Redskins not only kept the club in Baltimore but also, in his almost nine years in control, completely altered the style and image of the team from one of caution and conservatism to one of activism and, sometimes, impetuousness.

An attorney whose clients had included Senator Joseph McCarthy and Teamsters Union chief Jimmy Hoffa, Williams brought flair to a previously drab organization. His battles with city fathers for a new stadium began as early as 1980. While ultimately ignored in a suggestion to name the facility after Babe Ruth, whose father's saloon once stood in what became center field at Camden Yards, he was as responsible as anyone for the new facility, which opened in 1992, after his death. His marketing technique of eliminating any mention of Baltimore in plugging the Orioles and referring to the area between the city and Washington as Birdland angered local purists but also increased attendance. His early insistence that he had no interest in running a "Ma and Pa" franchise cost him points with the local media and boosters, but he backed up his bluster with cash

for free agents to make up for a farm system run dry.

The new owner and carryover general manager Hank Peters clashed repeatedly. Peters won the first major confrontation when Joe Altobelli was named manager to succeed Earl Weaver in 1983; despite a world championship that year, however, Altobelli was never Williams's idea of a high-profile pilot, and Weaver was back within a couple of years. Williams prevailed over the general manager with $12 million signings of outfielders Fred Lynn and Lee Lacy and reliever Don Aase; he was less successful in insisting on a trade for second baseman Alan Wiggins, whose drug problems followed him to Baltimore. The biggest battle between the two was over the appointment, in late 1985, of Doug Melvin as the owner's personal talent evaluator for a minor league system that had fallen so deeply into disrepair that not one of Peters's first-round draft picks in ten years had made it to the major leagues. Melvin's evaluation led directly to the firing of Peters and farm director Tom Giordano after the 1987 season.

A year later, Williams expressed surprise that there were no blacks employed in the front office (and surprised others by revealing that only 5 percent of the minor leaguers in the Baltimore system were black). Prompted by the public remarks the previous April of Dodger executive Al Campanis about the inadequacies of blacks to hold down managerial and front-office jobs, he brought in former Oriole slugger Frank Robinson as a special assistant and ex-NFL star Calvin Hill as a vice president charged with eliminating what the owner called "ethnic or gender insensitivity." At the same time, Williams appointed talent evaluator Melvin to direct the minor league operation and brought in Rollie Hemond as the new general manager.

The front-office overhaul turned out to be Williams's last major act for the club. Suffering from terminal cancer, he turned over daily operations to law firm associate Larry Lucchino in May 1988, and died the following August. In December his widow, Agnes Neil Williams, sold the club for $70 million to a group that included Eli Jacobs, a computer equipment millionaire; R. Sargent Shriver, a Kennedy brother-in-law; and Lucchino.

ELISA GREEN WILLIAMS

Williams was an official scorer for the Cubs who remained anonymous for many years. The wife of the team treasurer, she was offered the job in 1882 by owner Al Spalding, who was suspicious of some of the statistics submitted to his annual *Guide*. Her identity was kept secret—even from her own family—so as not to attract pressure from players.

GEORGE H. WILLIAMS

In October 1891, Chicago restaurateur Williams was granted a Chicago franchise in the American Association as part of the association's renewed warfare with the National League. Ignoring the fact that his club created an awkward nine-team circuit, Williams raised $50,000 and set about luring star players such as Fred Pfeffer, Amos Rusie, and Malachai Kittredge with impressive salaries. NL owners, unwilling to compete with such extravagance, absorbed four AA teams and bought out the others. Williams accepted $14,000 for his trouble, and his nameless team disappeared without ever playing a game.

KEN WILLIAMS

Williams was the founder of the 30-homer, 30-stolen-base club. A .319 career hitter, he had the best of his fourteen major league seasons with the Browns, for whom he played between 1918 and 1927 and for whom he averaged between .324 and .352 from 1921 and 1925. In 1922 he led the American League with 39 round-trippers and notched 37 thefts; he also paced AL hitters that year in RBIs and hit .332. His 30–30 feat was not matched until Willie Mays did it in 1956.

LEFTY WILLIAMS

Williams's dire performance in the 1919 World Series against the Reds made him one of the least sympathetic of the eight Chicago players outlawed from baseball because of the Black Sox scandal. After posting 23 wins during the season, the southpaw lost all 3 of his starts to Cincinnati, including a 1st-inning 3-run shelling in the final game. The only mitigating circumstance in his favor is that gamblers threatened both him and his wife prior to the concluding contest. He won

another 22 games in 1920 before Commissioner Kenesaw Landis issued his ban.

MITCH WILLIAMS

Williams earned his nickname of Wild Thing: Entering the 1995 season, the relief specialist had walked 516 batters in 674 major league innings, an average of 6.89 free passes every 9 innings—the highest of any pitcher in major league history. Despite driving managers for the Rangers, Cubs, Phillies, and Astros to distraction whenever he strolled in from the bullpen, the southpaw saved more than 30 games three times. In 1993 he reached a career-high 43 rescues, then added 2 more in the National League Championship Series against the Braves. In the World Series, however, Williams blew 2 games—most notably when he gave up a free pass and Joe Carter's 3-run homer to hand Toronto the world championship in the 9th inning of game six. So bitter was the reaction of Philadelphia fans that Phillies president Bill Giles traded his bullpen stopper to the Astros after the season. Houston released him midway through the 1994 campaign because of a combination of ineffectiveness and the southpaw's rising complaints that he wasn't regarded as the club's sole closer.

TED WILLIAMS (Hall of Fame, 1966)

Williams had few peers aside from Babe Ruth for hitting with both power and consistency. In nineteen seasons with the Red Sox between 1939 and 1960, he assaulted every offensive record standing; like the greatest entertainers, he also left fans hungry for more with the endless speculation about what else he might have accomplished if he hadn't lost three years to World War II and just about all of two others to the Korean War. His trophy case might also have been a little fuller if he hadn't put off sportswriters with tantrums that, while relatively mild by subsequent standards, were recalled with resentment when an MVP vote was held.

Boston got wind of Williams only after the Yankees and Cardinals had lost interest in him as a high-school prospect because of his demands for a $1,000 signing bonus. The Red Sox front office was also opposed to the bonus, but was talked into offering it by assistant general man-

Boston fans have always had a special interest in contending that Ted Williams was an even greater hitter than Babe Ruth. National Baseball Library, Cooperstown, N.Y.

ager Billy Evans. Williams's brashness became evident at a 1938 spring training trial when, informed that he was being sent to the minors, he told the veterans in the clubhouse that he would be back to make more money than they had ever dreamed of making. Once up with the Red Sox for good, he compiled statistics that verged on the eerie. A career .344 hitter and .634 slugger (second only to Ruth), the lanky left-handed hitter who was known as The Splendid Splinter took six batting titles, including one in 1941, when his .406 marked the last time that a big leaguer achieved the .400 plateau. He led the American League in homers four times, in RBIs four times, in runs scored six times, in doubles twice, in walks eight times, and in annual slugging average on nine occasions. For all his long-ball hitting, he struck out as many as 50 times only twice—in his first two years in the league. Such discrimination would help fuel stories—and some fables— about his extraordinary eyesight.

In 1941, while Joe DiMaggio was hypnotizing the country with his 56-game hitting streak, during which he batted .408, Williams was hitting .412 over the same period. In 1957 he set the record for the most consecutive times on base by putting together four home runs, two singles, nine walks, and one hit by pitch in 16 successive plate appearances. In 1958 he became the oldest player (forty years, twenty-eight days) to win a batting title. With the numbers went the drama. With his average standing at .3995 and eligible to be rounded off to .400 on the final day of the 1941 season, the outfielder insisted on playing both ends of a doubleheader so as "not to back in" to his achievement; he collected 6 hits and gained 6 points. In the 1941 All-Star Game, he hit a home run with two out in the 9th inning to provide the AL's winning margin. In the 1946 All-Star contest, he ran up on Rip Sewell's eephus pitch and deposited it over the wall. In his final at-bat in 1960, he tagged his 29th home run of the season, providing a fitting climax to John Updike's noted essay on his farewell performance.

Because of his perceived arrogance, Williams was constantly on the outs with the Boston press, which in turn never ceased to point out that he was no Gold Glove in left field. He only made matters worse one year by completing a tour of the bases on a home run, then spitting up at the press box. Struck out in a key situation in another game, he fired his bat at the screen behind home plate. On a third occasion, he went out to left field after failing in the clutch and punted his glove against the wall. Although he took MVP honors in 1946 and 1949, he was denied the prize in 1941, when he reached the .400 mark, and in 1942 and 1947, when he won the Triple Crown each time. In 1947, one vindictive sportswriter left his name off the ballot altogether, and DiMaggio ended up beating him by a single point.

Williams and DiMaggio were also co–stars of the Greatest Trade Never Made. The most popular account of the would-be exchange said that it was the Yankees who approached the Red Sox shortly after the end of World War II, proposing an exchange of the outfielders so that DiMaggio could take advantage of the outfielders of Fenway Park's Green Monster and Williams cavort with the short right-field porch in Yankee Stadium. The deal was said to have died when Boston owner Tom Yawkey, wary of DiMaggio's foot problems, insisted that New York add Yogi Berra to the swap. If Williams had any reason to envy DiMaggio, it was for the Yankee Clipper's appearances in postseason play; in his only World Series, against the Cardinals in 1946, the Red Sox slugger was held to 5 singles and a lone RBI over seven games. On the other hand, he has cited his 2,019 walks (the equivalent of four entire seasons of plate appearances) as his "proudest record."

Despite his often truculent manner as a player, Williams turned out to be both a successful batting coach and a surprisingly effective manager. As pilot of the expansion Senators in 1969, he exploded, at least temporarily, the myth that great players make bad managers by steering the club to its only above-.500 performance before moving to Texas. A good part of that success was due to the manager's unexpectedly deft handling of his pitching staff; ultimately, however, Williams was still being quoted in his midseventies as saying the same thing about the species as he had said in joining the Red Sox more than a half century before: According to Williams, pitchers were just "stupid."

NED WILLIAMSON

Called "the best all-around ballplayer the country ever saw" by Cap Anson, Williamson held the single-season record for home runs before Babe Ruth. Taking advantage of an 1883 renovation that reduced the dimensions of Chicago's Lake Front Park to 196 feet down the right-field line and to 180 feet to the foul pole in left, the third baseman set a new National League record of 49 doubles, many of them into the seats. In 1884, with the fences still temptingly close but the ground rules revised, Williamson clouted the ball into those same seats 25 times for homers. The 2 he hit on the road raised his year's tally to 27, the major league high until 1919. In no other season did Williamson reach double numbers in four-baggers.

MAURY WILLS

Wills restored the stolen base as a potent offensive weapon while with the Dodgers in the 1960s, paving the way for the even greater stardom of Lou Brock and Rickey Henderson. Although players from Ross Youngs to Jackie Robinson had shown the effectiveness of speed in general in the interim, the switch-hitting shortstop's 50 thefts in 1960 represented the first time that a National Leaguer had reached that level since Max Carey had in 1923. It was also the first of six straight seasons of leading the circuit in stolen bases. Wills's biggest year of all was in 1962, when he took MVP honors for becoming the first twentieth-century major leaguer to steal more than 100 times (he stole 104 bases). His baserunning was particularly crucial to the Dodgers of the early 1960s since, unlike his successors Brock and Henderson, he led off lineups that were usually weak in power and all the more reliant on the runs he could manufacture. Los Angeles won four pennants with him.

Wills's prime years with the Dodgers came to a somewhat abrupt end following the 1966 season, when Walter O'Malley ordered him traded for failing to accompany the club on a trip to Japan. Before closing his fourteen-year (1959–72) career, however, he returned to Los Angeles, winding up with 586 steals and a batting mark of .281.

Wills had a brief and stormy stint as manager of the Mariners at the end of 1980 and the beginning of 1981. Deeply dependent on drugs, he was given to sending out conflicting or no signals at all to his third-base coach, leaving the bench in the middle of games, or muttering to himself about the play of his charges while they sat only a few feet away. As if that weren't enough to get him fired, he showed up late for spring training in 1981 to keep a commitment in Japan, then went out of his way to make prize farmhand Dave Henderson uncomfortable. Wills was finally fired in early May.

WALT WILMOT

Nobody holds more obscure records that Wilmot, an outfielder for the Cubs in the 1890s. On September 30, 1890, he was called out twice in the same game for being hit by a batted ball. On August 22, 1891, he became the first player to be walked 6 times in a game. And in 2 consecutive games on August 6 and 7, 1894, he swiped 8 bases.

FRED WILPON

A New York real-estate millionaire, Wilpon teamed up with publisher Nelson Doubleday to buy the Mets in January 1980 for $21.3 million. Through most of the decade he stayed in the background, but then assumed a more visible role in club affairs with the advent of the 1990s and a gradual withdrawal of baseball operations chief Frank Cashen from the scene. It was Wilpon, for instance, who announced that Vince Coleman would ''never wear a Mets' uniform again'' even as the legalities were still being sorted out over the outfielder's hurling of fireworks outside Dodger Stadium in 1993. Wilpon was also prominent among the minority ownership forces that sought to keep Fay Vincent as baseball commissioner in 1992. In 1994, Wilpon confidently announced his intention of replacing Shea Stadium with a vast entertainment complex in Flushing that would require significant outlays from the city. By that time the franchise was being evaluated at some $200 million, almost ten times the original purchase price.

BILL WILSON

A reliever with the 1973 Phillies, Wilson was part of a club delegation that went to general manager Paul Owens demanding that manager Danny Ozark be fired. During the meeting Wilson got into a fight with ace Steve Carlton. When the brawl was reported by Bill Conlin of *The Philadelphia Inquirer,* Carlton instituted his years-long refusal to talk to the media.

HACK WILSON (Hall of Fame, 1979)

Wilson is one of the best arguments for Roger Maris's inclusion in the Hall of Fame. Although one of the National League's most prodigious sluggers as a member of the Cubs between 1926 and 1930, and the holder of both the single-season NL record for home runs (56) and the major league mark for RBIs (190), his fame rests largely on the year (1930) that he set those exceptional power standards—a season in which the exceptionally lively ball had the entire NL batting over .300. Moreover, while he topped Maris in batting consistency, the outfielder clouted 31 fewer home runs (275 to 244) over an identical twelve years, and was nowhere near as talented as the 1960s

star in fielding, throwing, and running. Be that as it may, the right-hand-hitting Wilson did set the league pace in homers four times and RBIs twice while playing in Chicago. From the start of his career, however, he was dogged by an alcohol problem; eventually it reduced him to a figure of ridicule as he sought to battle through hangovers while winding down his career with dreary Brooklyn and Philadelphia clubs.

Originally the property of the Giants, Wilson was sent down to the American Association Toledo Mud Hens in 1925, but through an administrative mixup in the New York front office his name was left off the club's reserve list. This left him eligible for the postseason draft, and the Cubs grabbed him on the recommendation of new manager Joe McCarthy, despite the protests of Giants' manager John McGraw that he was being robbed of a potential star.

JIM WILSON

Former pitcher Wilson resigned as general manager of the Brewers in 1974 to head the newly formed Major League Scouting Bureau. Intended as a cost-cutting tool for big league franchises, the scouting pool induced several clubs to decimate their internal staffs, with some franchises cutting their scouting complements by a third. When the bureau's product turned out to be pure vanilla, however, front offices in both leagues began to restaff. By the late 1980s, the number of scouts employed by the various teams was higher than it had been in the early 1970s.

JIMMIE WILSON

One of the National League's best defensive catchers for most of his eighteen-year (1923–40) career, Wilson gained his greatest notoriety after ostensibly retiring as an active player. As a coach with the 1940s Reds, he was pressed into service behind the plate in the final days of the season because of an injury to Ernie Lombardi and the suicide of backup receiver Willard Hershberger; in the ensuing World Series against Detroit, the forty-year-old Wilson not only threw out the only runner who tried to steal against him, but also swiped a base of his own while hitting .353. He had fewer glorious moments while managing the Cubs during World War II, spending most of the time feuding with general manager Jimmy Gallagher and declining to cooperate with beat writers even to the point of keeping secret his starting lineup until it was on the field. Wilson's less than sweet personality also manifested itself in his habit of removing the entire battery in a game if the Chicago pitcher and catcher didn't obey his sign to knock down an opposition hitter. The ploy became obvious enough for some teams to protest—futilely—to the league office when Wilson suddenly called time to bring in a new hurler and receiver.

MOOKIE WILSON

A grandstand favorite at Shea Stadium for his wild dashes around the bases, the equally wild-swinging Wilson astonished even his fans in the sixth game of the the 1986 World Series by managing to foul away one two-out, two-strike pitch after another, in a 10th-inning duel with Boston's Bob Stanley. The switch-hitting outfielder's tenacity finally paid off in a wild pitch that enabled New York to tie the Red Sox and in the grounder between Bill Buckner's legs that climaxed the Mets' dramatic comeback victory and pointed them to the world championship in the seventh game. When Wilson and Lee Mazzilli were dealt to the Blue Jays in August 1988, their positive impact on Toronto led local sportswriters to dub them Mazzookie; Wilson's influence on the division-winning club was considered so pivotal that he made the cover of the Canadian weekly *MacLean's*. The black Wilson's nickname—usually heard only in German-speaking countries—came from his grandmother, who once worked for a German.

OWEN WILSON

Wilson used the spacious alleys of Forbes Field to fashion the record for most triples in a season (36), while playing for Pittsburgh in 1912. Over the rest of his nine-year (1908–16) career with the Cardinals as well as the Pirates, the lefty-batting outfielder never collected more than 14 three-baggers in a season.

HOOKS WILTSE

On July 4, 1908, Giants southpaw Wiltse became the only pitcher in big league history to lose a perfect game by hitting the 27th man he faced. Taking first base on the pitch was Phillies hurler George McQuillan. Wiltse retired the next batter, completed a 10-inning masterpiece, then won the game when New York scored the game's lone run in the bottom of the 10th. Otherwise Wiltse won 139 games in twelve seasons (1904–15), all but one of them with the Giants.

DAVE WINFIELD

Winfield proved to be George Steinbrenner's most formidable baseball foe—so much so that his Hall of Fame credentials tended to be obscured by his headline skirmishes with the Yankees' owner. In fact, the right-handed slugger spent substantially less than half of his twenty-one-year career (between 1973 and 1994) in New York pinstripes.

Winfield started off with the Padres in 1973, going to San Diego directly from the campus of the University of Minnesota after choosing baseball over offers from the Atlanta Hawks of the National Basketball Association, the Utah Stars of the American Basketball Association, and the Minnesota Vikings of the National Football League. Through the 1994 season, he had accumulated 3,088 hits and 463 home runs; on the other hand, his .284 average is the lowest among players in the 3,000-hit club. The outfielder's consistency produced fifteen seasons of at least 20 homers; eighteen years of at least 20 doubles; and eight 100-RBI seasons, including a league-leading total in 1979. His run production (1,107 RBIs) in the decade from 1979 to 1988 was the highest of all major league hitters. Winfield was also a seven-time Gold Glove winner with a respected arm. His throwing ability gained continentwide attention when he killed a seagull with a warm-up throw between innings of a 1983 contest in Toronto; the death, of a member of a protected species in Canada, almost resulted in prosecution around claims that Winfield had taken deadly aim at the bird.

After signing as a free agent with the Yankees in 1981, Winfield took the customary top-dollar Steinbrenner contract followed by the equally customary abuse from the Bronx boss. Steinbrenner's attacks started with disparaging remarks about the outfielder's being ''Mr. May'' for going only 1-for-22 in the 1981 World Series against the Dodgers. But the true problems arose from Winfield's insistence that a percentage of his ten-year salary be put into the Winfield Foundation, a charitable trust intended to fund youth programs. When a cost-of-living escalator overlooked by Steinbrenner upped the full amount of the contract from $16 million to $23 million, the owner refused the foundation's funding until what he considered financial irregularities were straightened out. The depths to which the feud had degenerated became public in July 1990, when an investigation by Commissioner Fay Vincent's office revealed that Steinbrenner had paid Howard Spira, a professional gambler and a onetime employee of the foundation, $40,000 to provide information damaging to Winfield. Steinbrenner negotiated himself into a permanent removal from club affairs that lasted fewer than three years.

Even before the Steinbrenner-Spira connection had become known, Winfield was traded to the Angels, in May 1990. Signing with the Blue Jays as a free agent the following year, he provided a .290 average, 26 homers, and 108 RBIs toward a Toronto pennant, primarily as a designated hitter, but also as the club's moral leader. Not offered a contract for 1993, he signed with the Twins.

ERASTUS WINMAN

When entertainment impresario Winman bought the New York Metropolitans from John B. Day in December 1885, his plan was to add the team to the cluster of attractions, including Buffalo Bill's Wild West Show, that he offered on Staten Island. The promoter also looked to the Mets to increase the traffic on his Staten Island Rapid Transit Railway, which was in fact a ferry from Manhattan linking with a proposed Baltimore & Ohio Railroad terminal on Staten Island; Winman was to profit not only from his passengers' fares but also from the fee, based on ridership volume, that the B&O was going to pay him for use of the ferry. The rest of the American Association had other ideas, though, and expelled the club over suspicions that Day wanted to exile the Metropolitans and keep Manhattan exclusively for his other property, the National League Giants. Winman won a court battle to keep his franchise,

but lost so much money in his two-year big league venture that he sold the franchise to Brooklyn's Charles Byrne after the 1887 season.

TOM WINSETT

Outfielder Winsett was a model example of Branch Rickey's ability to palm off mediocre players on unsuspecting teams. As St. Louis general manager in the mid-1930s, Rickey boasted to one and all that Winsett was a "coming Babe Ruth." In December 1936, the Dodgers finally bit, sending the Cardinals Frenchy Bordagaray, Dutch Leonard, and Jimmy Jordan for the supposed phenom. After Winsett had retired some years later with the grand total of 8 home runs, Rickey defended his ballyhooing by declaring: "Woe unto the pitcher who throws the ball where the Winsett bat is functioning. But throwing it almost anywhere else in the general area of home plate is safe."

SAM WISE

Wise was the prize the first time major league baseball resorted to litigation to settle one of its intramural squabbles. After only a game with the National League Detroit Wolverines in 1881, the infielder signed an 1882 contract with the Cincinnati Reds of the new American Association, only to turn around and jump back to the NL, with the Boston Red Stockings. With association backing, the Reds sought—but were denied—an injunction from a Massachusetts court to prevent Wise from appearing for Boston. He remained with the Reds Stockings for seven seasons, during which time he became the first player to strike out more than 100 times in a season (104 in 1884).

WILLIAM ABBOTT WITMAN

A wealthy contractor and purveyor of coal and sand, Witman was a glutton for punishment when it came to attempting to establish third major leagues. His first effort, the United States League, got off the ground in 1912 with a sprinkling of former major leaguers (most notably the alcoholic Bugs Raymond and aging slugger Socks Seybold) and a few recognizable managers (among them outlawed Browns pilot Jack O'Connor). Although the circuit boasted six cities with existing major league teams, it also included Richmond and

Reading (Witman's hometown). Despite Witman's claims that the league had "enough money to pay salaries for the entire season even if not a single fan comes into our grounds," the venture fell apart precisely because of sparse attendance. In rapid succession in May, the Cincinnati club moved all its games to the road, Cleveland folded, and the Washington manager and players quit because they hadn't been paid. On June 1 Witman filed for bankruptcy.

Six months later, Witman was back to announce a second edition of the United States League, only this time, when the season opened in May 1913, there were no ex-big leaguers. Within days of the opening of the season, two clubs were unable to meet even the $75 guarantee to visiting teams, and the league collapsed. *The Sporting News* offered the observation that the second United States League was "the quickest and most ridiculous failure in the long history of baseball."

WHITEY WITT

The victim of one of the ugliest incidents ever to occur on a big league field, Witt exacted an appropriate revenge. Knocked unconscious by a bottle thrown from the grandstand of Sportsman's Park during a late September 1922 game against the Browns, the Yankee center fielder had to be carried off the field. The Browns offered a reward for information leading to the identification of the culprit, and American League president Ban Johnson went to St. Louis to investigate, but the efforts produced only a ludicrous tale that the bottle had been tossed by a small boy and had landed in the outfield grass, where Witt had stepped on it, sending it spinning upward to strike his head. The outfielder had the last word, however, when he returned to stroke a game-winning single in the third game of the series, sending the Yankees on their way to an eventual single-game margin over the Browns in the pennant race.

The lefty swinger averaged .287 in ten seasons, almost exclusively with the Athletics and the Yankees, between 1916 and 1926.

CHICKEN WOLF

The only player to hold down a roster spot in the American Association for all ten of its major league seasons, Wolf also holds the doubtful distinction of having been the lowest-paid big leaguer in history; in his rookie season of 1882, Louisville paid him a mere $9 a week—a paltry sum even by the standards of the time.

DICK WOODSON

Woodson was the first player to benefit from binding arbitration, when he was awarded a $20,000 raise from Minnesota in 1974. Twins owner Calvin Griffith angrily told newsmen that he would make up for the defeat by selling the southpaw, then, to avoid a fine, lied that he had ever made such a statement. Shortly afterward, he did indeed peddle Woodson, to the Yankees.

AL WORTHINGTON

Few players have been as rigid about their religious principles as Worthington, a reliever in the 1950s and 1960s. Early in the 1960 season, the right-hander, then a member of the White Sox, announced his retirement because of mortal objections to owner Bill Veeck's use of the scoreboard to steal signs. He stayed out of the game for almost three years while studying for the ministry, then came back in 1963 with the Reds, later going on to his best years as a bullpen specialist for the Twins.

GEORGE WRIGHT (Hall of Fame, 1937)

Wright is remembered primarily as the younger brother of fellow Hall of Famer Harry Wright; in fact, he was the star player on teams Harry managed, and when he tried his hand as a pilot, he outdid his brother—and every other major league manager. Wright was the highest-paid player for the 1869–70 Cincinnati Red Stockings, earning more than his manager-brother. With the National Association Boston Red Stockings from 1871 to 1875, George batted a composite .353 for the five seasons and was the best defensive shortstop of his day; Harry was able to convert this performance, among others, into four consecutive pennants. When the shortstop moved to the National League with the Red Stockings in 1876, his hitting fell off somewhat but his defensive skills were still sufficient to post an overall fielding mark of better than .900 for his seven major league seasons, a rarity in the preglove era; once again Harry piloted the club to pennants, in 1878 and 1879, as George sparked the club. Taking over in the dugout with the Providence Grays in 1879, Wright, separated from his brother for the first time in more than a decade, became the only one-year manager in major league history to win a pennant; the runner-up, by a 5-game margin, was Harry's Red Stockings.

Retiring to form the sporting goods firm of Wright and Ditson, George reemerged in 1884 as president of the Boston Reds, lending his prestigious name to the Union Association venture in exchange for adoption of his product as the league's official ball. For the most part, however, his firm concentrated on selling the paraphernalia of sports other than baseball. Wright is said to have played the first game of golf in the United States and to have manufactured the first tennis equipment in the country. (His son Beals became an early tennis star.) George gained entry to Cooperstown sixteen years before Harry.

HARRY WRIGHT (Hall of Fame, 1953)

The English-born Wright became the first professional manager when he assembled and piloted the Cincinnati Red Stockings of 1869–70; his emphasis on fundamentals became the hallmark of his subsequent twenty-three-year managerial career in the National Association and the National League.

An accomplished cricketer before switching to baseball, Wright was a competent outfielder and alternate pitcher with the Knickerbocker Club of New York, starting in 1858; on the mound, he was the first successful junkball specialist. As a manager, he was the first to win four consecutive pennants (with the NA Boston Red Stockings, from 1872 to 1875); added two more with the NL Red Stockings in 1877 and 1878; led the first baseball tour to England, in 1874, when a combination of his Boston players and some members of the Philadelphia Athletics beat local cricket players at both the American and British games; and was the first to employ coach's signals. In 1877 he had shown himself to be such an accomplished heckler of opponents that the NL considered barring managers from the bench just to get him off the field. His emphasis on team play

Harry Wright was one of several 19th-century major leaguers who took up baseball from cricket. National Baseball Library, Cooperstown, N.Y.

evolved into an insistence on morning practice sessions, a regimen of exercise, and pregame batting and fielding practice. After a two-year (1882–83) stint with the Providence Grays, he spent a final decade (1884–93) with the Phillies, producing profits with mediocre Philadelphia teams.

As respected for his amiability as for his business acumen, Wright was an easy mark for favor seekers; one such was Louisville crook Jim Devlin, who wrote to Wright for assistance in getting his banishment lifted. The reward for his decency came when Philadelphia had the fewest defectors to the Players League, enabling Wright to win one last pennant, in 1890. The punishment for it had come years before when his refusal to provide Al Spalding with gifts in addition to a salary contributed to the pitcher's decision to bolt the NA Red Stockings and join with Chicago owner William Hulbert in forming the National League.

TAFFY WRIGHT

Wright had the highest batting average in the American League in 1938, but was denied the hitting crown even through he qualified under the rules of the day. Appearing in the required 100 games for the Senators, the lefty-swinging outfielder averaged .350 in his rookie year, but because 39 of his appearances were as a pinch hitter and he had only 263 at-bats, the title went to Boston's Jimmie Foxx, who finished the season at .349. Wright never again reached the heights of his first season, but he did end up with a .311 average over nine seasons, most of them with the White Sox.

PHIL WRIGLEY

Wrigley's association with the nostalgic glories of day baseball at Wrigley Field during his forty-three-year (1934–77) ownership of the Cubs was merely part of the story. Not only was he ready to install lights in the Chicago ballpark in the early 1940s, but also several of his other organizational moves anticipated by decades the development of the major leagues into a corporate flowchart interrupted every so often by a single to right.

The deaths of his father, William, and team president Bill Veeck, Sr. left Wrigley in charge of the Cubs before he was ready for the job. His first solution was to surround himself with yesmen from his chewing gum company, and they were reinforced by such timid franchise souls as club president Boots Weber and chief scout Pants Rowland. The result was that Wrigley's own doubts (about purchasing a minor league prospect named Joe DiMaggio, for instance) and enthusiasms (for a modest Chicago outfielder named Tuck Stainback, for example) ended up being decisions no one dared to contradict. On the other hand, he didn't need fawners when it came to product research. Using the same techniques that had made Juicy Fruit and Doublemint successful, he brought in a battery of statisticians in the mid-1930s to break down every conceivable game situation involving pitchers and hitters, all in the interests of getting a better idea of individual productivity. Other specialists began filming Cub players for a closer look at their mechanics. It was also Wrigley who, at about the same time,

ordered field announcers and broadcasters never to refer to the home park without qualifying it as "beautiful Wrigley Field" and who then set about to make the claim true; in particular, he approved of Bill Veeck, Jr.'s proposal to pad the walls with ivy and of engineer Otis Shepard's suggestion to erect a hand-operated scoreboard.

Although usually depicted as baseball's chief foe of artificial lighting, Wrigley thought long and hard about introducing night games at Chicago in the late 1930s. By 1941 he had so convinced himself that night games were the future that he had light towers shipped to Wrigley Field for use the following season. But with the Japanese bombing of Pearl Harbor, he changed his mind again, mainly in apprehension that the government was going to eliminate baseball altogether during World War II; the light towers ended up being donated to the Great Lakes Naval Air Station for the war effort, and afternoon games remained the rule at Wrigley Field for another four decades.

Wrigley was far more opposed to minor league chains than he was to night baseball—to an almost bizarre degree. Despite owning the Los Angeles Angels of the Pacific Coast League, for instance, he did so personally and not as an extension of his holdings in the Cubs. The same was true of the American Association Milwaukee Brewers, which depended on his subsidies to survive but which were equally free to make the best deals possible with any major league team that came along. It was only with the arrival of Jim Gallagher as general manager in the early 1940s that he was talked out of his aversion to a farm system, and ultimately agreed to finance a chain that grew to twenty teams through working agreements or outright ownership within a few years.

In another financial hedge against the major leagues being shut down during the war, Wrigley bankrolled the All-American Girls Professional Baseball League in 1943. The league, which remained in operation until 1954, had teams in Illinois, Indiana, Wisconsin, and Michigan, with such names as the Kalamazoo Lassies and the Fort Wayne Daisies. Among the managers were Hall of Famers Jimmie Foxx and Max Carey.

As far as the Cubs were concerned, Wrigley spent much of the 1940s and 1950s hiring and firing managers and general managers who were alike only in their failure to raise the team much above seventh or eighth place. That the team still made money was due to a parade of home-run hitters (Bill Nicholson, Hank Sauer, Ralph Kiner, and Ernie Banks) who kept fans interested until the pitchers blew it all away. Then, in December 1960, the owner announced that he had become convinced that managers needed to be rotated as regularly as pitchers, and to that end was putting the Cubs under the command of a constantly moving octet that became popularly known as the College of Coaches. Officially the experiment lasted until Leo Durocher took over as pilot in 1966, but in practice it ended as soon as Bob Kennedy emerged as the first coach of coaches in 1963.

The Durocher years (1966–72) proved more wearying to Wrigley than the College of Coaches period—in part because of the manager's constant battles with his players, in part because of a politically motivated scheme in Chicago to embarrass a Durocher brother-in-law by suggesting that the pilot was involved with city racketeers. On both issues Wrigley stood behind Durocher, at one point taking out a full-page ad in Chicago papers to warn that what he called the "Dump Durocher Clique" was wasting its time. Eventually Durocher himself stepped down in 1972, but remained close enough to the franchise that Wrigley asked him back again as pilot in 1975. When Durocher said he would consider returning only as general manager, with Maury Wills coming in as manager, Wrigley said no.

Over the final years of his life, Wrigley showed a rising crustiness in his public appearances. When he wasn't blasting his players as "clowns," he was warning about the dire effects of free agency on the game and instituting various money-saving measures that often sounded as though they were in response to some front-office executive swindling. On the other hand, shortly before he died in April 1977 at age eighty-two, he insisted that neither he nor his son William would ever permit lights to be installed at Wrigley Field. He proved sincere insofar as it wasn't until William had sold the franchise to the *Chicago Tribune* that, on August 8, 1988, the first NL night game was played in the Windy City.

WILLIAM WRIGLEY

Aside from putting his name on what became baseball's most venerable ballpark, Wrigley helped shape the sport's administrative structure and beat Larry MacPhail to the intuition that broadcasting might be more of an incentive than a hindrance to attendance. The chewing gum king was also responsible for the involvement of the Veeck family in baseball's boardrooms.

Originally a junior member of the Charles Weeghman consortium that bought into the Cubs in 1916, Wrigley needed only five years to gain majority control of the franchise through a series of stock-for-loans arrangements. Even before then, however, he was the first to plump for the election of Chicago judge Kenesaw Landis as the first commissioner. His proposal of Landis followed a call by fellow Cub stockholder A. D. Lasker for a special commission of Three Wise Men to clean up the mess caused by various scandals, most notably that around the 1919 World Series; although hostile in principle to outsiders coming in to rule, Wrigley couldn't forget the involvement of some of his own players in thrown games, and considered the jurist, a highly visible Cub fan, a compromise.

Within his own organization, Wrigley's most important hire was that of sportswriter Bill Veeck, Sr., as vice president for baseball affairs; he hired the journalist as a put-up-or-shut-up challenge after months of seething at Veeck criticisms of the franchise. Although the club played respectably through most of the 1920s, it was also a period of frequent managerial changes until Joe McCarthy took over in 1926. Wrigley held his fire against Veeck mainly because the team began to draw well in 1925, chiefly due to the antics of Rabbit Maranville and the slugging of Hack Wilson. In 1927 the Cubs drew 1,163,347 spectators—making them the first NL franchise to go over the million mark. As far as Wrigley was concerned, another factor in the attendance was his decision to allow as many as five radio stations in the Chicago area to carry games at the same time. Statistical breakdowns showed that he had a point, insofar as roughly similar clubs studied over seven-year periods with and without air coverage indicated a 119 percent rise in attendance when fans had their interest whetted by play-by-play. It would be another decade, however, before MacPhail would make the same point more dramatically, and with more lasting effect, with Cincinnati.

Wrigley lived to see only one Cub pennant—in 1929. When the team lost to the Athletics in the World Series, he reprimanded McCarthy for some tactical moves, receiving such a testy reply that he soon afterward fired the manager in favor of Rogers Hornsby. Wrigley died in January 1932, just before the club returned to the World Series.

BUTCH WYNEGAR

Wynegar made two mistakes in his thirteen-year (1976–88) career—first playing for the wrong owner, then playing for the wrong team. After hitting a puny .229 for Minnesota in 1978, the switch-hitting catcher was blasted by a drunken Calvin Griffith for having spent too much of his time in spring training that year chasing his new wife around the bedroom. According to Griffith, Wynegar would have been better off picking up women for one-night stands since "love comes pretty cheap these days for ballplayers and they should take advantage of it." In 1986, while with the Yankees, Wynegar deserted the team for what was later diagnosed as a nervous breakdown caused by the pressures of playing in New York. Even as some teammates were sniping at him for being a "quitter," he was being put on medication for severe depression. The receiver finally escaped to the Angels for the 1987 season, but was already finished as a frontline player.

EARLY WYNN (Hall of Fame, 1972)

Wynn's prolonged quest for his 300th win in 1963 served as a bathetic ending to a twenty-three-year career in which he racked up five 20-victory seasons, paced the American League in wins and strikeouts twice apiece and in ERA once, and established the mark (later tied by Brooks Robinson and Carl Yastrzemski) for most seasons in the AL. Arriving in the majors with Washington in 1939, the right-hander labored through most of the 1940s with the perennial second-division club, not fashioning his first big year until he was with the Indians in 1951. In 1954 Wynn played a big part in a Cleveland pennant by pacing AL hurlers with 23 victories. With the White Sox in 1959, he took Cy Young honors for leading Chicago to a pennant with a pace-setting 22 triumphs. Forty-two years old in 1962, he was released by Chicago a win short of the magic 300. Although he had little left, he persuaded Cleveland to take him back for one more stab; it actually took numerous mound tries before he finally hurled 5 innings of a slugfest, then left the game in the hands of reliever Jerry Walker.

Wynn's tough demeanor on the hill spawned numerous responses to the question of whether he would brush back his son, his mother, or his grandmother: "It would depend on how well he was hitting," "Only if she were digging in," and "If she crowds the plate" are the most often-repeated versions of the story. After retiring, he was active in organizations for assisting needy former major leaguers.

BIFF WYSONG

Prior to his major league debut against the Phillies in 1930, Cincinnati southpaw Wysong was feted at a special Appreciation Day by hundreds of fellow residents of Clarkson, Ohio. He then went to the mound and suffered an 18–0 drubbing. He notched his only major league victory two years later.

Y

ABE YAGER

The sports editor of the *Brooklyn Eagle,* Yager took it upon himself to throttle a threatened strike by Dodger players in 1916 against owner Charlie Ebbets. The conflict had developed over Ebbets's move to slash salaries across the board for the season. Knowing that star outfielder Zach Wheat was one of the leaders of the uprising, Yager sent him a telegram in Ebbets's name, voicing regret for the impasse and inviting the future Hall of Famer to the team's Arkansas spring training site to talk over differences. Wheat fell for the ruse and, alone with Ebbets, gave in to his blandishments and agreed to a new contract. The revolt fell apart immediately afterward. Yager always denied sending the cable with Ebbets's knowledge, claiming that he simply needed daily coverage of the Dodgers to sell the *Eagle.* It was also Yager who first reported Willie Keeler's hitting formula as ''hit 'em where they ain't.''

HIROSHI YAMAUCHI

The president of Nintendo, Yamauchi became the target of baseball yahoos in 1992 for offering to buy the Seattle Mariners and keep them in the Northwest. Other owners and Commissioner Fay Vincent immediately began fretting about the dangers of a foreign ownership—not only failing to mention the Canadian interests behind the Blue Jays and Expos, but also trampling over Seattle fans who were only too aware that the most likely alternative to Yamauchi's proposal was the departure of the franchise for Florida. The transparent anti-Japanese attitude forced a bizarre compro-

mise under which Yamauchi put up 60 percent of the $125 million to buy the club, but held only a 49 percent of the stock and could have no hand in running the club. Although he represented less than 1 percent of the new capital, local businessman John Ellis took over as chief executive officer.

CARL YASTRZEMSKI (Hall of Fame, 1989)

Yastrzemski managed to be the thinking man's player without being a particularly thoughtful player. Identified throughout his twenty-three-year (1961–83) career with the Red Sox as one of the game's best performers under pressure, he also drew fire regularly for shortsighted tantrums and remarks that left teammates in the lurch, not least during management-labor wars in the 1970s. He was described by more than one contemporary as ''an all-star from the neck down.''

Yaz, as he was known popularly, was the rare case of one Hall of Famer directly succeeding another, taking over Ted Williams's left-field slot in 1961. In the years that followed in Fenway Park, he led the American League at least once in every significant offensive category except triples and steals. The lefty swinger's best season was 1967, when he became the last major leaguer to win a Triple Crown, with 44 home runs, 121 RBIs, and a .326 average, while also pacing AL batters with 189 safeties, 112 runs scored, and a .622 slugging percentage; he was an easy winner of that year's MVP award. He also won batting titles in 1963 and 1968 and topped the slugging numbers in 1965 and 1970. Yaz consolidated his reputation for timely hitting down the stretch of Boston's successful pennant drive in 1967, when he batted .444 with 26 RBIs over the last 19 games of the year; his home run on the next-to-last day of the season against chief rival Minnesota proved decisive for the flag.

Yastrzemski's lifetime numbers include a few anomalies. For instance, his 3,419 career hits make him one of only five players to collect that many safeties without averaging .300 (.285) and the first in that exclusive club who never had 200 hits in a season. His league-leading .301 average in 1968 was also the lowest ever for a batting champion. On the other hand, Yaz was one of only four players (with Willie Mays, Hank Aaron, and Stan Musial) to amass 3,000 hits and 400 home runs. Yaz also holds the AL record (and trails only Pete Rose overall) for most games, with 3,308.

As Boston owner Tom Yawkey's fair-haired boy, Yaz had more room than some of his teammates for dealing with managers. His biggest mistake in this area was taking on Dick Williams in 1969, after the pilot had accused him of not running out a ground ball. Although several other Red Sox players had been bridling for some time against Williams's dictatorial rule, Yastrzemski's involvement of Yawkey in the squabble and the subsequent firing of the pilot turned Fenway Park against the outfielder, perceived as being responsible for getting rid of the franchise's most successful dugout boss in decades. In 1972 he alienated many of his teammates by defending Yawkey during the players' strike, insisting that the Players Association was being too militant and would ultimately drive away "generous" owners such as the Red Sox boss; in turn, he was accused of elitism and worse by players in Boston and elsewhere aware of his special ties to Yawkey. In 1975, Yaz's nemesis was manager Darrell Johnson, who forbade the outfielder to leave the team for a one-day business trip after Boston had wrapped up the division title; he went anyway, defying Johnson to make an issue of it. Johnson didn't.

Over his final years, Yastrzemski willy-nilly became the symbol of the team in which regulars stayed away from bench players and, in the words of shortstop Frank Duffy, "twenty-five players took twenty-five cabs" after a game. For all his reputation as a clutch performer, he also had to retire without a world championship ring and with the knowledge of having made the last out in the 1967 World Series, the 1975 World Series, and the 1978 special playoff against the Yankees.

TOM YAWKEY (Hall of Fame, 1980)

Rarely photographed when he wasn't smiling or hugging his favorites Ted Williams and Carl Yastrzemski, Yawkey had an image of the most benevolent of baseball's midcentury owners. The image held against more than one ugly fray, but failed to extend to the Red Sox organization over which he presided for more than four decades (1933–76). In just about everything from racial integration to arbitration, Boston brought up the rear under his ownership.

The nephew of one-time Detroit owner William Yawkey and the heir to a family fortune built up in the lumber trade, Yawkey purchased Boston from Bob Quinn for little more than the $350,000 in debts that the outgoing owner had accumulated. Announcing his resolve to put an end to years of second-division finishes by the club, he hired Eddie Collins as general manager and went on a trading and buying spree that imported to Boston such future Hall of Famers as Joe Cronin, Lefty Grove, Jimmie Foxx, Rick Ferrell, and Heinie Manush. Of equal symbolic value, he opened his purse to the Yankees to acquire pitcher George Pipgras and third baseman Billy Werber. Although Pipgras was near the end of the line, no one in New England missed the significance of the Red Sox being the one to pay the Yankees for players after some fifteen years of New York's stripping Boston of its best players for quick cash.

Yawkey's deals made the Red Sox a respectable entertainment, and then a contender, but it wasn't until 1946 that the club got to a World Series. Even then, as in 1967 and 1975, however, he could not claim the world championship that he had targeted from the start as his major objective. On the other hand, thanks to the improved talent on the field and in a $750,000 renovation of Fenway Park, the Red Sox won back the city of Boston from the Braves and outdrew the National League entry regularly until its departure for Milwaukee in the early 1950s.

In the 1940s, Yawkey managed to pass the buck to Collins and then to Cronin whenever questions were raised about the organization's lack of interest in following the lead of the Dodgers and Indians in breaking the color barrier. The franchise remained lily-white until 1959—making it the last big league team to integrate. Instead, Yawkey continued his publicity romance with his future Hall of Fame left fielders—first Williams in the 1940s and 1950s, then Yastrzemski in the 1960s and 1970s—pointing them out as adopted sons who would never lack for anything as long as he was alive. His close relationship with Williams was tested often in the star's strained relationship with the local press. With Yastrzemski, the biggest crisis came in 1969, when tart-tongued manager Dick Williams included the outfielder on his list of jakers for not running out a ground ball. When Yawkey intervened to defend Yastrzemski, the Red Sox clubhouse split between factions siding with the pilot and with the star and owner. Two weeks before the end of the season, Williams was fired. Despite his previous popularity with the fans, Yastrzemski heard it loud and often from Fenway Park for the perception that he had invited Yawkey into a power struggle against the manager who had brought the city its Impossible Dream pennant in 1967.

The labor struggles of the early 1970s brought Yawkey new grief. Conceding that he had been stunned by the new militancy of the players and the failed impact of the owners' lockout during spring training in 1973, he began talking about selling the franchise. Although he backed down whenever he was approached by an interested buyer, he projected a constant uncertainty that was soon felt throughout the organization. It reached a critical stage in 1976, when general manager Dick O'Connell got into stubborn contract renewal negotiations with team stars Carlton Fisk, Fred Lynn, and Rick Burleson while at the same time announcing the club was ready to fork over $2 million to Charlie Finley for Oakland players Rollie Fingers and Joe Rudi. Not even Commissioner Bowie Kuhn's decision to kill the Oakland deal "in the best interests of baseball" arrived in time to prevent Minnesota owner Calvin Griffith from accusing Yawkey of doing more

to destroy baseball's salary structure than even Atlanta's Ted Turner and New York's George Steinbrenner. A month later, Yawkey died in a Boston hospital. Media loyalists, responsive to his image to the last, accused Fisk, Lynn, Burleson, and their agent Jerry Kapstein of killing the old man by not being satisfied with his generosity.

WALLY YONAMINE

A Hawaiian-born Nisei, Yonamine was the first American elected to the Japanese Baseball Hall of Fame. Known as the Jackie Robinson of Japan, he was a slash-hitting outfielder who initially scandalized Asian spectators with his rolling blocks into fielders and other aggressive tactics. Generally regarded as the finest leadoff batter in Japanese baseball history, Yonamine played only in the low minors for several years in the United States. Prior to joining the Yomiuri Giants in 1951, he had also been a member of the San Francisco 49ers football team.

RUDY YORK

York's name didn't begin with a G, but he was otherwise one of the offensive foundations of the Tigers in the late 1930s and early 1940s. A first baseman converted from catching because of defensive liabilities, the right-handed slugger hit at least 30 home runs four times and drove in 100 runs in five seasons; in 1943 he led the American League in both categories as well as in slugging percentage. His 18 home runs in August 1937 are the most by a player in any single month. Detroit got lucky twice over in retaining York's services in the middle of its lineup. The first time was when he was omitted from the long list of players Commissioner Kenesaw Landis released as free agents from the organization in 1940 because of paper scams aimed at holding them in the Tiger minor league chain; despite blatant manipulations in his case as well, York was allowed to stay in Detroit because he had already reached the majors. He was also one of the few AL stars to escape military service in World War II.

ANTHONY YOUNG

Young set the major league record for mound futility by losing 27 consecutive games for the

Mets between May 6, 1992, and July 24, 1993. The right-hander finally broke the streak with a relief win, but still went 1–16 in 1993.

CY YOUNG (Hall of Fame, 1937)

Young's combination of durability and longevity in a twenty-two-year (1890–1911) career, most prominently with the National League Cleveland Spiders and the Boston Red Sox, enabled him to set major league career marks for both wins (511) *and* losses (315). Although the right-hander was actually overshadowed at one point or another in his career by the likes of Amos Rusie, Kid Nichols, and Christy Mathewson, no one else has ever come close to his 16 seasons with at least 320 innings pitched or his other career records of most innings (7,356) and most complete games (750). Not that Young was just an arm that posted innings: In five seasons he won 30 or more games, and in ten others 20 or more. He was also the first hurler to toss no-hitters in both the National and American leagues. His most notable accomplishment was pitching 24 consecutive hitless innings over three contests, including the AL's first perfect game, against the Athletics, while a member of the Red Sox on May 5, 1904. The namesake of the Cy Young Award finally called it quits after the 1911 season, at age forty-four, not because his arm had given out but because he had gained so much weight that opposing batters could bunt their way on against him at will.

DICK YOUNG

For both good and bad, Young was one of the most influential reporters ever to cover baseball. As a beat writer for New York's *Daily News* in the late 1940s, he was one of the first to realize that radio had taken over much of the straightforward play-by-play repertorial function of newspapers, and stressed personal, behind-the-scenes angles through clubhouse interviews. He was also conspicuous in defending the arrival of Jackie Robinson in Brooklyn, often coming into conflict with some of the furrier heads in the press box and on his own paper. A few years later, however, the same Young was among the more transparently chagrined when Robinson stopped turning the other cheek, getting into field brawls and

Nobody will ever come close to Cy Young's 834 career decisions. National Baseball Library, Cooperstown, N.Y.

speaking out about baseball's racist establishment; like other New York writers, he began accenting the personal virtues of Dodger catcher Roy Campanella, viewed (in comparison with Robinson) as a genial black man who avoided ''making trouble.'' Although he cracked wise and often about the arrogance of what he called the Lords of Baseball, Young moved relentlessly toward a pro-owner stance on most issues affecting the sport in the 1960s and 1970s, even if he himself thought of it as a plague-on-both-your-houses attitude. He also occasioned considerable griping from other New York sportswriters for what was seen as an uncomfortably close relationship with Met manager Gil Hodges and team chairman M. Donald Grant. The ties enabled the *News* to gain exclusive photographs of Hodges after the manager's 1968 heart attack—coverage that was denounced by rivals as an organization public relations ploy aimed at assuring readers that the pilot would be back on the job the following year.

522

With the death of Hodges in 1973, Young's rising rancor about some Met players, in particular Tom Seaver, exploded in regular tirades, especially when it came to salary demands and voiced skepticism about the war in Vietnam. Given the fact that his son-in-law was employed by the Mets front office, the newsman was inevitably seen as using the *News* for mouthing the franchise's party line—a perception shared even by some of his colleagues on the daily.

Matters came to a head in July 1977 when Seaver, worn out by Young's innuendos and suspecting that they had been inspired by Grant, demanded a trade from the team. The breaking point for the pitcher had been a Young column suggesting that Seaver's wife was jealous that Nolan Ryan had received more money from the Angels than her husband had been offered by New York. When Seaver was traded to Cincinnati, on June 15, 1977, New York fans and other sportswriters blamed Young as much as Grant for what became known as the Midnight Massacre. For his part, the newsman brushed aside the charges, continuing to write increasingly sour pieces on the erosion of what he came to call "My America."

DON YOUNG

Young seemed to be everybody's scapegoat when the Cubs blew the pennant to the Miracle Mets in 1969. A good-glove-no-hit center fielder who had never played a full major league season, he was pressed into daily service by Leo Durocher mainly because the Chicago manager wasn't ready to admit that he had made a mistake in pressing for the trade of the more experienced Adolfo Phillips. When Young began sagging under the pressure down the stretch, even the normally team-spirited Ron Santo lashed out at him, losing some of his own credibility in the process. After the season, Durocher was suddenly the first to admit that the outfielder had been in over his head. Young never played in the majors again.

IRV YOUNG

There have been only two major league pitching staffs with four 20-game losers, and Young was the "ace" of both rotations. In 1905, Vic Willis, Chick Fraser, and Kaiser Wilhelm joined the left-hander in losing at least 20 for the Braves; the following year, Boston replaced that trio with Viva Lindaman, Jeff Pfeffer, and Gus Dorner, who turned in an almost identical performance. In neither year did Young's ERA go above 2.91.

NICK YOUNG

The fifth president of the National League (between 1885 and 1902), Young was the prototypical executive assigned the task of mouthing publicly the policy of the day, while the most powerful owners pursued diametrically opposed goals. Following strong chief executives like William Hulbert and A. G. Mills, he appeared pusillanimous in his habit of leaving league meetings whenever topics distasteful to him were discussed. In 1885, during the dissolution of the Union Association, Young defended the blacklist for players who had jumped their contracts, while the owners were working behind the scenes to reinstate them. In 1889, he refused to meet with the Players Brotherhood, calling it a "secret society," while Chicago owner Al Spalding was sitting down with Brotherhood organizer John Montgomery Ward. In 1890, during the Players League war, Young expressed outrage at the possibility that the NL would reward defectors by offering them more money than the PL, while, in only the most famous incident to the contrary, Spalding was offering King Kelly $10,000 to return to the fold. In 1891, after the American Association had followed the PL into extinction, he sounded resolute in his pronouncements that players could look forward to the same salaries they had been getting during the trade wars of the two previous seasons, while the owners were secretly meeting on the best way to slash their payrolls. When Amos Rusie held out for the 1896 season and took Giants owner Andrew Freedman to court in a suit that threatened to undermine the reserve clause, it was the other NL owners who stepped in to satisfy the pitcher's demands.

According to many observers of the period, Young was distracted by his other job, as a clerk for the U.S. Treasury Department in Washington; even when he left government service the following year, however, there was no discernible improvement in his ability to deal with the crises he confronted. In fact, he proved utterly overmatched by the obstreperous Freedman and his syndication plan of 1900, the ambitious Ban Johnson and his major league plans for the American League in 1901, and the wily Al Spalding and his coup aimed at Young's own office in 1902. Let go in favor of a troika of owners after the failure of Spalding's usurpation, Young returned to being league secretary-treasurer, the position he had held before his elevation to the presidency.

JOEL YOUNGBLOOD

On August 4, 1982, Youngblood became the only major leaguer to play for one team in one city in the afternoon (for the Mets in Chicago) and for another club in a second city in the evening (for the Expos in Montreal against the Phillies). Prior to the trade that enabled Youngblood to accomplish this feat, the theoretically versatile player had mainly been noted for his refusal to move from the outfield to the infield because, as he told a couple of managers, he didn't want to be knocked down by runners.

ROSS YOUNGS (Hall of Fame, 1972)

Next to Christy Mathewson, Youngs was New York manager John McGraw's favorite player. A short, slight speedster, the left-hand-hitting outfielder was the chief table-setter for the Giants throughout his ten-year (1917–26) career. In nine of those seasons, he batted over .300, reaching a high of .351 in 1920. Although he never stole more than 24 bases in a year, his daring running gained him the nickname of Pep among teammates, and McGraw was never reluctant to point out that he started more rallies than even the more well-known Hall of Famers on the club in the period. The one year in which Youngs failed to reach the .300 mark, 1925, was when he was feeling the initial effects of the kidney ailment known as Bright's disease that would kill him at age thirty. The following year, McGraw insisted that a male nurse accompany the outfielder on road trips. Although growing progressively weaker, Youngs still managed to hit .306 and steal 21 bases. He died the following year, sending

McGraw into a funk that he never truly recovered from.

ROBIN YOUNT

Only the third player (after Hank Greenberg and Stan Musial) to win the Most Valuable Player Award while playing two different positions, Yount was the franchise player for most of his twenty (1974–93) seasons with the Brewers. He reached that status despite an early-career decision to quit baseball for professional golf.

Yount arrived in Milwaukee in 1974 as an eighteen-year-old shortstop with unlimited potential and no idea where his throws to first were going to wind up. In his first six seasons, the infielder's only significant mark was to lead the American League in errors (44 in his sophomore year). Considering rumors of an imminent move to center field as early as 1977 an affront, he retired to go on the PGA tour. When his departure hastened the arrival of Paul Molitor to replace him at shortstop, Yount himself hastened back to Milwaukee to take up his old position and move the rookie over to second base.

The right-handed hitter's real career began after a winter on a Nautilus machine, the added strength from the workouts boosting his batting average from .267 in 1979 to .293 in 1980, and increasing his extra-base output from 26 doubles, 5 triples, and 9 homers to 49, 10, and 23. Two years later, Yount was the American League's Most Valuable Player on the strength of his single best year: career highs in hitting (.331), homers (29), and RBIs (114); league-leading totals in hits (210), doubles (46), slugging average (.578), and assists (578). Over the next decade, he reached the .300 level five more times, knocked in 100 runs two more times, and led the league in triples twice. Overall, he attained double numbers in round-trippers eleven times and in stolen bases on sixteen occasions.

A operation on his shoulder after the 1984 season fulfilled the earlier rumors about a shift to center field, and Yount became a good enough outfielder to top the league in putouts in 1990. He also won a second MVP trophy, in 1989, on the basis of a .318 average, 21 homers, and 103

RBIs, precipitating difficulties with a Milwaukee front office that felt it couldn't afford his salary demands and that let him enter the free-agent market before signing him to a five-year contract under pressure from Wisconsin fans and media. The club might have saved the money and taken the heat, since Yount's second MVP trophy proved a last hurrah. Over his final four seasons before retiring in 1993, he collected enough hits to give him 3,142 lifetime safeties but not enough to prevent his career batting average from slipping from .299 to .285.

Z

ADRIAN ZABALA

Reinstated by Commissioner Happy Chandler after being banned for jumping to the Mexican League, Zabala returned to the Giants in 1949 for 15 games. The southpaw's best effort that season was a 3–1 victory over the Cardinals on August 6, marred only by 3 balks; one of them, however, saved the game after St. Louis first baseman Nippy Jones knocked a pitch for what seemed to be a 2-run homer until, under the rules at the time, the home run was disallowed in deference to the balk. The Cardinals ended the year only a game behind the Dodgers. Zabala ended his major league career at the conclusion of the season.

ZIP ZABEL

On June 17, 1915, Zabel was called in from the Cubs' bullpen in the 1st inning of a game against the Dodgers because of an injury to starter Bert Humphries. The right-hander ended up pitching 18⅓ innings—allowing only 2 unearned runs and 9 hits—before being credited with a 4–3 victory. Zabel's stint is the longest ever by a relief pitcher.

TOM ZACHARY

Zachary spent nineteen seasons (1918–36) in the big leagues, with seven clubs, but is familiar almost exclusively for having served up Babe Ruth's 60th home run in 1927. The lefty's reaction, whenever asked about the precedent-setting clout, was to say, "If you really want to know the truth, I'd rather have thrown at his big, fat head."

JACK ZELLER

Zeller, an executive with the Tigers, cost his team the loss of more players than any other executive in baseball history. He gained the dubious distinction on January 14, 1940, when Commissioner Kenesaw Landis announced that he was releasing ninety-one Detroit farmhands as free agents because Zeller and Cecil Coombs, the business manager of a minor league club in Fort Worth, had been conniving for years on fake contracts and other paper shuffling to keep the players buried and under Tiger control even though the varsity had no need of them. In addition, Landis ordered Detroit to cough up indemnities to another fifteen minor leaguers who had been treated unfairly in the club's farm system. There were two surprising consequences to the commissioner's order. The first was that, of the released players, only outfielder Roy Cullenbine turned out to have an appreciable career for another team. The second was that Zeller wasn't fired from his post as Detroit general manager, but in fact survived until he himself resigned in 1945. Although there was never any evidence to support the speculation, baseball insiders attributed the general manager's survival to his denials that owner Walter Briggs had also been involved in the scheme. Zeller had been hired as farm director in 1926 to clean up another franchise scandal concerning scouts who had been recommending only prospects who had paid them a few dollars on the side.

CHIEF ZIMMER

The best defensive catcher of his day, Zimmer served as the first president of the Players Protective Association, a turn-of-the-century effort to unionize professional ballplayers. In a twenty-year (1884–1903) career with seven clubs, the right-handed hitter averaged .269, but left his mark defensively in the mid-1880s, while with the Cleveland Spiders, by abandoning the traditional practice of moving several paces behind the batter when there were no men on base and playing directly behind the plate on every pitch.

Zimmer was elected to head the players' group in January 1900 partly because, as one of the few players who had not joined the Players League a decade earlier, he was perceived as unthreatening to the owners. Tactically he walked a narrow line between the radicals and the conciliators, refusing help from Samuel Gompers, head of the American Federation of Labor, but hiring Harry Taylor, a former big leaguer and a relative militant on labor matters, as the organization's attorney. National League owners broke with precedent and agreed to negotiate with the group, if only to forestall massive defections to the new American League. Zimmer won a round by getting the owners to discuss several previously untouchable issues by promising to consider the expulsion from the union of any player who jumped his contract. It proved a hollow victory when the AL attracted large numbers of National Leaguers anyway and the union lost its leverage with the senior circuit.

DON ZIMMER

Zimmer's forty-plus years as player, coach, and manager have been filled with conflict, comedy, and near-tragedy. As a shortstop in the Brooklyn farm system, he was beaned so badly in 1951 that he remained unconscious for almost two weeks and had to be fitted with a cranial plate. With the varsity Dodgers, he never quite lived up to his billing as Pee Wee Reese's successor, but proved to be a valuable bit player in the club's 1955 World Series win, when he was removed for defense late in the seventh game, enabling Sandy Amoros to be inserted in the outfield just in time

for Yogi Berra's noted foul line drive. Wandering from team to team and from league to league for twelve years, Zimmer was the first of the Mets' innumerable third basemen in 1962, but failed to get a hit for the expansion franchise until he had been to bat more than 30 times; after he had finally broken his collar with a couple of safeties, he was dealt to Cincinnati behind a Casey Stengel crack that "we wanted to trade him while he was hot."

As of 1971, Zimmer began moving back and forth between coaching and managing positions, making stopovers in one capacity or another for eight different teams, several of them more than once. His first managerial experience, with the Padres in 1972, was relatively uneventful, but the same could not be said when he took over the Red Sox in 1976. Moving in to replace the unpopular Darrell Johnson after a pennant-winning season, Zimmer squandered much of his goodwill with Boston players by showing little talent for running a pitching staff. Since the Red Sox hurlers included the outspoken Bill Lee and Ferguson Jenkins, the result was almost daily quotes from the clubhouse on how the team was going down the drain. Zimmer's special nemesis was a clique of players (prominently Lee, Jenkins, and outfielder Bernie Carbo) who called themselves the Loyal Order of the Buffalo Heads because, according to its members, the buffalo was the dumbest animal on earth, as was anybody who played for Zimmer and the Red Sox. Lee also became noted for another zoological view that Zimmer resembled a "designated gerbil."

In the midst of battling a penurious front office over its failure to acquire some veteran players who would make the team more than a second-place finisher, Zimmer also pressed for the removal of his favorite thorns, eventually getting his way on Jenkins and Carbo. But even that victory proved decidedly Pyrrhic after Bucky Dent's 1978 playoff home run and vehement reminders that the Red Sox might not have been broken by the shortstop's blow if Carbo had been kept around on the bench. Even though he also stayed around long enough to see Lee packed off, Zimmer could never overcome the "gerbil" image fastened to him by the southpaw and easily ranked as New England's most unpopular sports figure until he was replaced near the end of the 1980 season.

After another humdrum tour as manager of the Rangers, Zimmer had a rebirth of sorts when he took over the Cubs in 1988 under his longtime friend general manager Jim Frey. The following year, Zimmer guided Chicago to division title, in the process becoming something of an attraction himself by his pudgy, pop-eyed appearance; volcanic explosions against umpires; and new tactics, which ran from the highly imaginative to the bizarre (e.g., hit-and-run plays with the bases loaded and fewer than two outs). Then, early in 1991, he was discharged for little apparent reason; after a couple of weeks of silence, the commissioner's office issued a cryptic statement saying that an investigation into Zimmer's noted racetrack betting had "produced insufficient evidence of any wrongdoing."

HEINIE ZIMMERMAN

Zimmerman was blackballed for conspiring with Hal Chase to throw games in 1919, making him the only Triple Crown winner without a Hall of Fame plaque. The third baseman played fourteen seasons (1907–19) in the National League, compiling a .295 average. The right-handed hitter's banner year came in 1912, for the Cubs, when he hit .372, stroked 14 home runs, and drove in 103 runners while pacing the league in hits, doubles, and slugging average. He also led the NL in RBIs in 1916 and 1917.

Traded to the Giants early in the 1916 season, Zimmerman was quietly dropped from the New York roster, along with Chase, in 1919. It emerged subsequently that the pair had offered outfielder Benny Kauff $500 to join them in intentionally losing a game against the Cardinals; the third baseman had approached pitcher Fred Toney with a similar proposition. Zimmerman is otherwise best known for chasing Eddie Collins across the plate with the world championship run in the sixth game of the 1947 World Series after a botched rundown.

RICHIE ZISK

Zisk was the prime example of both the advantages and the disadvantages of White Sox owner Bill Veeck's rent-a-player approach to free agency in the late 1970s. Knowing ahead of time that he would never be able to meet Zisk's contract demands after the season, Veeck acquired the outfielder from Pittsburgh for the his 1977 walk year. The good news was that Zisk responded with 30 home runs and 101 RBIs. The inevitable news was that he signed with Texas for the 1978 season. The bad news was that, to obtain the right-hand-hitting slugger, Veeck gave the Pirates future relief aces Goose Gossage and Terry Forster.

GEORGE ZOETERMAN

When the White Sox drafted Zoeterman out of prep school in 1947, they set in motion a series of events that culminated in the team's suspension from the American League, the only time in this century that such a sanction has been imposed. The contract, which violated the spirit, if not the letter, of a ban on signing high schoolboys, was voided almost immediately despite a hair-splitting defense offered by Chicago general manager Lester O'Connor; O'Connor, who had helped formulate the stricture while serving as an assistant to Commissioner Kenesaw Landis, had argued that his own handiwork failed to cover students in private schools not part of the National Federation of State Athletic Associations. The suspension of the franchise followed O'Connor's refusal to pay a $500 fine slapped on the club by Commissioner Happy Chandler as much for O'Connor's fastidious distinction as for the violation itself. The AL remained a seven-club circuit from October 24 to November 4, when majority owner Lou Comiskey, confronted with the possibility of a 1948 AL schedule that did not include Chicago, overruled O'Connor and agreed to pay the fine.

Selected Annotated Bibliography

Aaron, Hank. *I Had a Hammer.* New York: HarperCollins, 1991. A philosophical Aaron reviews his career.

Alexander, Charles C. *John McGraw.* New York: Viking Penguin, 1988.

———. *Ty Cobb.* New York: Oxford University Press, 1984. Definitive biographies of two of baseball's central figures.

Allen, Lee. *The Cincinnati Reds.* New York: Putnam, 1948. The best one-volume history of a franchise.

———. *The Hot Stove League.* New York: A. S. Barnes, 1965. An eclectic collection of ruminations on various facets of baseball, some trivial, some fascinating.

———. *100 Years of Baseball* New York: Bartholomew House, 1950. Less a history than a collection of essays on topics and personalities that interest the author, but highly readable and essential for a picture of early baseball.

Asinof, Eliot. *Eight Men Out* New York: Holt, Rinehart & Winston, 1963. Still the best account of the 1919 Black Sox scandal.

Barber, Red. *1947—When All Hell Broke Loose in Baseball.* Garden City, NY, 1982. Sometimes preachy, sometimes insightful look at Jackie Robinson's rookie season.

The Baseball Encyclopedia, 9th ed. New York: Macmillan, 1994. For all its statistical inconsistencies and seemingly trivial corrections from edition to edition, an essential part of any baseball library.

Beverage, Richard E. *The Angels.* Placentia, CA: The Deacon Press, 1981. A good early record of the Gene Autry ownership.

Blake, Mike. *Baseball Chronicles: An Oral History of Baseball Through the Decades.* Better Way Books, 1944. The most recent effort to mix history, nostalgia, and the gray area between.

Bouton, Jim. *Ball Four Plus Five.* Briarcliff Manor, NY: Stein & Day, 1982. The book that annoyed Bowie Kuhn and Billy Martin.

Bowman, Larry. "Moses Fleetwood Walker: The First Black Major League Baseball Player," *Baseball History,* ed. Peter Levine. Westport, CT: Stadium Books, 1988. Walker's life and career.

Brown, Warren. *The Chicago Clubs.* New York: Putnam, 1946.

———. *The Chicago White Sox.* New York: Putnam, 1952. Serviceable histories of the two Chicago franchises.

Chandler, Happy. *Heroes, Plain Folks, and Skunks.* Chicago Bonus Books, 1989. If only to get Chandler's version of events.

Creamer, Robert. *Babe: The Legend Comes to Life.* New York: Simon & Schuster, 1974. A superlative baseball biography.

———. *Stengel: His Life and Times.* New York: Simon & Schuster, 1984. Almost as good as his work on Ruth.

Dewey, Donald and Nicholas Acocella, *Encyclopedia of Major League Baseball Teams.* New York: HarperCollins, 1992. The best historical survey of big league franchises—if we do say so ourselves.

Durocher, Leo, with Ed Linn. *Nice Guys Finish Last.* New York: Simon & Schuster, 1975. Durocher trying to sound like St. Leo, but facts creep in anyway.

Falkner, David. *The Last Yankee: The Turbulent Life of Billy Martin.* New York: Simon & Schuster, 1994. If Martin deserves still another biography, this is the one to read.

Egenriether, Richard. "Chris Von der Ahe: Baseball's Pioneering Huckster," *Baseball Research Journal,* pp 27–31, 1989. An excellent account of Von der Ahe's escapades.

Gallagher, Mark. *The Yankee Encyclopedia.* New York: Leisure Press, 1982. Surprisingly frank entries on players, managers, owners, and front-office officials.

Gammons, Peter. *Beyond the Sixth Game.* Boston: Houghton Mifflin, 1985. Some entertaining tales about the end of the Tom Yawkey ownership.

Gibson, Bob, with Lonnie Wheeler. *Stranger to the Game.* New York: Viking, 1994. A noteworthy effort to fill the gap in generally neglected 1960s baseball.

Graham, Frank. *The Brooklyn Dodgers.* New York: Putnam, 1945.

———. *The New York Giants.* New York: Putnam, 1952.

———. *The New York Yankees.* New York: Putnam 1958. Graham's three team histories border on hagiography but contain important details.

Hailey, Gary. "Anatomy of a Murder: The Federal League and the Courts," *The National Pastime,* pp. 66–83, 1985. The best account of the Federal League's demise and the beginning of baseball's antitrust exemption.

Halberstam, David. *Summer of '49.* New York: Morrow, 1989. Readable retelling of one of baseball's dramatic pennant races, filled with nuggets about Casey Stengel, Joe DiMaggio, and Ted Williams.

Harshman, Jack E. "The Radbourn and Sweeney Saga," *Baseball Research Journal,* 1990. All the details of one of nineteenth-century baseball's most dramatic incidents.

Holway, John B. *Blackball Stars.* New York: Carroll & Graf, 1992. Biographical sketches of Negro leagues stars.

Honig, Donald. *Baseball Between the Lines.* New York: Coward, McCann, & Geoghegan, 1976.

———. *Baseball When the Grass Was Real.* New York: Berkley, 1975. A little bit of this sort of oral history goes a long way, but some of the players interviewed offer versions of events not found elsewhere.

Hynd, Noel. *The Giants of the Polo Grounds.* New York: Doubleday, 1988. Concise recapitulation of the McGraw years, though the book becomes scantier thereafter.

James, Bill. *The Politics of Glory.* New York: Macmillan, 1994. The strongest indictment to date of the nebulous criteria for inclusion in the Hall of Fame.

Kaese, Harold, and R. G. Lynch. *The Milwaukee Braves.* New York: Putnam, 1954. A history of the Braves in Boston and how they came to Milwaukee.

Kahn, Roger. *The Boys of Summer.* New York: Harper & Row, 1971. The most powerful microscope ever directed at one team.

Kerr, Jon. *Calvin: Baseball's Last Dinosaur.* Madison, WI: William C. Brown, 1990. Hilarious, if your humor runs to paleontology.

Kuhn, Bowie. *Hardball.* New York: McGraw-Hill. The commissioner's version of events, sufficiently well written as to be almost believable.

Lally, Dick. *Pinstriped Summers.* New York: Arbor House, 1985. The best of several books about George Steinbrenner's early years as owner of the Yankees.

Lang, Jack, and Peter Simon. *The New York Mets.* New York: Henry Holt, 1986. Believe it or not, many previously untold stories about a franchise that has generated almost as many books as runs.

Lansche, Jerry. *The Forgotten Championships.* Jefferson, NC: 1989. Dry but informative account of nineteenth-century postseason championship series.

Lee, Bill "Spaceman," with Dick Lally. *The Wrong Stuff.* New York: Penguin, 1984. Lee setting the record (almost) straight.

Lewis, Franklin. *The Cleveland Indians.* New York: Putnam 1949.

Lieb, Frederick. *The Baltimore Orioles.* New York: Putnam, 1955.

————. *Baseball As I Have Known It.* New York: Tempo Books, 1977.

————. *The Baseball Story.* New York: Putnam, 1950.

————. *The Boston Red Sox.* New York: Putnam, 1947.

————. *Connie Mack: Grand Old Man of Baseball.* New York: Putnam, 1948.

————. *The Detroit Tigers.* New York: Putnam, 1950.

————. *The Pittsburgh Pirates.* New York: Putnam, 1948.

————. *The St. Louis Cardinals.* New York: Putnam, 1944.

————. *The Story of the World Series.* New York: Putnam, 1950.

Lieb, Frederick and Stan Baumgartner. *The Philadelphia Phillies.* New York: Putnam, 1953. Lieb's team histories range from excellent (Baltimore) to ordinary (St. Louis); the Mack biography is still the best of the A's owner: *Baseball As I Have Known It,* a kind of summing up his sportswriting career, contains some rarely heard stories.

Linn, Ed. *Hitter: The Life and Turmoils of Ted Williams.* New York: Harcourt, Brace, 1994. Adds some shading to Williams's more popular *My Turn at Bat.*

Lowenfish, Lee, and Tony Lupien. *The Imperfect Diamond.* Briarcliff Manor, NY: Stein & Day, 1980. An important history of baseball labor relations.

Marazzi, Rich. *The Rules and Lore of Baseball. Briarcliff Manor, NY: Stein & Day, 1980.* A different approach to telling baseball stories (some hoary, some refreshingly new)—by relating them to the rule book.

Mead, William B. *Even the Browns.* New York: Contemporary Books, 1978. Baseball during World War II, and war rarely sounded as entertaining.

Mosedale, John. *The Greatest of All.* New York: Dial, 1974. The 1927 Yankees.

Murdock, Eugene. *Ban Johnson: Czar of Baseball.* Westport, CT: Greenwood, 1982. Overly scholarly but well-researched account of Johnson's career as American League president.

Oh, Sadaharu, and David Falkner. *A Zen Way of Baseball.* New York: Times Books, 1984. Less zen the reader bargains for.

Okrent, Daniel. *Nine Innings.* New York: Ticknor & Fields, 1985. Everything you ever wanted to know about the Milwaukee Brewers, cleverly presented as background to and digressions from an account of a single game.

Peterson, Robert. *Only the Ball Was White.* Englewood Cliffs, NJ. Prentice-Hall, 1970. The pioneering work on the Negro leagues.

Pietrusza, David. *Major Leagues.* Jefferson, NC: McFarland, 1991. Detailed account of the formation of every major league—including those that died aborning.

Players' National League. *The Players' National League Official Guide for 1890.* Chicago: F. H. Brunnell, 1998. Contemporary report on the Players League, unmatched by anything that followed.

Polner, Murray. *Branch Rickey.* New York: Signet, 1983. Straight from the Rickey files, but with some nice anecdotes.

Povich, Shirley. *The Washington Senators.* New York: Putnam, 1954. Sketchy account of the early years of Washington baseball; better on the first version of the Senators.

Reach Baseball Guides, 1883–1939. Indispensable reviews of each season.

Riley, James A. *The Biographical Encyclopedia of the Negro Baseball Leagues.* New York: Carroll & Graf, 1994. Monumental collection of every known fact about everyone who ever played in the Negro leagues.

Ritter, Lawrence S. *The Glory of Their Times.* New York: Random House, 1985. The original collection of interviews with old-time players.

Rizzuto, Phil, with Tom Horton. *The October Twelve.* Forge Books, 1994. The Scooter's idiosyncratic slant on his teammates who played on all five of the Yankee world championship teams of 1949–53.

Robinson, George, and Charles Salzberg. *On a Clear Day They Could See Second Place.* New York: Dell, 1991. Lively accounts of baseball's worst teams.

Seymour, Harold. *Baseball: The Early Years.* New York: Oxford University Press, 1960.

———. *Baseball: The Golden Age.* New York, Oxford University Press, 1971. Unquestionably the best history of baseball.

Spalding, A. G. *Baseball: America's National Game 1839–1915.* San Francisco: Halo Books, 1991. A reprint of Spalding's self-serving history of early baseball.

Spalding Official Baseball Guides, 1878–1939. The rival to the Reach guides.

Spink, J. G. Taylor: *Judge Landis and 25 Years of Baseball.* New York: Crowell, 1947. Surprisingly well-balanced biography of baseball's first commissioner.

Sporting Life, 1883–1903. A defunct weekly, essential for contemporary reporting on baseball events.

The Sporting News, 1886 to date. The baseball Bible—at various periods a house organ for the owners, a rehash of newspaper descriptions of games, and a source of original material.

The Sporting News Official Baseball Guides, 1940 to date (*Spink Official Baseball Guides* through 1979). The successor to the Spalding guides.

Thompson, S. C. *All-Time Rosters of Major League Baseball Clubs.* New York: A. S. Barnes, 1973). Full rosters, team by team, year by year; an excellent source for who played with whom and when.

Thorn, John. *The Relief Pitcher.* New York: Dutton, 1979. Some rarely told tales.

Thorn, John, and Pete Palmer, eds. *Total Baseball.* New York: HarperCollins, 1993. Livelier and more ambitious than the Macmillan *Encyclopedia,* but also in love with its own original statistics and requiring Ted Williams's eyesight to read.

Tiemann, Robert L. and Mark Rucker. *Nineteenth Century Stars.* Cooperstown, NY: The Society for American Baseball Research, 1989. Very good sketches of non-Hall of Fame players of the last century.

Titchener, Campbell B. *The George Kirksey Story.* Austin, TX: Eakin Press, 1989. Some good stories on the start of the Houston franchise.

Tuohey, George. *A History of the Boston Baseball Club.* Boston: M. F. Quinn, 1897. The prototype of the franchise history.

Tygiel, Jules. *Jackie Robinson and His Legacy.* New York: Random House, 1984. Far and away, the most incisive look at Robinson's impact.

Veeck, Bill, with Ed Linn, *Veeck as in Wreck.* New York: Signet, 1962. As irreverent, funny, and insightful as the author.

Voight, David Quentin. *American Baseball,* 3 vols. University Park, PA: The Pennsylvania State University Press, 1983. Useful but not in the same league with the Seymour history.

Ward, Geoffrey C. and Ken Burns. *Baseball: An Illustrated History.* New York: Knopf, 1994. Better than the movie.

Zimbalist, Andrew. *Baseball Billions.* New York: Basic Books, 1992. A primer that should be required reading for anyone who thinks major league owners are justified in all their whining.

Zoss, Joel, and John Bowman. *Diamonds in the Rough.* New York: Macmillan, 1989. One of the most entertaining catchall books about baseball ever put together. Most of it is marginal stuff, but you won't read it elsewhere.